Each new te[xt] exciting learn[ing] eBook contai[ns hundreds] of online links to **primary sources, images, web resources, simulations, maps, audio, and more.**

Teaching and Learning Styles

Each new text comes with access to **4ltrpress.cengage.com/world,** where we offer a suite of digital tools—including **interactive quizzing, flashcards, and more**—for the many different learning styles of today's students.

For instructors' different teaching styles, we offer Webtutor on Blackboard® and WebCT®, as well as PowerLecture™—a suite of PowerPoint® presentations, instructor's manual, and ExamView computerized testing.

Accessibility

At fewer than **550 pages each,** Volumes 1 & 2 of *WORLD* present all concepts, definitions, learning objectives, and study tools found in a book twice its size.

Value

WORLD offers full content coverage, review cards, and valuable material at **4ltrpress.cengage.com/world** – all for **$61.95 per split volume** and **$74.95 for the comprehensive edition.**

Comprehensive
978-0-495-80205-0

Volume 1: To 1500
978-1-439-08412-2

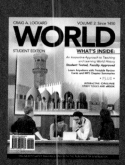

Volume 2: Since 1450
978-1-439-08413-0

WORLD
Craig A. Lockard

Senior Publisher: Suzanne Jeans

Senior Acquisitions Editor: Nancy Blaine

Development Manager: Jeff Greene

Senior Development Editor: Tonya Lobato

Assistant Editor: Lauren Floyd

Editorial Assistant: Emma Goehring

Senior Media Editor: Lisa Ciccolo

Senior Marketing Manager: Katherine Bates

Marketing Coordinator: Lorreen Pelletier

Marketing Communications Manager:
Christine Dobberpuhl

Senior Content Project Manager:
Carol Newman

Senior Art Director: Cate Rickard Barr

Print Buyer: Becky Cross

Senior Rights Acquisition Account Manager:
Katie Huha

Text Permissions Editor: Tracy Metivier

Senior Photo Editor: Jennifer Meyer Dare

Photo Researcher: Carole Frohlich

Production Service: Lachina Publishing Services

Text Designer: Dutton & Sherman Design

Cover Designer: Studio Montage

Cover Image: Angkor Wat © Kevin R. Morris/
Corbis

Compositor: Lachina Publishing Services

For product information and technology assistance, contact us at
Cengage Learning Customer & Sales Support, 1-800-354-9706

For permission to use material from this text or product,
submit all requests online at **cengage.com/permissions.**
Further permissions questions can be emailed to
permissionrequest@cengage.com.

Library of Congress Control Number: 2009929342

Student Edition:

ISBN-13: 978-0-495-80205-1

ISBN-10: 0-495-80205-0

Wadsworth
20 Channel Center Street
Boston, MA 02210
USA

Cengage Learning is a leading provider of customized learning solutions with office locations around the globe, including Singapore, the United Kingdom, Australia, Mexico, Brazil and Japan. Locate your local office at **international.cengage.com/region**

Cengage Learning products are represented in Canada by Nelson Education, Ltd.

For your course and learning solutions, visit **www.cengage.com.**

Purchase any of our products at your local college store or at our preferred online store **www.ichapters.com.**

Printed in the United States of America
1 2 3 4 5 6 7 13 12 11 10 09

Brief Contents

Kasuyoshi Nomachi/Pacific Press Photo; Ancient Art & Architecture Collection Ltd.; Erich Lessing/Art Resource, NY

iii

Amsterdams Historisch Museum; Visual Connection Archive; Wally McNamee/Corbis

Contents

v

Bildarchiv Preussischer Kulturbestiz/Art Resource, NY

Scala/Art Resource, NY

© Cultural Relics Press

The Nelson-Atkins Museum of Art, Kansas City,
Missouri. Purchase: William Rockhill Nelson
Trust, 34-7. Photography by Jamison Miller

PART V Global Imbalances: Industry, Empire, and the Making of the Modern World, 1750–1945 484

AP Images/STF

PART VI Global Systems: Interdependence and Conflict in the Contemporary World, Since 1945 686

Glenn Hunt/AAP

Maps

{ Explore It Your Way! }

"**What appeals to me is the fully virtual eBook with find/search feature which is absolutely irreplaceable and eternally helpful. I wish I had the eBook for when I was starting college.**"
William Manning, Student at Florida Atlantic University

We know that no two students read in quite the same way. Some of you do a lot of your reading online.

To help you take your reading **outside the covers** of **WORLD,** each new text comes with access to the exciting learning environment of an interactive eBook containing **tested online links to:**

- **Primary source documents**
- **Interactive maps**
- **Web links for further investigation**
- **Interactive quizzes**
- **Audio resources**
- **Historical simulation activities**
- **Profiles of key historical figures**

Access the eBook at 4ltrpress.cengage.com/world.

Foundations:
Ancient Societies, to 600 B.C.E.

NORTH AND CENTRAL AMERICA
The ancestors of Native Americans migrated into North America from Asia thousands of years ago. They gradually occupied the Americas, working out ways of life compatible with the environments they lived in. While many remained hunters and gatherers, the first American farming began in Mexico and spread to various North American regions. The Olmecs of Mexico built cities atop huge artificial mounds and created an alphabet and religious traditions that influenced nearby peoples. Other North Americans also built settlements around large mounds.

ARCTIC OCEAN

NORTH AMERICA

Mississippi R.

ATLANTIC OCEAN

OLMECS
MESOAMERICA

PACIFIC OCEAN

Amazon

PERU
ANDES

SOUTH AMERICA

SOUTH AMERICA
Some Native Americans reached South America thousands of years ago. Farming developed early along the Pacific coast and in the Andes Mountains region. The first cities, such as Caral in coastal Peru, arose around the same time as early cities in Egypt and India. Cities were later established in the Andes Mountains. The major Andean states influenced the art and religion of many other South American societies.

© Cengage Learning

EUROPE

Ancient cities and states formed on the Mediterranean island of Crete and in Greece. Minoans, the residents of Crete, were successful maritime traders. After their collapse, the Mycenaeans of mainland Greece traded widely and exercised regional power until they declined. Migrants into Greece mixed with the Mycenaeans to form the foundation for later Greek society. These southern European societies worked bronze and participated in trade networks linking them to North Africa, eastern Europe, and western Asia.

WESTERN ASIA

The world's first farmers probably lived in western Asia, east of the Mediterranean Sea, where the oldest known cities and states also arose. The diverse societies that formed in the Tigris-Euphrates River Valley in Mesopotamia developed bronzeworking, writing, science, and mathematics, and they also traded with India and Egypt. Western Asians perfected iron technology, which eventually spread around Eurasia. The Phoenicians were the greatest traders of the Mediterranean region and also invented an alphabet later adopted by the Greeks. Another notable people, the Hebrews, introduced a monotheistic religion, Judaism.

EASTERN ASIA

Farming developed very early in the Yellow and Yangzi River Basins in China, fostering the region's first cities and states. Chinese culture then expanded into southern China. The Chinese invented a writing system and worked bronze and iron. Mixing Chinese influences with their own traditions, Koreans took up farming and metalworking. Some Koreans migrated into Japan, where they and the local peoples mixed their traditions to produce the Japanese culture.

AFRICA

Farming appeared very early in North, West, and East Africa. Africa's earliest cities and states formed along the Nile River Valley in Egypt. The Egyptians invented a writing system and flourished from productive agriculture and trade with other African societies and Eurasia. Cities and states also arose in Nubia, just south of Egypt. Africans south of the Sahara Desert developed ironworking technology very early, and iron tools and weapons helped the Bantu-speaking peoples gradually expand from West Africa into Central and East Africa.

SOUTHERN ASIA AND OCEANIA

Farming and metalworking developed early in South and Southeast Asia. The people of the Harappan cities in the Indus River Basin grew cotton, made textiles, and traded with western and Central Asia. After the Harappan society collapsed, Aryan peoples from western Asia moved into India, and the mixing of Aryan and local traditions formed the basis for the Hindu religion. Meanwhile, Austronesian peoples migrated from Taiwan into the Southeast Asian and Pacific islands. Southeast Asians pioneered in maritime trade and formed their first states. Hunters and gatherers flourished in Australia.

3

CHAPTER 1

The Origins of Human Societies,
to ca. 2000 B.C.E.

Learning Outcomes

After reading this chapter, you should be able to answer the following questions:

LO¹ How have various human societies sought to understand the formation of the universe, earth, and humanity?

LO² According to most scientists, what were the various stages of human evolution?

LO³ How did hunting and gathering shape life during the long Stone Age?

LO⁴ What environmental factors explain the transition to agriculture?

LO⁵ How did farming and metallurgy establish the foundations for the rise of cities, states, and trade networks?

> **❝**We are long past the time when we could deal with the human story apart from the life story, or the earth story, or the universe story.**❞**
>
> —Cosmologist Brian Swimme and historian Thomas Berry[1]

The human story was already old when, at Abu Hureyra (AH-boo hoo-RAY-rah) in the Euphrates (you-FRAY-teez) River Valley, a group of villagers began to shape world history: they became some of humankind's first farmers. People who hunted game and gathered vegetables and nuts had occupied Abu Hureyra perhaps 13,000 years ago, when the area, in what is now Syria, was wetter and blessed with many edible wild plants and large herds of Persian gazelles. But a long cold spell brought a drought, and, to survive, the Abu Hureyra villagers began to cultivate the most easily grown grains. Gradually, they also began to raise domesticated sheep and goats. By 7600 B.C.E. they had stopped hunting and gathering completely.

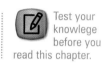 Test your knowlege before you read this chapter.

The Abu Hureyra farmers pursued a life that would be familiar to rural folk for millennia. Several hundred people crowded into a village of narrow lanes and courtyards. Families dwelled in rectangular, one-story, multiroom mud houses, studying the sky at night and pondering the mysteries of the universe. During the day, men did much of the farm work while women carried heavy loads on their heads, prepared meals, and ground grain by hand. Early farming life was not easy. Eventually Abu Hureyra was abandoned: the last villagers had left by 5000 B.C.E.

What do you think?

Scholarly theories on how the Americas came to be populated by humans have remained unchanged for centuries.

Strongly Disagree						Strongly Agree
1	2	3	4	5	6	7

Prehistory includes a vast span of time, from the earliest humans to the beginnings of agriculture and the emergence of complex societies with cities and states. Much of what we know about these millennia comes from archaeologists, who study the material remains of past cultures, and anthropologists, who study human biology and culture in relation to the physical and social environment. Societies are broad groups of people that share common traditions, institutions, and organized patterns of relationships. Over many millennia, humans evolved physically, mentally, and culturally, learning to make simple tools, developing societies, and then spreading throughout the world.

<< Tassili Archers Thousands of ancient paintings on rock surfaces and cave walls record the activities of African hunters, gatherers, and pastoralists. This painting of archers on a hunt was made in a rock shelter on the Tassili plateau of what is today Algeria, probably long before the Sahara region had dried up and become a harsh desert.

Later most societies, like the villagers at Abu Hureyra, made the first great historical transition from hunting and gathering to farming and animal herding. This transition profoundly changed the relationship between people and the environment and prompted the emergence of larger societies with cities and states. In turn this stimulated long-distance trade and the rise of social, cultural, and economic networks linking distant societies.

LO¹ Before Prehistory: The Cosmos, Earth, and Life

While most historians restrict their attention to the five or six millennia that can be examined through documentary sources, oral traditions, and archaeological findings, some scholars prefer to place the development of human societies and networks in a much longer and more comprehensive framework, the "universe story." Understanding prefarming peoples, these scholars argue, permits us to comprehend the rise of complex societies and networks. Going back further in time, we can also consider the ancestors of humans and, before that, the beginning of life on earth, and finally the formation of our planet within the larger cosmic order.

Perceptions of Cosmic Mysteries

Human development on earth constitutes only a tiny fraction of the long history of the universe, which most modern scientists think began in a cosmic Big Bang explosion some 14 billion years ago. As the universe expanded, matter coalesced into stars, and stars formed into billions of galaxies spread over vast distances. Our solar system emerged about 4.5 billion years ago out of clouds of gas. On our planet, earth, the developing atmosphere kept the surface warm enough for organic compounds to coalesce into life forms.

The Rig Veda
Read how Indra, "the thunderwielder," slew Vritra, "firstborn of dragons," and how Purusha created the universe through an act of ritual sacrifice.

Reflecting on Creation

Over the centuries, most human societies have crafted creation stories and cosmologies to explain their existence. The earliest known creation story, from Mesopotamia, claimed that heaven and earth were created as one in a primeval sea and then separated by the gods, humanlike beings unseen but far more powerful than mere mortals. Mesopotamian beliefs influenced the seven-day creation story in the Hebrew book of Genesis. Other cosmological traditions drew different conclusions. Ancient Hindu holy books, for example, describe the creation of a universe out of nothingness: "There was neither nonexistence or existence then; there was neither the realm of space nor the sky which is beyond. Darkness was hidden by darkness in the beginning, emptiness."² Then a Big Bang–like heat formed the cosmos and generated life. The ancient Chinese believed that the universe was created out of chaos and darkness and that the creator Pan Ku fashioned the sun, moon, and stars to put everything in proper order. The result was a unifying force in the universe, known as the "way," or *dao* (DOW). The Dogon (DOUGH-ghun) people of West Africa believed that the original germ of life emerged from a world egg and then expanded through the universe. Like other early peoples, the Dogon organized their society to reflect the working of the cosmic order as they perceived it.

The Natural Environment and Evolutionary Change

Living organisms that are able to consume food, grow, and reproduce with a genetic code have a long history. Life on earth has been influenced by natural forces such as geology and climate. A dozen or more large plates lie under the planet's surface and shift slightly each year. Over the ages, this moving of plates and the spread or contraction of sea floors reconfigured the land surface into continents, each with its unique plants and animals. Volcanic and earthquake activity caused by plate movements has shaped human societies and sometimes undermined them.

ArchNet Home Page (*http://archnet.asu.edu/*). This Arizona State University site contains links to information on human origins, prehistory, and archaeology.

The Darwinian Revolution

Most natural scientists agree that living things change over many generations through evolution, the process by which they modify their genetic composition to adapt to their environment. In the nineteenth century, the British biologist Charles Darwin, after observing the great variety of species around the world, explained the process with his theory of natural selection. He believed individuals developed variations that helped them compete for food and domination within their own species and to triumph over rival species. Those who competed successfully then passed on their genes to their descendants. Scientists still debate evolution's precise mechanisms, and some have modified Darwin's ideas, but modern biology has mostly confirmed Darwin's basic insights.

Mass Extinctions

In addition to gradual genetic adaptation, another force for change has been mass extinctions. A half-dozen massive species extinctions have occurred in the past 400 million years. The best-known extinction involved the dinosaurs, which flourished for 150 million years before dying out about 65 million years ago. It is believed that environmental changes resulting from the cooling of the planet from increasing volcanic activity, the cataclysmic impact of one or several large asteroids or comets smashing into the earth, or both, caused their demise. The end of the dinosaurs opened the door for mammals to rise and flourish.

The Ascent of Man

Eventually, after several billion years, evolutionary changes among one branch of mammals led to the immediate ancestors of humans. Humans are part of the primate order, the mammal category that includes the apes: in fact, more than 98 percent of human DNA is the same as that of chimpanzees. Today's two hundred primate species probably evolved from one common ancestor that lived some 20 million years ago.

Humans ultimately became dominant among large animal species by using their superior brain to gain an evolutionary edge. One key to their success was the ability to form complex social organizations that emphasized cooperation for mutual benefit. Humans also developed tools, mastered fire, and learned how to communicate, all of which gave them great advantages. Ultimately, they began using a more complex technology that enabled them to manipulate the physical environment in many ways to meet their needs.

LO² The Roots of Humanity

The history of humans is hardly a wink in the long history of earth and even modest compared to the long tenure of the dinosaurs. Hominids (HOM-uh-nids), a family including humans and their immediate ancestors, first evolved 5 to 6 million years ago from more primitive primates. The human story began in Africa, where the span of human prehistory is much longer than anywhere else. Most scientists agree that hominids evolved exclusively in eastern and southern Africa until at least 2 million years ago. Various evolutionary stages led up to modern humans and spurred their spread around the globe.

> **hominids**
> A family including humans and their immediate ancestors.

> ❝ Over 98 percent of human DNA is the same as that of chimpanzees. ❞

Early Hominids and Migrations out of Africa

Although scientists agree that the earliest humans originated in Africa, there is debate over the details and research methodology. The most extensive fossil evidence comes from the Great Rift Valley of East Africa, a wide, deep chasm stretching from Ethiopia south to Tanzania, but recent discoveries may mean that hominids evolved earlier and over a larger range than has been assumed. Heated disagreements have arisen over how to interpret the available evidence, and the archaeological record is full of gaps.

CHRONOLOGY

Hominid Evolution

20 million B.C.E.	Common ancestor to humans and Apes (Africa)
5–6 million B.C.E.	Earliest Proto-Humans
4–5 million B.C.E.	Australopithecines
2.5 million B.C.E.	*Homo habilis*
2.2–1.8 million B.C.E..	*Homo erectus/Homo ergaster*
400,000–200,000 B.C.E.	*Homo sapiens* (archaic humans)
135,000–100,000 B.C.E.	*Homo sapiens sapiens* (modern humans)

"Natural selection favored increased intelligence to deal with the challenges posed by this climate change."

Earliest Ancestors of Humans

Fossil discoveries point to several stages and branches in early human evolution. According to the available evidence, a common ancestral, apelike group lived in the woodlands and savannahs of East Africa. One division (the ancestors of most apes) began specializing in forest dwelling and climbing with all four limbs. Another division developed occasional and then permanent bipedalism, walking upright on two feet. This left the hands free for holding food or babies, manipulating objects, and carrying food back to camp. Bipeds, being higher off the ground, could also scan the horizon for predators or prey. These bipedal, apelike forms became the first hominids.

The First Hominids

Several hominid groups apparently coexisted at the same time, but only one led to modern humans. Beginning about 4 or 5 million years ago, several branches of early hominids known as **Australopithecines** (aw-strah-lo-PITH-uh-seens) lived in eastern and southern Africa. The brains of these erect bipeds, or proto-humans, were about one-third the size of our brains. One example was found in Ethiopia, where archaeologists unearthed the bones of a small female, named Lucy by anthropologists, who lived some 20 years and probably walked mostly on her feet.

Homo habilis

Some 2.5 million years ago, one branch of australopithecines evolved into our direct ancestor, a transition probably caused by environmental change and the resulting imbalances. The earth cooled, fostering the first of a series of Ice Ages, during which large areas of northern Eurasia and North America were covered with glaciers, and a drier climate and more open habitats began in Africa. Natural selection favored increased intelligence to deal with the challenges posed by this climate change. *Homo habilis* (HOH-moh HAB-uhluhs) ("handy human") was so named because of this species' larger brain size and its ability to make and use simple stone tools for hunting and gathering. Stone choppers and later hand axes made possible a more varied diet, more successful hunting, and larger groups that could cooperate to share food. The other branches of australopithecines died out, losing the competition to *Homo habilis*. As *Homo habilis* developed, males increasingly became the hunters or scavengers for meat and females the gatherers of nuts and vegetables. These early humans were probably mainly vegetarians, like many primates today. Cooperation between the sexes and group members was the key to survival and probably involved communication through gestures and vocal cries.

Homo erectus

Probably between 1.8 and 2.2 million years ago, some more advanced hominids evolved from *Homo habilis* in East Africa. Most scholars have termed these hominids *Homo erectus* (HOH-moh ee-REK-tuhs) ("erect human"). They were larger than *Homo habilis* and had a brain about two-thirds the size of ours. These people eventually developed a more complex and widespread tool culture that included hand axes, cleavers, and scrapers. They spread to other parts of Africa, preferring the open savannah.

Between 1 and 2 million years ago, as southern Eurasia developed a warmer climate, some *Homo erectus* bands began migrating out of Africa, carrying with them refined tools, more effective hunting skills, and an ability to adapt to new environments. Perhaps the first migrants were following game herds. This was the first great migration in human history, and it corresponded to the ebb and flow of the Ice Ages as well as the periodic drying out of the Sahara region. Over thousands of years, these hominids came to occupy northern Africa, the Middle East, South and Southeast Asia, China, Europe, and perhaps Australia.

Migrants spread widely. Some of the earliest non-African sites, perhaps 1.8 million years old, have been found in the Caucasus (KAW-kuh-suhs) Mountains of western Asia. Farther east, bones and tools discovered in Chinese caves and skulls from the island of Java in

The Laetoli Footprints Some 4 million years ago in Tanzania, three Australopithecines walked across a muddy field covered in ash from a nearby volcanic eruption. When the mud dried, their tracks were permanently preserved, providing evidence of some of the earliest upright hominids.

Indonesia suggest that *Homo erectus* may have been widespread in East and Southeast Asia by 1.5 million years ago. These hominids reached Europe later, living in Spain by 800,000 B.C.E., and in England and Germany by around 500,000 B.C.E. The hominid tool cultures of China and Europe, although equally complex, show different features, indicating cultural diversity.

By 500,000 years ago, *Homo erectus* in China lived in closely knit groups, engaged in cooperative hunting, and developed significant technologies. Most lived in caves, but some built simple wooden huts for shelter. The oldest hut so far found, in Japan, is 500,000 years old. Their hand axes were the Swiss army knives of their time, with a tip for piercing, thin edges for cutting, and thick edges for scraping and chipping. One of the key discoveries, how to start and control fire, was perhaps the most significant human invention

ever. Fire provided warmth and light after sunset, frightened away predators, and made possible a more varied diet of cooked food, which tasted better. In addition, control of fire fostered group living and cooperation as people gathered together around campfires and hearths. Fire also enabled ancestral humans to spread to cooler regions, such as Europe and eastern Asia.

Homo sapiens ("Thinking human") A hominid who evolved around 400,000 or 500,000 years ago and from whom anatomically modern humans (*Homo sapiens sapiens*) evolved around 100,000 years ago.

The Evolution and Diversity of *Homo sapiens*

The transition from *Homo erectus* to archaic forms of *Homo sapiens* (HOH-moh SAY-pee-enz) ("thinking human"), a species that was physically close to modern humans, began around 400,000 or 500,000 years ago

Evolution of Modern Humans (*http://anthro.palomar.edu/homo2/default.htm*). Valuable site maintained by Palomar College.

in Africa. By 200,000 years ago, a more complex tool culture was widespread, which serves as evidence for *Homo sapiens* occupation. Eventually, members of *Homo sapiens* were the only surviving hominids, and humanity became a single species.

**Homo sapiens:
Man, the Wise**

Members of *Homo sapiens* had many advantages over *Homo erectus*. With larger brains they were more adaptive and intelligent, and able to think conceptually. Archaic *Homo sapiens* may have used language, lived in fairly large organized groups, built temporary shelters, created crude lunar calendars, and killed whole herds of animals. They also raised more children to adulthood. Possession of symbolic language allowed *Homo sapiens* to share information over the generations, adjust to their environment, and overcome challenges not just individually but collectively.

Multiregional Origins Theory versus African Origins Theory

Scientists debate precisely how and where *Homo erectus* evolved into *Homo sapiens*, and several competing theories explain the transition. Some scholars, known as multiregionalists, argue that the evolution into *Homo sapiens* occurred in different parts of the Afro-Eurasian zone and that frequent interbreeding ensured that genes were exchanged and spread widely. This might, for example, explain a modern-looking and puzzling 60,000-year-old fossil from Australia. An alternative and more widely supported scenario, known as the African Origins theory, suggests that *Homo sapiens* evolved only in East Africa and then spread throughout Afro-Eurasia, displacing and ultimately dooming the remaining *Homo erectus* groups. The evidence for this theory includes the fact that (so far, anyway) the earliest *Homo sapiens* remains have been found in East Africa.

The most controversial tool in tracing human evolution is the study of genetic codes. The mutation history of mitochondrial (MY-tuh-CON-dree-uhl) DNA (DNA passed through generations by mothers) points to a common maternal ancestor to all present-day humans who lived in East Africa some 150,000 to 200,000 years ago. Other DNA studies and recent analysis of older fossil discoveries also mostly support the African Origins theory. However, in 2004, scholars were shocked by the discovery, on the small and remote Indonesian island of Flores, of the 18,000-year-old bones of diminutive hominids, 3 to 3-1/2 feet tall as adults. The Flores people may have been miniature versions of *Homo erectus* or of *Homo sapiens,* or perhaps constituted some unknown hominid species. Although the folklore of some modern Flores societies suggests that "little people" still lived in the recent past, scholars suspect they may have been wiped out in a massive volcanic explosion around 12,000 years ago.

> "Neanderthals were committed to social values, burying their dead, and caring for the sick and injured."

ical characteristics, but the race concept is dismissed by many experts for its inability to classify human populations. Observable physical attributes such as skin color and eye shape reflect a tiny portion of one's genetic makeup, and thus cannot always predict whether two groups are genetically similar or different. Most anthropologists argue that the idea of "race" is based not on biological facts but on social ideas and myths about the existence of real divisions between groups based only on the fact that they "look" different. Humans are much more similar than different.

Modern Humans and the Globalization of Settlement

Sometime between 130,000 and 100,000 years ago in Africa, anatomically modern humans, known as *Homo sapiens sapiens*, developed out of *Homo sapiens.* The brains of these modern humans were slightly larger than those of archaic *Homo sapiens.* With this biological change, language and culture expanded in new directions and developed many variations. Scholars debate whether creativity, intelligence, and even language abilities were innate to *Homo sapiens sapiens* or arose only some 50,000 years ago, possibly as a result of a genetic mutation. Whenever it occurred, with this great transition humanity reached its present level of intellectual and physical development, and established the foundation for the constant expansion of information networks to a global level.

The Human Race

Whether the evolution into *Homo sapiens* occurred only in Africa or on several continents, all humans came to constitute one species that could interbreed and communicate with each other. There were a few differences in physical features, such as skin and hair color and eye and face shape, but it remains unclear whether these developed earlier or later in *Homo sapiens* evolution. One controversial theory suggests that tropical peoples developed dark skins to protect themselves from the blistering sun and relatively little body hair because hair slows down heat loss, while others developed lighter skins and acquired more body hair as they moved into cooler climates.

The diverse groupings that evolved from *Homo sapiens* were once labeled "races," meaning large groups that shared distinctive genetic traits and phys-

Symbolic Thought, Aesthetic Expression

Human intellectual development included the development of languages as well as abstract, symbolic thought. Spoken language was the main method of communication for much of history; writing was used by only a small minority of people before modern times. Eventually, with expansion around the globe, some five thousand or six thousand languages emerged. Surviving artifacts of decoration and art reveal ancient symbolic thought. The gorgeous cave art of southwestern Europe, northern Africa, and western Asia has been traced back 30,000 to 40,000 years. The splendid rock art tradition found in southern Africa began by 30,000 B.C.E., and some recent discoveries suggest it may even be 75,000 years old. Indeed, several thousand engraved circles in rocks in northwestern Australia may be 60,000 to 75,000 years old. These creations reveal a genuine aesthetic sensibility and probably had ritual purposes, such as the celebration of spirits or valued animals.

The Dispersion of Humanity

Between 50,000 and 12,000 years ago, much of the world was settled by restless modern humans. As people spread, genetic differences grew and *Homo sapiens sapiens* proved able to adapt to many environments all over the world. By 100,000 years ago, some had already left Africa to settle in Palestine. Modern humans crossed to the eastern fringe of Asia before they populated Europe (see Map 1.1).

 Interactive Map

They lived in India and Southeast Asia between 50,000 and 40,000 years ago, in China between 35,000 and 50,000 years ago, and in Europe between 35,000 and 45,000 years ago. Dates for settlement in frigid eastern Siberia range from 28,000 to 14,000 B.C.E. By 40,000 years ago, they had migrated to Japan, which could then be reached by land bridges. To reach Australia from Southeast Asia across a very shallow sea required rafts or boats, but, according to controversial findings, modern humans had settled in Australia between 50,000 and 45,000 B.C.E.

The Neanderthals

Beginning around 200,000 years ago, a vibrant new tool culture developed in Europe that has been identified with the Neanderthals (nee-AN-der-thals), hominids who were probably descended from *Homo erectus* populations. By 100,000 B.C.E. the Neanderthals had spread to inhabit a wide region stretching from Spain and Germany to western and Central Asia; fossils have also been found in North Africa. Neanderthals were committed to social values, burying their dead, and caring for the sick and injured. In general, their cranial capacity equaled or even exceeded that of *Homo sapiens,* and they had larger bodies. Although they probably lacked spoken language, they were capable of communication. They also used tools, made bone flutes, and wore jewelry. They were skillful hunters, and their dietary protein came mainly from meat.

The relationship of the Neanderthals to *Homo sapiens sapiens* is unclear. By 70,000 years ago, both Neanderthals and modern humans lived in Palestine, and the two species apparently resided in the same areas for many centuries. When the modern, tool-using humans known as Cro-Magnons (krow-MAG-nuns) arrived in Europe, probably from western Asia, they also coexisted with Neanderthals for several millennia. DNA studies suggest that Neanderthals were a rather different species from Cro-Magnons, but a few fossil discoveries hint that interbreeding may have occurred at least occasionally. Around 28,000 years ago, the last Neanderthals died out or disappeared as a recognizable group. Whether they were ultimately annihilated, outnumbered, outcompeted, or assimilated by the more resourceful and adaptable *Homo sapiens sapiens,* who had better technology and warmer clothing, remains unknown.

The First Americans

Archaeologists long thought that the peopling of the Americas came very late and that the earliest migration into North America occurred only 12,000 to 15,000 years ago. But recent discoveries have led a few scholars to speculate that the pioneer arrivals may have crossed from Northeast Asia as early as 20,000 or possibly even 30,000 or 40,000 years ago. The scientific community is deeply divided on the antiquity of the first Americans (see Chapter 4). At various times a wide Ice Age land bridge connected Alaska and Siberia across today's Bering Strait, and the evidence for a migration chiefly from Asia over thousands of years is strong. The first settlers moved by land, or by boat along the coast. Gradually people of Asian ancestry settled throughout the Western Hemisphere, becoming the ancestors of today's Native Americans.

LO³ The Odyssey of Early Human Societies

For thousands of years, humans lived at a very basic level during what is often called the Stone Age, which included three distinct periods, each showing evidence of more efficient tools and stoneworking. The long Paleolithic (pay-lee-oh-LITH-ik) period (or Old Stone Age) began about 100,000 years ago.

Neanderthals Hominids who were probably descended from *Homo erectus* populations in Europe and who later spread into western and Central Asia.

Cro-Magnons The first modern, tool-using humans in Europe.

Paleolithic The Old Stone Age, which began 100,000 years ago with the first modern humans and lasted for many millennia.

Mesolithic The Middle Stone Age, which began around 15,000 years ago as the glaciers from the final Ice Age began to recede.

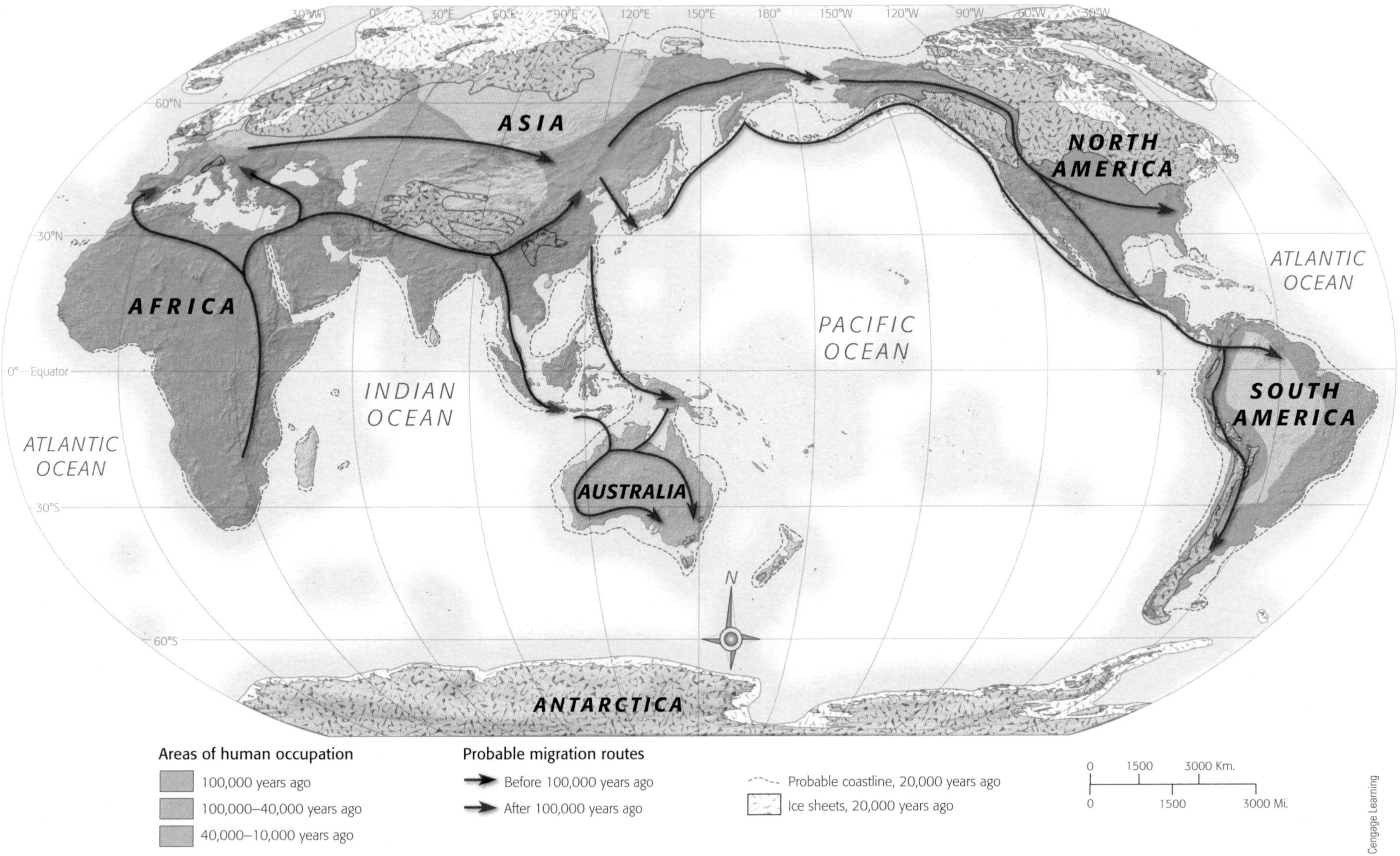
30°W
0°
30°E
60°E
90°E
120°E
150°E
180°
150°W
120°W
90°W
60°W
30°W
60°N
30°N
0°—Equator
30°S
60°S
ASIA
AFRICA
NORTH AMERICA
SOUTH AMERICA
AUSTRALIA
ANTARCTICA
ATLANTIC OCEAN
INDIAN OCEAN
PACIFIC OCEAN
ATLANTIC OCEAN
N
Areas of human occupation
100,000 years ago
100,000–40,000 years ago
40,000–10,000 years ago
Probable migration routes
Before 100,000 years ago
After 100,000 years ago
Probable coastline, 20,000 years ago
Ice sheets, 20,000 years ago
0 1500 3000 Km.
0 1500 3000 Mi.

Map 1.1
Spread of Modern Humans Around the Globe

Most scholars believe that modern humans originated in Africa and some of them began leaving Africa around 100,000 years ago. Gradually they spread out through Eurasia. From Eastern Asia some crossed to the Americas.

The Mesolithic (mez-oh-LITH-ik) period (Middle Stone Age) began around 15,000 years ago, when the glaciers from the final Ice Age receded. With this warming trend, the vast herds of large mammals that had flourished on the grasslands of Eurasia and North America began to thin rapidly. Major meat sources that were adapted to Ice Age climates, such as the woolly mammoth and mastodon, died out from warming climates, catastrophic disease, or zealous hunting by humans. The Neolithic (nee-oh-LITH-ik) period (New Stone Age) began between 9500 and 8000 B.C.E. in Eurasia, with the transition from hunting and gathering to simple farming. During the many centuries of the Paleolithic and Mesolithic eras, the various peoples organized themselves into small, usually mobile, family-based societies.

Hunting and Gathering Communities

The First Human Societies

Small groups of twenty to sixty members were the earliest and simplest forms of society. Their subsistence life depended on fishing, hunting live animals, scavenging for dead or dying animals, and gathering edible plants. Members cooperated in gathering or hunting to obtain food, usually just enough to ensure the group's survival. Improved tools made possible both more food options and better weapons against predators or rivals, especially when the bow and arrow were invented in Africa, Europe, and southwestern Asia at least 15,000 years ago. Now hunters could kill large animals at a safer distance, and men gained prestige from being the main hunters.

 !Kung Hunters and Gatherers

 Internet Ancient History Sourcebook (*http://www.fordham .edu/halsall/ancient/ asbook.htm*). Good collection of essays and links on prehistory.

The gathering by women of edible vegetation such as fruits and nuts was probably more essential for group survival than obtaining meat, and it gave women status and influence. Furthermore, women probably helped develop new technologies such as grinding stones, bone needles, nets (possibly used to catch small animals like rabbits and foxes), baskets, and primitive cloth. The oldest known woven-cloth clothing was made in eastern Europe some 28,000 years ago.

The hunting and gathering way of life may not have been as impoverished and unfulfilling as we sometimes imagine it was, with people continually searching for food in harsh environments. Many societies were creative, inventing fishhooks, harpoons, fuel lamps, dugout boats and canoes, and perhaps even beer. Studies over the past fifty years of groups who still hunt and gather, such as the Mbuti (em-BOO-tee) of the Congo rain forest and the !Kung of the Kalahari Desert, have found that they enjoy varied, healthy diets, surprisingly long life expectancies, considerable economic security, and a rich communal life. Many spend only ten to twenty hours per week in collecting food and establishing camps, leaving plenty of time for activities such as making music, dancing, and socializing. Although we cannot know for sure, the hunting and gathering life of millennia ago may have offered similar pleasures.On the other hand, hunters and gatherers have always faced serious challenges. Early humans had to make their own weapons and clothing and construct temporary huts. For some groups, life remained precarious and many died young, because not all enjoyed access to

Neolithic
The New Stone Age, which began between 10,000 and 11,500 years ago with the transition to farming.

CHRONOLOGY

The Spread of Modern Humans

135,000–100,000 B.C.E.	Eastern and Southern Africa
100,000 B.C.E.	Palestine
50,000–45,000 B.C.E.	Australia
50,000–40,000 B.C.E.	India, Southeast Asia
50,000–35,000 B.C.E.	China
45,000–35,000 B.C.E.	Europe
40,000 B.C.E.	Japan, Americas (disputed)
35,000–30,000 B.C.E.	New Guinea
20,000 B.C.E.	Siberia
15,000–12,000 B.C.E.	Americas (traditional view)
2000 B.C.E.	Western Pacific Islands
1500 B.C.E.	Samoa
200 B.C.E.	Marquesas Islands
400–500 C.E.	Hawaii
1000 C.E.	New Zealand

> "Women and men probably enjoyed a comparable status, as they do in many hunting and gathering societies today."

adequate food resources.

Hunting and gathering generally encouraged cooperation, which led to more closely knit communities based on kinship. Community members were able to communicate, and, as language developed, they also passed information from one generation to another. Gradually, humans increased in numbers, and societies, still based on kinship, became more complex. The mostly nomadic way of life made individual accumulation of material possessions impractical. Cooperative work and food sharing promoted the intense social life that is still common among hunting and gathering peoples today. But living close to others did not always result in harmony and mutual affection. Those who violated group customs could be killed or banished, temporarily or permanently, and sometimes groups split apart because of conflicts.

Most hunters and gatherers lived in small bands that had no system of government or leader. In these egalitarian social structures, all members in good standing often had equal access to resources. Everyone played a needed role, and social responsibilities linked people together. At the same time, groups often tended to reward the most resourceful members, and some societies had a headman who was chosen for his favored personal qualities. Yet early European explorers in the Americas and Australia were amazed at the degree to which many of the hunting and gathering peoples they encountered belittled or insulted their own leaders and could not comprehend the notion of high rank.

The Role of Women

Women and men probably enjoyed a comparable status, as they do in many hunting and gathering societies today. As key providers of food, women may have participated alongside men in group decision making. They also likely held a special place in religious practice as bearers of life.

Matrilineal (mat-ruh-LIN-ee-uhl) kinship patterns, which trace descent and inheritance through the female line, were probably common, as they are today in these societies. Although childbearing influenced women's roles, most hunting and gathering societies practiced birth control to limit group size. The practice of breast-feeding an infant for several years suppressed ovulation and created longer intervals between pregnancies. Plants and herbs were used as contraceptives or to induce abortions. If these schemes failed, unwanted babies might be killed. Paleolithic populations grew slowly, perhaps by only 10 percent a century.

Cultural Life and Violence

People and Their Gods

During the Paleolithic period, some aspects of culture were taking shape, such as religious belief. As people sought to understand dreams, death, and natural phenomena, they developed a perspective known as animism (ANN-uh-miz-um), the belief that all creatures, as well as inanimate objects and natural phenomena, have souls and can influence human well-being. Many early peoples also practiced polytheism (PAUL-e-thee-ism), the belief in many spirits or deities. Because spirits were thought capable of helping or harming a person, shamans (SHAW-mans), specialists in communicating with or manipulating the supernatural realm, became important members of the group and were sometimes women. The widespread practice of burying the dead suggests that many people believed in an afterlife. These societies may have had ample time for leisure, engaging in such group-oriented activities as storytelling. Some activities that promoted group unity developed early, including music, dance, and painting on rocks and cave walls. Primitive flutes can be traced back 45,000 years.

Violence and Conflict

Yet violence between and within different societies has been a part of human culture throughout history, and the seeds were planted in the Paleolithic period. People were hunters, but they were also hunted by predators such as bears, wolves, and lions. This reality may have instilled in early societies not only a terror of dangerous animals—apparent in myths and folklore—but also a tendency to justify violence. Men were often expected to prove their bravery to attract females, and some prehistoric peoples may have practiced cannibalism.

Social and cultural patterns that promoted certain behaviors, such as violence against neighboring groups, arose in response to environmental conditions. Anthropologists disagree about whether humans are inherently aggressive and warlike or peaceful and cooperative. Some primate species find ways to avoid conflict, and most engage in forms of reconciliation after fights. Humans may naturally seek self-preservation, but the influence of cultural patterns can channel behavior in one direction or another.

LO⁴ The Agricultural Transformation, 10,000–4000 B.C.E.

Between 10,000 and 11,500 years ago, people who had survived largely by hunting and gathering during the Mesolithic period began to develop simple agricul-ture. This momentous change marked the beginning of the Neolithic period, a time when humans began to master the environment in unprecedented ways. As agriculturalists, people now deliberately altered the ecological system by cultivating the soil, selecting seeds, and breeding animals that could help them survive. The shift from hunting and gathering to farming was one of the greatest transitions in history, and it changed human life all over the world. The earth's surface was also transformed as trees and grass were cleared from one-tenth of the planet for plowing. The production of a food surplus set the stage for everything that came later, including cities, states, social classes, and long-distance trade.

Environmental Change and Adaptation

Agriculture started with small, preliminary steps. Even before farming began, some people, like the villagers at Abu Hureyra in Syria, were settling alongside lakes or in valleys rich in wild grains that were easy to collect. Around the world, archaeologists have

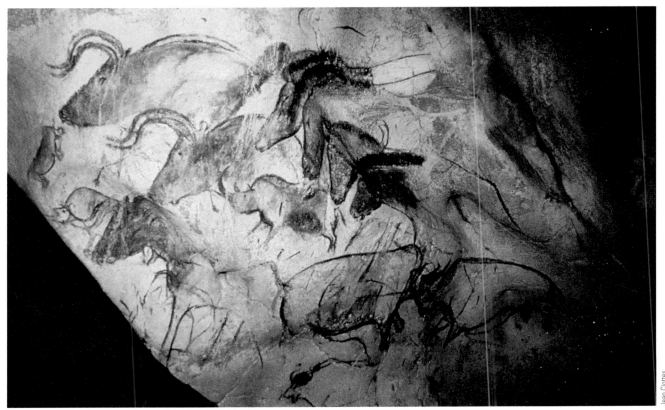

Cave Paintings in Europe This Ice Age painting of bison is from a cave at Altamira, Spain. Many paintings on cave walls have been found in France and Iberia. Paleolithic peoples all over the world painted pictures of the animals they hunted or feared as well as of each other, suggesting an increasing self-awareness.

horticulture
The growing of crops with simple methods and tools.

discovered clay-walled houses from the Neolithic period, as well as baskets, pottery, pits for storing grain, and equipment for hunting, fishing, and grain preparation. Probably the first farmers were simply reacting to environmental changes that were dooming the old ways. Documenting their steps taken in the transition to agriculture and settled life is not easy. Historical reconstruction depends largely on archaeological evidence, such as bones, artifacts, seeds, wild plants, tools, buildings, campsites, and the radiocarbon dating of the soils in which these things are discovered.

The Shift to Agriculture

Climate change and population growth were probably the most important factors in triggering the shift to agriculture. After the last great Ice Age, the earth entered a long period of unusual warmth, during which melting glaciers caused rising sea levels, covering about one-fifth of previously available land. Rising sea levels also covered over many land links, including those connecting the British Isles to continental Europe and Japan to Asia. Around 10,000 B.C.E., the world population had grown to perhaps 5 or 10 million, and in some regions, hunting and gathering could no longer meet the basic needs of everyone, especially as good land was submerged. But the warmer climate encouraged the spread of grasses, such as barley and wild wheat, which attracted grazing animals and food gatherers, who abandoned their nomadic ways to live near these rich food sources.

New Methods Emerge

The environment continued to change, posing new challenges. The earth cooled again briefly about 9000 B.C.E., reducing food supplies, and a drought in the Middle East presented a crisis for some food-gathering societies. Eventually it was no longer enough to just exploit local resources more efficiently. Responding to the challenges, hunters and gatherers like those at Abu Hureyra began to store food and learn how to cultivate their own grains. Former hunters and gatherers began to pioneer horticulture (HORE-tee-kuhl-chur), the growing of crops with simple methods and tools, such as the hoe or digging stick. Women were important to this process, because as the chief gatherers, they knew how plants grew and sprouted from seeds.

One major food-producing strategy was shifting cultivation, especially in wooded areas, where people could clear trees and underbrush by chopping and burning (hence the common term *slash and burn*). Once the area was cleared, they loosened the soil with digging sticks and finally scattered seeds around the

From A.M.T. Moore et al, *Village on the Euphrates: From Foraging to Farming at Abu Hureyra* (New York: Oxford University Press, 2000). © Oxford University Press
Photo: Andrew M.T. Moore

Ruins of Abu Hureyra The site of this ancient village overlooks the floodplain of the Euphrates River in northeastern Syria. The earliest settlement included intersecting pits that were turned into huts by roofs of reeds, branches, and poles.

area. Natural moisture such as rain helped the crops mature, but the soil became eroded after a few years, so shifting cultivators moved periodically to fresh land, returning to the original area only after the soil had recovered its fertility.

The Globalization and Diversity of Agriculture

Benefits and Challenges of the Settled Lifestyle

Farming promoted many radical changes in the way humans lived and connected with their environments. Agriculture could produce a much higher yield per acre and thus could support much denser populations in the same area. Permanent settlements also made possible the storage of food for future use, because the pots and buildings did not have to be moved periodically. Most people apparently believed farming was necessary for survival.

In some ways, however, farmers were more vulnerable to disaster from drought or other natural catastrophes. Food shortages may have become more rather than less common with farming. The earliest farmers could probably grow enough to feed themselves and their families with three or four hours of work per day. As they required more food to feed growing populations, they were forced to exploit local resources more intensively and to work harder in their fields. Some domesticated foods, like corn and bread, caused more dental problems and gum diseases than their wild counterparts. The Hebrew writer who recorded the biblical garden of Eden story blamed women for the hard work of farming: "Cursed is the ground for your sake; in toil you shall eat of it all the days of your life. In the sweat of your face you shall eat bread til you return to the ground."[3] Agriculture eventually depended on peasants, mostly poor farmers who worked small plots of land that were often owned by others.

Stonehenge and Other Megaliths

Whether for spiritual reasons or because of a new understanding of natural forces, some early farming peoples all over the world constructed megaliths, huge stone monuments. For example, Stonehenge was built in southern England in stages between 3100 and 1800 B.C.E. Some of the stone, weighing several tons, was obtained up to 140 miles away. Many scholars think Stonehenge was a ceremonial center where the community gathered at special times. It clearly served as an astronomical observatory, because its axis aligns with the summer solstice sunrise, an important time for Neolithic farmers.

The agricultural transformation eventually reached across the globe. Agriculture came first to Eurasia, where geography favored the movement of people to the east or west along the same general latitude, without abrupt climatic changes. Some peoples, such as those in Australia and the Arctic, did not or could not make the transition from food gathering because of environmental and geographical constraints. Nonetheless, the different regions all contributed significantly to the discovery and production of the food resources we use today (see Witness to the Past: Food and Farming in Ancient Cultural Traditions).

Agricultural Beginnings

Most archaeologists believe the earliest transition to farming occurred between 9500 and 8000 B.C.E. in the area of southwestern Asia known as the "Fertile Crescent." This includes what is today Iraq, Syria, central and eastern Turkey, and the Jordan River Valley. This region had many fast-growing plants with high nutritional value, such as wheat, barley, chickpeas, and peas. There is good evidence for the growing of grain crops by 8000 B.C.E., and scattered evidence for even earlier farming at a few sites such as Abu Hureyra. Food growing also began independently in several other parts of the world, although we still do not know precisely when (see Map 1.2). Clearly, several Asian peoples were among the earliest farmers: crop cultivation

Interactive Map

began around 7000 B.C.E. in China and New Guinea, 7000 or 6000 B.C.E. in India, 5000 or 4000 B.C.E. in Thailand, and 3000 B.C.E. in Island Southeast Asia.

Elsewhere the dates varied considerably. In the Mediterranean region, farming began in the Nile Valley by at least 6000 B.C.E., if not earlier, and in Greece by 6500 B.C.E. Agriculture reached northward to Britain and Scandinavia between 4000 and 3000 B.C.E. Farming may have spread into Europe with migrants from western Asia who intermarried with local people. People in Ethiopia were farming by 4500 B.C.E. In the Americas, cultivation apparently began in central Mexico between 7000 and 5500 B.C.E. and in the Andes (ANN-deez) highlands by 6000 B.C.E., if not earlier. Farming reached North America by 1000 B.C.E. The earliest crops that were grown varied according to local environments and needs. Millet dominated in cold North China, rice in tropical Southeast Asia, wheat and barley in the dry Middle East, yams and sorghum in West Africa, corn in upland Mesoamerica,

Food and Farming in Ancient Cultural Traditions

As agriculture became an essential foundation for survival, it became increasingly important in the traditions and mindsets of societies around the world. The following excerpts show three examples of how food and farming were reflected in the cultural traditions of ancient societies. The first, an Andean ritual chant many centuries old, is a prayer for successful harvests addressed to an ancient deity. The second is from a farmer's almanac from eighteenth-century B.C.E. Mesopotamia that offers guidance on cultivating a successful grain crop; this excerpt deals with preparing the field and seeding. The third reading, a song collected in China around 3,000 years ago, celebrates a successful harvest and explains how some of the bounty will be used.

Andean Chant

Oh Viracocha, ancient Viracocha, skilled creator, who makes and establishes "on the earth below may they eat, may they drink" you say; for those you have established, those you have made may food be plentiful. "Potatoes, maize, all kinds of food may there be."

Excerpt from Farmer's Almanac

Keep a sharp eye on the openings of the dikes, ditches and mounds [so that] when you flood the field the water will not rise too high in it. . . . Let shod oxen trample it for you; after having its weeds ripped out [by them and] the field made level ground, dress it evenly with narrow axes weighing [no more than] two thirds of a pound each. . . . Keep your eye on the man who puts in the barley seed. Let him drop the grain uniformly two fingers deep.. . . If the barley seed does not sink in properly, change your share. . . . Harvest it at the moment [of its fill strength].

Chinese Harvest Song

Abundant is the year, with much millet, much rice; But we have tall granaries, To hold . . . many myriads and millions of grain. We make wine, make sweet liquor, We offer it to ancestor, to ancestress, We use it to fulfill all the [religious] rites, To bring down blessings upon each and all.

Thinking About the Reading

1. Who did the Andeans believe determined the success of their harvest?
2. How did Mesopotamian farming depend on draft animals and cooperation?
3. How did ancient Chinese farmers use surplus grain and rice to fulfill obligations?

Sources: Brian M. Fagan, *Kingdoms of Gold, Kingdoms of Jade* (London: Thames and Hudson, 1991), p. 88; *The Book of Songs,* translated by Arthur Waley (London: George Allen and Unwin, 1954). Copyright by permission of the Arthur Waley Estate.

and potatoes in the high Andes. Some crops such as flax were grown for fiber to make clothing, while other plants had medicinal properties. Chinese were mixing herbs, acids, rice, and beeswax together to make a potent fermented alcoholic beverage by 7000 B.C.E. Southwest Asians began making wine from grapes and beer from barley between 6000 and 3000 B.C.E. The growing of fruits and nuts added variety to the diet.

Farming technology gradually improved. People living in highlands where slopes are steep, such as in Peru, Indonesia, China, or Greece, made their fields on terraces, which were laborious to construct and maintain. Then, as more people moved from highlands into valleys, they needed new techniques. Some people used water from nearby marshes or wells. On less well-watered plains, they built large-scale water projects such as irrigation canals.

The Domestication of Animals

The domestication of animals for human use developed in close association with crop raising and brought many advantages. As they continued to be bred in captivity, animals were gradually modified from their wild ancestors to supply meat and leather,

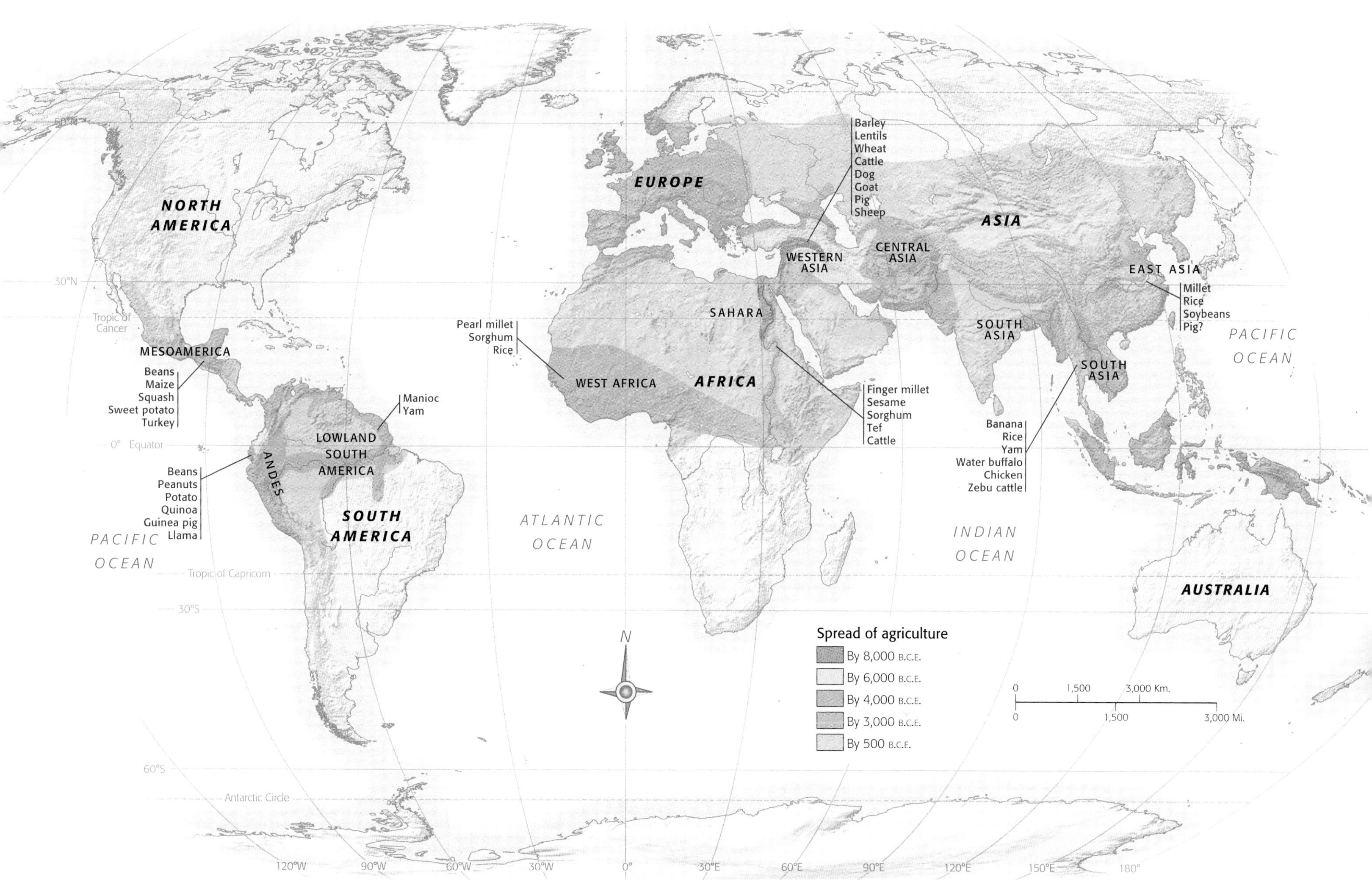

Map 1.2
The Origins of Agriculture

Between 11,500 and 7,000 years ago, people in western Asia, North and sub-Saharan Africa, southern Asia, East Asia, New Guinea, Mesoamerica, and South America developed agriculture independently and domesticated available animals. Later, most of these crops and some of the animals spread into other regions.

Spread of agriculture

- By 8,000 B.C.E.
- By 6,000 B.C.E.
- By 4,000 B.C.E.
- By 3,000 B.C.E.
- By 500 B.C.E.

WESTERN ASIA
Barley
Lentils
Wheat
Cattle
Dog
Goat
Pig
Sheep

EAST ASIA
Millet
Rice
Soybeans
Pig?

SOUTH ASIA
Banana
Rice
Yam
Water buffalo
Chicken
Zebu cattle

WEST AFRICA
Pearl millet
Sorghum
Rice

Finger millet
Sesame
Sorghum
Tef
Cattle

MESOAMERICA
Beans
Maize
Squash
Sweet potato
Turkey

LOWLAND SOUTH AMERICA
Manioc
Yam

ANDES
Beans
Peanuts
Potato
Quinoa
Guinea pig
Llama

© Cengage Learning

to aid in farming, to produce fertilizer, or to supply transportation. Horses and camels made long-distance travel and communication easier, while oxen pulled plows. Domesticated animals did pass on diseases to humans, but this eventually led to immunities among peoples in Eurasia. But Africa (except for cattle) and Australia lacked such animals, and most of the candidates in the Americas, such as the horse and camel, were extinct by 10,000 B.C.E. The only American possibilities were the gentle llamas and alpacas of the South American highlands, which Andean people used as pack animals by 3500 B.C.E.

CHRONOLOGY

The Transition to Agriculture, 10,000–500 B.C.E.

9500–8000	Southwestern Asia (Fertile Crescent)
8000	Vietnam (date disputed)
7000	Nubia (date disputed), China, Mexico, New Guinea
6500	Greece
6000	Northwestern India, Egypt, Andes, West Africa (disputed)
5000	Thailand (traditional view)
4900	Panama
4500	Ethiopia
4000	Britain, Scandinavia
3000	Island Southeast Asia, Tropical West Africa
1500	Amazon Basin
1000	Colorado
500	Southeast North America

Agriculture's Environmental Impact

At the same time that the environment influenced farming, the resulting population growth also contributed to environmental changes, some with negative consequences. Most hunters and gatherers, with limited technology and small numbers, left only a modest impact on their physical environment. Intensive agriculture more radically altered the ecology, especially as technology improved.

Technology: Blessing or Curse?

Technological innovation solved some problems for a while, but it did not always prove advantageous in the long run. For example, the invention of the plowshare made it easier to loosen dirt and eliminate weeds so that seeds could be planted deeper in nutrient-rich soil, but it also exposed topsoils to water and wind erosion. Similarly, vast irrigation networks provided the economic foundations for flourishing agriculture and denser settlement, but irrigation requires more labor than dry farming, and it can produce waterlogged land and also change the mineral content of the soil, eventually producing a thick salt surface that ruins farming. In Mesopotamia and the Americas, irrigation ultimately created deserts, leading to the rise and fall of entire societies.

Various activities contributed to environmental destruction. Farming and animal raising placed new demands on the land, as goats and cattle grazed on shrubs, tree branches, and seedlings, thus preventing forest regeneration. People exploited nearby forests for lumber to build wagons, tools, houses, furniture, and boats. Twenty-four centuries ago, the philosopher Plato bemoaned the deforestation of the Greek mountains, which he called "a mere relic of the original country. What remains is like the skeleton of a body emaciated by disease. All the rich soil has melted away, leaving a country of skin and bone."[4] Overgrazing and deforestation in the mountains feeding the main rivers produced silt that contained harmful salt and gypsum, which clogged canals and dams and transformed some fertile lands to salt desert.

The changing relationship of humans to their environment with farming generated new religious ideas. Early sacred and philosophical texts like the Hebrew book of Genesis often justified human domination over nature: its authors believed God told humans to "be fruitful and multiply; fill the earth and

Seated Goddess from Western Asia This baked-clay figure from one of the oldest towns in western Asia, Çatal Hüyük in Anatolia, shows an enthroned female, probably a goddess giving birth, guarded on both sides by cat-like animals—perhaps leopards.
C. M. Dixen/Ancient Art & Architecture Collection

subdue it; have dominion over the fish of the sea, over the birds of the air, and over every living thing that moves upon the earth."[5] Similarly, the Greek thinker Socrates argued that the gods were careful to provide everything in the natural world for human benefit.

LO⁵ The Emergence of Cities and States

Over time, farming hamlets in fertile areas grew into larger villages, and people began to see themselves as part of larger communities. Eventually these villages grew into the first cities, and in turn, cities established a foundation for the rise of states, trade networks, and writing.

New Technologies and the First Cities

Metalworking

While making possible complex societies, agriculture also fostered new technology. Many times in history, people came up against a serious resource problem, such as lack of food and water, and had to overcome the problem or perish. Often their solution was to develop some new technology, such as metalworking, which made possible a new level of human control over resources supplied by the environment. The first metalworking was done in Europe with copper for making weapons and tools as early as 7000 B.C.E., and in the Middle East by 4500 B.C.E. In fact, copper mining may have been the first real industry and commodity of the ancient world. Gold was also used and valued very early. These two soft metals could be fairly easily cut and shaped with stones.

Soon specialist craftsmen emerged to mine and work metals. By 3000 B.C.E. some of these specialists in western Asia had developed heating processes by which they could blend copper together with either tin or arsenic to create bronze. The bronze trade became a major spur to commerce in early Mesopotamia. By 1500 B.C.E. the technology for making usable iron had also been invented, although it took many centuries for people to perfect the new

alloy for practical use. Bronze and iron made better, more durable tools, but also more deadly weapons, and their use shaped many societies of the ancient and classical worlds (see "Societies, Networks, Transitions," page 91).

The Dynamics of Population

Agriculture also fostered population growth. By using cow's milk and grain meal for infant's food, women could now breast-feed for a shorter period and consequently bear children more frequently. In the Middle East, the population is believed to have grown in the space of 4,000 years (some 160 generations) from less than 100,000 in 8000 B.C.E. to more than 3 million by 4000 B.C.E. In more densely populated areas, farming villages grew into substantial, often prosperous towns. In one of the oldest towns, Çatal Hüyük (cha-TAHL hoo-YOOK) in central Turkey, roughly 10,000 residents lived in cramped mud-brick buildings from 6700 to 5700 B.C.E. The town's wealth derived from volcanic obsidian, which people converted into polished mirrors and traded around the region. Çatal Hüyük and similar towns became centers of long-distance trade and the basis for the first cities.

 Choose one of three identities in ancient civilization and explore what life was like through this interactive simulation.

The Urban Revolution

As people grouped together, they pioneered new ways of living. Through the process of urbanization, permanent settlements became larger and more complex, dominating nearby villages and farms. A city is a permanent settlement with a greater size, population, and importance than a town or village, and it usually contains many shops, public markets, government buildings, and religious centers. Cities emerged only where farmers produced more food than they needed for themselves and so could be taxed or coerced to share their excess crops. This surplus was critical to sustain nonfarming people such as priests, scribes, carpenters, and merchants.

What some call the urban revolution constituted a major achievement in different parts of the world,

> " Cities emerged only where farmers produced more food than they needed for themselves and so could be taxed or coerced to share their excess crops. "

Çatal Hüyük A view of rooms and walls in one of the first known towns, Çatal Hüyük in eastern Turkey. The ruins contained many art objects, murals, wall sculpture, and woven cloth.

perhaps as significant as the agricultural transformation. In southwest Asia, the first small cities were formed between 3500 and 3200 B.C.E.; they were administered by governments and dominated by new social hierarchies. Many cities were surrounded by walls, which the Greek philosopher Aristotle later called a city's "greatest protector [and] best military measure."[6] Many streets were lined by small shops and crowded with makeshift stalls selling foodstuffs, household items, or folk medicines. Craftsmen in workshops fashioned the items used in daily life, such as pottery, tools, and jewelry. Some of the goods made, mined, or grown locally were traded by land or sea to distant cities, fostering networks of communication and exchange.

The Rise of States

Food production and urbanization eventually led to the formation of states: formal political organizations or governments that controlled a recognized territory and exercised power over both people and things. The people within them—often from diverse ethnic and cultural backgrounds—did not necessarily share all the same values or allegiances. Nevertheless, complex urban societies organized into states developed at least 3,000 years ago on all of the inhabited continents except Australia.

Economic Diversification

These urban societies relied on diversified economies that generated enough wealth to permit a substantial division of labor and to support a social, cultural, and religious hierarchy. Farmers, laborers, craftsmen, merchants, priests, soldiers, bureaucrats, and scholars served specialized functions. Some states constructed monumental architecture, such as large temples, palaces, and city walls. While men dominated most of the hierarchies and heavy labor, women were responsible for textiles and other crafts, passing along their knowledge from mother to daughter.

Most urban societies were connected to elaborate trade networks extending well beyond the immediate region. The earliest known long-distance trade, by dugout canoes in Europe, dates to around 9000 B.C.E. By 4000 B.C.E. a network of merchant contacts linked India and Mesopotamia, 1,250 miles apart. Very crude mathematical calculations were being etched in bones by people in western Asia by 15,000 or 10,000 B.C.E., and clay counting tokens used for trade had appeared by 3100 B.C.E., if not earlier. By 5000 B.C.E. the first seafaring vessels had been built around the Persian Gulf to serve increased long-distance trade, and by 3500 B.C.E. these and other developments had set the foundation for more extensive networks linking diverse societies.

Bookkeeping and Storytelling

The early urban societies also introduced cultural innovations such as recordkeeping and literature. A system of recordkeeping could involve a written language, such as those developed by the Egyptians, Greeks, Arabs, Chinese, and Mayans, or records could be kept by a class of memory experts, as in some South American and African societies. Both nonliterate and literate societies created rich oral traditions of stories, legends, historical accounts, and poems, often nourished by specialists, that could be shared with all of the people.

Civilization: An Obsolete Term?

Some historians apply the term *civilization* to larger, more complex societies such as ancient Egypt and China, but this is a controversial concept with a long history of abuse. Modern historians may focus too much on societies that left more of an archaeological and written record, giving lesser attention to those societies that did not. The historian can cast a wide or narrow net in choosing which societies to consider "civilized." The term could refer to a large grouping of people with a common history and traditions, or it could be restricted to those large, complex urban societies that developed certain useful patterns such as bureaucratic governments, monumental architecture, and writing. Thus the term is too subjective to have much value, and many historians refuse to use it altogether. It is not used in this text.

Pastoral Nomadism

Some societies adopted an alternative to agriculture and cities known as pastoral nomadism, an economy based on breeding, rearing, and harvesting livestock. On the marginal land unsuitable for farming, some people began specializing in herding, moving their camps and animals seasonally in search of pasture. They traded meat, hides, or livestock to nearby farmers for grain. Both trade and conflict between the two contrasting groups, farmers and herders, became common. Pastoral nomadism was a highly specialized and developed way of life involving dispersed populations, yet some pastoral nomads exercised a strong influence on societies with much greater populations.

Pastoral nomads mostly concentrated in grasslands and deserts, which could sustain only small populations. Grasslands covered much of central and western Asia from Mongolia to southern Russia, as well as large parts of eastern and southern Africa. An even more inhospitable area was the Sahara region of northern Africa, which had become a huge, inhospitable desert habitable only by pastoralists by 2000 B.C.E.

Living along or beyond the frontiers of settled farming, the pastoralists lived very differently than farmers, but they were not culturally "unsophisticated." Herds had to be kept small and separated some distance from other herds to prevent overgrazing, so herders tended to live in small, dispersed kinship groups that were often part of tribes, associations of clans that traced descent from a common ancestor. Pastoralists domesticated horses in Central Asia around 4300 B.C.E. (Horses reached western Asia by 2000 B.C.E. Although camels were domesticated around 3000 or 2500 B.C.E. in Arabia, they were not widely used in western Asia until sometime after 1500 B.C.E.) Pastoralists were also capable of undertaking ambitious projects. Around 5000 B.C.E., Sahara cattle-herders built a remarkable megalithic ceremonial center of large stones to mark astronomical changes. Like other societies, pastoralists had humane values, a rich cultural life, and various networks to other peoples.

pastoral nomadism
An economy based on breeding, rearing, and harvesting livestock.

tribes
Associations of clans that traced descent from a common ancestor.

Indo-Europeans
Various tribes who all spoke related languages that derived from some original common tongue and who eventually settled Europe, Iran, and northern India.

The Structure of Pastoral Society

There were many differences among pastoralists. Whereas some societies maintained egalitarian social structures, others were headed by chiefs. In some of the pastoral societies of Central Asia, women seem to have held a high status and to even have served as warriors. Burial mounds in Turkestan contain the remains of what may be female warriors from 2,500 years ago, who were buried with daggers, swords, and bronze-tipped arrows. Some pastoralists became tough, martial peoples who were greatly feared by the farmers. As discussed in later chapters, Central Asian pastoralists like the Huns and Mongols played a central role in world history before modern times.

The Indo-Europeans

Among the pastoral nomads who had a great influence on world history were the various tribes known collectively as the Indo-Europeans (IN-dough-YUR-uh-PEE-uns). Historians derive this term from the original common tongue that spawned the many related languages spoken today by these peoples' descendants. Some scholars think these societies arose either in the Caucasus Mountains or in what is now southern Russia, whereas others place them in eastern Anatolia (modern Turkey). Eventually, because of the spread of these seminomadic and strongly patriarchal tribes and their languages, most people in Europe, Iran, and northern India came to speak Indo-European languages.

Indo-European expansion apparently occurred in several waves. According to recent studies, some Indo-Europeans may have moved into Europe and central Asia as early as 6500 or 7000 B.C.E., perhaps carrying with them not only their language but also farming technology, both of which they shared with, or imposed on, the local peoples. The culturally mixed people who resulted may have been the ancestors of, among others, the Celts and Greeks. Sometime between 3000 and 2000 B.C.E., many of the Indo-Europeans remaining in Anatolia and the Caucasus, most of them pastoralists, were driven from their homeland by some disaster, perhaps drought, prolonged frost, or plague. The various tribes dispersed in every direction, splitting up into smaller, more cohesive units and driving their herds of cattle, sheep, goats, and horses with them. As they encountered farming peoples, they turned to conquest in order to occupy the land (see Map 1.3).

Interactive Map

Map 1.3
The Indo-European Migrations and Eurasian Pastoralism

Some societies, especially in parts of Africa and Asia, adapted to environmental contexts by developing a pastoral, or animal herding, economy. One large pastoral group, the Indo-Europeans, eventually expanded from their home area into Europe, southwestern Asia, Central Asia, and India.

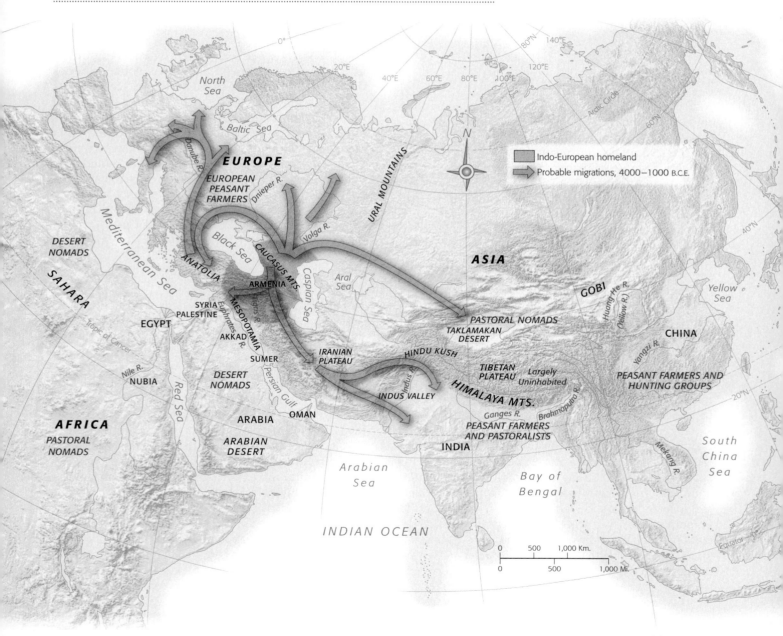

Listen to a synopsis of Chapter 1.

This dispersal of peoples from the Indo-European heartland set the stage for profound changes across Eurasia. The Hittites gained dominance in Anatolia and then, around 2000 B.C.E., expanded their empire into Mesopotamia. Other tribes pushed on between 2500 and 1500 B.C.E., some to the west across Anatolia into Greece, some to the east as far as the western fringe of China, some south into Persia (Iran). From Persia some tribes moved southeast through the mountain passes into northwestern India. Everywhere they went, the Indo-Europeans spread their languages and imposed their military power, eventually absorbing or subduing the peoples they encountered. Their spread opened a new chapter in the history of Europe, the Middle East, and India.

CHAPTER 2

Ancient Societies in Mesopotamia, India, and Central Asia,

5000–600 B.C.E.

Learning Outcomes

After reading this chapter, you should be able to answer the following questions:

LO¹ Why did farming, cities, and states develop first in the Fertile Crescent?

LO² What were some of the main features of Mesopotamian societies?

LO³ What were some of the distinctive features of the Harappan cities?

LO⁴ How did the Aryan migrations reshape Indian society?

LO⁵ How did Indian Society and the Hindu religion emerge from the mixing of Aryan and local cultures?

❝Inanna filled Agade [a Mesopotamian city], her home, with gold. She filled the storerooms with barley, bronze, and lumps of lapis lazuli [a stone used in jewelry]. The ships at the wharves were an awesome sight. All the lands around rested in security.**❞**

—Poem praising the goddess of love and generosity, written in 2250 B.C.E.[1]

Some 5,000 years ago in the Mesopotamian (MESS-uh-puh-TAIM-ee-an) city of Uruk (OO-rook), an unknown artist carved a beautiful narrative relief on a large stone-pedestaled vase, the first such sculpture known in history, and donated it to the city's temple for the goddess of love, Inanna (ih-NON-ah), the first known goddess in recorded history. The scenes of domestic and religious life celebrate a festival honoring the goddess, who, the sculptor believed, had blessed Uruk's people with growing herds and good crops. The Warka vase, as it is known today, reflects the artistic skill of a fine craftsman and depicts the social order and rituals of one of the world's earliest cities.

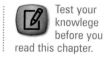

Test your knowlege before you read this chapter.

What do you think?

Trade and migration networks were the most significant influences in the development of early human societies.

Strongly Disagree   *Strongly Agree*
1   *2*   *3*   *4*   *5*   *6*   *7*

Sometime after the people in southwest Asia and India had become farmers, they began to make the next great transition by founding the first cities, like Uruk and Agade (uh-GAH-duh), and the first states. Various urban societies eventually formed in the Indus Valley in northwestern India and all along the **Fertile Crescent**, a large semicircle of fertile land that included the valleys of the Tigris (TIE-gris) and Euphrates (you-FRAY-teez) Rivers stretching northwest from the Persian Gulf, the eastern shores of the Mediterranean Sea, and, some scholars argue, the banks of the Nile River in Egypt. The Mesopotamians in the Fertile Crescent divided their labor into specialized tasks assigned to full-time farmers, professional soldiers, government officials, artisans, and priests. To the east, the people

Fertile Crescent
A large semicircular fertile region that included the valleys of the Tigris and Euphrates Rivers stretching northwest from the Persian Gulf, the eastern shores of the Mediterranean Sea, and, to some scholars, the banks of the Nile River in North Africa.

≪ **Bull's Head from Sumerian Lyre** This bull's head is part of the sound box of a wooden harp. The harp, made in Sumeria around 2600 B.C.E., is covered with gold and lapis lazuli and reflects the popularity of music in Mesopotamian society.

in ancient India also divided their society into social classes and established the foundations for Hinduism and Buddhism.

Among the Mesopotamians and Indians, the first dramatic changes in human life arose from contact through trade or warfare. Various Afro-Eurasian peoples built the foundations to sustain large populations. For at least three millennia, a large majority of the world's population has lived in an arc stretching from Egypt and Mesopotamia eastward through India and China to Japan. The people of western Asia created the first systematic use of writing, the first working of bronze, the first large states and empires, and the first institutionalized religions to worship deities like Inanna. These societies also constructed networks to exchange products and information over long distances. Agade, the hub for such a network, was visited by traders from near and far. Over time the Middle East, which includes North Africa and western Asia, became a crossroads between Europe, Africa, and southern Asia. And Mesopotamia was for centuries a great hub for trade and communication networks extending to distant lands.

LO¹ Early Mesopotamian Urbanized Societies, to 2000 B.C.E.

Geography and Cultural Development

The creation of small city-states around 5,000 years ago made Mesopotamia, and especially the southern part of the Tigris-Euphrates Valley, the home of some of the world's earliest urban societies. Geography played a key role in this region's transition to farming and then to urbanization and state building. Even in these early millennia, the connections between diverse peoples helped cultures change and grow. Over the centuries, various peoples moved into the area, building the first great cities and developing a written language. The cities were dominated by religious temples and had elaborate social class structures. As conquerors combined various city-states into a series of ever-larger states, empires were formed, and Mesopotamian societies were soon linked by trade to the Mediterranean and North Africa.

The Mesopotamian Environment

Life in these early societies owed much to the geographic features that brought people together. Most early urban societies began first in wide river valleys such as the Tigris-Euphrates, Indus, and Nile Valleys, because such places provided life-giving irrigation for the crops that supported larger populations. In the case of Mesopotamia (the Greek word for the "land between the rivers"), the first known cities and states arose in the Tigris-Euphrates Basin, a region stretching from the western edge of the Persian Gulf through today's Iraq into Syria and southeastern Turkey. The long river valley promoted interaction between peoples, both friendly and hostile. To the northwest the mountainous Anatolia (ANN-uh-TOE-lee-uh) Peninsula (modern Turkey) provided the key link between Asia and Europe. East of Mesopotamia lay Persia (present-day Iran), a land of mountains and deserts and the pathway to India and Central Asia. To the south the Arabian peninsula, largely desert, was characterized by oasis agriculture and nomadic pastoralism.

Although the rivers provided water, other characteristics of this region and its climate were not so generous. Ancient Mesopotamia had a climate similar to southern California today. Most rain fell in the winter, and summer temperatures in some places reached 120 degrees Fahrenheit. During the long, arid summer, the land, which was mostly composed of clay soils, baked stone-hard, and searing winds blew up a choking dust. Vegetation withered. The winter was little more comfortable, as winds, clouds, and the occasional rains made for stormy and bleak days. In spring the rains and melting snows in the nearby mountains flooded rivers, sometimes submerging the plains for miles around. Still, the annual but unpredictable floods created natural levees that could be drained and planted, and the nearby swamps contained abundant fish and wildlife.

 Exploring Ancient World Cultures (*http://eawe.evansville.edu/index/htm*). Excellent site run by Evansville University, with essays and links on the ancient Near East and Europe.

The Mesopotamian Melting Pot

Despite its harsh geography and climate, Mesopotamia saw the first transitions to settled agriculture and then to urbanization. Long before

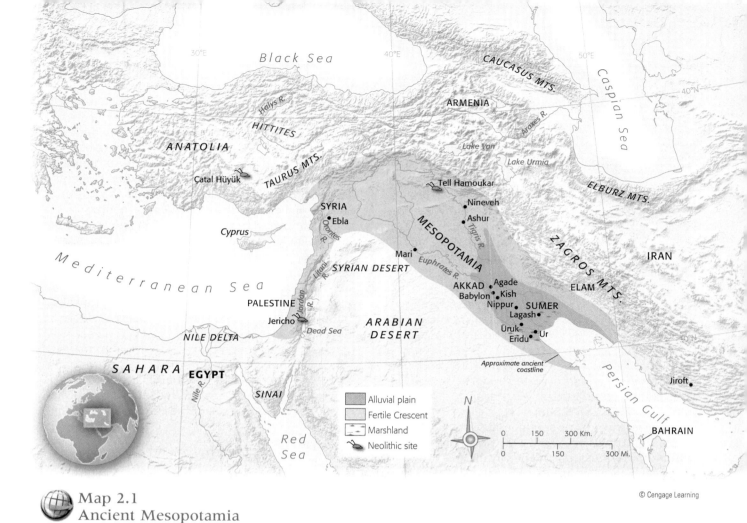

Map 2.1
Ancient Mesopotamia

The people of Mesopotamia and the adjacent regions of the Fertile Crescent pioneered farming, built the first cities, and formed the first states.

© Cengage Learning

Sumerians built the first cities at the head of the Persian Gulf, the transition to farming had taken place in various places of the Tigris-Euphrates Basin as well as in Palestine. By 9000 B.C.E., Jericho (JER-ah-ko), located near the Jordan River, was an agricultural community that had some two thousand people at its height. Excavated storage rooms, town walls, and a round storage tower indicate a complex town organization. Diverse peoples and languages contributed to the history and identity of the region, some of them speaking Semitic languages, including Arabic and Hebrew, which are related to some African tongues. Speakers of Turkic and of Indo-European languages such as Persian, Armenian, and Kurdish arrived later.

The Tigris and Euphrates Rivers fostered several Mesopotamian societies. Both rivers begin in eastern Anatolia and flow southeast more than one thousand miles to the Persian Gulf. The modern city of Baghdad is midway up the Tigris, and the ancient city of Babylon was only a few miles away on the Euphrates, where the two rivers flow closest to each other. Sometime after

6500 B.C.E., the population of farmers and herders in the fertile hills on either side of these rivers increased, and between 6200–5800 B.C.E., they left the hill country and created the first towns in the marshy, fertile areas near the head of the Persian Gulf. Although these people had been raising cattle and sheep and growing wheat and barley for several thousand years, after moving to the river valleys they worked together to build elaborate irrigation canals so they could grow food after the annual floods. Thus irrigation laid the foundations for organized societies and then cities, but the salts it added eventually created infertile desert.

The Pioneering Sumerians

People built the first Mesopotamian cities and states in Sumer (soo-MUHR), the lower part of the Tigris-Euphrates Valley in southern Iraq (see Map 2.1). By 3500 B.C.E., Uruk had grown into a city, eventually reaching a population of 50,000.

Interactive Map

From the archaeological discoveries at Tell Hamoukar, on the northern fringe of the Tigris-Euphrates Valley in modern Syria, some scholars suspect that other peoples may have been as important as the Sumerians in forging the first states, but our knowledge of the Sumerians is much more extensive.

Sumerian Infrastructure

The various settlers created elaborate canal systems and, by 3000 B.C.E., a network of city-states—urban centers surrounded by agricultural land controlled by the city and used to support its citizens. These earliest territorial political units allowed Sumerian societies to grow, to perhaps several million people, by 2500 B.C.E. Uruk was surrounded by 5 miles of fortified walls and had extended its influence through trade as far north as modern Turkey by 3500 B.C.E. A military attack by Uruk on the city of Tell Hamoukar in northern Mesopotamia is the world's oldest known example of large-scale organized warfare.

Myth and Urban Life

Sumerians had little sense of being citizens, as we understand that term, but they were clearly proud of their cities. A Sumerian myth begins with the lines "Behold the bond of Heaven and Earth, the city. Behold the kindly wall, the city, its pure river, its quay where the boats stand. Behold its well of good water. Behold its pure canal."[2] The city-dwellers lived in mud-baked brick houses constructed around courtyards. The largest building in any Sumerian city was the temple, or **ziggurat** (ZIG-uh-rat), a stepped, pyramidal-shaped building that was seen as the home of that city's chief god. One of these temples may have inspired the later Hebrew story of the tower of Babel (BAY-buhl/BAH-buhl).

Sumerian Economy and Culture

The social, political, and economic structures of Sumerian society became hierarchical, with some people having higher ranks than others. In the early years, decision-making assemblies of leading citizens governed the cities, appointing a city leader, sometimes a woman, with both secular and religious authority. However, with the waging of wars, male rulers, priests, and nobles came to dominate their populations. War leaders became kings and formed large armies, thus weakening the power of the assemblies and priests. Either the nobility or the priests controlled most of the land in and around the city, which was tilled by tenant farmers or slaves, and many of these common people became dependent on the nobles or priests for their survival. A Sumerian proverb claimed that "the poor man is better dead than alive; if he has bread, he has no salt; if he has salt, he has no bread."[3] The many slaves, who included captives taken in battles and criminals, were treated as personal property but allowed to marry. If a slave married a free woman, the children were free. Eventually royal officials, nobility, and priests controlled most of the economic life of the cities.

> ❝ The poor man is better dead than alive; if he has bread, he has no salt; if he has salt, he has no bread. ❞
>
> *Sumerian proverb*

Patriarchal Society

As it was the first of many male-governed societies, Sumeria introduced **patriarchy**, a system in which men largely control women and children and shape ideas about appropriate gender behavior. Sumerian women were generally subservient to men and excluded from government, but they could inherit property, run their own businesses, and serve as witnesses in court. A queen enjoyed much respect as the wife of the king. Sumerian religion also allowed a woman to be the high priestess if the city divinity was female. A proverb suggested the importance of women in the family but also the stereotypes they faced: "The wife is a man's future; the son is a man's refuge; the daughter is a man's salvation; the daughter-in-law is a man's devil."[4]

The Sumerian Trade Network

Because of their location and lack of natural resources, the Sumerian cities engaged in extensive trade, which helped form networks with neighboring societies and had significant consequences for world history. Even today, satellite images reveal the outlines of the 5,000-year-old road system that linked Mesopotamian cities. Sumerians imported copper from Armenia in the Caucasus Mountains and then discovered how to mix it with tin to make bronze. This alloy made for stronger weapons, which they often used against each other, thus launching the Bronze Age. The Sumerians also imported gold, ivory, obsidian, and other necessities from Anatolia, the Nile Valley, Ethiopia, India, the Caspian Sea, and the eastern shore of the Mediterranean.

The Persian Gulf became a major waterway, with many trading ports. Bahrain (bah-RAIN) Island served as a hub where various traders and travelers met. Mesopotamian merchants traveled to this port of exchange carrying cargoes of textiles, leather objects, wool, and olive oil, and they returned with copper, ivory, precious objects, and rare woods from various Western Asian societies and India. Already this early in history, trade helped people learn and profit from each other's skills and surplus goods.

The Sumerians also seem to have had some trade and other connections with another urban-based farming society known as Jiroft (JEER-oft), located in southeastern Iran. Jiroft seems to have emerged sometime between 3000 and 2500 B.C.E., with a rural economy based on cultivating date palms. Mesopotamian texts describe a state they called Aratta, a possible reference to Jiroft. Aratta's gaily decorated capital city had lofty red brick towers, and the rulers supplied artisans and craftsmen to Uruk.

> "Archaeologists have found the world's oldest known board games in the ruins of the farming society of Jiroft."

The ruins of the main Jiroft city, a regional commercial center, include a two-story citadel and a Sumerian-like ziggurat. Archaeologists have found the world's oldest known board games and staggering numbers of decorated vases, cups, and boxes there. The people adorned their products with precious stones from India and Afghanistan and decorations resembling the gods, plants, and beasts of Sumeria.

The First Written Records

The Sumerians were innovators in many areas. Although a few scholars think the Egyptians, Indians, or Chinese might have developed a simple writing system at least as early as the Sumerians, most still credit the Sumerians with producing the first written records. Trade and the need to keep accurate records of agricultural production and public and private business dealings led around 3200 B.C.E. to one of the most significant Sumerian contributions. This was their cuneiform (kyoo-NEE-uh-form) (Latin for "wedge-shaped") writing system, in which temple record-keepers, or scribes, began to keep records of financial transactions by making rough pictures (say,

Overview of Early City of Uruk This photo shows the ruins of one of the earliest Mesopotamian cities, a rich source of art objects and fine architecture. The best-known king of Uruk was the legendary Gilgamesh.

of an animal or fish) on soft clay with a stylus that made wedges in the clay. They then baked the bricks on which these pictograms were scratched. Writing provided a way of communicating with people over long distances and allowed rulers to administer larger states. Those who controlled the written word—like those who master electronic communication in our day—had power, prestige, and a monopoly over a society's official history. Because writing required mastery of at least three hundred symbols, those who learned to write largely came from the upper class. To teach writing the Sumerians created the world's first schools, where strict instructors beat students for misbehavior or sloppy work.

Writing became crucial in human history for several reasons. First, written language made it easier to express abstract ideas and create an intellectual life based on a body of literature. The oldest known signed poetry was composed by Enheduanna (en-who-DWAHN-ah), a Sumerian priestess, theologian, and princess living around 2300 B.C.E. Eventually writing also helped explain the physical world in rational instead of magical terms. In addition, a written language based on clearly understood symbols, whether phonetic or pictographic, allowed communication among people who spoke different languages but understood the same written symbols. Finally, writing was one key to the interaction among societies, encouraging the spread of trade and culture to those outside a particular homeland. Through this process, some people became multilingual.

Sumerian Innovation These first city-builders were innovative in many areas. They pioneered the first use of the wheel, glass, and fertilizer, and also created some of the earliest calendars, which were based on their observations of the movements of various celestial bodies. Theirs was one of the first mathematical systems, based on the number 60; remnants of this system can be seen today in our 60-minute hours and 60-second minutes. Later the

Cuneiform Tablet This letter, impressed on a clay tablet in Mesopotamia around 1900 B.C.E., records a merchant's complaint that a shipment of copper that he had paid for contained too little metal. Letters, written chiefly by merchants and officials, were enclosed in envelopes made of clay and marked with the sender's private seal.
Courtesy of the Trustees of the British Museum

Babylonians improved Sumerian mathematics by developing a simple calculator with tables of squares, cubes, reciprocals, square roots, and cube roots.

The Akkadian Empire and Its Rivals

Sargon and Akkad: The First Imperial State Eventually the political structure of the region changed. In the beginning, the Sumerian cities were related by a common culture but not a common ruler. Each city had its own king who ruled the people in the name of the city's god. This independence ended about 2350 B.C.E., when Sargon (SAHR-gone), the ruler of Akkad (AH-kahd), a region just north of Sumer whose capital was Agade, conquered Uruk as a prelude to uniting the other Sumerian cities under the rule of his family. Sargon formed the world's first known empire, a large state controlling other societies through conquest or domination. He declared, "I conquered the land, and the sea three times I circled."[5] The Akkadians enslaved many other people in addition to the Sumerians; in fact, slaves constituted perhaps one-third of the empire's population in 2300 B.C.E. Under Sargon, trade between Mesopotamia and India reached a peak, and Akkad became the major center for regional trade.

Struggles between rival cities became endemic, generating frequent warfare. Sargon's empire soon came into conflict with one created by another imperial city, Ebla (EBB-luh), in northern Mesopotamia. Ebla had a population of 30,000 and subject peoples totaling another 200,000 or more, its empire stretching from eastern Turkey to the ancient city of Mari (MAH-ree), several hundred miles north of Akkad.

The Akkadian Empire was destroyed by the twenty-first century B.C.E., probably from a combination of internal conflicts, external attacks, and climate change. Mesopotamian societies such as Sumer and Akkad were powerless against abrupt climate change that could reduce rainfall dramatically. Sumerian legends expressed dread of the periodic droughts: "The famine was severe, nothing was produced. The fields are not watered. In all the lands there was no vegetation [and] only weeds grew."[6] A disastrous drought began in 2200 B.C.E., affecting much of Eurasia, and lasted for 300 years. Irrigation canals silted up and settlements became ghost towns.

Ur and the Neo-Sumerian Empire

As the Akkadian Empire collapsed, a new Sumerian dynasty led by Ur took over much of the lower valley between 2100 and 2000 B.C.E., forming what historians term the Neo-Sumerian Empire. Some Ur kings boasted of their commitment to art and intellectual life, one ordering that the places of learning should never be closed. But Ur was devastated by a coalition of enemies and sacked and burned along with other Sumerian cities. A surviving lamentation describes the destruction of Ur in graphic detail: "Ur is destroyed, bitter is its lament. The country's blood now fills its holes like hot bronze in a mould. Our temple is destroyed, the gods have abandoned us, like migrating birds. Smoke lies on our city like a shroud."[7]

The Akkadians, Eblaites, and the later Sumerians established the first empires in history, even though their creations were short-lived and were not the large bureaucratic organizations we see in later empires. They were largely collections of city-states that acknowledged one city as overlord, especially

> **❝Our temple is destroyed, the gods have abandoned us, like migrating birds. Smoke lies on our city like a shroud.❞**
>
> *Sumerian lamentation*

when the ruler's troops were present. However, once the pattern of one city dominating others was established, it soon became clear that whoever had the best army would dominate Mesopotamia.

LO² Later Mesopotamian Societies and Their Legacies, 2000–600 B.C.E.

The Sumerians and Akkadians established a pattern of city living, state building, and imperial expansion. From 2000 B.C.E. and continuing for the next 1,500 years, a series of peoples, coming mainly from the north, successively dominated Mesopotamia and created new empires. The Babylonians, Hittites, and Assyrians made important contributions to the politics, laws, culture, and thought of the region. This pattern changed only when the entire area was incorporated into the Persian Empire in 539 B.C.E., launching a new era in the region's history.

 Internet Ancient History Sourcebook (*http://www.fordham .edu/halsall/ancient/ asbook.html*). Exceptionally rich collection of links and primary source readings.

The Royal Standard of Ur This mosaic from around 2500 B.C.E., made of inlaid shells and limestone, was found in a royal tomb. It depicts various aspects of life in the Mesopotamian city-state of Ur.

British Museum/Michael Holford

The Babylonians and Hittites

The Code of Hammurabi

Several states dominated Mesopotamia during the second millennium B.C.E., beginning with the Amorite kingdom of Babylon. In 1800 B.C.E. the Amorites (AM-uhr-ites), a Semitic people, conquered Babylon, a city about 300 miles north of the Persian Gulf on the Euphrates, and gradually extended their control in the region. Babylon's most famous king, Hammurabi (HAM-uh-rah-bee), who ruled from 1792 to 1750 B.C.E., reunified Mesopotamia. Hammurabi had nearly three hundred laws collected and "published" on a black basalt pillar erected near the modern city of Baghdad. These laws were designed, he said, "to make justice appear in the land, to destroy the evil and the wicked [so] that the strong might not oppress the weak."[8] Hammurabi's law code remains famous today because some of its principles appeared later in the laws of the Hebrews, and also because of its most noted principle, the law of retaliation: an eye for an eye and a tooth for a tooth.

The Hittites

Hammurabi's successors were able to hold his empire together for little over a century, but by 1595 B.C.E., the Babylonian Empire had been overcome by the Hittites (HIT-ites), an Indo-European people who moved into Mesopotamia from their base in central Anatolia. Much later, around 1500 B.C.E., the Hittites became famous for their later use of iron weapons, which were superior to those made of bronze, but these had not yet been invented when the Hittites invaded Mesopotamia. The Hittites may also have used the first known biological weapons, because one of their tactics was to send plague victims into enemy lands. The Hittite Empire dominated various parts of western Asia from 1600 to 1200 B.C.E. Despite their militarism, the Hittites established a tradition of religious tolerance and adopted many Mesopotamian gods.

CHRONOLOGY

Mesopotamia, 5500–330 B.C.E.

5500	First Sumerian settlements
3200	First cuneiform writing
3000–2300	Sumerian city-states
2750	Model for legendary Gilgamesh rules Uruk
ca. 2500–2100	Jiroft
ca. 2350–2160	Akkadian Empire unified Mesopotamia
ca. 2100–2000	Neo-Sumerian Empire led by city of Ur
ca. 2000	*Epic of Gilgamesh* written in cuneiform
ca. 1800–1595	Old Babylonian Empire
ca. 1790–1780	Hammurabi's Law Code
ca. 1600–1200	Hittite Empire
ca. 1115–605	Assyrian Empire
745–626	Height of Assyrian Empire
ca. 626–539	Chaldean (Neo-Babylonian) Empire
ca. 539–330	Persian Empire

The Rise and Fall of the Assyrian Empire

For several centuries after Hittite power declined, no one group dominated Mesopotamia for long. In 1115 B.C.E., however, the Assyrians (uh-SEER-e-uhns), named for their major city, Ashur, created an empire in western Asia larger than any before, the first that was more than a collection of city-states. They did this in three ways: (1) by creating a large, well-organized, and balanced military; (2) by systematically using terror against enemies; and (3) by devising methods of bureaucratic organization that later empires, especially the Persian, imitated. One of the greatest kings, Tiglath-pileser (TIG-lath-pih-LEE-zuhr) III (745–727 B.C.E.), conquered the entire eastern shore of the Mediterranean as far south as Gaza.

Assyrian kings ruled over their several million subjects by increasing the number of administrative districts and making local officials responsible only to the kings. To improve their administrative control, the rulers used horsemen to send messages hundreds of miles within a week. Some kings were both brutal and learned. Ashurbanipal (ah-shur-BAH-nuh-pahl) (680–627 B.C.E.) founded a great library and boasted of his learning, noting that he learned to solve complex mathematical problems and discovered the "hidden treasure" of writing. The Assyrians also tolerated other religions, a policy that allowed the Hebrew faith to survive the conquest of their state.

Weapons and Warfare

Assyrian armies made war serious business. Using iron weapons while their enemies still relied on softer bronze ones, the Assyrians launched armies of more than 50,000 men that were carefully divided into a core of infantrymen aided by cavalry and horse-drawn chariots. In addition, the Assyrians conducted sieges in which they used battering rams and tunnels against the city walls of their enemies, and employed guerrilla tactics when fighting in the forests or mountains.

Choose one of three identities in ancient civilization and explore what life was like through this interactive simulation.

The Assyrians' brutality ultimately contributed to their downfall. After destroying the state of Elam, King Ashurbanipal boasted that "like the onset of a terrible hurricane I overwhelmed Elam [a state in southwestern Iran]. I cut off the head of Teumman, their braggart king. In countless numbers I killed his warriors." As to the capital city, "I destroyed it, I devastated it, I burned it with fire."⁹ Soldiers routinely looted cities, destroyed crops, and both flailed and impaled their enemies. Such terror tactics understandably undermined Assyrian popularity.

The Chaldean Empire and Nebuchadnezzer

In 612 B.C.E., a coalition including the Chaldeans (kal-DEE-uhns) (also known as neo-Babylonians) captured the Assyrian capital at Nineveh (NIN-uh-vuh). The Chaldeans, who formed the last Mesopotamian empire, adopted the Assyrian administrative system and flourished from 626 B.C.E. until they were conquered by the much larger Persian Empire in 539 B.C.E. Their most memorable ruler, Nebuchadnezzar (NAB-oo-kuhd-nez-uhr) II (r. 605–562 B.C.E.), a brutal strongman, rebuilt Babylon and adorned it with magnificent palaces and the elaborate terraced "hanging gardens," which became famous throughout the ancient world. Nebuchadnezzar led the conquest of the remaining Hebrew kingdom in 586 B.C.E.

Mesopotamian Law, Religion, and Culture

Social Justice

Several different documents tell us much about Mesopotamian life and beliefs. The eighteenth-century B.C.E. law code of Hammurabi is one of the earliest systematic records we have of how ancient peoples viewed laws, government, and social norms. The code probably reflected a high crime rate in the cities, no doubt because of the tremendous gap between rich and poor, but it also addressed violations of social custom. Families were responsible for the crimes of any of their members. To keep lines of inheritance clear, Hammurabi prescribed harsh punishments for sexual infidelity and incest, as did many societies. Women who violated social norms generally suffered harsher punishments than men, just as the eyes and teeth of poor men or slaves were worth less than the same body parts among the upper classes.

Read about Hammurabi, the multitalented Babylonian king who came to personify Mesopotamian society.

Hammurabi's laws made clear that slaves could expect little sympathy, yet some slaves owned their own assets, carried on business, and even acquired their own slaves.

The code also addressed economic issues. In this class-conscious society, a surgeon could lose his hand if his patient failed to survive the operation. If a builder's house collapsed and killed its inhabitants, the builder could be executed. The existence of a thriving commercial class is confirmed by the existence of high interest rates on loans. One law limited an interest rate on loans to only 20 percent. In general, the punishments in Hammurabi's law code tell us how precarious life must have been in this society, where even a single small break in an irrigation canal wall could spell disaster.

Religion and Literature

Like most early people, the Mesopotamians believed in a host of gods and goddesses, such as Inanna, later called Ishtar (ISH-tar), the beautiful goddess of love who created desire. These divinities represented heavenly bodies or natural forces and came with human weaknesses, yet they were powerful enough to punish humans, who were created to serve them. People saw themselves as subject to the gods' whims. The gods were housed in massive and opulent temples, where ritual ceremonies were held. The Babylonians and later the Assyrians changed the names of some of the earlier Sumerian gods but maintained the basic Sumerian view of the universe.

The *Epic of Gilgamesh* (GILL-guh-mesh), first composed late in the third millennium B.C.E. but revised and retold by Mesopotamians for fifteen hundred years, reveals some of their religious values and attitudes. In one version of the Gilgamesh story, the hero—modeled after a real king in Uruk about

2750 B.C.E. and created to be two-thirds god and one-third man—engages in a series of adventures involving both the gods and men. Perhaps humanity's first epic adventure story, *Gilgamesh* echoes Hammurabi's view of the world as a dangerous place in which happiness is hard to find. Although only one part of a very rich legacy of imaginative literature and mythology from Mesopotamia, *Gilgamesh* probably had the most enduring and widespread influence, enriching the traditions of varied Eurasian societies. The stories probably originated in Sumerian times and were eventually written down around 2000 B.C.E. A Uruk master scribe lamented around 1300 B.C.E.: "Gilgamesh, what you seek you will never find. For when the Gods created Man they let death be his lot, eternal life they withheld. Let your every day be full of joy, love the child that holds your hand, let your wife delight in your embrace, for these alone are concerns of humanity."[10]

The *Epic of Gilgamesh* Find out how Gilgamesh's friend Enkidu propels him on a quest for immortality, and whether or not that quest is successful.

Many scholars have pointed out parallels between the Gilgamesh legend and Genesis and postulate that the Gilgamesh story became widely known far beyond Mesopotamia. Some motifs can be found in the literature of the Greeks, such as the Homeric epics. They also reappear in the much later Islamic period, such as the stories of Aladdin and Sinbad. Gilgamesh and other myths remained common in some parts of western Asia down to at least the tenth century C.E., and they are still found in the folk cultures of some villages. The Gilgamesh epic became one of the many unique traditions that shaped the societies of southwestern Asia and made them different from other early societies such as India and Egypt.

LO³ The Earliest Indian and Central Asian Societies, 6000–1500 B.C.E.

India developed a society with cultural features vastly different from those of the Middle East, Europe, or China. Aided by environmental factors, some Indians made the transition to farming very early, in 7000 to 6000 B.C.E., and the first cities and states east of Mesopotamia were founded around 2600 B.C.E. Most scholars trace the foundations of Indian urban society to the city-states and the widespread Bronze Age culture they shared, often called **Harappan** (huh-RAP-un), that were centered in the Indus (IN-duhs) River Valley and nearby rivers in what is now Pakistan and northwest India. Harappan culture eventually covered some 300,000 square miles, the largest in geographical extent of the ancient societies. To the north, an urban society also developed in Central Asia.

South Asian Environments and the Rise of Farming

River valley environments strongly shaped the early societies of India, just as they did Mesopotamia, Egypt, and China. The Indian subcontinent, about half the size of Europe, is rimmed by the Indian Ocean to the south and the Himalayan Mountains to the north, which boast the half dozen highest peaks in the world and inhibited regular communication between China and India. Just north of the Himalayas, the Tibetan Plateau is the source of great rivers, including the Indus and Ganges in India, the Yellow and Yangzi in China, and the Irrawaddy and Mekong in Southeast Asia, which eventually reach great plains and deltas. The land proved highly fertile in these river basins, allowing for productive farming and dense settlement. Rice and wheat became the staple crops for most peoples in both South and East Asia, and scavenging animals like chickens and pigs were important food sources.

As with all societies, India's distinctive features and cultural diversity resulted in part from its physical environment and tropical climate. The annual rains, which usually fell in torrents within a period of two or three months, sustained life, but seasonal flooding could be a chronic problem. Water has been an especially sacred commodity in Indian life and thought, and a frequent subject of literature. Extensive rain forests once covered large sections of India and the island of Sri Lanka, but they have rapidly diminished in recent centuries.

The early Harappan farmers lived in mud houses and raised domesticated sheep, goats, and oxen. Because they had many domesticated cattle, most Indians also learned to consume dairy products, including yogurt, a local invention. Thanks to sur-

Internet Indian History Sourcebook (*http://www.fordham.edu/halsall/india/indiasbook.html*). An invaluable collection of sources and links on ancient India.

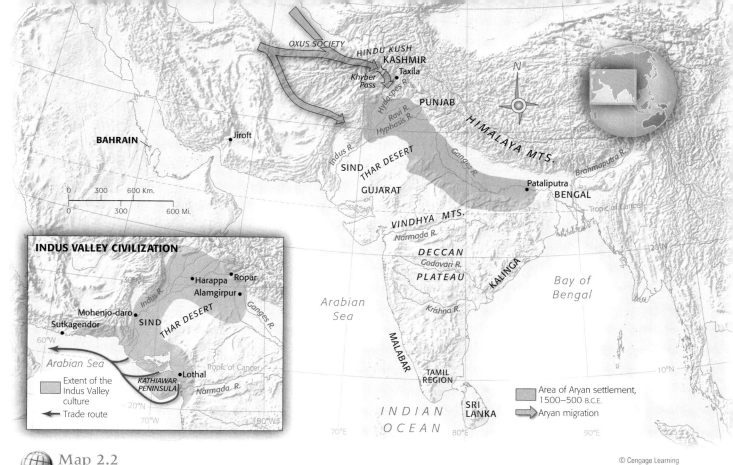

Map 2.2
Harappan Culture and Aryan Migrations
The Harappan culture emerged in the city-states of the Indus River Basin. They had collapsed by the time the Aryan peoples began migrating into India from Iran around 1500 B.C.E. and setting up states.

© Cengage Learning

 **Indus Valley Civilization** (*http:// ancienthistory.about .com/cs/indusvalley- civ/*). Gives access to many sites and links on ancient India.

pluses of wheat and barley, by 3000 B.C.E. the population of the Indus Valley may have reached 1 million, and regional trading networks emerged, setting the stage for the emergence of cities.

Around 2600 B.C.E., nearly a millennium after the rise of Sumer, the first Indian urban society emerged from regional cultures in the Indus River Valley, a semiarid region similar ecologically to the Nile and Tigris-Euphrates Valleys. Along the banks of the Indus, which later inspired the English term *India,* a vibrant urban-based culture thrived for hundreds of years and planted some seeds for the rich Indian culture that endures to the present. Silt spread by regular river floods served as a natural fertilizer, while nearby forests provided enough wood for baking the bricks used in building cities. Like the Nile in Egypt, the flat, easily navigable Indus and its tributary rivers gave Harappan society considerable uniformity.

Harappan Society and Its Beliefs

Over time cities grew up around the northwestern rivers, as well as along the coast (see Map 2.2). Most of the Harappan cities were in the Punjab (PUHN-jab) and Sind provinces of modern Pakistan, a crossroads of major trading routes, but some were hundreds of miles to the west or east. The two major Indus cities, called by archaeologists Harappa and Mohenjo-Daro (moe-hen-joe-DAHR-oh), stood 400 miles apart. More than 1,500 cities and towns contained a total population of perhaps 5 million people at the zenith of Harappan society.

 Interactive Map

Urban Planning

All of the cities had many common features in architecture, society, government, religion, and culture. The uniformity among Harappan cities suggests that the same central planning board designed them, and it reveals a society that valued order, organization, and cleanliness. Cities were rebuilt every half century or so, in a north-south grid pattern with wide streets and large rectangular city blocks. They built most buildings of sturdy baked brick molded to a standardized size. Residential and commercial districts were separated from a smaller area for public affairs. The Harappan cities were broken up into large blocks, which may have separated occupational or kinship groups. The largest city, Harappa, some 3-1/3 miles in circumference, contained perhaps 80,000 people at its height. Massive brick ramparts 40 feet thick at their base partially protected it from the river waters and attackers, and large ventilated warehouses could store voluminous supplies. People of all classes had exceptional, well-built housing for ancient times, with the most advanced sanitation system in the ancient world and strategically located public wells. Affluent residences had strong brick foundations with interior courtyards that provided considerable privacy, in a manner similar to elite Indian homes today.

Society and Governance

Although much is not known about Harrapan society and governance, each city was probably independent, perhaps governed by some powerful guild of merchants or a council of commercial, landowning, and religious leaders who maintained peace with neighbors. There is no Harappan counterpart to the glorification of Egyptian kings and little evidence for much warfare or militarism. The ruins contain few weapons, suggesting that, in contrast to Mesopotamia, peace was the norm. Some people owned beautiful objects of personal adornment, such as necklaces and beads, whereas others apparently lacked such valuable possessions. The ruins also contain many toys made from clay or wood, indicating a prosperous society that valued leisure for children.

Scholars debate many aspects of Harappan society. Most believe that those who created the society spoke

Josephine Powell, photographer. Courtesy of Special Collections, Fine Arts Library, Harvard College Library

Ruins of Mohenjo-Daro The photo shows the great bath at Mohenjo-Daro. Like modern Indians, the Harappans valued bathing for hygienic and possibly religious reasons.

a Dravidian (druh-VID-ee-uhn) language, although speakers of Iranian and possibly Indo-European languages may also have lived there. Harappans had unusual gender relations for that era: Apparently, Harappan husbands moved into their wives' households after marriage, a practice that suggests a matrilineal system. Yet, evidence suggests that at least some Harappans practiced a form of *sati* (suh-TEE), the custom of a widow killing herself by jumping onto the funeral pyre as her dead husband is being cremated.

Harappan city-dwellers developed an artistic appreciation, mixing art with religion and even commerce, and arguably creating a written language by 2600 B.C.E. Harappans made small clay seals, some of which contain brilliant portraits of indigenous animals like tigers, elephants, and rhinoceros. Pottery shows animal and geometric motifs; small bronze statues of dancers suggest the Harappans enjoyed dance. The seals, pottery, and various clay tablets contained some four hundred different signs that were completely unrelated to the scripts of Mesopotamia and Egypt, but unfortunately, modern scholars have not been able to decipher the Indus language.

Some Harappan religious notions contributed to Hinduism (HIN-doo-ism), a religion that developed after Harappan times. For example, one of the seals features a human figure sitting in a yogalike position, surrounded by various animals. The figure also appears to have multiple faces and may depict what later became the great Hindu god Shiva (SHEEV-uh). Harappans apparently already worshiped Shiva in his dual role as god of destruction and of fertility and the harvest. Mother-goddess worship seems also to have been prominent in Harappan religious life, as it was in the Fertile Crescent and ancient Europe. Some figurines with exaggerated breasts and hips may have represented the mother goddess.

Harappan Dynamism and Decline

The Harappan cities were hubs tied to surrounding regions, especially southwestern and Central Asia, through trade and transportation networks that fostered extensive contact. This foreign trade grew out of a vibrant and diverse local economy based on the cultivation of the staples barley and wheat and the production of cotton and metal products. Innovations helped Harappan society to remain stable and prosperous for hundreds of years.

Innovation and Trade

A highly sophisticated irrigation system and animal husbandry aided farming. Harappans or their ancestors domesticated the camel, zebu (oxen), elephant, chicken, and water buffalo. The raising of fowl enriched the diet, and water buffalo and zebu greatly aided farming as draft animals. Harappans also invented cotton cloth and learned to produce cotton textiles, one of ancient

Harappan Seal The seal from Mohenjo-Daro features a humped bull. The writing at the top has yet to be deciphered.

India's major gifts to the world. For many centuries, cotton spinning and weaving remained the most significant Indian industry, producing materials for eager markets both at home and abroad. Because there were few metals in the Indus Basin, the Harappans traded cotton and other products for copper, bronze, and stone.

The desirable Harappan agricultural and manufactured products led to extensive foreign trade that linked India with the wider world of western and Central Asia. A huge dock, massive granaries, and specialized factories at the coastal port of Lothal reflected a high-volume maritime trade. Some Harappan trade outposts have been found along the Indian Ocean coast as far west as today's Iran–Pakistan border. The Persian Gulf was a major crossroads for the Harappan–Sumerian trade. The Harappans exported surplus food, cotton, timber products, copper, and gold, as well as luxury items such as precious stones, ivory, beads, spices, and peacock feathers. Many of these items found their way as far west as Palestine.

A Mysterious Decline

Eventually, Harappan society declined, for reasons not altogether clear. Sometime between 1900 and 1750 B.C.E., a combination of factors disrupted the urban environment of this once wealthy, highly efficient, and powerful society. By 1700 B.C.E. most of the Harappan cities had been destroyed or abandoned, although a considerable rural population remained. The decay is obvious in the archaeological excavations. Seals and writing began to disappear around 1900 B.C.E. The careful grid pattern for city streets was abandoned, the drainage systems deteriorated, and even home sizes were reduced. Some evidence points to plundering and banditry.

Harappan decline may have resulted from several factors. Perhaps the Harappans overextended their economic networks, putting too much pressure on the land and exhausting their resources. Some evidence points to ecological catastrophes resulting from climate change, deforestation, increased flooding, excessive irrigation of marginal lands, and soil deterioration. Some scholars think that sometime between 1900 and 1700 B.C.E., volcanic or earthquake activity in the mountains to the north generated a mud slide that may have temporarily dammed the Indus River or one of its tributaries, changing its course and unleashing an awesome flood that quickly overwhelmed low-lying cities and their sur-rounding farms. The hoards of jewelry, skeletons buried in debris, and cooking pots found strewn across kitchens indicate hastily abandoned homes.

The fate of the Harappan people and their cultures is unclear. Many remained in the area, and some Harappan material technology and symbolism survive there today. Some cities well east of the Indus Valley remained populated for several more centuries, practicing modified but diverse forms of Harappan culture until around 1300 B.C.E. Whatever the causes of their decline, the remaining Indus peoples were left weak and unable to resist later migrations of peoples from outside.

Central Asian Environments and Oxus Cities

Central Asia is the vast area of plains (steppes), deserts, and mountains that stretches from the Ural Mountains and Caspian Sea eastward to Tibet, western China, and Mongolia. Before modern times, Central Asians played a role in history far greater than their relatively small populations would suggest, not only as invaders and sometimes conquerors but also as middlemen in the long-distance trade that developed on the land routes between China, India, the Middle East, and Europe.

The Nomads of the Steppes

Much of Central Asia offered a harsh living environment suitable only for the nomadic way of life. Many different peoples speaking Turkish or Persian languages lived in the region known as Turkestan, from east of the Caspian Sea to Xinjiang (SIN-john) on China's western frontier. Because of the geography and harsh living conditions, large-scale population movements and frequent warfare between competing tribal confederations became common. Most of the steppe societies were led by warrior chieftains, and many peoples were skilled horsemen and famous warriors, who used bronze and gold to make weapons and ornaments. The area's strategic location also promoted contact, and often conflict, with India and China. Some Central Asian peoples attacked and occasionally conquered northern China, and over the centuries various Central Asian peoples also migrated through the mountain ranges into northwest India.

The Oxus Society

Although much of Central Asia was steppe lands, some areas did support city life. In recent years archaeological discoveries have revealed an early urban society in Central Asia, which some call the Oxus (OX-uhs), after the river that runs through the area. The Oxus society apparently thrived between 2200 and 1800 B.C.E., about the time that the Harappan culture was at its height. The Oxus people built a number of walled cities with mud-brick buildings and possibly temples or palaces around desert oases in what is now Uzbekistan and Turkmenistan. Because they had a somewhat wetter climate than now, the people grew wheat and barley. They also forged bronze axes, carved figurines of women from stone and ivory, decorated pottery with elaborate designs, and may have developed their own written language. The cities, perhaps independent city-states, were situated along the "Silk Road" trade routes between India and China, suggesting that this trade may be older than is often thought. But the relationship of the Oxus cities to China, India, and Mesopotamia is unknown. Eventually the cities were abandoned and buried by sand.

LO⁴ The Aryans and a New Indian Society, 1500–1000 B.C.E.

Throughout India's long history, many people migrated from elsewhere into the subcontinent, and the assimilation of these various newcomers resulted in an increasingly diverse Indian society. One such group of invaders were the Aryans (AIR-ee-unzs), Indo-European-speaking nomadic pastoralists who migrated from Iran across northern India and introduced new traditions to the area. The Aryan Age, which lasted from around 1500 to 1000 B.C.E., built the foundation for a new society that mixed Aryan culture with the traditions of the indigenous peoples, including the Dravidians. The patterns that developed in the Aryan Age and the centuries that followed were so distinctive and enduring that India even today is unlike any other society.

The Aryan Peoples and the Vedas

Most scholars believe that the Aryans began migrating by horse-drawn chariot from Iran (the Persian word for "Aryan") or Central Asia into northwestern

> "The Aryans loved music and used such instruments as lutes, flutes, and drums."

Aryans
Indo-European-speaking nomadic pastoralists who migrated from Iran into northwest India between 1600 and 1400 B.C.E.

Vedas
The Aryans' "books of knowledge," the principal source of religious belief for Hindus: a vast collection of sacred hymns to the gods and thoughts about religion, philosophy, and magic.

India between 1600 and 1400 B.C.E., after the collapse of the Harappan cities. Other Indo-Europeans had already settled in Iran and Mesopotamia. The earliest arrivals were probably pastoralists, but later migrants might have been farmers. The migration to India came when rainfall in the Indus region was increasing again, improving economic conditions. The Aryans arrived in small groups over several centuries, bringing with them a rich oral literature and unusual ideas about government, society, and religion. For the next five hundred years, the Aryans expanded throughout northern India as more arrived from Iran and perhaps Central Asia.

Much of what we know about the ancient Aryans comes from their literature, the Vedas (VAY-duhs) ("books of knowledge"). A vast collection of sacred hymns to the gods and thoughts about religion, philosophy, and magic, the Vedas were based on oral accounts carefully preserved by bards through a vibrant oral tradition. The Vedas reflected the worldview of the priestly class and were already old when they were written down. They are the principal early source of Hindu religious belief.

From the Vedas we can infer that the Aryans were organized into tribes that frequently moved their settlements. Their class system consisted of warriors, priests, and commoners. Unlike the Harappans, before settling in India the Aryans apparently never fashioned sewer systems, baked bricks, developed writing, or crafted figurines. They raised cattle and were a militaristic people who harnessed horses to chariots and skillfully wielded bows and arrows and bronze axes. They had fought and trekked their way through blistering deserts and snowy mountains to reach India. Some Vedas celebrate Aryan victories against fortified settlements inhabited by other peoples, such as the Dravidians: "For fear of thee fled the dark-hued races, scattered abroad, deserting their possessions."[11] The various Aryan tribes could unite against a common enemy, but most of the time they fought against each other.

Sanskrit
The classical language of north India, originally both written and spoken but now reserved for religious and literary writing.

Mahabharata
("Great Bharata") An Aryan epic and the world's longest poem.

In India the Aryans mixed their language with those of local people, creating **Sanskrit** (SAN-skrit), the classical written and spoken language of north India, through which the Vedas were preserved during the first millennium B.C.E. By the fourth century B.C.E., however, vernacular (everyday) Indo-European spoken languages like Hindi and Bengali had become dominant in north India, and Sanskrit gradually became mostly a written language for religious and literary works.

Aryan Government, Society, and Religion

The early Aryan political and social structure was tribal and patriarchal, and marked by persistent conflict. Each tribe was governed by an autocratic male, known as a *raja,* who sought as much power for himself and his group as possible. The most powerful tribe seems to have been the Bharata (BAA-ray-tuh), which is also the official Sanskrit name for India today. Later the *Mahabharata* (MA-huh-BAA-ray-tuh) ("Great Bharata"), an Aryan epic and the world's longest poem, spun a complex and entertaining tale of many cousins and their titanic battles for supremacy.

The Aryan Family

The Vedas suggest that Aryan family structure, like the tribal organization, was patriarchal, with the father dominating his wives and children. In the centuries to follow, both male supremacy and a hierarchy based on age became the standard Indian family pattern. The Aryans developed a living pattern known as the joint family, also common in China, in which the wives of all the sons moved into the larger patriarchal household, which included members from three or even four generations. The status of Aryan women changed with time. The early Aryans educated both daughters and sons in the Vedas. One Vedic hymn encouraged women to speak publicly, and women may have composed some of the hymns. Several centuries later, women became more restricted and daughters less valued. They needed to obtain dowries (gifts for the prospective in-laws) in order to marry, could not participate in the sacrifices to gods, and did not inherit property.

The Aryans at Play

The Vedas also reveal something of Aryan recreational interests. The leading sports seem to have been horse-drawn chariot racing and gambling. Both dice and chess were invented in India, and many dice carved out of nuts have been found in the ruins of Mohenjo-Daro. Gambling features prominently in the *Mahabharata;* one raja loses his kingdom through his fondness for games of chance. The Aryans may also have used drugs like hashish, perhaps mixed into drinks, and were fond of wine. They loved music and used such instruments as lutes, flutes, and drums. In the centuries that have followed, song and dance have been an integral component of Indian religious worship and ritual.

The Vedic Religion

As sacred texts, the Vedas contained considerable information about the significance of various gods, the role of priests, and religious practices. Aryan religious views were similar to those of the Aryans' Hittite cousins in western Asia. Each Aryan tribe boasted its own bards, who had memorized the Vedic hymns and presided over sacrifices and rituals. The oldest and most important Veda, the *Rig Veda* ("Verses of Knowledge"), was probably composed between 1500 and 1000 B.C.E. It contains more than one thousand poems written in Sanskrit, most of them soliciting the favor of Aryan gods. The *Rig Veda* is the world's earliest surviving example of literature by any Indo-European people.

The Aryans worshiped a pantheon of nature gods, to whom they offered sacrifices. The *Rig Veda* describes some thirty-three deities, led by the thunderbolt-wielding war-god Indra (INN-druh), who is credited with defeating a demon and is ever youthful and heroic. There were also powerful gods of universal order and justice, fire, and immortality. Like the Hinduism that later developed, Aryan religion also included speculations on the deepest mysteries of existence. One poem, the "Hymn of Creation," questions the creation of the universe and the nature of knowledge: "Who really knows? Who will here proclaim it? Whence was this creation? The gods came afterwards, with the creation of the universe. Who then really knows whence it has arisen?"[12] This hymn also suggests a time before time when there was no space or sky, night or day, life or death. Then, in a kind of Big Bang, the cosmos was created by the power of heat.

It is unclear when or why many Indians began to consider the cow forbidden as food. The Aryans of

---

[12]Burton Stein, *A History of India.* Copyright © 1988 by Wiley-Blackwell Publishing Ltd. Reprinted with permission.

the Vedas consumed beef and held little reverence for these animals. Eventually, however, the practice of worshiping cows and avoiding beef became widespread even among later Aryans.

"The top class, the priests, enjoyed many special privileges as guardians and interpreters of sacred knowledge."

Indo-Aryan synthesis The fusion of Aryan and Dravidian cultures in India over many centuries.

Aryan Expansion and State Building in North India

Aryan Kingdoms Emerge

The Aryans eventually moved eastward, building kingdoms and mixing with local peoples. As the Indus region once again entered a cycle of reduced rainfall, many Aryans migrated into the wetter Ganges (GAN-geez) Valley, from 1000 to around 450 B.C.E. As the Aryans spread out and settled down, they eventually adopted Dravidian systems of farming, land tenure and taxation, village structure, and some religious concepts, but they also contributed their language, social system, and many religious beliefs to the mix. Throughout north India, city development and economic growth encouraged political consolidation. The tribes of early times became kingdoms. By the sixth century B.C.E., sixteen major Aryan kingdoms stretched from Bengal westward to the fringes of Afghanistan, and power had shifted from the Indus Basin to the central Ganges region, where most kingdoms were located. A unified government for all north India would not come until the establishment of the Mauryan Empire by a Ganges state in 321 B.C.E. (see Chapter 7).

The ancient Aryans never ceased engaging in military conflict. The *Mahabharata*, written down around 400 B.C.E. but reflecting life around 1000 B.C.E., was, like Homer's *Iliad* and Mayan records, drenched in the blood of endless struggles over succession and for supremacy between two rival kingdoms and their leaders. These epic battles suggest that states were continuously expanding and consolidating their control of nearby territories, which the rulers administered from their capital cities.

LO⁵ The Mixing of Dravidian and Aryan Cultures, 1000–600 B.C.E.

The encounters that resulted from Aryan migration brought together several distinctive peoples and cultures, reconfiguring Indian society. Over many centuries, a fusion of Aryan and Dravidian cultures occurred, a complex process that historians have labeled the Indo-Aryan synthesis. The mixing explains why many aspects of Aryan culture, such as the enthusiastic consumption of beef and liquor, differed dramatically from the traits of later Indian society. Enough cultural exchange between

Eliot Elisofon/Getty Images

Aryan Warfare Vedic stories remain popular in modern India. This scene from an old temple wall of Aryan warfare depicts embattled gods and demons from the *Mahabharata*.

brahmans
The Universal Soul, or Absolute Reality, that Hindus believe fills all space and time.

kshatriyas
Warriors and landowners headed by the rajas in the Hindu caste system.

vaisyas
The merchants and artisans in the Hindu caste system.

sudras
The mostly poorer farmers, farm workers, and menial laborers in the Hindu caste system.

caste system
The four-tiered Hindu social system comprising hereditary social classes that restrict the occupation of their members and their relations with members of other castes.

pariahs
The large group of outcasts or untouchables below the official Hindu castes.

Bhagavad Gita
("Lord's Song") A poem in the Mahabharata that is the most treasured piece of ancient Hindu literature.

north and south took place so that Indian society, despite great regional variety, developed many common features and considerable cultural unity. The mixing forged a distinctive new social system and Hinduism, a religion of diverse beliefs and traditions.

The Roots of the Caste System

The Indo-Aryan synthesis modified the social structure, which became increasingly complex as the expanding Aryans integrated diverse peoples into their network. A four-tiered class division emerged that comprised the **brahmans** (BRAH-munz), or priests; the **kshatriyas** (kuh-SHOT-ree-uhs), the warriors and landowners, who were headed by the rajas; the **vaisyas** (VIGH-shuhs), or merchants and artisans; and the **sudras** (SOO-druhs), mostly poorer farmers, farm workers, and menial laborers. The Aryans allocated the three highest categories to themselves. In fact, genetic studies suggest that upper-class Indians are more closely related to Europeans and Persians than to lower-class Indians. The top class, the priests, enjoyed many special privileges as guardians and interpreters of sacred knowledge. Over time the lowest tier, the sudras, mostly of non-Aryan origins, were locked into a permanent low status and were prohibited from reading the magically potent Vedic hymns.

The system was based on prejudice and religion. The Sanskrit term for a class division, or, in Hindu terms, ritual status, was *varna* (VARN-uh), which meant "[skin] color." The term suggests that the lighter-skinned Aryans wanted to maintain their domination over darker-skinned indigenous people. Many centuries later, Portuguese visitors referred to the system as *castas* ("pure"); hence the origin of the Western term *caste*. Aryans used religion to justify this class system. One of the hymns in the *Rig Veda* attributed the classes to the Lord of Beings, the originator of the universe: "When they divided the Man, into how many parts did they divide him? The brahman was his mouth, of his arms was made the kshatriya. His thighs became the vaisya, of his feet were born the sudra.[13]

Gradually, over many centuries, this four-tiered class hierarchy evolved into the complicated **caste system**. Each hereditary social class was restricted to certain occupations and constrained in their relations (such as marriage) with members of other castes. Below the caste system were a large group of **pariahs**, or untouchables, who performed tasks considered "unclean," such as tanning animal hides and removing manure. The division of most Indians into castes with different functions and status provided the basic structure of Hindu society for several millennia and was firmly in place by around 500 B.C.E.

Indo-Aryan Society, Economy, and Technology

The Vedas reveal some of the expectations and attitudes of ancient Indian society. For example, contained within the *Mahabharata* is a philosophical poem called the *Bhagavad Gita* (BAA-guh-vad GEE-tuh) ("Lord's Song"), the most treasured piece of ancient Hindu literature (see Witness to the Past: Hindu Values in the *Bhagavad Gita*). It encourages people to do their duty to their superiors and kinsmen resolutely and unselfishly. It also explains that death is not a time of grief, because the soul is indestructible. The other great ancient epic, the *Ramayana*, resembles the *Odyssey* of the Greek Homer in that it tells of a hero's wanderings while his wife remains chaste and loyal. The *Ramayana* conveys insights into the character of court life, which apparently involved endless intrigues.

Compared to the Aryan-dominated north, women seem to have enjoyed a higher status in mostly

> " Successfully let the good ploughshares' thrust part the earth, successfully let the ploughman follow the beasts of draft. "
>
> *Veda prayer*

Hindu Values in the *Bhagavad Gita*

The *Bhagavad Gita*, a philosophical poem in the *Mahabharata*, helped shape the ethical traditions of India while providing Hindus with a practical guide to everyday life. The following excerpt is part of a dialogue between the god Krishna (Vishnu) and the poem's conflicted hero, the warrior Arjuna (are-JUNE-ah), on the eve of a great battle in which Arjuna will slaughter his uncles, cousins, teachers, and friends. The reading summarizes some of Krishna's advice in justifying the battle. Krishna suggests that Arjuna must follow his destiny, for while the physical body is impermanent, the soul is eternal. The slain will be reborn. Furthermore, humans are responsible for their own destiny through their behavior and mental discipline. They also, like Arjuna, need to fulfill their obligations to society.

The wise grieve neither for the living nor for the dead. There has never been a time when you and I and the kings gathered here have not existed, nor will there ever be a time when we will cease to exist. As the same person inhabits the body through childhood, youth, and old age, so too at the time of death he attains another body. The wise are not deluded by these changes.

When the senses contact sense objects, a person experiences cold or heat, pleasure or pain. These experiences are fleeting; they come and go. Bear them patiently. . . . Those who are not affected by these changes, who are the same in pleasure and pain, are truly wise and fit for immortality. Assert your strength and realize this!

The impermanent has no reality; reality lies in the eternal. Those who have seen the boundary between these two have attained the end of all knowledge. Realize that which pervades the universe and is indestructible; no power can affect this unchanging, imperishable reality. The body is mortal but he who dwells in the body is immortal and immeasurable. . . . As a man abandons worn-out clothes and acquires new ones, so when the body is worn out a new one is acquired by the Self, who lives within. . . . Death is inevitable for the living; birth is inevitable for the dead. Since these are unavoidable, you should not sorrow. . . .

Now listen to the principles of yoga [mental and physical discipline to free the soul]. By practicing these you can break through the bonds of karma. On this path effort never goes to waste, and there is no failure. . . . When you keep thinking about sense objects, attachment comes. Attachment breeds desire, the lust of possession that burns to anger. . . .

They are forever free who renounce all selfish desires and break free from the ego-cage of "I," "me," and "mine" to be united with the Lord. This is the supreme state. Attain to this, and pass from death to immortality. . . . Strive constantly to serve the welfare of the world; by devotion to selfless work one attains the supreme goal of life. Do your work with the welfare of others always in mind.

Thinking About the Reading

1. What key aspects of Hindu thought are revealed in the poem?
2. How do the attitudes toward life, death, and desire influence the behavior of individuals?
3. What are some of the viewpoints in this ancient poem that might be considered universal in their appeal?

Source: From *The Bhagavad Gita*, trans. by Eknath Easwaran, founder of the Blue Mountain Center of Meditation, copyright 1985. Reprinted by permission of the Nilgiri Press, P.O. Box 256, Tomales, CA 94971, www.easwaran.org

Brahmanas
Commentaries on the Vedas that emphasize the role of priests (brahmans).

Upanishads
Philosophical writings that speculate on the ultimate truth of the creation of life.

Dravidian south India. There both matriarchal and matrilineal traditions persisted for centuries, and goddesses remained especially central to religious life. Dravidian women also exercised some economic power and owned property. But even in the north during the Vedic Age, some women mastered the Vedas and mixed freely with men.

Technology and Agriculture

The Indo-Aryan economy drew on technology derived from both foreign and local developments. Certainly the Aryans used iron, initially for weapons and horse harnesses, once they reached iron-rich districts in the Ganges region around 1000 B.C.E. Soon after they arrived, the Aryans made the transition from a largely nomadic pastoral economy to a combination of pastoral and agricultural pursuits that emphasized grains like barley and wheat. One Veda prays: "Successfully let the good ploughshares' thrust part the earth, successfully let the ploughman follow the beasts of draft."[14] The use of plows and the expansion of irrigated agriculture greatly increased the available food supply and thus fostered population growth. India's population in 500 B.C.E. has been estimated at 25 million, including 15 million in the Ganges Valley.

Hinduism: A New Religion of Diverse Roots

Although Indian religion has changed much since the Harappans, it has remained unique. Nothing in the Middle East or Europe remotely resembles basic Indian beliefs such as reincarnation. These are part of the bedrock of Indian society, molding thought and daily lives. What modern Indians would clearly recognize as Hinduism had probably not fully formed until the second half of the first millennium B.C.E., but the foundations were clearly established in ancient times. Hinduism can be seen historically as a synthesis of Aryan beliefs with Harappan and other Dravidian traditions that developed over many centuries.

The religious system became one of the richest and most complex in the world, with gods, devotions, and celebrations drawn from various regional and village cultures. The Aryans gradually turned from their old tribal gods to deities of probable Harappan origin such as Shiva. Hence the rise of the great gods of Hinduism: *Brahma* (BRA-ma) (the Creator of life);

Vishnu (VISH-noo) (the Preserver of life); and *Shiva* (among other functions, the Destroyer of life). Vishnu is a benevolent deity who works continually for the welfare of the world. Shiva personifies the life force and embodies both constructive and destructive power.

Hinduism loosely linked together diverse practices and cults that shared a reverence for the Vedas. The Vedic thinkers were influenced by pre-Aryan meditation techniques and mystical practices of possible Harappan origin, such as those that were later known as *yoga*. In the eternal quest for divine favor, the Hindus came to believe that everyone must behave properly so that the universe can function in an orderly manner. They came to see human existence as temporary and fleeting and only the realm of the gods as eternal.

From Vedism to Brahmanism to Hinduism

The Vedas underwent three major stages of development to become accepted as revealed literature. The earliest stage included the poems and hymns in the *Rig Veda* and several other collections. A half millennium later, from around 1000 to 700 B.C.E., a series of prose commentaries called the *Brahmanas* (BRA-ma-nus) appeared, emphasizing the importance of religious law as well as the central role of the priests, or brahmans, "those who chant the sacred words." Later still, between 800 and 600 B.C.E., a third group of more philosophical writings appeared, mostly in the form of 108 poetic dialogues known as the *Upanishads* (oo-PAHN-ih-shahds) ("sitting around a teacher"). These writings, which speculated on the creation of life, offered a striking contrast to the emphasis on ritual, devotion, and ethics in the older works and also gave women more importance.

The religious atmosphere of ancient India seems to have been dynamic, with growing tensions between competing ideas about the nature of existence and appropriate human behavior. The *Ramayana* contrasts the luxury-filled decadence of the royal courts with the austere existence of hermit-sages dwelling in the forest and practicing forms of meditation and mysticism. By the middle of the first millennium B.C.E., the debate and disenchantment that produced the *Upanishads* resulted in much more far-reaching critiques of the brahman-led system. The movements that developed out of this ferment included both Buddhism and the modified form of Brahmanism known today as Hinduism, as we shall see in Chapter 7.

 Listen to a synopsis of Chapter 2.

{ Speak Up! }

WORLD was built on a simple principle: to create a new teaching and learning solution that reflects the way today's faculty teach and the way you learn.

Through conversations, focus groups, surveys, and interviews, we collected data that drove the creation of the version of **WORLD** that you are using today. But it doesn't stop there—in order to make **WORLD** an even better learning experience, we'd like you to SPEAK UP and tell us how **WORLD** worked for you. What did you like about it? What would you change? Are there additional ideas you have that would help us build a better product for next semester's world history students?

At **4ltrpress.cengage.com/world** you'll find all of the resources you need to succeed in world history—flashcards, interactive online quizzes, an interactive eBook, the Wadsworth World History Resource Center, and more!

Speak Up! Go to **4ltrpress.cengage.com/world.**

Ancient Societies in Africa and the Mediterranean, 5000–600 B.C.E.

Learning Outcomes

After reading this chapter, you should be able to answer the following questions:

LO¹ What were some unique features of ancient Egypt?

LO² How did environmental factors help shape ancient sub-Saharan African history?

LO³ What were some achievements of the ancient Nubian, Sudanic, and Bantu peoples?

LO⁴ What were the contributions of the Hebrews, Minoans, Mycenaeans, Phoenicians, and Dorian Greeks to later societies in the region?

George Holton/Photo Researcher, Inc.

>> **Behold, the heart of his majesty was satisfied with making a very great monument; never has happened the like since the beginning. He made it as an everlasting fortress. It is wrought with gold and many costly stones.** <<

—Temple inscription at Thebes, Egypt, fourteenth century B.C.E.[1]

Around 1460 B.C.E., Queen Hatshepsut (hat-SHEP-soot), the powerful and gifted ruler of Egypt, issued a decree to build a temple in the city of Thebes on the banks of the Nile River for the glory of the highest god, Amon-Re (AH-muhn-RAY). To obtain fragrant myrrh trees for the temple's terraced gardens, the queen ordered an expedition to be sent down the Red Sea to the fabled land of Punt (poont) on the coast of northeast Africa, probably modern Somalia (so-MAH-lee-uh).

The new expedition was extremely successful, returning with myrrh trees for the temple, jewels, incense, and other treasures. Like other rulers, Queen Hatshepsut commemorated her achievements with inscriptions and pictures on the walls of her magnificent new temple, which declared, "Never were brought such things to any king, since the world was."[2] To continue to obtain such luxury products, Egyptians became shipbuilders and sailors, and they became connected to a much wider world. Foreign trade made Egypt the ancient world's wealthiest society.

Test your knowlege before you read this chapter.

What do you think?

Water and waterways such as the Nile River and Mediterranean Sea affected the development of ancient societies significantly.

Strongly Disagree						*Strongly Agree*
1	2	3	4	5	6	7

Among the Egyptians and some other African and eastern Mediterranean societies—including the Hebrews, Minoans (mih-NO-uhns), Mycenaeans (my-suh-NEE-uhns), Phoenicians (fo-NEE-shuhns), and early Greeks—we see the same kind of dramatic changes resulting from contact among different peoples that fostered urban life in Mesopotamia and India. Egypt greatly influenced neighboring peoples, and in turn it was influenced by commercially successful societies such as Kush (koosh) to the south and the Phoenicians of Lebanon. This interaction among neighbors promoted

<< **Abu Simbel** The great temple with its colossal statues at Abu Simbel overlooking the Nile River in Egypt was built as a monument to honor the powerful thirteenth-century B.C.E. pharaoh Rameses the Great.

cultural development in the Nile valley and the Mediterranean, much as it did in Mesopotamia and Harappa. Like the large river valleys of the Tigris-Euphrates and Indus, the Nile valley also made possible population growth, large state structures, and elaborate religious systems.

Ancient peoples also created unique and complex societies elsewhere in Africa and the eastern Mediterranean. Diverse sub-Saharan African societies developed farming and metal technologies and some built cities, but over the centuries many of the sub-Saharan people's monuments and buildings were covered by rain forest, blowing sand, or wayward rivers. This was not the case on the islands and shores of the eastern Mediterranean, where various peoples traded widely, built cities whose ruins still interest visitors, and developed religious concepts that endure to this day.

> "Because the floods came on an exact schedule, Egyptians formed a central government to organize large numbers of people to prepare the cropland in time to take best advantage of the flooding."

LO¹ Egyptian Society, Economy, and Culture

As in Mesopotamia, the formation of Egyptian society was a rich and complex process involving interactions among many different peoples. Egypt became an integrated society and was so successful that it survived in more or less its basic form for nearly 2,000 years. Perhaps because of the Nile inundation each fall, Egyptians of all social classes, blessed with many centuries of good crops, seemed to view themselves as favored. One writer celebrated the Nile Delta as "full of everything good—its ponds with fish and its lakes with birds. Its meadows are verdant, its melons abundant. Its granaries are so full of barley that they come near to

> 66 I know the Nile. When he is introduced in the fields, his introduction gives life to every nostril. 99
>
> *Temple inscription*

the sky."3 The river valley's African location allowed the Egyptians to develop many traditions, technologies, and ideas that were completely different from those in nearby Mesopotamia, Palestine, and Crete. Trading with many distant suppliers and markets contributed to Egypt's wealth and success.

The Environment and Foundations of Egyptian Society

North Africa, a region stretching from Morocco to the Red Sea, is bordered by water and desert. Its Mediterranean coastline, the Red Sea, and the Nile River provided access to other regions, while the vast Sahara Desert stretches all the way to the western coast of Africa on one end and the Red Sea and Ethiopian highlands on the other. In northwestern Africa (today's Tunisia, Algeria, and Morocco), mountain ranges separate the desert from the Mediterranean and Atlantic coastal plains, where farming is also possible.

The Gift of the Nile

The Nile River is the key to understanding the formation of Egyptian society (see Map 3.1). The settlers in the northern Nile valley enjoyed many centuries of uninterrupted development thanks to the deserts on both sides of the valley.

🌐 Interactive Map

The Egyptians referred to the small belt of fertile soil along the Nile as "the black land" and to the inhospitable deserts on either side as "the red land." This physical environment allowed Egypt to thrive for a thousand years without significant outside challenge. Because the Nile was navigable and slow moving, the river was a great highway that promoted political stability and uniformity. Although the Nile valley was grassland and rain forest in prehistoric times, by the fourth millennium the grassland had turned to desert, and "the black land" was fertile only because of the silt deposited by the fall flooding of the Nile.

The same process that transformed farming societies into urban societies in Mesopotamia took place a few centuries later, around 3100 or 3000 B.C.E., in the Nile valley, and also attracted a diverse population. Here too, with little rainfall, irrigation was necessary to take advantage of the rich silt. A temple inscription acknowledged the river's value: "I know the Nile. When he is introduced in the fields, his introduction gives life to every nostril."[4] But the river valley here was 10 miles wide, instead of 100 miles wide as in Mesopotamia. Thus people were more isolated than in Mesopotamia and concentrated in a smaller area.

A Cultural Melting Pot

The Nile valley began attracting immigrants well before the birth of cities. Many of the earliest settlers were migrants from a Sahara region that had been fertile but began drying out some 6,000 to 7,000 years ago. The Egyptian population eventually included peoples of Semitic (suh-MIT-ik), Berber (BUHR-bur), Ethiopian, Somali, black African, and, later, Greek origins. Egypt also enjoyed close relationships with the Nubians, black African peoples living along the Nile in what is today southern Egypt and northern Sudan. The ancient Egyptian language belonged to the Afro-Asiatic family. Before 600 C.E. most of the people in northwest Africa were Berbers, who spoke languages related to Egyptian.

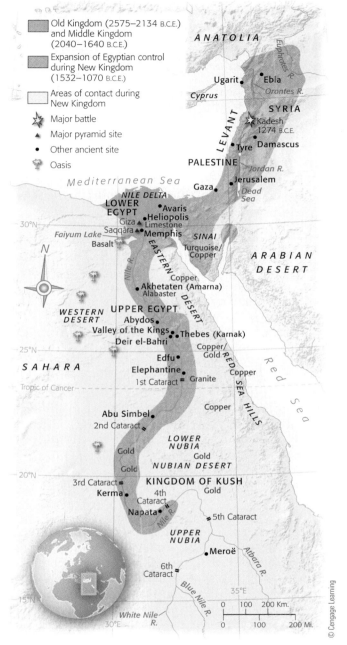

Map 3.1
Ancient Egypt and Nubia

The Egyptian and Nubian societies developed along the Nile River. Egypt traded with, and sometimes controlled, the peoples of the Levant on the eastern Mediterranean coast.

The Emergence of an Egyptian State

Because the floods came on an exact schedule, Egyptians formed a central government to organize large numbers of people to prepare the cropland

pharaohs
Rulers of ancient Egypt.

hieroglyphics
The ancient Egyptian writing system, which evolved from pictograms into stylized pictures expressing ideas.

in time to take best advantage of the flooding. This pattern differed from that in Mesopotamia, where the flooding was less predictable. In Egypt, as in Mesopotamia, it took back-breaking work to build dikes and irrigate the fields. If the floodwaters were not carefully channeled, little would grow. In periods of political disorder and weak central government, the desert spread and famine struck the land. When order prevailed and the dikes were maintained, the valley could support a high population. By 1000 B.C.E., the population had reached 3 or 4 million. Protected by the desert from foreign invasion until about 1500 B.C.E., Egyptians understandably worried more about domestic disorder. Given their general good fortune, it is not surprising that Egyptians saw themselves as the center of the world.

Most of Egypt's people lived along the Mediterranean coast or on the Nile River down to Aswan (AS-wahn), some 750 miles south at the river's first large waterfall (see Map 3.1). The 100-mile-long area from the modern city of Cairo down the Nile to the sea was considered Lower Egypt or the northern kingdom, at the end of which was the fertile Nile Delta. The area from Cairo south to Aswan was Upper Egypt or the southern kingdom. These two states were united by the legendary Upper Egyptian King Menes (MEH-neez) in about 3000 B.C.E.

Egyptian history from 3000 to 1075 B.C.E. is divided into periods called the Old Kingdom, the Middle Kingdom, and the New Kingdom. During each period various dynasties ruled Egypt, and the intermediate periods were marked by disorder or foreign conquest. After 1075 B.C.E., Egypt increasingly fell victim to the empire building of western Asian, Mediterranean, and other African peoples.

 Experience life as an ancient Egyptian through this interactive simulation.

The Old Kingdom: Egypt's Golden Age

Nothing better illustrates the Egyptian self-confidence of the Old Kingdom than the pyramids, perhaps the greatest, most enduring of the ancient world's construction projects. The Old Kingdom lasted from 2663 to 2195 B.C.E., and the first large pyramid tombs near Giza were built between 2600 and 2100 B.C.E. They reflected a powerful government, unsurpassed organizing talent, a prosperous society, and unique values and beliefs.

Pyramids and Pharaohs

The largest pyramid, that of the twenty-fifth-century B.C.E. Pharaoh Cheops at Giza, near modern Cairo, is nearly 500 feet high, covers an area of nearly 200 square yards, is almost exactly level, and remained the tallest building in the world until the twentieth century C.E. It was built with nearly 6 million tons of limestone. All of the limestone was moved into place on ramps and wooden rollers by tens of thousands of slaves, skilled artisans, and other workers without the benefit of winches, pulleys, or scaffolds. Work on the pyramids and other royal tombs took place in the fall, when the Nile flooded, allowing workers to use barges to float the stones close to the construction site.

The rulers of Egypt, who were eventually known as **pharaohs** (FAIR-ohs) (from per-o or "great house"), had the power to build such grand projects power because their subjects believed them to be the divine offspring of the sun-god Re, the creator of heaven, earth, and humans. Pharaohs also had soldiers, as well as the authority of priests and religion, to support their rule. Writing, invented by 3000 B.C.E., enabled the administration to function smoothly. The Egyptian writing system of **hieroglyphics** (hi-ruh-GLIF-iks), like Sumerian cuneiform, evolved from pictograms into stylized pictures expressing ideas. The surviving records give us a detailed view of ancient Egyptian society

The pharaohs were considered the owners of all the land and people in Egypt and governed a centralized state from the city of Memphis, strategically located where the Nile valley met the delta. Egypt was divided into about forty provinces, each headed by a governor appointed by the king. A chief minister supervised the administration and ensured that taxes were collected, grain properly stored in government warehouses, and salaries paid to government officials. During the Old Kingdom, the royal government also expanded trade through regional networks. The pharaohs dispatched expeditions east to Arabia, south to Nubia (NOO-bee-ah), and northeast to Lebanon, Syria, and Anatolia. The records from the Pharaoh Snefru (SNEF-roo) around 2600 B.C.E. provide the first known written accounts of international maritime trade. They describe the arrival of forty ships filled with cedar logs, probably from today's Lebanon, to make the cedar wood doors of the royal palace.

ma'at
Ancient Egyptian term for justice, the correct order of things.

Great Pyramid at Giza Three Egyptian pharaohs from the twenty-sixth century B.C.E. were buried in these magnificent pyramids, which symbolized the power of Old Kingdom Egypt. The rearmost pyramid, built for Pharaoh Cheops, remains the largest all-stone building ever constructed anywhere.

Demise of the Old Kingdom

Some historians believe that the expense of the great royal tombs (the pyramids) eventually impoverished the country during the final decades of the twenty-second century B.C.E. We do know that at this time the governors became more independent of the ruler at Memphis, whose authority weakened. Many peasants reasoned that if the power of the ruler lessened, it must mean that the gods were displeased. The Egyptian term for justice was ma'at (muh-AHT), which referred to the way the universe and human society are supposed to be. But environmental change may also have undermined the government. A dramatic and sudden drop in rainfall led to many years of poor harvests and starvation in Upper Egypt.

The Middle and New Kingdoms

After a century of social disorder, around 2080 B.C.E. the pharaohs of the Twelfth Dynasty restored strong government. They moved the capital from Memphis to the city of Thebes in the south and established stronger control over the governors. This Middle Kingdom lasted for 400 years and saw Egyptian influence extend to Palestine in the north and, briefly, to Nubia in the south. Amon-Re, a fusion of two great gods, now became Egypt's chief god and was proclaimed the ancestor of the divine pharaoh.

The Hyksos and the Nubians

However, foreign conquest and domestic disorder brought an end to the Middle Kingdom in 1640 B.C.E. The Hyksos (HICK-soes), an iron-using Semitic people from Syria and Palestine, conquered a portion of the Nile Delta region and established an independent kingdom. Hyksos rule led to further divisions: a separate dynasty began to rule Upper Egypt from Thebes, and the Nubians established yet a third state. Although regarded by Egyptians as invading barbarians, the Hyksos adopted Egyptian customs and brought several improvements to Egypt that would later pay dividends for the strong rulers of the New Kingdom. These benefits included increased trade with the Semitic and Indo-European peoples of the eastern Mediterranean and Mesopotamia, new methods of working bronze and making pottery, and military innovations, including the use of iron, smaller shields, body armor, and horse-drawn chariots.

The New Kingdom Revival

In 1570 B.C.E., a dynamic new set of rulers reestablished Egypt's regional power and became more active and expansionist in the western Asian and Mediterranean worlds. Using the new military technology, the pharaohs of the New Kingdom led armies on repeated campaigns into Palestine and Syria, as far east as the Euphrates River, and south into Nubia. Foreigners from as far away as Babylon in the east came to serve in the Egyptian court. During this time Egypt's power derived partly from its position as the major regional supplier of gold, which it obtained mostly from Nubia and Punt.

monotheism
The belief in a single, all-powerful god.

> "The Egyptians had no word for a female ruler and described a queen only as the "king's wife.""

Social Life and Urban Centers

For a certain period, Egypt was ruled by the female pharaoh introduced earlier. Hatshepsut (r. ca. 1479–1458), the daughter of Pharaoh Tuthmosis (tuth-MOE-sis) I, was the wife of another pharaoh and ruled in her own name between 1473 and 1458, supervising military campaigns in both the north and south and also sponsoring the marine expedition to Punt to collect luxury goods. The Egyptians had no word for a female ruler and described a queen only as the "king's wife." To ensure that she looked like a proper pharaoh, Hatshepsut apparently wore male clothing and the headdress and false beard that were symbols of royalty.

Akhenaton's Revolution

Another New Kingdom pharaoh, Amenophis (AH-meno-fis) IV (r. 1353–1333), rebelled against the priests of Amon-Re and promoted the worship of a new sun-god, Aton, who he claimed was the only god (other than the pharaoh himself). Amenophis changed his name to Akhenaton (AH-ke-NAH-tin) ("servant of Aton") and advocated monotheism, the belief in a single, all-powerful god, at roughly the same time that the Hebrews were developing their belief in a single god. At Akhenaton's death, however, the priests successfully pressured his successor to return to Amon-Re worship.

Climax and Decline of the New Kingdom

Despite this dispute, the New Kingdom continued its military successes for a while before faltering. In the thirteenth century, the high point of Egyptian empire building was reached when Rameses (ram-ih-SEEZ) II (r. 1290–1224) signed a treaty with the Hittites dividing Syria and Palestine between them. In 1208 B.C.E. Libyan tribes invaded the Nile Delta, probably to escape famine. Although they were pushed out, starting in about 1075 B.C.E. Egypt began its long decline as a power in the eastern Mediterranean. From about 750 to 650 B.C.E., a dynasty of pharaohs from the kingdom of Kush in Nubia ruled Egypt, adopting Egyptian customs and writing in hieroglyphics. Finally, Egypt was conquered by the Assyrians in the seventh century and by the Persians in the late sixth century B.C.E.

Like other societies with cities and states, Egypt was divided into classes. During the Old Kingdom, members of each social class had different responsibilities and roles. The head of this social hierarchy, the pharaoh, theoretically owned everything in the kingdom. The priests and nobles owned 80 to 90 percent of all the usable land. However, the scribe, or "writing man, " held the most honored upper-class occupation. Peasants maintained the irrigation works and paid taxes that could be as high as 20 percent of their crop. At the bottom of society were slaves, perhaps 10 or 15 percent of the population. They were mostly prisoners of war and foreigners, including Nubians and people from Palestine.

Learn about the daily life of an Egyptian Priest.

Influenced by the Nile environment, Egyptians valued security and regularity more than social equality. Because it was relatively easy to plant in the soft soil left after the floods, they did not need heavy plows. Despite occasional grueling labor on construction projects, peasants showed little discontent except during the troubled intermediate periods. Massive tombs and mummies were once bright with paint and gold, and people seemingly enjoyed life so much they wished to perpetuate it in the afterlife.

Gender Roles

Numerous temple paintings show men and women at work and play. Egyptians told bawdy stories, played musical instruments such as flutes, pipes, and harps, got drunk, and gave boring lectures to children. Both men and women used cosmetics to enhance their physical attractions, massaging themselves with scented oils and decorating their eyes with colorful eyeliners.

Gender roles were flexible, and women had more independence and rights, especially in law, than women in any other ancient society. Hatshepsut was the most famous of at least four women pharaohs. By the New Kingdom, legal distinctions among persons seemed to be based more on class than on gender. A woman could inherit, bequeath, and administer property, conclude legal settlements, take cases to court, initiate divorce, and testify. Some women could probably read and write. Many were involved in well-paying economic activities, and they were paid the same as men for the same work. Women weavers produced some of the finest cloth in world history. Wives also enjoyed rough equality with husbands and assumed the public and family responsibilities of their deceased spouses. Women served as doctors and priestesses, and a few women even held administrative positions.

Government and Trade

Egyptian cities were largely administrative centers created by the pharaoh to house tax collectors, artisans in government workshops, shopkeepers, and the priests who cared for the local temple. Even the larger cities such as Memphis and Thebes did not begin as centers for long-distance trade and commerce, because most trade involved the import of luxury goods by the wealthy. The Nile floods were more predictable than those along the unruly Euphrates, so fewer people were needed to manage the irrigation system. Therefore, more Egyptians lived in villages, and market towns were scattered up and down the river.

Although the cities were not commercial centers as they were in Mesopotamia, the Egyptians' long-distance trade systems were more wide-ranging than those of the Mesopotamians. Either directly or through intermediaries, Egyptians traded with sub-Saharan Africans as far south as the Congo River Basin, with the Berber peoples of Libya and Algeria to the west, with the societies along the Red Sea to the east, with Palestine, Phoenicia, and Mesopotamia to the northeast, and with southeastern Europe.

Science, Technology, and Religion

The geometrical precision of the pyramids tells us that the ancient Egyptians understood some mathematics and physics. They knew enough to make the pyramids level and to match the corners of each pyramid with the four points of the compass. The Egyptians also used a very accurate solar calendar that divided the year into 365 days, using twelve months of thirty days each and adding five days at the end. Egyptian arithmetic, however, was less sophisticated than their calendar might suggest. They understood fractions, but they had no concept of zero and dealt

 Egyptian Book of the Dead Read the number of potential sins that would likely tarnish a journeying spirit and prevent entrance into the realm of the blessed.

with numbers only by adding them; evidence suggests that they had much technical skill but little theoretical understanding.

In medicine, Egyptians used both surgery and herbal remedies to treat illnesses. They recognized that the heart was a pump, were able to cure some eye diseases, and did some dental work. Modern observers still admire Egyptian technical skill in treating the dead. Using a form of salt found abundantly in Egypt, and taking advantage of the extremely dry climate, Egyptian morticians were able to preserve human tissue well enough that the distinct features of individuals could be seen 4,000 years later.

Egyptian religious and moral beliefs included some two thousand gods and goddesses, most of them benevolent, many myths, and unique views of death.

> " Egyptians used both surgery and herbal remedies to treat illnesses. "

Like their Mesopotamian counterparts, the Egyptian gods were created to explain nature, but were also made in the image of humans and shared human weaknesses. Eventually they were seen as responsive to human needs. The emphasis on preserving bodies indicates another chief feature of Egyptian religion, the belief that a person's soul could be united with his or her body after death, but only if the body were properly preserved. In the Old Kingdom, only pharaohs could expect this afterlife, which mirrored life on earth. By the Middle Kingdom, however, all who could afford some form of mummification and whose souls passed a final moral judgment after death were candidates for immortality. As a result, people devoted vast resources to this quest.

The most dramatic and long-lived of the Egyptian myths is the story of Osiris (oh-SIGH-ris) and his wife Isis (EYE-sis). One version describes Osiris as the god-king who originally established peace and justice on earth. By this act he incurred the jealousy of his brother Set, who murdered him by sealing him in a box and throwing it into the sea. Isis, grief-stricken, found the body of her husband washed ashore. With the help of other gods, she revived Osiris long enough for him to impregnate her. Their son Horus later took revenge on Set, and Osiris descended to the underworld, where he established justice there as he had done on earth. A famous Egyptian drawing from the *Book of the Dead*, which depicts the afterlife, shows Osiris weighing the heart of a dead princess against the symbol of justice and truth.

Because of the *Book of the Dead*, the durability of the pyramids, other Egyptian tombs, and mummified remains, some scholars have viewed the ancient

Sudan

A grassland region stretching along the southern fringe of the Sahara Desert from the western tip of Africa to the Nile valley.

Egyptians as people preoccupied with death. However, the tombs are the only artifacts that remain because they were made of stone. The less durable mud-brick houses of most Egyptians, in which a great deal of activity took place, were washed away or dissolved into mud long ago. Thus the Egyptians were probably not as preoccupied with death as the physical remains suggest.

LO² The Roots of Sub-Saharan African Societies

Egypt was only the best-known of the early farming societies and states that emerged on the African continent. Africans fostered varied societies, built cities, formed states, and became linked to each other and the wider world by growing networks. Just as the annual Nile floods fostered Egypt's distinctive development, so the environment also influenced the varied traditions of sub-Saharan Africans and helped or hindered their early development of farming and technology.

African Environments

Africa, with one-fifth of the earth's landmass, is the second largest continent after Eurasia and occupies more space than the United States, Europe (excluding Russia), China, and India combined. The equator almost exactly bisects Africa, giving most of the continent a tropical climate. Lush rain forests have flourished along West Africa's Guinea coast and in the vast Congo River Basin in the heart of the continent. These forests and other areas near the equator are home to many insects, parasites, and bacteria that cause debilitating diseases like malaria, yellow fever, and sleeping sickness, the last of which is deadly to cattle and horses. Most of the continent has long been parched desert or savannah grasslands, including a huge dry zone that receives less than 10 inches of rain annually. African weather can be erratic, with fluctuating and often unpredictable rains. The deserts and some of the grasslands have largely been occupied by pastoral societies and herds of large wild animals. In some regions the poor-quality soil has been easily eroded by overuse, but early farmers managed to cultivate the grassland-covered region known as the Sudan (soo-DAN), which stretches along the southern fringe of the Sahara Desert from the western tip of Africa to the Nile Basin, south of Egypt.

CHRONOLOGY

Ancient Sub-Saharan Africa, 8000 B.C.E.–350 C.E.

8000–5000	Earliest agriculture in the Sahara and Nubia
5000–4000	Earliest agriculture in Ethiopia
3100–2800	First Nubian kingdom (disputed)
2500	Widespread agriculture in West, Central, and East Africa
2000	Beginning of Bantu migrations
1800–1500	Kerma kingdom in Nubia
1200	Early urbanization in western Sudan
1000–500	Bantu settlement of Great Lakes region
1000–500	Beginning of trans-Saharan trade
1000–500	Early ironworking technology
900–800	Mande towns
900–350 C.E.	Early Kush

Geographic Hindrances

Geography has often hindered communication. The eastern third of Africa includes extensive plateau and mountain regions, which in Ethiopia rise to 15,000 feet. Deep valleys and gorges complicate travel, but in some plateau districts, great lakes and volcanic soils have permitted denser populations. The eastern highlands also produced great river systems, including the Nile, the Congo (which drains the vast central African rain forests), and, in the south, the Zambezi (zam-BEE-zee), but all of these rivers have numerous rapids and waterfalls that have limited boat travel. Only the Niger (NIGH-jer) River, which flows mostly through the flat West African plains, is navigable over large distances. Nor was maritime transportation easy in the past. Prevailing winds made it difficult to sail along the West African coast, and much of the African coast has treacherous sandbars and few natural harbors, making it difficult to land a boat. Only along the eastern, Red Sea, and Mediterranean coasts did a few protected bays and prevailing winds favor seagoing trade.

Desertification

The catastrophic climatic change that created and expanded the Sahara Desert strongly shaped early African societies. The Sahara region was once a rich grazing land with lakes and rivers, occupied by a large human population that flourished from hunting, gathering, fishing, and some farming. Ancient rock art portrays people dancing, worshiping, raising children, riding chariots, and tending horses and cattle. Eventually, desertification, the process by which productive land is transformed into mostly useless desert, set in. For several millennia, the region became relatively wet. This pattern reached a peak in 3500 B.C.E., making settlement more attractive. Then, as rain patterns shifted southward again, the gradual "drying out" of the continent began. By 2000 B.C.E. the Sahara region was harsh desert, and animals and plants had disappeared along with the water. People contributed to this process by overgrazing marginal lands and burning forests to create grasslands.

> African Timelines (*http://web.cocc.edu:80/cagatucci/classes/hum211/timelines/htimelinetoc.htm*). Offers many links to essays and other sources on Africa; maintained by Central Oregon Community College.

Desertification influenced societies. The Sahara was left largely to nomadic herders of cattle and other animals, and most other inhabitants migrated to the north and south or into the lower Nile valley, perhaps generating ancient Egyptian development. Eventually the Sahara marked a general boundary between the Berber and Semitic peoples along the southern Mediterranean coast and the darker-skinned peoples in the rest of Africa. But the desert barrier did not prevent considerable social, cultural, and genetic intermixing and exchange.

The Origins of African Agriculture

Africa's geographic disadvantages did not prevent agriculture from developing early as the result of both local and imported discoveries. Recent discoveries suggest that, some 12,000 or 13,000 years ago, people in the eastern Sahara were perhaps the first in the world to make pottery, two centuries earlier than Middle Eastern people. Between 8000 and 5000 B.C.E., people in the north-central Nile (Nubia) and the

> "Between 8000 and 5000 B.C.E., people in the north-central Nile (Nubia) and the Sahara region had become among the world's first farmers."

> **desertification**
> The transformation of once-productive land into useless desert.

Sahara region had become among the world's first farmers. By 2500 B.C.E., farming was widespread in West, Central, and East Africa. In West Africa and the Sahara, almost all food crops developed from local wild African plants like sorghum, millet, yams, and African rice. Probably domesticated in the Niger River region, rice gradually spread south to become a major crop in the rainforest zone of the west coast. People in the eastern Sahara had also domesticated cotton and worked it into fabrics using spindles of baked clay, perhaps as early as 5000 B.C.E. Some crops came later from outside Africa, including wheat, barley, and chickpeas from the Middle East, while crops domesticated in West Africa, such as sorghum and sesame, reached India and China well before 2000 B.C.E.

Adapting and Overcoming

African peoples overcame geographic challenges in many ways. The major response to difficult climate and soils was to create a subsistence economy, rather than the high-productivity agriculture that was possible elsewhere. Pastoral nomadism became the specialty of some groups in dry regions. Others chose farming by shifting cultivation, a creative adaptation to prevailing conditions. As explained earlier, shifting cultivators moved their fields around every few years, letting recently used land lie fallow for a while to regain its nutrients. If not abused, this system worked well for centuries. Only in a few fertile areas was intensive sedentary agriculture possible, especially around the Great Lakes region of Central and East Africa and in the Ethiopian highlands. Animal domestication presented an additional challenge to sub-Saharan Africans, as few indigenous species were suitable. But by 6000 B.C.E., goats and sheep were brought in from the Middle East and utilized in the Saharan region by farmers and pastoralists.

Ancient African Metallurgy

Sub-Saharan Africans were among the world's earliest ironworkers. Iron smelters were built around 900 B.C.E. in the Great Lakes region of East Africa—

modern Burundi, Rwanda, and Tanzania (TAN-zeh-NEE-uh). This date makes them slightly older than the earliest Egyptian works. Between 600 and 300 B.C.E., iron was being mined, smelted, and forged in West, East, and North Africa, and by around 500 B.C.E. true steel was being made in Tanzania. Because most of the major iron ore deposits were located in far western Africa and Ethiopia, ore and iron artifacts had to be transported over long distances.

The technology gradually improved. Although some iron ore could be easily obtained from surface outcrops or riverbeds, in many places miners had to dig open pits or put down vertical shafts to reach deposits deep underground. Some of their furnaces for smelting were elaborate clay structures with blower systems that used animal skin bellows. The craftsmen made spear blades and arrowheads for warriors and hunters; hoes and knives for farmers and traders; bangles and rings for jewelry; hammers, hinges, and nails for household use; and iron bells for ceremonies and rituals.

The iron industry and its workers became a central feature of African life. The ruins of a 2,800-year-old village in Eritrea in the northeastern highlands revealed a people who lived in stone houses, drank beer, and ate cow and goat meat. They made gold jewelry as well as copper and bronze daggers and pottery jugs. Agriculture and metallurgy came to various African regions at different times, spreading to the southern half of the continent last. Originally much of this region was inhabited by expert hunters and gatherers such as the !Kung, the Khoisan-speaking people who flourished by skillfully exploiting the vegetation and animals of the harsh Kalahari Desert in southwestern Africa, fostering a community-minded, egalitarian society offering much time for leisure activities. The !Kung were successful adapters who had little incentive to develop agriculture or ironworking. Gradually most of these groups were pushed farther south by iron-using farmers.

LO³ Early African States, Networks, and Migrations, 1800–600 B.C.E.

Unlike the Egyptians and Nubians, many Africans rejected political centralization. Before the twentieth century, millions of people in sub-Saharan Africa remained by choice within loosely organized political structures, without kings, chiefs, or bureaucracies. In contrast to the citizens of most premodern kingdoms, these societies often enjoyed considerable democratic decision making and little tyranny. However, some sub-Saharan peoples were linked to societies in North Africa and western Asia, and thus participated in the iron and commercial revolutions of Afro-Eurasia. The Egyptians traded extensively with some peoples in northeastern Africa, probably helping to foster the rise of states, especially of Nubia just south of Egypt. But the complex societies in the Sudan, some of which may have fostered kingship by 600 B.C.E., probably owed less to Egyptian connections. Meanwhile, migrating Bantu (BAN-too)—African people who developed traditions based on farming and iron metallurgy—spread their languages, cultures, and technologies widely in the southern half of the continent. This migration brought farming and metallurgy to once-remote regions.

Nubia and the Rise of Kush

The first known urban African state after Egypt emerged in the region known in ancient times as Nubia, perhaps as early as 3100 B.C.E. (see Map 3.1). The Nubians occupied the land that today is the northern half of the country of Sudan and far southern Egypt. Like Egyptians, Nubians turned to the thin, fertile area along the Nile for survival. Today the region is mostly desert, and even several millennia ago it presented a difficult environment. By 6000 B.C.E., villages in the region were among the world's earliest pottery makers. Egypt enjoyed a long connection with Nubia and dominated the region for many centuries, occasionally through military occupations. Egypt and Nubia also established a two-way trade, with Egypt exporting materials such as pottery and copper items to Nubia and importing ivory, ebony, ostrich feathers, and slaves from the Nubians. This trade provided an economic incentive for local state building.

Kerma and Kush: Nubian Kingdoms

An independent Nubian kingdom, Kerma (CARE-ma), appeared between 1800 and 1600 B.C.E., as Egyptian power temporarily waned. Immigrants to this kingdom arrived from the Sahara and the south. Extensive ruins of massive cemeteries and large towers testify to a prosperous and well-organized society. Kerma was also distinguished for painted pottery and copper vessels and weapons. The Kerma religion mixed Egyptian and local African elements. Around 1500 B.C.E., Egyptian forces once again occupied Nubia and destroyed the Kerma state.

When Egyptian power declined around 900 B.C.E., after the end of the New Kingdom, a larger Nubian state known as Kush emerged, laying the foundations for a golden age of trade, culture, and metallurgy. The remains of many Kushite towns and cities have been found.

Kush Trade and International Relations

The Kushites conquered Egypt in the eighth century B.C.E. but were pushed out by the Assyrians after nearly a century of occupation. Kush became a major regional trading hub; overland caravan routes linked Kush with the Niger Basin, the Congo Basin, and the Ethiopian highlands. This enterprising society provided goods from central and southern Africa to the Mediterranean and Red Sea regions, as well as to markets as distant as India and China.

The Kush people's contacts with other societies added imported ideas to Nubian traditions, such as mechanical irrigation technology imported from Egypt. Kushite culture mixed Egyptian and local ideas: Kushites worshiped both Egyptian and local gods and buried their kings in Egyptian-style pyramids. A sixth-century B.C.E. inscription tells us that King Aspelta (as-PELL-ta), as the son of

> "The ancient Greek poet Homer described Kushites as "the most just of men; the favorites of the gods."

the Egyptian sun-god, Ra, built for his son a pyramid of white stone and made offerings of gold and silver. The unique Kushite society may have been matrilineal, and some women held key political positions, including that of queen.

Eventually Kush linked the peoples of Africa and the Mediterranean. By 600 B.C.E., Kush had become the major African producer of iron, a position that gave it an even more crucial economic influence on the ancient world. The ancient Greek poet Homer described Kushites as "the most just of men; the favorites of the gods. The lofty inhabitants of Olympus (oh-LIM-pus) (home of Greek gods) journey to them, and take part in their feasts."[5] Kush played an even more prominent historical role during the Classical Age (see Chapter 9).

The Sudanic Societies and Trade Networks

In ancient times, peoples in the Sudan grasslands also began developing towns and long-distance trade routes, and perhaps a few small kingdoms. Although trade extended to Nubia and Egypt, the Nubian and Egyptian influences in this region remain unclear. Urban societies existed in the Sudan three millennia ago, and perhaps earlier. By 1200 B.C.E., rice farmers in Mauritania (MORE-ee-TAIN-ee-uh) had built more than two hundred stone villages in what is now mostly uninhabited desert. By 900 or

From Derek A. Welsby, *The Kingdom of Kush* (British Museum Press). Reproduced with permission

Coronation Stela of Kushite King Aspelta (ca. 600 B.C.E.). The stela and inscription celebrate the coronation of King Aspelta. Related to the royal line through his mother, he was chosen from among many candidates by high priests acting in the name of the gods.

800 B.C.E., the population increase had changed walled villages into large, well-constructed towns. Then, between 500 and 300 B.C.E., this flourishing society was swallowed by the expanding Sahara, and the people probably moved south.

Long-distance trade, especially the caravan routes crossing the Sahara Desert dating back to 1000 or 500 B.C.E., aided the growth of Sudanic societies by forging enduring networks of communication. Some groups eventually took up commerce as their primary activity. The trans-Saharan trade depended on pack animals introduced by Berbers from North Africa, initially mules and horses and later camels. In time a large trade system spanned the Sahara, linking the Sudanic towns with the peoples of the desert and the southern Mediterranean coast as well as the forest zone to the south.

On the southern fringe of the Sudan, in what is now central Nigeria, the Nok people, mostly farmers and herders, were working iron by 500 B.C.E., and they also fashioned exquisite terra-cotta pottery and sculpture, including life-size and realistic human heads. The world-views of other peoples in the region, such as the ancestors of the Igbo (EE-boh) people in what is today southeastern Nigeria, may derive in part from Nok traditions.

Religious Beliefs

During the Ancient Era African societies, such as the people who later coalesced into the Mande and Igbo groups, were shaping their long-standing beliefs into complex religious traditions (see Witness to the Past: The World-view of an African Society). Many peoples, like the Mande and the Igbo, believed in one divine force or supreme being who created the cosmos, earth, and life, and then remained remote from human affairs. Africans needing immediate spiritual help appealed to secondary gods and spirits. By 6,000 or 7,000 years ago, some West Africans were

Nok Terra Cotta Sculpture of Head
Elaborate, life-size, technically complex sculptures reveal something of Nok material life in ancient Nigeria.
Werner Forman/Art Resource, NY

perhaps the world's first monotheists. Sub-Saharan African religion became a mix of monotheism, polytheism, and animism.

The Bantu-Speaking Peoples and Their Migrations

The Bantu-speaking peoples, who developed a society based on farming and iron metallurgy, spread these techniques widely by their great migrations. Today people who speak closely related Bantu languages occupy most of the continent south of a line stretching from Kenya in the northeast to Cameroon in west-central Africa. All of these societies can trace their distant ancestry back to the same location in west-central Africa. The Bantus incorporated many of the peoples they encountered and modified their own cultures to suit local conditions.

The Bantu occupation of central, eastern, and southern Africa is the result of one of the great population movements in premodern world history (see Map 3.2). During this process, the Bantu people multiplied and formed trade networks that spread technology. As the Bantus moved over a wider area, they gradually divided into more than four hundred different ethnic groups. The Bantus originated along the Benue (BAIN-way) River in what is now eastern Nigeria and western Cameroon (KAM-uh-roon). By 3000 B.C.E. they were already combining farming (especially of yams) with hunting, gathering, and fishing. But agricultural progress fostered overcrowding by 2000 B.C.E., spurring some to migrate eastward into the lands just north of the Congo River Basin. Bantus settled the Great Lakes region of East Africa between 1000 B.C.E. and 500 B.C.E., and by 1000 B.C.E. some Bantus from the Benue began moving south. Some moved up the Congo River, setting up small farms. As they settled in new areas, Bantus mixed with local peoples, exchanging technologies and cultural patterns.

Interactive Map

Technology and Agriculture

The Bantus benefited from metallurgy and agricultural technologies. Well before the Common Era, the

The World-View of an African Society

Few primary sources survive for the ancient period in sub-Saharan Africa. Although it is difficult to extrapolate the distant past from contemporary oral traditions, we can get some insight into ancient understandings of the natural and spiritual realms from such accounts. This excerpt on the world-view of the Igbo people in southeastern Nigeria was compiled by an Igbo anthropologist, who summarized Igbo thought. Many Igbo perspectives may well derive from the Nok and Bantu cultures, whose ancestral homelands are near the region where the Igbo live today.

There is the world of man peopled by all created beings and things, both animate and inanimate. The spirit world is the abode of the creator, the deities, the disembodied and malignant spirits, and the ancestral spirits. It is the future abode of the living after their death. . . . Existence for the Igbo is a dual but interrelated phenomenon involving the interaction between the material and the spiritual, the visible and the invisible, the good and the bad, the living and the dead. . . . The world of the "dead" is a world full of activities. . . . The principle of seniority makes the ancestors [in the world of the "dead"] the head of the [extended kinship system in the world of man]. . . .

The world as a natural order which inexorably goes on its ordained way according to a "master plan" is foreign to Igbo conceptions. Rather, their world is a dynamic one—a world of moving equilibrium. It is an equilibrium that is constantly threatened, and sometimes actually disturbed by natural and social calamities. . . . But the Igbo believe that these social calamities and cosmic forces which disturb their world are controllable and should be "manipulated" by them for their own purpose. The maintenance of social and cosmological balance in the world becomes . . . a dominant and pervasive theme in Igbo life. They achieve this balance . . . through divination, sacrifice, and appeal to the countervailing forces of their ancestors . . . against the powers of the malignant spirits. . . . The Igbo world is not only a world in which people strive for equality; it is one in which change is constantly expected. . . . Life on earth is a link in the chain of status hierarchy which culminates in the achievement of ancestral honor in the world of the dead. . . .

The idea of a creator of all things is focal to Igbo theology. They believe in a supreme god, a high god, who is all good. . . . The Igbo high god is a withdrawn god. He is a god who has finished all active works of creation and keeps watch over his creatures from a distance. . . . Although the Igbo feel psychologically separated from their high god, he is not too far away, he can be reached, but not as quickly as can other deities who must render their services to man to justify their demand for sacrifices. . . . Minor gods [can] be controlled, manipulated, and used to further human interests. . . . Given effective protection, the Igbo are very faithful to their gods.

Thinking About The Reading

1. How do the Igbo understand the relationship between the human and spiritual worlds?
2. What is the role of the supreme god in their polytheistic theology?
3. How might their beliefs about the relationship of the human and spiritual realms shape Igbo society?

Source: From Uchendu, THE IGBO OF SOUTHEAST NIGERIA, 1E © 1965 Wadsworth, a part of Cengage Learning, Inc. Reproduced by permission.

Bantus in the Benue region had learned to smelt iron, perhaps from the nearby Nok culture. Iron spread along the Bantu communication network. Metallurgy allowed the Bantus to use iron tools and weapons to open new land and subdue the small existing populations. They were also skilled farmers, and some raised cattle or goats. By 2,000 years ago, some Bantus living in northeast Africa had also learned to grow domesticated bananas and plantains (large bananas) imported from Southeast Asia, as well as sorghum (SOAR-gum) from the Nile valley. These high-yielding crops replaced yams as their primary staple food and stimulated population growth, encouraging new migration into southern Africa.

Map 3.2
Bantu Migrations and Early Africa
The Bantu-speaking peoples spread over several millennia throughout the southern half of Africa. Various societies, cities, and states emerged in West and North Africa.

LO⁴ Early Societies and Networks of the Eastern Mediterranean

During the second millennium B.C.E., smaller bronze- and then iron-using societies in the eastern half of the Mediterranean Basin developed influential ideas and states. Among these, the Hebrews created the base for three major religions. The Minoans became an economic bridge between western Asia and southeastern Europe, and the trade-oriented but warlike Mycenaeans built the first cities in Greece. The Phoenicians created an important new alphabet, established colonies in the western Mediterranean, and forged trade networks with people as far away as England. Greek migrants also began building a society that eventually nourished others in Europe, western Asia, and North Africa.

Eastern Mediterranean Environments

The history and diet of peoples living around the eastern Mediterranean were influenced by the regional climate, with its cool, rainy winters and hot, dry summers, and by the Mediterranean Sea and its coastal areas. On the narrow coastal or interior plains of the northern shores, grain was planted, and bread became a food staple. Olive trees and grape vines flourished, and both olive oil and wine became export crops for Greece and Anatolia. Because the Mediterranean topography made the development of large herds of cattle impractical, people raised pigs, sheep, and goats. Finally, the eastern Mediterranean Sea, a large, mostly placid body of water, fostered boat building, maritime trade, and interaction (see Map 3.3).

 Interactive Map

Greece and Geography

One of the densest populations emerged in Greece, an appendage of southern Europe located less than 100 miles from Anatolia across the Aegean (ah-JEE-uhn) Sea. Unlike western Asia and Egypt, where long and wide river valleys invited the creation of large political units, Greece consists of small valleys separated by numerous mountains, some 8,000 to 10,000 feet high. This physical separation encouraged small, independent city-states, which meant that people with unpopular or new ideas could move from one small state to another. This mobility encouraged intellectual diversity. Greece also has an extensive coastline with many good harbors, and Greeks could travel by sea east to Ionia (today Turkey's Aegean coast), south to Crete, or west to southern Italy more easily than they could establish connections with nearby inland towns. Thus the Mediterranean linked the societies of the Greek peninsula to the Minoans, Egyptians, Phoenicians, and others.

The Hebrews and Religious Innovation

For more than one thousand years, the Hebrews, a Semitic people, were one of many groups of pastoral nomads, led by powerful men known as *patriarchs* (from the Greek word for "rule by the father"). Although the united Hebrew monarchy lasted less than a century, their contribution to religious history was momentous. The various books of the Hebrew Bible contain the basic laws of the Hebrews and are the main source for their early history. The Hebrews trace their ancestry as a people back to Abraham, a patriarch (possibly mythical, many scholars suspect) who supposedly lived in Mesopotamia sometime between 2000 and 1500 B.C.E. Abraham and his two sons, Isaac and Ishmael, are considered the spiritual ancestors of three monotheistic religions—Judaism, Christianity, and Islam—which are often called the Abrahamic faiths and collectively have some 3 billion followers today.

The Bible

Historians and archaeologists, among them modern Israelis, have heatedly debated the historical reliability and antiquity of the Hebrew Bible; little of it can be confirmed by nonbiblical sources such as archaeology. Some scholars think the biblical books are quite old, whereas others argue that most or all of the books, even those offering accounts of very ancient events, were composed after 700 B.C.E. to support the claims of Hebrew political and religious factions. The earliest known material evidence for biblical passages are inscriptions found on silver scrolls dating from the late 500s B.C.E.

> **"The earliest known material evidence for biblical passages are inscriptions found on silver scrolls dating from the late 500s B.C.E."**

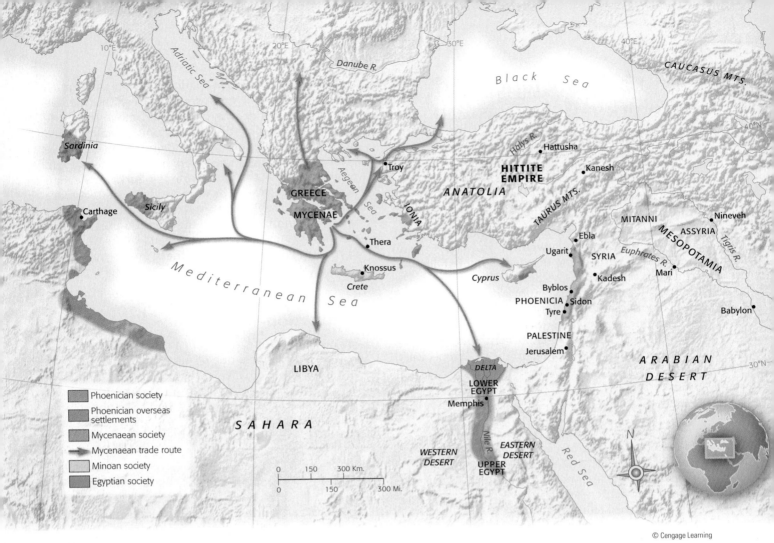

Map 3.3
The Ancient Eastern Mediterranean

The Hebrew, Minoan, Mycenaean, Phoenician, and Greek societies developed along the eastern shores of the Mediterranean Sea, interacting with each other and with other western Asians and the Egyptians.

© Cengage Learning

Some bible stories seem based on Mesopotamian and Egyptian traditions, such as the great flood in the *Epic of Gilgamesh*, suggesting the spread of ideas.

In the biblical account, during the second millennium Abraham led a small group of people on a migration from southern Mesopotamia to Palestine, an area on the Mediterranean coast between Egypt and Syria. Although born into a polytheistic world, Abraham recognized one supreme god. A group of Hebrews who had gone to Egypt to escape drought and been enslaved were freed and left Egypt, probably in the thirteenth century. This "Exodus" from Egypt and eventual return to Palestine was led by Moses, whom the later Hebrews believed to be the founder of their religion. Moses gave his name to a code of laws, including the Ten Commandments, by which the Hebrews governed themselves. The biblical account indicates that not all Hebrews were followers of Mosaic laws, but that around 1000 B.C.E., the Hebrews had enough unity to establish a monarchy centered in the small city of Jerusalem.

The End of Hebrew Unity

Hebrew unity proved short-lived. After the death of King Solomon in 922 B.C.E., the monarchy split into a northern kingdom of Israel and a southern kingdom of Judah. In 722 the Assyrians conquered Israel and resettled its inhabitants elsewhere in their empire. In 586 B.C.E. the Chaldeans conquered the

The Eastern Mediterranean,
2000–539 B.C.E.

2000–1500	Possible time frame for Abraham (biblical account)
2000–1400	Minoan society
1630	Volcanic eruption destroys Thera (Santorini)
1600–1200	Mycenaean society
1500–650	Phoenician society
1300–1200	Hebrew Exodus from Egypt led by Moses (biblical account)
1200–800	Greek "Dark Age"
1250	Destruction of Troy, possibly by Mycenaeans
1000	First Hebrew kingdom (biblical account)
922–722	Hebrew kingdoms of Israel and Judah
750	Carthage colony established by Phoenicians
722	Assyrian conquest of Israel
586	Neo-Babylonian (Chaldean) conquest of Judah
539	End of Babylonian captivity

kingdom of Judah and moved its leaders to the Euphrates near Babylon. The bitterness of the "Babylonian Captivity" was reflected in a Hebrew psalm: "By the rivers of Babylon, there we sat down, yea, we wept when we remembered Zion."[6] This exile ended in 539, when the Persians conquered the Chaldeans and allowed the Hebrews to return to Palestine. Later Palestine became part of the Roman Empire. The Jews (from the word *Yehudin*, a term Hebrews used to describe themselves by about 500 B.C.E.) were again dispersed after a revolt against Roman rule in 70 C.E. From that time until the establish-

> 66 There is no other God besides Me, a just God. Look to Me, and be saved, all you ends of the earth! 99
>
> *The Prophet Isaiah*

ment of modern Israel in 1948 C.E., there was no Hebrew or Jewish state.

The Contributions of Hebrew Religion

Over their long history both as nomads and as settled state-builders, the Hebrews developed or refined four religious concepts that made them stand out among ancient peoples and that later influenced the Western and Islamic traditions. These concepts are found in their sacred writings; they include monotheism, morality, messianism, and meaning in history.

The first concept, monotheism, developed out of the Hebrew belief that a single god, Yahweh (YA-way), had made an agreement, or covenant, with their earliest patriarchs and reinforced it when Moses received the Ten Commandments. If they would obey him, he would protect them. Gradually, the Hebrews asserted that there is only one God, Yahweh, for all peoples, as the prophet Isaiah proclaimed: "There is no other God besides Me, a just God. Look to Me, and be saved, all you ends of the earth!"[7]

Hebrew holy men known as prophets refined a second Hebrew religious concept, morality. Working in the troubled times between the end of the united monarchy and the fall of Israel to the Assyrians, these men emphasized that following Yahweh meant leading a moral life, that is, refraining from lying, stealing, adultery, and persecution of the poor and oppressed. Hebrew ethics emphasized mercy as well as justice, and compassion for the poor.

The third Hebrew contribution to religious thought was messianism, the belief that God had given the Hebrew people a special mission in the world. As the Hebrews faced their time of troubles after the division of Solomon's kingdom, and especially after the fall of Judah to the Chaldeans, messianism acquired a broad spiritual meaning of bringing proper ethical behavior to all peoples. This idea later inspired Christian missionary work.

The final important Hebrew religious contribution is the idea that history itself has meaning and that

messianism
The Hebrew belief that their God, Yahweh, had given them a special mission in the world.

Ancient Jewish History (*http://www .us-israel.org/jsources/ Judaism/jewhist.html*). Find useful information on Jewish history.

The Captivity of Israeli Women at Ninevah This relief comes from the palace of the Chaldean king Sennacherib in Ninevah. It was probably carved at the beginning of the seventh century B.C.E.

Erich Lessing/Art Resource, NY

it moves forward in a progressive, linear fashion and not in great repetitive cosmic cycles of thousands or millions of years. Sanctifying a linear view of time meant that the material, time-bound world was where human beings worked out their salvation by choosing good over evil. This belief stood in contrast to ideas enshrined in the Indian religions of Hinduism and Buddhism that the material world is illusory and that time is cyclical.

Minoan Crete and Regional Trade

An important urban society and network hub, now called Minoan (mi-NO-an), thrived on the island of Crete (kreet) between about 2000 and 1400 B.C.E. Crete lies just south of the Aegean Sea and the Greek peninsula, a strategic location that made it a logical center for sea trade between Egypt, western Asia, and southeastern Europe. Archaeologists who discovered the remains of an elaborate royal palace at Knossos (NAW-sus), on the northern shore of the island, named it Minos (MY-nus), after a Greek legend about a king who had once ruled in Crete. In the story, Minos "made himself master of the Greek waters, and for the safer conveyance of his revenues, he did all he could to suppress piracy."[8]

Minoan buildings had plumbing, and some towns had streets with drains and sewers, like the cities in ancient India. Paintings and sculptures show some Mesopotamian and Egyptian influences, but they are also different in style. Particularly interesting was the apparent worship of a large number of female deities and many paintings of flowers, animals, and bare-breasted females. The Minoans built no defensive walls, apparently relying on their fleet alone to protect them. Around 1630 B.C.E., many cities on the island were destroyed, perhaps from earthquakes that followed a massive volcanic explosion that blew apart the nearby island of Thera (THER-uh) (today's Santorini). The sinking of most of Thera and the dispersal of the survivors may have given rise to the legend of the lost continent of Atlantis.

Agriculture and Trade Routes
The first great Mediterranean sea power, the Minoans were innovators, pioneering a mixed agriculture of olives, grapes, and grain that was well suited to the region's sunny, dry climate. Already by 3000 B.C.E., they were using copper and trading intermittently with Egypt, and this trade became regular after 2000 B.C.E. Minoans traded extensively with Sicily, Greece, and the Aegean islands and sent wine, olives, and wool to Egypt and southwest Asia. Although their writing has not been deciphered, tablets found in the palace at Knossos appear to be written in two scripts, one of which may be related to a Mesopotamian language and the other to early forms of Greek. This suggests that ancient Crete served as a trading hub connecting western Asians and North Africans with various European societies. The Cretan ports were counterparts to the Persian Gulf ports that linked western and southern Asia.

Wall Painting from Thera, Crete The paintings in palaces and homes show slices of Minoan life. This one portrays female boxers, hinting that women played many roles in Minoan society.

The Mycenaeans and Phoenicians

The Mycenaeans and Phoenicians were two other influential Mediterranean societies. Mycenaeans—Indo-Europeans named after the city of Mycenae (my-SEE-nee) in southern Greece—became an important military power between 1600 and 1200 B.C.E. after migrating into the Greek peninsula Their graves, which contain swords and armor, show that they valued fighting and had a command of bronze technology. They had a state-controlled economy that was tightly organized from the top down by the king and his scribes. By the middle of the second millennium, the Mycenaeans controlled Crete, whose Minoan society had already collapsed. The Mycenaeans also conquered all of southern Greece and the Aegean islands, forming an empire from which they collected taxes and tribute. They continued the Minoan trading networks, dispatching ships to Sicily, Italy, and Spain and into the Black Sea and spreading bronze technology. Mycenaeans also engaged in war with rivals, operating, unlike the Minoans, out of strong fortresses.

According to legends, around 1250 the Mycenaeans conquered Troy, a prosperous Hittite trading port along the northwestern coast of Anatolia. This event inspired Homer's epic story, the Iliad, some 500 years later. Scholars differ as to whether an actual Trojan War ever took place, and some suspect that the Homeric stories combine oral accounts of various conflicts. Whatever their accuracy, they strongly influenced the later Greeks and Romans.

Decline of the Mycenaeans

By 1200 B.C.E., however, the Mycenaeans faced collapse, although the reasons remain unclear. A prolonged drought resulting from climate change or a possible series of earthquakes, which may also have destroyed Troy, may have been factors. Many historians blame civil wars and attacks by warlike Indo-Europeans known as the Dorian Greeks, who were migrating into the peninsula. In the several centuries after 1200, various groups known as "Sea Peoples" pillaged and disrupted trade throughout the Aegean and eastern Mediterranean, but eventually a creative society emerged in Greece that incorporated many influences from the Dorian Greeks, Mycenaeans, Phoenicians, and Egyptians, as will be discussed in later sections.

The Phoenician Trading Network and Alphabet

The Phoenicians, one of the greatest ancient trading societies, linked Mediterranean and southwest Asian peoples by trade networks and by their invention of a phonetic alphabet. Between 1500 and 1000 B.C.E., this Semitic people, known to the Hebrews as the Canaanites (KAY-nan-ites), established themselves along the narrow coastal strip west of the Lebanon mountains, where they built the great trading cities of Tyre (ti-ER), Sidon (SIDE-en), and Byblos (BIB-los). Described by Hebrew sources as the crowning city whose merchants were also princes, Tyre was a major hub, the place where luxury goods from many societies were collected and the finest artists and craftsmen worked.

Although sometimes dominated by Egypt, these cities were fiercely competitive independent states headed by kings. Although the Phoenicians spoke a common language and worshiped the same gods, they never united to form one country. The Greek word for book, *byblos*, was taken from the name of the Phoenician city that was famous for its high-quality papyrus, which was used to make written scrolls. The Phoenicians' relatively rich, well-situated land was the home of the now long-gone "cedars of Lebanon" prized by the tree-starved Sumerians, Egyptians, and Hebrews.

The most famous cultural achievement of the Phoenicians, their simplification of Mesopotamian cuneiform writing into an alphabet of twenty-two characters, became the basis of later European alphabets. The creation of this alphabet helped spread Phoenician influence in the Mediterranean and the networks they created. Between 1000 and 800 B.C.E., the seafaring Phoenicians began to replace the declining Mycenaeans as the leaders in Mediterranean trade with western Asia, becoming renowned as the great mariners of the Mediterranean. They established colonies or trading posts in North Africa, southern Italy, Sicily, Spain, and Morocco.

....

The Phoenician Legacy

Because the papyrus documents, which might have recorded their views on trade and daily life, have largely disappeared, most of what we know comes from Egyptian, Greek, and Hebrew sources. These peoples generally admired the Phoenicians' skills as scribes, seafarers, engineers, and artisans but also denounced them as immoral profiteers and cheaters. For example, an Egyptian report from around 1100 B.C.E. describes the difficult mission of a pharaoh's envoy, Wen-Amon, who was sent to Byblos to purchase some cedarwood for a new temple. On his sea journey, the hapless Wen-Amon was robbed. In Byblos he waited days for an audience with the Byblos king, Zakar-Baal, who wanted to sell timber but realized Wen-Amon now had little money left to purchase anything. After a chilly meeting, Zakar-Baal sold the demoralized Egyptian a small amount of wood, showing no mercy.

Between 1000 and 500 B.C.E., the Mediterranean Sea became a major source of goods and wealth, partly because of Phoenician efforts. Solid bars of precious metals served as currency until the seventh century B.C.E., when coins began to appear. Using their colonies as ports for resupply and repair, the Phoenicians traveled long distances to secure iron, silver, timber, copper, gold, and tin, all valuable commodities in western Asia and Egypt during the second and first millennia B.C.E. In 650 B.C.E., the Assyrians conquered the Phoenician home cities and brought an end to their dynamic power, but some Phoenician colonies lived on. The most famous colony was Carthage in North Africa, established around 750 B.C.E., which became the capital of a major trading empire and the chief competitor to the Romans in the western Mediterranean by the third century B.C.E. As great sailors the Carthaginians later explored far down the coast of West Africa.

The Eclectic Roots of Greek Society

The fall of the Phoenicians and the Mycenaeans set the stage for another seafaring people, the Greeks, to found an influential urban society. Historians have referred to the centuries from the destruction of Mycenae around 1200 B.C.E. down to around 800 B.C.E. as the Greek "Dark Age," because during this time organized states and writing disappeared, and social, economic, and political conditions were chaotic on the peninsula. Dorian Greeks, whose migrations had contributed to the fall of Mycenae, settled much of the Greek peninsula, and many Mycenaeans dispersed, some settling the offshore islands and others crossing the Aegean Sea to Ionia, where they established cities. The Greek world—scattered, as the philosopher Plato later put it, like frogs around a pond—became a mix of Mycenaean and Dorian peoples and traditions. In the absence of strong governments, various tribes struggled for power.

....

Homer: *Iliad* and *Odyssey*

The Homeric epics, which were written during this period, became an integral part of the Greek tradition in an era of much political and economic change. They were oral epics celebrating military conquests, written down between the eleventh and the eighth centuries B.C.E. Historians disagree as to whether Homer was an actual person or the collective name for several authors who compiled these epic poems into a narrative, and whether the epics reflect actual events from the Mycenaean era. Some scholars argue that many themes and plots in the epics reflect influences from Mesopotamian literature, such as the *Epic of Gilgamesh*.

The first Homeric epic, the *Iliad*, is set during an attack by some Greek cities, led by their king Agamemnon (ag-uh-MEM-non), on Troy across the Aegean in Anatolia. The poem emphasizes the aristocratic value of valor in war yet warns its readers against war's excesses and brutality. This poem and Homer's second epic, the *Odyssey* (ODD-eh-see), a story of the adventures of Odysseus (oh-DIS-ee-us) (or Ulysses (YOU-lis-eez)) returning home after the Trojan War, portrayed the Greek gods as superheroes who intervened frequently to help their human friends and hinder their enemies. The Homeric world measured virtue by success in combat. Both gods and men took more joy in competition and battle than they did in justice or mercy. Homer's emphasis on both human power and suffering remained a part of Greek literature throughout the following centuries. The Homeric epics and belief in the gods that they introduced greatly influenced the emerging Greek society.

Foundations of the Classical Era

As mentioned previously, Greek society eventually became a synthesis of Mycenaean and Dorian traditions. The Greeks also borrowed ideas from neighboring peoples, including the Egyptians and western Asians. Certainly the Mediterranean was a zone of interaction for peoples living around its rim. Phoenician ships, which had avoided a turbulent Greece for several hundred years, began to show up again, restoring Greek contact with the eastern Mediterranean and its regional trade networks. Soon the Greeks adopted and modified the Phoenician alphabet and began trading with western Asia again, as they had during the Mycenaean period. These centuries built a foundation for a dynamic Greek society in the Classical Era.

 Listen to a synopsis of Chapter 3.

Around the Pacific Rim:

Eastern Eurasia and the Americas, 5000–600 B.C.E.

Learning Outcomes

After reading this chapter, you should be able to answer the following questions:

LO¹ How did an expanding Chinese society arise from diverse local traditions?

LO² What were some key differences between the Shang and Zhou periods in China?

LO³ How did the traditions developing in Southeast and Northeast Asia differ from those in India and China?

LO⁴ How do scholars explain the settlement of the Americas and the rise of the first American societies?

> **❝**He encouraged the people and settled them. He called his superintendent of works [and] minister of instruction, and charged them with the building of the houses. Crowds brought the earth in baskets. The roll of the great drum did not overpower [the noise of the builders].**❞**
>
> —**Chinese poem from the second millennium B.C.E.**[1]

According to Chinese tradition, around 1400 B.C.E. a ruler named Pan Keng supervised the building of a new capital city, Anyang (ahn-yahng), on a flat plain alongside the Huan River. The king and his officials supervised the citizens in the hard construction labor, which was done to the beat of a drum. The king had high expectations for his new capital. Thanks to the rich soil, productive farms would stretch out into the distance. The river could supply water and aid in defense. People could find timber, hunt animals, or seek relief from the summer heat in the nearby mountains. Anyang was likely China's first planned city, and its system governed city planning for the next 3,000 years. Surrounded by four walls facing the points of the compass, it reflected the ancient adage that without harmony nothing lasts. Three-and-a-half millennia later, archaeologists digging at Anyang found exquisite ritual bronzes and "dragon bones," animal bones carved with some of the earliest Chinese writing. Although Anyang's buildings crumbled with time and ruling families came and went, the legacy of early China did live on for centuries.

Test your knowlege before you read this chapter.

What do you think?

Although ancient societies in Asia and the Americas were very distinct, both regions developed important trade networks.

Strongly Disagree						*Strongly Agree*
I	2	3	4	5	6	7

Cities, states, agriculture, and trade networks developed in various societies on both sides of the Pacific Ocean. On the Asian side, ancient cities like Anyang confirm that, as in India, Mesopotamia, and Egypt, distinctive urban societies appeared very early in China. People in East Asia were among the first people in the world to develop farming, metalworking, and maritime technology. The ancient Chinese established a foundation for a society that has retained many of its customs to the present day. Despite formidable geographic barriers, China and Southeast Asia also became connected very early to

Bildarchiv Preussischer Kulturbesitz/Art Resource, NY

<< Shang Axe Head The Shang Chinese made some of the ancient world's finest bronze tools. This axe head may have been used to behead rivals of the Shang rulers.

other parts of Eurasia by trade networks. On the American side of the Pacific, too, many peoples transitioned to farming, cities, and complex social structures, while others flourished by using other strategies for survival. Although environmental factors tended to isolate North, Central, and South American societies from each other, regional networks of exchange still formed even here during the ancient period.

LO¹ The Formation of Chinese Society, 6000–1750 B.C.E.

China was one of the first societies with cities and states, along with Harappa, Mesopotamia, Egypt, and Minoan Crete. Societies change in part through contact with each other, but forbidding desert and mountain barriers on China's western borders limited contact with the other ancient urban societies. But productive farming, creative cultures, and the rise of states laid the framework for a distinctive society, now at least 4,000 years old, that dominated a sphere of interaction in eastern Eurasia.

China and Its Regional Environments

The Chinese faced many challenges in communicating both with each other and with distant peoples. China's vast size, combined with a difficult topography, made transportation difficult and also encouraged regional loyalties. The Chinese were often divided into competing states, especially in early times, and governments struggled to enforce centralizing policies. The Himalayas (him-uh-LAY-uhs), the Tibetan Plateau, and great deserts inhibited contact with South and West Asia. However, the ancient Chinese did interact with the various peoples in Central Asia, North Asia, Southeast Asia, and Tibet, whose cultures, languages, and ways of life were very different from the Chinese. Over the centuries, the Chinese sometimes extended

Internet Guide for China Studies (*http://www.sino .uni-heidelberg.de/ igcs/*). A good collection of links on premodern and modern China.

political control over these peoples and sometimes were invaded and even conquered by them.

River Systems

Before modern times, most Chinese lived in inland river valleys rather than along the coast. As a result, maritime, or ocean, commerce was not very significant until 1000 C.E. In the interior, extensive mountains, deserts, and wetlands hindered transportation, and therefore communication, between regions. China's three major river systems helped shape Chinese regionalism. The Yellow, or Huang He (hwang ho), River; the Yangzi (YAHNG-zeh), or Yangtze, River; and the West, or Xijiang (SHEE-jyahng), River all flow from west to east and hence do not link the northern, central, and southern parts of China. The Yellow River flows some 3,000 miles through north China to the Yellow Sea, but it floods often and is easily navigable only in some sections. The more navigable but also flood-prone Yangzi, the world's fourth-longest river, flows through central China, a region of moderate climate that has had the densest population for the past thousand years. The shorter West River system helps define mountainous and subtropical south China.

Neighboring Cultures

China's neighboring regions had diverse environments and distinctive cultures. The deserts and grasslands of Central Asia, with their blazing hot summers and long, bitterly cold winters, were unpromising for intensive agriculture except in the Oxus River Valley (see Chapter 2). The rugged, pastoralist Central Asian societies that lived there traded with, warred against, and sometimes conquered the settled farmers of China, Korea, and India. South of the deserts, the Tibetans of the high plateau were subsistence farmers and herders. The ancient Chinese also forged occasional relations with people in mainland Southeast Asia, Manchuria, and Korea.

Early Chinese Farming Societies

Agriculture in China began around 7000 B.C.E., perhaps 1,000 years later than in Mesopotamia. The Yellow and Wei River Valleys in north China were major centers of early farming, probably because of their modest annual rainfall and somewhat predictable flooding. In addition, winds blowing in from the Gobi Desert of Mongolia to the northwest deposited massive amounts of dust, known as loess (LESS), which enriched the soils of north China. The people initially planted a highly drought-resistant grain called millet. Later, wheat, likely imported from India or Mesopotamia, became northern China's main cereal grain.

Agricultural Traditions

Further south, the Chinese in the Yangzi River Basin began cultivating rice by 5000 B.C.E. Thus, very early, two distinct agricultural traditions emerged. In the north, where the climate was cold and dry, drought-tolerant crops like wheat, millet, pears, and apricots were mainstays. In the wetter, warmer southern half of China, irrigated rice and more temperate crops came to predominate. But rice became so important that for several thousand years Chinese have greeted each other by asking, "Have you eaten rice yet?", and have described losing a job as breaking one's rice bowl.

Highly productive agriculture was always a key to China's success. Making wise use of the land, the Chinese sustained reasonably adequate diets over many millennia. As it was elsewhere, famine

> "The Longshan people built strong houses, lived in walled villages and towns, had weapons for warfare, and developed farming."

was fairly common, yet the Chinese people were basically well fed, well clothed, and well housed throughout much of history, beginning in ancient times. Productive farming also promoted population growth: northern and central China contained between 2 and 4 million people by 3000 B.C.E. The Chinese ate well enough and grew enough food that they came to perceive food as more than simple fuel. Cooking became an art form, an arena for aesthetic involvement and sensory delight, and an essential component of social life. A God of the Kitchen became an important deity of folk religion, and many distinctive regional variations in cooking developed. The use of chopsticks for eating meals probably goes back 4,000 years.

The Growth and Spread of Chinese Culture

Neolithic China

Neolithic China included several societies with distinctive regional traditions that established a foundation for Chinese cultural development. The best known of these societies is the Yangshao (YANG-shao) ("painted pottery") culture, which began in the middle Yellow River region around 5000 B.C.E. and covered an area of north China larger than Mesopotamia or Egypt. Several excavated villages from around 4000 B.C.E. reveal that people made fine painted pottery, used kilns, fashioned stone and bone tools, bred pigs and dogs, weaved thread, lived in timber houses, and buried their dead in cemeteries, suggesting belief in an afterlife. They also raised silkworms and fashioned the silk into clothes, establishing silk-making as a unique Chinese activity.

Farming life in this early society was hard, and probably much communal effort was needed to produce a small agricultural surplus. Village layouts suggest that people organized themselves into larger kinship groups such as clans, a feature of Chinese life thereafter. Some long-lasting cultural patterns developed (see Witness to the Past: The Poetry of Peasant Life in Zhou China). Music was popular; a 7,000-year-old

 Explore life in ancient China, as either a noble or a farmer, in this interactive simulation.

CHRONOLOGY

Ancient China, 7000–600 B.C.E.

7000	Agriculture begins in Yellow River Basin
5000	Agriculture begins in Yangzi River Basin
5000–3000	Yangshao culture in northern China
3000–2200	Longshan culture in northern China
2600	Copper mining
2183–1752	Xia dynasty in northern China (disputed)
1752–1122	Shang dynasty in northern China
1400	Beginning of bronze-casting industry
1122–221	Zhou dynasty

Witness to the Past

The Poetry of Peasant Life in Zhou China

We can learn something of the lives of ancient Chinese common folk, especially the peasants who worked the land, from *The Book of Songs*, a collection of 305 poems, hymns, and folk songs compiled between 1000 and 600 B.C.E.

Some songs address ordinary people at their labor. Men weed the fields, plant, plow, and harvest. Women and girls gather mulberry leaves for silkworms, carry hampers of food to the men in the fields for lunch, and make thread:

The girls take their deep baskets, And follow the path under the wall, to gather the soft mulberry-leaves.

Some of the songs deal with courtship and love, sometimes revealing strong emotion, as in this song by a girl about a prospective sweetheart:

That the mere glimpse of a plain cap, Could harry me with such longing, Cause me pain so dire. . . . Enough! Take me with you to your house. . . . Let us two be one.

Within the family, the father had nearly absolute authority over his wife and children. When the family patriarch died, his wife became the family head. Children were expected to obey their parents, but some songs reveal that mutual affection and gratitude were common:

My father begot me. My mother fed me, Led me, bred me, Brought me up, reared me, Kept her eye on me, tended me, At every turn aided me. Their good deeds I would requite.

Peasant lives were filled with toil and hardship, but they could find some relief from drudgery in friendship and kinship. Entertaining relatives and friends was a major leisure activity:

And shall a man not seek to have his friends? He shall have harmony and peace. I have strained off my liquor in abundance, the dishes stand in rows, and none of my brethren are absent. Whenever we have leisure, let us drink the sparkling liquor.

Peasants faced many demands on their time and labor. Songs complain and even protest about an uncaring government and its rapacious tax collectors:

Big rat, big rat, Do not gobble our millet! Three years we have slaved for you. Yet you took no notice of us. At last we are going to leave you, And go to the happy land . . . where no sad songs are sung.

Some songs record abject poverty and misery:

Deep is my grief. I am utterly poverty-stricken and destitute. Yet no one heeds my misfortunes. Well, all is over now. No doubt it was Heaven's [the supernatural realm's] doing. So what's the good of talking about it!

Zhou peasants needed all the help they could get and some songs seem to be prayers to Heaven to bless their lives:

Good people, gentle folk—Their ways are righteous. . . . Their thoughts constrained. . . . Good people, gentle folk—Shape the people of this land. . . . And may they do so for ten thousand years!

Thinking About The Reading

1. What do the songs tell us about the importance of families and friends to the Zhou Chinese?

2. What did peasants think about those who ruled them? Can you say why?

Source: The Book of Songs, translated by Arthur Waley (London: George Allen and Unwin, 1954). © copyright by permission of the Arthur Waley Estate.

seven-holed flute is the oldest still-playable musical instrument ever found anywhere in the world. The Chinese also created the first known numerical system. Because floods and earthquakes were common, the early Chinese speculated with techniques to predict the future.

By about 3000 B.C.E., the Chinese in the Yellow River Basin developed a society that was more complex than the Yang-shao society, with permanent settlements and irrigated farming, but there were also major achievements elsewhere. As late as 2000 B.C.E., many different societies existed in China, until gradually the societies in northern and central China merged their traditions into a common cultural zone.

The Yellow River Basin was always a major core of creativity. The Longshan (LUNG-shahn) ("black pottery") culture dominated the eastern Yellow River area between around 3000 and 2200 B.C.E. The Longshan people built strong houses, lived in walled villages and towns, had weapons for warfare, and developed farming. They also made pottery almost as hard as metal, carved high-quality jade, and created a simple pictographic writing system. Millennia before any other society, the Chinese of this era also used industrial diamonds to polish ceremonial ruby and sapphire axes. Other societies also developed traditions and technologies, such as the people in the Yangzi Basin, who produced techniques of agriculture, animal domestication, town building, and bronze metallurgy that were at least as old as those of north China.

Later, during the first millennium B.C.E., Chinese identity and customs gradually expanded from the Yellow and Yangzi Basins into south China. Later during the third millennium B.C.E., population growth and shared culture made possible the first states. The Chinese displaced or absorbed most of the indigenous peoples (the original inhabitants) in the south.

This mixing of different peoples produced a Chinese culture that encompassed many regional traditions and political systems, all held together by many common customs and values, as well as a standardized written language.

Xia Dynasty

The Chinese trace their political ancestry to several heroes who supposedly lived in north China during Longshan times and were models of behavior for all Chinese. Chinese historians labeled this era the Xia (shya) (Hsia) dynasty (2183–1752 B.C.E.), but its existence is still debated. A possible Xia capital city, one square mile in size, was built around 2000 B.C.E. near the Yellow River. The Xia may have presided over an occupationally diverse society including scribes, metallurgists, artisans, and bureaucrats. If the Xia were the first real Chinese state, the extent of their rule remains unclear.

Ancient China developed in such an original fashion as to almost create a world apart. Some influences filtered in from Central Asia, but in general, the Chinese built the ideas and institutions that gave their society the ability to expand, grow, adapt, and coordinate large populations. Many ancient traditions remain influential today.

LO² The Reshaping of Ancient Chinese Society, 1750–600 B.C.E.

China had made the great transition to cities and states when the Shang (shahng) dynasty established a powerful state and an expanding culture based on bronze technology. The Shang were followed by a more decentralized, iron-using system under

From Eleanor (von Erdberg) Consten, *Das alte China* (Stuttgart: Gustav Klipper Verlag., 1959)

Peasant Life in Zhou China The decorations on bronze vessels from Zhou China offer information on peasant life. This decoration, from the Warring States Period, shows people in varied activities: fighting, hunting, making music, performing rituals, and preparing food.

the Zhou (joe) dynasty, during which time the Chinese improved writing, developed a literature, and established some religious ideas of enduring influence. In addition, isolation from other Eurasian states convinced the Chinese that they needed little help from others, and a feeling of cultural superiority gradually developed. Indeed, strong governments, technological developments, and writing helped make China the most influential East Asian society for many millennia to come.

The Shang Dynasty of Northern China

The Shang (1752–1122 B.C.E.), the first fully documented Chinese dynasty, began around the same time that Hammurabi ruled in Babylon and the Harappan soci-ety was collapsing in India. A people from the western fringe of China, the Shang had adopted horse-drawn chariots for warfare and owed their success partly to networks linking them with Central Asian pastoralists. They conquered the eastern Yellow River Basin and imposed a hierarchy dominated by landowning aristocrats (see Map 4.1). Shang kings presided over a growing economy and the building of more cities, and their cultural influence reached far beyond their state. However, many Chinese maintained their own states and unique customs, particularly in places such as the western Yangzi Basin.

Interactive Map

Government

The Shang established an authoritarian state, perhaps in part to coordinate irrigation and dam building. Shang kingship was hereditary and was passed on to a monarch's male

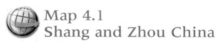
Map 4.1
Shang and Zhou China

The earliest Chinese states arose in north China along the Yellow River and its tributaries. The bronze-using Shang dynasty was succeeded by the iron-using Zhou, who governed much of north and central China.

© Cengage Learning

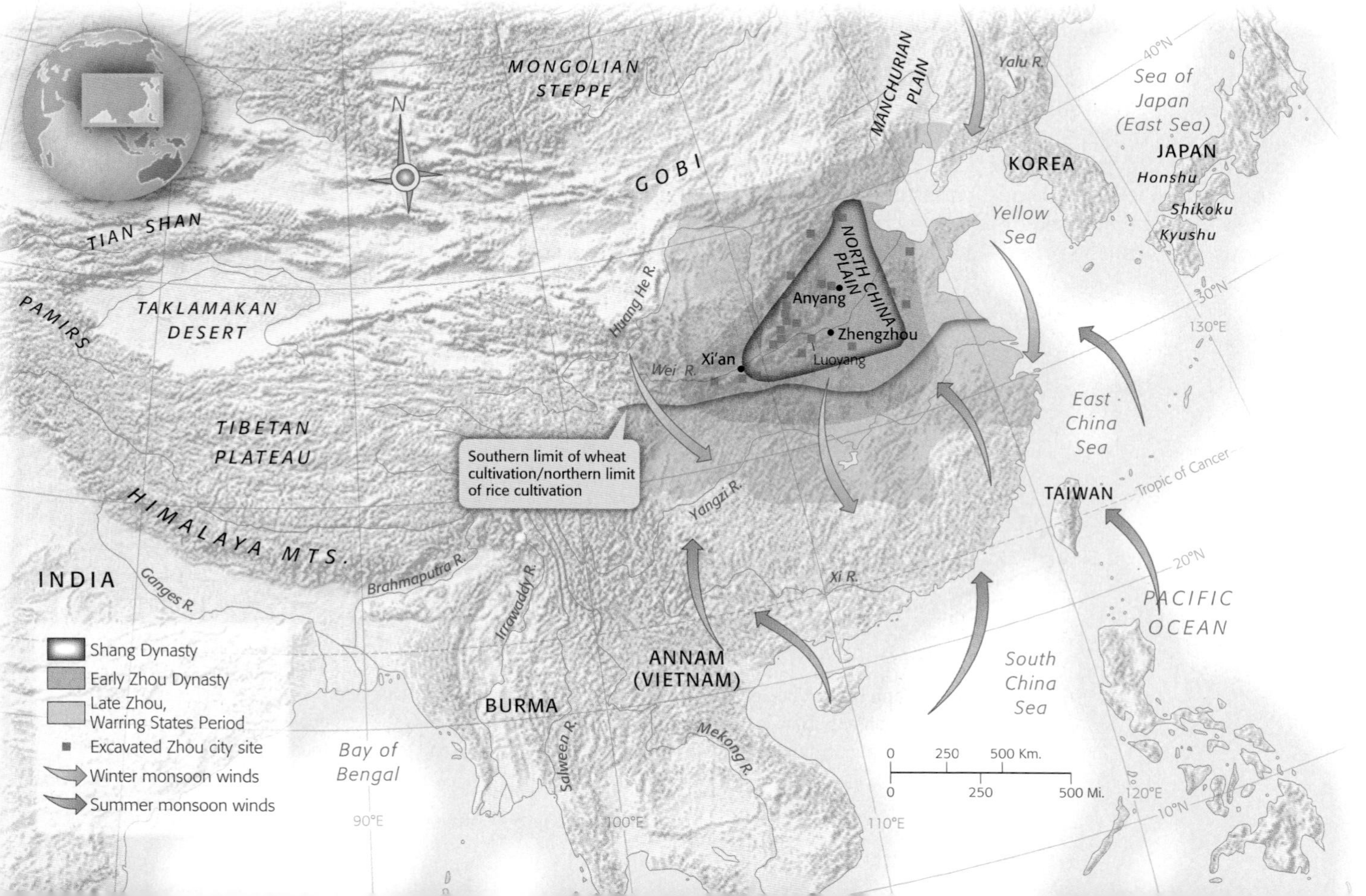

relative, usually a brother or son. Kings presented themselves as undisputed and even spiritual patriarchal figures who headed the country as a father did a family. Like the Aryans, who were then moving into India, they devoted much of their energy to military matters, using a lethal combination of archers, spearmen, and charioteers. One of their concerns was defending their northern borders, because China's relative prosperity in comparison to the marginal existence beyond the frontiers often prompted pastoral nomads to invade the Yellow River Valley. The largest of the successive Shang capital cities, Anyang, was the ruler Pan Keng's new capital city discussed in the opening to this chapter and spread out over some 10 square miles. It apparently took some 10,000 workers eighteen years to build Anyang, and the project reflected the considerable political and social organization of the time.

> "The Shang were harsh masters who practiced human sacrifice—usually of slaves—as part of their religious observances."

Technology

Technology improved, especially with the introduction of bronze and the earliest porcelain. The Chinese used copper by 2600 and bronze by 1400 B.C.E. This was the great age of bronze in the Afro-Eurasian Zone. The Shang and other Chinese are often considered the most skilled bronze casters the world has ever known. They used complex methods to produce flawless bronze arrows, spears, sculpture, pots, and especially ritual vessels for drinking wine. The Shang also produced glazed pottery that was the forerunner of the porcelain ("china") for which the Chinese would later become so famous.

Society and Culture

The Shang fostered a new social organization dominated by landowning aristocrats, many of whom also served as government officials. These elite individuals enjoyed luxurious residences and were buried in elaborate royal tombs surrounded by great quantities of valuable objects. The Shang middle class consisted of skilled artisans, merchants, and scribes, who may have formulated the world's earliest simple decimal system, around 1500 B.C.E. Farmers and laborers occupied the bottom of the social hierarchy. Many were war captives who had become slaves. The Shang were harsh masters who practiced human sacrifice—usually of slaves—as part of their religious observances.

Shang Bronze Pots These bronze ceremonial vessels, some featuring animal designs, were made during the Shang or early Zhou period.

> "Whatever their class status, women were expected to be meek and submissive."

The Shang's momentous contribution was an elaborate writing system. Some scholars believe that 4,800-year-old inscriptions on pottery can be considered writing, but most conclude that oracle bones from Shang times provide the earliest examples of Chinese writing. In an attempt to predict the future, influential people wrote questions addressed to the gods on bones of animals and tortoise shells. The writing found on oracle bones was clearly the forerunner of today's Chinese writing. In the later Shang period, people also wrote inscriptions on bronze vases.

Early Zhou Government, Society, and Economy

Zhou Decentralization

As Shang power faded, the Zhou, a state on the western fringe of China, invaded and overthrew the Shang. The new rulers formed a new dynasty, the Zhou (1122–221 B.C.E.), and established a different type of government from the Shang system. A relatively weak central government ruled over small, largely autonomous states that owed service obligations to the king, somewhat like the earlier Akkadian Empire in Sumeria. The royal family directly ruled the area around their capital, the present-day city of Xian (SEE-an), but parceled out the rest to followers, relatives, and Shang collaborators. This system allowed the Zhou kings to preside symbolically over a much larger land area than that of the Shang, from southern Manchuria to the Yangzi Basin (see Map 4.1). The decentralized system reflected the Zhou realization that, despite their impressive military technology, Chinese culture had spread too far for them to administer the entire society directly.

> ❝ We rise at sunrise, We rest at sunset. Dig wells and drink, Till our field and eat—What is the strength of the emperor to us? ❞
>
> *Peasant song*

The Mandate of Heaven and the Dynastic Cycle

The Zhou established two enduring political ideas for China. They justified their triumph over the Shang with a new concept: the Mandate of Heaven, declaring that rulers had the support of the supernatural realm ("heaven") so long as conditions were good. However, when there was war, famine, or other hardships, heaven withdrew its sanction and rebellion was permissible. The Duke of Zhou, credited for completing Zhou expansion, argued that the decadent Shang lost their right to rule, because their last kings mocked the gods by their behavior and "did not make themselves manifest to Heaven."[2] But over time this radical new concept was used against the Zhou and all later dynasties, because it added the criterion of morality to kingship.

Also during the Zhou period, Chinese scholars began to view their political history in terms of the dynastic cycle, a concept that would shape Chinese thinking for the next 2,500 years. Instead of seeing a straight line of progress in history, as the Hebrews did, the Chinese focused on dynasties of ruling families, all of which more or less followed the same pattern. The cycle always began with a new dynasty, which initially brought peace and prosperity but inevitably led to overexpansion, corruption, and rebellions. This disorder eventually resulted in a new dynasty, beginning the cycle anew.

Social Structure

Zhou government not only brought political fragmentation and a figurehead monarchy, but it also fostered a rigid social structure. Zhou society clearly divided aristocrats, commoners, and slaves. The nobility owed allegiance to the king as vassals but governed their own realms as they liked. Most aristocratic families owned large estates that were worked by slaves, and they hired private armies to defend their property. As influential commoners, the merchants and artisans were more insulated from the aristocracy. The majority of slaves were soldiers from rival mini-states who were captured in the frequent wars.

Peasants, the largest group of commoners, were mostly bound to the soil on aristocracy-owned land. Their superiors assigned them work and punished them if it was not done. Peasants were assigned houses, wore prescribed clothes to indicate their status, and had specified tax obligations. Their songs reflected resignation: "We rise at sunrise, We rest at sunset. Dig wells and drink, Till our field and eat—What is the strength of the emperor to us?"[3] Yet landowners did have to develop reasonably humane policies toward the common people on his lands, because workers and slaves often rebelled against exploitative land-lords, disrupting economic production.

Gender roles were also rigid in this patriarchal society. Both men and women were expected to marry, but all marriages were arranged by parents. Whatever their class status, women were expected to be meek and submissive, and they enjoyed no official role in public affairs, although some women exercised considerable informal influence. While many elite women were literate, few peasant women or men enjoyed opportunities to learn to read and write.

Technology and Economics

Zhou China nurtured many significant technological and economic develop-ments. Ironworking reached China over trade networks from Central Asia by around 700 B.C.E. From the Zhou states, iron reached southern Chinese, who improved the technology by 500 B.C.E. Iron made much better plows and tools than bronze but also improved weaponry. Newly introduced soy-beans provided a rich protein source and also enriched the soil. Chinese agriculture became so productive, and surpluses so common, that the population by 600 B.C.E. was around 20 million. Zhou social life often revolved around food: the Zhou-era Chinese clearly appreciated the culinary arts. The Chief Cook of the ruler was a high state official. Trade grew, merchants became more prominent, and copper coins were issued as China developed a cash economy.

Decline of the Zhou

But the Zhou system was unstable, plagued by chronic warfare between the various substates and outsiders. Over the centu-ries, larger substates conquered smaller ones. The worst warfare occurred during the Era of the Warring States, beginning around 500 B.C.E. (see Chapter 5). As a result, the 1,700 substates of the early Zhou years were reduced to seven by 400 B.C.E. These larger sub-states now had considerable power in counteracting the weakening Zhou kings. External pressures from Central Asians, who were obtaining faster ponies, also threatened political order.

Chinese Writing, Philosophy, and Religion

During the Shang and Zhou periods, a distinctive Chinese writing system arose to solve the problem posed by so many different spoken languages. Some six hundred dialects of Chinese are still spoken today, a heritage of many local cultures. Chinese from Guangzhou (GWAHN-cho), Shanghai (shahng-HIE), and Beijing (bay-JING) would not understand each other if they spoke only their local dialects. Another difficulty is that the monosyllabic Chinese languages are tonal: that is, the stress or tone placed on a sound changes its meaning. For example, depending on the tone employed by the speaker, in Mandarin the sound ma can mean "mother," "hemp," "horse," or the verb "to curse."

To overcome these problems, the Shang and Zhou Chinese gradually developed one written lan-guage based not on sound but on characters. The pictographs of early Shang times resemble crude pic-tures of an object, such as a man or bird. Over some centuries, they evolved into complex ideographs, in which characters stand for ideas and concepts. Some 50,000 new characters have been created since the Shang (see Figure 4.1).

As in Mesopotamia and Egypt, writing had vast social and cultural implications. The writing system promoted political and cultural unity, making pos-sible communication between people with different dialects. Without such a system, the Chinese might have split into many small countries. Thus writing helped create the largest society on earth, unifying rather than dividing peoples of diverse ancestries, regions, and languages. Chinese writing also rein-forced a strong feeling of historical continuity and a deep reverence for the past and one's ancestors. To be sure, the demands of memorizing and master-ing thousands of characters, as well as of acquiring acceptable brushwork skills, mostly limited literacy to those in the upper classes. Scribes gained special sta-tus as education, scholarship, and literature became valued commodities. Rulers and administrators also gained legitimacy through their literacy.

Tian, Yijing, and Yin-Yang

Chinese ideas on the deeper mysteries of life also developed in ancient times. The diverse Shang religion emphasized ancestor worship, magic, and mythology, as well as agricultural deities and local spirits. Gradually these ideas evolved by later Zhou times into distinctive notions such as the generalized supernatural force the Chinese called *tian* (tee-AN),

大	大	Large *(frontal view of "large" man)*
日	日	Sun
甴	曰	To speak *(mouth with protruding tongue?)*
日	口	Mouth
䜌	言	Speech *(vapor or tongue leaving mouth)*
戸	户	Door, house *(left leaf of double door)*
忄	心忄小	Heart, mind *(picture of physical heart)*
夕	夕	Evening, dusk *(crescent moon)*
朩	木	Tree, wood *(tree with roots and branches)*
鮫	魚	Fish
屮屮	艸屮	Grass *(growing plants)*
鼓	鼓	Drum *(drum on stand; hand with stick)*

Figure 4.1
Evolution of Chinese Writing
This chart shows early and modern forms of Chinese characters, revealing how pictographs, often recognizable, matured into increasingly abstract ideographs.

Yijing
The Book of Changes, an ancient Chinese collection of sixty-four mystic hexagrams and commentaries upon them that was used to predict future events.

which was believed to govern the universe. The first books probably appeared during the Shang period, including the *Yijing* (Yee-CHING) (Book of Changes), an ancient collection of sixty-four mystic hexagrams and commentaries upon them that were used to predict future events. The *Yijing's* main theme was that heaven and earth are in a state of continual transition.

The *Yijing* was closely related to Chinese cosmological thinking as expressed in the theory of *yin* and *yang*, which had appeared in simple form as early as the Shang period. To the Chinese, yin and yang are the two primary cosmic forces that make the universe run through their interaction. Neither one permanently triumphs; rather they are balanced, in conflict, and yet complementary in a kind of cosmic symphony. Many things were correlated with these principles:

> Yang: bright, hot, dry, hard, active, masculine, heaven, sun
> Yin: dark, cold, wet, soft, quiescent, feminine, earth, moon

Given the Chinese preference for hierarchy, yang was superior to yin, and male superior to female. Thus the philosophy justified inequalities in society. Chinese ideas such as yin-yang dualism strongly influenced their neighbors in Korea, Vietnam, and Japan, and over the centuries many Chinese ideas and institutions diffused to the peoples on their fringe.

LO³ Ancient Southeast and Northeast Asians

While the Chinese and Indians created some of the first urban societies, the neighboring societies of Southeast and Northeast Asia also made important early contributions in farming and technology in an environment that was somewhat different from their large neighbors. The resulting cultures, although influenced by China or India or both, demonstrated many unique characteristics. These societies and the networks of trade and migration that formed provided the foundations for enduring traditions.

Southeast Asian Environments and Early Agriculture

Geography and Climate

While historically linked to both China and India, Southeast Asian peoples developed in distinctive ways that were shaped in part by geography and climate. Southeast Asia, which stretches from modern Burma (or Myanmar) eastward to Vietnam and the Philippines and southward through the Indonesian archipelago, is separated from the Eurasian landmass by significant mountain and water barriers. The region has a tropical climate, with long rainy seasons and extensive rain forests. But the great rivers that flow through mainland Southeast Asia, such as the Mekong (MAY-kawng), Red, and Irrawaddy (ir-uh-WAHD-ee) Rivers, also carved out broad, fertile plains and deltas that could support dense human settlement.

The topography both helped and hindered communication. Shallow oceans fostered maritime trade, encouraging seafaring and fishing, and linking the peoples of large islands such as Sumatra (soo-MAH-truh), Java (JA-veh), and Borneo to their neighbors. But the heavily forested interior highlands of the mainland and the islands inhibited travel and encouraged cultural and economic diversity.

Agriculture and Technology

Agriculture arose early, but archaeologists still debate how early. Some think the transition to food-growing began in what is today Thailand and northern Vietnam by 8000 or perhaps even 9000 B.C.E. Certainly farming was widespread by 5000 B.C.E. Rice was apparently first domesticated in northern Southeast Asia or southern-central China 6,000 or 7,000 years ago; the two areas were closely linked in Neolithic times. Between 4000 and 3000 B.C.E., rice-growing became common. Southeast Asians may have been the first to cultivate bananas, yams, and taro and domesticated chickens, pigs, and perhaps even cattle.

Bronze-working appeared very early in Southeast Asia, sometime before 2000 B.C.E. By 1500 B.C.E., fine bronze was being produced in what is today northeast Thailand in villages like Ban Chiang (chang), founded around 3600 B.C.E., whose people lived in houses perched on poles above the ground. Ban Chiang women also made beautiful hand-painted and durable pottery. Village artists fashioned necklaces and bracelets as well as many household items of bronze and ivory.

Elsewhere in Eurasia, the Bronze Age was synonymous with states, cities, kings, armies, huge temples, and defensive walls, but in Southeast Asia bronze metallurgy derived from peaceful villages. Evidence for trade networks can be found in Dong Son village, Vietnam, where people made huge bronze drums that have been found

all over Southeast Asia. Tin mined in Southeast Asia may even have been traded to the Indus cities and Mesopotamia to be used in making bronze there. Southeast Asians worked iron by 500 B.C.E., several centuries later than northern China.

Migration and New Societies in Southeast Asia and the Pacific

Gradually new societies formed from local and migrant roots. The early Southeast Asians probably included the Vietnamese,

Dong Son Bronze Drum These huge Dong Son bronze drums, named for a village site in Vietnam, were produced widely in ancient Southeast Asia and confirm the extensive long-distance trade networks.
Erich Lessing/Art Resource, NY

Lapita
The ancient western Pacific culture that stretched some 2,500 miles from just northeast of New Guinea to Samoa.

> "Despite centuries of contact, the Koreans were never assimilated by the neighboring Chinese, in part because the Korean and Chinese spoken languages were very different."

Papuans (PAH-poo-enz), Melanesians (mel-uh-NEE-zhuhns), and Negritos (Ne-GREE-tos). Several waves of migrants came into mainland Southeast Asia from China sometime before the Common Era, assimilating local peoples or prompting them to migrate eastward through the islands. Migration fostered some of the oldest networks linking peoples over a wide area. The newcomers probably mixed their cultures and languages with those of the remaining indigenous inhabitants, shaping the region's societies. The ethnic merging produced new peoples such as the Khmers (kuh-MARE) (Cambodians), who later established states in the Mekong River Basin.

Austronesian Migration

Over the course of several millennia, peoples speaking Austronesian (AW-stroh-NEE-zhuhn) languages and possessing advanced agriculture entered island Southeast Asia from the large island of Taiwan, bringing new settlers and cultures and having a profound effect on other regions as well. Beginning around 4000 B.C.E., Austronesians began moving south from Taiwan into the Philippine Islands, and some later moved southward into the Indonesian archipelago (see Map 4.2). Sometime before 2000 B.C.E. they had settled Java, Borneo, and Sumatra, and by 1000 B.C.E. Indonesian islanders were the major seafaring traders and explorers of eastern Eurasia. Melanesians migrated eastward by boat into the western Pacific islands beginning around 1500 or 1600 B.C.E., carrying Southeast Asian domesticated crops, animals, house styles, and farming technology as far east as Fiji. Traveling in outrigger canoes and, later, in large double-hulled canoes, some Austronesians also sailed east into the open Pacific, mixing their cultures, languages, and genes with those of the Melanesians. By around 1000 B.C.E. Austronesian settlers had reached Samoa and Tonga.

These voyages were intentional efforts at discovery and colonization by fearless mariners who developed remarkable navigation skills, reading the stars with their eyes and the swells with their backs as they lay down in their canoes. The ancient western Pacific culture known as Lapita, stretching some 2,500 miles from just northeast of New Guinea to Samoa, was marked by a distinctive pottery style and a widespread trading network over vast distances. In Samoa and Tonga, Polynesian culture emerged from Austronesian roots. Some Polynesians eventually reached as far east as Tahiti and Hawaii, both 2,500 miles from Tonga (see Map 4.2).

The Austronesians, Vietnamese, and others established a foundation for societies based on intensive agriculture, fishing, and interregional commerce. By 1000 B.C.E. dynamic Austronesian trade networks stretched over 5,000 miles, from western Indonesia to the central Pacific, forming a commercial system that was unparalleled in the ancient world. Austronesians built advanced boats and carried out maritime trade with India by 500 B.C.E. The Vietnamese created the first known Southeast Asian states between 1000 and 800 B.C.E. and believed in a god that, according to their myths, "creates the elephants [and] the grass, is omnipresent, and has [all-seeing] eyes."[4]

Early Korean and Japanese Societies

The Chinese strongly influenced their neighbors in Northeast Asia, the Koreans and the Japanese, beginning in the Shang period and continuing for many centuries afterward. But the Koreans and Japanese already had complex societies. Over the following centuries, they integrated Chinese influences with their own ideas and customs, producing unique cultures and separate ethnic identities.

Korea and Japan are shaped by different environments (see Map 4.1). The 110 miles of stormy seas that separate them at their closest point made contact between the two societies sporadic. Korea occupies a mountainous peninsula some 600 miles long and 150 miles in width; Japan is a group of 3,400 islands stretching across

Interactive Map

The Ancient East Asia Website (*http://www.ancienteastasia.org/*). Offers useful essays and other materials on China, Japan, and Korea.

---

[4]*The Book of Songs*, translated by Arthur Waley (London: George Allen and Unwin, 1954), © Copyright by permission of The Arthur Waley Estate.

SOUTHEAST ASIA (Mainland)
Taiwan
Philippine Sea
Philippine Islands
Ban Chiang
Malay Peninsula MALAYSIA
Borneo
Sumatra
Sulawesi
Java
SOUTHEAST ASIA
AUSTRALIA
Coral Sea
New Guinea
New Britain
New Ireland
Solomon Islands
MELANESIA
Vanuatu
Fiji Islands
New Caledonia
Aotearoa (New Zealand)

MICRONESIA
Palau Islands
Caroline Islands
Marianas Islands
Marshall Islands
Kiribati

OCEANIA
PACIFIC OCEAN
POLYNESIA
Samoa
Tonga Islands
Cook Islands
Tahiti
Austral Islands
Marquesas Islands
Tuamotu Archipelago
Mangareva
Easter Island

Hawaiian Islands
Tropic of Cancer
NORTH AMERICA
20°N
Equator 0°
20°S
Tropic of Capricorn
40°S

Settled ca. 4000 B.C.E.
Settled ca. 2000 B.C.E.
Settled ca. 1500–1600 B.C.E.
Settled ca. 1000 B.C.E.
Settled ca. 300 B.C.E.

0   500   1000 Km.
0   500   1000 Mi.

© Cengage Learning

Map 4.2
The Austronesian Diaspora

Austronesians migrated from Taiwan into Southeast Asia, settling the islands. Later some of these skilled mariners moved east into the Western Pacific, settling Melanesia.

several climatic zones. Over 90 percent of the land is on three islands: densely populated Honshu (HAHN-shoo), frigid Hokkaido (haw-KAI-dow) in the north, and subtropical Kyushu (KYOO-shoo) in the south. Because mountains occupy much of Japan, only one-sixth of the land is suitable for intensive agriculture. The archipelago is also weak in all metals except silver.

Korean Distinctiveness

Despite centuries of contact, the Koreans were never assimilated by the neighboring Chinese, in part because the Korean and Chinese spoken languages were very different. Korean belongs to the Ural-Altaic language family and is therefore related to Mongol, Turkish, and the Eastern Siberian tongues. Ural-Altaic languages are polysyllabic and nontonal, unlike Chinese. Korean lives gradually changed as they began farming between 5000 and 2000 B.C.E., perhaps borrowing the technology from China. Later they creatively adapted rice-growing, which originated in warm southern lands, to their cool climate. As Korean agriculture became more productive, the population grew rapidly, generating migration across the straits to Japan. Growing occupational specialization led to small states based on clans, and female shamans led the animistic religion.

The ancient Koreans imported some useful ideas and also made several technological innovations. Sometime between the fifteenth and eighth centuries B.C.E., they adopted bronze, probably from China. Ironworking reached Korea from China or Central Asia between 700 and 300 B.C.E. Shang refugees fleeing in the wake of dynastic collapse brought more Chinese culture and technology, but Koreans also created their own useful products and technology, including some of the era's finest pottery. To contend with the frigid winters, the early Koreans invented an ingenious method of radiant floor heating, which is still widely used today.

Early Japan and the Ainu

The ancient Japanese were more isolated than the Koreans from China but no less creative. Human settlement began perhaps 40,000 years ago,

Jomon
The earliest documented culture in Japan, known for the ropelike design on its pottery.

before rising sea levels isolated Japan from the mainland. Pottery, for example, was produced on Kyushu by 10,700 B.C.E., which makes Japanese pottery among the oldest in the world. The identity of these early settlers and pottery-makers is unknown, but they were probably the ancestors of the Ainu (I-noo), who are genetically close to other East Asians despite their light skin and extensive body hair, which are unusual in the region. The ancestral Ainu seem to have built seaworthy boats, for they settled the Kurile (KOO-reel) Islands north of Japan and traded with the people of eastern Siberia. Several scholars think that ancestors of the Ainu were among the northeast Asians who settled the Americas.

Migration influenced Japan, but when Japan's non-Ainu ancestors arrived in the islands is unknown. Some may have come from northeastern Asia by way of Korea beginning 3,000 or 4,000 years ago. Genetic studies link modern Japanese to the Ainu, Siberians, and especially Koreans.

Jomon Society

The best documented early Japanese society is called Jomon (JOE-mon) ("rope pattern"), because of the ropelike designs on their pottery. The Jomon period began around 10,000 B.C.E. and endured until 300 B.C.E. The Jomon evidently had little contact with China but did trade some with Korea and Siberia. Most scholars suspect it was a primarily Ainu culture that was divided by various languages and regional customs. The Jomon and other ancient islanders were only partially the ancestors of the modern Japanese. They lived primarily from hunting, gathering, and fishing, and by 5000 B.C.E. they lived in permanent wooden houses containing elaborate hearths, probably the centers for family gatherings. A wide range of foods made up their highly

Dogu Figurine Jomon fired-clay figures, like this one, typically portray women, and may have been used in fertility rites. Many have a heart-shaped face and elaborate hair style.
Tokyo National Museum/The Art Archive

nutritious diet, including shellfish, fish, seals, deer, wild boar, and yams, but there is no evidence for complex agriculture until around 500 B.C.E.

As in Korea, a very different spoken language helped preserve cultural distinctiveness, despite much Chinese cultural influence over the centuries. At some point, probably between 500 B.C.E. and 500 C.E., most of the Ainu languages were overwhelmed by a Japanese language with diverse roots that was possibly based on a now-lost Korean dialect. As Japan's population grew, increasingly crowded conditions shaped the Japanese language, as its structure and vocabulary came to promote tact and vagueness. It is much more difficult to directly insult or provoke someone in Japanese than in most languages, a tendency that is part of Japan's unique heritage.

LO⁴ The Roots of Settlement in the Americas

After the migrations of humans from Eurasia to the Americas thousands of years ago, American societies developed in isolation from those in the Eastern Hemisphere. Early Americans created diverse cultures that often flourished from hunting and gathering, and later Americans in some regions developed agriculture, trade systems, religions, monumental architecture, and technologies to support them. These set the stage for more complex and diverse cultures, and eventually the first cities, states, and written languages.

 Ancient Mesoamerican Civilizations (*http://angelfire.com/ca/humanorigins/index.html*). Links and information about the Olmecs and other premodern societies.

The Environment and Movement of Native Americans

Most of the land area of the Western Hemisphere is found on two continents, North and South America, which are linked by the long, thin strand of Central America. A string of fertile islands also rings the Caribbean Sea from Florida to Venezuela. Unlike the east-west axis of Eurasia, the Americas lie on a north-south axis, with a large forest-covered tropical zone separating more temperate regions. Thus migrating peoples encountered very different environmental and climatic zones.

Geography and Climate

Although the total land area is smaller, the Western Hemisphere contains as much diversity of landforms and climate as that of the Eastern. Extensive tropical rain forests originally covered much of Central America and parts of the Caribbean islands as well as the vast Amazon and Orinoco (or-uh-NO-ko) River Basins of South America. Rain-drenched forests also once covered much of the northern Pacific coast and southern Chile, while the eastern part of what is now the United States had more temperate woodlands. Great mountain ranges shaped human life by discouraging communication, while river systems encouraged it. Like the Himalayas in Asia, the 5,000-mile-long Andes (AN-deez), which stretch from the Caribbean coast down the western side of South America, limited human interaction. Similarly, in North America, the Rocky Mountains provided an east-west barrier from New Mexico to northwestern Canada. Mountains also run along the Pacific coast from Alaska to southern Mexico. By trapping rain clouds, these formidable mountain complexes helped create huge deserts as well as extensive grasslands in the interior of the continents, while some of the great river systems, such as the Mississippi, drained fertile regions and fostered long-distance trade.

Native American Migration

The ancestry and antiquity of Native Americans generate exciting debate among scholars. Most anthropologists agree that modern Native Americans are descended chiefly from stone tool–using Asians who crossed the Bering Strait from Siberia to Alaska. Most likely entered North America when Ice Age conditions lowered ocean levels and created a wide land bridge. Seeking game like bison, caribou, and mammoths, migrants could have moved south through ice-free corridors or by boat along the Pacific coast, and gradually dispersed throughout the hemisphere. Waves of migrants from different cultural backgrounds in East and North Asia might account for the more than two thousand languages among Native Americans. The last wave some 5,000 years ago brought the Inuit (IN-oo-it) and Aleuts (AH-loots).

Much evidence supports the notion of ancient migration from Asia. The fact that no remains of any hominids earlier than modern humans have been found in the Americas suggests that all human evolution took place in the Eastern Hemisphere. Furthermore, the common ancestry of modern Native Americans is clear from the remarkable uniformity of DNA, blood, virus, and teeth types, which all connect them clearly to ancient peoples in East Asia and Siberia. Some early American flake tools and housing styles resemble those from northern Asia, and some American languages can also be linked distantly with northeast Asian languages.

The question of when the first migrants arrived in the Americas perplexes archaeologists. For many years, most traced the migration back to the Clovis (KLO-vis) culture some 11,500 to 13,500 years ago,

> **Clovis**
> A Native American culture dating back some 11,500 to 13,500 years.

CHRONOLOGY

The Ancient Americas, 40,000–600 B.C.E.

40,000–20,000	Possible earliest migrations to Americas (disputed)
11,500–9,500	Beginning of Clovis culture
8000	Beginning of agriculture in Mesoamerica and Andes
6000	Potato farming in Andes
4000	Early trade routes in North America
2500	Earliest mound-building cultures
3000–2500	Farming along Peruvian coast
3000–1600	Peruvian city of Caral
2500	Agriculture in lower Mississippi Valley
2000	Earliest agriculture in southwestern North America
1500	Agriculture in Amazon Basin
1200–300	Olmecs
1200–200	Chavín
1000–500	Poverty Point culture
650	Olmec writing

named after spear points discovered at Clovis, New Mexico. Clovis-type sites are widespread in North and Central America. However, human skeletons and artifacts have lately been discovered in North and South America that have much older radiocarbon dates. Monte Verde (MAWN-tee VAIR-dee), a campsite in southern Chile, which is more than 10,000 miles from the Bering Strait, may be at least 12,500 years old. Monte Verde people lived in two parallel rows of rectangular houses with wooden frameworks and log foundations, and they exploited a wide variety of vegetable and animal foods. A variety of other sites challenge the Clovis theory, but none offers conclusive evidence.

Hunting, Gathering, and Ancient American Life

The earliest Americans, known to scholars as Paleo-Indians, survived by hunting, fishing, and gathering while adapting to varied environments. Being skilled, spear-throwing hunters, they may have helped bring about the extinction of large herbivore animals such as horses, mammoths, and camels, which disappeared from the Western Hemisphere between 9000 and 7000 B.C.E. A similar die-off of animals also occurred in Eurasia at the end of the Ice Age, suggesting that environmental change may have been a contributing factor. In most places, these trends forced a shift to hunting smaller game, but on the North American Great Plains, many peoples existed for some 10,000 years hunting bison, without benefit of horses. Abundant deer fed hunters in other parts of North America.

Some people in favored locations flourished from hunting, fishing, and gathering for many millennia, even into modern times. This was the case in the Pacific Northwest, where coastal peoples built oceangoing boats and sturdy wood houses. Along the Peruvian coast, deep-sea fishermen were exploiting the rich marine environment by 7600 B.C.E. The Monte Verde villagers, who had extensive knowledge of the available resources, used more than fifty food plants and twenty medicinal plants. In the Santa Barbara channel region of southern California beginning between 6000 and 5000 B.C.E., the Chumash (CHOO-mash) society enjoyed a varied vegetation and meat diet that included large marine mammals such as seals. The Chumash built large, permanent villages headed by powerful chiefs, and they also used shell beads as a kind of currency.

The eastern third of what is now the United States provided an abundant environment for hunting, gathering, and trade. By 4000 B.C.E., extensive long-distance trade networks linked people over several thousand miles from the Atlantic coast to the Great Plains. Dugout canoes moved copper and red ocher from Lake Superior, jasper (quartz) from Pennsylvania, obsidian from the Rocky Mountains, and seashells from both the Gulf and East Coasts. Great Lakes copper was traded as far away as New England and Florida.

Early Societies and Their Cultures

Over many millennia, Americans organized larger societies and developed some distinctive social and cultural patterns that emphasized cooperation within family units, animistic religion, and, for some, building huge mounds. Most people lived in egalitarian bands linked by kinship and marriage. Hunting was often a communal activity.

Americans shared with people in the Eastern Hemisphere a belief in supernatural forces, spirits, or gods. Shamans claiming command over spirits or animal souls played an important role as vehicles to connect the human and spirit worlds, often through ceremonies fueled by their showmanship. Because the land furnished food, most Americans revered the earth as sacred. Some of them also adopted creation stories that were widely shared with other peoples.

Some ancient Americans organized communities around mound building, the construction of huge earthen mounds, often with temples on top. The oldest mound so far discovered, in Louisiana, dates to 2500 B.C.E. Beginning around 1600 B.C.E., some peoples in the eastern woodlands and Gulf Coast of North America developed a distinctive mound-building culture. One major site, Poverty Point in northeastern Louisiana, was occupied between 1000 and 500 B.C.E. by perhaps five thousand people at its height. Occupying about three square miles, Poverty Point had the most elaborate and massive complex of earthworks in all of the Americas at that time. The largest mound, an effigy of a bird that can only be seen from the air, was 70 feet high. Poverty Point served as the hub of a lower Mississippi River trading system extending as far away as present-day Florida, Missouri, Oklahoma, and Tennessee.

The Rise of Agriculture and Its Consequences

Americans became some of the earliest and most versatile farmers of the ancient world. Population growth and long-distance trade were key influences sparking this great transition. The ebb and flow of weather conditions made some hunting and gathering peoples vulnerable to devastating droughts. This may have prompted them to experiment with growing food sources, and eventually several quite different agricultural traditions emerged. Some of the chief crops, such as maize (corn), were much more difficult to master than the big-seeded grains of the Fertile Crescent. By 8500 or 8000 B.C.E., bottle gourds and pumpkins may have been raised in Mesoamerica, the region stretching from central Mexico southeast into northern Central America. Later crops included avocados, chili peppers, maize, sweet potatoes, and beans. Andes people cultivated chili peppers and kidney beans by about 8000 B.C.E. Later Andeans built elaborate irrigation canals that created artificial garden plots, and also grew potatoes and maize. Early communities in present-day Peru and Uruguay also made the shift to agriculture, and by 1500 B.C.E., farming had spread to the Amazon Basin.

Farming later spread over trade networks to North American societies, probably influenced by environmental change with a wetter climate. Maize and squash were grown in the Southwest by 2000 or 1500 B.C.E., and beans and cotton by 500 B.C.E. The southwestern peoples were particularly ingenious in adapting farming to their poor soils and desert conditions. Eventually maize, beans, and squash became mainstays from the Southwest to the northeastern woodlands, providing a nutritionally balanced diet.

Farming Patterns

Three basic farming patterns eventually shaped American societies. People in the highland and valley regions of Mesoamerica relied heavily on maize, beans, and squash. Difficult to grow, maize requires considerable labor. Another farming pattern was developed by people dwelling at the high altitudes of the Andes, who cultivated potatoes and other frost-resistant tubers. Tropical forest societies in South America evolved the third pattern, growing manioc, sweet potatoes, and root crops. The differing farming patterns proved significant for later world history, because the great diversity of crops later enriched modern food supplies. Americans domesticated more different plants than had all of the Eastern Hemisphere peoples combined, including potatoes, chocolate, quinine, and tobacco. The shifting cultivation used in most places also limited population densities and hence fostered smaller societies.

> "Some South American and several North American societies developed processes for mummifying the bodies of the deceased through drying."

Mesoamerica The region stretching from central Mexico southeast into northern Central America.

The Lack of Draft Animals

The Americans practiced less intensive agriculture than those peoples in the Eastern Hemisphere for one simple reason: the lack of draft animals. The only large herd animals available for domestication, the cameloids of the Andes like the llama and alpaca, were tamed by 3500 B.C.E., mostly for use as pack animals and wool sources. Americans domesticated dogs, but there were no horses, cattle, or oxen to aid in pulling a plow or wheel. However, people made other innovations, including various ingenious irrigation schemes like terracing and developing floating gardens. Perhaps most important, the lack of draft animals also meant that Americans were exposed to fewer infectious diseases. In the Eastern Hemisphere, domesticated animals passed diseases such as measles and smallpox to humans through infectious organisms such as germs and parasites, precipitating outbreaks that killed many people. This left Native Americans vulnerable to the diseases brought by Europeans and Africans beginning in 1492 C.E., for which they had no immunity.

Early Agricultural Cities and States

Archaeologists are learning more about the social and cultural patterns, such as village life and religion, of early farming peoples. Permanent lakeside villages may have appeared in Mexico's fertile central valley as early as 5500 B.C.E. Communal activity was essential in these early settlements as people cooperated

Olmecs
The earliest urban society in Mesoamerica.

for survival. In the northern Andes, people fashioned the oldest known ceramics in the hemisphere between 3000 and 2500 B.C.E. By 1600 B.C.E., societies in Baja (BA-ha) California made mural paintings on rocks and in caves.

Religion and Culture in Mesoamerica

Institutionalized religions began to take shape, led by a priestly caste. Some Mesoamericans may have practiced human sacrifice by 7000 B.C.E. Later human sacrifice became common in both Mesoamerica and the Andes to honor the gods and keep the cosmos in balance. Some South American and several North American societies developed processes for mummifying the bodies of the deceased through drying. Like the Mound Builders in North America, some societies in the Andes region and Mesoamerica began building permanent structures for religious, governmental, or recreational purposes. Pacific coast cultures in South America constructed some of the oldest monumental architecture, including stepped pyramids. Similar public buildings appeared in the Andes by the third millennium B.C.E., about the same time as monumental construction was taking place in Egypt, India, and China. A site in southern Mexico from 5000 B.C.E. contained a dance ground or ball court.

Learn about the life of the Mound Builders at Poverty Point, and why they did not need farming.

Agriculture, monumental construction, and long-distance trade provided a foundation for several societies to build the first cities and form the first states in the Americas (see Map 4.3). Between 3000 and 1000 B.C.E., farming people in Mesoamerica and the Andes made the technological breakthroughs and experienced the population growth that eventually led to urbanization. They worked metals like copper, gold, and silver to create tools, weapons, and jewelry, and they devised more productive farming systems, often including irrigation. Growing towns with public buildings became centers of political, economic, and religious activities. Massive ceremonial centers hundreds of feet long were constructed along the Peruvian coast, and huge mounds were erected in several places, laying the framework for the great pyramids that followed. Long-distance trade of commodities such as obsidian, mirrors, seashells, and ceramics also became more common by 1300 B.C.E.

Interactive Map

The First Cities

Growing populations and trade networks fostered the first cities. Between 4000 and 1 B.C.E., the population of the Americas grew from 1 or 2 million to around 15 million; more than two-thirds of this number were concentrated in Mesoamerica and western South America. The first settlements built around massive stone structures emerged around 3100 B.C.E. in the Norte Chico region of north-central Peru stretching from the western foothills of the Andes to the Pacific. The largest of these settlements, with some 3,000 residents and America's first known city, Caral, was built perhaps as early as 2500 or 3000 B.C.E., about the same time as the Harappan cities and the Egyptian pyramids. Caral was a 150-acre complex of plazas, pyramids, and residential buildings that probably required many thousands of laborers to build. The major pyramid is 60 feet tall and contained a sunken amphitheater capable of seating hundreds of spectators.

These findings show that the local economy was able to support an elite group of priests, planners, builders, and designers. The elite seem to have lived in large, well-kept rooms atop the pyramids, the craftsmen at ground-level apartments, and the workers in outlying neighborhoods. Eventually some twenty pyramid complexes occupied land for many miles around. The Norte Chico economy was based on obtaining marine resources such as fish and growing squash, sweet potatoes, fruits, and beans as well as cotton, which they traded to coastal fishermen for making nets. The Norte Chico people do not seem to have made ceramics, nor did they produce many arts and crafts. Caral was a major hub for trade routes extending from the Pacific coast through the Andes to the Amazonian rain forest. There is evidence for human sacrifice. The people evidently enjoyed music, and many animal bone flutes have been found in the ruins. Caral collapsed for unknown reasons around 1600 B.C.E.

Olmec Society

The Olmecs (OHL-mecks), a people who lived along the Gulf coast of Mexico, formed the earliest known urban society in Mesoamerica by 1200 or 1000 B.C.E., and they flourished until 300 B.C.E. (see Map 4.3). Each Olmec city was probably ruled by a powerful chieftain who made alliances with other chiefs. Olmec cities reflected engineering genius. The earliest city, known today as San Lorenzo, was built on an artificial dirt platform three-quarters of a mile long and situated above fer-

Map 4.3
Olmec and Chavín Societies
The earliest known American states arose in Mesoamerica and the Andes. The Olmecs and Chavín both endured for a millennium.

tile but frequently flooded plains. The stones for their sculptures and temples had to be brought from 60 miles away, and some of the blocks weigh more than 40 tons. The Olmecs studied astronomy in order to correctly orient their cities and monuments with the stars.

The Olmecs created remarkable architecture and art, as well as a writing system. The purpose of the huge sculptured stone heads they erected is unknown, but they might represent rulers. Olmec builders also constructed temples and pyramids in ceremonial centers and in palace complexes. By around 650 B.C.E., the Olmecs had also developed perhaps the first simple hieroglyphic writing in the Americas, which influenced other Mesoamerican peoples, especially the Mayan. Unlike in Mesopotamia, where writing developed from commercial needs, Mesoamerican writing kept records of kings, rituals, and the calendar, much as writing did in Egypt.

Commerce and the networks it created were a key to Olmec success and influence. The Olmecs traded with Mexico's west coast and as far south as modern

Costa Rica, importing jade, basalt, obsidian, and iron ore. The Olmecs may also have exploited cocoa trees for chocolate, which later became an important Mayan crop. Extensive communication between the Olmecs and neighboring peoples contributed to some cultural homogeneity in Mesoamerica, especially in religion. Olmec religious symbols and myths emphasized a pantheon of fearsome half-human, half-animal supernatural beings, the prototypes of later Mesoamerican deities. The developing religion required precise measurement of calendar years and time cycles, which fostered the development of mathematics and writing. Although Olmec society eventually disappeared, the Olmecs established enduring cultural patterns that influenced later peoples like the Maya (see Chapter 9).

Chavín Society

The earliest known Andean urban society, the Chavín (cha-VEEN), emerged 10,000 feet above sea level in northwestern Peru at the same time as the Olmecs, around 1200 or 1000 B.C.E., and collapsed by 200 B.C.E. The Chavín created flamboyant sculpture and monumental architecture, including the large pyramid that still sits in the ruins of their major city. They also developed a highly original art focusing on real animals and anthropomorphic creatures, and they knew how to work gold and silver.

Chavín lasted for a millennium and exercised considerable influence in surrounding regions. At its height, between 860 and 200 B.C.E., the main city probably had some three thousand inhabitants. Elaborate burial sites clearly reveal a pronounced class division. The Chavín people became a major regional power, trading widely with the coast and spreading their religious cult to distant peoples. Chavín helped establish or perpetuate some of the architectural

Listen to a synopsis of Chapter 4.

and religious patterns that became common in the Andes.

Olmec Head This massive head from San Lorenzo is nearly 10 feet high. The significance of such heads remains unclear, but they might represent chiefs, warriors, or gods.

Nathaniel Tarn/Photo Researchers, Inc.

Societies • Networks • Transitions

Ancient Foundations of World History, 4000–600 B.C.E.

Humans today live in the shadow of ancient peoples who began farming and later founded the Bronze Age cities in western Asia, Africa, South Asia, East Asia, and southern Europe. These innovative peoples constructed the foundations for organized societies and the growing networks that connected them.

After thousands of years of prehistory, some peoples congregated in villages and began to practice agriculture. This was perhaps one of the two greatest transitions in human history, the other being the Industrial Revolution of the eighteenth and nineteenth centuries C.E. Between 10,000 and 5000 B.C.E., early farmers invented pottery, cloth, and the plow. Agriculture was the essential building block that stimulated other major developments, in particular the founding of cities and states and the invention of metalworking. Better means of transportation allowed people, goods, ideas, and even diseases to travel longer distances in a shorter time. This increased movement became the basis for networks of trade and cultural exchange linking distant societies. A wider sharing of ideas helped bring about further social transformations.

Exploring Ancient World Cultures (*http://eawc.evansville.edu/*). Excellent site run by Evansville University, with essays and links on the ancient Near East, Egypt, India, China, and Europe.

Ancient transitions happened as the result of many influences, including disease, climate change, the availability of fertile land, and the annual flooding of rivers. Varying conditions helped shape such distinctive societies as Sumeria, Egypt, Nubia, Minoan Crete, Phoenicia, the Harappan cities, Shang China, and the Olmecs. At the same time, cross-continental interactions as well as long-distance migrations ensured that even largely distinctive societies shared certain common features.

Technological Foundations

Once developed, useful technologies such as metallurgy and vastly improved transportation had many consequences. Metallurgy became a key to economic growth: first bronze and later iron aided agriculture, transportation, and communication. Improvements in land and sea transportation helped move people and products over long distances, fostering trade networks. Expanded trade encouraged cities, and metal weapons and improved transportation allowed city rulers to build or expand states.

The Copper and Bronze Ages

The first metal to be worked was copper. Stoneworkers discovered that heating copper reduced it to liquid form and allowed it to be shaped in a mold. As it cooled, it could be given a good cutting edge. Many peoples in both hemispheres made copper tools and weapons, and they traded copper widely. Excavations of sunken trading ships from this era in the Mediterranean often discover large cargoes of copper. The Sumerian city-states were the first great metal-using society, followed soon after by the Egyptians, who used copper instruments to build the great pyramids. But metallurgy also led to deforestation, as forests were cut to make charcoal to fire the kilns. It took 140 pounds of wood to produce 1 pound of copper.

Geology Project (*http://www.unr.edu/sb204/geology*). Provides brief but useful information on the history of copper, bronze, and iron technology.

Beginning around 3000 B.C.E. in western Asia, metalworkers figured out how to mix copper with tin or arsenic to create bronze. This discovery launched the Bronze Age in Afro-Eurasia. Between 2600 and 2000 B.C.E., bronze technology was adopted or invented in Sumeria, Egypt, eastern Europe, Nubia, India, China, and Southeast Asia. The Chinese were the greatest users and mass producers of bronze. In South America, some peoples used another copper-arsenic alloy, as well as silver and gold.

Bronze technology affected life. Easier to make and more durable than copper, bronze was well suited for tools, drinking vessels, and weapons. Bronze making probably spurred both trade networks and warfare. Because tin deposits are less common than copper, tin was traded over great distances, and industries arose to obtain copper and tin and to manufacture bronze products. Metalsmiths were so valuable that invading armies often captured them. Finally, copper and bronze, as well as gold and silver, were used for the first coins, which gradually became the major medium of exchange.

The Iron Age

The making of iron provided the next technological break-through. Western Asia had little tin but large quantities of iron ore. Iron was much harder to work than copper: artisans needed to produce higher temperatures, and heating produced a spongy mass rather than a liquid. Eventually, inventive workers—possibly in the Hittite kingdom along the Black Sea or in Palestine—discovered a new but laborious technology that involved repeatedly heating and hammering the iron and plunging it into cold water.

The Iron Age began in western Asia and Egypt by around 1600 B.C.E. Between 900 and 500 B.C.E., iron technology was also adopted or invented in Greece, India, western and central Europe, Central Asia, China, Southeast Asia, and West and East Africa (see map). Some peoples acquired iron through trade, and others through contact with ironworking peoples like the Bantus. Ironworking never developed in the Americas or Australia, where contact with other peoples was limited; Eurasians and Africans may have benefited from having societies close enough to each other to regularly exchange ideas.

Ironworking brought many advantages. The metal was both more adaptable and cheaper to make than bronze. With it, people could produce better axes, plows, wagon wheels, and swords. For example, in Hebrew tradition, the Israelites could not drive the Canaanites out of the Palestinian lowland because they had iron chariots. Centuries later, metalworkers learned how to add carbon to iron to make steel. But like many technologies, iron proved a mixed blessing. While it improved farming, it also made for deadlier weapons, perhaps causing warfare to become more frequent.

Transportation Breakthroughs and Human Mobility

Metalworking was only one of several valuable technologies invented in ancient times. Land transport was dramatically transformed by the anonymous inventor of the wheel. Wheels were first used in pottery making, an activity that involved both men and women. But sometime between 3500 and 3200 B.C.E., probably in Mesopotamia, artisans found that fitting an axle to a cart allowed two wheels (often made of iron) to turn freely, and the wheeled cart was invented. Wagons followed rapidly, and then horse-drawn chariots. These wheeled vehicles made longer journeys with more cargo possible, increasing long-distance trade.

Increased travel inspired the first maps, drawn in Mesopotamia around 2300 B.C.E. These maps, drawn onto small tablets and then baked, recognized distant relationships in portraying agricultural land, town plans, and the world as known to Babylonians. One map from the sixth or seventh century B.C.E. shows the Babylonian world, including rivers, canals, cities, and neighboring states, in the center of a flat earth, with the remote lands on the fringe inhabited by legendary beasts. The mapmaker noted that his sketch showed the "four corners" of the earth.

The inventors of the first boats are unknown. The ancestors of Australian Aborigines and some of the first migrants to the Americas may have used boats to reach their destinations many thousands of years ago. Archaeologists have discovered the remnants of 10,000-year-old boats in northwest Europe. By 5000 B.C.E., people living in Mesopotamia and along the Nile had invented square sails, and wind could then be harnessed to drive boats through the water. The use of sails spread quickly. The Greek writer Homer reported how the Mycenaeans prepared ships for voyages: "they dragged the vessel into deeper water, put the mast and sails on board, fixed the oars in leather hoops, all ship-shape, and hauled up the white sail."[1] Austronesians were probably the first to construct boats capable of sailing the deep oceans. Better ships made it easier for distant peoples to come into contact with one another and share their ways of life. Some maritime trade networks stretched over vast distances.

The invention and spread of wheeled vehicles and boats also made it easier for people to migrate over longer distances. The ancient era saw several great migrations involving large numbers of people. Using seagoing boats, especially large outrigger canoes, Austronesians sailed to and settled most of the widely scattered Pacific islands. Using carts and chariots, Indo-European peoples occupied large areas of Eurasia. Traveling by foot or in canoes, and also possessing iron technology, Bantu-speaking peoples settled the forests and grasslands of the southern half of Africa.

Urban and Economic Foundations

The first cities, some of them with populations over 100,000, became the cultural focal points and organizing centers for surrounding regions. The first states formed around cities, which also fostered the first writing. The urban revolution also encouraged expanded economic activities, so that merchants become prominent members of society. In turn, merchants established the first long-distance trade networks that helped spread the influence of urban societies.

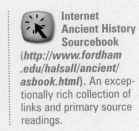

Internet Ancient History Sourcebook (*http://www.fordham .edu/halsall/ancient/ asbook.html*). An exceptionally rich collection of links and primary source readings.

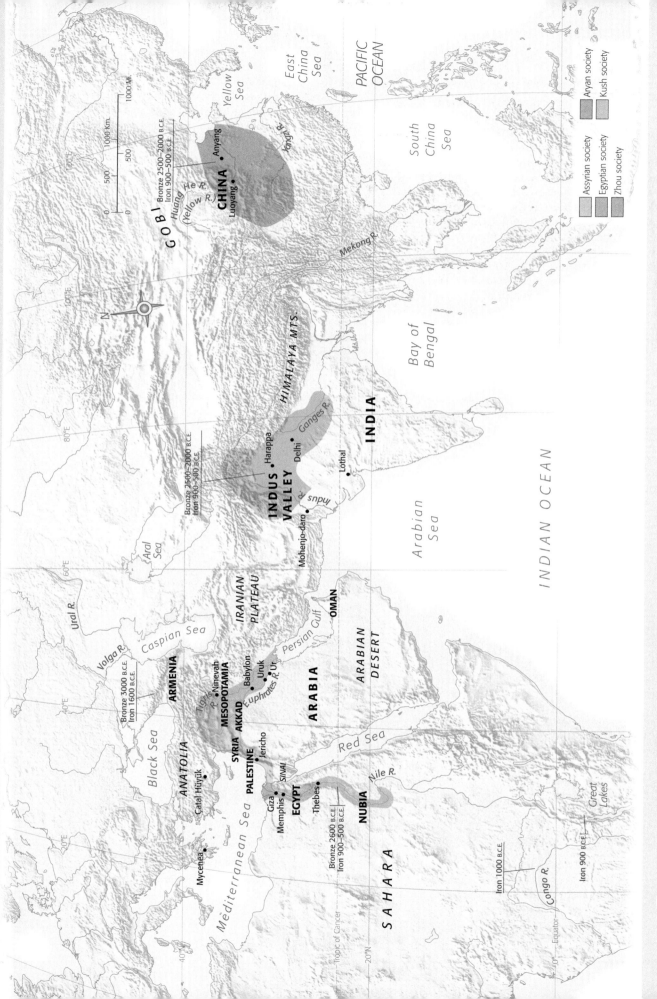

Metals and Great States ca. 1000 B.C.E.

The earliest states arose in river valleys—the Nile, Tigris-Euphrates, Indus, and Yellow—and these early states also worked metals, first bronze and then iron, to produce tools and weapons.

Legend:
- Assyrian society
- Egyptian society
- Zhou society
- Aryan society
- Kush society

Labels on map:

PACIFIC OCEAN

East China Sea

Yellow Sea

South China Sea

GOBI

Bronze 2500–2000 B.C.E.
Iron 900–500 B.C.E.

Anyang

CHINA

Huang He R. (Yellow R.)

Luoyang

Yangzi R.

Mekong R.

HIMALAYA MTS.

Bay of Bengal

Ganges R.

Harappa

Delhi

INDUS VALLEY

Bronze 2500–2000 B.C.E.
Iron 900–500 B.C.E.

Mohenjo-daro

Indus R.

Lothal

INDIA

Arabian Sea

INDIAN OCEAN

Ural R.

Aral Sea

Volga R.

Caspian Sea

IRANIAN PLATEAU

Black Sea

Bronze 3000 B.C.E.
Iron 1600 B.C.E.

ARMENIA

ANATOLIA

Çatal Hüyük

Mycenae

Mediterranean Sea

Ninevah

Tigris R.

MESOPOTAMIA

AKKAD

Babylon

Uruk

Euphrates R.

Ur

Persian Gulf

OMAN

SYRIA

PALESTINE

Jericho

SINAI

ARABIA

ARABIAN DESERT

Red Sea

Giza

Memphis

EGYPT

Thebes

Nile R.

NUBIA

Bronze 2600 B.C.E.
Iron 900–500 B.C.E.

SAHARA

Tropic of Cancer

Iron 1000 B.C.E.

Iron 900 B.C.E.

Congo R.

Great Lakes

Equator

20°N

20°E

40°E

60°E

80°E

100°E

N

1000 Mi.
1000 Km.
500
500
0
0

The Functions and Social Organization of Cities

From the very beginning, ancient cities served a variety of functions. Some, like several Mesopotamian cities and South American cities such as Caral and Chavín, developed as centers for religious ceremonies. An Akkadian text boasted that, in Uruk, "people are resplendent in festive attire, where each day is made a holiday."[2] Cities in Egypt and China, by contrast, seem to have been founded chiefly as administrative centers to govern the surrounding territories. Many others, including the Harappan, Nubian, and Olmec cities, formed around marketplaces. Many cities served all of these functions.

Cities fostered more elaborate class structures than could be found in the countryside. Political elites staffed the government bureaucracies such as the law courts, while religious leaders directed the temples. In Mesopotamian, Egyptian, Chinese, Harappan, and American cities, these upper-class groups generally lived in the center, around the temples and public buildings. Just outside this central zone, the middle-class merchants and skilled craftsmen lived with their families above their workshops and stores. In Mesopotamia, craftsmen accounted for 20 percent of the city population. On the city outskirts lived the laborers, including household servants, small farmers, and slaves. Cities also attracted people from neighboring societies, and ethnically diverse populations were common.

Most urban women led busy lives. As households awoke each morning, they prepared a quick meal for husbands and sons heading out to their work, perhaps as artisans, peddlers, soldiers, or laborers. Many used pots and pans made of copper or bronze to cook and serve the food. After cleaning their homes, many women walked through dusty streets to buy food grown on nearby farms. As they returned home, they may have passed children playing in the narrow alleys. In some societies, the wealthier women were increasingly restricted inside walled courtyards. The poorest women and men begged, searched through trash, or offered their services to those who were better off.

Cities, Trade, and Networks of Exchange

Making products available from near and far, merchants became prominent members of urban society. One of the most popular products was salt, which was used to preserve meat and add taste to food. Greeks, Pacific Islanders, Mesoamericans, and other peoples sought obsidian, a volcanic glass that made sharp tools and was found naturally only where volcanic activity had occurred. By 1500 B.C.E., long-distance traders supplied various Mediterranean and Middle Eastern societies with opium and other drugs, which were mostly used to ease the pain of illness or childbirth.

Growing trade required the creation of currencies. Simple forms of money, mostly varied weights of precious metals like silver, were invented between 3000 and 2500 B.C.E. in Mesopotamian cities. Legal codes were then writ-

Terra-Cotta Figures from Harappan Cities These terra-cotta figures found in the ruins of Harappa show the diverse hairstyles and ornaments popular in the city. Archaeologists believe that these indicate the diversity of social classes and ethnic groups that inhabited Harappa.

ten that specified fines, interest rates, and even the ideal price of some commodities. By 600 B.C.E., the first gold coins were struck in Anatolia. Money made exchange easier, and it may have stimulated the development of mathematics as a tool for calculating wealth in various ancient societies.

Trade networks moving objects of value linked major cities with distant societies. Between 4000 and 3000 B.C.E., traders began shipping minerals, precious stones, and other valued commodities over long distances, and Mesopotamia became a commercial hub linking southern Asia with Egypt. Beginning around 1200 B.C.E., heavily urbanized Phoenicia, which established many trading ports around the Mediterranean, became the first known society to flourish mostly through interregional commerce rather than farming. Gradually, trade routes expanded over long distances, increasing contacts between societies with different cultures and institutions. Goods traveled initially by riverboat and by animal caravans. By 2000 B.C.E., however, sea trading in the Mediterranean Sea, Persian Gulf, and Indian Ocean had become more important.

Trade fostered other developments. Some areas like Mesopotamia became trade centers. Its location as the hub of this network allowed it to draw ideas, produce, and people from a huge hinterland. Similarly, Egypt connected Africa and Eurasia. By 2000 B.C.E., cities like Dilmun on Bahrain Island in the Persian Gulf flourished as trade hubs located between major societies. The need to guide ships or caravans to distant destinations, as well as the belief that the changing skies could influence human activity (astrology), sparked the study of the stars.

Political Foundations

Closely related to urbanization was the emergence of the first states, with their bureaucratic structures and powerful ruling elites, marking a transition to more complex and organized societies. The first known states formed in Mesopotamia around 3500 B.C.E. and in Egypt by 3000 B.C.E. Between 3000 and 1000 B.C.E., states were also established in India, China, Vietnam, Nubia, and southeastern Europe, as well as in Mesoamerica and South America. Among the consequences of states was the rise of conflict between them, as well as with nearby pastoral peoples, resulting in increased warfare—a common pattern in world history.

Kings and Political Hierarchies

States were hierarchically organized political structures. The rulers—mostly kings and emperors, but sometimes queens, such as the Egyptian Hatshepsut—ruled over many rural peasants and city-dwellers living within the territories they controlled. These people paid taxes, in money or in agricultural products, in acknowledgment of the king's ability to keep order, promote justice, and protect his subjects from harm. The great law code associated with the Babylonian ruler Hammurabi is one illustration of this basis of ancient governments. Many kings sought the kind of support accorded to the Aryan kings in the Hindu sacred writings: "Him do ye proclaim, O men as kings and father of kings, the lordly power, the suzerain of all creation, the eater of the folk, the slayer of foes, the guardian of the law."[3] Bureaucracies were formed to administer the states and early empires. As royal power increased, the institutions that allowed merchants and other leading citizens to participate in government, such as the assemblies in Sumerian cities, lost their importance.

The rulers of large states had to possess legal and military power to reward their supporters and punish their enemies. This required sufficient income from either taxes or the spoils of war. Some of this money was also used to build monumental architecture, such as the Egyptian pyramids and Olmec mounds. Rulers also had to convince their subjects that they ruled either as gods themselves or with the permission of divine forces. Kingship was not always an easy job: officials might ignore their policies, rivals could challenge them, and disenchanted groups might rebel.

After states came empires, which were generally formed by conquest. The Akkadian Sargon in Mesopotamia established the earliest known imperial state around 2350 B.C.E. Sargon's use of a standing army set the pattern that prevailed in the Fertile Crescent for the next several millennia, as various states gained influence or control over their neighbors, often to secure scarce resources like silver, copper, or timber. Various ancient societies established empires, among them Assyrians, Egyptians, Mycenaeans, and Hittites. This expansion prompted states to set up forts on their frontiers to control the local population and the flow of traffic.

States and Warfare

With the rise of competing states and improved military technology, warfare became more common. As part of the rise of warfare as an institution, rulers were expected to be or honor heroic warriors. Even today people remember the legends of great ancient warriors (real or mythical) like Hercules at Troy or Arjuna in the Bhagavad Gita. To wage war, kings had to marshal resources such as food and metals as well as recruit soldiers. They also had to discourage dissent and convince the population that warfare was worthwhile. Opposition to the ruler and his policies was viewed as treason and could mean death or imprisonment. Yet soldiers were not always enthusiastic about their duties, as some conscripts in Zhou China complained: "What plant is not wilting? What man is not taken from his wife? Alas for us soldiers!"[4] Then as now,

 World Civilizations (http://www.wsu.edu/~dee/TITLE.HTM). A useful collection of materials on prehistory and ancient history, operated by Washington State University.

military technologies. Incursions into farming societies by nomadic pastoralists remained an important pattern in world history until the seventeenth century C.E.

Warfare became increasingly lethal as weaponry and strategy improved. When the Assyrians swept through Mesopotamia in the ninth century B.C.E., their advanced cavalry and siege weaponry enabled them to level and burn the great city of Babylon. Later the Assyrians experienced defeat, as their capital, Nineveh, fell to "the noise of the whip and of rattling wheels, galloping horses, clattering chariots!"⁵ Even though many cities were surrounded by defensive walls, they were still vulnerable to well-armed foes. But the costs of war, in treasure and people, also prompted rulers to make peace treaties with rival powers and prompted prophets to call for beating "their swords into ploughshares, their spears into pruning hooks; nation shall not lift up sword against nation."⁶ The quest for peace was as old as the urge to wage war.

Fragments of Egyptian–Hittite Treaty These carved stone fragments contain a treaty, signed around 1250 B.C.E., between Egypt and the Hittite kingdom in Anatolia that ended a war between the two states. The treaty is inscribed in the widely used cuneiform script of the Akkadian language. It eloquently demonstrates the reality of ancient warfare but also expresses the age-old quest for peace.

soldiering was a dangerous activity that required bravery and self-discipline.

In Afro-Eurasia, many wars matched states against pastoral nomads, who were attracted by the wealth of farming societies and cities. These mobile nomads, often viewed by the farming peoples as "barbarians," pioneered the development of chariot and cavalry warfare and possessed many horses or camels. Between 2000 and 1000 B.C.E., nomadic peoples occasionally conquered cities and states. Eventually many of these pastoralists, such as the Hittites in western Asia and the Aryans in India, adopted some of the ways of the conquered farmers, while the urban peoples acquired the pastoralists'

Social And Cultural Foundations

Beginning around 3500 B.C.E., the social forms common to hunters and gatherers began to change as more people settled down to farming and developed more organized societies. Perhaps the two most significant cultural innovations were writing, which allowed for record keeping and improved communication, and institutionalized religion, which shaped the values and behavior of societies. The social and cultural patterns that emerged in antiquity endured because they fulfilled basic human needs for group survival and personal satisfaction.

Inequality, Conflict, and Leisure

The shift from the relatively egalitarian ethos of hunting and gathering to a more hierarchical social organization changed people's lives. Increasingly, people were divided into social classes, with wealthier groups controlling the distribution and consumption of economic resources. Ancient graves reveal the differences in social status. Some graves were elaborate, filled with offerings of precious goods, and others were very simple. Legal codes usually favored the wealthy.

At the same time, with productive agriculture, populations grew. Between 8000 and 500 B.C.E., the world's

Bell of Marquies Music had a key function in the court life of Zhou China. This sixty-four-piece bell set was found in the tomb of a regional ruler, which also contained many flutes, drums, zithers, pan pipes, and chimes. Five men using mallets and poles were needed to play this set of bells.

population grew from 5 or 10 million to an estimated 100 million. The great majority of these people lived in Mesopotamia, Egypt, India, China, and southeastern Europe. People were also living longer than during the Stone Age, when one-third died before age twenty and only one-tenth lived past forty. Bronze Age peoples lived into their early forties, and probably 5 to 10 percent lived past sixty. With less equality but more people, the potential for social conflict increased. Most communities included haves and have-nots, landlords and landless, free citizens and slaves. The gap between rich and poor made theft and other crimes a serious problem that was addressed through harsh codes like that of Hammurabi.

Patriarchy was another source of inequality. Men increasingly believed that women were unsuited to run governments, and few of them were allowed to do so. Social changes that required heavy physical labor in farming, warfare, and long-distance trade influenced gender and family relations. An ancient Chinese saying asserted that "men plow and women weave."[7] Although women continued to produce some of the pottery and most of the cloth, they were no longer equal contributors to food needs, because they now spent more time at home. In farming families, women were also encouraged to bear a larger number of children to help in the fields. In many places, men had multiple wives or took concubines. In some societies, among them Sumeria, Egypt, and Shang China, older matrilineal family systems eroded, but middle-class urban women fought hard to retain their property and other rights. Sexual options became more limited for women, because men wanted

to ensure that their personal wealth would be passed on to their children of known paternity. Increasingly dependent on men for support, women became more preoccupied with physical appearance, hoping to attract male favor.

Despite the social inequality and long hours of toil, leisure activities developed. Sumerian city-dwellers enjoyed dancing and music and invented beautiful, elaborate harps and lyres for their pleasure. Zhou Chinese music-lovers preferred flutes and drums, and Egyptians preferred metal horns. Music was used for worship, festivals, and work, but the oldest known love songs had also appeared by 2300 B.C.E. in Egypt. Wrestling became a popular sport in many cultures. Alcoholic drinks like beer and wine were also common, often consumed in public taverns. Homer summed up the pleasures favored in early Greece: "The things in which we take a perennial delight are the feast, the lyre [a musical instrument], the dance, clean linen in plenty, a hot bath and our beds."[8]

Writing and Its Consequences

Although limited to a relatively small group of people for much of history, writing was a critical invention of several early societies. A Sumerian legend recalled a key discovery: "The High Priest of Kulaba formed some clay and wrote words on it as if on a tablet; with the sun's rising [to dry the clay], so it was!"[9] Initially developed to keep commercial accounts, codify legends and rituals, or record political proclamations, writing later gave birth to literature, historiography, sacred texts, and other forms of learning and culture that could now be transmitted and expanded. Writing helped spread the Sumerian epic of Gilgamesh so widely that it influenced the Hebrew book of Genesis and the *Iliad* and the *Odyssey* of the Greek Homer many centuries later. Writing also allowed rulers to communicate over long distances with district governors and foreign leaders, and it allowed merchants to make arrangements with merchants in other cities, enhancing the role of communication networks.

Writing, however, had contradictory consequences. On the one hand, it clearly stimulated creativity and intellectual growth while allowing for a spread of knowledge. But writing also often became a tool for preserving the social and political order, especially when literacy was restricted to a privileged elite such as bureaucrats, lawyers, or priests. A soldier in Zhou China complained that he and his colleagues wanted to return home, but they "were in awe of the [official] orders in the tablets."[10]

Institutionalized Religions

The rise of agriculture and then cities gradually transformed the belief that nature was alive with spiritual forces (animism) to more systematic theologies and organized religious observances. These beliefs and practices may have promoted cooperation and a sense of community. Ideas about the fate of individual humans after death as well as notions of morality differed widely as societies developed unique traditions and beliefs. While most ancient peoples were polytheists or animists, believing in many gods or spirits, a few, such as the Hebrews and some African societies, were monotheists, believing in one high god who presided over the universe.

Full-time religious specialists and mythologies emerged to help make sense of the supernatural and natural worlds. With the rise of agriculture and larger communities, a priestly class arose who were seen as able to communicate with the gods and interpret their will. They staffed the temples, which in some cities were massive buildings serving thousands of believers, and provided essential services such as writing or calculating the time of the annual floods. Myths, stories about the past or about the interaction of

Ancient and Lost Civilizations (*http://www.crystalinks.com/ancient.html*). Offers some useful essays on various world regions and ancient cultures.

gods with the human world, explained the birth of the universe, the progression of seasons, the uncertainties of agriculture, the flooding of rivers, and human dramas such as battlefield losses and victories. Many myths and legends were recorded in sacred books, and several thousand years later, some of these ancient books are still revered by many millions of people.

Institutionalized religions often became a powerful force for social control. Challenging the political or social system, which was seen as divinely inspired, now constituted blasphemy and condemned one to eternal punishment after death. Religious views also spread from one society to another. For example, Egyptian ideas of the afterlife and a final Day of Judgment were influential around the larger Mediterranean basin. Hebrews may have acquired their notions of a weekly Sabbath and a Garden of Eden from Mesopotamians. Many centuries later, all of these ideas were reflected in Christianity and Islam.

 Test your understanding of the material covered in Part I.

Suggested Reading

Adas, Michael, ed. *Agricultural and Pastoral Societies in Ancient and Classical History*. Philadelphia: Temple University Press, 2001. A useful collection of essays on various aspects of premodern world history.

Bogucki, Peter. *The Origins of Human Society*. Malden, MA: Blackwell, 1999. A detailed and up-to-date scholarly study of prehistory and the rise of ancient societies.

Casson, Lionel. *The Ancient Mariners: Seafarers and Sea Fighters of the Mediterranean in Ancient Times,* 2nd ed. Princeton, NJ: Princeton University Press, 1991. A fascinating study of ancient maritime trade and connections.

Christian, David. *Maps of Time: An Introduction to "Big History."* Berkeley: University of California Press, 2004. The most extensive presentation of the "big history" approach, with much on the ancient era.

Curtin, Philip D. *Cross-Cultural Trade in World History*. Cambridge: Cambridge University Press, 1984. A pioneering comparative study.

Diamond, Jared. *Guns, Germs and Steel: The Fates of Human Societies*. New York: W.W. Norton, 1997. A fascinating interpretation of prehistoric and ancient human societies, with emphasis on environmental influences.

Fagan, Brian. *The Long Summer: How Climate Changed Civilization*. New York: Basic Books, 2004. An up-to-date assessment of the connection between history and climate over the past 5,000 years.

Fagan, Brian M. *People of the Earth: An Introduction to World Prehistory*, 11th ed. New York: Longman, 2003. Contains much up-to-date material on the ancient societies and prehistory.

Manning, Patrick. *Migration in World History*. New York: Routledge, 2005. Provocative study, with much on prehistory and ancient history.

Matossian, Mary Kilbourne. *Shaping World History: Breakthroughs in Ecology, Technology, Science, and Politics*. Armonk, NY: M.E. Sharpe, 1997. A general examination of science, technology, and ecology, with much material on early farmers and the ancient societies.

Snooks, Graeme D. *The Dynamic Society: Exploring the Sources of Global Change*. London: Routledge, 1996. A challenging view of world history by an economist, with much on the ancient world.

Trigger, Bruce D. *Understanding Early Civilizations*. New York: Cambridge University Press, 2003. A detailed scholarly examination of ancient societies, including Egypt, Mesopo-

PART II

Blossoming:
The Classical Societies and Their Legacies, ca. 6000 B.C.E.– ca. 600 C.E.

NORTH AND CENTRAL AMERICA
The Maya established a long-lasting series of rival city-states in Mexico and Central America that flourished from creative farming, science, trade, and writing. Great cities based on trade also appeared elsewhere in Mexico. North of Mexico, town-dwelling farming societies emerged. Especially influential, the Mound Builders in eastern North America fostered long-distance trade networks stretching from the Atlantic Ocean and Gulf of Mexico to the Great Lakes.

SOUTH AMERICA
New states that used innovative agriculture emerged along the Peruvian coast and in the Andes highlands. The Moche, while warring with their neighbors, also created sophisticated pottery and art. In the Andes, Tiwanaku produced art and thought that influenced neighboring societies. Long-distance trade networks also connected various societies in South America.

© Cengage Learning

EUROPE
Greek city-states, notably Athens, experimented with democracy and fostered philosophy and science. By conquering a large empire, Alexander the Great spread Greek culture into western Asia and Egypt. The Romans built an empire that encompassed the Mediterranean Basin and much of Europe, spreading Roman influence. By late Roman times Christianity was becoming the dominant religion in the Mediterranean, and Germanic tribes migrated into southern Europe, contributing to the collapse of Roman power. To the east, Byzantium conquered a large empire while mixing Roman, Greek, and Christian traditions.

WESTERN ASIA
The Persians established a large empire over much of western Asia and Egypt, promoting Persian thought. After their collapse the Hellenistic Greeks dominated the region and spread Greek culture. The Hellenistic Greeks were then displaced by the Romans. In Roman-ruled Palestine the teachings of a Hebrew, Jesus, sparked a new religion, Christianity, which during the later Classical Era spread around the Mediterranean Basin. With Roman decline the Persians regained power over much of western Asia.

EASTERN ASIA
Chinese philosophies emerged during a time of rapid change, and Confucianism, Daoism, and Legalism became enduring influences. The Qin dynasty reunified China, and then the Han dynasty established a huge empire and overland trade with western Asia and Rome. When the Han collapsed, Buddhism filtered in from India. Chinese science and technology during this era were innovative. Koreans and Japanese formed states and imported Confucianism, Buddhism, and political models from China.

ARCTIC OCEAN

GERMANS
EUROPE
Danube R.

ROMAN EMPIRE
BYZANTIUM
GREECE
Carthage

ASIA

PERSIA
EGYPT
PALESTINE

HIMALAYAS
Ganges R.

CHINA

JAPAN

KUSH
INDIA

GHANA
Niger R.
AFRICA
AKSUM

CAMBODIA

Congo R.

ATLANTIC
OCEAN

INDIAN OCEAN

Mekong R.

INDONESIA

AUSTRALIA

AFRICA
Egypt fell successively under Persian, Hellenistic Greek, and finally Roman rule. Carthage was another major North African power and trade center until the Romans conquered the region. In northeast Africa, Kush was a trade center and major iron producer, and another trading state, Aksum, adopted Christianity. Trading cities and then empires, notably Ghana, emerged in the Sudan region. Elsewhere the Bantu peoples continued their expansion, settling much of central, eastern, and southern Africa. Long-distance trade networks connected West Africans with North Africa and East Africans with India and western Asia.

SOUTHERN ASIA AND OCEANIA
Buddhism arose in India, where it was later adopted by the kings of the region's first empire, the Mauryas. However, Hinduism remained India's majority faith, and Buddhism later split into rival schools. Indians traded with western Asia, Africa, Rome, and Southeast Asia. Various groups migrated into India from Central Asia. The Gupta kingdom made India a world leader in science, and Indian influence, including Buddhism and Hinduism, spread into Southeast Asia, helping foster states. Maritime trade linked Southeast Asia with China, India, western Asia, and East Africa. During this same time Austronesians continued settling the Pacific islands and traded with each other over vast distances.

CHAPTER 5

Eurasian Connections and New Traditions in East Asia, 600 B.C.E.–600 C.E.

Learning Outcomes

After reading this chapter, you should be able to answer the following questions:

LO¹ What were the distinctive features of the Chinese philosophies that emerged during the late Zhou period?

LO² How was Chinese society organized during the Han, and how was China linked to the rest of Eurasia?

LO³ What outside influences helped shape China after the fall of the Han?

LO⁴ How did the Koreans and Japanese assimilate Chinese influences into their own distinctive societies?

> 66 After the Han had sent its envoys to open up communications with the state of Da Xia [in today's Afghanistan], all the barbarians of the distant west craned their necks to the east and longed to catch a glimpse of China. 99

—Chinese diplomat Zhang Qian, reported by historian Sima Qian, ca. 100 B.C.E.[1]

In 138 B.C.E., the Han Chinese were being threatened by a Central Asian group known to the Chinese as the Xiongnu (SHE-OONG-noo). The Han emperor, Wu Di (woo tee), sought contact with another Central Asian society, the Yuezhi (yueh-chih), to forge an alliance. An attendant at the imperial court, Zhang Qian (jahng chee-YEN), a strong, congenial man known for his generosity, volunteered to undertake the dangerous diplomatic mission. He set off on the lengthy overland journey west with only a small escort. Zhang was captured by the Xiongnu and held prisoner for ten years, but he and his party finally escaped and continued their way west, following a route that soon became known as the Silk Road, one of the classical world's great networks of exchange. Although his diplomatic mission to ally with the Yuezhi failed, on his return to China after twelve years away, Zhang brought back useful products and knowledge about the lands to the west.

Test your knowlege before you read this chapter.

What do you think?

Chinese philosophies developed during the Classical Era had long-lasting influence throughout Asia.

Strongly Disagree   Strongly Agree
1   2   3   4   5   6   7

For more than a millennium after Zhang's journey, China traveled and traded continuously through Central Asia. Every year, merchants gathered just outside the walls of the main Chinese city, Chang'an (CHAHNG-ahn) (today's Xian (SEE-ahn)), to form a caravan loaded with bundles of silk and other goods on their horses and donkeys. From Chang'an they traveled west for weeks, skirting the southern side of the Great Wall of China. At the last outpost of Chinese society, marked by the Jade Gate, the horses and donkeys were exchanged for camels, which were better suited to the upcoming deserts. After weeks of travel across waterless wastes, the caravan still had to cross the snow-covered Pamir (pah-MEER) Mountains. Finally, several

<< **Fresco from Mogao Caves** The Mogao Caves, situated along the Silk Road in western China, contain many frescoes reflecting Silk Road life and the spread of Buddhism into the region. This fresco, painted in the third century C.E., shows a caravan resting at an oasis.

Courtesy, Dunhuang Academy/Lois Conner, photographer

thousand miles from Chang'an, they arrived at the Central Asian cities of Turkestan, where the merchants sold their precious commodities. Despite great distances and immense geographic barriers, this vast network of trails tied China to the world beyond.

China and its neighbors, Korea and Japan, had built their societies far away from the influence of the Middle East, India, and Europe. In doing so, and in responding to their particular environments, East Asian peoples developed many distinctive social, political, religious, and cultural traditions, but East Asians were also influenced by others. This was the time of the classical blossoming of East Asian cultures that established essential frameworks for the centuries to follow.

LO¹ Changing China and Axial-Age Thought, 600–221 B.C.E.

Chinese technology, science, and philosophical thought developed largely independently from outside influences. Yet Chinese originality was in part a response to many of the same challenges faced by other societies, especially during the Eurasian Axial Age of the early classical centuries. Like all societies, the Chinese needed ideas to explain the workings of the universe and to bring order to their lives. Such ideas appeared during the late Zhou (joe) period, when social and political conditions rapidly changed and produced unsettled conditions. Chinese philosophers seeking to restore order spawned several schools of thought that endured for several millennia.

Map 5.1
China in the Sixth Century B.C.E.

During the late Zhou era, China was divided into competing, often warring, states, only loosely ruled by the Zhou kings. Some, such as Ch'u and Wu, were large. In the third century B.C.E., the westernmost state, Qin, conquered the others and formed a unified empire.

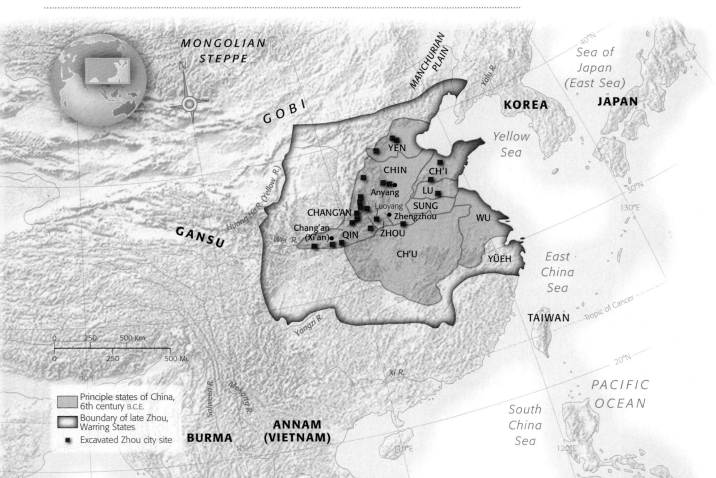

© Cengage Learning

Late Zhou Conflicts and Innovations

Warring States Period

The Zhou dynasty lasted for nearly 900 years (1122–221 B.C.E), but the later centuries, from around 600 to 221 B.C.E., experienced rapid change as well as chronic warfare (see Map 5.1). Military technology, improved through advances in iron making, contrib-

 Interactive Map

uted to the uncertainties of these times, a formative period for China. The era from 481 to 221 B.C.E., when the fighting was particularly intense, is known as the Warring States Period. Local lords did not challenge the Zhou king directly but increasingly ignored him, fighting instead among themselves for supremacy. The chronic warfare among ruthless local governments generated a long period of crisis.

The changes during the later Zhou were not all detrimental. For example, despite the fighting, by 250 B.C.E. China had become the most populous society on earth, with 20 to 40 million people. Improving technology and communications also fostered commerce and cities, and a cash economy developed in place of the old barter system. Political and economic power gradually shifted to the eastern part of the Yellow River Valley, while Chinese culture expanded south of the Yangzi River. The Yangzi River Basin became the major agricultural region because of its greater fertility and more favorable climate. Social mobility also increased. Many peasants and slaves moved to open land or to the fast-growing cities, as the merchant class grew in numbers and influence.

Science and Technology

During the late Zhou period, the Chinese joined the Iron Age, establishing an equal technological footing with western Asia. Chinese sources first mention iron use in 521 B.C.E., a millennium after the iron-using Hittites in western Asia and 500 years after the development of iron technology in India. By around 400 B.C.E., the Chinese became the first people to make the breakthrough to cast iron, which is much easier to shape into products. This technical advance made available superior axes, hoes, ploughshares, picks, swords, and chariots.

The Chinese also made major advances in water control and conservation. In 250 B.C.E., a vast complex of dikes, canals, and dams was constructed to control the fickle upper Yangzi River, a huge system that

CHRONOLOGY

Classical China

1122–221 B.C.E.	Zhou dynasty
550–350 B.C.E.	Height of Axial Age in China
481 B.C.E.	Beginning of Warring States Period
551–479 B.C.E.	Life of Confucius
221–206 B.C.E.	Qin dynasty
206 B.C.E.–220 C.E.	Han dynasty
141–87 B.C.E.	Reign of Wu Di
105 C.E.	Invention of paper
222–581 C.E.	Three Kingdoms and Six Dynasties Era
581–618 C.E.	Sui dynasty

worked so well that it is still used today. Soybeans, which were introduced in the seventh century B.C.E., provided a rich protein source and also enriched the soil. The late Zhou Chinese also invented the first compasses and became pioneers in mathematics, amending the Shang decimal system by adding a place for the zero in equations.

Philosophy: Taoism, Confucianism, and Legalism

Perhaps most significantly, the later Zhou was the most creative period in traditional Chinese thought, producing so many competing philosophies that it was called the era of the "hundred schools of thought." These diverse approaches were part of the period of widespread intellectual creativity throughout the Mediterranean world, western Asia, and India between 600 and 250 B.C.E. known as the Axial Age (see Chapters 6 and 7). During this turbulent period, philos-

 History of China (*http:// www.chaos .umd.edu/history*). Collection of essays and timelines on Chinese history maintained by the University of Maryland.

ophers across Eurasia emphasized ethical principles and generated new political ideologies. Later, powerful empires emerged in China, India, and the Mediterranean that reflected these new ideas.

> "Confucius maintained that education was the key to promoting morality; he stressed the study of history, philosophy, literature, poetry, and music."

The Axial Age in China provoked a questioning of philosophical, religious, and political issues. The hundred schools had resulted in part from the constant conflict during the Warring States Period. Another factor may have been increased knowledge of the outside world resulting from contact with Turkish pastoralists in Central Asia, who traded horses to China for grain, wine, and silks. But Chinese thought during the hundred schools era differed dramatically from that developed in other societies of this era, because it was humanistic and saw people as social and political creatures. Chinese philosophy also placed less emphasis on an afterlife and powerful gods than did the philosophies of many other societies.

This practical, down-to-earth approach had a basis in the early Chinese philosophers' position in society. Although literate and thoughtful, these philosophers were also pragmatic teachers who wandered from one Zhou state to another offering their services. Their disciples collected their sayings or thoughts into the classic texts that were venerated by later generations. The most significant philosophies that emerged were Confucianism, Daoism, and Legalism, all of which influenced China for the next two millennia.

Confucius and His Legacy

The most influential new philosophy of the late Zhou period was Confucianism (kun-FYOO-shu-NIZ-um), which emphasized the relations among people. Kong Fuzi (kong foo-dzu) ("Master Kung"), better known in the West as Confucius, probably lived from 551 to 479 B.C.E. Little is known of his life and ideas except indirectly, through the writings of his followers.

Confucius was born into a modest but aristocratic family in eastern China, the son of a soldier. As a young man he attempted unsuccessfully to gain appointment as a government official and then spent years as a teacher, apparently showing dazzling ability. Confucius left no direct writings, but his sayings were collected by his disciples and published a century or two after his death in a book called *The Analects*. Over his career he taught some three thousand students from all social classes. The sage claimed that he had "never refused to teach anyone, even though he came to me on foot, with nothing more to offer as tuition than a package of dried meat."[2] Confucius maintained that education was the key to promoting morality; he stressed the study of history, philosophy, literature, poetry, and music. Considering himself a transmitter of ancient wisdom, he revived traditional ideas and reorganized them into a coherent system of thought for the future.

The Confucian Ideal

The philosophy Confucius spawned, Confucianism, is a philosophy of social relations, a moral and ethical code designed to promote social stability. Human-heartedness, Confucius wrote, consists in loving others. In religious terms, Confucius could best be described as an agnostic; he said little about the spiritual world, arguing that, because people know little about life, they cannot know about death. Confucius developed a rationalist view opposed to superstition. The answer to the world's problems, Confucius argued, was virtue, ethics, and, above all, benevolence. Moderation in behavior was the ideal.

In forging a new harmonious order, Confucius advocated an autocratic but paternalistic form of government in which the ruler was responsible for the welfare of the people. The family constituted the model for the state. Just as children should respect and obey their parents, a rule known as filial piety, so citizens should obey a fair government. The philosopher talked about duty and obedience of inferiors to superiors: of wife to husband, son to father, younger to older, and citizen to king. In contrast to the inferior person, who covets profits and possessions, the cultivated person practices what he preaches, preaches what he practices, cherishes virtue, and understands

The Analects and Correct Confucian Behavior

The Analects is the main record of Confucius and his thought that survived the Warring States Period and the book burnings of the next dynasty. Compiled by his disciples many years after his death, it is presented largely in the form of questions from his followers and answers, short aphorisms, or long discourses by the sage. Divided into twenty chapters, the book covers many topics, mostly peoples' conduct and aspirations. It became the most important book in China from the Han dynasty down to modern times. These fragments present a few of Confucius's thoughts about the correct behavior of gentlemen (the rulers and other leaders), sons and daughters, and people in general.

[About the gentleman], Confucius said, "The gentleman concerns himself with the Way [the natural order that is also a moral order]; he does not worry about his salary. Hunger may be found in plowing; wealth may be found in studying. The gentleman worries about the Way, not about poverty. . . . The gentleman reveres three things. He reveres the mandate of Heaven; he reveres great people; and he reveres the words of the sages. Petty people do not know the mandate of Heaven and so do not revere it. They are disrespectful of great people and they ridicule the words of the sage. The gentleman aspires to things lofty; the petty person aspires to things base. The gentleman looks to himself; the petty person looks to other people. The gentleman feels bad when his capabilities fall short of some task. He does not feel bad if people fail to recognize him. . . ."

[About filial piety or respect for parents], Confucius said, "Nowadays, filial piety is considered to be the ability to nourish one's parents. But this obligation to nourish

even extends down to the dogs and horses. Unless we have reverence for our parents, what makes us any different? Do not offend your parents. . . . When your parents are alive, serve them according to the rules of ritual and decorum. When they are deceased, give them a funeral and offer sacrifices to them according to the rules of ritual and decorum. . . . It is unacceptable not to be aware of your parents' ages. Their advancing years are a cause for joy and at the same time a cause for sorrow. . . ."

[About humanity], Confucius said, "If an individual can practice five things anywhere in the world, he is a man of humanity. . . . [These are] Reverence, generosity, truthfulness, diligence, and kindness. If a person acts with reverence, he will not be insulted. If he is generous, he will win over the people. If he is truthful, he will be trusted by the people. If he is diligent, he will have great achievements. If he is kind, he will be able to influence others. . . . When you go out, treat everyone as if you were welcoming a great guest. Employ people as if you were conducting a great sacrifice."

Thinking About the Reading

1. What are some of the main qualities expected of a gentleman?
2. How might Confucian views on respect for parents have influenced the family system?
3. How did the advice reflect on Confucius's humanistic emphasis?

Source: Reprinted with permission of The Free Press, a Division of Simon & Schuster Inc., from Chinese Civilization and Society, A Sourcebook, Second Revised & Expanded Edition by Patricia Buckley Ebrey. Copyright © 1993 by Patricia Buckley Ebrey. All rights reserved.

what is right. But authority, he emphasized, must be wielded justly and wisely. When asked what thought should guide the conduct of both leaders and citizens throughout life, he replied: "Do not do to others what you yourself do not desire."[3]

Confucius helped set the common East Asian pattern of compromise. To promote harmony, Confucianism stressed strict adherence to rules of courtesy. For example, a book of etiquette from late Zhou times advised men on rules for visiting another

man of equal status: "The host goes to meet the guest outside the gate, and there bows twice, answered by two bows from the guest. Then the host, with a salute, invites him to enter."[4] The Confucian societies became noted for using ritual and etiquette to maintain stability and discipline, and, in the centuries to follow, they generally did. China became one of the most stable societies in history, and Confucianism contributed greatly to its cohesiveness. However, the ideas of Confucius became increasingly rigid in

Daoism
A Chinese philosophy that emphasized adaptation to nature; arose in the late Zhou era.

先師孔子行教像

德侔天地道冠古今
刪述六經垂憲萬世

Confucius Stone rubbing of a portrait of Confucius from an ancient temple. For 2,500 years, Confucius was the most honored and influential Chinese thinker, remembered in countless paintings, woodblock cuts, and carvings on walls.

spirit and application over the centuries, leading in some cases to a conservatism and inflexibility that Confucius might have condemned.

Mengzi and Xunzi

Two of the main followers of Confucius represented opposing schools of interpretation. Mengzi (MUNG-dze) (Mencius) (372–289 B.C.E.) advocated a liberal, even permissive government in which the ruler embraced benevolence and righteousness as his main goals. He dreamed of a united world state under a just king and was extremely optimistic about the prospects for society. Xunzi (SHOON-dze) (Hsun Tzu) (310–220 B.C.E.) disagreed; viewing human nature as essentially bad, he maintained that the state must enforce goodness and morality. Xunzi also contributed to the authoritarian tendencies of Confucianism by claiming that Confucian writings were the source of all wisdom.

Competing Philosophies: Daoism and Legalism

The second major philosophy to develop during the hundred schools period was Daoism (DOW-iz-um), which taught that people should adapt to nature. The main ideas of Daoism are attributed to Laozi (lou-zoe) (Lao Tzu or "Old Master"). However, we have no direct evidence that such a man ever lived. According to the legends about his life, Laozi was an older contemporary of Confucius and a disillusioned bureaucrat who became a wandering teacher. If such a man existed, he probably did not write the two main Daoist texts, which were most likely composed during the third century B.C.E.

Daoist Mysticism

Daoism was a philosophy of withdrawal for people who were appalled by the warfare of the age. It was mystical and romantic, fostering an awareness of nature and its beauties. This attitude became pronounced in Chinese poetry and landscape painting, which often recorded towering mountains, roaring waterfalls, and placid lakes. Daoist thinkers held that the goal of life for each individual was to follow the "way of the universe," or *dao*. Daoist teachers described the dao as "unfathomable, the ancestral progenitor of all things, everlasting. All pervading, dao lies hidden and cannot be named. It produces all things. He who acts in accordance with dao becomes one with dao."[5] Convinced that people could never dominate their environment, Daoist philosophy urged them to conform to the great pattern of the natural world rather than, as in Confucianism, to social expectations and governments. To the Daoists, societies were an obstacle and all governments corrupt and oppressive; they argued that Chinese rulers should maintain the balance between human society and nature, to govern well and follow correct rituals.

Daoism complemented Confucianism by enabling Chinese to balance the conflicting needs for social order and personal autonomy, adding the virtues of enjoyment, reflection, and a sense of freedom. Daoists advised Confucianists to flow with the spirit and the heart rather than struggle with the intellect. The man in power was a Confucianist, but out of power became a Daoist. The active bureaucrat of the morning became the dreamy poet or nature lover of the evening. Like all mystics seeking the heart of spirituality, Daoists found it difficult to express their basic ideas in words, claiming that "those who know do not speak; those who speak do not know."[6]

The Legalist Approach

Among the dozens of other competing philosophies of the Warring States Period, Legalism also had an enduring influence. Borrowing ideas from the Confucian Xunzi, who believed people were inherently selfish and power hungry, the Legalists emphasized the need for an authoritarian government to secure prosperity, order, and stability. To ensure the survival of the whole, they believed, the state must control all economic resources, and people should be well disciplined, subject to military duty and harsh laws.

Taken to extremes, Legalism led to unrestrained state power. The ruler needed to be strong and to have no regard for the rights or will of the people, because the larger goal was to maintain unity and stability. Legalists ridiculed Confucian humanism. One Legalist, in a pointed attack on the Confucians, argued that "the intelligent ruler does not speak about deeds of humanity and righteousness, and he does not listen to the words of learned men."[7] Although Legalism exercised a long-term influence on Chinese politics, the Chinese always balanced it with the more humane ideas of the Confucians and Daoists. Hence, the Chinese during the Classical Era did not follow one philosophy to the exclusion of others. In the resulting mix, leaders were to be obeyed but also ethical and benevolent.

LO² Han China: An Asian Empire

Chinese society, more than Indian, Middle Eastern, or European societies, was characterized by cohesion and continuity, as well as by the balancing of diverse influences. For example, although China was often attacked and even occasionally conquered by Central Asians, the invaders maintained continuity with China's past by adopting Chinese culture, a process known as Sinicization. But before modern times, one major transition set the pattern for centuries to follow: the replacement of the multistate Zhou system by a centralized empire. The new imperial China was forged by the harsh rulers of Qin (chin) and followed by the Han dynasty, which

> "The first Qin ruler assumed the new and imposing title of Shi Huangdi and prophesied that his dynasty would last ten thousand generations."

Legalism
A Chinese philosophy that advocated harsh control of people by the state; became the dominant philosophy during the Qin dynasty (221–207 B.C.E.) and was later tempered by Confucianism.

Sinicization
The process by which Central Asian invaders maintained continuity with China's past by adopting Chinese culture.

conquered a large empire, fostered foreign trade, and restored Confucianism as a guiding philosophy. The Han era was formative for many aspects of Chinese life and culture, and the economy grew dramatically.

The Qin Dynasty

Return to Centralization

The political turmoil of late Zhou times ended when the Qin dynasty (221–206 B.C.E.) conquered the other states and implemented repressive Legalist ideas, transforming China into an empire with a powerful and highly authoritarian central government. Located on the northwest borders, the state of Qin had gradually become the strongest state within the Zhou system. Some Legalist scholars had moved there and been appointed to high office. Under their policies, the state controlled the economy, establishing government monopolies over many trade goods. The prime minister, Li Si (lee SHE) (Li Ssu), a Legalist thinker, was a brutal man; he argued that those who used the past to oppose the present, the Confucians, had to be exterminated. Li Si was the chief deputy to the man who would eventually become the ruler, and first emperor, of all of China.

Shi Huangdi

In 221 B.C.E. the Qin, finally defeating and absorbing all the remaining Zhou states, established a new government that ruled most of the Chinese people. The first Qin ruler assumed the new and imposing title of Shi Huangdi (SHE hwang-dee) (first emperor) and prophesied that his dynasty would last ten thousand generations. The son of a Qin prince and his concubine, he was not yet forty years old when he became ruler of China. This extraordinary autocrat surrounded himself with mystery and pomp to enhance his prestige, living in carefully guarded privacy.

The new dynasty implemented dramatic policies, including military expansion. Not content with conquering the Chinese heartland, the Qin also sent armies to incorporate much of southern China and, for a while, Vietnam, into the empire, embracing nearly all regions where Chinese society was dominant. The first emperor also mandated a total reordering of China along Legalist lines, attempting to control all aspects of Chinese life. The growing bureaucracy that was needed to supervise these operations strengthened the centralized state system. Given this unification, the name *Qin* is quite fittingly the origin of the Western name for China.

Dynasty of Repression

Later Chinese historians viewed the Qin Empire as one of the most terrible periods in the country's long history. The common people hated the forced labor and strict laws. Spies, general surveillance, and thought control were paramount in the Qin police state, which closely monitored the citizenry. Intellectuals despised the Qin because the state launched attacks on all aspects of culture, including Confucianism. In the campaign to stamp out what they perceived to be subversive doctrines, the Qin burned thousands of books, sparing only practical and scientific manuals, and executed many scholars, often by burying them alive. In so doing the Qin ended the intellectual creativity of the hundred schools.

Qin Accomplishments

Yet despite the repression, Shi Huangdi's policies led to many achievements. A dazzling series of public works projects and state policies promoted communication, economic growth, and social change. The Qin standardized weights and measures, developed a postal service, unified economic and agricultural practices, and codified laws. They also standardized the written language, so that all literate Chinese anywhere in the empire could communicate easily. To foster economic growth, the Qin established state monopolies over essential commodities like salt. Taxes were high and often included devoting significant time to forced labor on government projects. The harsh Qin laws also ended crime, as a later Chinese scholar conceded: "Nothing lost on the road was picked up and pocketed, the hills were free of bandits, men avoided quarrels at home."[8] Finally, Qin land reform undermined the power of the old aristocracy, a mighty blow to the Zhou social structure.

The most famous public works project was the construction of an early and limited version of a Great Wall along China's northern borders. A few partial earthen walls had already been built in Zhou times, but the Qin consolidated these into a more formidable structure, later known as the Great Wall. As part of their tax obligation, vast numbers of laborers were drafted for building the wall, which became one of

The Great Wall This panorama from the region just north of Beijing shows a portion of the wall reconstructed in the fifteenth century C.E. The wall was an attempt to mark the northern boundary of China and to keep out nomadic invaders.

the greatest architectural feats of the ancient world. Later dynasties periodically rebuilt and added to the wall, which eventually stretched more than 1,400 miles across north China, with watchtowers placed every few miles. The wall was seldom as successful as the Chinese had hoped in curbing invaders. Still, it was a symbolic affirmation of empire and a statement of territorial limits.

Fall of the Qin Dynasty

But the Qin dynasty was short-lived. Shi Huangdi was a tyrant who fostered much general hatred, and his expansionist policies provoked conflict with neighboring peoples. The first emperor's death in 210 B.C.E was kept secret by his inner circle for fear of general revolt. He was buried in a huge underground mausoleum together with seven thousand astonishingly realistic life-size terra cotta horses and warriors brandishing real bronze weapons. When news finally spread of Shi Huangdi's death, peasant revolts broke out. In 206 B.C.E. the Qin forces were defeated by an alliance of various rebel armies. In the chaos that followed, a former peasant led his forces to victory, establishing a new dynasty, the Han (HAHN).

The Han Empire

The Han is the most respected dynasty in Chinese history, because during these four centuries (206 B.C.E.–220 C.E.), they built a huge empire stretching far into Central Asia (see Map 5.2). Trade across this area allowed greater contact Interactive Map

 Map 5.2
The Han Empire

The Han Empire fluctuated in size, but at its height controlled most of today's China, Korea, northern Vietnam, and a long corridor through Central Asia to Turkestan.

© Cengage Learning

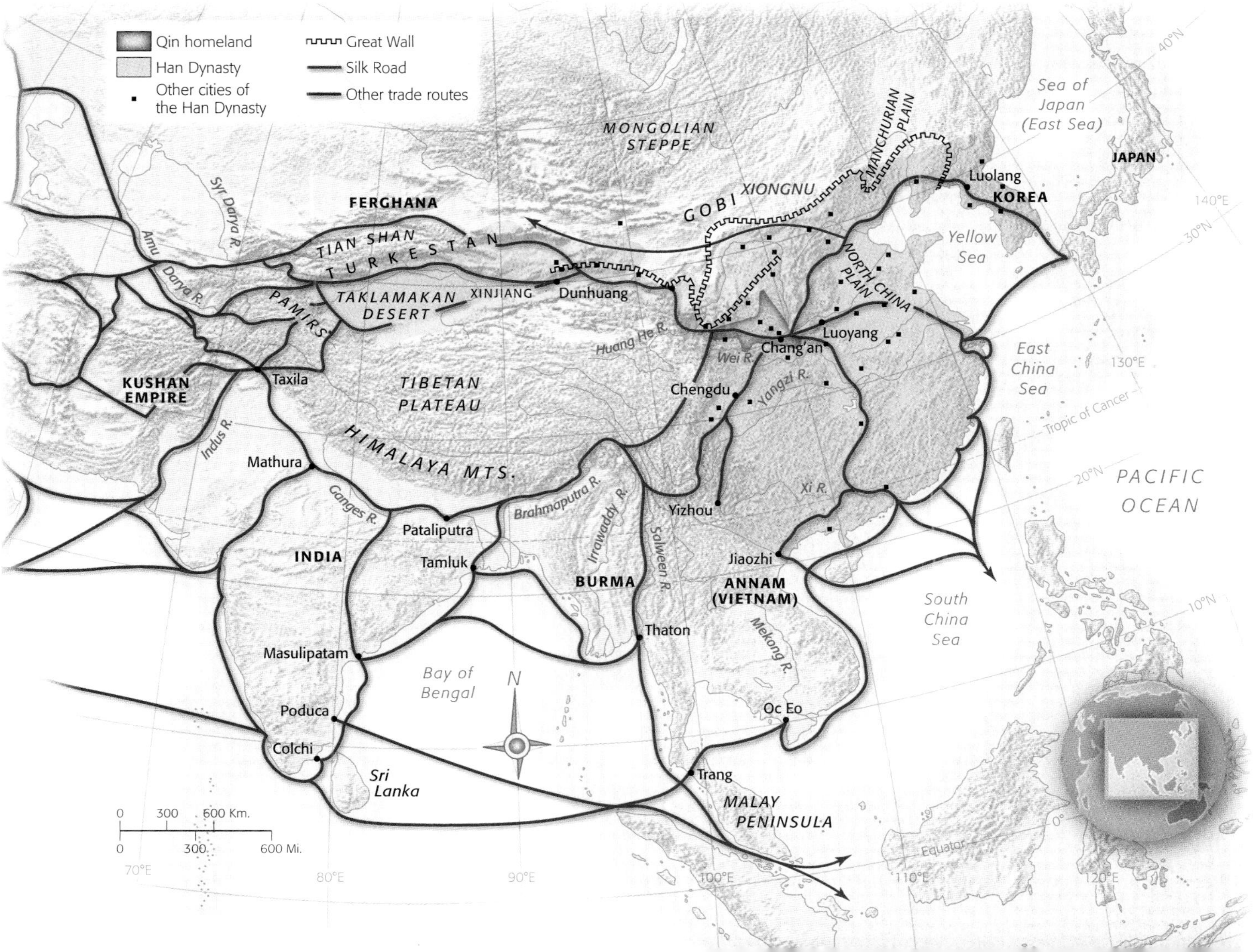

mandarins
Educated men who staffed the imperial Chinese bureaucracy from the Han dynasty until the early twentieth century.

with people to the west. Like the Qin, the Han built a strong state, but they also greatly modified the Qin's harsh Legalist structure. The brilliance of the Han and the expansion of Chinese society southward during this classical period set the pattern for later dynasties.

Imperial Han China

Large empires like the Han were common in the middle Classical Era, when large segments of the Eurasian landmass and North Africa came under the domination of large imperial structures. In organizing their societies, all of the empires built on the ideas of the Axial Age sages, resolving the crises that had sparked their rise. The Han and Roman Empires reached their zenith around the same time and resembled each other in population, although Rome's empire was larger in territorial size. In 2 C.E. the Han Empire contained at least 60 million people, and the Roman Empire ruled some 55 million. However, unlike the situation in the Roman Empire, most of the Han subjects lived in China, whereas the Romans were greatly outnumbered by their colonized populations.

Wu Di

The pinnacle of Han imperial power came under the emperor mentioned in the opening of this chapter: Wu Di, who ruled for over half a century (141–87 B.C.E.). Wu Di's imperialism came after several decades of national revival and dynastic consolidation. After he established firm control at home, Wu Di counteracted the encroaching pastoral nomads of the northern and western grasslands. In a series of bloody campaigns, Chinese forces pushed some nomads toward Europe, where they then disrupted the Roman Empire. Among the groups deflected toward the west were the Huns, including the branch the Chinese called Xiongnu, who had menaced China for centuries.

Empire building and diplomacy soon linked China to western Eurasia as well as to neighboring societies in East and Southeast Asia. To foster diplomacy, they sent ambassadors such as Zhang Qian to distant Central Asians seeking support against common enemies. But to neutralize nearby threats, Wu Di also dispatched a series of great armies, some numbering as many as 150,000 men, into the fringe areas of China and then beyond. Within a few years, they had conquered southwestern China, the Xinjiang (shinjee-yahng) region on China's western borders, Mongolia, and parts of Turkestan. Wu Di's armies also established colonial control over northern Korea and Vietnam. The Chinese ruled the former for four centuries and the latter for 1,000 years. Soon Chinese power extended even further, as states in today's Afghanistan sent tribute to Han emperors. By controlling the local peoples, Han military forces brought security to a narrow corridor that could be used for increased trade.

During this time, the Chinese even made contact with the Roman Empire. In later Han times a Chinese army of 90,000 men reached as far as the Caspian Sea in southeastern Russia, and a small force led by General Gan Ying apparently traveled through Parthia to the Persian Gulf in 97 C.E., the first Chinese known to reach there. On his return, General Gan reported on the Roman Empire, noting it was a massive state ruling many smaller ones, with many large cities.

Government and the Civil Service

The Han rulers developed a government structure that survived in its basic form until the early twentieth century. Whereas the Qin had sought to transform China in one brutal stroke, the Han were more pragmatic and cautious. The Han softened Legalism with Confucian humanism, demonstrating that Confucian philosophy could maintain stability in the wake of

Read about Sima Qian, the greatest Han dynasty historian.

momentous change. This Han pattern of mixing power with ethics characterized the Chinese political system for the next 2,000 years.

During Han times, the civil service developed. In the early Han era, the bureaucracy comprised some 130,000 officials, or 1 for every 400 to 500 people. Han officials boasted that they did not interfere in the daily lives of the people and kept public works to a minimum. The bureaucracy was staffed by educated men who were later called mandarins (MAN-duh-rinz). Chinese proverbs claimed that the country might be won by the sword but could be ruled only by the writing brush—in other words, by an educated elite. The Han Chinese invented the civil service examination system to select officials based on merit. Wu Di even established a national university, which by the late Han period trained up to 30,000 students who were studying for the exams. These exams tested knowledge of the Confucian writings, an indication that Confucianism was becoming the official ideology of the state.

The development of the Han bureaucracy marked the rise of the scholar-gentry, a social class based on learning and office holding but also on landowning, since many of the mandarins came from wealthy landowning families. Still, the social system was somewhat fluid. Scholars could not guarantee that their sons would be competent, and some poor men did rise by passing the civil service exams. Most of the scholar-gentry lived in towns, where they had some influence on local government officials.

Eurasian Trade and the Rural Economy

The Silk Road

The Han presence in Central Asia allowed for the establishment of overland trade routes between China and western Asia. A lively caravan route, known as the Silk Road for its most valuable cargo, linked China with India, the Middle East, and southern Europe. Central Asian cities such as Kashgar (kahsh-gar), Bactra (BAK-tru), and Samarkand (SAM-mar-kahnd) grew up along the overland route to service the trade and the merchants, becoming network hubs. Chinese silk, porcelain, and bamboo were carried west across the deserts and mountains to Baghdad and the ports of the eastern Mediterranean. Silk was the most desired product, and because it was lightweight and easily packed, large quantities were carried west by each caravan. Caravans then returned with horses and luxury goods, such as Egyptian glass beads, Red Sea pearls, and Baltic amber.

The Silk Road and the trade networks that it shaped greatly influenced the peoples who participated in the trade. To pay for Chinese luxuries, the Romans dispatched considerable quantities of silver to China. A serious trade imbalance ensued that contributed to the decline of the Western Roman Empire. Relations with Central and West Asians during the Han and later periods also brought new products to China, such as stringed musical instruments and new foods. Imperial power and foreign trade generated an economic boom and the rapid growth of commerce in China. The Silk Road network also fostered a Central Asian melting pot as peoples moved, met, and mixed.

Han Economy and Agriculture

Although trade became more significant, farming remained the basis of Chinese society, and landowning was the major goal of economic endeavor and investment. During the Han dynasty, China's economy was dominated by intensive farming, especially the growing of cereal crops. Peasants constituted the vast majority of the population and had to produce a food surplus for the 20 percent of the people living in towns and cities. The fertile Chinese land and peasant labor made this possible: Chinese peasants were able to achieve high yields, becoming some of the world's most efficient farmers. But Chinese agriculture also depended on hard physical labor, especially in growing rice.

Peasants did not lead easy lives. Most rarely went farther than the local market town to which they brought their produce. Family land and movable property were divided equally among sons, a form of inheritance that fragmented landholdings and stood in contrast to landholding patterns in pre-Han China, Japan, and Europe. In addition, a lack of capital kept many peasant families at the mercy of middlemen for advances until the crop came in, and often they were forced into tenancy. Population pressure and land shortage also created political instability. By the second century B.C.E., practically all

> 66 During the Han dynasty, China's economy was dominated by intensive farming, especially the growing of cereal crops. 99

sericulture
Silk making, which arose in ancient China.

of the good agricultural land in north and north-central China was being used. The dynastic cycle was partly a result of land shortage and population pressure, which fomented peasant rebellions.

The labor-intensive nature of the economy was also apparent outside agriculture. Transportation meant porters with carrying poles, men pushing wheelbarrows, and men bearing the sedan chairs of the elite. Men also walked along narrow paths pulling boats upriver through the narrow gorges of the Yangzi River. Even the famous silk industry required endless labor. Sericulture (silk making) produced silks and brocades of the finest weave by Han times, but

> "The amount of independence and influence women enjoyed depended on their age, social class, and local practices."

producing 150 pounds of silk required feeding and keeping clean the trays of 700,000 worms.

Social Life and Gender Relations

Han social life revolved around the family system, which became an elaborate institution, the central focus of allegiance for most Chinese for more than 2,000 years. Chinese were expected to honor their ancestors while also keeping in mind the welfare of future generations. The family provided great psychological and economic security, despite the inevitable tensions that disrupted family harmony. The Chinese ideal was the joint family—that is, three or four generations living together under one roof, even though only wealthy families could support the large houses and private courtyards that made such a way of life possible.

The family was led by a patriarch, or senior male, who commanded respect. Chinese traced descent exclusively through the male line. Children were expected to respect not only the senior male, but also both parents, and to venerate their elders. Because laws held the family accountable for the actions of its members, they discouraged disgraceful behavior by individuals.

From Patricia Buckley Ebrey, *The Cambridge Illustrated History of China*, 1996. Reproduced with permission of author.

Han Farmer Stone relief of Han farmer using an ox-drawn plow. These plows fostered the expansion of cultivated land during the Han.

Women in Han China: Ban Zhao

The family system increasingly put most women at a disadvantage compared to men. Women were expected to be devoted first to their parents, then later to their husband, and finally to their sons; care of the family and children was their central preoccupation. A young wife joined her husband's family and was subject to the authority of his parents. Parents arranged marriages with the goal of linking families. Although many marriages seem to have been happy, the sorrows of unhappy women became a common literary theme. Ban Zhao (ban chao), the most famous woman scholar in Han China and an accomplished historian, astronomer, and mathematician, wrote an influential book on women's place in society. Her advice to women

Lessons for Women
Discover what Ban Zhao, the foremost female writer in Han China, had to say about the proper behavior of women.

stressed the Confucian obligations of selfless behavior, devotion, and obedience.

Despite the preeminence of Confucian patterns, women's experiences were never standardized. The amount of independence and influence they enjoyed depended on their age, social class, and local practices. There were always women like Ban Zhao who achieved wide acclaim. Some elite women received an education, and some were celebrated for their poetry writing. In contrast, some peasant women, who worked in the fields alongside their men, were strong-willed and exercised influence in their families and villages. Indeed, male power was strongest at the elite level and often weaker among the lower classes.

Chinese Historiography, Science, and Technology

The Chinese developed one of the greatest traditions of studying and writing about history, known as historiography, among premodern societies. History writing in China goes back at least as far as the Zhou dynasty. One of the classics of Confucian learning, *The Spring and Autumn Annals,* attributed traditionally but probably inaccurately to Confucius, provided a largely factual and chronological recounting of political events in the eastern state of Lu (loo) from 722 to 481 B.C.E. But Confucians also read into the prose a moral assessment of history.

Sima Qian: Han Historian Beginning in Han times, most dynasties employed a group of professional historians, such as the Han era's Sima Qian (SI-mu tshen). Later Chinese historians were influenced by Sima Qian's belief that past events, if not forgotten, also taught about the future. The Chinese historians tended to ignore social and economic history in favor of political history, concentrating on personalities, stories, wars, and the doings of emperors while neglecting long-term trends. They aimed for objectivity, carefully separating their editorial comments from the narrative text, all in elegant prose. Historical literature served as a manual for government, because it discussed the success and failure of past policies with the goal of achieving wisdom and promoting morality.

Breakthroughs in Science and Mathematics China also developed one of the world's oldest and most influential scientific traditions, establishing along with the Indians, Mesopotamians, Egyptians, and Greeks the foundation for modern science. The Zhou and Han are credited with many important technical breakthroughs, such as porcelain ("china"), paper, the water-powered mill, the shoulder harness for horses, the magnetic compass, the seismograph, the wheelbarrow, the stern-post rudder for boats, the spinning wheel, and certain kinds of textiles, including linen. Most of these inventions did not reach western Eurasia over the trade routes until a few centuries—in some cases a millennium—later.

The Han also made great strides in mathematics and astronomy. Among the major achievements was the most accurate calculation of pi at the time. In addition, the Chinese were many centuries ahead of the rest of the world in the use of fractions, a simple decimal system, the concept of negative numbers, and in certain aspects of algebra and geometry. Around 190 C.E., Han Chinese invented the *abacus,* a primitive computer still used widely today, which proved to be an unparalleled tool for calculations. In the study of astronomy, the Han compiled catalogues of stars and speculated on sunspots. Around 100 C.E., the astronomer Zhang Heng (jang hoeng) explained the causes of lunar eclipses.

Medical Advances Chinese science, especially medicine, also owed much to the cosmological thinking exemplified in yin-yang dualism and also to Daoism, which inspired an interest in nature. An influential early Han book on medicine advised readers that when yin and yang are in proper harmony, a person is filled with strength and vigor. An enduring medical discovery, *acupuncture,* developed from the belief that good health was the result of proper yin-yang balance in the body. In this procedure, thin needles are inserted at predetermined points to alleviate pain or correct some condition. While pursuing acupuncture, Chinese experts learned the parts of the body and discovered how to read a pulse.

The Chinese pioneered many other medical innovations. They stressed good hygiene and preventive medicine, including proper dress, a well-balanced diet, and regular exercise. In their quest for the elixir of immortality, Daoist alchemists discovered many edible foods, herbs, and potions that improved health. They developed the greatest list of pharmaceuticals in the premodern world, which in turn promoted the study of botany and zoology.

Heavenly Mandates and Dynastic Cycles

During the Han, the Chinese came to view rulership in terms of the Mandate of Heaven, or sanction by the supernatural realm, and history in terms of the dynastic cycle (see Chapter 4). Most premodern Chinese scholars believed that emperors ruled as deputies of the cosmic forces, but only so long as they possessed the virtues of justice, benevolence, and sincerity. In each dynasty, able early rulers with these virtues were succeeded by debauched weaklings, who left government to the bureaucracy while they indulged their pleasures. Emperors had vast harems of wives, concubines, and sometimes boys, and usually enjoyed fine wine and foods. When an emperor misruled, he lost the Mandate of Heaven and rebellion was justified.

The rise and fall of dynasties also correlated with economic trends. A strong new dynasty initially generated security and prosperity, which led to population increase and additional tax revenues. However, these prospects lured ambitious emperors into overextending imperial power and squandering human and financial resources, not only on wars of expansion but also on palaces and court luxury. Overspending led to decline. Wasteful expenditures created financial difficulties and military stagnation. After a century or so, decay set in, and some bureaucrats became corrupt.

 The Book of Documents Read this Confucian classic to discover how rulers gain or lose the right to rule, an authority known as the Mandate of Heaven.

Wu Di and the Decline of the Han Dynasty

This pattern was illustrated by Han emperor Wu Di. His glorious empire came at a huge cost, straining the imperial treasury. The resulting inflation led to the world's first price stabilization board and generated a heated debate in China about the economic benefits of empire. Some Han scholars opposed military expansion as a senseless waste of lives and tax revenues, but higher government officials responded that the spending was necessary to protect the country from the Xiongnu and other invaders.

The Han dynasty finally collapsed in 220 C.E., not unlike the fall of Rome several centuries later. Critical factors for both empires included inadequate revenues, peasant revolts, powerful landed families contending for power, and raids by pastoralists from the borderlands. Across Eurasia the unusually warm conditions between 200 B.C.E. and 200 C.E. ended, and the colder weather affected agriculture. Both empires were also ravaged by epidemics in the second century C.E., which killed millions and thus reduced tax revenues further.

LO³ China After the Han Empire: Continuity and Change

After the collapse of the Han in 221 C.E., China experienced three-and-a-half centuries of disorder and political fragmentation. This period is known as the Era of the Three Kingdoms and Six Dynasties, a name that suggests its political diversity. China was divided into several states, some ruled by Chinese and others by invaders, and suffered frequent incursions by pastoral nomads from the north and west. By the seventh century, however, China had restored centralized government and reaffirmed the classical tradition.

Post-Han Innovation, Interactions, and Disunity

After the fall of the Han, the Chinese continued to develop innovative technologies. Printing was particularly crucial. Elementary block printing was in limited use in China by the sixth century C.E., and by the ninth century woodblock printing had become a major activity in East Asia. The Chinese also became some of the world leaders in shipbuilding, and some took up maritime trade. By at least the fifth century C.E., the Chinese had constructed oceangoing vessels with stern-post rudders for maneuvering, which permitted farther journeys. Some Chinese junks carried as many as three thousand sailors.

Isolationism and Resiliency

Despite such innovations, the post-Han period was a troubled one. Even more than in earlier times, pastoral nomads, including Mongols, Turks, and especially the Huns, crossed the Great Wall and attacked north China. These people were not unsophisticated herders; most used bronze and iron, and some may have had written languages. However, brutal winters and keen competition for good grazing land made them martial peoples scornful of the richer life available to the agriculture Chinese. Sometimes they succeeded in breaching the Great Wall by virtue of their skills in horseback warfare, especially when they united under strong chiefs.

Beginning during the Zhou and accelerating after the downfall of the Han, these invasions helped produce what historians have called the "Great Wall Complex": a natural Chinese paranoia about the security of borders and the perpetual fear of outside barbarians seeking China's wealth and glory. This fear prompted Chinese to rally to the cause of defeating invaders. A much-loved fifth-century ballad, perhaps based on an actual person, recalled the deeds of a young woman warrior, Mulan (moo-LAHN), who disguised herself as a man in order to fight invading Central Asians. These invasions also prompted many Chinese to move south, solidifying the Chinese character of the Yangzi Basin.

The Chinese learned to endure both division and invasion by outsiders. An ancient proverb reassured them by arguing that although the country may be defeated, the mountains and streams would endure. In dealing with invaders, the Chinese developed a remarkable defense mechanism: assimilation. Most of the barbarian conquerors were eventually forced to rule in a Chinese way, using the Confucian bureaucracy, while also adapting many elements of Chinese culture. As a result, the Chinese came to believe that rule by foreigners could be tolerated as long as Chinese culture was respected and protected. Chinese culture, social institutions, and economic patterns thus proved resilient, able to survive the shock of conquest.

> **66** China's openness to outside ideas led many Chinese to embrace an Indian religion, Buddhism. **99**

During the post-Han era, China became even more connected to the world outside, fostering a vital, cosmopolitan culture. Ideas and products continued to travel both directions along the Silk Road and by land and sea between China and Southeast Asia. In China, these foreign influences were reflected in post-Han art, which often showed Indian, Persian, Mesopotamian, Greek, or Roman influences, such as jade cups modeled on Roman goblets. China's openness to outside ideas also led many Chinese to embrace an Indian religion, Buddhism.

Buddhism and Chinese Society

During the later centuries of the Classical Era, universal religions—faiths that appealed to people from many cultures—became much more prominent in Eurasia and North Africa, spreading along the trade networks and marking another great transition. Christianity spread from western Asia to Europe, where it soon became the dominant religion; Hinduism spread throughout India and into Southeast Asia; and Mahayana (Mah-HAH-YAH-nah) Buddhism became influential in Central and East

Buddha Statue at Yungang This huge statue of the Buddha, created around 290 C.E., is 45 feet tall. It is one of thousands found along cliffs in western China and elsewhere along the Silk Road.

Asia. Frequently these universal religions merged with or incorporated existing local beliefs. The most pronounced synthesis took place in East Asia as Buddhism encountered earlier belief systems such as Confucianism.

The arrival of Buddhism was a momentous transition for East Asia; indeed, the fourth through the ninth centuries C.E. might well be called the Buddhist Age in both Chinese and, more generally, Asian history. Buddhism in some form became dominant in much of East, Central, and Southeast Asia, as well as in portions of South Asia (see Chapter 7). Basic Buddhist beliefs about overcoming suffering through good deeds and thoughts derived from the sixth-century B.C.E. teachings of the Indian sage Siddhartha Gautama, known to his followers as the Buddha ("the Enlightened One"), but the religion later split into several rival schools. One of these, Mahayana Buddhism, was carried by merchants and missionaries along the Silk Road into Central Asia. From there it spread into western China during later Han times, connecting China to distant India. Buddhism, a religion of compassion and gentleness, offered hope to people experiencing hardship, warfare, and instability. People sought inner peace if they could not find external peace. Buddhism appealed to Chinese because of its promise of salvation in an afterlife, which Confucianism and Daoism did not offer. But the Buddhist notion of reincarnation, which envisioned the soul passing through a long series of lives, clashed with Chinese beliefs in ancestor worship, so most Chinese never accepted this idea.

Because it had traveled from India through Central Asia, Chinese Buddhism acquired a cosmopolitan outlook, and its spread was accompanied by Indian artistic, literary, and cultural influences, such as the huge sculptures of the Buddha found along the Silk Road and in northwestern China. Many Buddhist missionaries entered China, and several hundred Chinese pilgrims went to India, either overland or along the sea route through Southeast Asia. The most notable in this era was Faxian (fah-shee-en), a monk who spent fifteen years in India and also visited Buddhist centers in Southeast Asia in the fifth century C.E. On their return to China, the pilgrims spread knowledge of the societies they encountered. Faxian's reports also provided modern historians with data on the Asia of his day.

> "Like the Qin, the Sui were builders who mobilized 6 million forced workers to construct the Grand Canal linking the Yangzi and Yellow Rivers."

China's Eclectic Religious Tradition

The Chinese philosophy and religion that were developing by the middle of the first millennium C.E. embraced three very different viewpoints—Buddhism, Confucianism, and Daoism—which were known as "the three ways." Over the next few centuries, the three schools interacted with and tempered each other, creating a rich synthesis, and many Chinese could no longer clearly differentiate between them. But despite the fusion of traditions, some distinctions were maintained. Only Buddhism developed a fully organized church, with monks and nuns, although there were also some Daoist orders. Confucianism, as a philosophy of social relations rather than a true religion, had no priests. Yet many Chinese sought answers in all three doctrines, not identifying themselves exclusively as Buddhists, Daoists, or Confucianists.

Gradually a gap between the relatively secular world-view of the educated elite and the popular religion of the common people widened over time. The intellectuals tended to favor a combination of Confucian humanism and Daoist naturalism, with moral perfection of humankind as the ultimate goal. For this reason, many intellectuals viewed popular religion, with its gods, spirits, ghosts, and magic, as superstition. Many peasants, artisans, and merchants believed in thousands of gods and goddesses of Buddhist, Daoist, or animist origin. Common people accepted notions of heaven and hell introduced into Chinese thought by Mahayana Buddhism. In addition, many peasants believed in astrology, ghosts, dream interpretation, and witchcraft.

The Sui Reunification of China

To an observer in the fourth century, it might have seemed that the Chinese empire was finished: overrun by "barbarian" invaders, broken apart, and turning to foreign, otherworldly religions. Yet, China was eventually reunified under a powerful, centralized government. Several factors contributed to China's reassembly. First, the high population density of the Chinese core area made reestablishment of a centralized state easier. By 400 C.E. the Chinese may have numbered 50 million, probably double the population of Europe. The nomadic invaders may have been easily absorbed in China, because the newcomers were so small in number compared to the Chinese. Culture and politics probably also played a role in Chinese reunification. Confucian ethical humanism provided cultural continuity, and Chinese writing encouraged linguistic unity, because it put hundreds of spoken dialects into a common system. Finally, in China the emphasis on rule by ethical men chosen by a merit system remained appealing and helped unify the country.

Recovery Under the Sui Dynasty

The Sui (sway) dynasty (581–618 C.E.) played the same role in history as the Qin, reuniting China after several centuries of turmoil and division. It was also nearly as ruthless. The Sui emperors were tyrants but also patrons of arts and letters, and they created the largest library at that time in the world (with 400,000 volumes). Like the Qin, the Sui were builders who mobilized 6 million forced workers to construct the Grand Canal linking the Yangzi and Yellow Rivers. At 1,200 miles long, the longest human-made channel ever constructed, this was one of the most formidable civil engineering projects in world history. The canal linked the economic power of central China with the political power of north China and ensured the prosperity of later dynasties.

Like earlier dynasties, the Sui overreached itself and collapsed. Exhausting campaigns of conquest temporarily extended imperial frontiers into Korea and Central Asia, but the Sui drove the Chinese people too hard, resulting in overwork and food shortages. Soon rebellions broke out. The victor in the ensuing struggles established the Tang (tahng) dynasty (618–907 C.E.), which launched China on its great golden age extending over many centuries and linked China more closely to Korea and Japan.

LO⁴ Korea, Japan, and East Asian Networks

Because the large, densely populated Chinese society persisted to modern times, it dominated East Asia for much of history. Consequently, eastern Asia did not develop the political diversity that prevailed in India, western Asia, or Europe after classical times. As intensive farming societies, Korea and Japan were receptive to Chinese cultural influence even as they creatively forged distinctive societies.

 Internet East Asian History Sourcebook (*http://www.fordham .edu/halsall/eastasia/ eastasiasbook.html*). An invaluable collection of sources and links on China, Japan, and Korea from ancient to modern times.

Korea and China

As a close neighbor, Korea experienced regular and extensive interaction with China, which brought both advantages and pressures. During the first millennium B.C.E., Chinese cultural and technological influences began permeating the Korean peninsula. Koreans adopted iron technology from the Chinese, and their increasing mastery of iron later fostered the rise of powerful, agriculture-based Korean states in the peninsula. Chinese influence soon overwhelmed these states. Chinese refugees from the Zhou wars and from Qin repression migrated across the frontier, bringing with them culture and technology. Then in 108 B.C.E., Wu Di's armies, reportedly 60,000 troops strong, conquered northern Korea against fierce resistance. China ruled the territory as a colony for the next four centuries, providing models to the Koreans in government structure, architecture, and city planning.

The end of Chinese colonization in 313 C.E. allowed three native kingdoms to emerge. These powerful states dominated Korea between the fourth and seventh centuries, occasionally warring against each other for control of fertile agricultural land. At the same time, however, Chinese cultural influences, including the writing system, spread more widely. Mahayana Buddhism, introduced from China into northern Korea in 372 C.E., had a strong influence on Korean painting, sculpture, and architecture. Confucian doctrines also became popular. But the

CHRONOLOGY

Classical Japan and Korea

300 B.C.E.–552 C.E.	Yayoi culture in Japan
18 B.C.E.	Rise of Koguryo in northern Korea
108 B.C.E.–313 C.E.	Han Chinese colonization of Korea
250 C.E.	Beginning of Yayoi tomb culture
350–668 C.E.	Koguryo Empire
514–935 C.E.	Silla state in southern Korea
538 C.E.	Introduction of Buddhism to Japan
552–710 C.E.	Yamato state in Japan
604 C.E.	First Japanese constitution

Koreans never became carbon copies of the Chinese. For example, unlike in China, an aristocracy of inherited position, living in considerable luxury, thrived for most of Korean history. Korean music remained distinctive, even if the instruments were adapted from Chinese models. And although most Koreans eventually adopted Buddhism, the animism that had long flourished never disappeared.

Emergence of the Koguryo State

Eventually, one Korean kingdom, Koguryo (go-GUR-yo), became the most influential (see Map 5.3). In the fifth century, with China divided, Koguryo expanded far to the north, annexing much of Manchuria and southeastern

 Interactive Map

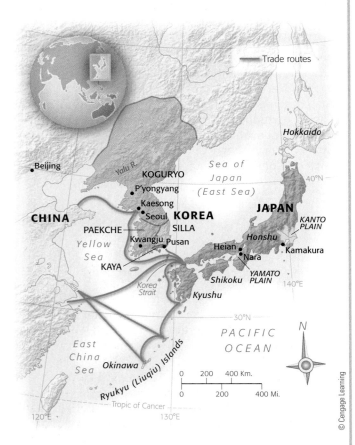

Map 5.3
Korea and Japan in the Fifth Century C.E.

During the Classical Era, Korea was often divided into several states. Koguryo in the north was the largest state, ruling part of Siberia. By the sixth century, the Yamato state governed much of the main Japanese island, Honshu.

Siberia in addition to the northern half of the Korean peninsula. In its expansion, Koguryo became one of the largest states in Eurasia at that time. The empire, which lasted from 350 to 668 C.E., also boasted a substantial population of several million people by the seventh century. At the same time, several much smaller Korean states controlled the southern part of the peninsula.

Koguryo proved a strong regional force. Its army repulsed seven major Chinese invasions by the Sui and Tang dynasties between 598 and 655 C.E., when a resurgent China was the most powerful state in the world. The great Koguryo generals commanded skilled and mobile legions. In 612 C.E., they routed an invading Sui army of at least 300,000 soldiers. The huge cost of the Chinese campaigns in Korea contributed to the collapse of the Sui dynasty. Finally, in 668 C.E., Chinese armies, allied with the southern Korean state of Silla (SILL-ah or SHILL-ah), overran Koguryo and destroyed the kingdom, carrying 200,000 prisoners back to China. This event allowed for the reunification of Korea under Silla, which then flourished for several centuries.

Yayoi Japan

Like Korea across the straits, Japan experienced dramatic change between 600 B.C.E. and 600 C.E. The prehistoric, pottery-making Jomon culture (see Chapter 4) persisted until around 300 B.C.E., when a new pattern emerged that archaeologists term Yayoi (ya-YOI). This emergence correlated with the rise of an exceptionally productive wet rice-farming society that established close links with Korea.

During the long Yayoi era (300 B.C.E.–552 C.E.), Korea remained a source of learning and population for Japan. A relationship between people in southwestern Japan and southeastern Korea promoted a continuous flow of Korean immigrants, as well as both Korean and Chinese ideas and technology from the mainland into the islands. Some Korean migrants brought horses, and the armored warrior on horseback later became a vivid feature of Japanese life. In addition, Koreans worked in Japan as skilled craftsmen, scribes, and artists. By 600 C.E., the Japanese people as we know them today had come together from the genetic and cultural mixing over many centuries of Korean immigrants with earlier settlers and the indigenous Ainu people.

The Yayoi also traded sporadically with China. A Chinese visitor in 297 C.E. left us much information about Yayoi society, reporting that the Yayoi were fond of dancing, singing, drinking rice wine, and eating raw vegetables; experienced no theft and little other crime; revered nature; practiced ritual cleanliness; and clapped their hands in worship. All of these behaviors characterize modern Japanese, suggesting that these early customs never eroded. The Chinese also noted that the Yayoi used the potter's wheel, were expert weavers, and had mastered both bronze and iron technology. Later they would fashion iron into highly effective swords and armor.

The Yayoi formed no centralized governments but did have a class structure. They were organized into a large number of clans, each ruled by a hereditary priest-chieftain. The clan elites were men who governed large numbers of farmers, artisans, and a few slaves and mobilized people to build hundreds of large earthen tombs, often surrounded by moats, all over south-central Honshu Island. The tombs housed the remains of prominent leaders, who were buried with prized possessions such as jewels, swords, and clay figurines.

Yamato: The First Japanese National State

Japan entered the light of written history in the sixth century C.E., with the beginning of the Yamato (YA-ma-toe) period (552–710 C.E.), named for the first state ruling a majority of the Japanese people. The Yamato was centered in south-central Honshu, where the cities of Kyoto (kee-YO-toe) and Osaka (oh-SAH-kah) now stand. The Japanese population had by then probably reached 3 million. Yamato leaders exercised some control from what is today Tokyo in the north to the southern tip of Korea. Yamato was not a centralized state like Han China or Koguryo, but rather a national government ruling over smaller groups based on clans and territorial control, each headed by a hereditary chief. Eventually Yamato extended its influence into southern Japan while expanding the northern frontier deep into Ainu territory.

Yamato was headed by emperors and occasionally empresses—all ancestors of the same imperial family that rules Japan today, fifteen centuries later. Political continuity under the same royal family gave the Japanese a strong sense of cultural identity and unity. The Japanese saw their history before the sixth century C.E. in mythological terms: they believed the imperial family descended from the Sun Goddess, *Amaterasu* (AH-mah-teh-RAH-soo). This female creator deity may have reflected a high status for women in early Japan. The Chinese reported that the Yayoi made no distinction in status between

men and women, and before the eighth century C.E., around half of the imperial sovereigns were women. But female power eventually eroded, and patriarchy became the common pattern by 1000 C.E.

Japanese Isolation and Encounters

The Japanese forged a particularly distinctive society in late classical times through a mixing of the local and the foreign. The islands were more than one hundred miles from the Eurasian mainland, which meant that communication with other societies was sporadic, mainly restricted to Korea and China, and their isolation made the Japanese expert at borrowing selectively from the outside during periods of intensive contact. Much of Japanese history can be understood as an interplay between the indigenous (native) and the foreign; ultimately, a native element survived despite a flood of borrowing from Korea, China, and, much later, the West. At the same time, physical isolation severely restricted the space and resources available to the steadily growing population on the mountainous islands. The result was a tightly woven society with intense social pressures.

> *"Harmony is to be cherished, and opposition for opposition's sake must be avoided as a matter of principle."*
>
> *Prince Shotoku*

Japanese Cultural Distinctiveness

The Japanese also created a large proportion of their own culture. Japan has been a leading technological innovator for millennia; for instance, it developed the best tempered steel of the classical world. This creative ability is particularly striking in the traditional arts, where the Japanese created forms and styles of universal appeal, such as carefully planned gardens and *bonsai* (bon-sigh) (miniature) trees, and in social organization, where they have evolved ingenious solutions to chronic problems such as urban crowding and limited resources. Thus, the Japanese house itself, containing thick straw floormats, sliding paper panels rather than interior walls, a hot tub for communal bathing, and charcoal-burning braziers, conserved building materials and minimized fuel needs for heating and cooking.

The importation of Chinese ideas into Japan began on a large scale in the middle of the sixth century C.E. Mahayana Buddhism was introduced around 538 and became a major medium for cultural change, bringing new forms of art and ideas about the

Shinto
("Way of the gods")
The ancient animistic
Japanese cult that empha-
sized closeness to nature;
enjoyed a rich mythology
that included many deities
(see animism).

cosmos and afterlife. Just as the Chinese maintained three distinct traditions of thought, in Japan Buddhism coexisted with the ancient animistic cult later known as **Shinto** (SHIN-toe) ("way of the gods"), which emphasized closeness to nature and enjoyed a rich mythology that included many deities.

During the sixth century, a growing awareness of Chinese and Korean strength among Japanese leaders led the Japanese to embrace new ideas. The adaptation of Buddhism as well as the Chinese written language launched an era of deliberate borrowing from China to reshape Japanese society. The Yamato state expanded relations with Sui China and began to reorganize government structures, integrating Confucian notions of social organization and morality.

Shotoku and Japanese Buddhism

The adoption of Chinese ideas accelerated at the beginning of the seventh century under the auspices of Prince Shotoku (show-TOW-koo) (573–621 C.E.), an ardent Buddhist who sponsored the building of temples, used Buddhism to unify the politically fragmented society, and also promoted Confucian values. "Harmony is to be cherished, and opposition for opposition's sake must be avoided as a matter of principle," he wrote.[9] Shotoku became one of the most revered figures in Japanese history. Over the next two-and-a-half centuries, many official embassies were exchanged between China and Japan, further promoting the exchange of ideas.

Listen to a synopsis of Chapter 5.

Imperial Household Collection

Prince Shotoku This painting from the eighth century C.E. shows Prince Shotoku, one of the major Yamato leaders, and his sons in the Japanese clothing style of the times. Prince Shotoku launched a period of intensive borrowing from China.

{ More Bang for Your Buck }

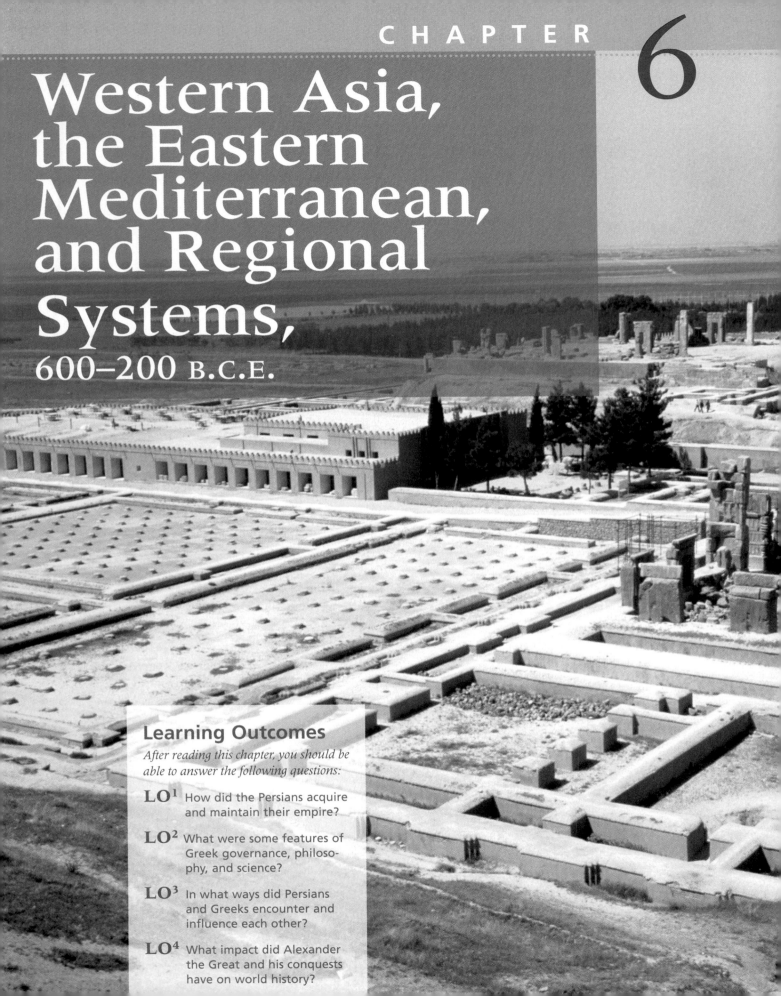

CHAPTER 6

Western Asia, the Eastern Mediterranean, and Regional Systems, 600–200 B.C.E.

Learning Outcomes

After reading this chapter, you should be able to answer the following questions:

LO¹ How did the Persians acquire and maintain their empire?

LO² What were some features of Greek governance, philosophy, and science?

LO³ In what ways did Persians and Greeks encounter and influence each other?

LO⁴ What impact did Alexander the Great and his conquests have on world history?

<blockquote>
❝Wonders are many on earth, and the greatest of these, is man, who rides the ocean. He is master of the ageless earth. The use of language, the wind-swift motion of brain he learned; found out the laws of living together in cities. There is nothing beyond his power.**❞**

—Chorus in *Antigone*, by the fifth-century Greek playwright Sophocles (SAHF-uh-Kleez)[1]
</blockquote>

The Greeks Thales (THAY-leez) and Anaximander (uh-NAK-suh-MAN-der) had the great fortune to grow up in the prosperous city of Miletus (my-LEET-uhs), a great commercial center on the southwestern coast of Anatolia (modern Turkey). For hundreds of years, Miletus was a crossroads for the entire region, mingling Greek and foreign cultures. Young men like Thales and Anaximander haunted the bustling docks and seaside bars, listening to the reports of sailors returning from distant shores and of travelers from foreign lands, as well as the ideas of Persian and other non-Greek residents. Along the shores of the Black Sea, Milesians (my-LEE-shuns) established settlements that supplied fish and wheat that enriched the city's traders.

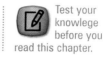

Test your knowlege before you read this chapter.

What do you think?

The greatest legacy of ancient Greece was the political concept of democracy.

Strongly Disagree					*Strongly Agree*	
1	2	3	4	5	6	7

Milesians benefited from cultural cross-fertilization fostered by trade. Some sailors brought scraps of learning from older societies such as Egypt and Mesopotamia, leading to new ideas in geography and cartography. Around 600 C.E., Thales worked out a geometrical system to calculate the position of a ship at sea. Fifty years later, his student, Anaximander, made the first map of the Mediterranean world and the first Greek chart of the heavens. Miletus matured into a great intellectual center and a meeting place for the Greek and Persian worlds.

The Greeks developed not only a penchant for maritime trade and an understanding of regional geography but also a unique society on the rocky shores of the Aegean Sea. In cities such as Miletus and Athens, they introduced many ideas and institutions that endured through the centuries. But their world included another creative

<< Persepolis During the height of their empire, Persian kings built a lavish capital at Persepolis, in today's Iran. This photo shows the audience hall, the part of the grand palace where the kings greeted their ministers and foreign diplomats.

Ancient Art & Architecture Collection Ltd.

125

society and even greater regional power, the Persian Empire, which dominated the eastern Mediterranean and western Asia and also developed innovations that affected the lives of many peoples. Ultimately the rival Greek and Persian societies were brought together in a political union that extended Greek culture into Asia and Africa but also added Persian culture to the mix. The resulting Hellenistic Age was an era of unprecedented cross-cultural sharing.

LO¹ The Persians and Their Empire

Although its period of influence lasted only two centuries, the Persian Empire was larger than any that came before it. It was also the first large multicultural empire in Eurasia, encompassing Anatolian Greeks, Phoenicians, Hebrews, Egyptians, Mesopotamians, and Indians. Domination of the east-west trade routes made the empire the meeting ground of the early classical world and generated influential new ideas. The Persians' wars with Greece and their empire building in western Asia paved the way for the Hellenistic ruler Alexander the Great and his successors.

Building a Regional Empire

Emergence of the Persians

The Persian homeland was located on a plateau just north of the Persian Gulf (see Map 6.1). Overland networks for traders and migrants connecting Mesopotamia and Anatolia to India and Central Asia passed through Persia, and cities emerged along the trade routes. Interactive Map

Travelers between Mesopotamia and India encountered many mountains and deserts, and various pastoral societies on the Persian plateau competed for power. Two of these, the Indo-European Medes (MEEDZ) and the Persians, had sent tribute payments to the powerful Assyrian Empire. By 600 B.C.E., the Persians were living in southeastern Iran under their own ruling family but were subjects of the Medes, who became the dominant regional power after they joined with the Babylonians in 612 B.C.E. to overthrow the Assyrians. But the Medes were soon overshadowed by the Persians.

Map 6.1
The Persian Empire, ca. 500 B.C.E.

At its height around 500 B.C.E., the Persians controlled a huge empire that included northern Greece, Egypt, and most of Western Asia from the Mediterranean coast to the Indus River in India.

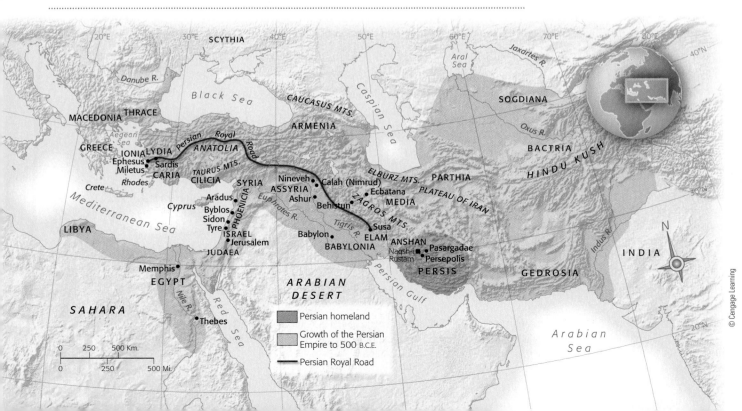

Imperial Persia

The Persian Empire, usually known as Achaemenid (a-KEY-muh-nid) Persia after the ruling family, was an extraordinary achievement. At its peak, it extended from the Indus Valley in the east to Libya in the west and from the Black, Caspian (KASS-pee-uhn), and Aral (AR-uhl) Seas in the north to the Nile valley in the south. This empire was created by a series of four kings: Cyrus (SY-ruhs) II (r. 550–530 B.C.E.), better known as Cyrus the Great; Cambyses (kam-BY-seez) II (r. 530–522 B.C.E.); Darius (duh-RY-uhs) I (r. 521–486 B.C.E.); and Xerxes (ZUHRK-seez) I (r. 486–465 B.C.E.). These leaders conquered vast territories and created an autocratic but effective and tolerant government, establishing a model for later Middle Eastern empires and challenging the Greeks in the west.

Cyrus the Great

Cyrus the Great began the expansion in 550 B.C.E. when he overthrew the Median king. By 539 he had conquered Mesopotamia, Syria, Palestine, Lydia (LID-ee-uh), and all of the Greek cities in Anatolia that had prospered under the pro-trade rule of the Lydians. In one decade, Cyrus built an empire stretching from the Aegean to Central Asia. As much diplomat as soldier, Cyrus followed moderate policies in the conquered territories, making only modest demands for tribute. After conquering Babylonia, Cyrus issued a proclamation on a cylinder, which some historians interpret as the world's first charter of human rights: "Protect this land from rancor, from foes, from falsehood, and from drought."

Under Cyrus's authority, the Jews taken to Babylon by the Assyrians were allowed to return to Palestine and rebuild their temple. Cyrus was killed in 530 B.C.E. while campaigning against nomads east of the Aral Sea. He was replaced by his son Cambyses II, who had learned to accept cultural differences while serving as governor of Babylonia. Cambyses II subjugated Egypt in 525 B.C.E. and wisely presented himself to the ruling class of priests as a new Egyptian ruler instead of a foreign conqueror, promising to bring stability, good fortune, health, and gladness.

Darius

Cambyses' successor and distant cousin, Darius I, began his reign by crushing a revolt in Egypt. He spread Persian power east and west, even annexing the Sind region in northwestern India, and promoted justice by supervising the organization and codification of Egyptian law. In 519 he fashioned a law code for Babylonia that basically reaffirmed Hammurabi's laws made almost 1,500 years earlier. To forge closer links with Egypt, Darius completed the first Suez Canal, an amazing engineering achievement that briefly connected the Mediterranean and the Red Seas. In 539 Darius began the building of a new capital at Persepolis (puhr-SEP-uh-luhs). The architecture of this spectacular city was drawn from many traditions and centered on a massive stone terrace, on which stood monumental royal buildings.

 Explore the Persian life through the eyes of a government official in the latter part of Cyrus's empire or as a soldier for Darius and Xerxes in this interactive simulation.

Darius and his successors eventually encountered major challenges. In 520 and 513, Darius campaigned unsuccessfully against the Scythians (SITH-ee-uhnz), warlike Indo-European pastoral nomads whose territory stretched from southern Ukraine and Russia eastward to Mongolia. Skilled horsemen and master workers of gold and bronze, the Scythians were among the Central Asians whose interactions with settled farmers helped shape Eurasian history. They had both fought and traded with the Greek trading cities. Later, the Scythians were one of the few peoples to defeat the formidable armies of Alexander the Great.

A more serious defeat at the beginning of the fifth century B.C.E. came with the first Greco-Persian War, in which the tiny disunited Greek states turned back the world's most powerful empire. Persians and peninsular Greeks were rivals for regional power, but many Greeks lived in Persian territories, including merchants and political exiles as far east as Mesopotamia. Inspired by Scythian resistance to Darius and concerned about losing trade to rivals, some Greek cities on the Ionian (eye-OH-nee-uhn) coast of Anatolia rebelled against Persian control (see Map 6.1), causing Darius to attack cities that supported the Ionian Greek rebels. While the Persians failed to occupy most of peninsular Greece, they reclaimed the Ionian Greek cities, brutally punishing

> "Persians and peninsular Greeks were rivals for regional power, but many Greeks lived in Persian territories."

Achaemenid
The ruling family of the Classical Persian Empire (ca. 550–450 B.C.E.).

the most rebellious, such as Miletus. Darius then cultivated democratic forces in Ionian cities, a tactical move he hoped would inspire cooperation with Persian aims.

His hopes proved unrealistic. Xerxes, the son of Darius, tried again to conquer the Greeks in 480 B.C.E. He attacked with a huge army and naval force, and a fierce two-year struggle resulted. Perhaps Xerxes' most effective ally was Queen Artemisia (AHRT-uh-MIZH-ee-uh) of the Ionian Greek city of Halicarnassus (hal-uh-kar-NASS-uhs), who was praised for her bravery, daring, and wise counsel to Xerxes. But the Persian thrust failed, and Xerxes returned home. He still held a large chunk of the Greek world and regained control of Egypt, but defeat in this second Greco-Persian war was a turning point in Persian history.

Imperial Policies and Networks

Unlike their Assyrian and Babylonian predecessors, Persian empire builders used laws, economic policies, and tolerance toward the conquered to rule successfully, and many people benefited from the peace that Persian rule provided for two centuries. Leading citizens came from many backgrounds, including Medes,

Persian Rhyton This gilded silver drinking cup, made in Persia in the fourth or fifth century B.C.E., has the figure of the ibex, a local animal, at the base. The cup is an example of the artistic treasures produced by classical peoples. Courtesy of the Trustees of the British Museum

Armenians, Greeks, Egyptians, or Kurds, a people living in the mountains just north of Persia and Mesopotamia. Such Persian strategies were imitated by their successors, including the Greeks and Romans, when they created even larger imperial structures centuries later.

Imperial Administration

The Persians followed and improved upon the systematic bureaucracy first used by the Assyrians. Although their power was in theory absolute, Persian kings were expected to consult with important nobles and judges. Each of the twenty-three Persian provinces was governed by a satrap (SAY-trap) ("protector of the kingdom"), an official who ruled according to established laws and procedures and paid a fixed amount of taxes to the king each year. The Persians had several grand capitals, including Babylon and Susa in Mesopotamia, before Persepolis was completed. Darius also set up courts with permanent judges.

Bas Relief of Darius and Xerxes Holding Court This relief was carved in one of the palaces at the Persian capital of Persepolis.

CHRONOLOGY

Persia, 1000–334 B.C.E.

ca. 1000	Life of Zoroaster
640	Persians become vassals of Medes
550–530	Kingship of Cyrus the Great
547–546	Conquest of Lydia
530–522	Kingship of Cambyses II
525–523	Conquest of Egypt
521–486	Kingship of Darius I
518	Persian conquest of Indus Valley
499	Rebellion by Ionian Greeks against Persian rule
499–479	Greco-Persian Wars
486–465	Kingship of Xerxes
404	Egyptian independence from Persia
334	Conquest of Persian Empire by Alexander the Great

Perhaps most crucial to their imperial success, the Persians generally treated the people they conquered with respect, allowing them to maintain their own social and religious institutions. In Egypt, for instance, Cambyses was a pharaoh, not a Persian ruler. The Persians prided themselves on their ability to unify the vastly different peoples of western Asia under the "king of kings," a title that recognized the existence of other rulers whose limited rights in their own territories were respected. For this reason, many Greeks fought for Persia in the Persian-Greek Wars. The Persians also utilized various official languages. Eventually, Aramaic (ar-uh-MAY-ik), spoken by many peoples of western Asia, became the official language. Most official documents were written in Aramaic using the Phoenician alphabet. Greek also became widely used as a written language in the western empire. The Greek historian Herodotus reported of the Persians that "there is no nation which so readily adopts foreign customs."[2]

Zoroastrianism and Persian Society

Zoroaster, the Persian Prophet

The Persians made another distinct contribution to later world history in their promotion of Zoroastrianism (zorr-oh-ASS-tree-uh-niz-uhm), a faith founded by Zoroaster that later became the state religion of Persia. Some ideas in Judaism, Christianity, and Islam are foreshadowed by, and perhaps even derived from, this early Persian religion. The prophet Zoroaster was one of the first non-Hebrew religious leaders to challenge the prevailing polytheism of his day. Although he is usually thought to have lived between 630 and 550 B.C.E.—at the beginning of the Eurasian Axial Age—many scholars believe he lived sometime between 1400 and 900 B.C.E.

In contrast to the polytheism of other Persians, Zoroaster had a monotheistic vision. He believed in one supreme god, Ahura Mazda (ah-HOOR-uh MAZZ-duh) (the "Wise Lord"), who was opposed by a Satan-like figure who was the source of lies, cowardice, misery, and other forms of evil. Zoroaster speculated that Ahura Mazda allowed humans to freely choose between heaven and hell. By serving Ahura Mazda, men and women were serving the spirit of ultimate goodness and truth while simultaneously improving the world. At the end of time, Zoroaster believed, there would be a final judgment at which Ahura Mazda would win a final victory over the spirit of evil. At that time, even hell would come to an end.

Many core Zoroastrian ideas, especially the notion of a contest between a good God and an evil devil and the corresponding belief in heaven and hell, were developed in later Jewish scriptures, and then in the sacred writings of both Christians and Muslims. The Jews may have adopted some of their ideas from Zoroastrians while the Jews were held captive in Babylon (586–539 B.C.E.). The Zoroastrian watchwords of "good thoughts, good words, good

Zoroastrianism
A monotheistic religion founded by the Persian Zoroaster that later became the state religion of Persia. Its notion of one god opposed by the devil may have influenced Judaism and later Christianity (see monotheism).

Ahura Mazda
(the "Wise Lord") The one god of Zoroastrianism.

Diotima: Women and Gender in the Ancient World (*http://www.stoa.org/diotima/*). Contains excellent materials on gender and women in the early Mediterranean world.

Witness to the Past

Good, Evil, and Monotheism in Zoroastrian Thought

The Persian thinker Zarathustra, better known today by the name given to him by the Greeks, Zoroaster, offered an ethical vision that, he believed, came from God. The early Persians apparently believed in three great gods and many lesser ones, but Zoroaster preached that only one of these, Ahura Mazda (The Wise Lord), was the supreme deity in the universe, responsible for creation and the source of all goodness. But a rival entity, Angra Mainyu (Hostile Spirit), embodied evil and was the source of all misery and sin. Zoroaster asked people to join the cosmic battle for good and worship Ahura Mazda while opposing evil and Angra Mainyu, referred to as the Liar. This excerpt outlining Zoroaster's beliefs comes from one of the devotional hymns, the Gathas, contained within the Zoroastrian holy scriptures. It was written down in final form centuries after Zoroaster's life, but was probably based on earlier writings by the prophet or his disciples.

Then shall I recognize you as strong and holy, Mazda, when by the hand in which you yourself hold the destinies that you will assign to the Liar [Angra Mainyu] and the Righteous [Ahura Mazda] . . . the might of Good Thought shall come to me.

As the holy one I recognized you, Mazda Ahura, when I saw you in the beginning at the birth of Life, when you made actions and words to have their reward—evil for the evil, a good Destiny for the good—through your wisdom when creation shall reach its goal. At which goal you will come with your holy Spirit, O Mazda, with Dominion, at the same with Good Thought, by whose action the settlements [human societies] will prosper through Right. . . .

"I am Zarathustra, a true foe to the Liar, to the utmost of my power, but a powerful support would I be to the Righteous, that I may attain the future things of the infinite Dominion, so I praise and proclaim you, Mazda. . . ."

As the holy one I recognized you, Mazda Ahura, when Good Thought [a good spirit created by Ahura Mazda] came to me, when the still mind taught me to declare what is best: "Let not a man seek again and again to please the Liars, for they make all the righteous enemies." And thus Zarathustra himself . . . chooses the spirit of thine that is holiest, Mazda. May Right be embodied, full of life and strength! May Piety abide in the Dominion where the sun shines! May Good Thought give destiny to men according to their works [good actions]!

This I ask you, tell me truly, Ahura. . . . Who determined the path of sun and stars? Who is it by whom the moon waxes and wanes again? . . . Who upheld the Earth beneath and the firmament from falling? Who the water and the plants? Who yoked swiftness to winds and clouds? . . .

This I ask you, tell me truly, Ahura—whether we shall drive the Lie away from us to those who being full of disobedience will not strive after fellowship with Right, nor trouble themselves with counsel of Good Thought. . . .

I will speak of that which Mazda Ahura, the all-knowing, revealed to me first in this earthly life. Those of you that put not into practice this word as I think and utter it, to them shall be woe at the end of life. I will speak of that which the Holiest declared to me as the word that is best for mortals to obey: he, Mazda Ahura said, "They who at my bidding render [Zarathustra] obedience, shall all attain Welfare and Immortality by the actions of the Good Spirit." In immortality shall the soul of the righteous be joyful, in perpetuity shall be the torments of the Liars [the followers of evil]. All this does Mazda Ahura appoint by his Dominion.

Thinking About the Reading

1. What supreme powers did Zoroaster attribute to Ahura Mazda?

2. How did Zoroaster expect individuals to work for good and combat evil?

3. What fate awaited those who chose the path of evil?

Source: Yasnas 43–45, in James Hope Moulton, *Early Zoroastrianism* (London: Williams and Norgate, 1913), pp. 364–370.

deeds" became key ideas of other religions, including Christianity and Buddhism. Darius I did much to spread Zoroastrianism, publicly attributing his victories to Ahura Mazda. While Zoroastrianism was displaced in western Asia by Christianity and, later, Islam, the faith lives on today among small groups in Iran and western India.

Social Structure and Gender Relations The Persians did not develop as politically diversified a society as did the Greeks. At the top of the system were the nobles, many of them warriors who had been granted large estates by the king, followed by priests, merchants, and bankers. In Babylonian cities ruled by Persia, these citizens met in formal assemblies to make important judicial decisions, and routine administration was done by councils of twenty-five leading men. Zoroastrian priests schooled the princes of the noble families to prepare for government careers. The middle class included brewers, butchers, bakers, carpenters, potters, and coppersmiths. Peasants and slaves constituted the bottom of the social structure. Over the centuries, many peasant farmers became poor renters or sharecroppers, bound to the land. There were also some slaves, mainly debtors, criminals, and prisoners of war.

Persian society was patriarchal and polygynous: many men, especially at upper levels, had several wives. Persian women were usually kept secluded in harems, and many probably veiled themselves, an ancient practice in western Asia. But some queens and other noble women exercised strong influences on their husbands, and many even controlled large estates. Egyptian women kept many of the rights they enjoyed before Persian rule, and most marriages there were monogamous.

The Decline of Achaemenid Persia

Although the Persian empire was not finally conquered until the army of Alexander the Great defeated Persian forces in 330 B.C.E., the seeds of decline were planted more than a century earlier when the policies of Xerxes I, especially a policy of heavy taxation of the satrapies, began to weaken support for Persian rule. Vast amounts of pure silver paid as taxes were sent to the Persian capital. By 424 B.C.E., the Persian Empire was suffering from civil unrest caused by fights within the Achaemenid family, currency inflation, and difficulty collecting taxes.

Under Xerxes and his successors, the wise policies of Cyrus and Darius, which promoted trade and treated non-Persians with respect, were gradually reversed. Many merchants and landlords were ruined by having to borrow money at very high interest rates. At the same time, fewer attempts were made to include other ethnic groups in the governing of the empire. Some regions like Egypt successfully rebelled and restored local rule. Thus support for the Persian kings weakened long before Macedonian conqueror Alexander's superior armies brought an end to Achaemenid Persia and its once great empire.

LO² The World of Greek City-States

The Mediterranean was a zone of interaction for peoples living around its rim, and by 700 B.C.E. the Persians' greatest rivals, the Greeks, had become active participants in maritime trade. Soon this activity led to prosperity for many Greek cities, new forms of government, and considerable intellectual achievement. The Greeks are often credited with inventing academic fields like history, biology, and geometry, but the Greek society modern people admire was also far from egalitarian and had many unattractive features.

Growth and Power

Greek Colonialism The Greek world was shaped by a geographic context of mountains, coastal plains, and islands that encouraged the development of a dozen or so major city-states rather than one centralized state. This geography also stimulated maritime trade, which led to growth and prosperity for most Greek cities between 800 and 500 B.C.E. A growing population, a shortage of good farmland at home, and commercial interests led many Greeks to leave their home cities. In what is called the Greek diaspora (dye-ASS-puh-ruh), meaning dispersion or spreading out, they established some 250 new settlements along the Ionian coast, around the Black Sea, in Italy, and even as far west as the Mediterranean coasts of what is today France and Spain (see Map 6.2). By the sixth century B.C.E., Greeks were even visiting and living in Egypt, where they worshiped Egyptian gods under Greek names.

 Interactive Map

Map 6.2
Classical Greece, ca. 450 B.C.E.

Greek settlements, divided into rival city-states, occupied not only the Greek peninsula but also Crete and western Anatolia. Two alliances headed by Athens and Sparta, respectively, fought each other in the Peloponnesian War (431–404 B.C.E.).

© Cengage Learning

The Greek *Polis*

Prosperity led to the development of a unique Greek political unit, the **polis** (POE-lis), a city-state that embraced nearby rural areas whose agricultural surplus helped support the urban population. The polis became the major institution of classical Greek life, a living community that gave citizens a sense of identity. All business, from building a new temple to making war, was decided by the free male citizens meeting in an open assembly. Even loyalty to one's family or clan was less important than loyalty to the polis. The worst punishment a Greek could suffer was being asked to leave the polis. Some Greeks committed suicide rather than face ostracism. City-states competed fiercely with each other, including in sports events. The Olympic Games, athletic contests begun in the eighth century B.C.E., were associated with a religious festival to honor the god Zeus (ZOOS).

Not all inhabitants of the polis were equal. Many cities developed into oligarchies (AHL-uh-gar-keez), rule by a small group of wealthy leaders. As much as 80 percent of the population in most Greek cities, including women, slaves, children, and resident foreigners, were not citizens and thus had no right to participate in political life by voting or holding office. Most Greek cities, despite their elected assemblies, were long dominated by a monarch or other executives who were supervised by a council of aristocrats.

Decline of the Oligarchy

By the seventh century, two factors had weakened aristocratic power. One was the growth of trade, which helped create wealth for merchants, allowing them to compete with the upper class. The second factor was the development of a new battle formation, the phalanx (FAY-langks), that relied on infantry more than the aristocracy-dominated cavalry. The phalanx consisted of a square of heavily armored soldiers eight wide and eight deep that moved in unison. With this development, Greek armies became citizen-armies, not paid professional forces. As men other than aristocrats risked their lives for their polis, they wanted a greater role in governing.

In sum, a new military system combined with population expansion and increased wealth from trade with the Greek cities in Ionia contributed to the rise of democracy, most notably in the city-state of Athens. But the Greeks also fought many wars with each other and other enemies, and these struggles undermined Greek political ideals.

Competing Cities: Athens and Sparta

Between 600 and 350 B.C.E., some Greeks tried to reconcile the contradictory ideas that people are politically free and that they owe their loyalty to the community. Some Greeks discovered how people could live with each other without being controlled by gods or kings, and many cities developed radical notions of political freedom and equality. These ideas had never been seen before.

> " Athenian men criticized Spartan women for their independence, portraying them as greedy and licentious. "

Athenian Politics

oligarchy
Rule by a small group of wealthy leaders.

The most dramatic political changes occurred in Athens, a polis on the eastern Greek peninsula of Attica. Athens became progressively more democratic, partly a result of a farming crisis caused by the overuse of the soil. As bad harvests occurred, farmers went deeply into debt, and many were reduced to selling themselves and their families into slavery. The poor demanded reform. Around 594 B.C.E., the Athenians elected Solon (SOH-luhn), a general, poet, and merchant, to lead the city and rewrite the old constitution. He canceled the debts of the poor, forbid enslavement for default of debts, and established a new Council of 400 to review issues before they came before an Assembly of Citizens, which now served as a people's court. Solon boasted of his attempts to gather back the common people and set straight laws alike for lowly and lords, in order to prevent mob violence and avoid civil war.

CHRONOLOGY

The Greeks, 750–338 B.C.E.

ca. 750–550	Greek colonization in Mediterranean, Black Sea
ca. 594	Solon's reforms in Athens
561–527	Peisistratus tyrant in Athens
507	Athenian democracy under Cleisthenes
499–479	Greco-Persian Wars
477	Founding of Delian League
469–399	Life of Socrates
ca. 460–429	Era of Pericles in Athens
431–404	Peloponnesian War
428–347	Life of Plato
384–322	Life of Aristotle
338	Philip of Macedonia's conquest of Greece

The Athenian path to a more democratic system came in several stages, from reform to tyranny to democracy. Solon's reforms failed to please either side in this social and economic struggle. The poor wanted him to take land from the rich and redistribute it, while the aristocrats resented their loss of power. After his death, Peisistratus (pie-SIS-truht-uhs) (r. 561–527 B.C.E.) seized power as a tyrant, not necessarily a brutal ruler but someone who ruled outside the law. Many Greek cities were governed by tyrants in this period. Peisistratus appealed directly to the poor, giving some of them land he had confiscated from aristocratic estates. He also launched a building program, one result of which was an aqueduct to bring water directly to the city center.

Another aristocrat, Cleisthenes (KLICE-thuh-neez), finally established genuine democracy in Athens in 507 B.C.E. by creating geographic units that chose people by lot to serve in a new Council of 500, which submitted legislation to the Assembly for approval. The Assembly consisted of 40,000 citizens; about 6,000 generally showed up for meetings, and these selected by lot the city officials. Cleisthenes' version of Athenian democracy was extended in the mid-fifth century when lower-income citizens were allowed to serve as officials. Euripides (you-RIP-uh-deez) described the system in his play, *The Suppliant Woman*: "The city is free, and ruled by no one man. The people reign, in annual succession. They do not yield power to the rich; the poor man has an equal share in it."[3]

Although the majority of people were excluded from political life, for those who were citizens, the system was more radically democratic than most modern governments. The Athenians chose representatives by lot rather than by election, believing the latter system was too divisive. But many Greeks did not think that democracy of any type was a good thing.

Narrative Drawing on Pottery The Francois vase, made around 570 B.C.E., is considered a masterpiece of narrative drawing on pottery, with fine detail and vivid coloring. It shows scenes of battle. Scala/Art Resource, NY

One disgruntled Athenian conservative complained that reforms gave more power to the common people than to the "respectable elements" of society.

The Spartan Ideal

In the Peloponnese (PELL-eh-puh-NEESE) peninsula, the landlocked city-state of Sparta (SPART-uh) followed a different course of development (see Map 6.2). In the eighth century B.C.E., when the Spartans found themselves short of land, they decided to conquer their neighbors rather than establish overseas colonies. Spartans saw military power as essential to their prestige and influence. After conquering neighboring Greeks, they made them agricultural slaves who worked the land for Spartan overlords, and then developed a rigid military state to control its subject population. Sparta's government limited participation. They were led by two kings and a Council of Elders composed of twenty-eight men over age sixty who were elected for life by an Assembly of all citizens over age thirty. Spartans older than thirty referred to themselves as equals and considered their system a perfect aristocratic democracy.

The Spartans discouraged independence of thought or behavior. Spartan boys who seemed physically unfit were generally taken to a remote rural area and allowed to die. The other boys were given a rigid military training in barracks from age six and taught that self-discipline and courage were the highest virtues. From ages twenty to thirty, Spartan males served in the army, and they were allowed to live at home with their wives only after this time. Spartan women acquired a higher status than other Greek women, and their husbands' frequent absences from home allowed some of them to acquire wealth. Athenian men criticized Spartan women for their independence, portraying them as greedy and licentious, and complained that Spartan women owned some 40 percent of all the city-state's land, giving them too much freedom from male control.

Religion, Rationalism, and Science

The Greeks may have been practical people, but they were also concerned with the supernatural realm and worshiped a multitude of gods. The gods and legends introduced by the Homeric epics profoundly shaped Greek thinking and values. Greek religion was similar to that of most other early Indo-European peoples and probably also owed something to the Egyptians and Phoenicians. A group of chief gods and goddesses, along with many lesser ones, represented various natural and human activities. The leader of the traditional Greek gods was Zeus, a sky-god who guaranteed the natural and social order. His wife, Hera (HEER-uh), represented legal marriage and the family. Poseidon (puh-SIDE-uhn), the brother of Zeus, was the lord of the sea. Athena (uh-THEEN-uh), Zeus's favorite daughter and the patron of Athens, was the goddess of wisdom. Many other notable deities included Apollo (uh-PAHL-oh), patron of music, philosophy, and other finer things in life, and Dionysus (DIE-uh-NYE-suhs), the god of wine. Although these gods and goddesses had human virtues and vices, they were seen as immortal and more powerful than humans. To defy the gods or overstep the bounds set by them was to invite disaster.

 Livius: Articles on Ancient History (*http://www.livius.org*). Very useful site with many short essays on the Greeks, Persians, Parthians, Romans, and other ancient and classical societies.

The Greek interest in the deeper meaning of life also led them to develop a rational approach to the search for truth, and in trying to understand the natural world, they joined the Mesopotamians, Egyptians, Indians, and Chinese in laying the ancient and classical foundation for modern science. By the sixth century B.C.E., some Greek thinkers in Ionia and the peninsula began to question supernatural explanations of natural events. Thales of Miletus (ca. 636–546), whom we met in the chapter opener, was the first person we know of to perceive the universe as orderly and rational and to seek a natural explanation of phenomena rather than attributing them to gods. The Ionian Pythagoras (puh-THAG-uh-ruhs) helped establish the foundations of modern mathematics by emphasizing the number 10 and developing the multiplication tables.

These early thinkers laid the foundations of natural science and philosophy by emphasizing the explanatory power of human reason. In the fifth century, Protagoras (pro-TAG-or-uhs) summarized the new understanding when he argued that human achievements should be measured by human, not divine, standards. However, some Greek thinkers also opened the door to the more troubling idea that human standards are relative rather

 Read about Archimedes, the famous Hellenistic mathematician and engineer.

than absolute. The Sophists (SAHF-uhsts) emphasized skepticism and the belief that there is no ultimate truth. One wrote that "since the criterion of truth has appeared to be unattainable, it is no longer possible to make positive assertions either about those things which seem to be evident and about those which are non-evident."[4] People have struggled with this twin legacy of Greek thinkers ever since.

Axial-Age Thinkers: Socrates, Plato, and Aristotle

Views of the Greek contribution to world thought often focus on the specific ideas of three major fifth- and fourth-century Athenian thinkers. The first two, Socrates (SOCK-ruh-teez) and Plato (PLAY-toe), studied the nature of truth; the third, Aristotle (AR-uh-staht-uhl), examined the truth to be found in nature. These men were part of an outpouring of philosophical and religious genius across Eurasia between 600 and 200 B.C.E. that historians often term the Axial Age. From Greece to India to China, the Axial-Age thinkers laid the groundwork for the beliefs of classical societies. The ideas of Buddha in India, Confucius in China, Hebrew prophets, Zoroaster, and various Greeks remained influential for many centuries.

Socrates

The earliest Greek philosophical giant, the Athenian Socrates (469–399 B.C.E.) famously asserted that "the unexamined life is not worth living." Shabbily dressed, eccentric, and passionate, he spent much time asking people leading questions that helped them examine the truth of their ideas, an approach called the Socratic Method. He asked questions to help people see what he considered the falseness of the Sophists' idea that truth and justice were relative, changing from one polis to another. Socrates believed in absolute truths that, if understood by people, would make them virtuous, but he also was suspicious of democracy, favoring government by the chosen few who had acquired

 Apologia Learn why Socrates was condemned to death, and why he refused to stop questioning the wisdom of his countrymen.

superior knowledge. Later in life, Socrates challenged the scientific perspective, arguing against the study of astronomy.

For asking so many challenging questions and "corrupting the youth," Socrates was condemned to death by the citizens of Athens in 399 B.C.E. Although he could have secured a lighter sentence or gone into exile, Socrates chose death: he drank the hemlock poison provided for his execution and defiantly proclaimed, "I shall obey God rather than you [and] never cease from the teaching of philosophy."[5] His death made him, in modern eyes at least, a martyr for truth and free expression.

Plato

At the time of Socrates' death, his leading pupil, Plato (428–347 B.C.E.), was twenty-eight years old. Plato became disillusioned with city politics after his mentor's execution. Most of what we know of Socrates comes from Plato, who interpreted and continued his inspiring teacher's explorations into the nature of truth. After a sojourn in Egypt, Plato founded a school in Athens that he called the Academy. Plato elaborated Socrates' belief in ultimate truth, beauty, and goodness. Most humans, he wrote in the *Republic*, are like men chained in a cave who mistake the shadows cast by a fire on the cave wall for reality. Because most of us are ruled by our emotions, we are unable to see that the fire is more real than the shadows it casts. Only a special class, the Guardians, trained to use reason to control the emotions and will, can understand ultimate truth and goodness.

Because he thought most people could not live according to the dictates of reason or distinguish knowledge from mere opinion, Plato favored a democratic government only if the Guardians headed it. Only they, he believed, could be trusted to treat others with justice. Later in his life, Plato retreated from this elitist conception and suggested that strong laws could control democratic excesses. Nevertheless, some charge that Plato's thinking sanctioned dictatorships in which a small group of men claimed special wisdom and virtue.

Aristotle

Aristotle (384–322 B.C.E.) was the Athenian philosopher whose ideas seem most similar to ours today. The son of a Greek physi-

Socrates This statue, made several centuries after his death, celebrates the Athenian philosopher Socrates, who had a strong influence on the thinking of Greek philosophers who came after him, including his student, Plato. HIP/Art Resource, NY

cian working for the king of Macedonia, Aristotle came to Athens to study philosophy with Plato and eventually founded a school of his own. Like Socrates, he was charged with impiety, but he chose to go into exile. Aristotle was more pragmatic than Plato and Socrates, because he emphasized how human nature and physical nature worked, rather than exploring the ultimate truths that lay behind our actions.

Aristotle's writings spanned many fields of what we today call the social sciences, humanities, and natural sciences. He was particularly interested in classifying and analyzing the world of nature and was the first to classify animals zoologically. As a philosopher, Aristotle was one of the first thinkers to examine metaphysics, the broad field that studies the most general concepts and categories underlying people and the world around them.

Aristotle on Politics Discover the strengths and weaknesses, as Aristotle saw it, of kingdoms, aristocracies, and democracies.

Greek Life and Literature

The literary creativity of Greece, especially of Athens, reflected an atmosphere of dynamism and freedom and provides many insights into social and gender relations of the time. The Greeks pursued their individual lives within the larger public sphere of the polis. The differences between social classes and genders were pronounced, and only some enjoyed formal citizenship. Freedom was reserved primarily for males, although women played a larger role than we might suspect. Athens attracted many of the great writers and artists, because the prosperity derived from a wealthy empire gave many people spending money for entertainment.

Drama

Perhaps the Athenians' most enduring contribution was in drama, which arose from annual religious festivals and was based on historical or mythological themes. Plays were usually performed in outdoor amphitheaters, accompanied by music played on flutes, trumpets, and stringed instruments. The dramatists had different styles. Aeschylus (525–456), who had fought in the Greco-Persian Wars, emphasized traditional values, probing the relationship of Greeks and their gods. He also explored issues of justice and portrayed the disasters brought by too much pride. Aristophanes (AR-uh-STAHF-uh-neez) (448–380) took a lighter approach, writing comedies that ridiculed Athenians' pretensions. For example, in *The Knights*, a general tries to convince an ignorant sausage seller to unseat the Athenian leader: "To be a leader of the people isn't for learned men, or honest men, but for the ignorant and vile. Don't miss the golden opportunity."[6]

Society

Such social satire belied the realities of class divisions in Greece. Greek society consisted, from top to bottom, of free men (only some of whom were citizens), resident foreigners, free women, and slaves. Most free men, if not wealthy landowners or small farmers, worked as laborers, artisans, or shopkeepers. In many Greek cities, noncitizens from other Greek cities and places like Phoenicia, Lydia, and Syria were primarily merchants, bankers, and artisans. Many acquired considerable wealth, and they were required to serve in the military. Free women could not vote, hold office, or serve on juries, and they were supposed to take no interest in public affairs.

About one-third of the population in a Greek city consisted of slaves, many of them non-Greeks. Most slaves were captives taken in battle or debtors. Slaves were often household servants or paid artisans, but many served as teachers, instructing generations of young people in how to write and play music. Slaves also built some of the great buildings and worked on agricultural plantations owned by aristocrats. Life for many slaves was harsh. They could be tortured and executed for mere suspicion of a crime.

Family and Gender Relations

Like the nuclear family system of the modern West, most Greek families consisted of a husband, a wife, and children. The principal tasks of women were to feed and clothe their families and to bear and raise children. Every woman brought to marriage a dowry, which a husband was legally required to use to support his wife and children. While a woman did not have the same sexual freedom as a man, she could own property, inherit it in the absence of male children, and divorce her husband. Women's partici-

pation was also essential in religious festivals. For example, the oracle at the temple of Delphi (DELL-fye), which many leaders consulted to determine the will of Apollo, spoke through a woman's voice.

But women also experienced strong prejudice in a patriarchal society. Some women expressed their discontent, as reflected in a tragic play by Euripides: "[Men] say we lead a safe life at home. What imbeciles! I'd rather stand to arms three times than bear one child."[7] In other works women are often powerful, such as the comedy *Lysistrata* (lis-uh-STRAH-tuh) by Aristophanes. In this bawdy play, a group of women organize to end war by refusing to have sex with their husbands until the men stop fighting.

Some Greek social customs might be considered controversial today. For example, free men could have sex with slaves or prostitutes. While their wives stayed at home, men attended parties and festive gatherings, sometimes enlivened by the presence of courtesans who were celebrated for their wit and charm. The most famous courtesan was Aspasia (ass-PAY-zhee-uh), a vivacious, literate Milesian who migrated to Athens and then operated a meetinghouse where educated men came for sex and conversation with intellectual women. An advocate of gender equality, Aspasia was a close friend of Socrates and became the mistress of the Athenian leader Pericles (PER-eh-kleez). But most prostitutes were slaves whose lives were far different from Aspasia's.

Same-sex sexual relationships, known today as homosexuality, have existed in all societies from earliest times, but Greek men were particularly open about these relationships. Homosexual behavior between older and younger upper-class men was accepted as part of a mentoring relationship for career preparation, and in Sparta some of the top military units comprised homosexual male couples. But the concepts of same-sex or even opposite-sex relationships 2,500 years ago were not the same as those today. In general, men of superior status took for granted that, with or without consent, they could have intimate relations with anyone of inferior status, including servants, slaves, and foreigners.

Poetry

Greek lyric poets also contributed to literary life, reflecting an individualistic and openly intellectual way of thinking. Perhaps the most intensely personal poet was Sappho (SAFF-oh), who lived on the Ionian island of Lesbos around 600 B.C.E. A director of a girls' school dedicated to Aphrodite, Sappho wrote passionate love lyrics to her students: "A host of horsemen, some say, is the loveliest sight upon the earth; some say a display of soldiery; some a fleet of ships, but I say it's whomever

Women Fetching Water The painting on this vase portrays everyday life in a Greek city. Women have congregated at a public fountain to fill jugs with water to be carried back home, where it will be used for drinking, cooking, and cleaning.

Scala/Art Resource, NY

one loves."[8] Sappho was seen in her times as the equal of Homer.

LO³ Greeks, Persians, and the Regional System

During the early fifth century B.C.E., Athens and allied Greek cities successfully fought a series of wars with the greatest power of western Asia, the Persian Empire. But the rival Greek states also fought ruinous wars with each other. The Greeks and Persians were also linked by trade and travel with many other societies, and both societies borrowed many ideas from neighboring peoples, including the Egyptians and western Asians.

The Greco-Persian Wars

The Battle of Marathon

The Greco-Persian conflict began in 499 B.C.E., when some Greek cities in Persian-held Anatolia rebelled against their Persian overlords. The Ionian Greeks were supported by Athens but were defeated by Persia in 494. To punish the Greeks in the peninsula, the Persian king Darius I dispatched a Persian fleet to Greece in 492. This first Greco-Persian War ended with a Greek victory at the Battle of Marathon in northern Greece in 490 B.C.E. It was a violent conflict with many deaths on both sides.

The Battles of Thermopyle, Salamis, and Plataea

The Persians made another attempt to conquer the Greeks in 480 B.C.E., sparking the second war. According to the Ionia-born Herodotus, who probably exaggerated the

scale, Persia's King Xerxes sent a huge army of nearly 200,000 men into Greece, supported by the entire Persian navy of perhaps one thousand ships. Although some northern Greek cities surrendered, were neutral, or even joined with the Persians, the two chief southern cities, Athens and Sparta, along with their allies, continued the fight. A Spartan force of three hundred fought to the death, holding a strategic pass, but they were betrayed by some Greeks who showed the Persians a path around them. Nothing could then stop the Persians from sweeping down into Athens and burning the city. Expecting final victory, the Persians attacked the Athenian fleet trapped in the Bay of Salamis (SAL-uh-muhs).

Surprisingly, the Greeks won the battle, destroying two hundred Persian ships while losing only forty of their own. Part of the reason for this victory was that the large Persian force was difficult to supply and control effectively. But the Athenians had also developed the world's most advanced fighting ship, the well-armored *trireme* (TRY-reem), which had three banks of oarsmen—two hundred crewmen in all—and deadly bronze rams. The Persians left an infantry force in Greece that was defeated at the battle of Plataea (pluh-TEE-uh) the following year (479). The Athenians reopened the Straits of Bosporus (BAH-spuh-ruhs) to Greek shipping and temporarily ended Persian rule in Ionia. But with the Persian threat ended, the old rivalries of the Greek cities reemerged.

Empire and Conflict in the Greek World

The period following the Greek victories against the Persians in the early fifth century B.C.E. was marked not only by great intellectual achievements by philosophers and playwrights but also by nearly constant warfare among Greek cities. Athens created an empire based on sea power, but its dominance led to a lengthy Peloponnesian War (431–404 B.C.E.) with Sparta during the last half of the fifth century. Sparta's defeat of Athens led to further political disunity in Greece.

The Acropolis The Acropolis dominated the surrounding city of Athens. The marble Parthenon at the center, dedicated to Athena, was built during the time of Pericles.

Athenian Ascendancy

To defeat the Persians, the Greek cities had organized a defensive alliance, called the Delian (DEE-lee-uhn) League, because the treasury was located on the island of Delos (DEE-lahs). The richest state and largest naval power, Athens led the league, while other cities contributed funds or ships to the alliance. But in 467 the island of Naxos (NAK-suhs) tried to withdraw from the league, and Athens refused; it was now clear that the Delian League had changed from a defensive alliance to an Athenian empire. In midcentury, Athens made its imperial control explicit by moving the treasury of the league from Delos to Athens and beginning to spend some of the money on Athenian civic improvements. Thus the Delian League became as much a commercial as a military alliance. Athenian weights, measures, and coinage spread to other league members.

Athens reached what historians have considered its golden age in the mid-fifth century under Pericles (ca. 495–429 B.C.E.), a visionary leader and spellbinding orator who brought more democracy to the legal system. Under Pericles' leadership, Athenians had many reasons to be proud of their city, especially of magnificent public buildings such as the Parthenon (PAHR-thuh-nahn), a temple dedicated to the city's patron goddess, Athena, on the hilltop known as the Acropolis (uh-KRAH-puh-luhs). Athenians also praised their city for fostering the self-fulfillment and individualism they believed increased their happiness. But Athenians feared that too much pride or self-expression spelled trouble. Playwrights, poets, and historians all taught how arrogance could lead to punishment by the gods and personal disaster.

Indeed, the Athenians' arrogance eventually brought disaster, as increasing resentment of Athenian power generated the long Peloponnesian War between Athens and Sparta and their respective allies, beginning in 431 B.C.E. Rivals considered Athens under its nationalistic leader Pericles too dominant. Pericles reportedly contrasted Athenian democratic

> **Delian League**
> A defensive league organized by Greek cities in the fifth century B.C.E. to defeat the Persians.

institutions and equality before the law with the "painful discipline" and lack of freedom found in Sparta. The underlying assumption—that because they had superior ideals, Athenians were superior to their neighbors—provided the spark that lit the war.

Sparta and Athens at War

The Peloponnesian War proved a disaster for Athens and a boon for Sparta. The Athenian strategy was to win the war at sea, fortifying themselves behind their city walls while using their navy to combat the superior land army of Sparta and its allies. But Athens was hit by a deadly plague. One-third of the population died, and Pericles succumbed to the disease in 429 B.C.E. The Athenians also blundered in an unwise attempt to capture Syracuse, a city founded by Greek settlers on Sicily. Later the Spartans, with Persian advice, destroyed the Athenian fleet. The Peloponnesian War ended with a Spartan victory in 404. The Spartans disbanded the Athenian navy, destroyed the city walls, and killed or exiled thousands of Athenians.

Although the war made Sparta the most powerful Greek state, several decades of instability followed. In alliance with another democratic city, Thebes (THEEBZ), Athens weakened Spartan power. In the end, the frequent conflicts between the Greek cities proved too destructive. Less than a century after the Peloponnesian War ended, Greece was conquered and became the base for a much greater empire led by the northern state of Macedonia.

Historiography: Universal and Critical

The Greeks were perhaps the first people to develop concepts of history that are still used today. Of course, the legends passed down through oral traditions, such as the Gilgamesh epic in Mesopotamia, the stories in the Hebrew Bible, and the Homeric epics, were narratives of history, although we cannot prove their accuracy. By the time of Confucius, the Chinese also wrote historical accounts. But the Greeks were the first to pursue critical, analytical, and universal history. The two most famous Greek historians were Herodotus and Thucydides (thyou-SID-uh-deez).

Herodotus

Herodotus (ca. 484–425 B.C.E.) wrote history on a scale never attempted before. Most of what we know of the Greco-Persian Wars comes from his account. Integrating information on geography and cultural traditions, Herodotus wrote vividly about neighboring societies such as the Persian Empire and Egypt. A sophisticated man with an inquiring mind, Herodotus lived for a time in Athens, where he was a friend of Pericles, and portrayed the Athenians favorably in his books. He attributed the Greek victory over the Persians to the Greeks' free society, which gave them more incentive than the armies of the absolute Persian monarch. Because his interests and travels went well beyond the Greek world, Herodotus might be considered the first world historian.

Thucydides

Much of what we know about Greek politics and wars during the fifth century B.C.E. comes from a single book, *The Peloponnesian War*, written by Thucydides (ca. 460–ca. 400 B.C.E.). A member of an aristocratic family that owned gold mines, Thucydides was an Athenian general who wrote his history after he was exiled from Athens for losing an important battle. Despite his exile, Thucydides objectively evaluated the strengths and weaknesses of his home city. He also added critical judgments to his narrative. For example, he was critical of the Athenians for ignoring the warnings of Pericles to attempt no new conquests. He also asked fundamental questions about the nature of power and wondered whether humans could use it wisely. Thucydides saw history as much more than a list of names, events, and dates. He looked for patterns and moral lessons in the past. Whenever historians seek to interpret the past, they are acknowledging a debt to Thucydides.

Interregional Trade and Cultural Diversity

The Mediterranean Basin remained a vast zone of exchange in which Greeks played the leading commercial role once dominated by Phoenicians. From the eighth to the fourth centuries B.C.E., Greeks established colonies and spread Greek culture throughout the Mediterranean and the Black Sea region. Athens exported wine and olive oil in beautiful painted vases, as well as luxury items such as gold cups, jewelry, and textiles. Like the Greeks, the Persians welcomed foreign traders. Persian gold coins were widely used in the Mediterranean basin. Persian leaders patronized Greek traders living in their domains, and tribute of various kinds flowed to the Persian capital, such as camels from Arabia and Bactria, gold from India, horses from the Scythians, bulls from Egypt, leather goods from Anatolia, and silver from Ionia.

Long-distance trade was crucial to the Mediterranean world in many ways. As the population of the Greek cities grew, merchants traveling elsewhere to trade eventually evolved into what historians call a trade diaspora, merchants from the same city or country who live permanently in foreign cities or countries. Most of the shipowners, traders, and moneylenders of Athens came from western Asia or from the Greek diaspora colonies such as Marseilles and the Crimea. Some Greeks specialized in carrying goods to and from Egypt, and communities of expatriate Greek merchants were established in Egypt, western Asia, and around the Black Sea.

Especially in Athens, trade contributed to the growth of a strong navy that helped the Greeks defeat the Persians. Capitalizing on this victory, Athens became the leading commercial and financial hub. Athens financed its rise to regional power through its control of rich silver mines, which were worked by more than 20,000 slaves. It was fed by huge amounts of wheat from Egypt, Sicily, and southern Russia. After the Peloponnesian War, bankers and traders became increasingly prominent in Athenian politics, and Athens developed a reputation as a place where even those of humble origins, including some slaves, could achieve wealth.

Cultural Fusion

Largely because of trade, the Mediterranean Basin provided a context for the intermingling of southern European, western Asian, and North African cultures. Persians, who were very open to outside influences, learned much from other peoples, blending Ionian Greek, Mesopotamian, and Scythian art styles and motifs with their own traditions. Like Persians, Greeks were highly creative and benefited from their connections with other societies. They were especially open to influences from the Phoenicians, Egyptians, and Mesopotamians. The Greeks adopted the Phoenician alphabet and several of their gods, and Ionian Greeks worshiped Anatolian

> "Like Persians, Greeks were highly creative and benefited from their connections with other societies."

trade diaspora
Merchants from the same city or country who live permanently in foreign cities or countries.

deities and borrowed artistic motifs, coins, and fashion trends from the Lydians. Greeks visited, worked in, or settled in other societies, in the process learning about other cultures. The Athenian lawgiver Solon visited Egypt as a merchant, studied with priests, and wrote poems about living at the mouth of the Nile. Cosmopolitan Ionia, where Greek and Asian cultures mixed, produced pathbreaking thinking in philosophy and science, often under Persian patronage. The Ionian-born mathematician Pythagoras (ca. 580–ca. 500 B.C.E.) may have visited Egypt and Babylon, and he seems to have learned Egyptian.

The Persian and Greek Legacies

Both the Persians and Greeks influenced the peoples around them while leaving a rich legacy for later societies. Persians built not only the world's first large empire but also the first international state, bringing together diverse societies under one unified monarchy. Two thousand years later, Persians still practiced many customs from Achaemenid times and looked back to Cyrus the Great for inspiration. Persians made many contributions to other cultures. Zoroastrian ideas influenced several religions, including Judaism, Christianity, and Islam. The Persians fostered an intellectually rich atmosphere in which science and mathematics continued to develop.

In the past several centuries, many historians have credited the Greeks with creating the Western tradition. They have admired the Greeks as the direct cultural, intellectual, and political ancestors of modern Europeans and North Americans, and perceived Greek society as culturally richer than any other before modern times. In particular the Athenian era of Pericles, Plato, and Aeschylus is viewed as the "golden age" that launched Western literature, history, philosophy, science, and the democratic ideal.

However, the view of Greece as the fountainhead of European culture has problems. Some historians suggest that the Greeks can be better understood as an extension of the western Asian and North African societies that influenced them. Many classical Greek

Hellenism

A widespread culture flourishing between 359 and 100 B.C.E. that combined western Asian (mainly Persian) and Greek (Hellenic) characteristics.

customs and social inequalities, especially their sometimes cruel treatment of women and slaves, appall people today. To critics, Greek thinkers were not as liberal and secular as is often claimed; their democracy was elitist and flawed; and what ideas western Europe derived from the Greeks came in modified form through the Romans. Moreover, they argue, modern science is based not only on Greek but also on Chinese, Indian, and Middle Eastern discoveries. The enduring debate indicates that the Greeks fostered ideas and institutions that were remarkable for their time.

LO⁴ The Hellenistic Age and Its Afro-Eurasian Legacies

Between 334 and 323 B.C.E., Alexander of Macedonia (MASS-uh-DUHN-ee-a), a student of classical Greek ideas, created the largest empire yet seen in the Afro-Eurasian zone, revitalizing Greek society and spreading its culture over a wide area. Alexander's legacy lived on for centuries in Hellenism (HELL-uh-niz-uhm), a culture that combined western Asian (mainly Persian) and Greek (Hellenic) characteristics. During the Hellenistic Age, Greeks ruled over large parts of western Asia and North Africa, a domination that ended only by the rise of the Roman Empire. Meanwhile, the impact of the Hellenistic Greeks spawned new empires based in Persia that continued to influence Middle Eastern history.

Alexander the Great and World Empire

The disunity into which Greece had fallen after the Peloponnesian War opened the door to the armies of Macedonia, whose rulers then conquered a vast empire. The war had so weakened all of the Greek cities that not one of them, not even Sparta, could unite the peninsula. That task, and the creation of a great Greek empire, was left to the state of Macedonia, on

> ❝ Alexander adopted the dress of a Persian ruler, wearing a purple and white cloak that had been previously worn by Persian royalty. ❞

the northern fringe of Greece. Led by King Philip II (382–336 B.C.E.), who developed a paid professional army and devised a more effective infantry phalanx, the Macedonian army defeated the combined armies of Thebes and Athens in 338 B.C.E. Two years later, on the eve of an expedition to Asia, Philip was assassinated.

After a power struggle, Philip's twenty-year-old son, Alexander (r. 336–323 B.C.E.), an intensely ambitious former student of Aristotle, became king. Alexander was a brilliant military strategist and leader of men. During his thirteen-year reign from 336 to his death in 323 B.C.E., Alexander used Macedonian, Greek, and mercenary troops to conquer the world from Greece east to western India, and from the Nile valley in the south to the Caucasus Mountains and the Black and Caspian Seas in the north. He employed ruthless tactics against enemies, sometimes destroying entire cities that resisted and slaughtering the inhabitants. The powerful Persian Empire was dismantled in three major battles between 334 and 331. The last Persian emperor, Darius III, was murdered by his own troops after Alexander had burned Persepolis and taken his place as Persian ruler. Alexander's empire eventually incorporated the remnants of most of the major ancient Afro-Eurasian societies, including Egypt, Crete, Mycenae, Phoenicia, Mesopotamia, and the Indus Valley.

From their base in Persia, Alexander's forces moved through Afghanistan, fighting difficult battles with the tough peoples of that mountainous region. The inhabitants pursued a scorched-earth policy, preferring to destroy their homes and farms rather than surrender. Many of Alexander's horses died and his grain ran out, and his soldiers were reduced to eating their baggage animals. Finally reaching the Indus Valley, the Macedonian wanted to move into the heart of India, but his exhausted troops refused to go farther.

The burning of Persepolis symbolized the end of one era of cultural exchange and the beginning of another. In Egypt, Alexander was accepted as a pharaoh, the physical son of god. Increasingly influenced by Eastern traditions, he married a princess from the eastern Persian province of Bactria and encouraged his soldiers to take Asian wives as well. He adopted the dress of a Persian ruler, wearing a purple and

Alexander Defeating Persians at Battle of Issus In this Roman copy of an earlier Greek painting, Alexander the Great is shown on his horse in the battle that brought defeat to Persian king Darius III in 333 B.C.E.

white cloak that had been previously worn by Persian royalty.

Hellenism's Legacies

When Alexander died in Babylon at age thirty-three, probably from a fever, his victories had already ensured that the conquered territories would retain a mixed Greek and Persian cultural flavor for centuries under the influence of Hellenism. The Hellenistic Age in the eastern Mediterranean and western Asia lasted several centuries, until these lands came under the control of the Roman Empire and a revived Persian Empire.

During this time, the legacy of classical Greece was passed on in a form that fifth-century Greeks might have found difficult to understand. Hellenistic culture placed less emphasis on individual freedom and the use of reason and more emphasis on the emotions than did earlier Greek society. Some of Alexander's soldiers settled in Afghanistan and western India, and Greek ideas had an enduring influence on the art of these regions. Even after the fall of the Hellenistic kingdoms, people as far away as Ethiopia, Nubia, and western India studied the Greek language and borrowed Greek artistic styles.

CHRONOLOGY
Hellenistic Age, 359–100 B.C.E.

359–336	Reign of King Philip of Macedonia
338	Philip's conquest of Greek states
336–323	Reign of Alexander the Great
332	Invasion of Egypt
330	Occupation of Persia
327–325	Invasion of India
306–30	Ptolemaic Egypt
238	Parthian state in Persia
141	Parthians' conquest of Seleucids

The Division of Alexander's Empire

By the end of the fourth century B.C.E., Alexander's empire had been fragmented by his former

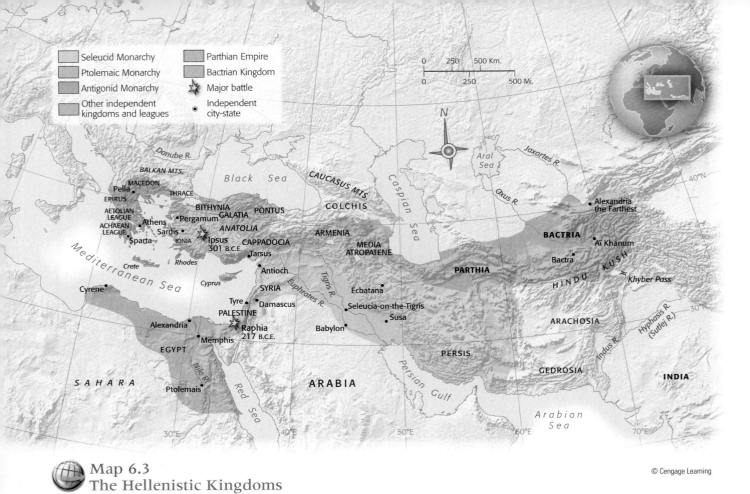

Map 6.3
The Hellenistic Kingdoms

© Cengage Learning

The empire conquered by Alexander the Great was divided into rival Hellenistic kingdoms on his death in 323 B.C.E. By 140 B.C.E., the Parthians had conquered some of the eastern territories.

Map legend:
- Seleucid Monarchy
- Ptolemaic Monarchy
- Antigonid Monarchy
- Other independent kingdoms and leagues
- Parthian Empire
- Bactrian Kingdom
- ☆ Major battle
- Independent city-state

generals, all Macedonians. A dynasty begun by Ptolemy (TAHL-uh-mee) controlled Egypt and the eastern Mediterranean coast; the family of Seleucus (suh-LOO-kuhs) controlled Persia, Mesopotamia, and Syria; and followers of Antigonus (an-TIG-uh-nuhs) controlled the Macedonian kingdom and northern Greece (see Map 6.3).

Interactive Map

These Greek-dominated kingdoms were based in cities that differed from the polis in Golden Age Greece, but they also enjoyed increased trade. Throughout his travels, Alexander had founded many cities named after him, the most famous of which was the still-surviving city of Alexandria, Egypt (see Map 6.3). Hellenistic cities were not politically independent city-states as in classical Athens but rather part of kingdoms, and their citizens did not enjoy much political freedom or participation in government. Wealthy aristocrats, professional soldiers, and bureaucrats ran the cities' governments.

Although the Hellenistic cities were centers of Greek culture, they were partly influenced by local traditions. Hellenistic monarchs relied on Greeks, Greek-speaking Persians, and others to rule their kingdoms, but these Greek leaders were vastly outnumbered by their Asian and African subjects. In addition, the cities were no longer the vibrant democratic communities they had been in the time of Pericles. The population of each city had less public spirit, and the urban culture glorified hedonism. The upper classes enjoyed high living, and poets celebrated activities like horse racing, lovemaking, and drinking.

Hellenistic Cosmopolitanism

Hellenistic cities were more cosmopolitan and ethnically diverse than their earlier Greek counterparts. Alexandria, Egypt, for example, was a city with large Egyptian, Greek, and Jewish populations. It was here that the Zoroastrian holy books and Hebrew Bible were translated into Greek, the latter to benefit

Greek-speaking Jews. Many poets and scholars moved there. The Syrian Greek poet Meleager expressed the cosmopolitan Hellenistic attitude: "Stranger, we live in the same motherland, the world."[9]

Alexander's conquests also linked the Mediterranean and western Asia in a vast trading network. Greek colonists introduced or expanded money-based economies. Long-distance trade expanded rapidly as silk from China and sugar from India were traded for onions from Egypt, wood products from Macedonia, and olive oil from Athens. As caravans of vegetables and wine moved eastward, they crossed caravans of spices and other goods moving westward out of India, Arabia, and northeast Africa. This trans-Eurasian trading network remained strong long after the Hellenistic states had disappeared.

Science, Philosophy, and Religion

Hellenistic thinkers maintained the classical Greek interest in scientific questions and made numerous contributions to our understanding of the natural world during the third and second centuries B.C.E. Although influenced by thinkers like Aristotle, Hellenistic scientists and mathematicians were more rigorous and professional in collecting and evaluating data, then offering hypotheses to explain mathematics problems, natural phenomena, and the workings of the universe.

Hellenistic Scholarship

Alexandria, Egypt, with the largest library in the ancient world (700,000 papyrus scrolls), was the research center of the Ptolemaic kingdom and the Hellenistic world. Much of the work of Alexandrian thinkers and inventors initiated or anticipated the scientific, mathematical, and technological developments of the modern world. Here in the third century, for example, Euclid (YOU-klid) wrote his text on plane geometry, a book used for 2,000 years. Aristarchus (AR-uh-STAHR-kuhs) first proposed that the sun rather than the earth was the center of the universe, an idea rejected for the next 1,000 years by most Europeans. A third-century B.C.E. geographer, Eratosthenes (ER-uh-TAHS-thuh-neez), calculated the circumference of the earth within about 200 miles, and the Alexandrian inventor Hero devised a steam turbine, although it was treated only as an amazing toy. The innovative mathematician and antiquity's greatest engineer, Archimedes, studied in Alexandria but made many of his contributions after returning home to Syracuse on Sicily.

Cynicism

Greek philosophical and religious thought went in new directions during the Hellenistic era. Some of the new ideas put less emphasis on the power of reason to solve problems and more on the importance of resigning oneself to life in ways that often seemed fatalistic. There was a new emphasis on simplicity and taking life as it comes. The school of thought known as Cynicism, made famous by Ionia-born Diogenes (die-AHJ-uh-neez) (ca. 412–ca. 323 B.C.E.), emphasized living a radically simple life, shunning material things and all pretense, and remaining true to one's fundamental values.

Cynicism
A Hellenistic philosophy, made famous by the philosopher Diogenes (fourth century B.C.E.), that emphasized living a radically simple life, shunning material things and all pretense, and remaining true to one's fundamental values (see Hellenism).

Stoicism
A Hellenistic philosophy begun by Zeno in the third century B.C.E. that emphasized the importance of cooperating with and accepting nature, as well as the unity and equality of all people (see Hellenism).

Mithraism
A Hellenistic cult that worshiped Mithra, a Persian deity associated with the sun; had some influence on Christianity.

Stoicism

Another Hellenistic-era philosophy, Stoicism (STOH-uh-siz-uhm), emphasized cooperating with and accepting nature, as well as the unity and equality of all people. Founded by Zeno (ZEE-noh) (ca. 334–ca. 265 B.C.E.) in Athens in the third century B.C.E., Stoicism, which is often misunderstood today as the belief in resigning oneself to fate, was actually a cosmopolitan and optimistic philosophy that accepted the ethnic diversity evident in the Hellenistic world. Stoics also taught that the law of nature governing human affairs transcended the limited human laws created by kings. The Stoic emphasis on basic human equality survived over the centuries to influence modern lawmakers.

Mystery Religions

Hellenistic religion, like its major philosophies, stressed personal satisfaction and offered people individual happiness or salvation. The religion of Isis, originally an Egyptian fertility goddess, promised personal salvation. In addition, various mystery religions valued faith and promised their followers eternal life. A very popular mystery religion was Mithraism (MITH-ruh-iz-uhm), a cult that worshiped Mithra, a Persian deity associated with the sun. Some historians believe that these Hellenistic religions help explain the appeal of the teachings and life of Jesus several centuries later. For example, Christianity borrowed from Mithraism the concept of purgatory as well as the winter solstice and birthday of Mithra (December 25). Hellenistic ideas remained important in western Asia and the eastern Mediterranean long after the end of the Hellenistic era.

Hellenistic Asia and Persian Revival

As mentioned earlier in this section, after Alexander's death, his empire was split into three parts ruled by the Ptolemies, Seleucids, and Antigonids. The dominance of the Hellenistic Seleucid kings, who governed a large territory in western Asia, including Persia and Mesopotamia, was short-lived. They were challenged by the Parthians (PAHR-thee-uhnz), originally Indo-European pastoral nomads who migrated from Central Asia into eastern Persia in the third century B.C.E. and initially became subjects of the Seleucids. In the middle of the second century B.C.E., however, the Parthians conquered large parts of Persia, Afghanistan, and Mesopotamia and seized the Seleucid capital on the Tigris River. Over the next few decades, they fought off Scythian invaders in the north, expanded their empire into the Caucasus, and then crushed an invading Roman army in 53 B.C.E.

The Parthians adopted many Hellenistic traditions and institutions, and they made Greek the official language of their state. Gradually, Persian influences grew stronger, and the Parthians adopted a form of Zoroastrianism, but frequent wars with Rome sapped their strength. In 224 C.E., the last Parthian ruler was defeated by a new Persian power, the Sassanians (suh-SAY-nee-uhnz). The Sassanians ruled much of western Asia for the next four centuries, coming into frequent conflict with the Romans, who replaced the Hellenistic kingdoms.

 Listen to a synopsis of Chapter 6.

{ Learning Your Way }

89% of students surveyed found the interactive online quizzes valuable.

We know that no two students are alike. **WORLD** was developed to help you learn world history in a way that works for you.

Not only is the format fresh and contemporary, it's also concise and focused. And, **WORLD** is loaded with a variety of supplements, like Chapter-in-Review cards, flashcards, an interactive eBook, the Wadsworth World History Resource Center, and more.

At **4ltrpress.cengage.com/world**, you'll find plenty of resources to help you study no matter what your learning style!

CHAPTER 7

Classical Societies in Southern and Central Asia,

600 B.C.E.–600 C.E.

Learning Outcomes

After reading this chapter, you should be able to answer the following questions:

LO¹ What ideas did Buddhism take from Hinduism, and what ideas were unique?

LO² How did the Mauryas shape Indian society, and how, in turn, did classical India influence the world beyond South Asia?

LO³ What were the main achievements of the Gupta era?

LO⁴ How did Southeast Asians blend indigenous and foreign influences to create unique societies?

> **"**The merchants used to move about in the rivers as they wished, in the forests as if in gardens and on mountains as if in their own houses. As [the King] used to protect the earth so it too gave him gems out of mines, corns from the fields, and elephants from forests.**"**
>
> —**Indian writer Kalidasa (Kahl-I-Dahss-Uh), fifth century c.e.[1]**

Sometime around 80 c.e., an unknown Greek boarded a trading ship that left the Egyptian port of Berenike (BER-eh-nick-y) headed for India. The ship sailed down the Red Sea, along the coast of Arabia, and to the Indus River, where the merchants exchanged clothing, silverware, and glassware for gems, Chinese silks, and Indian textiles. Proceeding down India's west coast, they stopped near present-day Mumbai, trading silverware, Italian wine, and slave musicians for pepper. Finally the travelers reached the great port of Muziris (MOO-zir-us) in southwest India. A second-century Indian poet recorded the arrival of such ships at Muziris: "The beautiful vessels stir white foam on the river, arriving with gold and departing with pepper."[2] After a stay in the port, which allowed the sailors to haunt the waterfront dives, the ship sailed around the southern tip of India and up the east coast, stopping to collect pearls, textiles, spices, and gems, finally reaching the mouth of the Ganges River before returning to Egypt.

Test your knowlege before you read this chapter.

What do you think?

Indian society and culture had little impact on other regions during the Classical Era.

Strongly Disagree   *Strongly Agree*

1   2   3   4   5   6   7

From the west—Arabia, Egypt, Persia, East Africa, Greece, Rome—ships like this one arrived annually at Indian seaports to trade. India also attracted sojourners such as Chinese Buddhist (BOO-dihst) pilgrims seeking new wisdom and adventure. Other people came to settle permanently. For those who arrived over the mountains from windswept Central Asia, the Indian sun was a blazing fury, the drenching summer rains a shock—and the Indian culture and religion were even more unusual than the climate. Indian society was adaptable and accommodating of diverse practices. Most immigrants, whatever their original religious views, were gradually enfolded into

<< **Gold Coin** This gold coin, showing a horseman, was made in India during the reign of King Chandragupta II, who presided over a great and prosperous Indian empire between 380 and 415 c.e.

Indian religions, which allowed for many paths to understanding. India remained confidently distinctive while also engaging with the world around it.

The Classical Era was a time of flowering in South and Southeast Asia. Several great empires and vibrant trading networks brought unusual political unity to South Asia and made India a leading world power. Hinduism developed new schools of thought, while Buddhism (BOO-diz-uhm) arose to become a major faith in many parts of Asia. Meanwhile, various Central and Southeast Asian peoples established distinctive societies.

LO¹ The Transformation of Indian Society and Religions

The forging of a new society from the synthesis of Aryan and local traditions that began in the second millennium B.C.E. (see Chapter 2) continued for centuries, affecting many aspects of life and thought. In particular, the distinctive caste system became a key part of the framework of Indian society, and Hinduism grew even more diverse and complex. In addition, Jainism and Buddhism were born out of the religious ferment of the Axial Age, that great philosophical awakening during the early Classical Age that spawned many new ways of thinking across Eurasia.

Caste and Indian Society

The Caste System

The social configuration known today as the caste system began to take shape early in the Classical Era, especially in North India. Members of a caste generally practiced a common occupation: some were priests, others warriors, merchants, artisans, or farmers. Caste membership was supported by Hindu values, including beliefs in

> "Pariahs worked as hunters, fishermen, butchers, gravediggers, tanners, leather workers, and scavengers, and they lived largely in their own villages or in shabby urban neighborhoods."

reincarnation and ritual practices. A political and legal document known as the Code of Manu (MAN-oo) and probably compiled sometime during the first or second century C.E., formalized many rules regarding caste relations. Gradually, during the first millennium of the Common Era, the four main castes (*varna*) were subdivided into thousands of subcastes known as *jati* ("birth group"), each with its own rules and, frequently, occupational specialization. Such rules produced an enduring social stability in India over many centuries.

Eventually the caste system became hereditary. Each person was born into a certain caste and expected to marry only within that caste. Caste members were required to eat and drink together, and strict food regulations prescribed the types of food that could be consumed, who could cook and serve the food, and who could accompany the diner. Some castes, especially those of higher rank, became vegetarian; others could eat meat. As vegetarianism became more common among the higher castes, cows were protected against being killed. A third-century B.C.E. book ordered that cattle should never be slaughtered. In Indian cities and villages, cows wandered at

CHRONOLOGY

Classical India

563–483 B.C.E.	Life of the Buddha
326 B.C.E.	Alexander the Great's army reaches western India
322–185 B.C.E.	Mauryan Empire
269–232 B.C.E.	Reign of Ashoka
200 B.C.E.–150 C.E.	Division of Buddhism into Theravada and Mahayana schools
ca. 50–250 C.E.	Kushan Empire in northwest India
ca. 320–550 C.E.	Gupta era

will, eating whatever grain they found and enjoying a pampered existence.

The mix of social and religious notions strongly influenced a group's placement in the caste system. The Hindu doctrine of *karma* held that one's caste status in the present life was determined by deeds in past lives. The three top caste groupings were considered further along the path of reincarnation. Low-caste Indians were held responsible for their status because of their presumed past sins. The *Bhagavad Gita* warned that ignoring caste destroyed the family: "When lawlessness prevails, the women of the family become corrupted. And to hell does this confusion [of caste] bring the family itself."[3]

> "Yoga was a system of physical and mental exercises that emphasized control of breathing to promote mental concentration, calmness, and a trancelike state that produced a mystical awareness of a universal soul."

Untouchables

Below the formal caste system were the untouchables, or *pariahs* (puh-RYE-uhz). Probably constituting some 10 percent of the Indian population, untouchables were generally condemned to trades regarded as unclean, because their function involved being polluted by filth or the taking of animal life. They worked as hunters, fishermen, butchers, gravediggers, tanners, leather workers, and scavengers, and they lived largely in their own villages or in shabby urban neighborhoods.

Assessing the Caste System

In several ways the caste system provided stability and security. It promoted mutual aid within each caste and regulated village life, as subcastes exchanged goods or services with other subcastes in the village. It also aided the assimilation process: new groups, such as invaders or immigrants, were integrated into the larger society by becoming new subcastes. Regional variations also developed: in South India, Bengal, and northwestern India, caste status remained ambiguous and the system was less complex. But elsewhere, caste became a pillar of Indian society, contributing to a group orientation, a passion for stability, and an acceptance of authority.

From A.L. Balsham, The Wonder That Was India (London: Sidgwick and Jackson, 1954)

Village Scene, Second Century C.E.
In classical times most Indians lived in villages. This drawing of a village scene is based on a relief made at Amaravati, a Buddhist temple complex built in the second century C.E. It shows members of different caste groups carrying out various village activities.

Brahman
The Universal Soul, or Absolute Reality, that Hindus believe fills all space and time.

Vedanta
("Completion of the Vedas") A school of Classical Indian thought that offered Hindus mystical experience and a belief in the underlying unity of all reality.

The Shaping of Hinduism

Hinduism faced increasing dissent during the Classical Era. Between around 1000 and 600 B.C.E., power was increasingly concentrated in the hands of the priestly class, the *brahmans*. Rituals presided over by priests were an essential feature of Hinduism. Enriched by gifts from the devout, many priests became wealthy landowners. Eventually, however, some Indians became resentful at what they viewed as priestly wealth and corruption. Out of these conflicts came new movements that emphasized spirituality over ritual, fostering new approaches to worship. The writings of critics of priestly power were collected in the *Upanishads*, the final portion of the vast Hindu scriptures.

Internet Indian History Source-book (*http://www.fordham.edu/halsall/india/indiasbook.html*). An invaluable collection of sources and links on India from ancient to modern times.

As a result of this new spirituality, the highest ideal of Hinduism came to be the escape from sensual and material pleasures and the joining of one's individual soul with Brahman, the Universal Soul that fills all space and time. To achieve this goal, some seekers turned to asceticism, rejecting society and seeking mystical unity with the divine through techniques known as *yoga* (YOH-guh) ("yoke" or "union"). Yoga was a system of physical and mental exercises that emphasized control of breathing to promote mental concentration, calmness, and a trancelike state that produced a mystical awareness of a universal soul. Union with the Universal Soul meant ending the cycle of reincarnation, called the "wheel of life." The *Bhagavad Gita* (see Chapter 2) identified three paths for achieving release from the wheel of life: devotion to God, selfless action, and knowledge achieved chiefly through intense meditation.

Whatever the path chosen, the ultimate goal was to escape from one's ego. Only by doing this could a person end reincarnation and finally achieve the ultimate bliss of merging with Brahman. New forms of worship stressing prayer made salvation more accessible to the lower castes, since members of these groups did not have time for intense meditative practices. Gradually, worship focused on personal devotion to specific gods such as Vishnu or Shiva, as well as to thousands of lesser deities represented by sacred stones and images. Every home had a shrine to worship such deities. Believers could also seek inspiration from many ancient stories about Hindu gods. Frequent religious festivals had mass appeal, and great throngs made annual pilgrimages to sacred places such as the River Ganges.

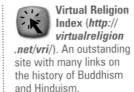
Virtual Religion Index (*http://virtualreligion.net/vri/*). An outstanding site with many links on the history of Buddhism and Hinduism.

New Schools of Hindu Thought

Eventually the quest for spiritual experience led to the formulation of new schools of Hindu thought. Perhaps the most influential was Vedanta (vay-DAHNT-uh), meaning the "completion of the Vedas." Vedanta offered mystical experience and a belief in the underlying unity of all reality. Members of Vedanta and similar schools found sophisticated ways of thinking about the deities found in popular Hinduism, a diversity often summed up by the phrase "33,000 gods."

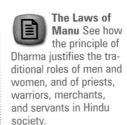
The Laws of Manu See how the principle of Dharma justifies the traditional roles of men and women, and of priests, warriors, merchants, and servants in Hindu society.

However, Vedanta thinkers perceived all of these gods and spirits as manifestations of the single Absolute Reality that pervades everything. The *Upanishads* states that Brahman is "God, all gods, the five elements—earth, air, fire, water, ether; all beings, great or small."[4]

Thanks to the great diversity of gods and beliefs, Hinduism developed a broad and tolerant approach to religious differences. Throughout history, many invaders swept into India, but most of them found a place in Hinduism, which incorporated a wide variety of other beliefs. In India, God could be worshiped in many forms and on many paths. From this time onwards, Hinduism developed not as a rigidly defined theology with a centralized church, but as a broad collection of loosely connected sects with some core beliefs but many variations. Indeed, before the nineteenth century C.E., Indians did not use the term *Hinduism* to refer to these sects collectively. Toleration and accommodation allowed Hinduism to retain its widespread popularity among both the better educated and the villagers, despite the clearly inequitable divisions of caste and the burdens of karma.

Jainism and Buddhism

Mahavira the Jain

Two dissident ascetics during the height of the Eurasian Axial Age eventually gave up on reforming Hinduism and founded new movements that became separate religions: Jainism (JINE-iz-uhm) and Buddhism. Jain ideas were organized by a famed teacher, Mahavira (MA-ha-VEER-a) ("Great Hero"), around 500 B.C.E. Mahavira grew up near Patna in north India, the pampered son of a tribal chief. At the age of thirty, he abandoned his affluent life to wander naked as an ascetic. A master of self-control, Mahavira practiced self-torture as the route to salvation, eventually starving himself to death. His ideas would be influential twenty-five centuries later when Mohandas Gandhi, a devout Hindu, utilized Jain ideas in developing his philosophy of nonviolence, out of which passive resistance and the fast-until-death developed as strategies for generating political change.

Sanctity of Life

The basic tenet of Jainism is that life in all forms must be protected, because everything in nature—including animals, insects, plants, and even sticks and stones—has a separate soul and is alive. A devout Jain is vegetarian and, while walking, sweeps the ground to avoid stepping on insects. Nonviolence is, in Mahavira's words, "the pure, unchanging law. All things living, all beings whatever, should not be slain, or treated with violence."[5] Because agriculture was difficult without killing some bugs and animals, most Jains became merchants and bankers, forming a relatively prosperous community.

Siddartha Gautama

More important in the long run than Jainism was Buddhism, a religion based on the teachings of a major Axial-Age thinker, the Buddha. Siddartha Gautama (si-DAHR-tuh GAUT-uh-muh) (563–483 B.C.E.) was born a prince of a small kingdom in what is now southern Nepal. As a youth, Siddartha led a privileged life but was shocked when he ventured from the palace and encountered the disease and miseries experienced by common people. Siddartha abandoned his royal life, wife, and family to search for truth as a wandering holy man. In his quest, he was

Setting in Motion the Wheel of Law
Siddartha's first sermon contains the core teaching of Buddhism: to escape, by following the Middle Path, the suffering caused by desire.

> **Jainism**
> An Indian religion that believes that life in all forms must be protected because everything, including animals, insects, plants, sticks, and stones, has a separate soul and is alive; arose in 500 B.C.E. as an alternative to Hinduism.

> **Buddhism**
> A major world religion based on the teachings of the Buddha that emphasized putting an end to desire and being compassionate to all creatures.

Worship of Buddhist Relics In the first century C.E., Buddhists erected a pillar containing this frieze of a stupa housing relics of the Buddha.

influenced by the critiques of brahman prayers and sacrifices that had led to the *Upanishads*. He also rejected the Hindu caste system as immoral. For several years he lived in the forest, practicing yoga, meditating, and nearly dying from fasting and self-torture. Eventually, around 528 B.C.E., Siddartha believed he understood cosmic truths, and was referred to as the Buddha ("The Enlightened One"). He began traveling to teach his new religion and attracted many disciples.

The Four Noble Truths

Giving his first sermon in the Ganges city of Benares around 527 B.C.E., Buddha laid out his Four Noble Truths (see Witness to the Past: Basic Doctrines in the Buddha's First Sermon). The first truth asserts that this life is one of suffering and ignorance. The second suggests that suffering stems from desiring what one does not have and clinging to what one already has for fear of losing it. The third truth is to stop all desire. The fourth truth provides the method of stopping desire, which is to follow the Noble Eightfold Path: correct views, intent, speech, actions, trade (or profession), effort, mindfulness, and concentration. Following this path means leading a good life that does no harm to others and realizing that one is but a tiny part of a larger chain of composite events. Buddhism is neither monotheistic nor polytheistic, and the Buddha was ambivalent as to whether a god or gods existed. If they did, he argued, they must follow the same four truths as mortals.

Buddhist Distinctiveness

Along with embracing nonviolence, moderation, and love for all creatures, Buddhists were encouraged to live moral, generous lives. Asked to summarize his beliefs, he replied: "Avoid doing evil deeds, cultivate doing good deeds, and purify the mind."[6] These teachings had economic consequences. The Buddha did not oppose acquiring wealth but believed that wealth alone did not bring happiness. He also condemned the irresponsible use of wealth, such as wasting it on drinking, gambling, and laziness rather than saving for emergencies and donating to worthy

causes. Buddha adopted many Hindu ideas but also modified them. Buddhists, like Hindus, believed in reincarnation: the idea that the individual soul progresses through a series of lives. But the goal for Buddhists was not unity with Brahman but rather nirvana (neer-VAHN-uh) (literally, "the blowing out"), a kind of everlasting peace achieved through perfection of wisdom and compassion. Buddha also urged his followers to avoid taking animal life if possible.

Buddha seems to have been the world's first religious leader to introduce the idea of monasticism (muh-NAS-tuh-siz-uhm), the pursuit of a life of penance, prayer, and meditation, either alone or in a community of other seekers. He advocated voluntarily adopting a monastic life that required chastity, poverty, and nonviolence. Buddha initially sanctioned only monks, but later nuns were also admitted to the order. Monks and nuns followed the rules of proper conduct and also used such techniques as yoga for concentration, thoughtful meditation, and self-discipline. They also begged for their food, which affirmed their humility.

Despite such deprivations, Buddha soon gained many followers, who believed his ideas established firm moral standards and pointed the way to ending the suffering of life. The Buddhist opposition to caste and priestly power also attracted followers. Eventually Buddhism became a major influence on the first great Indian imperial state, the Mauryan Empire, and spread out of India to become a major faith in Central, East, and Southeast Asia and Sri Lanka.

LO² The Mauryan Empire and Post-Mauryan Asia

The outstanding political development in the Classical Era was the emergence of India's first centralized empire, the Mauryan (MORE-yuhn) Empire, centered in the Ganges Valley. The rise of this powerful, prosperous state was in part a response to contact with peoples to the west. Indeed, the Mauryas were very much involved with the wider world, engaging in foreign trade and official sponsorship of Buddhist missions to neighboring societies. They also established a powerful army and government that brought unprecedented political unity to the subcontinent. Although the end of the Mauryas in the early second century B.C.E. was followed by 500 years of political fragmentation before the rise of the next empire, these centuries saw increasing contact between India and the outside world, causing repercussions for both sides.

Basic Doctrines in the Buddha's First Sermon

Buddhist tradition holds that, after achieving enlightenment, the Buddha preached his first sermon in a deer park in the outskirts of the Ganges city of Varanasi (Benares) around 527 B.C.E. The sermon became one of the most important sources of belief for all Buddhists. It laid out the framework of Buddha's moral message, including the Middle Way between asceticism and worldly life, the Noble Eightfold Path, and the Four Noble Truths. These are the most important concepts in all branches of Buddhism.

There are two ends not to be served by a wanderer. What are these two? The pursuit of desires and of pleasure which springs from desire, which is base, common, leading to rebirth, ignoble and unprofitable; and the pursuit of pain and hardship [asceticism], which is grievous, ignoble, and unprofitable. The Middle Way of the [Buddha] avoids both of these ends. It is enlightened, it brings clear vision, it makes for wisdom, and leads to peace, insight, enlightenment, and Nirvana. What is the Middle Way? It is the Noble Eightfold path—Right Views, Right Resolve, Right Speech, Right Conduct, Right Livelihood, Right Effort, Right Mindfulness, and Right Concentration . . .

And this is the Noble Truth of Sorrow. Birth is sorrow, age is sorrow, disease is sorrow, death is sorrow; contact with the unpleasant is sorrow, separation from the pleasant is sorrow, every wish unfulfilled is sorrow—in short, all of the five components of individuality are sorrow.

And this is the Noble Truth of the Arising of Sorrow. It arises from craving, which leads to rebirth, which brings delight and passion, and seeks pleasure from here, now there—the craving for sensual pleasure, the craving for continued life, the craving for power.

And this is the Noble Truth of the Stopping of Sorrow. It is the complete stopping of the craving, so that no passion remains, leaving it, being emancipated from it, being released from it, giving no place to it. And this is the Noble Truth of the Way which Leads to the Stopping of Sorrow. It is the Noble Eightfold Path . . .

Thinking About the Reading

1. What does the Buddha mean by the Middle Way?
2. What causes suffering, and how can people stop it?
3. What conduct do these ideas promote?

Source: Sources of Indian Tradition, Vol. 1 by William Theodore De Bary et al., eds. Copyright © 1958 Columbia University Press. Reprinted with permission of the publisher.

The Mauryan Empire and Indian Encounters

For several centuries, northwest India remained in close communication with societies to the west, first Persia and then Hellenistic Greece. Under their great king, Darius, the Persians conquered much of the Indus River Valley in what is now Pakistan in 518 B.C.E. This conquest brought India to the attention of the young Alexander the Great (see Chapter 6), whose forces conquered Persia and reached the Indus River by 326 B.C.E. The Macedonian conqueror was impressed with wealthy India and its systems of thought. He held numerous discussions with Indian scholars about religion and philosophy, apparently dispatching his notes back to his own teacher, Aristotle. Faced with a rebellion by his exhausted soldiers, however, Alexander turned back before entering the Ganges Valley. He died in Babylon in 323 B.C.E., but his legacy endured. Hellenistic cultural influence persisted in northwest India, and some Greeks remained behind, intermarrying with local women.

Chandragupta and the Mauryan Empire

The disruption by Alexander's invasion into western India created a political vacuum that was filled by the military forces of Chandragupta (CHUHN-druh-GOOP-tuh) Maurya, who established the first imperial Indian state, the Mauryan Empire (322–185 B.C.E.), and made himself the monarch of half the subcontinent. He reigned from 324 to 301 B.C.E., holding his empire together with a powerful army and an efficient administration (see Map 7.1). In 305 B.C.E., Chandragupta concluded a treaty with Alexander's heir that set the mutual border along the Hindu Kush Mountains. At its height the

 Interactive Map

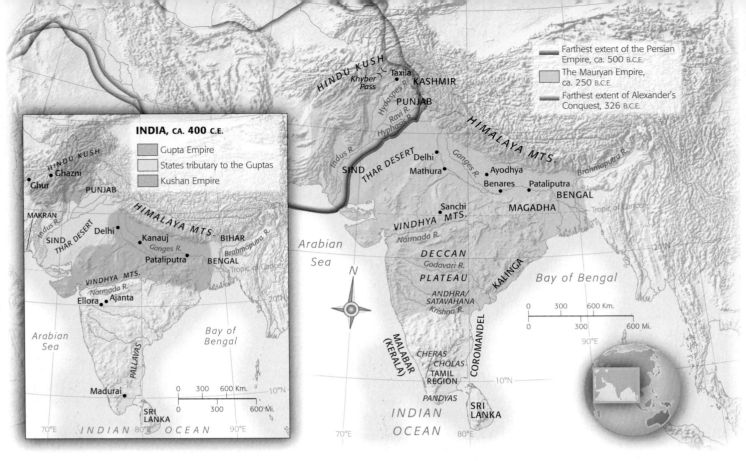

Map 7.1
The Mauryan Empire, 322–185 B.C.E.

During the Classical Era, major states arose in north India, most notably the Mauryan, Kushan, and Gupta Empires. The brief encounter with the Greek forces led by Alexander the Great, which reached the Indus River Valley in 326 B.C.E., may have stimulated the Mauryas to build India's first empire.

Mauryan Empire included parts of Afghanistan, most of north and central India, and large parts of south India. The Mauryas maintained diplomatic relations with many societies, including Greece, Syria, and Egypt.

Chandragupta was a cynical political realist who was skilled in manipulating power. His chief adviser, Kautilya (cow-TILL-ya), helped him to develop a powerful empire that probably offered the most efficient government in the classical world. A large army and secret police maintained order. The king closely supervised government officials, and spies kept them under constant surveillance. In the justice system, the king presided personally over court sessions and settled disputes. To maintain the expensive government, the state claimed between one-quarter and one-half of all agricultural production while also heavily taxing trade, mining, herding, and other economic activities. At the village level, councils composed of older men from leading families governed with considerable local autonomy, a pattern that became entrenched over the centuries. The Mauryan monarch claimed to be blessed by the gods and lived in great splendor, surrounded by an entourage of women who cooked his food, served his wine, and lulled him to sleep with music. Yet checks on autocratic power existed, such as the realization that excessive taxes and forced labor might drive the people into rebellion.

Mauryan Society and Economy

Many of the 50 to 100 million people in densely populated Mauryan India lived in cities, the centers for a prosperous economy. The Mauryan capital city, Patna (PUHT-nuh) (then called Pataliputra) on the Ganges River, was widely celebrated for its parks, public buildings, libraries, and a great university that attracted many foreign students. The accounts of Greek ambassadors suggest that Patna, with some 500,000 residents, was very likely the largest city in the world for that era, rivaled perhaps only by the capital of Han China. The circumference of the forti-

Ashoka Column This 32-feet-tall sandstone column, erected in northeast India around 240 B.C.E., weighs 50 tons. The inscriptions on the pillar outline Ashoka's achievements and offer advice on how citizens should behave.

ies, and well-kept highways fostered commerce. Products and merchants moved along the major east-west highway, which stretched from a seaport near present-day Calcutta (kal-KUHT-uh) to the borders of Afghanistan. Many foreign merchants resided in the empire, and an active exchange took place with China, Arabia, and the Middle East over trade networks. The government owned mines and forests and engaged in shipbuilding, arms manufacture, and textile production. Public granaries stored surplus food.

Ashoka's Reign and Mauryan Decline

A Warrior's Conversion

The Mauryas reached their height under the enlightened king Ashoka (uh-SHOH-kuh), one of the major political and religious figures in world history. The grandson of Chandragupta, the ambitious Ashoka became a general and rose to power through a bloody campaign of expansion. But this violence stopped when Ashoka underwent a spiritual experience and became a devout Buddhist. Ashoka spent his remaining years in power promoting the pacifist teachings of the Buddha. He pledged to bear wrong without violent retribution, to look kindly on all his subjects, and to ensure the safety, happiness, and peace of mind of all living beings.

To fulfill his pledge, Ashoka designed laws to encourage Buddhist virtues such as simplicity, compassion, mutual tolerance, vegetarianism, and respect for all forms of life. He also sponsored many public works, including hospitals, parks, and highways. Ashoka dispatched Buddhist missions to various foreign countries, spreading the religion into Sri Lanka, Southeast Asia, and Afghanistan. Despite his own devotion and strong beliefs, Ashoka neither made Buddhism the state religion nor persecuted other faiths. Public respect for his pacifist ideals and behavior discouraged rebellion. Ashoka styled himself "Beloved of the Gods," which in practice meant he was considered at least a semi-deity. For both Hindus and Buddhists, the Mauryas created a political legacy of the universal emperor, a divinely sanctioned leader with a special role in the cosmic scheme of things.

Demise of the Mauryan Empire

Ashoka ruled with popular acclaim, but his successors were less able.

fied timber wall around the city, which had 570 towers, was roughly 21 miles. Patna covered some 9 miles from one end to the other, and it was surrounded by a moat 900 feet wide.

Mauryan prosperity depended on the world's most advanced trading system and craft industries. The economy was a mix of private and public enterprise, which became a long-term pattern in India. Skilled artisans and merchants populated the cit-

Within a half century after his death, regions were seceding, the Mauryas were overthrown, and the empire destroyed. Perhaps Ashoka's policies had made India too peace-loving and had weakened Mauryan military forces. But difficult communications in a large empire also fostered local autonomy, and the mounting costs of a centralized bureaucracy drained the treasury. The end of the Mauryan Empire set a political pattern of brief periods of unity followed by prolonged fragmentation. But while India did not always possess political unity, it did possess a strong sense of cultural unity emphasizing loyalty to the family and caste rather than to the state.

Post-Mauryan Encounters and Networks

Despite internal political changes, India's relations with Central Asia, the area stretching from Russia eastward to the borders of China, were constant. Central Asia, especially the Turkestan region north of India, was a key contact zone stretching east to China, south to India, and west to Persia and Russia. As trade between China and western Asia developed, cities developed in Central Asia along the Silk Road through Turkestan. A Persian-speaking society, the Sogdians (SAHG-dee-uhns), mostly Zoroastrians or Buddhists, dominated the commerce of many cities and linked it to India.

Economic Expansion

The post-Mauryan era stands out as a time of unprecedented Indian communication and commerce. Even merchants from the Mediterranean visited India, trading gold coins, copper, tin, lead, and wine for Indian spices, cloth, silks, ivory, and works of art. The balance of trade seems to have favored India. Port cities were multilingual with special neighborhoods dominated by foreign trading communities. Trade with China continued through the Sogdian merchants along the Silk Road, while many Indian traders traveled to Southeast Asia.

Expanding foreign and domestic trade brought much wealth to the Indian commercial and artisan castes, fostering considerable economic growth in India. The increased use of gold coins prompted the emergence of banking and financial houses. but this commercial dynamism mostly occurred in the cities. Competition and business, as well as foreign products, did not often reach the villages, where the bartering of services between farmers, craftsmen, and servants continued to define social and economic relations.

> **66** The increased use of gold coins prompted the emergence of banking and financial houses. **99**

Silk Road Narratives (*http://depts.washington.edu/uwch/silkroad/texts/texts.html*). Explore cultural interaction in Eurasia through excerpts from Silk Road travelers.

Ethnic Diversity

Along with traded goods, the Silk Road fostered the migration of new peoples who added to India's hybrid character. The newcomers included invaders from the Hellenistic kingdom of Bactria in Afghanistan, a crossroads between east and west where Greek, Persian, and Indian cultures met and mixed. There Greeks and Indians exchanged knowledge of medicine and astronomy. Bactrian Greeks adopted Hinduism or Buddhism and inspired a Greek- and Roman-influenced form of Buddhist painting and sculpture, known as Gandhara, after the region where it emerged west of the Indus. Various other Central Asians such as the horseback-riding Huns settled in eastern Europe, the Caucasus, Persia, Afghanistan, and India.

Kushan Invasion

In the first century C.E., the Kushans (KOO-shans), an Indo-European people from Central Asia, conquered much of northwest India and western parts of the Ganges Basin, and they constructed an empire that also encompassed Afghanistan and parts of Central Asia, including many Silk Road cities. This expansion brought occasional conflicts with first the Parthians and then the Sassanians, two groups who successively dominated Persia (see Chapters 6 and 8). This empire building promoted communication and extensive trade between India and China, the Middle East, and the eastern Mediterranean. The Kushans were instrumental in spreading Buddhism into Central Asia, from which it then diffused to China. They promoted and spread a mix of Indian and Greco-Roman culture over a wide area.

South India and Sri Lanka

The Kushan Empire lasted from 50 to 250 C.E., gradually fading into a patchwork of competing states. Political instability occurred elsewhere in the subcontinent, but the post-Mauryan period also saw considerable political and cultural development in both south India and the large island of Sri Lanka.

Dravidian Revival North Indian influence spread south, in part because some Dravidian peoples extended their political power northward into the Ganges Basin. Aryan myths, values, rituals, and ideas, such as divine kingship, from north India appealed to south Indian rulers. South Indians also adopted a less-rigid caste system. These adaptations strengthened southern states, some of which had already flourished for centuries from maritime trade networks stretching from China to the Persian Gulf. However, Aryan influence did not destroy regional traditions in south India. For example, the Tamils, who speak a Dravidian language and inhabit India's southeastern corner, developed a vigorous cultural tradition distinct from that of the Ganges Basin. Poetry became the Tamils' most esteemed art. The mountain city of Madurai (made-uh-RYE), the temple-filled cultural center for the Tamils, developed into a major center of Hinduism, literature, and education.

Sri Lanka Just south of India, on Sri Lanka (Ceylon), a very different south Asian society developed even before Mauryan times. In the sixth century B.C.E., an Aryan prince and his followers had established the first Sri Lankan kingdom. Over the centuries, more migrants from India intermarried with the local people, in a mixing that eventually produced the Sinhalese (sin-huh-LEEZ) people. Beginning in the first century B.C.E., the Sinhalese began constructing one of the most intricate irrigation systems in world history to better grow rice. Over the next half millennium, they built canals dozens of miles long and artificial lakes covering thousands of acres. This sophisticated engineering project transformed Sri Lanka into one of the most skilled societies in water control, comparable to ancient China and Mesopotamia.

During Ashoka's reign, Buddhist missionaries converted much of the population, making Sri Lanka the first foreign land to adopt Buddhism. Buddhism became an integral part of Sinhalese identity, and in turn Sinhalese culture contributed to Buddhist art and thought. But Sri Lanka was not purely Buddhist. By the beginning of the Common Era, Tamil-speaking Hindus began to cross the narrow straits and settle in the northern part of the island. For the next two millennia, Sinhalese Buddhist and Tamil Hindu societies coexisted, sometimes uneasily, in Sri Lanka.

Buddhist Division, Hinduism, and Christianity

The post-Mauryan centuries saw considerable religious change, including the division and decline of Buddhism in India, the resurgence of Hinduism, and the arrival of both Christianity and Judaism. In addition, Indian philosophy and religious ideas gained a foreign audience. Some Indian philosophers seem to have visited western Asia, and their ideas may have influenced some of the religious and philosophical movements then percolating in the region. The idea of monasticism also expanded from India to western Asia, and Buddhist missionaries from India continued visiting neighboring regions to spread their message. Beginning in Ashoka's reign and continuing well into the Common Era, Buddhism and Buddhist art also spread into Central Asia, especially into the Silk Road cities.

The division of Buddhism into two major schools with competing visions occurred after Ashoka's reign, in the two centuries just before the Common Era. Some followers criticized the religion as it had developed as being remote from the real world, atheistic in its rejection of a conventional and personal god, excessively individualistic, and requiring too much self-discipline. In response, a canon outlining monastic rules and the structure of faith attempted to maintain orthodoxy. Critics, however, viewed the canon as neglecting the spirit of the original faith, and by the second century C.E., during the Kushan domination of northern India, the division into two schools, Theravada (THERE-eh-VAH-duh) and Mahayana (MAH-HAH-YAH-nah), became complete.

Theraveda Buddhism Theravada, which means "Teachings of the Elders," became one of the two main branches of Buddhism and clearly descended from the Buddhism promoted by Ashoka. To its followers, Buddha was not a god but rather a human teacher. The universe was in continuous change and had no supreme being or immortal soul. Because gods could not help or

> **Theravada**
> ("Teachings of the Elders") One of the two main branches of Buddhism, the other being Mahayana, that arose just before the Common Era. Theravada remained closer to the Buddha's original vision.

Mahayana
("the Greater Vehicle to salvation") One of the two main branches of Buddhism; a more popularized form of Buddhist belief and practice than Theravada. Mahayana Buddhism tended to make Buddha into a god and also developed the notion of the bodhisattva.

bodhisattva
A loving and ever-compassionate "saint" who has postponed his or her own attainment of nirvana to help others find salvation through liberation from birth and rebirth (see Buddhism, Mahayana).

hinder humans, believers could only take refuge in the wise and compassionate Buddha, his teachings, and the community of monks who maintained them. Theravadans emphasized that each believer was responsible for acquiring merit through devotion, meditation, and good works, such as feeding monks or supporting a temple. The only sure way to dramatically improve the chances of ending rebirth and reaching nirvana was to become a monk and abandon the temptations and responsibilities of normal life.

Mahayana Buddhism

Mahayana ("the Greater Vehicle" to salvation), a more popularized and less demanding form of Buddhist practice than Theravada, became the other major branch of Buddhism. Mahayana developed many sects, most of which transformed the Buddha into a god. Mahayana followers found comfort in devotional attachment to a loving deity (Buddha) and stressed charity and good works as paths toward salvation. A central feature in the faith is the bodhisattva (boe-dih-SUT-vuh) ("one who has the essence of Buddhahood"), an ever-compassionate saint who has died but postponed his or her own attainment of nirvana to help others find salvation. In China, Mahayanists converted the notion of nirvana into an appealing heaven, while the wicked were assigned to a terrifying hell.

Although several Buddhist monastic orders continued to exist and some believers remained, in India Buddhism was gradually absorbed into Hinduism. But Buddhism flourished abroad, often by providing spiritual support in times of rapid political change or instability (see Map 7.2). During the first millennium C.E., Buddhism spread widely along the trade routes, accommodating itself to local traditions and faiths. The Mahayana school eventually became the dominant form of Buddhism in Central Asia, including Tibet and Mongolia, from where it filtered into China, Korea, Vietnam, and Japan.

 Interactive Map

Mahayana Buddhism was also common in Southeast Asia for many centuries. The Theravada school became entrenched in Sri Lanka and, later, Southeast Asia.

Christianity and Judaism in India

New religions also arrived in India. According to local legends, the Christian apostle St. Thomas traveled to India around 52 C.E., establishing Christian churches and attracting followers along the Malabar (MAL-uh-bahr) coast of southwestern India. Although the role of St. Thomas cannot be proven, such a trip along active maritime trade routes was certainly possible. Large Christian communities still flourish in the Malabar state of Kerala (KER-uh-luh), especially in the ancient port cities. A few centuries after the arrival of Christianity, Jewish settlers also came to India's west coast, where they established permanent communities in Kerala and to the north at Bombay. The Jewish and Christian presence added two more elements to social and religious life in post-Mauryan India.

LO³ The Gupta Age in India

In the fourth century C.E., the great Gupta (GOOP-tuh) Empire was established, bringing political unity to India once again. The Gupta era (320–550 C.E.) was a brilliant period that saw the assimilation of both immigrants and foreign cultural influences that reshaped an ancient society. Today, Indians consider the Gupta their great golden age, a period of economic prosperity, tolerance, and major developments in science, medicine, mathematics, and literature. In comparison with the Roman Empire, by then in steep decline, and China between the Han and the Sui dynasties, Gupta India was perhaps the most dynamic society in the world.

Power and Society

The Gupta Empire

Between 320 and 409 C.E., the Gupta family and their allies conquered most of north India, carving out an empire covering roughly the same territory as Ashoka's domain. Like the Mauryan Empire before it, the Gupta Empire was somewhat decentralized, with relatively autonomous local rulers in outlying districts acknowledg-

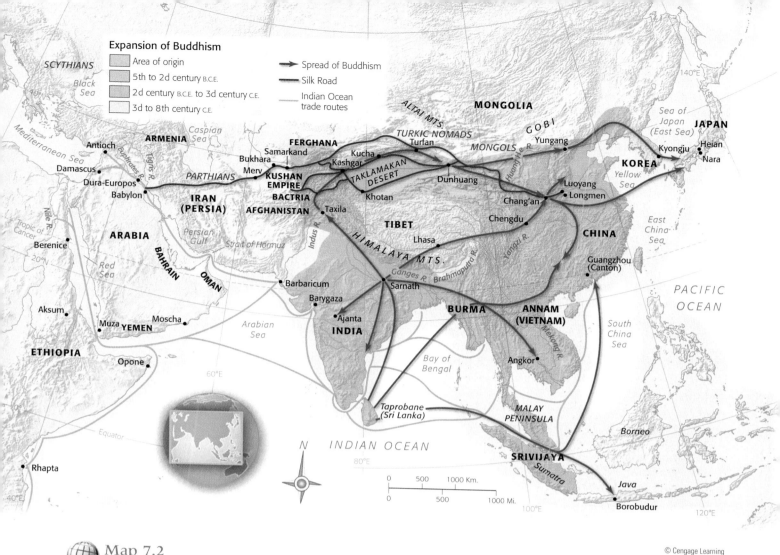

Map 7.2
The Spread of Buddhism in Asia, 100–800 C.E.
Buddhism originated in what is today Nepal and became a major religion in India during the Classical Era. From India it spread into Central Asia, China, Korea, Japan, and Southeast Asia as far east as Java.

© Cengage Learning

ing Gupta overlordship. Gupta rule reached its height under King Chandra Gupta II (r. 375–414), who became one of the most revered figures in Indian history. Although southernmost India remained outside of Gupta control, and many regional differences remained, Indian society became more uniform throughout the subcontinent under Gupta rule.

Gupta India enjoyed a considerable prosperity that was marked by significant internal and external trade, the widespread use of gold and silver coins, and highly productive agriculture. India increasingly became the textile center of the world, producing fabrics like calico, linen, wool, and cotton for export to the Middle East, Europe, China, and Indonesia. Jewels, pepper, spices, and timber were also important exports. Indeed, Gupta India stood at the center of a widespread commercial network. Taxes were relatively low, even for the peasants, and agriculture provided Indians and foreign visitors with a rich variety of foods, including mangos, pears, peaches, and apricots. Forced labor for one day per month to assist public projects remained common. The Gupta rulers, like the Mauryas, operated all metal and salt mines as well as various industrial enterprises such as arms factories and textile mills.

Guptan Exceptionalism

Gupta India enjoyed a remarkable degree of domestic peace, personal freedom, tolerance for minority views, and affluence. One Chinese Buddhist pilgrim, Faxian (FAH-shee-en) (Fa-hsien), who sojourned in Gupta India in the fifth century, observed: "The people are very well off. The king governs without corporal punishment. Criminals are fined according to circumstances, lightly or heavily. Even in cases of repeated rebellion, they only cut off the right hand. The people kill no living thing."[7] Chinese visitors noted that, while the rulers were Hindu, there was no official discrimination against Buddhists or Jains. The Guptas even helped build a great Buddhist monastery and university at Nalanda (na-LAN-da), where students from all over Asia explored Buddhist subjects as well as logic, medicine, and Hindu philosophy. A great university in Patna, the prosperous capital city, attracted ten thousand students, many from other Asian societies. However, as before the Gupta age, tolerance did not extend to the untouchables, who still occupied a degraded status.

Gender Relations

Indian social patterns were never stagnant, and patriarchy became more dominant over time as the status of women gradually declined throughout northern India. The *Mahabharata* warned men not to put "confidence in a woman or a coward, a lazybones, a violent man, a self-promoter, a thief, much less an atheist."[8] The Code of Manu tied women to the patriarchal family, urging that "in childhood a female must be subject to her father, in youth to her husband, and when her lord is dead, to her sons; a woman must never be independent."[9] The code also restricted women's property rights and recommended early marriage. The ancient custom of *sati* (suh-TEE), in which wives joined their late husbands on the funeral pyre, had been uncommon, but in the late Gupta became more widespread. Many Indian scholars and writers denounced it. However, patriarchy remained weaker in south India, where women often enjoyed more freedom and options. In contrast to the mostly male deities in the north, Hinduism in south India placed more emphasis on goddess worship, which may have given women higher status.

> "The greatest Gupta achievement was the formulation of the concept of zero and the consequent evolution of the decimal system."

Science, Mathematics, and the Arts

Intellectual pursuits flourished during the Gupta era, and India became the world's leading producer of scientific knowledge. One of the world's major astronomers, mathematicians, and physicists, Aryabhata (AR-ya-BAH-ta) (ca. 476–550), wrote his most influential work at the age of twenty-three. Aryabhata taught that the earth was round, rotated on its own axis, and revolved around the sun as one of a family of planets. He also correctly analyzed lunar eclipses, accurately calculated the moon's diameter and the circumference of the earth, and precisely determined the length of a solar year at 365.36 days. Many of his insights did not spread outside of India until many centuries later.

In mathematics, the Gupta Indians surpassed all other classical peoples, except in geometry. Aryabhata analyzed quadratic equations and the value of *pi*. The greatest Gupta achievement was the formulation of the concept of zero and the consequent evolution of the decimal system. The simple and logical Indian numbering system eventually reached the Middle East. Later still it was carried to Europe by Arab merchants and scholars, and hence became known misleadingly as Arabic numerals. Scorned in the West for centuries as pagan, Arabic numerals were not adopted by European scientists and mathematicians until the fifteenth century, opening the door to modern science and mathematics.

The Guptas were also remarkably creative in industrial chemistry. They discovered how to make soap and cement, and they produced the finest tempered steel in the world at that time. India's fine dyes and fabrics were later adopted by Europe, as was their process for transforming sugar-cane juice into granulated crystals for easy storing or shipping.

Medical Innovation

Gupta India also had the best medical system, drugs, and therapeutic methods in the world. The Guptas built on a long tradition of medical advances. Indian physicians discovered the function of the spinal cord and sketched out the structure of the nervous system. Medical experimentation was common. Through their studies, doctors learned to sterilize wounds, do Caesarian deliveries, and develop plastic surgery. Drugs the

Ajanta Cave Paintings This painting, made on a cave wall in central India during or just after the Gupta era, depicts one of the Buddha's earlier lives as a king listening to his queen.

Guptas discovered to control leprosy are still used today. Gupta doctors also vaccinated patients against smallpox by scratching a small amount of smallpox matter into the skin of children and inducing a mild case to give lifetime immunity. The effectiveness of the procedure is not known, but by 1000 C.E. it had traveled to China, and by the 1700s to Europe. Gupta doctors began to collect their knowledge of physiology, disease, and refined herbal medicines in medical textbooks by at least the second century C.E.

Literature and the Performing Arts

The Gupta era was also a great period for literature and performing arts. Writing mostly in Sanskrit, Gupta writers, many of them patronized by the royal court, produced religious works, poetry, and prose. The most popular writer, Kalidasa (kahl-i-DACE-uh) (ca. 400–455), rendered ancient legends and popular tales into drama and lyrics. His poem "The Cloud Messengers" uses a passing cloud surveying the panoramic landscape to capture the heartache of lovers separated by a vast distance: "I see your body in the sinuous creeper, your gaze in the startled eyes of deer, your cheek in the moon, your hair in the plumage of peacocks, and in the tiny ripples of the river I see your sidelong glances."[10] Theater, music, dance, and art flourished in the creative Gupta atmosphere. Instruments such as the lute, or *vina* (VEE-nuh), and zither, or *sitar* (si-TAHR), were adopted after being imported from western Asia. Gupta artists produced many religious sculptures and paintings, especially on cave or temple walls.

Decline of the Guptas

The arrival of Central Asian peoples brought an end to the Guptas and sparked many changes. In the last half of the fifth century C.E., Huns invaded the Indus Valley. Other Huns were then unsettling Europe during the fragmenting last days of the Roman Empire. The Huns conquered part of northwestern India before being blocked by Gupta power. But the Gupta state was in decline, and the cost of holding off the Huns badly depleted the treasury. Soon the empire disintegrated, and other Central Asian invaders followed the Huns into north India.

After the Gupta collapse, India lost its role as a major political power in South Asia. By 650 C.E., the region had entered a period of fragmentation, political instability, and frequent warfare that persisted for several centuries and left Indians open to conquest by Muslim peoples. Nevertheless, the many rival states that now constituted India remained part of the wider world. Cargo-laden Indian fleets from flourishing ports sailed with the monsoon winds far to the east, and Indian cultural influences, including Hinduism and Buddhism, diffused along the trade networks to Southeast Asia.

LO⁴ The Development of Southeast Asian Societies

In the tropical lands east of India and south of China, many societies borrowed political, religious, and cultural ideas from the two neighboring regions. When Southeast Asian states emerged, they were products of indigenous as well as outside forces. Most of the early Southeast Asian societies were centered on coastal plains and in river valleys, where they flourished from both productive agriculture and extensive foreign trade. The first cities and states were located

> 66 By the third century C.E., according to Chinese sources, Malay ships were able to carry seven hundred sailors and 6,000 tons of cargo. 99

in what is now Cambodia and Vietnam, and they established enduring patterns in government, religion, and trade.

Austronesian Trade and Migrations

Seafaring and maritime trade were major forces in the development of some Southeast Asian societies. As mentioned in Chapter 4, various Austronesian (AW-stroh-NEE-zhuhn) peoples were among the world's greatest mariners. Not only did they travel over hundreds of miles of ocean on trading ventures, but some also migrated thousands of miles away from Southeast Asia.

One group of Austronesians, the ancestors of the people known today as the Malays (muh-LAYZ), benefited from having a strategic position for maritime commerce and intercultural exchange. The Straits of Melaka (muh-LAK-uh), between Sumatra and Malaya (muh-LAY-a), became one of the most important contact zones of the world. The lands bordering the Straits of Melaka had for many centuries enjoyed a widespread reputation as a source of gold, tin, spices, and forest products, some of which were traded as far west as Rome. The prevailing climatic patterns in the

Relief of Indonesian Ship The Indonesians were skilled mariners. This rock carving, from a Buddhist temple in central Java, depicts a sailing vessel of the type commonly used by Indonesian traders in the Indian Ocean and South China Sea in this era.

Ancient Art & Architecture Collection

South China Sea and Indian Ocean allowed ships to meet in the straits, where their goods could be exchanged. By early in the Common Era, small coastal Malay maritime trading states had emerged in the Malay Peninsula and Sumatra. In the third century B.C.E., Malay ships visited the China coast using a sail that may have been the prototype for the revolutionary four-sided lateen (luh-TEEN) sail used soon after by Arabs and Polynesians, which allowed ships to sail directly into the wind.

Malays and other Austronesians became prominent in the expanding networks of exchange. Malays opened the maritime trade between China and India by obtaining cinnamon grown on the China coast and carrying it across the Indian Ocean to India and Sri Lanka. The Austronesian sailors returned to Southeast Asia from India with pottery, beads, and small luxuries, and possibly Indian ideas about government and religion. At the same time, other Austronesians from what is today central Indonesia introduced Southeast Asian foods, outrigger canoes, and musical instruments to East Africa. By the third century C.E., according to Chinese sources, Malay ships were able to carry seven hundred sailors and 6,000 tons of cargo.

Between the fourth and sixth centuries C.E., instability in Central Asia disrupted the overland trading routes along the Silk Road; as a result, the Indian Ocean connection became more crucial. Just as various Central Asian peoples had become important because of land-based international commerce, so some Southeast Asians, among them Malays, ben-efited from the growth of seagoing trade between China, India, and the Middle East. But the voyages held many dangers, including pirates and deadly typhoons.

Austronesian seafaring trade also led to migration. Between 100 and 700 C.E., some Austronesians from southern Borneo (BOR-nee-oh) and Sulawesi (soo-luh-WAY-see) migrated westward across the Indian Ocean. After sojourning along the East African coast, most of them settled on the large island of Madagascar (mad-uh-GAS-kuhr), off the southeast coast of Africa. Today their descendants account for the majority of the island's population, most of whom speak Austronesian languages. While some Austronesian emigrants moved westward, others moved eastward into the western Pacific. Eventually the descendants of these Austronesians, known today as the Polynesians and Micronesians, settled nearly all of the islands of the central and eastern Pacific (see Chapter 9). As a result of these movements in different directions, Austronesian-speaking societies stretched thousands of miles from Madagascar eastward through Indonesia and the Philippines to Hawaii and Easter Island in eastern Polynesia.

Indianization and Early Mainland States

Around the dawn of the Common Era, various states also arose on the Southeast Asian mainland, especially the lands bordering the lower Mekong River in what is now Cambodia and southern Vietnam. Indian culture influenced much of mainland Southeast Asia, as well as the western islands of the Indonesian archipelago. At the same time, Chinese colonization shaped a quite different society in Vietnam. Some outside influences were superficial, whereas others penetrated more deeply. However, many local traditions survived the centuries of borrowing and change.

Various states developed on the Southeast Asian mainland by early in the Common Era, but their foundations had been established a few centuries earlier. Land suitable for rice growing was an enormous environmental influence on Southeast Asia. The most populous societies emerged along the fertile coastal plains or in the valleys of great rivers like the Mekong, where irrigated rice cultivation was possible. Irrigated rice provided an ecologically sound, highly productive, and labor-intensive economic mainstay that could be sustained for many generations. By promoting social cooperation, this economy led to centralized kingdoms.

CHRONOLOGY

Classical Southeast Asia

111 B.C.E.–939 C.E.	Chinese colonization of Vietnam
39–41 C.E.	Trung Sisters' rebellion in Vietnam
ca. 75–550 C.E.	Funan
ca. 100–1200 C.E.	Era of Indianization
ca. 192–1471 C.E.	Champa
ca. 450–750 C.E.	Zhenla states

> "Perhaps the Vietnamese were able to avoid cultural and national extinction because they already had several centuries of state building and cultural identity behind them when the Chinese colonized."

Vietnam

By 500 B.C.E., a few small states had emerged that were based on irrigated rice agriculture as well as bronze and iron use. One of the earliest states was Van Lang in northern Vietnam. The Van Lang kings ruled through a landed aristocracy who controlled vast rice-growing estates worked by peasants. During the third century B.C.E., the earliest cities with monumental architecture appeared, most notably Co Loa in Vietnam. Here, near modern Hanoi, King An Duong built a huge citadel surrounded by a wall 5 miles long and 10 yards wide, to allow for chariot traffic on the top of the wall. By the first century C.E., urban societies had emerged in the river valleys among peoples such as the Khmers (kuh-MEERZ) (Cambodians), who carried on complex maritime trade.

Outside influences from China and India also generated change in Southeast Asia. A major transition came in the second century B.C.E., when Han China conquered what is today northern Vietnam, imposing a colonial rule that endured for a millennium (111 B.C.E.–939 C.E.) and spreading many Chinese cultural patterns into Vietnam. Although Chinese traders regularly visited many Southeast Asian states over the centuries, strong Chinese cultural and political influence was restricted to the Vietnamese. Elsewhere Indian influence was paramount in fostering a transition to a very different form of society. Around the beginning of the Common Era, Indian traders and brahman priests began regularly traveling the oceanic trade routes, bringing Indian concepts of religion, government, and the arts.

Indian Influence

The process by which Indian ideas spread into many Southeast Asian societies is often termed Indianization, a mixing of Indian with indigenous ideas. For a millennium, Southeast Asian peoples such as the Khmers in the Mekong Basin, the Chams along the central coast of Vietnam, and the Javanese (JAH-vuh-NEEZ) on the fertile island of Java were closely connected to the more populous and developed India. For example, Indian writing systems came to Southeast Asia and adapted to local spoken languages by 500 C.E.

Indian influence was particularly strong in religion and government. Mahayana Buddhism and Hinduism became important in Southeast Asia, especially among the upper classes. The imported religions fused with an indigenous animism that focused on communicating with spiritual forces to ensure bountiful harvests, address problems of daily life, and keep the cosmic order in balance. In politics, Southeast Asian rulers who were anxious to control increasing and diverse populations adopted the Indian concept of powerful kings who were supported by religious sanction, which made their positions difficult to challenge.

Southeast Asian Distinctiveness

Although centuries of borrowing and sometimes foreign conquest helped shape Southeast Asian cultures, Southeast Asians rarely became carbon copies of their mentors or conquerors. Like the Japanese and western Europeans, they took ideas that they wanted from outsiders and adapted them to their own use, creating a distinctive synthesis. For example, the Hindu and Buddhist architecture and temples of Burma, Cambodia, or Java differed substantially from the South Asian models, as well as from each other. The same diversity was true for the Indian heroes of Hindu epics, which Southeast Asian cultures shaped to their own liking.

Funan, Zhenla, and Champa

Funan

Productive agriculture, commerce, and Indianization helped foster most of the early mainland states. Funan (FOO-nan), founded by the first century C.E., flourished through the sixth century (ca. 75–550 C.E.). Funan was centered in the fertile Mekong Delta of what is today southern

Map 7.3
Funan and Its Neighbors

The first large mainland Southeast Asian states emerged during the Classical Era. The major states included Vietnam, which became a Chinese colony in the second century B.C.E., Funan, Zhenla, and Champa.

around the fifth century C.E. It played a major regional role until the eighth century C.E., when it succumbed to civil war. A fertile and strategic location, a vigorous and adaptive society, and a knack for political organization soon made the Khmer-speaking peoples who founded Funan and Zhenla the most influential society of mainland Southeast Asia.

Champa

But the Khmers had rivals. Dating from the second century C.E., the coastal Cham people of central Vietnam formed an Indianized state known as Champa (CHAM-pa). It was one of the oldest Indianized states and tried to control the increasingly dynamic coastal commerce between China and Southeast Asia. Like Funan, the Champa state did not have fixed territorial boundaries; rather, it was a fluctuating zone of influence. The kings excelled in pomp and circumstance but ruled uneasily over troublesome local chieftains. The Chams, who speak an Austronesian language, became renowned as sailors and merchants. Like many other maritime peoples, they sometimes resorted to piracy, and they frequently fought the Vietnamese, who continually pushed southward, forcing the Chams to shift their own settlements down the coast. Champa existed from 192 to 1471 C.E., when the Vietnamese finally conquered Champa and occupied its main city near modern Hue.

Vietnam. While the Khmer people who dominated the area for many centuries probably made up most of the population and the ruling group, some historians think Austronesians also lived and traded in Funan. The Funan people were in regular contact with the Chinese but also became Indianized. Their engineers built complex irrigation systems to turn swamps into productive agricultural land. Funan apparently extended some authority over much of

Interactive Map

what is today Cambodia and southern Thailand (see Map 7.3). With its access to major land and sea trade routes, it was part of large trading networks. Trade goods from as far as Rome, Arabia, Central Asia, and perhaps East Africa have been found in its ruins.

Zhenla

Another Khmer kingdom or grouping of city-states, Zhenla (CHEN-la), seems to have emerged inland in the Mekong River Basin

Vietnam and Chinese Colonization

During Chinese colonial times, Vietnamese society was largely confined to what is today the northern third of Vietnam. Vietnam developed a very different pattern than the Indianized kingdoms, because of the long period of Chinese colonial rule. China's final conquest and annexation of Vietnam, their southern neighbor, in 111 B.C.E. ended the independent evolution of one of the earliest Southeast Asian kingdoms. A relatively dense population already lived in the Red River Valley, where a Han dynasty census in 2 C.E. recorded a population of around 1 million.

Read about the rebel Vietnamese Trung Sisters and how they sparked rebellion throughout the country.

Chinese Assimilation Policies in Vietnam

Chinese policy was to assimilate the Vietnamese and implant Chinese values, customs, and institutions. Over the centuries, Chinese philosophies and religions like Confucianism, Daoism, and Mahayana Buddhism were adopted by most Vietnamese, and China's patriarchal family system, written language, and political ideas also sank deep roots into Vietnamese culture. Yet, while the Vietnamese adopted many of these Chinese patterns, they also sustained a hatred of Chinese rule and resisted cultural assimilation. The survival of the Vietnamese identity, language, and many customs during a millennium of colonialism constituted a display of national determination that was practically unparalleled in world history. Perhaps the Vietnamese were able to avoid cultural and national extinction because they already had several centuries of state building and cultural identity behind them when the Chinese colonized. Vietnamese desire for independence and collective identity reached through all social classes right down to the villages.

Vietnamese Resistance

Given these realities, the Chinese colonial period was punctuated by many revolts, all of them well remembered by the Vietnamese today as symbols of patriotism. The rebellions were sometimes led by women, the best known of whom are the Trung Sisters, who nearly forced out the Chinese before being defeated and committing suicide in 41 C.E. Rebel forces often fought for decades against hopeless odds. Chinese officials in the ninth century C.E. recommended harsh retaliation as the response to Vietnamese rebellion: "At every stream, cave, marketplace, everywhere there is stubbornness. Repression is necessary."[11] The Vietnamese qualities of patience, tenacity, and sense of a larger national community eventually generated a successful struggle for independence from the Chinese in the tenth century.

Economies, Societies, and Cultures

The social and cultural patterns established by these varied Southeast Asian societies between 100 and 600 C.E. established a framework for the centuries to come. Despite significant differences between societies like Champa, Funan, and Vietnam, many similarities existed throughout the region. For one, most of the larger Southeast Asian states were multiethnic in their population, including foreign merchants in temporary or permanent residence who were part of extended trade diasporas. Because many people in these states specialized in interregional commerce, the cities were frequently cosmopolitan.

Southeast Asian Prosperity

Many Southeast Asians lived well. Chinese envoys who visited Funan around 250 C.E. described walled cities, palaces, book-filled archives, and houses occupied by people who paid their taxes with gold, silver, perfumes, and pearls. Commerce was prevalent in most places, but rice agriculture was the basis for prosperity and survival. Funan's prominence resulted chiefly from its highly productive cultivation of the fertile land. Most Southeast Asians were farmers and fishermen living in self-sufficient villages and held together by ties of kinship and a communal spirit of cooperation.

Southeast Asian Social Order

The family system contrasted with those in China or India, where patrilineal and patriarchal systems prevailed. Although some Southeast Asians such as the Vietnamese followed a patriarchal pattern, others developed flexible systems incorporating both paternal and maternal kin. Some matrilineal systems also existed. The matrilineal Cham society was also matriarchal, and its women enjoyed considerable political influence. Both Cham men and women could have more than one spouse. In Southeast Asia, women generally enjoyed a higher status and played a more active public role than they did in China, India, the Middle East, and Europe.

Most Southeast Asians also blended diverse elements into a cultural unity. Animism was incorporated into or coexisted quite easily with Hinduism, Buddhism, Confucianism, and other imported religions. The result was a widespread tendency, as in East Asia, for religions to be inclusive and eclectic. This pattern of inclusion and blending, along with extensive trade, made Southeast Asian societies distinctive.

 Listen to a synopsis of Chapter 7.

{ Explore It Your Way! }

"What appeals to me is the fully virtual eBook with find/search feature which is absolutely irreplaceable and eternally helpful. I wish I had the eBook for when I was starting college."

William Manning, Student at Florida Atlantic University

We know that no two students read in quite the same way. Some of you do a lot of your reading online.

To help you take your reading **outside the covers** of **WORLD,** each new text comes with access to the exciting learning environment of an interactive eBook containing **tested online links to:**

- **Primary source documents**
- **Interactive maps**
- **Web links for further investigation**
- **Interactive quizzes**
- **Audio resources**
- **Historical simulation activities**
- **Profiles of key historical figures**

Access the eBook at 4ltrpress.cengage.com/world.

CHAPTER 8

Empires, Networks, and the Remaking of Europe, North Africa, and Western Asia,

500 B.C.E.–600 C.E.

Learning Outcomes

After reading this chapter, you should be able to answer the following questions:

LO¹ How did the Romans develop and maintain their large empire?

LO² What were some notable accomplishments of Roman life, and what factors contributed to Rome's decline?

LO³ How did Christianity develop and expand?

LO⁴ How did the Byzantine and Sassanian Empires reinvigorate the eastern Mediterranean world?

❝Remember, Roman, that it is for you to rule the nations. This shall be your task: to impose the ways of peace, to spare the vanquished and to tame the proud by war.❞

—Roman poet Virgil[1]

Around 320 B.C.E., Pytheas (PITH-ee-us), an adventurous scientist from the Greek colony of Massalia (ma-SAL-ya), today's city of Marseilles (mahr-SAY), on the Mediterranean coast of France, wrote a book about his remarkable travels in Europe. Some ten years earlier, Pytheas had reached the western coast of France, and from there he sailed on a boat owned by local Celtic (KELL-tik) people to southwest England. Pytheas continued north through the Irish Sea and may have reached Iceland. He then explored the North Sea coast as far as Denmark before retracing his journey home. Pytheas gave Mediterranean societies their first eyewitness account of the remote northern coast and its mysterious peoples, and his story tells us much about the western Eurasia of those times.

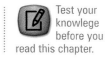 Test your knowlege before you read this chapter.

The people of the Mediterranean knew little of the lands and peoples north of the Alps and Balkans. However, the

What do you think?

The overextension of territory was a primary cause of the eventual fall of the Roman Empire.

Strongly Disagree						Strongly Agree
1	2	3	4	5	6	7

western Mediterranean was crisscrossed by trade networks: Greeks, Etruscans (ee-TRUHS-kuhns), Carthaginians (kar-thuh-JIN-ee-uhns), and the upstart Romans competed intensely for economic resources and political power. These societies were all part of an interdependent world incorporating southern Europe, North Africa, and western Asia, where commodities flowed and ideas were exchanged. Three hundred years after Pytheas's voyage, Europe was much more closely linked, thanks largely to the Romans, who in Pytheas's time were an ambitious but still minor power.

The Roman success in creating a large empire and rich society had a considerable impact on world history. As Rome flowered, diverse societies were changed in many ways, and networks were expanded. Roman expansion helped reshape much of Europe, marginalizing or incorporating the northern peoples while also

<< **Santa Sophia** The magnificent Santa Sophia Church in Constantinople, rebuilt during the reign of the emperor Justinian in the sixth century C.E., had interior walls covered in gold mosaics that glowed from reflected sunlight. This mosaic from the Zoe panel shows Jesus holding a Bible.

transforming North African and western Asian politics. When the Roman Empire finally ended after half a millennium, it left several legacies for later European, western Asian, and even African societies. The Romans passed on to later Europeans useful ideas on law and government, some of which derived from the Greeks. In addition, during Roman times, Christianity emerged to form the cultural underpinning of a new, post-Roman European society while also spreading in Asia and Africa.

A version of the Roman Empire, Greek-speaking Byzantium (buh-ZANT-ee-uhm), continued to exist in the eastern Mediterranean for a thousand years, a Christian society serving as an important center of transcontinental trade and a buffer between western Europe and the states of western Asia. The Romans and their successors had conflicts with societies in western Asia and North Africa, including a revived Persian Empire, which continued long after the Classical Age. These various struggles set the stage for the rise of another society, the Arabs.

LO¹ The Rise and Reign of Rome

By 300 B.C.E., the Mediterranean world was politically and culturally diverse. The Romans learned much from the older Etruscan society that they eventually absorbed, and they were influenced by Greek ideas in building their republic. The regional environment also played a part, as Roman political expansion was made possible by good access to the Mediterranean Sea. Eventually Rome conquered peoples in southern Europe and then beyond, establishing the framework of a huge empire. Athenians had pondered whether empire and democracy were compatible, and eventually they proved incompatible. Likewise, in Rome the rise of empire led to the decline and replacement of the Republic with a more autocratic and arrogant imperial system.

> "The Mediterranean climate was perfect for growing grapes and olives."

Regional Trade and Growing Roman Power

Geography and Climate

Geography and climate were influential in shaping Roman society. The rich agricultural Po Valley lies north of the Apennine mountain range, and smaller plains spread west from the Apennines to the Mediterranean. This topography directed the attention of the early settlers to the sea, where they took up maritime trade. In addition, Italy's geography, unlike the rocky hills of Greece, offered considerable fertile land suitable for intensive agriculture, especially along the west coast. The Mediterranean climate was perfect for growing grapes and olives, and as the Roman state grew, the Romans exported wine and olive oil while importing grain from the nearby islands of Sicily and Sardinia (sahr-DIN-ee-uh), and from northern Africa. The mild climate of Italy also encouraged frequent invasions through the Alps by the Indo-European Celtic and Germanic peoples living in western and northern Europe. As the Romans expanded beyond Italy, they drew upon the natural resources of the larger Mediterranean world (see Map 8.1) and beyond.

Interactive Map

CHRONOLOGY

The Roman Republic, 753–58 B.C.E.

753	Founding of Rome (traditional date)
ca. 616–509	Etruscan kings rule over Rome
509	Beginning of Roman Republic
265	Roman control of central and southern Italy
264–241	First Punic (Roman-Carthaginian) War
218–201	Second Punic War
149–146	Third Punic War
113–105	First German-Roman conflicts
60–58	Julius Caesar completes conquest from Rhine to Atlantic

Map 8.1
Italy and the Western Mediterranean, 600–200 B.C.E.

During the early Classical Era, the Etruscan cities in the north and the Greek city-states in the south held political power in Italy. Carthage held a similar status in northeast Africa. Eventually the Latins, from their base in Rome, became the dominant political force in the entire region.

patricians
The aristocratic upper class who controlled the Roman Senate.

Centuriate Assembly
A Roman legislative body made up of soldiers.

consuls
Two patrician men, elected by the Centuriate Assembly each year, who had executive power in the Roman Republic.

plebeians
The commoner class in Rome.

Etruscans

The Romans were greatly influenced by the Etruscans, who established the first urban society in the peninsula. A non-Indo-European people who may have originally come from western Asia, the Etruscans had founded a dozen or so city-states in central and northern Italy by the eighth century B.C.E. They were aggressive chariot warriors and sailors who traded with the western Mediterranean islands and Spain. Eventually Etruscans expanded their territory to include more of Italy as well as the nearby island of Corsica (KOR-si-kuh). They also had considerable contact with Greeks and Phoenicians, adopting a form of the Greek alphabet and Greek craft styles and myths. As more Greeks settled in Italy after 550 B.C.E., they had increased conflict with the Etruscans.

Although we do not know much about the Etruscans, their huge cemeteries with impressive, well-decorated tombs show that they were skilled artists and artisans. Their cities were well planned, ruled by individual kings, and were linked together by a good road system. The Etruscans' excellent iron axes, sickles, and tools were carried by merchants to every region. Their rigid social system included slavery, although Etruscan women apparently had a higher social status than women in most classical societies.

 Explore life in early Rome in this interactive simulation by choosing the path of either a senator in the Roman Republic or a soldier in the Roman Empire.

Roman Origins

Initially the relationship between the Romans and the Etruscans was peaceful, but it became contentious. Rome was established in the eighth century B.C.E. by a group of Indo-European pastoralists known as the Latins. Their city, Rome, built on seven hills along the Tiber (TIE-buhr) River, was originally founded as a base from which the early Romans could trade with the Etruscans. During the sixth century B.C.E., the Etruscans came to dominate Rome, and their influence was significant. The Romans adopted the twenty-six-character alphabet and the Etruscan phalanx infantry formation originally devised by the Greeks. Skilled Etruscan engineers taught the Romans to make the weight-bearing semicircular arch, which Romans used for building city walls, aqueducts to carry water, and doorways. But at the end of the sixth century B.C.E., the last Etruscan king was driven out for his brutality, and later the Romans conquered and assimilated the Etruscans.

Self-Governance and Expansion

The Roman Republic

The Romans borrowed many political ideas from the Greeks. As the Greeks did in Athens, the Romans built a system of self-government for their city-state. While doing so, however, they also began their territorial expansion. Again like Athens, Rome then faced the challenge of how to maintain its democratic aspirations while expanding an empire. After deposing the last Etruscan monarch, in 509 B.C.E., Romans established a republic—a state in which supreme power is held by the people or their elected representatives. Over the next three centuries, the Romans developed a system of representative government that introduced many enduring political ideas. Many modern English words taken from Latin—such as *senate, citizenship, suffrage* (the right to vote), *dictator* (a man given full power for a limited time, usually during a war), *plebiscite* (PLEB-ih-site), and even *republic*—reflect Roman influence.

Governmental Structure

The system changed over time. Initially, power rested entirely in the hands of the aristocratic upper class, or **patricians**. Patricians controlled the Senate—a small body that had previously advised the kings and later dominated foreign affairs—the army, and the legislative body made up of soldiers, known as the **Centuriate Assembly**. The Senate, composed of three hundred older men, all former government officials, claimed the right to ratify resolutions of the Centuriate Assembly before they became law. As the Republic developed, the Centuriate Assembly elected two men each year to serve as **consuls**, who had executive power. Consuls were assisted by other patrician officials, such as judges and budget directors.

 The Roman Empire (*http://www.roman-empire.net/*). Offers extensive materials and essays on the Romans.

The patricians were heavily outnumbered by the commoners, or **plebeians** (pli-BEE-uhnz), who were plagued by debts owed to the patricians. Wealth flowed into Rome as a result of military expansion in the peninsula and then beyond. As the soldiers who fought to make expansion possible, the plebeians wanted to share in this wealth. The long, hard-fought wars left many plebeians in debt, because long years of service in the army had taken them away from their farms, which were now in ruin. The plebeians therefore demanded a greater political voice, hoping that by gaining access to political power, they could secure economic equality.

Gradually social and political rights expanded. In 494 B.C.E., the plebeians selected two of their number, called tribunes, to represent their interests in the Centuriate Assembly. By 471 a separate Plebeian Assembly was established to elect tribunes and to conduct votes of the plebeian class, called plebiscites. In 451 the plebeians also demanded that the law code be carved on tablets and placed in the Forum, the public gathering place in Rome. In 367 B.C.E., plebeians also became eligible to serve as consuls, a major

> "Being a Roman citizen became a great honor entitling a person to special legal treatment."

tribunes
Roman men elected to represent plebeian interests in the Centuriate Assembly.

step that eventually led to their full acceptance into the political system. Full equality for plebeians was won by 267 B.C.E., when their assembly became the principal lawmaking body of the state.

Emerging Roman Imperialism

In the fourth century, the Roman Republic turned to imperialism, the control or domination by one state over another, as a way of resolving some of its problems. Roman political expansion began with a major defeat at the hands of the Gauls (gawlz), a Celtic people who plundered Rome in 390 B.C.E. Shocked by this defeat, Roman leaders decided to expand their territory to keep their frontiers safely distant from the city of Rome. During the rest of the fourth century, Romans successfully fought a series of wars with other Italian city-states. After victory,

The Roman Forum The Forum, located amidst various religious and governmental buildings, was the center of Roman political life.

they granted either full or limited Roman citizenship to the defeated peoples. Being a Roman citizen became a great honor entitling a person to special legal treatment. By treating former enemies fairly, the Romans spread their power without encouraging revolts and ensured that more men would enlist in their army. After securing their power in north and central Italy, the Romans then conquered the remaining Greek cities in southern Italy and Sicily. Across the Mediterranean, however, the Romans encountered their greatest enemy, the Carthaginians.

Carthage, Egypt, and the Punic Wars

Carthage

Both Carthage and Egypt played key roles in Mediterranean trade, and thus were destined to clash with Rome's emerging power. The city-state of Carthage was originally a Phoenician colony founded in 814 B.C.E. on the North African coast near where the city of Tunis is today. Egypt was ruled by the Hellenistic Greek Ptolemaic (taw-luh-MAY-ik) dynasty, which had fostered great prosperity for more than a century.

With a fine harbor and a strategic position, Carthage rapidly grew into the wealthiest and strongest Phoenician outpost. A Greek visitor reported that Carthage in the third century B.C.E. had "gardens and orchards of all kinds, no end of country houses built luxuriously, land cultivated partly as vineyards and partly as olive groves, fruit trees, herds of cattle and flocks of sheep."[2] However, differences between the Phoenician settlers, who owned most of the wealth, and the native Berbers created tensions, and the Carthaginians also fought frequent wars with their main commercial rivals, the Greeks.

 Livius: Articles on Ancient History (*http://www.livius.org*). Very useful site with many short essays on the Romans.

The Carthaginians were great sailors and used their maritime skills to develop trade and gradually create an empire along the southern and western shores of the Mediterranean Sea. Around 425 B.C.E., admiral Hanno (HAN-oh) led a naval expedition through the Strait of Gibraltar and down the coast of West Africa, establishing trading posts along the Morocco (muh-RAHK-oh) coast and sailing at least as far as the Senegal River. Other Carthaginian expeditions apparently reached the British Isles and perhaps Atlantic islands such as Madeira and the Canary Islands. By the third century B.C.E., they controlled a large part of Spain, much of the North African coast, and the islands of Corsica and Sardinia. In 264 B.C.E., they moved troops to Sicily to aid several Greek cities allied with them against Rome.

Ptolemaic Egypt

To the east there was Hellenistic Egypt. Although it had long flourished, the Ptolemaic hold on that country was becoming more tenuous by the second century B.C.E. The Ptolemies were hard-headed businessmen who worked to increase production by demanding more work from Egyptians. Egypt remained a major supplier of wheat and also exported papyrus, the preferred medium for texts throughout the region; textiles, including linen and woolen fabrics; and pottery and metal objects. Despite the economic growth, many Egyptians tired of foreign occupation, hardship, and high taxes, and several rebellions threatened the government. During this time, Egyptian rulers sought alliances with rising Rome in order to maintain their own independence. In 47 B.C.E., with Roman assistance, an ambitious eighteen-year-old woman became ruler as Queen Cleopatra VII, just as years of poor harvests and official corruption fostered more unrest. Her skills enabled the unstable state to maintain domestic peace and deflect Rome for nearly two decades.

The Punic Wars and Hannibal

In 264 B.C.E., the Romans began the first of three Punic Wars against their bitter trade rivals, the Carthaginians. The first Punic War (264–241 B.C.E.) resulted in several Roman naval expeditions against Carthage and finally ended with Roman occupation of Sicily, Corsica, and Sardinia. In the second of the wars (218–201 B.C.E.), the brilliant Carthaginian general Hannibal (HAN-uh-buhl) (247–182 B.C.E.) led his troops, and specially trained war elephants, through Spain and France to invade Italy across the Alps, defeating every Roman army sent against them. Hannibal's father had instilled in him an intense hatred of the Romans, and he used every tactic at his disposal to achieve victory, including drafting Celts from Spain and southern France into his army. But the elephants and Hannibal's troops were not used to the snow and ice of the mountains, and they perished by the thousands.

The arrival and early military success of Hannibal's still-formidable force alarmed the Romans. With his supply lines overstretched, however, Hannibal could not conquer the Italian cities. Eventually the Romans drove him out and defeated Carthage, which had to surrender all of its overseas possessions, including Spain. In the final Punic War (149–146 B.C.E.), Rome laid siege to the city of Carthage and destroyed it, spreading salt on the fields around the city to make it difficult to plant crops there in the future. Northwest Africa became a Roman province, a source of copper, grain, and West African gold.

Roman victory in the wars encouraged additional Roman imperial expansion in the Mediterranean region, aimed either at punishing Carthage's allies or at restoring stability. Rome went to war with Macedonia and ended Macedonian control of the Greek cities in 197 B.C.E. Few could resist the Roman infantrymen, who were armed with swords and rectangular shields, or the armor-clad Roman archers, who rode in carts carrying large crossbows, among the era's most feared weapons.

From Republic to Empire

Through these struggles, a Roman Empire was built that eventually commanded the entire Mediterranean and its vast resources, binding together Europe, western Asia, and North Africa. By the middle of the first century B.C.E., Roman power extended throughout the entire Mediterranean basin and beyond. The empire included most of Anatolia, Syria, and Palestine, as well as much territory in northern and western Europe. The Ptolemies still controlled Egypt, but the rulers were careful to do nothing to offend the Romans. The Romans absorbed much of the Hellenistic east, with its rich web of international commerce centered on several hubs, including Alexandria in Egypt, which distributed goods from as far away as India and East Africa.

Polarization of Roman Society

But imperial expansion provoked various crises that reshaped Roman politics and undermined the Republic, turning the representative institutions into window-dressing. Warfare gave excessive power to military leaders, weakening the influence of the Senate. In addition, growing Roman wealth increased the gap between rich and poor. As the empire expanded, upper-class families bought farmland from peasants who had become impoverished by long service in the army and the cheaper grain being imported from Sicily and North Africa. Many farmers moved to the city of Rome, where the government supported hundreds of thousands of displaced people to maintain their loyalty. Thus Roman society became polarized between the very rich and the desperately poor.

66 The Romans placed Egypt under a tighter grip than most of their colonies. 99

Militarization of the Republic

The changing nature of military power also undermined democracy. In 107 B.C.E., Gaius Marius (GAY-uhs MER-ee-uhs), who defeated Roman enemies in North Africa and southern France, was elected consul for five straight years, despite a law that prohibited a person from holding the office for more than one year. Marius set an undemocratic precedent for the future when he brought his military veterans to pressure the senators to vote for a law that gave the veterans public land. As a result, skillful military leaders thereafter used their armies to outmaneuver civilian leaders and the Senate. The result was a series of civil and foreign wars. Between 78 and 31 B.C.E., several ambitious military leaders used their power to expand Roman territory in Asia and Europe, while finally destroying republican institutions within Rome.

Julius Caesar

Julius Caesar proved to be the most ambitious of Rome's military leaders. During his years as Roman governor in Gaul (France), he completed the conquest of Europe from the Rhine River west to the Atlantic and sent the first Roman forces into Britain. These victories enhanced his influence. His power was further increased when he won a civil war against his former allies. In addition, Caesar weakened the Senate by enlarging it to nine hundred men, making it too large to be an effective governing body. Finally, in 44 B.C.E., he took charge of the state by having himself declared Perpetual Dictator. This act led to his assassination, made famous centuries later in the play *Julius Caesar* by the English author William Shakespeare.

Octavian, Mark Anthony, and Cleopatra

Caesar's death led to another civil war, the end of any pretence of democracy, and conquest of Egypt. Caesar's adopted son, Octavian (ok-TAY-vee-uhn), fought Mark Anthony, a general who had fallen in love with the Egyptian ruler Cleopatra. A remarkable personality who had borne a son by Julius Caesar, Cleopatra was described by the Greek historian Plutarch (PLOO-tark), who wrote that "her presence was irresistible; the

Pax Romana
("Roman Peace")
The period of peace and prosperity in Roman history from the reign of Augustus through that of Emperor Marcus Aurelius in 180 C.E.

attraction of her person, the charm of her conversation, was something bewitching. She could pass from one language to another."[3] The turmoil and the Republic itself ended when Octavian defeated Anthony and Cleopatra at the naval Battle of Actium (AK-tee-uhm), in Greece, in 31 B.C.E. Anthony and Cleopatra escaped to Egypt and eventually committed suicide. Soon their armies surrendered to Octavian, giving Rome control of Egypt. The Romans placed Egypt under a tighter grip than most of their colonies, passing laws to discourage Greek–Egyptian intermarriage, imposing heavy taxes, and encouraging more wheat production to feed the city of Rome.

"The Roman concept of law was influenced by the Greek Stoic belief in eternal truths that lay deeper in the human mind than the particular cultural practices found among many diverse societies."

Augustus and the *Pax Romana*

Rome and its empire were now ruled by emperors who controlled the military and much of the government bureaucracy. This trend was begun by Julius Caesar's nephew, Octavian (63 B.C.E.–14 C.E.), who called himself Augustus (aw-GUHS-this), a Latin term meaning "majestic, inspiring awe." Augustus became the empire's effective ruler in 31 B.C.E., and the Senate affirmed his exalted position in 27 B.C.E. During his long reign (r. 27 B.C.E.–14 C.E.), Augustus established a system in which the Senate appointed governors to the peaceful provinces, while he took charge of provinces where troops were stationed. Augustus gained the power to legally enact or veto legislation and to call the Senate into session. The writer Juvenal (JOO-vuhn-uhl) deplored the consequences of the lost popular voice: "The people that once bestowed commands now meddles no more and longs eagerly for just two things: bread and circuses."[4]

"The people that once bestowed commands now meddles no more and longs eagerly for just two things: bread and circuses."

Juvenal

The period in Roman history from the beginning of the reign of Augustus through that of Emperor Marcus Aurelius (aw-REE-lee-uhs) in 180 C.E. is known as the *Pax Romana* ("Roman Peace"). For the first and last time, the entire Mediterranean world was controlled by one power and remained at peace for two centuries (see Map 8.2). Whether in London or Paris, Vienna or Barcelona—all cities founded by the Romans—people lived under the same laws. Peace and prosperity encouraged trade and population growth. Trade flourished throughout the Mediterranean and along the Silk Road between Han China and Rome. Rome governed a huge population, which has been estimated at 54 million in the first century C.E., and its capital may have been the world's largest city, with a half million to 1 million inhabitants.

Interactive Map

In this diverse empire, the Roman ideal, like that of the Hellenistic Greeks, was cosmopolitan. Hence, Emperor Marcus Aurelius (r. 161–180 C.E.) wrote: "Rome is my city and country, but as a man, I am a citizen of the world."[5] Non-Romans were incorporated into the ruling class. By the second century C.E., half of the members of the Roman Senate were non-Italians from the provinces. Men of wealth and military skill, whatever their ethnic background, could rise to the highest levels in the army and civil administration. As the cosmopolitan trend continued, the empire slowly changed from a possession of the people of central Italy to a multinational state that fostered diversity within unity.

Map 8.2 >> The Roman Empire, ca. 120 C.E.

The Romans gradually expanded until, by 120 C.E., they controlled a huge empire stretching from Britain and Spain in the west through southern and central Europe and North Africa to Egypt, Anatolia, and the lands along the eastern Mediterranean coast.

© Cengage Learning

Legend

- Roman Empire by death of Augustus, 14 C.E.
- Territory added by death of Hadrian, 138 C.E.
- Territory gained and lost, with dates held
- Parthian Empire, ca. 200 C.E.
- ★ Major battle

N

ATLANTIC OCEAN

North Sea

Baltic Sea

Aral Sea

Caspian Sea

Black Sea

Mediterranean Sea

Adriatic Sea

Red Sea

Persian Gulf

ARABIAN DESERT

SAHARA

CAUCASUS MTS.

ALPS

Rivers: Volga R., Don R., Dnieper R., Dniester R., Vistula R., Elbe R., Danube R., Rhine R., Rhône R., Po R., Ebro R., Nile R., Euphrates R., Tigris R.

Regions and places:

CALEDONIA (85–105 C.E.)
Hadrian's Wall 122 C.E.
Eburacum (York)
BRITAIN
Camulodunum (Colchester)
Londinium (London)

GERMANIA (4–9 C.E.)
LOWER GERMANY
Colonia Claudia Agrippinensis
Moguntiacum (Mainz)
UPPER GERMANY
BELGICA
Alesia 52 B.C.E.
GAUL
LUGDUNENSIS
Lutetia Parisiorum (Paris)
Lugdunum (Lyons)
AQUITANIA
NARBONENSIS
Nemausus (Nîmes)
Narbo
Massilia (Marseilles)
Burdigala (Bordeaux)
Saguntum
TARRACONENSIS
Tarraco
SPAIN
LUSITANIA
Emerita Augusta (Mérida)
Corduba (Córdoba)
BAETICA
Balearic Is.

RAETIA
NORICUM
PANNONIA
Vindobona (Vienna)
Aquincum (Budapest)
DACIA (107–272 C.E.)
Singidunum (Belgrade)
DALMATIA
MOESIA
CISALPINE GAUL
Mediolanum (Milan)
ETRURIA
Arretium
ITALY
Ostia
Rome
Pompeii
Mt. Vesuvius
Brundisium
THRACE
Byzantium
MACEDONIA
EPIRUS
Thessalonica
Actium 31 B.C.E.
Corinth
ACHAEA
Athens
Crete
Sicily
Syracuse
Malta
Sardinia
Corsica

Carthage
AFRICA PROCONSULARIS
NUMIDIA
MAURETANIA
NORTH AFRICA
Leptis Magna
Cyrene
CYRENAICA

BITHYNIA AND PONTUS
GALATIA
CAPPADOCIA
ASIA ANATOLIA
Pergamum
Ephesus
PAMPHYLIA
LYCIA
CILICIA
Tarsus
Rhodes
Cyprus
Antioch
SYRIA
Damascus
Palmyra
JUDAEA
Jerusalem
Petra
ARABIA
EGYPT
Alexandria
Bahriya Oasis

ARMENIA (114–117 C.E.)
ASSYRIA (116–117 C.E.)
MESOPOTAMIA (115–117 C.E.)
Seleucia
Ctesiphon
Babylon
Susa
Ecbatana
PARTHIA
Nisa
Persepolis

BOSPORAN KINGDOM

Scale: 0 200 400 Km.
0 200 400 Mi.

LO² Roman Life, Rivals, and Decline

The Roman Empire lasted in the west for about five hundred years and in the east for many more centuries. This period of imperial rule saw the full development of Roman culture and of those elements of the Roman heritage, such as law, that formed a significant legacy to European society. Its decline began when a long period of internal and external disorder challenged the *Pax Romana*. The decline of Rome corresponded to the rise of northern European societies, the Celts and Germans, which pressured Roman borders. But the crises in succession to the imperial throne and social and health problems also sapped the Roman Empire from within, eventually leading to the empire's division.

Citizenship, Religion, and Society

Roman society owed much to other Mediterranean peoples, drawing, for example, on the Greeks' political, ethical, and metaphysical philosophies. But the Romans also made something distinctive from this Greek legacy by developing a more pragmatic way of looking at the world. In particular, the Romans extended the meaning of some of the classic Greek ideas, such as citizenship, and developed a concept of civic virtue. The Romans also developed a legal system and a polytheistic religion.

Roman Legal System Codified laws underpinned the Roman system and encouraged public responsibility. Several principles of Roman law have survived the centuries to become an accepted part of the laws of most modern nations and modern international law. For example, the Romans believed that all people, regardless of wealth or position, were equal before the law. They also developed the idea of crimes against the state, what we today call treason. Perhaps most important, the Romans promoted individual responsibility; a person's family could not be held responsible for one individual's misdeeds. Roman jurists also said that the burden of proof in a trial should rest with the person making the charge, and not with the defendant.

The Roman concept of law was influenced by the Greek Stoic belief in eternal truths that lay deeper in the human mind than the particular cultural practices found among many diverse societies. Leading Roman Stoics included the philosopher Seneca (SEN-i-kuh) (4 B.C.E.–65 C.E.), the great Roman lawyer and

CHRONOLOGY

The Roman Empire and Its Successors, 60 B.C.E.–526 C.E.

60–44 B.C.E.	Julius Caesar rises to dominance in Roman politics
31 B.C.E.–14 C.E.	Reign of Octavian (Caesar Augustus)
31 B.C.E.–180 C.E.	*Pax Romana*
6–7 B.C.E.–30 C.E.	Jesus's life and preaching in Palestine
64 C.E.	Death of Peter (first bishop of Rome) and of Paul of Tarsus
66–73 C.E.	Jewish revolt against Rome
251 C.E.	Germans defeat Roman armies and sack Balkans
306–337 C.E.	Reign of Constantine
313 C.E.	Legalization of Christianity
325 C.E.	Council of Nicaea
354–430 C.E.	St. Augustine of Hippo
391 C.E.	Paganism banned by Emperor Theodosius I
395 C.E.	Final division of eastern and western empires
410 C.E.	Alaric and Ostrogoths sack Rome
451–452 C.E.	Huns invade western Europe
455 C.E.	Vandals sack Rome
476 C.E.	Official end of western Roman Empire
481–511 C.E.	Clovis and Franks conquer Gaul
493–526 C.E.	Ostrogoths rule Italy

essayist Cicero (SIS-uh-roh) (106–43 B.C.E.), and the second-century emperor Marcus Aurelius (uh-REAL-yus), famous for his humanity and justice. Stoics promoted tolerance, moderation, and acceptance of life's travails. Because of such beliefs, the Romans generally allowed conquered cities and provinces to govern themselves.

Roman Religion

Roman religion comprised a pantheon of gods and goddesses, who were worshiped for practical reasons. Proper sacrifices, rituals, and prayers were crucial to ensure good fortune and to keep the gods and various spirits happy. As their control of the Mediterranean world increased, the Romans did not wish to offend any divinity who might help them. Hence, they adopted the gods and goddesses of other peoples. This was especially true of the Greek deities, which the Romans equated with their own gods. For example, the Greek leader of the gods, Zeus, became the Roman Jupiter; Zeus's wife Hera became the Roman Juno; and the Greek god of wine, Dionysus, became the Roman Bacchus (BAK-uhs). Roman religion was an integral part of civic life. Priests were part-time, unpaid state officials who performed public sacrifices to please the gods and promote the welfare of the state.

Imperial Society

Throughout all the political changes of the Roman Empire, Roman society remained stratified into sharply defined upper and lower classes (see Witness to the Past: The Voices of Common Romans). Below the upper classes were middle-class merchants and artisans. They ranked above the city-dwellers and peasants, who were the backbone of the Roman armies during the Republic. As in Greece, slaves occupied the bottom of the social ladder. By the first century B.C.E., one in every three persons in Italy was a slave. Most slaves were captured in the many wars, but some people were enslaved as payment for debt or as the result of a legal conviction for crime. Most of the gladiators who fought in the arenas to entertain the public were slaves. The Romans were generous in freeing slaves after years of good service, and they could then become Roman citizens.

Ara Pacis The Altar of Peace, commissioned by Caesar Augustus in 9 B.C.E., resided in a large enclosure, whose walls contain relief sculptures. This scene depicts Mother Earth and her children, with the cow and sheep at her feet representing the prosperity resulting from peace.

Scala/Art Resource, NY

The Voices of Common Romans

As with most premodern societies, we know much more from the surviving records and literature about the prominent and wealthy Romans than about the common people who constituted most of the population. But we can learn something about the middle and lower classes from the graffiti preserved in the ruins of ancient cities like Pompeii and the epitaphs on tombstones. Romans used graffiti and epitaphs to voice frank opinions on many matters and to summarize their lives. Like modern graffiti, some of the remarks address sexual activities and bodily functions or insult rivals with profanity. The following are some examples of less profane but often humorous graffiti and epitaphs from various Roman cities.

Graffiti

I'm amazed, O wall, that you've not collapsed under the weight of so much written filth.

A bronze urn has disappeared from my tavern. Whoever returns it will get 65 sesterces reward. Whoever informs on the thief will get 20 sesterces, if we recover it.

Perarius, you're a thief.

No loiterers—scram!

Livia, to Alexander: "If you're well, I don't much care; if you're dead, I'm delighted."

Samius Cornelius, go hang yourself!

Stronnius is an ignoramus.

Crescens is a public whore.

Whoever doesn't invite me to dinner is a barbarian.

Whoever is in love, may he prosper. Whoever loves not, may he die. Whoever forbids love, may he die twice over!

Marcus loves Spendusa.

If you haven't seen the Venus that Apelles painted, take a look at my girl—she's just as beautiful.

Thraex makes the girls sigh.

All the goldsmiths support Gaius Cuspious Pansa for public works commissioner.

The mule-drivers support Gaius Julius Polybius for mayor. Genialis supports Bruttius Balbus for mayor. He'll balance the budget.

I ask you to support Marcus Cerrinus Vatia for public works commissioner. All the late-night drunks back him.

Epitaphs

If you wish to add your sorrow to ours, come here and shed your tears. A sad parent has laid to rest his only daughter, whom he treasured with sweet love as long as the Fates permitted. Now her dear face and form are mere shadow and her bones mere ash.

For my dearest wife, with whom I lived two years, six months, three days, and ten hours. On the day she died, I gave thanks before gods and men.

I was once famous, preeminent among thousands of strong Bavarian men. I swam across the Danube in full armor. I once shot an arrow in the air and split it with a second in midair. No Roman or barbarian ever beat me with a spear, no Parthian with the bow. This tombstone preserves the story of my deeds. But I am still unique, the first to do such things as these.

Thinking About the Reading

1. What do these graffiti tell us about political life?

2. What do the graffiti and epitaphs reveal about what common people valued?

3. In what ways do the sentiments seem familiar to modern readers?

Source: *Lives and Times, A World History Reader, Volume I* 1st edition by HOLOKA/UPSHUR. © 1985 Wadsworth, a part of Cengage Learning, Inc. Reproduced with permission. www.cengage.com/permissions.

Like most classical societies, the Romans were patriarchal. Only men had a political voice, and they enjoyed extensive power over women, children, and slaves. Yet women held some legal rights. Although they had no recourse if their husbands committed adultery, early Roman laws did give an adult woman possession of her own property, even if she was married. Another law said a wife could sue her husband if he abandoned her. In addition, Roman women had more freedom to leave their homes and travel through the city than did their Greek sisters. Also giving them some freedom, abortion and contraception were common until they were outlawed around 200 C.E.

The Economy, Technology, and the Arts

Roman society flourished from expanding trade and industry. The Romans had industries, such as mining and pottery making, that produced wealth. But because the industrial workforce consisted mostly of slaves, the Romans had little incentive to produce labor-saving technologies. In addition, those who acquired wealth beyond that needed for public display invested it in land, the most prestigious form of investment, rather than in business or industry.

Roman Trade Networks

During the *Pax Romana*, many public works projects were completed, including the Roman road system. The Romans built more than 150,000 miles of roads, most of them 4 feet thick. The phrase "all roads lead to Rome" reflects these accomplishments, as well as the fact that Rome became a communications center for a large area of Afro-Eurasia. The roads allowed for the movement of armies, commercial traffic, and official mail. The Roman trade network became elaborate by the end of the Republic, and maritime trade provided a crucial foundation. Land and sea trade routes linked the Roman Empire to peoples in East Asia and sub-Saharan Africa. Roman merchants may also have sailed the Indian Ocean, and Roman coins have been found in the ruins of Funan, in what is now southern Vietnam. The longest land network, the Silk Road across Central and western Asia, allowed Chinese products to reach Rome. Romans shipped much gold and silver east in return for spices, jewelry, cut gems, glassware, and silk. Eventually the Roman economy was harmed by the expanding Roman appetite for Chinese goods.

Roman Literary Achievement

As in the realm of public works and trade, the achievements of Roman literary culture during the late republic and early empire were considerable. Virgil (70–19 B.C.E.) was Rome's greatest epic poet. His *Aeneid* (i-NEE-id) described the journey of the legendary Trojan hero Aeneas (i-NEE-uhs), who, according to the poem, left Troy and eventually founded the city of Rome. This Roman counterpart to the Greek *Iliad* and *Odyssey* was designed to promote Roman greatness and honor the ruler of Virgil's day, Augustus Caesar. Historians also made substantial contributions to Roman literature. For example, Tacitus (56–117 C.E.) wrote a history of the early emperors in which he lamented the end of the Republic's more open political atmosphere.

Roman Engineering

The Romans' quest to provide public services fostered creativity in other areas, including notable architecture. The Pantheon (PAN-thee-ahn), or temple to all the gods in Rome, provides testament to the Roman reputation for engineering. The great dome of this building has no interior-supporting pillars and forms a perfect sphere, as high as it is wide. Roman buildings were designed to impress. The famous Colosseum in Rome, for example, was the world's largest outdoor arena until the twentieth century. Aqueducts carried water hundreds of miles from the mountains of Italy and Spain into the Roman cities. In the capital, each person enjoyed an abundance of fresh water, encouraging the development of public baths as social centers.

The Decline of the Western Roman Empire

Imperial Incompetancy

The chief political problem causing the decline of the Roman Empire was succession. In 211, the dying Emperor Septimius Severus (suh-VIR-uhs), a former general, advised his successor to enrich the soldiers and ignore everyone else. The reliance on the army to decide who ruled resulted in twelve soldier-emperors between 235 and 260 C.E., none of whom died peacefully in old age. Temporary political stability was restored only at the end of the third century.

Economic Exhaustion

Other problems were economic. The Romans spent more and more of their wealth to support a growing bureaucracy and the military, pushing the state toward bankruptcy. At the same time, subjects in the western half of the Roman Empire struggled to pay their taxes. The Roman economy was stronger in the east, where the older, larger cities provided employment and a stronger tax base for the government. A serious "balance of payment" problem developed between the west and the east. The early third century was a turning point. At that time, Roman rulers were forced to end further conquests and merely defend the existing frontiers. In so doing, however, they cut themselves off from the income that conquest provided, thus further impoverishing the government. To make matters worse, some gold and silver mines in the western lands became exhausted, as did some of the fertile soil in Italy. Romans also suffered a steadily widening gap between rich and poor, a serious trade deficit with China, dropping levels of literacy, and growing corruption, apathy, and loss of public spirit.

Climate and Disease

Climate change and recurring epidemics brought additional challenges. A cooler climate may have diminished crop yields. Because of contacts with distant lands, Rome was also increasingly vulnerable to the spread of diseases. Epidemics that killed many thousands erupted from time to time. A plague in the empire from 251 to 266 C.E., which reached Europe from North Africa, caused dramatic population decline and weakened Roman military forces. At the height of the epidemic, five thousand people were said to have died each day just in the city of Rome.

The Rise of Celtic and German Societies

Celtic Culture

The Celtic (KELL-tik) and German peoples who occupied a large area of Europe posed a challenge to the expanding Romans. The Celtic culture had developed by the twelfth cen-

Roman Army Camp This carving shows a camp being built by Roman legionnaires during a military campaign. Some men build walls and dig ditches.

Alinari/Art Resource, NY

tury B.C.E. in the upper Danube River Basin north of the Alps. Early Celtic farmers used bronze and, around 750 B.C.E., adopted iron. Aided by these technologies, by 500 B.C.E. they had occupied large sections of central and western Europe, from Germany and France to southern Britain and Spain. Celtic migration continued westward into the British Isles and southeast into the Balkans. Fierce warriors and fine horsemen, Celtic warriors terrified their opponents. A Roman writer describing the Celtic armies in Gaul said that the many trumpeters and their war cries presented a very frightening scene.

Celtic society was hierarchical. Powerful chiefs ruled small states, and priests, known as *druids* (DROO-ids), organized the worship of the many gods. Many Celts lived in large fortified towns, and some had coins and writing. However, Celtic tribal rivalries caused much strife and contributed to Roman conquest. The well-drilled, disciplined Roman legions easily overwhelmed the Celtic fighters, despite their alarming war shrieks. In 225 B.C.E., the Romans overran the Celts in northern Italy. First the Carthaginians and then the Romans crushed Celtic power in Spain. By 100 B.C.E., the Celts were caught in a vise between northward-expanding Rome and westward-expanding Germans.

Boudica: Warrior-Queen

In 60–61 C.E., the Romans faced a temporary setback when Celts, led by a warrior-queen, Boudica (boo-DIK-uh) (d. 61 C.E.), destroyed several Roman settlements in England. Boudica had good reason to despise the Romans, who had pillaged her territory, flogged Boudica, and raped her daughters. According to legends, Boudica's forces killed some 70,000 Romans. A Roman historian lamented the defeat brought by a woman, which caused the Romans great shame. In retaliation, the Romans sent in a larger force, killing 80,000 of Boudica's subjects. The queen committed suicide rather than surrender to the Romans, but in most of mainland Europe and England, Celtic culture was gradually Latinized and Germanized. Celtic societies remained strong mostly in Ireland, the rugged hills of Wales, and the Scottish highlands, where harsh weather, rugged mountains, and the challenge of overcoming long lines of communication kept the Romans from extending their rule. The Roman emperor Hadrian (HAY-dree-uhn) had a remarkable 73-mile-long rock wall built across northern England to keep Celtic tribes out of Roman territory.

> **According to legends, Boudica's forces killed some 70,000 Romans.**

Germanic Resistance

The Germanic peoples posed another challenge to Roman rulers, pressuring the empire's northern borders and eventually migrating into the empire. Organized German societies speaking closely related languages seem to have originated in Scandinavia and the northern plains of Germany sometime during the first millennium B.C.E. No known German cities or states existed, as these societies were highly mobile. In military conflicts beginning in 113 B.C.E., Germans inflicted several defeats on Roman legions in Gaul. Although the Romans reorganized and crushed the Germans, fear of Germanic invasions was a major reason the Romans expanded northward. As a result, some Germans were brought into the Roman fold, but they were prone to rebellion and were largely viewed as dangerous "barbarians."

Unlike the Celts, the Germans successfully resisted the Romans, and for the next several centuries, conflicts intensified on the fringes of the empire. Contacts with Rome led to political change among the Germans between 10 and 300 C.E. Tribes joined to form confederations, whose combined strength made them a greater threat. Pushed by their own enemies such as the westward-moving Huns from Central Asia, many Germanic peoples began looking to the fertile Roman lands for new homes. This migration could not have happened at a worse time for Rome, whose empire and population were declining. In 251 C.E., a group of Germans defeated a Roman army and plundered the Balkans. But the Romans were unable to field enough high-quality soldiers to defeat the invaders because their shrinking population meant that men needed to farm could not be spared for the army.

The Division of the Roman Empire

Roman Roots of Feudalism

German expansion had a major impact on Roman society. The high taxes that were needed to support the Roman armies alienated all classes, but they fell primarily on the poor. Sometimes whole villages placed themselves under the protection of a wealthy landlord, who would then pay their taxes for them in return for agricultural labor. This system, in which men and women worked the land of their patrons, eventually reshaped the peasant class, as they gave

Life on a Late Roman Empire Estate The painting, of a fortified manor house and its surroundings, shows typical farming activity for each season.

up their freedom in exchange for protection. The upper classes also increasingly abandoned the government and cities, creating new private lives for themselves on their country estates. Roman cities slowly but steadily shrank in size.

Eastern and Western Empires

Mounting problems led to the division of the empire. At the end of the third century, Emperor Diocletian (DIE-uh-KLEE-shuhn) (r. 285–305) tried to stop the empire's evident decline by dividing it in half. He ruled the east from Nicomedia (NIK-uh-MEED-ee-uh) in Anatolia and appointed another man, Maximian, as emperor of lands west of the Adriatic Sea. A later emperor, Constantine (r. 306–337), temporarily reunited the empire under one ruler and established a new eastern capital on the Straits of Bosporus (BAHS-puhr-uhs). His new city, Constantinople (cahn-stan-tih-NO-pul)—today's Istanbul (IS-tahn-BUL)—in 395 became the capital of the eastern, or Byzantine (BIZ-uhn-teen) Empire, which survived the western Roman Empire by nearly one thousand years.

Goths, Huns, and Vandals

The worst military defeats suffered by Roman armies occurred in the fourth and fifth centuries C.E.. In 410 the Germanic Ostrogoths (AHS-truh-GAHTHS) (eastern Goths), led by their king, Alaric (AL-uh-rik) (370–410), plundered the city of Rome. Around 410 a branch of the Huns, fierce horse-riding Central Asian pastoralists who had occupied southern Russia, formed an empire in Hungary. They conquered some Germans and pushed others west into Gaul, Italy, and Spain. Led by the able warrior Attila (uh-TIL-uh) (406–453), the Huns ravaged the Balkans and Greece before plundering northern Italy in 452. After Attila's death in 453, Hun power collapsed, but Rome was again sacked by another German group, the Vandals (VAN-duhlz), in 455 C.E. The official end of the western empire came in 476, when Germans deposed the last Roman emperor.

Post-Imperial Europe

Various Germanic kingdoms, including the Vandals in Northwest Africa, the Visigoths (VIZ-uh-gahths) in Spain, and the Ostrogoths in Italy, now ruled the western Mediterranean world. Another German group, the Franks, under their leader Clovis, conquered what is now France and western Germany. Meanwhile, Germanic Angles and Saxons migrated into England. These Germanic peoples retained a considerable amount of Roman culture; moreover, some adopted local versions of Latin, which formed the basis for Romance languages such as French, Italian, and Spanish.

LO³ Christianity: From Local Sect to Transregional Religion

The one institution that was a vigorous part of the life of the Roman cities even in the final decades of the western empire was the Christian church. Christianity arose in Palestine in the first century C.E. as a Jewish sect (see Map 8.3). The religious and social

Interactive Map

institutions of Christianity accompanied Greco-Roman culture into the new Germanic kingdoms, and together they defined the culture that dominated Europe in the centuries following the Classical Age. The rise and values of Christianity are essential to understanding the history of these societies.

Roman Palestine and Jesus of Nazareth

Jesus of Nazareth

Christianity was founded on the teachings of Jesus of Nazareth, a Jewish teacher in first-century C.E. Roman-ruled Palestine. Palestine was one of the most restless Roman provinces and had a history of rebellion against Rome; it contained a mix of several traditions. Various ideas from Egyptian, Mesopotamian, Phoenician, Persian, and Greek traditions undoubtedly influenced the Jewish and then Christian faiths. According to Christian tradition, Jesus was a Jewish teacher and healer, a carpenter by trade, who probably lived from around 7 or 6 B.C.E. to 30 C.E. and inherited the prophetic tradition of the Jewish faith. As with Buddha and Confucius, our knowledge of Jesus and his career comes from the writings of followers, primarily through the four gospel accounts of the Christian New Testament.

The earliest of these narratives, the Gospel of Mark, was written around 70 C.E., some forty years after the death of Jesus. The gospels were written not as historical accounts but as faith statements; modern theologians and historians vigorously debate their accuracy since all were written several generations after the events described. Indeed, several dozen other gospels or fragments of gospels were not included in the Christian Bible, and some of them differ considerably from the official gospels.

From Jesus to Christ: The First Christians (*http://www.pbs.org/ wgbh/pages/frontline/ shows/religion*). Valuable essays linked to a documentary series on U.S. Public Broadcasting.

Romance languages

Languages that derive from Latin, such as French, Italian, and Spanish.

Teachings of Jesus

The gospels describe Jesus as, among other things, a moral reformer who confronted the Jewish leaders. Jesus favored a simple life that included love of others, forgiveness of enemies, acceptance of the poor and other despised groups, and opposition to excessive legalism and ceremony. According to the Gospel of Matthew, Jesus summed up his teachings in two commandments: "Love God with all your heart, soul, and mind; and love your neighbor as yourself."[6] Matthew also reported that Jesus angered influential Jews and Romans by advising the wealthy to give their money to the poor since, according to gospel accounts, he said that rich people were unwelcome in God's kingdom.

Death of Jesus

Jesus's enemies, especially the Roman governor but also a few Jewish religious leaders, accused him of treason against Rome, and Jesus was tried, convicted, and executed by crucifixion. After his death, followers of Jesus claimed that he was resurrected from death. Although historians cannot verify such a faith claim, this belief probably motivated his followers to stay together, preach his message to others, and honor his teachings by worshiping as a special sect within the first-century C.E. Jewish community.

Paul and the Shaping of Christianity

Paul of Tarsus The evolution of the religion of Jesus into Christianity was greatly affected by the works of Paul of Tarsus (TAHR-suhs), a port city in southeast Anatolia. Paul was a first-century Romanized Jew who said that he was miraculously converted to belief in Jesus as a young man, probably around 33 C.E. He then spent the rest of his life spreading this faith to non-Jews, traveling extensively from Palestine to western Asian and Greek cities before his death in a prison in Rome about 64 C.E.

Pauline Christianity Paul's teaching emphasized two things. First, he stressed that Jesus was a divine being, the "son of God" who earned forgiveness for the sins of humankind by his death on the cross. By accepting Jesus as the Christ ("anointed one"), Paul taught, a person could be saved from damnation. Second, Paul preached that a non-Jew who did not follow Jewish laws and ritual could become a follower of Jesus. By arguing for spiritual equality among followers, he was challenging fundamental Roman assumptions, such as those behind slavery. Paul's

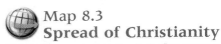

Map 8.3
Spread of Christianity

Christianity arose in Palestine in the first century C.E., and gradually gained footholds in parts of Western Asia, North Africa, and southern Europe by 300 C.E. Over the next five centuries, Christianity became the dominant religion in much of western and central Europe, and expanded its influence in western Asia and North Africa.

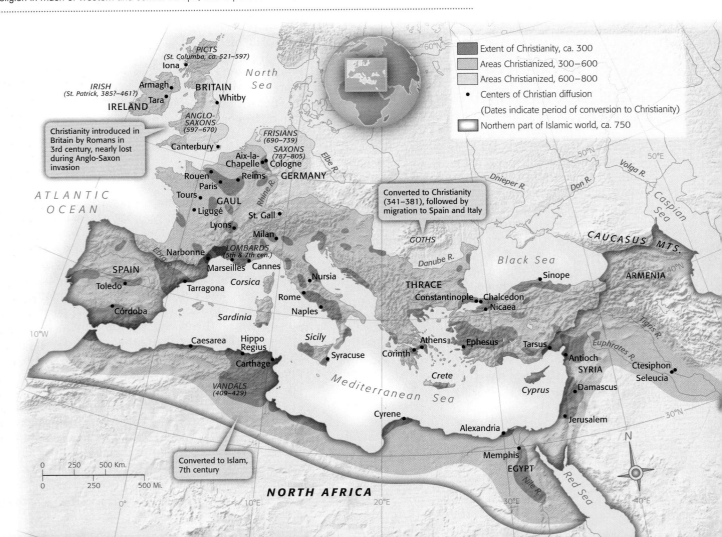

patriarchal views also strongly influenced Christian thinking. He urged wives to be subject to their husbands and remain silent in church.

Christian Differentiation and Jewish Rebellion

Paul disagreed strongly with those in Jerusalem who believed that Christians had to follow Jewish laws, thus creating something of a rift with the "Judaizers" (JOOD-uh-ize-uhrz) led by Peter, the chief disciple of Jesus who became the first bishop of Rome (and hence the first pope). Peter was probably killed in Rome during the persecution of Christians in 64. Eventually, most Christians believed they were saved by faith in Jesus, not by following any Jewish tradition. The victory of Paul in convincing Peter to include non-Jews was crucial in establishing Christianity as a world religion (see Map 8.3). A Jewish revolt from 66 to 73 C.E. resulted in the Roman destruction of the Jewish temple in Jerusalem and the dispersion of many Jews to other lands. After the Roman suppression, any Jew became discredited in Roman eyes, so it was fortunate for the early Christians that they had broken with Judaism. Meanwhile, while Jews scattered across Eurasia and North Africa, the number of non-Jewish Christians continued to grow throughout the empire as the religion spread along the networks of trade and occupation throughout western Asia, North Africa, and southern Europe.

Christianity in the Mediterranean Zone

Roman Christianity

The Roman context shaped Christian growth and institutions. The spread of this new religion was aided by its similarity to "mystery religions," many from western Asia, that were becoming popular in the Roman world at the same time. Christians believed in a life after death, a belief that became increasingly attractive as conditions in the Roman Empire worsened over the next several centuries, and in the spiritual equality of all people. In 313 C.E., Christianity became a legal religion by an edict of the Roman emperor Constantine, who

> "Christians believed in a life after death, a belief that became increasingly attractive as conditions in the Roman Empire worsened over the next several centuries."

believed he had won a battle because of the help of the Christian God. After this the organized church became more significant, although in the early centuries the bishop of Rome exercised limited authority over the wider church. By 400 C.E., paganism had been banned and Christianity had become the official Roman religion, thus uniting state and church in a troubled marriage for more than a millennium.

Resolving Doctrinal Differences

But Christians also had to contend with theological divisions. To combat what most Christians saw as heresies and to establish core beliefs, the emperor Constantine called a church council at Nicaea (nye-SEE-uh), in Anatolia, in 325 C.E., where he virtually ordered the bishops to resolve their doctrinal differences and determine which beliefs to follow. The Nicene (NYE-seen) Creed they produced became the official doctrine of the early church and is still recited in many denominations.

The early Christians did not live in a world of their own making but borrowed much Greco-Roman culture. They did not see themselves as enemies of the Roman Empire. Their only difference with the state was to refuse to acknowledge the emperor's official divine status, for which they sometimes were persecuted. Nevertheless, as the Christian religion spread, most Christians were left alone to worship as they wished, and they, in turn, acquired a Roman education and even celebrated traditional Roman festivals along with the new Christian ones. The Christians' celebration of the unknown birthday of Jesus on the date of the old Roman festival of the winter solstice is one example of how classical and Christian culture merged. Early Christians also generally adopted the Greco-Roman tolerance toward homosexuality, even

Nicene Creed
A set of beliefs, prepared by the council at Nicaea in 325 C.E., that became the official doctrine of the early Christian church.

The Capitulary on Saxony and a Letter to Pope Leo III Discover what punishments Charles established for worshiping at pagan shrines, and for other crimes committed in newly conquered Saxony.

within their own churches. Of course, there were also tensions between Christians and non-Christians, such as those that led to the murder of the philosopher Hypatia (hye-PAY-shuh) by Christian mobs in Alexandria around 416 C.E. In general, however, Christians adapted successfully to Roman life and institutions.

Christian Monasticism

By the early fifth century, the political and social leaders in most Roman cities were Christian, but some Christian leaders began to be troubled by their social and political success. After all, followers of Jesus were supposed to focus on spiritual instead of worldly success, and they claimed that their moral code differed from that of their pagan predecessors. One result of this questioning was monasticism, the pursuit of a life of penance, prayer, and meditation, either alone or in a community of other seekers. For early Christians this often meant leaving the cities. For instance, Benedict of Nursia (ca. 480–ca. 543) became so disillusioned by the hedonistic life in Rome that he moved into a cave and later founded western Europe's first monastic order, the Benedictines (ben-uh-DIK-teenz).

Augustine of Hippo

As Christianity expanded during the first centuries of the Common Era, it developed church institutions and produced thinkers who shaped the theology. A major Christian thinker, the North African bishop Augustine of Hippo (354–430 C.E.), defined Christian morality and history in a form that dominated western European culture for one thousand years. Born in North Africa, Augustine was a seeker after truth who had tried several faiths before becoming a convinced Christian. He became a priest and then, in 395, bishop of Hippo, a city near Carthage that had followers of many faiths, including various pagan and Persian traditions. After the sack of Rome by the Ostrogoths in 410, Augustine became troubled by pagan accusations that Christianity caused Roman society to wither. He felt compelled to defend his faith.

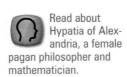 Read about Hypatia of Alexandria, a female pagan philosopher and mathematician.

In his book, *City of God*, completed in 427, Augustine defended Christianity against its critics. He argued that the "city of God" comprised all who followed God's laws (i.e., Christians), whereas the "city of man" consisted of non-Christians, who ignored God's teachings and would be damned in a final judgment at the end of time. Augustine contended that all of history was in God's hands, writing that human kingdoms are established by divine providence. Augustine's writings reached a wide audience, and his theology strongly influenced the Roman Catholic tradition. His beliefs also helped create a clearer separation between Roman morality and the new Christian culture, which increasingly saw itself as superior to hedonistic Roman traditions.

Dawn of a New Age

Christianity filled the vacuum in the western Mediterranean as Roman government collapsed and many people left the cities in the fifth century. For example, the population of the city of Rome fell from 800,000 in 300 C.E. to 60,000 in 530 C.E. The Christian clergy often provided the only semblance of order for those who remained. Church officials also achieved a huge boost when the Franks, a Germanic people, were converted to Latin Christianity under their ruler Clovis in the 490s. Then, in the late sixth century, Europe was hit by many disasters, which were enumerated in 599 by an alarmed Pope Gregory: "as the end of the world approaches, many things menace us which never existed before: inversions of the climate, horrors from the heavens and storms contrary to the season, wars, famine, plagues, earthquakes."[7] A new age was dawning in western Europe.

 **Saint Augustine Denounces Paganism and Urges Romans to Enter the City of God** In *The City of God,* Augustine uses sarcasm to condemn the rituals of Rome's pre-Christian religion.

LO⁴ Revival in the East: Byzantines, Persians, and Arabs

A century after Roman emperor Constantine dedicated his new capital city, later known as Constantinople, in 330 C.E., the western part of the empire fell to various German groups, while the eastern empire fostered a new and distinctive society, Byzantium. Byzantium saw itself as a continuation of the Roman Empire but developed a quite different political structure, as well as a culture and church that was more Greek than Latin. By taking the brunt of attacks by resurgent western Asian peoples such as the Sassanian Persians, Byzantium gave the struggling new states in western Europe time to develop into a separate Latin Christian culture. The conflict between the Persians

CHRONOLOGY

Byzantium and Western Asia,
224–616 C.E.

224–226	Sassanians overthrow Parthians
240–272	Sassanian Empire established
306–337	Reign of Constantine
330	Founding of Constantinople
395	Final division of eastern and western empires
527–565	Reign of Justinian
540–590	Plague of Justinian
607–616	Sassanians conquer Syria, Palestine, and Egypt

and Byzantines also helped shape the rising Arab society.

Early Byzantium and the Era of Justinian

Byzantium emerged as the most powerful state in the eastern Mediterranean region, a status it maintained for many centuries. Its capital, Constantinople, straddled the narrow waterway linking the Aegean and Black Seas and separating Europe from western Asia, symbolically linking diverse peoples and traditions. The large eastern Roman Empire initially encompassed the Balkans, Greece, Anatolia, Syria, Palestine, and Egypt, and some early Byzantine emperors expanded the borders even further. Few emperors in Rome enjoyed the power that the Byzantine government had over its people, economy, and religious institutions.

Justinian and Theodora

The most important early ruler of the Byzantine Empire was the Emperor Justinian (r. 527–565 C.E.). Spurred on and advised by his powerful and ambitious wife, Theodora, Justinian was determined to defeat the German states in the west and reunite the old Roman Empire, announcing that God would help him to reconquer the lost lands. Justinian and his

> 66 A splendid city, how stately, how fair. It would be wearisome to tell of the abundance of all good things. 99
>
> *Visitor to Constantinople*

brilliant general, Belisarius (bel-uh-SAR-ee-uhs), reconquered a large part of the western territories, including the Vandal kingdom in North Africa. They defeated the Ostrogothic kingdom in Italy in 563 after long years of fighting, but repeated battles for control of Rome left the city devastated. During the first half of the seventh century, Justinian's successors had to turn east to fight the Sassanian Persians, and the western lands were once again lost (see Map 8.3).

Byzantine Administration

Justinian established a political pattern of despotism in which the Byzantine emperors were treated as near-gods and wielded absolute power over nearly every area of national life. They presided over a centralized and complex bureaucracy; spies monitored the population. Justinian had many critics, among them the great Byzantine historian Procopius, who described the emperor as "at once villainous and amenable; as people say colloquially, a moron.... His nature was an unnatural mix of folly and wickedness."[8] But Justinian also collected all existing Roman laws into one legal code, preserving Roman laws and legal principles for later generations.

Justinian's fortunes gradually declined. In 540 the Byzantines encountered one of the most terrible epidemics in world history, often known as the plague of Justinian. The sickness, probably bubonic plague, began in Egypt and spread along the trade routes into western Asia before reaching Europe, and returned several times until 590. The misery hit remote villages as well as densely populated cities. At its height some 10,000 people per day perished. Ships were loaded with corpses, rowed out to sea, and abandoned. When Justinian died at age eighty-three, his empire was much poorer, weaker, and less populated than it had been when he took power.

Byzantine Society, Economy, and Culture

Despite its many political misfortunes, the Byzantine Empire survived for centuries because of its social and economic strengths. For example, the empire remained much more urban than western Europe. Constantinople grew to perhaps a million people and was described by a visitor as "a splendid city, how stately, how fair. It would be wearisome to tell of the abundance of all good things."⁹ As in most classical societies, a huge gap separated rich and poor, but Byzantine peasants faced unique restrictions. By the fifth century, laws required peasants who had lived many years in one place to remain there. They became bound to the soil, under the control of powerful landlords. In the early years, upper-class women in the large cities enjoyed respect and influence, and some queens exercised considerable power. Women had the legal right to control their own property and the return of their dowry if their husbands divorced them. However, men enjoyed greater legal safeguards, and wife-beating was common.

A Report on the Embassy to Constantinople
Read how a Catholic bishop was insulted by his Byzantine hosts—and how he insulted them back—after delivering a marriage proposal from emperor Otto I.

Byzantine Trade and Economics

The eastern lands were wealthier than the western Roman Empire, and the Byzantine economy flourished. Merchants and bankers, including many non-Greeks, were prominent members of the urban aristocracy and benefited from Constantinople's position astride the principal trade routes between Europe and Asia. It was difficult to go by land from western Asia to Europe without passing through Constantinople, where the government placed a 10 percent tax on all goods that passed through the capital (see Map 8.4). Byzantine currency was internationally recognized and retained its value for six centuries, a remarkable achievement. But most trade with China and India had to go through Persian-controlled lands, and the Persian–Byzantine relationship alternated between uneasy peace and armed conflict. Nonetheless, Constantinople served as a hub to which ships and caravans brought many products and resources: spices, cotton, and copper from India and Southeast Asia; jewels, silk, gold, and silver from China and Central Asia; gold, ivory, and slaves from Africa; cot-

Interactive Map

ton and grain from Egypt; grains, wool, and tin from northwestern Europe; olive oil and silver from Spain and Italy; and timber, fur, copper, hides, and slaves from Russia and Scandinavia.

Byzantine Culture

Byzantine culture was fundamentally Hellenistic Greek, and its religious practices diverged from the western Roman tradition. The Byzantines preserved and later passed on to the Latin west (often through the Muslims) the works of Plato, Aristotle, Homer, Sophocles, and other Greeks. The Christian church in the east also became separated from its Latin counterpart, over time evolving into a different branch of Christianity, the Greek Orthodox Church. This church developed many customs and viewpoints quite foreign to the Roman church in western Europe and permeated all aspects of Byzantine life. The church, especially monasteries, gained control of considerable land and hence wealth derived from the peasants. Religious questions were avidly discussed. Emperors took the lead in proposing church reforms and calling church councils to deal with what main-

Interior of Santa Sophia Cathedral The great cathedral of Santa Sophia in Constantinople, rebuilt for Byzantine emperor Justinian, was famous for its spectacular interior.

Werner Forman/Art Resource, NY

stream Christians considered heresies. A goddess figure who represented urban prosperity in the fourth and fifth centuries was replaced by the much-beloved Christian image of the Holy Virgin Mary, which gave women moral stature. But the church also viewed women as weak and easily tempted by sin.

Over time theological disputes between the eastern and western churches grew. In general, Greek Christians came to emphasize ritual and theological disputes to a greater extent than did their Latin brethren. They also refused to accept the notion that the bishop of Rome (later known as the pope) was superior in authority to the other bishops. Conflicts over author-

> "Persians produced some of the world's finest pottery, silver plates, pearls, brocades, carpets, and glassware, exchanging these for gems, incense, perfume, and ivory."

ity and doctrine contributed to the final split between the Latin and Greek churches in the eleventh century. Byzantine art and architecture, although quite original, reflected the cultural diversity of this huge empire. The fusion of some Persian and Greco-Roman influences can be seen, for example, in the great dome inspired by Persian models in the Church of Santa Sophia (Holy Wisdom) in Constantinople, built under Justinian. The church was designed to symbolize inner Christian spirituality in contrast to human pride. Hence, the external appearance was modest, but the interior was richly decorated with mosaics, marble columns, tinted glass, and gold leaf.

Map 8.4
The Byzantine and Sassanian Empires

By 600 C.E., the Byzantine Empire controlled much of southern Europe and the eastern end of the Mediterranean basin, and the Sassanian Empire dominated most of the rest of western Asia, part of Turkestan, and Egypt. Various Germanic kingdoms held political sway in far western Europe, northern Europe, and northeast Africa.

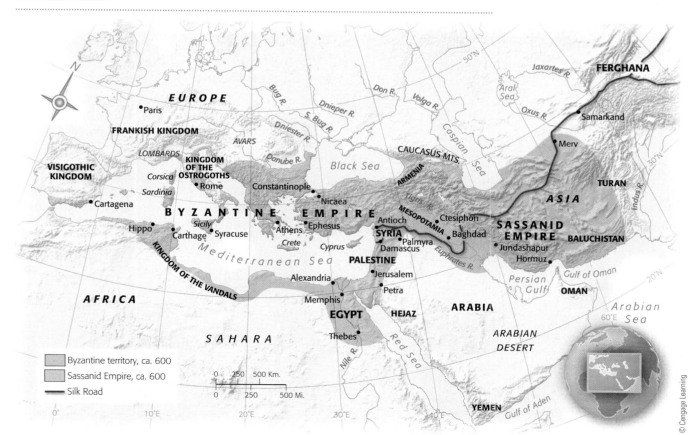

© Cengage Learning

Sassanian Persians and Their Culture

Sassanian Persian Revival

Both the Roman Empire and the Byzantines who replaced them in the east had to deal with a revived Persia under the Sassanian dynasty, which generated frequent conflict. The Sassanians, who took power in Persia in 224 C.E., were a high point of classical Middle Eastern history. Between 240 and 272 C.E., their rulers forged a large empire that would endure for four centuries. In the east they fought with the Kushans (KOO-shans), whose Afghanistan-based empire controlled parts of western India and Central Asia by the first century C.E. Eventually the Sassanians occupied much of Afghanistan and some of the Silk Road cities of Central Asia, but they lost these territories to the Huns in the fourth century C.E. To the west the Sassanians expanded into the Caucasus and Mesopotamia, creating chronic conflict with Rome in and around Syria. Considering themselves the successors to the Achaemenids a half millennium earlier, they also called themselves "king of kings."

Sassanian Trade

Controlling much of the Persian Gulf, Sassanian Persia became a contact zone for international trade. A Roman writer noted: "All along the coast [of the Persian Gulf] is a throng of cities and villages, and many ships sail to and fro."[10] Sassanian trade links stretched east as far as India, Central Asia, and China, and south as far as the Horn of Africa. Byzantine and Sassanian coins were used as currency in the Silk Road cities. Persians produced some of the world's finest pottery, silver plates, pearls, brocades, carpets, and glassware, exchanging these for gems, incense, perfume, and ivory.

Sassanian Religion and Culture

In contrast to the religiously tolerant Achaemenids, the Sassanians mandated a state religion, Zoroastrianism. The government imposed orthodoxy, supporting the priesthood and sometimes persecuting other religions. However, state religions tend to decay, and Zoroastrianism was no exception. The Zoroastrian establishment became corrupt and rigid, and by the fifth century the faith was losing influence and followers. Yet Zoroastrianism spawned various religions that combined this faith with others. One new religion, Manicheanism (man-uh-KEE-uh-niz-uhm), founded by the Persian Mani (MAH-nee) (216–277 C.E.), was a blend of Zoroastrianism, Buddhism, and Christianity that emphasized a continuing struggle between the forces of light and dark. Although Mani was executed for heresy, his religious dualism was later incorporated into Islam and some Christian sects.

As Zoroastrianism gradually lost influence, the state became more tolerant of diversity and turned the capital city, Jundishapur, into a cosmopolitan intellectual center. Foreign scholars migrated to the newly tolerant state, as did Jews and Christian minorities such as Nestorian Christians fleeing Byzantine repression. The Sassanians also collected scientific and literary books from many neighboring peoples, translated Greek writings, and established a renowned hospital and medical school. Sassanian Persia's multiculturalism provided a framework that enabled later Islamic governments to rule diverse peoples and faiths. But Zoroastrianism rapidly declined, becoming only a minor faith after Islam swept through the region. In 651 the last Sassanian king was murdered, and Arab Muslim armies gained control of all Sassanian territories.

Interregional Trade, Cities, and the Arabs

Rise of Arab Culture

The ebb and flow of long-distance trade in western Asia—often influenced by the activities of the Hellenistic Greeks, Romans, Byzantines, and Sassanians—helped foster the rise of Arab culture. Diverse Semitic societies lived in the Arabian peninsula, a dusty region of mountains, dry plains, and harsh deserts stretching from the Jordan River and Sinai southeast to the Indian Ocean. Most Arabian peoples were pastoral nomads divided into tribes, while others lived from trade or farming. Eventually all of these groups coalesced into the Arab society.

Petra and the Nabataeans

One of the peoples out of which Arab society arose were the Nabataeans (NAB-uh-TEE-uhnz), who traded all over the Middle East by land and sea. The Nabataean writing system became the inspiration for the Arabic script. They also established a kingdom and built a major trading city, Petra (PE-truh), in today's Jordan, astride the overland caravan routes. Built in a narrow gorge, Petra had a population of thirty thousand at its peak. The Petra residents developed an ingenious system for collecting and storing rainwater in this arid region. Beginning in the fourth century B.C.E., Petra flourished as a crossroads for goods moving between India, Arabia, Greece, and Egypt. But in 106 B.C.E., the Romans occupied Petra, and the city began a long decline as its trade shifted north to Palmyra (pal-MY-ruh), on the Euphrates River in today's Syria. Petra and Palmyra were two of the key trading cities that helped link east and west from their positions on the fringe of empires.

Queen Zenobia

Palmyra thrived until 273 C.E., when the Romans crushed a revolt led by the shrewd and ambitious Queen Septimia Zenobia (zuh-NO-bee-uh). When the Sassanians captured and killed the Roman emperor Valerian (vuh-LIR-ee-uhn) in 260 C.E., Odainat, the ruler of Palmyra and Zenobia's husband, earned Roman gratitude by defeating a Persian force. But in 267 Odainat was assassinated and the charismatic Zenobia took power. Taking advantage of Roman wars with the Goths, she sent her army into Egypt and then occupied much of Roman Asia, including much of Anatolia. After fierce battles, the Romans reoccupied Palmyra and took Zenobia to Rome, where she died. After another revolt, the Romans destroyed Palmyra.

Yemen

The farming-based kingdoms that rose and fell in Yemen in southern Arabia since the days of the fabled Queen of Sheba around 1000 B.C.E. constituted another source for Arab culture. Yemen included an area of high, cool mountains and well-watered valleys. The Yemenite people were highly skilled engineers who constructed splendid cities in valleys and along mountainsides. City-states emerged, among them Saba, possibly the Sheba of the Hebrew Bible. The Yemenites traded by sea with India and East Africa, as well as across Arabia by land with the eastern Mediterranean and Mesopotamia.

Political Disarray and the Emergence of Islam

In the sixth century C.E., Arabian conditions began to change. Political disarray, an Ethiopian invasion, and commercial depression began to undermine Yemenite society and power. To the north, renewed conflict between the Sassanians and Byzantines led both of them to actively seek allies in central Arabia. As a result, Arabia became a political pawn caught between Orthodox Byzantium, Zoroastrian Persia, and Coptic Ethiopia. This situation also increased the traffic over land trade routes and fostered the settlement of many Christian and Jewish merchants in desert towns like Mecca (MEK-uh). In the seventh century, all of these trends fostered the emergence of a new Arab faith, Islam, out of classical roots, and the dominance of Islamic armies over most of the Byzantine Asian territories and the Sassanian Empire.

 Listen to a synopsis of Chapter 8.

CHAPTER 9

Classical Societies and Regional Networks in Africa, the Americas, and Oceania,

600 B.C.E.–600 C.E.

Learning Outcomes

After reading this chapter, you should be able to answer the following questions:

LO¹ What were some of the similarities and differences between Kush and Aksum?

LO² How did the spread of the Bantus reshape sub-Saharan Africa?

LO³ What were some of the similarities and differences between the Maya and Teotihuacan?

LO⁴ How did the Mesoamerican, Andean, and North American societies compare and contrast with each other?

LO⁵ How were Australian and Pacific societies shaped by their environments?

> **❝**When the day dawns the trader betakes himself to his trade; the spinner takes her spindle; the warrior takes his shield; the farmer awakes, he and his hoe handle; the hunter awakes with his quiver and bow.**❞**
>
> —Ancient Yoruba proverb about daybreak in a West African town[1]

In the classical world, few settlements were as specialized as those serving the caravans that crossed the trackless sands of the vast Sahara Desert of Africa, a barren landscape of scorching sun and arid soil studded with isolated oasis towns. A later traveler commented that "the desert is haunted by demons, nothing but sand blown hither and thither by the wind."[2]

The round trip of many weeks between the cities of the North African coastal zone and those on the southern fringe of the desert held many dangers, including thirst, discomfort, and fierce raiders on horseback. Camels, the major beast of burden in the caravan trade, could travel many days without water. In the Sahara, wealth was measured more in camels than in gold. Thanks to these caravans and the brave men who led them, sub-Saharan African products reached a wider world, and goods and ideas from North Africa and Eurasia found their way along the trade networks to peoples living south of the Sahara.

The diverse societies that arose in sub-Saharan Africa, the Americas, and Oceania (the Pacific Basin) were all shaped by their environment and contacts with other societies. Connections such as the trans-Sahara trade routes ensured that few societies, regardless of where they were located, were completely isolated and unique. During the Classical Era, diverse societies developed in sub-Saharan Africa, the Americas, and Australia, and intrepid mariners settled most of the Pacific islands. Although they were distinct, these communities had much in common. In parts of Africa and the Americas, cities and states emerged that resembled each other, and in some societies there were many parallels to classical societies in Eurasia.

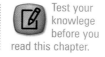

Test your knowlege before you read this chapter.

What do you think?

The economic systems of African, American, and Pacific societies had little in common with each other.

Strongly Disagree   *Strongly Agree*

| 1 | 2 | 3 | 4 | 5 | 6 | 7 |

<< **Aksum Stele** Early in the Common Era, the kings of the African state of Aksum, in what is today Ethiopia, decorated their capital city with tall, flat-sided pillars known as steles, some nearly 70 feet high, possibly as monuments to the royal family.

Werner Forman/Art Resource, NY

Meroitic
A cursive script developed in the Classical Era by the Kushites in Nubia that can be read only partly today.

This was truly a classical era, as societies and networks flourished and cultural influences spread over a wide area.

LO¹ Classical States and Connections in Northeast Africa

In classical times, tropical Africa and Eurasia were connected largely through intermediaries, including the North Africans linked to the trans-Saharan caravan trade and the maritime traders of the Indian Ocean who visited the East African coast. Two African societies, Kush (koosh) in Nubia and Aksum (AHK-soom) in Ethiopia, also served as intermediaries, becoming trading hubs and forming powerful states. Both enjoyed particularly close ties with Egypt and western Asia, fostering networks of exchange for other African societies.

The Kingdom of Kush

The kingdom of Kush, along the Nile south of Egypt (the region called Nubia in the ancient world—see Chapter 3), existed from about 800 B.C.E. to 350 C.E. From 600 to 100 B.C.E., Kush was the major African producer of iron and an important crossroads for the middle Nile region (see Map 9.1). Its capital city, Meroë (MER-uh-wee), became an industrial powerhouse of the classical world. The Kushites acquired iron technology either from Egypt or from the Africans who worked iron in Central and West Africa (see Chapter 3). Kush had many sources of iron ore, and heaps of iron slag litter the ruins of Meroë today. Kush linked various peoples of sub-Saharan Africa and the Mediterranean through trade networks, and hence played a central economic role in the Afro-Eurasian zone. Kush imported pottery, fine ceramics, wine, olive oil, and honey from Egypt and western Asia, and it exported both iron and cotton cloth. Both the Greeks and Romans admired the Kushites. Some Kushites seem to have visited Greece, and Roman sources report that Africans, possibly Kushites, came to Rome to trade or work. At its height Meroë was a grand city of perhaps 25,000 inhabitants. Built around a walled palace along the Nile, it contained massive temples, large brick-lined pools that may have been used for public

 Interactive Map

baths, and rows of pyramids, similar to those in Egypt, where kings and queens were buried in splendor.

Society and Culture

Although influenced by Egypt, Kushite society and the culture it produced were distinctive. At the top of the social hierarchy were absolute monarchs, including some queens, who both governed the state and served as guardians of the state religion, responsible for supporting and building the temples. In addition to worshiping some Egyptian gods, Kushites considered their monarchs, like those in Egypt, to be divine. Inscriptions testify to the piety of rulers and to the laws and traditions of the land.

Below the ruler were the military and bureaucratic elite. Kush's military officers led an army that was feared for both its weapons and the appearance of its soldiers. The Greek historian Herodotus described the soldiers of Kush:

> [They] were clothed in panthers' and lions' skins, and carried long bows made from branches of palm trees, and on them they laced short arrows made of cane tipped with stone. Besides this they had javelins, and at the tip was an antelope horn, made sharp like a lance; they also had knotted clubs. When they were going into battle they smeared one half of their body with chalk, and the other half with red ocher.[3]

Below the bureaucratic and military elite were free peasants and slaves. Women played a variety of economic roles, working in gold mines and engaging in farming and craft production. They also served as priestesses.

Kushites enjoyed a rich culture. Some Greek-speaking teachers apparently lived at Meroë, perhaps immigrants or the descendants of immigrants, and at least one Kushite king studied Greek philosophy. Meroë also had artists who produced highly polished, finely carved granite statues of their monarchs, and music played on trumpets, drums, harps, and flutes was a part of ceremonial and religious life. People of all classes wore jewelry made from gold, beads, iron, and copper alloy, and the presence of writing on numerous tombstones as well as graffiti suggests that literacy was widespread. Kushites developed their own alphabet, Meroitic (mer-uh-WIT-ik), a cursive script that gradually replaced Egyptian hieroglyphics in monumental inscriptions.

Kushite Decline and the Arrival of Christianity

After a millennium of power and prosperity, by 200 C.E. Kush was in decline, in part from environmental deterioration. Centuries of deforestation and overgrazing had

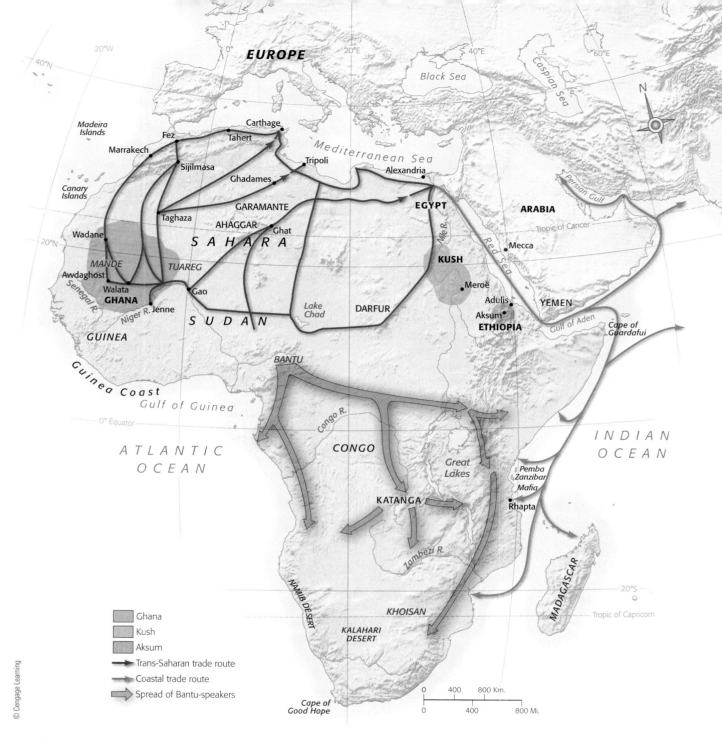

Map 9.1
Classical Africa, 1500 B.C.E.–600 C.E.

During this era, Kush, Aksum, and Jenne were major African centers of trade and government. Trade routes crossed the vast Sahara Desert, and the Bantu-speaking peoples expanded into central, southern, and eastern Africa.

Map legend:
- Ghana
- Kush
- Aksum
- Trans-Saharan trade route
- Coastal trade route
- Spread of Bantu-speakers

© Cengage Learning

History and Cultures of Africa (*http://www.columbia.edu/cu/lweb/indiv/africa/cuvl/cult.html*). Extensive links provided by Columbia University.

helped produce a drier climate. Chronic warfare with the Ethiopian state of Aksum also contributed to Meroë's problems. In 350 C.E., an invasion by the Aksum army destroyed what remained of the Kush kingdom. However, the culture of Kush was kept alive in some neighboring societies. Some West African societies developed political traditions not unlike those in Kush and have a folklore that identifies their origins to the northeast.

Several new kingdoms arose from the ashes of Kush, and contacts with the outside world eventually brought a new religion, Christianity, which became dominant in Nubia between the fourth and sixth centuries C.E. Nubian Christianity was a branch of the Coptic (KAHP-tik) Church, which had become influential in Egypt. Many Copts still live in Egypt. With its

patriarchal tendencies, Christianity seems to have replaced Nubian matrilineal traditions with patrilineal ones, but the religion's influence, isolated from other Christian communities to the north, gradually faded. Around 1400 C.E., Muslims conquered the last Christian Nubian state and converted most people to Islam. This religious change proved the most long-lasting transition for the societies of the middle Nile basin.

The Aksum Empire

Another literate urban African state, Aksum, emerged in the rocky but fertile Ethiopian highlands beginning around 400 B.C.E. Despite the difficult terrain and unpredictable climate of this area, its peoples traded

CHRONOLOGY

Classical Africa

2000 B.C.E.–1000 C.E.	Bantu migrations into Central, East, and South Africa
800 B.C.E.–350 C.E.	Meroë kingdom in Kush
500 B.C.E.–600 C.E.	Garamante confederation dominates trans-Saharan trade
400 B.C.E.–800 C.E.	Aksum kingdom in Ethiopia
300 B.C.E.	Beginning of maritime trade to East African coast
200 B.C.E.	Founding of Jenne-Jenno
300 C.E.	Introduction of Christianity to Kush and Aksum
ca. 500 C.E.	Founding of kingdom of Ghana

Queen Amanitere Queen Amanitere ruled Meroë along with her husband, King Natakamani, around 2,000 years ago. In this relief on the Lion Temple at Naqa, Kush, she holds vanquished foes by the hair while brandishing swords, thus demonstrating the power of the royal couple and the Kushite state.

From Graham Connah, *African Civilizations*, p. 44. Reproduced by permission of Cambridge University Press.

with Egypt from ancient times. They also benefited from proximity to the Red Sea, which linked northern Ethiopia to a widespread network of exchange and contact. At the Red Sea's narrowest point, only 20 miles of water separates the southern tip of Arabia from northeast Africa. Many Semitic people from Arabia crossed into Ethiopia and settled among the original inhabitants. Although many deep gorges inhibited communication across the plateau, the northern Ethiopians benefited greatly from accessibility to Arabia.

> "Aksumites built their first temples and palaces of masonry, as well as a city, dams, and reservoirs."

Solomon and the Queen of Sheba

Aksum sources and the Hebrew Bible testify to connections between Ethiopians and Hebrews. In these legends, the Queen of Sheba who met the Hebrew King Solomon was in fact an early Ethiopian monarch, Queen Makeda (Ma-KAY-da), who went to Israel in search of knowledge. According to an old Ethiopian book, Makeda supposedly told her people that "Learning is better than treasures of gold, better than all that has been created upon earth."4 Semitic immigrants from Yemen (YEM-uhn)—the probable location of the ancient Sheba (Saba) kingdom—may have brought the story with them to Ethiopia. The son of Solomon and Makeda, Menelik (MEN-uh-lik), supposedly founded a new kingdom, called Aksum.

One of the World's Four Great Kingdoms

The Aksum region, located on the northern edge of the Ethiopian plateau near the Red Sea, was already a center of agriculture and both bronze- and ironworking when Queen Makeda supposedly made her visit. It was inhabited by the ancestors of the Amharic (am-HAR-ik) people, who today dominate central Ethiopia. Between 400 B.C.E. and 100 C.E., Aksumites built their first temples and palaces of masonry, as well as a city, dams, and reservoirs. Irrigation and terracing supported a productive farming. The Aksumites also developed an alphabet.

For centuries Aksum enjoyed close economic and cultural exchange with the peoples of both southwestern Asia and eastern Africa, becoming something of a network hub between these regions. Soon Aksum had eclipsed Meroë and gained control of the trade between the Red Sea and the central Nile. Aksum became so well known that a Persian observer, the prophet Mani, included it with Persia, Rome, and China among the world's four great kingdoms. The Aksumites traded all over the Middle East, eastern Mediterranean, and East Africa (see Witness to the Past: A Shopper's Guide to Aksum). The Aksumites exported ivory, gold, obsidian, emeralds, perfumes, and animals and imported metals, glass, fabrics, wine, and spices. Aksumites used the Greek language in foreign commerce and were the first sub-Saharan Africans to mint their own coins.

Aksumite Society and Cultural Relations

The Aksum empire flourished from cultural interchange with many societies. Byzantium sent envoys to the court, seeking alliances against common enemies in Arabia. In addition, the Aksumites' extensive ties with the Semitic peoples of Yemen across the Red Sea led to considerable genetic and cultural intermixing between these two peoples. The classical Amharic language, Geez (gee-EZ), is a mixture of African and Semitic influences. The Jewish communities known as Falasha (fuh-LAHSH-uh) have lived in northern Ethiopia for many centuries.

Aksum's highly stratified social structure was dominated by kings, who largely had a paternalistic attitude toward their people. A fourth-century C.E. king left an inscription in which he claimed: "I will rule the people with righteousness and justice, and will not oppress them."5 Judging from their spectacular palaces, kings also enjoyed great wealth and power. Below the royal family was an aristocracy that supplied the top government officials. A substantial middle class included many merchants, and at the bottom of the social order were peasants and slaves, who could be conscripted for massive building projects.

The capital city of Aksum was a wealthy and cosmopolitan trading center, widely known for its monumental architecture. Its magnificent steles, thin stylized representations of multistoried buildings, were erected chiefly at burial grounds. The city also contained many stone platforms and huge palaces that required remarkable engineering skills.

Witness to the Past

A Shopper's Guide to Aksum

The following account of the trade of Aksum comes from the *Periplus of the Erythrean Sea,* written by an unknown Greek sometime in the second half of the first century C.E. The *Periplus* was a guide prepared for merchants and sailors that outlines the commercial prospects to be found in Arabia, the Indian Ocean, and the Persian Gulf. It also describes many of the bustling ports of this region. Hence, the *Periplus* is an excellent source for understanding Classical Era networks of exchange. In this excerpt, we learn about the port city of Adulis on the Red Sea. Adulis, now called Massawa (muh-SAH-wuh), was the chief Aksumite trade distribution center, where goods from the Ethiopian interior and from faraway places such as India, Egypt, and the Mediterranean were brought for sale or transshipment.

Adulis [is] a port . . . lying at the inner end of a bay. . . . Before the harbor lies the so-called Mountain Isla, . . . with the shores of the mainland close to it on both sides. Ships bound for this port now anchor here because of attacks from the land [by bandits]. . . . Opposite Mountain Island, on the mainland, . . . lies Adulis, a fair-sized village, from which there is a three day's journey to Coloe, an inland town and the first market for ivory. From that place to the [capital] city of the people called Aksumites there is a five day's journey more; to that place all the ivory is brought from the country beyond the Nile. . . .

There are imported into these places [Adulis], undressed cloth made in Egypt for the Berbers; robes from . . . [modern Suez]; cloaks of poor quality dyed in colors; double-fringed linen mantles; many articles of flint glass, and others of . . . [agate] made in . . . [Thebes, Egypt]; and brass, which is used for ornament and in cut pieces instead of coin; sheets of soft copper, used for cooking utensils and cut up for bracelets and anklets for the women; iron, which is made into spears used against the elephants and other wild beasts, and in their wars. Besides these, small axes are imported, and adzes and swords; copper drinking cups, round and large; a little coin for those coming to the market; wine of Laodicea [on the Syrian coast] and Italy . . .; olive oil . . .; for the King, gold and silver plate made after the fashion of the country, and for clothing, military cloaks, and thin coats of skin. . . . Likewise from the district of Ariaca [on the northwest coast of India] across this sea, there are imported Indian cloth [fine-quality cotton]. . . . There are exported from these places ivory, and tortoise-shell and rhinoceros-horn. The most [cargo] from Egypt is brought to this market [Adulis] from the month of January to September.

Thinking About the Reading

1. What were some of the societies that were linked to the trade at Adulis?
2. What does this reading tell us about the networks of exchange that connected Aksum to a wider world?

Source: W. H. Schoff (trans. and ed.), *The Periplus of the Erythraen Sea: Travel and Trade in the Indian Ocean by a Merchant of the First Century* (London, Bombay & Calcutta, 1912).

Christianity became influential just as Aksum reached its height of economic and military power in the fourth century C.E. Christian missionaries traveled the trade routes from western Asia, especially from the societies along the eastern Mediterranean coast with whom the Aksumites had long exchanged goods and ideas. Eventually Christianity became the official religion of the kingdom, perhaps in part to establish closer relations with Rome, Byzantium, and Egypt. But the Amharic population only slowly adopted the new faith. Ethiopian Christianity resembled the Coptic churches of Egypt and Nubia but also incorporated some of the long-entrenched spirit worship and various Hebrew practices, including the Jewish sabbath and kosher food.

The Aksum Legacy and Ethiopian History

Aksum eventually collapsed as a result of several challenges. By 400 C.E., reduced rainfall and the resulting pressure on the land had produced an ecological crisis. Political problems added to imperial decline. The conquest of southern Arabia by Aksum's enemy,

Sassanian Persia, in 575 diverted the Indian Ocean commerce from the port of Adulis. Then the rapid Islamic conquests of western Asia and North Africa beginning in the middle of the seventh century cut Aksum off from the Christian world. Aksum's trade withered, and it fell into economic stagnation, cultural decline, and political instability. By 800 C.E. the capital city was abandoned and the remnants of the kingdom had moved several hundred miles south.

Unlike Kush, however, Ethiopian society persisted in recognizable form. Indeed, the culture demonstrated a continuity for nearly 2,000 years, confirming that the Aksumite period was the Classical Age in northeast Africa. In particular, over the centuries Christianity became a deeply ingrained local religion among the Amharic and some of the neighboring peoples, producing the unique Ethiopian Christianity of today. Ethiopia remained relatively isolated in its mountain fastness for the next ten centuries.

LO² The Blossoming of Sudanic and Bantu Africa

While Kush and Aksum maintained the closest connections to Eurasia, complex urban societies also arose in the Sudanic region, on the Sahara's southern fringe, among peoples like the Mande (MAHN-day). These societies were linked to North Africa and beyond by trade networks. Meanwhile, Bantu-speaking Africans, first discussed in Chapter 3, continued to spread their languages, cultures, and technologies widely, occupying the southern half of the continent. Some became connected to trade networks linked to east coast port cities.

Sudanic Societies, Cities, and States

In the vast but dry grassland region known as the Sudan (soo-DAN), lying between the Sahara and tropical Africa, societies composed of farmers and city-dwellers germinated during classical times. The Sudanic peoples had long before adapted their economic life to the prevailing ecology. Most Sudanese became

farmers living in small, largely self-sufficient farming villages. Cereal crops suited to the dry soil, especially millet and sorghum, were the most basic food sources. West Africans also grew cotton and developed richly colored cotton clothing. The fertility of a large delta region along one stretch of the Niger (NYE-juhr) River made intensive farming possible there. The food grown in the delta, as well as the fish caught in the river, helped to feed the people of the trading cities.

Jenne-Jenno Some Sudanese congregated in large towns and cities reaching 30,000 or 40,000 in population, of which Jenne-Jenno was perhaps the major hub of a network of commercial centers along the Niger River. Located in what is now the nation of Mali (MAHL-ee), Jenne-Jenno developed as early as 200 B.C.E., and by the Common Era the city's people worked copper, gold, and iron, which they obtained from mines several hundred miles away. By 400 C.E. Jenne-Jenno had become the region's major trading hub and remained so for many centuries, closely tied, like other Sudanic cities, to hemispheric trade by the caravans across the Sahara. Eventually a wall more than one mile in circumference surrounded the city to protect the residents, most of whom lived in houses made from dried mud. Jenne-Jenno exported grain, fish, and animal products in exchange for metals. States of some sort may have existed around urban centers like Jenne-Jenno, but the ruins have yielded few clues as to political organization.

Large cities and states were less common in sub-Saharan Africa than in Eurasia and North Africa, in part because of the smaller population densities in Africa. The African agricultural system, mostly based on shifting cultivation, suited the soils but could not generally support the kinds of large settled populations that developed in parts of Eurasia and the northern Nile valley. At the beginning of the Common Era,

A Jenne Warrior This statuette, about two feet tall and made of a baked clay known as terra cotta, likely portrays a warrior in Jenne, probably of high status, although some experts believe it portrays a founding ancestor.

National Museum of African Art, Eliot Elisofon Photographic Archives, Smithsonian Institution. Photo by Frank Khoury

the African continent may have contained between 15 and 25 million people, much less than half that of China alone. About half lived in Egypt, Kush, and along the Mediterranean coast.

In the Sudan, kingdoms apparently grew out of markets and flourished from taxing the trade in gold and other commodities. The Soninke (soh-NIN-kay) people of the middle Niger Valley formed the first known major Sudanic state, Ghana (GAH-nuh). Ghana existed by at least 700 C.E. and reached its height as a trade-based empire in the ninth century and flourished until the thirteenth century.

The Mande Peoples

Diverse Mande (MON-day) peoples may have been typical of many classical Sudanic societies. The Mande spoke closely related languages, shared many customs, and dominated the western Niger River Basin and adjacent areas. Mande peoples combined farming with fishing along the Niger River. By 900 or 800 B.C.E., Mande farmers lived in large walled villages like Jenne-Jenno. Although divided into different groups, the Mande shared many common social, political, and religious traditions. They had highly stratified societies, with aristocratic, warrior, and commoner classes, and a special group of ritual and religious specialists. Political structures varied, but the Mande eventually developed a theocracy in which chiefs and village heads combined religious and secular duties. A respected class of oral historians and musicians known widely as griots (GREE-oh) memorized and recited the history of the community, emphasizing the deeds of leaders. The Mande and other Sudanic peoples also developed some common ideas about religion, including animism.

Trans-Saharan and Coastal Trade Networks

The establishment of caravan routes crossing the Sahara, which greatly aided the growth of Sudanic societies, began well before the Common Era.

Eventually a large trade system spanned the Sahara that linked the Sudanic towns with the peoples of the desert and southern Mediterranean coastal societies such as Carthage. From ancient times, Carthage sporadically carried on some trade with the Sudanic peoples, although the volume remains disputed.

The Garamante Confederation

Salt moving south to the Sudan and gold moving north to the Mediterranean drove the complex Saharan trade. The salt trade was mostly controlled by the Garamante tribal confederation, which inhabited the desert region in what is now southwestern Libya, southeastern Algeria, and northern Niger. These Berber (BUHR-buhr) people dominated the caravan trade routes as intermediaries from around 500 B.C.E. to 600 C.E., managing a vast commercial network. Sudanic cities shipped gold, cotton cloth, leather goods, pepper, and slaves to the north. Sudanic societies were largely self-sufficient, but they needed salt mined in the central Sahara and along the West African coast. The Garamantes used camels as pack animals and horses to pull light chariots. They made the parched desert livable by combining pastoral stock raising with irrigated farming; they constructed several thousand miles of underground canals to cultivate their farms; and they lived in walled cities and villages, built stone citadels as military outposts, and were apparently governed by royal families. Their state collapsed around the same time as the Roman Empire, and the remnants were later overrun by Muslims.

Guinea Coast Societies

Trade networks also developed along the Guinea (GIN-ee) coast, which stretches some 2,000 miles from modern Senegal (sen-i-GAWL) to southeastern Nigeria (nie-JEER-ee-uh), and was mainly covered by forest and swamp and had few edible plants or game animals. Over time various peoples, including some from the Sudan, migrated into the Guinea coast just south of the Sudan, a migration made possible by new tools and agricultural techniques.

The challenging life on the Guinea coast led to some pragmatic solutions. To survive, the people lived mostly in small, self-sufficient villages with rich social networks. They practiced cooperative subsistence agriculture, with yams and bananas as the staple crops. Furthermore, the Guinea peoples traded with Sudanic societies, over land or by boat up the rivers such as the Niger and Volta (VAHL-tuh), and thus became linked to wider networks of economic and cultural exchange. Over time, many of the coastal societies came to practice some common customs, including Sudanese traditions.

Bantu Migrations and Trade

Over several thousand years, many iron-using speakers of Bantu languages had migrated from their original homeland in eastern Nigeria into Central and East Africa (see Chapter 3). During the Classical Era, Bantu peoples accelerated their expansion to the south and east. They carried with them many traditions of art, music, farming, and religion that had originated in the Sudan, thus spreading Sudanese influence into other areas of Africa.

Some Bantu-speaking peoples moved into the southern Congo region now known as Katanga (kuh-TAHNG-guh), which they reached by 400 B.C.E. Katanga is an area of savannah grasslands like the region they had left, but it is less fertile and more prone to drought and disease. Much of the region south of the Congo Basin rain forest is relatively arid because of irregular rainfall. Fortunately, sorghum and millet from the Sudanic region and Ethiopia spread among the Bantus, who successfully adapted these cereal crops to the dry southern climate.

From Katanga many Bantus began moving to the west, south, and east. In the east they met Bantus migrating from the Great Lakes in the East African highlands. By 200 B.C.E. Bantu culture had reached the Zambezi (zam-BEE-zee) River Basin, and by the third century C.E. the first Bantu settlers entered what is now the nation of South Africa.

As Bantu-speaking migrants settled in a new location, they encountered local peoples and incorporated new influences. Because they worked iron, the Bantus possessed military and agricultural technologies that allowed them to push some of the local peoples into marginal economic areas suitable only for hunting and gathering. Many Bantus intermingled with, and probably culturally assimilated, those they met. Sudanese cultural forms carried by the Bantus, such as drums and percussive music, wood-

 Africa South of the Sahara (*http://www -sul.stanford.edu/depts/ ssrg/africa/guide.html*). A useful collection of links from Stanford University.

> "Sorghum and millet from the Sudanic region and Ethiopia spread among the Bantus, who successfully adapted these cereal crops to the dry southern climate."

Nilotes
Ironworking pastoralists from the eastern Sudan who settled in East Africa in the Classical Era and there had frequent interactions with the Bantus (see pastoral nomadism).

carving, and ancestor-focused religions, became widespread.

The contacts also influenced the Bantu cultures, especially in southern and eastern Africa. For example, the Xhosa (KOH-sah) and Zulu (ZOO-loo) peoples, who lived along the southeastern coast of today's South Africa by the fourth century C.E., mixed their languages and cultures with the local Khoisan cattle herders. Cattle herding was incorporated into Xhosa and Zulu economic life alongside farming and trade. The migrating Bantus also encountered and gradually absorbed various societies in East Africa, such as ironworking pastoralists from the eastern Sudan, the Nilotes (nie-LAHT-eez), who were also settling in East Africa. Although their interactions were not always peaceful, Bantus and Nilotes mutually modified their cultures as a result of contact.

Early in the Common Era, Indonesian mariners and migrants reached East Africa. Some of the Indonesian mariners settled along the coast and married local people, bringing crops such as bananas and sugar cane and domesticated chickens and pigs. These Indonesians and later arrivals also introduced Austronesian housing styles and musical instruments, which were incorporated into local cultures. They established trading posts to barter pottery, beads, and utensils for ivory and animal products. Indonesian influences reached as far west as the Congo River Basin. Between 100 and 700 C.E., Indonesians settled the large island of Madagascar, implanting there a mixed Indonesian–Bantu culture and language that still survives.

The East African coast thus developed a cosmopolitan society based on maritime trade. The winds and currents along the coast reverse direction every six months, allowing boats from southwestern Asia to sail to East Africa and back each year. The trading ports to which merchants from southern Arabia sailed were located along the coast from Somalia to present-day Tanzania. The main port city in this era, Rhapta (RAHP-ta) in Tanzania, had a large merchant community from southern Arabia.

The east coast trade grew slowly during the Classical Era. A first-century C.E. survey of maritime trade by an Alexandria-based Greek traveler reported that ships left Egypt's Red Sea ports and then visited Adulis and various Somalian ports before sailing to East African ports such as Rhapta. Growing numbers of traders came to the coastal towns. Various Roman accounts reported that East Africa exported ivory, rhinoceros horn, and tortoise shell to Egypt, India, and western Asia and imported iron goods, pottery, and glass beads. Egyptian, Roman, and West Asian coins found in the region date from 300 B.C.E. to 200 C.E., indicating trade with the Mediterranean area, and Persian pottery produced between 400 and 600 C.E. was distributed widely along the coast and inland. Eventually, the coast developed many large and flourishing port cities and a culture that mixed Bantu ideas with those of southwestern Asia.

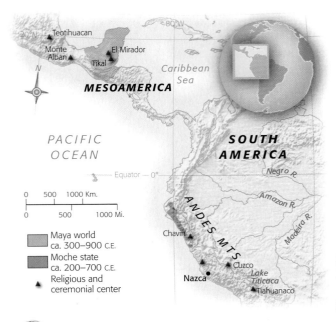

Map 9.2
Classical Societies in the Americas

The major American centers of complex agriculture, cities, and states emerged in Mesoamerica, where the Maya were the largest and longest-lasting society during the era, and the Andes regions, where Chavín, Moche, and Tiahuanaco were important societies.

LO³ Classical Mesoamerican Societies and Networks

As in Eurasia and Africa, the first cities and states in the Americas had developed during ancient times, including the Olmecs in Mesoamerica and the Chavín in the Andes (see Chapter 4). By the beginning of the Common Era, there may have been around 15 million people in the Americas. More than two-thirds of them were concentrated in Mesoamerica and western South America, where the most significant developments were taking place. The most long-lasting and widespread of these societies were the Maya (MIE-uh) of Mesoamerica, who forged a literate and prosperous urban culture.

> **❝**Hieroglyphic script was used for calendars, religious regulations, histories, and many sacred books. **❞**

The Emergence and Growth of the Maya

To the east of the pioneering Olmecs, in the lowland rain forests of Central America and the Yucatan (YOO-kuh-TAN) Peninsula in southeast Mexico facing the Caribbean Sea, a society coalesced that became the Maya (see Map 9.2). Farming

Interactive Map

by shifting cultivation and ceramic making dates back to at least 1100 B.C.E. Using innovative irrigation techniques, the Maya introduced the cultivation of maize (corn) and other foods into the tropical forests. As more productive agriculture led to more population, the Maya spread southward into the mountains and coastal zones of Central America.

As their power increased, the Maya elite organized ambitious building projects. The first Maya pyramids were constructed by 600 B.C.E. and were built for religious worship and ceremonies. By 100 B.C.E., notions of divine kingship became widespread, and the Maya began making stone statues and carvings of their rulers. By this time they also painted sophisticated murals on walls, illustrating Maya myths.

Urbanization and Cultural Innovation

Maya society was based on urbanization and cultural innovations such as writing. At the height of their culture, 150 B.C.E. to 800 C.E., the Maya built many

Maya History, Culture, and Archaeology (*http://www.hist.unt .edu/web_resources/ anth_mayas.htm*). Operated by the University of North Texas history department, this site offers links to innumerable resources concerning Maya history and culture.

cities, each boasting masonry buildings, large temples, spacious plazas and pyramid complexes, and elaborate carvings. The major early city was El Mirador, built between 150 B.C.E. and 50 C.E. The Maya developed the most comprehensive writing system in the Americas. Their hieroglyphic script was used for calendars, religious regulations, histories, and many sacred books. The Spanish who conquered the Maya lands in the 1500s marveled at the architecture. One wrote that "the buildings and the multitude of them is remarkable. So well built are they of cut stone that it fills one with astonishment."[6]

Tikal (ti-KAHL), in what is today eastern Guatemala near the border with Belize, was one of the major Maya cities between 200 and 900 C.E. and had a population of fifty thousand at its height. Tikal contained three hundred large ceremonial buildings dominated by temple pyramids 200 feet high and topped by temples. Leaders King Great Jaguar Paw and General Smoking Frog led Tikal to a great victory over the rival city Uaxactun in 378 C.E., ensuring Tikal's regional supremacy for the next two hundred years.

Maya identity was more cultural than political. There was much cultural uniformity among the competing cities, probably because of the region's dense population and the close proximity of the trading cities with one another. Perhaps 10 million people lived in the Maya lowlands by 600 C.E., and several cities had populations of between 30,000 and 50,000.

As Maya society grew, political structures changed, trade networks widened, and conflict increased. By around 500 C.E., many small city-states gave way to a few cities, such as Tikal, that asserted regional authority, but no united Maya state or empire ever existed. Warfare between kings of competing city-states was frequent and brutal, and prisoners of war were usually enslaved or sacrificed. As the larger cities fought for influence, smaller cities had to ally themselves with one of the major powers for survival. The kings were obliged to obtain needed goods and other resources for their people, either through trade or through conquest, as well as to contribute to agricultural expansion. Writing helped legitimize and celebrate the rulers, who erected stone monuments containing inscriptions glorifying their deeds and divine ancestry. Scribes, a respected and influential group, played an important role in this effort.

Trade Networks

Maya cities were linked in networks of interregional trade that were forged by hacking paths through the often-dense rain forests. The Maya also traded widely with non-Maya societies, some of them hundreds of miles away in central Mexico and deep into Central America. Through this trade they became influenced by other societies. The Maya did not work bronze or iron, but they did use copper and imported gold from Panama. One of the most prized materials obtained through long-distance trade was jade. Skilled artisans who could work this very hard stone were highly valued, and their products were traded widely.

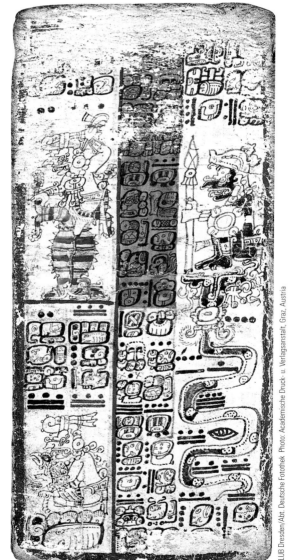

SLUB Dresden/Abt. Deutsche Fotothek Photo: Academische Druck- u. Verlagsanstalt, Graz, Austria

Maya Codex Only three Maya books (or codices) are known to have survived the Spanish conquest. This beautiful illustrated folding-screen book, the Dresden Codex, compiled around 1200 C.E., records astronomical calculations, tables of eclipses, and ritual detail. It is written on a long strip of bark paper coated with stucco.

Maya Society and Intellectual Achievements

The Maya maintained a hierarchical social structure. Below the ruling family, a class of nobles staffed the bureaucracy. The next rank included architects, priests, and scribes. Below them were many artisans, including sculptors, potters, painters, and stoneworkers. The laborers and farmers, who supplied manual work and food, occupied a lower rung still. At the bottom of the social structure were slaves.

Social Structure

The layout of city houses suggests that the Maya had an extended, multigenerational family structure. Although descent was patrilineal, they took genealogy seriously for both families. Maya society accorded men more rights, prestige, and privileges than women. Boys and young men often lived apart from their families in special communal houses, learning the arts of war. Mothers kept their daughters close at hand, giving them a strict upbringing; girls, but not boys, were severely punished

"The Maya were obsessed with placating the gods through ritual practices, which eventually included human sacrifice on a considerable scale."

for compromising their chastity. Yet, some royal women wielded considerable power behind the kings, and a few served as rulers.

City people had some time for leisure activities, including dancing festivals and ball games. Ball courts were built in all settlements. In the middle of each court was a stone ring, often 20 or 30 feet high. Players used a ball 6 inches in diameter, which they could only hit with their buttocks, fists, and elbows. Spectators probably gambled on the outcome. In an important match involving war captives, losers were sometimes sacrificed.

Each city was fed by thousands of peasants living around it, most of them growing maize and also *cacao* (kuh-COW), from which chocolate is made, by at least the fifth century C.E. Thus city and farm had a close relationship. Each farm family had its own plot, but clearing and cultivating were done communally with neighbors. The Maya and other Americans had no draft animals to assist in farming, so they could not practice the same kind of intensive agriculture as people did in the Eastern Hemisphere. Instead, Maya peasants had small plots, which they worked for a rather short time during the year, perhaps fifty days. They were also subject to military duty and provided labor for public works.

Religion

Maya religion, science, and mathematics were linked together. The Maya worshiped a paramount creator god and many other deities. The only surviving book of Maya religion, the *Popul Vuh* ("Book of Council"), claimed that the earth was sacred and that humankind was "given memory to count the days, [to be] bearers of respect for its divinity; to keep the rituals which connect humanity, nature and the heavens."[7] The Maya were obsessed with placating the gods through ritual practices, which eventually included human sacrifice on a considerable scale. The Maya also emphasized purification of the body. For this, there were many sweat baths, buildings fashioned to contain heat and steam generated by hot rocks.

Astronomy

The Maya's concern for using the correct times and seasons for religious celebrations motivated them to make calendars and to study astronomy. Cosmic phenomena determined

CHRONOLOGY

Classical Americas

1100–150 B.C.E.	Early Maya society
600 B.C.E.–1100 C.E.	Tiwanaku Empire in the Andes
400 B.C.E.–1000 C.E.	Monte Alban in Mexico
300 B.C.E.–1400 C.E.	Hohokam society in southwest North America
200 B.C.E.–600 C.E.	Hopewell mound-building culture in eastern North America
200 B.C.E.–700 C.E.	Moche in Peru
200 B.C.E.–750 C.E.	Teotihuacan in Mexico
150 B.C.E.–800 C.E.	Flowering of Maya city-states
100–900 C.E.	Anasazi society in southwest North America

Teotihuacan This overview shows the two largest pyramids at Teotihuacan, the Pyramid of the Moon (bottom center) and the Pyramid of the Sun. There were six hundred smaller pyramids in the city.

which days were best for war, marriage, trade, rituals, and other activities. Based on their observations, Maya astronomers correctly recorded the orbit of the planet Mars around the sun. The Maya secular calendar, based on a solar year at 365 days, was the most accurate calendar in the world before the sixteenth century. Their religious calendar, however, was based on 260 days. Every fifty-two years, the two calendars coincided, at which time great festivals and religious observances were held. The Maya were wise to study astronomy, because cyclical variations in the sun's energy brought on debilitating droughts roughly every two hundred years. Eventually increasing droughts probably contributed to the collapse of the Maya cities during the Intermediate Era.

Writing and Mathematics

The interest in time also contributed to writing and mathematics. The Olmecs probably created the first writing in Mesoamerica around the seventh century B.C.E., as well as the earliest calendar, and these may have influenced the nearby Maya. The earliest simple Maya writing dates from about 300 or 250 B.C.E. The Maya mathematical system was simpler and much easier to use than the Roman numerals of Europe. Like the mathematicians of India, the Maya also introduced the concept of zero. Unfortunately, all but a handful of the Maya books (known as codices) were destroyed by the Spanish invaders in the 1500s C.E. This terrible loss has made it much more difficult for historians to understand Maya history and culture.

Zapotec Society and Urban Teotihuacan

The Maya were not the only Mesoamerican peoples to develop cities and states in this era. By 400 B.C.E., small states were emerging among the Zapotec (ZAHP-uh-TEK) people in southern Mexico, especially around Monte Alban (MON-teh ahl-BAHN). This city atop a hill eventually became a large ceremonial

> "Teotihuacan boasted plazas, markets, apartment buildings, palaces, temples, and a complex water drainage system."

center extending over some 15 square miles; it also included several huge pyramid platforms. By 200 C.E., Monte Alban was the capital for a large state that was ruled by a hereditary elite of kings and priests deeply involved in religious observances. There is also some evidence of military activity, especially in the earlier centuries.

Monte Alban grew, developing distinctive cultural patterns. Thanks to population growth and migration, the capital city may have had a population of 25,000 to 30,000 people at its peak between 300 and 750 C.E., and satellite towns and villages contained many thousands more. One building may have been an astronomical observatory. The Zapotec developed writing sometime between 600 and 400 B.C.E. Their alphabet and calendar may have been derived from those of the Olmecs, whose influence had reached the area. Around 750 C.E., the Monte Alban city began a long decline and was later mostly abandoned.

The large Valley of Mexico (the site of present-day Mexico City) also became an important site for urban societies. The valley had long been a unified economic unit and a center for mining obsidian (uhb-SID-ee-uhn), a glassy, volcanic rock prized for its razor-sharp edges. By 200 B.C.E., Teotihuacan (teh-o-tee-wah-kahn) ("the City of the Gods") became the largest city in the Americas and the capital of an empire in central Mexico. Political and economic power allowed the city to extend its influence over much of Mesoamerica.

By 600 C.E., Teotihuacan had grown enormously and was home to between 120,000 and 200,000 inhabitants. Sprawling over 10 square miles, it was probably one of the half-dozen largest cities in the world at that time. Teotihuacan was built on a master plan that laid out the city on a north-south axis, bisected by wide avenues. The city boasted plazas, markets, apartment buildings, palaces, temples, and a complex water drainage system. Among the many monumental buildings, a huge pyramid rose more than 200 feet high in the ceremonial center of the city. It took some 3 million tons of volcanic rock—dug up and then transported to the city without benefit of iron tools or beasts of burden to pull wheeled vehicles—to build the Pyramid of the Sun. Like the settlements of the Maya and many peoples of Mesoamerica and North America, Teotihuacan contained ball courts for games played with rubber balls.

Teotihuacan was a political, religious, and economic center. The kings seem to have been viewed as divine and left administration to bureaucrats and aristocrats. The people of the city had writing and an ingenious numbering system, which no doubt assisted trade and administration. Many city people were engaged in special crafts, creating obsidian tools or ceremonial pottery. Workers lived in rooms in larger compounds linked by alleyways and patios. Teotihuacan may also have functioned as the hub for the many trade networks spanning Mesoamerica and extending far to the north and south. Teotihuacan merchants traveled widely, forging closer links between distant peoples like the Maya.

Teotihuacan society changed over time, and eventually it collapsed. The rulers seem to have become increasingly militaristic, and in later centuries human sacrifice became common. These trends earned Teotihuacan many enemies and may have harmed trade. In 750 C.E., invaders burned the city down, and the population scattered. The reasons for the collapse are unknown, but even in ruins the city's splendor lived on. A millennium later, the Aztecs who had settled the area told the Spanish conquerors of their reverence for the pyramids: "And this they call Teotihuacan, because it is where they bury the lords."[8]

LO⁴ New Societies of South and North America

The Maya and other Mesoamerican states were not the only societies that emerged and flourished in the Americas during the Classical Era. Various societies succeeded Chavín in the mountainous Andes region. Some North American farming peoples in deserts and river valleys built towns, and many societies all over the hemisphere participated in long-distance trading networks. Western Hemisphere peoples were also among the world's best farmers: by the fifteenth century C.E., they had domesticated more different plants than all of the Eastern Hemisphere peoples combined, including three thousand varieties of potatoes.

American societies developed diverse cultures and ways of life, some rooted in bureaucratic empires or states, and some based on villages and tribes.

Moche and the Peruvian Coast

The great Andes state of Chavín collapsed by 200 B.C.E., but some of the architectural and religious patterns it pioneered spread through the Andes and into adjacent lands. Perhaps the major society influenced by Chavín in the Classical Era was Moche (MO-che), a prosperous and powerful state that formed in the desert region along the northern Peruvian coast. In this dry, cool climate, farming required building irrigation canals to channel the runoff from the Andes. With irrigation, these people grew corn, beans, peppers, squash, and cotton, which they skillfully wove into textiles. The Moche also exploited the abundant, protein-rich maritime resources just offshore.

Moche Trade and Culture

The Moche were part of a distinctive, enduring culture that emerged among various societies on the north coast of Peru in the second century B.C.E. These societies built monumental architecture, with platforms and courtyards. They also fashioned beautiful jewelry, mirrors, and pottery. Coastal peoples traded some of their agricultural and maritime bounty to Andes societies for potatoes and other highland crops. Eventually trade networks linked distant societies over much of western South America. Some took up seagoing trade. For example, an urban society, known as the Manteno, living along the coast of what is today Ecuador, used balsa-wood rafts equipped with sails to forge a coastal trade network stretching from Mexico to Chile between 500 B.C.E. and the 1600s C.E. Because of such long-distance trade networks, coastal and interior peoples came to depend on each other. This trade encouraged the formation of states in both places.

 Read about the privileged but dangerous life of a Moche lord.

By 200 B.C.E., the Moche had established a capital city, some 200 miles north of the modern city of Lima, that centered around two massive brick pyramids, one dedicated to the sun, the other to the moon. The city, well planned with narrow streets and walled residential complexes, was home to perhaps ten thousand people. Separate and perhaps hostile city-based Moche kingdoms were spread over hundreds of miles, all with similar customs, buildings, and pyramids. The Moche were excellent gold workers and also made products from a copper and gold alloy as well as silver. In addition, the Moche devoted considerable effort and skill to constructing huge monumental platforms and temples, some rising 135 feet. They apparently also developed a mathematical system based on 10 and an effective irrigation system.

Moche
A prosperous, powerful state that formed along the northern Peruvian coast from 200 B.C.E. to 700 C.E.

Burial chambers and a huge assortment of clay pottery painted with highly realistic scenes of social activity provide much knowledge of Moche society, such as the sometimes elegant, sometimes brutal life of the elite. The wealth of the period is reflected in the enormous amounts of gold and silver artifacts that were buried with Moche dignitaries. Frequent wars helped them obtain captives who could be sacrificed in ritual ceremonies. The painted pottery shows that in these grisly ceremonies, the leaders drank the blood of their unfortunate victims. The painted pots also show midwives attending birthing mothers and women carrying babies on their backs in shawls. The paintings also show diverse sexual activities, erotic scenes of lovemaking between men and women and between gods and humans. Other scenes are gruesome to modern eyes, showing acts of ritual warfare and grisly executions.

Moche Decline

Eventually the Moche faced challenges they could not overcome. Between 500 and 600 C.E., they experienced a series of natural disasters, including periods of torrential rains, prolonged drought, and massive earthquakes. Moche leaders may have responded to the resulting food shortages with increasing warfare to obtain resources and human sacrifice to appease the gods. The ecological and political crises that these disasters generated brought the Moche to an end by 650 or 700 C.E.

Tiwanaku, Nazca, and the Andean Societies

At about the same time that the Moche dominated the northern Peruvian coast, various states continued to rise and fall in the Andes and along the southern Peruvian coast. In the Lake Titicaca (tit-i-KAHK-uh) region of the Andes highlands between 600 and 100 B.C.E., the ancestors of the Aymara (AYE-muh-RAH) people built a small state and constructed public architecture that included impressive stone sculpture. Even in ruins, the plazas, palaces, and gilded temples impressed the Spanish 1,500 years later; one wrote: "There is a hill made by the hands of men, on great foundations of stone. What causes most astonishment are some great doorways of stone, some made out of a single stone."⁹ The capital city of the Aymara state, known as Tiwanaku (tee-wah-NA-coo), emerged by 100 C.E. and reached its height in 600 C.E., when it had a population of perhaps forty thousand and controlled an empire over much of the southern Andes. Tiwanaku was the highest ancient city in all the Andes, over 10,000 feet above sea level.

Tiwanaku influenced a large region of western South America. The local art and religion, which probably involved human sacrifice, seem to have spread into neighboring societies. The lands around the capital, rich in llama herds and a center of copper technology, flourished from a system of raised field agriculture that was some 400 percent more productive than the farming in the region today. The Aymara, like other Andean peoples, were also skilled at using fibers. But by 1100 C.E., the capital and surrounding fields were abandoned, perhaps because of climate change that generated a drought so severe that rivers dried up.

The Nazca (NAHZ-kuh), a decentralized agrarian society that flourished in the harsh desert in southern Peru from 200 B.C.E. to 600 C.E., became most famous for creating geometric lines along their windswept plateau by clearing away surface stones to reveal the underlying rock and then laying the stones along the edges of the lines. Constructed on a huge scale, the lines depict either geometric shapes or animals such as monkeys and birds.

Pueblo and Mound-Building Societies of North America

Beginning just before the Common Era, several cultural traditions and permanent towns emerged among the desert farmers of the American Southwest, including the Hohokam (huh-HOH-kuhm), Anasazi (ah-nah-SAH-zee), and Mogollon (MOH-guh-YOHN). By around 300 B.C.E., the Hohokam of what is now southern Arizona and northwest Mexico were trading extensively with other southwestern peoples and the southern California coast. Farming success depended on water, and the peoples of this arid region used advanced irrigation, dams, terraces, and other strategies to grow maize, beans, squash, and cotton.

> " The Aymara, like other Andean peoples, were skilled at using fibers. "

The Hohokam

The Hohokam survived for some 1,500 years, building large towns holding one thousand or more people. The total Hohokam population in the vicinity of present-day Phoenix may have reached forty thousand. Ball courts and Mesoamerican-style platform mounds indicates some Mesoamerican influence over long-distance trade networks. Eventually overpopulation, deforestation, and drier climates increased conflict and put more stress on the society. By the fifteenth century, the Hohokam settlements had been abandoned, though some people remained. Their modern descendants include the Pima and Papago Indians of Arizona.

The Anasazi

The Anasazi and the closely related Mogollon culture were the direct ancestors of the Pueblo Indians in what is today Arizona and New Mexico. The Anasazi were once much more widespread and had towns in Utah and Colorado as far east as the western margins of the Great Plains. The Mogollon emerged around 200 B.C.E. and covered a territory stretching from central Arizona and New Mexico into northern Mexico. Although the Mogollon never built towns as impressive as those of the Anasazi and Hohokam, they flourished from a combination of corn growing and skillful gathering until the fifteenth century C.E. All of the southwestern societies traded with and adopted material traits from each other.

The Hopewell

In eastern North America, another great era of mound building emerged between around 500 B.C.E. and 400 C.E. (see Chapter 4). This new mound-building culture became widespread, encompassing the Mississippi, Ohio, Tennessee, and lower Missouri River Basins and their tributaries, as well as the South Atlantic coast. The most prominent mound-builder tradition, known today as Hopewell, was centered in the Ohio River region and arose between 200 and 50 B.C.E. Although there is no evidence for any large state, Hopewell artistic styles, maize cultivation, religious beliefs, ceremonial traditions, and burial customs spread throughout the eastern woodlands.

The Hopewell peoples supported their society through intensive agriculture and long-distance trade. They created extraordinary earthworks and other engineering projects, such as the Great Serpent Mound, built on a hilltop in Ohio around 2,000 years ago. Shaped like a snake, the mound ran 800 feet long from head to tail and was 4 feet tall and 20 feet wide. Members of the elite were buried in the mounds with goods that indicated their high status. The Hopewell and other mound-building cultures were supported by two major economic changes. First, agriculture became more intensive, especially after the spread of maize. Second, long-distance trade, which had existed for centuries, evolved into a network spanning a large section of North America. Along the river trade routes moved obsidian from the Rocky Mountains, copper from the Great Lakes, ceramics from the lower Great Lakes, ore from Kansas, silver from Ontario, shells from the Gulf of Mexico, freshwater pearls from the Mississippi, and marine products from the Gulf Coast. Hopewell artisans created ceremonial objects, from pan pipes to mirrors, from various metals, and they also manufactured large clay cooking pots.

The Hopewell culture began to decline around 300 C.E. and collapsed by 600 C.E. Overpopulation and the resulting competition for land might have put too much stress on the environment and economic system. Trade networks may have been disrupted, and evidence shows that the maize crop diminished, possibly in part because of a cooling climate. In addition, around 300 C.E. someone invented or imported the bow and arrow into the region, perhaps leading to warfare and the disruption of traditional alliances.

Changing States and the Spread of Cultures

While the traditions of the earliest urban societies, the Olmecs and Chavín, remained influential in Mesoamerica and the Andes region, much change occurred in these regions over the centuries. For example, around 200 or 300 C.E., various small states such as Monte Alban, Teotihuacan, Tikal, and Tiwanaku grew into larger states, and many societies developed more pronounced class divisions and occupational specialization. Long-distance trade increased, merchants became more influential, and ideas spread more widely. Artistic culture and thought flowered. Many American peoples revered the land, seeing both physical and spiritual life as coming from and returning to the land.

Except for the exceptionally enduring Maya and Tiwanaku, South American and Mesoamerican states exhibited a pattern of rise and fall after a few cen-

turies. Even the Maya cities were mostly abandoned long before European conquest in the sixteenth century C.E. Although the classical states established frameworks for later empires such as the *Toltec* (TOLL-tek), Aztec, and Inca, they did not survive into modern times in their original form, as the classical Chinese and Ethiopian states did.

The widespread presence of pyramids in Mesoamerica and South America has caused some observers to speculate about possible contacts across the Atlantic to North Africa and the Mediterranean long before the arrival of Norse Vikings around 1000 C.E. and, five centuries later, Spanish ships. A stray Phoenician, Egyptian, or West African boat crossing the Atlantic Ocean, perhaps swept off course by storms, cannot be ruled out. But there is no firm archaeological evidence for any ties to the Eastern Hemisphere, and most specialists are extremely skeptical that such contacts were ever made.

Along the American west coast, from California to Peru, are scattered hints of trans-Pacific contacts in pottery design, artwork, and plants, leading to occasional speculation about possible Chinese, Japanese, or Polynesian voyages to the Americas. Indeed, Polynesian voyagers, the world's most skilled mariners, were capable of trips over several thousand miles of uncharted ocean, and they could have occasionally visited the American coast and then returned home. This might explain the presence of the South American sweet potato in Polynesia. However, if any trans-Pacific contacts did occur, they left no obvious long-lasting influence.

LO⁵ Populating the Pacific: Australian and Island Societies

Although the original settlers of Australia and the Pacific islands migrated from or through Southeast Asia, the societies they developed remained largely isolated from the historical currents of Eurasia for many centuries. Australian Aborigines mastered a hostile environment, flourished from hunting and gathering, and enjoyed a complex ritual life. In extraordinary voyages, Austronesians migrated over thousands of miles of open ocean and were inhabiting most of the Pacific islands by the end of the Classical Era. They brought ancient Asian traditions into the Pacific but adapted them to new environments, creating diverse, distinctive cultures. The Pacific peoples organized societies that tapped island resources and developed long-distance trade networks.

Australian Geography and Aboriginal Societies

Australia was settled at least 50,000 years ago. As people spread out around this vast continent, they adapted to varied environments and organized themselves into many distinct societies. By 1000 B.C.E. most of Australia and the large offshore island of Tasmania were inhabited by Aboriginal tribes speaking some two hundred distinct languages. The environments that shaped the varied societies included the tropical, heavily forested coasts of the north and northeast, the temperate river basins and coasts of the southeast and southwest, and the vast deserts of the interior.

Hunting and Gathering

Aboriginal life was based largely on hunting and gathering. The Aborigines were skilled at exploiting many food sources, for example, by harvesting sea life along the coast and wild plants and insects in the harsh desert interior. As among other hunting and gathering peoples, Aboriginal women gathered plants and small animals, prepared meals for the family, looked after the children, made the clothing, and built the huts. Men fished, hunted large animals, and manufactured implements. In their food quest, Aborigines developed an intimate understanding of local weather patterns and their relationships to plants, animals, and land. Malnutrition and starvation were largely unknown.

Agriculture never developed in part because most of the land was infertile and the rains erratic. But there were also no native plants or animals capable of domestication. There was also no incentive for farming, because hunting and gathering were successful, and the climate changes that fostered the transition to farming elsewhere had less impact in Australia. Instead, Aboriginal societies developed excellent patterns of land management and usage that enabled them to conserve their resources over thousands of years. Many Aboriginal practices operated in tandem with the environment. For example, fire could be used to clear land to encourage regrowth of edible plants, and, of course, it could be used in cooking. Deliberately set fires may also have intentionally rejuvenated the natural ecosystem.

Center for Multilingual Multicultural Research (*http://www.bcf.usc.edu/~cmmr/Asian.html*). A useful collection to sources on Asian-Pacific Island languages and cultures.

Social Structure

Although they were diverse, Aboriginal societies also had many similar customs and beliefs. Because they had to move by foot with the seasons, most communities owned few possessions. Aboriginal men carried spear throwers and spears, while women carried digging sticks and baskets to hold foodstuffs. Their seasonal moves, designed to maximize food availability, were not random. Rather, they involved relocating to the same camps every year over regular trails. For example, peoples along the swampy, flood-prone northeast coast moved to high ground during the rainy season.

Aboriginal societies were divided into tribes organized either through the patrilineal or the matrilineal line. Nuclear families operated with considerable independence but regularly came together with other families. Few tribes had chiefs, but older males exerted considerable influence in religious and social life. At the same time, women made critical decisions about the campsite and controlled their own ceremonial life. Relations between the genders, though varying from tribe to tribe, were apparently flexible. Periodic disputes broke out between neighboring tribes and sometimes led to fighting, but they were more often settled by diplomacy involving the tribal elders.

Religious Life

Because most people had only to spend about three days per week in search of food, they had considerable time for ceremonial and religious matters, as well as rich social interactions. The highly ritualized cultures were dominated by religion and its ceremonial expression. Most Aboriginal societies shared a belief in the mythology of the dreamtime, the distant past when the spiritual ancestors gave order and form to the universe at the world's creation. Aborigines also recognized an animistic world inhabited by many spirits and ghosts. Their art had a religious base and took various forms, including body decoration, bark paintings, and especially rock carvings and paintings.

Australian Trading Networks

By 1000 B.C.E., a complex trade system spanned the continent. Pearls from northwest Australia have been found hundreds of miles away, and shells from the north coast reached southern Australia. Quartz, flint, and other stones to make tools, as well as animal skins, wood products, and ornaments, were exchanged over wide areas of the continent. By classical times Indonesian trading ships probably visited the northwest coast to obtain pearls from local people. Later, Chinese ships may have also engaged in such exchanges, but these outside contacts had little influence on the lives of most Australian societies.

Austronesian Migrations and Societies

Before the Classical Era, some Austronesian-speaking peoples moved from Southeast Asia into the western Pacific islands just northeast of Australia (see Chapter 4). There they encountered Melanesians (mel-uh-NEE-zhuhnz) who had earlier migrated from Southeast Asia. Over time the two traditions mixed, and Melanesians adopted Austronesian languages. Eventually some Austronesian-speaking peoples from the western Pacific sailed further east and north to colonize other islands, in the process fostering new groups later known as Polynesians (PAHL-uh-NEE-zhunz) and Micronesians (MIE-kruh-NEE-zhunz).

Navigating the Pacific

Sailing eastward and northward into the Pacific, and using only the stars, moon, sun, winds, and waves to guide them, the migrants endured the hardships of long open sea voyages to discover new lands and extend trade networks. Navigation and boatbuilding were a science; voyagers spent many days selecting the right tree for their canoes, because worm-ridden wood might prove disastrous at sea. An ancient Tahitian prayer reveals the voyagers' fears: "O gods! Lead us safely to land. Leave us not in the ocean. Give us a breeze. Let the weather be fine and the sky clear."[10]

These intentional migrations were spurred by overpopulation on islands, most of which had limited resources. Some Pacific islands were mountainous and often covered by dense rain forests, while others were flat atolls only a few feet above sea level, which left the inhabitants vulnerable to high waves resulting from fierce storms or tsunamis. Some islands lacked enough fresh water or fertile land to support many people. Islanders either learned to limit population growth or suffered the effects of deforestation and natural resource depletion, which generated conflict or migration. Excellent naval technology made the migrations possible: each double-hulled outrigger canoe, up to 100 feet long and consisting of two hulls with a platform lashed between them for living, cooking, work space, and storage, was capable of carrying up to eighty people, along with foods, plants, and animals.

The Austronesians known today as Micronesians, who settled many central and north Pacific islands, made ingenious navigation charts from cowrie shells tied together. The Austronesian-speaking ancestors of some Micronesians, apparently originating in the Solomon Islands, eventually colonized many small islands in the central Pacific, including the Carolines. The Marianas (MAR-ee-AN-uhz) may have been settled directly by Austronesians sailing east from the Philippines between 1500 and 1000 B.C.E. The Chamorro (cha-MOR-roe) people of the Marianas were the only Pacific society to grow Asian rice, suggesting they had continuing connections with the Philippines.

Populating the Pacific

Polynesian culture seems to have flowered first in the neighboring Fiji (FEE-jee), Tonga (TAHN-guh), and Samoa (suh-MO-uh) island groups around 500 B.C.E. Ancestors to the Polynesians had reached these islands between 1100 and 800 B.C.E. (see Map 9.3), and within a few centuries some were on the move again. The voyages must have involved incredible hardships, as men, women, children, animals, and precious seed plants were crammed into open canoes. Sometime in the early Common Era, Polynesians sailed from Samoa 1,500 miles north to the Kiribati (kear-uh-BAH-tee) Islands, and then on to the Marshall Islands. Later, between 400 and 600 C.E., mariners from the

Interactive Map

dreamtime
In Aboriginal Australian mythology, the distant past when the spiritual ancestors gave order and form to the universe at the world's creation.

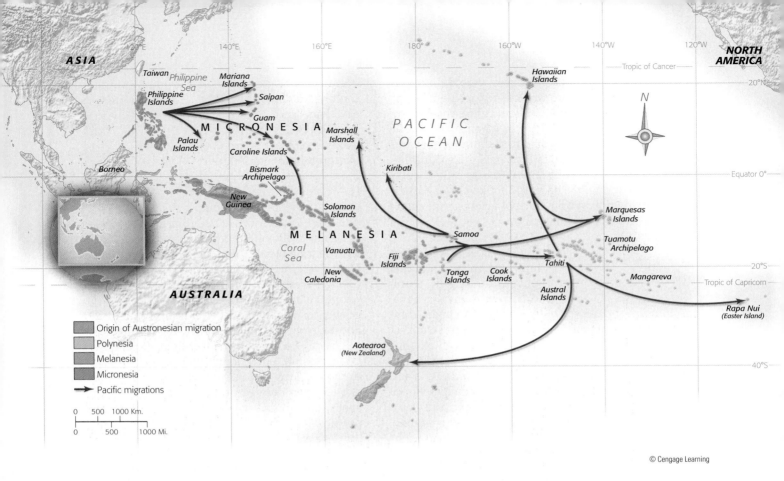

🌐 Map 9.3
Pacific Migrations in the Classical Era

During this era, Austronesian peoples scattered across the vast Pacific Basin, using ingenious canoes and navigation techniques to settle nearly all of the inhabitable islands. From bases in Tonga and Samoa in the west, the Polynesians settled a large expanse of the basin ranging from Hawaii in the north to Easter Island in the east and New Zealand in the south.

Marquesas settled Hawaii after crossing more than 2,000 miles of ocean, followed around 1100 or 1200 C.E. by a migration from Tahiti. Then Tahitians journeyed some 2,500 miles east to Easter Island. Finally, between 800 and 1000 C.E., some Tahitians moved west another 2,500 miles to Aotearoa (which a Dutch explorer much later named New Zealand), the largest landmass settled by Polynesians. These settlers, the ancestors of the Maori (MAO-ree) people, faced a very different environment from that of the tropical Pacific islands.

Polynesian Society

Polynesian settlement required adapting to such varied island environments. Their agriculture was based on Southeast Asian crops such as yams, taro, bananas, coconuts, and breadfruit, and animals including pigs, chickens, and dogs. Polynesians also exploited local food sources such as coconuts as well as the abundant marine life of the lagoons, coral reefs, and deep sea. But fragile island ecologies were easily unbalanced. For example, Easter Island, which was heavily forested when Polynesians arrived, was completely denuded over the centuries, and the people were reduced to poverty and chronic conflict over ever-scarcer resources.

Early Polynesians lived in clans that were generally dominated by hereditary chiefs. Conflict between rival clans and chiefdoms over status and land led to tensions and sometimes war. Those who felt aggrieved might seek a better life by sailing to new lands. Eventually the most elaborate social hierarchies emerged in Tonga, Tahiti, and Hawaii, where paramount chiefs ruled many thousands of followers and controlled much of the economy. While men held most political power, most Micronesian and some Polynesian societies were matrilineal, and Polynesian women often wielded significant spiritual and ritual authority.

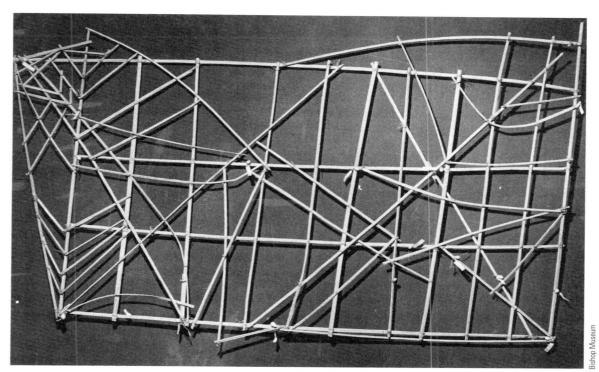

Polynesian Palm-Frond Navigational Map This nautical map, made in the Marshall Islands from palm fronds, shows distances between islands as measured by time traveled. The map may have originally had bits of shell or coral to mark islands. Polynesians and Micronesians often made such maps for their ocean voyages.

The Austronesian Dispersal in the Pacific and Beyond

Today some twelve hundred different Austronesian languages are spoken across the huge span of space from Madagascar eastward through Indonesia, Malaysia, and the Philippines to Easter Island, a few hundred miles off the west coast of South America. All of the Pacific islanders except those on and around New Guinea speak Austronesian languages. No premodern peoples migrated over as wide an area in so short a time as did the Austronesians. The huge triangle of Polynesia, anchored at the ends by Hawaii, New Zealand, and Easter Island, is one of the largest expanses of territory in the world. One of the first outsiders to explore the area, British captain James Cook, wrote in 1774 C.E.: "It is extraordinary that the same [people] should have spread themselves over all the isles in this vast Ocean, almost a fourth part of the circumference of the Globe."[11]

Migration over such vast distances did not necessarily mean isolation. The Austronesian languages may have been spread through the large maritime trading network that developed. As an example of this network, obsidian was mined on the island of New Britain, northeast of New Guinea. From there it was traded as far west as Borneo and as far east as Fiji, some 4,000 miles apart. On a smaller scale, nearby island groups traded with each other and maintained social links. The long-distance sailing could be treacherous and required remarkable observation. Even today Polynesian traditions honor great navigators such as Moikeha and Pa'ao, who sailed back and forth between the Marquesas and Hawaii over a millennium ago.

Regular trade and communication ensured that the far-flung Polynesian societies shared many linguistic and cultural traits, including elaborate facial and body tattooing (the word *tattoo* is of Polynesian origin), myths, reverence for ancestors, and art forms such as woodcarving. Many of these customs were also common in Melanesia and Micronesia, and all of these Pacific peoples derived not only their languages but also some of their culture, maritime prowess, and subsistence strategies from the Austronesians.

Listen to a synopsis of Chapter 9.

Classical Blossomings in World History, 600 B.C.E.–600 C.E.

In the second century B.C.E., a Greek historian, Polybius, observed that "the world's history has been a series of unrelated episodes, but from now on history becomes an organic whole. The affairs of Europe and Africa are connected with those of Asia and all events bear a relationship and contribute to a single end."[1] In his perception of increasing connections across cultures, Polybius identified a crucial transition. During the Classical Era, a vast exchange of ideas, cultures, and products grew in the Afro-Eurasian zone.

The commercial exchanges that were carried out along the trade routes represented the first glimmerings of a world economy centered on Asia. Greek merchants traveled as far as south India, and warehouses in the south Indian port of Pondicherry were filled with caskets of Roman wine. Goods from Persia and Rome reached Funan in Southeast Asia, while the statue of an Indian goddess was carried to the Italian city of Pompeii. Romans craved Chinese silk, Arabian incense, and Indian spices.

 Ancient and Lost Civilizations (*http://www.crystalinks.com/ancient.html*). Contains essays and other materials on ancient and classical societies.

Merchants near Kabul, in today's Afghanistan, dealt in Greek glass, Egyptian pots, Chinese lacquer ware, and Hindu carvings.

Thanks in part to greater interregional communication over widening networks of exchange, the Classical Era was a period of blossomings of many kinds. Creative philosophies established new value systems in the Mediterranean world and Asia. Between 350 B.C.E. and 200 C.E., the Afro-Eurasian world was also transformed by large regional empires. In the wake of these empires, universal religions such as Buddhism and Christianity crossed cultural boundaries, classical peoples refined their economic and social patterns, and each society was altered by contact with others.

The Axial Age of Philosophical Speculation

Between around 600 and 400 B.C.E., several societies of Eurasia faced a remarkably similar set of crises. People in China, India, Persia, Israel, and Greece were all beset by chronic warfare, population movement, political disruption, and the breakdown of traditional values. Improved ironworking technology produced better tools but also more effective weapons. Political instability was common,

as rival states competed with each other for power in China, India, the Middle East, and Greece. These troubled conditions led to a climate of spiritual and intellectual restlessness, provoking a questioning of the old order. Because of the many influential thinkers of this age, some scholars have called this an "axial period" or turning point, a crucial transition in history. This idea understates some crucial religious developments that occurred after 350 B.C.E., such as the reshaping of Hinduism, the division of Buddhism, and the rise of Christianity and

 Internet Ancient History Sourcebook (*http://www.fordham.edu/halsall/ancient/asbook.html*). An exceptionally rich collection of links and primary source readings.

Islam. Yet, the Axial Age produced enduring philosophical, religious, and scientific ideas that fostered new ways of thinking.

Axial-Age Thinkers

Many of the greatest thinkers in history were near-contemporaries; that is, they lived at roughly the same time, between 600 and 350 B.C.E. Laozi (credited by tradition as the inspiration for Daoism) and Confucius in China lived and taught in the sixth century around the same time as Buddha and Mahavira (the founder of the Jain faith) in India and the Greek thinkers Thales and Heracleitus. Other major Axial-Age thinkers included the Hebrew prophets Jeremiah, Ezekiel, and the second Isaiah, as well as Socrates, Plato, and Aristotle in Greece. Although he may have lived much earlier, the teachings of the Persian Zoroaster also became prominent in this era.

Some of these men were not only thinkers but also teachers. Confucius reflected the passion for education: "I am not someone who was born wise. I am someone who tries to learn [from the ancients]."[2] It was a time of exciting exchanges, as mystics and teachers traveled through India, dozens of philosophers spread their ideas in China, and students of Socrates competed with followers of the Stoics in the schools of Athens.

Causes and Characteristics of Axial-Age Thought

Some causes of the Axial Age were social and political instability, the effects of commercial exchanges along far-

Confucius and Laozi in Conversation This picture engraved on a stone tablet in an old Confucian temple shows Confucius visiting Laozi in the city of Loyang and amiably discussing with him views on ritual and music.

flung trade networks, relatively stable and prosperous economies, and the first glimmerings of the belief that individuals have intrinsic worth apart from their role in society. Other possible influences include the increase in cultural exchanges among Afro-Asian peoples with the spread of writing, iron tools and vehicles, and improved boats. These inventions helped stimulate human intellect and imagination.

Several themes became common to Axial-Age thinkers. First, especially in China and Greece, thinkers questioned the accepted myths and gods and promoted a humanistic view of life, one more concerned with the social and natural order than the supernatural order. Second, thinkers stressed moral conduct and values, a vision that often rejected the violent, selfish pursuit of material power they saw around them. Some, like the Buddha, Mahavira, and Laozi, were pacifists who denounced all violence. Third, Confucius, the Hebrew prophets, and several Greeks were among the first people to think about history and its lessons for societies. Fourth, while few of these thinkers favored social equality, many argued that rulers should govern with a sense of obligation to the powerless and less fortunate. Finally, all of the Axial-Age thinkers believed that the world could be improved, either by the actions of ethical individuals or by the creation of an ideal social order, or both. For example, Plato devised a model government led not by kings but by a special class of wise men.

But Axial-Age thinkers disagreed as to whether truth was absolute. Socrates and Plato, for example, argued for universal concepts, Plato writing that "those who see the absolute and eternal have real knowledge and not mere opinions." Yet, some Greeks and Chinese also explored the notion that truth was relative and dependent on circum-

stances. Philosophers still struggle with the question of universal or relative truth.

The Axial Age had not only philosophical and religious but also scientific and political consequences. Across Eurasia, people raised fundamental questions about many phenomena and answered them by systematic investigation. Greek thinkers such as Aristotle, who pondered and classified everything from political systems to animals, influenced European and Middle Eastern science, and their ideas inspired new discoveries by Hellenistic, Roman and, later, Islamic scientists. At the other end of Eurasia, Chinese influenced by Confucianism and Daoism also created another rich scientific tradition. Indians became some of the classical world's greatest mathematicians and astronomers. Axial-Age ideas built the foundation for modern science and also for new political ideologies. For example, in China, Confucianism mixed with Legalism provided the ideas for building stronger states, while Romans rose to power using modified Greek ideas of democracy. As a result of strengthening state institutions, in China, India, Persia, and Greece, the Axial Age ended in mighty empires that reflected a new order of technological and organizational planning.

The Age of Regional Empires

The empires that arose in much of Eurasia during or at the end of the Axial Age were greater in size and impact than those that had flourished in ancient times. The Persian Empire set the stage, thriving for nearly three centuries. More regional empires appeared between 350 B.C.E. and 250 C.E., from China in the East to Rome in the West, that were much grander in scale than earlier empires. In the Mediterranean Basin, Rome built on the heritage of Alexander the Great. The Parthians and then the Sassanian Persians governed some of western and Central Asia; the Chinese Han Empire dominated much of East and Central Asia; and in India the Mauryan state controlled much of the subcontinent for more than a century. Most of the empires built upon the ideas of classical sages and religious leaders, such as Confucius, Zoroaster, and Plato, in organizing society. In so doing they helped resolve the crises, such as political instability, that had sparked the rise of the Axial-Age reformers. Empires also appeared in sub-Saharan Africa and the Americas, including Aksum, Teotihuacan, and Tiwanaku, but on a smaller scale than in Eurasia.

The Rise of Empires

The first great regional empires in the Eastern Hemisphere developed during the Axial Age. The Achaemenid Empire of Persia (550–334 B.C.E.) dwarfed its Middle Eastern predecessors and was the first large empire that ruled many diverse societies. At its height it reached from Egypt and northern Greece across western Asia to Central Asia and the Indus Basin. Persian kings had reason to brag, as did Xerxes, that they were kings of lands containing many people, of the great earth far and wide; indeed, the Hellenistic Empire created by Alexander and the Macedonian Greeks built directly on the experiences of Persian imperial rule. The dynasties that succeeded Alexander dominated much of western Asia, Egypt, and southeastern Europe for the next two centuries.

 Exploring Ancient World Cultures (*http://eawc.evansville.edu/*). A very helpful collection of essays and other useful material.

By the end of the Axial Age, in the third and fourth centuries, new empires arose in Eurasia in part as a result of increased warfare. In each region one state eventually subdued its rivals; the Mauryan, Han, and Roman Empires were the results of these conflicts. Changing social and economic conditions also helped spur the rise of these empires. Rapid economic growth resulting from expanding long-distance trade networks made merchants more influential in all of these societies. The upper classes, such as the priestly brahman caste of India and the wealthy senatorial class in Rome, protected their own privileges while increasingly exploiting the peasants. The gap between rich and poor widened, causing increased tensions. Rulers surrounded themselves with the trappings of wealth and power, enjoying lavish ceremonies and giving themselves exalted titles.

But the move toward empire alleviated some social conflicts by providing large, stable environments in which resources could be acquired and distributed. During this period, the growing states required extensive administrative machinery, larger armies, standardized laws, and governing philosophies. Administrators collected taxes, organized social services, and served as judges. From China

to Rome, provinces paid taxes and supplied soldiers to the large armies needed to sustain and expand the empires. During the early Roman Empire, the armed forces received 58 percent of all government revenue; at the same time, the Han emperor stationed 300,000 troops along the Great Wall. Because everything was bigger and the stakes were higher, wars against competing states could be terribly destructive: after three wars with Carthage spanning more than a century, Rome razed that great city to the ground and laced salt into the soil to render it unfit for farming.

Philosophical and religious beliefs maintained community standards but were also used by rulers to sustain and legitimize their power. In China Confucian ideas urged people to respect leaders, and Legalist thinkers told leaders to exercise power ruthlessly. In Mauryan India, Ashoka enhanced his position by using Buddhist moral injunctions emphasizing peace, tolerance, and welfare to win popular support. Ashoka recorded his goals on pillars: "All men are my children, and just as I desire for my children that they should obtain welfare and happiness, so do I desire [the same] for all men."[3]

Increasing Cultural Unity and Contact

These new regional empires imposed peace and uniformity within their boundaries. Bureaucratic structures standardized practices throughout an empire so that the weights, measures, currencies, calendars, tax codes, and official languages used throughout its far-flung provinces were the same. Greek spread widely in the Hellenistic kingdoms of Asia; Latin became the common language in the Roman Empire, in the process fostering the western European "romance" languages, such as Spanish and French. But in Roman Asia, few outside the political elite spoke or read Latin. Similarly, the northern Chinese dialect of Mandarin became China's official spoken language even though, outside of the educated class, few in the southern half of China spoke Mandarin.

By stimulating commerce and communication, the empires fostered the spread of ideas and technologies into neighboring societies and increased contact among distant peoples. For example, Hellenistic Greeks and Mauryan Indians encountered each other in Afghanistan, a crossroads where Eurasian peoples both fought with each other and exchanged ideas. Spurred by imperial expansion, Roman culture and then Christianity permeated the Mediterranean Basin, Hellenistic Greek culture spread in western Asia and North Africa, and China influenced Japan, Korea, Vietnam, and Central Asia.

Great Empires and Trade Routes During the Classical Era, great empires often dominated East Asia, India, western Asia, North Africa, and southern Europe. Extensive land and maritime trade routes linked East Asia with western Eurasia, West Africa with the Mediterranean, and East Africa with southern Asia. >>

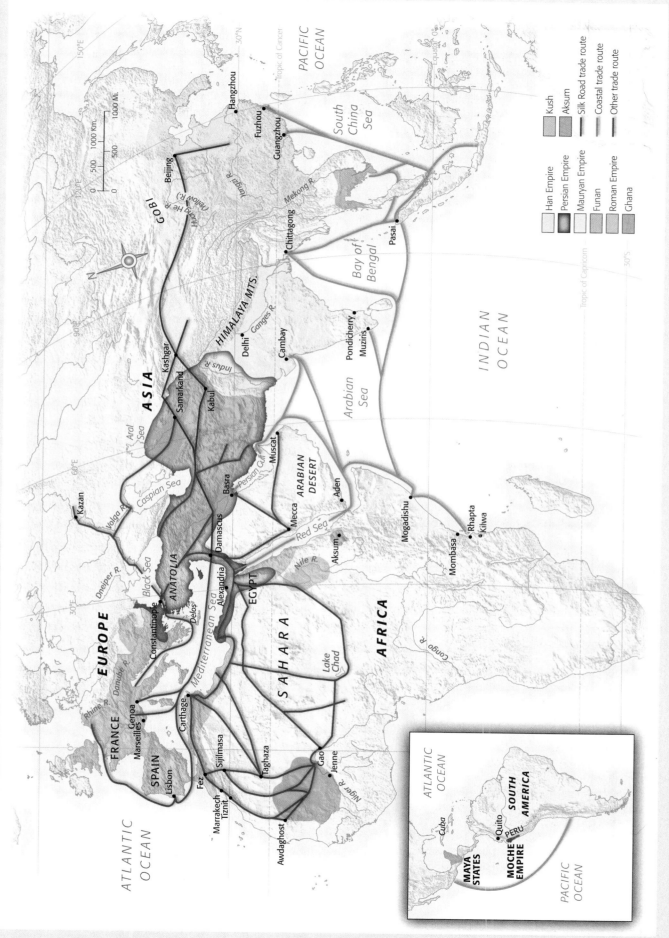

In Eurasia, trade routes grew out of transportation systems constructed to channel resources to imperial capitals. China built canals unprecedented in scale, Achaemenid Persia and Mauryan India constructed east-west highways, and the Romans developed 150,000 miles of paved roads. These roads and canals became linked to long-distance trade networks, which brought many societies, such as the Celts and Germans in northern Europe, the Sogdians in Central Asia, the Sudanic peoples of West Africa, the East African coastal dwellers, and the Japanese and Koreans, into closer contact with major empires.

Decline of Empires

While each of the great regional empires declined for different reasons, the Roman and Han Chinese Empires suffered from similar problems. Each empire expanded beyond its ability to support itself, weakening administrative structures and finances. Some conquered territories brought wealth to the empire, but others did not: the British Isles, for example, were a net drain on the imperial Roman treasury, and it was costly to maintain Chinese control in Central Asia. Both of these empires also suffered from civil wars and growing domestic unrest. Eventually both empires, unable to expand further, made economic cutbacks and raised taxes to sustain the imperial structure, which caused widespread resentment. The third-century C.E. Roman writer Cyprian recorded the decline, noting that "the World itself testifies to its own decline by giving manifold concrete evidence of the process of decay. This loss of strength and stature must end, at least, in annihilation."[4]

Both the Han and Roman Empires were also plagued by environmental problems. Because the empires formed as the global climate was warming, they could benefit from increased food supplies. Both the Han and Rome flourished during the peak of warmth between 200 B.C.E. and 200 C.E. With the return of colder weather after 200 C.E., however, agricultural production declined and the great empires collapsed or weakened. In addition, diseases traveled along the land and sea routes, undermining Rome and China in the second century C.E. Some outbreaks, like the terrible plague identified with Justinian's Byzantium, killed millions and made life miserable over wide areas. By the time the pandemic reached its end in the 590s, some 25 million West Asians, North Africans, and Europeans had perished.

When pastoral nomads began to put more pressure on the Roman and Chinese Empires, these states had been weakened so much by economic and environmental problems that they could no longer effectively resist. The Germanic tribes proved a long-term threat to Rome, and various Central Asians, among them Huns, Scythians, and Turkish peoples, continuously intruded along the fringes of Persia, India, and China. By 200 C.E., population growth and climate change pushed some of them to plunder in the declining Roman and Han Empires. In the end, the imperial orders were undermined in part by forces beyond their control.

Various peoples eventually conquered or displaced the great empires, although cultural influences endured. And the imperial idea never died: it proved particularly strong in Persia, where the Achaemenid, Hellenistic Seleucid, Parthian, and finally Sassanian Empires succeeded each other over a millennium. Even in India, where fragmented states were the norm, the Gupta rulers claimed kinship with the Mauryas five centuries earlier. The belief in the need for large regional empires also endured for centuries in China and served as a model for later dynasties. Hence, the China of the eighteenth century C.E., which incorporated many non-Chinese societies, clearly descended in recognizable form from the Han of 150 B.C.E. Similarly, the Byzantine Empire controlled vast European and western Asian territories that were once part of the old Roman Empire. After the fall of Rome, however, western Europeans never succeeded in reviving that empire, even though some Christian German kings centuries later claimed the title of Holy Roman Emperor.

World Religions and Their Influences

During the later centuries of the Classical Era, universal religions became more prominent in Afro-Eurasia, marking another great transition that reshaped societies. Instead of the gods of the ancient world, which were local and identified with particular cities or cultures, these new religions were portable and attracted believers far from their lands of birth. The Eurasian faiths with the most followers—Christianity, Buddhism, Hinduism, and Zoroastrianism—filled a vacuum created by political instability and cultural decline.

The Spread of Universal Religions

Religions spread along land and sea trade routes. A fourth-century C.E. Christian hymn in Syria implored: "Travel like merchants, That we may gain the world. Fill creation with teaching."[5] About six centuries after its founding in India, Buddhism reached China and Southeast Asia. Christianity, with roots in the eastern Mediterranean, spread to Rome, where it became prominent by the fourth century C.E.; it permeated northern Europe beginning around 500 C.E. Christianity also established roots in western Asia, Egypt, Nubia, and Ethiopia. Other faiths also established a presence. Manicheanism, a mix of Christian and Zoroastrian influences, attracted believers from North Africa to China. Judaism also gained some converts in Arabia, the Caucasus, and Ethiopia. By 500 or 600 C.E., small Christian and Jewish communities had even been established in Central Asia, western India, and northern China.

The universal religions gave people hope in the face of the political and social crises that marked the decline of the great regional empires from the second through the fifth centuries C.E. Sometimes these new religions merged with or incorporated existing beliefs. In East Asia, for example, Buddhism gradually blended with or accommodated Confucianism, Daoism, and Shinto, and, in northern Europe, Christianity acquired a Germanic or Celtic flavor over the centuries.

In sub-Saharan Africa and the Americas, some religious beliefs reached across many societies, becoming the counterparts to the organized Eurasian religions. The polytheistic beliefs of the Mande and other Sudanic peoples, for instance, gradually spread to the Guinea coast and Central Africa, and from there to eastern and southern Africa. In the Americas, the Olmecs introduced gods and views of the universe that contributed to the later religious beliefs of the Maya, and some Maya ideas may have spread to other Mesoamericans. Chavín religious traditions, including gods and shamanistic practices, probably influenced the views of other Andean peoples, such as the Moche and Tiwanaku. Some of the American peoples practiced human sacrifice, as did the Celts, Minoan Crete, ancient Egypt, and Shang China.

Bibliotheque nationale de France

King David For centuries, artists in the Christian Ethiopian kingdom, in the highlands of Northeast Africa, painted biblical figures on the pages of religious manuscripts. The artists often used Ethiopian motifs, and this painting of the Hebrew king, David, adorned in rich robes and crown and playing a harp-type instrument, resembles that of an Ethiopian king.

Religion, Culture, and Society

The universal religions became a major force in shaping the societies and regions in which they became dominant, eventually creating, for example, a largely Hindu India, a Buddhist Sri Lanka, and a Christian Europe. But after the regional empires collapsed into many rival states in the Mediterranean, India, and China, religious institutions transcended political divisions, fostering cultural unity across borders. Hindus, Buddhists, and Christians often saw themselves as part of larger communities. As a result, Chinese Buddhist pilgrims such as Faxian made the long and arduous journey to India to study with Indian Buddhists. Religion also offered the poor the hope that they might end their suffering and low status, if not in this life, then through reincarnation or in some form of heaven.

All of the universal religions, as well as the religions of urban American societies such as the Maya, had certain features, practices, and beliefs in common. They had sacred writings or scriptures, such as the Hindu Vedas and Christian Bible, strict moral codes, organized priesthoods, theologies laying out core beliefs, and some concept of existence after death. Most faiths also encouraged followers to treat others as they wanted to be treated themselves. The devout shared a belief in the universal truth of their faith. All of the religions were patriarchal to one degree or another, adding religious sanction to the growing suppression of women.

For all the spiritual comfort and insight they provided to believers, these new religions were also important as forces of social control. For example, Hindu ideas of reincarnation and karma underpinned the Indian caste system, encouraging people to accept their status. Christians focused on attaining heaven and were warned that questioning religious authority and beliefs might prevent salvation. Some of the religious establishments grew intolerant of dissent. For this reason, Christian bishops established a consensus on doctrine, excluding ideas considered to be heresy. Those who disagreed with Christian or Zoroastrian orthodoxy might be banned or punished, and they were expected to face retribution after death in hell.

Monasticism and Its Diffusion

Some of the universal religions spawned a new social and spiritual movement, monasticism. In Theravada Buddhist societies, most men spent some period as monks, bound by their rigid code of celibacy and poverty. But the concept then perhaps spread over the trade networks into western Asia. Whether or not inspired by Buddhist models, monasticism became a growing component of organized Christianity by the third century C.E.

Whether Christian or Buddhist, monasteries provided educational and charitable services while providing a focus for community religious life. In societies as far removed as England, Nubia, and China, a substantial number of men (and some women) joined monastic orders, abandoning the humdrum existence of everyday life for a focus on prayer and meditation. Most monks and nuns practiced austere religious practices such as sexual abstinence, fasting, and solitary contemplation. In the Hindu tradition, wandering holy men abandoned the comforts of settled life and families.

Changing Economic and Social Patterns

Increased migration and communication fostered major social and economic changes. Population growth encour-

Crossing the Pamir Mountains The Pamir Mountains, separating the deserts of what is now western China from the deserts and grasslands of Turkestan and Afghanistan, were one of the more formidable barriers faced by camel caravans traveling the Silk Road. To avoid the blistering summer heat of the desert, the caravans often traveled in winter, forcing them to maneuver through mountain snows.

Michael Fairchild/Peter Arnold

aged migration, which led to the intermixing of peoples and the exchange of ideas. Deadly disease epidemics moving along migration networks testified to this widespread contact between distant peoples. The long-distance trade routes also spread certain social practices, including attitudes toward women and slaves that lasted for centuries.

The Growth and Decline of World Population

Successful agricultural systems in the great empires allowed for substantial population growth from Europe to China. At the beginning of the Common Era, there were probably between 200 and 250 million people, more than 70 percent living in Asia and about 20 million each in Africa and the Americas. China was the largest society, with some 60 million people. In 450 B.C.E. the world's largest city was probably Babylon, with 200,000 people. By 100 C.E. Rome was the largest metropolis, with at least 500,000 people and perhaps 1 million.

But diseases began to limit population growth in the later Classical Era. Networks of exchange were often networks of contagion, with port cities the major hubs of transmission. Epidemics of smallpox and plague resulted from travelers unknowingly spreading new diseases into areas where people had not yet built up immunities to them. Epidemic diseases may have killed as many as 25 percent of the population of China and the Roman Empire during the second and third centuries C.E. Indeed, plague outbreaks contributed considerably to the decline of the classical empires. As a result, by 600 B.C.E. the world population remained between 200 and 240 million, similar to what it had been six centuries earlier.

Population growth led to increased movement, as people sought open lands and better opportunities. Responding to population pressures, Chinese migrants moved into central and southern China; Germanic and Turkish peoples spread into central Europe and western Asia, respectively; Bantu-speaking peoples occupied the southern half of Africa; and Austronesians settled remote Pacific islands. As groups migrated, they assimilated local peoples and adapted their lives to new surroundings.

Trade and Cultural Contact

The networks of trade, like those of imperial expansion and missionary activity, linked distant peoples while spreading the influence of cultures more widely. The Greeks picked up scientific and mathematical knowledge as well as some religious notions from the Egyptians and Phoenicians. Indian cultural influences, including Buddhism, spread over the trade routes into Central, East, and Southeast Asia, reaching as far

 Silk Road Narratives (*http://depts .washington.edu/uwch/ silkroad/texts/texts .html*). Explores cultural interaction in Eurasia through excerpts from Silk Road travelers.

as Korea, Japan, and Indonesia. Aksum was linked by commerce with the Mediterranean world and India, a link that brought Christianity to the Ethiopian highlands. Precious spices from southern Arabia, textiles from India, and gold from Malaya and West Africa found their way to the Mediterranean societies. Trade also connected Mesoamerica with neighboring regions and fostered networks of exchange in both eastern North America and western South America. Copper from the North American Great Lakes reached the Gulf Coast, Mesoamerican ball games spread far and wide, and tomatoes from the Andes carried into Central America and Mexico.

The Silk Road endured as a major overland long-distance network of exchange—in effect the first transcontinental highway—and allowed people, goods, and ideas to travel thousands of miles. As a Han dynasty history put it: "Messengers come and go every season and month, foreign traders and merchants knock on the gates of the Great Wall every day."[6] In Eurasia the introduction of coinage encouraged trade by offering widely recognized tokens of value. Indeed, the huge amounts of gold and silver exported by Rome to pay for Chinese silk and Indian spices did some damage to the Roman economy. Overland trade expanded with the growing use of camels, which became the trucks of the pre modern Afro-Eurasian zone. The merchants who used the camels carried not only bullion and products but also religions, especially Buddhism and Manicheanism, which spread along the Silk Road into Central Asia and China.

Cities grew up along the Silk Road across Central Asia to serve as suppliers and middlemen to the merchants. These cities, such as Kashgar in Xinjiang and Samarkand in Turkestan, became part of a contact zone linking many societies. Hubs at the eastern end of the Mediterranean, such as Petra, Palmyra, Alexandria, and Constantinople, served as transshipment points for goods traveling between China and Rome.

Maritime trade also flourished during this period, enriching various ports. Hence, both trade goods and cultural influences were carried by sea between eastern and western Asia. Sailing networks connected the entire Mediterranean Basin. For several centuries, one key network hub was the tiny Greek island of Delos (DEH-los) in the Aegean Sea, of which it was said, "Merchant, sail in and unload! Everything is as good as sold."[7] Merchants from all over, including Greeks from around the Mediterranean, Romans, Syrians, Jews, Phoenicians, Nabataean Arabs, and Yemenite Arabs, flocked to Delos to trade.

Eventually a vast maritime route linked China, Vietnam, and Cambodia in the East through Malaya and the Indonesian archipelago to India and Sri Lanka, and then stretched westward to Persia, Arabia, and the East African coast. Europe and North Africa were connected to this system through the Arabs, Aksumites, and Persians. The Greek geographer Strabo wrote that since merchants from Roman-ruled Alexandria had sent trading fleets to India, "these regions have become better known to us today."[8] Products from as far away as Java and Cambodia reached the markets of Berenike, and eleven different written languages, including Greek and Sanskrit, were used there. Berenike was also linked through Alexandria to the Mediterranean societies.

Maritime commerce faced serious limitations, however. Because of formidable currents, only the strongest oars would allow a boat to pass through the Strait of Gibraltar separating Spain from North Africa. This problem inhibited trade between Mediterranean and Atlantic societies for many centuries. Similarly, the vast distances of the Pacific Ocean, crossed in that day only by outrigger canoes, limited the volume and type of goods carried along the trading networks there.

Social Systems and Attitudes

The social systems and attitudes of the Classical Era set the patterns for centuries to come. In many places, gender roles hardened: in Greece and China, customs and laws allowed men far greater social freedom than women. Because the great empires were made through military conquest, they were very masculine in nature. In addition, patriarchal attitudes were encouraged by some of the new philosophies and religions. The faiths that replaced Greek and Roman religions removed goddesses as objects of worship in the Mediterranean world, although in southern Asia many Hindus continued to revere female deities. Earlier in the classical period, homosexuality was generally tolerated, especially in Greece and Rome. Chinese historians reported that many emperors of the era, including the empire-builder Wu Di of the Han dynasty, had male lovers in addition to their wives and concubines. But in many places official attitudes concerning gender roles and sexual behaviors became more rigid over time, pushing homosexuals to the margins of society.

Changing social and religious attitudes affected women. Although women had some legal protections in Greece and Rome, many also lived generally domestic and often secluded lives. When Roman women in 195 B.C.E. took to the streets to protest a law, passed during a costly war, that limited the amount of gold and finery a woman could wear, many men complained that women should stay home and out of politics. Women faced increasing restrictions in China and north India, where they were expected to be obedient to men. Patriarchy was also common in Africa, the Americas, and the Pacific islands. While there were notable exceptions, the leaders in Aksum and in the Maya city-states were mostly men.

But wherever they lived, women had varied experiences. Some were treated as property, assigned by their fathers to husbands, and many faced permanent dependency on fathers, husbands, and sons. Only a small minority of women anywhere were educated, Hypatia of Alexandria and Ban Zhao in China being notable examples. However, a few, such as Queen Zenobia in Palmyra, Cleopatra VII in Egypt, Queen Theodora in Byzantium, and several Kushite queens, attained great power. Some women asserted their own interests, a behavior reflected in some Greek plays. Thus, in Antigone (an-TIG-on-ee) by Sophocles, the main female character defies King Creon, who refuses to allow her to give her dead brother a proper burial.

Like patriarchy, slavery was practiced in many classical societies around the world. Most people saw slavery as a part of the natural order of things and essential to economic life. Slaves everywhere were bought and sold at the whim of the owner, and their lives and labor were controlled. In societies such as Han China, Mauryan India, Aksum, and the Maya society, slaves were only one segment of the lower class, whereas in Greece and Rome slaves constituted a large part of the population and were used in every area of the economy, from mining and construction to prostitution and domestic work. Slavery mostly died out in China and India during the first millennium C.E. and became less important in Europe after the collapse of the Roman Empire.

Test your understanding of the material covered in Part II.

Suggested Reading

Adas, Michael, ed. *Agricultural and Pastoral Societies in Ancient and Classical History.* Philadelphia, PA: Temple University Press, 2001. A useful collection of essays on various topics.

Bentley, Jerry H. *Old World Encounters: Cross-Cultural Contacts and Exchanges in Pre-Modern Times.* New York: Oxford University Press, 1993. An up-to-date survey of trade routes and the spread of universal religions.

Bulliet, Richard W. *The Camel and the Wheel.* Cambridge, MA: Harvard University Press, 1975. A classic study of the caravan trade in Asia and Africa.

Curtin, Philip D. *Cross-Cultural Trade in World History.* Cambridge, England: Cambridge University Press, 1984. Contains much material on long-distance trade in the Classical Era.

Fernandez-Armesto, Felipe. *Civilizations: Culture, Ambition, and the Transformation of Nature.* New York: Touchstone, 2001. A fascinating and wide-ranging survey across eras and regions that emphasizes adaptations to varied environments.

Foltz, Richard C. *Religions of the Silk Road: Overland Trade and Cultural Exchange from Antiquity to the Fifteenth Century.* New York: St.Martin's, 1999. Analyzes the spread of religions.

Lloyd, Geoffrey, and Nathan Sivin. *The Way and the Word: Science and Medicine in Early China and Greece*. New Haven, CT: Yale University Press, 2003. Compares these two great traditions of learning, arguing that modern science derives from both as well as from Indian, Islamic, and other cultures.

McClellan, James, and Harold Dorn. *Science and Technology in World History: An Introduction*. Baltimore, MD: Johns Hopkins University Press, 1999. A survey of science and technology traditions.

Pearson, Michael. *The Indian Ocean*. New York: Routledge, 2003. A history of the maritime connections.

Prazniak, Roxann. *Dialogues Across Civilizations: Sketches in World History from the Chinese and European Experiences*. Boulder, CO: Westview, 1996. Contains interesting comparative essays.

Smart, Ninian. *The Long Search*. Boston: Little, Brown and Co., 1977. A very readable introduction to the various universal religious traditions of Eurasia and their modern offshoots.

Super, John C. and Brian K. Turley. *Religion in World History*. New York: Routledge, 2006. Brief study of religious diffusion and change.

Wood, Frances. *The Silk Road*. Berkeley: University of California Press, 2002. Surveys 2,000 years of history.

PART III

Expanding Horizons:

Transformations in the Intermediate Era, ca. 600–1500

NORTH AND CENTRAL AMERICA
The Maya city-states flourished for centuries until the cities were abandoned. The Toltecs dominated central Mexico for two hundred years. In the 1400s the Aztecs conquered a large empire in Mexico and built a huge capital city. North of Mexico, societies such as the Anasazi lived in towns and farmed in the desert for centuries. To the east the Mississippian peoples built mounds and a grand city while trading over a vast area. Farming villages also dotted the east coast.

ARCTIC OCEAN

NORTH AMERICA

ANASAZI

MISSISSIPPI R.

MISSISSIPPIAN

AZTECS MAYA

ATLANTIC OCEAN

PACIFIC OCEAN

Amazon

SOUTH AMERICA

ANDES

INCA

SOUTH AMERICA
For most of the era Tiwanaku, in the Andes, and the Chimu Empire, based on the Peruvian coast, were the dominant powers in western South America. In the 1400s the Incas conquered most of the region, creating the largest empire in the history of the Americas. Skilled farmers, the Incas used a powerful but paternalistic state to rule millions of people.

© Cengage Learning

EUROPE

[I]n western Europe a rigid society, dominated by a powerful [C]hristian church, slowly emerged, reaching its zenith [a]round 1000 C.E. Dozens of small rival states fought each [o]ther. Urban and commercial growth, technological [i]nnovation, and the Black Death eventually undermined [f]eudalism and church power, and political, intellectual, [a]rtistic, and religious change began reshaping western [E]urope in the 1400s. At the same time, imported Chinese [a]nd Arab naval and military technology helped spur [m]aritime explorations. Meanwhile, Byzantium struggled to [h]old its eastern Mediterranean empire but also spread its [c]ulture to the Russians.

WESTERN ASIA

The rise of Islam in Arabia in the 600s transformed the region. Arab Muslim armies conquered much of Western Asia, and most of the region's peoples eventually embraced Islam. Islam also spread west through North Africa and into Spain, as well as east to India, Central Asia, and Indonesia, linking Western Asians with a vast Islamic community. Islam divided into rival Sunni and Shi'a schools. Muslim scholars fostered science and literature, and major Islamic states, especially the Abbasid Empire, dominated the region. Eventually the Ottoman Turks formed the most powerful Western Asian state, conquering Byzantium.

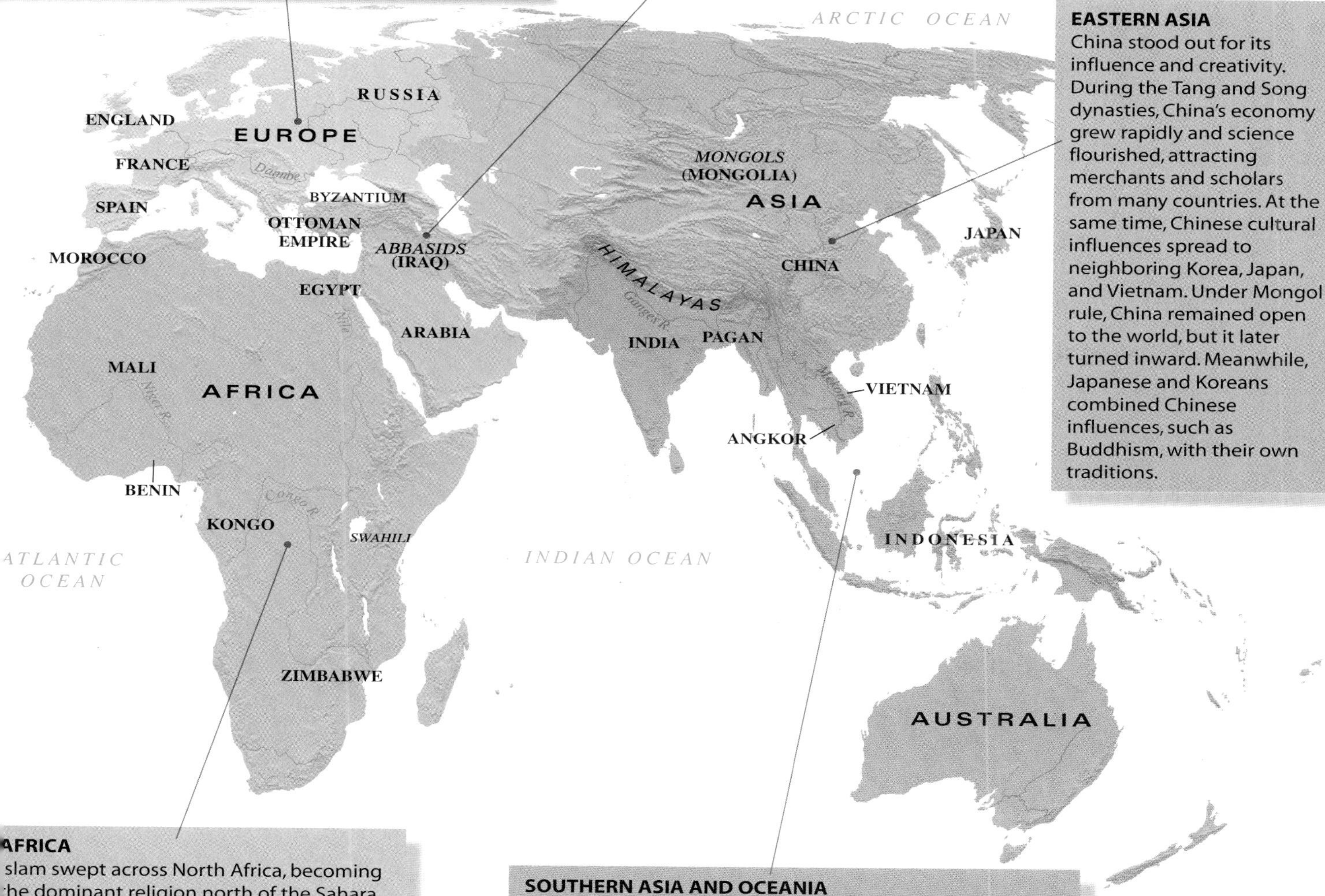

EASTERN ASIA

China stood out for its influence and creativity. During the Tang and Song dynasties, China's economy grew rapidly and science flourished, attracting merchants and scholars from many countries. At the same time, Chinese cultural influences spread to neighboring Korea, Japan, and Vietnam. Under Mongol rule, China remained open to the world, but it later turned inward. Meanwhile, Japanese and Koreans combined Chinese influences, such as Buddhism, with their own traditions.

AFRICA

[I]slam swept across North Africa, becoming [t]he dominant religion north of the Sahara. [I]t also reshaped societies as it spread into [W]est Africa and East Africa. Sub-Saharan [A]frican peoples formed large empires, such [a]s Mali, and flourishing states, such as [B]enin, Kongo, and Zimbabwe. West African [k]ingdoms and East African coastal cities [w]ere closely tied to world trade. In the [1]400s the Portuguese explored the West [A]frican coast and disrupted African states.

SOUTHERN ASIA AND OCEANIA

Although politically fragmented into diverse rival states, India remained a major commercial and manufacturing center. Muslims from West and Central Asia conquered parts of north India, spreading Islam there. In response, Hinduism became reinvigorated. Southeast Asians flourished from farming and maritime trade, and major kingdoms, notably Angkor and Pagan, emerged. Southeast Asians imported ideas from India, China, and the Middle East, and many people adopted Theravada Buddhism or Islam. Maritime trade, especially the export of spices, and the spread of Islam and Buddhism linked Southeast Asia to the wider Afro-Eurasian world. Meanwhile, Polynesians settled the last uninhabited Pacific islands, including Hawaii and New Zealand.

Map labels: ARCTIC OCEAN · RUSSIA · ENGLAND · EUROPE · FRANCE · SPAIN · MOROCCO · BYZANTIUM · OTTOMAN EMPIRE · ABBASIDS (IRAQ) · EGYPT · ARABIA · MALI · AFRICA · Niger R. · BENIN · KONGO · Congo R. · SWAHILI · ZIMBABWE · ATLANTIC OCEAN · INDIAN OCEAN · MONGOLS (MONGOLIA) · ASIA · HIMALAYAS · Ganges R. · CHINA · JAPAN · INDIA · PAGAN · VIETNAM · ANGKOR · INDONESIA · AUSTRALIA · Danube

CHAPTER 10

The Rise, Power, and Connections of the Islamic World,

600–1500

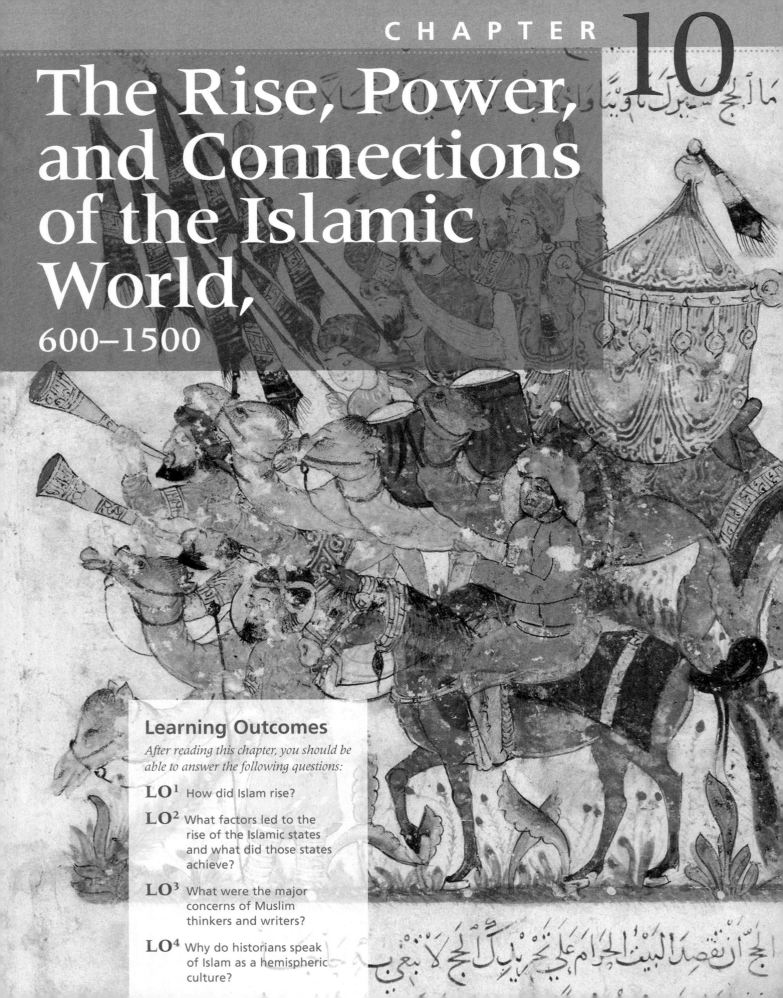

Learning Outcomes

After reading this chapter, you should be able to answer the following questions:

LO¹ How did Islam rise?

LO² What factors led to the rise of the Islamic states and what did those states achieve?

LO³ What were the major concerns of Muslim thinkers and writers?

LO⁴ Why do historians speak of Islam as a hemispheric culture?

Bibliothèque nationale de France

"Then came Islam. All institutions underwent change. It distinguished [believers] from other nations and ennobled them. Islam became firmly established and securely rooted. Far-off nations accepted Islam."

—Ibn Khaldun, fourteenth-century Arab historian[1]

In 1382 the author of these words, the fifty-year-old Arab scholar Abd al-Rahman Ibn Khaldun (AHB-d al-ruh-MAHN ib-uhn kal-DOON), left his longtime home in Tunis in North Africa and moved east to Egypt. He was already renowned as a thinker, and his work reflected the expansive cosmopolitan nature of Islamic society. After seven years of research and writing, he had recently completed his greatest work, a monumental history of the world known to educated Muslims that was the first attempt by a historian anywhere to discover and explain the changes in societies over time, especially those shaped by Islam.

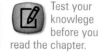

Test your knowlege before you read the chapter.

After growing up in Tunis, Ibn Khaldun visited and worked in various cities of North Africa and Spain. He served diverse rulers as a jurist, adviser, or diplomat. Now he was settling in Cairo (KYE-roh), Egypt, a city he praised as the "metropolis of the world, garden of the universe, meeting-place of nations, ant hill of peoples, high place of Islam, seat of power."[2] Cairo remained his home for the rest of his life as he served as a judge and a teacher, reading, writing voluminously, and traveling with high Egyptian officials to Palestine, Syria, and Arabia. Six centuries after his family left Arabia for the western Mediterranean, he could visit their ancestral homeland and feel at home.

The rise of Islam that produced Ibn Khaldun and his world was a major historical turning point that led to widespread change. The Islamic religion originated in seventh-century Arabia and eventually spread across several continents. Today Islam is, after Christianity, the second largest religion in the world, embraced by about one-fifth of the world's population. A dynamic faith, Islam adapted to a multitude of cultures while remaining close to its founding ideals. For

What do you think?

Islam spread rapidly because it readily absorbed cultural influences from other societies.

Strongly Disagree						Strongly Agree
1	2	3	4	5	6	7

<< **Pilgrimage Caravan** Every year caravans of Muslim pilgrims converged on Islam's holiest city, Mecca, in Arabia. This painting shows such a caravan led by a band. Pilgrims came from as far away as Morocco and Spain in the west and Indonesia and China in the east.

nearly one thousand years, Islamic peoples dominated much of the Eastern Hemisphere. Muslim thinkers salvaged or developed major portions of the science and mathematics that formed the basis for later industrial society, and Muslim sailors and merchants opened or extended networks that spread goods, technologies, and ideas throughout Afro-Eurasia.

LO¹ Early Islam: The Origins of a Continuous Tradition

The Islamic religion was founded in the seventh century in the Arabian peninsula, a land inhabited mainly by nomads who lived on the fringes of more powerful societies. Islam was inspired by the visions of a single influential man, Muhammad (moo-HAM-mad), and was influenced by Jewish and Christian thought. It quickly developed from a small Arab sect into the dominant faith of many millions of people throughout the Eastern Hemisphere.

The Middle Eastern Sources of Islam

Islam developed in a part of the Middle East known as the Arabian peninsula in southwestern Asia. Much of the Middle East, including Arabia, is a harsh, parched land that has long been a region of great cultural diversity. The peoples of Egypt, Mesopotamia, and Achaemenid Persia had produced flourishing societies in ancient times. Later the Hellenistic Greeks and Byzantine Empire influenced the region. Between 611 and 619, Sassanian Persia conquered Syria, Palestine, and Egypt, and during the sixth century the Persians, Byzantines, and Ethiopians all interfered in Arabian politics. By the end of the Classical Era, many Middle Eastern people were Christians, including sects such as the Monophysites and Nestorians, which were considered heretical by orthodox Christians. These diverse traditions eventually influenced Islam.

Islam's Arabian Cultural Matrix

Islam was also the product of a distinctive Arab culture and society. The Arabs, a Semitic people, occupied the desolate Arabian peninsula, where life was sustained by scattered oases and a few areas of fertile highlands. Survival in a sparsely populated environment depended on cooperation within small groups of related peoples divided into patriarchal clans and tribes. Many Arab tribes were tent-dwelling nomadic pastoralists, known as Bedouins (BED-uh-wuhnz), who wandered in search of oases, grazing lands, or trade caravans to raid. Poetry was central to Arabian life: one month a year, raids and battles were halted so that poets could gather and compete. The Arab romantic poetry tradition may have been taken to Europe centuries later by Christian crusaders, and there it may have influenced the chivalric love songs of medieval European troubadours.

Arabian Religion Before Islam

Arabia was saturated with ideas from diverse religious traditions, including Judaism, Christianity, and Zoroastrianism. Like their Hebrew neighbors, the Arabs believed that they were descended from Abraham, but through his son Ishmael, not Isaac, as the Hebrews claimed to be. While some Arabs had adopted Judaism or Christianity, most were polytheistic. Some tribes believed that the chief god was housed in a huge sacred cube-shaped stone, known as the Ka'ba (KAH-buh), in Mecca (MEK-uh), a bustling trading city in central Arabia near the Red Sea to which people made annual pilgrimages.

The Prophet Muhammad's Life and Message

The founder of Islam was Muhammad Ibn Abdullah (ca. 570–632). There is controversy among historians concerning Muhammad's life, how much Islamic thought arose out of older ideas, and the factors that shaped the expansion of the Arabs and Islam. But according to the traditional accounts by both Muslim and Western historians, Muhammad was a member of the Hashemite (HASH-uh-mite) clan of the prosperous mercantile Quraysh (KUR-aysh) tribe of Mecca. After becoming a merchant, Muhammad began shipping goods for a wealthy and prominent twice-widowed older woman, Khadija (kah-DEE-juh), who had capitalized on the opportunities that city life sometimes gave ambitious women. They soon married. Although Muhammad's business operating trade caravans flourished, he came to believe that Meccan merchants had become greedy, contrary to Arab traditions of generosity.

The Beginnings of Islam

In seeking answers to his concerns, Muhammad often retreated to meditate in the barren mountains around Mecca. His prophetic career began in 610, when he had a series of visions in which an angel revealed God's word. Alarmed, he consulted one of his wife's cousins, a monotheist who encouraged him to see the visions as authentic revelations from God. Fearing that he was possessed by demons, Muhammad often agonized about the visions, but he eventually came to be convinced of their truth, largely because of the support given by his wife Khadija, his closest spiritual adviser: "She believed in me when no one else did. She considered me to be truthful when the people called me a liar."[3] Muhammad began preaching the new faith of *Islam* ("submission to God's will") to a few followers, or *Muslims* (MUZ-limz) ("those who had submitted to God's will"), who were mostly drawn from among his middle-class friends and relatives. Muhammad insisted that he was human, not divine. To believers, Muhammad's visions were the last of several occasions in history during which God spoke to prophets, communicating through them from the divine to the human realm. The earlier prophets were Adam, Abraham, Moses, and Jesus, and Muhammad was considered the final voice superseding the others (see Witness to the Past: The Holy Book, God, and the Prophet in the Quran).

The Quran and the Hadith

In the 650s, several decades after Muhammad's death, his followers compiled his revelations into an official version, the Quran (kuh-RAHN), which became Islam's holiest book, to believers the inspired word of God. A second book revered by many Muslims as a source of belief, the Hadith (hah-DEETH), meaning "narrative," compiled by Muslim scholars into an official version during the ninth and tenth centuries, collected the remembered words and deeds of Muhammad himself. A source of religious guidance and law, the Hadith helped explain the principles of the Quran. Both Jews and Christians lived in Mecca, and many of the principle ideas of Islam clearly resemble some Judeo-Christian traditions. Like in these faiths, Muhammad's views were strictly monotheistic, and believers were assured of an afterlife. In Islam, Muhammad established principles of equality and justice, advocating for the sharing of all wealth, living simply, and guaranteeing women certain rights formerly denied them.

Rejection and the Hijra

Muhammad soon faced challenges. Mecca leaders rejected Muhammad's views and saw him and his followers as a threat to their position. He and his allies were harassed, and some enemies even plotted Muhammad's murder. In 619 his wife Khadija died, followed by the uncle who raised him, an influential tribal chief. The loss of his two most powerful supporters left Muhammad in despair. Meanwhile, the nearby city of Medina became engulfed in strife, and the contending factions invited Muhammad, respected for his fairness and honesty, to go there and arbitrate their disputes. Muhammad's life changed when he accepted the offer.

In 622 Muhammad led seventy Muslims and their families from Mecca to Medina, an event known as the hijra (HIJ-ruh), or "emigration." Hence, to believers, 622, which begins the Muslim calendar, represents humanity's response to God's message. In Medina the Muslims sought to form a new community of believers, or umma, united around God's message. Many of the Medinans came to accept Muhammad as the true Prophet, and he built his first mosque there, and took new wives. Because frequent warfare and raiding killed off many men, Arab men often had several wives so they could protect vulnerable women and procreate more children. Concerned for the welfare of women without husbands, Muhammad urged his men to marry widows, who had no protection or

Explore life in the middle ages through the eyes of a Muslim in this interactive simulation.

Quran
("Recitation") Islam's holiest book; contains the official version of Muhammad's revelations, and to believers is the inspired word of God.

Hadith
The remembered words and deeds of Muhammad, revered by many Muslims as a source of belief.

hijra
The emigration of Muslims from Mecca to Medina in 622.

umma
The community of Muslim believers united around God's message.

Witness to the Past

The Holy Book, God, and the Prophet in the Quran

The Quran is organized according to the length of individual chapters, so that early and later revelations are mixed together. That is, it does not follow a rigid organization of thoughts. In addition, the beauty of the powerful, poetic writing style is not always apparent in English translation, where most of the nuances of the Arabic language are lost. In Arabic the Quran clearly comes across as both a scripture and an elegant literature that has inspired millions. The following brief excerpts present some basic ideas about the holy book itself, the unity and power of the monotheistic God, and the recognition of Muhammad as a human prophet or apostle to God.

In the name of the Merciful and Compassionate God. That is the Book! There is no doubt therein; a guide to the pious, who believe in the unseen, and are steadfast in prayer, and of what we have given them expend in alms; who believe in what is revealed to thee, and what was revealed before thee, and of the hereafter they are sure. These are in guidance from their Lord, and these are the prosperous. . . .

God, there is no god but He, the living, the self-subsistent. Slumber takes Him not, nor sleep. His is what is in the heavens and what is in the earth. Who is it that intercedes with Him save by His permission? He knows what is before them and what behind them, and they comprehend not aught of His knowledge but of what He pleases. His throne extends over the heavens and the earth, and it tires him not to guard them both, for He is high and grand. . . . On Him is the call of truth, and those who call on others than Him shall not be answered at all, save as one who stretches out his hand to the water that it may reach his mouth, but it reaches it not! The call of the misbelievers is always in error. . . . In the name of the Merciful and Compassionate God, Say "He is God alone!"

Muhammad is but an apostle; apostles have passed away before his time; what if he die or is killed, will ye retreat upon your heels? He who retreats upon his heels does no harm to God at all; but God will recompense the thankful. . . . Muhammad is not the father of any of your men, but the Apostle of God, and the Seal of the Prophets; for God all things doth know!

Thinking About the Reading

1. What is the purpose of the Quran?
2. What are the powers of God?
3. What is the relationship between Muhammad and God?

Source: Excerpts taken from Chapters 2, 3, 13, and 33 of the Quran, as reprinted in L. S. Stavrianos, ed., *The Epic of Man to 1500* (Englewood Cliffs, NJ: Prentice-Hall, 1970), pp. 210–211.

---

support. He also required that all wives be treated equally and fairly.

Muhammad's growing popularity earned him more enemies. While some Medina Jews became allies, others mocked his beliefs. Muhammad urged his followers to respect sympathetic Christians and Jews, saying, "Dispute not with the People of the Book. We believe in what has been sent down to us, and what has been sent down to you; our God and your God is One."[4] But, believing he needed strong methods to preserve his umma in Medina, he expelled two Jewish tribes and had all the men of another killed because he suspected them of aiding his opponents. Muhammad's followers also fought and won various military skirmishes with his Meccan enemies, usually against much larger armies. In general, Muhammad was a merciful, pragmatic leader, usually willing to negotiate rather than shed blood.

Muhammad's Victory and the Emergence of the Caliphate

Muhammad's brilliant military victories and shrewd diplomacy made him the most powerful man in Arabia. After he was able to visit Mecca again, Muhammad pardoned most of his foes in the city, assumed power, and shared the taxes from trade with those who became Muslim. He then began building a confederacy to extend the influence and range of his umma. Gradually the Bedouin and Quraysh of the region converted to Islam. Muhammad's triumph in Mecca marked a shift of power in central Arabia.

Muhammad's message of monotheism, community, equality, and justice—concepts already familiar to some peoples in the region—proved a powerful attraction because it dissolved social barriers between tribes and encouraged assimilation into a larger spir-

Muhammad Enters a City in Triumph Although Islamic custom discourages painting images of the Prophet, Muslim artists, especially Persians and Turks, have done so over the centuries, such as this painting from an Islamic collection that shows Muhammad leading his followers into Mecca for the first time. An angel on the gate cries, "Thou are the prophet of God."

Courtesy, Nasser D. Khalili Collection of Islamic Art

itual community. In 632, in his last sermon at Mecca, Muhammad told his audience to deal justly with each other, treat women kindly, and consider all Muslims as brothers: "Know that every Muslim is a brother to every other Muslim and that you are now one brotherhood."[5] His message emphasized the one and only, all-powerful God, Allah (AH-luh).

A short time after his last sermon at Mecca, Muhammad died at age sixty-two. Islam faced a challenge with his passing. Muhammad had left little guidance on the umma's leadership after his death, and the issue provoked disagreements. The four men closest to him formed a caliphate (KAL-uhf-uht), an imperial state headed by an Islamic ruler, or caliph (KAL-uhf), considered the designated successor of the Prophet in civil affairs. In the earliest years after the Prophet's death, the umma was ruled from Medina by the Arab merchant aristocracy through Muhammad's four consecutive successors, known later as the Rashidun ("rightly guided") caliphs. These four men in succession constituted the first caliphate (632–661), but disagreements about succession continued.

Islamic Beliefs and Society

Muslims considered their faith the last revealed religion, believing that it built on and succeeded Judaism and Christianity. Like many Christians, Muslims believed their faith should be shared with all people, but Islam

> **66** Know that every Muslim is a brother to every other Muslim and that you are now one brotherhood. **99**
>
> *Muhammad*

offered more than a theology and a faith: the basic tenets of the religion, known as the five pillars, provided a framework for a new world-view.

The Five Pillars of Islam

The first pillar is the profession of faith: "There is no God but Allah and Muhammad is his messenger." Allah is said to be eternal, all powerful, all knowing, and all merciful. Second is the formal worship, performed five times daily as the worshiper faces toward Mecca. The third pillar requires giving assistance to the poor and disadvantaged, for which Muslims are expected to donate one-tenth of their wealth. The fourth pillar, the annual fast or Ramadan (RAM-uh-dahn), lasts thirty days, during which time Muslims have to abstain from eating, drinking, and having sex during daylight hours, to demonstrate sacrifice for their faith and understand the hunger of the poor. Finally, if possible, at least once in their lives believers make a pilgrimage, or haj (HAJ), to the holy city of Mecca, where they worship with

 The Quran: Call for Jihad Discover what the Quran says about the duty of Muslims to defend themselves from their enemies, and how this duty is qualified.

jihad
Effort to live as God intended; a spiritual, moral, and intellectual struggle to enhance personal faith and follow the Quran.

Jihad as a Spiritual Struggle

multitudes of other believers from around the world. Among other spiritual activities, pilgrims circle the great Ka'ba shrine, as Arabs had done before Islam.

Islam places other demands on believers. Its moral code prohibits adultery, gambling, usury (lending money with interest), or the use of intoxicating liquors, and Islam also has strict dietary laws, including a ban on eating pork. An important concept is jihad (ji-HAHD), or concerted effort to live as God intended. Most perceive this as a spiritual, moral, and intellectual struggle to enhance personal faith and follow the Quran. In recent centuries, however, a minority has reinterpreted jihad as involving military conflict or violent struggle with nonbelievers or enemies. Other Islamic beliefs, such as angels, heavenly servants who serve as God's helpers, a Devil who flouts God's command, and the anticipation of a last judgment, are similar to Judeo-Christian beliefs. In general, Muslims were asked to pursue justice, avoid excesses, and practice mercy.

Muhammad's Thoughts on Gender

Muslims applied the idea of unity to society, seeking to build a moral and divinely guided community. These ideas influenced gender relations. Most scholars think that Islam improved the position of women in Arab culture. Before Islam, most Arab women had few rights, and many were kept in seclusion. Under Islam, men could have up to four wives as long as they could support them and treated them equally, and men had more rights under the divorce and inheritance rules than women. However, women had some legal protection, could own property and engage in business, and were considered partners before God alongside men.

Scholars debate how Muhammad viewed women's roles in society. Muhammad enjoyed the company of women, helped out with household chores, listened with interest when his wives asserted their own opinions, and emphasized that men should treat women kindly. Muhammad had taken more wives after Khadija's death, and his favorite wife, A'isha, seems to have played a prominent political role. Muhammad also encouraged female modesty in dress, suggesting that they draw their cloaks about them when they went out. Whether this meant full

CHRONOLOGY
The Islamic World, 570–1220

ca. 570	Birth of Muhammad in Mecca
622	Hijra of Muhammad and followers to Medina
632	Death of Muhammad; Abu Bakr becomes first caliph
634	Muslim conquests begin
632–661	Rashidun Caliphate
636–637	Arab military victories over Byzantine and Sassanian forces
642	Arab conquest of Egypt
651	Completion of Arab conquest of Persia
661	Murder of Ali and establishment of Umayyad dynasty in Damascus
705–715	Arab conquests of Afghanistan and Central Asia
711–720	Arab conquest of Spain
732	European defeat of Arabs at Battle of Tours
750	Abbasid defeat of Umayyads and new caliphate
756–1030	Umayyad dynasty in Spain
825–900	Arab conquest of Sicily
969–1171	Fatimid dynasty in Egypt and neighboring areas
1061–1091	Norman conquest of Sicily from Arabs
1071	Beginning of Seljuk Turk conquest of Anatolia
1085	Spanish Christian seizure of Umayyad capital
1095–1272	Christian Crusades in western Asia and North Africa
1171–1193	Reign of Saladin in Egypt
1220	Beginning of Mongol conquests in Muslim Central Asia

veiling of the face remains a matter of dispute.

Quranic Tolerance

Islam also served to protect the freedom to worship as one pleased. Whatever Muhammad's differences with many Medina Jews, Muslims promoted toleration of Christians and Jews as "protected peoples." The Quran stated: "Lo! those who believe [in Islam], and those who are Jews and Christians, whoever believeth in Allah on the last day and doeth right—surely their reward is with their Lord, and no fear shall come upon them, neither shall they grieve."[6]

> "Muhammad encouraged female modesty in dress, suggesting that they draw their cloaks about them when they went out."

LO² Arab Expansion and Islamic Empires

Within 130 years of Islam's birth, Arab armies and navies had conquered much of the hemisphere from Spain to the Indus River Valley of India, and they had also penetrated India and China, in the process implanting Islam far from its homeland. These conquests and the adoption of Islam by millions of people dramatically reshaped many societies across the Afro-Eurasian zone. Arab language and culture spread, providing a new identity for the once-diverse Middle Eastern societies. Islamic expansion also established a framework by which powerful states could rule millions of Muslims and non-Muslims. For more than half a millennium, Arabic-speaking Muslims ruled a large segment of the Eastern Hemisphere. As new peoples were absorbed, non-Arab influences and leaders gradually became stronger in the Islamic community. But Islam also divided into rival sects, a split that created enduring tensions and that influenced Middle Eastern politics for many centuries.

 Internet Islamic History Sourcebook (*http://www.fordham .edu/halsall/islam/ islamsbook.html*). A comprehensive examination of the Islamic tradition and its long history, with many useful links and source materials.

Arab Conquests and the Making of an Islamic World

In 634, shortly after the Prophet's death, Muslim armies began their conquest of much of western Asia, North Africa, and Spain, in the process expanding Islam into the conquered territories. In 732, exactly a century after the Prophet's death, Islamic expansion in Europe was finally stopped in southern France, at the Battle of Tours (toor), by a combined Christian force led by the Frankish general Charles Martel. Had Arab forces won that conflict, the history of Europe might have been different. Within two centuries, Islam became the dominant religion in the Middle East and North Africa at the expense of Christianity and Zoroastrianism. In the centuries to follow, Islam spread across the Sahara to West Africa, down the East African coast, and north into Anatolia and then the Balkans.

Arabs also expanded eastward, carrying Islam with them (see Map 10.1). Arab armies completed the conquest of the Sassanian Empire in Persia in the mid-600s, and by 715 they had conquered a large swath of Interactive Map
Afghanistan and western India. By 751 Arab armies had reached the western fringes of the Tang Empire, where they defeated the Chinese in a fierce engagement at the Talas River. This momentous battle blocked Chinese westward expansion and helped turn Central Asian Turks away from China and toward the Islamic world, a decisive turning point. Muslims now controlled most Silk Road network hubs, such as Samarkand and Bukhara. In the eleventh century, Muslims began ruling large parts of India. Later, in the fifteenth and sixteenth centuries, Islam spread through the islands of Southeast Asia.

Motives of Islamic Expansion

Internal and external factors contributed to such rapid Arab expansion. Conditions in Arabia, including long-term drought, poverty, and overpopulation, may have motivated leaders to seek new lands and lucrative trade routes to support the growing Islamic umma. In addition, the Byzantine and Sassanian Empires, exhausted from warfare and infighting, made an easy target for conquest. Furthermore, the Arab fighters were often highly motivated by religious faith. Yet, most historians agree that Muslims made no systematic attempt to impose their religion on the conquered.

The dynamics within the socially fragile Islamic community itself provided a motive for expansion. Muhammad's death confronted his followers with a

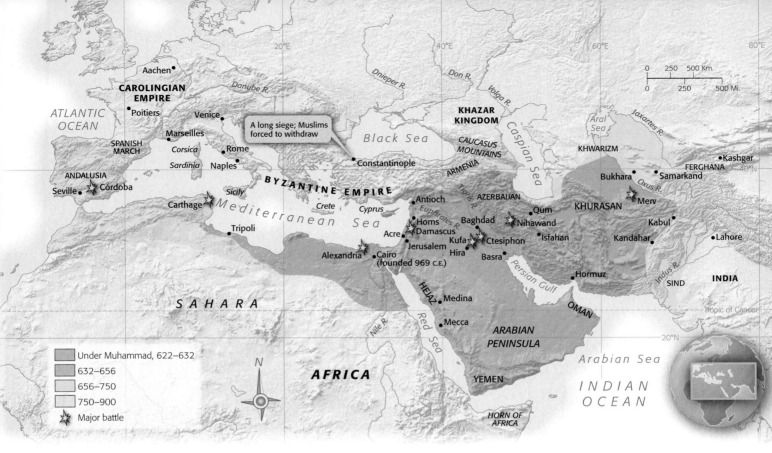

A long siege; Muslims forced to withdraw

Map 10.1
Expansion of Islam, to 750 C.E.
The Arabs rapidly conquered much of western Asia, North Africa, and Spain, in the process expanding Islam into the conquered territories. By 750 their empire stretched from Morocco and Spain in the west to western India and Central Asia.

crisis, because they had lost their charismatic spiritual leader. By providing a common cause, war and conquest discouraged tribal fighting. Under Muslim direction, Arab armies, though small, were cohesive, mobile, and well led. To prevent the rise of rival factions, Muhammad's first successor, his best friend Abu Bakr (ab-boo BAK-uhr), forbade people from leaving the umma and declared Muhammad God's final prophet. Arab fighters divided up the spoils of conquest, spreading wealth within the community and thus maintaining unity. Sharing the new wealth kept the allegiance of the many Muslims who believed strongly in a radical egalitarianism.

Arab expansion spread not only Islam but also Arab identity and the Arabic language to many peoples in western Asia and North Africa. This was often a gradual transition: it probably took three centuries for Arabic to

completely replace the Egyptian (Coptic) and Greek languages in Egypt. Adoption of the Arabic language and Islam provided cultural coherence for diverse peoples.

66 Many found the religion and the increasingly cosmopolitan community of believers an attractive alternative to their old traditions. **99**

Establishing Religious, Political, and Legal Traditions

By the eleventh century, Islam had attracted enough followers to become the dominant religion over a wide area of Afro-Eurasia, joining older universal religions such as Buddhism and Christianity. Conversion to Islam was easiest for those peoples whose own cultural ideas, attitudes, and institutions were already similar. Muslims shared animal sacrifice with animists and Zoroastrians, ritual slaughter of food animals and covering heads in worship with Jews, and circumcision

© Cengage Learning

with Jews and Christians. The Muslims' month-long fast followed by a festival was common in the region, and their ritual prayer resembled that of Nestorian Christians.

The Islamic Empire

Late-seventh-century Muslims thought of themselves as carriers of a global movement and new religion encompassing many peoples, rather than an Arab cult. They ruled over self-governing religious communities of Greek Orthodox Christians, Nestorians, Copts, Zoroastrians, Manicheans, and Jews, but began encouraging conversion and cultural synthesis. Contrary to Western myth, conversion by force was the exception rather than the rule. Many found the religion and the increasingly cosmopolitan community of believers an attractive alternative to their old traditions.

Shari'a Law

Muslims also developed unique concepts of government and law. In theory many Muslims viewed government and religion as the same, and political and religious power were often combined in a theocracy headed by a caliph or more commonly a **sultan** (SUHLT-uhn), a Muslim ruler of only one country. Although such far-reaching power could be easily abused, the moral authority of respected religious scholars could sometimes check any abuses of political power. Muslim leaders established a legal code, or **Shari'a** (shah-REE-ah), for the regulation of social and economic as well as religious life. These laws institutionalized the ethical concerns of Middle Eastern societies forged over the previous 3,000 years. Because Islam was viewed as a complete way of life, the Shari'a provided a comprehensive guide, covering areas such as divorce, inheritance, debts, and morality. It was based chiefly on the Quran and the Hadith, but competing interpretations of the scriptures led to the rise of several traditions that differed slightly in their emphasis.

Religious scholars played a major role in elaborating the Shari'a and in sustaining Islamic culture.

 Islam and Islamic History in Arabia and the Middle East (*http://www.islamicity.com/education*). A comprehensive site sponsored by a moderate Muslim organization.

"The Umayyad's laxness in religious devotion, as well as their legendary drinking and womanizing, shocked the more pious and generated civil war and division."

sultan
A Muslim ruler of only one country.

Shari'a
The Islamic legal code for the regulation of social, economic, and religious life.

madrasas
Religious boarding schools found all over the Muslim world.

Some of these scholars were judges, and others served as prayer leaders or preachers in the mosques. These scholars' legal decisions and writings provided cohesion and stability over the centuries. Muslims valued education based on studying with renowned religious and legal scholars. By the tenth century, religious boarding schools, known as **madrasas** (muh-DRAH-suhz), headed by a religious scholar, began appearing. Today thousands of these schools can be found all over the Muslim world.

Unity, Strife, and the Sunni–Shi'a Split

Muslim political history revolved around the imperial caliphates, beginning with the Rashidun, who attempted to maintain unity but also faced challenges. After 661, the end of the Rashidun era, political power shifted outside of Arabia with two successive imperial dynasties, the Umayyad (oo-MY-ad) and the Abbasid (ah-BASS-id). Both dynasties were installed by members of Muhammad's Quraysh tribe. While Mecca and Medina remained spiritual hubs, reinforced by annual pilgrimages, new cities emerged as more important political and economic centers for the Islamic world.

The Rashidun Caliphate

The sense of social and religious unity within a growing umma, achieved with the expansion of Islam and represented by the Rashidun Caliphate, did not prevent political conflict. The early conquests greatly enriched Medina and Mecca, but some Muslims grew critical of the new materialism that enticed the young. A full revolt against the Islamic leadership erupted, and dissidents murdered the unpopular third caliph, Uthman (ooth-MAHN), and installed Ali (ah-LEE) (ca. 600–661), Muhammad's son-in-law, as the fourth caliph. Although well qualified, pious, and generous, Ali proved weak. To reform the

> "Over time Shi'ites provided an alternative religious vision to Sunni Islam and eventually divided into three rival schools."

system, he moved the capital from Medina to Kufah (KOO-fa), in what is today Iraq, but others soon challenged Ali for leadership. Muhammad's widow, A'isha, helped rally the opposition to Ali, resulting in a civil war. Ali was finally killed by Uthman's relatives, who blamed him for their leader's murder. With Ali's death, the Rashidun era ended, but the divisions generated a permanent split in the Islamic world.

The Great Umayyad Mosque in Damascus This mosque, built between 709 and 715, is the oldest surviving monumental mosque.

Jane Taylor/Sonia Halliday Photographs

The Umayyad Caliphate

With the end of the Rashidun period, the caliphate moved to Damascus (duh-MAS-kuhs), in what is today Syria, under the leadership of the Umayyad dynasty (661–750). The Islamic empire was now led by men with no direct connection to, or descent from, the Prophet. With the move to Damascus, Arab politics came to be defined by large bureaucratic states with remote leaders who passed on their rule to their sons. Military expansion continued, and the Umayyad caliphs extended the Islamic empire deep into Byzantine territory, but their system soon experienced unrest. Although the rulers encouraged their subjects to adopt Islam, they did not practice the morality that they preached. In response, devout Muslims opposed to the Umayyads emphasized Muhammad's role as God's prophet, clearly setting Islam apart from rival monotheistic religions. The Umayyad's laxness in religious devotion, as well as their legendary drinking and womanizing, shocked the more pious and generated civil war and division. Among the challengers was the Prophet's only remaining male heir, his grandson Husayn (hoo-SANE), who attracted support from those who believed the caliph must be a direct descendant of Muhammad. Husayn's rebellion in 680 failed, however, and he was killed in the Battle of Karbala (KAHR-buh-LAH), a city in Iraq. In death he and his father Ali, the murdered caliph, became martyrs against the Umayyads.

Sunnis and Shi'ites

After the Rashidun turmoil, Islam began to split into two main branches, although this division was not fully formed for several centuries. At the heart of the split was disagreement over the nature of the umma and the full meaning of Muhammad's revelations. The main branch of Islam, **Sunni** (SOO-nee) ("The Trodden Path"), comprised those who accepted the practices of the Prophet and the historical succession of caliphs. Today about 85 percent of all Muslims are Sunni. Sunni embraces a wide variety of opinions and practices and was probably not named until the ninth or tenth century. It was more political than theological, suggesting adherence to one of four main schools of Islamic law and a broad view of who qualifies for political power.

The other main branch of Islam was the Shi'a (SHEE-uh), or "Partisans" of Ali. They emphasized only the religious leaders descended from Muhammad through his son-in-law, Ali, whom they believed was the rightful successor to the Prophet. Karbala and nearby Najaf (NAH-jaf), where Husayn and Ali are buried, respectively, became holy Shi'ite pilgrimage centers. Over time Shi'ites provided an alternative religious vision to Sunni Islam and eventually divided into three rival schools. The main concentrations of Shi'ites are found today in Iran, where most Persians adopted the school after 1500, and also in Iraq and Lebanon. Although they shared many commonalities, the differences and antagonism between these two branches were deep. Sunni majorities sometimes persecuted Shi'ite minorities, producing a Shi'ite martyrdom complex and tradition of dissent against Sunni rulers. Over the centuries, Shi'ite movements established various states, often ruling uneasily over Sunni majorities.

The Abbasid Caliphate, Urbanization, and Agriculture

The Abbasid Caliphate (750–1258), the next dynasty after the Umayyad, enjoyed great power and fostered a dynamic society for several centuries, surviving for half a millennium. As leaders of the most powerful Islamic state between 750 and the 940s, the Abbasid caliphs embodied the unity of the Islamic umma and established a style for later Muslim rulers. The Abbasids, a Sunni branch of the Quraysh tribe descended from Muhammad's uncle, Abbas, had capitalized on dissent against the Umayyads to attract support from both Sunnis and Shi'ites, and they rallied a military force that defeated the Umayyad army. The lone Umayyad survivor fled to Spain, where he established a separate state that flourished for three centuries. The Abbasid Empire expanded to encompass some 30 million people by 800 C.E. (see Map 10.2).

 Interactive Map

The Abbasid Dynasty and the Rise of Baghdad

In 756 the Abbasid capital was moved to Baghdad (BAG-dad), located where the Tigris and Euphrates Rivers come closest together in today's Iraq. This placed the capital strategically along major trade routes and in the middle of a farming district made fertile through irrigation. Baghdad became one of the world's greatest hubs, and its bazaars were filled with goods from as far away as China, Scandinavia, and East Africa. The Abbasid government employed thousands of people in public works projects, building palaces, schools, hospitals, and mosques in Baghdad. The Abbasids made a public show of their piety and generosity, such as by endowing religious buildings in the capital.

Baghdad reflected the cosmopolitan flavor of Islamic society. In the 1160s, a rabbi from Muslim-ruled Spain, Benjamin of Tudela, visited Baghdad and noted its atmosphere of tolerance: "This great Abbasid [caliph] is extremely friendly towards the Jews, many of his officers being of that nation. Baghdad contains about one thousand Jews, who enjoy peace, comfort, and much honor".[7] Indeed, Islam became a far-reaching world culture because of its ability to receive and absorb culture and technology from all parts of the Eastern Hemisphere. Persian influence on the new system was strong, and many Persians came to occupy high positions in the government. Muslims learned papermaking technology from Chinese who had been captured in the Battle of Talas of 751. By 800 Baghdad had its first paper mill. Papermaking allowed for a wider distribution of the Quran, helping to spread Islam.

The height of the Abbasids in Baghdad conjures up images of flying carpets and magic genies, based on the affluence and romance reported in *The Arabian Nights*, a cycle of stories probably collected from the tenth through twelfth centuries that influenced European writers, artists, and composers. During the reign of the greatest Abbasid caliph, Harun al-Rashid (hah-ROON al-rah-SHEED) (786–809), there were no flying carpets, but many people enjoyed a comfortable life. Like some other caliphs, Harun had a large harem of wives, concubines, and slave girls and a reputation for heavy drinking.

The Urbanization of Islam

As they adopted the ways of the conquered, Arabs were gradually transformed from desert

> **" Baghdad contains about one thousand Jews, who enjoy peace, comfort, and much honor. "**
> *Benjamin of Tudela*

Shi'a
The branch of Islam that emphasizes the religious leaders descended from Muhammad through his son-in-law, Ali, whom they believe was the rightful successor to the Prophet.

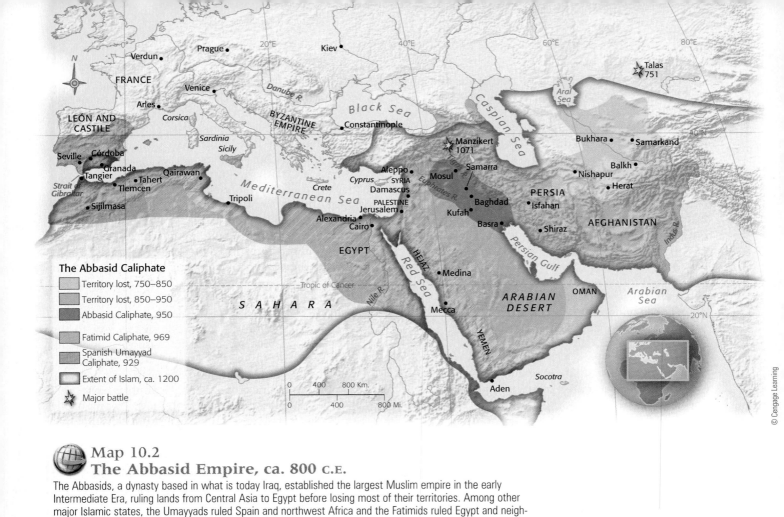

Map 10.2
The Abbasid Empire, ca. 800 C.E.

The Abbasids, a dynasty based in what is today Iraq, established the largest Muslim empire in the early Intermediate Era, ruling lands from Central Asia to Egypt before losing most of their territories. Among other major Islamic states, the Umayyads ruled Spain and northwest Africa and the Fatimids ruled Egypt and neighboring lands.

The Abbasid Caliphate
- Territory lost, 750–850
- Territory lost, 850–950
- Abbasid Caliphate, 950
- Fatimid Caliphate, 969
- Spanish Umayyad Caliphate, 929
- Extent of Islam, ca. 1200
- ★ Major battle

herders and traders into imperial rulers. Like the Sassanians, the caliphs patronized a state religion, now shifted from Zoroastrianism to Islam, and lavishly supported arts and crafts. Caliphs appointed Muslim judges and built mosques. The centralized caliphate was quite contrary to the egalitarianism of original Islam, but it worked.

The growth of cities followed Islamic conquests. New cities like Cairo and Basra, a port at the head of the Persian Gulf in modern Iraq, began as Muslim garrisons. The caliphates needed administrative centers, however, and these drew in surrounding people seeking work. Hence the Abbasid capital, Baghdad, rapidly swelled, becoming the world's largest city by 900 C.E. with perhaps 1 million people. The caliphs adopted the Sassanian system of dividing cities into wards marked by ethnic and occupational groups and of governing these groups through their own leaders. In doing so, they tolerated cultural diversity. Hence Muslim-ruled Toledo (tuh-LEED-oh) in Spain absorbed an influx of ten thousand Jews in the eleventh century without opposition.

Muslims and Agricultural Growth

To support its populations, between the eighth and thirteenth centuries Islamic societies proved agriculturally innovative. Enhanced farm productivity in turn spurred more population growth. Arab conquests opened the door to India, allowing Arabs to bring South Asian crops such as cotton, hard wheat, rice, and sugar cane as well as a variety of fruits and vegetables to the Middle East. These imports from wetter lands encouraged better irrigation, including the use of enormous water wheels to supply water. The spread of agricultural products was one of the Islamic peoples' major contributions to world history. Most of these crops filtered westward to Spain, where they thrived. Some crops moved by ship to southern Africa and Madagascar, and many reached Christian Europe, but they were adopted there only slowly.

Abbasid Decline and the End of Arab Empire

Like all empires, the Abbasids eventually faced mounting problems, and they gradually lost their grip on power by the tenth century. One factor was that Turkish soldiers, assigned to guard the caliphs, became more powerful in the government. Furthermore, Shi'ites became disaffected from the weakening caliphate and fomented bloody revolts. Some Persians challenged the system as well. Soon parts of the empire began to break away. In the tenth century, anti-Abbasid Shi'ites established the Fatimid (FAT-uh-mid) Caliphate in Egypt and North Africa. The Fatimids claimed descent from Muhammad's daughter Fatima and chose Cairo as their capital. The university founded in Cairo by the Fatimids in 970, Al-Azhar, became the most influential in the Islamic world and remains so today. Shi'ites also ruled various smaller states, where most of the population remained Sunni or non-Muslim yet generally enjoyed religious freedom.

Invasions and rebellions continued to undermine the Abbasids. The Mongols—Central Asian nomads who built a great regional empire stretching from East Asia to eastern Europe in the thirteenth century (see Chapter 11)—were attracted by the wealth of the Abbasid realm. In 1258 Mongol armies sacked and destroyed Baghdad and executed the last Abbasid caliph. This event shattered the symbolic unity of the Muslim world and the Islamic umma. Throughout the Middle East, Arab dominance was challenged by Persians, Berbers, Kurds, and Turks as well as by Mongols.

Yet, although few later Muslim rulers could match the power of the early Abbasids, Islamic society, though politically fragmented, continued to flourish. Furthermore, Islam accelerated its diffusion to new peoples. Between 1258 and 1550, the territorial size of the Islamic world doubled, and its scholars, saints, and mystics assumed leadership roles, establishing traditions and ideas that helped define the vital core of Islamic culture.

Cultural Mixing in Muslim Sicily and Spain

Islamic culture also flourished in Sicily and Spain in the western Mediterranean, fostering a cosmopolitan mixed culture that brought prosperity and the sharing of scientific knowledge. Between 825 and 900, Muslim

> "At its height, the Muslim capital of Sicily, Palermo, was larger than any other city in Europe except Constantinople."

forces conquered Sicily, the largest Mediterranean island. Under Muslim rule, Sicily benefited from close ties to the Arab-dominated maritime trade system and light taxation. Muslim rulers repaired long-decayed Roman irrigation works and vastly increased agricultural production. Many Arabs, Berbers, Africans, Greeks, Jews, Persians, and Slavs gravitated to the island. At its height, the Muslim capital, Palermo (puh-LEHR-moh), was larger than any other city in Europe except Constantinople. But by the eleventh century, political divisions among Muslims left the island open to a gradual Christian reconquest. By 1200 Christian German rulers had established a Sicilian state and were persecuting Muslims and Jews, gradually ending an era of tolerance and cultural fusion.

Umayyad Spain

A more enduring Muslim society emerged in Spain, much of which was first conquered by Islamic forces between 711 and 720. The ruling Umayyad family made their capital at Cordoba (KAWR-duh-buh), which became the largest city in Europe by 1000 C.E., home to half a million people. Under Umayyad rule, Spain was for several centuries the most powerful state in Europe and a famed center of culture and learning. A great meeting of traditions occurred in Muslim Spain, with Christian, Muslim, and Jewish thinkers working together to share and advance knowledge. Scholars and thinkers from all over Europe and the Islamic world were drawn to its schools and libraries. Cordoba's library held 400,000 volumes when libraries in Christian Europe owned only several hundred. An Arab poet called Cordoba the garden of the fruits of ideas.

The Christian Reconquest of Spain

By 1000, decline had begun to set in, marked by civil wars and factionalism. Many people remained loyal to Catholicism, providing a base of support for efforts at reconquest. Much of northern Spain gradually came under Christian control. In 1085, Christian knights conquered Cordoba, the center of Islamic power. Constant Christian military pressure gradually pushed Muslim rule into southern Spain. By 1252, Christian princes, some of whom persecuted all non-Christians, controlled much of Spain and Portugal. Finally, in 1492, Christians took

Alhambra, Court of Lions The Alhambra, or Palace of Lions, built in Granada in southern Spain in the fourteenth century, is one of the finest architectural treasures from Muslim Spain. It features a courtyard with a fountain.

Sufism
A mystical approach and practice within Islam that emphasized personal spiritual experience.

the last Muslim stronghold at Granada (gruh-NAHD-uh). The new Christian rulers, militant and intolerant, forced Muslims and Jews to either convert to Christianity or face expulsion. Thousands fled, usually to Muslim countries in North Africa or to Anatolia.

LO³ Cultural Hallmarks of Islam: Theology, Society, and Science

Islamic expansion launched a thousand-year era, from the seventh to the seventeenth century, that brought many Afro-Eurasian peoples into closer contact with one another and allowed for a mixing of cultures within an Islamic framework. Muslims synthesized elements from varied traditions to produce a new hybrid culture that was rooted in theol-

ogy, social patterns, literature and art, science, and learning. Islamic theology continued to develop, fostering several distinct strands of thought and behavior. In western Asia and North Africa, Islamic societies fashioned a distinctive social system and a renowned cultural heritage.

Theology, Sufism, and Religious Practice

From the very beginning, Muslims' debates over theological questions led to divergent interpretations of the Quran. As in all religions, a variety of views about the great questions of life and death developed within Islam, reflecting the mixing of intellectual traditions. Some Muslim thinkers emphasized reason and free will, while others believed that Allah preordained everything.

Islamic Philosophy and Mysticism

Influential thinkers appeared throughout the Islamic world, some of whom had mastered several fields of knowledge. Among the greatest was Abu Yusuf al-Kindi (a-BOO YOU-suhf al-KIN-dee) (ca. 800–ca. 870), an Arab who lived in Iraq. Al-Kindi praised the search for truth and popularized Greek ideas, emphasizing logic and mathematics. Another Muslim scholar, Abu Ali al-Husain Ibn Sina (a-BOO AH-lee al-who-SANE IB-unh SEE-nah) (980–1037), known in the West as Avicenna (av-uh-SEN-uh), was both a philosopher and a medical scholar who spent most of his career in Persia. Afghanistan-born Abu Hamid al-Ghazali (AH-boo HAM-id al-guh-ZAL-ee) (1058–1111), a teacher in Baghdad, used Aristotelian logic to justify Islamic beliefs. As an advocate of mysticism, he also opposed the rationalism of thinkers like Ibn Sina. The rationalistic approach remained influential in Shi'a thinking but lost support in Sunni circles from the fourteenth century onward.

Sufism

Among both Sunnis and Shi'ites, a variant of Islam developed and gained many followers. **Sufism** (SOO-fiz-uhm) was a mystical approach and practice that emphasized personal spiritual experience rather than nitpicking theology. Through asceticism and mysticism, Sufis sought a personal, spiritual communion with God. A famous Sufi poet in Persia, Baba Kuhi, saw God in everything: "In the market, in the cloister—only God I saw; In the valley and on the mountain—only God I saw. Him I have seen beside me oft in tribulation; in favor and in fortune—only God I saw."[8] Many Sufis exchanged information with Christian, Hindu, and Jewish mystics and were willing to synthesize Islam with other ideas as long as the central spirit was maintained. Sufis congregated in orders led by masters who taught prescribed techniques and who attracted devoted followers. The whirling *dervishes* (DUHR-vish-iz) of Turkey are one of the most famous Sufi orders. Several Sufi orders were renowned as peace-loving and tolerant of different views and customs. Followers credited some Sufi masters with magical powers. Although popular, Sufism remained a controversial movement.

Islamic Studies, Islam, Arabic, and Religion (*http://www .uga.edu*/islam). A comprehensive collection of links and resources maintained at the University of Georgia.

Three Patterns of Islamic Practice

As the religion of Islam spread into diverse cultures, it developed three distinct patterns of practice. The adaptationists, the most liberal in defining the faith, showed a willingness to make adjustments to changing conditions. These Muslims have provided the base for reform and for secular and modernizing movements. Conservatives, on the other hand, strove to preserve established beliefs and customs, such as the rigid division of the sexes, and mistrusted innovation. Finally, some Muslims, including many Sufis, stressed the personal aspects of the faith. These three patterns still have large followings among both Sunnis and Shi'ites, sometimes causing political and social conflict in Muslim societies.

Social Life and Gender Relations

Most Muslims were settled farmers, craftsmen, and traders. As Islamic culture expanded and matured, the social structure became more complex and marked by clear ethnic, tribal, class-occupational, religious, and gender divisions, especially in the Middle East. Arabs generally had a higher social status than Turkish, Berber, African, and other converts. The descendants of the Prophet and members of the Hashemite clan to which he belonged held an espe-

> "Arabs generally had a higher social status than Turkish, Berber, African, and other converts."

cially honored status. In addition, because the first Muslims were merchants, the religion had a special appeal for people in the commercial sector, providing spiritual sanction of their quest for wealth. This wealth could finance their pilgrimage to Mecca and also help the poor through almsgiving.

Slavery in Islamic Societies

Slavery was common in Islamic societies. Slaves were bureaucrats and soldiers, factory workers and farm laborers, household servants and concubines. One Abbasid caliph kept 11,000 slaves in his palace. Islamic law encouraged owners to treat slaves with consideration, and many slaves were eventually freed. Many slaves were war captives and children purchased from poor families, but Christian European states like Byzantium and Venice also sold slaves to Muslims. For more than a dozen centuries, perhaps 10 to 15 million African slaves were brought to the Middle East across the Sahara or up the East African coast by an Arab-dominated slave trade. The Islamic religion imposed some other divisions in society, as Christian and Jewish communities did not always have the same rights as Muslims, but these non-Muslim communities did enjoy some protection under the law. Although the level of that protection varied, on the whole these communities were allowed to follow their own laws, customs, and beliefs and to maintain their own religious institutions.

Islamic Family Life

Families were at the heart of the social system. Marriages were arranged, with the goal of cementing social or perhaps business ties between two families. Although law allowed men to have up to four wives at a time, this situation remained fairly rare and largely restricted to the rich and powerful. Many poor men never married at all, because they could not afford the large bridal gifts they were expected to provide. Parents expected children to obey and respect them, even after they became adults. Social gatherings, which were usually segregated by gender, often involved poetry recitations, musical performances, or Quran readings. Islamic law harshly punished homosexuality; yet, homosexual relationships were not uncommon, and same-sex love was often reflected in poetry and literature.

Persian Women at a Picnic This miniature from sixteenth-century Persia shows women preparing a picnic. The ability of women to venture away from home varied widely depending on social class and regional traditions.

The Status of Women

The status of women in Islamic society has been subject to debate by both Western and Islamic observers in modern times, and by Muslim thinkers for centuries. The philosopher Ibn Rushd (IB-uhn RUSHED) (1126–1198), known in the West as Averroes (uh-VER-uh-WEEZ), attacked restrictions on women as an economic burden, arguing that "the ability of women is not known, because they are merely used for procreation [and] child-rearing."⁹ Although the Quran recognized certain rights of women, prohibited female infanticide, and limited the number of wives men could have, it also accorded women only half the inheritance of men and gave women less standing in courts of law. Scholars have disagreed over whether restrictions such as veiling and seclusion were based on Quranic mandates or on patriarchal pre-Islamic Arab, Middle Eastern, and Byzantine customs. Some Muslim communities in the Middle East, and many outside the region, never adopted these practices. In fact, women played diverse roles in Muslim societies. Some wives of Abbasid caliphs played political roles, albeit mostly behind the scenes. While formal education for girls in the Middle East was generally limited, women monopolized certain occupations such as spinning and weaving, and they also worked in the fields or in some domestic industries beside men. And in some Muslim societies, particularly in sub-Saharan Africa and Southeast Asia, women often maintained their relative independence and were free to dress as they liked, socialize outside the home, and earn money.

Achievements in the Arts, Sciences, and Learning

During the Islamic golden age, many creative thinkers emerged. Muslims borrowed, assimilated, and diffused Greek and Indian knowledge and were familiar with some Chinese technologies. By the seventh century, certain classical and Hellenistic Greek traditions of philosophy and science had been nearly forgotten in Europe, but they survived in the Middle East. Thanks to the mixing of ideas as cultures encountered each other, science and medicine flourished, and Muslims also made many contributions to mathematics and astronomy.

Islamic Literacy

Although Islamic societies became identified with literacy and literature, the Arabic alphabet originated in South Arabia long before Muhammad's time. In Mecca the script had been used chiefly by merchants to keep their books, but Islam enhanced the script further by emphasizing literacy. The Quran stated: "Read, and thy Lord is most generous, Who taught with the pen, Taught man what he knew not."¹⁰ Muslims adopted the Arab poetic tradition but modified romantic ideas into praise, not for a lover but for the Prophet and Allah. Islamic culture also developed a written and oral prose literature, including tales of Alexander the Great.

One of the greatest writers of Abbasid times, also an astronomer and mathematician, was the Persian Omar Khayyam (OH-MAHR key-YAHM). In his famous poem *Rubaiyat* (ROO-bee-AHT), he noted the fleeting nature of life: "O, come with old Khayyam, and leave the Wise, to talk; one thing is certain, that Life flies; one thing is certain, and the rest is Lies; the

Bodleian Library, Oxford University, MS Elliot 189

flower that once has blown forever dies."[11] The most famous Sufi poet was the thirteenth-century Persian Jalal al-Din Rumi (ja-LAL al-DIN ROO-mee). Born in what is today Afghanistan, Al-Din Rumi blended liberal spirituality with humor in writings about love, desire, and the human condition. His vision was optimistic, joyful, and ecumenical: "I am neither Christian, nor Jew, nor Zoroastrian, nor Muslim."[12]

Calligraphy and Architecture

Some Muslims emphasized the visual arts. Since Arabic is written in a flowing style, the artful writing of words, or calligraphy (kuh-LIG-ruh-fee), became a much admired art form, appearing in manuscripts and on the walls of public buildings. Islamic Persia, India, and Central Asia also fostered a tradition of painting, especially landscapes. In addition, Muslims produced world-class architecture, some of it monumental, that included lavishly decorated buildings such as the Taj Mahal in India. Some architecture, such as mosques with domes and towers, reflected Byzantine church influence.

Science and Medicine

Many advances in science and medicine were made in the Islamic world as experts synthesized the learning of other societies with their own insights. Some knowledge was carried into the Middle East by Nestorian Christians, who taught Greek sciences under Abbasid sponsorship and helped make Baghdad a center of world learning. The Abbasid caliphs opened the House of Wisdom in Baghdad, a research institute staffed by scholars charged with translating Greek, Syrian, Sanskrit, and Persian works into Arabic. Aristotle's writings were particularly influential. The institute also included schools, observatories, and a huge library. Another massive library of 2 million books, The House of Knowledge, was built in Cairo by the Shi'ite Fatimids.

After the ninth century, Arab and Persian scholars were not just translating but also actively assimilating the imported knowledge. As the influential eleventh-century Persian philosopher Al-Biruni (al-bih-ROO-nee) wrote: "The sciences were transmitted into the Arabic language from different parts of the world; by it [the sciences] were embellished and

> "The scientific revolution that later occurred in Europe would have been impossible without Arab and Indian mathematics."

penetrated the hearts of men, while the beauties of [Arabic] flowed in their veins and arteries."[13] The dialogue resulting from a diversity of ideas produced an open-minded search for truth among scholars. In the eleventh century, Christian Europe became aware of the Muslim synthesis of Greek, Indian, and Persian knowledge from libraries in Spain.

Muslims also turned their attention to medicine, where they enjoyed considerable success. Although much influenced by Greek ideas, Muslim medical specialists developed an empirical tradition, and Baghdad hospitals were the world's most advanced. Muslim surgeons learned how to use opium for anesthesia, extract teeth and replace them with false teeth made from animal bones, and remove kidney stones. After many Islamic medical books were translated into Latin in the twelfth century, they became the major medical texts in Europe for the next five centuries.

Doctors Abu Bakr al-Razi (aboo BAH-car al-RAH-zee) (ca. 865–ca. 932) and Ibn Sina (also known as Avicenna) compared Greek ideas with their own research. Al-Razi, a Persian, directed several hospitals and wrote more than fifty clinical studies as well as general medical works. The latter included the *Comprehensive Book*, the longest medical encyclopedia in Arabic (eighteen volumes), which was used in Europe into the 1400s. A century later, Ibn Sina, who was born in Central Asia, placed considerable stress on psychosomatic medicine, treated depression, and pioneered the study of vision and eye disease.

Mathematics, Astronomy, and Geography

As with science, Islamic mathematics moved well beyond the imitative, and it also helped spur astronomy. The scientific revolution that later occurred in Europe would have been impossible without Arab and Indian mathematics. In Baghdad the Persian Zoroastrian al-Khuwarizmi (al-KWAHR-uhz-mee) (ca. 780–ca. 850) developed the mathematical procedures he called algebra, building on Greek and Indian foundations. Omar Khayyam, the beloved Persian poet, helped formulate trigonometry. Meanwhile, Arab thinkers also made advances in geometry. From Indian math books, Muslims adopted a revolutionary system of numbers. Today we know

Dar al-Islam
("Abode of Islam") The Islamic world stretching from Morocco to Indonesia and joined by both a common faith and trade; arose between the eighth and the seventeenth century.

them as Arabic numerals, because Europe acquired them from Muslim Spain. The most revolutionary innovation of Arabic numerals was not just their greater convenience, but also the use of a dot to indicate an empty column, which eventually became the zero. Advances in mathematics and physics made possible improvements in water clocks, water wheels, and other irrigation apparatus that spread well beyond the Islamic world.

The Muslim world also improved astronomical observations. Muslim astronomers combined Greek, Persian, and Indian knowledge of the stars and planets with their own observations. Applying their knowledge of mathematics to optics, Muslim scholars constructed a primitive version of the telescope, and one astronomer reportedly built an elaborate planetarium that reproduced the movement of the stars. A remarkable observatory built at Samarkand in Central Asia in 1420 produced charts for hundreds of stars. Some astronomers noted the eccentric behavior of the planet Venus, which challenged the widespread notion of an earth-centered universe. Indeed, many Muslim astronomers accepted that the world was round.

Finally, the modern study of geography and history owes much to Muslim research and writing. With the expansion of Islam and Arab trading communities to the far corners of the Eastern Hemisphere, Muslims were able to travel long distances and record their observations. Aided by travel accounts, geographers and cartographers such as Al-Idrisi (al-AH-dree-see) from Muslim Spain produced atlases, globes, and maps. Ibn Khaldun (1332–1406), the well-traveled North African introduced at the beginning of the chapter, was apparently the first scholar anywhere to look for patterns and structure in history. His recognition of the role in history of "group feeling" (what today we call ethnic identity) and the powerful role of religion was pathbreaking. Ibn Khaldun put the Arab expansion into the broader flow of regional history, in the process focusing on various regional cultures.

LO⁴ Globalized Islam and Middle Eastern Political Change

The major theme of early Islam was the transformation of a parochial Arab culture into the first truly hemisphere-wide culture that was connected by many

CHRONOLOGY
The Islamic World, 1095–1492

1095–1272	Christian Crusades in western Asia and North Africa
1250–1517	Mamluk rule in Egypt and Syria
1258	Mongol seizure of Baghdad and end of Abbasid Caliphate
1260	Mamluk defeat of Mongols in Battle of Ayn Jalut
1260–1360	Mongol Il-Khanid dynasty in Persia and Iraq
1300–1923	Ottoman Empire
1369–1405	Reign of Tamerlane in Central and Southwest Asia
1371	Ottoman conquest of Bulgaria and Macedonia
1396	Ottoman defeat of European forces at Battle of Nicopolis
1453	Ottoman capture of Constantinople and end of Byzantine state
1492	Christian seizure of Granada; expulsion of Muslims and Jews from Spain

religious and commercial networks. From this expansion was created Dar al-Islam (the "Abode of Islam"), the Islamic world stretching from Morocco to Indonesia and joined by both a common faith and trade. Networks fostered by Islam spread Arab words, names, social attitudes, and cultural values to diverse peoples. Eventually, several powerful military states rose to power and ruled over large populations of Muslims and non-Muslims. The Islamic world also faced severe challenges that set the stage for the rise of new political forces in the fifteenth and sixteenth centuries.

The Global Shape of Dar al-Islam

To identify the Muslim world with the Arab world is misleading. More than half of the world's 1.3 billion Muslims today live outside the Middle East, and Arabs are significantly outnumbered by non-Arab believers. This chapter largely focuses on the Middle East, but this is only a part of a larger global whole of Islam. After the destruction of the cosmopolitan Abbasid Caliphate in 1258, Arab political power diminished, but Islam grew rapidly in both Africa and South Asia. Beginning in the thirteenth century, Muslims constructed a hemisphere-spanning system based not just on economic exchange but also on faith. This system, built on a shared understanding of the world and the cosmos, was linked by informal networks of Islamic scholars and saints advocating for the Quran's message of a righteous social order. One of those scholars, the fourteenth-century Moroccan Ibn Battuta, spent thirty years traveling the length and breadth of Dar-al-Islam from West Africa and Spain to China and Southeast Asia.

 Read about the great journeys of famous Muslim traveler, Ibn Battuta.

 Ibn Battuta's Rihla (http://www.sfusd.k12.ca.us/schwww/sch618/Ibn_Battuta/Ibn_Battuta_Rihla.html). A useful site on Ibn Battuta and his wide travels.

Trade in the Islamic World

The spread of Islam corresponded with the growth of Muslim-dominated long-distance trade and the travel it fostered, especially the maritime trade around the Indian Ocean Basin. Except for the Chinese, Arabs enjoyed the world's most advanced shipbuilding and navigation between 1000 and 1450. The lateen sails that Arabs devised, or perhaps adapted from classical Southeast Asians, allowed European ships to undertake long-distance voyages in the 1400s. Throughout the first millennium of the Common Era, an increasingly integrated maritime trading system gradually emerged that linked the eastern Mediterranean, Middle East, East African coast, Persia, and India with the societies of East and Southeast Asia (see Map 10.3). Muslim peoples soon became the most prominent traders on this route.

 Interactive Map

Between 1000 and 1500 C.E., the Straits of Melaka in Southeast Asia and Hormuz (HAWR-muhz) at the Persian Gulf entrance stood at the heart of what became the key mercantile system of the Intermediate

world. Over these sea routes, the spices of Indonesia and East Africa, the gold and tin of Malaya, the textiles of India, the gold of southern Africa, and the silks, porcelain, and tea of China traveled to distant markets. The maritime network achieved its height in the fifteenth and sixteenth centuries, when Muslim political power was reduced, but Muslim economic and cultural power remained strong.

Turks and Crusaders

Between the eleventh and fifteenth centuries, the Muslim peoples of the Middle East faced a series of interventions by outsiders that helped reshape the region politically. The rise of the Turkish peoples in Central Asia eventually led to Turkish conquests in western Asia. During these same centuries, Christian crusaders occasionally attempted to control Palestine and displace Muslim rule. Although Europeans eventually failed, the crusading thrust left a heritage of Muslim bitterness and wariness toward Christian Europe.

The Rise of the Turks

The rise of the Turks in this period was a major development. Originally pastoral nomads from Central Asia, for centuries the Turks had intruded into Chinese, Indian, and western Asian societies, and by 550 C.E. some had established a vast confederation stretching from the Ukraine to Mongolia. Some Turks adopted such religions as Nestorian Christianity, Judaism, and Buddhism. Gradually they drew closer to Middle Eastern social and cultural patterns, and most eventually embraced Islam when they cooperated militarily with the Abbasids. Late in the tenth century, a group of Muslim Turks, the Seljuks (SEL-jooks), achieved regional power in Central Asia, expanding and recruiting other Turkish tribes into their confederation. By the mid-eleventh century, they had swept westward through Afghanistan and Iran into Iraq. Allied with the declining Abbasids, Seljuk forces continued to expand, eventually creating a large empire stretching from Palestine to Samarkand. The weakening of an aging Byzantine state allowed the Seljuks in 1071 to seize much of Anatolia, which had for many centuries been populated largely by Greek-speaking Orthodox Christians. Now it was ruled by Turkish-speaking Muslims.

> 66 The final six crusades, the last one ending in 1272, failed to wrest control of North Africa, Jerusalem, and Anatolia from Muslim hands. 99

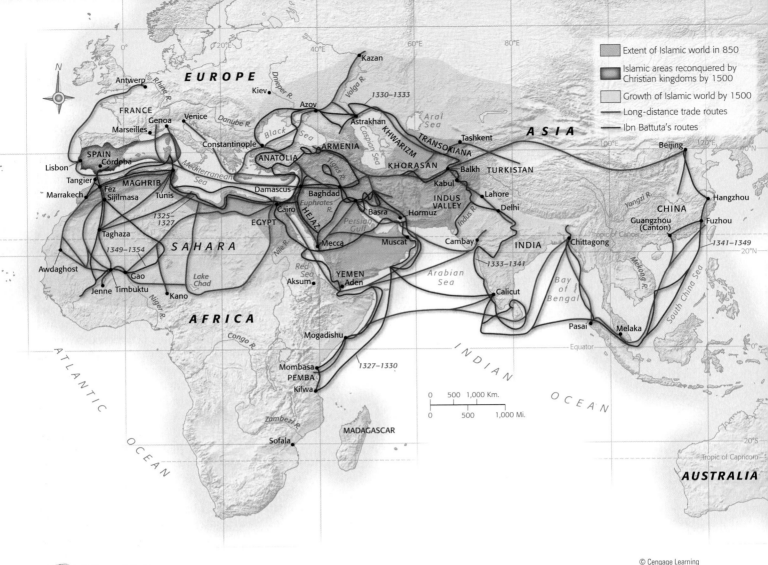

Map 10.3
Dar al-Islam and Trade Routes, ca. 1500 C.E.
By 1500 the Islamic world stretched into West Africa, East Africa, and Southeast Asia. Trade routes connected the Islamic lands and allowed Muslim traders to extend their networks to China, Russia, and Europe.

The Crusades

By the eleventh century, some Islamic states faced increasing challenges from European Christians. Between 1095 and 1272, Christians from various European societies launched a long series of Crusades to win back what they saw as the Judeo-Christian Holy Land from Muslim occupation (see Chapter 14). The First Crusade (1095–1099) was triggered by the encroachment of Seljuk Turks on Byzantine territory and a division of the Christian church into two rival branches in 1054. Roman popes—worried about Seljuk expansion and anxious to assert their primacy over the leaders of the breakaway Greek Orthodox Church based in Constantinople—promoted the idea of positive vio-

lence to defend the faith. Using untrue or exaggerated stories of Arab and Seljuk atrocities against Christians in Palestine and Syria, Pope Urban II called on Christians to reclaim the Holy Land and protect the churches and relics of Jerusalem. His plea attracted some 100,000 European volunteers, some pious, others just hungry for booty. Capitalizing on Muslim divisiveness, the crusaders reached Jerusalem in 1099. They took the city and then killed thousands of Muslims, Jews, and even local Christians. Some crusaders stayed on to guard the sites, and four small crusader states were established in what is today Israel and Lebanon. As Muslim forces regrouped, another pope dispatched the Second Crusade (1147–1149), in which the crusaders mostly slaughtered Jews in Europe and pillaged the Byzantine Empire.

In the mid-twelfth century, Muslims effectively counterattacked, pushing back Christian forces and prompting the Third Crusade (1189–1192). The Muslim armies were led by General Salah al-Din, or Saladin (SAL-uh-din) (1138–1193), an Iraqi-born Kurd who once served the Fatimid rulers of Egypt, then deposed them and became sultan, replacing Shi'ite with Sunni rule. Saladin's forces stopped a crusader invasion of Egypt and then, between 1187 and 1192, captured Jerusalem from the crusaders and extended his power into Syria. A tolerant leader, Saladin spared the Christians who surrendered in Jerusalem, and he is still revered today. The final six crusades, the last one ending in 1272, failed to wrest control of North Africa, Jerusalem, and Anatolia from Muslim hands.

Historians still debate the heritage of the Crusades. Many crusaders were undoubtedly inspired by a sincere religious zeal to preserve access to Christian holy sites, but many also looted captured cities and sacked the Orthodox Christian capital, Constantinople. Likewise, Muslim armies often showed little mercy on their enemies. Some believe that this militant Christian challenge to Islam ultimately made both religions less tolerant and more zealous, complicating relations between the two groups. Even today, Islamic militants still capitalize on lingering resentment against Western "crusaders."

Mongol Conquests and the Black Death

Another people from outside the region, the Mongols (MAHN-guhlz), also swept into western Asia, destroying various states, creating instability, and unwittingly laying the foundation for a hemisphere-wide disease that caused much devastation and death in the Middle East. The Mongols, Central Asian pastoral nomads, constituted a much greater threat to Islam than the Christian crusaders. Led by Genghis Khan (GENG-iz KAHN) (ca. 1162–1227), the Mongols—prompted perhaps by environmental stress and overpopulation—first extended their control over several rival groups in Central Asia. Between 1218 and 1221, they fought their way through the lands inhabited mostly by Turkish-speaking Muslims just north of Afghanistan, destroying several great Silk Road cities.

Hulegu and the Mongol Empire Mongol atrocities were legendary. In one vicious attack, they killed 700,000 mostly unarmed residents and even family pets in the Persian city of Merv. Their goal was to paralyze the Muslim societies with fear; it usually worked. After Genghis Khan's death in 1227, the Mongols turned to conquering China, Russia, and eastern Europe but also put pressure on the Caucasus and Anatolia. In 1243 they defeated the remnants of the Seljuk Turks. In 1256 a grandson of Genghis Khan, Hulegu (hoo-LAY-goo) (1217–1275), led new attacks on the Middle East that had more lasting consequences for the region. Crossing the mountains into Iraq, Hulegu's brutal army pillaged Baghdad in 1258, burning schools, libraries, mosques, and palaces, killing perhaps 1 million Muslims, and executing all of the Abbasids. Hulegu's forces pushed on west from Baghdad, occupying Damascus and destroying the key eastern Mediterranean port of Aleppo (uh-LEP-oh). In addition to destroying cities, the pastoralist Mongols badly disrupted western Asian agriculture.

But the Islamic tradition proved resilient. In 1260, Hulegu's armies tried to invade Egypt but were defeated by the Mamluks (MAM-looks), ex-slave soldiers of Turkish origin who had taken power in Egypt. The Mamluk occupation of Palestine halted the Mongol march westward, but Hulegu's Mongols were content to stay in Iraq and Persia, calling themselves the Il-Khanid (il-KHAN-id) dynasty and eventually adopting Islam. Hulegu's Muslim descendants practiced religious toleration and encouraged monumental architecture, learning, and a literary renaissance. Under their rule, Persian scholars opened a huge library of 400,000 volumes, built a great observatory, produced enduring poetry, and wrote pathbreaking histories of the world that tell us much about the Mongol empire. Il-Khanid rule lasted a century before fragmenting in 1360.

The Black Death By building a large empire across Eurasia, the Mongols fostered long-distance overland trade and travel, but in so doing they provided a path over which deadly diseases could spread. Like Europe and China, much of the Islamic world was deeply affected by the devastating fourteenth-century pandemic known in the West as the Black Death. The Black Death was a catastrophic disease, probably bubonic plague, that killed quickly and spread rapidly over the networks of exchange. Initially carried into the Black Sea region from eastern Asia by fleas infesting rats that stowed away on caravans along the Mongol-controlled Silk Road or on board trading ships, the pandemic hit the Middle East repeatedly over the course of a century, reducing the population of Egypt and Syria by two-thirds. Ibn Khaldun wrote that "cities and towns were laid waste, roads and way signs were obliterated, settlements and mansions became empty. The entire inhabited world changed."[14] Major cities like Cairo lost half their population, but by the 1400s the Middle East had stabilized.

The Rise of Mamluks, Timurids, and Ottomans

In the thirteenth and fourteenth centuries, several powerful Muslim military states arose, including those of the Mamluks in Egypt and the Timurids in Central Asia. By this time, gunpowder—a Chinese invention that filtered westward along the Silk Road—had reached the Middle East, where it forever changed the nature of warfare and politics. Because recruiting, arming, and training soldiers to use cannons and muskets was expensive, the use of firearms led to the rise of stronger, more bureaucratic states.

The Mamluks in Egypt and Syria

The Mamluks, who had thwarted Mongol expansion, ruled Egypt and Syria from 1250 to 1517 and drove the crusaders out of Palestine in 1293. The Mamluks made Egypt the richest Middle Eastern state. They also extended their power into Arabia, capturing Mecca and Medina. This conquest allowed them to control and tax the flow of Muslim pilgrims. For many years the Mamluks also enjoyed an active trade with the two major Italian trading cities, Genoa and Venice, supplying valuable Asian goods to Europe.

Map 10.4
The Ottoman Empire, 1566

Between 1300 and the mid-1500s, the Ottoman Turks expanded out of western Anatolia to conquer a large empire in western Asia, Egypt and North Africa, and eastern Europe, making the Ottomans one of the world's largest states.

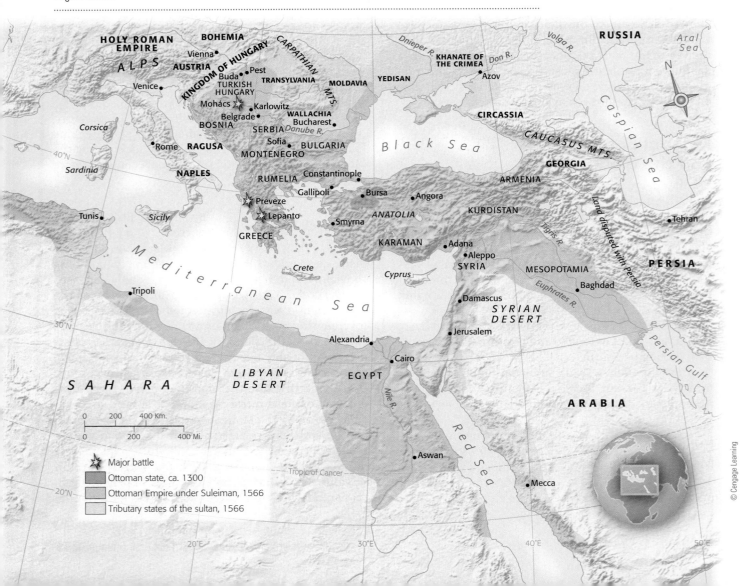

Venetian Ambassadors Visiting Mamluk Damascus Venetians and Genoese merchants, fierce rivals, regularly visited the Middle East to acquire silks, spices, and other valuable products. This painting from the 1400s shows Venetians being received by the Mamluk governor of Damascus, who wears a horned hat and sits on a low platform, in today's Syria.

 Interactive Map

Eventually, however, corruption grew among the Mamluk leaders, prompting seafaring European merchants to seek an alternate maritime route to the East, and in 1516–1517 another Turkish group, the Ottomans, defeated the Mamluks and absorbed their lands into the growing Ottoman Empire (see Map 10.4).

Tamerlane

To the east, in Central Asia, the Timurid state became the dominant regional power for more than a century. The state's ruthless founder, Tamerlane (TAM-uhr-lane) (1336–1405), a Muslim prince of Turkish and Mongol ancestry, hoped to emulate Genghis Khan. From his capital at Samarkand, Tamerlane's army rampaged through the Caucasus, southern Russia, Persia, Iraq, and Syria starting in 1369, killing thousands of people and destroying cities. He then turned against India, wreaking havoc in the north (see Chapter 13). Only Tamerlane's death in 1405 halted his forces from invading China and Ottoman Turkey. His legacy was largely one of smoking ruins and mounds of human heads, but his successors built mosques and patronized scholars.

The Ottoman Empire

The most powerful and enduring military state was established by the Ottoman (AHT-uh-muhn) Turks, who were the most successful Muslim people in exploiting the possibilities of gunpowder. The Ottomans originated as a small Anatolian state led by a chief, Osman (ohs-MAHN), who came under the influence of Sufis dedicated to the destruction of Byzantium. By the late 1200s, Byzantium was reeling from temporary occupation of Constantinople by crusaders. The Ottomans capitalized on this vacuum and, by 1300, began raiding and then annexing the remaining Byzantine strongholds in Anatolia. Ultimately the Ottomans conquered much of the Byzantine Empire, creating one of the most dynamic states in western Eurasia and a link between Middle Eastern Islam and European Christianity. The once great Byzantium became a shell of a state surrounding Constantinople.

Soon the Ottomans moved into the Balkans, where they challenged the strongest Christian power in southeastern Europe, Serbia (SUHR-bee-uh). In 1389, in the Serbian region of Kosovo (KOH-suh-voh), the Ottomans routed a Christian army comprising many Balkan ethnic groups, among them Serbs, Albanians, and Bulgars. The Ottomans eventually incorporated Serbia in 1459. Over the next several centuries, many Albanian and Serb-speaking Christians adopted Islam, perhaps partly for economic reasons, creating a division in the Balkans between Catholic, Orthodox, and Muslim peoples that complicated politics for centuries to come. Other battles in the fourteenth and fifteenth centuries led to eventual

Ottoman triumph. At the Battle of Nicopolis (nuh-KAHP-uh-luhs) in 1396, the Ottomans defeated a Hungarian-led force of Europeans opposed to further Ottoman expansion. In 1453 Sultan Mehmed (MEH-met) (1432–1481) the Conqueror finally took Constantinople and converted the city into the Ottoman capital, eventually renamed Istanbul.

The Ottoman Empire had become the major regional power. The imperial capital, Istanbul, attracted a diverse population and remained a major trade hub through which many networks passed. Mehmed the Conqueror, who patronized the arts, launched a major rebuilding project in Istanbul, which by 1500 was Europe's largest city. As in other Muslim states, Ottoman sultans used the millet ("nationality") system, allowing leaders of religious and ethnic minorities to administer their own communities. Thus the millet system allowed the Turks to divide and rule diverse peoples and faiths.

Under a dynamic and militarily powerful state, the Ottomans continued to expand. By 1500 they had solidified control over Greece and the Balkans (see Map 10.4). In the 1500s, the so-called Ottoman golden age, Ottoman rule was extended over much of western Asia as far east as Persia and also through North Africa from Egypt to Algeria. However, the Ottomans were defeated when they attempted to take Hungary in 1699. This event was the high-water mark of Ottoman, and Islamic, expansion in western Eurasia, but the Ottoman Empire continued until 1923.

Islamic Contributions to World History

By linking peoples of varied cultures, ideas, religions, and languages, the Arab conquests fostered intellectual and artistic creativity. In the west, the Arabs passed on to Europe some of the fruits of the advanced science, mathematics, and technology of the Middle East and Asia transported over the networks of exchange. In addition, the Arabs served as the critical link between the classical Greeks and Indians and the late medieval Europeans. The transmission of Greco-Roman and Islamic learning to Europe, where it was studied in medieval universities, came mainly through Spain and Sicily from the ninth through the eleventh centuries.

Islamic Cultural Synthesis

Mixing Arab, Persian, Turkish, Byzantine, Christian, Jewish, African, and Indian influences, Muslims created a hemispheric-wide Islamic world that connected culturally and politically diverse societies sharing a common faith. While most people, in what is today Iraq, Syria, Egypt, and North Africa, adopted the Arabic language and called themselves Arabs, the Persians and Turks continued to speak their own languages, which they now wrote using the Arabic script. Non-Muslims played key roles in the Islamic world, especially in commerce. From the eighth through eleventh centuries, Jews were the key trade middlemen between Christian Europe and the Muslim world, but after the eleventh century they lost ground to the Italians in the west and the Armenian Christians in the east.

The Decline of Islamic Influence

Several powerful Islamic states, including the Ottoman Empire, continued to exercise political and economic influence in the sixteenth and seventeenth centuries. But, with the occasional exception of Ottoman Turkey, technological innovation, scientific inquiry, and the questioning of accepted religious and cultural ideas fell off in the Middle East after 1500. The madrasas, while training Muslim clerics and providing spiritual guidance, tended to have narrow, theology-based curriculums that deemphasized secular learning. Some historians believe this undermined the humanist, tolerant tradition of Islamic scholarship, such as the open-minded approach of Baghdad's House of Wisdom and the schools in Muslim Spain. Over the next three centuries, most of the Middle Eastern peoples who had boasted innovative and cosmopolitan traditions for a millennium gradually lost power, while Europeans surged.

Listen to a synopsis of Chapter 10.

{ Test coming up? Now what? }

CHAPTER 11

East Asian Traditions, Transformations, and Eurasian Encounters,

600–1500

Learning Outcomes

After reading this chapter, you should be able to answer the following questions:

LO¹ What role did Tang China play in the Eurasian world?

LO² Why might historians consider the Song dynasty the high point of China's golden age?

LO³ How did China change during the Yuan and Ming dynasties?

LO⁴ How did the Koreans and Japanese make use of Chinese culture in developing their own distinctive societies?

LO⁵ How did Korean and Japanese society change in the late Intermediate Era?

66China is a sea that salts all rivers that flow into it. 99

—Italian traveler Marco Polo (1275)[1]

Early in the twelfth century, the Chinese artist Zhang Zeduan painted a massive scroll of people at work and leisure throughout the city of Kaifeng (KIE-FENG), then China's capital and home to perhaps 1 million people. The scroll portrays life during one of premodern China's most prosperous eras and reveals the grandeur of the city, from its riverside suburbs to the towering city gates to the downtown business district. In Zhang's scroll, Kaifeng's streets are crowded with people going about their daily activities. Foreign merchants and other visitors can be seen, as well as streetside hawkers touting their goods, fortune tellers, scholars, and monks. Zhang's record of Kaifeng's commercial life is particularly vivid: warehouses, arsenals, shipyards, and textile firms share space with hotels, food stalls, teahouses, and restaurants. Cargo barges cruise the river, while camels heavily laden with foreign goods enter the city.

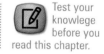 Test your knowlege before you read this chapter.

Much of the prosperous city life Zhang portrayed was familiar to Chinese of earlier and later generations, for Chinese society showed considerable continuity over time. The Han's eventual succession by the Sui and then by the Tang (tahng) and Song (soong) dynasties ensured that Chinese society continued along traditional lines, in contrast to the dramatic changes that took place elsewhere during the Intermediate Era. Once the Tang adopted a modified version of the Han system, the seventh through the eighteenth centuries proved to be a golden age, broken only occasionally by invasion or disorder. Some scholars call the Intermediate Era in world history the "Chinese Centuries." China became the world's richest and most populous society, enjoying a well-organized government and economy, a flourishing artistic and literary culture, and creativity in technology and science. Many commercial and cultural networks connected China to the rest of Eurasia. China's neighbors in Korea and Japan adopted many aspects of Chinese culture, though they also forged

What do you think?

In this era, China's emperors were more successful at controlling their people than the Japanese and Korean rulers were.

Strongly Disagree   Strongly Agree
1   2   3   4   5   6   7

Rafael Macia/Photo Researchers, Inc.

<< **Giant Japanese Buddha at Kamakura** During this era, most Japanese adopted Buddhism, some expressing their faith in art. This gigantic statue, erected in the city of Kamakura in 1252, shows the Buddha in meditation.

their own highly distinctive societies during this period. China did indeed, as Marco Polo recognized, influence or awe all those with whom it came into contact.

LO¹ Tang China: The Hub of the East

The harsh Sui dynasty that united China after the disintegration of the Han ruled for only a short time (581–618 C.E.) before rebellions brought it to an end. The victor in the struggles between rival rebel forces established the Tang dynasty (618–907). The three centuries of Tang rule set a high-water mark in many facets of Chinese life and provided a model for neighboring Asian societies. The Tang made important advances in political organization, economic production, science, technology, art, literature, and philosophy.

Tang China's Government, Networks, and Growth

In the seventh and eighth centuries, Tang China—an empire of some 50 or 60 million people—was the largest and most populous society on earth, and it had an immense influence in the eastern third of Eurasia (see Map 11.1). Like the Han before them, the Tang launched a series of ambitious campaigns that brought Central Asia, Tibet, Mongolia, Manchuria, and parts of Siberia under Chinese rule. Vietnam had already long been a colony. The Koreans became a vassal state, and the Japanese established close ties. Kingdoms as far away as Afghanistan acknowledged Chinese leadership, and Chinese garrisons protected the Silk Road, fostering the flow of goods and people across Eurasia. In western Asia, the powerful Abbasid caliph Harun al-Rashid testified to China's diplomatic clout by signing a treaty with the Tang.

Interactive Map

Map 11.1
The Tang Empire, ca. 700 C.E.

The Tang dynasty forged a large empire across Central Asia into Turkestan before their expansion was halted by Muslim armies at the Battle of Talas in 751. Control of Central Asia allowed the Tang to protect the Silk Road trade route. The Tang also controlled Vietnam and dominated Korea.

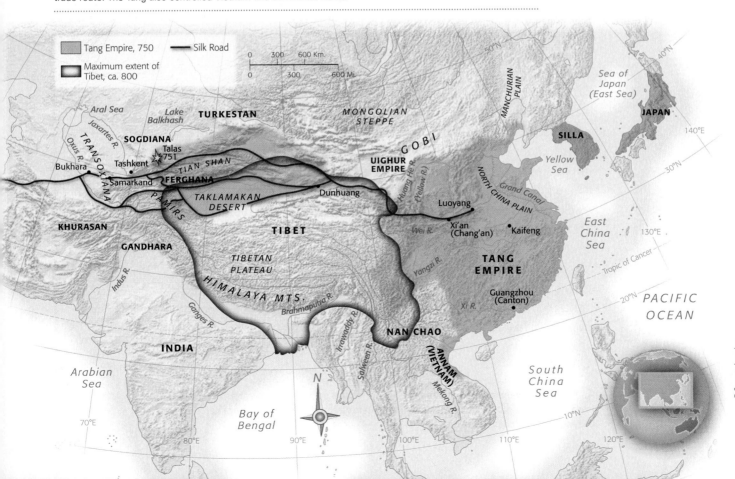

Trade and Commerce

The Tang were the most outward-looking of all Chinese dynasties, and during these years China became an open forum of ideas, people, and things arriving over the networks of exchange. The Silk Road, established during the Han era, remained a transcontinental highway. Along this network, traders, adventurers, diplomats, missionaries, and pilgrims traveled, many making their way to China. Others arrived by sea: perhaps two-thirds of the 200,000 inhabitants of the southern port of Guangzhou (gwahng-jo)—also known as Canton, a great trading hub—were immigrants, including Arabs, Persians, Indians, Cambodians, and Malays. For the many Muslim residents, the city boasted both Sunni and Shi'ite mosques. Indian astronomers and mathematicians joined the Tang government as scientific officials, while several hundred Chinese scholars visited India, most of them seeking Buddhist literature.

Tang wealth and power stimulated commerce throughout Eurasia. A lively sea trade linked China with Southeast Asia, India, Persia, and the Arabs. By land or sea, many Chinese inventions and treasured Chinese silk and porcelain reached western Eurasia. This multicultural exchange also benefited China. New products appeared, most notably tea from Southeast Asia, which became the national drink. Teahouses selling boiled tea opened in every marketplace. Another new arrival was the chair, probably from the Middle East. Diverse societies in places such as Burma, Java, and Nepal regularly sent embassies to the Tang court bearing gifts. Renewed contacts with India and the Middle East as well as many other peoples helped foster China's creativity, despite the criticism of some Chinese scholars, who complained about excessive foreign influences.

A Visual Sourcebook of Chinese Civilization (http://depts.washington.edu/chinaciv/). A wonderful collection of essays, illustrations, and other useful material on Chinese history.

Chang'an: The World's Largest City

The Eurasian exchange during the Tang fostered dynamic and culturally rich cities. Tang China boasted many cities larger than any contemporary cities in Europe or India, and the capital, Chang'an (CHAHNG-ahn), present-day Xi'an (SHEE-ahn), was home to 2 million inhabitants. The world's largest city, Chang'an was a model of urban planning, with its streets carefully laid out in a grid pattern and the city divided into quadrants. The broad thoroughfares were crowded with visitors from many lands. Many foreign artists, artisans, merchants, and entertainers worked in the capital. To serve the non-Chinese, the city contained four Zoroastrian temples, two Nestorian Christian churches, and several mosques. The only contemporary cities that could nearly match its size and amenities were Baghdad, the center of the powerful Abbasid Caliphate, and Byzantine-ruled Constantinople.

Silk Road Narratives (http://depts.washington.edu/uwch/silkroad/texts/texts.html). Explores cultural interaction in Eurasia through excerpts from Silk Road travelers.

Imperial Structure

Under the Tang, the centralized imperial structure, with the emperor at the top of the system, reached a high level of efficiency and maintained one of the world's most productive economies. Despite bloody rebellions, invasions, assassinations, palace coups, and dynastic upheavals, the hallmark of China's political system for many centuries was stability, the result of mixing a strong institutional structure with innovative political ideas. According to Confucian theory, the family was the model for the state, so the emperor was viewed as the symbolic father of the people and was expected to govern by moral example, not physical force. As during the Han, the Chinese considered the emperor the Son of Heaven and the first scholar of the land. He held daily audiences, during which diplomats from distant lands sometimes presented gifts as a symbol of their submission to his authority. In return the emperor bestowed on them a title, state robes, and gifts. While women sometimes had power behind the throne,

© Cultural Relics Press

Musicians on the Silk Road This glazed pottery figurine, one of many similar pieces from the Tang era, shows musicians playing Persian musical instruments while riding a camel along the Silk Road to China, demonstrating China's ties to the Middle East.

only one, the Empress Wu Zhao (woo chow) (625–705), a former imperial concubine who maintained power for more than fifty years, ever officially led the government. While Empress Wu generally ruled ably, Chinese scholars viewed her as an evil usurper.

In theory the emperor held absolute power, but he was watched by the Censorate, an agency unique to China that monitored the workings of the government, rooted out corruption, proposed changes in state policies, and criticized the government for failings. In addition, the doctrine of the Mandate of Heaven—that people have a right to overthrow an evil, corrupt, or ineffective government—meant that emperors had to consider the consequences of their policies and behavior.

> "The 80 percent of Chinese who tilled the soil were generally able— though often just barely— to produce a food surplus for the other 20 percent in towns and cities."

> 66 Chinese poems usually contained balance and symmetry and blended emotion with restraint. 99

Civil Service Exam

Because administering such a large and diverse empire required a competent bureaucracy, the Tang revived the competitive civil service exams from Han times. The civil service merit exam system was one of the greatest achieve-

ments of Chinese society and the most important institution that contributed to the long duration of the political system. The Chinese believed that government officials, known as mandarins, should be the wisest and ablest men in the land, and developed merit-based exams, a national university, and hundreds of local-level academies. During the Tang and the succeeding Song periods, perhaps 15 percent of the mandarins did not come from upper-class backgrounds, indicating that the examinations led to some social mobility. By passing the highest-level examination, a man received the equivalent of a Ph.D. degree, the prerequisite to hold office. The exams largely tested knowledge of Confucian literature, giving the ruling elite a shared Confucian ideology emphasizing ethics and loyalty. The Tang bureaucracy numbered around fifteen thousand officials, an extraordinarily small number for a country as huge as China. Clearly they ruled with the cooperation of the local people.

Tang officials had to pursue policies that maintained economic growth, especially agricultural production. The 80 percent of Chinese who tilled the soil were generally able—though often just barely—to produce a food surplus for the other 20 percent in towns and cities. They worked hard to achieve better yields and became one of the world's most efficient farming peoples. The Tang also attempted to circumvent the power of powerful landowning families and ensure stability by assigning each peasant family their own plot of land, under the "equal field system." For a time the reforms brought the peasantry some prosperity, but powerful families maintained control of much of their land. When the Tang declined after some 120 years of prosperity, the equal field system also disintegrated.

 The Craft of Farming Look inside a twelfth-century Chinese treatise on farming, with advice on when to plow, which crops to plant, and how to use compost as fertilizer.

CHRONOLOGY

China During the Intermediate Era

589–618	Sui dynasty
618–907	Tang dynasty
751	Battle of Talas
868	First books from woodblocks on paper
907–960	Five Dynasties
960–1279	Song dynasty
1167–1227	Life of Genghis Khan
1279–1368	Yuan dynasty (Mongols)
1368–1644	Ming dynasty
1405–1433	Voyages of Admiral Zheng He

Religion, Culture, and Technology

The early Intermediate Era was the golden age for Buddhism in Central Asia, Southeast Asia, and East Asia. It was also a time of cultural flowering and technological innovation. The first woodblock print books were produced, and some of China's greatest painters and sculptors lived in Tang times.

Buddhist Dominance

Under the Tang, Buddhism, which had spread into China early in the Common Era, grew to be a dominant faith, while Confucianism and Daoism remained influential. However, Buddhism presented the government with some problems. It divided into numerous competing sects, causing discord, and the Buddhist monasteries, which came to control vast amounts of tax-exempt land and wealth, constituted a challenge to the government as an alternative power center. In the mid-ninth century, the government cracked down on Buddhism. Emperor Wuzong (woo-chong) (840–846), in desperate need of more revenues, closed and seized 4,600 monasteries and defrocked all monks under the age of fifty. Although Wuzong's successors reversed his policies and restored the monasteries, this brief crackdown led Chinese Buddhism to lose some of its dynamism.

Meanwhile, new religions flowed east along the Silk Road. Nestorian Christianity, a sect considered heretical in Byzantium, gained a small following, and Islam became strong in northwest China and in pockets of southwest and southern China. Jewish merchants also settled in several north China cities, founding small Jewish communities that lived there for centuries. Except for Wuzong, the Tang court generally took a tolerant, ecumenical view of religion; indeed, religious persecution is rare in Chinese history. As one Tang emperor proclaimed: "The Way [truth] has more than one name. There is more than

one sage. Doctrines vary in distant lands, their benefits reach all mankind."[2]

Scientific and Technological Achievements

In this era of tolerance, Tang scholars and craftsmen made significant scientific and technological achievements. Tang astronomers established the solar year at 365 days and studied sunspots, and some argued that the earth was round and revolved around the sun. They were also the first to analyze, record, and then predict solar eclipses. Around 600 C.E., Chinese engineers built the first load-bearing segmental arch bridge, and Tang chemists perfected gunpowder. Chinese military forces could now use primitive cannon and flaming rockets to protect their borders or resist rebels.

Paper had been developed a millennium earlier, but the Tang made great strides by inventing woodblock printing as demand for copies of religious and Confucian texts outpaced supply. The first known book printed on paper with this method was a Buddhist text from 868. The Chinese had an insatiable desire to classify the wisdom of the past for use by future generations. Aided by printing, they could now compile encyclopedias to record their accumulated knowledge.

Literary and Artistic Achievements

Poetry was highly valued in this era. Annual literary festivals were held in Chang'an to select prizewinners, and one anthology of Tang poetry contains 49,000 poems by 2,300 poets. Many poems depicted the blessings and hardships of life: poverty, war, friendships, romantic

Song Landscape This painting, completed around 1000 C.E., shows a Buddhist temple dwarfed by towering mountain peaks.

The Nelson-Atkins Museum of Art, Kansas City, Missouri. Purchase: William Rockhill Nelson Trust, 47-71. Photograph by John Lamberton

love, the passing of time, the imminence of death. Chinese poems usually contained balance and symmetry and blended emotion with restraint, reflecting their Daoist and Buddhist influences. Poet Wang Wei (wahng way) wrote: "Walking at leisure we watch laurel flowers fall. In the silence of this night the spring mountain is empty. The moon rises, the birds are startled, As they sing occasionally near the spring fountains." His words invoke Daoist feelings of peace, detachment, and purity.

The two giant figures of Tang poetry were Li Po (lee po) and Du Fu (too foo), who were close friends but very different in their personalities and styles. Li (701–762) was romantic, disrespectful of authority, and humorous but often melancholy. Influenced by Daoism, Li said that a good person must be carefree, maintaining the heart and mind of a child. Many of Li's poems were composed during drinking sessions. In "The Joys of Wine" he wrote: "Since Heaven and Earth love wine, I can love wine without shaming Heaven. With three cups I penetrate the Great Dao. Take a whole jugful and I and the world are one. Such things as I have dreamed in wine, Shall never be told to the sober."[3] The opposite of Li Po, Du Fu (712–770) was a Confucian humanist, the preeminent poet of social consciousness and deeply concerned with the human condition. If Li's poems reflected his eccentric personality, Du Fu's held up a mirror to his times. His antiwar poems remain powerful even a millennium later: "When will men be satisfied with building a wall against the barbarians? When will the soldiers return to their native land?"[4]

Painting, which was an activity pursued by scholars and government officials, was closely associated with calligraphy, which also used brush and ink on silk or paper. Chinese paintings used color sparingly and were generally philosophical in presentation. Being influenced by Daoism, many painters specialized in landscapes, while other Chinese arts reflected Confucian influence, stressing order, morality, and tradition. Poetry and painting shared the stage with other art forms. The traveler to Tang China experienced art when he sipped tea from nearly transparent porcelain cups, the most sanitary utensils in the world at that time. China also became famous for splendid lacquerware, furniture made with mother of pearl, gold and silver inlay, fine musical instruments, and luxurious brocades.

Changes in the Late Tang Dynasty

Significant changes took place in China between the eighth and tenth centuries. For one, the overwhelm-ing majority of Chinese now lived in central and south China, where the fertile Yangzi Basin was the most productive economic region. For another, new crop strains were introduced from Southeast Asia that eventually made it possible to harvest two crops of rice per year. This led to more trade and substantial increases in the urban population. Crafts and merchant guilds and the world's first paper money appeared, and Chinese traders visited Southeast Asia to obtain luxury goods.

Eventually the Tang Empire collapsed, as it became too expensive to maintain and too difficult to defend. After a bitter defeat by Arab forces at the Battle of Talas (near Samarkand) in 751, Tang military power declined, and Muslim forces filled the vacuum. Islam became the dominant religion in Turkestan and in the Xinjiang (shin-jee-yahng) region just west of China proper. Finally the Tang lost control of China itself. The country broke apart, and in 907 Chinese rebel bands, spurred by famine and drought, sacked Chang'an. The Tang demise allowed Vietnam to finally free itself from the long yoke of Chinese rule.

During the next five decades after the Tang collapse, China was divided into several competing states known as the Five Dynasties. But Chinese society was now too massive and deeply rooted to experience the centuries of anarchy that occurred between the Han and Sui, and from the Tang onward the interludes of disorder between great dynasties proved brief. In addition, the Chinese came to deplore disunity. A proverb stated: "Just as there cannot be two suns in the sky, there cannot be two rulers in China."

LO² Song China and Commercial Growth

The next great dynasty, the Song (sung) (960–1279), founded by an able general, presided over a sophisticated period of achievement. Although lacking the Tang's grandeur, empire building, and world leadership, the Song was more accomplished in technological development and material richness. Late Song China contained perhaps 120 million people, with some two-thirds of them living in the Yangzi Basin or in the south. This Chinese population—between one-quarter and one-third of the world's total—lived in an area that stretched one thousand miles east to west and north to south, all of it linked by rivers and an extensive canal system. Clearly the Song continued the golden age begun by the Tang.

---

[3]Poem by Wang Wei "Bird-singing Stream" as seen in *The White Pony: An Anthology of Chinese Poetry* by Robert Payne (NY: Mentor, 1960). Poem by Li Po "Joys of Wine" as seen in *The White Pony: An Anthology of Chinese Poetry* by Robert Payne (NY: Mentor, 1960)

[4]"A Song of War Chariots" by Tu Fu from ANTHOLOGY OF CHINESE LITERATURE, VOL. 1 edited by Cyril Birch, copyright © 1965 by Grove Press, Inc. Used by permission of Grove/Atlantic, Inc.

Economic Prosperity and Song Society

During the Song, cities grew rapidly and economic growth was renewed. Song China boasted the world's largest cities. At least five cities had populations over 1 million, and nearly fifty other cities contained more than 100,000 people. Chinese urban residents enjoyed a high quality of life.

In the later Song era, when the government had been pushed south of the Yangzi River by nomadic invaders, the capital was Hangzhou (hahng-jo), a city of several million on the southern end of the Grand Canal (see Witness to the Past: Life in the Chinese Capital City). A later and well-traveled visitor, Marco Polo, called Hangzhou unquestionably the greatest city in the world. Social life in Hangzhou and other cities coalesced around the wine shops, restaurants, theaters, entertainment houses, and brothels. Hangzhou would be followed by Nanjing in the fifteenth century, and then Beijing from the sixteenth into the nineteenth centuries, as the world's largest cities.

> "Song China had the world's most advanced farming, and its expanding productivity met the needs of a flourishing market economy."

The Song also marked the high point for Chinese commerce and foreign trade. The flourishing merchant class grew substantially, and tax revenues were three times higher than for the Tang. The Grand Canal, which linked the Yellow and Yangzi River Basins, provided an economic cornerstone, allowing the mass movement of goods between north and south. China also developed the world's first fully monetized economy, putting paper money and silver coins into wide use. In addition, Song China had the world's most advanced farming, and its expanding productivity met the needs of a flourishing market economy for agricultural products. Foreign trade was now based more on maritime networks. Chinese merchants regularly visited Southeast Asia and traded around the Indian Ocean, and the coastal seaports of Guangzhou (Canton) and

 East and Southeast Asia: An Annotated Directory of Internet Resources (*http://newton.uor.edu/Departments&Programs/AsianStudiesDept/index.html*). Varied collection of links, maintained at University of Redlands.

Scroll of Kaifeng This segment from the scroll "Spring Festival on the River," discussed in the chapter opening, shows people thronging the Rainbow Bridge while boatmen lower their masts to pass under the cantilevered structure. Along the streets and bridge, people in stalls sell their goods.

Werner Forman/Art Resource, NY

Quanzhou (Zayton) in the south were home to thousands of foreigners, including many Arab, Indian, Persian, and East African merchants.

Redefining Gender Roles

During the Song era, Chinese society changed as a common elite culture spread among the educated. Printed books fostered the spread of education, as did the government's establishment of schools in every district. Although only a small percentage of these students ever became mandarins, a degree or some educated background became a certificate of status. The cultivated gentleman, whether or not in government service, was expected to be proficient in music (especially lute playing), chess, calligraphy, poetry, and painting.

However, while educated men enjoyed many options, women experienced more restrictions than they had known earlier. Women had been involved in public life during the Tang, but during the Song era, women's status began to decline as conservatives sought to limit women's economic roles. Men more often took concubines in addition to their official wives, and families increasingly frowned upon remarriage for widows. Peasant wives had the most equitable position, because they were crucial to family economic livelihood, but children belonged to the father's family, and the wife was ruled by her husband's mother.

Still another source of suffering for women was footbinding, which was introduced during the Song period among the elite and some of the common folk. Mothers tightly bound the feet of their five- or six-year-old daughters to prevent normal growth. This practice crippled a girl's feet and gave her a dainty walk, which enhanced what Chinese men viewed as her beauty and eroticism. But many peasants rejected the practice as too physically debilitating, and footbinding was not widespread until later dynasties.

Industrial and Intellectual Achievements

Song China's industry was the world's most advanced, and its manufacturing sector grew dramatically.

> "Although the Chinese had the technology to sail the seas and colonize other lands, they lacked the incentive because China was largely self-sufficient."

Chinese porcelain was traded all over Asia, the Middle East, and parts of Africa, and the name *china* became synonymous with the very finest porcelain products. China's iron industry was the world's largest before the eighteenth century, producing the finest steel for tools, weapons, stoves, ploughshares, cooking equipment, nails, building materials, and bridges. Spurred by domestic and foreign trade, Song China also developed a significant shipbuilding industry. Its huge compartmentalized ships had four decks and four to six masts and were capable of carrying five hundred sailors and extensive cargo. This maritime technology was the world's best at that time.

Technology, Science, and Medicine

During the Tang and Song periods, Chinese technological development outstripped that of other Afro-Eurasian societies. Some studies suggest that, between the first and fifteenth centuries C.E., the Chinese produced a majority of the world's major inventions. Song Chinese invented new agricultural and textile tools and machines, built the world's longest bridge (2.5 kilometers), and expanded the use of water-powered clocks and mills. Major Chinese inventions of the era that later spread throughout Eurasia included the magnetic compass, the sternpost rudder, and the spinning wheel. Song craftsmen also made movable type, first from fired clay and then from tin or copper, an invention that greatly facilitated the printing of books. Song weapons technicians developed the fire lance, a bamboo tube filled with gunpowder that was the precursor of the metal-barrel gun. Song engineers also invented the world's first industrial machines, a mechanized spinning process for the reeling of silk and later hemp thread.

The Song had notable achievements in astronomy and medicine. Today astronomers still use data the Song collected from observation of the skies, such as on the supernova that created the Crab Nebula. A Song calendar precisely measured the solar year (365.2425 days). In medicine, Chinese doctors inoculated against smallpox, a disease that ravaged much of Afro-Eurasia. Some Chinese medical ideas reached the Middle East and Europe by the thirteenth century.

Life in the Chinese Capital City

The following excerpts are from a description of Hangzhou, the capital city of China during the southern Song dynasty, written by a Chinese observer in 1235. It reveals the life of urban people in China during one of its most creative eras. The writer describes the city's many amenities, including shops, restaurants, and taverns, and also its cultural and social activities. The many specialized enterprises and diverse clubs indicate a highly complex society.

During the morning hours, markets extend from . . . the palace all the way to . . . the New Boulevard. Here we find pearl, jade, talismans, exotic plants and fruits, seasonal catches from the sea, wild game—all the rarities of the world. . . . In the evening . . . the markets are as busy as during the day. . . . In the wine shops and inns business also thrives. . . . In general the capital attracts the greatest variety of goods and has the best craftsmen. For instance, the flower company at Superior Lane does a truly excellent job of flower arrangement, and its caps, hairpins, and collars are unsurpassed in craftsmanship. Some . . . famous fabric stores sell exquisite brocade and fine silk which are unsurpassed anywhere in the country.

Among the various kinds of wine shops, the tea-and-food shops sell not only wine, but also various foods to go with it. However, to get seasonal delicacies . . . one should go to the inns, for they also have a menu from which one can make selections. The pastry-and-wine shops sell pastries with duckling and goose fillings. . . . In the large teahouses there are usually paintings and calligraphies by famous artists on display. . . . Most restaurants here are operated by people from the old capital [Kaifeng], like the lamb rice shops which also serve wine. . . . There are special food shops such as meat-pie shops and vegetable-noodle shops. . . . The vegetarian restaurants cater to [Buddhist] religious banquets and vegetarian dinners. . . . There are also shops specializing in snacks. Depending on the season, they sell a variety of delicacies. . . . In the evening, food vendors of all sorts parade the streets and alleys . . . chanting their trade songs. . . .

The entertainment centers . . . are places where people gather. . . . In these centers there are schools for musicians offering thirteen different courses, among which the most significant is opera. . . . In each scene of an operatic performance there are four or five performers who first act out a short, well known piece. . . . Then they give a performance of the opera itself. . . . The opera is usually based on history and teaches a moral lesson, which may also be a political criticism in disguise. . . . There are always various acting troupes performing, and this usually attracts a large crowd.

For men of letters, there is a unique West Lake Poetry Society. Its members include both scholars residing in the capital and visiting poets from other parts of the country; over the years, many famous poets have been associated with this society. . . . Other groups include the Physical Fitness Club, Angler's Club, Occult Club, Young Girl's Chorus, Exotic Foods Club, Plants and Fruits Club, Antique Collector's Club, Horse-Lover's Club, and Refined Music Society. . . . There are civil and military schools inside . . . the capital. Besides lineage schools, capital schools, and country schools, there are at least one or two village schools, family schools, private studios, or learning centers in every neighborhood.

Thinking About the Reading

1. What do the main goods sold in the markets say about economic prosperity?

2. What does the reading tell us about popular pleasures and entertainments in Hangzhou?

3. What do the main recreational and educational activities available suggest about leisure time and societal values?

Source: Reprinted with permission of The Free Press, a Division of Simon & Schuster Inc., from *Chinese Civilization and Society*, A Sourcebook, Second Revised & Expanded Edition by Patricia Buckley Ebrey. Copyright © 1993 by Patricia Buckley Ebrey. All rights reserved.

Neo-Confucianism

The Song also saw the rise of neo-Confucianism, a form of Confucianism that incorporated many Buddhist and Daoist metaphysical ideas. Neo-Confucianism was associated particularly with Zhu Xi (JOO shee) (1130–1200), a child prodigy and one of the most influential thinkers in Chinese history. He believed that the original ideas of Confucius had become rigid and altered over the centuries, and he advocated rediscovering the essence of the sage's ideas and writings. The influence of Daoism can be seen in Zhu Xi's rational and humane approach, which recognized a dualism between the material world and the energizing force thought by Chinese to pervade the universe, qi (ch'i). In the spirit of Confucius, Zhu identified reason or principle as the unchanging law, and morality as the measure of all human affairs: "For every person in the society the most important thing is the cultivation of himself as an ethical being."[5] Yet, Zhu was indifferent to natural science; hence, although he seemed to advocate a scientific method, his ideas did not help regenerate or sustain scientific inquiry. Over time neo-Confucianism dominated China's universities, a force for stability but not innovation.

The Song in World History

In many ways the Song could have been a turning point in Chinese and world history, but it did not foster a major transition. Profound Song developments remind some historians of eighteenth-century Europe at the dawn of rapid industrialization. But unlike that revolution's transforming impact in the West, the Song's commercial and agricultural dynamism never revolutionized Chinese society. Instead, these developments were contained and absorbed; although the Chinese had the technology to sail the seas and colonize other lands, they lacked the incentive because China was largely self-sufficient. The highly bureaucratic empire easily maintained its dominance over merchants and kept them from disrupting China's social order and hierarchy. With enough agricultural production to feed a huge population, convenient transportation, and many natural resources, the Chinese had no great need to develop additional mechanized technologies. Furthermore, the Mongol conquest of the Song, a cooler climate by the thirteenth century, a growing land shortage, and the Black Death pandemic in the fourteenth century, undermined economic dynamism.

In its domination of the merchants, the imperial government played a central role in containing economic growth. Many essential commodities remained government monopolies, such as iron, grain, cloth, and salt. In part this socialist policy reflected the low esteem accorded merchants in Confucian ideology. Monopolies over essential products helped enrich the state and also protected the population from price and supply problems, but they restricted merchants to handling nonessential products. One ambitious Song prime minister with socialist leanings, Wang Anshi (wahng ahn-shee) (1021–1086), experimented with guaranteed state loans to farmers, fixed commodity prices, unemployment insurance, and old-age pensions to promote equality, but these innovations ultimately proved unsuccessful.

The Song government devoted resources to weapons but was generally disinterested in military expansion. Prosperity, trade, and urban living made peace more attractive than conquest. Although it maintained the world's largest army, the Song, unlike the Han and Tang, took steps to reduce the power of military leaders so they could not threaten civilian authority, which had been a chronic problem in the Tang. As a result, the Song adopted a passive attitude toward controlling the pastoral nomads across the border, attempting to appease them with generous payments. Ultimately the policy failed. In the twelfth century, a nomadic people, the Jin (chin), conquered north China, forcing the Song court to move south across the Yangzi, where it continued to rule central and south China from Hangzhou until the invasion by the Mongols.

LO³ Mongol Conquest, Chinese Resurgence, and Eurasian Connections

From the thirteenth through the nineteenth centuries, the Chinese way of life showed great stability. Three ruling houses—the Yuan, the Ming, and the Qing (see Chapter 18)—held power between the downfall of the Song and the end of the imperial system in the twentieth century. Yet this almost unprecedented record of political stability has a puzzling aspect, because two of the three dynasties were conquest dynasties imposed by non-Chinese nomadic peoples. The two dynasties that held power between the thirteenth and seventeenth centuries were the Yuan (yu-wenn), established by invading Mongols, and the Ming, which marked a return to Chinese rule.

The Mongol Empire and the Conquest of China

For several millennia the Chinese had feared what they considered the northern "barbarian" scourge, fast-riding horsemen who came out of the Central Asian grasslands and deserts killing, looting, and taking captives. The ever-threatening Central Asian influence on China's political life was based on a major geographic fact: the close proximity of the arid grasslands north and west of China, which, compared to the lush farmlands of China, were suitable only for mobile herding. These contrasting environments had produced very different societies. In the grasslands a pastoral economy produced tough, self-reliant herding peoples: few resources necessitated seasonal migration, chronic poverty, and small temporary settlements. When China was weak, the Great Wall proved no major barrier to militant invaders. In the thirteenth century, a new confederation of warlike peoples, the Mongols, conquered all of China.

Genghis Khan

Before invading China, the Mongols conquered much of Eurasia, including eastern Europe and western Asia. Traditionally divided into often feuding tribes, the Mongols became united under Temuchin (ca. 1167–1227), a ruthless but brilliant man who changed his name to Genghis Khan (GENG-iz KAHN) ("Universal Emperor"). He had simple motives: "A man's greatest pleasure is to defeat his enemies, to drive them before him, to take from them that which they possessed, to see those whom they cherished in tears, to ride their horses, to hold their wives and daughters in his arms."[6] Skilled horse soldiers, the Mongols were formidable opponents. Their powerful bows could kill at 600 feet, and they boasted the world's most advanced siege weaponry, including catapults.

Khubilai Khan and the Yuan Dynasty

Because of China's strength, it was one of the last countries to fall to Mongol control. Genghis Khan had conquered parts of northern China in 1215. The Mongol conquest of the rest of China, which came fifty years after the death of Genghis, was accomplished by his grandson, Khubilai Khan (koo-bluh KAHN) (r. 1260–1294). The Mongol conquest resulted in a new dynasty, which took the name Yuan (1279–1368), and China became part of a great world empire, one that stretched from eastern Europe to Korea and from the Black Sea to the Pacific Ocean (see Map 11.2).

Interactive Map

The Mongols under Khubilai Khan made major changes in China, imposing a distinctive government system and fostering new cultural forms. By Mongol standards, Khubilai Khan was a rather enlightened ruler who patronized Buddhism. The Mongols also built granaries for food storage, operated an efficient postal system, and improved the transportation network. But Chinese historians have condemned Khubilai Khan for the sins committed by the Mongols generally, in particular their resistance to assimilation into Chinese society. Later Chinese viewed the Yuan as China's darkest hour, an intolerable rule by aliens who would not be absorbed. Khubilai Khan moved the capital to Beijing (bay-JING) ("Northern Capital"), before this a provincial city close to the Great Wall. Beijing was a hub situated alongside the major highways leading north and west; it symbolically tied China to the borderlands. Except for brief periods since, Beijing has remained the capital of China, politically eclipsing more ancient cities like Chang'an and Hangzhou.

Description of the World
Follow Marco Polo, and hear him relate the natural—and sometimes supernatural—wonders he encountered on his journey to Khubilai Khan.

Although Khubilai Khan made some determined attempts to win Chinese support by modeling his government along Chinese lines and dutifully performing Confucian rites, the Mongols failed to get the cooperation of most scholars and bureaucrats. To rule the vast country, they were forced to rely administratively on foreigners who came to China to serve in what was effectively an international civil service. These included many Muslims from Central Asia, western Asia, and even North Africa, as well as a few Europeans who found their way to "fabled Cathay," as they called China.

Mongol Culture and Networks

The Mongols did not patronize intellectuals—indeed, they mistrusted them—but they were tolerant in religious matters. In part this was because Khubilai Khan and his successors ruled over a religiously diverse society and wanted to avoid conflict. However, the Mongols had more rigid gender expectations and

Mongol campaigns before 1240

Mongol campaigns after 1240

Route of Marco Polo

Map 11.2
China in the Mongol Empire

After the Mongols conquered much of Central Asia, western Asia, and eastern Europe, they added China and Korea to their huge empire, the largest contiguous land empire in world history. During the Mongol era, many Asians and some Europeans, including the Italian Marco Polo, visited or worked in China.

marriage practices than the Chinese, and women's roles became more circumscribed. In response to occasional Mongol mistreatment of Chinese women, Chinese men now expected women to remain at home and emphasize feminine behavior, including the growing fashion of tightly bound feet to set them apart from non-Chinese women.

Culturally the Mongol period proved relatively sterile in comparison to the brilliance of the Tang and Song, but there were some innovations. Musical drama (Chinese opera) became a popular form of entertainment, appealing mostly to the Chinese common folk rather than the elite. In addition, some Chinese intellectuals who refused to work for the Mongols began writing novels, an elaboration of age-old storytelling.

> 66 Marco Polo's reports astonished Europeans, because China in this era was far more developed in many fields than the rest of Eurasia. 99

Commerce in the Yuan Dynasty

The Mongols paved the way for enhanced global communication, opening China's doors to the world. By protecting the Silk Road, which had languished for several centuries from chronic warfare between Central Asian societies, the Mongols fostered networks for the exchange of not only goods but also ideas and technology between East and West. During the Mongol era, Chinese inventions like gunpowder, printing, the blast furnace for cast iron, silk-making machinery, paper money, and playing cards moved westward, as did many medical discoveries. Bubonic plague, which killed millions of Chinese during Mongol rule, probably traveled the overland trade routes, fostering the Black Death that ravaged the Middle East and Europe in the fourteenth century (see Chapters 10 and 14).

Marco Polo

One visitor to Yuan China was the Italian merchant Marco Polo (ca. 1254–1324), who initially went to China seeking trade goods but spent seventeen years there, mostly in government service. Eventually Polo returned to Italy and wrote of the wonders he had

Khubilai Khan and His Entourage Hunting This painting by a Chinese artist of the time shows Khubilai Khan, dressed in ermine, and Mongol colleagues, including a woman, hunting on horseback, a popular activity among Mongols.

encountered. When Polo's book was published, most Europeans dismissed it as full of lies, but the general accuracy of his account has been confirmed by historians. He recorded the resentment of the Chinese people toward the Mongols, who imposed their rule by sometimes-brutal force. For example, they once slaughtered a city's entire population for the killing of one drunk Mongol soldier. Polo also wrote of China's great cities. Standing along the shores of Hangzhou's beautiful West Lake, the Italian wrote that "the city is beyond dispute the finest and noblest in the world in point of grandeur and beauty as well as in its abundant delights. The natives of this city are of peaceful character, thoroughly honest and truthful and accustomed to dainty living."[7]

Polo's reports astonished Europeans, because China in this era was far more developed in many fields than the rest of Eurasia and had the world's highest standard of living. Polo noted, for example, that the Chinese had for a thousand years burned black stones (coal) for heat and that they took regular baths. This latter information was astounding, since medieval Europeans seldom if ever bathed.

Fall of the Yuan Dynasty

While the Mongol conquests had enormous consequences for Central Asia, the Middle East, and Europe, Mongol rule in China lasted only a century and did not leave a deep imprint. For one thing, they were always unpopular, even hated. The Mongols in China had a difficult time adjusting to peace: they lost their fighting toughness and came to desire luxury more than sacrifice. As Mongol unity fragmented, corruption and power struggles grew rampant. Then, a terrible plague outbreak raged and the Yellow River flooded severely, bringing famine and challenges to the Mongols' claims to the Mandate of Heaven. The turmoil was ended by a Chinese commoner who established a new Chinese dynasty, the Ming. Mongol military forces left China and returned to Central Asia.

Ming Government and Culture

The new Ming dynasty (1368–1644) became a great period of orderly government and social stability, with a rich culture. The founder, Zhu Yuanzhang (JOO yu-wen-JAHNG) (1328–1398), like the founder of the Han, rose from abject poverty through sheer ability and ruthless behavior in a time of opportunity. Under the Ming, China's people lived for nearly three centuries in peace and prosperity, with living standards among the highest and mortality rates among the lowest of anywhere in the world. China more than doubled in

population, from around 80 million to between 160 and 180 million.

The Ming installed a government similar to that of the Han and Tang but were somewhat more despotic. Perhaps because of the bitter experience of Mongol rule, the Ming emperors exercised more power than Song or Tang emperors and placed the bureaucracy under closer imperial scrutiny. Yet, the bureaucracy was still small, some twenty thousand officials, 25 percent of whom were from nonelite backgrounds. The Ming eliminated the office of prime minister, which had been traditional since the Han, and the Censorate became more timid, reducing the checks on royal abuses. As a result of these changes, the Ming emperors became more isolated from the real world.

Still, Ming rulers encouraged intellectual pursuits, expanding the Hanlin Academy, which was established in the Tang. Research fellows there were paid to

A Ming Imperial Workshop Printer's shops, such as the one shown here, used movable type to publish encyclopedias with information on engineering, medicine, agriculture, and other practical topics.

read and write whatever they liked, and Ming scholars compiled an 11,000-volume encyclopedia and a 52-volume study of Chinese pharmacology. A sense of order infused the arts, which saw several genres mature during the Ming. Theater reached its highest level in this period: each performance of a play aimed at harmonizing all the elements: song, speech, costume, makeup, movement, and musical accompaniment. The most popular form of theater at the peasant level, Chinese operas, were often witty and unrealistic. Much Chinese music was composed for operas or for ritual and ceremonial purposes. String, wind, and percussion instruments were popular, especially the flute, lute, and zither. Although most Ming scholars considered fiction worthless, it had a large audience. Most novels had a Confucian moral emphasizing correct behavior, but some offered social criticisms or satires. Perhaps the greatest Ming novel, *The Water Margin* (also known as *All Men Are Brothers*), presented heroes who were also bandits, driven into crime by corrupt officials.

Ming China: Looking Outward and Inward

Rather than building a new empire, the Ming turned to overseas exploration, which resulted in closer political and economic relations with Southeast Asia. The emperor dispatched a series of grand maritime expeditions to southern Asia and beyond to reaffirm China's preeminence in the eastern half of Asia by, as official sources put it, "showing off the wealth and power of the Central Kingdom."[8] Admiral Zheng He (jung huh) (Cheng Ho) (ca. 1371–1435), a huge man and a trusted court eunuch of Muslim faith, commanded seven voyages between 1405 and 1433. The world had never before seen such a large-scale feat of seamanship: the largest fleet comprised sixty-two vessels carrying 28,000 men, and the largest "treasure ships," as they were known, weighed 1,500 tons, were 450 feet long, boasted nine masts nearly 500 feet high, and carried a crew of five hundred. Zheng He's extraordinary voyages carried the Chinese flag through Southeast Asia to India, the Persian Gulf, and the East African coast (see Map 11.3). The ships had the capability of sailing around Africa to Europe or the Americas but had no incentive to do so. Even though the Chinese came mostly in peace, some thirty-six countries in southern and western Asia officially acknowledged Chinese preeminence. Even the ruler of the East African city of Malindi sent ambassadors bearing tribute, including a giraffe.

 Interactive Map

The Voyages of Zheng He

Historians still debate the causes and effects of Zheng He's great voyages. Some argue that the emperor wanted foreign countries to reaffirm his position as the Son of Heaven; others suspect the ambitious emperor wanted to demonstrate China's military capabilities. Some historians, however, see commercial motives as primary, because these voyages occurred at a time of increased activity by Chinese merchants in Southeast Asia, thousands of whom had settled or were sojourning in the Philippines, Indonesia, Siam, and Vietnam. The voyages of Zheng He may also have helped revitalize the traditional tribute system. Under this system, China considered the various East, Southeast, and Central Asian states as vassals or tributaries and granted them trade relations and protection. In return, the tributary states sent periodic envoys bearing gifts to the emperor, confirming his superiority in ritual form. The vassal states played along, whatever their true feelings, because they desired China's goodwill and trade goods.

Beginning in the Han, the Chinese never recognized any other society as an equal, at least not symbolically. They developed the notion that they were superior not just materially but also culturally: for the Chinese, to be civilized was to embrace Chinese culture. When a tribute mission arrived in the capital, part of the rite was the kotow, the tribute-bearers' act of prostrating themselves before the emperor. This practice left little doubt as to who was superior and who was inferior, reflecting a Confucian sense of hierarchy.

Ming Isolationism

In the early Ming, China remained at the cutting edge, perhaps the world's wealthiest and most developed country. Commercially vibrant and outward-thrusting, Ming China had the capability to become the dominant world power. But world dominance never came: instead, China turned inward. The grand voyages to the west and the commercial thrust in distant lands were suddenly halted by the Ming emperor, and soon the state outlawed Chinese emigration altogether. The causes of the stunning reversal of official Chinese engagement with the world that, in the perspective of later history, seemed so counterproductive remain subject to debate. Some causes were economic. Perhaps Zheng He's voyages were too costly even for the wealthy Ming government. Another cause for stagnating

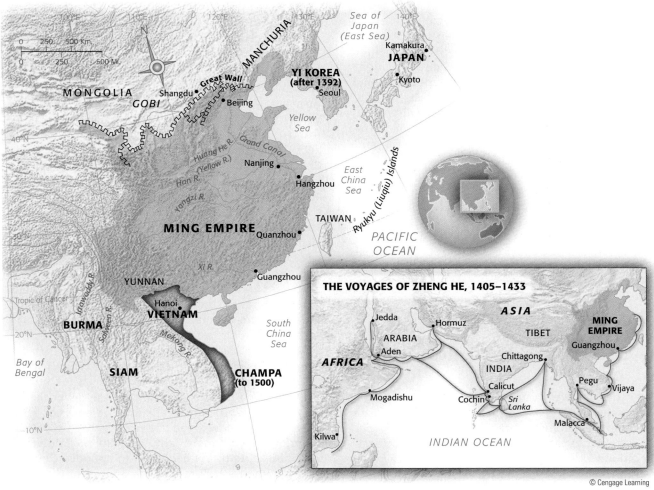

 Map 11.3
The Voyages of Zheng He

After replacing the Mongols, the Ming reestablished a strong Chinese state, attempted to recolonize Vietnam, and rebuilt the Great Wall. Ming emperors dispatched a series of grand maritime expeditions in the early 1400s that reached the Middle East and East Africa.

© Cengage Learning

international interaction may have been that merchants held a low status in the Confucian social and ideological system, despite their flourishing guilds and frequent wealth. Indeed, Ming leaders were even more convinced than their predecessors that profit was evil, and mercantile interests inevitably conflicted with social and political ones.

Military and economic factors also influenced the turn inward. With the Mongols regrouping in Central Asia,

A Description of Foreign Peoples
Discover the rich commodities and exotic customs of Arabia and southern Spain, as seen by a thirteenth-century Chinese trade official.

the Ming court shifted its resources to defense of the northern borders and the pirate-infested Pacific coast, spending millions rebuilding and extending the Great Wall. But military operations along the northern border and an ill-fated invasion of Vietnam generated a fiscal crisis that weakened the government. Finally, the turn inward can be seen as a reaction to the Mongol era, as the Chinese became more ethnocentric and antiforeign. But despite its growing isolation, China remained powerful, productive, largely self-sufficient, and mostly prosperous, enjoying generally high living standards well into the eighteenth century.

LO⁴ Cultural Adaptation in Korea and Japan

As the cultural heartland of East Asia, China strongly influenced its three large neighbors of Vietnam (see Chapter 13), Korea, and Japan. At the same time, all of these societies adapted these Chinese influences to their indigenous customs. Both Vietnamese and Koreans retained their sense of cultural identity, and Japan produced a variant of East Asian culture that was even more distinctive, especially in its political and social structures.

> "The involvement of monks in political life fostered religious corruption and a more worldly orientation that alienated some believers."

Silla Korea and the Koryo Era

As Korean society developed, several strong states emerged on the peninsula. In the mid-seventh century, the southern Korean state of Silla (SILL-ah) defeated its main rival, Koguryo, and united all Koreans, but at the price of becoming a vassal of China. Political unity, which Koreans enjoyed into the 1900s, allowed Korean culture to became homogenized. But Silla also borrowed Chinese culture and institutions: Buddhism triumphed, and the Tang system became the model in government, with Confucianism used as a political ideology. However, the Korean social structure placed more emphasis than the Chinese did on inherited status instead of merit, and Korean peasants faced many legal restrictions. In addition, the gap between rich and poor was much wider than in China. Yet, among Silla's rulers were three queens, two of them among the state's most effective rulers, suggesting less gender bias than in China. Silla women generally shared in the social status of their menfolk, enjoyed many legal rights, and could even head families.

During the Silla era (688–918), Koreans mixed influences from Tang China with their own traditions to produce a distinctive culture, and also formed connections with the rest of the world. They adapted Chinese writing to their own very different spoken language and began creating a distinctive literary tradition, composing works of history, religion, and poetry. To mass-produce these works, Silla craftsmen also developed woodblock printing as early as China. The oldest still extant example of woodblock printing in the world, a Korean Buddhist writing, dates from 751. Perhaps influenced by the Chinese, Koreans also studied astronomy. A great observatory built in this era is the oldest still standing in East Asia. Buddhist pilgrims came from as far away as India, and many Arabs traded at Silla. One Arab wrote that "seldom has a stranger who has come there from Iraq or another country left it afterwards. So healthy is the air there, so pure the water, so fertile the soil and so plentiful of all good things."[9]

Gradually Silla declined, damaged by elite rivalries, corruption, and peasant uprisings, and it was replaced by a new state, Koryo (KAW-ree-oh), which lasted for more than four centuries (918–1392). Chinese influence continued in politics and philosophy: Koreans set up an examination system like that of China and Confucian schools, and neo-Confucianism became popular. But Korean kings, who were never as strong as Chinese emperors, were more influenced by the court, military, and aristocratic landowning families. In contrast to Silla, Koryo women played a lesser role in public affairs and faced more restrictions than Silla women. Unlike in China, Korean farming relied on large estates. These patterns persisted long after the Koryo dynasty ended.

Thanks to the continued mixing of Chinese and Korean influences, substantial religious, cultural, and technological change characterized the Koryo

CHRONOLOGY

Korea and Japan During the Intermediate Era

645	Taika reforms in Japan
688	Destruction of Koguryo
688–918	Domination of Korea by Silla
710–784	Nara period in Japan
794–1184	Heian period in Japan
918–1392	Unification of Korea by Koryo
1180–1333	Kamakura Shogunate in Japan
1274, 1281	Mongol invasions of Japan
1338–1568	Ashikaga Shogunate in Japan
1392–1910	Yi dynasty in Korea

years. Buddhism gradually became a more powerful economic and political force but also assimilated many elements from animism. The involvement of monks in political life fostered religious corruption and a more worldly orientation that alienated some believers, and the religion gradually lost influence. More secular artistic trends emerged, including landscape painting and some of the world's finest porcelain. Wide interest in literature fostered a publishing industry. The first movable-type printing made of clay came from China in the eleventh century, and Koreans invented the world's first metal movable-type printing by 1234.

Like China, Korea had to occasionally fend off northern pastoralists. The Mongols conquered the peninsula in the early 1200s, making Koryo a colony in their vast empire. When Koreans resisted, the Mongols devastated the land, carrying off hundreds of thousands of captives and imposing heavy taxes on peasants. Yet, thanks to trade networks, more Chinese and western Asian learning and technology reached Korea during the Mongol era.

Nara Japan: Government and Culture

Although using many Chinese and Korean influences, Japan, like Korea, produced a distinctive, robust, and sophisticated society. In the mid-sixth century, the Japanese embarked on three centuries of deliberate cultural borrowing from China. The changes began with the *Taika* (TIE-kah) ("Great Change") reform of 646 C.E. The country was divided into provinces that were ruled by governors who derived their power from the emperor. Japanese leaders also established a governmental system made to resemble the Chinese centralized bureaucracy. Moreover, the Japanese were now able to record their history and conduct their daily activities using the Chinese writing system. Finally, the adoption of Buddhism from China brought with it a rich constellation of art and architecture.

Ancient Japan (*http://www.wsu.edu:8080/~dee/JAPINRES.HTM*). A useful site from Washington State University offering many essays and links on premodern Japan.

The height of the period of conscious borrowing from China (710–784) takes its name from Nara (NAH-rah), Japan's first capital city, which was built on the model of the Tang capital, Chang'an. Nara had a population of some twenty thousand, half of them government officials and their families. During the Nara period, land was nationalized in the name of the emperor and, using Tang models, reallocated on an equal basis to the peasants. In return, the peasants paid a land and labor tax. This system was abandoned as unworkable after a few decades, but it illustrated that in agrarian societies like Japan, land control is the key to political power.

Although these changes were designed to strengthen imperial authority, the Japanese emperor never became an unchallenged and activist Chinese-style ruler. Powerful aristocrats maintained control of the bureaucracy and also retained large tax-exempt landholdings. In practice Japan became a dyarchy, a form of dual government whereby one powerful family filled the highest government posts and dominated the emperors, whose power was mostly symbolic. The emperors passed their lives in luxurious seclusion, with the main goal of guaranteeing an unbroken succession through having sons. This dyarchical system, so different from China's, remained the pattern in Japan into the nineteenth century.

Economic unrest characterized the late Nara period. Peasants resented corvée (forced labor) and military conscription, which often resulted in economic ruin. Many abandoned their fields, becoming wandering, rootless ronin (ROH-neen) ("wave people"), some of whom were hired by large landowners as workers. To stop people from becoming ronin, the government abolished compulsory service and gave the responsibility for defense to local officials. Eventually the ronin these officials hired as troops were transformed into the provincial warrior class.

Chronicles of Japan These guidelines for imperial officials show how the Soga clan welcomed Chinese influence in an attempt to increase the authority of the Japanese imperial family.

Nara leaders promoted aspects of Chinese culture but blended them with Japanese traditions. The rituals and ceremonies of the imperial court, largely based on Tang Chinese models, included stately dances and orchestral music using Japanese versions of Chinese musical instruments; they are still maintained at the Japanese court today. Also, the Chinese written language gained great prestige, and Chinese ideographs were adapted to Japan's very different nontonal spoken language, in what must have been a difficult conversion process. Chinese literary forms, including poetry and calligraphy, became popular. The Japanese also adopted and reshaped Chinese philosophical and religious doctrines that they found appealing, including Confucianism and Mahayana Buddhism, whose world-view that all things are impermanent greatly influenced their art and literature.

But the Japanese also retained their original animist religion known today as Shinto, a kind of nature worship. Shinto and Buddhism addressed different needs and easily blended into a synthesis. The deities of Shinto were not gods but beautiful natural phenomena such as Mt. Fuji (FOO-jee), waterfalls, thunder, or stately trees. Shinto stressed ritual purity, encouraging bathing and personal cleanliness, and the Japanese became the world's best-scrubbed people. Shinto worshiped the land and ancestors but had no coherent theology or moral doctrine, no concept of death or an afterlife. The faithful flocked to shrines, such as the famous Ise (EE-say), for festivals or to seek help from spirits.

Heian Renaissance and Decline

The period of imitation and direct cultural borrowing from China ended during the Heian (HAY-en) period (794–1184). After the capital moved from Nara to Heian, or Kyoto (kee-YO-toe), 28 miles north, Japan gradually returned, over some decades, to a period of relative isolation. The leaders discontinued foreign contacts in the ninth century and set about consciously absorbing and adapting the Chinese cultural patterns imported during the Nara era under the slogan "Chinese learning, Japanese spirit." The centralized government gave way to a resurgence of aristocratic rule, and Buddhism gradually harmonized with Shinto beliefs and practices while generating new sects, art, and temple building.

A rich and uniquely Japanese court society arose, and in turn supported the development of purely Japanese art and literary styles. The modification of Chinese influence was exemplified in the

 Read about the great Heian novelist, Lady Murasaki, and her very famous novel *The Tale of Genji.*

development of kana (KAH-nah), a phonetic script consisting of some forty-seven syllabic signs derived from Chinese characters. Now Japanese could write their language phonetically. This allowed more freedom of expression, especially when the kana letters were combined with Chinese characters.

Heian elite culture, a world enormously remote from us today in time, attitudes, and behavior, reached its high point around 1000 C.E. It flourished among a very small, highly inbred group of privileged families in Kyoto, which then had a population, including both the elite and commoners, of around 100,000. Many elite residents derived their incomes from bureaucratic jobs and land ownership. The Kyoto aristocracy became extraordinarily withdrawn from the realities of the outside world, creating a culture that was governed by standards of form and beauty and in which the distinction between art and life was not clearly made. Passionately concerned with their rank and status in society, they created some of Japan's greatest literature and art. The Heian period was probably unique in world history for the careful attention spent in choosing an undergarment, or the time writing a love note, always exquisite down to the last detail. The Heian aristocrats were not interested in pure intellect or social morality; their value system was superficial. They were obsessed by mood, especially the sense of the transience of beauty, but they left a wonderful cultural legacy.

Women from affluent families had their highest position in Japanese history during the Heian, at least in the capital city. They were free to have romantic affairs and spent their days playing games, writing diaries, listening to romantic stories, or practicing art. Some women, such as the novelist Lady Murasaki (MUR-uh-SAH-kee), gained a formal education and learned to write poems and prose. In poetry, a writer might deftly turn a scene of nature into one of emotion: "The flowers withered, their color faded away, while meaninglessly, I spent my days in the world, and the long rains were falling."[10] Heian standards of feminine beauty were distinctive: women wore their hair long to the ground, applied white skin powder and lipstick, plucked their eyebrows, and blackened their teeth with dye.[11] Men also used cosmetics and were equally concerned with their personal dress and appearance.

Heian culture was perhaps too removed from real life to survive. Only a tiny fraction of Japan's population could afford this hedonistic way of life. The common people outside of Kyoto were mostly illiterate and saddled by unremitting work, their rural lives brightened only by the occasional festival or family activities. Aristocrats feared leaving Kyoto; they called peasants "doubtful, questionable creatures" and the provinces "uncivilized, barbarous, wretched" places.[12] The Kyoto elite became aware that their world of aesthetic perfection was a fleeting phenomenon that might soon vanish. Indeed, by the twelfth century, the Heian era had ended and Japan had moved into a new phase of its history.

kana

A Japanese phonetic script developed in the Heian period (794–1184) that consisted of some forty-seven syllabic signs derived from Chinese characters.

LO⁵ Changing Korea and Japan

During the second half of the Intermediate Era, the Koreans came under the sway of a new dynasty while the Japanese changed substantially, producing a very different way of life. For all its cultural brilliance, the Heian aristocracy was not the prototype of later Japanese society. Instead, another vigorous group, the provincial warrior class, would shape the future of Japan.

Korea During the Early Yi Dynasty

In 1392 a new Korean dynasty took over from the Mongols, the Yi (yee), whose state was known as

Interactive Map

Choson (cho-suhn) (see Map 11.4). They lasted until 1910, an incredible longevity of 518 years. Yi rulers sought good relations with China and maintained a tribute relationship with their large neighbor. During this time, Koreans learned to better use Chinese social and political models. To Koreans, Confucianism provided a philosophical justification for government by a benevolent bureaucracy under a virtuous ruler. Education expanded to prepare students for the civil service exams, which tested for both Confucian and scientific knowledge, and gradually this knowledge came to define the intellectual elite. Confucian influence also remade Korean social institutions such as the family. The Yi believed that Korean women had too much freedom; they introduced policies to encourage women's seclusion at home and imposed arranged marriages, veiling of the face when out in public, female chastity, and strict obedience to husbands and fathers.

Aided by extensive use of movable-type printing, Yi Korea continued to develop literature, technology, and science, including mathematics and astronomy. King Sejong (SAY-jong) (r. 1418–1450) was a particularly strong supporter of scientific progress. Respected by his people for improving the Korean economy and military, helping poor peasants, and prohibiting cruel punishments, Sejong wrote books on agriculture and formed a scholarly think tank, the Hall of Worthies. Aided by Sejong, fifteenth-century Yi scholars invented a phonetic system for indicating Korean pronunciation of Chinese characters and for writing the Korean language. These years also saw a renaissance of intellectual activity, including a 365-volume encyclopedia of medical knowledge. Choson was

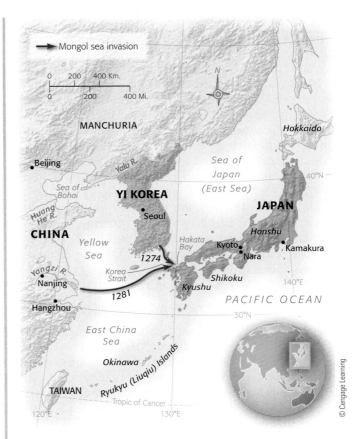

Map 11.4
Korea and Japan, ca. 1300

Japanese society developed in an archipelago, the major early cities rising in central Honshu. In 1274 and 1281, the Japanese repulsed Mongol invasions by sea. Throwing off the Mongols, Korea was unified under the Yi dynasty in 1392.

among the more creative and sophisticated of the late Intermediate Afro-Eurasian societies.

The Samurai and Shogunates

When the Heian period ended, a new warrior class gradually became the dominant force in Japanese politics and society, helping to produce a very different Japanese government and culture. The warrior class triumphed for several reasons. First, Heian provincial governors, who were too fond of the refinements of Kyoto, had a growing tendency to delegate their powers and responsibilities to local subordinates. Second, rural society was changing. Powerful local families and Buddhist communities were always hungry for land and often able to seize it by force. In the Heian era, estates were replaced by a system of scattered landholdings

King Sejong This modern painting portrays the Yi dynasty King Sejong, revered by Koreans for his political, economic, and scientific achievements, observing stars, supervising book printing, and contemplating a musical instrument he commissioned.

Courtesy, Yushin Yoo

in which a lord ruled over the villages on his parcel of land. This system led to more direct ties between peasants as vassals and the warrior class as lords.

The net result was that, by the end of the twelfth century, tax-paying land amounted to 10 percent or less of the total cultivated area, and local power had been taken over by the new aristocracy in the rural provinces. As this aristocracy expanded their landholdings, soldiers and ronin signed on as military retainers to aristocratic families. Conscription had ended earlier because it was too burdensome for the peasants, so imperial forces were weak. In this way political and military power dispersed to rural areas.

As this warrior class moved to the center of the historical stage, it led Japan into a type of social and political organization that was more like that of Zhou China or medieval Europe than the centralized Tang state. Historians disagree as to when between the twelfth and fourteenth centuries the transition to a new, warrior-based system—Japanese called it the Age of Warriors—was completed, but it continued in some form up to the nineteenth century. During this time, military power absorbed into itself political and economic authority, and all three became defined in terms of rights to land and relations between lords and vassals.

Bushido and the Samurai

The warrior class, or samurai (SAH-moo-rie) ("one who serves"), moved gradually into a position of military supremacy over the emperor and the court. The samurai resulted from a relationship formed between the rural lords and their military retainers, based on an idealized feudal ethic later known as Bushido (boo-SHEE-doh) ("way of the warrior"), which was not completely developed until the seventeenth century. The samurai had two great ideals derived from Bushido: loyalty to leaders, and absolute indifference to all physical hardship. They enjoyed special rights in return for unquestioning service to their lords. Although only a few women of the samurai class, most famously Tomoe Gozen in the twelfth century, engaged in combat, most received some martial arts training. The samurai occupied the highest level of the social system, but they were a

samurai
("One who serves") A member of the Japanese warrior class, which gained power between the twelfth and fourteenth centuries and continued until the nineteenth.

Bushido
("Way of the Warrior") An idealized ethic for the Japanese samurai.

small percentage of the population. If they failed to do their duty or achieve their purpose, suicide was a purposeful and honorable act by a man who could be respected for his physical courage, determination, and sincerity.

Kamakura Shogunate

The periodic fighting of the warrior society resulted in part from overpopulation: too many people competing for too little land. By the twelfth century, Japan was controlled by competing bands of feudal lords, and a civil war broke out between two powerful families and their respective allies. One lord, Minamoto-no-Yoritomo (MIN-a-MO-to-no-YOR-ee-TO-mo), emerged victorious and set up a military government in Kamakura (kah-mah-KOO-rah), near Tokyo (TOE-kee-oh), which lasted from 1180 to 1333. The emperor commissioned him shogun (SHOW-guhn) ("barbarian-subduing generalissimo"), in effect a military dictator controlling the country in the name of the emperor, who remained in seclusion in Kyoto. The shogun was responsible for internal and external defense of the realm, and he also had the right to nominate his own successor.

Although the imperial house, which traced its origins back to the Sun Goddess in an unbroken line, had become politically impotent, no shogun seriously attempted to abolish it. To many Japanese, the emperors symbolized the people and the land. The Kamakura shoguns were nominally subordinate to the emperors but had real power in many parts of the country. However, before 1600, the system was not very centralized.

During the Kamakura Shogunate the Mongols failed twice, in 1274 and 1281, to invade Japan. The 1281 Mongol attempt involved the largest force, in some accounts up to 150,000 men transported by more than 4,000 conscripted Chinese ships. These ships were armed with ceramic projectile bombs, the world's first known seagoing exploding projectiles. On both occa-

sions, the Mongol armies landed, met fierce resistance, and were destroyed when great storms scattered and shipwrecked their fleets. These divine winds, or *kamikaze* (KAHM-ih-KAHZ-ee), convinced the Japanese of special protection by the gods. Japan was never successfully invaded and defeated until 1945. Any inferiority complex toward China had ended.

Japanese Social, Political, and Economic Change

The new Japanese society and culture, shaped by the warrior class, differed substantially from Heian culture. Japanese society had always been hierarchical, but now the special status of the samurai reflected a more rigid structure than before. Inequality started in the family: children owed obedience to their parents, and the young honored the old. Women now commonly moved into their husband's household, where they were expected to be dutiful, obedient, and loyal to their menfolk. Marriages were arranged for the interest of the family, not from romantic love. Yet, while women lost some freedom, marriage became more durable and divorce more difficult, giving married women more security. Furthermore, women from aristocratic families also dominated the staff of the imperial court and ran the emperor's household, giving them some political influence. As in China, the interest of the group always took precedence over that of the individual.

> **"** Marriages were arranged for the interest of the family, not from romantic love. **"**

Sects Within Japanese Buddhism

The Japanese developed new forms of religion and the arts between 1200 and 1500. Many Buddhist sects emerged, but three became the most significant and enduring. The largest, the *Pure Land,* emphasized prayer and faith for salvation and stressed the equality of all believers, minimizing distinctions between monks and laypeople. It also rejected the notion of reincarnation, maintaining that believers went straight to nirvana. Another Buddhist sect, *Nicheren* (NEE-chee-ren), has sometimes been compared to Christianity and Islam because of its militant proselytizing and concern for the afterlife. Nicheren was angry and outspoken, seeing rival views as heresy.

The third major Buddhist sect originated in China under Daoist influence. Zen is called the meditation sect because it emphasized individual practice and discipline, self-control, self-understanding, and intuition. Knowledge came from seeking within, deep into the mind, rather than from outside assistance. One Zen pioneer wrote, "Great is mind. Heaven's height is immeasurable but Mind goes beyond heaven; the earth's depth is unfathomable, but Mind reaches below the earth. Mind travels outside the macrocosm."[13] The Zen culture was devised over the centuries to bring people in touch with their nonverbal, nonrational side.

Religious perspectives, especially Zen, affected the arts. Zen values can be seen in Japanese rock gardens, landscape gardening, and flower arrangements. Whereas the Chinese preferred their nature unspoiled, the Japanese liked it ordered. Japanese gardens, ponds, and buildings, such as the beautiful Golden Pavilion of Kyoto, built in the thirteenth century, were all constructed in harmony with their natural surroundings. The tea ceremony, which also resulted from Zen, emphasized patience, restraint, serenity, and the beauty of simple action involving the commonplace. Other arts also flourished in this era. Japanese ceramics later became famous throughout the world for their subtlety and understated beauty, and they are considered by some to have been the world's greatest. Japanese painting emphasized skill and technique through self-discipline. The Noh drama, plays that presented stylized gestures and spectacular masks, appeared in this era.

The Ashikaga Shogunate and Rise of the Daimyo

Although a samurai-dominated hierarchical society became well established, these centuries also saw considerable political and economic change. In 1333 the Kamakura Shogunate was ended through intrigues and civil wars and replaced by a government headed by the Kyoto-based Ashikaga (ah-shee-KAH-gah) family (1338–1568), but the Ashikaga shoguns never had much power beyond the capital. Furthermore, a growing population, which reached 5 million by the 1300s, became harder to control. Political power became increasingly decentralized, as local lords struggled to obtain more land. This competition led to the rise of great landowning territorial magnates called daimyo (DIE-MYO) ("great name"), who monopolized local power. Each of the several hundred daimyo had his supporting samurai and derived income from the peasants working on their land.

By the 1400s, Japan had experienced rapid change in both economic and political spheres. Agriculture became more productive, an increasingly active merchant class lived in the fast-growing towns, and Japanese ships traveled to China and Southeast Asia. The rigid political and social system strained to accommodate these new energies. In the next century, civil war and the arrival of Europeans aggravated these problems and resulted in a dramatic modification of the political system.

Noh
Japanese plays that use stylized gestures and spectacular masks; began in the fourteenth century C.E.

daimyo
("Great name") Large landowning territorial magnates who monopolized local power in Japan beginning during the Ashikaga period (1338–1568).

Listen to a synopsis of Chapter 11.

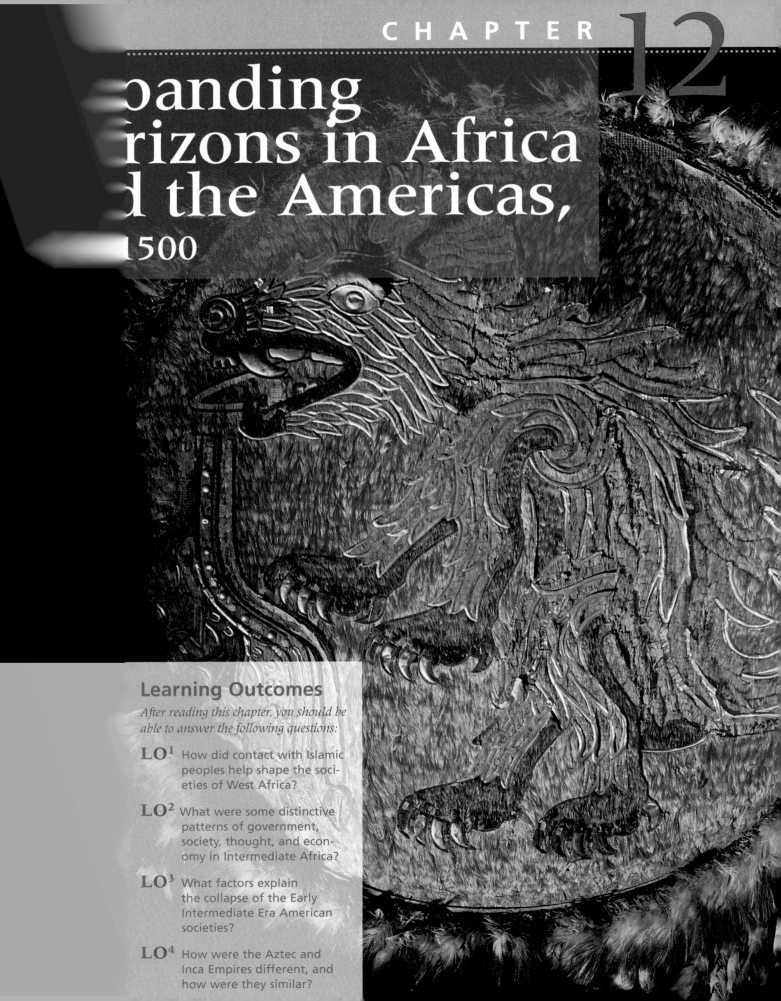

CHAPTER 12

Expanding Horizons in Africa and the Americas, 1500

Learning Outcomes

After reading this chapter, you should be able to answer the following questions:

LO¹ How did contact with Islamic peoples help shape the societies of West Africa?

LO² What were some distinctive patterns of government, society, thought, and economy in Intermediate Africa?

LO³ What factors explain the collapse of the Early Intermediate Era American societies?

LO⁴ How were the Aztec and Inca Empires different, and how were they similar?

> **❝**A long time ago, when the Arabs arrived in Lamu [a port in today's Kenya, East Africa], they found local people there. The Arabs were received with friendliness and they wanted to stay on. The local people offered to trade land for cloths. Before the trading was finished, the Arabs had the land, and the [local people] had the cloth.**❞**
>
> —**A Lamu oral tradition**[1]

Around 912, the Baghdad-born Arab geographer Abdul Hassan Ibn Ali al-Mas'udi sailed to East Africa with mariners from Oman (OH-mahn), in eastern Arabia, on their regular trading expedition to what Arabs described as *Zanj* ("the land of black people"). Al-Mas'udi discovered that traveling along the East African coast could be perilous, with reefs and high waves that "grow into great mountains and open deep gulfs between them." Al-Mas'udi spent three years traveling from port to port, venturing as far south as Sofala (so-FALL-a), a city in what is today Mozambique (moe-zam-BEEK). After further travels to Persia, India, and China, al-Mas'udi finally returned to Africa to settle in Cairo, where he wrote several books before his death around 956.

Test your knowlege before you read this chapter.

What do you think?

Religion had little influence in Africa and the Americas during the Intermediate Era.

Strongly Disagree						Strongly Agree
1	2	3	4	5	6	7

Al-Mas'udi's informative account pictured East African society in a key period of state formation and economic connection through the Arabs to other Eurasian societies. He praised the energetic traders and skilled workers of the coast, reported that the Sofala region produced abundant gold for export, and provided details about the international ivory trade. Arabs carried ivory from Zanj to Oman, from where they shipped it to India and China. He wrote that "in China the Kings and military and civil officers use ivory [to decorate furniture]. In India ivory is much sought after. It is used for the handles of daggers. But the chief use of ivory is making chessmen and backgammon pieces."[2]

<<**Feathered Shield** This brightly colored feathered mosaic shield, used for ceremonial purposes by an Aztec warrior in the fifteenth century, has an image of the Aztec water god, a monster that resembled a coyote, outlined in gold.

Erich Lessing/Art Resource, NY

281

Many sub-Saharan Africans became connected to the vast Eurasian network through trade and the spread of world religions. As al-Mas'udi's reports confirm, transregional trade was significant. As trade networks expanded, some African peoples, such as the gold producers near Sofala, became integral parts of hemispheric commerce while remaining part of networks within Africa. But the American societies across the Atlantic Ocean had no known links at all to these busy Afro-Eurasian networks of exchange.

Despite lack of contact with each other, Africans and Americans shared some patterns of social and political development. Using their own creativity, some of these peoples thrived in forbidding environments. Between 600 and 1500, African and American states rose and fell, among them a few regional empires. However, in contrast to the more densely populated areas of Eurasia, for many Africans and Americans, politics was mainly a matter of self-governing villages rather than large, centralized governments. In the Western Hemisphere, trade routes existed over wide areas, but geography inhibited the growth of long-distance networks. Only after 1492 did maritime exploration permanently connect African, American, and Eurasian peoples.

LO¹ The Power and Maturation of African States

After 600, major changes took place in West Africa that resulted in the rise of several kingdoms in the Sudanic region (the area stretching from west to east just below the Sahara Desert) and along the Guinea (GINN-ee) coast. As in Eurasia, empires sprouted, flourished, and decayed. Networks of exchange and travel helped shape societies. The rise of great kingdoms in the Sudan coincided with the expansion of both a global religion, Islam, and a global commerce that linked West Africa with North Africa, the Mediterranean Basin, and western Asia. The movement of Bantus into central, eastern, and southern Africa also continued in this era. Some Sudanic-style kingdoms were formed, while commercial cities tied to Indian Ocean trade emerged on the East Coast.

Islam and the First Sudanic Kingdom

For hundreds of years, camel caravans had plied the trackless, barren Sahara sands, transporting valuable products such as gold, salt, ivory, slaves, and ceramics between West and North Africa. The people benefiting the most from these networks lived in the Sudan (soo-DAN), the largely grasslands region just south of the Sahara. Because its flat geography and the long but sluggish Niger River allowed for easy communication, the Sudan became a meeting place of people and ideas. Beginning in the 800s, Islam filtered down the Saharan trade routes, carried peacefully by merchants, teachers, and mystics. As Muslim merchants settled in towns involved with the trans-Saharan trade, they helped form stable governments, and their religion was absorbed into the Sudanic societies. Islam introduced a complex, literate tradition to the Sudan, producing changes in customs, names, dress, diet, architecture, education, and festivals. The Sudanic religious atmosphere promoted tolerance, by Muslims toward animists and vice versa. Still, Islamic practice was often superficial, and it took several centuries for the religion to permeate into the villages.

A few kingdoms with similar features already existed by the time Islam reached the Sudan. Reflecting their peoples' animist beliefs, the kings in these societies were considered divine and enjoyed direct access to the spirits, but their power was often limited. Many kings had to consult councils of elders to approve their decisions, and some kings were elected by elders or chiefs. The women of the royal families also had great power, sometimes as queens. While some kingdoms became regional empires, states had no fixed territorial boundaries, only fluctuating spheres of influence, and they often included diverse ethnic groups. Their lack of political, ethnic, and cultural cohesion made them inherently unstable.

Civilizations in Africa (*http://www.wsu.edu:8080/~dee/AFRINRES.HTM*). Contains useful essays concerning premodern Africa.

Kingdom of Ghana

The earliest known Sudanic kingdom was Ghana (GON-uh), centered on the northwestern part of the Niger River (see Map 12.1). Founded by Mande speakers of the Soninke (soh-NIN-kay) ethnic group, Ghana reached its golden age in the ninth and tenth centuries, prospering from its control of the trans-Saharan gold trade between

Interactive Map

Map 12.1
Major Sub-Saharan African Kingdoms and States, 1200–1600 C.E.

Many large kingdoms and states emerged in Intermediate Africa. Large empires dominated the Sudan in West Africa. Prosperous trading cities sharing a Swahili culture dotted the east coast.

West and North Africa. For generations, gold and various tropical crops had been traded northward for salt, dates, textiles, and horses. The Ghana capital, Koumbi, was a major trade center located near gold deposits. Many of the city's twenty thousand inhabitants were immigrants, including Arab and Berber merchants.

By the tenth century, Ghana's rulers, at their pinnacle of power, had converted to Islam, a move that apparently increased the wealth and splendor of the royal court. An Arab visitor in 1067 said that the king's attendants had gold-plaited hair and carried gold-mounted swords, and that even the guard dogs wore collars of gold and silver. But early in the eleventh century, a civil war erupted, and Berbers from North Africa took advantage of the turmoil to attack the kingdom. Perhaps the empire had lost its cohesion by incorporating so many different peoples; it collapsed in 1203. The court was destroyed and the merchants moved away.

Sudanic Empires: Mali and Songhai

The next great Sudanic empire, Mali (MAHL-ee), was formed in 1234 by another Mande-speaking group,

the Malinke (muh-LING-kay), led by the Keita (KAY-ee-tah) clan. The Keita leader, Sundiata (soon-JAH-tuh), became the mansa (MAHN-suh), or king, of Mali. Famed farmers and traders, the Malinke conquered much of the western Sudan, including the territory once controlled by Ghana. The empire's total area stretched some 1,500 miles from east to west and incorporated dozens of ethnic groups. The Malinke *mansa* was both a secular and religious leader who surrounded himself with displays of wealth and ceremonial regalia and expected his subjects to approach him on their knees. At some point Sundiata apparently converted to Islam, perhaps to secure better relations with North Africa, but he also used Malinke animism, developing a reputation as a magician.

Mansa Musa

Islamic influence gradually grew stronger, and some of the later Mali emperors made glittering pilgrimages to Mecca. When Sundiata's descendant, Mansa Musa (MAN-sa MOO-sa) (r. 1312–1337), went to Mecca in 1324 riding a white Arab horse, he took fifty slaves bearing golden staffs, one thousand followers, and one hundred camels, each loaded with 300 pounds of gold. According to an Arab official writing of Mansa Musa's stop in Egypt, he "spread upon Cairo the flood of his generosity; there was no person, officer of the court, or holder of any office who did not receive a sum of gold from him. The people of Cairo earned incalculable sums from him, whether by buying and selling or by gifts."[3] Mansa Musa reportedly spent so much money in Cairo that the Egyptian currency was devalued. But whatever attention Mansa Musa lavished on Islam, the majority of the Mali people continued to follow animism, and Mali remained an essentially secular state.

Mali's Commercial Network

Mali's economic base included farming, commerce, and control of the gold and salt trade across the desert. The kingdom supplied about two-thirds of the world's gold supply in this era. In the thirteenth century, the Mali trading city of Timbuktu (tim-buk-TOO) emerged as the major southern terminus of the trans-Saharan caravan trade. Cities and towns like Timbuktu were filled with craftspeople, but most Malians lived in small villages and cultivated rice, sorghum, or millet, sup-

Chronicle of the Seeker
Learn more about the famous journey that King Musa of Mali made to Mecca in the fourteenth century and why he and his entourage were remembered well by Muslims along the route.

CHRONOLOGY

Africa in the Intermediate Era

ca. 500–1203	Kingdom of Ghana
1000–1200	Rise of Hausa city-states
ca. 1000–1450	Zimbabwe kingdom
1200–1500	Golden age of East African coastal cities
1220–1897	Kingdom of Benin
1234–1550	Mali Empire
ca. 1275	Rise of Yoruba kingdom of Oyo
1324–1325	Mansa Musa's pilgrimage to Mecca
ca. 1375	Rise of Kongo kingdom
1464–1591	Songhai Empire
1487	Bartolomeu Dias rounds Cape of Good Hope

plemented by herding or fishing. Rulers like Mansa Musa may have dazzled the world, but most Malians lived simply.

Mali benefited from network connections. The international links provided by Islam and the trans-Saharan commerce enticed many visitors and sojourners to the Sudan, including poets, architects, teachers, and traders from places such as China, Spain, and Egypt. The fourteenth-century Moroccan traveler Ibn Battuta spent months in Mali and had mixed feelings about the empire. He admired the Malians' many "admirable qualities" and peaceable atmosphere, commenting that there was "complete security in the country. Neither traveler nor inhabitant in it has anything to fear from robbers or men of violence."4 But the pious Muslim frowned on what he considered the immodest dress and independent behavior of women and the custom of eating dogs.

Mali rapidly declined in the 1400s because of internal factionalism and raids by other peoples. By 1550, the Mali of former days was gone. A much smaller Mali kingdom limped into the 1600s, one of numerous small states in the western Sudan.

Songhai Empire

The third great Sudanic empire was Songhai (song-GAH-ee), a kingdom formed by several ethnic groups that seceded from Mali in 1340. Over the next decades, Songhai increased its power, and by 1464 it was roughly as large as the former Mali Empire. The most revered Songhai leader was Aksia (ACK-see-a) the Great (1483–1528), a humane, pious, and tolerant man who was devoted to learning. The imperial capital at Gao (ghow) on the Niger River was a substantial city containing perhaps 100,000 people. As demand for gold and slaves increased in both North Africa and Europe, Songhai flourished from the trans-Saharan caravan trade, even more than Ghana and Mali had done before. Slaves were obtained from nearby peoples and sold in the Gao slave market, and many were taken on the arduous journey across the Sahara to the Mediterranean societies. In exchange, Songhai received glass, copperware, cloth, perfumes, and horses.

Under Songhai rule, Timbuktu flourished. The city on the Niger became a major Islamic intellectual center with a famous Islamic university that specialized in teaching astronomy, astrology, medicine, history, geography, Arabic, and Quranic studies. The thousands of scholars in the city patronized

> 66 Corn, cattle, milk, and butter were available in great abundance. 99

bookstores and libraries containing thousands of books, many in African languages using Arabic script. In recent years, more than thirty thousand lost books, hundreds of years old, on many subjects have been unearthed. Corn, cattle, milk, and butter were available in great abundance. Songhai flourished until 1591, when Moroccans destroyed its military power.

The Hausa and Guinea Kingdoms

Another dynamic area of the Sudan developed further east. Between 1000 and 1200 C.E., the Hausa (HOUSE-uh) people of the region erected a series of flourishing and fiercely competitive city-states, ruled by kings, that came to dominate some of the trans-Saharan trade into the eighteenth century. The prosperity of these city-states attracted many non-Hausa immigrants, including Arabs and Berbers, many of whom were assimilated into the Hausa society. Hausa cities such as Kano (KAHN-oh) were centers for manufacturing cotton cloth and leatherwork, some of which was sold as far away as Europe. The Hausa were also farmers, famed craftspeople, and skilled traders.

Hausa Society

Hausa society combined features from several cultural traditions, including Arab, Berber, and West African influences. Today Hausa is the most widely spoken African language. Like many Sudanic peoples, the Hausa possessed a strong class system. At the top were the royal families, and below them was the traditional aristocracy. In the villages a strong sense of mutual obligation and cooperation prevailed. Hausa women enjoyed a high status compared with women in many African societies. In the fifteenth century, a queen, Amina, ruled one of the major Hausa states, Zaria (zah-REE-uh). An oral poem praised her as "like the moon at its full, like the morning star. She is a lion as precious as gold among all women."5

Read about Sundiata, the "Lion Prince" and founder of the great Mali Empire.

Yoruba Society

West African political development was also occurring just south of the Sudan, along the Guinea coast, a region of rain forest and grasslands. By about 1000 C.E. the Yoruba (YORE-uh-buh) peoples of what is now western

Hausa Houses in Kano Hausa towns and cities feature houses with large courtyards behind high walls. Structural beams made from local palm trees protrude from the walls.

Werner Forman/Art Resource, NY

Nigeria had developed several states, each based on a large city ruled by a king or prince. The kings were powerful and considered sacred, but they were controlled by powerful elders and aristocrats, and Yoruba identity was more cultural than political. One Yoruba kingdom, Oyo (OY-oh), rose rapidly after 1275 and was soon the most powerful state in the area, flourishing for centuries under able kings and a strong administrative structure.

Yoruba society had an urban and mercantile orientation. Many towns dotted Yoruba country, serving as both commercial and political centers and ruled by elaborate bureaucracies. Yoruba women were not expected to work in the fields, so many developed wealth and influence as traders. Artisans worked iron, wood, leather, ivory, and cloth. One thousand years ago, the Yoruba at Ife (EE-fay) were already casting beautiful bronze portraits of their rulers. Because the Yoruba prized submissiveness to superiors and discouraged conflict, crime was rare.

King Ewuare and Benin

Another great Guinea kingdom, Benin (buh-NEEN), situated just east of Yoruba territory, emerged around 1220, and under King Ewuare (ee-WAHR-ee) the Great it established a sizable empire in the mid-1400s. Early kings like Ewuare were warriors, but later they became more spiritual leaders, subject to influence by powerful local chiefs. Benin artists cast beautiful bronzes and carved ivory to glorify the accomplishments of the king and state.

Benin was located near the Atlantic coast, where Europeans began to explore in the late 1400s; therefore, it was one of the first African kingdoms to be visited by Europeans, who wrote of the prosperous society they admired. Benin city was 25 miles in circumference, was protected by high walls, and included an elaborate royal palace, neat houses with verandas (porches), and neighborhoods linked by broad avenues. The king enjoyed vast wealth and had a large, lavish court, and an elite commercial

Benin King and Musicians
This bronze plaque shows the king, preparing for war, wearing beads and royal musicians on both sides. Such plaques were hung on palace walls and pillars to glorify the ruler.

The Nelson-Atkins Museum of Art Kansas City, Missouri. Purchase: William Rockhill Nelson Trust, 58-3. Photograph by Jamison Miller

class traded with the Hausa, Yoruba, and Songhai. Bini merchants dealt in woodcarvings, foodstuffs, ironwork, farm tools, weapons, and later cloth. Because they produced most of the cloth, Bini women also benefited from this trade. Those unable to work were supported by an innovative welfare system. This society flourished until 1550, when it began to decline. Nonetheless, the Benin kingdom extended until 1897.

The Bantu Diaspora and Islamic Influence

Considerable movement of Bantu peoples persisted during the Intermediate Era, bringing encounters with other groups. In East Africa and the Great Lakes region, the migrating Bantus came into contact with the Nilotic speakers, who had migrated to the region from north-central Africa. Bantus and Nilotes (NAI-lots) competed over resources such as good grazing land and salt, but they also traded, coexisted, and sometimes mixed together.

Over time the Bantu peoples scattered over thousands of miles of forest, savannah, and highlands in the southern half of Africa, creating diverse cultures, languages, political systems, and economic patterns but also maintaining many common traditions. Most Bantu speakers were farmers, practicing shifting cultivation where necessary but using more complex methods in the fertile East African highlands and elsewhere. Bananas became the staple crop of East Africa. Some Bantus lived in towns of fifteen thousand to twenty thousand residents, such as those

among the Sotho (SOO-too) and Tswana (TSWAHN-uh) of southern Africa. Some centralized kingdoms on the Sudanic model appeared, especially in the Great Lakes region, but the village usually remained supreme.

While Bantus were settling along the East African coast in the first millennium C.E., the expansion of both Islam and global commerce integrated the East African coastal peoples into Dar al-Islam and the wider world. The 1,200 miles of coast stretching from present-day Somalia down to central Mozambique was a cultural melting pot, where a growing trade network linking East Africa with the societies around the rim of the Indian Ocean and beyond brought diverse cultures, languages, and religions to the region. Egyptians, Greeks, Persians, Indonesians, and Romans made occasional voyages. Eventually Arabs from the Persian Gulf, Oman, and Yemen came to dominate the East African coastal trade, seeking products such as ivory, tortoise shell, leopard skin, gold, and copper.

As trade increased, many city-states developed along the coast. Among the largest were Mogadishu (mo-ga-DEE-shoo), Malindi (ma-LIN-dee), Mombasa (mahm-BAHS-uh), Zanzibar (ZAN-zuh-bahr), and Sofala. Each city-state was politically independent, and city leaders were chiefly interested in trade, not military expansion. As the maritime networks improved, settlers came from Arabia, Persia, and India. Each city-state was dominated by a royal court, often claiming Persian or Arab ancestry, and powerful trading families. Trade networks from the coast into the interior expanded with the discovery of gold in what is now Zimbabwe (zim-BOB-way). Because of its access to the goldfields of the interior, the port of Sofala at the mouth of the Zambezi (zam-BEE-zee) River became a major trade hub and a wealthy state.

The tenth-century Arab traveler al-Mas'udi left a record of a largely Bantu coastal society that also had many Sudanic customs. He reported that farmers grew sorghum as their chief crop, and he described

"By 1500 some ten thousand Arab and Swahili traders lived inland along the river, buying and then exporting gold."

the people as elegant orators with animist beliefs: "Everyone worships what he pleases, a plant, an animal, a metal."[6] Yet, they also had a concept of a supreme deity or great god. Two centuries later, many Bantu customs had been reshaped by increasing Arab and Islamic influences.

East African Commerce and Swahili Culture

The golden age of the East African coast, which boasted royal courts, stone palaces, coral-carved mosques, and imported luxury goods, began about the ninth century and reached its peak from the twelfth through the fifteenth centuries as Islam became entrenched. Ships from Arabia, Persia, and India regularly visited the coast. One passenger, the Moroccan jurist Ibn Battuta, traveled as far south as Kilwa, a prosperous city on an island off what is today Tanzania, which he described as "one of the most beautiful and well-constructed towns in the world, elegantly built [with] good buildings of stone and mortar, entirely surrounded by a wall and towers."[7] Kilwa, which had perhaps twenty thousand people, was a collection hub for goods coming in from north and south.

By Ibn Battuta's time, the coast had become largely Muslim, and the Moroccan traveler felt at home. He described the Kilwa Muslims as virtuous and its rulers, a family claiming Yemenite descent, as humble and pious. The East African city-states became an integral part of the greatest maritime trading network of the Intermediate world, a system that linked economies around the rim of the Indian Ocean and stretched from Indonesia to East Africa. This network was generally dominated by seafaring Arab and Indian Muslims, but it did bring the East

African coastal people considerable prosperity, as evidenced by the many beautiful homes of the coastal cities, some with tropical gardens, fountains, and pools.

Over time the blending of Bantu, Arab, and Islamic influences in the coastal cities produced a distinctive new African people and culture, Swahili (Arab for "people of the coast"). Arab settlers had come in such numbers that they could not be absorbed into the dominant Bantu culture. Instead, intermarriage and a fusion of cultures and language occurred. Mixing Bantu and Arabic tongues created a new Swahili language. The Swahili people began writing their language in the Arabic script and produced poetry, historical legend, and religious speculation, in addition to commercial accounts. Its influence reached as far inland as the eastern Congo River Basin. Today Swahili is second only to Hausa as a first or second language in sub-Saharan Africa.

But Swahili identity involved more than language. The Swahili tended to favor Arab dress, including long gowns for men and modest attire for women. Yet, according to a visitor around 1500, women from wealthy families "wear many jewels of fine gold, silver too in plenty, earrings, necklaces, bangles, bracelets, and good silk garments."[8] Arab architectural styles dominated the cities. The Swahili also adopted Arab ideas of inheritance, becoming firmly patrilineal. Islam became dominant along the coast by the twelfth century, spreading in part because it was a flexible religion, willing to tolerate the incorporation of Bantu beliefs in spirits and ancestor worship.

Zimbabwe and the Kongo Kingdom

The East African trading cities were only a part of the wider Bantu diaspora, which also included various kingdoms in central and southern Africa. On the fertile plateau of south-central Africa, one of the greatest kingdoms, Zimbabwe, which means "houses built of stone," emerged, flourishing

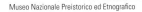
Museo Nazionale Preistorico ed Etnografico

The Great Zimbabwe Complex Great stone enclosures, most probably used as royal residences or religious sanctuaries, were built around the Zimbabwe kingdom. This one, surrounded by high walls, was at the center of the kingdom's capital city.

from trade with the coast. Today little remains of the kingdom's monumental buildings except for dozens of impressive stone ruins that dot the landscape for hundreds of miles. The Shona (SHO-nah) people, who still live in the area today, had lived on the plateau since at least 1000 C.E. and had constructed these buildings and a great state between the thirteenth and fifteenth centuries, eventually controlling much of the plateau.

Shona Prosperity

Mining was the key to Zimbabwe's prosperity. The Shona were already advanced in mining technology, and they extracted gold, copper, and iron ore on the plateau from open-pit and occasionally underground mines. They traded these minerals with the Arabs and Swahili along the coast, using the Zambezi River as the route between plateau and coast. By 1500 some ten thousand Arab and Swahili traders lived inland along the river, buying and then exporting the gold to the Middle East and India through Sofala and Kilwa. The Shona mined perhaps one thousand pounds of gold annually in the early 1500s, and in exchange Zimbabwe received Indian textiles and Chinese ceramics. Some residents were skilled artists who produced copper, bronze, and gold ornaments.

But Zimbabwe's prosperity did not endure. In the 1400s, the empire broke up into two rival states, and the capital city was largely abandoned by 1450. Because the Shona economy mixed farming and pastoralism, perhaps Zimbabwe was a casualty of overpopulation and soil exhaustion. As Zimbabwe declined, the trade routes and then the government may have shifted north to the upper Zambezi River Valley, which was closer to sources of gold, copper, ivory, and salt.

The Kongo Kingdom

Another great Bantu kingdom, Kongo, emerged 1,400 miles northwest of Zimbabwe, near the Atlantic coast of what is today northern Angola and western Congo. Kongo was established by the Bakongo (bah-KOHNG-goh) people in the 1300s at the hub of intersecting trade routes. Eventually its population reached 2.5 million. The king's compound, nearly 1 mile around, was located in the capital city of Mbanga (um-BAHN-ga). Royal musicians bearing drums and ivory trumpets announced visitors and ceremonies. The king and other high-status people wore finely woven cloth fabrics, beautifully dyed, which European visitors compared to velvet, silk, and brocade. Although in theory absolute and divine, the king was limited by logistical challenges and was obligated to seek advice from the heads of the leading clans.

The common Bakongo lived much differently than the elite. Each village consisted of a few closely related families together with some domestic slaves. A village chief settled disputes but referred serious quarrels or crimes to district judges. Villagers lived in houses with walls of palm matting and thatch roofs. Each homestead had its own granary, where people stored the annual harvest of millet, the staple crop. Meat such as chicken or fish and bananas, yams, and pumpkins provided some variety. Trade flourished, and people used a seashell-based currency. Local markets sold salt, colored cloth from India, palm cloth, palm belts, and animal skins.

LO² African Society, Thought, and Economy

Although societies across Africa shared many common patterns of social organization, religion, culture, and economy, they also varied considerably. Intensive agriculture did not develop to the same extent in Africa as in Eurasia, but trade was widespread. During the fifteenth century Africa's trade with the wider world attracted European explorers to the region.

Stateless Societies

The powerful kingdoms such as Mali, Benin, and Zimbabwe have usually received the most attention from historians, marking Africa as a continent of major states. But many sub-Saharan Africans lived in decentralized, village-based political systems, which modern anthropologists have called "stateless societies." These societies featured generally self-sufficient, self-governing villages. A council of elders normally assisted the chief and applied customary law to regulate conduct.

The Tiv (tihv), a West African people of what is today eastern Nigeria, developed an egalitarian society in which legal and economic rights were based on kinship. They taxed no crops and allowed no exploitation of others. Elders provided land to all according to need but allocated particular fields to families. Women controlled their own fields and did much of the farm work, but they were aided by men in harvesting and planting. Tiv politics can be described as local democracy. Although no central government existed, village elders administered justice and organized community activities, and customs compelled citizens to behave.

Like the Tiv, the Gikuyu (kee-KOO-you), a Bantu people living in farming villages in the temperate, green highlands around Mt. Kenya in East Africa, had no local chiefs. Whereas most Tiv resided in multifamily villages, most Gikuyu lived in individual family homesteads, and each extended family was headed by the senior male. Village councils elected representatives to district councils of elders, and at the local level, younger Gikuyu formed a special council that handled military affairs. All government positions were elective, and officeholders could be dismissed. This democratic Gikuyu system relied heavily on group discussion and the power of public opinion.

Social Patterns and Religious Traditions

Although African social patterns were diverse, some commonalities also existed. Individuals were connected to others through varied social networks and anchored by the family unit. The family often consisted of several households, including all the members of living generations and their spouses and children. Various societies practiced matrilineal kinship, and where societies had kings, the queen sister or queen mother was usually a highly respected figure. The Bini people still revere Idia, an early-sixteenth-century queen mother who raised an army and used her magical powers to aid her son in overcoming his enemies. Some queens ruled in their own right: oral traditions suggest that the founder of the East African city-state of Mombasa was a woman, Mwana Mkisi (MWAHN-a em-KEE-see). Like family patterns, however, women's status varied widely. Older men dominated most families, even in many matrilineal societies, and powerful men often had multiple wives. Because the chief goal of marriage was children, a woman's status with her husband and the community depended on her child-bearing ability.

African communities were controlled by a web of associations that defined socially acceptable behavior. The family was part of a clan or lineage, which included many closely related people tracing descent to a particular ancestor. Most people lived in villages, and people related to other villagers through work or music groups, secret societies, religious cults, and age cohorts. Most groups prized collective effort and responsibility instead of individual initiative. A larger community than the clan and village was the *ethnic group*, often mistakenly called the "tribe" by modern observers. The ethnic group included people, not necessarily related by kinship ties, who had some cultural unity and usually lived in the same general territory. Distinct cultures, languages, and religions marked off groups such as the Yoruba, Hausa, Shona, and Gikuyu.

Sub-Saharan Slave Trade

Some sub-Saharan peoples, especially in the kingdoms, condoned slavery and engaged in slave trading. Slaves were often war captives or debtors. Ibn Battuta wrote that, in many Sudanic cities, the wealthy "vie with one another in regard to the number of their slaves and serving-women. They never sell the educated female slaves, or but rarely and at a high price."[9] Some slaves, such as the palace advisers in the Hausa states, enjoyed a high social status, whereas others were considered members of households. Slaves could usually marry and have children. Slave life was often hard, but among many African peoples, slaves had more rights and could expect better treatment than slaves in most other societies.

African Religious Beliefs

African religion included not only Muslim and Christian believers but also many millions who practiced monotheism, a rich polytheism with many gods and spirits, animism, or a mix of the three. Africans often recognized a supernatural world of sorcery, magic, spirits, ancestors, and multiple gods. Most African societies had shamans, male or female healers who were skilled in curing disease and had knowledge about the spiritual realm. Some male elders,

> "African musicians emphasized percussion, using many types of drums, but they also played various wind and string instruments."

oral traditions
Verbal testimonies concerning the past; the major form of oral literature in cultures without writing.

considered sages, collected and pondered wisdom and also challenged individuals to become better and more knowledgeable.

Reverence toward cosmic forces blended into a sense of worship and spirituality. Many Africans believed in a life force that was part of all living and material entities. Deceased family members and ancestors, believed to be present in spirit, were also revered. Most societies envisioned an unapproachable high god, such as the Arab traveler al-Mas'udi described for Sofala. For example, the Shona at Zimbabwe believed in a supreme being-creator, but because he held himself aloof from daily affairs, the people prayed to ancestors and spirits.

Literature and the Arts

Africans developed various forms of oral and written literature, as well as various arts. Most societies relied on oral traditions, verbal testimonies concerning the past that were passed down through the generations. Many African societies had a class of professional rememberers, known as *griots* in West Africa, who served as local historians and recordkeepers. As a modern griot explained: "We are vessels of speech, the repositories which harbor secrets many centuries old. We are the memory of mankind."[10] These specialists were trained after a long apprenticeship, and over time they became walking libraries, "speaking documents" who transmitted knowledge to their successors.

 Learn what life was like for early African residents in this interactive simulation by exploring either West or East Africa in the fifteenth century.

Some peoples in West and East Africa had written languages, the most widespread of which were Arabic, Hausa, Amharic, and Swahili. However, writing spread slowly, for two reasons. Most Africans relied on well-defined customs instead of written laws, and because they had communal ownership, they did not need to record facts about land use and inheritance. As in Mesopotamia and India, merchants in the Sudanic and East African cities found it valuable to record their transactions, which they could do in Arabic or Swahili, but merchants elsewhere faced serious barriers to writing. Paper deteriorates quickly in the tropical African climate, especially in the rain forest zone, which also lacks stone or clay to make writing tablets.

Africans produced a rich artistic heritage, including sculpture, dance, and music. Sculpture in wood, clay, ivory, or metal became the major visual art form: while the Benin and Yoruba people produced sculpture in bronze, many Africans used wood to make masks for religious festivals. Perhaps the greatest cultural traditions were music and dance, both closely integrated into work, leisure, and religion. African musicians emphasized percussion, using many types of drums, but they also played various wind and string instruments. Later, African musical traditions spread widely and filtered into the Middle East along the trade routes, influencing Islamic music. Beginning in the 1500s, African slaves carried their musical traditions to the Americas, where they blended with European and Native American styles.

> " Between 650 and 1500, trans-Saharan caravans transported perhaps 2 to 4 million slaves from West Africa to the Mediterranean societies. "

Economic Diversity and the Slave Trade

Sub-Saharan Africans successfully exploited the resources of the tropical environment, overcoming many obstacles to foster farming and trade. Whereas Eurasian societies had horses and oxen, in much of tropical Africa, these animals could not be bred or survive because of various tropical diseases or insect pests that killed draft animals. For many peoples, economic production and transportation had to rely on human muscles.

Agriculture and Commerce

Agriculture reflected African realities. Most Africans, like most Chinese, Indians, or Europeans, were peasants, small farmers who produced food primarily for their own use. With often poor soils, irregular rainfall, and no manure from draft animals for fertilizer, most Africans could not match the intensive, highly productive agriculture found in China, India, and Europe. Hence many Africans practiced shifting cultivation, a practical adaptation to local conditions. This system worked well as long as population densi-

ties remained small. By 1500 there were probably some 40 million people in sub-Saharan Africa, compared to more than 100 million in China. More sophisticated techniques such as irrigation or terracing were used where possible.

As already discussed, trading networks interlaced tropical Africa, though the extent to which they constituted a single continental economic system rather than sporadic contacts remains debatable. Still, great markets emerged, especially in the Sudan, at cities such as Gao and Timbuktu. Here traders bought and sold ivory, ebony, and honey from the Guinea coast and books, wheat, horses, dates, cloth, and salt from the north. Throughout sub-Saharan Africa, most market traders were women and most traveling merchants were men. Some peoples were renowned as long-distance traders, such as Muslim Mandinka traders from Mali who set up permanent operations in the Akan states to exchange gold for cotton, leather, and other goods. Various commodities were exported from tropical Africa to North Africa, Asia, and Europe. Both gold and cowry (KOW-ree) shells, collected on the Indian Ocean coast and spread around in Africa, were used as local currency.

Local trade was often more essential than international commerce. People bought and sold things needed for everyday life, such as cloth, salt, ironware, and copper. Because salt was rare in tropical Africa, it commanded a high price, and traders sometimes had to obtain it from hundreds of miles away. Iron ore was more common, but African miners lacked the tools to dig far underground. Smelting of iron ore took place in areas that had the best wood for making charcoal. Copper was valued from ancient times, but there were few good sources: the most extensive copper mining occurred south of the Congo Basin and in South Africa.

The Slave Trade

Africa was connected to Eurasia primarily across the Sahara Desert or along the East African coast. By the later Intermediate centuries. trade, especially in slaves, increased. As international trade expanded, Arab, Berber, and African traders shipped more African slaves north, where they were sold in North Africa, Muslim Iberia, Arabia, Persia, India, and Christian Europe. Between 650 and 1500, the trans-Saharan caravans transported perhaps 2 to 4 million slaves from West Africa to the Mediterranean societies, while up to 2 million were shipped from East Africa. African slaves in the Middle East, like the slaves of European, Turkish, and other backgrounds, became domestic servants, laborers, soldiers, and even administrators.

The trans-Saharan slave trade acquainted western Europeans, especially the Portuguese, with the prospects of eventually procuring slaves directly in West Africa, spurring Portuguese exploration down the West African coast. In search of Asian spices and African gold as well as slaves, the well-armed Portuguese began sailing south along the West African coastline in the early 1400s. By the later 1400s, they had reached as far as the modern nation of Ghana on the west coast. As they visited more of Africa, the Portuguese became involved in African affairs, colonizing the Cape Verde (VUHRD) Islands in the Atlantic and the nearby coastal region of Guinea-Bissau (GIN-ee bis-OW). Some West Africans picked up artistic and religious ideas from the Portuguese merchants and Christian missionaries, integrating these into their own traditions.

Arrival of the Europeans

In 1487, a Portuguese expedition led by Bartolomeu Dias (DEE-ahsh) rounded the Cape of Good Hope at the tip of Africa and sailed into the Indian Ocean, thus opening up a whole new chapter in African history. In 1497, Portuguese ships commanded by Vasco da Gama, having rounded the Cape of Good Hope, sailed up the East African coast to the great trading city of Malindi and on to southern India. Da Gama had discovered the fastest oceanic path to the great Indian Ocean maritime trading network.

In the 1480s, the Portuguese began a long relationship with the Kongo kingdom, where they sent Catholic missionaries and skilled craftsmen. The resulting blend of Christian and Kongolese traditions profoundly reshaped the region. In 1491, after two court officials claimed that the Virgin Mary appeared to them in dreams and a stone shaped like a cross was discovered near the capital, the Kongolese king, Nzinga a Nkuwu (en-ZING-a ah en-KOO-WOO), and some of the aristocracy adopted Christianity and sent their children to Portugal for study. By the early 1500s, after they realized the economic possibilities of the Americas, the Portuguese became far more interested in obtaining slaves than in treating the Kongolese as equals. In 1514, they began exporting Kongolese slaves, some going to the Americas. This began a new era for Africa and a direct relationship with the peoples of Europe and the Americas.

LO³ American Societies in Transition

As in Africa, most Americans creatively exploited their environments. Whereas many Africans had direct or indirect contact with Eastern Hemisphere networks, Americans remained a world apart. Furthermore, these American societies were often separated from each other by great distances and geographic barriers. Yet cultures, technologies, and trade goods spread over a wide area. At the center of some of these major networks were the powerful states and complex agricultural societies of Mesoamerica and the Andes, which arose after some long-standing American societies, such as the Maya, declined or collapsed. Less centralized or village-based governments formed elsewhere.

The Collapse of the Classical States

Unlike their Afro-Eurasian counterparts such as Rome, Kush, Sassanian Persia, Gupta India, Han China, and Funan, most of the major American states of the Classical Era survived into the early Intermediate Era. Great cities flourished for centuries, such as Teotihuacan (teh-oh-tee-WALK-aun) in central Mexico, Monte Alban in southern Mexico, Tikal in the Maya lands, the Moche settlements on the Peruvian coast, and Tiwanaku in the southern Andes. Their success was based on a combination of productive and often innovative farming, trade, and metalworking, combined, in some cases, with warfare. Americans became creative plant breeders, a talent that aided population growth. Maize, the main crop domesticated in Mesoamerica, combined with beans, squash, and fish or game, provided many Americans with a well-balanced, healthy diet. Americans were also experts in pharmacology, discovering many plant drugs that are still used today, including quinine.

 **Ancient Mesoamerican Civilizations** (*http://www.angelfire.com/ca/humanorigins/*) Links and information about the premodern American societies.

However, substantial cultural and political change occurred during the Early Intermediate Era, as older centers of religious, economic, or political power were replaced by newer ones. In Mesoamerica, Monte Alban, the capital of the Zapotec state, began its decline around 750 but remained inhabited for several more centuries. To the north, Teotihuacan collapsed in the eighth century, removing a unifying commercial and political hub for central Mexico. The reasons for such rapid reversals of fortune remain somewhat unclear, but climate probably played a role.

Late Maya Society

The Maya of Yucatan and northern Central America, who declined rapidly and then suddenly collapsed, reflected the transition of the era, opening the way for new powers to rise. Maya society reached its peak between 600 and 800, with growing populations and massive monument building. Across 36,000 square miles of territory, population densities reached a staggering 600 people per square mile, similar to China today. Maya farmers used complex irrigation systems to cultivate their poor land, which enabled them to support a population of 3 to 5 million people between 600 and 900.

The Maya remained dynamic in the early Intermediate Era. A half-dozen major Maya states existed between 300 and 800. Warfare was frequent, but victories were short-lived and resulted in no large, permanent empires. The Maya were also in close commercial contact with the peoples of central Mexico and benefited from networks of exchange. Excellent sculptors, builders, astronomers, and mathematicians, the Maya also had a well-developed writing system. Thousands of folding-screen books called codices, made of bark paper, were produced, although only a handful survived after the Spanish arrival in the early 1500s.

Maya Decline

Eventually this society, which had survived for so many centuries, faced the same transition as other classical states. Between 800 and 900, most of the Maya cities in the southern lowlands were deserted, and the whole region lost perhaps two-thirds of its population over several decades. The reasons are unclear. Climate change seems to have caused a drought lasting more than a century, with dry weather emptying the Mayas' complex system of canals and reservoirs. Overpopulation may have prompted frantic attempts to increase agricultural productivity on marginally fertile land. Combined with military defeats and possibly natural disasters, these problems may have led to a questioning of the system; governments may have become more unstable, prompting revolts. As people abandoned the southern Maya cities, the political and religious hierarchy may have dis-

> 66 In Toltec tradition, Quetzalcoatl was a human leader who was banished to sea by the war-gods. 99

CHRONOLOGY

The Americas in the Intermediate Era

200 B.C.E.–700 C.E.	Moche
300–1450	Mogollon culture
600 B.C.E.–1100 C.E.	Tiwanaku
300–1400	Hohokum culture
600–800	High point of Maya
700–1400	Anasazi culture
700–1700	Mississippian culture
800–900	Abandonment of southern Maya cities
800–1475	Chimu Empire
900–1168	Toltec Empire
ca. 1000	Norse settlement in Newfoundland
1050–1250	High point of Cahokia
1200	High point of Chimu Empire
1428–1521	Aztec Empire
1440–1532	Inca Empire
1492	Columbus reaches Caribbean

appeared, and merchants, scribes, and craftsmen ceased their work. The complex agriculture system probably then fell into disuse, and people returned to shifting cultivation.

However, these dramatic developments seem not to have affected the northern, and often newer, Maya cities such as Uxmal (oosh-MAHL), which flourished until around 1000, when they also declined. Only the northern Yucatan coast enjoyed continuity after 900. But more frequent warfare also engulfed this region, and human sacrifice increased. By the 1500s, the Yucatan Maya were fragmented into small states in chronic conflict with each other. The remnants of the Maya people still existed over a wide area of Mesoamerica, but their once brilliant history was past.

The Toltecs and Chimu

> "Chimu's impressive engineering skills were illustrated by its 25-foot-wide main roads."

As the older Mesoamerican and Andean states declined or collapsed, other peoples completed the transition by establishing powerful states not unlike the kingdoms that flourished in West Africa, such as Mali. In Mesoamerica, the Toltecs (TOLL-teks) moved into Mexico's central valley from the desert north and, led by King Mixcoatl (MIX-coat-el) ("Cloud Serpent"), created an empire that lasted from 900 to 1168. The Toltec Empire seems to have been a loose military alliance involving newcomers from the north mixing with the local people, whose roots lay in Teotihuacan, located near today's Mexico City. The Toltecs adopted the cult of Quetzalcoatl (kate-zahl-CO-ah-tal), the feathered serpent, which goes back deep in Mesoamerican history. In Toltec tradition, Quetzalcoatl was a human leader who was banished to sea by the war-gods. Historians think that the story is based on Topiltzin (to-PILLT-sen) (b. ca. 947), a cult high priest who succeeded his father, Mixcoatl, as Toltec king but whose opposition to human sacrifice and promotion of peace angered more warlike leaders. Forced into exile, the man gradually blended into the god in myth. But the legend also said that the banished man-god, bearded and of fair complexion, would return to seek revenge, and this prophecy haunted later Mesoamericans.

The Toltecs achieved considerable power and influence throughout the region, even over some of the northern Maya cities. The capital city, Tula (TOO-la), built by Topiltzin, was filled with ceremonial architecture and was a center for obsidian mining and processing; it reached a population of 30,000 to 60,000. The Toltecs maintained the active trade networks around the region, and some reached as far away as southern North America. But in the twelfth century the Toltec state, weakened by

Ancient Mexico.com (*http://www.ancientmexico.com/*). Contains useful features on art, culture, and history.

Pyramid at Tula Each figure on this pyramid at the Toltec capital is made of fitted stone sections and represents a warrior carrying a throwing stick in one hand and a bag of incense in the other.

Robert Harding World Imagery

long-term drought, famine, and war, collapsed and Tula was abandoned. Several centuries of political fragmentation followed.

A powerful new state also emerged in South America. Beginning around 800 the Chimu (chee-MOO) Empire, based at Chan Chan (CHAHN CHAHN) in the old Moche region along the Peruvian coast, began its rise to prominence. By 1200 the Chimu controlled a sizeable empire stretching some 600 miles north to south. Chan Chan was a substantial city, filled with many adobe-walled compounds and a population of 25,000 to 50,000. The Chimu lords, who lived in seclusion in magnificent walled palaces up to three stories high, had elaborate funerals in which several hundred men and women were sacrificed to serve as attendants in the afterlife.

Like other Andean peoples, the Chimu were great builders. Workers drafted into the army labored on vast construction and irrigation projects. Chimu's impressive engineering skills were illustrated by its 25-foot-wide main roads. To irrigate the fields, they constructed hundreds of miles of terraces and large storage reservoirs that controlled the flow of water down the mountainsides. Indeed, the Chimu linked five separate river valleys into a single agricultural complex, an amazing feat. These activities allowed the Chimu to achieve two or three crops a year.

Eventually the Chimu faced challenges they could not overcome. Even with the productive farming, the Chimu faced a constant challenge from disruptive El Niño climate changes. By the fourteenth century, the Chimu were in decline, perhaps because of overpopulation and increased salinization of the soil. Around 1475 they were conquered by the Incas and incorporated into a vast Andean empire.

Pueblo Societies

While only a few American societies formed kingdoms or built large cities such as those of the Maya, Toltecs, and Chimu, many peoples creatively farmed in challenging environments and supported towns and long-distance trade. Some of the most successful societies developed in the southwestern desert of North America, where maize had been grown for many centuries. These southwestern people and their modern descendants are called Pueblo Indians because of their permanent towns, known as *pueblos* in Spanish. By learning to farm this dry region, they survived and sometimes flourished. To overcome a climate that was too dry for maize, the Pueblo peoples became experts at selecting just the right soils. Southwestern peoples also grew cotton and were famed for their weaving of cotton cloth. Towns were often built around riverbeds and human-made dams, terraces, irrigation canals, and reservoirs. The Pueblo peoples also traded over long distances with societies in central Mexico and on the Pacific coast. They mined turquoise and exchanged it with the Toltecs for craft goods.

Several distinct cultures emerged in the North American Southwest (see Map 12.2). By 700 the Hohokum (huh-HOH-kuhm) and Mogollon (MOH-guh-YOHN) societies dominated parts of southern Arizona, New Mexico, and northern Mexico. Hohokum artists were probably the first anywhere to etch intricate designs on shells. They also built large buildings, like the neighboring Mogollon people, who by 1000 had developed masonry technology. But climate change caused drought in the 1300s, and both the Hohokum and Mogollon settlements were eventually abandoned.

Interactive Map

The Anasazi

The Anasazi (ah-nah-SAH-zee), meaning "ancient ones" in the Navaho (NAH-vuh-ho) language, flourished between 700 and 1400 and reached their height of town building and prosperity between 900 and 1250. Using huge sandstone blocks to construct masonry houses, they constructed towns over large sections of today's U.S. Southwest, including major centers at Mesa Verde and Chaco (CHAHK-oh) Canyon. Mesa Verde probably housed 2,500 people and was ingeniously built into steep cliff walls. The Anasazi constructed their pueblos with wood beams, stone, and clay carried from distant forests. Wide roads connected the Chaco pueblos with Anasazi towns a hundred miles away. The total Anasazi population, dispersed over a large area, probably numbered 100,000. The Anasazi, like many Pueblo Indians, lived in egalitarian communities that practiced matrilineal kinship and matrilocal residence, with a husband moving into his wife's household.

Environmental challenges eventually proved overwhelming for the Anasazi, precipitating collapse. By 1200 their agriculture had declined, probably because of a severe drought. By 1300 many Anasazi had moved south to the Rio Grande River Valley, where they mixed with other newcomers. By 1400 the older Anasazi culture had collapsed, and the pueblos of Chaco and Mesa Verde had long been abandoned. Surviving Anasazi were probably the ancestors of southwestern tribes like the Hopi (HOH-pee) and Zuni.

Map 12.2
Major North American Societies, 600–1500

Farming societies were common in North America. The Pueblo peoples such as the Anasazi in the southwestern desert and the Mound Builders in the eastern half of the continent lived in towns. The city of Cahokia was the center of the widespread Mississippian culture and a vast trade network.

Approximate extent of mound-building cultures

Approximate extent of the Mississippian culture

Approximate extent of the Anasazi culture

Approximate extent of the Hohokam culture

Approximate extent of the Mogollan culture

The Mississippian and Eastern Woodland Societies

In the vast Mississippi and Ohio River Basins of eastern North America, where the land was more fertile than in the southwest, a series of mound-building cultures flourished for centuries. The Mississippian culture, the most widespread between 700 and 1700, displayed urban features like those elsewhere in the world: several cities, monumental architecture, social hierarchies, ethnic diversity, and religious art. The main Mississippian center, Cahokia (kuh-HOH-kee-uh), was strategically located near the juncture of the Mississippi

and Missouri Rivers, a few miles from today's St. Louis. At its peak between 1050 and 1250, the city and suburbs probably had a population of between 30,000 and 60,000. The downtown covered 200 acres, and the suburbs of thatch houses another 2,000 acres.

Cahokia

Cahokia was the North American counterpart to Mesoamerican cities such as Teotihuacan and Tula, and Mesoamerican influences are clear. Cahokia and most Mississippian communities were built around central plazas that included platform mounds topped by temples and elite houses, probably surrounded by markets. The largest pyramid, 1,000 feet long, 700 feet wide, and 100 feet long, was much larger than the great pyramids of Egypt. Circles of standing timbers tracked the seasons by marking the sun's position. As in Mesoamerican cities, Cahokia's priest-rulers probably presided over lavish rituals atop the pyramids, perhaps worshipping some Mesoamerican gods. The Mississippian peoples shared a common religious symbolism of mythical creatures, which appeared in their art.

We have only limited knowledge of Cahokia society. The society was matrilineal and divided into several distinct classes. Both men and women nobles were required to marry commoners. At the death of a ruler, some commoners were sacrificed to accompany him on the voyage to the hereafter. The Cahokia state seems to have administered many other settlements over a wide area. Early Spanish explorers recorded an oral tradition in which a lord rode in a flotilla of large canoes decorated with gold objects. Warfare over territory may have been common. Cahokia had many artisans, who made baskets, pottery, shell beads, leather clothes, copper ornaments, wooden utensils, and stone tools.

Cahokia was the major hub of a vast trade network that, at its high point, encompassed much of the North American midsection, from the Great Lakes to the Rockies, along the Mississippi, Missouri, and Ohio Rivers. Cahokians imported copper from the Great Lakes to make jewelry and other objects. The network must have reached south to the Gulf of Mexico, because many marine shells, shark, and barracuda jaws have been found at Cahokia. Cultural influences from Cahokia, including maize farming, also spread through the eastern woodlands. Many smaller versions of Cahokia were scattered around the Mississippi Basin, such as Moundville in Alabama, home to three thousand people.

By the time of European arrival, the Mississippian culture had collapsed. Overpopulation, soil depletion, climate change, and epidemics, including the first appearance of tuberculosis, may have been partly responsible. In some places, the Mississippian culture continued until the early 1700s but was then devastated by diseases such as malaria and smallpox brought by European invaders.

> 66 [The land was] so planted with gardens and corn fields, and so well inhabited with a goodly, strong people [that] I would rather live here than any where. 99
>
> *Englishman visiting present-day Massachusetts in 1614*

Woodland Societies

To the northeast, few states developed in the eastern woodlands of North America before 1500, and most farming communities resembled the African stateless societies such as the Tiv and Gikuyu in their political structure. Some eastern woodlands people lived in walled villages. While warfare using bows and arrows was common, it generally led to few casualties. Individual villages had chiefs, but consensus politics was more common. Because most people depended on farming for survival, there were few full-time craftsmen and only limited intergroup trade. An English observer visiting what is today Massachusetts in 1614 noted that the land was "so planted with gardens and corn fields, and so well inhabited with a goodly, strong people [that] I would rather live here than any where."[11]

We know a little about woodlands society in this era. The men cleared the fields but were often gone for long periods, hunting or fighting. Women working in groups did most of the farm work, and their social and political status was high. The relative freedom of women resulted in a stronger emphasis on romantic courtship among some peoples. Many societies were matrilineal, with residence based on affiliation with senior females. Women elders often had the power to approve or prohibit warfare and nominate new chiefs.

LO⁴ The American Empires and Their Challenges

Several rich and powerful empires formed in Mesoamerica and the Andes in the 1300s and 1400s. The transition that accompanied the collapse of the Maya and the decline of the Toltecs and Chimu had resulted in the rapid rise of the great Aztec (AZ-tek) and Inca (IN-kuh) Empires. These empires had been the products of political fragmentation and continuous military conflict in the thirteenth and fourteenth centuries. Thanks to strong armies and well-organized governments, both empires gained widespread dominance, but both also rapidly collapsed when confronted in the 1500s with Spanish

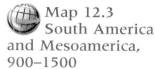

Map 12.3
South America and Mesoamerica, 900–1500

The Maya and Aztecs in Mesoamerica and the Incas in the Andes forged the most densely populated societies, the most productive farming, and the best organized governments. Other urban societies also flourished in Mexico and South America.

© Cengage Learning

Interactive Map

military forces and epidemics. The Aztecs and Incas created the largest empires and most sophisticated states ever seen in the Americas before 1500 (see Map 12.3).

The Aztec Empire, Religion, and Warfare

The Mesoamerican Aztec society was created in the 1300s by the Mexica people, immigrants from the north known for their military skills. Many of them had served as mercenaries in other states' armies but felt mistreated. The Mexica took pride in their repu-

tation as warriors and identified themselves as successors to the Toltecs. By 1325 they had established a strong state that soon controlled much of the Valley of Mexico, the lake-filled basin where Teotihuacan had once flourished. The city of Tenochtitlan (teh-noch-TIT-lan) became the Mexica capital. The Mexica and other Nahuatal (NAH-waht-uhl)-speaking people in the Valley of Mexico came to be known as Aztecs.

Soon the Aztecs turned to conquest. In 1428 they expanded into neighboring regions. Their greatest ruler, Moctezuma (mock-teh-ZOO-ma) I (1440–1468), was a war hero who also used diplomacy to establish the imperial foundations. By 1519 the Incas controlled much of central and southern Mexico and even

Witness to the Past

An Aztec Market

The Spanish conquistadors who made their first visit to the Aztec capital of Tenochtitlan in 1519, two years before their conquest, were impressed with the wealth of foods and other trade goods available in the markets in and around the city. This account by Bernal Diaz del Castillo (DEE-as del kah-STEE-yoh), a Catholic priest who observed the Spanish conquest, describes the great market of Tlatelolco, near Tenochtitlan. Every day the market was thronged with as many as 25,000 people, and special market days might have attracted twice that number.

We were astounded at the number of people and the quantity of merchandise that [the market] contained, and at the good order and control that was maintained, for we had never seen such a thing before. . . . Each kind of merchandise was kept by itself and had its fixed place marked out. Let us begin with dealers of gold, silver, and precious stones, feathers, mantles, and embroidered goods. Then there were other wares consisting of Indian slaves, both men and women. . . . Next there were other traders who sold great pieces of cloth and cotton, and articles of twisted thread. . . . There were those who shod cloths of hennequen [a tough fiber] and ropes and the sandals with which they are shod. . . .

    Let us go and speak of those who sold beans and sage and other vegetables and herbs, . . . and to those who sold fowls, cocks, . . . rabbits, hares, deer, mallards, young dogs and other things of that sort in their part of the market, and let us also notice the fruiterers, and the women who sold cooked food, dough and tripe; . . . then every sort of pottery made in a thousand different forms from great water jars to little jugs; . . . then those who sold . . . lumber, boards, cradles, beams, blocks and benches. . . . Paper . . . and reeds scented with liquid [amber], and . . . tobacco, and yellow ointments. . . .

    I am forgetting those who sell salt, and those who make the stone knives, . . . and the fisherwomen and others who sell some small cakes . . . [and] a bread having a flavor something like cheese. There are for sale axes of brass and copper and tin, and gourds and gaily painted jars made of wood. I could wish that I had finished telling of all the things which are sold there, but they are so numerous and of such different quality and the great market place with its surrounding arcades was so crowded with people, that one would not have been able to see and inquire about it all in two days.

Thinking About the Reading

1. What does the reading tell us about Aztec society and its material culture?

2. In what ways does the Aztec market remind you of a modern supermarket or department store?

Source: Bernard Diaz del Castillo, "The Discovery and Conquest of Mexico," trans. by A. P. Maudslay (NY: Farrer, Straus and Cudahy, 1956).

---

collected tribute from people far to the south, in what is today Guatemala and El Salvador. Tribute from the conquered became an important revenue source.

Religious Practices   The Aztecs imposed a state religion that reinterpreted many ancient Mesoamerican rituals and beliefs. The Mexica believed the sun to be a warrior-god who daily battled his way across the skies and required blood from non-Aztec warriors captured in their frequent fighting. In Aztec myths, their god Huitzilopochtli (wheat-zeel-oh-POSHT-lee) ("The Hummingbird Wizard") commanded them to feed him with human hearts torn from the recently sacrificed. The Aztec practiced human sacrifice on a greater scale than any other major society ever did, sacrificing several thousand captured warriors per year throughout the empire. Other central Mexican people practiced blood sacrifice as well, sometimes with Aztec captives.

Society and Agriculture   The Aztecs developed a prosperous economy and a dynamic social system. The capital city, built on a swampy island in the middle of a large lake, became a major trade center. By the early 1500s, Tenochtitlan (the site of today's Mexico City) was one of the world's

Aztec Warrior These drawings, made by a sixteenth-century Aztec artist, show Aztec warriors, wearing costumes that reflect their status, who have defeated their opponents and forced them to kneel in submission. Many such captives would later be sacrificed.

General History of the Things of New Spain

Read an account of the Spanish conquest of the Aztec Empire, compiled from eyewitness testimony by the Aztecs themselves.

The Aztecs/ Mexicas (*http://www .indians.org/welker/ aztec.htm*). Essays and information on the Aztecs.

great cities: large palaces, temples, forty pyramids, and diverse markets served some 150,000 to 300,000 residents. The Spanish marveled at the order of the markets, where each kind of merchandise was sold in its respective street (see Witness to the Past: An Aztec Market). Traversing the city were six major canals, used daily by thousands of canoes. The first Spaniards to reach the city in 1519, even those from big cities, were awed by the sight: "These great towns and buildings rising from the water, all made of stone, seemed like an enchanted vision.

Indeed, some of our soldiers asked whether it was not all a dream."[12]

The Aztec economy was based on highly productive farming and trade. The Aztecs grew their food on artificial islands, called chinampas, that were built on the lakes of the central valley, a technique that dated back hundreds of years before the Aztecs. An elaborate system of dikes, canals, and aqueducts increased the area available for farming. The Aztecs were also the core of a regional trade system that stretched into North America and Central America. Merchants were organized into guilds but were careful to maintain the state's goodwill, and some probably served as spies in outlying areas.

chinampas

Artificial islands built along lakeshores of the central valley of Mexico and used by the Aztecs for growing food.

Like most centralized American states, the Aztecs had a hierarchical social structure. At the top were the emperors, true despots who were considered semigods. They were selected by a group of high officials, priests, and warriors and advised by an elected council of four princes. Then came the warrior-noble caste, followed by priests and merchants. The priesthood, mostly celibate, played a key role in Aztec life. As the intellectual elite, they prepared the calendars and most of the books. Aztec artists served the elite, creating beautiful representations of the human figure. Aztec sculpture, painted codex books, and murals influenced artists all over Mesoamerica. The great number of Aztec commoners were held in contempt by the elite classes. At the bottom of society were many slaves, often debtors or criminals.

Men and women led very different lives. While their men-folk served the state, elite women enjoyed wealth but faced many restrictions. They largely had two roles: childbearer and weaver. Noble fathers advised their daughters "to learn very well the task of being a woman, which is to spin and weave. It is not proper for you to learn about herbs or to sell wood, peppers, [or] salt on the streets"[13] like the commoner women. Boys of all classes went to school to learn religion, history, rhetoric, and the arts of war. In schools or at home, girls were taught domestic skills and religion, and they prepared for marriage at around age sixteen.

Arrival of the Spaniards

Eventually the Aztecs' brutal imperialism led to collapse. The need for a regular supply of captives for sacrifice fostered a permanent state of war and terror, causing instability and fierce resistance. The conquered peoples paid tribute, but rebellions were frequent, which provided an excuse to fight and obtain more captives. By 1500 the Aztecs faced growing economic, political, and military problems as well as many enemies, some of whom were willing to cooperate with the newly arrived Spanish in the early 1500s to invade Tenochtitlan. Even before this, Aztec leaders seem to have been haunted by bad portents. As Aztec scribes later reported, these worries increased in 1518, when word reached Tenochtitlan of winged towers (Spanish ships), bearing white men with beards, landing on Mexico's east coast. The Spanish arrival coincided with the prophesied return of Quetzalcoatl. Seeking to explain their defeat, Aztec nobles claimed that fear of retribution by this god may have sapped Emperor Moctezuma II's will to resist the Spanish. Although the Spanish encountered a vigorous Aztec society, it might have soon collapsed even without Spanish conquest and occupation in 1521.

The Inca Imperial System

The Incas began to build an empire in the Andes even larger than the Aztec Empire around 1200. In the early 1400s a new leader, Viracocha (VEE-ruh-KOH-chuh) Inca, who claimed to be a living god, launched a new era of conquest. The army, led by professional officers, was efficient and effective. Viracocha's son, the pragmatic and visionary Pachacuti (PA-cha-koo-tee) ("World Remaker"), was the major empire builder. Under Pachacuti (r. 1438–1471) the Incas eventually conquered the Lake Titicaca Basin and the Chimu Empire. As a result, both the Peruvian highlands and coastal zone were united under one government for the first time in history. By 1525 the Incas dominated nearly the whole of the Andes region from what is today southern Colombia to central Chile, ruling from their capital city, Cuzco (KOO-skoh), which contained between 60,000 and 100,000 people. Their empire stretched for nearly 3,000 miles, much of it above 8,000 feet in altitude.

Imperial Administration

The Inca state became the most politically integrated and dynamic in all of the Americas, geared for conquest. But Incas treated conquered peoples much more generously than the Aztecs, incorporating them into their armies, rewarding their service, and tolerating their religions and cultures. Inca empire building derived in part from the Inca religion and ideas of royalty. Kings were believed to be divine, offspring of the sun and responsible for defending the order of the universe. On their death the kings' bodies were mummified and became the center of a cult. Because deceased kings were still considered to be the owners of their property and land, their successors had an incentive to seek new conquests so as to acquire their own property and land. Beliefs such as these supported imperial expansion.

The Incas conquered or frightened into submission nearly all the farming societies in the region but then reached their geographic limits. In contrast to the brutal Aztecs, the Incas faced relatively few rebellions, because they used resettlement and festivals to promote unity. The Incas encouraged sons of non-Inca leaders to attend school with the sons of Inca nobles in Cuzco. The Incas also practiced human sacrifice on a vastly smaller scale than the Aztecs, and only on special ceremonial occasions. But, like the Aztecs and most Eastern Hemisphere empires, the Inca system was also hierarchical and rigid. The royal family kept their bloodline undiluted by having siblings marry each other. The elite held anyone outside the Inca ruling caste in contempt. After some time, rebellions became more frequent, and many regional leaders dreamed of independence. When the Spanish arrived in 1532, a civil war had just ended, weakening Inca resistance and allowing the Spanish to triumph.

> "The Incas' vast agricultural engineering projects, such as terraces and irrigation canals, generated widespread prosperity."

Economy and Gender Roles

The Inca economy, like the imperial government, was authoritarian. While most rural people remained self-sufficient, food collected by imperial storehouses was distributed as needed to others. Trade within the empire was more limited than in Mesoamerica, though some products were exchanged between coastal, lowland, and highland peoples. In contrast to the Aztecs, who allowed merchants to trade freely, the Inca state operated the imperial economy, taking the place of merchants in collecting and distributing goods. The state also required subjects to serve in the army, work state-owned farms, or serve on public works projects.

Although royal women enjoyed great influence, Inca society was patriarchal. Most Inca commoners practiced patrilineal kinship and were part of large extended families. The ancient Andean creator-god and chief Inca deity, Viracocha, had both male and female characteristics, and the Incas worshiped

Machu Picchu This dramatic mountaintop settlement in the high Andes was probably built as a spiritual retreat for Inca royalty, who enjoyed its well-constructed drains, baths, fountains, and administrative buildings.

several female deities, including the Earth Mother.

Incan Engineering

Whereas the Aztecs mainly pursued sacrificial victims, the Incas wanted control of labor and land. To secure this they built administrative centers throughout their territories. Some of these centers were retreats for the elite, such as Machu Picchu (MAH-choo PEE-choo), a spectacular collection of buildings built high atop a narrow mountain ridge. The empire was divided into administrative provinces that were ruled by local families. In this way non-Inca leaders were taken into the governmental system. Because communications were a priority in ruling conquered lands, the Incas linked this vast empire with 14,000 miles of graded, paved roads radiating out from Cuzco. Inca engineers tunneled through rocks and built suspension bridges across gorges and pontoon bridges of reeds across rivers. The road system awed the Spanish, one of whom wrote, "I believe there is no account of a road as great as this, running through deep valleys, high mountains, banks of snow, torrents of water, living rock, and wild rivers. It was swept free of refuse, with lodgings, storehouses, temples, and posts along the route."[14]

Unlike the Mesoamericans, the Incas had no formal writing system, but they did have an efficient and sophisticated form of recordkeeping that involved the use of differently colored knotted strings, called quipus, to record commercial dealings, property ownership, and census data. The Incas also created an oral literature with narrative power, including tales, prayers, and plaintive love songs, all passed down through the generations. They were particularly skilled in technology and science, paving the way for impressive material accomplishments. The Incas' vast agricultural engineering projects, such as terraces and irrigation canals, generated widespread prosperity. Farming was a social and cooperative activity, and men and women sang and chanted while together they worked the land, growing potatoes, maize, peanuts, and cotton. Famine was rare.

Chronicles
Learn how the Incas used mysterious knotted ropes called quipus as record-keeping devices which helped them govern a vast empire.

Science and Technology

The Incas developed sophisticated medicine and surgical techniques, including simple anesthesia procedures. They also fashioned beautiful metal objects using copper and bronze technology as well as gold and silver. In addition, the Incas were among the world's greatest weavers. Weavers wove luxurious woolen fabrics from the fleece of the alpaca, and they made bridges from cords and roofs from fibers. The Incas also developed some of the best civil engineering in the Intermediate Era world: engineers built fortresses and temples with great blocks of stone so perfectly joined that even a knife could not be inserted between them.

American Societies and Their Connections

The various American societies exchanged ideas and goods with each other over extended networks. As a result of trade and conquest, some ideas, commodities, and peoples reached far beyond their originating regions. But the Andean and Mesoamerican societies were separated by thousands of miles of forests and mountains, which limited direct contact. The only known direct communication between the two regions was undertaken by traders known as the Manteno, from coastal Ecuador, who for centuries had sailed large balsa rafts carrying cargo up and down the Pacific coast from Chile to Mexico.

However, geographic barriers did not prevent the Andean and Mesoamerican societies from developing some common social and political features. Gender relations were very similar: these were patriarchal societies in which men dominated central governments, village life, and households. Unlike the kings and nobles, who might have several wives, most commoners practiced monogamy. Most of the empires respected local cultural practices, religions, and languages. In both regions, warfare was common but ritualized. Because most battles occurred far from cities, civilians, settlements, and fields were largely left alone.

The Americas, which encompassed a huge land area, had far fewer people than the Eastern Hemisphere, but even so some societies fostered relatively dense populations. Historians debate the size of the Western Hemisphere population in the late 1400s, some arguing that the population may have exceeded 100 million, more people than in Europe or Africa. Recent studies place the total population at between

60 and 75 million; Mesoamerica had the most people, perhaps 20 to 30 million. Compared to the Eastern Hemisphere, Americans faced few deadly diseases. Periodic famine, often caused by climate change, was a problem, however, and could kill millions.

Europeans in the Western Hemisphere

Eventually the American societies faced a challenge coming from the Eastern Hemisphere. The only known European visits to the Americas before the voyage led by Christopher Columbus took place north of the eastern woodlands, in Newfoundland and Labrador. Around 1000 C.E. a small group of Greenland-based Norse (Norwegian) Vikings led by Leif Ericson visited the area and established a base camp (see Chapter 14). Ericson's Vikings alienated the local people and abandoned their settlement after a few years, but occasional Norse trading visits to the area may have continued for decades, even centuries. The isolated Norse did not publicize their discoveries to Europe, although Portuguese fishermen who visited Iceland may have picked up some information.

Five centuries later, a more enduring connection between the hemispheres was forged. In search of Asia, a Spanish expedition led by an Italian mariner, Christopher Columbus, ventured out in three small ships in 1492, eventually reaching the Bahamas. In later voyages, Columbus visited  Listen to a synopsis of Chapter 12. more parts of the Caribbean and the coast of South America. The new oceanic link altered American history forever, as epidemics wiped out millions of people, great empires fell, and Europeans colonized the hemisphere.

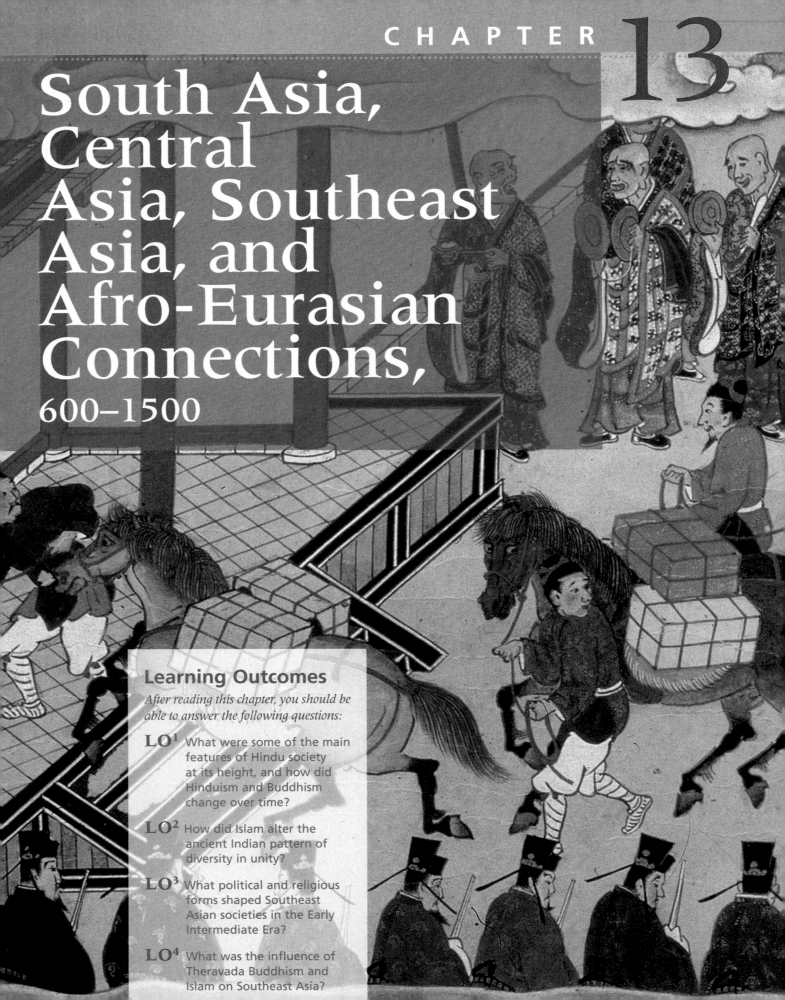

South Asia, Central Asia, Southeast Asia, and Afro-Eurasian Connections,

600–1500

Learning Outcomes

After reading this chapter, you should be able to answer the following questions:

LO¹ What were some of the main features of Hindu society at its height, and how did Hinduism and Buddhism change over time?

LO² How did Islam alter the ancient Indian pattern of diversity in unity?

LO³ What political and religious forms shaped Southeast Asian societies in the Early Intermediate Era?

LO⁴ What was the influence of Theravada Buddhism and Islam on Southeast Asia?

"India's shape is like the half-moon. The administration of the government is founded on benign principles. The taxes on the people are light. Each one keeps his own worldly goods in peace. The merchants come and go in carrying out their transactions. Those whose duty it is sow and reap, plough and [weed], and plant; and after their labor they rest awhile.**"**

—Xuan Zang, seventh-century Chinese visitor to India[1]

In 630 c.e., a brave and determined Chinese Buddhist monk, Xuan Zang (swan tsang) (ca. 600–664), traveled the Silk Road to India on an extended pilgrimage and ended up spending fifteen years there, visiting every corner of the sub-continent. He found much to admire in India. Even though Hinduism had become dominant, Buddhism enjoyed protection and royal patronage. Xuan Zang's writings described an Indian society that had a rigid social structure but was also creative, diverse, and open to foreign influences. Xuan Zang was much impressed with India's high standard of living, efficient governments, and generally peaceful conditions. But some dietary customs troubled him, as did the caste restrictions, especially the confinement of untouchables within their own neighborhoods. After covering some 40,000 total miles in his many years of travel, Xuan Zang returned to China in 643, taking with him hundreds of Buddhist books to be translated into Chinese. He became a confidant of the Tang emperor and fostered closer relations between India and China.

The cultural diversity and openness to foreign influence that Xuan Zang admired in India was partly the result of repeated invasions by Central Asian peoples, who brought with them diverse beliefs and customs. Over the centuries, Hindu religion and society absorbed these newcomers and their ideas (see Witness to the Past: The Songs of Kabir). Groups with differing customs generally lived

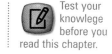

Test your knowlege before you read this chapter.

What do you think?

Compared with China, India exerted far greater influence on Southeast Asian nations such as Thailand, Burma, and Vietnam.

Strongly Disagree | | | | | | Strongly Agree
1 | 2 | 3 | 4 | 5 | 6 | 7

◀◀**Xuan Zang Arriving in China** A seventh-century c.e. Buddhist Chinese pilgrim, Xuan Zang, spent many years traveling in India, collecting Buddhist wisdom and observing Indian life. This Chinese painting shows him and his caravan returning to China with pack-loads of Buddhist manuscripts.

Fujita Art Museum

> "The Rajput code emphasized respect for women, mercy toward enemies, and precise rules of conduct in warfare."

peacefully side by side, and Indian ideals were spread through trade with neighboring peoples. But Hindu political domination faced a particularly severe challenge with the arrival of Muslims, who gained control over large parts of the subcontinent. Having their own strong religious ideas, Muslims were not easily absorbed into the complex world of Hindu culture. The coming of Islam constituted a great turning point in the region's development, a transition comparable to that initiated by the Aryan migrations into India several millennia earlier.

Like Indians, Southeast Asians also adopted new political systems and religions. Powerful kingdoms emerged—some of them strongly influenced by Indian culture—and by the fifteenth century new faiths, Theravada Buddhism and Islam, had reshaped the political map. Cultural and religious diversity, as well as trade, became hallmarks of Southeast Asian societies.

LO¹ Hinduism, Buddhism, and Indian Society

Political disunity and regional diversity marked the Early Intermediate Era in India. No Hindu leaders were able to recreate an empire like the earlier Maurya or Gupta, and India became a region of many states, cultures, and languages. Hinduism experienced a renaissance in the Early Intermediate centuries, growing in popularity and increasingly shaping Indian life, yet most South Asians were split into many microcultures. Buddhism faded in India but found new influence in neighboring societies at the same time that Islamic peoples and ideas exerted growing influence in India. These pronounced regional distinctions within a widely shared Hindu culture demonstrated one of the great themes in Indian history: diversity in unity.

Hindu Politics: States, Cities, Villages

The political disunity following the fall of the Gupta state in the fifth century proved to be a long-term pattern of political fragmentation. King Harsha Vardhana (600–647) briefly united parts of north India, but this consolidation proved short-lived. Harsha came to power at the age of sixteen and ruled for forty-one years. A man of enormous energy, he put together a formidable army that, at its strongest point, included 100,000 cavalry and 60,000 elephants, together with many thousands of infantrymen. Much more than a warrior-king, Harsha was a Buddhist who loved philosophy and was renowned as a poet; as king, he promoted tolerance of all faiths and was attentive to the concerns of his humbler subjects. Harsha skillfully held together his small empire while cultivating close relations with Tang China, but his empire collapsed on his death. Despite Harsha's brilliant reign, in the post-Gupta centuries, hundreds of small states proliferated in the subcontinent. The Hindu states had varied types of government, including many absolute monarchies. Rulers owned many economic resources, such as irrigation works, forests, mines, and spinning and weaving operations. Kings tried to control outlying regions through appointed governors or patronage over local leaders. Because they occupied a precarious position of power, they attempted to claim a divine mission and employed Brahmans (Hindu priests) as court advisers for legitimacy.

Rajput States of Northern India

North and south India developed somewhat different political patterns. Rajputs ("King's sons"), members of a warrior caste formed by earlier Central Asian invaders who adopted Hinduism, controlled some of the north Indian states. This military aristocracy was raised in traditions of chivalry, honor, and courage not unlike those of Japanese samurai or medieval European knights. The Rajput code emphasized respect for women, mercy toward enemies, and precise rules of conduct in warfare. However, the Rajput-led kingdoms never united and often fought wars against each other for regional power. In contrast to the north, many south Indian states were oriented to the sea and continued their lucrative maritime trade with Southeast Asia, China, and the Middle East.

606–647	Empire of Harsha in north India
620–649	First Tibetan kingdom and introduction of Buddhism
711	First Muslim invasion of northwest India
846–1216	Chola kingdom in south India
1192–1526	Delhi Sultanate
1336–1565	Kingdom of Vijayanagara in south India
1398–1399	Devastation of Delhi by Tamerlane

Village and Urban Life

With an absence of strong centralized government, the village remained the basic unit of Indian life. Farmers had to feed an Indian population that reached around 100 million by 1500. Rulers also depended on villages for income, as the land tax remained the main source of state revenue. This was a collective responsibility, because the village paid as a unit. As long as they regularly met their tax obligations, villages ran themselves and remained economically self-sufficient. A well-entrenched pattern of village government included a council, elected annually from among village elders and caste leaders, which dispensed local justice and collected taxes. The typical Hindu village organized itself through the caste system, which promoted stability. Within the village the individual served his or her caste. Each village had a potter, carpenter, blacksmith, clerk, herdsman, teacher, astrologer, and priest, as well as many farmers. Each individual had a recognized status as well as certain rights and duties. The village structure probably did not change substantially during the Intermediate Era.

A large number of Indians also lived in towns and cities, many of which were commercial hubs. Urban merchants helped administer the towns, but they were heavily taxed and not allowed to become too powerful. Some merchant groups were immigrants, such as the Zoroastrians, who fled to western India to escape the Islamic conquest of Persia and formed the distinctive *Parsee* (PAHR-see) community, known for its commercial prowess in several cities of western India. Over the centuries, the Parsees adopted local languages and traditions. Manufacturers also lived in the cities. Indeed, India and China provided most of the world's industrial goods until the eighteenth century. Workshops located mainly in or near cities and towns produced cloth, textiles, pottery, leather goods, and jewelry for local use or export. Some artisans spun and wove cotton to be sold as far away as China, Africa, or eastern Europe.

polyandry
Marriage of a woman to several husbands.

Hindu Society and Science

The Hindu social system demonstrated great continuity over the centuries and, as in China, subordinated the individual to the group. The Indian owed an even more basic social obligation to the extended family than to the caste. The family, which included people of several generations, lived together in the same compound, enforced caste regulations among its members, and also collectively owned economic assets, such as farmland. Because families shared their wealth, they constituted an effective source of social security. Most families, especially in north India, were patriarchal, headed by a senior male with strong authority, although older women held considerable influence. Child-rearing became a group obligation, and children enjoyed great security.

Diverse Marriage Customs

Marriage customs often reflected regional differences. In north India, parents arranged marriages for their children and hoped that love would follow marriage. Girls were married off young, sometimes by the age of seven or eight, usually to a boy in a neighboring village, and the bride's family was obligated to pay for the wedding and dowry. In south India, girls were more likely than in north India to marry boys whom they already knew, often a cousin. In Kerala (CARE-a-la) in southwestern India, one large group practiced polyandry, marriage of a woman to several husbands. Most Indian families discouraged divorce, viewing it as a humiliation. Views about sexuality were more diverse than in other cultures. Many books commended celibacy and advised married men to exercise their sexual prerogatives sparingly if they wanted health and virtue. Yet, the worldly views of many, especially among the elite, are reflected in many Indian texts such as the *Kama Sutra*, a manual of lovemaking and related matters written around the third century C.E.

Coming from a Hindu family that had recently converted to Islam, Kabir was well acquainted with both religious traditions. His mystical poems of passionate love for a monotheistic god rejected religious prejudice, rigid dogmatism, and the caste system. Modern Indian intellectuals seeking to bridge the gap between the two faiths particularly admired his attempt to see beyond the limitations of the two religions and his absolute opposition to violence. The following poem argues that individuals must experience God for themselves.

O servant, where dost thou seek Me? Lo! I am beside thee.

I am neither in temple nor in mosque; I am neither in Kaaba [Muslim shrine] nor in Kailash [abode of Shiva].

Neither am I in rites and ceremonies, nor in Yoga and renunciation.

If thou art a true seeker, thou shalt at once see Me. . . .

It is needless to ask of a saint the caste to which he belongs; For the priest, the warrior, the tradesman, and all the thirty-six castes, alike are seeking for God.

It is but folly to ask what the caste of a saint may be; The barber has sought God, the washerwoman, and the carpenter. . . .

Hindus and Muslims alike have achieved the End, where remains no mark of distinction. . . .

O brother! when I was forgetful, my true Guru [teacher] showed me the Way.

Then I left off all rites and ceremonies, I bathed no more in the holy water: . . .

From that time forth I knew no more how to roll in the dust in obeisance:

I do not ring the temple bell; I do not set the idol on its throne; I do not worship the image with flowers.

It is not the austerities that mortify the flesh which are pleasing to the Lord,

When you leave off your clothes and kill your senses, you do not please the Lord,

The man who is kind and who practices righteousness, who remains passive amidst the affairs of the world, who considers all creatures on earth as his own self,

He attains the Immortal Being, the true God is ever with him.

Kabir says: "He attains the true Name whose words are pure, and who is free from pride and conceit."

If God be within the mosque, then to whom does this world belong?

If Ram [God] be within the image which you find upon your pilgrimage, then who is there to know what happens without?

Hari [Lord Vishnu] is in the East; Allah is in the West. Look within your heart, . . .

All the men and women of the world are His Living Forms. Kabir is the child of Allah and of Ram [God]: He is my Guru [Hindu teacher], He is my Pir [Sufi saint].

Thinking About the Reading

1. Why would someone of mixed religious background be open to questioning rigid doctrines?

2. What does Kabir think about the traditions of organized religions?

3. Where does Kabir believe that God is to be found?

Source: William Theodore De Bary, ed., *Sources of Indian Tradition, Vol. 1.* Copyright © 1958 Columbia University Press. Reprinted with permission of the publisher.

Gender Roles

In the Indian social system of the Intermediate Era, men enjoyed many privileges. Women by and large led lives marked by obedience, sacrifice, and service. In ancient India, especially in merchant families,

women often chose their own husbands and circulated freely in local society, but by 600 C.E., customs had become more conservative. Females of all castes were now taught to keep a distance from all men except their closest relatives. From an early age they were taught to sacrifice themselves for parents, husband, and children. The stereotypical role model was the loyal and submissive wife who always followed her husband's lead. Yet, husbands often treated their brides indulgently and tenderly. Indians also revered motherhood and equated childbearing with success. As a woman grew older, she gained more influence within the family.

Women faced a complex situation. They enjoyed some legal rights, and ill-treatment of women, including physical brutality, was condemned, although it was undoubtedly common. In practice not all wives were silent and subservient, but widowhood could prove catastrophic, particularly if a woman had no son to care for her. Because Hindu custom frowned on remarriage, to be a young and childless widow was to face an especially difficult situation. This helps to explain the practice of *sati*, whether voluntary or coerced. To avoid surviving their deceased husband, some women, especially in north India, died on their husband's funeral pyre.

> "Women by and large led lives marked by obedience, sacrifice, and service."

Bhaskara: Indian Mathematician

Another distinctive feature of Indian cul-

ture was its creative investigation of mathematic and scientific problems. One of the greatest Indian mathematicians, Bhaskara (bas-CAR-a), lived in the twelfth century. In addition to proving that zero was infinity, he also designed a perpetual motion machine by filling a wheel rim with quicksilver, in the process demonstrating the Hindu belief in perpetual change in the universe. Bhaskara's book on the subject was later translated into Arabic and reached Europe by 1200 C.E. Soon after, drawings of quicksilver wheels appeared there, and the first weight-driven clocks, built in Europe after 1300, may have been based in part on Bhaskara's ideas. A seventh-century Syrian astronomer said that "no words can praise strongly enough" the Hindus'

Benoy K. Behl

Sculpture of Two Lovers from Konarak Temple This sculpture of two embracing lovers comes from the Konarak temple in the north Indian state of Orissa. The Hindu temple, dedicated to the sun-god, was built in the thirteenth century and featured many erotic sculptures.

discoveries in astronomy and their rational system of mathematics.[2] Some Indian astronomers and mathematicians found employment in Tang China, fostering a fruitful exchange of knowledge between the two societies.

But later, such intellectual creativity lessened as the indifference of the higher castes to applied or practical inquiry hindered the development of science after Gupta times. The Brahmans became more powerful and controlled education, while those who pursued technical activities or physical labor sank lower in the status system. By the tenth century, some visitors reported a growing disdain among Hindu thinkers for foreign ideas: an astute Muslim observer wrote that "the Hindus believe that there is no country, king, religion, [or] science like theirs."[3]

Hindu Diversity and Renaissance

Hinduism provided the spiritual framework for the great majority of South Asians until the coming of Islam. Its strength lay in its diversity, which could accommodate all classes, personalities, and intellects. Recognizing that individuals varied in their spiritual and intellectual capacities, Hindus tolerated many different practices and relied on no fixed and exclusive theology or set of beliefs. Concepts of spiritual power ranged from an indescribable but all-pervading, omnipotent God, to personal gods with human attributes, to demons and spirits. An Indian proverb welcomed all to sample the essence of Hindu ideas: "Life is a river; virtue is its bathing place; truth is its water; moral convictions are its banks; mercy is its wave. In such a pure river, bathe."[4] As a result, Hinduism remained undogmatic, a philosophy and way of life with no central church to monitor the faith. During the Intermediate Era, Muslims introduced the collective term *Hindu,* from the Persian term for "Indians," to describe the varied Indian sects, and in the nineteenth century C.E., Europeans began referring to the diverse collection of Indian beliefs as "Hinduism."

A Tradition of Tolerance

The tradition of tolerance suggested that all approaches to God were equally valid. Mother goddess worship was particularly common among the lower castes living in thousands of villages, especially in south India, but was less popular among the higher castes. Although India was a patriarchal society, men and women often believed that the wives and companions of the main male gods were more responsive to their needs than the male gods themselves. For example, many cults worshiped Shiva's wife, Shakti (SHAHK-tee), who was a composite of opposites: kind and beautiful but also cruel and fearsome.

> **Hindus tolerated many different practices and relied on no fixed and exclusive theology or set of beliefs.**

Hinduism helped establish a common culture throughout India. For all their diversity of beliefs, most Hindus perceived the universe as a collection of temporary living quarters inhabited by individual souls going through a succession of lives. The most devout had the ultimate goal of liberation from finite human consciousness, which freed one from the endless cycle of birth and rebirth. Yet most Hindus were obligated to meet their social obligations to family, caste, and village. Brahmans served as advisers to kings, ensuring a certain standardization of political ideas and rituals in Hindu states, but the Hindu classics were available to all through storytellers. Legends and traditions from the ancient Vedas were also handed down through the generations by word of mouth, and by around 1000 C.E. were being translated from Sanskrit into various regional languages.

Shankara and the Vedanta Tradition

Many thinkers who embellished or revitalized Hindu traditions lived during the Intermediate centuries, creating what has been called the Hindu Renaissance. Perhaps the greatest was Shankara (shan-kar-uh) (788–820), a south Indian Brahman who helped refine Hindu thinking. Through his itinerant preaching, debates with rivals, and written commentaries on the *Upanishads,* Shankara revitalized the mystical *Vedanta* tradition, with its belief in the underlying unity of all reality. To Shankara, all of the Hindu gods were manifestations of the impersonal, timeless, changeless, and unitary Absolute Reality, *Brahman,* and the individual soul was only a tiny part of the whole unity of the universe. While accepting the Hindu scriptures as divine revelation, Shankara wanted to prove them through logical reasoning and debate. Yet, contradictorily, he also argued that all knowledge was inconclusive and relative, impaired because humankind's grasp of reality is warped by ignorance and illusion.

The Bhakti Tradition

Other philosophers offered different visions

of Hinduism. In the eleventh century, Ramanuja (RAH-muh-NOO-ja) rejected both reliance on Brahman priests and Vedanta meditation and instead emphasized bhakti, devotional worship of a personal god, arguing that the gods should be accessible without priestly help. As a Hindu poet-saint put it: "The lord comes within everyone's reach."[5] The bhakti tradition emphasized pilgrimage to holy places such as the city of Benares (buh-NAHR-uhs) (Varanasi), alongside the Ganges. Hindus who died in Benares, it was believed, had their sins washed away. Ramanuja and other early bhakti thinkers, most of them non-Brahmans, also opposed or downplayed the caste system. The bhakti tradition appealed particularly to women, who were marginalized in brahmanic worship. Later the bhakti movement became part of mainstream Hinduism.

The Hindu Renaissance included the building of increasingly flamboyant temples, whose sculptural art was designed to illustrate the intricate mythology of the faith. One of the best examples of such a temple was constructed in the tenth century by a prince in his home city of Khajuraho (kah-ju-RA-ho). Dedicated to Vishnu, sculptures carved into the temple walls suggested the delights enjoyed by the gods, including lovemaking.

Decline and Change in Indian Buddhism

During the first half of the Intermediate Era, while Hinduism was resurging, the influence of Buddhism gradually declined in much of India. However, it retained considerable support in northeast India, where many Buddhist holy sites were located. Pilgrims from distant lands, such as Xuan Zang of China, showed how much Buddhism was becoming a major influence in the eastern half of Eurasia, a trend that continued throughout the Intermediate Era. The intellectual and cultural environment of northeast India promoted a dialogue between Hinduism and Mahayana Buddhism that fostered new schools of thought. One new Buddhist school, the Vajrayana ("Thunderbolt"), featured female saviors and the human attainment of magical powers. It spread during the eighth century into Nepal and Tibet, where it became the predominant form of faith.

Tantrism

In Bengal the continued contact between Mahayana Buddhists and Hindu followers of Shiva—many of whom revered his consort, the goddess Shakti—led to a new approach called Tantrism (TAN-triz-uhm), which worshiped the female essence of the universe. Both the Tantric and Vajrayana schools exalted female power as the highest form of divine strength. Tantric sects developed within both Hinduism and Buddhism. Some were mystical and presented sexual union as an action form of worship, whereas other sects promised release from life's pain in a single lifetime to those who cultivated hedonism and ecstasy. Most Hindus and Buddhists denounced Tantrism as an excuse for debauchery and sexual desire, however, and Tantrism gradually became a minor strand in the two religions.

bhakti
Devotional worship of a personal Hindu god.

Vajrayana
("Thunderbolt") A form of Buddhism that featured female saviors and the human attainment of magical powers; developed in the Intermediate Era and became the main form of Buddhism in Nepal and Tibet.

Tantrism
An approach within both Buddhism and Hinduism that worshiped the female essence of the universe; developed in the Intermediate Era.

State Building and Buddhism in Tibet

While Buddhism declined in India, the remote high plateau of Tibet became a refuge for the religion. The first known pre-Buddhist Tibetan state emerged when Songsten-gampo (SONG-sten-GOM-po) (r. 620–649 C.E.) unified several tribes. Interested in connecting to an Asian world where Buddhism was expanding, Songsten-gampo married a Chinese princess and established close relations with Tang China, and although not a Buddhist, he tolerated Buddhism's spread. Several trade routes linked Tibet to the Silk Road and China, and some young Tibetans went to China for study. Tibetans also borrowed the Sanskrit script from India and made it their written language.

Buddhism in Tibet

By the eighth century, Buddhism had become the dominant Tibetan faith, but many Tibetans also continued to follow the ancient folk religion, bon. The two faiths competed for popular support and political influence for the next several centuries, and late in the ninth century, violent religious conflicts destroyed the unified state. However, both Buddhism and state building were reinvigorated later. In the thirteenth century, many Buddhist monks fled to Tibet to escape Islamic persecution in India. Political relations with the predominantly Buddhist Mongols, who had established loose

> "The pillaging and destruction by the early Muslim invaders fostered long-term Hindu antipathy toward Muslims."

control over parts of Tibet, also boosted Tibetan Buddhism. A unified Tibetan government was established in 1247 under the leadership of one Buddhist sect allied to the Mongols, but the end of Mongol rule in China brought a return to aristocratic lay leadership in Tibet, which persisted into the seventeenth century.

Lamaism

Tibetans developed a distinctive religious system in their harsh highlands environment, and many of their customs differed from those of East and Southeast Asian Buddhists. Tibetan Buddhism, which is divided into four sects, is often termed Lamaism (LAH-muh-iz-uhm) because of the centrality of monks, or *lamas* (LAH-muhz), and huge monasteries. Perhaps one-quarter to one-third of male Tibetans became career monks, and Buddhism permeated every aspect of Tibetan life. Tibetans also blended Buddhism with strong beliefs in the supernatural, including evil spirits. People spun handheld or roadside prayer wheels, carved prayers into stones, and performed elaborate death rites to propel the soul to the next rebirth.

LO² The Coming of Islam to India and Central Asia

The spread of Islamic religion and government in India was a major transition in Indian history, as important as the coming of the Aryans several millennia earlier. Muslims and Hindus were almost exact opposites in their beliefs, so Islam created a great divide in South Asian society. For centuries Hinduism had absorbed invaders and their faiths, but Islam, a coherent and self-confident religion, could not be assimilated. Although tension between the two faiths sometimes resulted in conflict, Islam enriched Indian culture, establishing new connections with western Asia while also promoting the spread of Indian ideas. Many Indians embraced the new faith, and Muslims also gained political dominance over large parts of India, though Hindu power remained strong in south India.

Early Islamic Encounters

Islamic forces reached Central Asia and India through the Silk Road and other trade networks within a few decades of the religion's founding. Initially Indian and Central Asian encounters with Islam were sporadic and often peaceful, but Islamic rulers sought to dominate these valuable regions, and military conflict increased.

Islam in Central Asia

During the seventh century, Arab forces expanded through Persia into what is today Afghanistan. By 673, Arab armies were moving into Silk Road cities such as Bukhara and Samarkand, dominated by the Sogdians (SOG-dee-uhnz), an ethnic group famed for their commercial skills. The rival Central Asian city-states, which were geared more toward trade than toward battle, could not easily come together against the dynamic Arabs. The Sogdians, most of whom were Zoroastrian or Buddhist, resisted and sought Chinese and Turkish help, but by the early eighth century, Arabs had conquered most of the cities. The Arab defeat of Chinese forces at the Battle of Talas in 751 marked the end of serious resistance to Muslim dominance in Central Asia. Eventually most Central Asians adopted Islam.

Mahmud of Ghazni in India

In neighboring India, conflict between Hindus and Muslims began slowly, with attacks by Hindu pirates on Muslim shipping in western Asia. In 711 C.E., Indian pirates plundered an Arab ship near the mouth of the Indus River, and Arab armies responded by briefly conquering the western Indus Basin, in the first of many incursions to follow. The subsequent expansion of Islam into Central Asia presented a challenge to India. By the eleventh century, various Turkish peoples had formed independent Islamic sultanates in Afghanistan, of which Ghazni (GAHZ-nee) was the most powerful. Between 997 and 1025, Sultan Mahmud (MACH-mood) of Ghazni (r. 997–1030) led his soldiers on seventeen campaigns through the passes into India, as much for plunder as for conquest. Seeing the multitude of Hindu idols as an abomination to Islamic monotheism, the invaders destroyed Hindu temples while they looted cities. The

The Kutb Minar Tower in Delhi The 240-foot-high Kutb Minar temple in Delhi was built between the twelfth and fourteenth centuries to celebrate Muslim victory in north India.

vast wealth they took to Ghazni helped that city become a great center of Islamic learning and arts.

India's Ineffective Opposition

The Rajputs led the major Indian opposition to Muslim invaders, maintaining a spirited Hindu resistance for many decades that kept Islam from spreading into the Hindu heartland. But Rajput military tactics were outdated, based on relatively immobile war elephants, and the military forces were increasingly divided in their political loyalties. In addition, Indian wars had been fought by rulers, not by citizen-soldiers. The caste system allowed only warriors such as the Rajputs to be trained in arms, so they could not effectively mobilize other Indians to help in the fight. Eventually the Rajput armies were defeated by the more mobile, horse-riding Muslims.

The pillaging and destruction by the early Muslim invaders fostered long-term Hindu antipathy toward Muslims. Many Hindus were killed, enslaved, or robbed. Mahmud's most famous exploit involved a long march across the desert to attack the revered Hindu temple of Somnath. Hindu sources reported, probably with some exaggeration, that the attack killed fifty thousand Hindus. Even the Muslim scholar Al-Biruni admitted that Mahmud "utterly ruined [India's] prosperity."[6] The Muslim newcomers zealously persecuted Buddhists as well; thousands of monks either were killed or fled to sanctuary in the Himalayas or Tibet. This repression helped eradicate Buddhism from the land of its birth.

Islamic Expansion and the Delhi Sultanate

A new chapter in Muslim expansion began in 1191 when a Turkish prince, driven by religious fervor and lust for the region's riches, conquered most of northern India and founded the Delhi (DEL-ee) Sultanate (see Map 13.1). The sultanate (1192–1526) reached its height in the 1200s and 1300s and brought political unity to north India for the first time in centuries. Under the Delhi regime, Islamic authority and religion spread throughout north India, but the Delhi system was unstable and experienced frequent bloodshed and treachery.

Interactive Map

The Delhi Sultanate

The Delhi sultans had diverse ruling styles. Some were patrons of the arts, supporters of science, experts in Greek philosophy, and builders of architecturally splendid structures. Many others, however, were tyrannical and cruel, routinely killing rivals and spending recklessly. All of the sultans employed Persian-style ritual and royal pomp, but in some ways they also outdid Hindu monarchs in demanding prostration and toe-kissing from subordinates. Some sultans expanded Delhi's power into central India and, briefly, south India, creating an empire larger than the Gupta realm. The most militarily successful sultan, Alauddin Khalji (uh-LAH-ud-DEEN KAL-jee) (1296–1316), was also politically creative. For instance, because he was unhappy with the high living of local officials while the poor suffered, he introduced wage and price controls to help citizens meet rising costs.

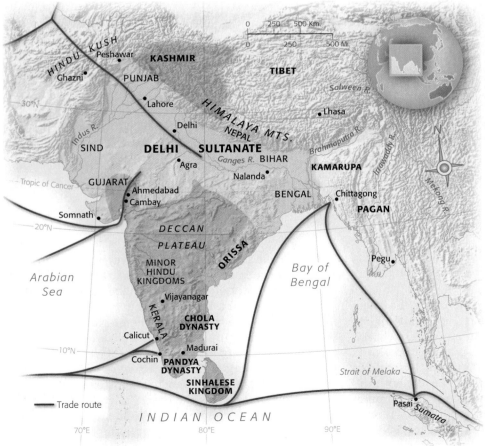

 Map 13.1
India and the Delhi Sultanate, ca. 1300 C.E.

At its height, the Delhi Sultanate controlled much of northern India. South India was divided into many major states, with the Cholas and Pandyas the largest. Indian ports were connected by a vigorous maritime trade to the Middle East, East Africa, and Southeast Asia.

© Cengage Learning

Iltutmish and Raziya Two of the most able Delhi sultans were Iltutmish (il-TOOT-mish) (1211–1236), who made the Delhi Sultanate the most powerful state in north India, and his remarkable daughter, Raziya (r. 1236–1240). Iltutmish kept out the Mongol armies of Genghis Khan by skillful diplomacy and gradually followed more tolerant policies toward Hindus, allowing Hindu princes to rule their own domains as long as they paid generous taxes. During his reign, many Muslim refugees fleeing the Mongol conquest of western Asia arrived, among them scholars and artists. Iltutmish's chosen successor, Raziya, became the only female Muslim ruler in Indian history and proved exceptionally able, fostering trade, building roads, planting trees, supporting poets and artists, and opening schools. A male Muslim observer described her as "a great monarch, wise, just and generous."[7] But Raziya was resented as a female leader in a patriarchal society, and she further offended Muslim conservatives by abandoning the veil, dressing in male garb, and having a close, perhaps romantic, relationship with a male attendant, a former slave of African origin. She died defending her position from male rivals.

Hindu Politics and Culture

While the Delhi Sultanate governed northern India, various Hindu monarchies survived elsewhere. Like post-Heian Japan and medieval Europe, these states featured local economic self-sufficiency and political decentralization, with warriors receiving land from the monarch in exchange for military service. Commerce flourished in some places, especially in south India: merchants on the southwest coast, including Jews and Arabs, maintained close ties to western Asia and North Africa and enjoyed great influence and wealth. Ports such as Cochin (KOH-chin) and Calicut (KAL-ih-cut) in Kerala and Cambay (kam-BAY) in Gujarat (GOO-jur-ot) played major roles in Indian Ocean trade.

> " By the mid-fourteenth century, north India was humbled by severe drought and famine caused in part by climate change. "

The Tamil People and the Chola Dynasty

For many centuries, the Tamil (TAA-mill) people of southeast India, controlled by a Hindu dynasty known as the Cholas (CHO-luhs) (846–1216), profited from both piracy and foreign trade. The powerful Chola navy controlled the eastern Indian Ocean and conquered both Kerala and Sri Lanka (Ceylon). Merchant castes, which played a prominent role in Chola society, organized a dynamic maritime trade that brought great wealth to the society and revenue to the kings. Some Chola rulers established close diplomatic and trade ties to Burma, Cambodia, and China. The Tamils developed an outstanding artistic tradition, including many fabulous Hindu temples featuring magnificent bronzes. Perhaps the greatest creation was made by some unknown tenth-century genius, a bronze figure of Shiva portrayed as "Lord of the Dance," ready to commence the cosmic dance of life and restore vitality to the world.

The "City of Victory"

The Cholas declined politically in the thirteenth century, and the power vacuum was eventually filled by another Hindu kingdom, Vijayanagara (vij-uh-yuh-NUHG-uhr-uh) ("City of Victory"), established in 1336. This militarily powerful state, which eventually dominated much of south and central India, was destroyed by rivals in 1565. During its existence, huge temple cities arose, including the capital, which was one of the most magnificent cities of the Intermediate Era. The persistence of Hindu rule in southern India preserved Hindu customs and institutions, which were disappearing in some northern areas.

Shiva as Lord of the Dance This famous bronze statue of Shiva as Lord of the Dance was made by Chola artists in southeast India. Displaying himself as a god of many qualities, Shiva grasps the flame of destruction in one hand and the drum of creation in another. The small figure under his foot represents the illusions that Shiva undermines.

The Nelson-Atkins Museum of Art, Kansas City, Missouri. Purchase: William Rockhill Nelson Trust, 34-7. Photography by Jamison Miller

Tamerlane and Muslim Rule

> "By the fifteenth century, India was fragmented into dozens of Muslim and Hindu states."

Eventually Delhi's power ran its course. By the mid-fourteenth century, north India was humbled by severe drought and famine caused in part by climate change. The state went into a rapid decline and was devastated by increased rebellion and civil war. While conflict raged internally, a new threat appeared in the northwest, the Mongol and Turkish forces of Tamerlane (TAM-uhr-LANE) (1336–1405). Tamerlane's branch of Mongols had become Muslim. From his base in Samarkand along the Silk Road, the ruthless warrior had already conquered Central Asia and Persia, creating the Timurid Empire based at Samarkand (see Chapter 10). In 1398 his forces invaded India, looting Delhi and killing perhaps 100,000 inhabitants in the city, mostly Hindus. Tamerlane and his army returned to Central Asia, leaving Delhi's few surviving inhabitants to perish by plague or starvation. In 1401–1402, Tamerlane's armies invaded Egypt and Anatolia but were repulsed. He died attempting to invade China.

Tamerlane and the Political Fragmentation of India

Tamerlane's invasion had a great impact on India, destroying the grand city of Delhi and all semblance of political unity in north India. The Delhi Sultanate survived, but in a shrunken form. Various Muslim sultans ruled small states scattered around the plains, and occasional invasions by Afghans unsettled the northwest. Some new states rose to prominence: one distinctive region, Bengal in the northeast, remained independent, incubating a unique Bengali language and its own forms of Islam and Hinduism. By the fifteenth century, India was fragmented into dozens of Muslim and Hindu states.

Muslim Control, Hindu Resistance

This growing Islamic political power caused a long history of conflict between Muslims and Hindus. To Muslims, Hinduism—with its many deities, elaborate rituals, powerful priests, fondness for images, and preference for eating pork but not beef—constituted the exact opposite of all Islam held sacred. At the same time, Hindus despised the intolerance of some Muslims and desperately resisted Muslim political control. Yet Muslim governments could not afford to permanently alienate their Hindu subjects, who constituted a huge majority of the population. This reality fostered some compromises. Although Muslim rulers often confiscated the wealth of rich Hindu nobles, the common people were less affected, and life in the villages went on largely undisturbed. While some Muslims continued to view Hindus as infidels requiring conversion, eventually many Muslim scholars and leaders came to respect Hindus and the Parsee Zoroastrian community, but non-Muslims still faced second-class status and special tax payments.

Over the centuries, many Indians on the periphery of India, in the northwest and in Bengal in the northeast, converted from Hinduism to Islam. A much smaller proportion of southerners embraced the new faith. Converts included rich Hindus who wanted to safeguard their positions and secure government offices in Muslim-ruled states, as well as many poor Hindus who converted to escape low or untouchable status and to avoid the heavier taxes levied on non-Muslims. Sufi mystics, who sought personal union with god, were the key to many Hindus' conversion to Islam, especially in places like Bengal. People respected the intensity of the Sufis' spiritual discipline and the depth of their religious understanding. Perhaps Sufi practices became popular because they closely resembled devotional bhakti Hinduism and Mahayana Buddhism, which also emphasized emotional commitment.

Some people attempted to mix the faiths, building on the similarity between Sufi mysticism and the bhakti tradition. In the later fifteenth century, some Hindu and Muslim mystics came together to form a group emphasizing a love of god. Some poets, honored later as saints, promoted a mixture of Sufi and bhakti ideals that appealed to mystics in both religious communities. The cultural mixing also fostered a new language, Urdu (ER-doo), a combination of Persian, Turkish, Arabic, and Indian words superimposed on a Hindi grammar and written with the Arabic script, that was used by many Muslims in north and northwest India.

The Indian Muslim Custom of Secluding Women

Muslims and Hindus also engaged each other culturally. Muslim influences, including Persian words and Persian food, were incorporated into Hindu social life, and many Hindu males adopted Muslim clothing styles. In north India, some Hindus began practicing the local Muslim custom of purdah, seclusion of women. Hinduism became more conservative, emphasizing tradition and priestly leadership. Some intermarriage also occurred, and, at the village level, Muslims fit themselves into the caste system to some extent. Thus the Muslim society that developed in India, like the Hindu society, was not egalitarian but rather was led by an upper class who descended from immigrants.

Despite some mixing, from the thirteenth century onward, the life of India became two distinct currents flowing side by side. Most Muslims refused to be assimilated into Hinduism and remained disdainful of Hindus and of the caste system, but Hinduism was not destroyed either. Unlike Buddhism, which was centered in vulnerable monasteries, Hinduism's decentralized structure proved stable. Thus Hindus and Muslims mingled to some extent but never united to form a single stream.

LO³ Cultural Adaptation and New Southeast Asian Societies

Owing partly to the stimulus from India and, to a lesser extent, China, several great Southeast Asian kingdoms developed near the end of the first millennium C.E., establishing their main centers in what is today Cambodia, Burma, the Indonesian islands of Java and Sumatra, and Vietnam. These Southeast Asian states mixed outside influences with their own

 Interactive Map

traditions to produce new societies (see Map 13.2).

Indianized Kingdoms and Societies

From early in the Common Era until around the fourteenth century C.E., many Southeast Asian societies made selective use of Indian models in shaping their political patterns, a process known as Indianization. For example, the rulers declared themselves god-kings, or devaraja worthy of cult worship. In theory absolute rulers, in reality their power faded with distance from the capital cities. Warfare was no less frequent in Southeast Asia than in other areas of the world, as rulers fended off rivals and sought more land and labor to supply revenues.

The Indianized kingdoms of Southeast Asia were not all alike, and the economic foundations of their

prosperity differed. Some were based largely on agriculture, whereas others depended heavily on maritime trade. In many respects these contrasting patterns represented skillful adaptations to the environment. In the agriculture-based economies, rice-growing technology improved considerably beginning in the ninth

purdah
The Indian Muslim custom of secluding women.

devaraja
("god-king") The title used by Indianized Southeast Asian rulers, who wished to be seen as a reincarnated Buddha or Shiva worthy of cult worship.

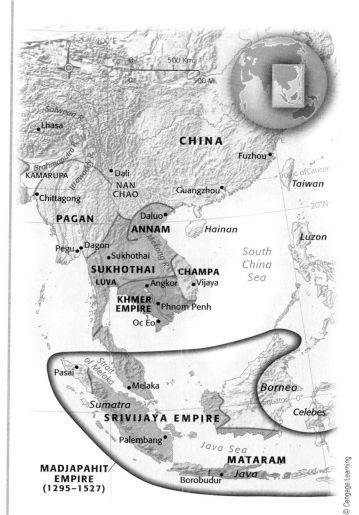

Map 13.2
Major Southeast Asian Kingdoms, ca. 1200 C.E.

By 1200 the Khmer Empire (Angkor), which once covered much of mainland Southeast Asia, had declined. Sukhothai, Pagan, Srivijaya, Champa, and Vietnam were other major states.

century, becoming productive enough to sustain large centralized states. But in places with large areas of swampland, such as Malaya and Sumatra, people maximized their access to the open frontier of the sea and became traders.

Indian Religion in Southeast Asia

The migration and mixing of peoples and their cultures were significant themes in Southeast Asia, as they had been in India, Europe, and Africa. Following in the footsteps of earlier arrivals, peoples such as the Burmans (BUHR-muhnz) in the ninth century and the Tai (tie) peoples in the seventh to thirteenth centuries immigrated from Tibet and China into mainland Southeast Asia and reshaped the region. For example, the Burmans established the dynamic state of Pagan (puh-GONE) in central Burma after assimilating Buddhism and Hinduism from local people.

Religion played a central role in these states. Although the peasantry remained chiefly animist, Southeast Asian elites adopted Mahayana Buddhism and Hinduism from India. At its height in the twelfth century, the city of Pagan, the capital of a great kingdom, was one of the architectural wonders of the world, a city filled with Buddhist and Hindu temples. At Pagan and elsewhere, religion infused government and the arts, and Hindu priests became advisers on ritual in the courts. Hindu Indian epics such as the *Ramayana* and *Mahabharata* became deeply imbedded in both the folk and elite culture, and Hindu kings, gods, and demons animated the arts.

> 66 An enduring gap separated the social and cultural traditions of the royal families, administrations, and capital cities from those of the villages. 99

Southeast Asian Societies

Southeast Asian societies shared many common features. Extensive trade networks, both land and maritime, had linked the region from earliest times, and many people specialized in local or foreign commerce. Most of the larger states were multiethnic in their population, fostering a cosmopolitan attitude in many cities. Still, most Southeast Asians were farmers and fishermen and lived in villages characterized by a spirit of cooperation. An enduring gap separated the social and cultural traditions of the royal families, administrations, and capital cities from those of the villages. The two traditions differed significantly in religious orientations, worldviews, and ways of life. Southeast Asian family patterns were diverse, ranging from flexible structures to a few patriarchies and matriarchies. In contrast to India and China, women held a relatively high status in most Southeast Asian societies, and some, like the Burmese queen Pwa Saw, wielded great power.

The Angkor Empire

The Khmer people created the greatest Indianized state, the kingdom of Angkor (ANG-kor), in what is today Cambodia. It was established by a visionary king, Jayavarman (JAI-a-VAR-man) I (r. 802–834), in 802 C.E., who identified himself with the Hindu god Shiva. His successors extended and consolidated the kingdom, which persisted until 1432. Angkor was notable for its substantial empire, advanced architecture, and unique social system. By the twelfth century, the bustling capital city, Angkor Thom (ANG-kor tom), and its immediate environs contained perhaps 1 million people. It was much larger than any medieval European city and comparable to all but the largest Chinese and Arab cities. Trade with China and other

---

CHRONOLOGY

Southeast Asia, 600–1500

192–1471	Kingdom of Champa
600–1290	Srivijaya Empire
802–1432	Angkor Empire
939	End of Chinese colonization in Vietnam
1044–1287	Pagan kingdom in Burma
1292–1527	Madjapahit kingdom on Java
1238–1419	Sukhotai kingdom in Siam
1350–1767	Ayuthia kingdom in Siam
1403–1511	Melaka kingdom and Sultanate
1428–1788	Le dynasty in Vietnam (founded by Le Loi)

---

countries flourished, and many Chinese merchants lived in the kingdom.

Administering the Angkor Empire

The Angkor kings presided over a vigorous imperial system. At its height in the twelfth and thirteenth centuries, Angkor had an empire controlling much of what is now Cambodia, Laos, Thailand, and southern Vietnam. The Khmers acquired and maintained their empire by a skillful combination of warfare, diplomacy, and pragmatism. Only the most ruthless kings wielded unchallenged power, and many were art patrons and builders. Jayavarman VII (r. 1181–1219) was a devout Buddhist who expanded the empire, commissioned important artworks, built roads, and sponsored the construction of many monuments and temples.

 Read about Pwa Saw, the admired Burmese Queen who exercised her political influence for forty years.

The Angkor government structure resembled a theocratic state: it presided over a well-developed cult for the popular worship of the god-kings, and priestly families held a privileged position. Perhaps as many as 300,000 Hindu priests lived in the empire at its height, and the numerous temples controlled massive wealth. Hindu values were also reflected in many aspects of culture, including theater, art, and dance. The state held much power over the population and often used that power to enrich the society, maintaining hospitals, schools, and libraries. It also constructed an extensive canal network for efficient water distribution, exhibiting some of the most advanced civil engineering in the premodern world. The Khmers may have had the most productive agriculture in world history, producing three to four crops per year.

Angkor Wat

Many magnificent stone temples were built during the Angkor period. They were designed to represent the Hindu conception of the cosmos centered on the abode of the gods. The most famous temple was part of the largest religious complex in the premodern world, Angkor Wat (ANG-kor waht). The complex, containing buildings, towers, and walls, was built by some seventy thousand work-

> "The Khmers acquired and maintained their empire by a skillful combination of warfare, diplomacy, and pragmatism."

ers in the twelfth century. Angkor Wat dwarfed other Intermediate Era monumental religious buildings, including the magnificent cathedrals of Europe and the grand mosques of Baghdad and Cairo.

In exchange for considerable material security and the protection of a patron to whom they owed allegiance, Khmer commoners tolerated a highly inequitable distribution of wealth and power as well as substantial labor demands, such as the draft of workers to build Angkor Wat. Like many hierarchical societies of the era, Angkor had numerous slaves, and although no Indian-style caste system existed, the social structure was similarly rigid. Each class had its appointed role: below the king were the priests, and below them were the trade guilds. The vast majority of the population were of the farmer-builder-soldier class, which had labor obligations to the sovereign. Peasants were tied to the soil they plowed, the temples they served, and the king's army.

Women in Khmer Society

Khmer women played a much more important role in society and politics than women did in most other places in the world. According to Zhou Daguan (joe ta-kwan), a Chinese ambassador, women operated most of the retail stalls: "In this country it is the women who are concerned with commerce."[8] Jayarajadevi (JAI-ya-RAJ-adeh-vee), the first wife of King Jayavarman VII, took in hundreds of abandoned girls and trained and settled them. After her death, the king married Indradevi (IN-dra-deh-vee), a renowned scholar who was acclaimed as the chief teacher of the king. Women dominated the palace staff, and some were even gladiators and warriors. Chinese visitors were shocked at the liberated behavior of Khmer women, who went out in public as they liked. Khmer society in this era was matrilineal, giving women status in the family.

Indianized Urban Societies in Java and Sumatra

Of the other important Indianized states in Southeast Asia, several developed in the Indonesian archipelago, on the large islands of Java and Sumatra. The

Angkor Wat Temple Complex This photograph shows the inner buildings of the Angkor Wat temple complex in northern Cambodia. The towers represented the Hindu view of the cosmos. Mount Meru, the home of the gods, rises 726 feet in the middle.

wayang kulit
Javanese shadow puppet play, developed during the Intermediate Era, based on Hindu epics like the *Ramayana* and local Javanese content.

encounters between Indian influence and local traditions produced a distinctive religious and political blend known as Hindu-Javanese, which was based on an agricultural economy and included many unique beliefs. Among these were the notions that the earthly order mirrored and embodied the cosmic order and that people must avoid disharmony and change at all cost. The duty of the god-king was to maintain order in a turbulent human world.

Madjapahit

As in Angkor, the capitals and palaces of Javanese kingdoms were built to imitate the cosmic order. The greatest Javanese kingdom of this era was Madjapahit (MAH-ja-PA-hit)

(1292–1527). Madjapahit reached its peak in the fourteenth century under the fabled Prime Minister Gajah Mada, when it loosely controlled a large empire embracing much of present-day Indonesia. Hindu-Buddhist ideas can be seen most vividly in the temple complexes of that time, such as the famous temple mountain of Borobodur (BOR-uh-buh-door) in central Java. They were also reflected in the arts, such as the shadow puppet play, or **wayang kulit** (WHY-ang KOO-leet), which was based on the Hindu epics like the *Ramayana* but had much local content as well.

Social inequality permeated Hindu-Javanese society. A complex etiquette regulated the relations between those of varied status, and hence confirmed the social hierarchy. The aristocracy expected deference from commoners, most of whom lived in villages whose ways of life differed substantially from those of the royal capital. The villagers' main link with the government was through tax and labor obligations. Peasants identified more with their village community than with distant kings in their palaces.

Srivijaya and the Straits of Melaka

Coastal states on Sumatra were shaped much more heavily by international trade than were the inland agricultural kingdoms of Java and Cambodia. The Straits of Melaka separating Sumatra from the Malay Peninsula was a major contact zone throughout history and a passageway for trade and religious networks. Throughout the first millennium of the Common Era, a complex maritime trading system gradually emerged that linked the eastern Mediterranean, Middle East, East African coast, Persia, and India with the societies of East and Southeast Asia. Between 600 and 1290, many of the small trading states in the Straits region came under the loose control of Srivijaya (SREE-vih-JAI-ya), a federation of trading ports based in southeastern Sumatra and a fierce rival of the Cholas in South India. Srivijaya exercised considerable power over the international commerce of the region, maintaining both a strong navy and a close trade relationship with powerful China. Besides being a trading hub, Srivijaya was also a major international center of Buddhist study, attracting thousands of Buddhist monks and students from many countries.

International Influences and the Decline of the Indianized States

The great Indianized states of Southeast Asia ended between the thirteenth and fifteenth centuries, for a variety of complex reasons, but the changes were mostly gradual. Some causes of decline were internal, but international influences also played a major role in the disintegration of Angkor and neighboring states. These included the migrations of the Tai peoples, the intervention of the Mongols, and the arrival of Theravada Buddhism and Islam.

Arrival of the Tai Peoples

Over several centuries, various Tai-speaking groups from mountainous southwestern China migrated into Southeast Asia. By the thirteenth century, the Tai began setting up their own states in the middle Mekong valley and northern Thailand. These were the ancestors of the closely related Siamese (SYE-uh-meez), today known as the Thai, and the Lao (laow) peoples. As they moved south, the Tai conquered or absorbed the local peoples while also adopting some of their cultural traditions. Eventually they came into conflict with Angkor, and by the mid-1400s they had seized much of the empire's territory. The Khmer Empire soon disintegrated, and the Angkor capital was abandoned. The Khmers became pawns perched uneasily between the expanding Vietnamese and Siamese states.

Meanwhile, the Mongols encountered Angkor's neighbors, but their impact was smaller than that of the Tai. After conquering China, in 1288 they attacked Pagan because the Burmans refused to recognize Mongol authority. Although the Mongols soon withdrew, in their wake they left instability in Burma as rival groups competed for power. Elsewhere in Southeast Asia, the Mongols found mostly frustration; Southeast Asians were among the few peoples to successfully resist Mongol conquest and power.

Theravada Buddhism and Islam in Southeast Asia

Another force for change was religion. By early in the second millennium of the Common Era, two new universal religions began filtering peacefully into the region from outside: Theravada Buddhism and Islam. Theravada Buddhism had been present in the region for several centuries, but a revitalized form came from Sri Lanka and provided a challenge to the Indianized regimes. The Buddhist message of tolerance, egalitarianism, pacifism, and individual worth proved attractive to peasants who were weary of war, public labor projects, and tyrannical kings. Furthermore, Theravada Buddhism was a tolerant religion that was able to exist alongside the rich animism of the peasants, who could honor the Buddha while worshiping local spirits. By the fourteenth century, most of the Burman, Khmer, Siamese, and Lao peasants had adopted Theravada Buddhism, while the elite mixed it with the older Hindu–Mahayana Buddhist traditions.

About the same time, from the thirteenth through sixteenth centuries, Sunni Islam filtered in from the Middle East via India and spread widely. Like Buddhism, Islam also offered an egalitarian message as well as a complex theology that appealed to peasants and merchants in the coastal regions of the Malay Peninsula, Sumatra, Java, and other islands. Some Southeast Asians adopted Sunni Islam in a largely orthodox form, while others mixed it with animism or Hinduism-Buddhism. Mystical Sufi ideas embedded in missionary Islam also blended well and fostered conversion by promoting an emotional spirituality rather than dry, dogmatic theology.

As Theravada Buddhism and Islam spread across Southeast Asia, only a few scattered peoples maintained Indianized societies, among them the Balinese (BAH-luh-NEEZ). On the Indonesian island of Bali, Hinduism and other classical patterns remained vigorous, emphasizing arts like dancing, music, shadow plays, and woodcarving.

> "Buddhist states like Sukhothai and Ayuthia were monarchies, and Siamese kings were considered semidivine reincarnated Buddhas."

LO⁴ Changing Southeast Asian Societies

By the fifteenth century, Southeast Asia had experienced a major transition. The Indianized kingdoms, such as Angkor, Pagan, and Srivijaya, had gradually been replaced by new states with less despotic governments and more dynamic economies. Networks of trade and religion linked the region even more closely to wider areas of Afro-Eurasia. In these centuries the major Southeast Asian societies began to diverge from the earlier Indian and Chinese-influenced patterns, and by the fifteenth century, three broad but distinctive cultural patterns had developed: the Theravada Buddhist, the Vietnamese, and the Malayo-Muslim or Indonesian.

 WWW Southeast Asia Guide (http://www.library.wisc.edu/guides/SEAsia/). An impressive, easy-to-use site from the University of Wisconsin at Madison.

Theravada Buddhist Society in Siam

The Siamese formed one of the most influential Theravada Buddhist societies, establishing several states in northern and central Thailand. The first major Siamese state, Sukhotai (SOO-ko-TAI), was founded in 1238 by former Angkor vassals and controlled much of the central plains of what is today Thailand. According to Siamese tradition, Sukhotai's glory was established by Rama Kamkheng (RA-ma KHAM-keng), a shrewd diplomat who established a close tributary relationship with the dominant regional power, China. Under Rama's leadership, Siam adopted the Khmer script and other Khmer influences in literature, art, and government. Rama made Theravada Buddhism the state religion and adopted laws that were humane by world standards; he was heralded as a wise and popular ruler.

Ayuthia: A Regional Empire

By 1350 Sukhotai was eclipsed by another Siamese state that emerged in the southern Thai plains, with its capital at Ayuthia (ah-YUT-uh-yuh). While Sukhotai declined and finally collapsed in 1419, Ayuthia developed a regional empire whose influence extended into Cambodia and the small Lao states along the Mekong River. Its rivalry with the Burmans and Vietnamese for regional dominance occasionally led to war. Buddhist states like Sukhothai and Ayuthia were monarchies, and Siamese kings were considered semidivine reincarnated Buddhas. They lived in splendor and were advised by Brahman priests in ceremonial and magical practices. They had many wives and therefore many sons, all of whom could be rivals for the throne. This problem meant that the top levels of government were plagued with instability. But these rivalries generally had little impact in the villages, which had substantial autonomy; royal power lessened as distance to the capital increased.

Siamese Society

Siamese society and culture had many similarities to those of other Theravada Buddhist peoples, such as the Khmer, Burmans, and especially the Lao. Like them, the Siamese social order was divided into a small aristocracy, many commoners, and some slaves. Although women did not enjoy equality with men, free Siamese women enjoyed many rights. They participated in the markets, inherited equally with men, and could initiate marriage or divorce. Male slaves did a variety of jobs, from farming and mining to serving as trusted government officials. Slave women were often concubines, domestic servants, or entertainers. Deference to higher authority and recognition of status differences were expected among the Siamese people. In contrast to the extended families of China or India, small nuclear families were the norm. While Theravada peoples encouraged cooperation and mutual obligations within the family and village, they also valued individualism.

Siamese society reflected Theravada Buddhist values, such as gentleness, meditation, and reincarnation, as well as the concept of *karma*—the idea that one's actions, either in this life or a past life, determined one's destiny. To escape from the endless round of life, death, and rebirth, believers were expected to devote themselves to attaining merit by practicing merciful and generous deeds, with the ultimate goal of reaching *nirvana*, or release from pain. Buddhist monks played key roles in local affairs, operating many village schools. Hence Theravada societies had some of the highest literacy rates (especially for males) in the premodern world.

Vietnamese Society

A Chinese colony for more than one thousand years, Vietnam also constituted a major Southeast Asian society. In 939 C.E., with the Tang dynasty collapsing, a Vietnamese rebellion finally succeeded in pushing the Chinese out and establishing independence, but China remained a permanent threat. Vietnamese leaders wisely continued to borrow ideas and institutions from China and even became a vassal state, sending regular tribute missions to the Chinese emperor. By the fourteenth century, Vietnam, which was still strongly influenced by Chinese political and philosophical ideas, offered a striking contrast to Theravada Buddhist societies.

The Le Dynasty of Vietnam

Despite Vietnam's formal subservience, Chinese forces occasionally attempted a reconquest, inspiring the Vietnamese to become masters at resisting foreign invasions. In 1407 the new Ming dynasty invaded and conquered Vietnam in an attempt to restore China's control. In response to harsh Chinese repression, Le Loi (lay lo-ee) (1385–1433), a mandarin from a landlord family, organized a Vietnamese resistance movement that struggled tenaciously for the next two decades. After it finally expelled the Chinese in 1428, Le Loi became founding emperor of a new Vietnamese dynasty, the Le (1428–1788). His efforts to launch social and economic reforms to reduce the power of the traditional elite, as well as his struggle against Chinese domination, made him one of the

heroes of Vietnam's long struggle for independence and self-determination. As Le Loi told his people: "Over the centuries, we have been sometimes strong, sometimes weak; but never yet have we been lacking in heroes. In that let our history be the proof."[9]

> ❝ By the fourteenth century, Vietnam, which was still strongly influenced by Chinese political and philosophical ideas, offered a striking contrast to Theravada Buddhist societies. ❞

Following the Chinese Imperial Model

Vietnam had an imperial system modeled on China's. For example, the Vietnamese considered the emperor a "son of heaven," not a god-king but an intermediary between the terrestrial and supernatural realms, ruling through the Mandate of Heaven. As in China, emperors governed through a bureaucracy staffed by scholar-administrators (*mandarins*) chosen by civil service examinations designed to recruit men of talent. The emperor and his officials followed the official ideology of Confucianism, which stressed ethical conduct, social harmony, and social hierarchy. Vietnam also adopted the Chinese model of tributary states and sought to influence or control the peoples of the highlands as well as the neighboring Cham, Khmer, and Lao states.

Peasant society differed considerably from the Chinese-influenced culture of the political elite. In the villages, religious life mixed Mahayana Buddhism, Confucianism, and Daoism with the preexisting Vietnamese spirit and ancestor worship. Villages were autonomous and closely knit communities. The Vietnamese social system was patriarchal and patrilineal, giving family and village power to senior males, but women dominated the town and village markets, doing most of the buying and selling of food and crafts, and their influence increased with age.

The "Drive to the South"

Beginning in the tenth century, some Vietnamese left the overcrowded Red River Valley and Tonkin Gulf to migrate southward along the coast in a long process known as the Nam Tien, or "Drive to the

Nam Tien

("Drive to the South") A long process beginning in the tenth century in which some Vietnamese left the overcrowded north to migrate southward along the coast of Vietnam.

South." Over the centuries these Vietnamese settlers, supported by imperial forces, overran the Cham people and their states, in what is today central Vietnam. By the sixteenth century, they were pushing toward the Khmer-dominated Mekong River Delta in southern Vietnam. As a result, the Vietnamese became more involved with Southeast Asia, and the central and southern dialects and cultures gradually diverged from those in the northern part of Vietnam.

> "Southeast Asian people had excelled as seafaring traders since the beginning of their history, trading as far away as East Africa."

Islam, Maritime Networks, and the Malay World

Southeast Asian people had excelled as seafaring traders since the beginning of their history, trading as far away as East Africa. During the Intermediate Era world, trade more closely connected diverse Eurasian and African peoples, and Southeast Asian port cities became essential intermediaries in the Indian Ocean trade between China, India, and the Middle East. Peoples like the Malays and Javanese played active roles in this maritime trade.

Islamic Dominance in Indonesia

Trade also brought Southeast Asians into contact with the Muslim traders who dominated interregional commerce. As Islamic merchants from Arabia, Persia, and India spread Islam along the Indian Ocean trading routes, Islam became a major influence in the Malay Peninsula and Indonesian archipelago. By the fourteenth century, Islam was well established in northern Sumatra, and some Hindu-Buddhist rulers of coastal states in the Malay Peninsula and Indonesian islands adopted the new faith to attract Muslim traders. The increased trade fostered by the spread of Islam sparked the growth of cities and increasing influence of merchants in local politics. In addition, a new type of maritime trading state emerged to handle the growing commerce. Revenue from trade became more important than agricultural tribute in many states. This transformation in the international maritime economy created an unprecedented commercial prosperity and cosmopolitan culture in Southeast Asia. At the same time, more intensive agricultural growth, including new crops and varieties of rice, spurred population increase, migration, and more bureaucratic states, some large and many small ones.

The Great Port of Melaka

The spread of Islam in the region coincided with, and was spurred by, the rise of the great port of Melaka (muh-LACK-uh) on the southwest coast of Malaya facing the Straits of Melaka. In 1403 the Hindu ruler of the city, Parameswara, adopted Islam and transformed himself into a sultan. In Southeast Asian fashion, the Melakans blended Islamic faith and cul-

Le Dynasty Ruler This Vietnamese drawing shows the Le emperor being carried in state, accompanied by his mandarins, parasol- and fan-bearers, and a royal elephant. The drawing was printed in an eighteenth-century British book, with an English description of the procession.

From Churchill, *A Collection of Voyages and Travels*, 1732

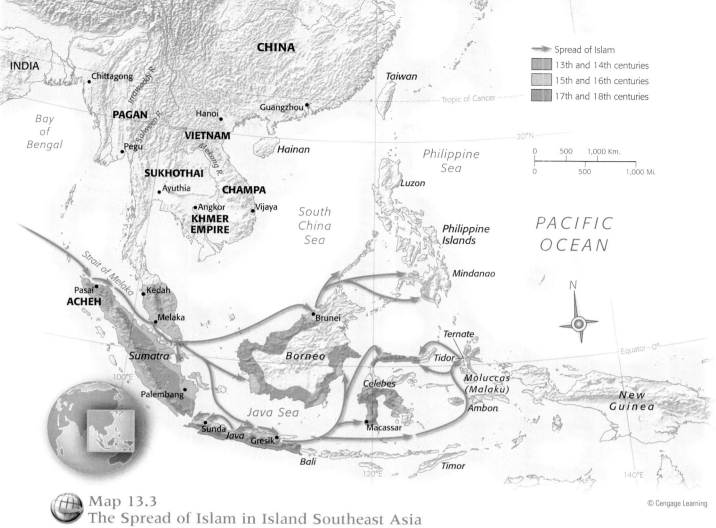

Map 13.3
The Spread of Islam in Island Southeast Asia

Carried by merchants and missionaries, Islam spread from Arabia and India to island Southeast Asia, eventually becoming the major faith on many islands and in the Malay Peninsula.

© Cengage Learning

The Book of John Mandeville

Scholars are skeptical about the truth of the first-hand accounts of Sir John, a knight and trans-Eurasian explorer in the fourteenth century, although no less entertained by his adventures; Sir John claimed to have served both the sultan of Egypt and the Mongol khan of China.

ture with the older Hindu-Buddhist (and, for peasants, animist) beliefs, creating a cultural pattern that remained eclectic for generations. Because Islam in the region was closely identified at first with the Malay people of the Melaka region, historians often refer to the Muslim Southeast Asian societies as Malayo-Muslim. Malay identity spread to many societies in Malaya, Sumatra, and Borneo, where the people practiced Islam and spoke the Malay language.

Melaka became one of the major commercial hubs of the world, flourishing as a vital link in world trade until 1511. An early sixteenth-century

Portuguese visitor wrote that it had "no equal in the world" and extolled the importance of Melaka to peoples and trade patterns as far away as western Europe.[10] Merchants from all over were attracted to Melaka: by the late 1400s, Melaka's 100,000 to 200,000 people included 15,000 foreign merchants, including Arabs, Egyptians, Ethiopians, Jews, Burmese, Indians, Filipinos, Japanese, and Chinese. Visitors claimed that more ships crowded the Melaka harbor than at any other port in the world, attracted by its stable government and free trade policy.

Melaka also became the main center for the spread of Islam in the peninsula and western archipelago (see Map 13.3), spurring political change and economic growth. Sultanates appeared in many districts

Interactive Map

and islands as rulers embraced the new faith for religious, political, and commercial reasons. Some

Islamic states, such as Acheh (AH-chay) in northern Sumatra, became regional powers. Gradually, many in the region followed the example of their rulers and adopted Islam. As a result, the Malay Peninsula and Indonesian archipelago were joined to the great Islamic world, but there also remained many village-based societies in more isolated areas such as the Philippine Islands, with no political authority higher than local chiefs.

Islamic Fusion in Indonesia

As Islam was grafted onto different cultures, various patterns of Islamic belief and practice, more diverse than elsewhere in the Islamic world, emerged in the scattered island societies. In most cases, Islam did not completely displace older customs. On Java, Indianized kings and courts combined Islamic beliefs with older Hindu-Buddhist practices, while many peasants maintained their animist beliefs under an Islamic veneer. At the same time, others, especially merchants, adopted a more orthodox Islamic faith. This complexity mirrored a hierarchical social system. The sultans in their palaces remained aloof from the people, and the aristocracy, obsessed with practicing refined behavior rooted in mystical Hinduism, disdained the common folk.

Southeast Asia and the Wider World

Southeast Asia had long been a cosmopolitan region where peoples, ideas, and products met, and that attracted visitors and sojourners from many lands. The intrepid Italian traveler Marco Polo passed through in 1292 on his way home from China. He wrote admiringly that "Java is of unsurpassing wealth, producing all kinds of spices, frequented by a vast amount of shipping. Indeed, the treasure of this island is so great as to be past telling."[11] The Southeast Asia that Marco Polo and other travelers encountered had become one of the world's more prosperous and urbanized regions. Major cities like Ayuthia, Melaka, and Hanoi (huh-NOY) (Vietnam) each probably contained around 100,000 residents, and thus were as large as the major European urban centers like Naples and Paris. Still, though having perhaps 15 to 20 million people, Southeast Asia was dwarfed by the dense populations of nearby China and India, but Southeast Asians often enjoyed better health, more varied diets, and adequate material resources.

Arrival of the Portuguese

Southeast Asia's connections to the wider world, as well as its famed wealth, eventually attracted arrivals who were not welcome. By the beginning of the sixteenth century, a few Portuguese explorers and adventurers, with deadly weapons, state-of-the-art ships, Christian missionary zeal, and desire for wealth, reached first India and then Southeast Asia seeking "Christians and spices." They were the forerunners of what became a powerful, destabilizing European presence that gradually altered the region after 1500.

 Listen to a synopsis of Chapter 13.

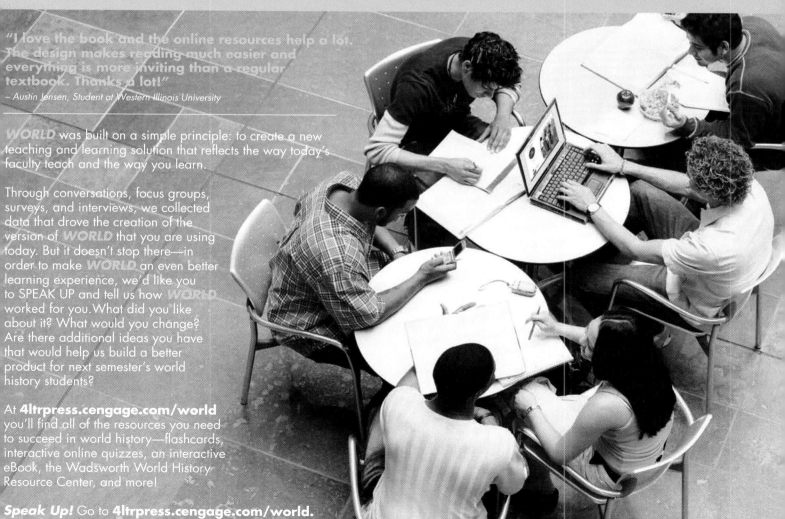

{ Speak Up! }

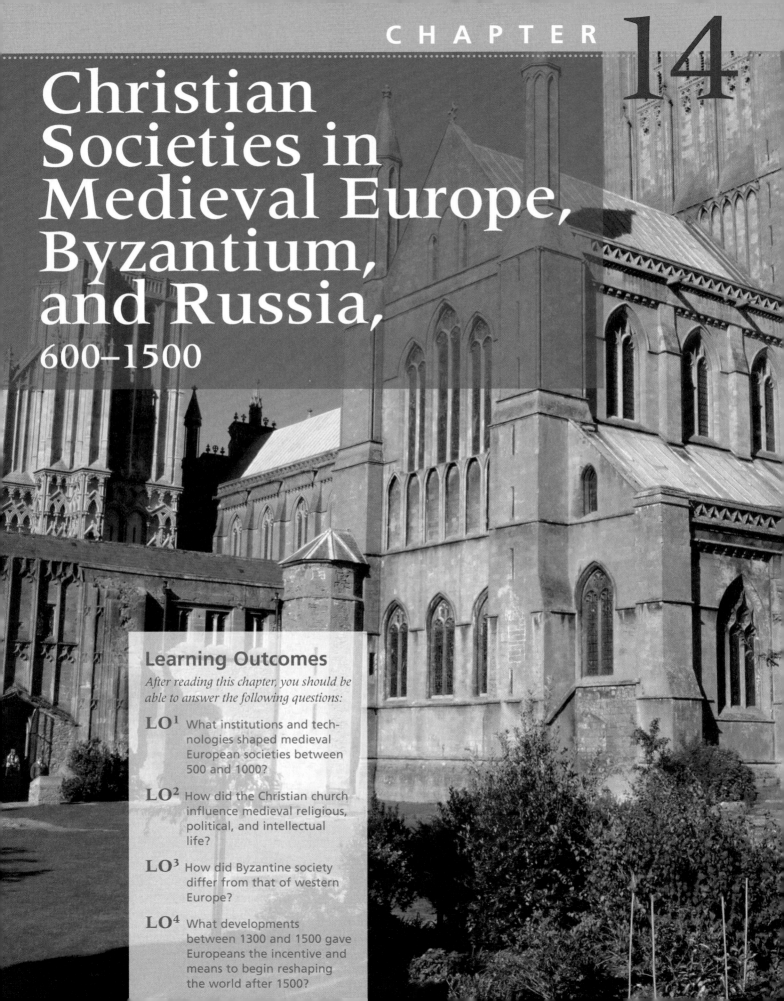

CHAPTER 14

Christian Societies in Medieval Europe, Byzantium, and Russia,
600–1500

Learning Outcomes

After reading this chapter, you should be able to answer the following questions:

LO¹ What institutions and technologies shaped medieval European societies between 500 and 1000?

LO² How did the Christian church influence medieval religious, political, and intellectual life?

LO³ How did Byzantine society differ from that of western Europe?

LO⁴ What developments between 1300 and 1500 gave Europeans the incentive and means to begin reshaping the world after 1500?

> **"**The most Christian man beloved by God, the glorious king of the Franks, while he was building this [Christian] monastery, wished that [its] consecration and the battles which he [waged] should not be consigned completely to oblivion.**"**
>
> —Monastery dedication attributed to Charlemagne, ninth-century Frankish Emperor[1]

It was Christmas, 800 c.e. in the city of Rome, the center of Roman Christendom. Along one of the many roads that connected the metropolis to a wider Europe, the most powerful ruler in Europe, Charlemagne (SHAHR-leh-mane), the Christian king of the Franks, traveled from his capital of Aachen (AH-kuhn) some 700 miles away in what is now northwest Germany. He came to celebrate Christmas mass with Pope Leo III.

 Test your knowlege before you read this chapter.

A towering man, 6 feet 4 inches tall, Charlemagne entered the spectacular St. Peter's cathedral. When the Christmas service ended, the pope placed upon Charlemagne's head a golden crown encrusted with sparkling jewels. Led by the pope, the crowd chanted, "Crowned by god, great and peace-loving Emperor of the Romans, life and victory."[2] For the next few centuries, popes influenced secular affairs, while kings like Charlemagne used religion—even the building of monasteries—for their own purposes. The complex relations between the Roman church and diverse European states helped shape the tapestry of European life in this era.

What do you think?

Europe was the most contentious region in the world during the Intermediate Era.

Strongly Disagree   Strongly Agree

| 1 | 2 | 3 | 4 | 5 | 6 | 7 |

medieval
A term first used in the 1400s by Italian historians to describe the centuries between the classical Romans and their own time.

In the 1400s, Italian historians first coined the term **medieval** to describe the centuries between the classical Romans and their own time. In their view, it was a superstitious and ignorant "Dark Age." But the reality of what later scholars often called the "Middle Ages" in Europe was more complex, and always in flux. Linked by networks of faith and culture, medieval western Europeans combined Christianity with practices inherited from both the Romans and Germanic groups like the Franks. In both western Europe and Byzantium to the east, the strong influence of the Christian churches in all aspects of society, including politics, was an innovation.

<< **Wells Cathedral** The importance of Christianity in European life was symbolized by magnificent cathedrals. This cathedral, built in the town of Wells in England in the thirteenth century c.e., was designed to reflect the glory of God.

The role and spread of Christianity were only one aspect of a Europe that changed considerably over the millennium between 500 and 1500. Europeans made their own history but borrowed much from other cultures, especially Muslims. In addition, the many tensions of European life fostered a competitive spirit that helped spur overseas exploration in the fifteenth century.

> "Although classical unity was lost, Europe's favorable geography enabled many areas to develop similar religious, social, economic, and political patterns."

LO¹ Forming Christian Societies in Western Europe

The disintegration of the western Roman Empire in the fifth century C.E. led to political and social instability, which cleared the ground for the rise of new societies between 500 and 1000. These were centuries of considerable creativity, spurred partly by the mixing of Roman and Germanic traditions as well as by relations with non-European peoples. While the societies of western Europe varied, they also developed many common features, including a dominant Rome-based Christian church and similar social, political, and economic systems. Economic change, technological development, and a rural society based on feudalism and manorialism also set the foundation for a new Europe.

Environmental and Christian Influences

Climate change and disease were two of the factors that shaped post-Roman Europe. In contrast to the warmer weather of the middle Classical Era, a cooling climate brought shorter growing seasons between 500 and 900, after which warmer trends returned. The terrible plague that devastated Europe during Justinian's time reappeared occasionally throughout the eighth century. Between 200 and 800, western Europe also suffered repeated and prolonged incursions by migrating peoples. Various Germanic groups occupied much of the region, destroying forever the western Roman Empire and much of its culture.

Given these challenges, it was not surprising that people turned to religion for support.

The Church Replaces the Empire

Although classical unity was lost, Europe's favorable geography enabled many areas to develop similar religious, social, economic, and political patterns. Much of western and central Europe was blessed by fertile, well-watered plains rich in minerals, while a long coastline offered many fine harbors along the Mediterranean and Baltic Seas as well as along the Atlantic Ocean. Long navigable rivers such as the Danube (DAN-yoob) and Rhine and accessible mountain passes through the Alps made communication within the region much easier than for Asia, Africa, and South America. Hence, land and sea networks fostered the movement of ideas, products, peoples, technologies, and diseases. In addition, the Christian church exerted tremendous influence over medieval politics, society, and culture. As Roman power melted away, the church became the major source of authority, and local bishops and monasteries were often the only government in rural areas. Over time the bishops of Rome gained authority and prestige, eventually establishing the papacy and asserting power over kings.

Monasteries

The popes led a church that also included religious orders. From Christianity's earliest centuries, some men and women had tried to escape what they felt were the corruptions of cities by moving to isolated places to pray and prepare for Heaven. Many early monks were lonely hermits, but others joined monasteries, Christian communities for men who had taken holy orders. Similar places where women devoted their lives to prayer and service were known as convents. With the slogan "to work is to pray," monks and nuns filled their lives with activity to avoid idleness. They divided the day into periods of communal prayer and song, work in the fields, and intellectual labor such as copying manuscripts, eventually creating the bound book. By 850 one German monastery boasted a library of one thousand titles, all of them hand-copied.

Missionaries

During this time, Christians also became more interested in converting "nonbelievers." The popes continued their efforts to spread the faith to those Germanic peoples who remained pagan and followed their ancient gods, such as the gods of war and weather and the goddess of love and fertility. As a result of missionary efforts, the Anglo-Saxon kingdom of Kent in England converted, and Canterbury (KAN-tuhr-bare-ee) became the headquarters of the new church in England. From there, missionaries—the most famous of whom was Boniface (BON-uh-face) (ca. 675–754), a member of the Benedictine order who won many converts—were sent to German lands. But as the Christian religion spread north of the Alps, it began to change as Christians helped spread the faith by blending German values and practices into their religion.

For instance, Germans emphasized the presence of gods in nature and set up shrines in the woods where they could worship them. Christians changed these to special places where people could pray to particular holy men and women whose behavior while on earth merited their being acclaimed saints, such as Boniface. However, because the church was led by bishops who were upper-class members of the new German states, many Christian leaders began valuing warriors and fighting, which had not been a prominent feature of early Christianity.

The Frankish and Holy Roman Empires

Between 500 and 1000, the political map of Europe changed. Muslim armies conquered North Africa, the eastern shore of the Mediterranean, and most of Spain during the seventh and early eighth centuries (see Chapter 10), and small Muslim bands raided Italy and France. The victory of the Frankish ruler Charles Martel (SHARL mahr-TEL) at the Battle of Tours (TOO-ers) in 732 finally stopped these raids. Following this victory, the Franks created a large state in western Europe.

> 66 To enhance his power, Charlemagne also sent diplomatic missions to Byzantium and various Islamic states, thus fostering a communications network with eastern Europe and the Middle East. 99

The "Donation of Pepin" and the Papal States

In 753 Pope Stephen sought the aid of the Franks against the Germanic Lombard kingdom in northern Italy, which was threatening papal control of central Italy. He then anointed the Frankish king Pepin (PEP-in) the Short as the special protector of Italy. In return, Pepin defeated the Lombards and, in 756, donated land in central Italy to the pope. This "Donation of Pepin" became the basis of the Papal States, a collection of small states surrounding Rome that remained under the control of popes for more than 1,000 years. From this time on, the attention of western Europe's chief religious leaders became divided between their spiritual and earthly concerns.

Charlemagne

A new dynasty of Frankish rulers—known as the Carolingians (kah-roe-LIN-gee-uhnz) after their greatest ruler, Charlemagne (r. 768–814)—soon controlled the Frankish kingdom. The special relationship between the popes and the Franks grew during the reign of Charlemagne, who was crowned by the pope in Rome. In return, Frankish kings were obligated to protect the Roman church. Charlemagne spread Frankish power from France and northern Italy deep into the lands inhabited by another Germanic people, the Saxons, in north and central Germany. His Carolingian empire temporarily united the heart of western Europe (see Map 14.1). Charlemagne used the church to strengthen his empire, appointing bishops and priests, influencing ceremonies and doctrines, and controlling monasteries. He took great interest in the religious lives of his people and pursued uniformity in church ritual, preaching, and presentation of scripture. On one occasion, he issued instructions to the Saxons that anyone deliberately breaking the Lenten fast by eating meat should be executed. To enhance his power, Charlemagne also sent diplomatic missions to Byzantium and various Islamic states, thus fostering a communications network with eastern Europe and the Middle East.

 Interactive Map

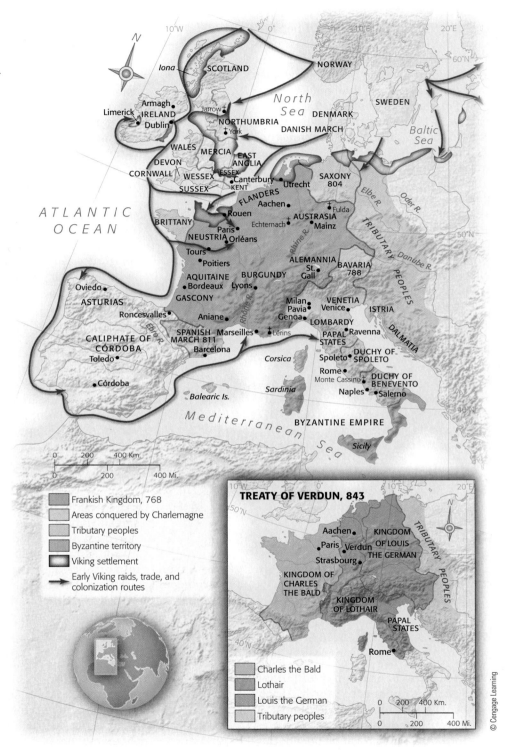

Map 14.1
Europe During the Carolingian Empire

At the height of their power under Charlemagne, the Carolingian rulers of the Franks controlled much of northwestern Europe, including what is today France, the Low Countries, western and southern Germany, and northern Italy.

Map legend (main map):
- Frankish Kingdom, 768
- Areas conquered by Charlemagne
- Tributary peoples
- Byzantine territory
- Viking settlement
- Early Viking raids, trade, and colonization routes

Inset: TREATY OF VERDUN, 843
- Charles the Bald
- Lothair
- Louis the German
- Tributary peoples

Labels on inset: Aachen, Paris, Verdun, Strasbourg, KINGDOM OF LOUIS THE GERMAN, KINGDOM OF CHARLES THE BALD, KINGDOM OF LOTHAIR, PAPAL STATES, Rome, TRIBUTARY PEOPLES

© Cengage Learning

The Carolingian Empire after Charlemagne

Charlemagne's empire did not long outlive him; it was divided among his three grandsons in the Treaty of Verdun (vuhr-DUN) in 843. Eventually other Germanic peoples challenged the Franks for influence. The Saxon ruler Otto I—known as Otto the Great (r. 936–973), a Saxon who had replaced the Frankish king in East Francia—was responsible for the creation of a new German empire. Otto established his control over rebellious princes in Germany, and the next year took an army into northern Italy. In 962 the pope, grateful for Otto's help against the Lombards, declared Otto "Roman Emperor." From this point until 1806, rulers in Germany retained this title, eventually proclaiming their lands to be the "Holy Roman Empire." But this empire had little in common with the classical Roman Empire: most Germans, Italians, Slavs, Czechs, and Hungarians within its domains had little sense of common citizenship beyond the local level. Still, Otto

> "The European heartland continued to attract other peoples seeking wealth—both traders and outright invaders."

and his successors continued to both defend and dominate the church.

Invaders and Traders

The European heartland continued to attract other peoples seeking wealth—both traders and outright invaders. The biggest threat came from the Vikings, or Northmen, who faced population pressures that led them to launch raids out of Scandinavia, a region with limited productive farmland. Viking warriors burned and looted Christian towns and monasteries in England, France, Holland, and Ireland. People prayed: "From the violence of the men from the north, O Lord, deliver us."[3] In addition to being fearsome raiders, the Vikings were skilled craftsmen who built ingenious shallow-draft boats. Between 750 and 1200, various Vikings raided, traded, and settled around Europe, establishing settlements from the Black Sea and Russia to the British Isles to western France. Normans who descended from the Vikings in Normandy, France, conquered England in 1066.

Viking Longship This longship from the ninth century, excavated from a burial mound in Norway in 1904, boasted intricate decorations and carvings. Probably used for ceremonial purposes, it became the burial chamber of a royal Viking woman.

Iceland and Greenland

Eventually the Vikings both at home and abroad became part of mainstream European society, giving up raiding for trade and farming. Those Vikings who settled outside Scandinavia adopted the cultures and faiths of the local Celtic, Latin, Germanic, or Slavic peoples, adding their own heritage to local languages and culture. One of their most impressive accomplishments was the Norse Vikings' settlement of Iceland in 874 and Greenland around 986.

The Bulgars and Magyars in Central Europe

Two other warlike peoples, the Bulgars (BUL-gahrz) and Magyars (MAG-yahrz), migrated from Russia into central Europe. The Slavic Bulgars created a large state between the Byzantine and Frankish empires during the ninth century. However, they were contained by Byzantine armies, and eventually they converted to Eastern Orthodox Christianity and settled in the eastern Balkan region known today as Bulgaria. The Magyars, excellent horsemen who spoke a Ural-Altaic language related to Turkish, moved from north of the Black Sea into the Hungarian plain, threatening Germany and Italy. This threat was contained when German forces under Otto the Great crushed a large Magyar army in 955. The Magyars then settled permanently in Hungary and adopted Roman Christianity.

In addition to invasions, trade also shaped the new Europe. While most Europeans were peasants, growing food or raising livestock for sale at local markets, some were merchants who traded products over long distances. As it had for centuries, trade continued briskly in the eastern Mediterranean, where it was tightly controlled by the Byzantine rulers. Trade between the Franks and Constantinople flourished at various times, and as time passed the east-west trade grew dynamic. The northeastern Italian city of Venice, built on its lagoons in the fifth century, was an active trading center throughout the Middle Ages, and Venice and Genoa were other centers of trade with the Middle East and Byzantium. By 800, multiple networks were reconnecting western Europeans to eastern peoples.

Trade and Cultural Dialogue

As trade increased, Europeans benefited from growing connections with the Muslim world. Islamic expansion stimulated a wider movement of people, goods, and information, such as Asian science and classical Greek thought, that gradually influenced many Afro-Eurasian societies. The exchange of products and ideas between Islamic Spain and Sicily, where various cultures met, and Christian Europe proved especially fruitful for European intellectual life. In the eighth and ninth centuries, Arab Muslims conquered Sicily and much of Spain, where they created cosmopolitan societies and several strong states. The meeting of Christian, Jewish, and Muslim traditions in Muslim-ruled Spain and Sicily allowed the philosophical, scientific, and technological writings of many Classical Greek and Indian, as well as Persian and Arab, thinkers to spread among educated Europeans. In the 1140s, an Italian translator of Arabic texts wrote that "it befits us to imitate the Arabs especially, for they are our teachers and the pioneers."[4]

Technology, Agricultural Growth, and Industry

The development of new technology helped establish the economic foundations of medieval Europe, especially in farming and power generation. Various technological improvements, some originating in Asia, came into common use in western Europe during

---

CHRONOLOGY

The Early Middle Ages, 500–1000

529	First Benedictine monastery
732	Battle of Tours
750–1200	Viking attacks in Europe
756–1492	Muslim states in Spain
768–814	Reign of Charlemagne over Franks
800	Papal crowning of Charlemagne
843	Division of Carolingian Empire in Treaty of Verdun
874	Viking settlement of Iceland
955	Defeat of Magyars
962	Revival of Holy Roman Empire by Otto the Great
986	First Norse settlements in Greenland

"Tilling the Fields" Most medieval Europeans were peasants growing food. This French painting from the 1400s shows peasants working land on a manor.

these early centuries, laying the basis for European expansion after 1000.

Agricultural Innovations

Some of the major technological innovations improved agriculture. Three devices or practices spurred the higher grain yields that sparked population growth in Europe: the moldboard plower, the horseshoe, and the three-field system. The new plow and horshoe enabled farmers to turn and drain the heavy, wet soil of northern Europe. The three-field system meant that Europeans divided their fields into three parts and let only one-third lie fallow each year; they then increased their yield by planting winter and summer wheat in the other two fields. Peasants were also learning to plant more beans and other nitrogen-fixing crops, which returned nutrition to the soil and produced a better-balanced diet. All of these measures multiplied the food supply.

Harnessing Natural Power: Watermills and Windmills

Other innovations fostered the growth of industry. First invented in Roman times, watermills were built along rivers and streams to generate power. This technology spread widely in early medieval times, freeing up human and animal labor for other tasks. By 1056 more than 5,600 watermills in England provided power for such activities as sawing logs and grinding wheat into flour. By the 1100s, Europeans also used windmills, invented in Persia around 650, to generate power for such industries as grinding grain.

Feudalism and Manorialism

Historians define feudalism as a political arrangement characterized by a weak central monarchy ruling over smaller states or influential families that were largely autonomous but owed service obligations to the monarch. The ruler was a "lord," and his subordinates were vassals. Monarchs were lords to nobles, and nobles were lords to most of the common people. In medieval Europe, noble families often held large estates in exchange for paying homage and offering military service or labor to the royal governments. Likewise, warriors in a landowner's service and farmers living and working on the land also owed obligations to the landowner. Supported by Church leaders, this basic political and social formation was strongest in France, England, and parts of Italy.

Political Fragmentation in the Early Medieval Period

Despite the unifying role of the Christian church in creating a common culture and the accomplishments of strong rulers such as Charlemagne and Otto the Great, certain forces worked toward the fragmentation that characterized feudalism during the early medieval period. Roman roads had fallen into disrepair, disrupting transportation, and Europe remained largely rural. The most densely populated region, France, boasted a population of only 8 or 9 million people, and, as late as 1000, England had only 1.5 million. Europe as a whole was home to around 40 million by 950. By contrast, early Song China had around 100 million. These conditions made it difficult for even a strong ruler to maintain a powerful central government. Because both money and talent were scarce and land was the source of wealth, Charlemagne often rewarded his best soldiers and administrators

by giving them control over large areas of land. Vassals who held such grants of land, called benefices, took an oath of personal loyalty to the king and promised him military service. In return they had a virtually free hand to govern the territory, which led to political fragmentation.

Historians often use the concept of feudalism in a narrow sense of legal relations between lords and vassals. The term *fief* described the thing granted in a feudal contract, usually land. The vassal might also be obliged to provide hospitality to the ruler when he traveled around his kingdom. If a fief of land were large enough, as many were, the vassal could subdivide it and have vassals of his own. Thus feudalism allowed a king to rule a large country without personally administering it through his own paid officials.

Lectures in Medieval History (*http://www.vlib.us/medieval/lectures/*). Many useful essays for the general reader by a leading expert.

The Structure of Feudal Society

Feudal society included knights, armored military retainers who swore allegiance to their lord and who fought mostly on horseback. A large peasant class that was, for the most part, denied military and therefore political power, supported the warriors at the top. Knights had a rigid code of behavior, including a sense of duty and honor known as chivalry. A thirteenth-century French writer explained the chivalric ideal: "A knight must be hardy, courteous, generous, loyal and of fair speech; ferocious to his foe, frank and debonair to his friend. [He] has proved himself in arms and thereby won the praise of men."[5]

States and rival lords fought each other regularly, so knights were kept busy. But despite the dangers, the rewards could be great. For instance, one of the most renowned English knights, William Marshall (1145–1219), became very wealthy, an adviser to kings, and married a woman from an aristocratic family. The mounted cavalry was medieval Europe's chief fighting force, and the innovation that made it possible was the stirrup, which enabled the knight to stand when delivering a blow and contributed greatly to the knight's fighting power.

Manorial Economy and Serfdom

The rural medieval economy was based on manorialism, a system of autonomous, nearly self-sufficient agricultural estates. The roots were laid in late Roman imperial practices. As the Roman cities became expensive places to live, wealthy Romans retreated to their country estates and hired low-wage agricultural workers, who were also seeking security during dangerous times. Eventually these Roman states became the manors, the combination of farms and villages into which each territorial fief was divided.

The manors, often organized around a castle, were owned by nobles who had the right to the produce grown by the large class of hereditary serfs, peasants who were legally bound to their lord and tied to the land through the generations. Serfs tilled the lord's fields as well as their own and were given, instead of money, the use of the manor's resources, such as farming tools or crafts, and protection in the manor house or castle in case the settlement was attacked. Although serfs were not allowed to change their status or leave without permission, they were not the personal property of their lords, and they could not be dispossessed unless they failed to live up to their obligations. Serfs' security and stability were paid for with compliance and a lifetime of drudgery. Occasional peasant revolts, sometimes targeting the noblemen, indicated some dissatisfaction.

Slavery in Medieval Europe

Although serfdom gradually became far more pervasive, slavery did not disappear, and slave trading was a key part of the medieval economy. Slaves were used in England, where they constituted perhaps 10 percent of the population until the eleventh century, and in Italy and Spain. Complex networks of trade transported slaves all over Europe and the Middle East. The Carolingians and Venetians sold slaves from various European societies to the Arabs, while Vikings enslaved captives and also sold English and French slaves to Byzantium and Islamic Spain. By the 1400s, Arabs and Portuguese were selling some enslaved West Africans in southern Europe. The Church did not condemn slavery; indeed, leading Christian thinkers like St. Thomas Aquinas argued that slavery was morally justified and an economic necessity.

LO² Medieval Societies, Power, and Thought

The pluralism of religious, social, political, and economic institutions forged in early medieval Europe, combined with an unusually warm climate, spurred many changes between 1000 and 1300, centuries historians term the "High Middle Ages." Europeans experienced both exuberance and turmoil during this period: massive cathedrals with lofty spires were built, and the first universities were established. The power of the Roman church and its popes grew, fostering conflict with rulers and intellectuals. Varied conflicts, including the growing divergence between cities and countryside, helped reshape European society.

> ❝ City life and the money to be made attracted many people to places such as London and Paris. ❞

Medieval Cities, Towns, and Trade

European societies experienced considerable change during the High Middle Ages, including the growth of population, towns, and cities. Compared to Byzantium, Tang China, and the Islamic world, early medieval western Europe was economically underdeveloped, a reality reflected in the size of its cities: by 1000 Rome had only 35,000 people, Paris around 20,000, and London an insignificant 10,000. By contrast, the world's largest city, Baghdad, had 1 million people. However, between 1000 and 1300, improved nutrition spurred Europe's population to double to about 75 million, and western European cities increased in both population and importance. Milan and Paris grew to almost 100,000 during these three centuries.

Medieval Urban Life

A variety of characters inhabited the medieval city, and they increasingly operated outside the feudal structure. City life and the money to be made attracted many people to places such as London and Paris. A traditional German expression, "city air makes one free," referred to the fact that a serf who left the manor and was able to spend "a year and a day" in a city without being caught was considered legally free. City craftsmen and merchants organized themselves into guilds, collective fraternal organizations designed to protect members' economic interests and win exemptions from feudal obligations. Eventually cities had their

serfs
In medieval Europe, peasants legally bound to their lord and tied to the land through generations.

guilds
In medieval Europe, collective fraternal organizations of craftsmen and merchants designed to protect the economic interests of their members.

Organization of Feudal Society

own courts and other privileges of self-government. Rulers granted such privileges because of the great wealth that city commerce brought them.

In feudal society, people belonged to one of three categories, in order of importance: (1) "those who prayed" (churchmen, priests, and monks), (2) "those who fought" (aristocratic warriors and knights), and (3) "those who worked" (peasants and serfs). No matter how successful, merchants and bankers had no place in this hierarchy. People resented merchants for several reasons. For one, some traveled long distances to strange places that were inhabited by foreigners who might corrupt their integrity. For another, greed was considered a serious sin. Medieval people were particularly upset at merchants' and bankers' practice of loaning money at interest, which was regarded as usury because the lender was making a profit without doing any labor. But money lending was necessary to commerce, and even popes borrowed money at interest on occasion. While Italians became renowned as bankers, money-lending elsewhere was left largely to Jews, allowing Christians to benefit from borrowing money without committing the sin of usury.

A Medieval Town This painting shows a variety of town enterprises, including a tailor's shop, barbershop, and an apothecary.

Bibliothèque nationale de France

Broadening Trade Horizons

One of the clearest signs of economic expansion, and of declining prejudice against merchants, was the growth in trade and commerce around Europe and with Byzantium and Asia, which reached its peak between 1100 and 1350. Western Europeans shipped textiles, wines, olive oil, fruit, and timber to the East in return for luxury goods such as spices, silk, perfumes, and precious gems. Eastern Europeans exported grain, honey, fish, fur, and slaves, as well as raw materials such as iron, copper, tin, and lead. Major trading centers were located on the Mediterranean (Constantinople, Venice, Genoa), in the Low Countries (Bruges [broozh] and Amsterdam), and in Strassburg in the Rhineland, Nuremberg (NOOR-uhm-burg) in south Germany, and Basel (BAHZ-uhl) in Switzerland.

The wealth created in Europe fostered a commercial revolution and made merchants and bankers more influential. By the 1200s, commerce had become more central to the European economy than agriculture. Never again would western Europe have an economy that relied primarily on farming. The broad repercussions of the commercial revolution—(1) the rise of capitalism; (2) the incorporation of merchants as a vital social class; (3) stronger monarchies; and (4) the weakening of both feudalism and the Christian church—became clear only centuries later.

> "Western Europeans shipped textiles, wines, olive oil, fruit, and timber to the East in return for luxury goods such as spices, silk, perfumes, and precious gems."

CHRONOLOGY

The High Middle Ages, 1000–1300

987–1328	Capetian kings in France
1066	Norman conquest of England
1095–1272	Christian Crusades to reclaim Holy Land
1198–1216	High point of medieval papacy under Innocent III
1215	Signing of Magna Carta
1231	Beginning of Inquisition
1265	First English Parliament

courtly love
A standard of polite relationships between knights and ladies that arose in the 1100s in medieval Europe. Courtly love was celebrated in song by wandering troubadours.

Medieval Society: Insiders and Outsiders

Medieval society was patriarchal, though family life and gender relations varied with social status and local customs. Generally, men supported the family and women ran the household and raised children. Legally, marriage existed to protect legitimate children and guarantee property rights. Sons were considered more important than daughters, because sons passed on the family line, property, and name. Parents arranged most marriages. Relationships between men and women reflected the tensions between the church and secular society. From the church's point of view, marriage was a necessary evil that legitimized sex only for procreation, not pleasure. But rulers often flouted custom: Charlemagne enforced rigid Christian morality on his people while also marrying four times, having five mistresses, and siring eighteen children. By the 1100s, courtly love—a new standard of passionate but pure relationships between knights and ladies and celebrated in song by wandering troubadours—brought romance to male-female relations and elevated the status of aristocratic women. This model probably originated in Muslim Spain, where women poets flourished, and was passed on to French and Italian authors.

 **Medieval and Renaissance Europe: Primary Historical Documents** (*http://eudocs.lib.byu.edu/index.php/History_of_Medieval_%26_Renaissance_Europe:_Primary_Documents*) Many links to primary sources.

Women in Medieval Society

Medieval society had an almost contradictory view of women. On the one hand, gender stereotypes in the Bible led people to believe that women were subordinate to men and also led them into sin, as Eve did Adam. On the other hand, Mary, the Virgin Mother of Jesus, became one of the most popular objects of devotion. Many cathedrals were named after Notre Dame (NO-truh DAHM) ("Our Lady"). Furthermore, women could inherit property and pass it on to their children. Women worked in many occupations, including farming, ale making, small-scale trade, glassmaking, and the textile industry.

Pagans, Infidels, and Heretics

Medieval society was tightly ordered but also rife with tensions. Daily life was precarious for rich and poor alike, and violent crime remained common throughout the period, with disputes often ending in murder. Many tensions, however, arose because medieval society made a major distinction between Christians and "outsiders"—pagans, Muslims, Jews, heretics, and, eventually, homosexuals. No matter how poor or overworked medieval serfs were, they considered themselves superior to outsiders. By the High Middle Ages, Christians used the term *pagan* to describe Muslims, who reciprocated by calling Christians *infidels* (unbelievers). The drive to destroy all beliefs outside of the Christian mainstream eventually led to a long series of crusades against Islam and persecution of Jews.

Although Christians mostly tolerated the Jews before 1150, anti-Semitism soon increased dramatically as more Christians took up banking and marginalized Jewish rivals, and as Christians became more militant in asserting their faith. In 1182 the Jews were ordered to leave France, an expulsion imitated in other countries during the next three centuries. Numerous expelled Jews migrated to Poland and Byzantium, which developed large Jewish populations.

The disdain shown to Muslims and Jews was also directed at people considered to be heretics. Christians struggled with defining what was correct belief and what was heresy from the early centuries onward, and this concern intensified after 1200. Some devout Christians criticized church corruption, but church leaders tended to view any reformers challenging their power as heretics. As a result, they organized military attacks on the Albigensians (AL-buh-JEN-shunz), a group in southern France who criticized the church's material wealth, urged clerical poverty, and wanted the Bible to be translated from Latin into vernacular languages so that ordinary people could read it for themselves. The church's crusade destroyed the Albigensians.

The early Christian tolerance of homosexuality survived through the Early Middle Ages, but beginning in the thirteenth century, the church launched a violent campaign against heresy and unconventional behavior that often targeted people who were suspected of homosexuality. In 1250 homosexual behavior was legal in most of Europe; by 1300 it had become a capital offense everywhere except Germany and south Italy.

The Church as a Social and Political Force

The medieval Christian church claimed to help its members reach Heaven and avoid Hell, but the church of the High Middle Ages, contrary to today's understanding of the separation of church from state, was also a powerful social and political force. Indeed, the strong bonds that linked people to their clergy allowed popes, for a time at least, to challenge kings. The basis of clerical power was the administration of sacraments, rites that were the source of divine grace. Most medieval Christians measured the stages of their lives by sacraments such as baptism and matrimony. Medieval priests certified births and marriages and also collected taxes. They had enormous power, because they controlled both individuals' privileges in this life and their salvation in the next. The faithful believed that a person who had committed a serious sin without confessing it to a priest went straight to Hell. Priests and bishops had the power to deny someone the sacraments, and they could also excommunicate, or expel, a person from the church and its sacraments.

Clerical Deficiencies and Corruption

However, not all priests lived up to their responsibilities or growing expectations for celibacy, leading many people to have ambivalent attitudes toward the clergy. Many priests had so little education that they could barely recite the Latin necessary for the celebration of the Catholic liturgy, while others were corrupt and took bribes. Many priests and monks were married, a practice that reformist church leaders attempted to end between the eleventh and thirteenth centuries, because they felt priests should not be distracted by families or inheritance obligations. Nonetheless, even after the final ban, some priests were married in violation of church law while others kept mistresses.

In the eleventh century, reformers intensified their efforts to purify the church. New religious orders insisted that all monks remain celibate, while several German rulers revived the papacy by appointing a series of reform-minded men to the position. In addition to mandating clerical celibacy, these popes tried to end simony (SIGH-muh-nee), a common practice whereby wealthy families paid to have their sons appointed bishops. In an attempt to keep European rulers from interfering in papal elections, in 1059 the College of Cardinals was established to elect the pope. Roman law was made the basis of church law, because it referred all matters to the person at the top, which fit the Church's hierarchy well.

The Growth of Papal Authority

The growing political power of the papacy was made clear during the eleventh and twelfth centuries, when a major church–state conflict erupted over the appointment of bishops. For centuries, rulers had appointed their leading nobles to key church offices. But in 1075, Pope Gregory VII (ca. 1020–1085), hoping to change this custom, excommunicated the German emperor for appointing the archbishop of Milan (mi-LAHN) in north Italy. The struggle was not resolved until 1122, when the two leaders agreed that both emperor and pope would invest new bishops with the symbols of authority. Eventually, increasing papal power led to decentralized government and political warfare in the German-speaking lands.

Another pope, Innocent III (r. 1198–1216), dramatically extended papal authority over secular rulers. He used his sacramental authority to control many rulers of western Europe, for example, by requiring the king of France to take back a wife he had divorced. This pope also received as honorary fiefs various states, among them Aragon (AR-uh-GON) (in Spain), Denmark, England, and Poland. In 1215 Innocent III moved against non-Christians by requiring Jews to wear distinctive clothing, and he also aggressively punished "heretical depravity."

The Holy Inquisition

The papal drive to investigate and eliminate heresy led to the Holy Inquisition, a church court created in 1231. Friars from several religious orders tried thousands of people with views outside the mainstream, and popes sanctioned torture and starvation to induce confessions. Those found guilty faced a range of punishments, including penances, banishment, prison, mutilation, and death. Over the next two centuries, several thousand people were executed. The most notorious inquisition began, under state rather than church control, in Spain in 1478, and perpetrated brutal persecution of Jews and Muslims; at least two thousand people were burned at the stake. The inquisitions continued into the 1600s and also included bans on books that were viewed as dangerous to the faith.

Church and Environment

To many Christian thinkers, God planned and ordered the world, including the natural environment, explicitly for human benefit, and human progress necessitated exploiting nature. Thus, they believed, it was God's will that people improved land by clearing forests and wetlands, which some monasteries did with great enthusiasm. The crass medieval attitude toward nature gave ideological justification for the great technological and economic development to later emerge in the West, but also caused environmental problems. Some Christian and Jewish thinkers, such as the eighth-century English theologian Bede, dissented from these views and affirmed that nature was also God's creation and required care and stewardship.

New European States and Crusades

Threatened by the increase in papal power, and with less need for feudal vassals as economies grew, rulers sought to gain more control over their lands (see Map 14.2). The English kings were most successful at this. After leading the Norman conquest of England in 1066, William of Normandy (1027–1087) had divided the land among his chief vassals. But by the 1100s, William's successors were taking authority away from the local nobility and shifting it to the king's representatives. Kings appointed justices and officials to collect taxes and closely supervise local officials. One of the strongest kings, Henry II (r. 1154–1189), expanded the power of the royal courts over feudal and church courts. He also invaded Ireland in 1171 and established English control of the eastern region centered on Dublin.

Interactive Map

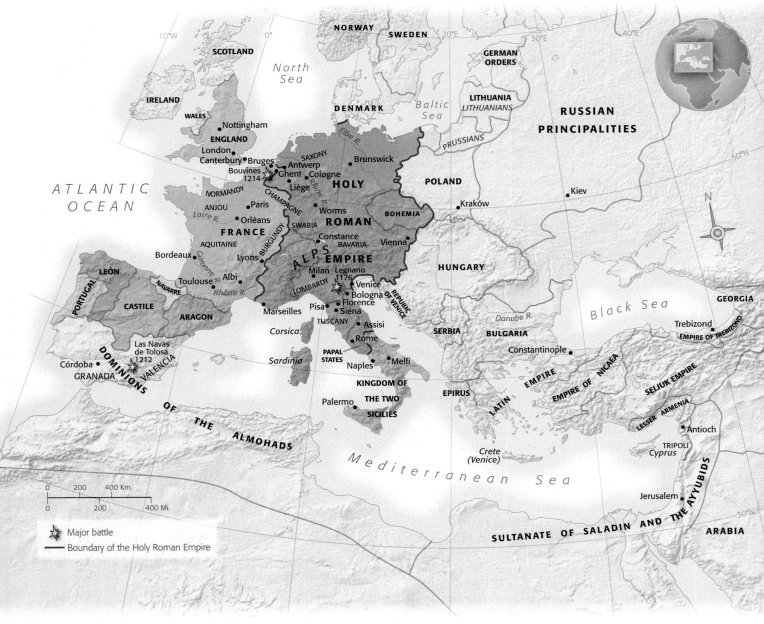

Major battle

—— Boundary of the Holy Roman Empire

Map 14.2
Medieval Europe, 900–1300

During the High Middle Ages, the Holy Roman Empire, comprised of dozens of smaller states, covered much of what is today Germany, Austria, eastern France, and northern Italy. France, England, Hungary, and Poland were also major states.

© Cengage Learning

The Seed-plot of Representative Government

However, while seeking to strengthen royal power, some of Henry II's successors unintentionally laid the foundations for a later representative government in England. John weakened royal power in 1215 by signing the Magna Carta (MAG-nuh KAHR-tuh), or "Great Charter," an agreement that

Magna Carta: The Great Charter of Liberties Learn what rights and liberties the English nobility, on behalf of all free Englishmen, forced King John to grant them in 1215.

limited the feudal rights of the king and his officials while protecting the rights of the church, lords, and merchants. King John promised not to tax his vassals unless the taxes were sanctioned by custom or approved by his barons. The Magna Carta was later used to support the notion that rulers had to have the consent of their subjects, one of the foundations of modern English constitutional monarchy.

Henry III (r. 1216–1272) also contributed unwittingly to representative government. His incessant demand for taxes to fight foreign wars made him unpopular and, in 1265, rebellious barons called together a parliament (literally, a "speaking place") that included non-aristocrats to demand that the king consider their views. This parliament became the model for later meetings called by kings to secure approval of their policies.

The Avignon Papacy and the Ascendance of France

In France, the Capetians (kuh-PEE-shuhnz), a dynasty that succeeded the Carolingians (987–1328), expanded their territory and increased control over their many vassals. King Philip II (r. 1180–1223), for example, gained control over Normandy and strengthened the royal bureaucracy. Louis IX, or St. Louis (r. 1226–1270), a pious man who curbed the power of the nobility while persecuting heretics and Jews, appointed inspectors to report to him any injustices inflicted by his officials. But Philip the Fair (r. 1285–1314) may have had the most impact on France and Europe. He added to the list of lands held directly by the French monarchy, and raised money for his wars by arresting all Jews and seizing their property before expelling them from the kingdom. He also had the leaders of a militant religious order,

Explore the Middle Ages as either a Crusader or a Muslim in this interactive simulation.

the Knights Templar (TEM-plahr), burned at the stake as heretics so that he could default on a loan they had given him.

When Pope Boniface VIII (r. 1294–1303) challenged Philip's growing power, Philip accused the pope of sexual perversion and murder and sent a force to Italy to arrest him. Townspeople rescued the pope by driving French troops away, but Boniface died soon after. For the next seventy years (1305–1377), the College of Cardinals, bowing to French pressure, elected popes, most of them French, who chose to live in the papal territory of Avignon (ah-vee-NYON) in southern France. Philip's ruthless action showed that the days of papal control over European rulers were ending. By the late 1200s, France had emerged as the strongest kingdom in western Europe.

The Fragmentation of Germany and Italy

German rulers had the least success in centralizing their lands, largely because they spent too much time trying to control Italy. In addition, the feudal nobility in Germany remained powerful. Several members of the Hohenstaufen (HO-uhn-SHTOU-fuhn) dynasty, who served as Holy Roman Emperors between 1152 and 1254, made the last attempt to establish a strong monarchy. Frederick I (r. 1154–1190) reasserted his authority as Holy Roman Emperor over the wealthy cities in northern Italy, but this involved full-scale war with the pope, who organized an Italian coalition that defeated Frederick's forces. Frederick I's successors gradually lost power to German princes, and German lands became more divided than ever. It would be seven hundred years before Italy and Germany finally achieved territorial unity.

The Crusades

Perhaps the most significant military initiatives of the medieval period were the Crusades, a series of military expeditions or holy wars between 1095 and 1272 to reclaim the Christian "Holy Land," Palestine, from Muslim control (see Chapter 10). Affluent European Christians had long made pilgrimages to Jerusalem and considered the city part of their world. The crusading began after the Byzantine emperor sought Christian help to dislodge his rivals, the Muslim Seljuk Turks, who had gained domination over much of western Asia. Medieval Christians had a militant zeal to spread their faith and destroy Islam, but while many crusaders were undoubtedly motivated by sincere religious beliefs, these often became mixed with economic motives and political rivalries.

In 1095 Pope Urban II urged Christian rulers to unite to protect the Christian holy sites, prompting the first of nine crusades by land and sea. Fabricating or exaggerating stories of Muslim atrocities against Christians, he proclaimed that the Turks "have completely destroyed some of God's churches and they have converted others to the uses of their own cult. They ruin the altars with filth and defilement. They are pleased to kill others. And what shall I say about the shocking rape of the women."[6] Various kings, nobles, and bishops joined the cause. Some crusaders temporarily occupied parts of the Holy Land, such as Jerusalem, even establishing crusader-led states, but eventually they were forced out. Other crusaders were diverted to ransacking Constantinople or Egypt.

Annals Read a harrowing, firsthand account of the pillage of Constantinople by western crusaders on April 13, 1204.

While they looted and pillaged cities, in many cases the crusaders also slaughtered thousands of people, including Muslims, Jews, and Byzantine Christians. They burned mosques and synagogues, sometimes with hundreds of people inside. The Muslim defenders often responded by killing local Christians. The streets of Jerusalem, it was said, ran ankle-deep in blood. Crusaders even slaughtered twelve thousand Jews in Germany in 1096. As a result of their depredations, they were often viewed by non-Christians as pirates and terrorists rather than the religious idealists they believed themselves to be. In the thirteenth century, the crusades dissipated, but they left a bitter heritage between Christian and Muslim societies.

Read about Heloise, the French scholar and nun who had a scandalous love affair with her teacher, Peter Abelard, at the school of the Notre Dame Cathedral.

Intellectual Life and Literature

Some of the tensions of the High Middle Ages derived from robust intellectual debates involving theologians, philosophers, and writers. By the twelfth century, guilds of scholars were forming centers of higher

> "In the thirteenth century, the crusades dissipated, but they left a bitter heritage between Christian and Muslim societies."

learning in some medieval cities. Universities existed earlier in India and the Islamic world, but they mostly specialized in religious studies; in the European universities, students gathered to study not only religion but also secular knowledge, such as the pagan ideas of Aristotle as passed on by Jewish and Arab scholars. The most famous European universities were at Paris, France; Oxford, England; and Salerno (suh-LUR-no) and Bologna (boe-LOAN-yuh) in Italy. They grew out of cathedral or monastic schools where students had learned the "seven liberal arts": astronomy, geometry, arithmetic, music, grammar, rhetoric, and logic. At the new universities, students also then specialized in higher study of medicine, law, or philosophy.

Thomas Aquinas: Reconciling Reason and Faith

The medieval study of philosophy, especially the heated debates over the relative importance of faith and reason, contributed much to later Western thought. Some thinkers reclaimed the classical tradition of rational thought, often against church opposition. The most elaborate attempt to reconcile faith and reason was made by Thomas Aquinas (uh-KWINE-uhs) (1225–1274), an Italian monk of the Dominican (duh-MIN-i-kuhn) order and professor at the University of Paris who believed that much could be determined by reason, even the existence of God, but that at some point a believer had to accept on faith many mysteries. Reflecting medieval views, he also argued that human domination over nature was part of a divine plan and that women were passive and incapable of moral perfection.

Literature and Court Life

Literature, like many other aspects of life during the High Middle Ages, was diverse and contradictory. For example, the *Song of Roland*, written down in France in the twelfth century, described the great deeds of a loyal knight who died while guarding the rear of Charlemagne's army. But the warlike and masculine tone of the epic *Song of Roland* contrasted with the many contemporary French lyric poems and stories that exalted romantic love as an ideal in a society that generally arranged marriages for distinctly non-romantic reasons. Writers all over Europe took up the Celtic legend of the British King Arthur and his court. In some versions, Arthur's wife, Guinevere (GWIN-uh-veer), and his best friend, Lancelot, followed their hearts and became doomed lovers.

LO³ Eastern Europe: Byzantines, Slavs, and Mongols

Byzantium, and the eastern European societies it influenced, remained very distinct from western Europe, despite their shared belief in the Christian religion and long-standing trade connections. Byzantine society demonstrated a remarkable longevity against the odds. From the sixth century onward, the Byzantine Empire fought for its life and, beginning in the eleventh century, experienced steady political decline until its final defeat by the Ottoman Turks in 1453. In the meantime, however, it served as a buffer zone protecting central and western Europe against

> 66 Byzantium faced nearly continuous pressure from neighboring peoples. 99

Muslim, Slavic, and Mongol invaders. Most of the Slavic societies in eastern Europe adopted Eastern Orthodox Christianity, and one of these, the Russians, eventually created a powerful state.

Byzantium and Its Eurasian Rivals

Byzantium faced nearly continuous pressure from neighboring peoples. In the sixth and seventh centuries, the Sassanian Persians and Byzantines fought a series of wars that weakened both empires and made Arab conquest easier. The Arabs were at the walls of Constantinople in 673 and 717, but the Byzantines survived both attacks. Eventually the Byzantines stabilized their frontier with the Arabs but were faced with other enemies. Various Slavic peoples had begun moving into eastern Europe in late Roman times, and by the early Middle Ages, they were the dominant population in a vast region stretching north from Greece to the eastern Baltic and eastward through Russia.

The major Slavic challenges to Byzantium came from the Bulgars and Serbs. One of the Byzantine rulers, known as "Basil the Bulgar-slayer," defeated a Bulgar army in 1014 and blinded 15,000 Bulgarian prisoners of war before releasing them to return home. The defeat of the Bulgars, who had controlled considerable territory, opened the door to the Serbs, who set up several small states in the Balkans. During the eleventh century, one Serbian state expanded its power, bringing it into conflict with Byzantium. After a series of wars, the Ottoman Turks conquered the Serbs in 1441.

 Byzantium: Byzantine Studies on the Internet (http://www.fordham.edu/halsall/byzantium/index.html) Contains useful texts, images, essays, and bibliography.

Decline and Fall of Byzantium

Byzantine political fortunes began to decline seriously by the late eleventh century. In 1071, Byzantine forces were driven from southern Italy by Norman knights, and in 1091, at the Battle of Manzikert (MANZ-ih-kuhrt), they were defeated by Seljuk Turks in eastern Anatolia. From that point on, the shrunken Byzantine territories faced attacks from both east and west. Turks soon completed the conquest of Anatolia and left Constantinople a beleaguered fortress. Despite

---

CHRONOLOGY

Byzantium, Russia, and Eastern Europe, 600–1500

632	First Arab expansion into the Byzantine Empire
825	First Swedish Viking bases in Russia
863	Cyrillic alphabet created
988	Conversion of Vladimir of Kiev to Christianity
1054	Schism between Roman and Byzantine churches
1091	Battle of Manzikert
1237–1241	Mongol invasions of Russia and eastern Europe
1389	Ottoman Turk defeat of Serbs
1453	Ottoman Turk conquest of Constantinople

An Orthodox Church in Novgorod, Russia The distinctive architecture of this church represents the fusion of Slavic, Byzantine, and Viking influences.

RIA Novotsi

A merchant class remained a vital and accepted part of Byzantine life, because Constantinople lay astride the principal trade routes between Europe and Asia. Slave traders thrived by shipping eastern European slaves, many of them Slavs from the Black Sea region, from Constantinople to be sold in the Mediterranean. Taxes from this commercial activity enriched the treasury, and Byzantine coins were used around Eurasia.

Byzantine Distinctiveness Church and state were intertwined, and Christianity and its rituals influenced all aspects of Byzantine society. Unlike in western Europe, rulers dominated the church and regularly interfered in church affairs. The culture was artistically rich, filled with lengthy religious ceremonies and an intense prayer life, especially in the monasteries. Byzantines engaged in hair-splitting theological disputes, bitterly disagreeing over the use of icons, painted images of holy figures, and the origin of the Holy Spirit. Byzantine Christians also refused to recognize the supreme position of the bishop of Rome over other bishops. These conflicts were critical issues in the final split between the Roman Catholic and Greek Orthodox Churches, which came when the pope and the patriarch of Constantinople angrily excommunicated each other in 1054. Like the Roman church, the Byzantine church supported male power, but a few women were influential, including Empress Irene, who ruled Byzantium for two decades (780–802), and Byzantium's best-known historian, the princess Anna Comnena (1083–1148).

the divide between the Roman and Greek churches, the Byzantines requested the help of western knights to defend Byzantine territories against the Turks. In 1204, bribed by the Venetians (who were Byzantine trading rivals), western crusaders conquered Constantinople and governed it until forced out in 1261. Capitalizing on these disasters, the expanding Ottoman Turks finally conquered Constantinople and the surrounding territory in 1453, ending the Byzantine state and renaming the capital city Istanbul.

> 66 Church and state were intertwined, and Christianity and its rituals influenced all aspects of Byzantine society. 99

Byzantine Economy, Religion, and Society

Despite its many political and military misfortunes, the Byzantine Empire survived as long as it did in part because of its economic and religious strengths.

The Spread of Byzantine Culture The Byzantines held off political foes long enough so that Byzantine culture, stimulated by trading contacts as well as war, could spread north and east. This achievement allowed Byzantine religion and culture to survive the defeat of the empire. The differences between eastern and western versions of Christianity gave some of the eastern European peoples a choice. In the ninth century, two Byzantine brothers, known later as Saints Cyril and Methodius (mi-THO-dee-uhs), traveled east of the German lands to convert the Slavs to eastern Christianity. The brothers devised an alphabet, now known as Cyrillic (suh-RILL-ik), for the Slavs, and Cyril began translating the Bible and other church writings from Greek into Slavic. Some Slavs eventually adopted aspects of Byzantine culture, including Orthodox Christianity, while others adopted Roman Catholicism. Byzantium greatly influenced the Russians and other Slavs. They learned their Christian culture and their politics from a society in which an autocratic emperor dominated and in which church and state remained closely connected. Eastern and western European cultures remain distinct even today.

Russians and Mongols

The Russians descended from a people known as the Rus (roos), whose capital was at Kiev (KEE-yev), in today's Ukraine (you-CRANE). Swedish Vikings, who founded trading cities in the Slavic regions beginning around 825, had become the Rus ruling class, both trading with and raiding the Byzantines and neighboring societies. Viking trade networks connected various states situated on the great Russian and Ukrainian plains, and by the tenth century the Vikings had been assimilated by the majority Slavs. From the tenth to the twelfth centuries, the Russian people expanded. Their settlements went northward as far as Novgorod (NOHV-goh-rod), from which timber was shipped south through Kiev to the Black Sea. The Rus ruler Vladimir (VLAD-ih-mir) I (ca. 956–1015) in Kiev opened the doors to Byzantine influence. Vladimir had several wives and eight hundred concubines but sought marriage to a Byzantine prin-

> "The Byzantines held off political foes long enough so that Byzantine culture, stimulated by trading contacts as well as war, could spread north and east."

> 66 By the time western Europeans were beginning to hear rumors about the brutal Mongols, the Russians were already encountering Mongol armies. 99

cess. After she refused to marry a pagan polygamist, he agreed to accept Orthodox Christianity in 988 and make her his only wife. When Vladimir ordered his men to the Dnieper (d-NYEP-er) River in Kiev to be baptized, he unwittingly guaranteed that a large part of eastern Europe would become Eastern Orthodox.

The Mongols in Russia

By the time western Europeans were beginning to hear rumors about the brutal Mongols, the Russians were already encountering Mongol armies. Under their great leader Genghis Khan, Mongol armies conquered Central Asia, much of Russia, and parts of China and the Middle East (see Chapters 10 and 11). Mongol armies repeatedly sacked Russian cities beginning in 1237. Until the fifteenth century, most Russians remained subject to the Mongols, and especially to the Golden Horde, a Mongol state on the lower Volga River.

The World of the Vikings (*http://www .worldofthevikings .com*). Contains many links to texts, images, and essays on the Vikings.

Western Europe was fortunate to escape Mongol conquest. In 1241, several large Mongol armies moved far into Europe, crushing both Polish and Hungarian forces sent against them. Soon they stood on the banks of the Danube contemplating an invasion into German lands. But the Germans and European societies farther west were spared, perhaps because Mongol generals decided to return to Mongolia when they heard of the death of the Mongol leader, Ogodei, the son of Genghis Khan. Had the Mongols continued westward, the history of Europe might have been very different.

Moscow: The Third Rome

Eventually Muscovy became the dominant Russian state as Mongol political power declined and the head of the Russian Orthodox Church, appointed by the patriarch of Constantinople, moved from Kiev to Moscow. During the reign of Ivan III (1440–1505), Muscovy escaped Mongol control and established domination over other Russian states. Ivan began to call himself *czar* (meaning "Caesar") to indicate his superiority over lesser rulers, and he married the niece of the last Byzantine emperor. The Russian Orthodox Church had broken its connection with the patriarch of Constantinople even before the fall of the Byzantine capital, and during Ivan's reign, Russian clergy began referring to Moscow as the Third Rome, successor to Constantinople and Rome, and the home of the purest version of Christianity. The Russians also expanded into the territories of their most powerful rivals, the Catholic Lithuanians, adding religious antagonisms to other tensions between states and ethnic groups in eastern Europe.

LO⁴ Late Medieval Europe and the Roots of Expansion

The Late Middle Ages, between 1300 and 1500, were a period of transition in western Europe. For a century the population shrunk dramatically as a result of famine, plague, and warfare, which contributed to the gradual end of feudalism. Politically, royal power increased in many places at the expense of the feudal nobility. The Roman church also lost influence as a profound moral crisis led to a questioning of church practices and beliefs. Many shared the pessimism of the French writer who lamented that "all mirth is lost. All hearts have been taken by storm, by sadness and melancholy."[7] Yet, the ferment fostered intellectual and cultural creativity, European trade rose, and brave mariners began exploring the world beyond Europe.

The Black Death and Social Change

Late medieval Europe was not a happy place, ravaged as it was by several disasters, including famine, disease, and war. Europe's climate turned colder about 1300, fostering what scholars call "the Little Ice Age." As a result, for example, the Norse farming settlements in Greenland collapsed from deforestation, expanding glaciers, and conflict with the local Inuit for scarce resources. Cooler temperatures also shortened the European growing season by several weeks, causing serious food shortages and famine.

> 66 Late medieval Europe was not a happy place, ravaged as it was by several disasters, including famine, disease, and war. 99

The Black Death

Between the mid-fourteenth and early fifteenth centuries, Europe also repeatedly suffered from the Black Death, a terrible *pandemic*, or massive epidemic that crossed many regions. The Black Death was named for the black bruises that appeared under the skin in one form of the disease. In 1347, a trading ship coming from the Black Sea limped into the harbor of Messina (mi-SEE-nuh) in Sicily with all of the crew either dead or dying. It had picked up a deadly infection spread by fleas that lived on black rats aboard ship. Most historians believe the infection was bubonic plague, perhaps mixed with pneumonic (noo-MON-ik) plague. The pandemic caused unprecedented death and suffering as it spread along and disrupted the networks of exchange all over Eurasia and North Africa. Within a year, this plague had spread throughout southern Europe, and by 1349 it had reached the Baltic Sea.

The Black Death, during its peak years from 1348 to 1350, had terrible effects, killing one-third of all Europeans. More than 65 percent of the population in some congested cities (such as Venice, Florence, and Paris) died, and Europe's overall population in the fourteenth century dropped from around 70 to 75 million to some 45 to 50 million people. Many millions were killed by either a severe and fast-acting respiratory infection or by swelling and internal bleeding. Pope Clement VI wrote about the 1348 outbreak that "the living were barely sufficient to bury the dead, or so horrified as to avoid the task. So great a terror seized nearly everyone."[8] Those who survived developed some immunity: although the Black Death recurred for decades, up to about a century, it killed fewer people each time.

Reconfiguring European Society after the Plague

The troubles reshaped European social patterns. The plague struck all classes, but the upper classes, already weakened by royal centralization, may have suffered the greatest long-term effects. With far fewer peasants alive to

A Literary View of Late Medieval People

The English writer Geoffrey Chaucer (ca. 1340–1400) wrote one of the best-known books of the Late Middle Ages, *The Canterbury Tales*, set in the time of the Black Death. Born in London, Chaucer was a cosmopolitan poet, soldier, and diplomat who served in the English Parliament and was familiar with French and Italian intellectual and cultural trends. His writings reflected these trends while also strongly influencing spoken and written English. *The Canterbury Tales* also offered a witty and sophisticated picture of English society. This excerpt presents stereotypical and satirical views of various pilgrims on their way to visit Canterbury, the seat of church power in England.

The knight there was, and he was a worthy man, Who, from the moment that he first began To ride about the world, loved chivalry, Truth, honor, freedom, and all courtesy. . . . Of mortal battles he had fought fifteen . . . And always won he sovereign fame for prize . . . He never yet had any vileness said [about him] in all his life . . . He was a truly perfect, gentle knight. . . .

There was also a nun, a prioress, Who, in her smiling, modest was and coy . . . At table she had been well taught withal, And never from her lips let morels fall, Nor dipped her fingers deep in sauce, but ate With so much care the food upon her plate That never driblet fell upon her breast. In courtesy she had delight and zest. . . .

A monk there was, one made for mastery [and loved hunting] . . . A manly man, to be an abbot able. Full many a blooded horse had he in stable: And when he rode men might his bridle hear A-jingling in the whistling wind as clear, Aye, and as loud as does the chapel bell Where this brave monk was of the cell. . . . This said monk let such lowly old things [strict old monastic rules] slowly pace And followed new world manners in their place. What? Should he study as a madman would Upon a book in cloister cell? Or yet, go labor with his hands and . . . sweat [as St. Augustine commanded]? . . .

There was a merchant with forked beard, and girt . . . Upon his head a Flemish beaver hat; His boots were fastened rather elegantly. He spoke [his opinions] pompously, Stressing the times when he had won, not lost [his profits] . . . At money changing he could make a crown. This worthy man kept all his wits well set; There was no one could say he was in debt, So well he governed all his trade affairs. . . .

There was a good man of religion, too, A country parson, poor . . . but rich he was in holy thought and work. He was also a learned man also [a scholar] . . . who Christ's own Gospel truly sought to preach. Devoutly his parisoner's would he teach . . . Benign he was and wondrous diligent, Patient in adverse times and well content . . . But rather would he give . . . unto those poor parishioners about, Part of his income, even of his goods . . . That first he wrought and after words he taught [first he practiced, then he preached]. . . .

Thinking About the Reading

1. What are the various clerical stereotypes presented?
2. How is the merchant portrayed?

Source: General Prologue to Geoffrey Chaucer's *Canterbury Tales*, electronic edition prepared by Edwin Duncan (http:www.towson.edu/~duncan/chaucer/titlepage.htm)

Tande p̄ ꝑ ꝼragem lpīm marimā luct ieiunia et
pīnas graues ꝑ ꝓcessionalē cunta ꝑ roma cum
unuila plebe et clero apparet angelus sanguino
lenai ense inagina reponens sup palaciu magn⁹

Praying for Relief This image of survivors carrying away plague victims in Rome was commissioned by a French duke for an illuminated book in the early 1400s. It illustrates the despair and devastating loss of life caused by the Black Death, especially in cities.

till the fields, those who were left asked for more privileges or more money or both. Peasant revolts demanding an end to serfdom increased, most notably in France in 1358 and in England in 1381. Although not successful, these uprisings demonstrated that the lower classes had some collective power.

Meanwhile, some people challenged social norms. For example, in addition to writing works of history, ethics, and poetry, the French author Christine of Pisan (1364–ca. 1430) criticized women's position in society, writing that "those who blame women out of jealousy are those wicked men who have seen many women of greater intelligence and nobler conduct than they themselves possess."[9] Some literature, such as the fiction of the fourteenth-century English writer Geoffrey Chaucer (CHAW-suhr), reflected the changing social customs (see Witness to the Past: A Literary View of Late Medieval People).

As the Black Death took its toll, the impact on western and eastern Europe proved quite different. Because eastern Europe had fewer cities and more villages, fewer peasants died. Indeed, Poland, Lithuania, and eastern Germany experienced little labor shortage after 1350. Also, because the ruling monarchs in these eastern areas were weaker, the aristocracy was able to impose serfdom on many of their peasants, creating large agricultural estates in northeast Europe. The eastern European nobility were actually strengthened socially and politically by the Black Death, while their western European counterparts were weakened by labor shortages and higher costs. In western Europe, as cities recovered, rulers strengthened their central governments, because the landed aristocrats were too weak to stop them.

Warfare and Political Centralization

Warfare in late medieval Europe, which was common, generally increased the power of kings and states as opposed to the nobility (see Map 14.3). The intermittent fighting between English and French troops known as the Hundred Years' War (1337–1453) increased royal power in France and also, eventually, in England. This war, caused by the English kings' desire to hold on to their feudal lands in France, went through several phases before the French finally claimed victory. At first the English were victorious by using their new weapon, the longbow, which launched arrows powerful enough to pierce the armor of French mounted knights. This weapon, used by trained commoners, diminished the knights as an effective fighting force.

 Interactive Map

During the war's final stage (1429–1453), the French recovered their land, aided by Jeanne d'Arc (zhahn DAHRK) (Joan of Arc, ca. 1412–1431), a sixteen-year-old peasant who believed that voices from saints told her to lead troops into battle. Led by Jeanne, the French broke the English siege of the city of Orleans (or-lay-AHN) and slowly recovered most of the English-held territory in France. Jeanne, meanwhile, was captured, tried by the English as a witch, and burned at the stake.

"Late medieval Europe was not a happy place, ravaged as it was by several disasters, including famine, disease, and war."

The French kings were the clearest victors in the Hundred Years' War. During the conflict's final stages, the monarchs introduced new direct taxes and reorganized the royal armies, weakening the aristocracy. In England, military defeat fostered a long conflict between two rival royal houses, the War of the Roses (1455–1485), which ended with Henry VII founding a new Tudor (TOO-duhr) dynasty. The Tudors established England as a world power during the 1500s.

The Reconquista: Driving the Muslims from Spain

Royal power also increased during the late 1400s in Spain. In 1085 Christians began the long reconquest of the peninsula from Muslims. By 1249 they had reclaimed Portugal, and by the 1300s, Spanish Christians had displaced all of the Muslim states except for Granada (gruh-NAH-duh) in the far south. In 1469 the two largest kingdoms were united when King Ferdinand of Aragon married his cousin, Isabella of Castile (kas-TEEL). These monarchs finally crushed Granada in 1492, the same year that, obsessed with religious uniformity and heresy, they expelled the Jews from Spain. It was also the year they sponsored the first trans-Atlantic voyage by the Italian mariner, Christopher Columbus.

The House of Habsburg

In contrast to France and England, the nobility remained strong in the Holy Roman Empire, which included much of the German-speaking lands and parts of Italy. The Habsburg (HABZ-berg) family, who took power in 1273, were unable to create a strong centralized state. In 1356 they issued an imperial edict that reduced the pope's influence over the election of Holy Roman Emperors, but that also confirmed the power of the princes over the emperor. During the coming centuries, Habsburg rulers concentrated on increasing the personal territorial holdings of their family instead of strengthening their political power. In the later 1400s, by royal marriage alliances, they gained control of the Netherlands and, through their links to the Spanish throne, much of southern Italy.

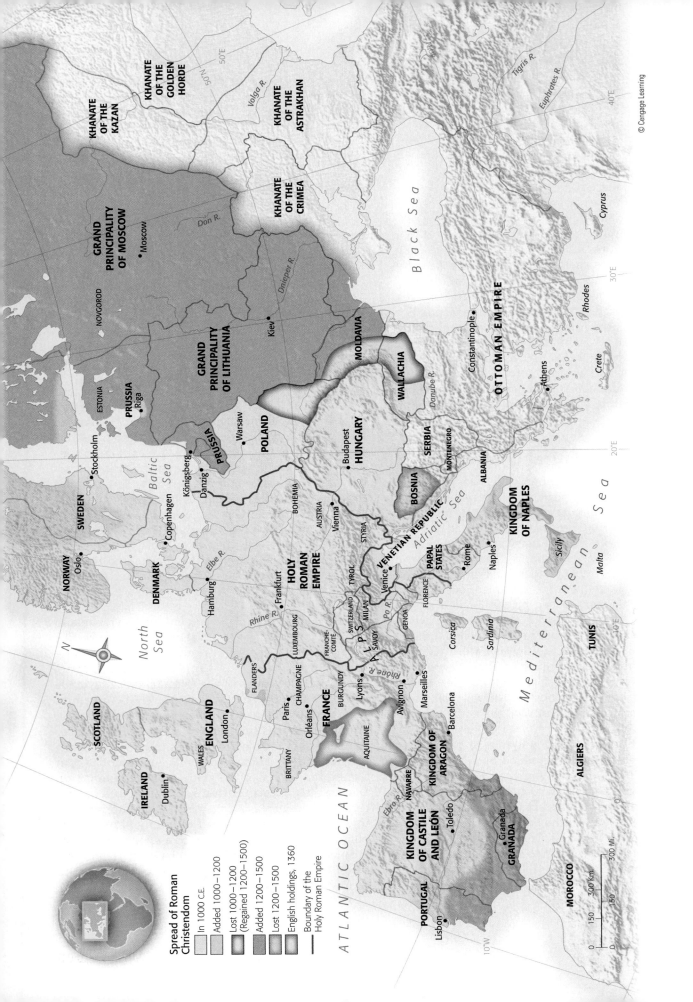

Spread of Roman Christendom

In 1000 C.E.

Added 1000–1200

Lost 1000–1200 (Regained 1200–1500)

Added 1200–1500

Lost 1200–1500

English holdings, 1360

Boundary of the Holy Roman Empire

© Cengage Learning

Crisis and Renaissance

Between 1300 and 1500, papal political power and the Roman church entered a period of decline, partly because of moral and political corruption. Many within the church complained about the buying of church offices and favoritism to relatives. These led to other abuses, such as absenteeism. When a man became bishop of more than one diocese so that he could collect the extra revenue, he was necessarily absent from one or other of his jobs. In addition, skeptics viewed practices such as venerating holy relics associated with Jesus, Mary, or saints and going on pilgrimages as superstition that encouraged fraud. Cynics muttered that there were enough pieces of the "true cross" around to build a cathedral.

The "Great Schism"

Papal prestige steadily declined after the popes moved to Avignon in southern France (1309–1377). The Avignon popes increased their revenues by requiring that candidates for bishop had to pay a large sum to the papal treasury in advance. When the papacy finally returned to Rome, two men claimed to be the rightful pope: one claimant moved back to Avignon and was supported by the French, and the other stayed in Rome, supported by the English. Europeans picked sides in this Great Schism (1378–1417), as the split between popes was called. Although the split ended in 1415, much damage had been done to the papacy's remaining prestige. After a council of bishops in the mid-1400s tried to replace papal monarchy with a reformed church government, popes refused to call any further councils.

Opening the East

The Late Middle Ages was also a time of new innovations, some of which derived from European contacts with Asia and Africa. The Mongols reenergized the Silk Road and Eurasian trade, allowing many useful inventions and ideas to flow west to Europe from China and western Asia. Some of these inventions, such as printing, gunpowder, and the compass, eventually revolutionized European technology. Furthermore, Muslims and Europeans vigorously traded not only goods but also ideas and art. Europeans, especially Italians, imported spices, carpets, silks, porcelain, glassware, and even painting supplies from the bazaars of Muslim Spain, Ottoman Turkey, Mamluk Egypt, and Persia. The cosmopolitan Ottoman ruler Mehmed (MAY-met) the Conqueror (1430–1481), whose armies had seized Constantinople, read and published Greek and Latin books, encouraged mapmaking, and invited Italians to work in the new Ottoman capital, Istanbul (formerly Constantinople). By the later 1400s, the Portuguese brought back artworks and fabrics from West Africa and the Kongo that also influenced European artists.

Some of these imported ideas and products may have contributed to the dramatic flowering of arts and learning later known as the Renaissance, or "rebirth," which began in the Italian city-states around 1350 and intensified throughout the 1400s and 1500s, spreading to other societies (see Chapter 15). In the main Renaissance center in the 1400s, Florence, artists and thinkers rediscovered the ideas of the Classical Greeks and Romans. Because it emphasized humanity, worldly concerns, and reason rather than religious ideals, Renaissance philosophy was called humanism.

The books of Dante Alighieri (DAHN-tay ah-lee-GYEH-ree) (1265–1321), especially *The Divine Comedy*, promoted vernacular language, in this case Italian, rather than Latin, and attacked the pope. The writer Giovanni Boccaccio (jo-VAH-nee boh-KAH-chee-oh) (1313–1375), in his novel *Decameron*, emphasized love and reason rather than faith. In the 1400s, painters in Italy and the Netherlands depicted space and the human figure realistically. Renaissance artists and writers emphasized tolerance of diverse views and new ideals of beauty, thus weakening the influence of the church among many educated people. The Renaissance, which brought hope to a gloomy time, eventually spread into northern Europe in the 1500s.

> ❝ The Late Middle Ages was also a time of new innovations, some of which derived from European contacts with Asia and Africa. ❞

Map 14.3 <<
Europe, 1400–1500

During this period, France became western Europe's strongest kingdom, but Spanish kings gradually reunified much of the Iberian peninsula. The Holy Roman Empire remained decentralized. Meanwhile, Lithuania, Hungary, and Poland controlled much of eastern Europe.

Renaissance ("Rebirth") A dramatic flowering in arts and learning that began in the Italian city-states around 1350 and spread through Europe through the 1500s.

humanism The name for the European Renaissance philosophy, which emphasized humanity, worldly concerns, and reason rather than religious ideals.

Technological Importation and Innovation

Another manifestation of the dynamism of later medieval Europe was the extraordinary technological development spurred by imports from other regions. During the twelfth and thirteenth centuries, European scholars translated Arab and Greek scientific writings in Muslim Spain, while Asian and Muslim technologies reached Europe over the trade routes. During the fourteenth and fifteenth centuries, western Europeans developed better ships, in part by improving Chinese inventions such as the compass and by adapting the Arab lateen sails. By the 1490s, Europeans were masters of the oceans. Europeans also devised time-measuring devices, including mechanical clocks in the 1300s. Imported technology, especially gunpowder from China, also made for more lethal warfare. Gunpowder weapons killed many knights and nobles in European wars and would give Europeans a huge military advantage over societies that did not have them.

Perhaps the most crucial late medieval invention was printing by movable type, which allowed information to be produced and spread in unlimited quantities. The Chinese had invented woodblock printing and then movable type made of clay centuries earlier, and in the 1200s they introduced metal type (see Chapter 11). Block printing was used in Europe by the 1400s for books and playing cards. In 1455 the German goldsmith Johann Gutenberg (yoh-HAHN GOO-ten-burg) (1400–1468) introduced the first known metal movable type outside of East Asia, using it to print a Bible. From then on the printed word became an essential medium of mass communication.

Expansion and Exploration

Technological advance was matched by population and economic growth. Europe's population increased by 40 to 50 percent between the tenth and fourteenth centuries. This growth rate, the highest in the world, was supported by increased agricultural development that provided more food. After the devastation of the Black Death, Europe's population again increased rapidly, grain production doubled, and many peasants moved into eastern Europe to open lands.

> "As foreign trade became more economically important and trade networks widened, commerce became a part of everyday life."

Venice Leads the Way

Commerce also grew. As foreign trade became more economically important and trade networks widened, commerce became a part of everyday life. Valuable spices from India and Southeast Asia were distributed by merchants from Venice, who had trading posts all over the Middle East and around the Black Sea, as well as from Genoa. Observers were awed by the vast quantity of merchandise available in fifteenth-century Venice; one commented, "It seems as if the whole world flocks here."[10] Gold from West Africa, used in coins, treasuries, and jewelry, also stimulated the European economy. To keep track of their businesses, European merchants borrowed and used Arab trading practices and mathematics. In the early 1200s, Fibonacci (fee-bo-NACH-ee), a merchant from Pisa in Italy, wrote of the Arab and Indian numerals and calculations he had studied abroad. Soon the mathematical innovations he learned were adopted in Venice, Genoa, and Florence.

The Hanseatic League

Western European cities were unique in their growing political power and autonomy. Unlike in centralized China or the Ottoman Empire, these cities existed in a politically fragmented region and thus could bargain with kings for advantages and autonomy. In 1241 various North German cities expanded a trade alliance of more than 165 member cities known as the Hanseatic (han-see-AT-ik) League. Eventually it had its own army and navy, making it almost an independent political power. The league existed for more than 500 years.

These developments gave European merchants a status and power unique in the world. In China, for instance, merchants, while often prosperous, had a low ranking in the Confucian social system, were heavily taxed, and faced many restrictions. By contrast, in western Europe, merchants became mayors and political leaders in cities and towns, and in turn gave support to merchant interests. These late medieval Europeans laid the foundation for an economic revolution that would fundamentally alter world history.

The lively caravan trade that developed along the Silk Road had other consequences too. Over the centuries many Chinese inventions, such as gunpowder, wheelbarrows, and the compass, were transported westward over the Silk Road and profoundly changed Western society. The trade even influenced food preferences. Chinese noodles, for example, spread widely in Asia, and Arabs may have brought Chinese-derived pasta to Italy. But the exchange was not entirely one-way: one Chinese scholar sojourned in Baghdad around 900, learned Arabic, and made copies of important medical texts to take back to China.

The Silk Road was not the only major land trade network. Others linked West Africa and the Mediterranean across the Sahara Desert, allowing the movement of commodities such as salt and gold. Land and riverine routes also tied northern and eastern Europe into the broader Eurasian trade system. Between 800 and 1000, Swedish Vikings established a trading network stretching from Scandinavia through Russia to Byzantium. Persia, Mali in West Africa, Byzantium, the northern Italian city-states, and Muslim Spain also prospered from their strategic locations along major trade routes.

At about the same time that these routes were expanding in Eurasia and Africa, in the Americas overland trade also carried Mesoamerican influences deep into North America while spreading Andean technologies, crops, and religious cults widely around South America. Although oceanic exchange in the Americas was limited, a lively canoe and raft trade linked the Caribbean islands, and some traders sailed along the Pacific coast on rafts.

The Rise of Maritime Trade

By 1000 an increasingly lucrative maritime trade, perhaps spurred by improving naval technology, grew in the

Silk Road Travelers The Silk Road remained a key trade route during this era. This painting, from a fourteenth-century atlas made in Spain, shows one of the horse and camel caravans that traveled between China and Central Asia.

Bildarchiv Preussischer Kulturbesitz/Art Resource, NY

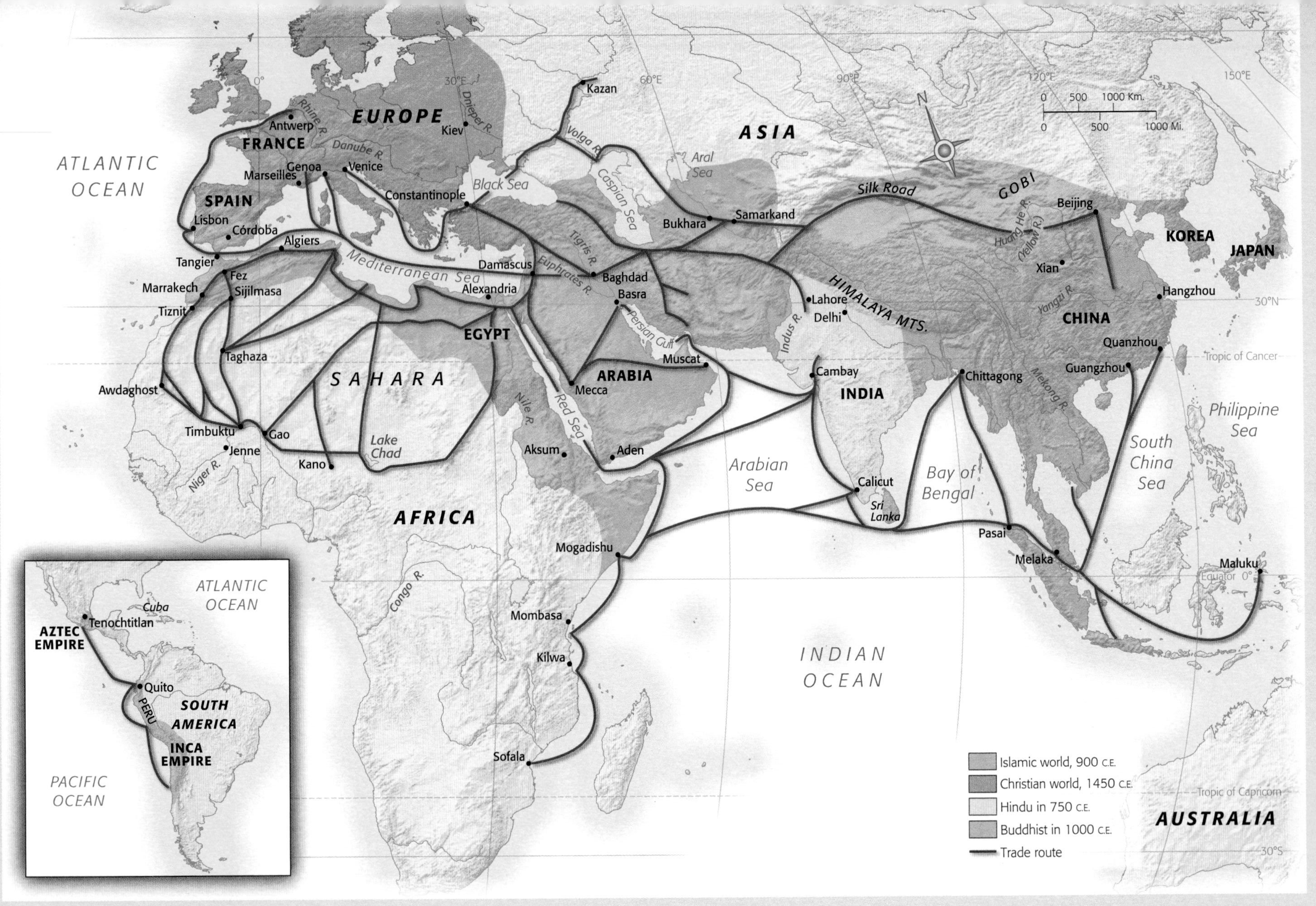
ATLANTIC OCEAN
EUROPE
FRANCE
SPAIN
Antwerp
Marseilles
Genoa
Venice
Kiev
Lisbon
Córdoba
Algiers
Tangier
Fez
Marrakech
Sijilmasa
Tiznit
Taghaza
Awdaghost
Timbuktu
Jenne
Gao
Kano
Lake Chad
SAHARA
EGYPT
AFRICA
Constantinople
Black Sea
Mediterranean Sea
Damascus
Alexandria
Baghdad
Basra
Persian Gulf
Muscat
ARABIA
Mecca
Red Sea
Nile R.
Aksum
Aden
Mogadishu
Mombasa
Kilwa
Sofala
Congo R.
Niger R.
Rhine R.
Danube R.
Dnieper R.
Volga R.
Kazan
Caspian Sea
Aral Sea
Tigris R.
Euphrates R.
ASIA
Bukhara
Samarkand
Silk Road
GOBI
HIMALAYA MTS.
Lahore
Delhi
Indus R.
Cambay
INDIA
Calicut
Sri Lanka
Arabian Sea
Bay of Bengal
INDIAN OCEAN
Chittagong
Mekong R.
Pasai
Melaka
Beijing
Huang He R. (Yellow R.)
Xian
Yangzi R.
CHINA
Hangzhou
Quanzhou
Guangzhou
KOREA
JAPAN
South China Sea
Philippine Sea
Maluku
Equator 0°
Tropic of Cancer
Tropic of Capricorn
30°N
30°S
0°
30°E
60°E
90°E
120°E
150°E
N
0 500 1000 Km.
0 500 1000 Mi.
AUSTRALIA
Islamic world, 900 C.E.
Christian world, 1450 C.E.
Hindu in 750 C.E.
Buddhist in 1000 C.E.
Trade route
ATLANTIC OCEAN
Cuba
Tenochtitlan
AZTEC EMPIRE
Quito
PERU
SOUTH AMERICA
INCA EMPIRE
PACIFIC OCEAN

© Cengage Learning

Silk Road Narratives *(http://depts. washington.edu/uwch/ silkroad/texts/texts .html).* Explores cultural interaction in Eurasia through excerpts from Silk Road travelers.

Eastern Hemisphere, despite the dangers from pirates and storms. At one end of the Afro-Eurasian zone, much trade crisscrossed the Mediterranean, while sailing networks along Europe's Atlantic coast later linked the Baltic and North Seas to Mediterranean ports and helped foster the Hanseatic League of Baltic ports.

Farther east, the Indian Ocean routes became the heart of the most extensive maritime trade network in the Intermediate world. The Abbasid caliph al-Mansur, writing from Baghdad, boasted that "there is no obstacle to us and China; everything on the sea can come to us on it."[2] The Indian Ocean system linked China, Japan, Vietnam, and Cambodia in the east through Malaya and the Indonesian archipelago to India and Sri Lanka, and then westward to Persia, Arabia, Russia, the eastern and central Mediterranean, and the East African coast as far south as Mozambique. Over these routes, spices, tea, precious metals, silk, ivory, coffee, carpets, and porcelin moved to distant markets. Many of these products reached Europe, sparking interest there in reaching the sources of the riches of the East.

Spices grown in tropical lands were among the main products moving from east to west. Black pepper was cultivated chiefly in India, Siam, and Indonesia, while cloves, nutmeg, and mace came from the Maluku (Moluccan) Islands of eastern Indonesia. Cinnamon was grown in Indonesia and Sri Lanka. In addition, red pepper from West Africa was traded to the Middle East and reached Europe in the 1300s. Intermediate Era people treated a range of illnesses and aided digestion with spices, and many cultures used them in cooking. Asian spices such as almonds, ginger, saffron, cinnamon, sugar, nutmeg, and cloves improved late medieval European diets. An English book from the early 1400s reported that "Pepper is black and has a good smack, And every man doth it buy."[3]

World Religions and Trade Routes, 600–1500 <<

Much of the Eastern Hemisphere was linked by land and maritime trade routes. Along with goods and travelers, Buddhism, Christianity, and Islam spread along these trade routes, attracting believers from many societies.

Various states around the Persian Gulf, Indian Ocean, and South China Sea were closely linked to maritime trade. However, no particular political power dominated the Indian Ocean trading routes. Trade dynamism depended on cosmopolitan port cities, especially hubs such as Hormuz in Persia, Kilwa in Tanzania, Cambay in northwest India, Calicut on India's southwest coast, Melaka in Malaya, and Quanzhou (chwan-cho) in southern China. The thirteenth-century traveler Marco Polo was fascinated by the coming and going of ships at Quanzhou: "Here is a harbor whither all ships of India come, with much costly merchandise. It is also the port whither go the [Chinese] merchants [heading overseas]. There is such traffic of merchandise that it is a truly wonderful sight."[4]

A hemispheric trade system developed in which some people came to produce for a world market. This system was fueled by China and India, the great centers of world manufacturing in this era. Together China and India probably produced more than three-quarters of all world industrial products before 1500. China exported iron, steel, silk, refined sugar, and ceramics, while India was the great producer of textiles. Their industrial products might be transported thousands of miles. The Muslim soldiers who resisted the Christian crusaders used steel swords smelted in India from East African iron. Merchants from all over Afro-Eurasia traveled great distances in search of profits, often forming permanent trade diasporas. One Cairo-based Jewish family firm had branches in India, Iran, and Tunisia. Most of the goods traded over vast distances were luxury items, but some, including pepper and sugar, also reached consumers of modest means.

Universal Religions and Social Change

The power and reach of universal, or world, religions such as Buddhism, Christianity, and Islam increased during the Intermediate Era. Religion dominated the lives of millions around the world and fostered globalization, propagating ideas and generating trade across regional boundaries. By 1500 the religious map of the Eastern Hemisphere looked very different than it had in 600. Universal religions promoted moral and ethical values that helped preserve harmony in societies that were increasingly cosmopolitan. The Christian injunction to "love thy neighbor as thyself," the Buddhist emphasis on good thoughts and actions, and the Muslim ideals of social justice and the equality of believers fostered goodwill and cooperation. Religious beliefs also spurred the emergence of new values and social forms.

The Triumph of Universal Religions

During the Intermediate Era, most people in Eurasia and many in Africa eventually embraced one or another universal religion. Islam became the most widespread, rapidly expanding through the Middle East and eventually claiming Central Asia and parts of Europe, while gaining a large following in West Africa, the East African coast, South Asia, China, and Southeast Asia. Islam fostered religious, social, and economic networks that linked peoples from Morocco and Spain to Indonesia and the Philippines with a common faith, values, and trade connections. Some Muslim scholars and jurists, such as the Moroccan Ibn Battuta, traveled, sojourned, and even settled thousands of miles from their homelands.

Older faiths also spread in this era, changing societies in varied ways. Theravada Buddhism was established in Sri Lanka and then expanded into mainland Southeast Asia, where it gradually displaced earlier faiths and reshaped cultures by teaching moderation, pacifism, unselfish acts, and individualism. To the north, Mahayana Buddhism first reached Central Asia and then China early in the Common Era, and during the Intermediate Era, it became entrenched in Japan, Korea, Vietnam, Mongolia, and Tibet. In most places, Buddhism existed alongside rather than replacing earlier religious traditions, such as animism in Siam and Tibet, Shinto in Japan, and Confucianism in China. By 1000 a Buddhist world incorporating diverse societies and several sects stretched from India eastward to Vietnam and Japan, but the temples, pagodas, and statues constructed to honor the Buddha reflected local styles and taste. Buddhist networks tended to facilitate the movement of pilgrims, such as the seventh-century Chinese monk Xuan Zang (swan tsang), who sojourned in India.

Christianity expanded to encompass nearly all of Europe by 1200, filtering north into the Germanic and Celtic lands and east among the Slavs, but the original Christian church divided. The Roman church dominated the west, while the Orthodox church claimed Russia and much of eastern Europe. Although Christianity was pushed back by Islam in western Asia and North Africa, sizeable Christian communities sometimes flourished in these regions, aided by the tolerance Muslims usually accorded to Christian practice. Nonetheless, chronic tensions arose between Christian Europe and the Islamic world, derived from political and economic conflicts as well as a clash between the strong missionary impulses of both religions.

Tensions between the two rival faiths generated the European Crusades to regain the Holy Land, which left a legacy of bitterness on both sides.

All universal religions nurtured a respect for learning. An admiring Arab described a great library, the House of Knowledge, opened by the Shi'ite Fatimid caliph in Egypt in 1005: "People could visit it, and whoever wanted to copy something that interested him could do so. Lectures were held there by the Quran readers, astronomers, grammarians, philologists, and physicians."[5] Some Buddhist centers of higher education, such as the university at Nalanda in India and the monasteries in Srivijaya, in Sumatra, attracted students from all over Asia. In Europe, various Christian orders and thinkers encouraged the preservation of knowledge, laying the foundation for universities such as Paris and Oxford. Chinese rulers patronized centers of scholarship such as the Hanlin Academy, and scholars across Africa were drawn to the university at Timbuktu.

Gender Roles and Family Patterns

The expansion of universal religions during the Intermediate Era, combined with increasing trade, also influenced many aspects of social life, thought, and attitudes. All of the religions had patriarchal institutional structures that were led by men who promoted notions of female inferiority. A fifteenth-century Italian warned that "it would hardly win us [men] respect if our wife busied herself among the men in the marketplace. It also seems somewhat demeaning to me to remain shut up in the house among women when I have manly things to do among men."[6] Islam incorporated many Arab and Persian customs that constrained women, but seclusion and veiling became the main pattern primarily in Muslim societies that already had a strong patriarchal tradition, such as Arabia, Egypt, north India, and the former Byzantine territories. Where pre-Islamic cultures had less rigid gender roles, as in Spain, Southeast Asia, and West Africa, Islamic patriarchy was considerably modified.

The status of women varied around the world. As Confucianism dug deeper roots in East Asia, patriarchy became a stronger force there than it had been in classical times. By Ming times it was more common to seclude upper-class Chinese women, and even bind their feet. Japanese society also became more patriarchal, as the warrior culture replaced the Heian culture in which elite women had flourished. In mainland Southeast Asia, Theravada Buddhism proved a generally moderating force in gender relations, although men had more opportunity than women to acquire the merit needed to reach nirvana, because only men could become monks. In societies as different as Byzantium, Carolingian France, West Africa, Southeast Asia, and the Inca Empire, individual women, such as the Burmese queen Pwa Saw, could still gain power as queens or as powers behind the throne. But in most societies, formal education, religious hierarchies, and military organizations remained mostly male.

Religious values influenced family patterns and sexual attitudes. Islam allowed men to have four wives, but polygamy for some men meant that women were unavailable to others, who then could not marry. Christian teachings favored monogamy and marriage, but many men and women joined clerical orders or for other reasons never married. And European kings often flouted church teachings by having concubines and mistresses. In many societies around the world, men of elite status had multiple wives and concubines.

Attitudes toward homosexuality varied widely: followers of Christianity, Judaism, Islam, and Confucianism all shared an aversion to homosexual relations, in part because they did not produce children. But this sexual behavior had long been practiced and even tolerated in all of these traditions. Christian tolerance turned to fierce repression only in the thirteenth century, and such repression was not a global pattern. Perhaps because there were many unmarried Muslim men, and also because of the rigid segregation of the sexes, some Islamic societies ignored homosexual activity. The Japanese, Chinese, and some Southeast Asian and Native American societies also tended to accept homosexuality as part of life.

Slavery and Feudalism

Most societies were hierarchical, and many people lived in slavery or faced severe restrictions on their freedom. Slavery had long been common throughout the world and remained so in the Intermediate Era, except for East Asia, where it largely died out by 1000. Islam permitted slavery but encouraged owners to treat slaves well. Many Muslim African societies, and some that were non-Muslim, had slaves, including the West African kingdoms and East African city-states, although their status varied widely. Africans had been shipped north for centuries to work in the Islamic world, and some African slaves in the Persian Gulf region revolted.

Slaves were also common in Southeast Asian societies such as Angkor and Siam. A Persian observer wrote that, in Indonesia, the people "reckon high rank and wealth by the quantity of slaves a person owns."[7] Various American peoples also enslaved prisoners of war, debtors, and criminals. In Europe, slavery's decline and gradual replacement by serfdom, a less restrictive form of bondage, did not end the slave market there. An active Mediterranean slave

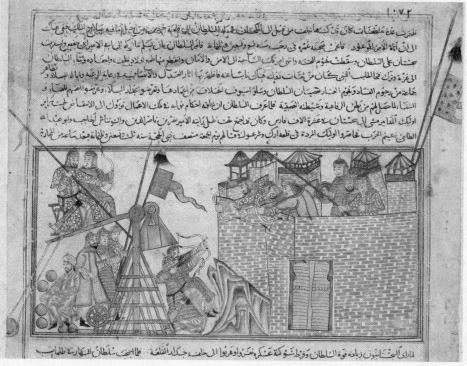

Catapults The Mongols used advanced military technology, including catapults, to conquer cities. This battle scene, painted by a Persian artist, shows the Mongols attacking a city around 1300.

Edinburgh University Library, Orms. 20. fol. 124v

trade shipped Slavs, Greeks, and Turks from the Black Sea region to southern Europe and North Africa. By the fifteenth century, Africans appeared in southern European slave markets.

Although some scholars question the usefulness and scope of the concept of feudalism, others identify it as a major new social and political pattern in the world in the Intermediate Era. The feudal model, which included lords and knights, independent manors, serfdom, small states, and chronic warfare, was best represented by some medieval European societies between 800 and 1300. Some historians also apply feudalism to post-Heian Japan under the warrior class and shogunates, and others to parts of India and Southeast Asia, where many small states competed for power. Feudal societies such as Norman England, the Carolingian realm, and perhaps Ashikaga Japan differed in many ways from the large centralized states such as Song China, Abbasid Iraq, Mali, or the Inca Empire, where emperors or kings exercised great power through bureaucracies.

In most hierarchical societies, whether feudal or centralized, workers were more or less controlled by, and owed obligations to, those in power, such as Inca kings and Chinese emperors. In medieval Europe, the dominant Christian church encouraged people who wanted to reap rewards in Heaven to accept the social order, and some governments standardized work requirements. Hence, in 800 the Frankish king Charlemagne proclaimed that the peasant living on church and royal estates "must plow his lord's land a whole day [but not also be asked] to do handiwork service during the same week. The dependent shall not withdraw from these services and the lords shall not ask more from them."[8] In both western Europe and Japan, feudalism built up intense pressures that eventually erupted.

The Mongol Empire and Hemispheric Connections

Between 1250 and 1350, the Mongols established the largest land empire in world history, stretching from lands on the western shores of the Black Sea east to the Pacific coast of China and Korea. The building of the Mongol Empire was a ruthless but amazing feat. Within the span of a century the Mongol armies, supported by a Mongol population of less than 2 million, swept out of their arid Central Asian grasslands to put more than 200 million people under their control. By reopening Central Asian trade routes closed by political turmoil and by connecting with many different peoples and countries, the Mongols fostered communication networks and the transfer of technology between once-remote parts of the Eastern

Hemisphere. In doing so, they were major catalysts of change.

The Mongol Empire

The forces prompting the Mongols to build their empire are not altogether clear. Warfare was common among the Mongols, who were tough steppe herders of horses and camels. Historically, various other Central Asian pastoralists, including Turks, Huns, and Tibetans, had forged large but short-lived empires or confederations. Various factors in Central Asia, including ecological instability, climate change, population growth, and the spread of Mahayana Buddhism and Nestorian Christianity, may have prompted the Mongol expansion. These forces led to the emergence of Genghis Khan (ca. 1162–1227), a visionary leader who effectively united the Mongol tribes. His warriors, mounted and well armed, and aided by siege weaponry and innovative military strategies of rapid attack, made a formidable fighting force.

Within a few decades, Mongol armies conquered Central Asia, Tibet, Korea, Russia, part of eastern Europe, Afghanistan, and a large part of western Asia, including Persia and Anatolia. The Mongols were at the Danube, preparing to sweep through Hungary into western Europe, when Genghis Khan's successor, his son Ogodei (1185–1241), died, aborting that thrust. Thus western Europe was spared. In the mid-1200s, the Mongols expanded their domination in western Asia, overpowering the Arab Abbasid Caliphate. The widespread destruction they caused in the Middle East and Central Asia ended the Islamic Golden Age and reshaped politics and agriculture in these regions. Later, China and Korea were also eventually added to the Mongol-ruled realm. Contemporary accounts credit the Mongols with massacring hundreds of thousands, perhaps millions, of people and burning many cities, but some historians doubt that many civilians were killed en masse, since they were needed for production and transportation.

The Mongol Empire proved short-lived, partly because the Mongols never connected with maritime commerce. They were also victims of their success. Before he died, Genghis Khan worried that his successors would forsake the rigorous life for the comforts of wealthy conquered peoples such as Arabs and Chinese, predicting that "after us, [our] people will wear garments of gold; they will eat sweet, greasy food, ride splendid coursers, and hold in their arms the loveliest women, and they will forget that they owe these things to us."[9] This warning proved prophetic. The Mongols' harsh and increasingly corrupt rule provoked rebellions that would end their domination.

The Heritage of the Mongols and Their Networks

Some historians consider the Mongols the great equalizers of history by facilitating the transfer of technology and ideas from East Asia to western Europe and the Middle East. The Mongols unwittingly set in motion changes that allowed Europeans to acquire and improve Chinese innovations such as printing, gunpowder, and the magnetic compass while developing new inventions of their own. Chinese inventions had a major impact in Europe. In the seventeenth century, the English philosopher Francis Bacon noted that Chinese printing, gunpowder, and the magnet "changed the whole face and state of things" in European literature, warfare, and navigation.[10] Europeans improved on Chinese military technology, making late medieval warfare far deadlier. These weapons, coming by way of routes opened by the Mongols, also helped reshape Middle Eastern politics and fostered the rise of the Ottoman Empire.

Because of the Mongols, travel from one end of Eurasia to the other became easier than ever before. During Mongol times, many men of talent moved from west to east. In China the Mongols relied administratively on a large number of foreigners who came to serve in the civil service. These included many Muslims from West and Central Asia and a few Europeans such as Marco Polo who found their way to the fabled land the Europeans called Cathay. Polo's reports on his travels increased European interest in Asia and inspired later explorers, such as Christopher Columbus, to seek a sea route to East Asia.

Disaster and Dynamism in the Late Intermediate Era

A combination of natural disasters, including a terrible pandemic and abrupt climate change, also helped reshape Eurasian societies. Increased trade by land and sea and the migration of peoples such as the Turks, Germans, and Mongols fostered the spread of diseases across the Eastern Hemisphere. Many regions also experienced much cooler climates beginning around 1300, which caused agricultural failures, and with them, widespread famine. But these disasters also sparked dynamic new energies that revived trade and maritime exploration.

The Spread of Diseases

The worst pandemic in world history, known in the West as the Black Death, may have resulted from the Mongol conquests, in particular the greater contact they brought among Eurasian societies. Climate change may also have been a factor. Eurasia was unusually wet during the 1300s,

perhaps increasing the number of fleas and rats. The Black Death, which most scholars think was chiefly caused by bubonic plague carried by flea-infested rats, apparently originated in China or Central Asia. By the mid-1300s, it had been carried by merchants and soldiers along the Silk Road to southern Russia. Ships leaving the Genoese trading colony at Calfa, on the Crimean peninsula at the north end of the Black Sea, carried it unwittingly to the Middle East and Europe, where it raged through cities and towns. In the affected societies, from China to Egypt to England and even to fishing villages in remote Greenland, perhaps one-third of the total population died in the first outbreak. Surveying the damage, the Italian writer Petrarch wrote that future generations would be "incredulous, unable to imagine the empty houses, abandoned towns, the squalid countryside, the fields littered with dead, the dreadful silent solitude which seemed to hang over the whole world. Physicians were useless, philosophers could only shrug their shoulders and look wise."[11]

Ultimately the Black Death disrupted the complex system of interregional trade and communication that had flourished around Eurasia in the thirteenth and fourteenth centuries. Agricultural and industrial production declined, and financial crises and labor shortages wrecked economies from China to France. The huge population losses also helped undermine Mongol rule in East Asia and the Middle East. When the Black Death ended, a spurt of growth saw population levels soar from East Asia to Europe. By 1500 the world population had reached between 400 million and 600 million people, about twice the population of 1000. China accounted for one-fourth of the total, and India for at least one-fifth. Europe, including Russia, grew rapidly to 70 to 95 million. The Black Death did not affect sub-Saharan Africa or the Americas, each of which probably had 60 to 80 million people by 1500.

Climate Change and Societies

Climate change has affected societies since the dawn of humankind. It spurred the transition to farming in western Asia 10,000 years ago, undermined the Mesopotamian and Indus societies 4,000 years ago, and hastened the decline of the Chinese Han and Roman Empires around 200 C.E. Eurasian weather became more erratic during the 1200s, perhaps prompting Mongol expansion. In the Americas, climate change during the Intermediate Era probably contributed to the collapse of various societies, including Tiwanaku, Moche, Teotihuacan, the southern Maya, and the Anasazi.

Around 1300 an unusually warm period gave way to much cooler weather that lasted until 1850, sparking what scientists call the "Little Ice Age," with serious results for societies. Whatever the causes, which are still debated, longer and more frigid winters periodically affected Europe, North America, Central Asia, and China. Bitter cold drove the Norse Vikings out of Greenland, and Icelandic farming floundered. Severe storms and flooding in Europe were followed by drought and crop failures, causing widespread famine. Rivers and canals froze, inhibiting boat traffic. Between 1315 and 1317, perhaps 15 percent of Europe's population starved to death. In addition, rainfall declined in India and Africa, drying up many lakes.

In North America great droughts in the late 1200s may have contributed to Cahokia's decline and caused the dispersal of the Anasazi. Pueblo peoples responded to hard times by migrating, as they said in their songs and poems: "Survival, I know this way. It rains. Mountains and canyons and plants grow. We traveled this way."[12] The North Atlantic climate became even colder from the mid-1600s to mid-1700s, and such discomfort may have inspired some adventurous Europeans to seek greener pastures abroad, in the Americas.

The Roots of Oceanic Exploration

The Mongol conquests had connected distant peoples and fostered trade. With the Mongol Empire's demise, however, and the security of Silk Road travel reduced, maritime trade became more crucial and naval technology improved considerably. As a result, late in the Intermediate Era there was a trend toward oceanic exploration over vast distances. The fame of Melaka, Calicut, Hormuz, and other Asian ports as commercial hubs for valuable goods had reached Europe, and by the late fourteenth century, some European merchants were beginning to dream of an easier sea route to the East.

By the early 1400s, the Chinese had the most advanced ships and navigational techniques, and most outward-looking attitude. The Chinese took the initiative of exploration, dispatching unprecedented voyages of discovery led by Zheng He that sailed as far as the Middle East and East Africa on long-established maritime networks. This Chinese thrust did not have lasting effects on the world, however. Although they had the naval capability, the Chinese, unlike the Europeans, lacked the economic incentive and religious zeal, and hence never sailed around Africa in search of Europe. However, some historians think a few Arabs and Indians may have. A navigation manual written by the Arab navigator Shihab al-Din Ahmad Ibn Majid (SHE-hob al-DIN AH-mad ibn MA-jeed) in the later 1400s, and probably based on earlier voyages, gives quite detailed, and mostly accurate, instructions for sailing down the East African coast, around the Cape of Good Hope, up the West African coast, and then into the Mediterranean.

The Portuguese and then the Spanish, both peoples with long maritime traditions and coastal locations, used Chinese, Arab, and European naval technology to construct ships and equip crews for successful long-distance voyages. In search of gold, spices, slaves, and other resources, Portuguese ships sailed to West and Central Africa, where they established outposts and eventually colonies. By the end of the fifteenth century, the Portuguese had rounded the Cape of Good Hope to reach the Indian Ocean, the East African trading ports, and finally India, inspiring other European mariners. An historian in the early 1500s reported:

> Christopher Columbus, a Genoese, proposed to the Catholic King and Queen [of Spain] to discover the islands which touch the Indies. He asked for ships, promising not only to propagate the Christian religion, but also certainly to bring back pearls, spices and gold beyond anything imagined.[13]

The Spanish expedition led by Columbus landed in the Americas in the 1490s, profoundly altering the history of the world.

Test your knowlege of the material covered in Part III.

Suggested Reading

Bentley, Jerry H. *Old World Encounters: Cross-Cultural Contacts and Exchanges in Pre-Modern Times.* New York: Oxford University Press, 1993. An up-to-date survey of trade routes and the spread of universal religions.

Curtin, Philip D. *Cross-Cultural Trade in World History.* Cambridge: Cambridge University Press, 1984. A sweeping examination of world trade and cross-cultural exchange.

Fernandez-Armesto, Felipe. *Millennium: A History of the Last Thousand Years.* New York: Scribner, 1995. An idiosyncratic but interesting overview of the world over the past millennium, for the general reader.

Gilbert, Erik, and Jonathan Reynolds. *Trading Tastes: Commodity and Cultural Exchange to 1750.* Upper Saddle River, NJ: Prentice Hall, 2006. A readable survey of the salt, silk, spice, and sugar trades and their impacts.

Hobson, John M. *The Eastern Origins of Western Civilisation.* New York: Cambridge University Press, 2004. A fascinating, well-researched study offering an Asia-centric history of the era.

Larner, John. *Marco Polo and the Discovery of the World.* New Haven, CT: Yale University Press, 1999. A readable study of the impact of Marco Polo's writings on European exploration.

McNeill, William H. *Plagues and Peoples*, rev. ed. Garden City, NJ: Anchor, 1998. One of the best studies of the history and role of diseases, including the Black Death.

Morgan, David. *The Mongols.* New York: Basil Blackwell, 1986. A fine study of the Mongols and their empire.

Pacey, Arnold. *Technology in World Civilization.* Cambridge, MA: MIT Press, 1990. Discussion of Asian and European technologies in this era.

Pearson, Michael. *The Indian Ocean.* New York: Routledge, 2000. A comprehensive look at the role this ocean played in world history.

Ringrose, David R. *Expansion and Global Interaction, 1200–1700.* New York: Longman, 2001. Explores the relationship between expansion and global interaction that began with the Mongols.

Risso, Patricia. *Merchants and Faith: Muslim Commerce and Culture in the Indian Ocean.* Boulder, CO: Westview, 1995. A readable survey of Islam-centered commerce from the beginning through the nineteenth century.

Stearns, Peter. *Gender in World History.* New York: Routledge, 2000. A brief but general study with good material on this era.

Super, John C., and Briane K. Turley. *Religion in World History.* New York: Routledge, 2006. A brief overview of religious traditions and change.

Weatherford, Jack. *Genghis Khan and the Making of the Modern World.* New York: Crown, 2004. A readable and provocative examination of the Mongol role in world history.

Whitfield, Susan. *Life Along the Silk Road.* Berkeley: University of California Press, 1999. A readable portrait of Silk Road life through the experiences of travelers and residents.

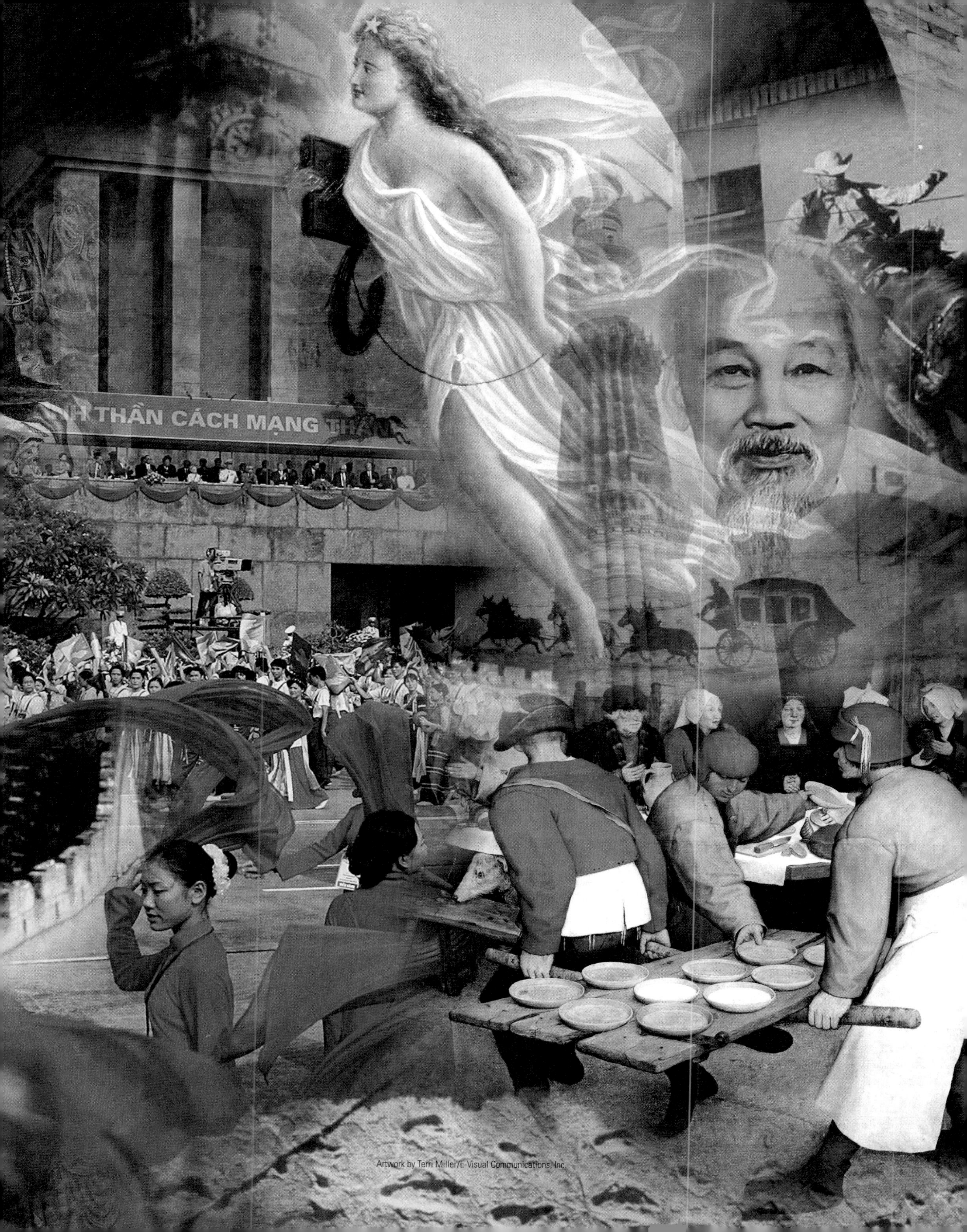

Artwork by Terri Miller/E-Visual Communications, Inc.

PART IV

Connecting the Globe:

Forging New Networks in the Early Modern World, 1450–1750

NORTH AND CENTRAL AMERICA
The bridging of the Atlantic by a Spanish expedition led by Christopher Columbus in 1492 had major consequences. In the century to follow, the Spanish conquered various Caribbean islands, Mesoamerica, and southwestern North America. The English and French established settlements and then colonies along the Atlantic coast and gradually expanded westward, at the expense of Native American societies that were devastated by diseases brought from Eurasia. In the southern colonies and the Caribbean islands, plantations worked by African slaves became the major economic activity.

ARCTIC OCEAN

NORTH AMERICA

Mississippi R.

BRITISH AMERICA (13 COLONIES)

SPANISH AMERICAN EMPIRE

MEXICO

ATLANTIC OCEAN

PACIFIC OCEAN

Amazon

PERU

BRAZIL

ANDES

SOUTH AMERICA

SOUTH AMERICA
The arrival of the Spanish and Portuguese changed the politics, economies, and demographics of the region. The Spanish toppled the Inca Empire and colonized much of South and Central America, while the Portuguese dominated Brazil. The European colonizers established mines, ranches, and plantations. After diseases from Eurasia killed much of the Native American population, the colonizers imported African slaves as workers. As a result, European, Native American, and African peoples and cultures blended to foster unique Latin American societies.

EUROPE

Several European societies emerged as major world powers. The Portuguese and Spanish in the 1500s, followed by the Dutch, English, and French in the 1600s and 1700s, established footholds and colonies in Africa, the Americas, and Asia. The resources obtained abroad, especially the minerals and plantation crops of the Americas and Southeast Asia, brought wealth to Europe. Exposure to a wider world fostered capitalism, science, technology, and a questioning of long-standing religious doctrine, resulting in the Protestant Reformation and the Enlightenment.

WESTERN ASIA

The Ottoman Empire became the world's major Islamic power, controlling not only much of Western Asia but also much of North Africa and southeastern Europe. Rivals of the major European powers, especially the Russians, the Ottoman Turks prospered by fostering learning, accommodating ethnic minorities, and importing military and technical expertise. To their east, the Persians under the Safavid dynasty dominated parts of Central Asia and flourished for several centuries.

EASTERN ASIA

While experiencing dynastic changes, China remained a major world power and the key Eurasian manufacturing center and commercial economy. China dealt with European traders and governments on its own terms, setting strict limits on trade and diplomatic relations. In both China and Japan, Western missionaries were at first tolerated and then expelled. Likewise, the Tokugawa government in Japan maintained a rigid social order and secluded the country from the West.

ARCTIC OCEAN

NETHERLANDS

BRITAIN

FRANCE

SPAIN

EUROPE

OTTOMAN EMPIRE

RUSSIA

ASIA

JAPAN

PERSIA

CHINA

HIMALAYAS

MUGHAL INDIA

PHILIPPINES

Danube

Nile

AFRICA

SONGHAI

HAUSA

ETHIOPIA

CONGO R.

KONGO

Niger

SWAHILI

ATLANTIC OCEAN

INDIAN OCEAN

INDONESIA

AUSTRALIA

SOUTH AFRICA

AFRICA

Many African societies experienced dramatic change. The need by European powers for cheap labor in their American colonies fostered the trans-Atlantic slave trade, which disrupted much of the West and Central African coast as millions of Africans were enslaved and shipped to the Americas. Although some African states, such as Ashante and Benin, flourished from the slave trade and other commerce, warfare between states became more common. The Portuguese conquered the states of Angola and Kongo and destabilized the East African coastal cities, while the Dutch established a foothold in South Africa.

SOUTHERN ASIA AND OCEANIA

India, ruled by the Islamic Mughal dynasty, was one of the world's major powers, with a flourishing economy that attracted merchants from many societies. After obtaining footholds in India, Europeans then sought wealth in nearby Southeast Asia. First the Portuguese and then other European powers gained a modest presence in Southeast Asia, the Spanish colonizing the Philippines and the Dutch parts of Indonesia. While Europeans began exploring the Pacific Basin, their impact on Oceania was slight. Nonetheless, the Spanish trade across the Pacific between the Philippines and Mexico laid a foundation for the global economy.

obal
nnections
d the Remaking
Europe,
–1750

Learning Outcomes

After reading this chapter, you should be able to answer the following questions:

LO¹ How did exploration, colonization, and capitalism increase Western power and wealth?

LO² How did the Renaissance and Reformation mark a crucial cultural and intellectual transition?

LO³ What types of governments emerged in Europe in this era?

LO⁴ How did major intellectual, scientific, and social changes help to reshape the West?

> **"O, wonder! How many goodly creatures are there here! How beauteous mankind is! O brave new world That hath such people in't!"**
>
> —Miranda, in *The Tempest* by William Shakespeare, 1611[1]

The European and world economy changed rapidly in the sixteenth century, and few places exemplified change more than the port city of Antwerp (AN-twuhrp), on the River Scheldt (skelt) in what is now Belgium. In 1567 an Italian diplomat and historian, Ludovico Guicciardini (loo-do-VEE-ko GWEE-char-DEE-nee), visited the mostly Flemish-speaking city and its fabulous Bourse (boors), a huge, multistory building that served as a marketplace and stock exchange. Guicciardini observed that "all of these persons being people who are earning money, invest it not only in commerce but also in building, in buying lands and properties, and thus the city flourishes and increases marvelously."[2] From the late 1400s until the late 1500s, Antwerp was the European hub for ever-widening world networks of commerce. Every week, fabulous merchandise arrived from all over the world: as many as 2,500 ships anchored at one time in the harbor, many laden with gold and silver from the Americas, and the Bourse became the clearinghouse for their cargo. Antwerp represented a postmedieval Europe shaped by the fruits of overseas exploration, conquest, and expanding commerce. The new economic thrust was one aspect of the many changes that the English playwright Shakespeare referred to as a "brave new world."

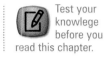

Test your knowlege before you read this chapter.

What do you think?

European exploration and colonization would have been improbable without the technologies and influences of Islamic and Asian societies.

Strongly Disagree					Strongly Agree	
1	2	3	4	5	6	7

In 1500, as the Early Modern Era began, western Europeans were still medieval in many respects: they were dominated by the multinational Roman church, their countries had little sense of national identity, they were skeptical of science, and they were minor participants in hemispheric commerce and barely aware of distant lands. By the mid-1700s, however, Europe and parts of the wider world had undergone a profound economic, intellectual, and political transition: Europeans conquered and settled the Americas and established colonies or trading networks in Asia and Africa. As a result, wealth

<<**Amsterdam Stock Exchange** During the seventeenth century, the Dutch port city of Amsterdam was the center of European commerce and played a key role in the world economy. The Amsterdam stock market, shown here in a painting by Dutch artist Job Adriaenz, attracted merchants and financiers from all over Europe.

> "For the first time since the Roman Empire and Charlemagne, large centralized states developed in Europe, particularly in England and France."

flowed into Europe, fostering investment in science and technology. New knowledge of, and influences from, non-European cultures reshaped European thinking and cultures. The Catholic Church faced severe challenges as some European thinkers were influenced as much or more by secular ideas. Although such changes often resulted in strains that produced long and bloody wars, they nevertheless remade Europe's political and social systems. By 1750 Europeans had left many of their medieval institutions and beliefs behind and were on the verge of introducing even more profound changes to the world.

LO¹ Transitions: Overseas Expansion and Capitalism

The foundations for the dramatic changes that reshaped many Early Modern European societies were established in late medieval times and embellished by developments after 1500. The European encounter with America, the growth of a trans-Atlantic slave trade, and the opening of direct trade with Asia all increased European wealth and stimulated the development of capitalism, an economic system in which property, exchange, and the means of production are privately owned. Inherently dynamic, capitalism gradually expanded its scale of operation to a global level. The economic revolution fostered stronger European states and reshaped the daily lives of nearly all Europeans.

The Roots of Europe's Transformation

Significant economic changes accelerated during the 1400s. Commerce and merchants flourished, cities grew larger and more numerous, and the feudal social systems and the values that supported them broke down. Commerce, with its widening trade networks, became a part of everyday life. The ability of the middle classes to buy more luxury goods spurred the growth of industries like textile manufacturing. However, most Europeans were still neither urban nor middle class; 80 percent were peasants who worked the soil. Although many peasants were now free or tenant farmers rather than serfs, most were still heavily burdened with taxes and service obligations to lords. They also tithed crops and livestock to the church. Only a few received any formal education.

Yet, despite being rooted in farming, the economy was changing, partly as a result of population growth and climate change. The European population (excluding Russia) increased from 70 to 100 million between 1500 and 1600, and then to 125 million by 1750, making for larger commercial markets. The global cooling that began around 1300 intensified, reached its height in the late 1600s, and then began to thaw around 1715, finally ending in the mid-1800s. This "Little Ice Age" brought winter freezing to canals and rivers, caused poor harvests, and helped motivate overseas explorers to seek better conditions and food sources elsewhere. Importing foods from the Americas, such as corn and potatoes, helped avert mass famine.

The Advent of Capitalism

Political and economic changes were felt more strongly by urban populations, especially merchants. By 1500, cities such as Paris and London had grown to over 200,000 and were unique in the world for their growing political power and autonomy. Unlike Chinese or Ottoman cities, European cities existed in a politically fragmented region rather than a centralized empire. Not having to answer to centralized authorities, city leaders could bargain with kings for advantages and autonomy. More favorable attitudes toward commerce gave some European merchants unusual power. Western European banks also favored economic growth. Blessed with these advantages, late medieval Europeans developed capitalism, a dynamic system that was highly oriented to economic growth. In the 1400s, cities such as Venice and Genoa in Italy, and Bruges (broozh) and Antwerp in what is today Belgium, became centers of capital-

Antwerp Marketplace The marketplace at the center of Antwerp, in what is today Belgium, was the main hub for European trade in the 1500s, the place where goods from all over Europe and from Africa, the Americas, and Asia were bought and sold. Musées Royaux Beaux-Arts de Belgique

istic enterprise. But early capitalism was limited by the Catholic Church's condemnation of usury and by cumbersome business methods. Not until after 1500 did the scope and nature of capitalism, fostered by overseas exploration and conquest, change dramatically.

Large, Centralized States

Political systems of western Europe also began to shift in the 1500s. After the ending of the Roman Empire in the Late Classical Era, western Europe had remained politically fragmented, but in the 1500s, some small states were gradually transformed into integrated monarchies, which became enriched by resources obtained by their merchants and adventurers in Africa, the Americas, and Asia. Both merchants and monarchs resented the independence of the landed aristocracy and cooperated to destroy their influence in a series of bloody wars. For the first time since the Roman Empire and Charlemagne, large cen-

tralized states developed in Europe, particularly in England and France. The growth of these strong but competitive states made the political system dynamic and unstable.

Mapping the Globe

New intellectual currents also emerged that fostered broader horizons, especially improvements in mapmaking. In 1375 Abraham Cresques (kres-kay), a Jewish cartographer on the Spanish island of Majorca (muh-JOR-kuh), used Christian, Muslim, and Jewish traditions and travelers' accounts to produce a map that placed Jerusalem rather than Europe at the center of the world. In the 1400s, Portuguese mapmakers drew innovative maps that influenced Flemish mapmakers of the 1500s, such as Gerardus Mercator (muhr-KAY-tuhr). But these maps were also misleading and, unlike Cresques' effort, did not de-center Europe.

 Explore new encounters in the early modern world in this interactive simulation.

Eastern Inspiration, Western Innovation

Developments in technology and mathematics, many inspired by earlier Arab, Chinese, and Indian innovations, were also important. Between 1450 and 1550, Europe's technology surpassed that of the Arabs and was catching up to China's. The major improvements came in shipbuilding, navigation, weaponry, and printing. European ships took advantage of lateen sails developed by Arabs and sternpost rudders from China, and they also used the Chinese magnetic compass to navigate. Facing much rougher waters than the placid Mediterranean and Indian Ocean, the people along Europe's Atlantic coast also had to build sturdier ships, giving them a naval advantage. Europeans also greatly improved gunpowder weapons and printing processes, both invented in China. The introduction of the European printing press in the mid-1400s made possible the dissemination of both Christian and secular knowledge to an increasingly literate audience. Some 13,000 books were published in Europe by 1500. Europeans also blended imported mathematical concepts, such as the Indian numerical system and Arab algebra, with their own insights to improve quantification.

"Gold, God, and Glory": Explorations and Conquests

During these centuries, the rise of Europe as a world power took place within a context of European overseas expansion and conquest (see Chapters 16–18). Historians use a standard shorthand, "Gold, God, and Glory," to describe European motives. "Gold" was the search for material gain by acquiring and selling Asian spices, African slaves, American metals, and other resources. "God" refers to the militant crusading tradition of Christianity, including the rivalry with Islam and the hatred of non-Christian religions. "Glory" describes the goals of the competing monarchies, who sought to establish their claims to new territories so as to strengthen their position in European politics. Motivated by these three aims, various western European peoples expanded overseas during the Early Modern Era, gaining control over widening segments of the globe.

> "Between 1450 and 1550, Europe's technology surpassed that of the Arabs and was catching up to China's."

Portugal and Spain Lead the Way

During the 1400s, the seafaring peoples of the Iberian peninsula, the Spanish and Portuguese, ventured out into the Atlantic and discovered the Azores (A-zorz), Madeira (muh-DEER-uh), and Canary island chains off northwest Africa (see Map 15.1). Several factors pushed Iberians to pioneer in overseas expeditions: a favorable geographic location facing the Atlantic Ocean and North Africa, a maritime tradition of deep-sea fishing, an aggressive Christian crusading tradition, and possession of the best ships and navigation techniques in Europe by the 1400s. The Iberians also had economic motives. Early Iberian exploration sought a way to circumnavigate the Venetian monopoly over the valuable trade from southern Asia through Persia and Egypt. The Iberians also sought gold from West Africa as well as new food sources, because Iberia did not produce enough meat and wheat to feed its growing population.

 Interactive Map

This maritime exploration and conquest required new technologies, such as a new type of ship to sail the rough Atlantic. Building on Chinese and Arab innovations, the Portuguese invented the caravel, an easily maneuverable type of ship designed to travel long distances. Later the Iberians built larger ships such as galleons, which provided much more room for cargo and larger crews. To chart the position of the sun and stars, Iberian sailors used the astrolabe (AS-truh-labe), invented by tenth-century Arabs. Some Europeans also learned how to mount weapons on ships, which enabled them to overwhelm coastal defenses and defeat lightly armed ships. By the late 1500s, the English were building the most maneuverable ships and the best iron cannon, and by the 1700s, European land and sea weapons greatly outclassed those of once militarily powerful China, India, Persia, and Ottoman Turkey.

Driven by Competition

The intense competition between major European powers led to increased exploration, the building of trade networks, and a scramble for colonies, subject territories where Europeans could directly

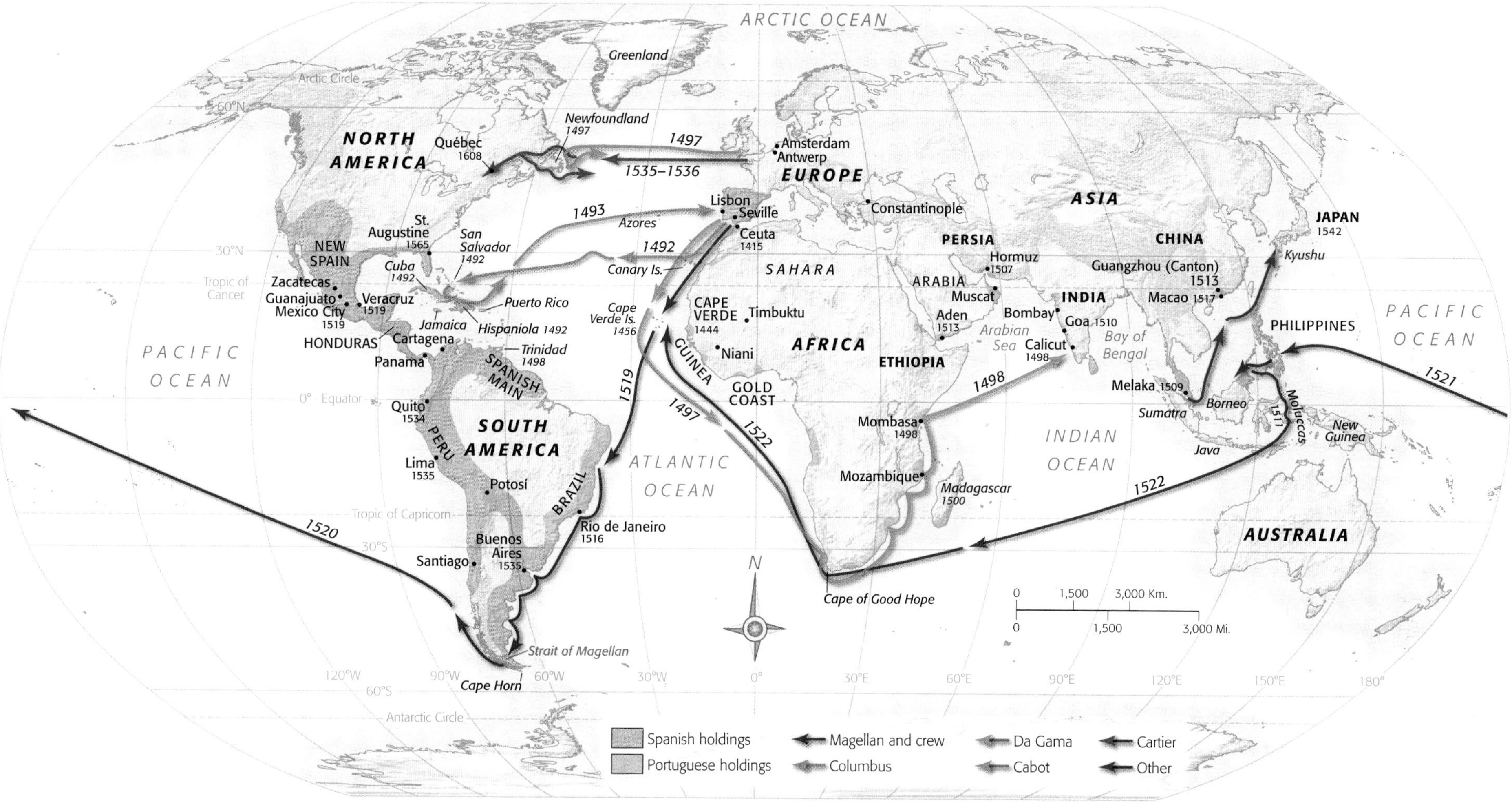

Map 15.1
European Exploration, 1450–1600

Between the early 1400s and mid-1600s, explorers sponsored by Portugal, Spain, France, Holland, and England discovered the sea route around Africa to South and Southeast Asia, crossed the Atlantic to the Americas, and sailed across the Pacific Ocean from the Americas to Asia.

© Cengage Learning

control primary production. In the 1400s, the Portuguese began direct encounters with the peoples of coastal Africa, and by 1500, Portuguese explorers had reached East Africa and then sailed across the Indian Ocean to India. Soon, they seized key Asian ports such as Hormuz on the Persian Gulf, Goa in India, and Melaka in Malaya. Meanwhile, the Spanish discovered that a huge landmass to the west, soon to be named America, lay between Europe and East Asia. By the later 1500s, the Spanish had conquered much of the Americas, including the great Inca and Aztec Empires, making them the most powerful European state for some decades. Portugal, England, France, and Holland had also established American colonies by the early 1600s.

At the same time, Europeans established colonies in Africa and carried increasing numbers of enslaved Africans to the Western Hemisphere to work on plantations growing cash crops for European consumption. In the sixteenth and seventeenth centuries, the Portuguese, Dutch, and Spanish colonized several Asian port cities and various Southeast Asian islands, including the Philippines, Java, and the Spice Islands of Indonesia. American minerals, especially silver, supported a great expansion of the European economy and allowed Europeans to buy into the rich Asian trade. These conquests and economic activities enabled the transfer of vast quantities of resources to Europe.

The Foundations of Colonial Imperialism

During the Early Modern Era, Europeans gradually brought various peoples into their economic and political sphere, laying the foundations for a system of Western dominance in the world after 1750. The Portuguese and Spanish prospered in the 1500s from their overseas activities, while in the 1600s the overseas trade of the Dutch, English, and French enabled them to become the most powerful European countries. But European influence was still limited in many autonomous regions, including China, Siam, Japan, and Morocco. Nonetheless, overseas trade and exploitation provided some European societies with valuable human labor and natural resources and contributed to the growth of capitalism.

The Rise of Capitalism

Arising first in western Europe, capitalism has taken many forms and fostered new values around the world. Under capitalism, the drive for profit from privately owned and privately invested capital has largely determined what goods are produced and how they are distributed. Capitalism was unique when it first arose in Europe because, on a much greater scale than ever before, money in the form of investment capital was used to make profits. The various forms of capitalism that emerged as the economic system spread had certain common features: the need for constant accumulation of additional capital, economic self-interest, the profit motive, a market economy of some sort, and competition. These features shaped both economic and social relations between people. For example, individual carpenters who once shared their services with the community on a barter basis, or who belonged to a guild that operated for the benefit of all local carpenters, began to charge fees instead, competing for customers with other carpenters. By the 1800s, capitalism also included private ownership of the means of production, such as factories, businesses, and farms.

The Economic Center Shifts to Amsterdam

Capitalism was not necessarily inevitable. The profit motive and competition were incompatible with certain traditional cultures that disapproved of individuals accumulating more wealth than their neighbors. In precapitalist societies, governments siphoned off surplus wealth, and the elite spent their resources on conspicuous consumption of luxuries, such as the building of magnificent cathedrals, palaces, and pyramids. In medieval Europe, merchant and craft guilds emphasized ethics, accepting a strict regulation of economic activity for the greater good. By contrast, capitalists invested some profits in further exchange or production, reinvestment that differentiated capitalism from earlier economic systems. During the 1500s, the English and the people of the Low Countries, especially the Flemish and Dutch, developed the most dynamic forms of capitalism, and soon they eclipsed Italy, shifting the economic balance of power in Europe from the Mediterranean to the north. By the 1620s, Amsterdam in Holland had emerged as Europe's capitalist powerhouse, dominating much European and Asian trade. This clean, orderly, and prosperous Dutch city boasted amenities that were rare elsewhere, such as street lamps and watch patrols to prevent crime.

> " Expanding capitalism fostered new economic ideas, social groups, and consumption patterns. "

Emergence of the Bourgeoisie

Expanding capitalism fostered new economic ideas, social groups, and consumption patterns. Spurred by increasing trade, old concepts of investing wealth in land ownership gradually gave way to the view that capital should instead be invested in business and industry to help increase production of ships, armor, arms, and textiles, and thus create more capital. The increase in available capital began to change business methods, especially the use of credit on a large scale, which fostered banking. Capitalism also produced a new social group known as the bourgeoisie, an urban-based, mostly commercial, middle class of merchants, financiers, and other businessmen. The new materialism of the cities encouraged more people of all backgrounds to purchase consumer goods, from tea, coffee, and sugar to clocks, china, and glassware.

CHRONOLOGY

Political, Economic, and Intellectual Developments, 1500–1750

1500–1770	Era of commercial capitalism
1533–1586	Reign of Ivan the Terrible in Muscovy
ca. 1600–1750	Scientific Revolution
ca. 1600–1750	Baroque era
1609	Dutch independence
1618–1648	Thirty Years' War
1641–1645	English Civil War
1648	Congress of Westphalia
1661–1715	Reign of Louis XIV in France
1675–1800	Enlightenment
1682–1725	Reign of Peter the Great in Russia
1688	English Bill of Rights
1688–1689	Glorious Revolution and Declaration of Rights in England
1700–1709	Great Northern War
1701–1714	War of the Spanish Succession
1707	United Kingdom of England, Scotland, and Wales

Economic Secularization

As a new capitalist order emerged, many Christian Europeans changed their attitudes toward charging interest for loans and seeking profit. The medieval church had denounced charging interest as usury, a mortal sin, and had also opposed commercial profit, leaving much commerce and banking to the Jewish minority. By the late 1500s, however, many rejected these church teachings and instead heeded the cynical saying that "he who takes usury goes to hell; he who doesn't goes to the poorhouse." This reflected a gradual shift toward an entirely different type of society in western Europe. Jacob Fugger (FOOG-uhr) (1459–1525) of Augsburg (AUGZ-burg), a southern German city, was one European who prospered from the new economic trends, eventually becoming Europe's richest man. He wrote the epitaph for his own tomb, praising himself as "behind no one in attainment of extraordinary wealth, in generosity, purity of morals and greatness of soul."[3]

Agricultural Backlash

While western Europe became increasingly capitalist, parts of eastern Europe discouraged capitalism. In the 1500s, as the demand for agricultural products increased while cooler climates hindered farming, eastern European nobles faced a labor shortage on their estates. Allied with the landowning aristocracy, kings in Poland, Lithuania, Prussia, and Russia mandated serfdom on the peasantries and imposed new laws forbidding people to leave the land. At the same time, by providing little support to the local merchant classes, these governments thwarted capitalist expansion and diminished the political influence of cities.

Commercial Capitalism and Mercantilism

As a dynamic, flexible economic system, capitalism continually evolved and expanded. Under the form of capitalism that was dominant in western Europe between 1500 and 1770, commercial capitalism, most capital was invested in commercial enterprises such

> "Renaissance philosophy, known as humanism, emphasized humanity and its creations rather than God."

as trading companies, including the world's first joint-stock companies. To increase their efficiency and profits, these precursors of today's giant multinational corporations pooled their resources by selling shares, or stocks, to merchants and bankers. Joint-stock companies encouraged investment and mobilized great capital. They employed cashiers, bookkeepers, couriers, and middlemen skilled in various languages, and invested in diversified economic activities such as real estate, mining, and industry. Few Asian or African merchants could compete with this collective power.

Mercantilism

Commercial capitalism was strongly shaped by the cooperation of the state and big business enterprises, which worked together for their mutual benefit. States practiced mercantilism, an economic approach based on a government policy of building a nation's wealth by expanding its reserves of gold and silver bullion. The Atlantic states of England, Holland, France, and Spain particularly pursued mercantilism. Trading was controlled by semi-military, government-backed companies protected from competition. To attract bullion held by other nations, these governments tried to limit imports and increase exports. Spurred by mercantilism, during the 1500s commercial capitalism expanded out of western Europe and into Africa, Asia, and the Americas.

LO² The Renaissance and Reformation

Two major movements, the Renaissance and the Reformation, reshaped European thought and culture in the 1500s. During the Renaissance—a dramatic flowering in arts and learning that began in Italy around 1350 (see Chapter 14)—new philosophical, scientific, artistic, and literary currents paved the way for more creative, secular societies. The movement reached its peak in the 1500s, as economic expansion provided more people with money to purchase art and books. In the same century, the Reformation—the movement to reform Christianity—spawned new Christian churches that provided alternatives to the Roman Catholic Church. Both movements transformed western European cultural and religious life.

Renaissance Philosophy and Science

Medieval, Renaissance, Reformation: Western Civilization, Act II (*http://www.omnibusol.com/medieval.html*) A treasure trove of links on many aspects of society in these centuries.

The Renaissance fostered new ideas in philosophy and science. During this spurt in knowledge, thinkers and artists rediscovered the ideas of the Classical Greeks and Romans while absorbing inventions and ideas from the Islamic world and China. The Renaissance promoted values such as individualism, secularism, tolerance, beauty, and creativity. Renaissance philosophy, known as humanism, emphasized humanity and its creations rather than God.

Humanism and the Church

Humanism also focused on problems in the church. A growing crisis of confidence in the Roman Catholic Church, with its abuses by leadership and clergy, became more serious after 1400. Some Renaissance thinkers favored gradual church reform and less rigid ideas. The French humanist writer François Rabelais (RAB-uh-lay) (ca. 1494–1553) went so far as to call monks "a rabble of counterfeit saints, hypocrites, pretended zealots, who disguise themselves like masquers to deceive the world."[4] By spurring freedom of thought and offering critical insights, humanists began to topple the authoritarian medieval attitudes that had crippled scientific investigation, but popes rejected any significant changes.

Machiavelli: The Study of Power

In the area of political thought, Niccolò Machiavelli (MAK-ee-uh-VEL-ee) (1469–1527), the Florentine author of a political manual, *The Prince*, was perhaps the first European to study power as

CHRONOLOGY

The Renaissance and Reformation, 1350–1615

ca. 1350–1615	Era of Renaissance
ca. 1517–1615	Protestant Reformation
1532	Formation of Church of England (Anglicans)
1534	Founding of Society of Jesus (Jesuits)
1536	Move of John Calvin to Geneva
1545–1563	Council of Trent
1558–1603	Elizabethan era in England
1562–1589	Wars of religion in France
1571	Defeat of Turks at Lepanto by "Holy League"
1588	English defeat of Spanish armada
1598	Edict of Nantes

something separate from moral doctrine. *The Prince* argued that the ruler must always keep end goals in mind and apply ruthless policies, such as deception and violence, in pursuing vital national interests. But the exercise of power did not necessarily require tyranny, because the ruler must avoid being hated. Rulers ignored popular moral values at their peril. Machiavelli also argued that it was not necessary for a leader to have piety, faith, integrity, and humanity— only the appearance of such values. Machiavelli's writings became very influential as a guide for European leaders.

Leonardo da Vinci

Although Greco-Roman traditions greatly influenced Renaissance thought, some thinkers developed more interest in science, often employing experimentation and observation. For example, the Florentine Leonardo da Vinci (lay-own-AHR-doh dah VIN-chee) (1452–1519) argued that simply repeating classical traditions without verifying them placed emphasis on memory more than intelligence. A painter, sculptor, architect, scientist, mathematician, and engineer, da Vinci exemplified the versatile Renaissance personality and openness to varied influences.

The Copernican Revolution

Another influential scientist, Polish astronomer Nicolaus Copernicus (koh-PUR-nuh-kuhs) (1473–1543), studied the skies and Islamic scholarship on astronomy, especially the influential writings of the Arab mathematician Ibn al-Shatir (1304–1375), whose research suggested that the earth might not be the center of the universe. Copernicus then transformed astronomy and physics when he devised his revolutionary "heliocentric," or sun-centered, theory of the solar system in 1507. Copernicus refuted the traditional European idea that earth was the center of the universe, arguing that earth and the planets revolved around the sun. He did not dare publish his findings until after his death, fearing persecution by the church.

The Prince: Power Politics During the Italian Renaissance Learn from the man himself what it means to be "Machiavellian."

Late Renaissance Art and Literature

The Renaissance reshaped European art and spread Italian artistic influence. The art of this period was founded on a desire to reflect the deepening knowledge of humanity by more accurately representing human concerns in sculpture, painting, architecture, and literature. Some of the inspiration came from the growing contacts with Islamic, Asian, and African cultures. Italians such as the Venetian painter Giovanni Bellini (ca. 1430–1516) worked in or visited Muslim cities such as Istanbul and Cairo, spreading Italian influences but also returning with new perspectives. In the early 1500s, Rome replaced Florence as the new capital of Italian art. Among those who worked in Rome, the eccentric Florentine Michelangelo Buonarroti (mi-kuhl-AN-juh-loh bwawn-uh-RAW-tee) (1475–1564) became famous for his realistic sculptures, paintings, and frescoes. He paid keen attention to the attitudes and gestures of each figure he painted on the ceiling of the Vatican's Sistine Chapel.

The Renaissance also spread well beyond Italy. In the Low Countries, Pieter Bruegel (BROY-guhl) the Elder (ca. 1525–1569) integrated Renaissance and local traditions, painting realistic landscapes and sympathetic scenes of peasant and town life. El Greco (ell GREK-oh) (1541–1614), a native of Crete who studied in Italy before settling in Spain, blended Venetian, Byzantine, and Spanish traditions.

Read about how Dutch artist Rembrandt Van Rijn earned his livelihood in the free market as a painter.

The Literary Heritage of the Renaissance

As in art, the Renaissance had literary consequences throughout Europe. In England during the brilliant reign of Queen Elizabeth I (r. 1558–1603), playwright William Shakespeare (1564–1616) wrote histories, comedies, and tragedies that many literary scholars have believed transcend time and place. Some of his plays, such as *Henry V* and *Julius Caesar*, addressed English or ancient history, while others, such as *Othello*, *Hamlet*, and *The Merchant of Venice*, commented on the world beyond England. One of his best-known characters, Hamlet, voiced Renaissance exuberance: "What [a] piece of

> "Growing knowledge about other cultures forced some Europeans to reconsider their assumptions about the world, and their new ideas helped reshape literature and social thought."

work is a man, how noble in reason, how infinite in faculties."[5]

In Spain in 1615, Miguel de Cervantes (suhr-VAN-teez) Saavedra (1547–1616) published one of the era's great novels, *Don Quixote* (kee-HO-tee). His book painted a vast panorama of society at the end of Spain's golden age. The main character, Don Quixote, sets out to battle dragons and evil men, right injustice, and protect the innocent, but he mainly makes a grand nuisance of himself. Cervantes reflected Renaissance attitudes by dignifying the human spirit but also, like some classical Greek playwrights, making fun of its plight.

Growing knowledge about other cultures forced some Europeans to reconsider their assumptions

Bruegel's *Peasant Wedding* Painted around 1567, Pieter Bruegel's *The Peasant Wedding* celebrates the rituals of peasant life, in this case a wedding dinner for a village. The Flemish artist may also have intended the painting of the feasting villagers as a satire on self-indulgence.

Musée de la Ville de Paris, Musée Carnavalet/The Bridgeman Art Library International

about the world, and their new ideas helped reshape literature and social thought. The French writer Michel Eyquem de Montaigne (mon-TANE) (1533–1592) idealized Native American societies, popularizing the notion of a "Noble Savage" uncorrupted by "civilization." Shakespeare took up the theme in his 1611 play *The Tempest*, where he mocked the idea of the Noble Savage. In the play he creates a contrast between the civilized Prospero and the savage Caliban (KAL-uh-ban) (an anagram for *cannibal*). His Caliban is fierce and brutal, a far cry from the Noble Savage.

The Reformation and Religious Change

Changing societies and a questioning of the old order also spawned the Reformation. To critics, the Roman church had become corrupt, often led by incompetent popes and clergy who blatantly violated priestly requirements for celibacy and poverty. In addition, the spread of literacy and printed books inspired some individuals to interpret Christian writings for themselves. Throughout the 1500s, various groups sought church reform. Some, later called Protestants, eventually broke completely with Roman Catholicism and established their own churches. The Reformation

 Interactive Map

(1517–1615) transformed the religious makeup of Europe and profoundly reshaped Western thought (see Map 15.2). By 1600 almost 40 percent of non-Orthodox Europeans, mostly in the north, had renounced the Catholic faith and adopted some form of Protestantism, such as Lutheranism, Calvinism, and Anglicanism.

Martin Luther

Martin Luther (1483–1546), a German, launched the movement that ended the unity of Western Christianity. Luther studied law, then became an Augustinian monk, and later earned a doctorate in theology, after which he taught at the University of Wittenberg. Eventually Luther con-

 Table Talk Read Martin Luther in his own words, speaking out forcefully and candidly— and sometimes with humor—against Catholic institutions.

cluded that nothing in scripture justified papal power and elaborate church rituals, and that only faith, not good works, could wipe away a person's sin and ensure salvation. Luther's break with the church was prompted by the lucrative church practice of selling indulgences, clerical statements that canceled punishment due for sins in exchange for cash contributions to the church. In 1517 Luther distributed a paper containing ninety-five statements in Latin attacking indulgences. Soon his statements caused an uproar, and Pope Leo X excommunicated Luther in 1520. Luther then translated the Bible into German and condemned Rome as "the greatest thief and robber that has ever appeared on earth or ever will."[6] Lutherans formed a church rooted in the Augsburg Confession, a doctrinal statement issued in 1530 that argued for the Bible as the only source of faith, stated that every believer had the freedom to interpret scripture, and attacked the cults of the Virgin Mary and the saints, priestly celibacy, and the monastic orders.

> 66 Luther's break generated unrest and divided Western Christianity. 99

Consequences of Luther's Reforms

Luther's break generated unrest and divided Western Christianity. Lutheranism spread widely in northern Germany, Scandinavia, and the eastern Baltic coast. In the 1520s, many Germans threw their support to Luther and the reform cause. But in 1524, a major conflict split the reform movement when peasants, inspired by Luther's challenge to Catholic Church power, revolted against the lords and church leaders who owned the land. Luther, opposed to mixing religion and social protest, unsuccessfully mediated between the sides and then supported the nobles, who crushed the uprisings. The result was more than 100,000 deaths. Many German princes became Lutheran, while their overlord, the Holy Roman Emperor, remained staunchly Catholic.

John Calvin in Geneva

Non-Germans were also inspired by Luther's example. One Protestant movement, Calvinism, was more radical than Lutheranism in rejecting Catholic doctrine. Its founder, John Calvin (1509–1564), was forced to leave France for supporting Luther's ideas and settled in Geneva (juh-NEE-vuh), Switzerland. Unlike Luther, Calvin believed not in human free will but in predestination, the doctrine that an individual's salvation or damnation was already determined at birth by God. Because good

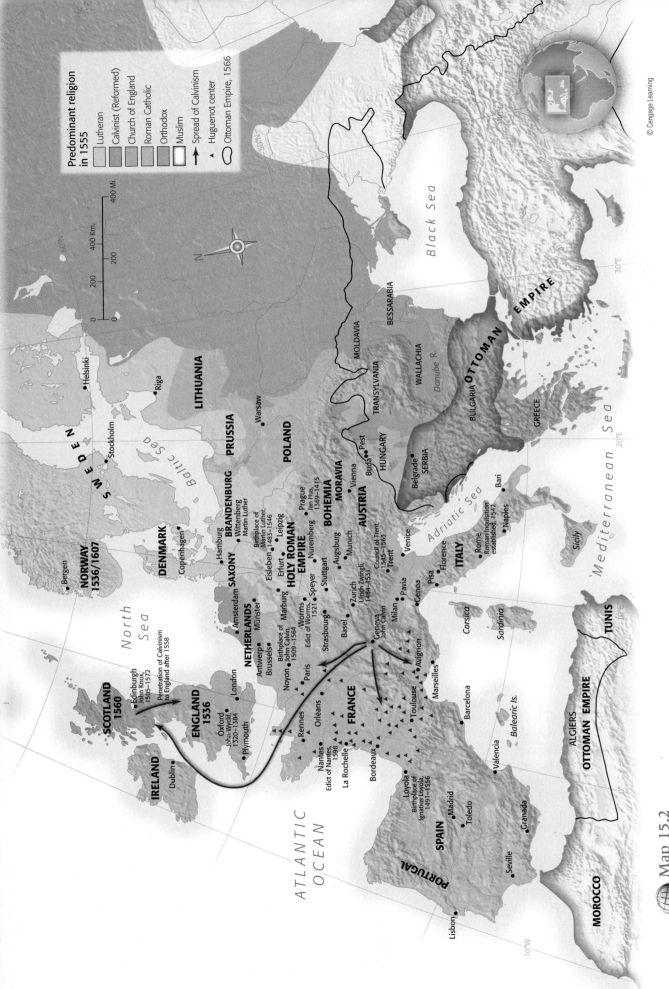

Map 15.2
Reformation Europe

The Protestant Reformation reshaped Europe's religious landscape in the 1500s and early 1600s. By the mid-1550s, some form of Protestantism had become dominant in much of northern Europe, England, and Scotland. Catholicism remained predominant in the southern half of western Europe and parts of eastern Europe.

Predominant religion in 1555
- Lutheran
- Calvinist (Reformed)
- Church of England
- Roman Catholic
- Orthodox
- Muslim
- Spread of Calvinism
- Huguenot center
- Ottoman Empire, 1566

© Cengage Learning

ATLANTIC OCEAN

North Sea

SCOTLAND 1560
Edinburgh
John Knox, 1505–1572

IRELAND
Dublin

ENGLAND 1536
Oxford
John Wyclif, 1320–1384
London
Plymouth
Penetration of Calvinism to England after 1558

NORWAY 1536/1607
Bergen

SWEDEN
Stockholm
Helsinki
Riga

Baltic Sea

DENMARK
Copenhagen
Hamburg

LITHUANIA

PRUSSIA
Warsaw

BRANDENBURG

POLAND

SAXONY
Wittenberg
Birthplace of Martin Luther
Eisleben, 1483–1546
Martin Luther
Erfurt
Leipzig

HOLY ROMAN EMPIRE
Prague
Jan Hus, 1369–1415

BOHEMIA

MORAVIA

Nuremberg

AUSTRIA
Vienna

HUNGARY
Buda
Pest

BESSARABIA

MOLDAVIA

TRANSYLVANIA

WALLACHIA
Danube R.

BULGARIA
OTTOMAN EMPIRE
Belgrade
SERBIA

GREECE

Black Sea

NETHERLANDS
Amsterdam
Münster
Antwerp
Brussels

Marburg
Speyer
Worms
Edict of Worms, 1521
Strasbourg

Augsburg
Munich
Stuttgart

Basel
Zurich
Ulrich Zwingli, 1484–1531

Geneva
John Calvin
Council of Trent, 1545–1563
Trent

Venice
Milan
Pavia
Genoa

Adriatic Sea

ITALY
Florence
Pisa
Rome
Roman Inquisition established, 1542
Naples
Bari

Sicily

Corsica
Sardinia

Mediterranean Sea

Noyon
Birthplace of John Calvin, 1509–1564
Paris
Rennes
Orléans

FRANCE
Nantes
Edict of Nantes, 1598
La Rochelle
Bordeaux
Toulouse
Avignon
Marseilles

Barcelona
Valencia
Balearic Is.

SPAIN
Madrid
Toledo
Granada
Seville

PORTUGAL
Lisbon

Loyola
Birthplace of Ignatius Loyola, 1491–1556

MOROCCO

ALGIERS
OTTOMAN EMPIRE

TUNIS

0   200   400 Km.
0   400 Mi.

N

behavior and faith could not guarantee reaching Heaven, the authorities must enforce morality to maintain order. Under Calvin, Geneva became a theocratic society, ruled by church leaders who demanded strict morality and attacked worldly pleasures such as swearing, dancing, rolling dice, and playing cards. Calvinism spread rapidly in Switzerland, England, and Holland and also developed centers of strength elsewhere; in Scotland, the Calvinist John Knox founded the Presbyterian Church in 1561.

Henry VIII: A Different Kind of Reformation

In England, unlike Germany and Switzerland, the initiative for religious change came from the king, Henry VIII (r. 1509–1547), who was then a Catholic. Henry had no male heir with his wife, Catherine of Aragon, so he asked the pope to annul his marriage so that he could marry Anne Boleyn (1501–1536). When Rome refused the annulment, Henry chose to break with the church in 1532, rejecting papal supremacy. He announced his divorce, married Anne Boleyn, and arranged to be made head of the Church of England, later known as the Anglican Church. Henry quickly moved to suppress both Calvinism and the Catholic Church. He closed the English monasteries and distributed their lands to his allies among nobles and businessmen. However, the Anglicans largely retained Catholic dogma. Ironically, Henry grew disenchanted with Anne Boleyn, who also bore him no sons, and had her beheaded in 1536. Henry married four more times.

Henry's moves generated religious strife in England. His only male heir, the sickly Edward VI (r. 1547–1553), came to the throne at age ten but died at sixteen of tuberculosis. The Catholic reaction was led by Henry's daughter by Catherine of Aragon, Queen Mary Tudor (TOO-duhr) (r. 1553–1558), who suppressed the Anglican Church. But she was succeeded by Elizabeth I (1533–1603), the daughter of Henry VIII and Anne Boleyn, who restored the Anglican Church. Calvinist influences then began reshaping Anglican dogma. English Calvinists (known as Puritans) were at first tolerated by Anglicans but later persecuted by Elizabeth's successors for opposing moves toward Catholic–Anglican reconciliation. Some Puritans emigrated to Holland. From there one small Puritan group, the Pilgrims, moved to North America in 1620 to seek more religious freedom, helping plant Puritan influence in the New England colonies.

Protestantism and Capitalism

Some scholars believe that Protestant doctrines contributed to, and supplied religious underpinnings for, capitalist values. Some forms of Protestantism were certainly congenial to the thriving new economic attitudes. Like Calvinists and other Protestants, capitalists favored productive labor, frugality, sobriety, and accumulation of wealth as good in themselves. Both Protestantism and capitalism also encouraged individualism, thus undermining the medieval values that the Catholic Church defended. Indeed, capitalism flourished in several Protestant societies, especially Holland, England, and northern Germany. The strongest capitalist societies were also the most Protestant; they were also the most intellectually diverse and gave rise to some secularized free thinkers. Protestantism opened the doors to democracy: once people had freely voiced their opinions on religion, they moved on to seeking a voice in government.

> **Counter Reformation** A movement to confront Protestantism and crush dissidents within the Catholic Church.

The Counter Reformation and Catholic Reform

The Protestant challenge generated a reaction, the Counter Reformation, a movement to confront Protestantism and crush dissidents within the Catholic Church. The church used varied strategies to fight Protestantism, including the Holy Inquisition, the church court formed in medieval times to combat heretical ideas (see Chapter 14). Persecution of dissidents became especially ferocious in Spain, where several thousand people who were believed to hold dissident ideas were burned at the stake. The pope also formed the Congregation of the Index to censor books, and promoted increased missionary activity abroad. The Spanish Basque former soldier, Ignatius of Loyola (loi-OH-luh) (1491–1556), founded the Jesuit order, or Society of Jesus, in 1534, which boasted strict discipline. One prominent Jesuit, the Spanish Basque St. Francis Xavier (ZAY-vee-uhr) (1506–1552), became a pioneering missionary in India, Southeast Asia, and Japan.

The Council of Trent

For all the harsh punitive measures, dissidence within the church persisted, prompting the pope to sponsor a series of conferences, the Council of Trent, to reconsider church doctrines. Although the council (1545–1563) mostly reaffirmed Catholic dogma, it did bring about some reform, imposing more papal supervision of priests and bishops and mandating that all clergy be trained

Witness to the Past

Queen Elizabeth I Rallies Her People

Few women have ever enjoyed the power and respect of England's Renaissance queen, Elizabeth I. Her forty-five years of rule (1558–1603) marked a brilliant period for English culture, especially in literature and theater. On her death, the admiring playwright Ben Jonson wrote her epitaph: "For wit, features, and true passion, Earth, thou hast not such another." The queen may have been, as her detractors claimed, deceptive, devious, and autocratic, but her intelligence and formidable political skills helped her maneuver successfully through the snake pit of both English and European politics. But English–Spanish relations deteriorated, prompting war. In 1588, as the powerful Spanish armada sailed toward the English coast, Elizabeth launched the English ships with a speech to her subjects that ironically played off her gender to reinforce her link with the English people. With the help of foul weather, the English defeated the Spanish, changing the fortunes of both countries.

My loving people. We have been persuaded by some that are careful for our safety, to take heed how we commit ourselves to armed multitudes, for fear of treachery, but I assure you, I do not desire to live to distrust my faithful and loving people. Let tyrants fear; I have always so behaved myself, that, under God, I have placed my chiefest strength and safeguard in the loyal hearts and good will of my subjects, and therefore I am come amongst you, as you see, at this time, not for my recreation and disport, but being resolved in the midst and heat of the battle, to live or die amongst you all, to lay down for my God, and for my kingdoms, and for my people, my honor and my blood, even in the dust.

I know I have the body of a weak and feeble woman; but I have the heart and stomach of a king, and of a king of England too; and I think foul scorn that . . . Spain, or any prince of Europe should dare to invade the borders of my realm; to which rather than any dishonor shall grow by me, I myself will take up arms, I myself will be your general, judge, and rewarder of every one of your virtues in the field.

I know already for your forwardness you have deserved rewards and crowns; and we do assure you in the word of a prince, they shall be duly paid you. In the meantime my lieutenant general shall be in my stead, than whom never prince commanded a more noble or worthy subject; no doubting but by your obedience to my general, by your concord in the camp, and your valor in the field, we shall shortly have a famous victory over those enemies of my God, of my kingdoms, and of my people.

Thinking About the Reading

1. How did Elizabeth justify the forthcoming battle with Spain?
2. What personal qualities did this Renaissance monarch suggest she could offer to her people in their time of peril?

Source: Charles W. Colby, ed., *Selections from the Sources of English History* (Harlow: Longmans, Green, 1899), pp. 158–159. Quotation in introduction from A. L. Rowse, *The Elizabethan Renaissance: The Life of the Society* (New York: Charles Scribner's, 1971), p. 59.

---

in seminaries. The Trent reforms enabled Catholicism to recover some lost ground, and the Catholic Church endured in a modified form. Catholics gradually turned from confronting Protestants to converting the peoples outside of Europe.

But religious passions continued to foster intolerance. Indeed, in Europe, religious minori-

ties, such as Jews, French Protestants, and English Catholics, faced discrimination and sometimes violence; many emigrated to escape such persecution. Several popes pursued anti-Jewish policies, as did some Protestants: Luther advocated burning synagogues, arresting rabbis, and confiscating Jewish property.

Religious Wars and Conflicts

Religious divisions contributed to a series of European wars and other conflicts from the late sixteenth through early eighteenth centuries. The Spanish Empire, ruled by a branch of the Habsburg family, was particularly troubled by religious tensions. During the 1500s, Spain emerged as a major European power, which, thanks to exploration and conquest, controlled a vast empire in the Americas and Southeast Asia. The Spanish Habsburgs also ruled other Europeans, including Portugal, the Low Countries, and parts of Italy. King Philip II of Spain (r. 1556–1598), known as "the most Catholic of kings," put the resources of the Spanish crown toward defending and spreading the Catholic faith.

The Spanish Armada and the Birth of the Netherlands

Philip faced one of his biggest challenges in the Low Countries, where his suppression of Calvinism antagonized businessmen and the nobility. Inflamed Protestants attacked Catholic churches, and Spain's execution of dissident leaders spurred a general revolt in 1566, in which both Catholics and Protestants rallied behind the Calvinist leader, the Dutchman William of Nassau (NAS-au), Prince of Orange. Philip dispatched an occupation army that executed more than 1,100 Protestants and, in 1576, sacked Antwerp, Europe's wealthiest city. In 1579, hoping to divide his opponents, Philip promised political liberty to the ten largely Catholic Flemish- and French-speaking southern provinces of the Low Countries, thereby forging the foundations of modern Belgium and Luxembourg. Because of English assistance to the Low Country rebels and English attacks on Spanish shipping in the Americas, Philip II tried to invade England by sea in 1588 but faced a determined foe in Queen Elizabeth I (see Witness to the Past: Queen Elizabeth I Rallies Her People). The English ships outmaneuvered Spain's armada of 130 ships and then triumphed when a fierce storm in the English Channel devastated the Spanish fleet. The mostly Protestant, Dutch-speaking northern provinces of the Low Countries broke away from Spain in 1588 and became fully independent in 1609, forming the country that became the Netherlands.

The Edict of Nantes

Between 1562 and 1589, religious conflicts also raged across France. The French Calvinists, known as Huguenots (HYOO-guh-nauts), were led by the powerful Bourbon (BOOR-buhn) family. In 1572, after the assassination of Calvinist leaders on royal orders sparked Huguenot rioting in Paris, Catholic forces massacred 30,000 Huguenots. In 1593 Henry of Bourbon (1553–1610), remarking that "Paris is well worth a mass," renounced Calvinism for Catholicism in order to become King Henry IV. Remaining a Protestant sympathizer, in 1598 he signed the Edict of Nantes (nahnt), which ended the religious conflicts by recognizing Roman Catholicism as the state church of France but giving Huguenots the right to freely practice their religion.

Turkish Expansion, European Resistance

While Protestant–Catholic tensions in Europe were intense, Christian–Muslim conflicts also simmered and often translated into political and military conflict. Many Europeans were concerned about the growing power of the Muslim Ottoman Turks (see Chapter 16), who sought to expand their empire, which already included Greece, much of the Balkans, and Bulgaria. When some people in the Balkans abandoned Christianity for Islam, Christian leaders became alarmed, and the Holy Roman Emperor Charles V marshaled allies to defeat the Turks at Vienna in 1529. Then in 1571 the so-called Holy League of Spain, Rome, and Venice used advanced naval gunnery to destroy the Turkish fleet at the Battle of Lepanto (li-PAN-toh), off Greece, ending Turkish ambitions for a while. In 1683 the Turks besieged Vienna, and Austria was saved only by Polish intervention. Finally, the Austrians pushed the Turks out of Hungary. Ottoman expansion in Europe had ended.

LO³ Changing States and Politics

The encounters with the wider world, capitalism, Renaissance humanism, and the Protestant Reformation reshaped Europe and challenged old beliefs. European politics also changed, as bloody wars drew much of Europe into conflict: kingdoms were torn asunder and reconfigured, old states declined, and new states gained influence. Many of these states used mercantilist policies to strengthen their power, and in some states, some form of royal absolutism flourished. A few other states developed representative governments with elements of democracy.

Regional Wars and National Conflicts

Various wars raged during the Early Modern Era, some prompted by religious divisions, and others spawned by tensions between rival states and empires. Even after religious tensions subsided, warfare remained a constant reality, involving most European societies at one time or another.

> "Even after religious tensions subsided, warfare remained a constant reality, involving most European societies at one time or another."

The Thirty Years' War and the Treaty of Westphalia

The major conflict was the Thirty Years' War (1618–1648), a long series of bloody hostilities that claimed millions of lives and involved many countries. This complex struggle for regional power started in the Holy Roman Empire, as Czech (check) Protestants revolted against oppressive Habsburg Catholic rulers. Eventually the fighting also drew in German princes and two mostly Lutheran countries, Denmark and Sweden. Finally France, although a mostly Catholic country, went to war against its Habsburg rivals who ruled Austria and Spain. In 1648 the conflict ended after a four-year-long European congress in Westphalia (west-FALE-yuh), a German province. The Treaty of Westphalia reaffirmed freedom of religion but did not permanently end Protestant–Catholic conflict. The new balance of power in Europe favored France and curbed the Habsburgs, and France enjoyed unrivaled prestige after 1659. The Holy Roman Emperor lost influence to German princes, Sweden gained territory, and the conference recognized Swiss independence from Habsburg rule. The wars of the later 1600s and early 1700s were fought with well-drilled professional soldiers, large warships, and more deadly gunpowder weapons. Consequently, the human costs of war increased: in the 1709 Battle of Malpaquet, 40,000 French soldiers were killed or wounded.

The War of Spanish Succession

The most widespread conflict, the War of the Spanish Succession (1701–1714), brought together England, Holland, Austria, Denmark, Portugal, and some German states to battle France and Spain over who would inherit the Spanish throne from the last Habsburg king. The Treaty of Utrecht (YOO-trecht), which ended the war, forced Spain to transfer its ter-

Soldiers' Return In the early 1600s, the French artist Jacques Callot made a series of moving etchings about the Thirty Years' War called "Miseries of War." This etching shows a group of discharged soldiers, so impoverished and brutalized by war that they either beg for food or die alongside the road.

ritory in Belgium and Italy to Austria. The once-prosperous Dutch had overextended themselves in the war, damaging their economy, and Venice became a peripheral, declining state. Now a major maritime power, England received most of the spoils of war, including the strategic Gibraltar peninsula at Spain's southern tip. Utrecht resulted in a new balance of power among European states, and most of Europe entered a period of calm.

Absolutist and Despotic Monarchies

States changed during the Early Modern Era, with many governments moving far from medieval forms. New ways of thinking, as well as political, social, and religious strife, set the stage for diverse patterns of government by the seventeenth century. One trend among states was the rise of absolutism, a system of concentrated monarchial authority best represented by the French kings and the Russian czars.

The Sun King

For a time, absolute monarchies dazzled Europe, with King Louis XIV (r. 1661–1715) of France serving as the widely envied model. By the mid-1600s, France, with 18 million people, was western Europe's largest country, was self-sufficient in agriculture, and had some thriving industries. Louis XIV believed that his power derived from God, thus he was a monarch by divine right. Known as the Sun King for the brilliant extravagance of his court, Louis enjoyed great power, demanding obedience from all at the expense of the nobility.

The king tried to control everything. He imposed mercantilism, fostering industries and companies subject to royal domination, and he revoked the Edict of Nantes, forbade Protestant pastors to preach, and closed Protestant schools and churches. His repression of Protestantism led 200,000 Huguenots to emigrate to England, Holland, and North America. Louis also ordered a spectacular palace built at Versailles (vuhr-SIGH), a Paris suburb. Versailles became the center of French life, and French nobles and foreign leaders were compelled to spend time there. The king patronized the arts and literature, and in turn artists celebrated the king, comparing him to classical Greek and Roman leaders.

Louis XIV's search for power elsewhere in Europe caused four major wars aimed at preventing Habsburg dominance. Marrying his dreams of personal glory to his goal of state prestige, he built up an effective military force. French power reached its height around 1680, but the wars proved financially ruinous and fell short of their objectives. The War of the Spanish Succession sapped the French treasury and military and enabled Austria, England, and Holland to counterbalance French power. Although France remained a major state after 1715, it had lost some of its glory.

> **absolutism**
> A form of government in which sovereignty is vested in a single person, the king or queen; monarchs in the sixteenth and seventeenth centuries based their authority on the theory of the divine right of kings (i.e., that they had received their authority from God and were responsible only to Him).

> 66 New ways of thinking, as well as political, social, and religious strife, set the stage for diverse patterns of government by the seventeenth century. 99

Ivan IV

Russia also developed a strong and often tyrannical government led by czars. Ivan (ee-VON) IV (r. 1533–1584)—known as Ivan the Terrible because of his paranoia and brutality—built a centralized Russian state while fighting wars with neighboring Poland and Sweden and conquering the Tartar states, founded by Mongols and Turks three centuries earlier, along the lower Volga River. Ivan also ordered the death or torture of many thousands of Russians whom he considered enemies. Muscovite czars after Ivan imposed a rural economy based on serfdom to gain support from the landed nobility. Lords could sell their serfs, making them little better than slaves. The czars imposed tight control over the Russian Orthodox Church after it broke officially from the Greek Orthodox Church in the late 1500s and pursued expansion toward the southeastern Baltic region, where they came into conflict with the Poles and Lithuanians.

Peter the Great

Russia gradually developed an even more powerful state, especially during the reign of Peter I the Great (r. 1682–1725), an enlightened but despotic czar who encouraged Russia's integration with the West. Nearly 7 feet tall and possessed with tremendous energy, Peter saw Russia's only hope as copying Western technology

St. Petersburg This painting, made around 1760, shows the Winter Palace, inhabited by the Russian royal family, occupying the left side of the Neva River in St. Petersburg, a major port that attracted many trading ships. Michael Holford

and administrative techniques. In 1698, the czar launched ambitious political, economic, military, and educational reforms and hired foreign specialists to advise him. Some of Peter's policies to promote western European practices were superficial and unpopular, such as banning beards. He increased royal power at the expense of the church and nobility, and expanded Russia's frontiers, established industries, strengthened autocracy and serfdom, put together a navy to protect his Baltic flank, and developed a more efficient government. Because he hated gloomy Moscow, with its medieval feel, in 1713 Peter began building a new capital on the Baltic, modeled on Amsterdam and Venice, and named it St. Petersburg.

 Russian History Index: The World Wide Web Virtual Library (http://vlib.iue.it/hist-russia/Index.html). Contains useful essays and links on Russian history, society, and politics.

Peter also had many foreign achievements. In 1699 he forged a secret alliance with Sweden's rivals, Denmark and Poland, and battled the Swedes in the Great Northern War beginning in 1700. Only in 1709 did an exhausted Sweden abandon the eastern rim of the Baltic to Russia. Russia's growing power unsettled European rivals, as Peter and other Russian czars pursued expansion to the south and east. Anxious to forge permanent access to the warm Mediterranean Sea, because it was open to shipping twelve months a year, Russian forces pushed south toward the Black Sea and the Straits of Bosporus (see Map 15.3). They also began acquiring territory in Siberia and Muslim Central Asia (see Chapter 16). By eventually creating a huge colossus of an empire and exploiting the resources of the newly colonized areas, Russia developed a largely self-sufficient economy. Despite Peter the Great's Westernization policies, most later czars were wary of foreign influence.

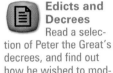 **Edicts and Decrees** Read a selection of Peter the Great's decrees, and find out how he wished to modernize, and Westernize, Russia.

 Interactive Map

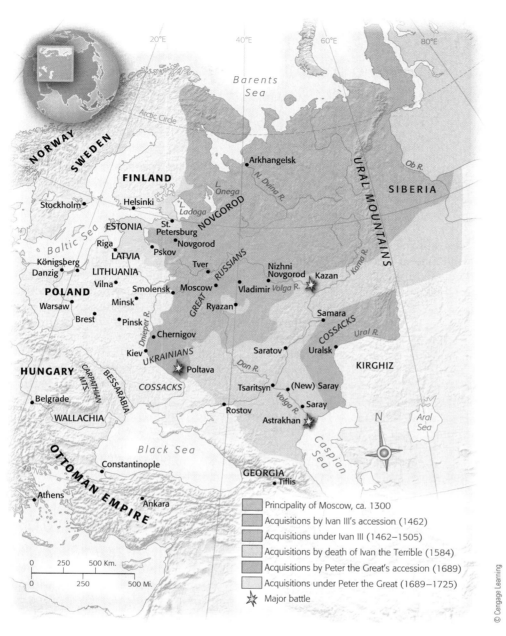

Map 15.3
Russian Expansion, 1300–1750

Beginning in the 1300s, the Russians expanded from a small remote northern state, based in Moscow, into an empire. By the mid-1700s, the Russians had gained political domination over western Siberia, the northern Caucasus, and part of what is today the eastern Baltic region and the Ukraine.

Legend:
- Principality of Moscow, ca. 1300
- Acquisitions by Ivan III's accession (1462)
- Acquisitions under Ivan III (1462–1505)
- Acquisitions by death of Ivan the Terrible (1584)
- Acquisitions by Peter the Great's accession (1689)
- Acquisitions under Peter the Great (1689–1725)
- ✦ Major battle

© Cengage Learning

The Rise of Representative Governments

Some European countries moved toward greater political freedom in this era. Iceland enjoyed self-rule for several centuries, while Switzerland was a multilingual, decentralized, and constitutional confederation of self-governing Catholic and Protestant districts. Among the more powerful states, the Netherlands and England developed the most open and accountable governments: the Netherlands became a republic and England a constitutional monarchy.

The Dutch East India Company

The Netherlands enjoyed a golden age during much of the 1600s. It built a colonial empire, including holdings in the Americas, South Africa, Sri Lanka, and Southeast Asia, and also dominated the Atlantic, Baltic, and Indian Ocean trade. Large Dutch joint-stock companies like the Dutch East India Company controlled the overseas market. The Netherlands became Europe's most prosperous society, with Amsterdam serving as a major hub of world trade. The flow of wealth from overseas activities influenced Dutch political life, fostering an innovative republican system. Holland had long enjoyed a climate of freedom and tolerance, attracting people who sought a more open intellectual atmosphere. After breaking away from Spanish domination, the predominantly Protestant Netherlands became a republic and confederation linked by common institutions such as the assemblies of delegates. But the system was troubled by tensions among elite families, and in 1619 the country entered the Thirty Years' War. Although the peace in 1648 favored business and banking interests, a French invasion of the Netherlands in 1672 shattered the accord.

The Ascendancy of England

Over several centuries, the English forged a colonial empire. England already held Ireland as a colony and sent Protestant settlers to some districts of the mostly Catholic island. Following the 1601 establishment of the English East India Company in Asia, England also founded a colonial empire in North America and the Caribbean. By 1700 it overtook the Dutch as major international traders.

> "Holland had long enjoyed a climate of freedom and tolerance, attracting people who sought a more open intellectual atmosphere."

The English Civil War and Oliver Cromwell

England also experienced profound political changes. In the 1600s, two political upheavals secured first a republic and then a constitutional monarchy. Hostile to absolutism, the English had long struggled to define the relative rights of kings and parliaments. Even one of the most effective European monarchs in history, Queen Elizabeth I, had to tolerate parliamentary influence while using her astute political skills to get her way. However, the Stuarts—the Scottish royal family who became the monarchs of both Scotland and England after Elizabeth I died without an heir—had absolutist ambitions. Stuart king Charles I's decision to make Anglicanism the only recognized faith in both Scotland and England antagonized the Puritans and Presbyterians. In 1641, Parliament condemned despotic Stuart policies, prompting the English Civil War. The parliamentary troops were led by Oliver Cromwell (1599–1658), a member of the rural gentry and a zealous Puritan whose army defeated the royalist forces by 1645. To the great shock of many observers, King Charles I was beheaded.

Parliament abolished the monarchy and proclaimed a republican Commonwealth (1649–1660) dominated by Cromwell. Although the Puritans inclined toward capitalism and protected property rights, their majority in Parliament were fanatics determined to root out what they considered heresy and "godlessness," even expelling the Presbyterians from Parliament. To maintain order, Cromwell became dictator and imposed Puritan morality: he banned newspapers, executed dissidents, and crushed a Catholic rebellion in Ireland by burning crops and massacring thousands. On Cromwell's death, Parliament restored the Stuarts to the throne after they agreed to guarantee individual freedom of religion.

The Glorious Revolution

After the Stuart restoration, the Protestant–Catholic conflicts resumed and eventually led to a broad-based government with a stronger Parliament. Because Stuart king James II (r. 1685–1688) favored absolutist and pro-Catholic policies, Parliament, now dominated by Anglicans, offered the kingship to Dutch leader William of Orange (r. 1689–1702), a champion of the Protestant cause. In 1688 James II was forced to abdicate and flee to France. In what came to be known as the Glorious Revolution (1688–1689), Parliament decreed William and his wife, Mary, sovereigns after they accepted a Bill of Rights recognizing the right of petition and requiring parliamentary approval of taxes. The Toleration Act, establishing freedom of religion, followed.

After the Glorious Revolution, England moved only partway toward a democracy involving all the people. Although royal power was modified, the government represented only the factions that had political influence and wealth: the nobility, wealthy merchants, and property owners. English kings now had far less power than absolutist monarchs, and the great landed aristocratic families, elected from towns and counties, dominated Parliament. Only Parliament could vote the money for the king and his army. In 1707, England, Scotland, and Wales officially combined as the United Kingdom, often known as Great Britain. To control ethnic minorities, the Scottish highlanders were cleared from their lands and forced to move to coastal cities or emigrate, and their Celtic language, Gaelic (GAY-lik), was banned. In colonized Ireland, Protestant English and Scottish settlers acquired land, and Irish Catholics became second-class citizens, denied the right to education, property, and political office.

Rising New States, Declining Old States

The forces unleashed by capitalism, religious change, warfare, and shifting political power caused powerful new states to emerge and longtime powers to decline (see Map 15.4). Among those that emerged was Catholic and German-speaking Austria, which, under the Habsburg monarchs, became a major power after the Thirty Years' War, outshining the German states to the west. The new centralized Austrian empire governed diverse societies: Czechs, Croats, Slovenians, most Hungarians, and some Italians, Romanians, and Serbs.

Interactive Map

Gustavus Adolphus and the Rise of Sweden

Much of Sweden, another emerging power, became independent of once-mighty Denmark in 1520. Swedish society was distinctive: its peasants had never been serfs, many owned their own land, and peasant representatives served in the national assembly. The Swedish state became a hereditary but not absolutist monarchy, with an efficient administration and Lutheranism as the state religion. Soon Swedes dominated Baltic trade, but eventually lost their economic position to the Dutch. Under King Gustavus Adolphus (r. 1611–1632), a brilliant military strategist and creative administrator, Sweden became one of Europe's most influential states, and by the mid-1600s controlled much of Poland and part of Denmark. By 1721, however, the Swedes had lost all of their possessions in the eastern Baltic except Finland to Russia or Prussia (PRUH-shuh).

The Militarization of Prussia

A third state on the rise in Europe was Prussia, which originated as a small, mostly German-speaking state along the eastern Baltic coast, on the borderlands between the Holy Roman Empire and Poland. Long under Polish rule, the state became independent in 1660. In the mid-1700s, Prussia built one of the most formidable military forces in Europe under an authoritarian but constitutional monarchy. Under King Frederick II the Great (r. 1740–1786), Prussia rapidly expanded its territory at the expense of Poland, Austria, and the Holy Roman Empire. A brilliant leader and strategist, Frederick had many dimensions: he was warlike and ruthless but also a fine musician who enjoyed conversations with philosophers.

A Shifting European Landscape

As new states emerged in Europe, several older states declined. By the 1500s, the Holy Roman Empire had become a political entity without much coherence. The emperors, elected by leading princes, were little more than figureheads presiding symbolically over a collection of some three hundred diverse states. The empire was effectively swept away in 1740, when Austria and Prussia began a 130-year struggle for dominance in the region. Italians also remained divided into small states. Poland and Lithuania, major states in medieval times, also faced change. In 1569 the two predominantly Catholic states combined to form a republican commonwealth, launching a golden age of economic prosperity and tolerance of religious diversity. Jewish communities in Poland and Lithuania, in contrast to the rest of Europe, enjoyed many legal rights and some self-government. Elected kings and noble-dominated national and local assemblies presided

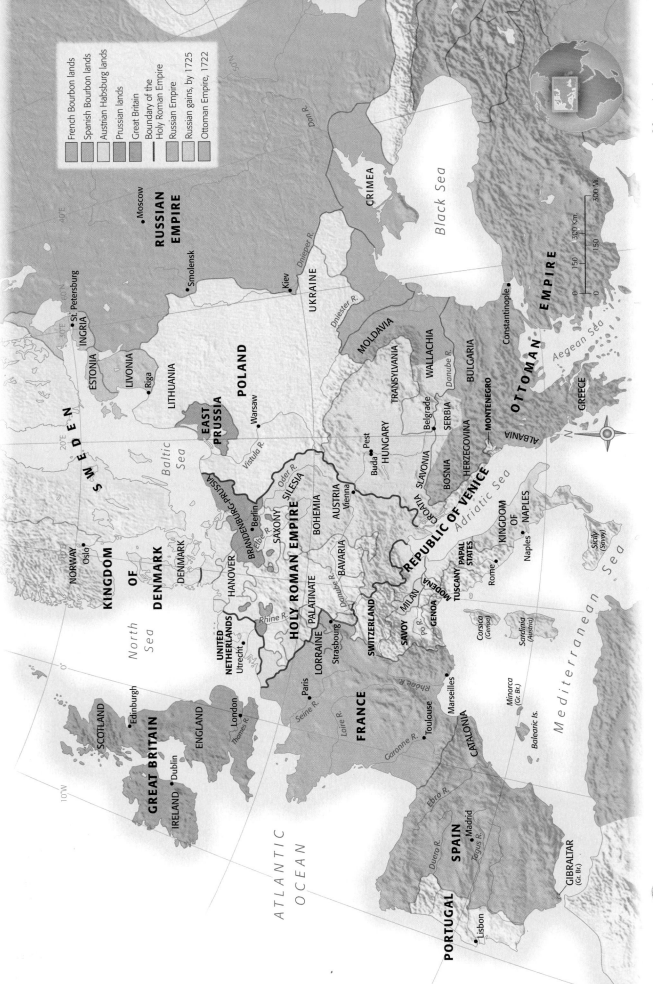

Map 15.4
Europe in 1740

By the mid-1700s, France and Great Britain were the most powerful western European states. While once-powerful Spain and Portugal had lost influence and the Germans and Italians remained divided, Prussia, Sweden, Russia, and Habsburg-ruled Austria were gaining strength.

Legend:
- French Bourbon lands
- Spanish Bourbon lands
- Austrian Habsburg lands
- Prussian lands
- Great Britain
- Boundary of the Holy Roman Empire
- Russian Empire
- Russian gains, by 1725
- Ottoman Empire, 1722

Labels on map:

ATLANTIC OCEAN

North Sea

Baltic Sea

NORWAY
Oslo

KINGDOM OF DENMARK
DENMARK

SWEDEN

St. Petersburg
INGRIA
ESTONIA
LIVONIA
Riga
LITHUANIA

RUSSIAN EMPIRE
Moscow
Smolensk
Kiev
UKRAINE

SCOTLAND
Edinburgh

GREAT BRITAIN

IRELAND
Dublin

ENGLAND
London
Thames R.

HANOVER
UNITED NETHERLANDS
Utrecht

BRANDENBURG-PRUSSIA
Berlin
Elbe R.
SAXONY
Oder R.
SILESIA
BOHEMIA

EAST PRUSSIA
Warsaw
Vistula R.

POLAND

Paris
Seine R.
Loire R.

FRANCE

LORRAINE
Strasbourg
Rhine R.
PALATINATE
HOLY ROMAN EMPIRE
Danube R.
BAVARIA
AUSTRIA
Vienna
SWITZERLAND

Marseilles
Rhône R.
SAVOY
MILAN
Po R.
GENOA
MODENA
TUSCANY
PAPAL STATES
Rome

CATALONIA
Ebro R.

SPAIN
Madrid
Tagus R.
Duero R.

PORTUGAL
Lisbon

GIBRALTAR (Gr. Br.)

Corsica (Genoa)
Sardinia (Austria)
Minorca (Gr. Br.)
Balearic Is.

Mediterranean Sea

Sicily (Savoy)

KINGDOM OF NAPLES
Naples

REPUBLIC OF VENICE
Adriatic Sea

CROATIA
SLAVONIA
HUNGARY
Buda Pest
BOSNIA
HERZEGOVINA
SERBIA
Belgrade
MONTENEGRO
ALBANIA

TRANSYLVANIA
WALLACHIA
Danube R.
BULGARIA
MOLDAVIA
Dniester R.

GREECE

OTTOMAN EMPIRE
Constantinople

Black Sea

CRIMEA
Don R.
Dnieper R.

Aegean Sea

Toulouse
Garonne R.

N

0 150 300 Mi.
0 150 300 Km.

over a somewhat decentralized semi-democracy. But by the mid-1600s, the commonwealth was struggling amidst rebellion and invasion. After 1717, Poland became little more than an appendage to the expanding Russian empire, and Lithuania became a Russian province.

LO⁴ The Transformation of Cultures and Societies

Europeans' sixteenth- and seventeenth-century voyages of discovery and the colonization that followed altered their view of the world and its peoples, broadened their horizons, and contributed to intellectual change within Europe. In some seventeenth-century societies, a measure of religious tolerance added to the ferment of ideas. New ways of perceiving the natural world fostered an emphasis on reason, while capitalism spurred by overseas expansion reshaped social patterns, creating a transition from a largely rural to an increasingly urban society.

Arts and Philosophy

The expanding horizons of thought opened by the Renaissance and Reformation led to an extravagant artistic movement in the 1600s known as the baroque, a term that originally meant "contorted" or "grotesque." Baroque artists emphasized movement, tension, exaggerated lighting, intense emotions, and decoration. In Italy, baroque art, such as the marble statues and fountains of the Roman architect and sculptor Gianlorenzo Bernini (buhr-NEE-nee) (1598–1680), was expressive and sensuous, rejecting restraint and emphasizing freedom.

A Broader Audience for the Arts

In contrast to Renaissance artists such as Michelangelo, Dutch artists saw their work as a capitalist enterprise and often produced for the wider market rather than for individual patrons. Painters such as Rembrandt van Rijn and Jan Vermeer (1632–1675), influenced by baroque approaches, conveyed an impression of emotion and immediacy in their portraits and other works. Their paintings communicated personality, the thoughts and feelings of individuals, even of ordinary people in Amsterdam. Some music composers also created works to appeal to a wide audience. The German Lutheran composers George Frederick Handel (1685–1750) and Johann Sebastian Bach (1685–1759) produced work of enduring popularity. Handel settled in London, where he wrote his famous choral work, *The Messiah*. Bach wrote pieces for both Protestant and Catholic churches and for many instruments.

> **baroque**
> An extravagant and, to many, shocking European artistic movement of the 1600s that encouraged release from restraints of thought and expression.

> 66 Baroque artists emphasized movement, tension, exaggerated lighting, intense emotions, and decoration. 99

The Birth of Modern Science, Philosophy, and Political Science

The rise of baroque art corresponded to the greatest era of philosophical and scientific speculation in Europe since the classical Greeks. The Englishman Francis Bacon (1561–1626) built some of the foundations for this intellectual growth. Bacon sought to eliminate intellectual restraints on science by separating philosophy from theology and advocating the use of reason. He developed a famous maxim: "Knowledge is power." Bacon's scientific method—probably based in part on the ideas of earlier Islamic thinkers—encouraged systematically studying things that need understanding. The scientist should develop an idea, test it experimentally, and then draw conclusions.

Another key thinker and the founding father of modern philosophy, René Descartes (DAY-cart) (1596–1650), promoted pure reason and a rationalist view of the world. Descartes believed that human rationality was founded on a distinction between mind and body. He sought to sweep away traditional learning and establish a new system of knowledge embracing all aspects of reality. The only thing he could not doubt was his own existence: "While I wanted to think everything false, it was absolutely necessary that I, who was thinking thus, must be something. I think, therefore I am."[7] Just as science brought order to the physical world, Descartes intended to bring order to thought.

The English political thinker Thomas Hobbes (1588–1679), a friend of Descartes, believed that society was not perfectible, even with the use of reason or Christian teachings. Hobbes, a pessimist, held that, in the state of nature, with no government to control humanity's anarchic, power-seeking instincts, the life of man was "solitary, poor, nasty, brutish, and short."[8]

His disturbing book, *The Leviathan*, provided a new view of the state and its relationship to the individual. Because war and conflict were inherent to human society, Hobbes believed, people needed despotic power to control them. Values such as truth, reason, or justice, however useful, were just artificial attributes of human society created by social convention and language. People could either give in to violent, selfish human nature or erect a powerful state to ensure harmony.

Science and Technology

The Scientific Revolution (ca. 1600–1750), an era of rapid advance in knowledge, built on the work of thinkers like Bacon and Descartes to gain a new understanding of the natural and physical world and to create several technological innovations. European scientists demolished the medieval view of the earth's position in the cosmos and laid the groundwork for later intellectual and industrial transitions. Although offering new ideas could be dangerous in a continent full of religious conflicts and despotic monarchs, advances occurred in many areas.

The Scientific Revolution derived in part from imported Asian and Islamic ideas and technologies. European scientists were quite familiar with the writings of earlier Muslim thinkers. They also learned from China. The Jesuits who sojourned in China in the sixteenth and seventeenth centuries sent back reports that praised Chinese scientific traditions and inventions. As Europeans assimilated and improved imported models while creating new ones, the general dynamism of science and technology shifted from China and the Middle East to Europe. Between the seventeenth and nineteenth centuries, western Europe caught up with and then surpassed China technologically.

Foundations of Modern Astronomy and Physics

Astronomers made some of the most significant scientific discoveries. The German mystic Johannes Kepler (1571–1630) used mathematics to amplify the discoveries of Copernicus, showing that all of the planets revolved around the sun. The era's greatest astronomer, the Italian Galileo Galilei (gal-uh-LAY-oh gal-uh-LAY-ee) (1564–1642), proved experimentally that Copernicus's theories were correct. Galileo built the first telescope in 1609 and discovered that the moon had mountains, Jupiter had four large moons, and our solar system was but a small part of a Milky Way galaxy containing thousands of stars that could not be seen with the naked eye. These findings were dangerous, however: in 1615 the Catholic Church summoned the scientist to Rome to be tried as a heretic, and he was forced to publicly recant his views in order to leave prison, but he continued publishing his findings. As punishment, Inquisition officials placed him under house arrest for the last decade of his life.

Scientific activity reached its height with Sir Isaac Newton (1642–1727), a mathematics professor at Cambridge University whose development of fundamental laws of physics was the culmination of a century's observations and scientific findings. Newton's importance to the world was proclaimed in a famous epitaph by his contemporary, the poet Alexander Pope: "Nature and Nature's laws lay hidden in night; God said, 'Let Newton be!' and all was light."[9] In 1687, Newton published his *Mathematical Principles of Natural Philosophy*, which accounted for all the motions of the planets, the comets, the moon, and the sea. He found the connection, especially the law of universal gravitation, that tied together varied parts of the physical world into an ordered whole. Newton's ideas dominated Western scientific thinking for the next two hundred years.

 Letter to the Grand Duchess Christina Read Galileo's passionate defense of his scientific research against those who would condemn it as un-Christian.

In the wake of scientific discoveries, and sometimes borrowing from advances made in other societies, technology improved. During the 1500s, more advanced gunpowder weapons and such useful items as the watch, lead pencil, thermometer, and concrete became available. In the 1620s, an English mathematician developed the first slide rule, and a German mathematician invented the first mechanical calculator. These devices performed multiplication, divi-

> "European scientists demolished the medieval view of the earth's position in the cosmos and laid the groundwork for later intellectual and industrial transitions."

sion, and much more. The Dutch scientist Christian Huygens (HYE-guhnz) introduced a more accurate clock in 1657. Innovations in industrial machinery led to many advances; by the 1730s, the English textile industry became more efficient with spinning machines, similar to those introduced in China in the 1200s, for making cotton products.

"The Enlightenment helped replace unquestioning religious faith with observed fact and suggested that objective truth could be established through reason."

Enlightenment
A philosophical movement based on science and reason that began in Europe in the late seventeenth century and continued through the eighteenth century.

Newton, the Enlightenment would have been unthinkable. But the movement also owed something to growing European knowledge of egalitarian Native American societies and of Chinese thought. The Enlightenment helped replace unquestioning religious faith with observed fact and suggested that objective truth could be established through reason. The scientific investigation of the natural world could now be separated from religious doctrines. In England, France, Scotland, and elsewhere, fresh ideas emerged, including new notions of tolerance, individual rights, and the relationship between

The Enlightenment

The Enlightenment, which began in 1675 and continued until 1800, was a philosophical movement based on science and reason that was perhaps the most fertile period in the history of Western philosophy. Without the earlier achievements in the study of science and human reason by scholars like Bacon, Descartes, and

Painting of Madame Geoffrin's Salon This mid-eighteenth-century painting by French artist Lemoinnier shows a gathering of Enlightenment thinkers and artists at the elegant Paris salon operated by Madame Geoffrin, seated toward the right.

Reunion des Musées Nationaux/Art Resource, NY

citizens and the state. Overall, the Enlightenment spread a humanistic secularism, promoted critical approaches to knowledge, and aimed at increasing human happiness. It also provided a forum for addressing gender issues.

John Locke and Empiricism

The Englishman John Locke (1632–1704), a physician who lived for a decade in France and Holland, was one of the first major Enlightenment philosophers. Locke made experimental studies of medicine and science that led him to proclaim the value of empiricism, an approach that stressed relying on experience and testing propositions rather than using reason alone to acquire knowledge. Locke became particularly influential as a political theorist, his work providing a foundation for the modern democratic state and notions of human freedom. In contrast to Thomas Hobbes, Locke condemned absolute monarchy and urged people to defend their freedom by uniting in a civil society where people cooperated for common goals but the state enjoyed only limited powers over the individual. The state, he conceded, was needed to protect popular desires but had to preserve self-governance and freedom. If the state transgressed these rights, people had the right to oppose it. He favored individual rights, such as the separation of church and state, but also favored some limits, such as restricting political participation to people with property. Many of Locke's ideas became influential not only in England but also among the founders of the United States, especially Thomas Jefferson.

Voltaire and the Philosophes

The French Enlightenment was fostered by intellectuals known as philosophes (fill-uh-SOHFZ) (philosophers). The best-known philosophe, Voltaire (1694–1778), a poet, dramatist, and historian, believed that science and rational social behavior led people to live happier lives. He was occasionally imprisoned in France for resisting the system, and he spent many years in exile in England, Switzerland, and Prussia. Growing European knowledge of China and Confucianism led him to view China as an admirable political model of a despotic but secular and benevolent state, in contrast to absolutist France. Although he supported tolerance, Voltaire and some other Enlightenment thinkers fiercely attacked established religion and also disliked the Jews for their separation, often involuntary, from mainstream society and their commitment to tradition.

Capitalism's Impact on European Society

Capitalism gradually reshaped rural society. In many places, a changing economy turned many peasants into a displaced labor force. England experienced this change in the 1500s, when King Henry VIII seized the lands of the Catholic Church and distributed them to his cronies, including wealthy businessmen, who began buying land as an investment. The new hardhearted landowners increased demands on peasants or shifted land use from agriculture to more profitable sheep raising, ejecting peasants from the land. With a policy known as enclosure, landlords, claiming ownership rights, also fenced off common lands once used by the public for grazing livestock and collecting firewood. As their options dwindled, the English peasantry mostly disappeared and were replaced by tenant farmers working for big landlords.

The Dark Side of Capitalism

The transition to capitalism brought poverty to English rural dwellers and other economic consequences. Thousands of English peasants became landless. Some found jobs in towns, creating a labor pool for fledgling industries, and some became rural craftsmen such as weavers, but many could not find steady work and became rural vagabonds. Whereas under feudalism people saw individual well-being as socially controlled, a product of the manor, under capitalism it became individually controlled: people were responsible for their own condition. Capitalism also undermined guilds as businessmen gave crafts production to displaced peasants and paid them for each item they made. In exploiting desperate peasants, businesses destroyed medieval concepts of economic justice. Eventually these trends spread to other western European societies. The great contrast between the few rich and the many poor, amplified by famine and the devastations of war, brought on uprisings in England, especially after the Civil War of the 1640s.

Life was increasingly dangerous and unhealthy for both rural and urban people. Between wars and rebellions, bandits prowled the roads and mercenary soldiers roamed the countryside, attacking merchant convoys and plundering villages. The cities were overcrowded and filled with beggars. Trash-filled streets, polluted water, the stench of human waste, and disease made life deplorable for most people. In the 1600s, one-third of London's children died before the age of one. Reflecting on the difficulties of coping with such misery, an observer in 1751 called gin the principle sustenance of more than 100,000 Londoners.

Redefining the Family

Family life and gender relations also changed in the Early Modern Era. For the growing middle classes of northern Europe, the nuclear family of parents and their children, which was rare in medieval times, increasingly became common. Unlike medieval times, when children were viewed as small adults, societies increasingly recognized childhood as a distinct phase of life, inventing toys and games for children and opening more schools, mostly for boys. However, half or more of children left their families by their early teens, many to become apprentices or servants with other families. The economic roles and status of women also shifted. In contrast to medieval times, when many women never married and also worked in a wide variety of occupations, western European women were now encouraged to look chiefly to marriage and motherhood; their place was in the home.

Women and Sexuality in the Early Modern Era

The experiences of women varied across Europe. For instance, many Dutch women enjoyed liberated lives, some becoming merchants. Elsewhere, some women also engaged in trade. The German Jewish merchant Glukel of Hameln (HAH-muhln) (1646–1724), the mother of eight, traveled widely to trade fairs and wrote memoirs of her experiences. But in most European societies, few women controlled enough financial resources to become major traders. Women's paid work and unpaid housework were increasingly devalued in much of Europe. But some women faced even worse problems as a fear of witchcraft spread throughout Europe and colonial New England in the Early Modern Era. For centuries, people had feared witches, who were thought to be capable of destroying crops and causing personal misfortunes. As wars and religious conflicts raged in the sixteenth and seventeenth centuries, official persecution of alleged witches provided a diversion. Many thousands of women, most of them single, were suspected of being witches and were executed, tortured, or banished from their communities.

Nonconformity to social standards faced increasing hostility. More restrictive views of sexuality led to punishment of women and men who defied convention. Often prompted by churches, governments became more concerned with regulating sexual and moral behavior, partly to encourage family life. Yet, many people ignored such laws, and premarital pregnancy rates ranged from 10 to 30 percent. In addition, Catholic and Protestant churches condemned homosexuality, and men or women engaging in homosexual behavior faced severe sanctions, including execution. Yet, laws were enforced erratically, especially in tolerant England and Scandinavia, and male homosexuals congregated in large cities.

 Listen to a synopsis of Chapter 15.

CHAPTER 16

New Challenges for Africa and the Islamic World, 1450–1750

Learning Outcomes

After reading this chapter, you should be able to answer the following questions:

LO¹ How did the larger sub-Saharan African societies and states differ from each other in the sixteenth century?

LO² What were the consequences of African–European encounters in this era, especially the trans-Atlantic slave trade?

LO³ What factors made the Ottoman Empire such a powerful force in the region?

LO⁴ How did the Persian and Central Asian experience differ from that of the Ottomans?

> 66 Warriors will fight scribes for the control of your institutions; wild bush will conquer your roads; your soil will crack from the drought; your sons will wander in the wilds. Yes, things will fall apart. 99
>
> —Igbo ancestral curse[1]

Confirming the Igbo curse, things fell apart for many Africans in the Early Modern Era. Among the many Africans caught up in unprecedented new challenges was Ayuba Suleiman Diallo (ah-YOO-bah SOO-lay-mahn JAH-loh). In 1731 the thirty-year-old educated son of a leading family in the West African kingdom of Bondu was captured by enemies while on a trading mission and sold to the British as a slave. Eventually he was shipped to Maryland, where he was put to work on a plantation growing tobacco. After an attempted escape, he was taken in by Thomas Bluett, an English entrepreneur who recognized both Diallo's talents and his connections to West African commercial life. Diallo's Islamic faith and ability to read and write Arabic reflected the influence of Islam and Arab traditions in parts of West Africa. Bluett emancipated Diallo and then took him to London and presented him at the English court. The British hoped he might help them to increase their commercial and slaving activity in the Senegambia, and he agreed to act as middleman in obtaining more slaves. Finally, after pledging friendship with the British, Diallo was able to return to Bondu and resume his life. Until his death in 1773, Diallo profited from his connection to British merchants as a trading partner. He had been both victim and beneficiary of the new economic forces of his times.

Ayuba Suleiman Diallo's story reflects the changing Atlantic world of the Early Modern Era. African life was transformed, in part because of contact with Europeans, whose presence in Africa gradually increased. The West African trading world that produced Diallo now included English, Portuguese, Dutch, and French companies seeking gold, gum, hides, ivory, and especially slaves. Diallo gained freedom quickly and eventually returned home, but the ancient Igbo

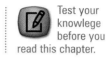
Test your knowlege before you read this chapter.

What do you think?

The overseas expansion of Europe during the Early Modern Era had little impact on Africa and the Middle East.

Strongly Disagree | | | | | | Strongly Agree
1   2   3   4   5   6   7

<< **Glassblowers' Procession** The Ottoman rulers periodically had the members of several hundred occupational guilds in Istanbul parade before them, including storytellers, taxidermists, potters, and even executioners. This painting, from an illuminated manuscript finished around 1582, shows the glassblowers, some of them on a wheeled cart demonstrating their skills.

curse proved prophetic for the many other Africans who were shipped off as slaves.

Not all Africans were affected by European activities: some, like the Fulani, remained untouched by the various slave trades and other disruptive European activities and continued to pursue their ways of life as they always had. Still, Diallo's experience illustrates the expanding influence of Europe in Africa and the Americas during the early modern centuries. Encounters with Europe reshaped parts of Africa and drew them into an emerging Atlantic world, as first the Portuguese and then other Europeans established trading posts along the West African coast. Soon these trading posts, such as Goree Island, became centers for acquiring and shipping slaves. The Portuguese and Dutch also began to conquer and settle several African regions.

Growing European power also gradually affected some of the Islamic lands of the Middle East and Central Asia, though not to the same extent. By the 1500s, Islam had spread from the westernmost fringe of Africa to central Indonesia and the southern Philippines. Islamic political ideas, trade networks, and literary traditions linked many millions of people, and several large and dynamic Islamic states dominated much of the Middle East and South Asia, the successors to the great Islamic empires of earlier centuries. The powerful Ottoman Empire, which included much of western Asia, North Africa, and southeastern Europe, and a new Persian state, the Safavid Empire, had increasing connections of trade and conflict with non-Islamic societies. But while these Islamic societies experienced some changes, they also maintained long-standing traditions and remained largely autonomous.

> "For nearly two centuries, Timbuktu remained the greatest Islamic city in sub-Saharan Africa."

LO¹ Sub-Saharan African Societies

At the beginning of the Early Modern Era, African societies reflected considerable political, economic, and cultural diversity, and many flourished. Some, especially in West and East Africa, formed great empires and states, engaging in extensive long-distance trade, fostering intellectual debate, and connecting with the wider Eastern Hemisphere. Many people in the Sudanic region of West Africa and along the East African coast had adopted Islam. But many other Africans had decentralized political systems based on villages and religions mixing monotheism, polytheism, and animism. Whatever their ways of life and thought, many African societies possessed valuable human and natural resources that attracted Europeans as the era progressed, posing new challenges and changing Africa's relationship to the world.

Early Modern West African States

The last of the great Sudanic empires, Songhai (song-GAH-ee), became the major power in interior West Africa during the 1400s and flourished through much of the 1500s (see Map 16.1). From its capital of Gao (ghow) on the Niger River, Songhai built an empire stretching some 1,500 miles from east to west. The people of Songhai blended Islam with local customs: the women of Songhai and some other Islamic states in the Sudan held a high social position and enjoyed considerable personal liberty, much to the shock of Arab visitors. Many women engaged in small-scale commerce, and in some Sudanic cities, women were free to have lovers as they desired. Some Sudanic societies were matrilineal.

 Interactive Map

Timbuktu

The Songhai city of Timbuktu became a major terminus for the trans-Saharan trade that shipped to North Africa large supplies of gold and ivory as well as slaves for Arab and European markets. For nearly two centuries, Timbuktu remained the greatest Islamic city in sub-Saharan

Buganda
Kongo
Monomotapa
Kingdom of Songhai, ca. 1500 C.E.
Kingdom of Kanem-Bornu, ca. 1500 C.E.
Hausaland
Kingdom of Ethiopia
Main coastal trading areas

© Cengage Learning

Map 16.1
African States and Trade, 1500–1700

Some African states, such as Songhai, Kanem-Bornu, Benin, Lunda, Buganda, and Ethiopia, remained powerful in this era. West African coastal societies were increasingly drawn into world trade, while the East African coastal cities remained significant in Indian Ocean trade.

Africa. An early-sixteenth-century Arab visitor, Leo Africanus, reported that Timbuktu had "numerous judges, doctors of letters, and learned Muslims. The king greatly honors scholarship. Here too, they sell many hand-written books. More profit is had from their sale than from any other merchandise."[2] The Islamic University of Sankore at Timbuktu was modeled after the respected University of Cairo, and its faculty and the student body came from throughout the Islamic realm.

History and Cultures of Africa (http://www.columbia.edu/cu/lweb/indiv/africa/index.html). Provides valuable links to relevant websites on African history.

But Songhai did not remain a dominant state in West Africa. After several strong kings ruled the empire, Songhai's leadership deteriorated and succession struggles emerged. In 1591, when an army from Morocco seized much of the Niger River territory from Songhai, the kingdom collapsed. The end of Songhai marked the end of the era of huge imperial states in the western Sudan.

Other West African States

Besides Songhai, other Sudanic and Guinea Coast societies exercised regional influence and flourished from trade. The Dyula (JOO-lah), a large Mandinka-speaking Muslim mercantile clan, became the most important trading group, with operations throughout West Africa. Dyula merchants moved goods such as gold and salt through the forest with caravans of porters, down the rivers in canoe fleets, and across the grasslands in donkey trains. Women usually dominated the village markets. In fact, many Sudanic and Guinea societies were matrilineal, and some had women chiefs or queens. The Igbo people of southeastern Nigeria worshiped female deities, and some had female leaders. Africans often venerated women elders for their wisdom and closeness to the ancestors.

Idrus Aloma and the Kanem-Bornu Kingdom

Several strong Islamic kingdoms and states arose to the east of the Niger River. Kanem-Bornu (KAH-nuhm-BOR-noo), centered on Lake Chad, had formed in the ninth century and prospered from trans-Saharan trade, especially from trading slaves to North African Arabs for

> "Several strong Islamic kingdoms and states arose to the east of the Niger River."

horses. The kingdom reached its height in the late 1500s and early 1600s under King Idrus Aloma (IH-dris ah-LOW-ma), who extended his territories northward deep into the Sahara and imported guns from the Ottoman Empire. A devout Muslim, Idrus Aloma reformed the easygoing local customs by imposing Islamic law.

The Hausa and the Trans-Saharan Trade

Among other flourishing West African trading states were the city-states of the Hausa (HOUSE-uh) people, of what is now northern Nigeria, eastern Niger, and southern Chad. Headed by kings, these fiercely competitive states dominated some of the trans-Saharan trade into the eighteenth century. Hausa cities were centers for trade and manufacturing cotton cloth and leatherwork, some of which was sold as far away as Europe. Places such as Kano (KAH-no) and Katsina also attracted Muslim scholars in the 1400s and 1500s, and Islam gradually became the dominant faith throughout the Hausa lands. But, in contrast to women in the patriarchal Muslim soci-

CHRONOLOGY
Africa and the Atlantic World, 1482–1750

1482	First Portuguese-Kongo encounter
1487	Portuguese discovery of Cape of Good Hope
1497	Vasco da Gama's first voyage to East African coast
1505	Portuguese pillage of Kilwa
1514	First African slaves to Americas
1507–1543	Rule of Alfonso I in Kongo
1526–1870	Trans-Atlantic slave trade
1652	Dutch settlement of Cape Town
1575	End of Portuguese technical assistance to Kongo
1591	Destruction of Songhai

Sankore Mosque Built in the fourteenth century, the Sankore Mosque in the Sudanic city of Timbuktu, a center of commerce and scholarship in the Songhai Empire, symbolized the spread of Islam in the region but also the adaptation of the faith to West African traditions, reflected in the mosque's unique architecture.

eties in the Middle East, Hausa women continued to play vital political and social roles. For instance, Queen Amina of Zaria (ZAH-ree-uh) extended her city's power while building effective walled defenses against rival states and raiders.

Trade on the Guinea Coast

Important non-Muslim states occupied the Guinea Coast from today's Ghana to eastern Nigeria. The Akan (AH-kahn) peoples of the Volta (VAWL-tuh) River Basin, farmers with a matrilineal social structure, were organized into several small states that prospered from mining and trading gold to the north. In western Nigeria, the Yoruba (YORE-a-bah) peoples developed a series of states, each based on a large city ruled by a king or prince. Yet, women also exercised political influence through the position of *Iyalode* (literally, "mother of the town"), elected by women to the council of chiefs. Many Yoruba towns served as both commercial and political centers and were ruled by elaborate bureaucracies. One great Guinea kingdom, Benin (buh-NEEN), in what is now south-central Nigeria, shared many cultural and political traditions with the Yoruba. European visitors in the 1500s and 1600s admired the prosperous society they encountered, including the capital city of wide streets and large wooden houses with verandas.

Europeans in West Africa

As Arab merchants did before them, the first European explorers and merchants in West Africa could tap into well-established trade networks and markets. At Guinala (gwee-NAH-la)—a Mandinka-governed district in what later became Guinea-Bissau (GIN-ee-bi-SOU)—the Portuguese encountered in 1591 a huge weekly market where more than 12,000 men and women gathered to trade. As one Portuguese merchant wrote, "All that is available in this land and in surrounding lands is offered for sale, that is, slaves, cloth, provisions, cows, and gold."[3] Undoubtedly, some of the merchants at Guinala were Dyula and Hausa.

Bantu Trading Cities and Kingdoms

By the sixteenth century, various Bantu peoples had settled much of eastern, Central, and southern Africa, and some were closely linked to the wider world. The closest ties to hemispheric networks were forged by various city-states along the East African coast, where Bantu settlers and Arab immigrants had created the Swahili (swah-HEE-lee) culture mixing African and Islamic traditions. For nearly two millennia, Indonesians, Indians, Persians, and Arabs had regular contact with East Africa, bringing ideas, products, technologies, and immigrants to enrich the African mosaic. The varied city-states, all thriving centers of trade, achieved considerable grandeur.

Three Traders This bronze plaque, from the sixteenth century, shows three Benin merchants, possibly appointed by the king to negotiate with the Europeans who were then arriving in the region. The merchant in the center holds a staff signifying his royal appointment and royal authority over commerce with non-Benin people.

Trade on the East African Coast

The golden age of the East African coast, with its royal court, mosques, and luxury goods, reached its peak from the twelfth through the fifteenth centuries. Ships from Arabia, Persia, and India regularly visited the coast, and Chinese voyagers explored the area in the early 1400s. East African city-states, such as Kilwa and Malindi, became a significant part of the great trading network around the Indian Ocean, a network generally dominated by seafaring Arabs and Indian Muslims. These Swahili ports functioned as trade centers, collecting goods from the African interior to be exchanged for Asian goods.

The Shona and the Ganda

Other major Bantu states emerged in south-central Africa. On the plateau bordering the great Zambezi (zam-BEE-zee) River, the Shona people flourished from gold mining, exporting gold as well as ivory to the Middle East and India through the coastal city-state of Sofala (so-FALL-a), the southernmost Swahili-speaking city. Swahili boats carried these exports from Sofala to Kilwa, where they were plugged into the international trade networks. By 1500 the once-great Shona kingdom of Zimbabwe (zim-BAH-bway) had collapsed and was replaced by several competing Shona kingdoms. Another Bantu people were the Ganda, who established a small kingdom, Buganda (boo-GON-da), in the 1500s just west of Lake Victoria. By the 1700s, Buganda had a well-developed bureaucracy and a powerful military, as well as an extensive trade network with the East African coastal cities.

The Kingdom of Kongo

In the Congo River Basin as well, several influential Bantu states flourished. The large Kongo kingdom arose in the 1300s along the Congo River in what is today northern Angola and western Congo. Kongo became one of the first great African states to be visited by European explorers. Described by the first Portuguese visitors as powerful and having many vassals, the Kongo kingdom ruled a population of around 2.5 million people by 1500. To the east, the Luba (LOO-buh) and Lunda kingdoms were established around 1350 and 1600, respectively, and built substantial empires in the southern Congo. Their location far inland and their access to trade networks running through Central Africa allowed them to remain independent of European power into the nineteenth century.

The Xhosa and the Zulu

Various Bantu-speaking groups had been migrating into southern Africa for centuries. Most of the Bantu societies formed small states led by chiefs and combined farming with cattle herding. The largest societies, the Xhosa (KHO-sa) and Zulu, mostly lived along or near the Indian Ocean coast of what is today South Africa. Some non-Bantus also lived in the area. Around 50,000 Khoikhoi (koi-koi) pastoralists, also called Hottentots (HOT-n-TOTs), lived in and around the Cape of Good Hope at Africa's southern tip. They were a branch of the Khoisan (KOI-sahn) peoples, long resident in southern Africa, who also included the !Kung (Bushmen) of the Kalahari Desert.

Africa in the Hemispheric System

Africans had long played key roles in the Eastern Hemisphere economic system, but the rapid rise of European power between 1450 and 1600 soon presented them with serious challenges and reshaped their role in the world. Sub-Saharan Africans were vulnerable to European and Arab power, because they did not enjoy the same environmental advantages and interregional connections that had benefited parts of Eurasia and North Africa. By 1500, various Eurasian and North African societies had invented or borrowed from each other cutting-edge technologies such as printing and gunpowder weapons, and they had also created more productive economies. Most sub-Saharan Africans never encountered the Chinese technology and Indian mathematics that spurred Middle Eastern and European development. In addition, much of sub-Saharan Africa had marginally fertile soils, scarce exploitable minerals, and few good harbors.

Africa the Unknown

Although West and East Africans had been major suppliers of gold, ivory, and other commodities to the Middle East and Europe for centuries, only a few Europeans and Africans had made direct contact with each other. During the Intermediate Era, several Italian merchants braved the Sahara Desert to reach the Sudanic trading cities by camel caravan, and the few remaining Christian Nubian kingdoms in the central Nile valley may have maintained a few links with Christian leaders in Europe. But by the 1300s, these kingdoms had been conquered by Muslims, and Christianity died out in Nubia. Only in remote Ethiopia, where the Amharic (ahm-HAHR-ik) people had adopted a form of Christianity related to Eastern Orthodoxy early in the Common Era, did the religion flourish. Ethiopia's state, led by kings who traced their ancestry to the ancient Hebrew king Solomon, had survived 1,500 years in the highlands of Northeast Africa, where it built splendid churches, often on steep mountainsides. But the expansion of Islam cut off the Ethiopians from Europe. Because of these intermittent contacts, Africans and Europeans knew little of each other.

The "Opening" of Africa

Direct contacts between Europe and Africa only began in the early 1400s, when the Portuguese began exploring down the West African coast in search of gold, Christian allies against Islam, and a hoped-for sea route to China and Southeast Asia, the sources of the silk and spices that were so valued in Europe. The Europeans' ignorance of black Africa helped create the myth of Darkest Africa, those areas of the African continent least known to Europeans but, in European eyes, awaiting to be "opened" to the "light of Western civilization." At the same time, Europeans also perplexed Africans. According to the traditions of Niger River Delta peoples in what is today southern Nigeria, the first appearance of white men around 1500 shocked the local fisherman who spotted them: "Panic-stricken, he raced home and told his people what he had seen; whereupon he and the rest of the town set out to purify themselves, [to] rid themselves of the influence of the strange thing that had intruded into their world."[4]

> **"** Europeans did not invent the African slave trade, but they soon transformed it. **"**

The Beginning of the African Slave Trade

Eventually, after they began establishing control in the Americas, Europeans became particularly interested in

> "As they visited more of Africa, the Portuguese shifted from exploration to exploitation."

enslaving Africans. Slavery existed in many African societies, just as it had in other areas of the world, and in East Africa, over the course of twelve centuries, perhaps 10 to 15 million enslaved Africans were taken to the Middle East and beyond by Muslim slave traders. In Europe, societies such as Spain, Portugal, Italy, and France enslaved many of their own people in the 1500s, making them work as domestic servants, plantation laborers, and prostitutes. Thus slavery had no particular "racial" identity yet, but the growing knowledge of Africa combined with the forging of plantation economies in the Americas focused more attention on Africa as a source of slaves. Europeans did not invent the African slave trade, but they soon transformed it.

LO² European Imperialism and the Trans-Atlantic Slave Trade

As Portuguese ships began making ever-longer journeys down the West African coast in search of gold, the encounters that followed fostered trade, conflict, and destruction. By the later 1400s, the Portuguese had made contact with the Kongo, located near the Atlantic coast, which they eventually colonized. Then during the 1500s, the Portuguese became active in East Africa, undermining the coastal trading cities and affecting interior societies. Meanwhile, the Dutch gained a foothold in South Africa. These developments contributed to a new global system of trade and empire that created a wide gulf in wealth, power, and development between Africa and Eurasia by the 1700s.

 Explore new encounters in the early modern world in this interactive simulation.

Racism—a set of beliefs, practices, and institutions based on devaluing groups that are supposedly biologically different—can be traced to early Western relations with sub-Saharan Africa and the exploitation of Africans. The most prominent factor in these relations, the trans-Atlantic slave trade, fostered both commerce and cultural change in West Africa.

The Portuguese and African Encounters

The Portuguese were the first Europeans to have direct encounters with many African societies. Having the world's most advanced and well-armed ships, the Portuguese began exploring the West African coastline in the early 1400s. By 1471 they had reached as far as the modern nation of Ghana on the west coast, where they tapped into the gold trade from the Akan states, calling the region the Gold Coast. As they visited more of Africa, the Portuguese shifted from exploration to exploitation. They colonized the Cape Verde Islands and the nearby coastal region of Guinea-Bissau, and they established various trading forts to obtain gold, ivory, and slaves. In the 1480s, the Portuguese began a long relationship with the prosperous Kongo kingdom of south-central Africa, sending Christian missionaries and skilled craftsmen. Over the next century, they expanded their operations in Africa.

Bartolomeu Dias and Vasco de Gama

Soon Portuguese explorers sailed farther south and then east. In 1487 Bartolomeu Dias (ca. 1450–1500) led an expedition that sailed round the Cape of Good Hope, the southern tip of Africa, into the Indian Ocean, intensifying Portuguese interest in both Africa and Asia. Dias believed that he had discovered the best route to eastern and southern Asia, and his explorations soon intensified contact with South African peoples. More Portuguese exploration followed, eventually reshaping the hemispheric trade system. In 1497 four ships commanded by the zealous Portuguese captain Vasco da Gama (VAS-ko dah GAH-ma) (ca. 1469–1525) left Portugal. Surviving hurricanes and mutinies, da Gama and his remaining crew sailed south around the Cape and then up the East African coast, visiting the Swahili trading cities of Mozambique, Mombasa, and Malindi. Da Gama was disappointed to discover that the merchants in these cities had no interest in his meager trade goods. Shifting his strategy, da Gama engaged a skillful pilot in Malindi and sailed eastward across the Indian Ocean to southwestern India. Even though the Indians told him his merchandise could not compete with better-made products from India, China, Indonesia, and Persia, da Gama had located the sea route to the East. He acquired a small cargo of spices

A Kongolese King Protests the Slave Trade

In the early sixteenth century, the Kongolese king Alfonso I, who had embraced Catholicism and welcomed the Portuguese to his kingdom, wrote more than twenty letters in Portuguese to the king of Portugal, creating the earliest known African commentary on European activities in Africa. Some letters complained of aggressive Portuguese activities and asked that the king halt the slavers from obtaining Kongolese citizens. They also requested educational, medical, and religious assistance from Portugal. The letters, usually polite in tone, revealed gradually diminished hopes as friendly early encounters turned into Portuguese plunder and exploitation. These are excerpts from several letters written in 1526.

Sir, Your Highness should know how our Kingdom is being lost in so many ways that it is convenient to provide the necessary remedy, since this is caused by the excessive freedom given by your factors and officials to the men and merchants who are allowed to come to the Kingdom to set up shop with goods and many things which have been prohibited by us. . . .

And we cannot reckon how great the damage is, since the mentioned merchants are taking every day our natives, sons of the land and the sons of our noblemen and vassals and our relatives, because the thieves and men of bad conscience grab them wishing to have the things and wares of this Kingdom which they are ambitious of; they grab them and get them to be sold; and so great, Sir, is the corruption and licentiousness that our country is being completely depopulated, and Your Highness should not agree with this nor accept it as in your service. And to avoid it we need from . . . [your] Kingdoms no more than some priests and a few people to teach in schools. . . . It is our will that in these Kingdoms there should not be any trade of slaves nor outlet for them. . . . And as soon as they are taken by the white men they are immediately ironed and branded with fire. . . .

It happens that we have continuously many and different diseases which put us very often in such a weakness that we reach almost the last extreme; and the same [thing] happens to our children, relatives and natives owing to the lack in this country of physicians and surgeons who might know how to cure properly such diseases. And as we have got neither dispensaries nor drugs which might help us in this forlornness, many of those who had already been confirmed and instructed in the holy faith of Our Lord Jesus Christ perish and die; and the rest of the people in their majority cure themselves with herbs and breads and other ancient methods, so that they put all their faith in the mentioned herbs and ceremonies if they live. . . . And this is not much in the service of God. . . . We beg of you to be agreeable and kind enough to send us two physicians and two apothecaries and one surgeon, so that they may come with their drug-stores and all the necessary things to stay in our kingdoms, because we are in extreme need of them all.

Thinking About the Reading

1. What do these examples of letters tell us about Portuguese slaving activities and growing power in the Kongo?
2. What did Alfonso believe his kingdom needed from the Portuguese?
3. Why were the Portuguese unlikely to grant Alfonso's requests?

Source: Basil Davidson, ed., *African Civilization Revisited: Chronicles from Antiquity to Modern Times* (Trenton, N.J.: Africa World Press, 1991), pp. 223–226. This excerpt has been reprinted with the permission of Africa World Press in Trenton, NJ.

and precious stones and returned home in triumph. Soon the Portuguese set up trading bases around the Indian Ocean and attempted to limit the maritime commerce of their Arab, Ottoman, Persian, and Indian rivals.

The Portuguese in the Kongo

On the Atlantic coast, the Portuguese had a major impact in the Kongo and the surrounding region. During the early sixteenth century, an enlightened,

Christian king, Alfonso I (r. 1507–1543), ruled the Kongo. He outfought rivals for power after the death of the former king and, the Portuguese claimed, credited his victory to the intercession of a Christian saint, St. James, the brother of Jesus. Initially, the Kongolese were open to foreign influence: the monarch adopted Christianity and clearly wanted to modernize the kingdom along Western lines with Portuguese help. He might have succeeded had the Portuguese not become far more interested in acquiring enslaved Kongolese.

The Portuguese began shipping slaves from Kongo in 1514. Slavery was traditional in Kongo, where owners had a responsibility to treat slaves well. Even Alfonso, who was opposed to slavery in principle, was willing to sell slaves to the Portuguese in exchange for goods and services he regarded as essential to his kingdom's progress. However, in the 1500s, the Portuguese established a colony in Brazil, across the Atlantic from Kongo, and began setting up plantations to grow sugar and other tropical crops, multiplying the need for enslaved labor. Alfonso and his successors permitted only a modest trade in slaves, so the Portuguese resorted to forceful tactics. Alfonso repeatedly asked the Portuguese to halt their armed raids, which were damaging and depopulating his country, but his pleas were unsuccessful (see Witness to the Past: A Kongolese King Protests the Slave Trade). He eventually grew disillusioned with the rapacious Portuguese and wary of their ulterior motives.

> 66 Slavery was traditional in Kongo, where owners had a responsibility to treat slaves well. 99

Queen Nzinga and African Resistance

Halting their cooperation with the Kongo government in 1575, the Portuguese turned to outright conquest. After setting up a base at Luanda (loo-AHN-duh) in 1580, they began a war against a fringe state in the Kongo region, Ndongo (uhn-DONG-go), whose ruler was called the Ngola, hence the Portuguese name for the region, Angola (ahng-GO-luh). Like the Kongolese, the Ndongo warriors were skilled but armed only with arrows, lances, and swords against Portuguese guns, cannons, and steel swords. But the Portuguese encountered a formidable adversary in Queen Nzinga (en-ZING-a) of Ndongo (1624–1663), one of the most remarkable women in African history. A brilliant diplomat, eloquent debater, and skilled warrior who dressed as a man, she shrewdly negotiated with the Portuguese to preserve her kingdom, demanding to be treated as an equal with Europeans. After years of diplomacy alternating with war, the pragmatic Nzinga recognized a lost cause and made peace, a victim of Portugal's superior arms and ruthless quest for gold and slaves. Late in life, she adopted the Christian faith and abandoned her harem of men, many of them slaves. After her death, Ndongo became the foundation for the Portuguese colony of Angola.

In the early seventeenth century, the Portuguese and groups of displaced Africans they had hired and armed began raiding southern Kongo. The Christian Kongolese kings sent a series of moving appeals to the papacy for help, but they were mostly ignored. Kongo soon became engulfed in a long series of civil wars, which only generated more captives to be sold as slaves. During the late 1600s and early 1700s, an unusual Kongolese woman, Dona Beatriz Kimpa Vita, led a spiritual movement combining Catholic and traditional elements in an attempt to reform Kongolese political life. She threatened many powerful government and church interests, however, and in 1706 Catholic missionaries had her burned at the stake. Eventually most of the old Kongolese kingdom was incorporated into Portuguese Angola, and Christianity gradually lost support. The Kongolese kings had cooperated with the Portuguese in good faith, but the Portuguese proved unworthy allies.

Made increasingly vulnerable by occasional warfare and deteriorating economic conditions, Angola and Kongo became deeply enmeshed in the transatlantic slave trade, which, by the later 1600s, had grown much larger than the Arab and Black Sea slave trades. Angola and Kongo were the major suppliers of slaves to Brazil—indeed, the largest single source of enslaved men and women to the Americas, accounting for some 35 to 40 percent of the total. The decline of Kongo allowed its rival, the Lunda kingdom, to expand westward and engage the Portuguese in trade, exchanging slaves and ivory for woolen cloth and guns. These guns gave the Lunda kings control over much of the regional trade.

Portuguese activity extended into the eastern side of Africa after Vasco da Gama's first voyage. In 1502 da Gama led a squadron of twenty ships to supervise an occupation of the trading ports of Mozambique and Sofala. To establish commercial control of the East African coast, Portuguese forces attacked several major Swahili trading cities, plundering them of

Queen Nzinga This drawing by an Italian priest, Father Cavazzi, shows the formidable Queen Nzinga of Ndongo, in Angola, sitting on her throne, wearing a crown topped by a Christian cross while giving an order to attendants.

Courtesy, Luigi Araldi

their riches and burning some of them to the ground. Their East African conquests gave the Portuguese bases from which to extend their power in the Indian Ocean. During the next several decades, the Portuguese conquered or established control of several trading ports in the Persian Gulf, India, Malaya, Indonesia, and China, and they also seized the Spice Islands of eastern Indonesia, the main source for the priceless clove and nutmeg supplies. Using ruthless methods, such as attacking and sinking Arab, Persian, and Indian ships, they were able to gain partial control of the Indian Ocean maritime commerce.

The Decline of Portuguese Influence

The Portuguese became nominal masters of the East African coast, controlling key ports such as Mombasa, but they never really prospered, because the city-states declined into poverty. Merchants quit coming, and many traders fled elsewhere. The fanatically Christian Portuguese suppressed the Islamic Swahili culture and destroyed much of its literary heritage. The Portuguese dominated the coast and what commerce remained for a century, but they gradually lost their ability to control the Indian Ocean maritime trade. By the mid-seventeenth century, their influence was waning all over the coast except in Mozambique. Arabs from Oman, on the northeast Arabian coast, overran the Portuguese settlements in the late 1600s, established a sultanate on Zanzibar (ZAN-zuh-BAHR), and supervised the lucrative slave and ivory trade to the Middle East and India.

New Challenges for the Shona States and Ethiopia

Eventually the Portuguese sought influence inland from the East African coast. In the early 1500s, they

> "The available solution to the labor shortage, African slaves, provided the lowest available cost option and thereby created the racial basis of trans-Atlantic slavery."

built forts at the old coastal trading cities of Sofala and Mozambique as a base for locating and acquiring the rich source of gold on the plateau occupied by the Shona people. Portuguese adventurers seeking wealth began moving up the Zambezi River to the fringes of the largest Shona kingdom, then known as Monomotapa (MO-no-mo-TOP-a). The Portuguese gradually took control of the lower Zambezi valley and its gold trade, establishing a colony later called Mozambique. They dispatched Catholic missionaries upstream, but these had little success in finding converts. In addition, because the Portuguese died in large numbers from tropical diseases such as malaria, the Shona were able to hold out for many years. By 1628, however, a decaying Monomotapa had become a virtual Portuguese puppet state, but in trying to control the gold trade, the Portuguese ended up destroying it. Monomotapa dwindled in size and was eventually overrun by neighboring African states, which forced the Portuguese out of the plateau. Eventually the goldfields became less productive. The Portuguese then began concentrating their efforts on coastal Mozambique. Those Portuguese who settled there, especially in the Zambezi valley, tended to marry African women and adopt many aspects of local culture and customs.

Ethiopian Civil War

The Portuguese also intervened briefly in Ethiopia, where Christians maintained traditions that had been forged many centuries earlier. In the 1520s, the Portuguese sent a small force to help Ethiopians successfully repulse an invasion by Muslim neighbors backed by the rising Ottoman Turkish Empire. In the early 1600s, the Portuguese renewed their contacts with Ethiopia, sending Jesuit missionaries to convert the king, Susenyos (soo-SEN-yos) (r. 1607–1632), from the state church to Catholicism. At Portuguese urging, Susenyos began an effort to reform Ethiopian society and the Ethiopian Church. When both the church and the Amharic population resisted, civil war erupted. In the end, the pro-Portuguese king abdicated, the missionaries and other Portuguese were expelled, and Ethiopia went back to its old ways and faith.

South Africa and Dutch Colonization

European activity also affected the peoples living at the southern tip of Africa, where social, political, and economic developments differed greatly from most of the rest of Early Modern Africa. In 1652 the Dutch established a settlement, Cape Town, on the Cape of Good Hope, to provision the Dutch ships sailing between Europe and Indonesia. After a government was set up, Dutch settlers arrived in Cape Town and took up farming. At first they traded with the local Khoikhoi people for meat, but because they had guns, they soon began seizing what they wanted. In 1659 the Khoikhoi rose against the Dutch. After crushing the poorly armed resistance, the Dutch declared that the Khoikhoi "could not expect to get the land back."[5] Eventually the Dutch enslaved or killed all the Khoikhoi living near the Cape and began imposing white supremacy rule over Africans in the lands they controlled. To obtain a labor supply for their farms and households, the Dutch imported slaves from Madagascar, Mozambique, and Indonesia. Soon enslaved Africans and Asians far outnumbered the whites as the agricultural economy developed. Masters and slaves lived close together, but whites always held a politically, legally, and economically superior status.

The Boers and "Trekking"

Continued Dutch immigration led to rapid population growth, and some Dutch, chafing at governmental rules, began looking eastward for new land to settle. The Dutch settlers, later called Boers ("farmers"), began a movement not unlike the Bantu migrations centuries earlier. To survive, many Boers adopted the sheep- and cattle-herding economy of the Bantus. As some Boers expanded east along the coast and into the interior in search of farmland in the 1700s, they encountered the Xhosa and later the Zulu peoples. These encounters—plus Boer attempts to take over the land—produced a series of deadly

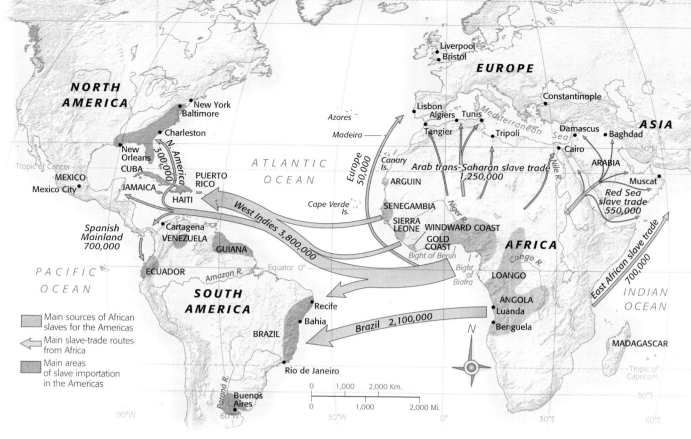

![Map legend]
Main sources of African
slaves for the Americas

Main slave-trade routes
from Africa

Main areas
of slave importation
in the Americas

Map labels (North America): New York, Baltimore, Charleston, New Orleans, MEXICO, Mexico City, CUBA, JAMAICA, PUERTO RICO, HAITI, Spanish Mainland 700,000, Cartagena, VENEZUELA, GUIANA, ECUADOR, SOUTH AMERICA, BRAZIL, Recife, Bahia, Rio de Janeiro, Buenos Aires

Map labels (Europe/Africa/Asia): Liverpool, Bristol, EUROPE, Constantinople, Lisbon, Algiers, Tunis, Tangier, Tripoli, Damascus, Baghdad, Cairo, ASIA, ARABIA, Muscat, Azores, Madeira, Canary Is., ARGUIN, SENEGAMBIA, SIERRA LEONE, WINDWARD COAST, GOLD COAST, Bight of Benin, Bight of Biafra, LOANGO, ANGOLA, Luanda, Benguela, AFRICA, MADAGASCAR

N. America 300,000
West Indies 3,800,000
Europe 50,000
Arab trans-Saharan slave trade 1,250,000
Red Sea slave trade 550,000
East African slave trade 700,000
Brazil 2,100,000

© Cengage Learning

Map 16.2
Trans-Atlantic Slave Trade, 1526–1870

While the Arab-run slave trade from West and East Africa to North Africa and western Asia continued, the trans-Atlantic slave trade was far larger in scope. Millions of Africans were transported across the Atlantic, the greatest number ending up in Brazil and the West Indies. The majority of slaves came from what is today Angola, Congo, and Nigeria.

conflicts that lasted for nearly half a century. The migrations of Boer settlers in cattle-drawn wagons, known as **trekking**, became a tradition, occurring whenever a Boer group wanted to flee government restraints.

The Trans-Atlantic Slave Trade

The economic growth of the American lands colonized by Europeans created a tremendous market for labor that could not be filled by free men and women, coerced Native Americans, or the small number of available European slaves. Newly opened American farms and mines badly needed labor after the massive decline of the Native American population during European conquest and colonization. The available solution to the labor shortage, African slaves, provided the lowest available cost option and thereby created the racial basis of trans-Atlantic slavery. Europeans may have more easily rationalized the ruthless exploitation of Africans because of their different culture and appearance.

trekking
The migrations of Boer settlers in cattle-drawn wagons into the interior of South Africa whenever they wanted to flee government restraints.

The Slave Trade Expands

In the early 1600s, the English, Spanish, French, Dutch, and Danes began following the Portuguese by obtaining enslaved people in West Africa and shipping them across the Atlantic to meet the limitless demands of the new American plantation economies (see Map 16.2). Because the West African coastal region was so fragmented politically, resistance to European slavers

Interactive Map

Middle Passage
The slave's journey by
ship from Africa to the
Americas.

was difficult. Furthermore, the region contained a population that was highly skilled in both tropical agriculture and mining, the enterprises for which labor was needed in the Americas.

Profits from the slave trade soared along with the volume of transported Africans, and European forts to obtain, store, and ship slaves soon dotted the West African coast from Senegal down to Angola. Many merchants bought slaves at various ports and then transported them all to one West African holding center, such as Accra (ah-CRAW) in today's Ghana, for sale to slave ships, a system known as "bulking." Europeans traded cotton goods, guns, iron, rum, and tobacco for slaves, often with the cooperation of local African chiefs, but sometimes they acquired Africans directly by force, as the Portuguese did in the Kongo. How many Africans were originally enslaved for the trade is uncertain, but they probably added up to some 25 to 30 million people. Between one-third and one-half survived to be sold at auction in the Americas. Most studies conclude that between 9 and 12 million Africans were landed in the Americas over four centuries. Perhaps one-third were women. Millions of slaves died in holding cells in West Africa or on the notorious Middle Passage, the slaves' journey by ship from Africa to the Americas. The trans-Atlantic slave trade reached its peak between 1700 and 1800, with perhaps 100,000 Africans per year being shipped to the Americas.

Horrors of the Middle Passage

Both the Middle Passage and the fate of the enslaved Africans who survived the trip were horrific. Depending on the weather, the trip from Kongo to Brazil took one month and from West Africa to the Caribbean and North America around two months. The slaves on board faced harsh and cruel conditions. Olaudah Equiano (oh-LAU-duh ay-kwee-AHN-oh), an Igbo seized in Nigeria in the 1750s, described the intolerable stench of the hold, which made him ill, and of floggings on the deck for misconduct that sometimes resulted in death, after which the bodies were thrown overboard. Many slaves committed suicide before reaching the Americas. Equiano recounted a case when two other Igbos, in despair, jumped overboard while chained together. Many crews installed nets along the sides of slave ships to catch jumpers. There were also many mutinies, in which slaves attempted (occasionally with success) to gain control of the ship, such as the celebrated 1839 incident aboard a small Spanish ship, the *Amistad,* bound from Sierra Leone to Cuba.

Those who survived the hardships of the Middle Passage faced a bleak future in the Americas. When they arrived, they were sold without regard to personal ties. Equiano wrote of his landing in Barbados: "Without scruple, are relations and friends separated, most of them never to see each other again."[6] The majority of slaves were sold to sugar, cotton, or coffee plantations and endured brutal, exploitative working conditions.

The Middle Passage This painting from the era vividly shows the overcrowded conditions on the ships that carried African slaves, packed like sardines, on the "Middle Passage" across the Atlantic to the Americas. Such brutal conditions resulted in the deaths of many slaves and eventually prompted reformers to demand the end of the slave trade.

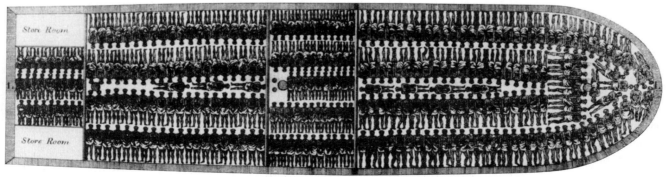

From a Parliamentary Report

Rationalizing the Slave Trade

During the slave trade, Europeans quickly developed feelings of superiority to Africans that resulted in racism. In 1589 the English adventurer Richard Hakluyt described Africans as "a people of beastly living, without a God, law, religion, or common wealth."[7] The English had long seen the color black as signifying "soiled, dirty, foul, malignant, deadly, sinister." Now they contrasted white and black skin color as connoting, as one observer put it, "purity and filthiness, virginity and sin, virtue and baseness, beauty and ugliness, beneficence and evil, God and the devil."[8] Some Westerners thought slavery helped Africans by exposing them to Western values and Christianity.

The Slave Trade and African Societies

The impact of the trans-Atlantic slave trade on Africa varied from region to region. Some coastal regions of West and Central Africa succumbed to chronic raiding and kidnapping as well as occasional warfare, in an "enslave your neighbor or be enslaved" syndrome. European guns traded for slaves made some regions dangerous, leaving plundered villages and broken families. Some peoples, among them Kongolese, Angolans, Yorubas, Igbos, and Akans, were disproportionately transported to the Americas, and their societies were badly disrupted. By linking parts of Africa closely to Europe and the Americas, the slave trade also created an Atlantic System, a large network that spanned western and Central Africa, the east coast and southern region of English North America, the Caribbean Basin, and the northern and eastern coastal zones of South America.

The Impact of the Slave Trade on Africa

The slave trade fostered economic change in Africa. While their major target was slaves, Europeans also coveted gold and cloth, and Western merchants soon monopolized the African coastal trade. But some Africans and people of mixed African and European ancestry also flourished as merchants and slave traders. Others refused to cooperate in slave trading and dealt with Europeans on their own terms. Hence, until the 1700s, the kings of Benin, located inland, prohibited the sale of male slaves and instead obtained the firearms needed to protect the state by trading cotton textiles, pepper, ivory, and beads. Some states prospered by cooperating with the slave trade at the expense of their neighbors, like Dahomey (duh-HO-mee), which formed in the seventeenth century as a dependency of a Yoruba kingdom and grew powerful in the eighteenth century as a major supplier of slaves.

The most far-reaching changes were found in the coastal regions stretching from Senegambia down to Angola, sometimes reaching several hundred miles inland. Some states, such as Kongo, declined, while others, such as Ashante, rose in power. Except in the interior of Angola, most West and Central African societies far from the coast had little direct contact with the European slavers. On the other hand, the Arab slave trade badly disrupted some East African regions, even reaching as far inland as the eastern Congo River Basin. The Sudan region, such as the Hausa states, remained a source of slaves for North Africa.

The activities of Europeans had a long-term impact on Africa. The trans-Atlantic slave trade created economic imbalances that hindered the evolution of local industries and integrated Africa into the world economy as a supplier of resources. The exchange was not entirely one way: American food crops, such as corn and peanuts, became important to African diets, and the slave trade spurred some African states, such as Dahomey, to develop commercially.

Early Imperialism and Colonialism in Africa

One of the main results of European intrusion was imperialism, the control or domination, direct or indirect, of one state or people over another. Often imperialism led to colonialism, government by one society over another society. A few areas, such as Angola, Mozambique, and South Africa, became Western colonies. But the full-blown Western colonial scramble for Africa only began with rapid industrialization in Europe, which

Atlantic System A large network that arose with the trans-Atlantic slave trade; the network spanned western and Central Africa, the east coast and southern region of English North America, the Caribbean Basin, and the northern and eastern coastal zones of South America.

imperialism The control or domination, direct or indirect, of one state or people over another.

colonialism Government by one society over another society.

A Voyage to New Calabar River in the Year 1699 Learn about the slave trade in West Africa, from a Frenchman on an English slave-trading expedition.

contributed to the end of the slave trade in the 1800s but accelerated the need for natural resources for commercial products.

The heritage of racism made Africans and their descendants in the Americas a permanent underclass, treated with contempt by people of European ancestry. Racism became a pervasive ideology supporting bad treatment of particular groups. The first Europeans to encounter great African states like Benin, Kongo, and Kilwa in the late 1400s and early 1500s were awed by their prosperity and marveled at how even the poorest were treated with dignity. By the 1700s, those views had changed profoundly.

LO³ The Ottomans and Islamic Imperial Revival

The Islamic societies of the Middle East, the large region including North Africa and western Asia, did not experience the jarring transitions felt by many Africans during the Early Modern Era. While European nations established supremacy of the seas, Islamic states remained major land powers. The greatest of these, the Turkish Ottoman Empire, began in 1300 and survived until 1923, eventually ruling much of southeastern Europe, the western fringe of Asia, and much of North Africa, including Egypt. By the 1700s, however, the Ottomans and other Middle Eastern states were suffering from chronic warfare, poor leadership, a growing rigidity, and a superiority complex in relationship to the upstart Europeans. Their decline came as Europeans were on the rise.

The Ottoman Empire: Government and Economy

From their base in central Anatolia, the Ottoman Turks gained power over much of the once-great Byzantine Empire in the 1300s. The Ottoman conquest of the Byzantine capital, Constantinople, in 1453 demonstrated conclusively the power of Islamic society, as the capital of Orthodox Christianity was transformed into Muslim-ruled Istanbul. By 1512 the Ottomans controlled all of Anatolia and what is today Bulgaria, Greece, Albania, Serbia, and much of Romania. Between 1514 and 1517, the Ottomans defeated Persian forces and added Syria, Lebanon,

> "From their base in central Anatolia, the Ottoman Turks gained power over much of the once-great Byzantine Empire in the 1300s."

Palestine, and Egypt to their domains. During the sixteenth century, they controlled the Mediterranean, even raiding coastal Spain and Italy.

Suleiman the Magnificent

The Ottoman golden age came under the leadership of Sultan Suleiman (SOO-lay-man) the Magnificent (r. 1520–1566), a just, lawful man but also a merciless conqueror to his enemies. Under Suleiman, the Ottomans pushed north of the Danube River and into the eastern Balkans, defeated the Hungarians, and besieged Vienna. They also gained control of Egypt and then the North African coast. Suleiman's empire now stretched from Algeria to the Persian Gulf and from Hungary to Armenia (see Map 16.3). But the Ottomans never controlled much of the Arabian Peninsula, enabling independent sultanates such as Oman to extend their own power to the East African cities. Omani Arabs and other coastal Arabs remained active in the Indian Ocean trade network.

 Interactive Map

CHRONOLOGY

The Middle East, 1500–1750

1501–1736	Safavid dynasty in Persia
1514–1517	Ottoman conquest of Syria, Egypt, and Arabia
1520–1566	Reign of Ottoman sultan Suleiman the Magnificent
1529	First Ottoman siege of Vienna
1554–1659	Sa'dian dynasty in Morocco
1682–1699	Ottoman wars with Habsburg Austria
1715	Beginning of Russian conquest of Turkestan
1722	Afghan invasion of Safavid Persia
1736–1747	Rule of Nadir Shah in Persia

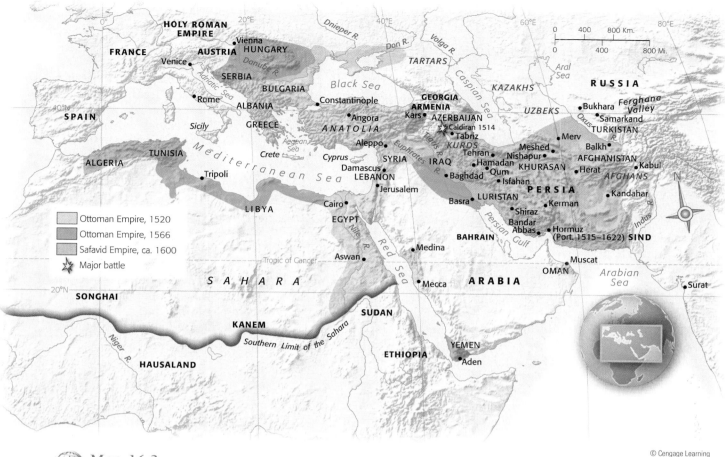

Map 16.3
The Ottoman and Safavid Empires, 1500–1750
By the later 1500s, the Ottoman Empire included large parts of western Asia, southeastern Europe, southern Russia, and North Africa. Their major rivals, the Safavids, controlled Persia and parts of Iraq, the Caucasus, Afghanistan, and Central Asia.

© Cengage Learning

Suleiman's reign revived the Islamic glory that had faded with the downfall of the Iraq-based Abbasid Empire in the 1200s. Suleiman and other Ottoman sultans claimed to have restored the caliphate, the governing system of early Islamic times that was thought to be ordained by God and that blended political and religious power. In 1538 the Ottoman ruler could boast proudly: "I am God's slave and sultan of this world. I am head of Muhammad's community."[9] Suleiman's position at the center of an extensive international political system often involved him in European conflicts, but his broad empire also gave him large commercial benefits. Spices and other products from India, Southeast Asia, and China were shipped to the Ottoman-ruled port of Basra (BAHS-ruh), at the head of the Persian Gulf, and then transported to Ottoman-controlled markets for sale to European merchants. Ottoman ships also controlled the Black Sea trade.

Ottoman Imperialism

Ottoman political success owed much to military power and immigration. The Ottomans adopted gunpowder weapons, especially cannons, which were often built and operated by mercenary Hungarian Christians in Ottoman service. These weapons equaled the best of European gunnery until the late 1600s. The Ottomans also developed an effective navy, often led by Muslim refugees from Spain. These refugees included Jews, who were expelled from Spain in the 1400s and 1500s and who brought valuable expertise and international connections.

> "Istanbul and other major cities served as centers for transregional trade, and artisan and merchant guilds with elected leaders became central to urban life."

Ottoman imperialism supported an effective state led by very able men. The Ottomans chose officials based on merit, allowing Arabs and other non-Turks to serve in the government and military, often in high positions. The sultans governed through an imperial council headed by a prime minister. The ruling elite lived in luxury, residing in beautiful palaces with large harems and many servants. Christian princes remained the major landowners in Ottoman Europe, and the Ottomans especially recruited administrators and soldiers from Christian peoples. At regular intervals, the sultan's agents swept through the provinces selecting Christian youth for training. Essentially becoming slaves, they were required to embrace Islam. The most talented were sent to the palace school to be trained for administration, while the other conscripts joined the elite military corps of infantrymen known as janissaries ("new troops"), who lived in barracks and were not allowed to marry but were well paid.

Under this dynamic state, the Ottoman commercial economy flourished. Istanbul and other major cities served as centers for transregional trade, and artisan and merchant guilds with elected leaders became central to urban life. But the dynamic international trade mostly involved luxuries such as Indian textiles and Chinese porcelain, and the empire was largely self-sufficient in necessities such as food.

Ottoman Society and Culture

The diverse Ottoman society thrived in this era. The empire's multiethnic population, about evenly divided between Christians and Muslims, was large, containing some 50 million people at its peak and dwarfing the largest European country of the time, France, which had less than one-third of the Ottoman total. The size and diversity of the Ottoman population posed administrative challenges, however. Following the pattern in most multicultural Muslim states, the sultans governed the Jewish, Greek Orthodox, and Armenian Christian communities through their own religious leaders. Each religious group had its own laws and courts and enjoyed a toleration rare in the world at that time. The Ottomans attracted many immigrants, among them European merchants and technicians and Christian peasants from the Balkans. Ottoman cities, where varied peoples mixed, were vibrant: urban social life revolved around coffeehouses, public baths, and taverns.

Women in the Ottoman Empire

Women had a higher status in Turkish society than in Arab tradition, and this pattern continued under the Ottomans. Women in the royal family exercised considerable political clout, and upper-class women often owned land, managed businesses, and controlled wealth. Throughout the empire, the courts protected women's rights to inheritance and property. Turkish society was patriarchal, but older women had control of both the young males and females in their families. Yet, women could also be abused by men and more easily divorced, and women who were suspected of illicit sexual activity could be punished or killed.

Ottoman Arts and Sciences

The Ottomans stimulated literary and artistic creativity, often with royal patronage. Istanbul attracted artists and artisans from all over Europe and the Middle East. The Sultan Mehmed II (1432–1481) arranged with the Venetians to have their most famous artist, Giovanni Bellini, spend two years (1479–1480) decorating his palace with paintings. Suleiman the Magnificent welcomed humanist thinkers from Italy to the capital. Ottoman poets wrote ornate verse in Persian or Turkish, and architects, such as the

Read about Pasha Sinan, an Ottoman architect, and one of the most innovative in world history.

highly innovative Pasha Sinan, designed beautiful domed mosques and other public buildings. Artists also produced beautiful painted tiles and pottery.

Although the Ottomans pursued science, by the 1700s they were falling behind some rival states. Ottoman medicine remained vibrant, and scholars published many volumes on astronomy, mathematics, and geography. Muslim geographers also produced world maps more sophisticated than those of

Europe, but the emphasis on law and theology rather than science in Ottoman higher education inhibited technological innovation.

Conservative Islam and the Sufi

The Ottomans drew the religious establishment close to the state, which was headed by a leader who saw himself as anointed by God. Religious leaders emphasized rote learning and memorization rather than analysis of the sacred texts, and some punished deviation from orthodoxy. Furthermore, Islamic leaders were increasingly conservative and hostile to technological innovation. Yet various mystical Sufi sects, seeking a personal experience of God, had large followings. Seyh Bedreddin (SAY beh-DREAD-en), a famous mystic, founded an order of practitioners known as dervishes, who feverishly danced to achieve a trance-like state. Although some Sufi sects operated with official approval and financial support, others were suspected of political disloyalty and of modifying too many Islamic principles.

> **Eventually the Ottomans faced new challenges that undermined the state and reduced the size of the empire.**

Ottoman Challenges and Decline

Eventually the Ottomans faced new challenges that undermined the state and reduced the size of the empire. Well into the 1600s, however, Ottoman armies continued to effectively wage battles against European and Persian rivals. Only in 1683, when Austria and its allies repulsed the last Ottoman attack of Vienna, did European observers begin to perceive the Ottoman decline. In the next few years, the Ottomans were pushed out of many areas in eastern Europe, and by 1699 the Ottomans were forced to cede Hungary to the rival Habsburgs. Although in the early 1700s the Ottomans did reclaim some of these territories, Ottoman power was no longer feared. Some of the decline resulted from failing Ottoman military practices and technology: the discipline among the janissary military forces weakened, and eventually the whole training system for young men was eliminated. The Ottomans' technology also fell behind. The development of Ottoman weaponry, especially artillery, stagnated just as European military technology was rapidly improving.

Internal Conflicts

Problems of governing also stressed the empire. Compared to China or the emerging European states, the Ottoman state was not very centralized, and imperial control was difficult to maintain. In the early 1500s, the Ottomans had conquered the Kurds—a Sunni Muslim ethnic group occupying a large region from what is today eastern Turkey, northern Iraq and Syria, and northwest Iran—and many Kurds increasingly resented Turkish control. At the same time, many Arabs and Balkan Christians who once welcomed Ottoman rule for providing stability and justice began to think of their own peoples as nations repressed by the empire. Ottoman citizens also disliked higher taxes, growing corruption and poverty, and a bloated bureaucracy.

Meanwhile, in Istanbul the ruling elite was able to exercise more power over a weak or incompetent sultan. Potential successors to the throne were often kept locked up in the palace as prisoners until chosen to take the throne. Ottoman sultans had increasing difficulty controlling restless provinces in North Africa and western Asia. Occasional rebellions were met by brute force, but during the 1600s, some areas broke away from the empire. By the mid-1700s, Ottoman influence was deteriorating in large parts of the empire, and the Russians were putting pressure on Ottoman territory north of the Black Sea.

External Challenges

While beginning to deteriorate from within, the Ottomans also faced increasing economic and military challenges from western European nations, the Habsburg realm, and Russia. Increasing European participation in Asian trade weakened Anatolia's historic position as a middleman, undermining economic conditions, and Ottoman rulers did little to support the empire's merchant class, most of whom were Greeks, Armenians, and Jews. With its own industries growing less competitive, the once self-sufficient empire became increasingly dependent on imports from Europe. Western merchants thus gradually bested their Ottoman rivals, reducing the Ottomans to a secondary region in the emerging global trade system. Large Western trading firms, armed with both great capital and better business methods and backed by their own governments, became increasingly influential.

The resurgence of European power led to fierce debates in the empire. Reformers became interested in European products and customs and favored the importing of some European technology. But reformist forces struggled for influence against conservatives, who preferred the status quo, and reformers also found it difficult to overcome an Arab and Turkish superiority complex regarding the once-upstart Europeans.

> "Eventually Persians came to view Shi'ism as central to Persian identity."

caused many Sunni families to emigrate to the Ottoman Empire and elsewhere. Eventually Persians came to view Shi'ism as central to Persian identity.

The Safavids established a strong political system, but their imperial prospects were limited. Safavid armies rode on horseback and viewed guns as both awkward and unmanly, an attitude that left them vulnerable to the gunpowder weapons possessed by their Portuguese and Ottoman enemies. The Portuguese seized and held the strategic port of Hormuz (hawr-MOOZ), on Persia's southeast coast, for decades in the 1500s. In 1514 the Ottomans drove deep into Safavid territory, acquiring Safavid lands in Armenia and Anatolia. The battle losses to the hated Ottomans demoralized Safavid military leaders and stalled expansion.

LO⁴ Persia, Morocco, and Central Asia

Other Islamic societies from Morocco to Central Asia also underwent significant changes during the Early Modern Era. East of the Ottoman Empire, in Persia, a Shi'ite dynasty known as the Safavids became an internationally recognized power. Persian leaders, thinkers, and officials had long played a significant role in Islamic society, and Persian, widely spoken by elites from Istanbul to Delhi, India, was the closest thing to a hemispheric language. The Safavids developed a prosperous economy linked to international trade and fostered a brilliant artistic culture. In northwest Africa, Morocco became notable for its military prowess. Meanwhile, northeast of Persia, various Islamic societies in Central Asia emerged from the ashes of the Mongol Empire but struggled to maintain the ancient Silk Road trade networks.

The Safavid Empire

The Safavid dynasty came to power in Persia at the beginning of the sixteenth century. It was founded by a Turkish group from what is today Azerbaijan (AZ-uhr-bye-ZHAHN) in the Caucasus Mountains. The Safavids belonged to a militant Sufi order that had shifted from the Sunni to the Shi'a branch of Islam. From their base in Azerbaijan, the Safavid movement grew rapidly in alliance with other Shi'ites in the region.

Ismail and the Conquest of Persia

In 1501, the Safavids, led by a charismatic thirteen-year-old boy, Isma'il (1487–1524), invaded and conquered Persia, then a center of Sunni practice and home to a variety of small Sunni Turkish and Persian states. Isma'il, who claimed descent from Mohammad and Sassanian princes, and his dedicated followers wanted to unite the region both politically and religiously. Within ten years, the Turkish Safavids controlled all of Persia. Isma'il thought of himself as an agent of God and mandated the conversion of the Persians to Shi'ism, which took a long time and

The Safavid Zenith under Shah Abbas

Safavid rule reached its peak under Shah (king) Abbas (ah-BAHS) I (r. 1587–1629), who consolidated his power by manipulating or executing his enemies. His capital, Isfahan (is-fah-HAHN), became a beautiful, tree-shaded city of some 1 million people, filled with 160 mosques, 273 public baths, many parks, and a great bazaar that one visitor described as "the surprisingest piece of Greatness in Honor of Commerce that the world can boast of."¹⁰ Shah Abbas planned the city with the help of Shaikh Baha al-Din Muhammad Amili, a famed Persian philosopher, judge, poet, astronomer, and engineer. Abbas maintained good relations with European powers, welcoming ambassadors from a half-dozen European nations and importing English advisers to help train his military forces and manufacture modern cannon and muskets, marking a change in Safavid military strategy. With these weapons, Shah Abbas waged successful wars against the invading Ottomans and Uzbeks and recaptured Hormuz from the Portuguese. For their part, Europeans sought Persia as an ally against their mutual Ottoman enemy. To earn revenue for the government, Abbas and his successors also gradually placed more land under state control. Peasants worked on land owned by the king and received a share of the crop for their labors.

The Safavid Trading Network

The Safavid economy flourished for several centuries. Persia remained a major exporter of silk, a trade increasingly dominated by Armenian settlers from the Caucasus, who also operated the lucrative gold and silver crafts industries. Networks extending all over the Eastern Hemisphere, and long-distance trade by land and sea, had flowed through Persia since ancient times and continued during the Safavid era. Safavid trade with Europe gradually increased: during the 1600s, English, Dutch, and French merchants visited Persian ports to obtain silk, carpets, brocades, cotton, wool, and other products. Foreign merchants from all over were attracted by the great bazaar that developed in Isfahan, where artisans produced fine carpets, textiles, metalwork, and ceramics. Some 25,000 people worked in Isfahan's textile industry.

Armenians, who flourished from Safavid trade, also competed fiercely with Dutch, English, Portuguese, and Indian merchants in parts of Eurasia. The Armenian network radiated outward from New Julfa (JOOL-fa), a mostly Armenian city built by the Safavids near Isfahan. A central council of Armenian merchants in New Julfa coordinated local councils in the Armenian trade diaspora. Armenians shared a common culture and the Christian religion, and their merchants played a key role in the overland trade from India to Central Asia and the Middle East. In the 1660s, New Julfa merchants also negotiated trade agreements with Russia, which allowed them to bypass the Ottoman Empire and reach northern Europe through Russia and the Baltic.

> " By the eighteenth century, the Safavid sultans had become weaker, the Shi'ite religious officials had become stronger, and the empire's economy had declined. "

Women in Safavid Society

Safavid society was patriarchal, with men having more rights than women, who were often restricted to the home and expected to veil themselves when they went out of the household. Yet, as in Ottoman Turkey, Persian women often had more influence than was the case among Arabs. Royal women in harems raised royal sons and also at times tried to shape government policies. As in classical Persia two millennia earlier, some women became wealthy and owned land and businesses.

Safavid Culture and Decline

The Safavids patronized art and literature as well as commerce. The major cities, especially Isfahan, became centers for artists, poets, writers, and craftsmen. Safavid artists became especially famous for miniature paintings, which combined the harmony of color with the rhythm of design, often to illustrate great Persian literature. In 1525 the Safavid sultan commissioned an ambitious project to produce an illustrated version of an old epic poem recounting Persian history. The completed version contained 258 paintings by many artists. This was also a golden age for crafting carpets, textiles, and ceramics, for which Persians became famous. Carpet weaving became both an art form and a national industry, with government-run factories producing a range of silks, brocades, velvets, and other fabrics.

Transformations in Shi'ism

Persian Shi'ism underwent some changes over the years. The Safavids encouraged passion plays and religious processions commemorating the tragic death of the prophet Muhammad's grandson, Husayn, in the Battle of Karbala in 680, the event that split the Islamic community. Sufi influence gradually declined, while religious teachers increasingly emphasized their own authority over that of the Quran and other sacred texts. The result was increasing belief in the infallibility of Islamic leaders, who enjoyed greater power than was common elsewhere in the Islamic world. Even the shahs claimed to represent divine power, giving the state a theocratic cast, but tensions over religious power between the shahs and Shi'ite leaders continued to simmer.

Safavid Decline and the Rise of Nadir Shah

By the eighteenth century, the Safavid sultans had become weaker, the Shi'ite religious officials had become stronger, and the empire's economy had declined. Unable to control the clergy or trust their sons who were plotting for the throne, later Safavid rulers often turned to alcohol for comfort, and corruption grew rampant. In 1722, Afghans seized Isfahan and then repulsed Ottoman forces invading from the west. Isfahan, once one of the world's most beautiful cities, was nearly destroyed. In 1736, a new Persian leader, Nadir Shah (1688–1747), led a force that drove

Letter to Shah Ismail of Persia The Ottoman sultan Selim I, a Sunni Muslim, threatens war against the Persian shah, his Shi'a enemy.

Persian Tiles As Isfahan flourished under Shah Abbas I, wealthy Persians decorated their homes and mosques with tiles featuring scenes, often gardens, painted by local artists. This tile painting shows a woman at leisure in her garden, holding a vase while her servant offers her fruit.

out the Afghan invaders. Casting aside the remaining Safavids, he launched a vigorous new state. His armies went on the offensive, marching into Ottoman lands and north India, where his forces plundered the major city, Delhi. But Nadir Shah's ruthless tactics antagonized many, and economic collapse exposed millions to famine. After ill-advised efforts to reconvert the Persians from Shi'a to Sunni Islam, Nadir Shah was assassinated in 1747. In the decades to follow, Persia was again divided into smaller states, and Western pressure intensified.

Moroccan Resurgence and Expansion

While the Ottomans and Safavids dominated much of the Islamic world, the Moroccans on the far northwestern fringe of Africa forged a strong state, conquered an empire, and linked themselves to various networks of exchange. Moroccan society comprised Berbers, Arabs, and an influential Jewish community, many of whom had been forced out of the Iberian Peninsula. Some Spanish Muslims joined Moroccan military forces, while Jews invigorated commercial life. During the 1400s and 1500s, ships from Europe regularly visited Moroccan ports, exchanging metals, textiles, spices, hardware, and wine for leather, carpets, wool, grain, sugar, and African slaves.

The Sa'dian Dynasty of Morocco

During the later 1400s and early 1500s, Moroccan encounters with the Portuguese eventually brought the Sa'dians to power. Portugal's cultivation of sugar on the Atlantic islands began undermining the Moroccan economy, and the establishment of Portuguese forts along the coast posed a military threat. In response, growing mystical Sufi movements organized tribal coalitions to resist the Portuguese. In 1554 the Sa'dians, a Moroccan family who claimed descent from the prophet Muhammad and had fought against the Portuguese forts, conquered much of Morocco with the support of Sufi and tribal leaders, launching a new era.

The Sa'dians ruled Morocco until 1659, forging a powerful military and a regime quite different from those of the Ottoman territories. The greatest Sa'dian leader, Sultan al-Mansur (man-SOOR) (r. 1578–1603), recruited foreign mercenary soldiers who knew how to use firearms. By 1603 the army of 40,000 included 4,000 Europeans, 4,000 Spanish Muslims, and 1,500 Turks, armed with modern artillery. The Netherlands and England, both rivals of the Portuguese, sold Morocco ships, cannons, and gunpowder. The resulting military power allowed the Moroccans to capture the Portuguese ports along the Atlantic coast, and in 1591 Moroccan forces seized the Songhai city of Timbuktu, gaining control of the trans-Saharan trade linking West and North Africa. In the later 1600s, the Sa'dian system broke down, and a new Moroccan dynasty, the Alawis (uh-LAH-wees), who also claimed descent from the prophet Muhammad, came to power in 1672. This dynasty still rules Morocco today.

Central Asia and Russian Expansion

The most direct and long-lasting confrontations between Muslims and Europeans resulted from Russian imperial expansion into Central Asia and Ottoman territories. Islam had a strong foothold in Central Asia, and many places had large Sufi communities where Sufi masters often gained political power. But as the remnants of the Mongol Empire broke up into various rival societies by the 1400s, Russia capitalized on the political vacuum to extend its own power first into Siberia and then into the Black Sea region and Central Asia. While several western European nations built maritime empires, Russia transformed itself into a great land-based territorial empire. A key role in this Russian expansion was played by the Cossacks (KOS-aks), tough, hard-drinking adventurers and fierce warriors from southern Russia who were descendants of Russians, Poles, and Lithuanians fleeing serfdom, slavery, or jail.

Russian Expansion to the East and South

The expansion east across sparsely populated Siberia began in the 1500s and accelerated during the seventeenth and eighteenth centuries. By 1637 Russian explorers had reached the Pacific Ocean. In 1689, conflict with China forced the Russians to temporarily abandon settlements in the Amur (AH-moor) River Basin north of China (see Chapter 18), but they continued to add other Siberian territory. The Russians also began acquiring territories on their southern fringe, coveting access to the Black Sea and the Straits of Bosporus bisecting Istanbul, through which Russian ships could reach the warm Mediterranean. The southward thrust meant confronting the Tartars (TAHR-tuhrz), Muslim descendants of Mongols and long a threat to the Russians. In the 1400s and 1500s, Tartars, Russians, Ottoman Turks, Poles, and Lithuanians fought for control of today's southern Russia. Between 1552 and 1556, the Russians seized the Tartar state of Kazan (kuh-ZAN), slaughtering many residents in the capital, and then gradually gained more land. Russian commerce benefited from Russia's new domination of the northern Caspian Sea.

Russian Conquests in Central Asia

Soon the Russians turned toward Muslim Central Asia, settled largely by Turkish peoples and often known as Turkestan. By the early 1700s, the Russians had gained territory occupied by the Kazakhs (kah-ZAHKS), a pastoral people who had once ruled a large area, and by 1864 they controlled all of the Kazakh lands to the eastern border with China. They then targeted the Silk Road cities, where the Uzbeks (OOZ-beks)—a people of mixed Turkish, Persian, and Mongol ancestry—proved a formidable threat. But the Sunni Uzbeks, enemies of the Shi'ite Safavics, eventually were weakened. When Safavid hostility closed Persia to Uzbek trade, the prosperity of the Silk Road cities declined, and the roads saw fewer travelers. Eventually the Uzbeks and their neighbors earned smaller revenues and their merchants lost profits. In the early 1700s, the Persians gained control of some Uzbek territory and much of Afghanistan, and by the later 1800s, an expanding Russia was able to conquer all of southern Turkestan.

Cossacks
Tough adventurers and soldiers from southern Russia who were descendants of Russians, Poles, and Lithuanians fleeing serfdom, slavery, or jail.

Listen to a synopsis of Chapter 16.

CHAPTER 17

Americans, Europeans, Africans, and New Societies in the Americas, 1450–1750

Learning Outcomes

After reading this chapter, you should be able to answer the following questions:

LO¹ How did encounters between Europe and the Americas increase in the 1500s?

LO² How did Europeans conquer and begin settling the American societies?

LO³ What were the major consequences of European colonization of the Americas?

LO⁴ What impact did the trans-Atlantic slave trade and emerging Atlantic system have on European and American societies?

> **❝**Truly do we live on earth? Not forever on earth; only a little while here. Although it be jade, it will be broken. Although it is gold, it is crushed.**❞**
>
> —**Aztec poem on the meaning of life, ca. 1500**[1]

In the sixteenth century, Spanish colonists in Mexico trained an Aztec historian, Chimalpahin Cuahtlehuanitzin (chee-MAL-pin QUAT-al-WANT-zen), how to read and write in the Western alphabet. Using this alphabet but writing in his native Nahuatl (NAH-waht-ell) language, the Aztec historian created one of the best records of the Mexican world at the moment of contact. He wrote of Aztec military triumphs over neighboring people, and also of the reports that began to reach Tenochtitlan in 1519 of pale-skinned men in huge boats arriving on the eastern coast from the sea, where gods might come from. In fact, Aztec legends claimed that, centuries earlier, a Toltec king driven into exile by rivals had become a god, Quetzalcoatl (kate-zahl-CO-ah-tal), who promised to return some day seeking revenge. These strange men on the coast seemed suspiciously godlike: they dressed in metal, had unfamiliar but lethal metal weapons, rode on large animals as tall as houses—and they arrived around the year some believed that Quetzalcoatl would return.

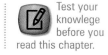 Test your knowlege before you read this chapter.

What do you think?

The most important factor in Europeans' domination of the Americas was the inadvertent spread of disease to Native American communities.

Strongly Disagree   Strongly Agree
1   2   3   4   5   6   7

Cuahtlehuanitzin wrote that, nearly three decades earlier, 13-Flint in the Aztec calendar (1492 in the Gregorian calendar) had been an unusually bad year, bringing an eclipse of the sun, volcanic eruptions, and widespread famine. The Aztec philosophy of life understood such occasional setbacks, but the Aztecs were not prepared for the troubles the Europeans would provoke. The leader of the pale men was the Spanish explorer Hernán Cortés. The invaders arrived in the Aztec lands, Cuahtlehuanitzin remembered, when a terrible and unknown disease, smallpox, began killing off the people. And within two years, these men from afar, with horses, metal armor, and gunpowder weapons, had conquered the Aztec Empire.

The first Europeans to arrive in the Americas claimed to have discovered a "new world," but it was actually an old one, long populated by a mosaic of peoples. The voyages of Christopher Columbus and

◀◀A Mestizo Family The intermarriage of Europeans and Indians was common in Latin America, especially in Mexico. This Mexican painting, by the eighteenth-century artist Las Castas, shows a Spanish man, his Indian wife, and their mixed-descent, or *mestizo*, daughter.

the conquests of such adventurers as Cortés in Mexico often destroyed long-existing American societies and reshaped them, in reality *creating* a "new world." In fact, the whole Western Hemisphere changed. During the 1500s, the Spanish and Portuguese conquered and colonized large areas of what we now call Latin America. A century later, in North America and the Caribbean, the English, French, and Dutch followed, gradually extending their power. As a result of these incursions, few regions experienced more changes than the Americas. Later, European exploration in Southeast Asia also led to the first encounters between Europe and the diverse island societies of the Pacific Ocean.

The transitions that resulted from European encounters with Native Americans affected both sides of the Atlantic. Among the most important consequences was a complex global exchange of crops, animals, peoples, and cultures, while diseases carried from the Eastern Hemisphere set off a demographic disaster for Native American peoples. The societies that emerged from the European colonization of the Americas reflected diverse influences from all over the Atlantic world. Perhaps most important, in some regions of the Americas a plantation economy developed that engaged enslaved Africans and their descendants in agonizing circumstances.

LO¹ Early American–European–Pacific Encounters

American peoples had developed a wide variety of societies, economies, and styles of governing by the fifteenth century, but they faced a great challenge from the coming of the Europeans. Christopher Columbus

> "By 1500 the Aztecs, based in central Mexico, were the most powerful Mesoamerican society, and the Incas, centered in central Peru, controlled most of the Andes region."

began the historic change in 1492. In his wake, various European nations first explored and then conquered, colonized, and settled the entire Western Hemisphere, drawing the Americas into commercial, travel, and religious networks. The exploration of the Americas also spilled over into the Pacific Ocean, though few Pacific islanders encountered the West in this era.

American Societies in 1500

In 1500 the Western Hemisphere contained many societies with distinctive institutions, customs, and survival strategies. Those who lived by hunting, gathering, and fishing could be found in the North American Great Plains, the Pacific Northwest coast, Alaska, northern Canada, and some of the tropical forest regions of Central and South America. Other peoples developed small-scale farming, especially in eastern North America, parts of the North American desert and Amazon Basin, and southeastern Brazil.

The Meso-American Empires For millennia the most complex Native American societies flourished from intensive farming in Mesoamerica (Mexico and northern Central America) and the Andes region of western South America. By 1500 the Aztecs, based in central Mexico, were the most powerful Mesoamerican society, and the Incas, centered in central Peru, controlled most of the Andes region. The Aztec state, through military conquest by a strong army and well-organized government, completed its empire building in 1428. But the Aztecs only loosely controlled the various peoples in their empire, and by the early 1500s, they faced mounting military confrontations with rivals. Cruel Aztec imperialism, including the widespread use of human sacrifice, had created enemies, some of whom were later willing to cooperate with the Spanish to overthrow Aztec power. The Incas had completed the conquest of their empire in 1440: it was larger than the Roman or Han Chinese Empires of the Classical Era, stretching nearly 2,500 miles north to south, much of it above 8,000 feet in altitude. The Inca state was the most dynamic and integrated of all the American states.

Cultures in Decline Probably in part as a result of climate change, some Native American societies had long passed their peak by 1500. By 1440 the last Maya states of Central America had collapsed, but some 5 to 6 million Maya-speaking people, living mostly in villages, remained as examples of a once-vibrant society, more than 2,000 years old. In North America the mound-building and trade-oriented Mississippian culture had reached its peak in the 1100s, and the major Mississippian town, Cahokia (kuh-HOE-key-uh), had been deserted by 1250. The once-vast Mississippian trading system was in steep decline by the 1400s, by which time the Anasazi (ah-nah-SAH-zee) and other societies of the Southwestern desert had already abandoned their major settlements.

Flourishing Native American societies besides the Aztecs and Incas remained, however, such as the Taino (TIE-no) in the Caribbean islands and the diverse farming peoples along the Atlantic coasts of North America and Brazil. While the first European settlers wrongly considered the Americas to be largely empty land, some

> **Probably in part as a result of climate change, some Native American societies had long passed their peak by 1500.**

regions were densely populated. By 1492 the population of the Western Hemisphere probably numbered between 60 and 75 million people, but because of many millennia of isolation from the Eastern Hemisphere, American peoples had no immunity to the diseases brought by Europeans and later African slaves. Native Americans also had no metal swords or firearms to resist Europeans, rendering them doubly vulnerable.

Bridging the Atlantic Barrier

The Atlantic Ocean was the major barrier between the hemispheres, but Europeans steadily overcame the challenge. In the later tenth century C.E., some Norse Vikings sailed west and established small farming settlements in several glacier-free coastal valleys in southern Greenland. By around 1000, a few of these hardy Norse, perhaps blown off course, reached the Canadian coast and built a small village in Newfoundland, but abandoned it soon thereafter, largely because of conflicts with local Native Americans. The Greenland Norse, however, apparently sent occasional trading and lumbering expeditions to eastern Canada for several hundred years. The Greenland settlements also collapsed by 1450, perhaps as a result of deforestation and colder climates that made the already difficult farming impossible.

The Norse may not have been the only people from the Western Hemisphere to spot the North American coast before 1492. The winters of the Little Ice Age in Europe brought poor harvests and reduced fish catches along Europe's Atlantic coast, pushing some desperate fishermen farther from home. For many years, European and Moroccan fishermen had worked the waters of the North Atlantic in search of cod, whales, and sardines. Perhaps a few of the fishermen saw North America, but if there were any landings, they apparently went unreported in Europe.

Different motives, including the quest for riches, national glory, and Christian converts, encouraged other Europeans to venture out into the Atlantic. While early Portuguese expeditions concentrated on the African route to the East, others, led by Christopher Columbus, hoped to sail westward from Europe to Asia. Contrary to myth, many educated people in Europe accepted that the earth was round and hence could be circumnavigated.

Arawak Women This woodcut, made in the sixteenth century, shows Arawak women on a Caribbean island preparing tortillas and stew.

Courtesy of John Carter Brown Library at Brown University

Columbus's Voyages to the Americas

The first explorers to brave the Atlantic directly from Europe with the purpose of reaching Asia came under the Spanish flag, beginning with Christopher Columbus. Columbus (1451–1506), born in the Italian port of Genoa, had lived for many years in the Portuguese capital, Lisbon, where he married Donha Felipa Moniz. She died soon after giving birth to their son, Diego, but the marriage gave Columbus social status and access to her family's navigational charts and records. Soon Columbus, inspired by the writings of the thirteenth-century Italian adventurer Marco Polo, began planning to sail to China to find the sea route to the silk- and spice-rich lands of China and Southeast Asia, but his inaccurate maps vastly underestimated the size of the earth and the distance to Asia.

Columbus eventually convinced the Spanish monarchs, King Ferdinand and Queen Isabella—fresh from their final triumph over the last Muslim state in southern Spain—to finance his voyages of exploration in hopes of establishing direct ties to Asia. Commanding ships far smaller than the great junks of the Chinese explorer Zheng He in the early 1400s,

Columbus surveyed much of the Caribbean and some of the South American coast in four voyages over the next decade, and believed that he had discovered outlying regions of Asia. When Ferdinand and Isabella realized he was wrong, they were at first disappointed. America was a heartbreaking obstacle on the route to eastern Asia.

On his first voyage in 1492, Columbus encountered the Taino, an Arawak (AR-uh-wahk)-speaking people who lived on Caribbean islands (see Map 17.1). When Columbus and his crew sailed into the Bahamas, they were greeted by curious Taino islanders. The Taino proved friendly, and they may have desired to cultivate a potential ally. Interactive Map
Even before the arrival of the Spanish, they had often had to resist incursions by the Caribs (KAR-ibs), a more warlike Native American group that had originated in South America.

Taino Society

The Taino had a flourishing society; they smoked cigars, slept in hammocks, possessed a little gold, and some of them lived in

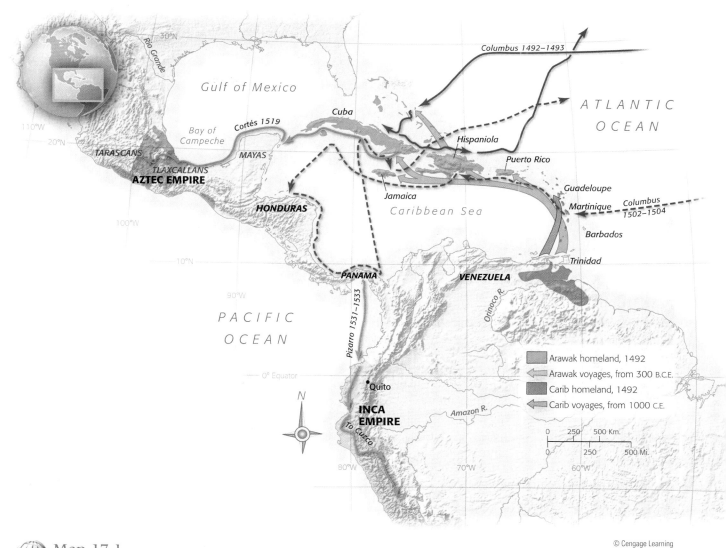

Columbus 1492–1493

Gulf of Mexico

Cuba

ATLANTIC OCEAN

Cortés 1519

Bay of Campeche

Hispaniola

Puerto Rico

TARASCANS

MAYAS

TLAXCALLANS

AZTEC EMPIRE

Guadeloupe

Columbus 1502–1504

Martinique

HONDURAS

Jamaica

Caribbean Sea

Barbados

Trinidad

PANAMA

VENEZUELA

PACIFIC OCEAN

Pizarro 1531–1533

Orinoco R.

Arawak homeland, 1492
Arawak voyages, from 300 B.C.E.
Carib homeland, 1492
Carib voyages, from 1000 C.E.

0° Equator

Quito

INCA EMPIRE

Amazon R.

To Cuzco

N

0   250   500 Km.
0   250   500 Mi.

110°W 30°N 20°N 100°W 10°N 90°W 80°W 70°W 60°W

© Cengage Learning

Map 17.1
The Americas and Early European Exploration

The several voyages across the Atlantic led by Columbus explored the Caribbean Basin and set the stage for Spanish conquest of many American societies, most notably of the Aztec and Inca Empires.

sizeable towns built around Mesoamerican-style plazas and ball courts. They combined fishing with highly productive cultivation of corn and manioc, and they carried on extensive interisland trade in large canoes that were not much smaller than Columbus's ships and capable of holding up to 150 people. The women did the farming and often served as community leaders, a status that confounded the Spanish. Columbus developed favorable views of the Taino, seeing them as innocent children of nature: "They are a loving and uncovetous people. They love their neighbors as themselves."[2] Later, however, when Columbus encountered Taino noncooperation or armed resistance to Spanish demands, he modified his views.

Hispaniola

Columbus then moved onto the island he called Hispaniola (HIS-puhn-YO-luh), today the home of Haiti and the Dominican Republic but then dominated by six Taino chiefdoms. Leaving a small colony of Spaniards there, Columbus began his return voyage to Europe by way of Cuba, which Columbus believed might be China. There he dispatched a small party, led by a Jew who spoke Hebrew, Chaldean, and Arabic, to search the interior for, and possibly communicate with, the Chinese ruler. They returned only with some mysterious dried leaves called *tobacos*, which local people smoked. Columbus and his crew sailed back to Spain with six

Taino Indians from the Bahamas to present at court. He was greeted as a hero and promoted to admiral.

The Treaty of Tordesillas

Although he did not find China, Columbus's discovery of the wind patterns that could push ships back and forth across the Atlantic launched a new era of exploration. Spanish authorities quickly planned a second voyage and, to counteract a possible Portuguese challenge, persuaded the pope to issue an order, the Treaty of Tordesillas (tor-duh-SEE-yuhs) in 1494, that divided the newly discovered Atlantic lands into Spanish and Portuguese spheres. Ultimately, the treaty gave Spain the rights to most of the Americas, while the Portuguese received Africa and Brazil. Both Iberian countries promised the pope that they would evangelize the "heathen" peoples they encountered.

Taino Exploitation

During his four voyages, Columbus explored much of the Caribbean region. He brought Spanish colonists with him on his second voyage in 1493 and established on Hispaniola the first permanent European settlement in the Americas. The success of the Spanish colony depended on exploiting the Taino through forced labor. Estimates of the Taino population in the Caribbean in 1492 range from 100,000 to 1 million, but within thirty years all of the Taino on Hispaniola, and many elsewhere, had been wiped out. The Hispaniola colony Columbus governed was a failure economically, and he returned to Spain in 1496. On his third voyage, in 1498, Columbus found Trinidad and the Venezuela coast. Queen Isabella allowed Columbus one final voyage to find a strait that might lead to India. This expedition explored the coast of Central America, from what is today Honduras to Costa Rica. Although Columbus encountered a Maya trading raft he thought might be Chinese, he also began to speak of the Caribbean islands as the "West Indies" as separate from the eagerly sought "East Indies" (India and Southeast Asia). After he and his crew were shipwrecked for a year on Jamaica, he returned to Spain and died in 1506, a broken man.

Eventually some Europeans began referring to the Native Americans as "Indians," a European name that confuses American peoples with those of India. Because of this, some scholars and activists prefer terms such as "Native American" or "First Nations" to Indian. The term *America* derives from an Italian merchant, Amerigo Vespucci (1454–1512), who claimed to have made several voyages to the Western Hemisphere. His letters to powerful European princes described two separate continents in a "new world" that was soon known as "Amerigo's land."

> "Columbus's encounters inspired others, and exploration soon became a multinational effort involving the English, French, Portuguese, and Spanish."

The Continuing Search for Wealth

Columbus's encounters inspired others, and exploration soon became a multinational effort involving the English, French, Portuguese, and Spanish. By 1525 a series of European expeditions had explored the Atlantic and Caribbean coasts of the Americas from eastern Canada to the southern tip of South America. Some explorers sought to enrich themselves and the European monarchs who sponsored them, while others hoped to gain God's favor through Christian missionary activity.

These exploring expeditions stimulated still further European voyages and claims. Following an expedition led by another Genoese, John Cabot, the English claimed the Atlantic coast of North America in 1497. This action set off a fruitless search for a northwest passage, a sea route that might lead from the Atlantic Ocean through North America to the Pacific, but no practical route existed. In 1500 Portugal established its claim to Brazil, which fell within the longitudes awarded to it by the pope in the Treaty of Tordesillas, and by 1502 Portuguese settlement of Brazil had begun. By 1511 the Spanish controlled Cuba, Puerto Rico, and Jamaica and had a presence on the northern coast of South America. In 1513 a Spanish expedition led by Vasco Nunez de Balboa (bal-BOH-uh) crossed Panama and sighted the Pacific Ocean, which he claimed for Spain. The French claimed eastern Canada in 1524 with a voyage led by an Italian captain from Florence, Giovanni da Verrazano.

The only practical sea route to Asia via the Americas was finally discovered in 1520, in a Spanish expedition led by a Portuguese captain, Ferdinand Magellan (muh-JELL-un) (1480–1521). From Spain his ships sailed down the Atlantic and rounded the southern tip of South America; they then survived a torturous trip through the stormy strait that today bears his name and leads to the Pacific Ocean: the Strait of Magellan. Magellan continued on across the Pacific. It was a long, difficult journey during which no inhabited islands were spotted before Guam, with the crewmen living off rat meat and boiled leather for months. Eventually the expedition landed in the Philippine Islands, where Magellan was killed in a clash with local people. Magellan's one remaining ship continued on westward around Africa, limping into Europe three years after they had left Spain. Europeans now had a better idea of world geography and turned to the conquest and settlement of the Americas.

New Horizons and Exploration in the Pacific

Exploration of the Americas, and the continued search for a sea route to Asia, led to European exploration of the Pacific basin. Long before Europeans arrived, the Pacific islanders, scattered across many island chains, had evolved distinctive traditions and social systems. The Polynesian people living on mountainous islands had varied food sources from farming and fishing that supported denser settlement and states led by kings or powerful chiefs, such as the eight inhabited Hawaiian Islands, divided into four rival chiefdoms, which had a population of perhaps 200,000. By contrast, many peoples living on small atolls only a few feet above sea level relied chiefly on resources from the sea and had smaller populations. Many island societies traded over vast distances, and so were linked into widespread sea networks. Warfare between rival islands and states was also common. Some islanders also faced increasing destruction of their fragile environments. Most Pacific islanders had not been in direct touch with Asia for millennia, making them vulnerable to Eurasian diseases later brought by Europeans.

Although Spanish ships annually sailed across the Pacific Ocean between the Philippines and Mexico beginning in 1565 (see Chapter 18), Europeans made little effort to colonize the vast Pacific region in this era. The first European expedition into the Pacific, led by Magellan in 1521, encountered no island societies before finally chancing on Guam, where they clashed with the local Chamorro (chuh-MOR-oh) people, the first of many unhappy encoun-

> 66 With its gleaming temples and network of canals, the Aztec capital city, Tenochtitlan, astonished the Spanish, and Cortés called it the world's most beautiful city. 99

ters between Pacific islanders and European visitors. In the 1500s and 1600s, Spanish, Portuguese, English, and Dutch expeditions visited many islands, but they looked unpromising for exploitation.

Spain established the first successful Pacific colony in Guam in 1663, founding a Catholic mission there, but 90 percent of the Chamorros died over the next two decades, mostly from disease brought by the Spanish. In 1671 a demoralized Chamorro chief, though careful not to provoke retaliation, complained to a missionary that "the Spanish would have done better to remain in their own country. We have no need of their help to live happily. They treat us as gross barbarians."[3]

LO² The European Conquest of the Americas

European explorations and the search for riches soon led to colonization in the Americas. Native Americans lacked guns to resist the invaders and were also weakened by division. Thousands of Spanish adventurers roamed the Americas seeking wealth in the 1500s. Many were soldiers engaged in armed conquest, whose leaders were known as conquistadors (kon-KEY-stuh-dorz). The main town established by the Spanish on Hispaniola, Santo Domingo (SAN-toe duh-MING-go), became the early Spanish base for exploration and conquest. The major Spanish conquests came in Mexico and the Andes, while the Portuguese annexed Brazil. Later, the English, French, and Dutch obtained footholds in North America, the Caribbean, and the northeast coast of South America. By 1750 many American societies were under firm colonial control.

 Early America (*http:// earlyamerica .com/earlyamerica/ index.html*). Offers primary sources on the thirteen North American colonies in the eighteenth century.

The Fall of the Aztec and Inca Empires

In 1519 Hernán Cortés (kor-TEZ) (1485–1547) and 550 soldiers from Spanish-controlled Cuba landed on Mexico's east coast, where they founded a settlement that later became the city of Veracruz (VER-uh-KROOZ). Cortés' major target was the rich Aztec Empire. First Cortés defeated and then forged an alliance with the Tlaxcalans, a people who had long resisted the Aztecs. Impressed by Spanish power, the Tlaxcalan nobles adopted Christianity and joined Cortés. Marching inland, Cortés fought and defeated several other peoples on the empire's perimeter, and then marched through the mountains into the Valley of Mexico, the heart of the Aztec Empire. With its gleaming temples and network of canals, the Aztec capital city, Tenochtitlan (teh-noch-tit-lan), astonished the Spanish, and Cortés called it the world's most beautiful city. The Aztec leader, Moctezuma II (mock-teh-ZOO-ma), warmly greeted them. Moctezuma (r. 1502–1520) may initially have identified Cortés with Quetzalcoatl and believed the Spaniards to be gods. Taking advantage of the confusion, the Spanish arrested Moctezuma. With sixty Spanish soldiers supplied with horses and guns, and many Indian allies, Cortés had taken temporary control of the capital of an empire of 25 million subjects. His force was soon joined by a thousand more Spanish soldiers arriving from Cuba.

Cortés and the Aztecs

Soon violence erupted, precipitating war. Spanish thievery and arrogance created hostility, and Aztec mobs killed or captured some Spaniards. Moctezuma, no longer a credible leader, was killed, and the Spanish had to fight their way out of the city, at great cost in Spanish life. Some fleeing Spaniards, loaded down with stolen Aztec gold, fell into the canals and drowned. Forced to return to the coast, Cortés proceeded to make alliances with more Aztec enemies and recruited more Spanish soldiers from Cuba. His enlarged army, numbering around one thousand Spaniards and ten thousand Tlaxcalans and other Indian allies, now laid siege to Tenochtitlan, where thousands of Aztecs resisted fiercely while a smallpox epidemic, inadvertently spread by the Spanish, ravaged their population. In 1521 the Spanish occupied the city and captured the last emperor, Moctezuma's nephew Cuauhtemoc (KWA-the-mock), while Tlaxcalans took revenge on an old enemy by massacring thousands of Aztecs.

Pizarro and the Incas

The Spanish now ruled the Aztec Empire, using the efficient Aztec administration to collect the tribute from the former Aztec subjects. As his people died from disease or faced

demands for harsh labor, one poet lamented that "broken spears lie in the roads; we have torn our hair in our grief. The houses are roofless now, and their walls are red with blood."[4] Spanish conquerors next pushed south to seize Central America, Panama, and, a few years later, the northern part of South America that eventually became Colombia and Venezuela. Later others moved north to what is now Florida, New Mexico, and northern California. From his base in Panama, the Spanish conquistador Francisco Pizarro (ca. 1476–1541) began a long exploration down the west coast of South America. In 1531, as his forces marched into the Andes Mountains, he launched his campaign of conquest. As in Mexico, the first Spaniards arrived after smallpox had already wiped out millions of Incas, including much of the leadership. In 1532, with only 160 Spaniards but with the advantages of artillery and horses, Pizarro ruthlessly defeated the Incas, ignoring pleas from Catholic priests to be more merciful.

The Spanish quickly expanded their territory. By 1534 the conquistadors had seized the Inca capital, Cuzco (KOOZ-ko), and had begun converting it into a Spanish settlement. Pizarro also founded the city of Lima (LEE-muh) along the Pacific coast. Over the next few years, the Spanish gained control over much of what is today Peru, Ecuador, Bolivia, and Chile and brutally crushed Indian uprisings. As Cortés had done

Codex of Aztec Resistance Illustrations in a book published around 1580 revealed a local perspective on the Spanish conquest of the Aztec Empire. This illustration shows Aztec warriors besieging a Spanish force in Tenochtitlan and the difference in weapons technology.

in the Aztec lands, Pizarro and his men placed themselves at the top of the efficient Inca administrative system, but Pizarro was later murdered in Lima by rivals.

The Conquest of Brazil and the Caribbean

While the Spanish concentrated on Mexico and the Andes, the Portuguese established small trading posts along the Brazilian coast. The land seemed promising. The Portuguese began obtaining and shipping brazilwood, which made an excellent dye for European textiles, but they remained more focused on exploiting the wealth of Africa and Asia. After a French effort to establish a foothold in Brazil, the Portuguese founded a permanent colony along the southern Brazilian coast in 1532 and began awarding land grants to private entrepreneurs for settlement.

Facing not the large, settled societies of Mexico and the Andes, but rather

> ❝While the Spanish concentrated on Mexico and the Andes, the Portuguese established small trading posts along the Brazilian coast. ❞

seminomadic food collectors and small farmers, the Portuguese viewed the Indians as potential slaves who had to be compelled to work for Portuguese enterprises. Portuguese slavers from the southern Brazilian settlement at São Paulo (sow PAU-low) pushed deep into the interior raiding for slaves. The colonial government began to combat these activities, and expand its control in the interior, only in 1680. The Dutch also set up plantations that grew huge quantities of sugar for the European market. But the Portuguese eventually expelled their rivals and soon took over the profitable northeast, building a city, Salvador da Bahia, at Bahia (ba-HEE-a).

In the Caribbean, the Spanish competed with the Portuguese, Dutch, English, and French, all of whom founded settlements in the Caribbean from the later 1500s until the late 1600s. The Dutch moved to several small Caribbean islands and also established a foothold in the northwestern South America region known as the Guianas (ghee-AHN-as), founding the colony of Dutch Guiana (now Suriname). The

French seized Haiti, the western half of Hispaniola, which became a center for plantations and a major source of wealth for France, as well as the islands of Guadeloupe (GWAD-eh-loop) and Martinique (mahr-ten-EEK) and a portion of Guiana. Meanwhile, the English made Jamaica, Barbados, British Guiana (now Guyana), and later Trinidad the linchpins for their colonial activity.

> "The English and French focused their colonizing efforts on the eastern seaboard of North America, expanding their settlements at the expense of Native American societies."

In the Caribbean, piracy by Europeans against other Europeans became a major economic activity, much of it directed at prosperous Spanish settlements or at the Spanish galleons hauling rich cargoes of silver, sugar, or imported Asian goods to Europe. In 1670 the English pirate Sir Henry Morgan undertook a particularly brazen attack, leading a force of 1,400 men to sack Panama City, where warehouses stored wealth from Asia and Latin America. The Spanish burned the city rather than allow it to fall to the buccaneers. Some pirates, such as the Englishmen Morgan, John Hawkins, and Sir Francis Drake, became influential and respected figures in their homelands, celebrated for the wealth they captured at the expense of rival countries. As a French buccaneer boasted in 1734, "Fortune is to be found on the sea, where one must go to collect it."[5]

The English, French, and Indians in North America

The English and French focused their colonizing efforts on the eastern seaboard of North America, expanding their settlements at the expense of Native American societies. These societies, which were often matrilineal, were mostly based on farming. Their chiefs held little power in comparison to Eurasian leaders or Inca kings. The Indians soon came to disdain the Europeans as unintelligent, physically weak, and smelly—in contrast to Indians, who valued personal cleanliness, the British and French seldom bathed. Nonetheless, the Indians usually offered hospitality and eagerly traded with and sought allies among the newcomers, but the settlers soon wore out their welcome.

The English

Hoping to outflank rival countries, the English planted a series of settlements up and down the Atlantic coast. In 1587 they founded a small English colony at Roanoke, in what is today North Carolina, but it did not survive. In 1607 the first successful English settlement in North America was established at Jamestown, in today's Virginia, which struggled to survive in the unfamiliar land. The English began sending families from England to farm and establish communities, but in many cases, only the generosity of Native Americans enabled the colonists to survive. By the middle of the seventeenth century, English settlements dotted the coast. The Dutch settlement at New York, founded in 1624, also came under English control once the sponsoring Dutch West India Company concluded it could not compete with English immigration.

The French

Equally ambitious, the French established their first settlement in Acadia in 1604, followed by outposts at Quebec City in 1608 and Montreal in 1642. New France was formally established as a colony in 1627 and covered much of eastern Canada. French Jesuit missionaries (known as "Black Robes") undertook campaigns to convert the Native Americans to Catholicism and traveled widely, as far west as today's Illinois, in their pursuit of conversions. By the 1670s, French explorers and trappers mapped and established trading outposts throughout the Great Lakes and Mississippi River Basin. To counter English and Spanish expansion, in 1699 the French founded New Orleans, which then became the base for French territorial claims in Louisiana and the Mississippi Valley.

The English colonies north of Maryland developed largely as agricultural economies of free white settlers. Although most colonists were farmers, many English and French settlers also came to North America to exploit two valuable commodities, fish and fur. The seas off New England and eastern Canada teamed with cod, which became a major part of the European diet. Later some English and French immigrants moved inland in search of beaver pelts; fur remained the major Canadian export until the rise of wheat farming in the nineteenth century. Although both French and English settlement disrupted the Indian tribes, the French generally maintained better relations with local peoples. Nonetheless, in both French and English colonies, the Native Americans died from either disease or armed conflict or were pushed north and west.

The Iroquois Confederation

Some Indian groups were well organized and proved formidable opponents. The most complex political structure among North American Indians was the Iroquois (EAR-uh-coy) Confederation, a coalition formed in the 1500s to unite five once-warring tribes living in what is today upstate New York. These longhouse-dwelling tribes shared a common enemy in the Huron (HYOOR-uhn) of southern Ontario, who established a rival confederation of allied groups. By the 1630s, the Iroquois numbered some 16,000. Initially the Iroquois alliance was primarily a nonaggression pact among the members. Later, in the 1690s, it became a pantribal government with a council of chiefs and an oral constitution. Some scholars credit Iroquois political ideas, such as a representative congress and freedom of speech, as an influence on the later constitution of the United States. The Iroquois were an effective military alliance, outmaneuvering European arrivals for many years.

LO³ The Consequences of American Colonization

By the late sixteenth century, the Spanish had explored and claimed a massive empire stretching from northern California and the Rocky Mountains southward to southern Chile and Argentina, including parts of the Caribbean. Meanwhile, the English, French, and Dutch established settlements in the Caribbean region and in North America. Despite many similarities in conquest, the American colonies were very different from each other. However, the results almost always came at the expense of the Native American peoples, who suffered especially from the colonists' diseases. Colonization also involved Christian missionary activity and violence.

The Columbian Exchange

One result of European exploration and conquest was the transfer of diseases, animals, and plants from one hemisphere to another, what historians refer to as the Columbian Exchange. A chief consequence was demographic: virulent microbes brought from the Eastern Hemisphere caused massive depopulation and suffering in the Americas. Of course, although often healthier than Eastern Hemisphere peoples, the Native Americans before 1492 did not live in a disease-free paradise. They suffered from such maladies as polio, hepatitis, some varieties of tuberculosis, many intestinal parasites, and syphilis. Only syphilis, a sexually transmitted disease, seems to have made any serious impact when carried to Europe, but it was more an unpleasant nuisance than a mass killer.

The Native Americans had no immunity to diseases brought by Europeans and Africans, such as measles, typhus, influenza, and smallpox; these claimed millions of victims. Within two centuries, the Native American population was reduced by around 90 percent. No group remained untouched, and some were completely eliminated as the diseases spread destruction and havoc. A Maya writer reported that "great was the stench of the dead. The dogs and vultures devoured the bodies. We were born to die!"[6] The American population numbers began recovering as the most resistant individuals survived and as immigrants from Europe and Africa intermarried with Native Americans, producing less susceptible children. Eventually Native American populations grew, particularly in more isolated areas.

The Columbian Exchange affected both sides of the Atlantic. From the one side, Europeans brought their political, cultural, and social institutions, as well as plants such as wheat, orange trees, and grape vines, and domesticated animals. Some imports were useful for American peoples, such as horses brought by the Spanish that enabled some tribes in the North American Great Plains to hunt buffalo more effectively. From the Americas, gold and silver had a major impact on the Eurasian economy. American crops such as tobacco, rubber, American cotton, potatoes, and maize (corn), as well as drugs including quinine and coca, spread across the Atlantic. Some of these crops, such as potatoes, corn, and tomatoes, became diet staples in Europe and Asia. South American chilies became a mainstay of South and Southeast Asian cooking, making the spicy foods even hotter.

The Spanish Empire in the Americas

The conquered Americans were forced to pay the costs of the conquest. In Spanish America and

Columbian Exchange The transportation of diseases, animals, and plants from one hemisphere to another that resulted from European exploration and conquest between 1492 and 1750.

The Columbian Exchange (http://nationalhumanitiescenter.org/tserve/nattrans/ntecoindian/essays/columbian.htm). Links to essays by Alfred Crosby and more.

Portuguese Brazil, some Europeans made great fortunes by exploiting people, land, minerals, animals, and plants. Gold and silver from the Americas financed the building of the Spanish empire. Once in power, the Spanish and Portuguese seized all the riches they could locate, forced or persuaded the Indians to adopt Christianity, destroyed their religious centers, and murdered Indian leaders who refused to cooperate. While many local peoples resisted the occupying powers, these efforts were usually futile in the long run. While taking the local peoples' material wealth, disturbing cultures, and spreading disease, the new settlers also learned survival skills from the people. They also intermarried or had sexual relations with local women, producing people of mixed descent.

In building their American empire, the Spanish appropriated American political structures but also introduced their own institutions. The Spanish colonists established settlements that became large cities, such as Havana, Buenos Aires, Lima, and Mexico City, the last-mentioned built on the site of the Aztec capital, Tenochtitlan. In the 1500s, Spain divided its vast empire into two smaller divisions (viceroyalties): New Spain (governed from Mexico City) and Peru (governed from Lima). The top Spanish official in each was the viceroy, a deputy to the king who was always Spanish-born and held great power. Later two more viceroyalties were created in South America. Given the huge territories, each viceroyalty had to be subdivided into smaller political units known as **audiencias**, judicial tribunals with administrative functions.

In building their empires, the Spanish and other Europeans sometimes faced considerable resistance. Maya Yucatan fell to the Spanish only in 1545 after a long, bitter military struggle. In the 1530s, many Indians rose up in rebel-

> **Complaint of the Indians of Tecama Against Their Ecomendero, Juan Ponce De León** This summary of judicial proceedings in Mexico City in 1550 confirms that legislation designed to protect Indians from abuse was often ignored.

lion in Peru, and sporadic resistance continued for two centuries. In New Mexico, resentment by some Pueblo peoples against the Spanish and Catholic missionaries, which held little tolerance for Native American customs, led to several revolts. The most serious came in 1680, when a respected shaman, Popé (PO-pay), led a force that pushed the Spanish out of the area. Although the Spanish returned and reestablished authority in 1692, the revolt prompted them to adopt more cooperative policies.

New Latin American Societies

Gradually, distinctive societies and cultures began to emerge in Spanish America and Brazil, a huge area later known as Latin America. A key group in most of these societies were the **creoles** (KREE-awlz), people of Iberian ancestry who were born in Latin America. Other groups stemmed from the mixing of peoples, creating **mestizos**, a blend of white and Indian ancestry, and **mulattos**, a mix of African with white or Indian ancestry or both (see Witness to the Past: Spanish Men and Inca Women). While most creoles enjoyed positions of high status, the two mixed groups held a status between Europeans at the top of the social system and Indians and Africans at the bottom. By the 1700s, the mixed groups also represented a sizeable portion of the population in many colonies. Europeans tended to view the creoles, mestizos, and mulattos with either condescension or contempt: in the 1600s, a creole scholar born in Mexico of Spanish parents complained that people in Europe "are hardly able to discover anything rational in us."[7]

> **66** Within two centuries, the Native American population was reduced by around 90 percent. **99**

Emergence of Latin American Culture

Many writers and artists were born and educated in the Americas. Perhaps the greatest colonial American poet was the creole Mexican nun Sor (Sister) Juana Inez de la Cruz (1651–1695), who also won renown as a playwright, philosopher, and scientist. As a young woman she mastered Latin and Aztec while studying logic, history, mathematics, and literature. To pursue her intellectual and literary interests, the well-born Sor Juana chose life in a convent over marriage, eventually collecting the largest private library in Mexico, some four thousand volumes.

Latin American culture actually remained more closely connected to the Catholic Church than was the case in western Europe, which was reshaped by the Renaissance and Enlightenment. To screen out what they considered dangerous ideas, the church had to approve all printed matter entering the colonies. Church-controlled universities, which were set up to train creole men for careers as colonial officials and priests, taught largely in Latin and employed clerics as instructors. Spanish officials also brought the ruthless, counter-reform Holy Inquisition to the colonies to root out heresy. People suspected of having secret Jewish or Protestant sympathies were tried. In particular, those of *converso* background—Jews who were forced to convert to Christianity in Spain and their descendants—were subject to investigation, imprisonment, and sometimes gruesome executions.

Latin American societies exhibited dramatic contradictions: while many of the elite looked toward Europe for inspiration, the majority of the population wanted to preserve the languages, beliefs, and ways of life from pre-Columbian times. Latin American writers often examined the conflicted relationship between Spain and Latin America, describing a mix of good and evil or, as one put it, sun and shadow. Such a mix might also describe the experiences of people in the Portuguese, English, and French colonies.

Women in Latin America

Women faced the greatest dilemmas in Latin America, often both accepting and repudiating Spanish rule. They now enjoyed new food sources, but they also clung to their native dress and pride. Despite patriarchal traditions, some Indians and mestizo women engaged in commerce while others worked in domestic service, tended animals, or made clothing, including carding, spinning, and weaving wool from sheep.

Native Americans: Missions and Mistreatment

Both the Spanish and the Portuguese were committed to spreading Catholicism as part of their imperial enterprise. Although they enjoyed only mixed success, missionaries were frequently militant in their faith and often had a profound influence. The mission impact on Latin American Indians came in different forms. Sometimes missionaries altered

people's settlement and even economic patterns, requiring seminomadic hunters and gatherers, like the Chumash (CHOO-mash) on the California coast, to live in towns and cultivate crops imported from Europe. In Yucatan, a few missionaries gained control over many Maya people. Although these missionaries sometimes admired Maya culture, such as the ancient writing system, they were also intolerant of non-Christian beliefs and destroyed Maya books and religious symbols, which they considered pagan. In 1562 some priests, who suspected that certain converts continued to secretly worship Maya gods, launched a terrible inquisition and tortured 4,500 Indians, 158 of whom died. The church punished the priest in charge but later made him a bishop.

Christianity in the New World

As the Maya account illustrates, the missionaries often faced resistance. In the former Inca territories, for example, many women openly rejected Catholicism in the 1500s. According to a Spanish observer: "They do not confess, attend catechism classes, or go to mass. Returning to their ancient customs and idolatry, they do not want to serve God or the [Spanish] crown."[8] Native Americans could also put their stamp on Christianity: in 1531 an Aztec peasant supposedly saw a vision of the Virgin Mary at a shrine to the Aztec mother goddess. A church was later built there to honor "Our Lady of Guadalupe," and the image of the virgin as an Indian woman became a symbol of Mexican nationalism.

Spanish actions led to the Black Legend, the Spanish reputation for brutality toward Native Americans, including the repression of native religions, execution of rebels, and forced labor. The Spanish were particularly zealous in persecuting homosexuals. Although the Black Legend exaggerated Spanish atrocities, Spain's enemies in Europe eagerly passed along such stories. Actually, disease killed far more Indians than murder and brutality. Nor were the Spanish the only culprits; the other European settlers could be just as intolerant and forceful in their dealings with local peoples.

> **Black Legend**
> The Spanish reputation for brutality toward Native Americans, including the repression of native religions, execution of rebels, and forced labor.

> 66 Both the Spanish and the Portuguese were committed to spreading Catholicism as part of their imperial enterprise. 99

Witness to the Past

Spanish Men and Inca Women

In many parts of Latin America, Spaniards married or cohabitated with Native American women, fostering a mixed, or mestizo, population. In Peru, some Spaniards deliberately sought to marry Inca princesses, perhaps to establish local connections in a factionalized colonial society. In this account from the early seventeenth century by the Peruvian historian Garcilaso de la Vega, himself the product of such a match, we learn of an Inca princess who was less than enthusiastic about her Spanish suitor, a captain from a modest background. Her ambivalent response has been viewed by some historians as representing a mixed attitude common in Latin America toward the imposition of European culture: contempt for many European customs and the brutal conquest but also admiration of some European values and Europeans' military power.

. . . a daughter of [Inca leader] Huaina Cápac and herself . . . the owner of the Indians [workers], was married to a very good soldier called Diego Hernández, a very worthy man, who was said in his youth to have been a tailor. . . . [Before the marriage] the princess learned this and refused the match, saying that it was unjust to wed the daughter of Huaina Cápac with a . . . tailor. Although the Bishop of Cuzco as well as . . . other personages who went to attend the ceremony of betrothal, begged and pleaded with her, it was all to no purpose. They then sent to fetch her brother. . . . When he came, he took his sister into a corner of the room and told her privately that it was impolitic for her to refuse the match, for by doing so she would render the whole of the [Inca] royal line odious in the eyes of the Spaniards, who would consider them mortal enemies and never accept their friendship again. She agreed, though reluctantly, to her brother's demands, and so appeared before the bishop, who wished to honor the betrothed by officiating at the ceremony.

When the bride was asked through an Indian interpreter if she consented to become the bride and spouse of the aforesaid, the interpreter said "did she want to be the man's wife?" for the Indian language had no verb for consent or for spouse, and he could therefore not have asked anything else. The bride replied in her own tongue: . . . "Maybe I will, maybe I won't." Whereupon the ceremony continued. . . . They were still alive and living as man and wife when I left Cuzco.

Other marriages of this kind took place throughout the empire, and were arranged so as to give allocations of Indians to [Spanish] claimants and reward them with other people's properties. Many, however, were dissatisfied, some because their income was small and others because their wives were ugly; there is no perfect satisfaction in this world.

Thinking About the Reading

1. What does the reading tell us about social attitudes among Incas and Spaniards in colonial Peru?
2. What do we learn about the treatment of women?
3. How might the princess's attitude be seen as a form of resistance?

Source: Garcilaso de la Vega, *Royal Commentaries of the Incas and General History of Peru,* Part Two. Translated by Harold V. Livermore (Austin: University of Texas Press, 1966), pp. 1229–1230. Copyright © 1966 by the University of Texas Press. Reprinted with permission.

Bartolomé de Las Casas

While many Spaniards saw the Native Americans as savages, some Catholic clerics advocated humane policies and sought to protect them. The Dominican friar Bartolomé de Las Casas (lahs KAH-suhs) (1474–1566), although an ardent missionary for Catholicism, proclaimed that Indians were humans like the Spanish and bemoaned the destruction they experienced. In 1637 the Jesuits, in what is today Uruguay (YOOR-uh-gwye), even armed the Indians to help protect them against slave raiders.

But the battle over how to treat Indians was won by intolerant people, reflecting the values of a Europe engulfed in religious conflict between Catholics and Protestants (see Chapter 15). Most Spaniards considered the Indians justly conquered and favored exploitation of people they considered born for servitude, enhancing the Black Legend. These harsh attitudes often affected women even more than men. In 1625, an Indian writer in Peru charged that white men exploited both women's labor and their bodies: "In the mines, Indian women are made into concubines, daughters of Indian men are kidnapped. . . . There is no one who takes these women's side."[9] Missionaries gave Indian men and women a superficial Christianity, changing local gods into Christian saints, but many Indians continued to secretly worship old gods and ancestors. After the initial violence, the church treated Indians paternalistically, as children needing guidance. But, as a result of conquest, the Indian quality of life—health, morale, leisure, and joy—mostly declined. Demoralization and disease generated alcoholism and despair.

English and French Colonies in North America

The English and French competed for control in North America while expanding their settlements

Interactive Map

(see Map 17.2). By the mid-1700s, the territory from New England south to Georgia was divided into thirteen separate English colonies, each administered by an appointed English governor. Immigrants came from England and also from Scotland, Ireland, Germany, and the Netherlands. Some from poor or criminal backgrounds emigrated as indentured laborers, signing contracts to work on farms or in households to repay their passage. Many immigrants took up farming, especially in the northern colonies. By 1730 the thirteen colonies contained around 500,000 European settlers. African slaves or their descendants, constituting 20 percent of the total colonial population, were concentrated in the South but were also found in the northern colonies such as New York.

Intellectual and religious diversity characterized English colonial life. Educated colonists were often influenced by English and French Enlightenment thinkers and espoused democratic ideals and reason. Many early English immigrants were Protestant

religious dissenters seeking freedom of religion. The Puritans had an important influence on the colonial culture, especially in the north, implanting Calvinist attitudes about the value of work and commerce.

The French and English in Canada

North of New York and New England, the English and French clashed for decades over control of Acadia (Nova Scotia) and New France, in what is today eastern Canada. This conflict resulted in part from a larger English–French competition for influence throughout the world. Eventually England triumphed over France in North America. In 1713 the English

Map 17.2
The English and French in North America, ca.1700

While the English colonized much of the Atlantic coast of North America, the French concentrated on what is today eastern Canada and the interior of North America, including the Great Lakes and the Mississippi and Ohio River Basins.

Indian Slavery Spain's enemies publicized cases of Spanish brutality toward Native Americans. This sixteenth-century engraving, by the Dutch observer Theodore de Bry, portrays the misery of Native Americans subjected to slavery and forced labor.

Metis
People in Canada of mixed French and Indian descent.

took control of Acadia, and in 1755 they deported much of the Acadian French population to the French colony of Louisiana, forming the basis for the French-speaking Cajun (KAY-juhn) community there, which today numbers nearly 1 million. In 1759 English forces defeated the French near Quebec City, and in 1760 captured Montreal, gaining control over New France. French cultural influence was eventually confined chiefly to the large area of eastern Canada now known as the province of Quebec. In 1774 the English, recognizing the tenacity of French culture, allowed the French in Quebec to hold public office, speak their language, and freely practice Catholicism. Both the French and

A Dominican Voice in the Wilderness: Preaching Against Tyranny in Hispaniola A Dominican friar, and former landholder, expresses his outrage at the injustices committed against the native people of "New Spain."

English Canadians settled down to farming, like their neighbors in New England.

Europeans and Indian Societies in North America

At the same time, relations between European settlers and Indian societies in North America remained complex. Indians resented and often resisted the foreigners' occupation of their land, and the English and French had to deal carefully with the better-organized tribes and federations. But some Indians, becoming dependent on trading partnerships with Europeans, were inevitably drawn into the often violent English–French competition. Indians such as the Huron allied with the French; some, including the Iroquois, allied with the English; and some opposed both. The fur trade had an additional social impact: as French fur traders set up trading posts far from the cities, they tended to intermarry with Indians, producing the **Metis** (may-TEES), people of mixed French and Indian

Courtesy of John Carter Brown Library at Brown University

Johnson Hall by Edward Lamson Henry (1841–1919). 1903. Oil on canvas 21-1/4 X 37 inches. Albany Institute of History and Art Purchase 1933.44

Johnson Hall This grand house, built in the mid-eighteenth century by American fur trader William Johnson in what is now upstate New York, became a meeting place for Native American tribes, such as the Iroquois, allied with the British against the French.

descent. In contrast, English colonists tended to immigrate as families, reducing the rates of intermarriage with Indians.

The encounter with Europeans made living much more difficult for North American Indians. In 1705 an English observer, Robert Beverley, noted that "they have on several accounts to lament the arrival of the English [who] have taken away great part of their country, and consequently made everything less plenty among them."[10] The Indians mistrusted colonists, who often broke treaties, but they also desired European trade goods, especially met-

alwork and guns. A few tribes, like the Cherokee in the Carolinas and Georgia, who probably numbered some 30,000 in the mid-1500s, actively adopted European influences, such as new farming methods and patriarchal social traditions. Christian missionaries had less success in North America than in Latin America, although social patterns among Native Americans were irrevocably changed, often forcibly, by European influence.

LO⁴ Slavery and the Atlantic System

Quite different economic and social systems emerged in Latin America and northern English America. In much of Latin America, the Caribbean, and some of the southern colonies of North America, European rule produced an inequitable economic relationship between the colonies and their colonizing countries. In North America, English colonists emphasized commerce and family farming, eventually moving toward economic independence. Perhaps the major impact of American colonization was to link West Africa, the Americas, and Europe into a larger Atlantic System, a vast network that saw the movement of enslaved Africans to the Americas, where they labored on plantations growing sugar, cotton, and tobacco for shipment to Europe. European merchants then used the lucrative proceeds from slave labor to purchase guns, rum, textiles, and other commodities for shipment

CHRONOLOGY

The Americas, 1650–1760

ca. 1605–1694	Palmares maroon state
1713	English control of Acadia
1739	Stono Rebellion in South Carolina
1755	Deportation of French Acadians to Louisiana
1759	English defeat of French in Quebec

haciendas
Vast ranches in Spanish America.

encomienda
("Entrustment") The Crown's grant to a colonial Spaniard in Latin America of a certain number of Indians from whom he extracted tribute.

monoculture
An economy dependent on the production and export of one chief commodity.

development
Growth in a variety of economic areas that benefits the majority of people; the opposite of monoculture.

Interactive Map

to Africa to obtain more enslaved labor. As a result, African slavery reshaped the economies, social patterns, and cultures of many societies.

Economic Change in Latin America

From the beginning, Latin American colonies were largely geared to export natural resources (see Map 17.3). In the Andes and Mexico, the Spanish developed rich gold and silver mines. The silver mines discovered by the Spanish in 1545 in today's Bolivia became some of the richest in the world. Drafted to labor in the mining economy, Indian mine workers in the main Andean mining center, Potosi (po-tuh-SEE), found life difficult, "working twelve hours a day, going down seven hundred feet, down to where night is perpetual, the air thick and ill smelling. When they arrive at the top out of breath, [they] find a mineowner who scolds them because they did not bring enough load."[11] For much of the eighteenth century, Brazil supplied more than half of the world's gold. While providing few benefits to the Native Americans, mining brought prosperity to colonial cities such as Lima, enriched merchants, filled royal treasuries, and linked the colonies to the world economy. Most of the wealth was exported, ultimately passing through Spain and Portugal to northern Europe as payment for manufactured goods. This transfer enriched first Flanders, then Holland, and later England, helping to finance English industrialization. American silver also bought Europeans access to other world markets, especially in Asia.

Ranching and the *Encomienda*

While mining flourished in only a few mountainous areas, ranching became a major economic activity in many other regions. Cattle and horses brought from Europe enabled many settlers to take up ranching, especially in the grasslands of what is today Argentina and Venezuela. Vast cattle ranches, known in Spanish America as haciendas, were often more than 1 million acres in size. Like the mines, the ranches provided great incomes for monarchs, merchants, and investors.

During the early 1500s, to ensure Indian labor the Spanish imposed some version of the encomienda ("entrustment"), the Crown's grant to a colonial Spaniard of a certain number of Indians from whom he extracted tribute. In exchange for providing labor, such as in the gold and silver mines, the Indians were instructed in Christianity by clergy. While in theory this system protected Indians, in fact it fostered many abuses. A Spanish Franciscan reported that "The Indian slaves who up to the present have died in these [gold] mines cannot be counted."[12] Because of the abuses, by the mid-1500s the institution had been reformed considerably, but the system still allowed temporary conscription of Indian labor.

Economic Stagnation

Despite the early Spanish and Portuguese successes in developing their colonies, Latin America eventually fell behind North America in economic development, a contrast that became dramatic by the 1800s. At the outset, Latin America had many advantages that British North America lacked: rich gold and silver mines, abundant fertile land, and a much larger population. By the 1700s, Latin Americans, unlike North Americans, had built a half-dozen large cities and many fine universities, and the region produced great wealth. But the failure of Latin American and Caribbean societies to match the economic vigor of North America resulted in part from the system of monoculture, an economy dependent on the production and export of one chief commodity. Monocultures were usually based on slave or coerced labor and were completely dependent on the colonizing country to buy the resource, such as sugar, silver, or beef, they produced. In return the colonizing country supplied food and other necessities to the colonized society.

Plantation, mining, or ranching-based economies, however, cannot generate overall development, growth in a variety of economic areas that benefits the majority of people. Monoculture economies generally benefit only one segment of a population, and they prosper or decline depending on world prices for their export commodity. With few alternatives

> **❝** From the beginning, Latin American colonies were largely geared to export natural resources. **❞**

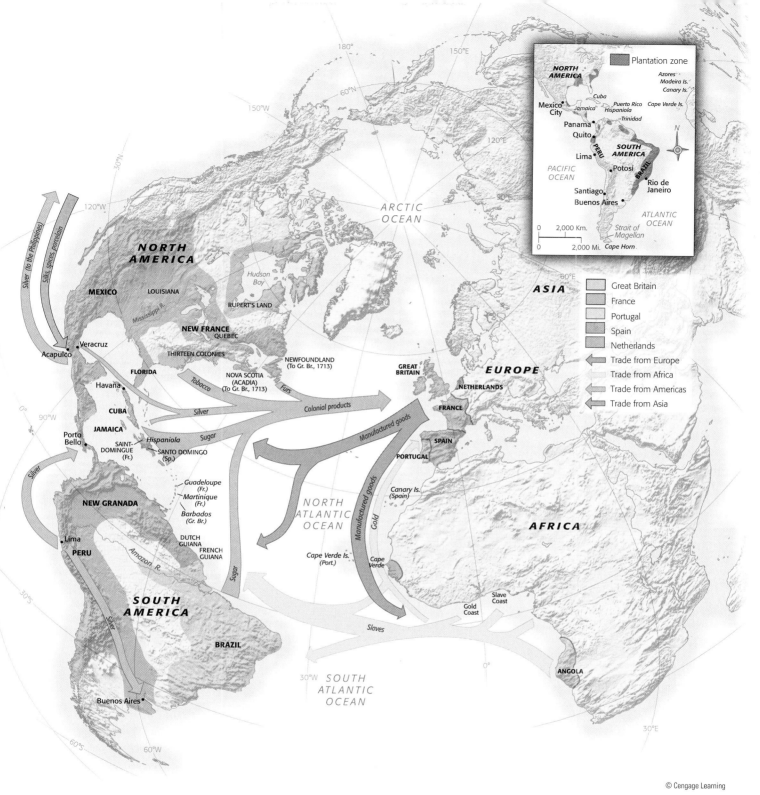

Map legend:

- Great Britain
- France
- Portugal
- Spain
- Netherlands
- Trade from Europe
- Trade from Africa
- Trade from Americas
- Trade from Asia

Plantation zone

Map 17.3
The Atlantic Economy

The Atlantic economy was based on a triangular trade in which African slaves were shipped to the Americas to produce raw materials that were chiefly exported to Europe, where they were turned into manufactured goods and exported to Africa and the Americas.

© Cengage Learning

"The first American plantations emerged in Brazil, where sugar was grown along the coast by the early 1500s."

The Sugar Industry

The growing sugar industry fostered transitions in Europe as well as the Americas. With the rise of the American plantations and cheaper supplies, sugar was transformed from a rare luxury to an everyday necessity, becoming a staple of the European diet. Sugar sweetened bland foods and provided more calories for the often undernourished working classes. In England, the use of sugar in foods allowed people to take their lunches with them and stay at work all day, in this way helping to foster an industrial economy in Britain.

The plantation economies of the Caribbean islands and some coastal districts were essentially sugar "factories," relying on mass production of raw sugar by enslaved workers. A seventeenth-century saying noted that "without sugar, no Brazil; without slaves, no sugar; without Angola, no slaves."[13] The southern English colonies of North America differed from these Caribbean and Latin American economies only in that the crops were more varied: cotton, rice, and tobacco were grown as well as sugar. The populations of all the plantation-based societies were composed chiefly of enslaved people of African ancestry. Slavery as a key institution stretched from the southern half of what became the United States through the Caribbean Basin and down the South American coast to central Brazil in the east and coastal Peru in the west.

Africans in America: America's Journey Through Slavery (*http://www.pbs.org/wgbh/aia/home.html*). A useful website offering materials relevant to a documentary series broadcast on Public Television.

to generate wealth, plantation and mining societies remained dangerously specialized, leading to the economic stagnation of Latin America and the Caribbean as the North American economy was on the rise.

The Plantation Zone and African Slavery

At first, mines and ranches dominated the Latin American economy, but the plantation soon became the key economic institution in much of the tropical and subtropical areas of the South American mainland, the Caribbean islands, and southeastern North America. The first American plantations emerged in Brazil, where sugar was grown along the coast by the early 1500s. By the later 1600s, plantations were flourishing in many regions, growing sugar, coffee, cotton, bananas, and sisal (a tough fiber used to make rope) for shipment to North America and Europe. The plantations depended on the labor of African slaves and their descendants.

Plantation Economies

The transition to a plantation economy created the plantation zone, a group of societies with economies relying on enslaved African labor and stretching from Virginia and Kentucky southward through the West Indies and the east coast of Central America to central Brazil and the Pacific coast of Colombia. The changes were particularly striking in the Caribbean islands, where sugar planting transformed whole economies. European settlers were first attracted to Caribbean islands such as Jamaica, Barbados, Hispaniola, Cuba, and Puerto Rico, and in the later 1500s and early 1600s, they set up self-sufficient farms that grew diverse crops. But in the mid-1600s, the growing of sugar, which was much more profitable than the other crops, expanded. Because sugar growing needed plentiful land and cheap labor, white farmers were gradually displaced by plantations using slave labor, while laws that prevented plantation owners from growing anything but sugar protected the profits of the colonial elite.

Africans in the New World

The needs of the plantation economy, and the high mortality rates of enslaved labor, required the constant importation of slaves from Africa. Between 1500 and 1850, some 9 to 12 million Africans were brought into the Americas as slaves. Most went to the Caribbean islands, where they became the majority population, and to Brazil, which today has the largest population of African descent in the Americas. African slaves were also used outside the plantation zone, in northern English colonies and as far south as Argentina, though on a much smaller scale. By 1850, Brazil received some 40 percent of all

Caribbean Sugar Mill On a West Indian plantation, this windmill crushed sugar cane into juice, which was boiled down in the smoking building on the right to produce sugar granules. Such plantations were the dominant economic activity on the Caribbean islands and in parts of South America, Central America, and southeastern North America.

In turn, economic conditions contributed to differing administrative policies. In contrast to the Latin American colonial administrations, the British allowed their colonies from New Jersey north through New England considerable freedom to build diversified economies for local and trans-Atlantic markets. Merchants from Boston, Providence, and New York competed with the English in the Caribbean to obtain sugar and molasses, which was converted to rum and shipped to Africa for slaves. Some North Americans, like Europeans, amassed huge profits from the slave trade, profits that were then invested in their own broad-based economies. In sum, those Latin American and Caribbean colonies with the most abundant natural and human resources to exploit enjoyed greater short-term economic growth but less eventual development. By contrast, the northern English colonies, with fewer resources, had the opposite experience.

Read about Caetana, the brave slave rebel who challenged patriarchy.

enslaved Africans, followed by the British Caribbean (21 percent), French Caribbean (15 percent), Spanish America (15 percent), and British North America (5 percent). About one-third of all people of African descent eventually lived in the Western Hemisphere. As the number of transported Africans increased in the later 1600s and early 1700s, many areas were transformed into societies in which slaves constituted a majority. Yet Africans occupied the bottom of the social ladder, where life was extremely harsh. On some sugar plantations, as many as half the slaves died within two or three years of arrival.

> 66 The lives of African slaves and their unfree descendants in the Americas were governed by the imperatives of the marketplace. 99

Economic Growth in English North America

Conditions in the northern English colonies created economies that were strikingly different from the monocultures that were common elsewhere in the Americas. The northern colonies lacked the mineral resources, soil, or climate for profitable mining, plantation farming, or ranching. Slaves in the north mostly worked for farms, businesses, or households. In addition, the immigrant population was largely composed of working farmers, artisans, and merchants, making the northern economies less dependent on slave plantations and the severe social inequality they fostered.

Slave Life and African-American Cultures

The lives of African slaves and their unfree descendants in the Americas were governed by the imperatives of the marketplace. In contrast to the treatment of slaves in many African societies, colonial America gave enslaved people few, if any, rights. Because the markets for sugar and other plantation crops expanded, slave owners sought maximum profit regardless of the human consequences. In Brazil, for example, the majority of enslaved Africans and their unfree descendants worked in agriculture, especially on sugar, coffee, and tobacco estates. The average Brazilian sugar plantation in the seventeenth and eighteenth centuries owned between eighty and one hundred enslaved workers. Most were field hands who were each expected to produce three-quarters of a ton of sugar per year. The slave owner recovered the cost of purchasing and maintaining slaves after about three years of such production. With two men for every woman, the Brazilian population with African ancestry did not grow very rapidly and required constant replenishment from Africa. Encouraged by the Catholic Church to marry, many Brazilian slaves formed families, even though they could be broken up by sale.

Slave Revolts

Africans and their descendants often resisted the slave system. Slave revolts erupted in Haiti, Mexico, the North American colonies, and elsewhere, but they were brutally crushed and the leaders executed. For example, the 1739 Stono Rebellion in South Carolina, the deadliest of the North American uprisings, largely involved recently imported, frequently Catholic, Kongolese. The captured rebels were beheaded. Some slaves, known as maroons (muh-ROONS) in the English Caribbean, escaped from plantations and set up African-type societies in the interior of several American colonies, including Brazil, Colombia, Jamaica, Haiti, Dutch Guiana, and some of the southern colonies in North America. The largest maroon community was formed in northeast Brazil, where rebellious slaves established a state around 1605, Palmares (paul-MARYS), with a government led by an African-style king and chiefs. With a population of perhaps 30,000, mostly of African ancestry, Palmares flourished, and resisted nearly annual Portuguese assaults, for nearly a century before being crushed by the Portuguese in 1694.

Africans and their descendants, free or unfree, became a part of local societies. Some slaves were eventually freed, a process known as manumission. Manumission was rare in the English colonies and more common in Latin America, especially Brazil, where women, mulattos, and local-born children were most likely to be freed. In both English and Latin America, a few slaves earned enough to buy their own freedom, and some slave owners gave favored slaves an inheritance. As a result, a slowly growing class of free blacks filled niches in American life. Together the enslaved and freed people of color constituted some two-thirds of the population in parts of Brazil and Cuba. While racism—judging people based on observable physical traits such as skin color—remained influential throughout the Americas, Latin Americans tended to rank people according to their occupation and status as well as skin color, making for a flexible social order. In contrast, the English colonies rigidly divided people largely by skin color and whether they had any African ancestry.

Emergence of an African American Culture

The harsh conditions of slave life notwithstanding, unique, new African American cultures emerged. Africans in the Americas and their descendants frequently mixed Western and African customs, and some created hybrid religions based on both African and Christian beliefs. Combining African rhythms with local European and sometimes Native American musical traditions, African Americans also invented musical forms that won wide appeal in the twentieth century, including jazz, blues, salsa, reggae, calypso, and samba. A few African Americans even developed new languages, such as the Gullah (GULL-uh) dialect of the Georgia Sea Islands, which mixed English and African words. African American cultures also influenced other ethnic groups in the Americas. Many non-Africans enjoyed various folktales and traditions of African origin. Africans introduced several crops from their homelands, including watermelons, black-eyed peas, okra, and rice, and contributed their invaluable knowledge of blacksmithing and iron-working to colonial life.

The Atlantic System's Impact

Trans-Atlantic migration, voluntary and forced, and increasingly close economic ties among Europe, Africa, and the Americas created an Atlantic System by which cargoes of plantation crops were shipped east across the Atlantic to Europe, while cargoes of slaves moved west to the Americas. The Atlantic System comprised a large network that spanned western and Central Africa, the east coast and southern region of English North America, the Caribbean Basin, and the northern and eastern coastal zones of South America. Plantations, slavery, and the numerical prominence of Africans and their descendants in the Americas defined this system, which ultimately helped spur major developments in modern world history, including the rise of European capitalism and wealth.

Economic Impact of the Slave Trade

As key economic activities in the Atlantic System, the slave trade and plantation economies provided enormous capital to Europeans and North Americans. Slave trading became a hugely profitable enterprise that was operated on a sophisticated business basis and attracted large amounts of capital, which allowed for rapid expansion of the trade. The prosperity of eighteenth-century European cities such as Bristol and Liverpool in England, and of North American cities such as Boston, Providence, Charleston, and New Orleans, depended heavily on the slave trade. Because the slavers, the cooperating African chiefs and merchants, the plantation owners, the shipbuilders, and the other groups linked directly or indirectly to the trade were all reluctant to abandon a lucrative activity, the trade endured for four hundred years.

The Atlantic System also contributed to European industrialization. Some of the profits from the slave trade and American plantations were invested in enterprises and technology in England, the Netherlands, France, and North America, helping to bring economic development to these societies and later spurring rapid industrialization in England. Some of the investment capital for inventing industrial technologies came from individuals and companies linked to the slave trade and plantations. For example, Glasgow merchants known as the "tobacco lords"—because of their ties to North American tobacco plantations—set up industries in Britain, such as printing companies, tanneries, and ironworks, and also invested in cotton textile plants and coal mines.

Economic Decline of Spain

However, some Europeans made wiser use of American profits than others. However vast the profits earned from overseas commerce, mercantilist economic strategies could not necessarily convert the incoming wealth into a growing domestic economy. Spain, the most powerful European country for most of the 1500s, had reaped vast riches from colonization, but the Spanish did not ultimately use this wealth in ways that promoted their own economic improvement. In fact, much of the exploitation of the Americas hurt Spain. For example, the flood of American bullion into Spain caused severe inflation, resulting in the need to import lower-priced products from other European countries. In addition, the large investments in the colonies were

obtained in part by heavily taxing peasants and merchants in Spain. Because most Spanish merchants aspired to be large landowners in Spain, they used their profits to buy land rather than investing in trade or industry. By 1600 Spain was bankrupt, and a Spanish official charged that the country had wasted its wealth on frivolous spending rather than manufacturing. Similarly, the Portuguese squandered their colonial wealth through nonproductive investments, such as building magnificent churches and monasteries rather than financing local industry.

Dutch and British Successes

The Dutch and English did much better investing their profits than the Spanish and Portuguese. Enriched by its strong trade position in northern Europe, the Netherlands became a major banking center and also boasted the world's largest commercial fleet. During the 1600s, Dutch merchants earned vast profits from selling Indonesian coffee and spices to other Europeans, and they invested much of these profits in their domestic economy. The Dutch were the strongest European power for most of the seventeenth century, until they were finally eclipsed by England, which enjoyed the most long-term success. In the 1700s, England held the most powerful position in the Atlantic System, with large amounts of wealth flowing into Britain from the slave, tobacco, and sugar trades. The colonial wealth enriched businessmen and bankers, who could now easily mobilize capital for investment in trade, technology, and manufacturing. These factors gave England unique advantages that it fully exploited in the 1700s and 1800s.

During the Early Modern Era, the Americas were transformed and linked to the rest of the globe, forever reshaping world history. The conquest and exploitation of Native Americans and the acquisition of American resources enriched Europe and shifted economic power in the world. Ultimately, this economic power also added to European political and military strength. By the late 1700s or early 1800s, several European countries, especially Britain, had surpassed a declining China in wealth, living standards, and power.

Listen to a synopsis of Chapter 17.

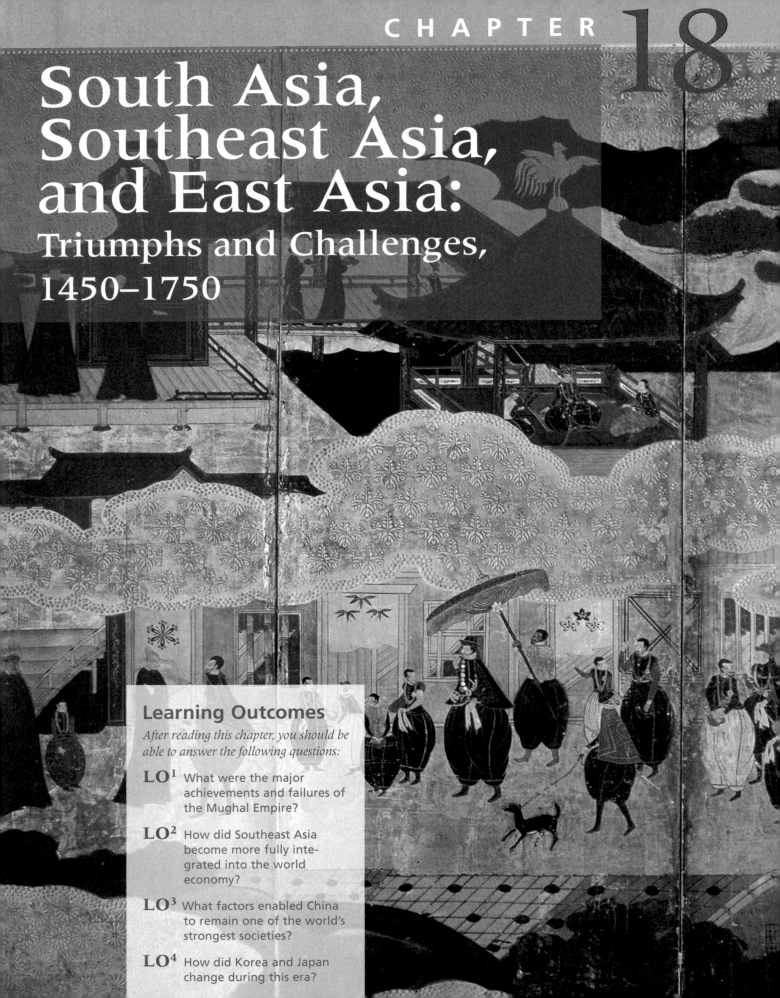

CHAPTER 18

South Asia, Southeast Asia, and East Asia:
Triumphs and Challenges, 1450–1750

Learning Outcomes

After reading this chapter, you should be able to answer the following questions:

LO¹ What were the major achievements and failures of the Mughal Empire?

LO² How did Southeast Asia become more fully integrated into the world economy?

LO³ What factors enabled China to remain one of the world's strongest societies?

LO⁴ How did Korea and Japan change during this era?

> **"** The Portuguese saw that Melaka was magnificent, and its port exceedingly crowded. The people gathered around to see what the Portuguese looked like, and they were all surprised by their appearance. [But] these [Portuguese] know nothing of manners. **"**

—**Malay Chronicles**[1]

Sultan Mahmud Shah (MA-mood Shah) (r. 1488–1511), the Malay ruler of the great trading state of Melaka (muh-LAH-kuh), on the southwest coast of the Malay Peninsula, had a problem. In 1509, five unknown but well-armed ships, each with a banner bearing a cross and full of menacing pale-skinned men, lowered anchor off his capital. Portuguese intentions were unclear to the sultan. They did not act like the peaceful Asian merchants who arrived regularly in trading ships, nor did they bring the customary valuable gifts for the sultan and his officials. Initially, as the Malay chronicles reported, curious Melakans gathered around a Portuguese envoy who came ashore, but the ill-mannered Portuguese violated local customs, antagonized Melaka officials, and alarmed influential local Indian traders. As tensions rose, fighting between Portuguese sailors and Malay visitors to their ship broke out. The Portuguese, unprepared for a full-scale assault on the heavily defended city, sailed away, vowing revenge.

Two years later, in 1511, a Portuguese fleet of some forty ships, mounted with cannon and carrying hundreds of soldiers armed with deadly muskets, sailed back to Melaka to capture the city. The sultan led the defense mounted on his elephant. As the Portuguese gained the upper hand after a bloody month-long assault, they slaughtered much of the population and looted the city. Melaka became the first Southeast Asian society to be severely disrupted by European power.

Many eastern and southern Asians had better success than the Melakans in deflecting the Europeans, who were beginning to arrive in the 1500s seeking markets and resources. The Portuguese in the

Test your knowlege before you read this chapter.

<<**"Southern Barbarians"** This painting on a sixteenth-century Japanese screen, decorated with gold leaf, depicts a Portuguese sea captain, shaded by a parasol carried by his black servant, being greeted by black-robed Jesuit missionaries in the port of Nagasaki. His porters carry gifts for the Japanese merchants.

The Namban Bunkakan, Osaka

449

> "Babur was a gifted leader whose new dynasty restored the imperial grandeur of India."

1500s, the Dutch in the 1600s, and the English in the 1700s established some degree of control over the Indian Ocean maritime network and colonized a few areas, such as Melaka. But, for all their deadly gunpowder weapons, the Europeans did not yet have a clear military and economic advantage over the stronger Asian states, and as a result their influence was modest. Various Asian leaders manipulated the rival Europeans and sometimes forced them to leave. Asian countries were also protected by distance, because they could be reached only by long and dangerous voyages from Europe. As a result, most Asian societies did not undergo the transitions that were reshaping the Americas and parts of Africa in this era.

Some Asian states also remained politically and economically strong. A Muslim kingdom dominated much of India, many Southeast Asian states flourished from trade, China was still a major power, and the Japanese fiercely defended their interests. As in western Eurasia, connections to networks of exchange stretching around the world helped various Asian states grow commercially. As late as 1750, China and India together still accounted for more than half of world manufacturing, but by the mid-1700s, most of the great Asian states were under stress or collapsing from a combination of internal problems and destabilizing Western activities.

LO¹ Mughal India, South Asia, and New Encounters

During its long history, India's culture was shaped by the Hindu religion. During the Intermediate Era, however, Muslims had become politically influential and had introduced major changes. During the Early Modern Era, a powerful Muslim dynasty, the

Mughals (MOO-guhlz)— Central Asians of mixed Mongol-Turkish descent— ruled much of India and the Hindu majority. At their height in the later 1500s and early 1600s, the Mughals presided over one of the world's most creative societies, and also fashioned a prosperous economy that allowed many Indians, both Muslims and Hindus, to flourish. In the early 1700s, however, the Mughal system rapidly declined and began to collapse, just as pressures came from European societies.

The Mughal Empire

In 1526, Babur (BAH-bur) (1483–1530), a Muslim descendant of Genghis Khan and Tamerlane, led 12,000 troops from Afghanistan and conquered much of north India to form a new ruling dynasty called the Mughal, a corruption of *Mongol* (see Map 18.1). Babur was a gifted leader whose new dynasty restored the imperial grandeur of India. The wealth displayed at the Mughal court prompted a French visitor to wonder whether any other monarch possessed more gold, silver, and jewels. Mughal India had few rivals in military strength, government efficiency, economic power, and royal patronage of the arts.

Interactive Map

Society and Religion

The Mughals, like earlier Indian governments, managed a highly diverse society. The majority of people shared many traditions and practiced Hinduism, but since the ninth century, a succession of Muslim states had ruled parts of the subcontinent, and perhaps one-quarter of the Indian population embraced Islam. Polytheistic Hinduism and monotheistic Islam offered starkly different visions of the cosmic and social order, and Hindus and Muslims often disagreed and competed for influence in Indian society. Yet at the village level, Hindus and Muslims lived side by side, sharing many customs.

By 1500, Buddhism, which had thrived for centuries, had nearly died out in India, but most people in Tibet and on the island of Sri Lanka (Ceylon) remained Buddhists. Indian society was also fragmented by caste divisions and hundreds of different regional languages. While proud of their Central Asian origins and influenced by Persian culture, the Mughals adapted to Indian conditions. For example, they used **Urdu**, a mix of Hindi, Arabic, and Persian

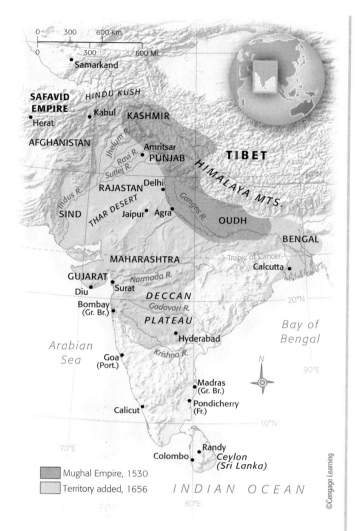

Mughal Empire, 1530
Territory added, 1656

©Cengage Learning

Map 18.1
The Mughal Empire, 1526–1761

By the mid-1600s, the Mughals controlled much of the Indian subcontinent, but some ports fell under European rule. The Portuguese had a colony at Goa and, by the early 1700s, the British had established outposts at Bombay, Calcutta, and Madras, and the French-occupied Pondicherry.

written in the Persian script, as their language of administration. Urdu had developed earlier as a common language among many Indian Muslims.

Akbar the Great   Akbar (AK-bahr) (r. 1556–1605), a grandson of Babur, pursued innovative policies and became the most outstanding Mughal ruler. Akbar, whose name means "Very Great," expanded Babur's

empire over all of north India, including Bengal, and deep into south India. To ensure stability and defuse opposition, Akbar gave Hindus high positions in the government and removed the extra taxes that earlier Muslim rulers in India had imposed, policies that brought him wide popularity. He also reformed the government, cracked down on corruption, and promoted religious toleration and compromise between communities. Akbar tried to abolish what he considered the most pernicious social customs, such as *sati* (burning the wife on the husband's funeral pyre), child marriage, and trial by ordeal, but was unable to curb such practices. Still, Akbar's India enjoyed an enlightened criminal code for the era, and all citizens had the right of appeal to the ruler if they believed themselves wrongly convicted of a crime or mistreated in the courts. Peace and prosperity prevailed during his reign.

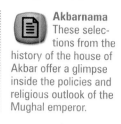

Akbarnama These selections from the history of the house of Akbar offer a glimpse inside the policies and religious outlook of the Mughal emperor.

Jahangir and Shah Jehan

Akbar presided over a golden age, but many of his successors were less tolerant and wise. The Mughals never worked out a stable pattern of succession, and because Muslim rulers in India had many wives and concubines, succession was often wildly contentious. Akbar was poisoned by a rebellious son, who then occupied the throne as Jahangir (ja-HAN-gear) ("World Seizer"). Although Jahangir generally pursued Akbar's public policies, his son, Shah Jahan (r. 1628–1658), promoted Islam relentlessly and destroyed several Hindu temples. He also took extravagant living to new heights, assembling a harem of five thousand concubines. Sitting on his splendid jewel-encrusted Peacock Throne in Delhi, Shah Jahan doubled the tax bills, and launched extensive building projects that virtually bankrupted the state. Unsuccessful military campaigns in Afghanistan and Central Asia added to the problems. Eventually, Shah Jahan was imprisoned by his ambitious, even more intolerant son, Aurangzeb (ow-rang-ZEB) (r. 1658–1707), who greatly expanded the empire in the south, but also set in motion the forces that began to undermine the Mughal state.

Read about Akbar, the Mughal ruler, who came to power at age 13 and was one of the most respected political leaders of India.

Indian Economy and Society

Under the Mughals, India flourished, as it had for centuries, from industry, farming, and trade. Thanks to manufacturing, especially of textiles and iron, India had long been one of the world's most industrialized societies. By 1750, India still accounted for one-quarter of the world's industrial output, and it remained the largest producer of textiles. Its highly efficient farming, which benefited from investments in reservoirs and irrigation, produced large yields of wheat and rice. Cash crops, including cotton, indigo, pepper, sugar, and opium, found ready markets. The productive Indian economy and agriculture supported a doubling of the population between 1500 and 1750.

Foreign trade spurred the economy, and the bullion it brought to India benefited the Mughal treasury. Indian merchants and bankers maintained and even expanded some of the largest commercial networks in the Early Modern world. By the 1400s, the Indian maritime trade diaspora stretched from Arabia, Persia, northeast Africa, and the Red Sea to Melaka, Sumatra, Siam, and China. In the 1600s, an influx of American silver, used by European merchants to obtain textiles and other products, stimulated a tripling of the money supply. Revenues from commerce and industry allowed the Mughals to build an extensive network of imperial roads, support a luxurious court life, and fund ambitious building projects.

The Indian merchant networks enjoyed vast amounts of capital, as well as sophisticated credit and financing arrangements. Heavily capitalized family- and caste-run firms competed successfully against European and Asian rivals. Some merchants in Surat (SOO-raht), the Gujerat (goo-juh-RAHT) region's main port, were among the world's richest entrepreneurs. Other ports also had successful merchants. A Dutch diplomat wrote that the merchants of Bengal were "exceptionally quick and experienced. They are always sober, modest, thrifty, and cunning in identifying the source for their profit."[2]

Caste and Gender in Mughal India

The Indian traders came from a society divided by caste and gender divisions. Most of the Hindu merchants belonged to various subcastes (*jati*) of the larger caste grouping known as the *vaisya*, who ranked below the priests (*brahmans*) and warriors in a caste system that had been evolving for more than two thousand years. Caste remained dynamic, and subcastes moved up or down in the system. Nor did caste necessarily correspond to wealth, since many traders were affluent. Women's influence depended on their caste and family situation. In north India, where both Muslim and Hindu women were often kept in seclusion, they were expected to be chaste and obedient to fathers and husbands in a patriarchal, patrilineal society. Yet some women in the Mughal court exercised influence. For instance, Khanzada Begum (1478–1545), Babur's oldest sister, successfully interceded with rebellious brothers to end a family split and keep Babur's son, Humayun, on the throne. The Mughal women had financial resources, which they often devoted to endow mosques and support religious scholars.

> "The Indian traders came from a society divided by caste and gender divisions."

Indian Religion and Arts

The coming of Islam in the centuries before 1500 dramatically changed India's religious and cultural environment. Muslims remained religiously distinct and were often disdainful of Hindus and of the caste system; the two groups never united to form a single people. Nonetheless, Muslim customs, such as veiling and secluding women, influenced upper-class Hindus in north India. The early Mughals, especially Akbar, mostly left the Hindus free to live as they wished, but less-tolerant policies emerged in later years.

Sufism

Mysticism became increasingly popular among both Muslims and Hindus. Sufi influences grew in the Islamic communities beginning in the 1300s, when Muslim rulers welcomed Sufi masters, some of them renowned poets, to their courts. Akbar and Jahangir were particularly sympathetic to Sufism, horrifying Muslim dogmatists, who regarded the mystics as heretics. Sufis argued that a personal bond existed between each believer and God, and they denied that either religious or political institutions could replace that bond. As a result, some Sufi movements, such as the Chishtiya (CHIS-tee-ya), avoided association with secular powers.

Bhakti

Meanwhile, many Hindus, particularly from lower castes, gravitated toward the mystical bhakti (BUK-tee) devotional movement, which had first emerged

in the Intermediate Era. Some bhakti groups challenged accepted wisdom by opposing the caste system, ignoring the high-caste brahmans and their traditional ritual practices, and sympathizing with the poor. Bhakti worship often involved dances, poems, and songs, as in Sufism, and focused on commitment to a particular Hindu god, such as Shiva or Vishnu.

Mysticism helped forge a gradual accommodation between some Muslims and Hindus but appealed more to women than to men. The barriers between the contrasting mystical approaches blurred, and many Muslims and Hindus venerated both Sufi and bhakti saints, making pilgrimages to their tombs. Many bhakti poets were women. The most famous, Mirabai (MEERA-buy) (ca. 1498–ca. 1546), a Rajput who was widowed at a young age, refused the pleas of her in-laws to commit sati and spent the rest of her life writing praises to Vishnu. Some historians view her life as a partly successful struggle against the patriarchal system and the brahmans (Hindu priests).

Sikhs

While many Sufi and bhakti mystics found common ground, other Indians tried to blend or transcend Hinduism and Islam by forming new sects. The largest of these sects, the Sikhs ("Disciples"), adopted elements from both Hinduism and Islam while creating a new religion. Eventually the Sikhs numbered several million people, mostly living in the Punjab region of northwest India. The religion was founded by Guru Nanak (GOO-roo NAN-ak) (1469–1539), born a Hindu, who had been strongly influenced by Hindu bhakti movements. But he argued that devotion was not enough: "God will not ask a man his tribe or sect, but what he has done. There is no Hindu and no Muslim. All are children of God."[3] Nanak was followed by nine spiritual leaders who refined the faith during Mughal times. Akbar respected the faith and granted Sikhs land for a great temple in Amritsar (uhm-RIT-suhr) in the Punjab.

Sikhs shared numerous beliefs and a mystical approach with other faiths but also had distinctive customs. Like Muslims, they worshiped one universal and loving God, rejected the caste system and priests, promoted egalitarianism, forbade alcohol and tobacco, and stressed discipline, hard work, and charity for the needy. Like Hindus, they offered devotional hymns to their god, but Sikhs also differed in significant ways: observant Sikh men adopted a look very different from that of Hindus or Muslims. Prohibited from cutting their hair, many wore turbans. Sikh women enjoyed great freedom compared to Hindus and Muslims, but persistent persecution by Mughal leaders after Akbar led Sikhs, once pacifists, to become militaristic.

Sikhs ("Disciples") Members of an Indian religion founded in the Early Modern Era that adopted elements from both Hinduism and Islam, including mysticism.

Art in the Mughal Empire

Early Modern Indians also made significant achievements in the arts. Based on Persian models, the distinctive Mughal school of miniature painting flourished under royal patronage. The Mughals were also great builders of tombs, mosques, forts, and palaces. Their architectural style, known as Indo-Islamic, blended Indian and Persian influences and made lavish use of mosaics, domes, and gateways. In the audience hall of his spectacular Delhi palace, the ruler Shah Jahan had inscribed: "If on earth be an Eden of bliss, it is this, it is this, it is this!"[4] East of Delhi, at Agra (AH-gruh), Shah Jahan left another legacy, the Taj Mahal (tahzh muh-HAHL). Often considered the world's most beautiful building, the Taj took 22,000 workers twenty-two years to complete. It was the final resting place for Shah Jahan's beloved favorite wife, Mumtaz Mahal (MOOM-taz muh-HAHL).

Mughal Decline and Portuguese Influence

Eventually the Mughals' endless wars of expansion and extravagant royal spending drained state coffers, reducing their ability to maintain power. Before the eighteenth century, the military strength of the Mughal state had been sufficient to keep Europeans and other enemies at bay. Although the state lacked naval power, the Mughal army, numbering some 1 million soldiers, was equipped with gunpowder weapons, such as muskets and field artillery, that rivaled European arms, and it had thousands of elephants to ride into battle and large cavalry units. By the early 1700s, however, the once-vaunted Mughal military machine was faltering, and the Mughals lacked the money to match European military capabilities.

Aurangzeb's Policies

Poor leadership also contributed to the decline. Aurangzeb's ruthless and intolerant policies alienated both Muslims and non-Muslims alike. A man with a more dogmatic view of

Islam and less generous viewpoints than his predecessors toward non-Muslims, Aurangzeb placed higher taxes on non-Muslims and persecuted—sometimes even executed—Hindu and Sikh leaders he saw as a threat to his power. His cruelty toward opponents and toleration of corruption also alienated many pious and tolerant Muslims. Revolt undermined Aurangzeb's later years, eventually leading to the dismantling of the Mughal state as regions broke away. The Marathas (muh-RAH-tuhz), a Hindu group from western India who had long resisted Mughal power, began raiding into the empire in the later 1600s and cutting Mughal supply lines. Some Hindu merchants, disenchanted with Mughal corruption, provided the Marathas with guns. When Safavid Iran conquered much of the Mughal-controlled areas of Afghanistan in the early seventeenth century, Mughal leaders were too busy plotting against each other to respond. They were finally defeated in 1761 by Hindu and Sikh insurgents.

The decline and demise of the powerful Mughal state left India open to penetration by Europeans. The anti-Mughal forces could not unite, leaving India fragmented and vulnerable. The division between Muslims and Hindus, a split intensified by the intolerance of later Mughal rulers, played a critical role in gradual European encroachment. Europeans had long been interested in southern Asia as a source of spices and textiles, and this interest spurred the Portuguese to seek a sea route around Africa and the Spanish to sponsor the Columbian voyages westward across the Atlantic in search of "the Indies." The Portuguese explorers came from a country with superior naval technology, missionary zeal, and a compelling appetite for wealth, but a standard of living little if any higher than that enjoyed by many Indians, Southeast Asians, and Chinese.

Vasco de Gama: The Portuguese in India

The Portuguese were the first Europeans to arrive in India directly from Europe by sea around Africa. Following the Indian Ocean maritime trade route from East Africa, the pioneer Portuguese explorer, Vasco da Gama (ca. 1469–1525), reached the southwestern Indian port of Calicut in 1498 with the help of a pilot hired in East Africa. At Calicut, Da Gama quickly realized the economic potential of Asia and learned that the European goods he carried had little value. Da Gama had one military advantage over the Indians—mounted cannon on his ships—but he was able to obtain a cargo of spices without force, which he sold in Europe at 3,000 percent profit. In 1500 a second Portuguese fleet returned to Calicut,

and, after fighting broke out ashore between the Portuguese and some local people, the Portuguese used their cannon to bombard Calicut, blasting the city to rubble and destroying bigger but less maneuverable Indian and Arab ships that were helping defend the city.

Like all the European powers that followed them to Asia, the Portuguese resorted to violence when they believed it necessary to enforce their power and acquire wealth. Seeking to control the trade from Asia to the West, the Portuguese established fortified settlements at strategic locations around the Indian Ocean in the early 1500s. In 1515 they also occupied Colombo (kuh-LUM-bow) in western Sri Lanka, a source of cinnamon. Soon the Portuguese used their warships to exercise partial control over the maritime trade of the western Indian Ocean, extorting payments from Ottoman, Arab, Indian, and Indonesian merchant ships. Sometimes they used terrorism: in 1502, to take revenge for the Portuguese killed earlier in Calicut, Vasco da Gama attacked, plundered, and burned an Arab passenger ship bound for Calicut carrying more than three hundred people, including several of Calicut's richest merchants and many women and children, killing all of the people aboard. But, despite devoting vast resources, including some eight hundred ships, to the effort, and despite controlling several key ports, the Portuguese never completely dominated the Indian Ocean commerce. Asian merchants often

---

CHRONOLOGY

South Asia, 1450–1750

1498	Arrival of Vasco da Gama in India
1510	Portuguese conquest of Goa
1515	Portuguese occupation of western Ceylon
1526–1761	Mughal India
1556–1605	Reign of Akbar
1600	Founding of British East India Company
1640s	Dutch conquests in Ceylon
1717	British settlement in Calcutta and Madras

found ways to outmaneuver or evade Portuguese ships, and Asian states resisted Portuguese demands. The Portuguese still had to compete for Asian goods with Asian merchants.

"Christians and Spices"

Although chiefly interested in trade, the Portuguese were also zealous missionary Christians. Da Gama had told Calicut leaders that the Portuguese sought "Christians and spices," a useful shorthand. Hostility to Islam was a cornerstone of Portuguese policy, sometimes leading to persecution of Islamic institutions and repression of believers in Portuguese-held territories. Portuguese men settled in Goa and Colombo, marrying local women and fostering mixed-descent communities, but they also brought rigid gender roles to their Asian colonies, limiting the role of women.

South Asia's New Challenges

Before the mid-1700s, European influence on India and its trade remained relatively modest. Only some 10 percent of the silk and other cloth produced in Bengal in 1750 ended up in Europe. But the Portuguese activity foreshadowed an increasingly active European presence. The Dutch, French, and English followed the Portuguese to Asia, and all attempted to impose their influence on parts of South Asia. The overextended Portuguese were hard-pressed to sustain their power against these European rivals, who had larger populations and were developing better ships and gunpowder weapons.

The Dutch East India Company

The Dutch challenged the Portuguese for domination of the Indian Ocean trade in the early 1600s, eventually destroying their power in South and Southeast Asia and gaining partial control over Indian Ocean commerce. In 1602 Dutch merchants in Amsterdam, with the goal of tapping into the Asian trade, formed the Dutch East India Company, a private company with government backing that had its own armed fleet and operated in conjunction with other Dutch activities. In South Asia the Dutch concentrated their attention on Sri Lanka, gaining control of some of the coastal regions from the Portuguese in the 1640s. They remained in Sri Lanka, often intermarrying with local people, until they were ousted by the British in the early 1800s.

Soon the French joined the competition, forming their own East India Company in 1664. In the later 1600s and early 1700s, the French established a trading presence at Surat and Calcutta, and they built a military and commercial base at the southeast coast town of Pondicherry (pon-dir-CHEH-ree). Vigorous French competition for Indian merchandise generated tensions with the English. The two countries were also bitter rivals in Europe, and the resulting antagonisms sometimes spilled over into conflict in India: in 1746, the English and French fought fierce battles for dominance in southeast India that drew

A Goa Market A Dutch traveler, Jan Huygen Van Linschoten, made this plate while living in the Portuguese-ruled port city of Goa in the 1580s. It shows a street scene, including market stalls and, on the far right, a Portuguese woman walking with two Indian maids. Some Indians, wearing crosses, have become Christians.

in local Indian states and destabilized the region's politics.

The British East India Company

The English became the main threat to the Mughals, Dutch, and French in Asia. In 1600, British investors formed the British East India Company in London. They also built a fort at Madras (muh-DRAS) (today known as Chennai) and established a stable commercial base at Surat in northwest India, with Mughal permission. At Surat the English forged a commercial alliance with the Parsis (PAHR-seez), the Zoroastrian descendants of Persian refugees who were leading traders in India. By the late 1600s, the English were increasing their presence in India and, in 1717, they established bases at Bombay (today called Mumbai) and Calcutta, soon controlling these towns. But outside of Bombay, Calcutta, and Madras, English officials still had to negotiate with the Mughals or local princes for trading privileges. When piracy and banditry grew rapidly as Mughal authority collapsed, the law and order in the three English-run towns, secured by an increasing English military presence, attracted Indian settlers. English and Indian merchants in the three English bases prospered. The growing English presence in India also had consequences in England, where competition from Indian textile imports spurred local textile manufacturers to cut costs, helping stimulate English industrialization.

By the mid-eighteenth century, the English were strong enough to treat local rulers with less deference and expand their control from their three bases into the surrounding regions. When local Indian governments resisted this encroachment, the English resorted to military force. By the 1750s, this had resulted in a war in Bengal, where, from their Calcutta base, the English now began their long period of military conquest in South Asia. Eventually they controlled nearly all of South Asia except for a few small enclaves, such as Portuguese Goa and French Pondicherry. With the English, India faced a major new challenge.

LO² Southeast Asia and Global Connections

Southeast Asia had long been a cosmopolitan center where peoples, religions, ideas, and products

> "Increased trade encouraged political centralization, the growth of cities, and the spread of world religions."

met. Southeast Asians participated in the wider hemispheric trade and most adopted Theravada Buddhism, Confucianism, or Islam. The Portuguese arrival at Melaka inaugurated a new era of transregional contacts during which European adventurers, traders, missionaries, and soldiers were active in the region. Several areas were influenced by the West before 1750, particularly Malaya, the Philippine Islands, and parts of Indonesia. However, in most parts of Southeast Asia, including strong kingdoms such as Siam, Burma, and Vietnam, Western influence remained weak until the nineteenth century.

Southeast Asian Transitions and Trade

In the Early Modern Era, Southeast Asia was undergoing a transition that included commercial growth, political change, increasingly productive agriculture, and expansion of Islam and Buddhism. Partly because of increasing connections with European, Chinese, Arab, and Indian merchants, commerce increased between the 1400s and 1700s, and Southeast Asia remained an essential hub in the maritime trade network linking East Asia with India and the Middle East. Sailing ships still stopped in the region's ports to exchange goods or wait for the monsoon winds to shift.

Increased trade encouraged political centralization, the growth of cities, and the spread of world religions. Larger, more centralized states absorbed neighboring smaller states: on the mainland some twenty states in the fourteenth century had been reduced to less than a dozen by the early eighteenth century, with Siam, Vietnam, and Burma being the most influential. Thanks to the increased amounts of products being obtained and transported, regional ports flourished, and urban merchants became powerful in local politics. Although revenue from trade became more crucial than agricultural taxes in many states, agriculture remained a major activity, and new crops and varieties of rice spurred population growth. At the same time, Theravada Buddhism dug deeper roots on the Southeast Asian mainland, and Islam continued to spread throughout the Malay Peninsula and the islands of Indonesia and the southern Philippines. As a result of increased trade and exposure to new religions, cultures were opened to the outside world.

European Colonialism in Southeast Asia

Southeast Asia's wealth and resources, especially spices such as cloves, nutmeg, and pepper, attracted European merchants and conquerors to the region. The Portuguese who occupied Melaka were the forerunners of a powerful and destabilizing European presence that transformed Southeast Asia between 1500 and 1900. By controlling Melaka, the Portuguese gained an advantage against their European and Malay rivals. A few years later they brutally conquered the Spice Islands, known as Maluku (muh-LOO-ku), in northeast Indonesia, thus gaining control of the valuable spice trade to Europe.

But, as in India, Portuguese power in Southeast Asia proved short-lived. Like the East African ports they occupied earlier, Melaka languished under Portuguese control, since fewer Muslim merchants chose to endure the higher taxes and Portuguese intolerance of Islam. Portuguese policies often involved brute force, and their effort to convert subject peoples to Christianity made them unwelcome. Although the Dutch replaced the Portuguese in Melaka in 1641, for several centuries Portuguese became a language of trade and commerce in some coastal regions of Asia, from Basra in Iraq to ports in Vietnam.

Portuguese activities spurred the Spanish, Dutch, English, and French to compete for markets, resources, Christian converts, and power in Southeast Asia. The Spanish conquered the Philippines, and the Dutch gained some control of the Indian Ocean maritime trade by force and conquered Java and the Spice Islands. Preoccupied with India and the Americas, the English mainly sought only trade relations in this era. The French became involved in Vietnam, beginning in 1615, seeking trade but also dispatching Catholic missionaries, who recruited a small following of Vietnamese. But European power had its limits: Southeast Asian states such as Siam, Vietnam, Burma, and Acheh were strong enough to resist more than three hundred years of persistent effort by Westerners to gain complete political, social, and economic domination, which they achieved only by 1900.

Buddhist and Islamic Societies

Despite such incursions, various Southeast Asian societies remained vigorous in this era, in both the Buddhist and Islamic realms (see Map 18.2). Among the strongest states with a mostly Theravada Buddhist population was Siam, governed from 1350 to 1767 by kings based at Ayuthia. Siam was involved in maritime trade and developed a regional empire, extending its influence into Cambodia and some of the small Lao (laow) states along the Mekong River. Its competition with the Burmese, Vietnamese, and the largest Lao state, Lan Xang (lan chang), for regional dominance occasionally led to war. Indeed, in the 1560s, a Burmese army ravaged Siam and sacked Ayuthia, carrying back to Burma thousands of Siamese prisoners and their families.

Interactive Map

> **Portuguese activities spurred the Spanish, Dutch, English, and French to compete for markets, resources, Christian converts, and power in Southeast Asia.**

Siamese Society

Siam eventually recovered from Burma's conquest and flourished. For example, during the reign of King Narai (na-RY) (r. 1656–1688), the king used some of his revenues to promote literature and art, often with a Buddhist emphasis, thus fostering a cultural renaissance. Because Theravada Buddhist monks sponsored many village schools, Siam had one of the highest literacy rates in the premodern world. Siamese society was hierarchical but tolerant by the world's standards at that time. The royal family and the aristocracy that administered the government were mostly Buddhist, and they remained aloof from the commoners and a large class of slaves. Women enjoyed rights, including that of operating village and town markets. Theravada Buddhism encouraged tolerance toward other faiths

CHRONOLOGY

Southeast Asia, 1450–1750

1350–1767	Ayuthia kingdom in Siam
1511	Portuguese conquest of Melaka
1565	Spanish conquest of Philippines
1619	Dutch base at Batavia
1641	Dutch seizure of Melaka from Portuguese
1668	Siamese expulsion of French

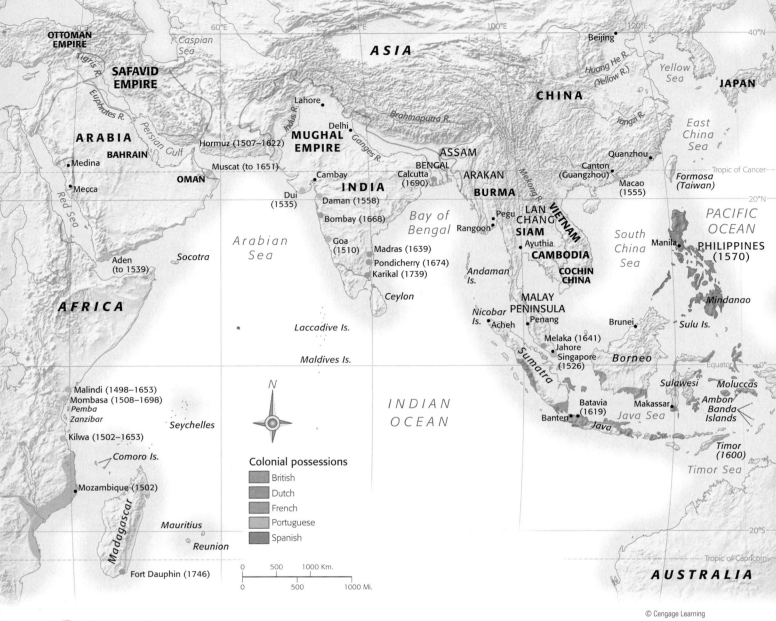

Map 18.2
Southeast Asia in the Early Modern Era

Much of Southeast Asia remained independent, able to deflect European ambitions, but the Portuguese had captured the port of Melaka, Timor, and the Moluccas (Maluku), and the Spanish had colonized the Philippines. In the 1600s, the Dutch displaced the Portuguese from Melaka and the Moluccas, and ruled part of Java from Batavia.

© Cengage Learning

WWW
Southeast Asia Guide (*http://www.library.wisc.edu/guides/SEAsia/*). An impressive, easy-to-use site from the University of Wisconsin—Madison.

and cultivated a more liberal society. Ayuthia's openness to merchants and creative people from all over Eurasia made it a vibrant crossroads of exchange and influence.

However, Siam had to contend with increasing European activity. English, French, and Dutch traders all established operations in Ayuthia. King Narai, who had regularly sent missions to Persia, India, and China, sent three diplomatic missions to the French court of Louis XIV to obtain Western maps and scientific knowledge, and employed several foreigners as officials. One of these, Constantine Phaulkon, was discovered to have plotted with the French to convert Narai to Christianity and station French troops near the capital in 1688.

When the Siamese learned of the plot, they expelled all French diplomats, missionaries, and merchants from Siam and executed Phaulkon. For decades after, the Siamese mistrusted Europeans and refused to grant them any special trading privileges.

> "Trade networks fostered the expansion of Islam and increased its influence throughout the Indonesian islands and the Malay Peninsula."

Hispanization
The process by which, over nearly three centuries of Spanish colonial rule beginning in 1565, the Catholic religion and Spanish culture were imposed on the Philippine people.

Ferdinand Magellan

Islam in Southeast Asia

Some Muslim societies also flourished in Southeast Asia. Trade networks fostered the expansion of Islam and increased its influence throughout the Indonesian islands and the Malay Peninsula. Various societies adapted Islam to their own cultural traditions. Many Javanese superimposed Islam, often with a Sufi flavor, on the existing foundation of Hinduism and mystical animism, producing an eclectic and tolerant mix of faiths. Other peoples embraced a more orthodox version of Islam. As more Muslim merchants called at ports with Muslim rulers, the strengthening of trade ties enriched states. The mixing of Islam and maritime trade encouraged mobility and connections to the wider world.

Islam also changed gender relations. As in most of Southeast Asia, women in Indonesia had often enjoyed independence. However, Islam, rooted in patriarchal Arab traditions, diminished women's rights in some Indonesian societies. For instance, in Acheh (AH-cheh) in northern Sumatra, where four successive women had ruled in the later 1600s, women were eventually prohibited from holding royal power, but elsewhere women often continued to play key roles. Muslim courts on Java and other islands were often filled with hundreds, sometimes thousands, of women. Some were wives and concubines, but most were attendants, guards, or textile workers.

The Philippines Under Spanish Colonization

The greatest Western impact in Southeast Asia before 1800 came in the Philippine Islands, which were conquered by Spain. For nearly three centuries of its colonial rule, beginning in 1565, Spain imposed the Catholic religion and many aspects of Spanish culture with a policy known as Hispanization. However, the Filipinos managed to mix their indigenous customs with the Spanish influences. Under Spanish rule, the Philippines became a key participant in the new world economy.

Spanish interest in the Philippines was a result of their activities in the Americas and their quest for a sea route to Asia. The first Spanish ships to reach the islands in 1521, commanded by Ferdinand Magellan, were part of the first successful effort to circumnavigate the world, though Magellan himself did not complete the voyage. Magellan pressured the Filipinos he encountered to adopt Christianity. He ordered a local chief to burn all his peoples' religious figures and replace them with crosses, which every villager should worship every day on their knees. Magellan's arrogant demands inspired opposition, and he was killed in a skirmish with hostile Filipinos. Today, on the beach on Cebu Island where Magellan died, a memorial honors Lapulapu (LAH-pu-LAH-pu), the chief who led the attack, as the first Filipino to repel European aggression.

Filipino Society

Magellan had chanced upon an island group inhabited by some 1 to 2 million people divided into many distinct ethnic groups and speaking more than one hundred Malay languages. The population was scattered across 7,000 islands, although the majority lived on the two largest islands, Luzon (loo-ZON) and Mindanao (min-duh-NOW). Muslims occupied the southernmost islands, and Islam was slowly spreading northward, but most Filipinos mixed belief in Allah with animism. Remote from the mainland and western Indonesia, the islands had historically received relatively little cultural influence from India or China, but a few hundred Chinese traders lived in the major towns, and some Filipinos traveled as far as Melaka and Burma as maritime traders. Unlike the kingdoms of Java or Siam, the largest Filipino political units were villages led by chiefs.

The Spanish in the Philippines

When, four decades after Magellan's death, the Spaniards returned to conquer and evangelize,

Moros
The Spanish term for the
Muslim peoples of the
southern Philippines.

they renamed the islands the Philippines after their monarch, Philip II, known as "the most Catholic of kings." Given the ethnic divisions and lack of a dominant Philippine state, the militarily superior Spanish had little trouble conquering the islands and co-opting local chiefs. But the Muslims in the south, called Moros by the Spanish, were never completely pacified, and Spanish authority there remained mostly nominal. The Spanish set up their colonial government and trading base in Manila (muh-NIL-uh), located on a fine natural harbor.

The Catholic Church took a major role in the colonial Philippine enterprise. The church governed various regions outside of Manila and acquired great wealth. In many districts, priests collected taxes and sold the crops, such as sugar, grown by Filipino parishioners. Catholic friars, accompanying the soldiers, began the process of conversion, and several religious orders competed to gain the most converts. Indeed, the Spanish colonial regime gave the missionaries special authority, and the Spanish crown financed the conversion efforts. Missionaries concentrated on the children of village leaders but, to better control and evangelize the Filipinos, they also required people to move into towns. Few schools were opened outside Manila, and what education existed was in church hands. To control competing ideas, the Spanish destroyed nearly all of the pre-Spanish writings, which they considered pagan. Eventually around 85 percent of the Filipinos adopted Roman Catholicism, but many incorporated their own animist traditions into the religion. Friendly spirits became Christian saints, and miracles attributed to Jesus or the Virgin Mary became the new form of magic. Some Filipinos even used religious festivals to subtly express opposition to Spanish rule.

Inequality also showed up in economic and social patterns. The colonial economy forged a rural society based on plantation agriculture and tenant farming, implanting a permanent gap between the extraordinarily rich landowners, who emphasized lucrative cash crops, and the impoverished peasants. Filipinos, once masters of the land, mostly became tenants working for a few powerful landowning families or the church. Priests and landowners told them their religious duty was to labor hard for others—they would get their just rewards later in heaven.

Although the Spanish created a country and expanded the economy, they did not construct a cohesive society. Regional and ethnic loyalties remained dominant. The Spaniards occupied the top spots, controlling the government and church. The great majority of Spanish lived in Manila, often in luxury, and few outside the church ever learned to speak local languages. Below them were mixed-descent people, known as mestizos, and a few Filipino families who descended from chiefs. Below them were Chinese immigrants, who worked as merchants and craftsmen and mostly remained middle class. But while the Spanish needed the Chinese as middlemen, they also despised, persecuted, and sometimes expelled them. On occasion, when their resentment of Chinese wealth or concern with growing Chinese numbers became intense, Spanish forces slaughtered the residents of Manila's large Chinatown.

From Edgar Wickberg, *The Chinese in Philippine Life 1850–1898* (New Haven, CT and London: Yale University Press, 1965)

Chinese Mestizo Couple This painting by a French artist shows two wealthy, well-dressed Chinese mestizos riding in Manila. Chinese mestizos, products of marriages between Chinese immigrants and Filipino or Spanish women, played a key role in colonial life.

The lowest social status was held by the vast majority of Filipinos, whom the Spanish called Indios. They faced many legal restrictions; for example, they were prohibited from dressing like Spaniards. The Filipinos retained their traditionally strong communal orientation, including powerful kinship networks. However, because the Spanish culture and church devalued women, Filipinas lost the high position they had enjoyed in pre-Spanish society and now faced restrictions on their activities. But despite male prejudice and a narrowing of gender roles, Filipinas continued to control family finances and engage in small-scale trade.

Indonesia and the Dutch

In the seventeenth century, the Dutch arrived, displacing the Portuguese from most of their bases and becoming the dominant European power in Southeast Asia. Dutch ships had long carried spices from Portugal to northern Europe. The Dutch gradually expanded their influence from the Spice Islands to other islands, notably Java. Because they built their empire in the Indies over a period of three hundred years, their impact varied widely over time. The Dutch sought wealth but, unlike the Portuguese and Spanish, cared little about spreading their culture and religion. In 1595 a Dutch fleet visited the Spice Islands of Maluku and brought back spices to Holland. Over the next several decades, the Dutch, after bloody battles, dislodged the Portuguese from most of their scattered outposts, capturing the Portuguese-controlled port of Melaka in 1641.

Over the next several centuries, the Dutch gradually gained control of the islands of Indonesia, except for the Portuguese-ruled eastern half of the island of Timor. They quickly became hated for their ruthlessness and slaughtered their Indonesian opponents by the thousands. After Dutch forces attacked and occupied the prosperous trading city of Makassar (muh-KAS-uhr), in southeast Sulawesi (SOO-la-WAY-see), in 1659, the sultan's secretary, Amin, ruefully observed, "Never make friends with the Dutch. No country can call itself safe when they are around."[5] The Dutch were well-organized, resourceful, and shrewd diplomats, allying themselves with one state against a rival state. While exploiting local conflicts, however, they sometimes were drawn into civil wars or were faced with stiff resistance.

The Dutch in Java

With trade as their major goal, for several centuries the Dutch left administration of their Indonesian bases to the Dutch East India Company, which had great capital and large resources for pursuing profit. Holland was ten months away by boat, so there was little guidance and few restraints on the company's power, and it used its goal of gaining a monopoly of trade in Southeast Asia to justify ruthless policies. If the people of a Spice Island grew restless, Dutch forces might exterminate them or carry them off as slaves to Java, Ceylon, or South Africa. For instance, in 1621 the entire population of the spice-producing Banda (BAN-duh) Islands—some 15,000 people—were killed, taken away as slaves, or left to starve.

Eventually the Dutch concentrated on the rich island of Java, which had a flourishing mercantile economy tied to maritime trade and several competing sultanates. In the 1600s, Java boasted at least two cities with more than 100,000 people, and their population was a cosmopolitan mix drawn from throughout Asia. Javan artisans were noted for fine craftsmanship; the island's smiths made perhaps the finest steel swords in the world. Their commercial prowess was renowned in the region, and Javanese women were prominent in business. The Dutch did not come into an underdeveloped society, but one with living standards comparable to those in western Europe.

Capitalizing on Java's political instability and divisions, the Dutch slowly extended their power across the island after establishing a military and commercial base at a village they renamed Batavia, on the northwestern coast, in 1619. Batavia later grew into a city, today known as Jakarta. Most of Java came under direct or indirect Dutch control by the end of the eighteenth century. Soon the Dutch concentrated on making Java a source of wealth. In the highlands of west Java, and later in Sumatra, peasants were forced to grow coffee for export through a system of annual quotas. Coffee—domesticated centuries earlier in Ethiopia and then grown in southern Arabia—had become a popular beverage in both the Middle East and Europe. The huge sums from this process financed much of Holland's industrialization in the nineteenth century. The Dutch co-opted local elites and governed some districts through local rulers. Dutch and Chinese entrepreneurs slowly displaced the Javanese merchant class, once major players in the world economy.

Javanese Social Structure

Through their political and economic activities, the Dutch gradually transformed Javan society and life. As in other colonies, inequality characterized the society. Europeans occupied the top rung, followed by

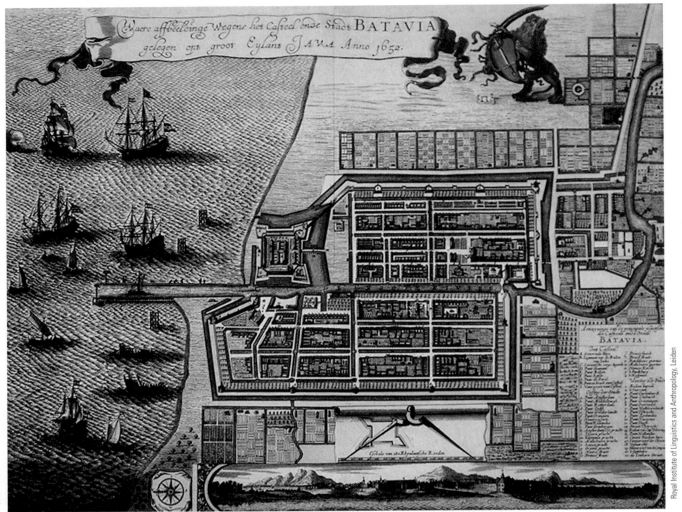

Batavia The Dutch built a port they called Batavia on the northwest coast of Java. Batavia, shown on this map from 1652, grew rapidly as the political and commercial center of the Dutch empire in Southeast Asia.

those of mixed-descent, known as Eurasians, and the co-opted local aristocracy. Javanese now became even more preoccupied with social status, and the peasants were encouraged to treat the aristocratic officials with great awe and respect. The middle class was mostly Chinese. Like the Spanish in the Philippines, the Dutch came to fear the growing Chinese community, a fear that sometimes led to a massacre of Chinese in Batavia. The lower class included not only the peasants but also Javanese merchants.

Denied real power, the Javanese royal courts turned inward to refine the traditional culture. Many Dutch found Javanese culture seductive and took local wives, owned slaves, dressed in Javanese clothes, and indulged in the delicious spicy curries, now enriched by American chilies. Other Dutch, however, criticized this behavior. Whatever their attitude toward

local customs, most Dutch lived in Batavia, which was built to resemble a city in the Netherlands. The Dutch, who recognized religious freedom at home, spent little money on Christian missions.

Southeast Asians and the World Economy

During the Early Modern Era, Southeast Asia became even more crucial to the developing world economy. Some historians point to the significance of the Philippine city of Manila in 1571, which became the first hub linking Asia and the Americas across the Pacific. Each year, Philippine crops and other Asian products, including Chinese silk and porcelain, were brought to Manila for export to Mexico. From there, some products were shipped on to Europe on Spanish galleons. These ships symbolized the new global reality. More than half the silver mined in the Americas ended up in China, giving the Asian economy a great push and encouraging increased production of Philippine sugar, Chinese tea, and Indian textiles. The Manila galleon trade was highly speculative, since Spanish businessmen bet their fortunes that the galleons would arrive in Mexico safely. Pirates, storms, and other obstacles made the voyages dangerous. The unpredictable galleon trade fostered a "get-rich-quick" mentality rather than a long-term strategy to bring prosperity to the Philippines.

Despite all the economic changes, Southeast Asians retained considerable continuity with the past. The West was not yet dominant, except in a few widely scattered outposts such as Melaka, the Spice Islands, and the Philippines. European interlopers had to compete with Chinese, Arab, Indian, and Southeast Asian merchants. Nor were Europeans the only growing political power. The Vietnamese, continuing their long expansion down the Vietnamese coast, had annexed the Mekong Delta by the late 1600s, and the Siamese forced the French to leave. In brief, the European powers had entered a wealthy, open, and dynamic region. Only by the eighteenth century did the Southeast Asian commercial society begin to collapse under the weight of accelerating Western activity and internal strife.

LO³ Early Modern China and New Challenges

Two dynasties, the Ming followed by the Qing (ching), ruled China for more than half a millennium, between the overthrow of the Mongols and the advent of a republic in 1912 (see Map 18.3), marking one of the great eras of orderly

Interactive Map

Map 18.3
Qing China and East Asia in the Early Modern Era

Qing China remained the colossus of eastern Eurasia, controlling a huge empire that included Tibet, Xinjiang, and Mongolia. Korea and Vietnam remained tributary states of China, but the Russians expanded into eastern Siberia. The Japanese partly secluded themselves from the outside world.

© Cengage Learning

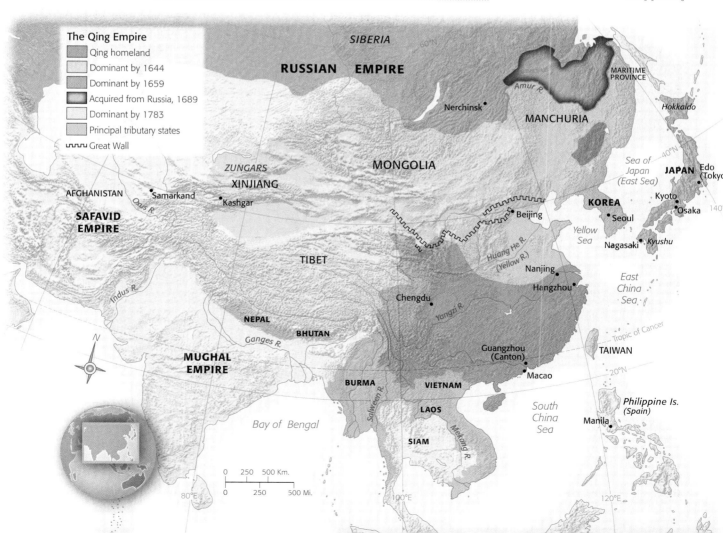

government and social stability in history. Like western Europeans at this time, the Chinese enjoyed widening market networks and more cultivation of cash crops. China still remained one of the strongest, most industrialized societies through the eighteenth century, boasting a vibrant culture and economy. Although encounters with Europeans indicated the challenges ahead just as China began to experience political and technological decay, no other country could match the size, wealth, and power of Early Modern China.

The Later Ming Dynasty

China under the Ming (1368–1644) remained strong and dynamic. The imperial political system administered by the mandarins was supported by a highly productive agriculture and the world's largest, most diversified commercial economy. Although heavily regulated, commercial activity provided the people with numerous products and services, and the Mings' rebuilding of the transportation network centered on the Grand Canal made it easier to ship

Internet Guide for China Studies (*http://www.sino.uni-heidelberg.de/igcs/*). A good collection of links maintained at Germany's Heidelberg University.

goods. Cotton, silk, and tea were exported to Japan and Southeast Asia for silver and spices.

For centuries, China had been among the world leaders in scientific thought and technological invention. This inventiveness continued: late Ming and early Qing Chinese developed better cotton gins, spinning wheels, and other technologies for textile and silk production, which fostered growth and the employment of many more workers. Chinese also continued to publish scientific books. At the same time, however, Ming China turned somewhat inward. Always self-sufficient and self-centered, China became increasingly ethnocentric, even anti-foreign; the great maritime voyages of the early fifteenth century had ended, and the Ming court increasingly concentrated on home affairs and the defense of the northern borders. Although some foreign merchants continued to come to China, and Chinese merchants still went to Southeast Asia, the Ming launched a period of increased isolation, in contrast to the cosmopolitanism of the earlier Tang, Song, and Yuan periods. Misrule and other mounting problems helped undercut the Ming and led to dynastic change.

> **❝** The imperial political system administered by the mandarins was supported by a highly productive agriculture and the world's largest, most diversified commercial economy. **❞**

During the later 1500s, crop failures, which caused famine, and a terrible plague killed millions in north China. In the 1590s, the Ming had to dispatch soldiers and ships to defend their Korean vassal from the Japanese, at a huge cost to the treasury. Adding to the pressure, Japanese pirates ravaged the southern coast and peasant revolts broke out. These problems opened the doors to the Manchus (MAN-chooz), a seminomadic pastoral people from Manchuria who were angry at the migration of Chinese settlers into their homeland. United under a strong chief, the Manchus found collaborators among Chinese who were tired of the Ming failures. While peasant rebellions rocked the country, Manchu forces swept into China on horseback, routing the Ming; however, it took several decades to occupy and pacify the country.

The Qing Empire: Society and Culture

The new Manchu rulers installed the Qing dynasty, which ruled from 1644 to 1912. The first Qing rulers were exceptionally competent overseers. Although they retained their ethnic identity, forbidding Manchu intermarriage with Chinese, the Manchus knew that to be successful they would have to adopt Chinese institutions and culture to win the support of the Chinese people. Hence, like most earlier foreign rulers, the Manchus underwent voluntary assimilation to Chinese ways. Chinese served in high offices, and many villagers scarcely knew China had foreign rul-

CHRONOLOGY	
China, 1450–1750	
1368–1644	Ming dynasty
1557	Portuguese base at Macao
1610	Death of Matteo Ricci in Beijing
1644–1912	Qing dynasty
1689	Treaty of Nerchinsk

ers. Like earlier dynasties, the Qing relied on the mandarins, scholars educated in the Confucian classics, for administration.

Kangzi and Yongzheng

Some Qing emperors were outstanding managers and hard workers, aware of their awesome responsibility and willing to temper arbitrary power. The most admired Qing ruler, the reflective Kangzi (kang-shee) (r. 1661–1722), loved to tour the provinces inspecting public works and joining hunting expeditions. Like other emperors, he was also a noted writer and painter, exemplifying the Confucian ideal of the virtuous ruler. His son and successor, Yongzheng (young-cheng) (r. 1723–1735), tried to improve social conditions. For example, he ordered that anyone held in hereditary servile status anywhere in the empire be freed. The law was aimed at groups in remote regions who still practiced forms of slavery.

The Manchus created the greatest Eurasian land empire since the Mongols, making China one of the world's major political powers. Qing armies reasserted Chinese control of the western and northern frontier, annexing Xinjiang (shin-chang) ("New Dominions"), a desert region largely inhabited by Turkish-speaking Muslims, and Mongolia. For the first time in Chinese history, peace prevailed along the northern and western borderlands. Tibet, long a tributary state to China, was brought into the Manchu fold. The Qing also incorporated Taiwan, off the east coast. This large, fertile island's original inhabitants were Malay peoples, but Chinese began immigrating there in large numbers in the 1600s.

> "The Manchus created the greatest Eurasian land empire since the Mongols, making China one of the world's major political powers."

Qing Social Order

Ming and Qing China owed their political and social stability in part to the Chinese gentry, whose power was based on their combined possession of land and office in an agrarian-based bureaucratic empire. As landlords and moneylenders, the gentry had dominated economic life in villages since the Tang dynasty. Because they owned land and could afford tutors, the gentry men also received a formal education and held scholarly degrees. Under the Ming, a close relationship had developed between the local gentry and the imperial bureaucracy, a relationship that continued under the Qing. Together the Chinese gentry and the Manchu rulers sought to preserve the status quo.

Women had a complex status in the patriarchal society of Qing China. The education of women was frequently debated among the elite and was encouraged by some intellectuals. Some women from

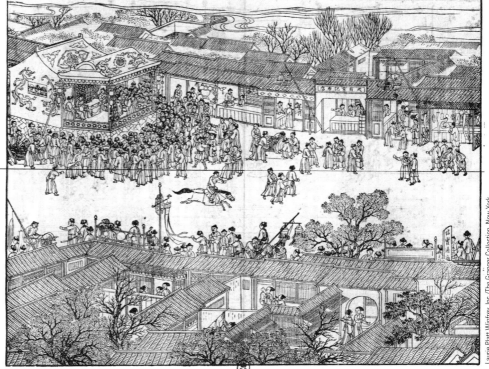

Emperor Kangxi The Qing emperor Kangxi had one of the longest reigns in Chinese history, and his birthdays were given lavish public celebrations. In this print of Beijing, a crowd gathers around the royal dais, while women observe the festivities from courtyards (foreground) and shopkeepers look on from their businesses.

Laurie Platt Winfrey, Inc./The Granger Collection, New York

gentry and merchant families were educated informally, reading and even writing literature. However, elite women also had limited physical mobility because of foot-binding, a custom that was introduced half a millennium earlier but that only became widespread during the Ming. Peasant women were usually illiterate but nonetheless played a key economic role. In the cloth industry, the men planted the cotton, but the women picked the crop, processed it into yarn, and wove the finished product for sale. In many districts, however, peasant women were gradually marginalized as their menfolk or large commercial farmers took over their livelihood.

Neo-Confucianism

Along with social conditions and steady leadership, philosophy also contributed to the stability of the Ming and Qing period. A renaissance of Confucian thought flourished during the Ming and early Qing, when changing times seemed to call for something more than mere memorization of Confucian classics written in the Classical Era. In response to these changes, some scholars developed an interpretation of Confucianism, known as neo-Confucianism, that incorporated elements of Buddhism and Daoism, stressed rational thinking, and reemphasized the natural goodness of people. Some Ming and Qing philosophers offered ideas similar to those of such European philosophers as Sir Francis Bacon, René Descartes, and John Locke. Like Bacon, the neo-Confucian Wang Yang-Ming (1472–1529) pondered the unity of knowledge and conduct, concluding that the first necessarily required the second. Like Descartes, Wang wondered how people know the external world and concluded that "whatever we see, feel, hear, or in any wise conceive or understand is as real as ever."[6] Like Bacon and Locke, many scholars espoused the idea that the mind is reason. A few Chinese scholars, such as the philosopher and poet Tai Chen, studied knowledge from other societies.

 **A Visual Sourcebook of Chinese Civilization** (*http://depts.washington.edu/chinaciv/*). A wonderful collection of essays, illustrations, and other useful material on Chinese History.

However, as neo-Confucianism became more influential, it turned into a new orthodoxy, limiting Chinese interest in alternative ideas. Some Qing scholars wrote that no more writing was needed, because the truth had been made clear by ancient thinkers: all that was left was to practice their teachings. By the 1700s, fewer Chinese intellectuals showed much interest in practical inquiry or technological development. Neo-Confucianism reinforced a grow-ing social rigidity, including increasing male dominance over women. Thus, although it contributed to the unparalleled continuity of Chinese society, Neo-Confucianism was hostile to originality or ideas from outside.

Art and Literature in Qing China

While intellectual inquiry began to stagnate, China's art and literature, in contrast, remained creative. As they had for centuries, artists painted landscapes featuring misty distances, soaring mountains, and angular pine trees. However, many innovative painters drew on Daoist mysticism to create fanciful scenes at odds with tradition, such as Zhu Da (ca. 1626–1705), who painted bizarre conceptions of nature. Qing authors wrote some of China's greatest fiction. In the early 1700s, the novel *The Scholars,* by Wu Jingzi (woo ching-see), satirized the examination system and revealed the foibles of the pompous and the ignorant. Likewise, *The Story of the Stone* by Cao Xueqin (tsao swee-chin), often considered China's greatest novel, used a large and declining gentry family to discuss, and sometimes satirize, Qing life.

China and the World Economy

China in the later Ming and early Qing had commercial vitality, flourishing industrial production, and extensive foreign trade. Indeed, the Chinese, whose goods often sold hundreds of miles from where they were produced, enjoyed the world's largest and best-integrated commercial economy (see Witness to the Past: A Mandarin's Critique of Chinese Movements). Government taxation policies encouraged both agriculture and industry. A Chinese official wrote in 1637 that there was at least one cotton loom in every ten houses. Gradually, the fertile lower Yangzi (yahng-zeh) Basin, linked by the Yangzi River and Grand Canal to west and north China, became China's industrial heartland, commercial hub, and most prosperous region. Throughout the 1700s, the people of the Yangzi Basin enjoyed living standards comparable to those of the world's other wealthiest regions, England and the Netherlands, both enriched by overseas colonization.

Ming and early Qing China remained a major force in an international economy. China exported such products and resources as porcelain, cotton textiles, silk, tea, quicksilver, and zinc, and was a market for and source of valuable products. As Europeans shipped silver to China to pay for Chinese products, Chinese production increased in response. Chinese population growth was also due to China's link to the international economy, a result of the introduction by Spanish merchants of new crops from the Americas as well as Chinese development of a new fast-growing rice. The thriving economy served a population that reached 250 or 300 million by 1750, one-quarter of the world total. Several major cities had more than 1 million residents, including Nanjing (nahn-JING), Beijing, and Guangzhou (gwong-joe) (known in the West as Canton).

However, despite Ming and Qing China's economic dynamism, full-scale capitalism and industrialization did not develop, a result that has puzzled historians. The commercial revolution and technological advances of the Tang, Song, and Ming failed to bring about in China the revolutionary changes that transformed western European feudalism into capitalism. One reason was that, unlike the English and Dutch, the Chinese lacked an overseas empire that could be exploited to acquire capital for investment. Another basic difference from Europe was the continuity of Chinese traditions. The Han pattern was continued in essentials by the Sui, the Sui by the Tang, and so on in unbroken succession until 1912. In addition, with a fast-growing population,

Courtesy of the Trustees of the British Museum

China had no labor shortage and hence no great spur for technological innovation. Its economy met its basic needs well.

The relations between the imperial government and the merchants may also have been a factor in preventing full-scale capitalism. The imperial system heavily restricted and taxed the merchant class, a major difference from early modern Europe, where big business enterprises and the commercial middle class had a growing influence in politics. During the Song commercial revolution, many mandarins came from merchant backgrounds and tended to protect their family's enterprises as well as business generally, but by the Qing this was no longer true. The government also deprived the merchants of valuable goods, and ultimately inhibited capitalism, by maintaining monopolies over the production and distribution of essential commodities, including arms, textiles, pottery, salt, iron, and wine.

Indeed, few opportunities for unrestricted entrepreneurship existed in Ming and Qing China. Government policies reflected China's priorities as a

Chinese Porcelain Like other peoples around Eurasia, people in southwestern Asia prized Chinese porcelain like the bowl shown above. The Turkish miniature painting below shows several valued pieces of Chinese porcelain, probably part of a bride's dowry, being carried in a decorated cart for display during a wedding procession.

Topkapi Palace Museum

Witness to the Past

A Mandarin's Critique of Chinese Merchants

In the late sixteenth century, a Ming official, Zhang Han (chang han) (1511–1593), wrote an essay criticizing merchants. Because he was from a wealthy merchant family, Zhang had the ambivalent attitude toward merchants that was typical of the Confucian elite of the day. He asserted that merchants were greedy, self-serving, arrogant, and pampered, but he also admired the products provided by commerce and the efficiency with which they were distributed throughout the empire. And he suggested that China could benefit from lower taxes on mercantile activity.

Money and profit are of great importance to men. They seek profit, then suffer by it, yet they cannot forget it. They exhaust their bodies and spirits, run day and night, yet they still regard what they have gained as insufficient. Those who become merchants eat fine food and wear elegant clothes. . . . Opportunistic persons attracted by their wealth offer to serve them. Pretty girls in beautiful long-sleeved dresses and delicate slippers play stringed and wind instruments for them and compete to please them. Merchants boast that their wisdom and ability are such as to give them a free hand in affairs. They believe that they know all the possible transformations in the universe and therefore can calculate all the changes in the human world, and that the rise and fall of prices are under their command. They are confident that they will not make one mistake in a hundred in their calculations. These merchants do not know how insignificant their wisdom and ability really are. As [the *Chuang Tzu*, an ancient Daoist text] says: "Great understanding is broad and unhurried; little understanding is cramped and busy."

Because I have traveled to many places during my career as an official, I am familiar with commercial activities and business conditions in various places. . . . Those who engage in commerce, including the foot peddler, the cart peddler, and the shopkeeper, display not only clothing and fresh foods from the fields but also numerous luxury items such as priceless jade from [K'un-lun], pearls from the [southern] island of Hainan, gold from Yunnan (in southwest China), and corals from Vietnam. These precious items, coming from the mountains or the sea, are not found in central China. But people in remote areas and in other countries, unafraid of the dangers and difficulties of travel, transport these items step by step to the capital, making it the most prosperous place in the empire. . . . The profits from the tea and salt trades are especially great, but only large-scale merchants can undertake these businesses. Furthermore, there are government regulations on their distribution. . . .

Turning to the taxes levied on Chinese merchants, though these taxes are needed to fill the national treasury, excessive exploitation should be prohibited. . . . But today's merchants are often stopped on the road [at checkpoints] for additional payments and also suffer extortions from the [marketplace] clerks. Such exploitation is hard and bitter enough but, in addition, the merchants are taxed twice. How can they avoid becoming more and more impoverished? . . . Levying taxes on merchants is a bad policy. We should tax people according to their degree of wealth or poverty.

Thinking About the Reading

1. What criticisms does Zhang make of merchants?
2. In Zhang's view, what benefits does China gain from merchant activity?
3. How does Zhang believe merchant activity could be stimulated?

Source: Reprinted with permission of The Free Press, a Division of Simon & Schuster Inc., from *Chinese Civilization and Society*, A Sourcebook, Second Revised & Expanded Edition by Patricia Buckley Ebrey. Copyright © 1993 by Patricia Buckley Ebrey. All rights reserved.

centralized, agriculture-based empire. Those from Fujian (fu-JEN) province, on the southeast coast, remained prominent in Asian trade throughout the Early Modern Era, especially in Southeast Asia.

These fundamental differences from European patterns deflected Chinese energies inward at a fateful turning point in world history, leaving the world's oceans open to Western enterprise.

Confronting Western Challenges

Although it turned inward, China did not cut itself off completely from the outside world. In the 1500s and 1600s, European ships seeking to acquire silk, tea, porcelain, lacquer ware, and other products reached Chinese shores. The Portuguese landed on the China coast in 1514 and began a troubled relationship with China by failing to request permission from imperial officials to trade. They earned reputations as pirates and religious fanatics. With their naval forces spread thinly around Asia and Africa, the Portuguese were no match for Chinese armed junks. In 1557, to stop the piracy, the emperor allowed the Portuguese to establish a trading base at a small unpopulated peninsula, Macao (muh-cow), near Guangzhou on the southeast coast. By the 1580s, Macao had a population of 10,000, including some 500 Portuguese, several hundred African slaves, and Chinese and Japanese merchants.

> "Although it turned inward, China did not cut itself off completely from the outside world."

Matteo Ricci: The Jesuits in China

Christian missionaries from Europe, especially Jesuits, also became active in the late Ming and early Qing. The most influential Jesuit missionary, the Italian Matteo Ricci (ma-TAY-o REE-chee) (1552–1610), was a brilliant scholar and linguist trained in law, mathematics, and geography. In 1583 he entered China from Macao to study Confucianism and foster an interest in Christianity among Confucian scholars. Ricci impressed Chinese officials, and he began training young scholars for the civil service exams. Eventually the emperor allowed Ricci and his Jesuit colleagues to settle in Beijing. Armed with his knowledge of European Renaissance science, Ricci became a scientific adviser to the imperial court, helping improve clocks, calendars, and astronomical observations. On Ricci's death, the Chinese buried him with honors in Beijing. Despite earning Chinese respect, Ricci attracted only a few converts to his faith.

 Journals: Matteo Ricci This story about Jesuit missionaries in China provides an interesting look at the nexus of religion and politics in the early seventeenth century.

For their part, the Jesuits, chiefly well-educated Italians, were much impressed with a China that seemed to have more wealth and a more impressive technology than did Europe. Jesuits wrote letters home describing Chinese ideas and advanced technology, knowledge that circulated widely in Europe. Enjoying their status, the Jesuits lived like mandarins and wore Chinese clothing. Their admiration of Chinese traditions led them to attempt to harmonize Christianity with Chinese philosophy as a way of attracting support from Chinese scholars. The encounter between the Jesuits and the Chinese certainly expanded the horizons of both parties. A few Chinese even visited Europe, including the Christian convert Michael Alphonsus Shen, who demonstrated chopstick techniques for French king Louis XIV and catalogued Chinese books in the Oxford University library.

The efforts of Ricci and his colleagues laid some groundwork for introducing Roman Christianity to China, and by the end of the seventeenth century, some 100,000 Chinese had become Catholics. But this was a tiny percentage of the vast population, and the less-tolerant Catholic missionaries who followed the early Jesuits made even less progress. After the pope prohibited any attempt at mixing Christianity and Confucianism, the faith had less appeal. In the early 1700s, the Qing banned Christianity for undermining such Chinese traditions as ancestor worship, persecuted converts, and expelled missionaries.

China and Russia

China faced other challenges from Western countries in the 1600s. Before 1800, Europeans could be rebuffed because China was militarily and economically strong, but relations with the Dutch and Russians suggested changes to come. The Dutch had established a base on Taiwan in 1624 but were expelled in 1662 by the militarily stronger Ming resistance forces that had moved to the island. In 1683 the Qing took control of Taiwan, but the Dutch remained active in the China trade. In the late 1600s, Russian expeditions crossed Siberia, seeking trade with China as well as sable fur. Over time they consolidated control of the sparsely populated regions north of Xinjiang and Mongolia. In the late 1600s, Russian and Chinese forces fought several battles in Siberia. The Chinese won these conflicts but granted Russians commercial privileges in the Treaty of Nerchinsk of 1689, the first treaty between China and a European power and a symbol of things to come. Russia maintained its ambitions in eastern Siberia, occasionally testing Qing resolve and power.

Western Influence and Chinese Resistance

Needing little from outside, China still had considerable control of the relations with European powers before the 1800s. The Qing minimized contacts by restricting foreign trade to a few border outposts and southern ports, especially Guangzhou (Canton), and politely but firmly refused diplomatic relations on an equal basis with the Western nations. The Chinese were willing to absorb useful technologies to improve mapmaking and astronomy, as reflected in the fruitful relationship between Emperor Kangzi and the early Jesuits, but they were less interested in foreign ideas like Christianity. China's internal problems, such as overpopulation, mounted just as Western economic, industrial, and military power increased and foreign pressures on China intensified in the later 1700s. Having lived under foreign rulers such as the Mongols and Manchus, the Chinese understood political subjugation but could not comprehend that foreign forces might compel them to rethink their cultural traditions. In late imperial China, culture and nation were one, but during the later 1800s, the 2,000-year-old imperial system declined rapidly.

> 66 The Koreans had learned over the centuries how to mix Chinese influences with local traditions, adapting and modifying Chinese political models, Confucian social patterns, and Mahayana Buddhism. 99

LO⁴ Continuity and Change in Korea and Japan

For much of the Early Modern Era, Korea and Japan remained more isolated than China from the wider world, although both maintained trade relations with China. Korea faced little Western pressure, local issues and conflicts with Japan being far more important. Japanese history also largely revolved around the country's changing economic and social patterns. For a brief period, Japan encountered a significant European presence, but when the experience proved destabilizing, the Japanese became aloof from the West.

Choson Korea

The Koreans had learned over the centuries how to mix Chinese influences with local traditions, adapting and modifying Chinese political models, Confucian social patterns, and Mahayana Buddhism. The Yi (yee) dynasty, which called its state Choson, came to power in 1392 and survived until 1910, a longevity of more than five centuries. Strongly Confucian in orientation, the Yi maintained close relations with China. The early Yi era enjoyed progress in science and technology as well as in writing and literature. However, Choson began to decline in the 1500s, damaged by factional disputes and a Japanese invasion that proved most disastrous for Korea.

In 1592 a Japanese army of 160,000 captured the capital, Seoul (soul); however, the Koreans, aided by China and their invention, in 1519, of the first ironclad naval vessels, fought back and soon prevailed. Forced to the peace table, the Japanese agreed to withdraw, but the Japanese invasion destroyed infrastructure, weakened the central government, and generated severe economic problems.

After these invasions, while the Yi maintained their power, Koreans abandoned or modified some customs borrowed from China. In theory the Yi government remained Confucian, but practice varied considerably. The rigid old class system was modified, with class lines becoming more open. The society also enjoyed economic development and change: agriculture became more productive, and population grew, reaching 7 million by 1750. Commerce and the merchant class also expanded. Growing dissension fostered change after the mid-1700s, laying the foundations for a new era.

CHRONOLOGY

Korea and Japan, 1450–1750

1338–1568	Ashikaga Shogunate
1392–1910	Yi (Choson) dynasty in Korea
1549	Beginning of Christian missions in Japan
1592–1598	Japanese invasions of Korea
1603	Founding of Tokugawa Shogunate
1637	Christian rebellion against Tokugawa
1639–1841	Japanese seclusion policy

Ashikaga Japan and the West

> "During the Ashikaga years, rapid economic and population growth had major consequences for Japanese society."

Japanese society, with its samurai (SAH-moo-rie) warrior class, distinctive mix of Buddhism, Confucianism, and Shinto, and long history of adapting foreign influences, differed dramatically from those of Korea and China. But by 1500, Japan under the Ashikaga (ah-shee-KAH-gah) Shogunate (1338–1568), was experiencing rapid change that strained the samurai-dominated political and social system. The Kyoto-based Ashikaga shoguns, military leaders who dominated the imperial family in Kyoto and the central government, never had much power beyond the capital. A long civil war, during which Western powers intruded into Japan, unsettled conditions even more.

Economic Development

During the Ashikaga years, rapid economic and population growth had major consequences for Japanese society. As technological advances improved agriculture, production per acre tripled, and Japan's population doubled from 16 million in 1500 to perhaps 30 million in 1750. The increased productivity in turn stimulated trade and the gradual development of cities and towns. By 1600 the largest city, Kyoto, may have grown to some 800,000 people. In the cities and towns, merchants and craftsmen organized themselves into guilds that protected their interests.

 Nakasendo Highway: A Journey to the Heart of Japan (http://www.nakasendoway.com/). This website, hosted at Hong Kong University, uses a famous highway to introduce Tokugawa Japan.

As merchants became more active and assertive, they spurred foreign and domestic trade. Japanese traders and pirates began visiting Korea, China, and Southeast Asia, and Japanese settlers immigrated to Vietnam, Cambodia, Siam, and the Philippines. Several thousand Japanese lived in Manila, and one Japanese even became a governor in Siam. Japan also became a major supplier of silver, copper, swords, lacquer ware, rice wine, rice, and other goods to Asia.

Civil War in Japan

If the Ashikaga economic and military expansion had continued, the Japanese might have been in a position to challenge the Portuguese and other Europeans for influence in Southeast Asia. Instead, political power became increasingly decentralized and unstable, as great territorial landowning magnates, called daimyo, increasingly dominated the regions outside of Kyoto. At the beginning of the 1500s, there were several hundred of these daimyo, each with a supporting samurai force. The most powerful hoped to one day rule Japan. However, the rise of the daimyo precipitated a civil war that raged for more than a century, from the mid-1400s into the late 1500s. The military engagements during the centuries of warrior dominance were mainly matters of hand-to-hand conflict between samurai wielding long, slightly curved, two-handed swords with great efficiency, supported by commoner spearmen.

Ashikaga Decline and Rise of the Tokugawa Shogunate

During the late sixteenth and early seventeenth centuries, three men who successively became shogun gradually restored order. All were brutal warlords but also devotees of the refined tea ceremony and pragmatists willing to challenge powerful institutions. The first, Oda Nobunaga (OH-da no-boo-NAG-ga) (1534–1582), was so wild as a youth that a family servant committed suicide hoping this desperate act might settle the young man down. With the slogan "rule the empire by force," Oda, from a minor daimyo family, became a brilliant military strategist who once defeated an army of 25,000 with his own small force of 2,000 men. Oda deposed the last Ashikaga shogun. Hideyoshi Toyotomi (1536–1598), the second warlord and of peasant origins, had ambitions abroad and dreamed of conquering China. When the Koreans refused his request to use Korea as a staging base for the China invasion, he instead sent a large army into Korea in 1592. The fierce Korean resistance forced the Japanese to abandon the effort on Hideyoshi's death. The last of the three, Tokugawa Ieyasu (ee-yeh-YAH-soo) (1542–1616), one of Hideyoshi's chief generals, ended the warfare and became shogun in 1603.

Europeans in Japan

During the civil war, European traders and missionaries arrived in Japan, and their encounter with the Japanese sparked cultural exchange but also conflict. In 1542 the Portuguese reached Japan, starting an encounter that troubled both sides. The European arrivals caused a sensation among Japanese, and the Europeans were equally astonished at what they found. An Italian

Jesuit in the 1500s put it simply: "Japan is a world the reverse of Europe. Hardly in anything do their ways conform to ours."[7] But for all the mutual astonishment, the Europeans had an economic, religious, and military impact. The Portuguese traded Chinese silk for Japanese gold, and soon Spanish and Dutch merchants arrived to compete in the Japanese market.

Francis Xavier (1506–1552), a Spanish Jesuit missionary, began to preach Christianity in 1549. As a result of energetic Spanish and Portuguese missionary efforts, by 1600 perhaps 300,000 Japanese were Christians, out of a total population of some 18 million. But many Japanese grew increasingly suspicious of the missionaries, resented their intolerance of Japanese faiths and local customs, and could not comprehend the fierce competition between rival Catholic orders. Japanese leaders viewed the armed Christian communities as posing a threat to their power.

The Japanese adopted what was useful to them: Western technologies. Major consequences often followed. They acquired, then quickly improved, muskets from the Portuguese and Spanish, and developed new tactics for using them. European guns sharpened warfare and, because even nonsamurai could obtain them, contributed to the breakdown of social class lines. The increasingly common and deadly violence resulting from guns often prompted peasants to seek solace in religion, and some adopted Christianity.

The Tokugawa Shogunate: Stability and Seclusion

The civil war brought on by the rise of the daimyo, and intensified by gunpowder weapons, ended with the Tokugawa Shogunate, which ruled Japan from 1603 to 1868. Tokugawa Ieyasu was a great warrior and able administrator, but also cruel and treacherous. He subdued his rivals and established a shogunate at Tokyo, then known as Edo (ED-doe), presiding over the most centralized state in premodern Japanese history, in striking contrast to the weak Ashikaga shoguns a century earlier.

The Tokugawa leaders imposed a government mixing authoritarian centralization with the rigidly hierarchical social system that emerged in the later Intermediate Era, which resembled medieval European feudalism in some respects. Japan now had a more powerful shogunate than ever before, while the imperial family in Kyoto remained powerless. To discourage rebellion, some members of each daimyo family were required to live in Edo as hostages. The Tokugawa restored the pre–civil war social structure, with the samurais at the top.

> "The civil war brought on by the rise of the daimyo, and intensified by gunpowder weapons, ended with the Tokugawa Shogunate, which ruled Japan from 1603 to 1868."

The Closing of Japan

To stop the conflict between the various Europeans and Catholic orders, Tokugawa closed off Japan from the West and ordered home Japanese traders in Southeast Asia. In the process he ejected the feuding Catholic missionaries and merchants, and broke the power of the Christian communities. This led to a rebellion by Japanese Christians in 1637, to which Tokugawa responded by massacring 37,000 Japanese Christians. But trade with China, Korea, and Southeast Asia continued, with Japan paying for silk with its main mineral resource, silver. In addition, after 1639 a few Dutch traders were allowed to remain and set up a base on a small island, Deshima (DEH-shi-ma), in Nagasaki (nah-gah-SAH-kee) Bay. The Dutch were only interested in commerce, not religious conversion, and for the next two centuries the Dutch base served as Japan's only link to the European world.

Tokugawa Rigidity

Tokugawa leaders believed that society could be frozen in a hierarchical pattern, but under the surface of the rigid Tokugawa rule, new social forces simmered. For example, even though the rulers restricted travel between cities or regions, merchants found ways to evade the rules and move their wares. The Japanese population grew rapidly, straining the country's resources. Thousands of local peasant protests, riots, and uprisings reflected more dramatic discontent. Tokugawa Japan also boasted several large cities, with Tokyo and Osaka each more than 1 million in population by 1800. The cities became centers of complex commercial networks, and their demands fostered agricultural productivity and economic prosperity, especially in the Edo region. Merchants and their values became more influential. By the mid-1700s, Japan was a well-organized country, with rising living standards but growing tensions.

The Tokugawa tried to restrict Japanese women. In contrast to some Asian societies, Japanese women had never been secluded and participated in community life. Some women were literate, and a few became noted writers. Nonetheless, like women in most societies, Japanese women had few legal or property rights, faced arranged marriages, and were encouraged to be dependent on men, all patriarchal customs reinforced during the early Tokugawa period. As a result, severe laws against adultery only punished women. Women in samurai families were raised to be courteous, conciliatory, and humble toward their husbands; however, gender expectations and relations among urban merchant and artisan families were less rigid.

Art and Entertainment

In Tokugawa culture, distinctive new forms also emerged in the 1600s. In the major cities, entertainment districts known as the "floating world" were filled with restaurants, theaters, geisha houses, and brothels. The writer Ihara Saikaku (ee-HAR-oo sigh-KOCK-oo), from a merchant family, chronicled the floating world and satirized urban merchant life in often erotic novels. The master artist Moronobu (more-oh-NOH-boo) introduced the colorful woodblock prints known as ukiyo-e (oo-kee-YO-ee), which celebrated the life of the floating world. Later, landscapes, such as views of Mt. Fuji, became popular themes for woodcuts. By the 1800s, many European artists collected and were influenced by these prints. New theater forms included the bunraku puppet theater and the racy kabuki drama. Aimed particularly at the merchant class, kabuki featured gorgeous costumes, beautiful scenery, and scripts filled with violent passion. Men played all the roles. Professional female impersonators were highly honored and spent years mastering the voice, gestures, and other aspects of femininity.

A new literary device, the seventeen-syllable haiku poem, also became popular. Haiku proved an excellent vehicle for discussing the passage of time or briefly summarizing some action or scene through a series of images, such as the famous presentation by the samurai turned wanderer and greatest haiku poet, Matsuo Basho (BAH-show) (1644–1694), of a sudden event on a quiet pond: "An old pond. Frog jumps in. Sound of water."[8]

ukiyo-e
Colorful Japanese woodblock prints that celebrated the life of the "floating world," the urban entertainment districts of Tokogawa Japan.

bunraku
The puppet theater of Tokugawa Japan.

kabuki
The all-male and racy drama that became the favored entertainment of the urban population in Tokugawa Japan.

haiku
The seventeen-syllable poem that proved an excellent vehicle for discussing the passage of time and the change of seasons in Early Modern Japan.

Kabuki Theater The urban middle classes, especially the merchants and samurais, enjoyed kabuki drama. This eighteenth-century print by one of the most acclaimed artists, Moronobu, shows the audience enjoying a play about a vendetta involving two brothers.

Werner Forman/Art Resource, NY

Tokugawa Stability and Its Costs

Tokugawa Japan largely enjoyed security and peace for 250 years, but it came at a price. Although commerce thrived, Japan, like China, experienced no political transformation or social rejuvenation, because Tokugawa policies preserved rigid social divisions and shielded Japanese from outside influence. The lack of political and social dynamism left the Tokugawa vulnerable to a later return of Western power, as several Western nations rapidly acquired wealth and resources and improved their technology between 1500 and 1850.

When the West intruded in the mid-nineteenth century, the latent tensions between samurai and merchants and between daimyo and shoguns boiled over, and the Tokugawa lost their grip on power. But Japan, unlike China, was able to respond creatively. Japan's history of borrowing from abroad made it uniquely prepared to make the necessary adjustments, and the Japanese could assimilate Western techniques and customs to Japanese traditions, as they had done with Chinese and Western imports in earlier eras. These differences meant that China and Japan eventually met the challenge from the West in very different ways.

Listen to a synopsis of Chapter 18.

Connecting the Early Modern World, 1450–1750

The permanent connecting of the hemispheres that followed Columbus reshaped the world. In the Early Modern Era's new global age, greatly increased communication and mobility resulted in encounters between societies that were once remote from each other. As a result, the exchange among societies of people, diseases, ideas, technologies, resources, and products occurred on a greater scale than ever before. Europeans forged a new world economy, while disrupting, changing, and sometimes destroying the societies they encountered, especially in the Americas and parts of Africa and Southeast Asia. Because of the growing contacts spanning the two hemispheres, for the first time in history an interconnected world became a reality.

But the encounters between Europeans and peoples they could reach only after long sea voyages were only part of the story. The world had many political and economic centers between 1450 and 1750. In the Afro-Eurasian zone, Morocco, the Ottoman Empire, several western European societies, Safavid Persia, Mughal India, China, and a few Southeast Asian societies such as Siam were wealthy, populous, and linked to each other by trade networks and diplomatic ties. They all enjoyed military prowess, had effective states, and fostered creative thinkers. Some African kingdoms, such as Ashante and Buganda, also enjoyed influence and connections to hemispheric trade. No single country or region dominated world politics or the world economy. Yet, the links forged during the Early Modern Era laid a foundation for an even more integrated global system, encompassing even the most remote peoples, in the Modern Era.

 Columbus and the Age of Discovery (http://muweb.millersville.edu/columbus/main/html). This site, maintained by Millersville University, offers many sources related to the linking of the hemispheres during this era.

New Empires and Military Power

From the dawn of recorded history, some peoples have used military power to impose their will on others and create empires. Increasing wealth and power, as well as more deadly weapons, led some Early Modern Era societies to build large empires. Some, such as Safavid Persia, Mughal India, Qing China, and Russia, ruled land empires.

In contrast to these empires, which annexed nearby and often sparsely populated territories, the Ottoman Turks controlled large areas of southeastern Europe, western Asia, and North Africa, and the Omani Arabs established footholds in East Africa. The Portuguese, Spanish, Dutch, English, and French empires were even more ambitious, incorporating distant peoples in Africa, Asia, and the Americas. These conquests created empires on a geographic scale never imagined before.

Gunpowder Empires

Historians characterize most Early Modern empires as "gunpowder empires" because they depended on bigger and better gunpowder weapons, including cannon mounted on ships, field artillery, and guns. Gunpowder empires dominated Eurasia and the Americas. Various Asian and European societies sought to acquire resources in neighboring societies by building empires rather than relying chiefly on trade. Only a few European countries, however, had the means to dominate very distant societies, and also the incentive: the quest for "gold, god, and glory." The worldwide exploration and conquest that took place during this era resulted from the transformation of European societies by various forces—the rise of capitalism, powerful merchants, and competitive, centralizing states, as well as by rivalry among Christian churches—while improved military and maritime technology provided the means.

Europeans took advantage of their economic growth and military expansion to improve their position in the world and to compete more effectively for resources in the East, where Islamic societies, India, and China had long enjoyed the most political, economic, and cultural power. Advanced naval and military technology, including gunpowder weapons unknown in the Americas and in much of Africa and Southeast Asia, allowed the Portuguese to seize various African and Asian trading ports, and the Spanish to construct a huge empire in the Americas. The Dutch, English, and French soon followed, establishing footholds in North America, the Caribbean, coastal Africa, and southern Asia. Europeans controlled Atlantic shipping and also gained considerable power over Indian Ocean trade, which brought them great wealth. As the English adventurer Sir Walter Raleigh recognized in 1608, "Who so commands the sea commands the trade of the world;

who so commands the trade of the world commands the riches of the world."[1]

A Polycentric World

Despite the growth of empires, the Early Modern world had varied centers of political and economic power, a situation known as polycentrism. Despite their weaponry, Europeans did not become dominant all over the world during this era. European power was limited in Asia, the Middle East, and parts of Africa and South America, and much of North America and the Pacific remained untouched by European exploration. For much of the era, the Ottomans, Mughals, and Chinese were more politically, economically, and culturally influential in Eurasia than European societies. Many Muslims admired Mughal India, which became a destination for merchants, writers, and religious scholars. A Persian poet proclaimed: "Great is India, the Mecca of all in need. A journey to India is of essence to any man made worthy by knowledge and skill."[2] The major Asian states also collected far larger tax revenues than did any European government. Societies in Eurasia, from China to England, and in Africa, from Buganda to Songhai (song-GAH-ee), extended their power into nearby territories, centralized their governments, fostered commerce, and worked to integrate ethnic minorities into the broader society.

The era was dynamic, as encounters fostered compromises and information exchange. Across Eurasia, varied societies experienced economic innovation, free markets, industrialization, and rising living standards, and cities such as Amsterdam in Holland, Isfahan (is-fah-HAHN) in Persia, and Ayuthia (uh-YUT-uh-yuh) in Siam became bustling trade crossroads. Foreign merchants, such as the Dutch and Persians at Ayuthia or Surat, had to adapt to local customs to succeed. Sometimes, as in Siam, Tokugawa Japan, and Morocco, Europeans who disregarded local customs or threatened local governments were expelled. Many Asians and Africans adapted ideas from other cultures to meet their own needs. Among other leaders, the Chinese emperor Kangzi (KANG-see), the Siamese king Narai (na-RY), the Mughal sultan Akbar (AK-bahr), and the Kongo king Alfonso I showed a keen interest in Western ideas and technologies. Narai also borrowed architectural styles and medical knowledge from the Persians and Chinese.

The main European advantage had been in acquiring the resources of the Americas for exploitation, often using enslaved African labor. But the large-scale trans-Atlantic slave trade became possible because the kings or chiefs of some African states, such as Ashante (ah-SHAN-tee) and Dahomey (da-ho-MAY), profited by collaborating with it. Similarly, Spanish rule in the Americas survived only because the conquerors ultimately made compromises with Indian societies. In the Spanish empire, as well as in other empires of the era such as the Ottoman and Mughal, laws recognized local customs, and different groups often maintained their own legal codes.

Innovative thought reflected the vigor of many societies. Science and technology remained creative all over Eurasia. The Chinese and British, for example, published important scientific books and invented new technologies, especially for the textile industry. New astronomical observatories were built in China, India, and the Middle East, although Europeans had by now developed a much keener interest than Asians in clocks and mathematics.

Dutch Diplomats In this print, a Dutch delegation, eager to make an alliance with the Kongolese against the Portuguese, prostrate themselves before the Kongolese king, sitting on his throne under an imported chandelier, in 1642.

From Olfert Dapper, *Beschreibung von Africa,* Amsterdam, 1670

Japan's fostering of schools gave it the world's highest literacy rate, and Siam and Burma also enjoyed high rates of literacy. Leaders of the European Renaissance, Reformation, and Enlightenment, Sufi mystics in the Ottoman and Mughal Empires, the Hindu bhakti (BUK-tee) movement in India, and some Chinese thinkers challenged accepted wisdom. Various European and Chinese philosophers emphasized reason, as did some Latin Americans, such as the Mexican nun and scientist Sor Juana Ines de la Cruz. Indeed, some participants in the European Enlightenment were inspired by their growing knowledge of secular China, which was ruled by emperors who dabbled in philosophy. A French ambassador in 1688 praised Qing China for promoting "virtue, wisdom, prudence, good faith, sincerity, charity, gentleness, honesty [and] civility."[3]

European achievement of global power was not inevitable: in this era China also had a sizeable empire and considerable potential. Early Modern China, boasting the world's largest commercialized economy, remained the engine of the Eurasian economy. China and Europe experienced commercial growth, increases in cash cropping, growing industrial production, and widening marketing networks. The maritime expansion of Europe, however, contrasted sharply with that of the Chinese. Just as western Europeans turned outward, competing with each other for strategic advantage, the Chinese pulled back from their grand maritime expeditions of the early 1400s; their government enjoyed huge budget surpluses until the late 1700s and did not need colonies or foreign trade to prosper. In addition, the Chinese government treated rich merchants warily, viewing commerce as a threat to Confucian values. In contrast, western European merchants had the support of their mercantilist governments, especially in England, the Netherlands, Spain, and France.

Gunpowder and Warfare

Gunpowder weapons were not new. The Chinese invented gunpowder and then made the first true guns in the tenth century C.E., primarily for defensive purposes. The Mongols improved these Chinese weapons into a more effective offensive force, to blow open city gates; by 1241 gunpowder had reached Europe. Early Modern Europeans, Turks, Mughals, and Chinese owed their strength in part to improvements in gunpowder weaponry.

As they spread around Eurasia and North Africa, gunpowder weapons changed warfare. Europeans learned how to make particularly deadly weapons, improving the technology in part because they had easier access to metals. In Europe—full of competitive, often hostile states—no ruler had a monopoly on weapons, so rulers had an incentive to constantly improve their armaments to maintain the balance of power. As a result, warfare among Europeans became far more deadly. The Portuguese, Dutch, and English slaughtered each other in Southeast Asia, and the English and French fought long

wars in North America. A similar increase in battlefield casualties came in Japan in the civil war era of the 1500s, when Japanese sword-smiths learned how to replicate Portuguese and Spanish guns and cannon. Japanese small arms soon proved superior to European rifles. In contrast, the Ottomans did not create a class of Turkish and Arab craftsmen and instead relied heavily on hiring European craftsmen to manufacture their military and naval technology.

But Asians took the development of their gunpowder arsenals only so far. With gunpowder weapons, the Qing greatly expanded China's land frontier deep into Central Asia and Tibet, thereby stabilizing their border regions. After that, secure in their power, the Manchu emperors had little need to increase their offensive capability, while the land-oriented Mughals saw little gain in developing naval armaments. The Chinese, Japanese, and Koreans all had some naval power but no interest in challenging the Europeans in the Indian Ocean. When the Chinese came into contact with foreign firearms in 1500s, they found them superior to their own. Nonetheless, Chinese firearms proved adequate for ejecting the Dutch from Taiwan and the Russians from the Amur Valley in the 1600s. But two centuries later, superior European military technology dramatically changed the hemispheric balance of power.

The Emerging World Economy

With the opening of the Atlantic and Pacific Oceans to regular sea travel, a global network of economic and political relationships emerged that increasingly shaped the destinies of people around the world. Rather than the luxuries of earlier times, such as silks and spices, long-distance trade increasingly moved bulk items: essential natural resources, such as sugar and silver from the Americas, and manufactured goods, such as textiles from Europe and Asia. Traders moved commodities and capital faster and more cheaply over greater distances than ever before. These trends wove together different societies into a world economy. Western Europeans usually benefited the most, and Europeans laid the foundations for a new global system to emerge after 1750.

The New Trading System

The capitalist market economy that gradually developed was increasingly centered on northwestern Europe, especially England and the Netherlands, but a half-dozen other European countries were also enriched by trade (see map). The Spanish conquest of the Americas provided huge quantities of silver from Peru, Bolivia, and Mexico, which financed expansion of the European economy and enabled Europeans to gain access to Asian markets. The Spanish establishment of a base at Manila in 1571

Interactive Map

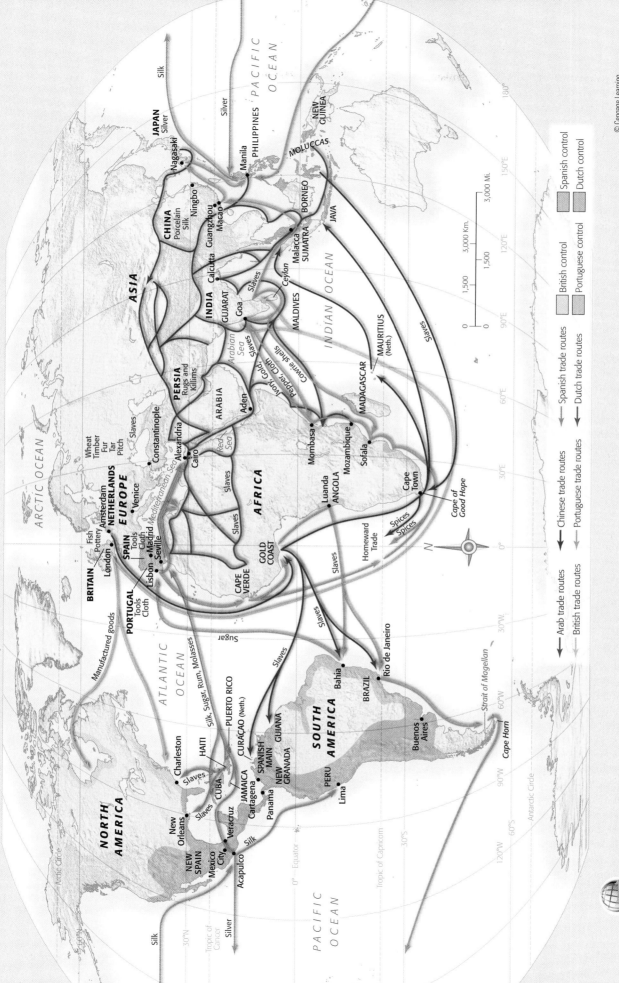

Early Modern Trade Routes

Between 1500 and 1700, the world economy developed and new trade routes proliferated. Major maritime routes linked Asia and the Americas across the Pacific; Europe, Asia, and the Americas across the Atlantic; and eastern and southern Asia with Africa and Europe across the Indian Ocean.

© Cengage Learning

Map legend:

Spanish control
Dutch control
British control
Portuguese control

Arab trade routes
British trade routes
Chinese trade routes
Portuguese trade routes
Spanish trade routes
Dutch trade routes

Labels on map:

ARCTIC OCEAN
ATLANTIC OCEAN
PACIFIC OCEAN
INDIAN OCEAN
Mediterranean Sea
Arabian Sea
Red Sea

NORTH AMERICA
SOUTH AMERICA
EUROPE
AFRICA
ASIA

BRITAIN — London
NETHERLANDS — Amsterdam
SPAIN — Madrid, Seville
PORTUGAL — Lisbon
Venice, Constantinople
Cairo, Alexandria
ARABIA — Aden
PERSIA — Rugs and Kilims
INDIA — Gujarat, Goa, Calcutta
Ceylon
MALDIVES
CHINA — Porcelain, Silk, Ningbo, Guangzhou, Macao
JAPAN — Silver, Nagasaki
PHILIPPINES — Manila
MOLUCCAS
BORNEO
SUMATRA
Malacca
JAVA
NEW GUINEA

AFRICA
Mombasa
Mozambique
Sofala
Luanda — ANGOLA
GOLD COAST
CAPE VERDE
Cape Town — Cape of Good Hope
MADAGASCAR
MAURITIUS (Neth.)

NEW SPAIN — Mexico City, Acapulco, Veracruz
New Orleans
Charleston
CUBA, HAITI, JAMAICA, PUERTO RICO (Neth.), CURAÇAO (Neth.)
Cartagena, Panama
SPANISH MAIN
NEW GRANADA
GUIANA
PERU — Lima
BRAZIL — Bahia, Rio de Janeiro
Buenos Aires
Strait of Magellan
Cape Horn

Trade goods labels: Silk, Silver, Porcelain, Spices, Slaves, Gold, Ivory, Pepper, Cloth, Cowrie shells, Manufactured goods, Sugar, Silk, Sugar, Rum, Molasses, Wheat, Timber, Fur, Tar, Pitch, Fish, Pottery, Tools, Cloth, Homeward Trade

Arctic Circle
Tropic of Cancer
Equator
Tropic of Capricorn
Antarctic Circle

30°N, 60°N, 0°, 30°S, 60°S
120°W, 90°W, 60°W, 30°W, 0°, 30°E, 60°E, 90°E, 120°E, 150°E, 180°

0 1,500 3,000 km.
0 1,500 3,000 Mi.

provided an essential economic link between eastern Eurasia and the Americas. European exploration and settlement in the Americas brought access to resources such as timber, marine mammals, fish, and wildlife.

Growing commercial activity stimulated production for the market, in mining and manufacturing but especially in tropical agriculture. Highly profitable plantations that sprung up around the Caribbean Basin, along the Atlantic coast of North and South America, and on the Atlantic and Indian Ocean islands and the Philippines reflected the expansion of production. A growing trans-Atlantic slave trade provided cheap labor to the American plantations, enabling them to produce inexpensive calories for Europe in the form of sugar and, after 1700, abundant cotton for English mills. Thousands of slaves obtained in eastern Europe, East Africa, Sri Lanka, and Indonesia also labored for European and Muslim enterprises in the Middle East, South Africa, and Southeast Asia.

As a result of the growing commercial activity, by 1750 millions of people worked thousands of miles from their place of birth or otherwise experienced lives very different from those of their ancestors. Chinese merchants lived on Java; Persians served in the Siamese government; Turkish soldiers fought for the sultans of Acheh (AH-cheh) in Sumatra; Portuguese settled in Mozambique; Kongolese labored in Brazil; and French traders explored the Mississippi Basin.

Asia and Europe in the New World Economy

The transition to a European-dominated trading system took place over several centuries. Before the 1800s, Asia boasted the bulk of world economic activity. Asians produced some 80 percent of goods as late as 1775, and this production had probably increased since 1500. The industries of China and India remained the twin pillars of Asian commerce well into the 1700s. Indian textiles such as cashmere and cotton cloth were so popular in Asia, Africa, and Europe that they almost constituted a form of currency. Handicraft industries also flourished in the Ottoman Empire, Persia, Sri Lanka, Burma, Siam, and Java during the sixteenth and seventeenth centuries. These societies imported raw materials from India (including raw cotton), China (especially silk), and Japan (copper) for production into exportable consumer goods. The economies of India and China dwarfed those of any other country. The most economically developed regions within China, Japan, India, and northwestern Europe probably enjoyed comparable standards of living.

Asian merchants, enjoying lower overhead and shrewd business skills, could often outcompete those from Europe. After 1670, Indian merchants even took the Indonesian textile market away from the Dutch. Like Europeans, Asians also traded over long distances. In the 1600s, for example, Arab and Persian traders remained influential at the main Mughal port, Surat, while north Indian merchants were found all over the Persian Gulf.

Many wealthy Asian trading magnates had huge capital resources. A European visitor to Goa in 1510 was amazed at the competition provided by fabulously rich Arab and Indian merchants: "We [Europeans] believe ourselves to be the most astute men that one can encounter, and the people here surpass us in everything. And they can do better calculations by memory than we can do with the pen."[4] European merchants competed best when they were, like the Dutch East Indies Company traders, supported by military force.

European–Asian trade relations often favored Asians. Because Asians had little interest in European manufactured goods such as clothing, which they considered inferior, Europeans bought Asian goods and resources with American silver and gold. For example, Europeans traded with China for products such as tea, so vast amounts of American silver ended up in China, where it served as the basis of the monetary system and promoted economic growth. The Ottoman, Safavid, and Mughal Empires also willingly traded goods for silver, and their goods found a ready market around the world. While European ships carried a growing amount of seaborne trade, European merchants accounted for only a small proportion of trade from India and China. Mughal India traded far more with Central Asians and Ottomans than with the Dutch or English. Asian exports to Europe grew slowly; intra-Asian trade was far larger.

Expanding Trade Networks

The growth of long-distance trade corresponded to the expansion of trade networks operated by different commercial communities. Dutch, English, and French merchants established themselves in India, Southeast Asia, West Africa, eastern Europe, Russia, and the Caribbean Basin. At the same time, Sephardic Jews, originally from Iberia, spread their trading networks throughout western Europe, flourishing particularly in Antwerp, Amsterdam, Seville, and Geneva. Eventually, Jews also became active as merchants in parts of South America, the Caribbean, and the Indian Ocean. The Mendes family, for instance—expelled from Spain in 1492 and eventually based in Istanbul—had business connections in several European cities and helped finance the gem and spice trades across Asia, Europe, and Africa.

Groups specializing in trade were prominent in many lands, and some maintained commercial networks over vast distances. Chinese remained active all over Southeast Asia, establishing permanent settlements in many cities and towns. For example, the Spanish in the Philippines depended on the Chinese merchant class to supply many consumer goods. Traders of French or mixed French and Indian descent traveled deep into the North American continent contacting local peoples. In East Africa, the Omani Arabs had a leading role. In West Africa, Hausa (HOUSE-uh) merchants increasingly dominated the trade networks of the Sudan by the 1600s. The Indian maritime trade network stretched from Arabia, Persia, northeast Africa, and the Red Sea to Melaka, Sumatra, Siam, and China, while their Indian overland trade networks extended across Central Asia, Afghanistan, Tibet, Persia, the Caucasus states, and much of Russia. Armenian merchants based in Safavid Persia flourished in the overland trade from India to Central Asia and the Middle East, and from Persia to Russia, England, and the Baltic. Growing Eurasian trade clearly involved, and often benefited, varied groups.

Environmental Changes

Human activity reshaped the natural world and was influenced by it in turn. As they had for millennia, people tapped the Earth for underground resources, such as coal and iron ore, but large-scale manufacturing, which often pollutes the environment, was found in only a few widely scattered countries, mostly in Eurasia. For farming and light industries, Early Modern economies relied chiefly on traditional power sources, such as people, animals, water, and wind. Nonetheless, natural systems came under more stress as the global population nearly doubled, putting severe pressure on land and resources. Expanding settlements and farming in frontier regions displaced woodlands, grasslands, and wetlands and reduced the variety of plant and animal life. More spectacularly, the exchange of diseases, plants, and animals across the Atlantic altered entire environments and resulted in huge population losses in the Americas.

Climate Change and Population Growth

Between 1300 and 1850, much of the world experienced a fluctuating "Little Ice Age," probably caused by a dimming sun and increased volcanic activity, that had significant consequences for many societies. In North America and Eurasia, this period brought cool temperatures, shorter growing seasons, and famine. The coldest years came between 1570 and 1730, and then through the early 1800s. The lands bordering the North Atlantic saw much colder and wetter conditions, which diminished agricultural production and resulted in widespread starvation in much of Europe. Indeed, harsh weather conditions, combined with occasional outbreaks of bubonic plague, may have been one of the factors that spurred Europeans to seek new lands abroad. Climate change also affected topical regions: West Africa had abundant rain until 1700, when rainfall began diminishing, allowing desert to claim much of the Sahel and pushing savannah farming southward by several hundred miles.

Nonetheless, despite the poor weather, the distribution of new food sources and other resources was widening. For instance, western European societies obtained more food, particularly grain, from eastern Europe, and thus became more linked to that region. Seaborne trade, especially from the Americas, also provided valuable resources, especially to coastal maritime states such as the Netherlands and Britain. Indeed, American crops such as the potato helped Europe stave off even worse climate-related famines. To the east, the Mughals cleared the forests and wetlands of Bengal to create a large area for rice growing, and around the world the expansion of farming came at the expense of shifting cultivators, pastoralists, and food collectors. Some peoples, such as the pastoral Khoikhoi (koi-koi) in South Africa, died off or were enslaved or killed.

Partly because of the spread of food crops, especially from the Americas to Afro-Eurasia, world population increased significantly. In 1500 the earth contained between 400 and 500 million people. Perhaps 60 percent lived in Asia, with China and India each accounting for nearly a quarter of the world total. By 1750 the world population had grown to between 700 and 750 million, probably 80 percent of them peasants living on the land. China and India together, totaling perhaps 400 million, still accounted for over half, while Europe held perhaps 20 percent and Africa 10 percent of the world total.

The Exchange of Diseases, Animals, and Crops

In this era, people, chiefly Europeans and Africans, moved to distant lands, carrying with them species of animals, insects, bacteria, and plants that reshaped local ecosystems. These biological invasions, what historians have termed the Columbian Exchange, particularly accompanied the encounter between Eurasia and the Americas. The European settlers in the Americas brought with them horses and food animals: pigs, chickens, sheep, and cattle. To raise beef cattle, Europeans introduced ranching. Ships returning to Europe carried with them American turkeys, which enriched Eurasian diets.

 The Columbian Exchange (*http://national humanitiescenter.org/ tserve/nattrans/ntecoin- dian/essays/columbian .htm*). Links to essays by Alfred Crosby and more.

The exchange of diseases between the Eastern and Western Hemispheres was not one-way, but it had a greater impact on the Americas than on Eurasia and Africa. Native Americans had never experienced, and hence had no immunity to, Afro-Eurasian diseases such as smallpox, diphtheria, measles, chicken pox, malaria, bubonic plague, cholera, typhoid fever, and influenza. These diseases devastated the Americas. Smallpox brought the greatest known demographic catastrophe in world history, killing off around 90 percent of the peoples of the Americas. This was a much greater percentage of population than that destroyed by the terrible Black Death, which ravaged much of Eurasia and North Africa in the 1300s. The demographic disaster for the Americas emptied productive land and hence paved the way for Europeans to settle the Americas and to import captive Africans for labor. Only in the highlands, such as the Andes Mountains in South America, did European diseases have a smaller impact. In contrast, only a few American diseases, especially syphilis, brought suffering to people in Europe and Africa.

Crop exchanges also proved momentous. Eurasian and African crops transformed some American regions, and required the introduction of new agricultural practices. Most Native Americans had grown crops such as corn (maize) and potatoes on small plots, but settlers found that Afro-Eurasian crops such as wheat, rice, coffee, barley, and sugar were most successfully grown on large farms or estates. Among these imported crops, sugar had the most impact on the Americas, and vast acreage was devoted to its growth, mostly on plantations. Much of the sugar was exported to Europe for use to sweeten foods such as jam and breads, and beverages such as tea and coffee.

American crops spread widely in the Eastern Hemisphere, where they diversified European diets and habits. Tobacco, for instance, gained popularity in China and Europe, generating both avid devotees and opponents who considered it unhealthy or immoral. Many imports, such as tomatoes, made once-bland European meals more varied. Potatoes became a mainstay of the European diet and the major crop grown in several societies, including Ireland and Scotland. Maize could be grown on marginal land and proved a boon in Africa, southwest Asia, and China, where it was planted on unused hillsides. Corn also fed livestock, and the stalks could be used to make huts and sheds. American chilies, hotter than Asian black peppers, proved hugely popular in South and Southeast Asian cooking, and peanuts became a key crop in West Africa. The new foods offered not only a more varied diet but also a healthier one. By 1750 a diner in many cities in the world could enjoy a fruit salad mixing pieces of Southeast Asian bananas and mangos, Chinese peaches, Southwest Asian pears, African watermelons, Mesoamerican papayas, South American pineapples, and Mediterranean grapes.

European expansion and colonization owed much to the spread of the Eurasian biota, a distinct package of plants, animals, and germs that overwhelmed the rest of the world, especially the Americas and, later, Oceania. Eurasian plants, such as wheat and apple trees, and animals, such as cattle, often replaced indigenous ones in the temperate zones of the Americas and, after 1800, Australia and New Zealand. These changes occurred in part because Europeans viewed animals, plants, and land largely as commodities, to be exploited for their own benefit. The English scientist Sir Francis Bacon expressed these attitudes well: "The world is made for man, not man for the world."[5]

Social and Cultural Change

During the Early Modern Era, the growing networks of trade, information, and technology fostered changes in societies all over the world. Some changes resulted from the increasing migration of peoples, voluntarily or by force. Intermarriage or sexual contact between people from different ethnic groups produced new peoples with mixed cultural backgrounds. Other

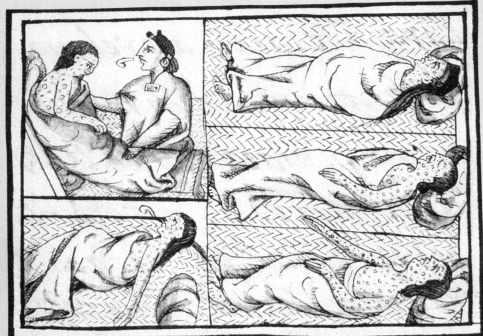

Smallpox Victims in the Americas Eurasian diseases accompanied the Europeans to the Americas, causing a catastrophic loss of life for the Native Americans, who had no immunity. As shown in this print from the 1500s, millions of people sickened and died from smallpox.

Biblioteca Medicea Laurenziana

contributing factors were changing economic systems, the growth of international trade, and the exchange of ideas. Encounters with other ways of living stimulated curiosity and fostered rethinking. Several religions expanded their boundaries and sought converts, challenging ancient, indigenous faiths.

Migration and Hybrid Groups

Improved maritime technology made it possible for people to cross vast oceans, leading to a new system of global migration that brought people with very different customs and values together, not always happily. The largest population movement involved Europeans settling in the Americas and bringing with them enslaved Africans but few European women. Women comprised perhaps only one-fifth of the Spanish and Portuguese who went to the Americas; men thus frequently sought partners among Native American and African women.

Intermarriage and sexual relations across social boundaries led to the creation of American societies that contained many mixed-descent people. By 1750, in Latin America and in French colonies such as Haiti and Louisiana, a large part of the population blended European and Native American backgrounds, creating mestizos, or European and African ancestries, fostering mulattos. For example, many people in Mexico City were mestizo, while in New Orleans blacks and mulattos predominated. In turn, these groups' cultures often mixed the varying social influences, as in northeast Brazil, where people blended African religions and Catholic traditions. Unlike English North America, where any African ancestry usually meant classification as black, in much of Latin America, a complex hierarchy of social categories developed based on gradations of skin color.

Migration and intermarriage also occurred in the Eastern Hemisphere. Dutch and Portuguese adventurers and merchants, most of them men, settled in southern Africa and the port cities of South and Southeast Asia, often taking wives from the local population. Some of the Russians who moved into Siberia and the Black Sea region mixed with local peoples. As had been true for centuries, Arab and Indian traders relocated to distant lands in Africa and Eurasia, often settling permanently. Many Chinese also migrated, usually with their families, and moved into nearby territories such as Taiwan, and male merchants settled in Southeast Asia, in trading centers like the major Siamese city, Ayuthia. Many of the Chinese married Ayuthia women and stayed permanently, their descendants mixing Chinese and Siamese culture. More Chinese also arrived, and by 1735 some 20,000 lived in the kingdom.

Groups of mixed European and Asian ancestry appeared in European colonies in Asia. For instance, the Portuguese men who settled in Goa, Colombo, and Melaka married local women and raised their children as Portuguese-speaking Catholics, but their descendants adopted many local customs. Hence, in Melaka today,

while Catholic churches, schools, and festivals remain at the heart of Portuguese community life, the local Portuguese language contains many Malay words, the cuisine has borrowed extensively from Malay and Chinese cooking, and, unlike their merchant, sailor, and soldier ancestors, most men work as fishermen. Throughout the era, Portuguese was the lingua franca of maritime Asia, spoken in many ports, and some of its words were incorporated into local languages such as Malay.

In Africa too—South Africa, Mozambique, Angola, and along the West African coast—the mixing of Europeans and Africans led to hybrid social groups. The offspring of relations between Dutch men and African or Asian women were so common in South Africa that they became a distinct racial group, known as the Coloreds. Prominent slave-trading and merchant families of West Africa often descended from Portuguese men who married women from local chiefly or royal families. Like Brazilian mulattos and many Asian mestizos, African mulattos often spoke a version of Portuguese, the first language with a global reach.

Changing Gender Relations

Although men were much more likely than women to join overseas ventures or cross oceans, women were also affected by the changes of the era. In the Americas, many European men sought Indian women, often by force. One-third of enslaved Africans taken to the Americas were women, some of whom were brought into close contact with slave-owning men, mostly white, who exercised control over their lives. The result was forced sexual activity and mixed-descent children. Christian missionaries working among North American Indians often pursued policies that marginalized women in once-egalitarian cultures, such as the Algonquians of eastern Canada and the Iroquois of New York.

Gender patterns were modified around the world, including in Africa. For instance, in the parts of Africa most affected by slave trading, the absence of men in their productive years encouraged the remaining men to take multiple wives. The traditional role of West African women in local commerce, however, also meant that, along the coast, some became active as slave traders. A few of these, such as Senhora Philippa, who in the 1630s controlled the trading center of Rufisque (ROO-feesk) in today's Senegal, became immensely wealthy. Women also played powerful roles in some of the newer kingdoms fostered by the trans-Atlantic slave trade, such as Dahomey, where queen mothers wielded extraordinary power. A Portuguese missionary to one Senegambia kingdom described a powerful woman, the king's aunt, who was "so respected and obeyed that nothing of importance took place in the kingdom without her knowledge."[6]

In much of Eurasia, women experienced increasing subordination by men, although there were exceptions. Women generally became more restricted in Mughal

India, China, and Japan as patriarchal attitudes strengthened, largely as a result of internal factors. For example, Qing leaders turned more socially conservative, imposing harsher laws against behavior that was considered deviant, such as homosexuality, and stressing the purity of women, which meant less freedom for women to leave home. Indeed, in Southeast Asia, the Spanish and Portuguese were often appalled at the relative freedom of women. Spanish officials criticized Filipinos for tolerating adultery and premarital sex, and they punished those who engaged in these activities. Yet in China, Qing women from elite families published essays and poetry that were widely read and admired. One Chinese poet recalled how her father nurtured her talent: "Understanding that I was quite intelligent, He taught his daughters as he taught his sons, [advising us to] Develop together, support, and do not impede each other."[7]

Missionaries and Religious Change

The encounters between widely differing cultures around the world also had a religious dimension, forcing people to confront different belief systems while widening or sparking divisions in established faiths. Tensions simmering for several centuries in Europe finally fragmented Western Christianity into Catholic and diverse Protestant churches in the 1500s, spurring religious wars, militancy, and hostility toward non-Christians. Scientists such as the Italian astronomer Galileo Galilei were tried by the Holy Inquisition, a Catholic Church institution organized to root out heresy.

Meanwhile, other religious traditions also dealt with tensions and divisions. Mystical Sufi orders became more influential in Islamic societies from Indonesia to West Africa. For example, the early Mughal emperors Babur (BAH-bur) and Akbar were fervent Sufis. Babur wrote in a poem that "I am a king, but yet a slave [follower] of the Dervishes [mystics]."[8] But the Sufis' popularity distressed dogmatists, fostering debate on Sufism's value among Ottoman, Mughal, and Central Asian Muslims. Islamic division hardened in Persia, too. Ordered by their Safavid rulers, Persians shifted from the Sunni to the Shi'a branch of Islam, causing many Sunnis to emigrate. But tensions sometimes led to secular approaches: one such movement, neo-Confucianism, became a strong influence in China, helping secular values to triumph there while Buddhism lost influence among the elites. To comprehend a world charged with diverse and changing ideas, Chinese thinkers, European Enlightenment philosophers, and several Mughal emperors questioned religious dogmas and sought to broaden intellectual horizons.

In contrast, many became religious zealots and engaged in missionary activity. Christians actively sought converts in the Americas, Africa, and Asia. Christian missionaries were often intolerant of local traditions and scornful toward the people they were trying to reach. Catholicism eventually triumphed in Latin America, Kongo, and the Philippines, and it found a few thousand converts in East Asia. Protestant missionaries mostly concentrated on Catholic Europe, Southeast Asia, and North America, where they particularly targeted Native Americans and slaves. But the Christian missionary enterprise faced challenges, including stiff resistance. To gain acceptance, missionaries often had to blend Christianity with local traditions, often against the opposition of church leaders. The intolerance of many Christian missionaries toward other faiths led to their expulsion from Japan and China. East Asians assimilated some useful Western technical and scientific knowledge from the missionaries, such as clock-making and mapmaking, but most rejected Christianity. Christian missionary efforts had little success among Muslims, Theravada Buddhists, and Hindus.

Christianity was not the only missionary religion: millions of Europeans, Africans, and Asians embraced Islam. Islam spread into the Balkan societies under Ottoman control, and many Serbs, Albanians, and Bulgarians adopted the faith, forging a permanent divide between Christians and Muslims in the region. Islam continued to gain strength in sub-Saharan Africa, Mughal India, and Island Southeast Asia. Unlike Christianity, Islam was not identified with unpopular Western conquest, and it continued to link distant societies. For instance, in the 1600s, Nuruddin al-Raniri, (new-ROOD-in al-RAN-eer-ee) from Gujerat in India, studied in Mecca and then traveled widely, finally settling in Acheh, Sumatra, and becoming an adviser to the king.

Some trends promoted accommodation between divergent faiths. For example, in India the Mughal emperor Akbar preached tolerance and cultural diversity. Akbar's more zealously Islamic successors, however, repressed Hinduism, reviving a long conflict between the two faiths. Theravada Buddhists generally respected all religions. Hence, when the French king, Louis XIV, sent a mission to King Narai of Ayuthia requesting that he and his people adopt Roman Catholicism, the Siamese monarch sent a letter back, arguing that God rejoiced not in religious uniformity but in theological diversities. Meanwhile, Muslims and animists lived side by side without conflict in parts of Africa. Similarly, in some European societies, notably the Netherlands and Poland, Protestants and Catholics learned to live in peace. And growing European knowledge of Chinese society, including Confucianism, led some leaders of the European Enlightenment, such as Voltaire, to view China as an admirable, secular alternative to the religious divisions and orthodoxies of Europe. In this way, Asian ideas influenced some Europeans just as European power expanded, a testament to an increasingly connected world.

Test your understanding of the material covered in Part IV.

Suggested Reading

Adas, Michael, ed. *Islamic and European Expansion: The Forging of a Global Order*. Philadelphia: Temple University Press, 1993. Contains excellent essays by William McNeill, Alfred Crosby, and Philip Curtin on major developments in this era.

Black, Jeremy. *War in the World: Military Power and the Fate of Continents, 1450–2000*. New Haven, CT: Yale University Press, 1998. A global history of land and sea warfare and its contexts.

Brandon, William. *New Worlds for Old: Reports from the New World and Their Effect on the Development of Social Thought in Europe, 1500–1800*. Athens: Ohio University Press, 1986. Examines the impact on Europe of the American discoveries and cultures.

Crosby, Alfred W. *Ecological Imperialism: The Biological Expansion of Europe, 900–1900*. Cambridge: Cambridge University Press, 1993. A pioneering exploration of the environmental changes in the past millennium.

Curtin, Philip D. *The World and the West: The European Challenge and the Overseas Response in the Age of Empire*. Cambridge: Cambridge University Press, 2000. Explores relevant themes in world history since 1500.

Eltis, David. *The Rise of African Slavery in the Americas*. New York: Cambridge University Press, 2000. Overview of slavery and the Atlantic system.

Gunn, Geoffrey C. *First Globalization: The Eurasian Exchange*. Lanham, MD: Rowman and Littlefield, 2003. An idiosyncratic but absorbing study of East–West encounters.

Hobhouse, Henry. *Seeds of Change: Five Plants That Transformed Mankind*. New York: Harper and Row, 1985. A fascinating study of how quinine, sugar, tea, cotton, and the potato changed the world.

Marks, Robert B. *The Origins of the Modern World: A Global and Ecological Narrative*. Lanham, MD: Rowman and Littlefield, 2002. A stimulating, readable, and concise account of how the modern world emerged.

Pacey, Arnold. *Technology in World Civilization*. Cambridge: MIT Press, 1990. Provides a global overview of technological change in this era.

Pilcher, Jeffrey M. *Food in World History*. New York: Routledge, 2006. Examines changing food cultures around the world.

Pomeranz, Kenneth, and Steven Topic. *The World That Trade Created: Society, Culture, and the World Economy, 1400 to the Present*, 2nd ed. Armonk, NY: M. E. Sharpe, 2006. Contains dozens of brief esasys written for the general public.

Richards, John F. *The Unending Frontier: An Environmental History of the Early Modern World*. Berkeley: University of California Press, 2003. A detailed but stimulating study of environmental change, with many case studies.

Smith, Alan K. *Creating a World Economy: Merchant Capital, Colonialism, and World Trade, 1400–1825*. Boulder, CO: Westview Press, 1991. A valuable survey of the world economy in this era.

Wiesner-Hanks, Merry E. *Christianity and Sexuality in the Early Modern World: Regulating Desire, Reforming Practice*. New York: Routledge, 2000. A wide-ranging study of the impact of spreading Christianity on sexual practices.

Wills, John E. *1688: A Global History*. New York: W.W. Norton, 2001. A very readable and informative exploration of various peoples and societies around the world in the late seventeenth century.

PART V

Global Imbalances:
Industry, Empire, and the Making of the Modern World, 1750–1945

NORTH AND CENTRAL AMERICA
In the later 1700s, the thirteen British colonies along the Atlantic coast revolted and established a new democratic nation, the United States, that gradually expanded across the continent. After a civil war ended slavery, the United States rapidly industrialized; as it became the world's major political and economic power in the later 1800s, it attracted immigrants. U.S. military power proved decisive in World Wars I and II. Meanwhile, Canada spread west to the Pacific and achieved self-government. After overthrowing Spanish rule, Mexico was reshaped by liberalism, dictatorship, and revolution.

ARCTIC OCEAN

CANADA

NORTH AMERICA

UNITED STATES

MEXICO

ATLANTIC OCEAN

VENEZUELA

PACIFIC OCEAN

Amazon

PERU

BRAZIL

SOUTH AMERICA

ANDES

ARGENTINA

SOUTH AMERICA
During the early 1800s the Latin American societies overthrew colonialism by force and became independent nations, but they also retained close economic links to Europe, reinforcing their natural resources-based economies and limiting industrialization. The struggles between liberal reformers and conservatives often led to military dictatorship. As European and Asian immigrants reshaped Latin American societies, Latin Americans created distinctive cultures by combining imported and local traditions.

EUROPE

The Industrial Revolution, which began in Britain in the later 1700s, sparked dramatic economic, social, and political change. The French Revolution and the rise of parliamentary democracy in nations such as Britain benefited the middle classes and fostered new national loyalties. Russia conquered Siberia and Central Asia. Britain, France, and Germany renewed imperialism in the later 1800s, forging large empires in Asia and Africa. After 1914 Europe was reshaped by World War I, communist revolution in Russia, economic collapse, the rise of fascism, and World War II.

WESTERN ASIA

Although gradually losing its grip on southeastern Europe and North Africa, the Ottoman Empire maintained control of much of western Asia until after World War I, when Britain and France acquired the Arab territories and the Ottomans collapsed, replaced by a modernizing Turkish state. Persia attempted reforms but still fell under Western domination. Arab nationalism challenged Western power, while secular reformers and pro- and antimodern Muslims struggled for influence throughout the region.

EASTERN ASIA

China remained strong until the early 1800s, when, unable to reform and thwart Western ambitions, it lost several wars to the West and experienced rebellions. After a revolution ended the imperial system in the early 1900s, China lapsed into warlordism and then civil war, opening the door for Japanese invasion. Fearing Western power, the Japanese had rapidly industrialized and modernized their society in the later 1800s but, ravaged by economic depression, came under military rule in the 1930s, which eventually led to their defeat in World War II.

Map labels

ARCTIC OCEAN

RUSSIA

BRITAIN
GERMANY
FRANCE
EUROPE
ITALY
Danube

TURKEY
PERSIA
EGYPT

ASIA

HIMALAYAS
Ganges R.

JAPAN
CHINA

INDIA

THAILAND
VIETNAM

AFRICA

NIGERIA
Niger R.
ASHANTE
Congo R.
CONGO
BUGANDA

ATLANTIC
OCEAN

INDIAN OCEAN

INDONESIA

AUSTRALIA

SOUTH
AFRICA

AFRICA

Although some African states, such as Ashante, Buganda, and Egypt, remained strong into the 1800s and instituted reforms, they could not halt increasing Western power. The ending of the trans-Atlantic slave trade by the mid-1800s opened the door to Western colonization of the entire continent. The British and French built large empires in both sub-Saharan Africa and North Africa. Western imperialism created artificial countries, undermined traditional societies, and drained Africa of resources. After World War I African and Arab nationalist movements struggled against Western domination.

SOUTHERN ASIA AND OCEANIA

Overcoming local resistance, the British gradually conquered India, and their rule exploited India's resources, reshaped Indian life, and generated opposition from Indian nationalists seeking independence. Dynamic Southeast Asian states repulsed the West until the mid-1800s, when the British, French, and Dutch colonized all of these resource-rich societies, except Thailand, often against fierce resistance, and the United States replaced Spanish rule in the Philippines, crushing a local independence movement. To the east, Western powers colonized the Pacific islands and Europeans settled in Australia and New Zealand.

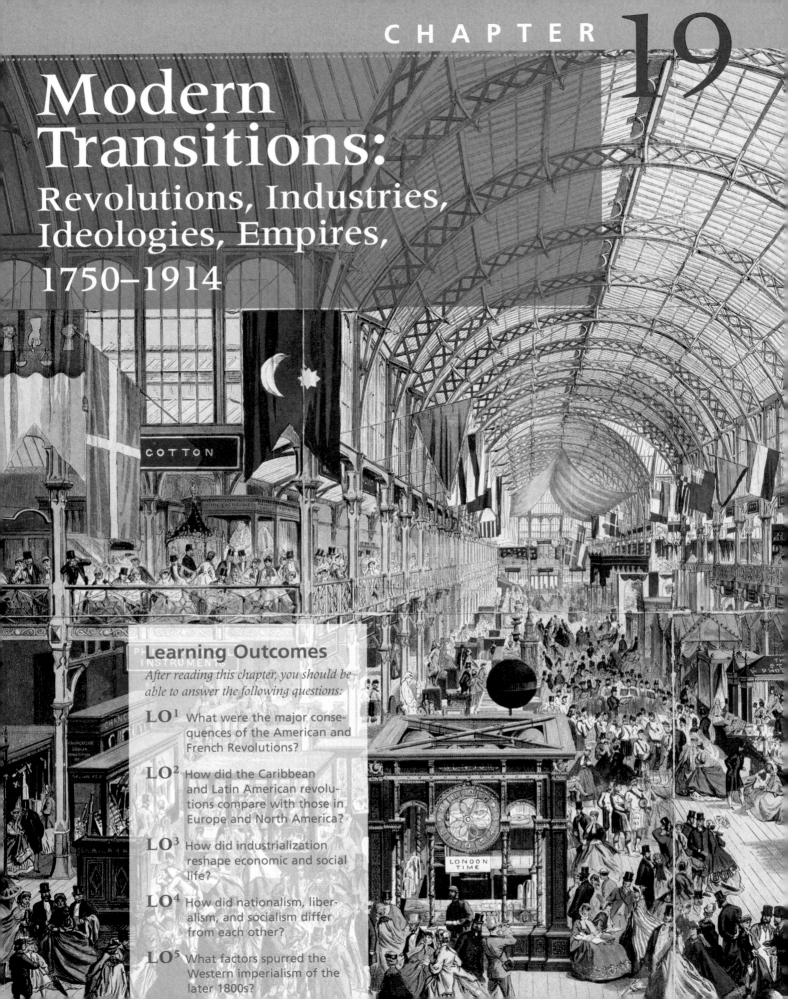

19

Modern Transitions:
Revolutions, Industries, Ideologies, Empires, 1750–1914

Learning Outcomes

After reading this chapter, you should be able to answer the following questions:

LO¹ What were the major consequences of the American and French Revolutions?

LO² How did the Caribbean and Latin American revolutions compare with those in Europe and North America?

LO³ How did industrialization reshape economic and social life?

LO⁴ How did nationalism, liberalism, and socialism differ from each other?

LO⁵ What factors spurred the Western imperialism of the later 1800s?

> **❝**From this foul drain the greatest stream of human industry flows out to fertilize the whole world. From this filthy sewer pure gold flows. Here humanity attains its most complete development and its most brutish.**❞**
>
> —**French writer Alexis De Tocqueville on Manchester, England, 1835[1]**

On a spring day in 1851, Britons of all social classes headed for the spectacular new Crystal Palace in Hyde Park to see the official opening, led by Queen Victoria herself, of the Great Exhibition. All shared in the excitement of an exhibition designed to celebrate "The Works of Industry of All Nations," with Progress as the organizing theme. The first "world's fair," the Great Exhibition was dazzling. Some 14,000 firms participated in the displays, showcasing British industrial leadership in particular. The hall of machinery contained power textile looms, marine engines, locomotives, and other inventions that had revolutionized British life. Another hall lavishly presented industrial products that British merchants sold all over the world, including fine textiles made from wool, cotton, linen, and silk. Nearly half of the exhibitors represented other countries of Europe and North America.

Test your knowlege before you read this chapter.

What do you think?

The Great Exhibition of 1851 celebrated the industrialization that had begun three-quarters of a century earlier and was already dramatically transforming the social and physical landscapes in Britain, the United States, and parts of Europe. The age of the machine had arrived: modern industry, a growing economy, and science meant humanity's triumph over the natural world. Industrialization gave Britain and other Western countries the economic and military power to increase their influence around the world.

Along with industrialization, political revolutions and new ideologies were also defining developments in Europe and the Americas between 1750 and 1914. The economic and political changes resulting from industrialization and political revolutions fostered new ideas about politics and government and about the relationship of citizens to the state. Great Britain, France, Germany, and Russia emerged as the main powers in Europe, while the United States became the

≪≪Crystal Palace Exposition of 1851 Attracting more than 6 million visitors, the Great Exhibition, held at the Crystal Palace in London in 1851, showcased industrial products and the companies that produced them from all over the world, but especially from Europe.

Laurie Platt Winfrey, Inc./The Granger Collection, New York

> "Revolutions have been momentous events in modern world history, erupting on every inhabited continent except Australia."

strongest American country. But by the later 1800s, these trends had also yielded mixed blessings, including a renewal of the imperialism, begun in the 1500s, that resulted in various European nations acquiring or expanding empires in Asia and Africa.

LO¹ The Age of Revolution: North America and Europe

Some historians use the phrase "the Age of Revolution" to refer to the period from the 1770s through the 1840s, when revolutions rocked the Atlantic world. During these years, revolutionaries employed armed violence to seize power and forge fundamental changes. Two types of revolutions emerged in modern times. Political revolutions, notably the one resulting in the United States, changed the personnel and structure of government, while social revolutions, such as France's tumultuous upheaval that began in 1789, transformed both the political and social order. For the next two centuries, revolutions transformed states, ideologies, and class structures, especially in Europe, Latin America, and Asia.

Modern Revolutions

Revolutions have been momentous events in modern world history, erupting on every inhabited continent except Australia. In the late 1700s, Europeans and Latin Americans watched fascinated as the disaffected citizens in the thirteen British colonies in North America struggled to overthrow British rule and then established an independent federation that soon became the United States. The American revolutionary leaders proclaimed Enlightenment political theories formulated in Europe, such as democracy and personal freedom, and then sought to apply these theories to their new representative government. The French Revolution electrified Europe by violently replacing the monarchy with a republic and spreading the new values of liberty and social equality. But

the French Revolution also generated terrible violence, the rise of despotic leaders, long years of war, and a transformed nineteenth-century European continent.

Revolutions often shared common features. Revolutionary leaders were frequently well-educated and privileged, but in many cases, they mobilized followers from among disenchanted peasants and urban workers. Many revolutions, including the French, moved from moderate to more extreme actions, such as purging dissidents, rivals, or opponents. And though most revolutions replaced incompetent and oppressive governments, they were also destructive and brutal, and few ultimately satisfied the demands of their people. The majority of these revolutions were sparked by one or more causes, most commonly hunger, poverty, war, overpopulation, the spread of destabilizing capital-

CHRONOLOGY

The North American and European Revolutions, 1770–1815

1770s–1840s	Age of Revolution
1773	Boston Tea Party
1776	American Declaration of Independence
1783	Britain's recognition of United States' independence
1787	United States constitutional convention; Northwest Ordinance for forming new states
1789–1815	French Revolution
1791–1792	Constitutional state in Poland-Lithuania
1804	Crowning of Napoleon as emperor of France
1810–1811	Height of Napoleon's empire
1815	Defeat of Napoleon at Battle of Waterloo; Congress of Vienna

ism, or, as in British North America, the desire for more personal freedom and self-government.

British Colonialism and the American Revolution

The successful political revolution in British North America resulted from resentments that had festered for decades between British colonists and the imperial government. Britain had forged a foothold on the eastern seaboard of North America in the 1600s, establishing a presence in Canada and in thirteen colonies stretching from New Hampshire south to Georgia. Each colony had unique institutions and economies: the southern colonies depended largely on plantation slavery, whereas the northern colonies combined commerce and manufacturing with farming, a more balanced mix of economic activities. Only 2 million persons lived in the colonies in the 1760s, and the largest town, Boston, had only 20,000 residents. One-fifth of the colonial population was African American, most of who were enslaved.

Given these conditions, the white colonists seemed to have little to rebel against. Except for enslaved African Americans, the American colonists were generally prosperous and enjoyed considerable self-government and religious toleration. The majority of adult white males, if they owned sufficient property, could vote for local assemblies and mayors. The colonists also faced much lighter taxes than did people in Britain. Most colonists were proud to be British subjects, and by the mid-1700s, the British hold on these colonies seemed strong.

But after the Seven Years' War (1756–1763), tensions increased between the British—who needed American help to pay their war debts—and the colonists. Many colonists felt divorced from Britain and increasingly resented British policies, such as taxation without representation in the British Parliament. Clumsy British attempts to raise taxes, enforce

 The American Revolution (*http:// revolution.h-net.msu .edu/***).** An excellent collection of links, essays, and other resources.

> "Many colonists felt divorced from Britain and increasingly resented British policies, such as taxation without representation in the British Parliament."

> 66 We hold these truths to be self-evident, that all men are created equal . . . 99
> *from the Declaration of Independence*

long-ignored laws, and reserve the coveted land west of the Appalachians for Indians angered many colonists, some of whom began tarring and feathering tax collectors. Both men and women also mounted boycotts of British goods. In 1773, to protest a higher tax on tea, outraged colonists, dressed as Indians, raided three British ships in Boston harbor and dumped their cargo of tea overboard, an event known as the Boston Tea Party. Colonists favoring independence, known as Patriots, and those opposed, called Loyalists, increasingly clashed.

Declaration of Independence

The Patriot supporters of independence admired progressive European thought. Deeply influenced by European Enlightenment thinkers such as John Locke in England and Baron de Montesquieu in France, they favored democracy and a republic (see Chapter 15). The Patriots were also stirred by recent English immigrant Tom Paine's (1737–1809) passionate pamphlet *Common Sense*, which urged Americans to oppose tyranny and free themselves by force in order to "begin the world over again." A series of American–British skirmishes escalated in the 1770s, leading to the Second Continental Congress, at which delegates from all thirteen colonies met and declared that the colonies ought to be free and independent states. On July 4, 1776, the delegates approved the Declaration of Independence, written largely by Thomas Jefferson (1743–1826), a Virginia planter, which stated, "We hold these truths to be self-evident, that all men are created equal, that they are endowed by their Creator with certain inalienable Rights, that among these are Life, Liberty and the pursuit of Happiness."[2]

The United States Declaration of Independence, Thomas Jefferson, (1776) Did you know that Thomas Jefferson was influenced by Enlightenment thinkers? Look for overtones of this philosophy in his United States Declaration of Independence.

Patriots vs. Loyalists

With conflict unavoidable, a revolutionary army organized and commanded by George Washington (1732–1799), a respected Virginia planter and veteran of the Seven Years' War, then fought the British and their Loyalist allies for six bitter years. Although one-third of the colonists remained staunchly loyal to Britain, the revolutionary effort reached to the grassroots as women and men from all quarters raised funds, supported Washington's army, and sabotaged British efforts. Britain's rivals, France and Spain, also aided the Patriot cause. The British were supported by many Indians, who resented the colonists for aggressively occupying Indian lands, and by some black slaves, who were promised their freedom if they helped the Loyalist cause. Some accused the Patriots of hypocrisy, wanting freedom for themselves while maintaining slavery for nonwhites.

The American defeat of British forces at Yorktown, Virginia, in 1781 proved decisive, and, after negotiations, Britain recognized the independence of the thirteen colonies in 1783. Despite their democratic values, the Patriots treated the Loyalists harshly, confiscating their land and jailing them. Ultimately 100,000 Loyalists were expelled or fled to Canada, and many others left for England.

The Legacy of the American Revolution

During the war of independence, the thirteen colonies joined to form an independent federation, the United States of America. The first confederation, which required the unanimous consent of every state for major political changes, proved unworkable. Seeking a stronger central government, delegates from each state met in 1787 at a convention in Philadelphia and approved a constitution for a national government that was mostly written by James Madison (1751–1836), a shy, well-educated Virginian. The constitution called for an elected president and congress presiding over a federal system that granted many powers to the states. The delegates then elected the war hero George Washington as the first president of the republic. Unlike Jefferson and Madison, Washington was not a talented speaker or writer, but Americans admired the general's integrity and suc-

> "The French Revolution was perhaps the world's first true social revolution, traumatic but also inspiring in its message of 'liberty, equality, and fraternity.'"

cess, and they considered him a man who embodied American virtues. The first elected Congress approved ten constitutional amendments, known as the Bill of Rights, which enshrined Enlightenment values such as freedom of speech, assembly, press, and religion.

Despite their rhetoric of liberty and equality, the Patriot founders did not challenge slavery, recognize Native American claims to land, or expand voting rights beyond white men. Most northern states gradually abolished slavery, but the institution was maintained in most of the south. Indians could only watch bitterly as the new national government claimed most of the land east of the Mississippi River and made plans to survey and settle it. Nor did the nation's founders give women equal rights with men, despite their significant contributions to the cause of independence.

American Exceptionalism

Nevertheless, Americans believed they had formed a society unique to history. This idea of a distinctive character and history, known as American "exceptionalism," was intensified after the Revolution. Americans viewed theirs as the most democratic, individualistic, enterprising, and prosperous society on earth. The new country seemed unhindered by the burdens of history that held down other peoples. Americans also argued that their ideas and institutions were relevant for the whole world, echoing the Puritan Massachusetts governor, John Winthrop, who had claimed in 1630 that his new colony constituted a "City upon a Hill, [with] the eyes of all people upon us."[3] Thomas Jefferson, who became the third president of the new republic, declared that America was a standing monument and example for the world.

The French Revolution

The French Revolution was perhaps the world's first true social revolution, traumatic but also inspiring in its message of "liberty, equality, and fraternity." With fair distribution of wealth as a popular principle, the French middle classes took over the government in the name of the common people. But the Revolution also plunged Europe into a prolonged crisis that

Storming the Bastille This painting celebrates the taking of the Bastille, a castle prison in Paris that symbolized hated royal rule, by armed citizens and soldiers. The governor and his officials are led out and will soon be executed.

resulted in a series of wars between France and its European rivals, who feared the spread of radicalism. Ironically, these wars actually helped to spread French revolutionary ideas to other European societies.

Revolutionary Causes

The Revolution had many causes. France's participation in the American War of Independence worsened the government's long-standing financial problems. Included in these problems was an unjust economic system that badly needed reform. For example, the Roman Catholic clergy and the privileged nobility were exempt from most direct taxes, and thus the entire burden was put on artisans and peasants. Several bad harvests increased the common peoples' hunger and misery. To calm rising passions, King Louis XVI (1754–1793), a member of the long-ruling Bourbon family, called the Estates General, a long-dormant consultative body that included the clergy, the nobility, and a Third Estate comprising the middle classes and peasants. Every town debated political issues, drew up lists of complaints, and then elected delegates to the Estates General. High prices, food shortages, and high unemployment spurred resentment of the government and privileged classes; one Third Estate pamphlet called them a malignant disease preying on a sick society.

The leaders of the Third Estate, who represented more than 90 percent of the French population, demanded influence in the Estates General that reflected their numbers. Stalemated in the Estates General, the Third Estate delegates formed a rival national assembly and began writing a new French constitution. In response, the king called in the army to restore order and fired a popular reformist official. These actions provoked anger and violence in 1789 when armed crowds stormed the Bastille, the royal prison and a hated symbol of tyranny, to release the prisoners and seize gunpowder and cannon. The Bastille attack, which resulted in many deaths on both sides, proved so inspirational that the date (July 14) later became France's national holiday.

The Declaration of Rights of Man and Citizen, National Assembly of France (1789) Do you see similarities in France's Declaration of Rights of Man and Citizen and the United States Declaration of Independence? Do you think one was influenced by the other?

As unrest spread through France, the terrified nobility fled. Members of the Third Estate formed a new Constituent Assembly, which voted to destroy the social order and adopted the Declaration of the Rights of Man and of the Citizen, a document strongly influenced by the English Bill of Rights of 1689 and the new United States constitution. The Declaration announced that all people everywhere had a natural right to liberty, property, equality, security, religious toleration, and freedom of expression, press, and association. A new constitution preserved the monarchy but made the king bound by laws and subject to an elected assembly. The leaders also outlawed slavery and targeted corruption in the church.

Counterrevolution and War

Counterrevolution supported by rival countries soon embroiled France in a long series of wars. France's neighbors, fearing the radicalism that the Revolution unleashed, sought a restoration of royal power in France. To preempt an invasion, French leaders declared war in 1792. A national convention, elected by universal male suffrage, now made France a republic, ending the monarchy. In the name of all the world's people, the French began a revolutionary crusade for self-determination and the end of absolute monarchies in Europe. With patriotic enthusiasm, the French public rallied behind the revolutionary government, and in 1793 the revolutionaries executed King Louis XVI for treason. Most European states declared war on France's revolutionary government, but poor leadership on both sides prevented any decisive victory.

Jacobins

As military conflict intensified, so did dissension in France. The country faced not only foreign enemies but also internal dissent and worsening economic problems. Some leaders had emphasized preserving the Revolution's libertarian principles, such as freedom of speech and assembly. However, a more radical faction known as Jacobins (JAK-uh-binz) prioritized order over freedom, imposing a dictatorship to promote internal security. The Jacobins set up the Committee of Public Safety, which used terror against real or imagined opponents by ordering mass executions, often cutting off their victims' heads in public using the gruesome guillotine. Perhaps 40,000 French citizens, mostly rebellious peasants and provincial leaders, were executed, and tens of thousands more were arrested, often on flimsy evidence. Even some Jacobin leaders were executed in factional disputes. The terror abated when the Jacobins lost power in 1795, but their discordant legacy included innovative laws guaranteeing universal public education and public welfare for the poor.

The Legacy of the French Revolution

Although not all of its accomplishments proved long-lasting, the French Revolution showed that an old regime could be destroyed and a new order created by its own people, providing both a model and an inspiration for generations of revolutionaries to come. The Revolution not only installed the middle class in power in France but also ultimately constructed a modern bureaucratic state. The French example also inspired other Europeans to adopt political reform. For example, in 1791, reformers in Poland-Lithuania reshaped the state and expanded voting rights. But a year later, Russia, supported by the Polish nobility, invaded Poland-Lithuania and crushed the reformist government. Ultimately, the terrible violence of the French Revolution dampened its appeal as the Jacobins' terror undermined personal liberty. Indeed, the French trauma and terror turned many westerners against revolutions, which they now feared too often degenerated into anarchy and then despotism.

The declaration of the French "Rights of Man" inspired some to raise the question of women's rights. Olympe de Gouges (1748–1793), a French butcher's daughter, published a manifesto complaining that women were excluded from decision making and tried to organize a female militia to fight for France. For her efforts she was executed. A British campaigner for women's rights, Mary Wollstonecraft (1759–1797), whose outrage was spurred by watching her merchant father abuse her mother, moved to Paris and wrote the *Vindication of the Rights of Women* in 1792, calling for equal opportunities for women in education and society. But despite the efforts of reformers such as de Gouges and Wollstonecraft, women remained excluded from citizenship in France and nearly everywhere else.

The Napoleonic Era and a New European Politics

Although the republican system had inspired many within and outside of France, the end result in France was a military dictatorship. The terror and the shifting fortunes of war led to a resurgence of pro-monarchy feelings in France and prompted antiroyalists to turn to the ambitious General Napoleon Bonaparte (BOW-nuh-pahrt) (1769–1821), a brilliant military strategist from the French-ruled island of Corsica. Bonaparte's ambitions and deeds would shake up the politics of France and Europe.

Bonaparte's Rise to Power

Bonaparte's rise to power was astounding. In 1795 he was a lowly artillery officer just released from prison for alleged Jacobin ties. Through political connections and his forceful personality, he rapidly rose through the ranks to command major military victories in France, Italy, Austria, and Egypt, becoming the most influential French leader of his day. In 1804, responding to growing sentiment that only a dictator could provide stability, Bonaparte crowned himself emperor in a regal coronation and then quickly began to promote reconciliation and economic progress. He also upheld the equality of all citizens before the law, thus making permanent the Revolution's core values. However, the Corsican's general dictatorial tendencies betrayed French liberty, and his militarism led to near-constant warfare with other European nations.

British Coalition

In 1805, Britain, the world's dominant sea power and longtime rival of France, forged a coalition with Austria, Prussia, and Russia to defeat Napoleon. In the following years, France won most of the land battles, enabling it to occupy much of western Europe. By 1810, Bonaparte's family ruled Spain, Naples, and some German states, but their power eventually waned. Armed resistance, a costly French invasion of Russia resulting in humiliating retreat, and an invasion of France by rival powers all sapped Bonaparte's military strength. He was finally overcome by British and Prussian armies at Waterloo, a Belgian village, in 1815. While the Bourbon family reclaimed the French throne, Bonaparte, for a decade the most powerful man in Europe, spent his remaining years in exile on a remote, British-ruled South Atlantic island.

The demise of revolutionary France and the dismantling of Napoleon's empire allowed for a partial return to the political status quo in Europe. The victorious allies met in 1815 at the Congress of Vienna to remold the European state system (see Map 19.1). Dominated by Austria, Britain, Russia, and the revived royalist government of France, the Congress reaffirmed pre-Napoleonic borders and restored most of the former rulers who had been displaced by revolutionaries and reformers. It also led to the confederation of thirty-nine German states, laying the foundation for modern Germany.

 Interactive Map

Uprising and Revolt

In the following decades, revolutionary ideas combined with popular discontent continued to unsettle Europe, and various revolutions broke out in 1830–1831 because of discontent with despotic political systems. The French overthrew the increasingly despotic Bourbon king, Charles X, and installed his more progressive cousin and former Jacobin, Louis-Philippe (1773–1850), as a constitutional monarch who recognized democratic liberties. Uprisings in several German and Italian states and in Poland sought voting rights, and a peasant rebellion caused by poverty and unemployment rocked Britain.

Even more turbulent European revolts erupted in 1848, a result of poor harvests, rampant disease, trade slumps, rising unemployment, massive poverty, and a desire for representative government. These upheavals again began in France, forcing the increasingly unpopular King Louis-Philippe to abdicate, and soon spread to Austria, Hungary, and many German and Italian states. But around Europe, conservative regimes crushed the dissident movements within a few months, often causing great bloodshed. A French observer said that "nothing was lacking" in the repression in Paris, "not grapeshot, nor bullets, nor demolished houses, nor martial law, nor the ferocity of the soldiery, nor the insults to the dead."[4] Still, the uprisings helped further spread democratic ideas, and monarchies lost ground as parliamentary power increased in countries such as Denmark and the Netherlands. To prevent revolutionary outbursts, many European governments also began to consider social and economic reforms, such as higher wages, to improve people's lives.

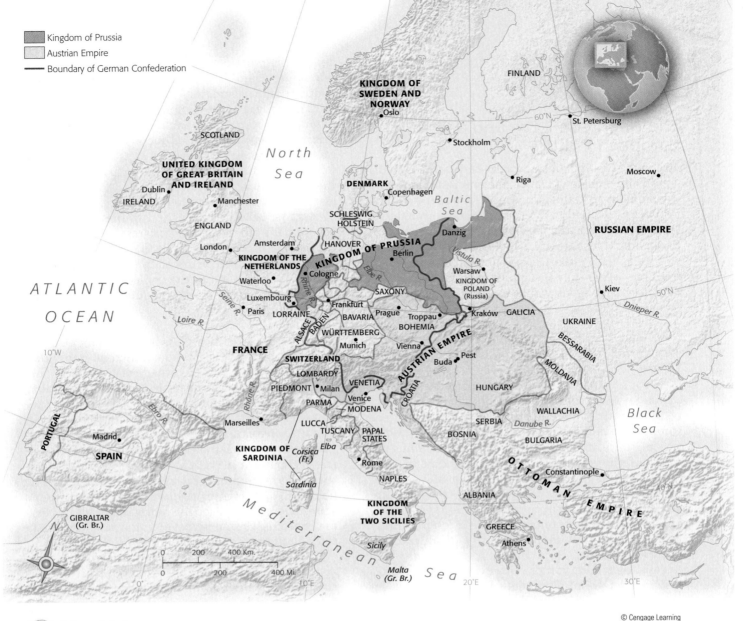

Map 19.1
Europe in 1815

With the Napoleonic wars ended, the Congress of Vienna redrew the map of Europe. France, Austria, Spain, Britain, and a growing Prussia were the dominant states, but the Ottoman Turks still ruled a large area of southeastern Europe.

Map legend:
- Kingdom of Prussia
- Austrian Empire
- — Boundary of German Confederation

LO² The Age of Revolution: The Caribbean and Latin America

The Age of Revolution was not confined to North America and Europe. Just as in British North America, dissatisfaction with colonialism was common in the Caribbean and Spanish America, and it led to revolutions and wars of independence in these regions in the early 1800s. The first successful movement to overthrow colonialism came in Haiti, where slaves of African ancestry fought their way to power. Many Central and South American countries also eventually won their independence by the 1820s.

Spanish and Portuguese America's Colonial Heritage

The Spanish and Portuguese ruled much larger American empires than did the British. By 1810, some 18 million diverse people lived under Spanish rule from California in the north to the southern tip of South America. This population included Europeans, Indians, Africans, and people of mixed descent. The empire was divided into four administrative units based in Mexico, Colombia, Peru, and Argentina, each supervised by Spanish governors. Corruption ran deep, but the planters, ranchers, mine owners, bureaucrats, and church officials who benefited from Spanish rule or profited from exploiting the economic resources opposed any major change. They preferred a system that sent raw materials, such as silver and beef, to Spain rather than one that developed domestic institutions and markets.

> 66 By 1810, some 18 million diverse people lived under Spanish rule from California in the north to the southern tip of South America. 99

CHRONOLOGY

The Caribbean and Latin American Revolutions, 1750–1840

1791–1804	Haitian Revolution
1808	Move of Portuguese royal family to Brazil
1810–1826	Wars of independence in Spanish America
1810–1811	First Mexican revolution
1816	Argentine independence
1819	Founding of Colombian republic by Bolívar
1822	Mexican independence; Dom Pedro emperor of Brazil
1830	Independence of Colombia, Venezuela, and Ecuador
1839	Division of Central American states

Political Structure

The Spanish ruled their colonies differently than did the British in North America, allowing little self-government, maintaining extractive monocultures, and imposing Roman Catholicism. Only a small minority shared in the wealth produced by the mines, plantations, and ranches. Latin American social conditions did not promote unity or equality. The creoles—whites born in the Americas—resented influential newcomers from Spain, but they also feared that resistance against Spain might get out of control and threaten their privileges. The great majority of the population, a dispossessed underclass of Indians, enslaved Africans, and mixed-descent people, faced growing unemployment and perhaps the world's most inequitable distribution of wealth.

In contrast to British America, Latin America, dominated by a rigid Catholic Church that was wary of dissent, enjoyed little intellectual diversity. The Inquisition denounced as seditious any literature espousing equality and liberty for all people and punished people it considered to be heretics. Local critics accused the government and church of "placing the strongest fetters on Enlightenment and [keeping] thought in chains."[5] Yet one successful dissenter was the Mexican creole Jose Antonio Alzate y Ramirez (1738–1799), who published a magazine that promoted science and Enlightenment rationalism.

Colonial Revolts

Given the political and social inequalities, various revolts punctuated Spanish colonial rule. The largest revolt spread over large parts of Peru in the 1700s and was led by Tupac Amaru II (1740–1781), the wealthy, well-educated mestizo who claimed to be a descendant of an Inca king. Although the better-armed Spanish defeated the rebel bands and executed Tupac and his family, the Tupac Amaru revolt paved the way for larger upheavals across South America several decades later.

Portuguese Brazil also experienced dissent. By the late 1700s, Brazil was the wealthiest part of the Portuguese colonial realm, but only a small, mostly white minority enjoyed the prosperity. Because Brazil was the major importer of slaves, accounting for one-quarter to one-third of all Africans arriving in the Americas, blacks vastly outnumbered Native Americans in Brazil, in contrast to Spanish-ruled Mexico and South America. Disgruntled

Afro-Brazilians demanded a better life, but they faced many setbacks; in 1799, one revolt seeking social equality and political freedom was crushed in the northeastern state of Bahia (buh-HEE-uh).

> "The Afro-Caribbean peoples appropriated European cultural forms and languages, welding them with retained African forms."

Caribbean Societies and the Haitian Revolution

Most of the small Caribbean islands and the Guianas in northeast South America were colonies of Britain, France, or the Netherlands and were inhabited chiefly by African slaves and their descendants, most of whom worked on sugar plantations. The Afro-Caribbean peoples appropriated European cultural forms and languages, welding them with retained African forms. In British-colonized islands such as Jamaica, Barbados, and Antigua, most slaves adopted Christianity and Anglo-Saxon names. The African influences that shaped slave life included musical influences such as drumming, improvisation, and varied rhythms.

Slave Revolts   Slave revolts were common throughout the colonial era, but only one, the Haitian Revolution, overthrew a regime. In 1791, some 100,000 Afro-Haitian slaves, inspired by the French Revolution and its slogans of liberty and equality, rose up against the oppressive society presided over by French planters, thus beginning years of war and bloodshed. Toussaint L'Ouverture (too-SAN loo-ver-CHORE) (1746–1803), a freed slave with a vision of a republic composed of free people, became the insurgent leader.

Haitian Revolution   The Haitian revolution went from triumph to tragedy. For a decade the Afro-Haitians fought the French military, and by 1801, Toussaint's forces had gained control over Haiti and freed the slaves. But Napoleon Bonaparte sent in a larger French force to restore order, and in 1803, French soldiers captured Toussaint, who soon died in a French prison. In 1804, Afro-Haitians defeated Napoleon's army and established the second independent nation in the Western Hemisphere after the United States. Slaves elsewhere in the Americas were cheered by the Haitian Revolution, but horrified planters became more determined to preserve slavery, and the United States, still a slave-owning nation, withheld diplomatic recognition of the black Haitian republic. In Haiti, French planters were either killed or fled, and the ex-slaves took over sugar production, but the promise of a better life for Haiti's people proved short-lived. Toussaint's successor as revolutionary leader, the Africa-born Jean Jacques Dessalines (de-sah-LEEN) (1758–1806), became emperor and ruled despotically, beginning two centuries of tyranny.

South American Independence Wars

As in North America and Haiti, dissatisfaction in Spanish-ruled South America exploded into wars of national independence. In 1800, the Spanish colonial hold on its empire seemed secure, but resentments simmered, especially among creoles, who criticized Spain for its commercial monopoly, its increasing taxes, and the colonial government's favoritism toward those born in Spain. Creoles also often felt more loyalty toward their American region than to distant Spain, and some were influenced by the Enlightenment and the American and French Revolutions. The British, who were pressuring the Spanish and Portuguese to open Latin American markets to British goods, also secretly aided anticolonial groups. At the same time, Spain was experiencing political problems at home, including French occupation during the Napoleonic wars, which weakened the country's ability to suppress unrest in Latin America.

Simón Bolívar   Because Spain refused to make serious political concessions, creole revolutionaries of middle-class backgrounds waged wars of independence between 1810 and 1826, forming new countries. Two separate independence movements began in 1810–1811 in Venezuela and Argentina, and they soon came under the leadership of Simón Bolívar (bow-LEE-vahr) in the north and Jose de San Martin (san mahr-TEEN) in the south. Born into a wealthy Caracas family, Bolívar (1783–1830) had studied law in Spain, admired rationalist Enlightenment thought, and had a magnetic personality that inspired loyalty. He expressed sympathy for

Simón Bolívar The main leader of the anti-Spanish war of independence in northern South America, Bolívar came to be known as "the Liberator," a symbol of Latin American nationalism and the struggle for political freedom.

blacks in Haiti and Jamaica and offered an inclusive view of his Latin American people: "We are a microcosm of the human race, a world apart, neither Indian nor Europeans, but a part of each."[6] In 1812, Bolívar formed an army to liberate northern South America, offering freedom to slaves who aided his cause. After many setbacks, Bolívar's forces liberated the north in 1824. San Martin (1778–1850), a former colonel in the Spanish army, led the southern forces against Spain and its royalist allies, helping Argentina gain independence in 1816 and Chile in 1818. In 1824, San

Martin and Bolívar cooperated to liberate Peru, where royalist sympathies were strongest.

Consequences of Victory

But these victories over the colonial regimes did not always meet the expectations of the liberated or the liberators. The wars damaged economies and caused people to flee the fighting. In addition, the creoles who now governed these countries often forgot the promises they had made to the Indians, mestizos, mulattos, and blacks, who had often provided the bulk of the revolutionary armies. And although some slaves were freed, slavery was not abolished. Women also experienced disappointment, especially those who had enthusiastically served the revolution as soldiers and nurses, such as Policarpa Salavarrieta, who was captured by the Spanish. Before she was executed in Bogota's main plaza, she exclaimed: "Although I am a woman and young, I have more than enough courage to suffer this death and a thousand more."[7] Despite such sacrifices, women soon found that they still lived in patriarchal societies that offered them few new legal or political rights. Finally, unlike the founders of the United States, Latin America's new leaders were largely unable to form representative and democratic governments. Simón Bolívar could not hold his own country together, and in 1830 it broke into Colombia, Ecuador, and Venezuela. Meanwhile, Uruguay and Paraguay split off from Argentina, and Bolivia separated from Peru. Disillusioned, Bolívar concluded that Latin America was ungovernable.

 The Jamaica Letter, Simón Bolívar Did you know that Simón Bolívar was a pivotal leader of the Latin American independence movement against Spain? Read his thoughts on the prospects of the liberation movement after a major setback against the Spaniards.

Independence Movements in Mexico and Brazil

Political change also came to Mexico and Brazil (see Map 19.2). In 1810, two progressive Mexican Catholic priests, the creole Manuel Hidalgo (ee-DAHL-go) and the mestizo Jose Maria Morelos (hoe-SAY mah-REE-ah moh-RAY-los), mobilized peasants and miners and launched a revolt promoting independence, the abolition of slavery, and social reform to uplift the mestizos and Indians. Conservative royalists

 Interactive Map

Map 19.2
Latin American Independence, 1840

By 1840, all of Latin America except for Cuba and Puerto Rico, which were still Spanish colonies, had become independent, with Brazil and Mexico the largest countries. Later the Central American provinces and Gran Colombia would fragment into smaller nations, and Argentina would annex Patagonia.

suppressed the revolt and executed Hidalgo and Morelos. But a compromise between various factions brought Mexico independence in 1822 under a creole general, Agustín de Iturbide (ah-goos-TEEN deh ee-tur-BEE-deh) (1783–1824), who proclaimed himself emperor. However, although initially the anti-Spanish struggle had united creoles, mestizos, and Indians against a common enemy, the alliance unraveled, and a republican revolt soon ousted Iturbide. The Central American peoples split off from Mexico and, after several attempts at unity, by 1839 had splintered into five states.

Internet Resources for Latin America (*http://lib.nmsu.edu/subject/bord/laguia/*). An outstanding site with links to many resources.

Brazil escaped many of the bloody conflicts bedeviling Spanish America. In 1808, the Portuguese royal family and government sought refuge in Brazil to escape the Napoleonic wars, and in the following years, Brazilians increasingly viewed themselves as separate from Portugal. When the Portuguese government tried to reclaim the territory, a member of the royal family still in Brazil, Dom Pedro (1798–1834), severed ties with Portugal in 1822 and became emperor of Brazil as Pedro I, Latin America's only constitutional monarch. However, although a parliament was set up and elections were held, most Brazilians had no vote, and Pedro I governed autocratically.

LO³ The Industrial Revolution and Economic Growth

Along with political and social revolutions, the Industrial Revolution, a dramatic transformation in the production and transportation of goods, was a major force reshaping the economic, political, and social patterns of Europe and later of North America and Japan. For the first time in history, people became capable of the rapid, constant, and seemingly limitless increase of goods and services. This revolution was perhaps the greatest transformation in society since settled farming, urbanization, and the first

> "The wars damaged economies and caused people to flee the fighting."

> ❝ We are a microcosm of the human race, a world apart, neither Indian nor Europeans, but a part of each. ❞
>
> *Simón Bolívar*

Industrial Revolution A dramatic transformation in the production and transportation of goods that transformed western Europe from the 1770s to the 1870s.

states arose thousands of years ago. The transition began in Britain and then spread to western Europe and North America, eventually helping transform the West to dominate much of the world by 1914.

The Roots of the Industrial Revolution

The Industrial Revolution and the changes it generated had deep roots in Early Modern Europe. The Renaissance, Reformation, and Enlightenment had generated new ways of thought, including the expanded quest to understand the natural world reflected in the Scientific Revolution (see Chapter 15). The commercial capitalism that arose in the 1500s and 1600s generated trade and conquest overseas, forming political and economic links between the Americas, the African coast, some Asian societies, and western Europe by 1750. These connections allowed Europeans to acquire natural resources and great wealth overseas, which provided capital for investment in new technologies and incentives for producing more commodities for the world market.

British Advantages Great Britain became the world's leading trading nation in the 1700s. By the 1730s, spinning machines were making the English textile industry more efficient and causing the nation to replace India as the world's leading supplier of cotton textiles. Britain had many advantages over rival countries, including an open intellectual atmosphere, a reasonably democratic political system that included the middle classes in government, a productive economy, favorable terrain on which to build transportation networks, abundant raw materials like coal and iron, and many water sources to run machines. Between the 1780s and 1830s, Britain dominated European industrialization.

Because of its earlier overseas activities in the Americas and Asia, Britain acquired one of the prerequisites for industrialization: adequate capital. Profits from the British-controlled Caribbean islands, North American colonies, and trading posts in India were particularly crucial in funding the Industrial Revolution. Some British companies made vast fortunes from the trans-Atlantic slave trade and the slavery plantations in the Americas. The English region east of Liverpool and northern Wales known as the Midlands, near rich coal and iron ore fields, became the center of British industry. Concentrating production in large factories in or near cities such as Birmingham and Manchester in the Midlands lowered transport costs and tapped a ready labor supply.

Industrial Capitalism

Beginning around 1770, commercial capitalism, dominated by large trading companies, transformed into industrial capitalism, a system centered around manufacturing. During this era, European industrial firms made and exported manufactured goods to other countries and in return imported raw materials, such as iron ore, to make more goods. The Industrial Revolution gave businesses marketable products and a powerful compulsion to market them in ever-increasing quantities. Because of the heavy investments in machines, success depended on a large and steady turnover of goods. Advertising developed to create demand, and banking and financial institutions expanded their operations to better serve business and industry. The industrialists, bankers, and financiers were also supported by political leaders who pursued policies of maximizing private wealth.

Adam Smith

As economic and government efforts were made to support industrial capitalism, some intellectuals felt the need to justify it. Economic philosophers emerged to praise British-style capitalism. The most influential, the Scottish professor Adam Smith (1723–1790), was a friend and supporter of Enlightenment thinkers. In his book *The Wealth of Nations* (1776), Smith helped formulate modern economics theory, known as neoclassical economics. In examining the consequences of economic freedom, Smith concluded that the market should be left alone. He advocated laissez faire, the restriction of government interference in the marketplace, such as laws regulating business and profits. Smith believed in self-interest, arguing that the "invisible hand" of the marketplace would turn the individual greed of the entrepreneur into a rising standard of living for all. Smith also introduced the new idea of a permanently growing economy and ever-increasing wealth as time went on. Smith's free trade ideas helped end the protectionist mercantilism of the Early Modern Era, when several European states worked closely with large commercial enterprises to accumulate wealth.

But Smith saw the potential for both good and evil in industrial capitalism. He championed free trade but also found areas where government regulation might be useful and even essential. Smith acknowledged that free enterprise did not necessarily generate prosperity for all, since the interests of the manufacturers were not necessarily those of society or even of the broader economy. To ensure these larger interests, he encouraged businesses to pay their employees high wages, writing that "no society can surely be flourishing and happy of which the far greater part of its members are poor and miserable. [They should be] well fed, clothed and lodged."[8]

CHRONOLOGY

European Politics and Economy, 1750–1914

1770s	Beginning of Industrial Revolution in England
1774	James Watt's first rotary steam engine
1776	Adam Smith's *The Wealth of Nations*
1800	British Act of Union
1821–1830	Greek war of independence
1830–1831	Wave of revolutions across Europe
1831	Formation of Young Italy movement by Mazzini
1845–1846	Irish potato famine
1848	Wave of revolts across Europe; *The Communist Manifesto* by Marx and Engels
1851	Great Exhibition in London
1859–1870	Unification of Italy
1862–1871	Unification of Germany
1870s–1914	Second Industrial Revolution

The Age of Machines

The Industrial Revolution introduced an era in which machines produced the goods used by people and increasingly performed more human tasks, reshaping peoples' lives. These machines were moved by energy derived from steam and other inanimate sources rather than human or animal sources. As a result, the Industrial Revolution created great material wealth. Between the 1770s and 1914, a Europe of peasant holdings, country estates, and domestic workshops became a Europe of sprawling and polluted industrial cities such as Manchester, with a wide gap between the few rich and the many poor (see Map 19.3). During the Industrial Revolution, the material culture of Europe and North America changed more than it had in the previous 750 years.

Interactive Map

Technological Innovation

The Industrial Revolution triggered continual technological innovations as inventions in one industry stimulated inventions in others. The cotton industry mechanized first: new cotton machines created a demand for more plentiful and reliable power than could be provided by traditional water wheels and horses. The steam pump invented by the Englishman Thomas Newcomen in 1712, possibly based on an earlier Chinese model and used mostly for pumping water out of mines, was innovative but inefficient. Seeking more efficiency, James Watt (1736–1819), a Scottish inventor, produced the first successful rotary steam engine in 1774. Steam engines ultimately provided power not only for the textile mills but also for the iron furnaces, flour mills, and mines. When used in railroad engines and steamships, steam power conquered time and space, bringing the world much closer together.

After a while technological and economic growth came to be accepted as

> "Beginning around 1770, commercial capitalism, dominated by large trading companies, transformed into industrial capitalism, a system centered around manufacturing."

> 66 The Industrial Revolution introduced an era in which machines produced the goods used by people and increasingly performed more human tasks, reshaping peoples' lives. 99

Luddites Anti-industrialization activists in Britain who destroyed machines in a mass protest against the effects of mechanization.

normal, provoking admiration and wonder. The British novelist William Thackeray celebrated the changes in 1860: "It is only yesterday, but what a gulf between now and then! *Then* was the old world. Stagecoaches, riding horses, pack-horses, knights in armor, Norman invaders, Roman legions—all these belong to the old period. But your railroad starts a new era."[9] In others, however, mechanization provoked fear, causing them to turn against industrialization. Between 1815 and 1830, anti-industrialization activists in Britain known as Luddites, mostly skilled textile workers, invaded factories and destroyed machines in a mass protest against the effects of mechanization. The British government sent in 12,000 troops to stop the destruction and made the wrecking of machines a crime punishable by death.

The Spread of Industrialization

For decades Britain was the world's richest, most competitive nation, with a reputation as the workshop of the world. The new factories and machines mass-produced goods of better quality and lower price than traditional handicrafts, helping the British to overcome the old problem of finding commodities to trade to the world. By the mid-1800s, Britain produced two-thirds of the world's coal, half the iron, and half the cotton cloth and other manufactured goods. The British enjoyed political, military, and economic supremacy in Europe and significant power in other regions of the world.

However, the British invested some of their huge profits in western Europe, spreading the Industrial Revolution across the English Channel between the 1830s and 1870s. As iron-smelting technology improved, industrial operations became concentrated in regions rich in coal and iron

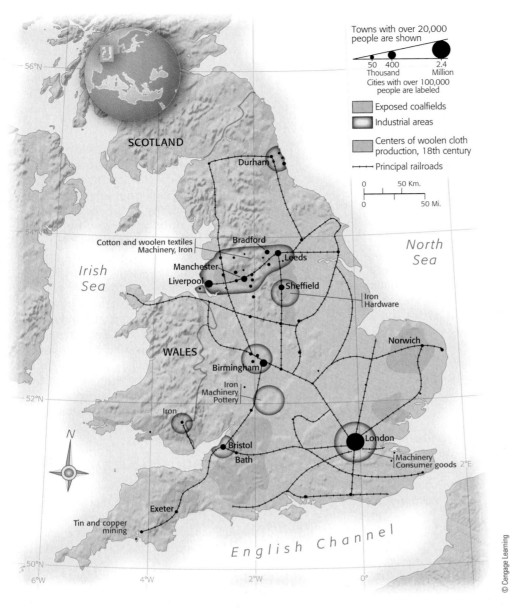

Towns with over 20,000
people are shown

50 400   2.4
Thousand   Million
Cities with over 100,000
people are labeled

Exposed coalfields

Industrial areas

Centers of woolen cloth
production, 18th century

Principal railroads

0   50 Km.

0   50 Mi.

SCOTLAND

Durham

North
Sea

Cotton and woolen textiles
Machinery, Iron

Bradford

Leeds

*Irish
Sea*

Manchester

Liverpool

Sheffield

Iron
Hardware

WALES

Norwich

Birmingham

Iron
Machinery
Pottery

Iron

London

Bristol
Bath

Machinery
Consumer goods 2°E

Exeter

Tin and copper
mining

English Channel

© Cengage Learning

Map 19.3
Industrial Transformation in England

British industrialization mostly occurred near coalfields and iron ore deposits, spurring the rise of cities
such as Birmingham, Leeds, Liverpool, and Manchester.

ore, such as in Belgium. Capitalizing on its reserves of these resources, prosperous trading cities, and a strategic location between France, Holland, and Germany, by 1850 the Belgians had tripled their coal production and increased the number of steam engines from 354 to 2,300. Belgium also capitalized on the transportation revolution, building an ambitious railroad system to transport coal, iron, and manufactured goods and connecting it to neighboring countries.

By the 1830s, France had also begun constructing a national railroad network. In contrast to Britain and Belgium, France had to import coal, and, since it had fewer rich merchants than Britain, the government helped fund industrial activity. In the German states, political fragmentation before 1870 discouraged industrialization, except in several coal-rich regions such as the Ruhr Valley in western Germany and Silesia in Prussia. Some countries, including Portugal,

Industrial Sheffield This painting of one of the key British industrial cities, Sheffield, in 1858 shows the factories, many specializing in producing steel and metal goods, that dominated the landscape.

Spain, and Austria-Hungary, remained largely agricultural. By 1914, however, industrialization was widespread around Europe and had also taken root in North America and Japan, and large numbers of people lived in cities and worked in factories.

Second Industrial Revolution

From about 1870 to 1914, technological change, mass production, and specialization accelerated, causing what some historians call the Second Industrial Revolution. The increasing application of science to industry spurred expansion and improvement in the electrical, chemical, optical, and automotive industries and brought new inventions such as electricity grids, radio, the internal combustion engine, gasoline, and the flush toilet. The United States and Germany led in implementing these changes, and by 1900 Germany was Europe's main producer of electrical goods and chemicals. By the early 1900s, factory production was often done on the assembly line, with work broken down into separate specialized tasks.

 Learn about how songwriter and miner Tommy Armstrong used his song-making talent to address the issue of workers' rights during the Industrial Revolution.

The Second Industrial Revolution promoted a shift to a form of capitalism in which giant monopolies, led by tycoons with unprecedented wealth, replaced the more competitive economy of industrial capitalism. The concentration of capital in what became known as "big business" gave a few businessmen and bankers, such as the Krupp family in Germany and the Rockefellers in the United States, vast economic power and control over many industries. The monopolies emerged because the huge capital investment needed for new factories and important innovations such as electric power eliminated many of the small businesses. A long depression in the late 1800s undermined competition, and spurred a drive to colonize more of the world to ensure access to resources and markets.

ideology
A coherent, widely shared system of ideas about the nature of the social, political, and economic realm.

LO⁴ Nationalism, Liberalism, and Socialism

Besides the political and economic revolutions, the Modern Era also produced three new ideologies—nationalism, liberalism, and socialism—that influenced the European and American political order and that continue to shape our world. An ideology is a secular faith or philosophy: a coherent, widely shared

nationalism
A primary loyalty to, and identity with, a nation bound by a common culture, government, and shared territory.

nation-states
Politically centralized countries with defined territorial boundaries.

> "The Second Industrial Revolution promoted a shift to a form of capitalism in which giant monopolies, led by tycoons with unprecedented wealth, replaced the more competitive economy of industrial capitalism."

system of ideas about the nature of the social, political, and economic realm. In the Modern Era, nationalism fostered unified countries, liberalism encouraged democratic parliamentary governments in various nations, and socialism sparked movements to counteract the power and social impact of industrial capitalism.

Nations and Nationalism

Between 1750 and 1914, many societies in Europe and North America sought to form nations, communities of people united by a common culture and organized into independent states. The ideology that sparked this transition was nationalism, a primary loyalty to, and identity with, a nation bound by shared culture, history, government, and territory. Nationalists insisted that support for country transcended loyalty to family, village, church, region, social class, monarch, or ethnic group. Often appealing more to emotion than reason, nationalism particularly interested the rising middle classes and intellectuals struggling to gain more political power. A Swiss newspaper articulated the ideology well in 1848, declaring that the "nation [Switzerland] stands before us as an undeniable reality with her own voice and equipped with extensive powers. The Swiss of different cantons [small self-governing states] will henceforth be perceived and act as members of a single nation."[10] Some historians conceive of the nation as an "imagined community" that grew in the minds of people living in the same society.

Nationalism helped to cause political solidarity, but it also fostered conflicts and wars, becoming an explo-

 Extract from *History of Germany in the Nineteenth Century*, Heinrich von Treitschke Read about influential historical thinker Heinrich von Treitschke's view that militarism, authoritarianism, and war was the path to German greatness. Does his thinking remind you of other influential leaders? Why do you think his views were appealing?

sive force throughout the world. Most historians credit the birth of modern nationalism to France and Great Britain in the late eighteenth and early nineteenth centuries. The French revolutionaries, in "The Declaration of the Rights of Man," proclaimed that all sovereignty emanated from the nation, rather than from individuals or groups, and the Jacobins identified themselves as custodians of French nationhood. The British also began to conceive of themselves as one nation composed of several peoples as the spread of English power led to the deliberate suffocation of Scottish, Welsh, and Irish cultures and languages in the 1800s.

Nationalism transformed Europe's political landscape. In 1750 large parts of Europe were dominated by multinational states that had ethnically diverse populations. For instance, one royal family, the Vienna-based Habsburgs, ruled Austria, Hungary, the Czech lands, Belgium, and parts of Italy. Sweden ruled Finland, and Denmark ruled Norway. But during the 1800s, nationalism fostered the emergence of nation-states, politically centralized countries with defined territorial boundaries, such as Italy, Belgium, and Norway. By 1914 only the Russian and Habsburg-ruled Austro-Hungarian empires remained major multinational states in Europe.

Unified Nations, Frustrated Nations

In the 1800s, some of the most dramatic efforts to create unified nations were made in Greece, Italy, and Germany. The Greeks, long a part of the Turkish-dominated Ottoman Empire, were one of the first modern European peoples to claim nationhood through violence. Many Greeks served in the Ottoman government, and Greek merchants dominated commerce in Ottoman-ruled western Asia. Wealthy Greek merchants sent their sons to western Europe to study, where they picked up nationalist ideas. Some organized a secret society that began an uprising for independence in 1821, killing many Turks. The Ottomans responded by massacring Greek villages, pillaging churches, and hanging the leader of the Greek Orthodox Church in Istanbul, acts that inflamed western Europeans. In 1827 the intervention of Britain, France, and Russia on the Greek side led to the destruction of the Turkish fleet. In 1830 Greece became independent, and in 1843 a rebellion against Greek royal absolutism resulted in a parliamentary government. Inspired by Greek nationalism, Romania also became independent in 1862.

Italian Unification

While the Greeks wanted independence, Italians wanted to realize a long-held dream of unity. For centuries they were divided into many small states, some of them part of the Habsburg and Holy Roman Empires, some ruled by the pope. In 1831 Giuseppi Mazzini (jew-SEP-pay mots-EE-nee) (1805–1872), a fiery Genoese, founded the Young Italy movement as a brotherhood of Italians who believed that Italy was destined to become one nation. Mazzini promoted a republican form of government and women's rights, radical ideas in Italy, and inspired nationalists elsewhere in Europe. In 1859, Italian nationalists began an armed struggle for unity and drove the Habsburg forces out of the north. By 1861, Mazzini had lost influence, but Giuseppi Garibaldi (gar-uh-BOWL-dee) (1807–1882) helped create the kingdom of Italy, which included all of the states except papal-dominated Rome. In 1870, Italian troops entered Rome, reuniting Italy for the first time since the Roman Empire.

German Reunification

German reunification also came in stages. In 1862, Otto von Bismarck (BIZ-mahrk) (1815–1898), the prime minister of Prussia, brought together many northern German states under Prussian domination. Bismarck shared with the Prussian king William I a dislike of business and professional leaders, who favored expanding democratic political rights. Instead Bismarck looked to uniting the Germans through warfare, a policy he characterized as "blood and iron." A series of wars with Denmark, Austria, and France between 1864 and 1870 significantly expanded Prussia's borders. In 1871, King William I of Prussia was declared *kaiser* (emperor) of a united Germany, by now one of Europe's major powers.

Jewish Minorities

Some peoples, such as the Poles and Jewish Europeans, were unable to satisfy their nationalist aspirations. The Jewish minorities faced difficult barriers, scattered as they were around Europe. Many Jews, especially in Russia, Poland, and Lithuania, had been restricted to all-Jewish villages and urban neighborhoods known as ghettoes, and they often maintained conservative cultural and religious traditions. Other Jews, especially in Germany, France, and Britain, often adopted a more secular approach and moved toward assimilation with the dominant culture. Reacting against widespread anti-Semitism, other Jews gravitated to revolutionary groups or to Zionism (ZYE-uh-niz-uhm), a movement founded by Hungarian-born journalist Theodor Herzl (HERT-suhl) (1860–1904) that sought a Jewish homeland.

> **Zionism**
> A movement arising in late-nineteenth-century Europe that sought a Jewish homeland.

> ❝ Nationalism helped to cause political solidarity, but it also fostered conflicts and wars, becoming an explosive force throughout the world. ❞

Irish Struggle for Independence

The Irish were also frustrated in their desire for nationhood. Ireland had been a colony of England for centuries, and Irish opposition to harsh English rule simmered, sometimes erupting in violence. The English attempted to destroy the language, religion, poetry, literature, dress, and music of the Irish people and came to control much of the best farmland in Ireland. Conditions worsened after 1800, when the English mounted even more severe laws to restrict Irish rights, deporting thousands who resisted to Australia. Many Irish men, with few job prospects, were recruited into the British army to fight in England's colonial wars abroad. Then during the 1840s, the potato crop failed for several successive years. One and a half million Irish died from starvation, while English landlords ejected Irish peasants from the land for more profitable sheep raising. Millions of Irish people sought escape from poverty and repression by emigrating to the Americas and Australia.

But the Irish who remained rebelled against British rule every few years. In the mid-1800s, resistance became more organized, led by the Fenians (FEE-ni-ans), a secret society dedicated to Irish independence. By 1905 the Fenians were transformed into Sinn Fein (shin FANE) (Gaelic for "Ourselves Alone"), which first favored peaceful protest and then turned to violence against English targets. Sinn Fein extremists formed the Irish Republican Army, which organized the 1916 Easter Uprising, in which some 1,500 volunteers seized key buildings in Dublin and

liberalism
An ideology of the Modern Era, based on Enlightenment ideas, that favored emancipating the individual from all restraints, whether governmental, economic, or religious.

parliamentary democracy
Government by representatives elected by the people.

proclaimed a republic in Ireland. The English quickly crushed the rising, shot the ringleaders, and jailed 2,000 of the participants, but Sinn Fein and the IRA would continue to bedevil their English colonizers.

Liberalism and Parliamentary Democracy

While nationalism reshaped states, another ideology emerged to offer a vision of democracy, freedom, and representative governance. Influenced by Enlightenment thinkers such as John Locke and Baron de Montesquieu, liberalism favored emancipating the individual from all restraints, whether governmental, economic, or religious. Liberals supported the sovereignty of the people, representative government, the

right to vote, and basic civil liberties such as freedom of speech, religion, assembly, and the press. The liberal Scottish philosopher John Stuart Mill (1806–1873) offered the most eloquent defense of individual liberty and free expression, writing that no one should restrict what arguments a legislature or executive should be allowed to hear.

Liberal politicians fought against slavery, advocated religious toleration, and promoted constitutional democracy. Liberalism proved particularly popular in Britain and the United States, and it provided the bedrock for the United States Constitution and Bill of Rights. Many historians argue that democratic decision making is an old and widespread idea. Village democracies that allowed many residents to voice their opinions and shape decisions had long existed in various tribal and other stateless societies of Asia, Africa, and the Americas. But in the nineteenth century, liberalism led to political systems like parliamentary democracy, government by representatives elected by the people. Britain became the most successful parliamentary democracy in Europe

Battle of Langhada The Greek war for independence from the Ottoman Turks gained strong support from liberals and nationalists all over Europe. This painting, by the Greek artist Panagiotis Zographos, uses Byzantine art traditions to show Greek soldiers riding to fight the Turks in the Battle of Langhada.

Gennadeion Library, Athens/Visual Connection Archive

as royal power declined. By the 1800s, the British monarch, even one as popular as Queen Victoria (r. 1837–1901), was no longer very powerful. Instead, prime ministers, elected by the majority of Parliament members, had become the major power holders. The Reform Act of 1832 increased the number of voters to about 650,000, all upper- and middle-class males, but this left out many men and all women.

> "Liberal politicians fought against slavery, advocated religious toleration, and promoted constitutional democracy."

Socialism and Marxist Thought

In contrast to liberalism's promotion of individual liberty, socialism focused on equality and the common ownership of economic institutions such as factories. It grew out of the painful social disruption that accompanied the Industrial Revolution, as utopian socialists in Britain, France, and North America offered visions of perfect societies shaped by the common good. For example, British industrialist Robert Owen (1771–1858) set up a model factory town around his cotton mill and later moved to the United States to found a model socialist community, New Harmony, in Indiana. Some proponents of women's rights, such as Emma Martin (1812–1851) in Britain and Flora Tristan (1801–1844) in France, promoted socialism as the solution to end female oppression. Utopian communities tended to be insular and were viewed with suspicion by many citizens.

Karl Marx

Karl Marx (1818–1883) had the most significant influence on socialist thought, and his ideas, known as Marxism, became one of the major intellectual and political influences around the world. Marx, a German Jew with a passion for justice, came from a wealthy family, studied philosophy at the University of Berlin, and then worked as a journalist in several European cities before settling in London. Marx wrote his classic works in the middle and late 1800s. In England he worked closely with his German friend, Friedrich Engels (1820–1895), who collaborated in writing and editing some of Marx's books and introduced Marx to the degraded condition of English industrial workers.

The Communist Manifesto

> ❝ Marx called himself a communist to differentiate himself from earlier socialists, whom he dismissed as naive utopians. ❞

In *The Communist Manifesto* (1848), Marx developed a vision of social change in which the downtrodden could rise up in a violent socialist revolution, seize power from the capitalists, and create a new society (see Witness to the Past: The Communist View of Past, Present, and Future). Marx argued that, through revolution, workers could change their conditions and alter the inequitable political, social, and economic patterns inherited from the past. He also criticized nationalism, writing that working people had no country, only common interests, and needed to cooperate across borders.

Marx was a product of his scientific age and considered his socialist ideas as laws of history. He argued that historical change resulted from class struggle, in which the confrontation between antagonistic social classes produced change. All social and economic systems, he suggested, contain contradictions that doom them to conflict, which generates a higher stage of development. Eventually, Marx predicted, this process would replace capitalism with socialism, where all would share in owning the means of production and the state would serve the interests of the masses rather than the privileged classes. Finally would come communism, where the state would wither away and all would share the wealth, free to realize their human potential without exploitation by capitalists or governments. Such a vision of change proved attractive to many disgruntled people in Europe and later around the world.

Marx's ideas have been hotly debated by economists and historians ever since. He believed that the nature of the economic system and technology determined all aspects of society, including religious values, social relations, government, and laws. Marx also argued that religion was the "opiate of the

proletariat
The industrial working class.

people," encouraging people to fatalistically accept their lot in this life in hopes of earning a better afterlife rather than protesting or rebelling. He criticized capitalism for creating extremes of wealth and poverty and for separating workers from ownership of the means of production—the farms, mines, factories, and businesses where they labored—to furnish wealth to the owners as well as to the urban-based, mostly commercial, middle class that Marx called the bourgeoisie. Under capitalism, workers had become tenants and employees rather than self-employed farmers and craftsmen. Marx observed that the industrial working class, the proletariat, grew more miserable as wealth became concentrated in giant monopolies in the later 1800s.

With its promise of a more equitable society, Marxism became a major world force. Socialist parties were formed all over Europe in the late 1800s and early 1900s, and, in some cases, more radical socialists soon split off to establish parties that called themselves communist. Marxism also influenced the founding of labor unions in the late nineteenth and early twentieth centuries in Europe and North America. But not all poor people or industrial workers in Europe gravitated to Marxism. While many envied the rich and thought life was unfair, they were also inhibited by family, religion, and social connections from joining radical movements or risking their lives in a rebellion that might fail. Marxism never became as influential in the United States or Great Britain as in parts of Europe. The first successful socialist revolution came, over three decades after Marx had died, in Russia.

Social Democracy and Social Reform

Eventually a more evolutionary version of socialist thought gained influence in many European societies. In contrast to the call by radical Marxists for revolution, some socialists favored a more evolutionary approach of effecting change, establishing a system mixing capitalism and socialism within a parliamentary framework. The first Social Democratic Party was formed in Germany in 1875, and soon others emerged in western and eastern European countries. Criticizing Marxist revolutionaries, a German Social Democratic leader, Eduard Bernstein (1850–1932), argued that socialists should work less for the better future and more for the better present.

Labor Unions

Social Democrats, Marxists, and other socialists actively supported labor unions and strikes to promote worker demands. Although most employers were opposed, unions gradually gained recognition as representatives of the workforce. Between 1870 and 1900, unions gained legal status in many nations, and in Britain, France, Germany, the Netherlands, and Sweden, trade unions and labor parties acquired enough political influence to improve working conditions.

In the later 1800s, governments implemented social reforms to address the ills of the Industrial Revolution, creating the interventionist, bureaucratic state with state-run welfare systems. Many European nations passed laws regulating the length of the working day, laws regarding working conditions, and safety rules. Reformers pushed for nationalizing landed property, state inspections of housing, town planning, and slum clearance. To tackle the problem of poverty, Germany and Britain passed social legislation introducing health and unemployment insurance and creating old-age pensions. Contrary to Marx's expectations, life for many European workers improved considerably by the early 1900s, but many people, including children, still worked in dangerous and unhealthy conditions.

LO⁵ The Resurgence of Western Imperialism

The Industrial Revolution provided economic incentives, and nationalism provided political incentives, for European states to exploit the natural and human resources of other lands. In the nineteenth century, European nations colonized and dominated much of Asia and Africa, an explosion of imperialism that reshaped the global system. As a result, industrial capitalism became a genuine world economy. With the entire world connected by economic and political networks, history from now on transcended regions and became truly world history.

 His Story, Ndansi Kumalo Read a firsthand account of the hardships suffered by the Ndebele, a people of southeastern Africa, in their dealings with European colonists.

Industrialization and Imperialism

The quest for colonies diminished somewhat in the first phase of the Industrial Revolution, even for the strongest European power, Great Britain. From the later 1700s through the mid-1800s, the British feared no competitor in world trade because they had none.

The Communist View of Past, Present, and Future

In 1848, Karl Marx and Friedrich Engels published *The Communist Manifesto* as a statement of beliefs and goals for the Communist League, an organization they had founded. In this excerpt Marx and Engels outlined their view of history as founded on class struggle, stressed the formation of the new world economy, and offered communism as the alternative to an oppressive capitalist system.

A specter is haunting Europe—the specter of communism. All the powers of old Europe have entered into a holy alliance to excise this specter. . . . Where is the party in opposition that has not been decried as communistic by its opponents in power? . . . The history of all hitherto existing society is the history of class struggles. . . . Oppressor and oppressed stood in constant opposition to one another, carried on in an uninterrupted, now hidden, now open fight, a fight that each time ended, either in a revolutionary reconstitution of society at large, or in the common ruin of the contending classes.

In the earlier epochs of history, we find almost everywhere a complicated arrangement of society into various orders, a manifold gradation of social rank. In ancient Rome we have patricians, knights, plebeians, slaves; in the Middle Ages, feudal lords, vassals, guild-masters, journeymen, apprentices, serfs; in almost all these classes, again, subordinate gradations. The modern bourgeois [middle class] society that has sprouted from the ruins of feudal society has not done away with class antagonisms. It has but established new classes, new conditions of oppression, new forms of struggle in place of the old ones.

Our epoch, the epoch of the bourgeoisie, possesses, however, this distinctive feature: it has simplified the class antagonisms. Society as a whole is more and more splitting up into two great hostile camps, into two great classes directly facing each other: bourgeoisie and proletariat (working class). . . . The discovery of America, the rounding of the Cape [of Good Hope], opened up fresh ground for the rising bourgeoisie. The East Indian and Chinese markets, the colonization of America, trade with the colonies, the increase in the means of exchange and in commodities generally, gave to commerce, to navigation, to industry, an impulse never before known, and, thereby, a rapid development to the revolutionary element in the tottering feudal society. . . . Meantime the markets kept ever growing, the demand ever rising. Even manufacture no longer

sufficed. Thereupon, steam and machinery revolutionized industrial production. The place of manufacture was taken by the giant, modern industry, the place of the industrial middle class, by industrial millionaires. . . .

Modern industry has established the world market, for which the discovery of America paved the way. . . . The bourgeoisie, by the rapid improvement of all instruments of production, by the immensely facilitated means of communication, draws all, even the most barbarian, nations into civilization. The cheap prices of its commodities are the heavy artillery with which it batters down all Chinese walls. . . . It compels all nations, on pain of extinction, to adopt the bourgeois mode of production. . . . It creates a world after its own image. . . .

[The Communists] have no interests separate from those of the proletariat as a whole. . . . The immediate aim of the Communists is . . . the formation of the proletariat into a class; the overthrow of the bourgeois supremacy; and the conquest of political power by the proletariat. . . . The Communists disdain to conceal their views and aims. They openly declare that their ends can be attained only by the forcible overthrow of all existing social conditions. Let the ruling classes tremble at a Communistic revolution. The proletarians have nothing to lose but their chains. They have a world to win. WORKING MEN OF ALL COUNTRIES, UNITE!

Thinking About the Reading

1. What did Marx and Engels identify as the opposing classes in European history?

2. What developments aided the rise of the bourgeoisie to power?

3. What is the goal of the Communists?

Source: From *The Communist Manifesto,* trans. 1880. http://www.anv.edu.au/polisci/marx/classics/manifesto.html.

Britain already controlled or had gained access to valuable territories in the Americas, Africa, Asia, and the Pacific. While Britain lost its thirteen North American colonies, it took control of French Canada and Australia. Furthermore, the collapse of Spain and Portugal during the Napoleonic wars led to most of their Latin American colonies becoming independent in the 1820s, opening doors for British commercial activity.

> "From the later 1700s through the mid-1800s, the British feared no competitor in world trade because they had none."

the top, followed by Germany and then a fading Britain and France.

As they industrialized, Germany, France, and the United States became more competitive with Britain, and growing economic and political competition renewed the quest for colonies abroad. The shift to domestic economies dominated by large monopolies was a major factor in the new push for colonies in Africa and Asia. The monopolies stimulated empire building by piling up huge profits and hence excess capital that needed investment outlets abroad to keep growing. Furthermore, by the 1880s, some of the wealth generated by the industrial economy began to filter down to the European working classes, stimulating new consumer interests in tropical products such as chocolate, tea, soap, and rubber for bicycle tires. To satisfy the need for resources and markets, Western businessmen looked for new opportunities to exploit in Africa, Asia, and the Pacific, and then pressured their governments to assist their efforts.

New Technologies

British merchants also benefited from new technologies that enabled them to compete all over the world. Steam power meant that British ships could reach distant shores faster. The first exclusively steam-powered ships appeared in 1813 and took 113 days to travel from England around Africa to India, in contrast to eight or nine months by sailing ships. Then in 1869, the completion of the Suez Canal linking the Mediterranean Sea and the Red Sea dramatically cut the travel time between the Indian Ocean and Europe. Britain, the canal's major shareholder, now found it easier to extend its influence to East Africa and Southeast Asia.

> ❝ Western imperialism forged networks of interlinked social, economic, and political relationships spanning the globe. ❞

Shifts in Economic Advantage

Despite a pragmatic preference for peaceful commerce, Britain did obtain some colonies between 1750 and 1870. The British took over territories or fought wars when local governments, such as India, Malaya, and Burma, refused to trade or could not protect British commerce by establishing law and order (see Chapter 22). However, the British economic advantage in world markets gradually diminished as economic leadership in the world changed during the later 1800s. The British invested many of the profits that they earned from India and their Caribbean colonies in other nations, much of it in the United States, Canada, and Australia. Because British investors found it more profitable to invest abroad rather than at home, British industrial plants became increasingly obsolete. In 1860, Britain had been the leading economic power; by 1900, the United States was at

National rivalries also motivated imperialism. Nations often seized colonies to prevent competitors from gaining opportunities. The result was the greatest land grab in world history: between 1870 and 1914, a handful of European powers divided up the globe among themselves. The national rivalries and intense competition for colonies also planted the roots of conflict in Europe. By the early 1900s, Germany and Austria-Hungary had forged an alliance, and this prompted Britain, France, and Russia to do likewise, setting the stage for World War I.

The Scramble for Empire

With the resurgent Western imperialism, millions of people in Africa, Asia, and the Pacific Islands were conquered or impacted by Western nations and thus brought into the Western dominated world economic system. However, many peoples fiercely resisted conquest. The Vietnamese, Burmese, and various Indonesian and African societies held off militarily superior European armies for decades, and even after conquest, guerrilla forces often continued to attack European colonizers (see Chapters 21 and 22). Countless revolts punctuated colonial rule, from West Africa to the Philippines, and Western ambitions were sometimes frustrated. In Africa, Ethiopians defeated an Italian invasion force bent on conquest. A few Asians maintained their independence by using creative strategies. The Japanese prevented Western political domination by modernizing their own government and economy, and the Siamese (Thai) used skillful diplomacy and selective modernization to deflect Western power.

Imperial Expansion

New technologies permitted and stimulated imperial expansion. The Industrial Revolution gave Europeans better weapons, including the machine gun to enforce their will. A British writer boasted: "Whatever happens we have got the Maxim Gun, and they have not."[11] These weapons gave Europeans a huge advantage against Asians and Africans, and the discovery of quinine to treat malaria enabled European colonists and officials to survive in tropical Africa and Southeast Asia. Later, better communication and transportation networks, such as steamship lines, colonial railroads, and undersea telegraph cables, also helped consolidate Western control.

As the scramble continued, old European empires grew and new ones were founded (see Map 19.4). By 1900, Western colonial powers controlled 90 percent of Africa, 99 percent of Polynesia, and 57 percent of Asia. By 1914, the British Empire, the world's largest, included fifty-five colonies containing 400 million people, ten times Britain's population, inspiring the boast that "the sun never sets on the British Empire." France acquired the next largest empire of twenty-nine colonies. Germany, Spain, Belgium, and Italy joined in the grab for African colonies. Between 1898 and 1902, the United States took over Hawaii, Samoa, Puerto Rico, and the Philippines. Russia also continued its expansion in Eurasia, which began in the Early Modern Era (see Chapter 23).

Interactive Map

Increasing Globalization

Western imperialism forged networks of interlinked social, economic, and political relationships spanning the globe. Hence, decisions made by a

Lipton Tea European imperial expansion brought many new products to European consumers. Tea, grown in British-ruled India, Sri Lanka (Ceylon), and Malaya, became a popular drink, advertised here in a London weekly magazine.

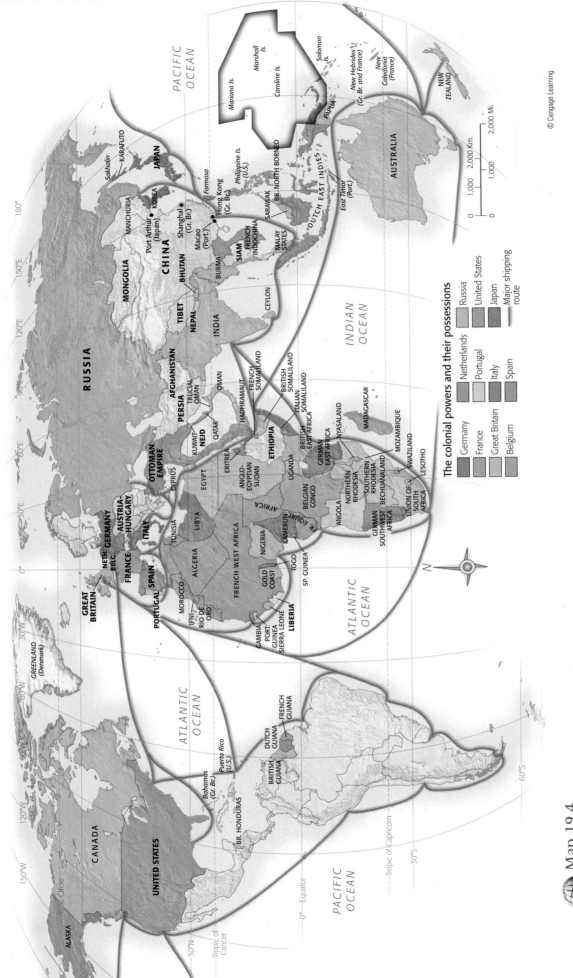

Map 19.4
The Great Powers and Their Colonial Possessions in 1913

By 1913, the British and French controlled huge empires, with colonies in Africa, southern Asia, the Caribbean zone, and the Pacific Basin. Russia ruled much of northern Eurasia, while the United States, Japan, and a half-dozen European nations controlled smaller empires.

The colonial powers and their possessions

- Germany
- France
- Great Britain
- Belgium
- Netherlands
- Portugal
- Italy
- Spain
- Russia
- United States
- Japan
- Major shipping route

© Cengage Learning

government or business in London or Paris soon affected people in faraway Malaya or Madagascar, and silk spun in China was turned into dresses worn by fashionable women in Chicago and Munich. Westerners had the strongest position in this network, ruling many subject peoples and enjoying advantageous trade relations with or strong influence over neocolonies such as China, Siam, Persia, and Argentina. Yet various Asian, African, and Caribbean peoples also challenged the colonial regimes (see Chapters 21, 22, and 25).

The scope of Western imperialism changed world power arrangements. In 1750, China and the Ottoman Empire remained among the world's strongest countries, but by 1914 they could not match Western military and economic power. In 1500, the wealth gap between the more economically developed and the less developed Eurasian and African societies was small, and China and India dominated world trade and manufacturing. By 1914, the gap in total wealth and personal income between industrialized societies, whether in Europe or North America, and most other societies, including China and India, had grown very wide.

Social Darwinism and Imperial Ideology

By the late 1800s, a new ideology known as Social Darwinism supported the revival of imperialism and colonialism. Supporters of imperialism used the ideas about the natural world developed by the British scientist Charles Darwin, who described a struggle for existence among species (see Chapter 20). This idea led other thinkers to conclude that this struggle led to the survival of the fittest, a notion that they then applied to the human world of social classes and nations.

Industrialized peoples considered themselves the most fit and saw exploited peoples as less fit. A German naval officer wrote in 1898 that "the struggle for life exists among individuals, provinces, parties and states. The latter wage it either by the use of arms or in the economic field. Those who don't want to, will perish."[12] Social Darwinists stereotyped Asian and African societies as "backward" and held their own nations up as "superior" peoples who had the right—and obligation—to rule.

....

Racism

As a result of this ideology, Western racism and arrogance toward other peoples increased. For example, in the 1600s and 1700s, many Western observers had admired the Chinese, and Enlightenment thinkers saw China as a model of secular and efficient government. But by the 1800s, Europeans and North Americans had developed scorn for "John Chinaman" and the "heathen Chinee." Most Western peoples accepted these stereotypes; the British imperialist Cecil Rhodes boasted, "I contend that we British are the finest race in the world, and that the more of the world we inhabit the better it is for the human race."[13]

Speech Before the French National Assembly, July 28, 1883, Jules Ferry Read French imperialist Jules Ferry's reasons for supporting French expansionism.

> " Industrialized peoples considered themselves the most fit and saw exploited peoples as less fit. "

This perceived superiority legitimized the effort to "improve" other people by bringing them Western culture and religion. The French proclaimed their "civilizing mission" in Africa and Indochina; the British in India claimed that they were "taking up the white man's burden"; and the Americans colonized the Philippines claiming condescendingly to "uplift" their "little brown brothers." Western defenders argued that colonialism, despite much that was shameful, gave non-Western societies better government and drew them out of isolation into the world market. A British newspaper in 1896 claimed that "the advance of the Union Jack means protection for weaker races, justice for the oppressed, liberty for the down-trodden."[14] However, most people in Asia, Africa, and the Pacific opposed colonialism, seeing it only for the terrible toll it took on their lives. The Indian nationalist leader Mohandas Gandhi, educated in Britain, reflected the resentment. When asked what he thought about "Western civilization," he replied that civilizing the West would be a good idea.

Listen to a synopsis of Chapter 19.

CHAPTER 20

Changing Societies in Europe, the Americas, and Oceania,

1750–1914

Learning Outcomes

After reading this chapter, you should be able to answer the following questions:

LO¹ How and why did European social, cultural, and intellectual patterns change during this era?

LO² How did westward expansion, industrialization, and immigration transform American society?

LO³ What political, economic, and social patterns shaped Latin America after independence?

LO⁴ Why did the foundations for nationhood differ in Canada and Oceania?

❝At present, all of the European countries shine with the light of civilization and have an abundance of wealth and power. Their trade is prosperous, their technology is superior, and they greatly enjoy the pleasures and comforts of life. Upon observing such conditions, one is apt to conclude that these countries have always been like this, but such is not the case. The wealth and prosperity one now sees in Europe date to a considerable degree from the period after 1800. It has taken forty years to produce such conditions.**❞**

—**Kume Kunitake**[1]

In 1871, a thirty-three-year-old Japanese samurai and Confucian scholar, Kume Kunitake (1839–1931), boarded an American steamship at Yokohama and began a three-week voyage to San Francisco as a member of an information-gathering delegation sent from Japan to the United States and then Europe. Hoping to avoid conquest, the government had asked Kume's group to assess the factors behind growing Western power in the world. Kume's delegation traveled across America, visiting factories, museums, schools, churches, public parks, and scenic mountains. Kume filtered his perceptive impressions of Western life through the cultural lens of Japan, concluding that "the customs and characteristics of East and West are invariably different." Kume admired U.S. democracy but noted that Americans were "careless about official authority, each person insisting on his own rights." Kume recorded the Americans' friendliness but also their brashness, ambition, and sense of destiny.

After leaving the United States, Kume's delegation traveled to Europe, where Kume was delighted to see how Europeans treasured and even imitated Japanese art. He loved the culture, but as an ardent Confucian rationalist, he disliked Christianity, which he saw as irrational. Kume contrasted the splendor of the churches with the poverty of the people, criticizing what he saw as the "unbounded

Test your knowlege before you read this chapter.

What do you think?

Unlike European nations, the United States never colonized other regions.

Strongly Disagree						Strongly Agree
1	2	3	4	5	6	7

<<**Australian Gold Rush** The discovery of gold in southeastern Australia set off a gold rush in the 1850s. Hoping to strike it rich, miners, often from other countries, among them Chinese, flocked to the goldfields, and immigration to Australia boomed.

greed" of Western rulers and merchants. Finally, returning by ship to Japan, Kume's delegation passed through the colonies of Ceylon, Singapore, and Hong Kong, where he noted ruefully, "Ever since the Europeans began to travel to distant places, the weak countries of the tropics have all been fought over and devoured, and their abundant products taken. They treated the natives with arrogance and cruelty."[2] Kume later became a distinguished professor of history at Tokyo University, and his journals continue to provide insights about the Modern Era's imbalances of wealth and power.

Although Europe, the Americas, and Oceania were geographically and historically distinct, their societies were shaped by similar patterns of capitalism, migration, overseas imperialism, and nation-building between 1750 and 1914. By 1914 the United States, Canada, and Mexico occupied all of North America, while Latin American and the Caribbean societies divided into many countries. In the Pacific Ocean Basin, the Europeans also settled the region known today as Oceania, which comprises Australia and New Zealand, while colonizing other, smaller islands. The United States, Canada, Australia, and New Zealand, and some Latin American countries all became settler societies that were colonized chiefly by European immigrants, who planted European institutions and ideas after indigenous populations were largely wiped out. Europeanization also occurred in societies such as Mexico, Cuba, Venezuela, and Peru, where nonwhite and mixed-descent peoples were a larger percentage of the population. European influence in American and Oceanic settler societies varied by time, circumstances,

> "Expanding economies, better public health, and the introduction of new crops such as potatoes from the Americas lowered Europe's mortality rate and fostered population growth."

and the cultures of ethnic minorities.

In the Americas, the United States and Canada gradually diverged from Latin America in their economic and social patterns and cultures. As Kume observed, many in the United States held vast expectations for their nation's global influence and wealth. By expanding its frontiers and rapidly industrializing in the 1800s, the United States became the colossus of North America and a world power, extending its political and economic influence into Latin America and the Caribbean.

LO¹ The Reshaping of European Societies

Thanks to destabilizing revolutions in political and economic life (see Chapter 19), modern Europeans lived in a world of cities, new forms of work, and temptations to abandon home villages for urban areas or faraway lands in search of work and a better life. Industrialization led to changing social structures and family systems. The world of thought, the arts, and science reflected the new Europe that emerged in the Modern Era, and the resulting innovations influenced peoples around the world.

Population Growth, Emigration, and Urbanization

Expanding economies, better public health, and the introduction of new crops such as potatoes from the Americas lowered Europe's mortality rate and fostered population growth. People married earlier and more frequently, increasing the birthrate. Europe's population (including Russia) grew from 100 million in 1650 to 190 million in 1800 and to 420 million in 1900, one of the world's highest growth rates at that time.

The Threat of Overpopulation

Rapid population growth created new problems, however. Thomas Mal-

CHRONOLOGY

European Society and Culture,
1750–1914

1859	Publication of Charles Darwin's *On the Origin of Species*
1860s	Beginning of impressionist artistic movement in France
1896	Women's suffrage in Finland
1905	Publication of Albert Einstein's general theory of relativity

thus, an English clergyman and economist, argued in 1798 that population growth was checked by poverty, disease, war, and famine, but if these problems were eliminated, the gains in human security would soon disappear as the world's population outgrew its means of subsistence. Throughout Europe, many were compelled to move overseas or migrate to urban areas. Poles, for example, moved to the mines of northern France and western Germany, and emigration cut Ireland's population by half between 1841 and 1911. Jews, too, migrated as the tensions caused by competition for scarce resources increased. In some areas, they were victims of coordinated mob attacks known as *pogroms* (from the Russian word meaning "round-up"). Some 45 million Europeans emigrated to the Americas, Australia, New Zealand, Algeria, and South Africa to escape poverty (see Map 20.1).

 Interactive Map

Europeans also moved from rural areas to cities, which increased social problems. The larger European cities grew spectacularly between 1800 and 1900: London increased from 900,000 to 4.7 million, Paris from 600,000 to 3.6 million, and Berlin from 170,000 to 2.7 million. Rapidly expanding cities lacked social services such as sanitation, street cleaning, and water distribution. Huge numbers of people lived in poverty, crammed into overcrowded housing with high disease rates. Millions lived in crime-ridden slums. As the English poet William Blake wrote: "Every night and every morn, some to misery are born." The standard of living did not rise much for most Europeans until the 1880s, when incomes began to improve and several countries, including Britain and Germany, developed social welfare programs for their citizens.

Advances in Agriculture

While cities grew dramatically, western European rural life also changed. Agricultural technology and practices developed rapidly, resulting in better yields, more mechanization, and improved animal breeding. Market agriculture largely displaced the subsistence production of earlier times. But even with improved farming methods, peasants often earned low wages, and many small farmers lost their land to more highly capitalized and mechanized operations. Occasional famines also occurred, notably in Ireland and Russia, but by the 1850s, such disasters were rare except as a result of war. In contrast to western Europe, some feudal traditions remained influential in eastern countries like Russia and Poland, where the landed gentry retained authority over peasant lives.

Society and Family Life

Population movement and urbanization were only two manifestations of much broader changes resulting from industrialization. After 1870, the rise of mass-distribution newspapers, organized football (soccer) leagues, more widespread vacation travel, and other activities connected peoples within and between nations. People enjoyed a growing range of options in areas of life that were once fixed by tradition, such as where to live, work, or go to church and whom to marry, but such choices increased moral anxiety and social instability. For example, the middle class increasingly discouraged sexual activity before marriage and limited sexual intercourse within marriage, while the working classes experienced higher rates of illegitimacy, infidelity, and more frequent sexual relations than ever before. Thus, a British factory girl in 1909 complained, "I wanted no one to know that I was a factory girl because I was ashamed at my position. I was always hearing people say that factory girls were loose-living and corrupt."[3]

Families still provided the framework of social life, but changes occurred. During the Early Modern Era, some people in northern Europe, especially England and the Low Countries, began to marry later and live in nuclear families, which were

> " Families still provided the framework of social life, but changes occurred. "

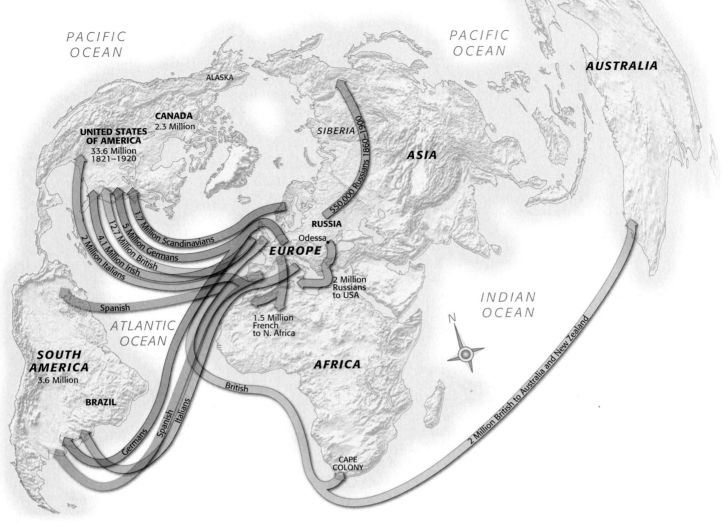

PACIFIC OCEAN

PACIFIC OCEAN

AUSTRALIA

ALASKA

CANADA
2.3 Million

UNITED STATES
OF AMERICA
33.6 Million
1821–1920

SIBERIA

ASIA

550,000 Russians 1860–1900

1.7 Million Scandinavians
5 Million Germans
12.7 Million British
4.1 Million Irish
2 Million Italians

RUSSIA
Odessa

EUROPE

2 Million
Russians
to USA

INDIAN
OCEAN

Spanish

ATLANTIC
OCEAN

1.5 Million
French
to N. Africa

SOUTH
AMERICA
3.6 Million

AFRICA

N

BRAZIL

Germans
Spanish
Italians

British

2 Million British to Australia and New Zealand

CAPE
COLONY

© Cengage Learning

Map 20.1
European Emigration, 1820–1910

Pushed by rapid population growth and poverty, millions of Europeans left their homes to settle in the Americas (especially the United States), North and South Africa, Siberia, Australia, and New Zealand. The British and Irish accounted for the largest numbers of emigrants, nearly 17 million combined. (Reprinted by permission of HarperCollins Publishers, Ltd. © *Times Atlas of World History*, 3rd. ed. Some data from Eric Hobsbawm, *The Age of Empire, 1875–1914* [New York: Pantheon, 1987]).

smaller than extended families of just parents and their children. During the 1800s, the nuclear pattern became common in most of northern Europe, especially among the middle classes, while large extended families remained the norm in southern and eastern Europe. In the 1700s, western Europeans began to adopt the notion that people should have the freedom to choose their partner and marry for love, rather than to meet family demands or economic need. At the same time, middle-class men often assumed that women belonged at home as submissive helpmates and encouraged them to cul-

tivate their beauty and social graces to please their menfolk.

The industrial economy was hard on working families, particularly on women and children. Most Europeans assumed that women were not breadwinners and hence should be paid less than men. Women typically earned only 25 percent of men's wages. Women and children also often did hard manual labor in cotton mills and mines. In 1838, a liberal member of the British parliament reported: "I saw a cotton mill, a sight that froze my blood, full of women, young, all of them, some large with child, and obliged to stand twelve hours each day. The heat was excessive in some of the rooms, the stink pestiferous. I nearly fainted."[4] Increased mechanization and labor reforms, however, meant that fewer women and far fewer children worked full-time in the industrial sector by the early 1900s.

Challenges to Societal Norms

The dynamism of industrializing societies led some to challenge social norms. By the later 1800s, some men and women criticized marriage as stifling and old-fashioned. Prominent people in the artistic and political worlds, such as the popular French actress Sarah Bernhardt and the fiery German socialist Rosa Luxemburg, lived openly with same-sex partners out of wedlock. Homosexuals could be found at all levels of society, but they often faced discrimination and persecution, as did the Irish poet, novelist, and playwright Oscar Wilde (1854–1900), the married father of two, who was tried and imprisoned in 1895 for engaging in homosexual relationships, known as sodomy. The increasing attention to homosexuality and the first scientific studies of it sparked heated and ongoing debates.

Nevertheless, men remained dominant in the political, social, economic, and religious spheres, and women's roles were increasingly restricted to marriage, motherhood, and child rearing. Often women had no legal standing and could not divorce their husbands. Women struggled to adapt to the changing circumstances. Upper- and middle-class women practiced artificial birth control and had fewer children than in earlier eras. In the later 1800s, European women gained more legal rights and economic opportunities. Leading professional women, such as the influential German composer and pianist Clara Schumann (1819–1896) and the British nurse Florence Nightingale (1820–1910), provided role models, and schools for girls grew in number. In 1867 the University of Zurich in Switzerland became the first university to admit women and was soon followed by universities in France, Sweden, and Finland.

feminism
A philosophy that became strong in the twentieth century, promoting political, social, and economic equality for women with men.

suffragettes
Women who press for the same voting rights as men.

The Emergence of Feminism

Some women began movements promoting what later became known as feminism, a philosophy promoting political, social, and economic equality for women with men. One leader of the British movement, Harriett Taylor, wrote bitterly that "all that has been said respecting the social condition of women goes on the assumption of their [innate] inferiority. People do not complain of [women's] state being degraded at all."[5] Inspired by pioneers such as Mary Wollstonecraft in the late 1700s, the first feminist movements emerged in Britain and Scandinavia, with some women, later known as suffragettes, such as the British Emily Pankhurst (1858–1928), pressing for the same voting rights as men. In 1896, Finland became the first European nation to accept female suffrage.

SHE. IT IS TIME I GOT OUT OF THIS PLACE. WHERE SHALL I FIND THE KEY ?

CONVICTS LUNATICS AND WOMEN! HAVE NO VOTE FOR PARLIAMENT

Library of Congress

"Convicts and Lunatics" The movement for women's right to vote, or suffrage, was particularly strong in Britain. This poster, "Convicts and Lunatics," designed by the artist Emily Harding Andrews for the Artist's Suffrage League around 1908, shows a woman graduate, deprived of basic political rights, treated similarly to a convict and a mentally disturbed man.

Thought and Religion

The industrial and political revolutions, and the social changes they sparked, fostered new directions in European thought. Philosophers such as the Germans Immanuel Kant (KAHNT) (1724–1804) and Friedrich Nietzsche (NEE-chuh) (1844–1890) contested the values of the Enlightenment, a movement based on reason that began in the 1600s and continued through the 1700s. Kant believed that experience alone was inadequate for understanding, because the perceptions it fosters are ultimately shaped by the mind, which imposes a structure on the sensations we see and converts these sensations into knowledge. He doubted that a perfect society could ever be achieved, arguing that "man wishes concord, but nature, knowing better what is good for his species, wishes discord."[6] To Nietzsche, there was no fundamental truth, including moral and scientific truth, as the Enlightenment philosophers had thought, but rather misconceptions developed by each culture as its members tried to understand the world. With no absolute truth, absolute good and evil cannot exist. In the twentieth century, extreme nationalists and racists distorted Nietzsche's ideas to persecute ethnic minorities.

For many Europeans, religion also changed with the times. Gradually, Protestants and Catholics learned to tolerate each other, but religious passions did not diminish. In the later 1700s and early 1800s, an evangelical revival inspired many English Anglicans and Baptists to seek personal relations with God, as well as social reform and missionary activity. Soon new faiths emerged, such as charismatic British Anglican preacher John Wesley's (1703–1791) Methodist movement, which sought a more emotional faith and appealed particularly to miners and factory workers.

In contrast to evangelical movements, some Europeans embraced secular approaches, as the relevance of religion declined for many. Some middle-class Protestants sought a liberalized faith stressing social tolerance rather than the hellfire and damnation preached by some evangelicals. Thus, by 1851, only half of the English population attended church. The divide between the more liberal and the more devout resulted in public debates across Europe about the role of religion in society. The Roman Catholic and Greek Orthodox Churches also faced challenges. Spurred by the French Revolution, the Catholic clergy in France and Belgium lost the privileged status they had enjoyed for centuries, such as control of education and exemption from taxes. France opened a public school system in the 1890s and mandated state neutrality toward religion in 1905. At the same time, however, the Catholic Church remained important in Austria, southern Germany, Poland, Spain, Portugal, and Italy. The Greek Orthodox world fragmented into national churches in Greece, Serbia, Romania, and Bulgaria.

New Directions in Culture, Science, and Technology

Literature and the arts also reflected the changing times. The growth of a literate public liberated writers, composers, and artists from dependence on wealthy patrons, but they now had to satisfy the new commercial world of a consuming public.

Romanticism

Inspired by the political revolutions of the late 1700s and early 1800s, some thinkers and artists adopted romanticism, a philosophical, literary, artistic, and musical movement that questioned the Enlightenment's rationalist values and instead glorified emotions, individual imagination, and heroism. The German Friedrich Schiller (1759–1805), a former soldier, offered intense romantic images with a nationalist tinge, such as a poem that turned the story of William Tell, a legendary hero of Swiss resistance against foreign invasion, into a manifesto for German political freedom. In contrast to romanticism, writers and artists embracing another movement, realism, portrayed a grimy industrial world filled with uncertainty and conflict. For example, the liberal Spanish painter Francisco de Goya (GOI-uh) (1746–1828) produced a moving series on the Napoleonic invasion of Spain that portrayed not warfare's glory and heroism but its horrors: orphans, pain, rape, blood, and despair. The British novelist and former factory worker Charles Dickens (1812–1870) revealed in detail the hardships of industrial life, the injustices of capitalism, and the miseries of the poor.

European classical music enjoyed a golden age during this period. Influenced by the Enlightenment, the Austrian Wolfgang Amadeus Mozart (MOTE-sahrt) (1756–1791) wrote thirty-five symphonies, eight operas, and many concertos. Romanticism inspired many later composers, most famously the German Ludwig van Beethoven (BAY-toe-vuhn) (1770–1827), whose much admired Ninth Symphony set Schiller's poem, "Ode to Joy," to music.

The Influence of Modernism

Between 1880 and 1914, Europe was swept by a quite different movement, modernism, a cultural trend that openly broke with romanticism, realism, and other traditions by welcoming the future and new ideas. Several significant movements influenced by modernism shaped the visual arts in the later 1800s, sparked in part by the increasingly connected world and European exposure to Asian, African, and Pacific art. One such movement was impressionism, whose practitioners such as Claude Monet (moe-NAY) (1840–1926) and Pierre Renoir (ren-WAH) (1841–1919) sought to express the immediate impression aroused in momentary scenes, bathed in changing light and color.

In the 1880s, other French artists experimented with a return to elemental shapes and compositions. The most influential included Paul Cezanne (say-ZAN) (1839–1906), famous for his landscapes and portraits; the prolific Dutch-born Vincent Van Gogh (van GO) (1853–1890), who introduced intense primary colors and thick brushstrokes; and Paul Gauguin (go-GAN) (1848–1903), whose richly colored paintings often featured idyllic scenes of Polynesian life, stimulating European interest in the wider world. By the early 1900s, Pablo Picasso (pi-KAH-so) (1881–1973), a young Spaniard who settled in Paris, was already revolutionizing Western art with his new approaches, such as integrating ideas from African sculpture and masks.

Medicine, Darwin, and Einstein

Europeans also made spectacular achievements in science and technology. Some major breakthroughs came in medicine and public health, such as the development of effective vaccines against deadly diseases such as smallpox that had ravaged the world for centuries. Improved sanitation led to better public health and the prevention of many diseases such as cholera, which was eradicated from Europe's industrial cities by 1874. Scientists also made major contributions to the understanding of nature. British naturalist Charles Darwin (1809–1882)—after years spent traveling around the world studying plants, animals, and fossils in many lands—formulated the theory of evolution emphasizing the natural selection of species. In his book, *On the Origin of Species*, Darwin argued that all existing species of plants and animals, including humans, had either adapted to their environment over millions of years or died out. Eventually evolution became the foundation for the modern biological sciences, but many religious leaders saw it as a degradation of humanity.

The German-born Jewish physicist Albert Einstein (1879–1955) also transformed western science. His papers on the theory of relativity, published in the early 1900s when he worked as a clerk in the Swiss patent office, provided the basis for modern physics, our understanding of the universe, and the atomic age. Einstein offered a new view of space and time, showing that distances and durations are not, as Newton thought, absolute but are affected by one's motion. He also proved that matter can be converted into energy and that everything is composed of atoms, insights that provided the basis for atomic energy. His papers electrified the scientific world and continue to influence modern science.

> ❝ New and rapid technological discoveries all over Europe improved people's lives. ❞

modernism
A cultural trend that openly broke with romanticism and other traditions by embracing progress and welcoming the future.

Radios, Automobiles, and Greenhouse Gases

New and rapid technological discoveries all over Europe improved people's lives. In the early 1800s, electric batteries, motors, and generators emerged as new sources of power. In the 1890s, the Italian Guglielmo Marconi (mahr-KO-nee) (1874–1937) introduced wireless telegraphy: in 1901 he used his invention to communicate between England and Canada, opening another network connecting the world. Various inventors worked on building internal combustion engines, and two Germans, Gottlieb Daimler and Karl Benz, became the "fathers of the automobile," producing the first petroleum-powered vehicle in the 1880s. Meanwhile, some scientists worried about the effects of industrial pollution on the environment. The observation that carbon-dioxide emissions from coal-burning factories heated the atmosphere led the Swedish scientist Svante Arrhenius to speak of a "greenhouse effect" that potentially threatened modern societies, an issue that continues to engage scientists.

LO² The United States: A Rising Global Power

After the American Revolution, in which the thirteen colonies successfully overthrew British control, the newly minted citizens turned to building their nation. The United States became an ongoing experiment as Americans learned how to balance regionalism and national unity, freedom and order, individualism and social obligation, and national autonomy and world leadership.

During the early republic, Americans established new forms of government, reshaped economic patterns, fostered a new culture, and began the movement westward. Later, after the Civil War (1861–1865),

> "During the early republic, Americans established new forms of government, reshaped economic patterns, fostered a new culture, and began the movement westward."

the United States changed dramatically, as slavery ended and the federal government asserted more authority over the states. This centralization, combined with economic protectionism and an abundance of resources, allowed the United States to expand its territory, economy, population, and international influence dramatically.

CHRONOLOGY

The United States and the World, 1750–1914

1787	U.S. Constitution
1803	Louisiana Purchase
1812–1814	U.S.-British War of 1812
1823	Monroe Doctrine
1825	Completion of Erie Canal
1846–1848	U.S.-Mexican War
1848	U.S. acquisition of Texas, California, and New Mexico
1849	California gold rush
1861–1865	Civil War
1862	Lincoln's Emancipation Proclamation
1867	U.S. purchase of Alaska from Russia
1869	Completion of transcontinental railroad
1898	U.S. incorporation of Hawaii
1898–1902	Spanish-American War
1902	U.S. colonization of Philippines
1903	First powered flight by Wright Brothers

Government and Economy

After the War of Independence ended in 1783, its leaders were divided over many issues, including the power of a national government and the comparative autonomy of the separate states. The Constitution and Bill of Rights, approved in 1787, established a relatively powerful central government, elected by voters in each state, within a system, known as federalism, that ensured the sovereignty and recognized the lawmaking powers of each member state. White Americans gained many civil liberties, and white adult males were granted the right to vote, but the government maintained slavery and excluded nonwhites and women from political activity.

The American republic reflected a mix of liberalism and fear of disorder. Inspired by a hatred of despotic government in Europe, the founders made tyranny difficult through the separation of powers into executive and legislative branches and an independent judiciary, with each institution having defined roles. But wary of potential radicalism and shocked by the excesses of the French Revolution, the nation's leaders also discouraged attacks on the interests of the upper classes by limiting voting rights. The indirect election for the presidency through the Electoral College, in which each state chose electors to cast their

 **WWW-VL: History: United States** (*http://vlib.iue.it/history/USA/*). A virtual library that contains links to hundreds of sites.

votes, also reduced popular sovereignty and produced results that did not always reflect the choice of the majority of citizens.

American leaders also had to establish a sound economic foundation for the new nation. The southern plantation interests favored free trade to market their crops abroad without obstacles, especially cotton, tobacco, and sugar. Many northerners, meanwhile, hoped to foster an Industrial Revolution like Britain's. The first treasury secretary, the West Indian–born Alexander Hamilton (1757–1804), laid the basis by establishing a national bank, favoring tariffs to exclude competitive foreign goods, and providing government support for industry.

The War of 1812

Hamilton's policies and protectionism encouraged manufacturing but led to another conflict with Great Britain. Tensions over trade, the nebulous U.S.–Canada border, and other issues led to the War of 1812 (1812–1814). The British captured Washington, burning down the White House, and repulsed a U.S. invasion of Canada, but after some U.S. victories, the two sides negotiated peace. Industrialization proceeded in the U.S. Northeast, and in 1813 the first large textile mills to convert raw cotton into finished cloth opened in New England. The northern industrialists who favored protectionist policies soon prevailed over the southern planters who wanted free trade. Meanwhile, to move resources and products, Americans also built more than 3,300 miles of canals by 1840. The longest of these was the Erie Canal, completed across New York State in 1825, which linked the markets and resources of the Midwest and Mississippi Basin to the port of New York City.

> 66 The American republic reflected a mix of liberalism and fear of disorder. 99

> 66 Gradually Americans forged a society distinct from Britain's. 99

Society and Culture

Gradually Americans forged a society distinct from Britain's. The French writer Alexis de Tocqueville (TOKE-vill) (1805–1859), who visited the United States in the early 1830s, noted the American commitment to democracy and individualism, the "blending of social ranks," and Americans' "unbounded desire for riches."[7] But he also considered slavery and racial prejudice a dark blot on American claims to equality, and he feared that too much individualism and greed for riches undermined community.

Slavery shaped the society of the southern states. Enslaved African Americans endured brutal conditions: beatings were a constant threat, families were frequently torn apart on the auction block, and some white masters felt entitled to use their female slaves as concubines. Slaves' resistance included escape, sabotage, infrequent but potent uprisings, and the sustaining of African traditions and culture. After

1830, an abolitionist movement led by whites and freed African Americans in the North launched relentless critiques of the slave system. Women such as Sarah and Angelina Grimke, two southern sisters who grew to hate the society in which they were raised, were active in the movement and flouted custom by speaking out publicly (see Witness to the Past: Protesting Sexism and Slavery).

While some Americans, especially on the East Coast, still looked to Europe for cultural inspiration, the nation increasingly created its own distinctive literary and intellectual traditions. Later-nineteenth-century writers such as Walt Whitman and Mark Twain helped forge a uniquely American literature that examined society and its problems. Whitman (1819–1892), a journalist influenced by European romanticism, celebrated democracy, the working class, and both heterosexual and homosexual affection while addressing the transformations of the Industrial Revolution. In 1855 Whitman described his ethnically diverse and dynamic nation as "a newer garden of creation, dense, joyous, modern, populous millions, cities and farms. By all the world contributed."[8] Twain (1835–1910), a former printer and riverboat pilot from Missouri turned journalist, was inspired by European realism and sought material for his essays, short stories, and novels all over the country and the world. Unlike the optimistic Whitman, Twain shed light on the underside of American life and character.

American philosophy and religions also went in new directions. Leading American philosophers broke with the European tradition by claiming that ideas had little value unless they enlarged people's concrete knowledge of reality, an approach known as pragmatism developed by William James. While many Americans embraced secular and humanist views, many others were influenced by the religious revivals that periodically swept the country. The Protestant missionary impulse, inherited from the first settlers and augmented by the growth of evangelical churches, fostered religious and moral fervor. As a result, Americans became active as Christian missionaries around the world. At the same time, the nation became more religiously diverse. In 1776, most Americans were Protestant, often Calvinist. By 1914, the United States contained followers of many faiths, including some Buddhist and Muslim immigrants from Asia.

Witness to the Past

Protesting Sexism and Slavery

Sarah Grimke and her younger sister, Angelina, were the daughters of a wealthy slaveholding family in Charleston, South Carolina. Adopting the Quaker faith, which emphasized human dignity, and rejecting their positions as members of the state's elite, they dedicated their lives to advocating women's rights and the abolition of slavery. In 1837 they moved north and began giving lectures before large audiences. Because they spoke out so publicly, they were often criticized by churches for violating gender expectations. Sarah Grimke responded in 1838 by writing letters to her critics that often used Christian arguments to defend women's right and obligation to voice their views. When the letters were published together in one volume, they became the first American feminist treatise on women's rights. The following excerpts convey some of Grimke's arguments:

Here then I plant myself. God created us equal; he created us free agents; he is our Lawgiver, our King and our Judge, and to him alone is woman bound to be in subjection, and to him alone is she accountable for the use of those talents with which her Heavenly Father has entrusted her. . . . As I am unable to learn from sacred writ when woman was deprived by God of her equality with man, I shall touch upon a few points in the Scriptures, which demonstrate that no supremacy was granted to man. . . . [In the Bible] we find the commands of God invariably the same to man and woman; and not the slightest intimation is given in a single passage, that God designed woman to point to man as her instructor. . . .

I hope that the principles I have asserted will claim the attention of some of my sex, who may be able to bring into view, more thoroughly than I have done, the situation and degradation of women. . . . During the early part of my life, my lot was cast among the butterflies of the fashionable world; and of this class of women, I am constrained to say, both from experience and observation, that their education is miserably deficient; that they are taught to regard marriage as the one thing needful, the only notice of distinction; hence to attract the notice and win the attentions of men, by their external charms, is the chief business of fashionable girls. They seldom think that men will be allured by intellectual acquirements, because they find, that where any mental superiority exists, a woman is generally shunned and regarded as stepping out of her "appropriate sphere," which, in their view, is to dress, to dance, to set out to the best possible advantage her person. . . . To be married is too often held up to the view of girls as [necessary for] human happiness and human existence. For this purpose . . . the majority of girls are trained. . . . [In education] the improvement of their intellectual capacities is only a secondary consideration. . . . Our education consists almost exclusively of culinary and other manual operations. . . .

There is another class of women in this country, to whom I cannot refer, without feelings of the deepest shame and sorrow. I allude to our female slaves. . . . The virtue of female slaves is wholly at the mercy of irresponsible tyrants, and women are bought and sold in our slave markets, to gratify the brutal lust of those who bear the name of Christians. . . . If she dares resist her seducer, her life by the laws of some of the slave States may be . . . sacrificed to the fury of disappointed passion. . . . The female slaves suffer every species of degradation and cruelty, which the most wanton barbarity can inflict; they are indecently divested of their clothing, sometimes tied up and severely whipped. . . . Can any American woman look at these scenes of shocking . . . cruelty, and fold her hands in apathy, and say, "I have nothing to do with slavery"? She cannot and be guiltless.

Thinking About the Reading

1. What do the letters tell us about the social expectations and education for white women from affluent families?
2. In what way do Grimke's letters address the issue of slavery?

Source: Sarah M. Grimke, *Letters on the Equality of the Sexes, and the Condition of Woman* (Boston: Issac Knapp, 1838).

Westward Expansion and U.S. Influence in the Americas

The nation's boundaries gradually expanded westward, providing a counterpart to European imperialism in Asia and Africa (see Chapter 19) and allowing the acquisition of abundant fertile land and rich mineral deposits. As they expanded westward, Americans developed the potent notion of Manifest Destiny, the conviction that their country's institutions and culture, which they regarded as unmatched, gave them a God-given right to take over the land, by force if necessary. Although Americans avoided interference in European affairs until World War I, the belief that they had God's favor, along with the quest for resources and markets, led ultimately to territorial expansion into Latin America and the formation of a new kind of empire.

Expansion to the Pacific coast was achieved during the 1800s. After acquiring the Ohio territory, in 1787 the new nation extended from the Atlantic to the Mississippi River, and it was further enlarged in three expansionist waves. In the first, President Thomas Jefferson (g. 1800–1809) astutely bought from France, in the Louisiana Purchase (1803), a huge section of the Midwest and South that doubled the size of the country. In the second wave, the United States acquired Florida and the Pacific Northwest from Spain. In the third wave, the United States obtained from Mexico in 1848 Texas, California, and New Mexico as a result of the U.S.-Mexican War. The discovery of gold near what is today Sacramento in 1849 prompted more than 100,000 Americans, known as "49ers," to board sailing ships or covered wagons and head for California from the distant east, hoping to strike it rich. The 1867 purchase of Alaska from Russia eliminated all European rivals from North America (see Map 20.2). In less than a century, the United States went from a mostly rural nation along the Atlantic coast to a transcontinental powerhouse.

 Interactive Map

....

The Frontier and American Individualism

The gradual migration west shaped a pioneer society different from that on the eastern seaboard.

American Progress This 1893 painting by the American artist John Gast extols progress and shows Americans, guided by divine providence, expanding across, and bringing civilization to, the forests and prairies of the Midwest and West. The painting reflects views held by many Americans of their destiny and special role in the world.

Library of Congress

The vast North American frontier offered conditions where settlers could develop new ways of life and ideas. For example, the rise of ranching, especially of cattle, on the Great Plains fostered the growth of a new occupation, that of the cowboy. Cowboys on horseback were needed to guide herds of several thousand cattle on long drives, sometimes hundreds of miles, to railroad towns for shipment east. Some historians argue that the frontier helped democratize the United States as individualists sought adventure and a better life, but life on the frontier was often hard. An Illinois farm wife, Sara Price, lamented her hardship in poetry, writing that "life is a toil and love is a trouble. Beauty will fade and riches will flee. Pleasures will dwindle and prices they double, And nothing is as I would wish it to be."[9]

The Native American Question

Westward expansion also came at the expense of the people already there, including Mexicans, Spaniards, and especially Native Americans. Indians saw whites as invaders in their territory and often resisted violently. To whites, Indians represented an alien way of living and thinking and needed to be controlled, that is, restricted to reservations. The U.S. Supreme Court ruled in 1831 that the Indians' "relation to the United States resembles that of a

 Map 20.2
U.S. Expansion through 1867

The United States expanded in stages after independence, gaining land from Spain, France, Britain, and Mexico, until the nation stretched from the Atlantic to the Gulf and Pacific coasts by 1867. During the same period, Canadians expanded westward from Quebec to British Columbia.

© Cengage Learning

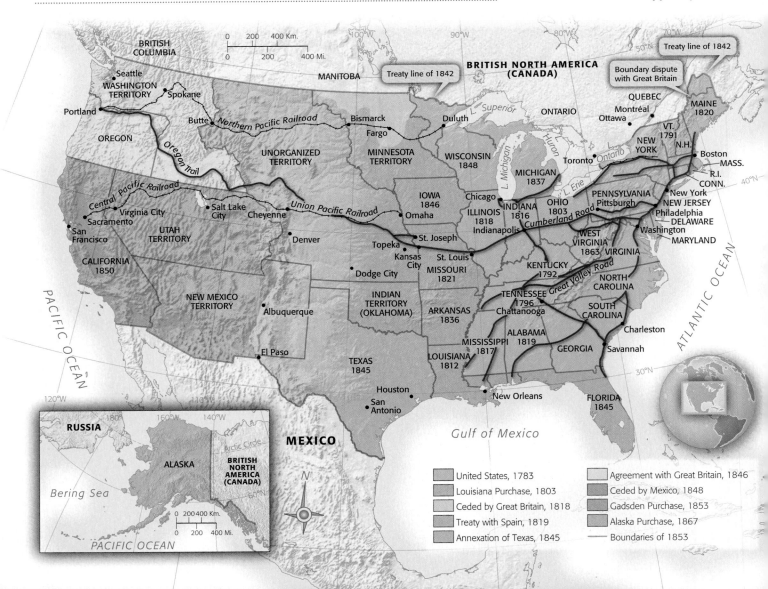

United States, 1783
Louisiana Purchase, 1803
Ceded by Great Britain, 1818
Treaty with Spain, 1819
Annexation of Texas, 1845

Agreement with Great Britain, 1846
Ceded by Mexico, 1848
Gadsden Purchase, 1853
Alaska Purchase, 1867
Boundaries of 1853

ward to his guardian."[10] Over time many Indians were removed from their native lands, even tribes who lived in peace with whites and had adopted aspects of European culture. For example, the Cherokee—farmers who had developed their own written language, published a newspaper, and had a written constitution—had long cultivated good relations with their white neighbors. Yet, after gold was discovered on their land, 15,000 Cherokee from Georgia were forced into concentration camps and then in 1838 sent on a forced march of 1,200 miles, the "Trail of Tears," to Oklahoma. Four thousand Cherokee died from starvation or exposure on the journey.

The Monroe Doctrine

The expansionist impulse also influenced U.S. foreign policy. In 1823 James Monroe (1758–1831), the fifth president of the United States, delivered the Monroe Doctrine, a unilateral statement warning European nations against interfering in the Western Hemisphere and affirming U.S. commitment to shape Latin America's political future after the overthrow of Spanish colonialism. The doctrine claimed that the United States enjoyed a special political and economic status in the Americas, and it effectively marked Latin America as an American sphere of interest, an area in which one great power assumes exclusive responsibility for maintaining peace and attempts to monopolize the resources of that area. Nearly a century after the Monroe Doctrine, Secretary of State Robert Lansing reaffirmed this pattern, claiming that the United States "considers its own interests. The integrity of other American nations is an incident, not an end."[11] As a result, the Monroe Doctrine forged complex links between the United States and the rest of the Americas, often provoking hostility in Latin America, and it set the stage for the rise of the United States as a world power.

War with Mexico and American Military Interventionism

The U.S.-Mexican War of 1846–1848 was a war of expansion that led to a doubling of the U.S. national domain by seizing territory from Mexico. Some 35,000 Americans and their slaves had settled in the Mexican province of Texas. Chafing at Mexican taxes and its antislavery policies, the Americans rebelled and pushed the Mexican forces out, declaring themselves an independent republic in 1836. Soon the Texans sought annexation to the United States, a move favored by the pro-slavery southern states and opposed by the antislavery northern states. In 1844 the U.S. president and Congress moved to admit Texas to statehood, provoking the ire of Mexicans, who now reasserted their claims.

The war that followed stirred politically divisive and passionate debate among politicians and the media in the United States. After President James Polk (1795–1849) ordered military action, the United States Congress went along, but the war badly divided Americans. A Massachusetts legislative resolution proclaimed "that such a war of conquest, so hateful, unjust and unconstitutional in its origin and character, must be regarded as a war against freedom, against humanity, against justice, against the Union."[12] The war ended when 14,000 U.S. troops invaded Mexico and captured Mexico City. This victory allowed the United States to annex Mexican territories from Texas to California. However, the conflict killed 13,000 Americans and 50,000 Mexicans, and it also fostered an enduring Mexican distrust of the United States.

The war sparked a debate over the political and economic ramifications of extending Manifest Destiny to Latin America and Asia. In 1853 Senator William Seward placed expansion in global perspective, advising Americans: "You are already the great continental power. But does that content you? I trust that it does not. You want the commerce of the world. The nation that draws the most from the earth and fabricates most, and sells the most to foreign nations, must be and will be the great power of the earth."[13] Americans soon engaged in the lucrative China trade, including opium smuggling, while the U.S. Navy led the way in opening up reclusive Japan (see Chapters 22–23).

Many historians argue that during the nineteenth century, the United States began to build a new kind of empire, not a territorial one like the British, French, Spanish, and Russian Empires, but chiefly an informal one based on using financial controls and military operations to extend U.S. power rather than gain formal political control. Hence, American naval forces intervened in Southeast Asia almost annually from the 1830s through the 1860s, often arrogantly. Throughout the nineteenth century, various presidents also sought to obtain nearby Cuba from Spain or helped to finance Cuban revolts to overthrow Spanish rule.

sphere of interest An area in which one great power assumes exclusive responsibility for maintaining peace and attempts to monopolize the area's resources.

The Civil War and Social Change

The Civil War (1861–1865), a major transition for the United States, reshaped U.S. society by ending slavery. Like Sarah Grimke, many Americans had believed that slavery mocked liberal democracy. Slavery had largely disappeared from northern states by the early 1800s, and the U.S. government outlawed the slave trade in 1810, although it continued elsewhere. Economic disparities exacerbated the North-South conflict. By 1860, the North was the home of industry, banks, and great ports such as New York, Boston, and Philadelphia. By contrast, the South was largely a monocultural plantation economy supported by 350,000 white families and 3 million black slaves. The northern leaders mostly favored high customs tariffs to protect their industries, but this policy threatened the South, which depended on exports to survive.

In 1860–1861, eleven southern states seceded from the union, forming the proslavery Confederate States of America. President Abraham Lincoln (1809–1865), a lawyer from Illinois who wanted to end slavery and preserve the union, mobilized the military forces of the remaining states to resist the secession. In 1862 he issued the Emancipation Proclamation, freeing all slaves. After four years of war, the North defeated the South, mainly because of the North's dynamic economy and population advantage of nearly four to one.

The Civil War was in many respects a social and political revolution. Not only did it end slavery, but it also crushed the southern struggle for self-determination, destroyed the South's economic link to Britain, firmly established protectionism as economic policy, and fostered a much stronger federal government. The war resulted in more deaths than all other wars combined that were fought by Americans before or since, killing 360,000 Union and 258,000 Confederate troops, and it devastated the southern countryside. The South began to enjoy balanced economic development only with the growth of industry in the twentieth century, largely paid for by northern investors.

Ethnic Minorities in the Years Following the Civil War The Civil War emancipated African Americans from slavery but did not eliminate the disadvantages faced by them and other ethnic minorities. Determined to overcome barriers, many former slaves taught themselves to read—usually forbidden under slavery—and some opened schools to expand opportunities for young blacks. Many African Americans left the plantations to find work elsewhere, but their prospects were chiefly limited to sharecropping, such as growing cotton, or physical labor, such as mining or longshoreman work. Long after slavery ended, African Americans faced discrimination reflected in laws restricting their rights and were often prevented from voting. Skin color became the major determinant of social class, and segregation based on this physical feature remained the norm in the South until the 1960s. African Americans attended separate schools, were largely confined to their own neighborhoods, and could not use public facilities, such as parks, restaurants, and drinking fountains, reserved for whites. Those who violated these laws and customs faced jail, beatings, or even executions, known as lynchings (some 235 in 1892 alone), by white vigilantes.

In the aftermath of the Civil War, as peace brought a resumption of westward American expansion into central and western North America, more Native Americans suffered. After 1865, whites subdued the Great Plains and its people and rendered the territory unfit for Indian survival. Settlers, railroad builders, and fur traders massacred 15 million bison, the chief source of subsistence for Indian tribes on the Great Plains, while farmers and ranchers reshaped the environment of the prairies and northern woodlands. In 1886, the Apache of Arizona, under their chief, Geronimo (juh-RON-uh-moe) (1829–1909), finally surrendered after years of fighting. In 1890, the United States Army's massacre of three hundred Lakota Sioux followers of the Ghost Dance, an Indian spiritual revival movement, at Wounded Knee in South Dakota marked the triumph of U.S. colonization of the west. Defeated by the army, decimated by epidemics, and reduced to poverty, Indians were put on reservations controlled by the federal government. They experienced the American dream in reverse, as democracy became tyranny and liberty became confinement.

Industrialization

The northern victory in the Civil War and economic policies of protectionism spurred the great industrial growth in the later 1800s, which fostered a better material life but also generated changes in American class structure and ways of living. The industrial economy in the United States resembled those in Europe but became more productive. In 1860, the United States ranked fourth among industrial nations, but by 1894 it ranked first; in addition, American exports had tripled, and the nation was second only to Britain as a world trader. A surge in technological innovation changed economic life. Electricity as a power source, combined with improved factory production methods, turned out goods faster, more cheaply,

Women Textile Workers In both Europe and North America, women became the largest part of the workforce in the textile industry. These women, working in a New England spinning mill around 1850, endured harsh work conditions and the boring, often dangerous, job of tending machines.

and in greater quantities than ever before, increasing U.S. competitiveness in the world. American and European inventions such as portable steam engines and the internal combustion engine revolutionized industry, leading to a tripling of U.S. factory output between 1877 and 1892.

American life and population patterns were also shaped by an improved transportation and communication network; by 1890 the U.S. railroad network was larger than all European railroad systems combined. Railroad construction owed much to ethnic minorities and immigrants, because many of the workers who drove the spikes and blasted the passages through rocks and mountains were African-Americans, Chinese, or Irish. The transportation revolution continued when Henry Ford (1863–1947) started a motor company in 1903 and began turning out the first affordable cars and refining the mass-production assembly line. In another transportation breakthrough, Orville and Wilbur Wright became the first men to achieve powered flight in 1903, launching the age of aviation.

But industrialization also led to monopoly capitalism, a concentration of industrial and financial resources similar to Europe's that worsened the inequitable distribution of wealth. A few fabulously wealthy tycoons, such as John D. Rockefeller and J. P. Morgan, known to their critics as the Robber Barons, had great influence over politicians, controlled much of the economy, and expected workers to labor at subsistence wages. Using Social Darwinist thinking (see Chapter 19), Rockefeller claimed that "the growth of large business is merely survival of the fittest and a law of God."[14] Although some Americans prospered, industrial workers in cities, factories, and mines often experienced tough conditions and little job security. The work was dangerous, the hours long, and the wages low; children often worked alongside their parents.

Immigration, Urbanization, and Social Movements

This era was also marked by social change, including the influx of millions of immigrants. Some 25 million Europeans immigrated to the United States between 1870 and 1916, and by 1900 more than 1 million Europeans entered the nation each year in search of a better life. At first they came largely from northwestern Europe, especially English, Irish, Germans, and Scandinavians. Later many arrived from southern and eastern Europe, including Italians, Greeks, Serbs, and Poles. The population of European ancestry in the United States increased from 2.5 million in 1770 to 32 million in 1860 and 92 million by 1910. Meanwhile, thousands of Chinese and Japanese immigrants landed on the Pacific Coast in the later 1800s, followed by Filipinos after 1900. Most of these newcomers, both European and Asian, typically faced discrimination and violence, particularly during economic downturns.

The decades between 1865 and 1914 were also marked by movements seeking economic and social change. Economic depression, panics, and bloody labor conflicts fostered working-class radicalism, which threatened the wealthy and the middle class. Farmers and workers resented the wealth of the Robber Barons and the power of large corporations and railroads. Even while increased agricultural output made the United States the world's leading agricultural producer, in the 1890s many farmers went bankrupt, losing their land to banks. Political leaders worried that an inflamed public mood would spark a revolution.

The Emergence of Labor Unions

Although outright revolution did not occur, workers and farmers fought those with power and privilege. Labor unions had first appeared in the 1820s, when women and men campaigned for better conditions and a shorter workday in the textile mills of Lowell, Massachusetts. In 1860 female strikers in the textile mills of nearby Lynn chanted, "American ladies will not be slaves." Eugene Debs (1855–1926), the socialist leader of the railway union, explained in 1893 that "the capitalists refer to you as mill hands, farm hands, factory hands. The trouble is he owns your head and your hands."[15] By the early 1900s, the radical, Marxist-influenced International Workers of the World (better known as the Wobblies) were gaining influence among industrial workers, miners, and longshoremen. Employers and their political allies disparaged union members as communists and fought their demands, eventually destroying the Wobblies as a mass movement.

The Suffrage Movement

Women also struggled for their civil rights. The republic excluded more than half of the population from democracy for the first 150 years. During the 1800s, although large numbers of women worked in factories, shops, and offices, they also managed their homes. Despite their increasing economic roles, women were also urged by religious leaders to be more pious, self-sacrificing, and obedient to men. Women gained basic privileges more on a par with men only after a long effort. The suffrage movement for the vote was born in 1848, when women meeting in Seneca Falls, New York, declared, in a reference to the U.S. Declaration of Independence, that "all men and women are created equal." They opposed a system in which women had no rights to property or even to their own children in case of divorce. After seven decades of marching, publicizing their cause, and lobbying male politicians, suffragettes convinced Congress to give women the right to vote in 1920.

American Capitalism and Empire

As in Europe, industrial capitalism fostered imperialism and warfare. A series of economic depressions from the 1870s through the 1890s spurred public demand for foreign markets and for extending Manifest Destiny to other parts of the world. As a result, by the later 1800s, many American businessmen, farmers, and workers favored acquiring territories overseas to improve national economic prospects. Others hoped to spread American conceptions of freedom, which they increasingly equated with individualism, private property, and a capitalist marketplace economy.

These pressures led to military interventions. The United States sent military forces to at least twenty-seven countries and territories between 1833 and 1898 to protect the economic interests of American businesses during insurrections or civil strife or to suppress the piracy that threatened U.S. shipping. Troops were dispatched at various times to nearly a dozen Latin American nations, China, Indonesia, Korea, and North Africa. U.S. forces also brought the Hawaiian Islands—a Polynesian kingdom where Americans had long settled as traders, whalers, planters, and missionaries—into the U.S. empire. The growing American population in Hawaii, led by sugar planters, resented the Hawaiian monarchy, and in 1893 they overthrew beloved and talented Hawaiian queen Liliuokalani (luh-lee-uh-oh-kuh-LAH-nee) (1838–1917). Aided by

150 U.S. troops, American settlers formed a provisional government and effectively made Hawaii a neocolony. The end of the monarchy transformed the islands not only politically but also socially, as thousands of Japanese, Chinese, Korean, and Filipino immigrants became the main labor force, mostly working on plantations owned by American settlers and companies. By the 1930s, Asians constituted the large majority of Hawaii's population.

The Spanish-American War

The major imperial conflict involving the United States was the Spanish-American War (1898–1902), which pitted American against Spanish colonial forces. The war was a watershed in U.S. foreign affairs that helped make the United States an empire. On the eve of the war, President William McKinley (1843–1901) argued for the necessity for obtaining foreign markets for America's surplus production, linking expanding markets with the maintenance of prosperity. In what Secretary of State John Hay called a "splendid little war," the United States fought with Spain over that country's remaining, restless colonies: Cuba, Puerto Rico, Guam, and the Philippines.

The war unleashed American nationalist fervor as the United States quickly triumphed against the hopelessly outmatched Spanish. A future president, Woodrow Wilson, boasted about America's emergence as a major power in the global system: "No war ever transformed us quite as the war with Spain. No previous years ever ran with so swift a change as the years since 1898. We have witnessed a new revolution, the transformation of America completed."[16] However, to colonize the Philippines, the United States had to brutally suppress a fierce nationalist resistance by Filipinos opposed to U.S. occupation (see Chapter 22). The U.S. struggle against Filipinos, while ultimately successful, resulted in the deaths of thousands of Filipinos and Americans and indicated the challenges and costs of exercising power in the world. The colonization of the Philippines, Puerto Rico, and Guam, and economic and political domination over nominally independent Cuba, also transformed the United States from an informal into a territorial empire much like the Netherlands and Portugal.

> "Creating stable political systems among remote regions proved to be a struggle, and wars and military dictatorships were frequent."

LO³ Latin America and the Caribbean in the Global System

Brazil and most of Spain's Latin American colonies won their independence in the early 1800s, although the Caribbean islands mostly remained colonies (see Chapter 19). But most Latin Americans experienced considerable turmoil, including political instability, economic decline, and regional conflicts. However, by the 1870s, conditions stabilized somewhat. Expanding European markets by then had created a greater demand for Latin American exports and stimulated economic growth. Black slaves gained their freedom, and waves of European immigrants poured into some nations, changing the social and cultural landscape; meanwhile, the United States increasingly exercised power in the region.

Latin American Nations

After winning their independence from Spain and Portugal, Latin Americans faced new challenges. Some countries, such as Argentina, Brazil, and Mexico, were large and unwieldy, while others, such as El Salvador and the Dominican Republic, were small and had limited resources. Except for Brazil, which was governed by an emperor, the new countries were republics.

Creating stable political systems among remote regions proved to be a struggle, and wars and military dictatorships were frequent. Civil wars for dominance continued into the 1860s, often pitting those favoring regionalism against partisans of a strong centralized government. In addition, various frontier disputes fostered occasional wars. For example, Chile fought Peru and Bolivia in 1837 and again in 1879–1884, acquiring territory from those two countries as a result.

Caudillos and Social Structure

Although the Latin Americans achieved political independence, most leaders did not favor dramatic social and economic change. The wealthy upper class largely consisted of creoles who owned

> "Social and economic inequalities in Latin American countries often led to reforms and sometimes to revolutions."

large businesses, plantations, and haciendas or had seized them from the departing Spaniards. The small middle class of shopkeepers, teachers, and skilled artisans was mainly composed of mestizos and mulattos. More than half of the population, including most Indians and blacks, remained at the bottom of the social structure. Politics usually remained chiefly an affair for the wealthy, and political and economic leaders often restricted the political participation of the poor nonwhite majority. To contain or prevent unrest resulting from the severe gap between rich and poor, military strongmen,

known as caudillos, who acquired and maintained power through force, gained control of many Latin American countries. Some of these, such as the dictator Juan Manuel de Rosas (huan man-WELL deh ROH-sas) (1793–1877) in Argentina, were tyrants who used violence, torture, and murder to maintain power.

Most Latin American nations established some stability by the 1850s, although politics remained highly contentious. Many countries sought both "progress and order," which often led to caudillo rule. But a few fostered multiparty systems in which competing parties sought access to national power in order to reward supporters. The political elite often disagreed on policies. Liberals generally favored federalism, free trade, and the separation of church and state. Conservatives sought centralization, trade protectionism, and maintenance of church power. Conflicts between these groups were sometimes violent.

Internet Resources for Latin America (*http://lib.nmsu.edu/subject/bord/laguia/*). An outstanding site with links to many resources.

Brazil's Quest for Political Order

Brazil was the only Latin American nation to maintain a monarchy rather than a republic. By the 1880s, Brazilians had begun debating both slavery and the legitimacy of the monarchy. As tensions simmered, the army seized power in 1889, exiled Emperor Dom Pedro II, and replaced the monarchy with a republic. However, although a federal system on the U.S. model emerged, suffrage was highly restricted, the majority of Brazilians gained neither property nor civil rights, and many remained desperately poor. In the end, Brazil maintained an authoritarian tradition, but rebellions and regionalism constantly challenged the government.

Revolution in Mexico and Cuba

Social and economic inequalities in Latin American countries often led to reforms and sometimes to revolutions. Revolution was most notable in Mexico; however, the birth of the Mexican republic in 1824 did not bring stability to the vast country. Between 1833 and 1855, a caudillo, General Antonio Lopez de Santa Anna (SAN-tuh AN-uh) (1797–1876), led a series

CHRONOLOGY

Latin America and the Caribbean, 1750–1914

1842	End of trans-Atlantic slave trade by most nations
1861–1872	Benito Juarez president of Mexico
1862–1867	French occupation of Mexico
1876–1911	Diaz dictatorship in Mexico
1879–1884	War between Chile and Peru-Bolivia
1885–1898	Cuban revolt against Spain
1886	Abolition of slavery in Cuba
1889	Abolition of slavery in Brazil
1889	Brazilian republic
1898–1902	Spanish-American War
1901	Platt Amendment to Cuban constitution
1910–1920	Mexican Revolution
1912	U.S. intervention in Nicaragua
1914	Completion of Panama Canal

Experience the Latin American revolutionary era through the eyes of either the Spanish monarchy or the independent movement in this interactive simulation.

of dictatorships punctuated by civil war. By leading his country into the disastrous U.S.-Mexican War (1846–1848), Santa Anna also lost half of Mexico's territory, including Texas and California, to the United States.

Benito Juarez: The Man of Bronze

Santa Anna's misadventures and growing social problems sparked upheaval. In 1861 Mexican liberals led by Benito Juarez (WAHR-ez) (1806–1872), a pragmatic lawyer and Zapotec Indian, defeated the conservatives and suspended repayment of the foreign debt. In 1862 this provoked a short-lived occupation by France, whose ruler, Napoleon III, dreamed of renewed American empire. The French made a member of the Habsburg family, Maximilian of Austria (1832–1867), emperor of Mexico. However, under pressure from Mexican liberals and the United States, France withdrew its troops, and Maximilian's regime collapsed in 1867. Juarez again served as president from 1867 until his death in 1872, seeking social justice, fighting corruption and the privileged classes, freeing peasants, and subordinating the church to the secular state. His reformist policies and his Indian ancestry—his admirers called him the "man of bronze" because of his dark skin—made Juarez Mexico's most honored national leader.

The Dictatorship of Porfirio Diaz

In 1876 Mexico came under the dictatorship of Porfirio Diaz (DEE-ahs) (1830–1915), a caudillo of mestizo ancestry who ruled until 1911. Diaz brought stability and economic progress, allowing the country's population to grow from 9 million in 1874 to 15 million in 1910. But Diaz also allowed foreign business interests and investors to take over much of Mexico's economy, and he did little to help the growing mass of impoverished people, as much of the land became owned by large haciendas and land companies.

Emiliano Zapata and the Mexican Revolution

Eventually, Diaz's economic policies led to civil war and revolution. In 1910

various forces coalesced to fight the unpopular Diaz regime in the Mexican Revolution (1910–1920). One faction was led by political rebels such as the creole Francisco Madero (muh-DER-oh) (1873–1913), a landowner's son who was educated in France and the United States. In the south, the mestizo Emiliano Zapata (zeh-PAH-teh) (1879–1919), a charismatic former peasant, organized a peasant army that seized haciendas and fought the federal army. With the defeat of Diaz, largely by Zapata's forces, the idealistic Madero was elected president but proved a weak leader, and was murdered by a rival. Madero's death caused sporadic violence as all factions used ruthless tactics, and alliances formed and collapsed. Zapata

Archivo General de la Nación, Mexico, courtesy of Martha Davidson

Women Revolutionaries in Mexico. Hoping for social change and more rights, women joined men in fighting, and sometimes dying, for one or another faction during the Mexican Revolution.

The Plan of Ayala Read the accusations leveled by Emiliano Zapata and his followers against Francisco Madero, whom they had just helped come to power in Mexico.

was assassinated by a rival in 1919, but his reputation lived on in death, making him the most celebrated revolutionary hero.

The ongoing violence raised expectations for social change and fostered a yearning for peace. For example, hoping to gain more rights and influence, women played a critical revolutionary role as soldiers, spies, and couriers. Some of their hopes seemed realized in a constitution introduced in 1917, which set forth progressive goals such as an eight-hour workday and paid maternity leave, while ignoring other goals like women's suffrage. In 1920 the revolutionary conflict wound down after claiming 1 million lives. While most Mexicans remained impoverished, a new party led by former revolutionaries formed a government and brought political stability and some progress on women's rights.

José Martí and Cuba

In the Caribbean, Cuba also experienced revolt. The Spanish retained a tight control of Cuba and its valuable sugar plantations, but by the later 1800s, an independence movement had developed. Its major spokesman, the journalist José Martí (mahr-TEE) (1853–1895), was a true citizen of the world who had travelled and lived in Europe, the United States, and various Latin American nations. Martí's writings helped inspire a Cuban revolt in 1895, but he was killed in the fighting, and eventually the revolution was sidetracked by U.S. intervention during the Spanish-American War, which turned Cuba into a U.S. neocolony.

Latin American Economic Patterns

Like North Americans, Latin Americans debated the benefits of free trade as opposed to protectionism, of heavy involvement in the world economy as opposed to self-sufficiency. After the destructive wars of independence, Latin American exports and investments declined. However, in contrast to the protectionist United States, this decline did not prompt Latin American leaders to move toward economic independence. Instead, they largely pursued free trade and maintained the export of raw materials such as Ecuadorian cocoa, Brazilian coffee, Argentine beef, Cuban sugar, and Bolivian and Chilean ores.

> 66 The decision to concentrate on exporting natural resources left Latin American societies economically vulnerable. 99

Export-based Economies

The decision to concentrate on exporting natural resources left Latin American societies economically vulnerable. Around the region, earnings from minerals and cash crops like rubber and coffee ebbed and flowed with the fall or rise of world commodity prices. By the twentieth century, the economic fate of Brazil and other Latin American countries became closely tied to fluctuating world prices for those countries' exports, but many countries may have had few viable alternatives to free trade. The impoverished state of most Indians and blacks gave them little purchasing power to support any local industries that might be developed, and attempts to foster industrialization failed in Brazil, Colombia, and Mexico in the 1830s and 1840s because of competition from European imports. Only Argentina made modest progress in manufacturing in the later 1800s.

Foreign Investment and Domination

Investment by North Americans and Europeans in mines and plantations drew Latin America more firmly into the global market, exposing the region's peoples to continued exploitation by outsiders. Independence opened Latin America to U.S., French, and especially British merchants and financiers, who used their economic power to dominate banking and the import trade for industrial goods such as cotton textiles and who also invested in mines and plantations. By the mid-1800s, British businessmen and bankers controlled the imports and exports of both Brazil and Argentina. Argentina was sometimes called an informal member of the British Empire; in 1895, an Argentine nationalist complained that "today our country is tributary to England."[17]

Foreign investment and domination had several consequences for Latin Americans. First, foreign corporations increasingly owned the plantations and mines. Such companies sent their profits to the United States or Europe rather than investing further in Latin America. Second, Latin America became a major contributor to world commodity markets, producing some 62 percent of the world's coffee, 38 percent of the sugar, and 25 percent of the rubber by World War I. Third, by the later 1800s, increased communication and transportation, as well as growing

U.S. demand for markets and raw materials, fostered economic expansion in many countries. Despite this growth, however, inequalities grew between powerful landed families and peasants and workers. Throughout Latin America, powerful families or foreign corporations increasingly owned the usable land, creating imbalances that produced political unrest in the twentieth century.

Social and Cultural Change

The abolition of slavery brought social change in Latin America. Some of the leaders who overthrew Spanish rule, such as Simón Bolívar and Jose de San Martin, had favored emancipation and freed slaves who fought in the wars of independence. Between 1823 and 1854, slavery was legally abolished in most of Latin America and the Caribbean. Most European and American countries outlawed the trans-Atlantic slave trade by 1842, and by the 1880s, only Cuba and Brazil still maintained legal slavery. The Spanish rulers finally granted Cuban slaves their freedom in 1886, and abolitionists became more outspoken in Brazil, where slavery remained common in the sugar and coffee industries until 1889. However, economic conditions for freed slaves did not dramatically improve. Many blacks shifted from being slaves to sharecroppers, tenant farmers, and laborers, experiencing little change in their low social status.

Latin America and Immigration

Latin American Resources (*http://www.oberlin.edu/faculty/svolk/latinam/htm*). An excellent collection of resources and links on history, politics, and culture.

Meanwhile, the immigration of millions of Europeans and Asians reshaped many Latin American societies. European immigrants, especially Italians, Spaniards, Germans, Russians, and Irish, sought better economic prospects in new lands, particularly in Argentina, Brazil, Chile, Uruguay, and Venezuela. People from overcrowded lands in Asia and the Middle East also immigrated to the Americas in the later 1800s and early 1900s. In Trinidad, British Guiana, and Dutch Guiana, the abolition of slavery prompted the import of workers from India, and Indians eventually accounted for around half of the population in these colonies. Japanese settled in Brazil, Peru, and Paraguay as farmers and traders. Arab immigrants from Lebanon and Syria developed trade diasporas throughout Latin America, and Indonesians moved to Dutch Guiana as plantation workers. Chinese flocked to Peru and Cuba and, in smaller numbers, to Jamaica, Trinidad, and the Guianas. Latin America's richly diverse population doubled between 1850 and 1900 to more than 60 million.

Despite the newcomers, Latin America remained more conservative than North America in social structure. The creole elite dominated most countries, while European and Asian immigrants and mixed-descent people constituted the middle class. Many mulattos and most blacks and Indians remained in the lower class. Indians in countries such as Mexico, Guatemala, Peru, Bolivia, and Colombia often withdrew into their rural village communities. In 1865 a Mexican described the wide gap between whites and Indians: "The white is the proprietor; the Indian the worker. The white is rich; the Indian poor and miserable."[18]

Brazilian Culture

Read about respected Brazilian writer, Euclides da Cunha, a spokesman for rising Brazilian nationalism.

Because of its large populations of European, African, and mixed-descent people, Brazil developed a society and culture different from those of other Latin Americans countries. Brazilians considered their nation's unique, multiracial society to be less obsessed by skin color than other countries. Unlike in the United States, economic class and skin color did not always coincide, and marriage and cultural mixing between members of different groups was common. Yet blacks were also more likely than whites to experience prejudice and to be poor, a fact reflected in Rio de Janeiro's largely black hillside shantytowns.

Cultural forms reflected the Latin American struggle to reconcile indigenous with imported traditions. Rejecting European models, novelists focused on social themes, such as the Brazilian writer Euclides da Cunha (KOO-nyuh) (1866–1909), who wrote about the country's poor. In contrast, the cosmopolitan, well-traveled Nicaraguan poet Ruben Dario (1867–1916) rejected the expression of ideas in art in favor of escapist and fantastic images and a stress on beauty as an end in itself.

Especially creative cultural innovations came in music and dance. For example, the sensuous dance called the tango emerged in the bars and clubs of poor neighborhoods in Buenos Aires, Argentina, which had more than 1.6 million people by 1914. Its music was based partly on rhythms derived from the drumming of African slaves and featured the accordion-like *bandoneon*, invented in Germany and carried to Argentina by Italian immigrants. The tango became a symbol of lower-class identity and was popular in Europe by the 1900s. Brazil's unique music blended European

samba
A Brazilian popular music and dance that arose in the early twentieth century.

calypso
A song style in Trinidad that often featured lyrics addressing daily life and topical subjects.

melody and African rhythms. The abolition of slavery and the migration of Afro-Brazilians from Bahia State in the northeast to Rio de Janeiro gave rise to samba, a popular music and dance developed by Bahian women that became an integral part of Carnival, the three-day celebration before the long Christian period of penitence known as Lent, which was first organized in Rio de Janeiro in the 1890s. Samba emerged as the soul of Brazil, popular with all classes.

Caribbean Traditions
Like Brazilians, Caribbean peoples also mixed African and European influences to produce distinctive cultures, but often in defiance of colonial restrictions. On Trinidad, British colonial officials who feared the black majority passed laws to prohibit African-based musical forms, but two traditions emerged nevertheless. The first was calypso, a song style that often featured lyrics addressing daily life and topical subjects and that eventually became the major popular music in the English-speaking islands of the eastern Caribbean. The second tradition was the pre-Lent Carnival, which, as in Brazil, assumed great social significance while providing a forum for calypso songs that often questioned colonial policies. A song in the 1880s protested colonial restrictions on music during Carnival: "Can't beat my drum, In my own native land. Can't have Carnival, In my native land."[19]

The United States in Latin America

Latin Americans faced challenges from the increasingly powerful United States, a nation they both envied and feared, whose citizens and military forces occasionally intervened in Central America and the Caribbean. For example, in 1856, William Walker—an American adventurer financed by influential U.S. businessmen who were interested in acquiring natural resources and markets—invaded Nicaragua with a well-armed mercenary force of three hundred Americans and temporarily seized the country. Walker proclaimed himself president, and, despite opposition by Central American leaders, the United States granted his government diplomatic recognition. Walker introduced slavery and tried to make English the official language before being forced out in 1857, becoming a hated symbol in Central America of what Latin Americans often called Yankee imperialism.

The Spanish-American War led to U.S. domination in Cuba, which became a U.S. neocolony. The Platt Amendment to the Cuban constitution, imposed by the United States in 1901, integrated the Cuban and U.S. economies and required that the United States Congress approve any treaties negotiated by Cuban leaders. The American military governor summarized the consequences of the Platt Amendment: "There is little or no real independence left to Cuba. She is absolutely in our hands, a practical dependency of the United States."[20] U.S. businessmen soon owned much of Cuba's economy, including railroads, banks, and mills, and the United States acquired a naval base at Guantanamo (gwahn-TAH-nuh-moe) Bay. Later, Cuban nationalists blamed Cuba's squalid condition not on the often-despotic Cuban governments but on the United States. The Platt Amendment was finally repealed in 1934.

The World of 1898: The Spanish-American War (*http://www.loc.gov/rr/hispanic/1898*). A Library of Congress site that provides excellent documents and resources.

In the early 1900s, the United States became more deeply involved in Central America and the Caribbean. To build a canal across Central America linking the Pacific and Atlantic Oceans, the United States helped Panama secede from Colombia in 1903 and convinced its leaders to lease a 10-mile-wide zone across the isthmus in perpetuity to the United States. Several thousand workers from Panama and elsewhere died in the ten arduous years of construction. In 1914 the Panama Canal, 51 miles long, was completed, one of the great engineering feats of history and a boon to maritime commerce and travel. In 1912 the United States overthrew the president of Nicaragua, who was suspected of inviting the British to build a rival canal across his country. U.S. soldiers also occupied Haiti (1915–1933) and the Dominican Republic (1916–1924) to quell unrest or maintain friendly governments. These interventions set the stage for a more active U.S. imperial policy in Latin America and the Caribbean.

LO⁴ New Societies in Canada and the Pacific Basin

The United States was not the only European-settled colony to build a democratic nation and foster economic strength. To the north of the United States, Canada also expanded across the continent to the Pacific and formed a federation of states. During

this era, Western nations also located and colonized the island societies scattered around the Pacific Basin. Meanwhile, in Australia and New Zealand, British immigrants established settler colonies that helped to transform these South Pacific territories (see Map 20.3).

Making a Canadian Nation

France originally colonized most of what is today eastern Canada, but by 1763, the British had defeated the French forces and gained control of this large region. The victorious British now had to forge a stable relationship with 80,000 French-speaking people who resisted assimilation into British culture. By 1774, the British pragmatically recognized the influential role of the Catholic Church and French civil law in Quebec, while British colonists settled chiefly in the Atlantic coastal region. Although the British governed Quebec and the English-speaking regions separately until 1841, relations between British and French Canadians, with different cultures and languages, remained uneasy, causing a British official in the 1830s to conclude that Canada was "two nations warring in the bosom of a single state."[21]

Relations with the United States

Whatever their ethnic backgrounds, Canada's peoples had to deal with the ambitions of the United States, whose leaders hoped that Canada might eventually join the Union. In a U.S.-British

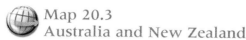
Map 20.3
Australia and New Zealand

The British colonized and gradually settled Australia and New Zealand between the late 1700s and 1914. In 1901 the six Australian colonies became a federation, with a capital eventually built in Canberra.

© Cengage Learning

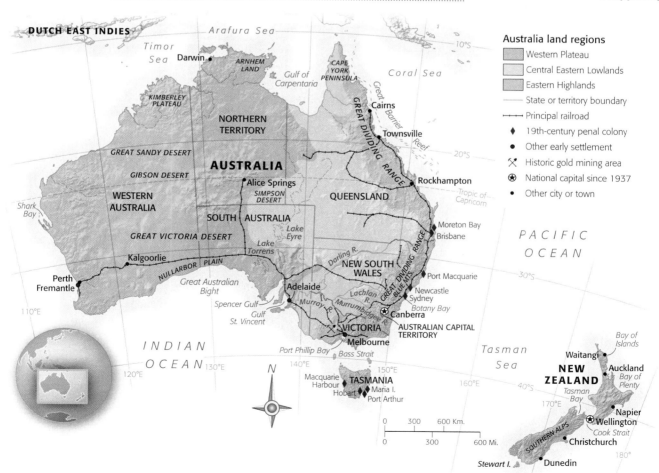

treaty in 1783, the United States recognized British control north of the Great Lakes and the Saint Lawrence River. After the American Revolution, many Loyalists, who had supported continued British rule, moved north to Canada, increasing the English-speaking population substantially and promoting reforms and representative assemblies.

The relations between the United States and British-ruled Canada remained tense for years. Americans suspected that, from their Canada base, the British supported Native Americans, such as the powerful and charismatic Shawnee chief Tecumseh (teh-CUM-sah) (1768–1813), who gathered a large alliance of tribes to drive the white settlers out of Ohio and reinvigorate Indian ways. When conflict between the United States and Britain led to the War of 1812, Tecumseh served with the British. During the war, Americans repeatedly invaded Canada with hopes of annexing the territory but were repulsed. The war ended U.S. attempts to expand north and also laid the seeds for a Canadian identity separate

> "Whatever their ethnic backgrounds, Canada's peoples had to deal with the ambitions of the United States, whose leaders hoped that Canada might eventually join the Union."

from the United States and Britain. In 1846 another treaty fixed the U.S.–Canada boundary in the west.

The Dominion of Canada

Canadians could now turn to building a diverse society and democratic nation in peace, welcoming 800,000 British immigrants between 1815 and 1850 while working to modify British control. Growing popular sentiment prompted the British to consider reforms that eventually brought a unified Canada and an elected national parliament. But Canadians rejected complete independence in favor of self-rule within the British Empire as a strategy to help Canada maintain stability, settle the west, foster economic development, and resist U.S. power. In 1858 Canadians built a national capital at Ottawa, and in 1867 leaders negotiated a Canadian Confederation that guaranteed strong provincial rights and preservation of the French language wherever it was spoken. Under this arrangement,

Along the Canadian Pacific Railroad During the late nineteenth century, both native-born Canadians and European immigrants from many lands followed the Canadian Pacific Railroad to settle the newly opened lands of the Midwestern prairies and Western mountains. Some people set up temporary tent villages by railroad stops before taking up farming, mining, logging, trade, or fishing.

Saskatchewan Archives Board #RA 2309

Canada became a dominion, a country having autonomy but owing allegiance to the British crown.

The confederation soon faced new challenges. Expansion of white settlement and political power to the West fired resentment among Indians and people of mixed descent, the French-speaking Metis (may-TEES), which sometimes led to violence. The combative Metis leader, Louis Riel (ree-EL) (1844–1885), who had once studied to be a Catholic priest, led two rebellions before being executed for treason. Eventually, however, Manitoba and British Columbia joined the confederation, and the federal government promised to build a transcontinental railroad. Canada's first prime minister and Riel's chief opponent, Scottish-born John MacDonald (g. 1867–1873, 1878–1891), hoped the railroad would transform the 4 million Canadians into a unified nation; it was completed in 1885. The government negotiated treaties with Native Americans, allocating reservations to many. Although they faced some Indian resistance, white settlers increasingly moved to the western provinces, and towns sprung up along the railroad. By 1905, Canada included all of the present provinces except Newfoundland.

The Canadian economy and ethnic structure were transformed between the 1860s and 1914. Beaver fur and fish had been the major exports of Canada since the 1600s, but now wheat grown in the Great Plains surpassed fur as the major export. Gold strikes in the Yukon and the offering of free land in western Canada attracted immigrants from many lands, including the United States. From 1896 until 1911, more than 2 million British and other European immigrants arrived, often settling in the west, where many built sod houses and grew wheat. Immigrants from eastern and southern Europe as well as China and Japan enriched the ethnic mosaic. Increasingly critical of British imperialism in the world, by 1911 Canadians took control of their own foreign affairs and diplomacy, fostering increased industrialization and warmer relations with the United States, while maintaining the British monarch as symbolic head of state.

Exploration and Colonization of the Pacific Islands

The peoples who lived on the small mountainous islands and flat atolls scattered across thousands of miles in the vast Pacific Ocean Basin were the last to experience European expansion, but when it came, the impact was significant.

By the mid-1700s, the British and French had begun a race to explore what they considered the last frontier, the Pacific Ocean. Eventually these two countries, along with Spain, Germany, Russia, and the United States, had colonized all of the inhabited islands.

The Explorations of James Cook

The English captain James Cook (1728–1779) led some of the most extensive explorations, greatly aided by the learned Polynesian high priest, Tupaia (ca. 1725–1771). Cook reached the eastern Polynesian island of Tahiti in 1769, where he recruited Tupaia, whose skills as a navigator and speaker of several Polynesian languages greatly aided the expedition. Tupaia drew up the charts that helped Cook map Polynesia, including New Zealand and the coast of Australia, but then died on Java of fever. Cook made two more expeditions to the Pacific in the 1770s; after becoming the first known person to circumnavigate Antarctica, he located the Hawaiian Islands in 1778 and then sailed to Alaska. His early reports created an image of the South Sea islands as paradise, a "Garden of Eden" with amiable people, but Cook was killed in Hawaii after antagonizing local leaders.

> 66 By the mid-1700s, the British and French had begun a race to explore what they considered the last frontier, the Pacific Ocean. 99

Traders and Missionaries in the Pacific

European explorations eventually sparked economic exploitation and Christian missionary activity. In the late 1700s, the Russians established a foothold in Alaska and the Aleutian Islands as a base for hunting seals and sea otters for their fur. By the 1850s, both animals had been hunted to near extinction, and thousands of Aleuts had died from exposure to European diseases. Deep-sea whaling lasted longer, attracting Western and Polynesian sailors. Western traders also sought resources such as sandalwood, greatly valued in Asia for building furniture. It took only ten years to cut and export all of Fiji's sandalwood. Meanwhile, Protestant and Catholic missionaries went to the islands seeking converts, with varied results. The Samoans welcomed the missionaries, often adopting Christianity. Fijians initially rejected missionaries, but later, desiring trade with the West, tolerated them. Fijian converts often pragmatically mixed Christianity with their own traditions. Some peoples, like the inhabitants of New Hebrides, rejected missionaries violently.

Traders and missionaries opened the way for colonization, and between the 1840s and 1900, Western powers colonized all of the Pacific societies. Between the 1840s and 1870s, the French gained domination over many island chains, such as the Society Islands, which included Tahiti, and the Marquesas, while the British colonized various others, among them the Fijian archipelago. By 1898, the Germans and Americans had divided up Samoa, and the British imposed a protectorate over the kingdom of Tonga. By 1900, the Germans had acquired most of Micronesia, and Britain and France controlled much of Melanesia. Hawaii was seized by the United States in 1893.

The Rise of Australia and New Zealand

The British colonized the continent they named Australia and the two large islands they called New Zealand, landmasses in the western Pacific whose human histories long predated the arrival of Europeans. European settlement in Australia began in the 1780s, when the British began transporting convicts, often Irish, from overcrowded British jails to penal colonies they founded at Botany Bay and Sydney Harbor. Agriculture, ranching, and mining became the basis for the Australian economy.

The Aborigines of Australia

British colonization came at the expense of the Aborigines, indigenous peoples who had lived on the continent for thousands of years. Divided into hundreds of scattered tribes and numbering somewhere between 500,000 and 3 million in 1750, Aborigines lived chiefly by fishing and nomadic hunting and gathering and were considered primitive and inferior by European settlers. Many Aborigines resisted encroachments on their land by raiding British settlements; in response, British settlers killed as many as 20,000 Aborigines. As was the case for Native Americans and Pacific

> "Creating a common Australian identity and nationhood took more than a century."

Islanders, diseases brought by Europeans devastated the Aboriginal population, and many were further destabilized by having their land forcibly settled by white newcomers. Eventually, to survive, many Aborigines moved to cities or European cattle and sheep ranches, while others remained on tribal reservations, where they maintained many of their traditions and beliefs.

Creating the Commonwealth of Australia

Creating a common Australian identity and nationhood took more than a century. Throughout the 1800s, Europeans clung to the coastal regions suitable for farming and ranching and avoided the desert interior. The discovery of gold in southeastern Australia in 1851 attracted settlers from Europe, and by the 1860s, more than 1 million whites lived in Australia. Gold mining also prompted Asians to seek their fortunes in Australia, creating resentments among the Europeans. In 1899, one European leader charged that Asians "will soon be eating the heart's blood out of the white population."[22] Violence between Europeans and Asians led to laws restricting Asian immigration, which ended only in the later twentieth century. Another social challenge was the female struggle for influence. By the 1880s, white women's movements were pressing for moral reform and suffrage, and white women gained the right to vote in 1902, but women still enjoyed little political power at the local or national level. Aborigines only gained the right to vote in 1962.

Gradually, Australia became a nation. By 1890, Britain had turned all six of its Australian colonies into self-governing states, which formed the Commonwealth of Australia in 1901, with the British monarch remaining symbolic head of state, like Canada. A transcontinental railroad system, completed in 1917, connected the vast country, but the majority of the 4 million Australians lived in or near five coastal cities. In 1908 Canberra became the nation's capital. Distance from European supplies fostered some local manufacturing, including steel production, and white Australians enjoyed prosperity.

New Zealand and the Maoris

The British also colonized the two large mountainous islands of New Zealand, 1,200 miles east of Australia, at the expense of the Polynesian Maori people, numbering around 100,000 in 1792. The Maori had lived on the islands, which they called Aotearoa, for a millennium, gradually dividing into sometimes warring tribes headed by chiefs and surviving by hunting, fishing, and horticulture. As more British settlers came, territorial disputes with the Maori occurred. The Treaty of Waitangi in 1850 between the British and five hundred Maori chiefs seemingly confirmed the Maori's right to their land while acknowledging British sovereignty. But the British asserted the treaty gave them political and legal power and usurped the chiefs' authority over their lands and people, leading to a series of wars that ended only in the 1870s and resulted in an even sharper decline in the Maori population. Eventually, Maori resistance subsided, and an 1881 peace agreement accorded Maori control over some districts.

Gradually, the European identity in New Zealand grew stronger. Immigrants were attracted by the discovery of gold in 1861, higher living standards than they enjoyed in Europe, a colonial economy based on farming and sheep raising, and a growing government welfare system. New Zealand prospered after 1882, when steamships acquired refrigerated holds to carry lamb and dairy products from the islands to Europe. A parliamentary government including Maori representatives was formed in 1852, and by 1893 both men and women of all communities enjoyed universal suffrage. New Zealand gained self-government as a British dominion in 1907, but it proudly remained an outpost of the British Empire well into the twentieth century.

 Listen to a synopsis of Chapter 20.

CHAPTER 2

Africa, the Middle East, and Imperialism,
1750–1914

Learning Outcomes

After reading this chapter, you should be able to answer the following questions:

LO¹ How did Western nations obtain colonies in sub-Saharan Africa?

LO² How did white supremacy shape South Africa?

LO³ What were some of the major consequences of colonialism in Africa?

LO⁴ What political and economic impact did Europe have on the Middle East?

LO⁵ How did Middle Eastern thought and culture respond to the Western challenge?

66 The power of these Europeans has advanced to a shocking degree and has manifested itself in an unparalleled manner. Indeed, we are on the brink of a time of [complete] corruption. As for knowing what tomorrow holds, I am blind. 99

—Moroccan historian Ahmad Ibn Khalid Al-Nasri, 1860s[1]

Fresh from his victories in Italy and Austria, in 1798 the French general Napoleon Bonaparte vowed to add his name to the list of illustrious European conquerors who had achieved glory and riches before him in the Middle East, the region encompassing North Africa and western Asia. First he planned to invade Egypt, and then he intended to reduce the Ottoman Turks and Persians to French vassals.

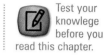

Test your knowlege before you read this chapter.

Eventually he hoped to reach India and found a new religion. With an armada of four hundred ships carrying 50,000 soldiers, Bonaparte quickly established control over northern Egypt. He also took with him some five hundred French scholars to gather valuable information on Egyptian history, society, lan-

What do you think?

Europeans typically considered Africans unfit to rule them-selves and badly in need of Western leadership.

Strongly Disagree						Strongly Agree
1	2	3	4	5	6	7

guage, and environment. Near a town in the Nile River Delta, they dis-covered the Rosetta stone, a tablet made in 196 B.C.E. that contained writings in several languages. One of those languages was Greek, so for the first time, scholars could translate ancient Egyptian hiero-glyphics into Western languages.

Bonaparte acted like a Muslim ruler and even hinted that he might embrace Islam. In a bid for popular support, the French gen-eral confidently announced: "People of Egypt, I come to restore your rights; I respect God, His Prophet and the Quran. We are friends of all true Muslims. Happiness to the People!"[2] But Bonaparte's poli-cies soon alienated Egyptians, and conquest proved a burden. The French army, small and ill-equipped, withered in the desert heat. An attempt to conquer Syria having failed, Bonaparte left for Paris in 1799, becoming another example of a Western ruler failing to control Muslim peoples.

<< **Tomb of Muhammad Ahmad in Khartoum** Muhammad Ahmad ibn 'Abd Allah, known to history as the Mahdi ("Divinely Guided One"), used Islamic appeals to recruit a large army and lead opposition to the joint British and Egyptian rule in Sudan. He died soon after routing the Brit-ish forces in 1885, but his tomb remains a symbol of Muslim resistance to Western power.

Although unsuccessful, the French invasion of Egypt provided a harbinger of more invasions of the kind feared by the Moroccan historian Ahmad ibn Khalid al-Nasri, through which Europe would extend its domination in the world. Bonaparte's expedition was a turning point in Western relations with sub-Saharan Africa and the Middle East, the cutting edge of a European thrust that also overwhelmed India, Southeast Asia, and the Pacific islands. The Industrial Revolution, new technology, and capitalism in Europe had greatly accelerated Europe's need for natural resources that could be processed into industrial products, as well as for new markets to consume these goods. These economic factors combined with European political rivalries caused a ruthless policy of incorporating territories in sub-Saharan Africa and the Middle East. While the sub-Saharan and North Africans often resisted European imperialism, their societies' economies, cultures, and political systems were transformed.

> "By 1800 British bankers could make more money investing in manufacturing than in plantations and the slave trade."

LO¹ The Colonization of Sub-Saharan Africa

During the nineteenth century, various Western nations colonized most of sub-Saharan Africa. Although Europeans had established a few small, scattered outposts in West Africa and colonized coastal regions of Angola, Mozambique, and South Africa in the sixteenth and seventeenth centuries, the full-blown quest for colonies began only with the end of the trans-Atlantic slave trade and the spread of the Industrial Revolution in Europe in the mid-1800s. At this time, European imperial ambitions fostered what a British newspaper called the "scramble for Africa," during which the European powers divided up the African continent among themselves, often against fierce resistance, and commenced the full-scale economic penetration of Africa.

The End of the Slave Trade

For more than three centuries, the trans-Atlantic slave trade (1520–1870) dominated relations between Africa, Europe, and the Americas, but growing opposition in all three regions eventually brought it to an end. In the West, especially in Britain, abolitionists were prompted largely by religious and moral outrage at slavery, while others were influenced by the Enlightenment vision of human equality. One sympathizer wrote that people "are not objects. Everyone has his rights, property, dignity. Africa will have its day."³ Africans and African Americans also struggled against slavery. Slave revolts in the Americas, including the successful revolution in Haiti (see Chapter 19), as well as attempts by slaves to seize control of slave ships conveying them to the Americas, indicated the willingness of many slaves to risk their lives for freedom and also forced many Europeans to rethink their views on slavery.

Another force working against slavery was the Industrial Revolution, which made slavery uneconomical. Overseas markets for factory-made goods became more desirable than cheap labor for plantations. Furthermore, so many colonies produced sugar that the market was flooded and the price fell, making the plantations less profitable at the same time that African states were charging more to provide slaves. By 1800 British bankers could make more money investing in manufacturing than in plantations and the slave trade.

As a result of this combination of moral and economic factors, the slave trade from Africa to the Americas and the slavery era came to an end in the Atlantic world in the nineteenth century. The slave trade was first outlawed in Denmark in 1804, then in Britain in 1807, and then in all British-controlled territories, including their plantation-rich Caribbean colonies, in 1833. Many Latin American nations and Haiti outlawed slavery in the early 1800s, forcing planters to shift to free labor. By 1842 most European and American countries had made it illegal to transport slaves across the Atlantic. The Civil War ended the practice of slavery in the United States in 1865, and in the later 1880s, Brazil and Cuba also finally outlawed slavery.

The East African trade that sent slaves to the Middle East and the Indian Ocean islands—run chiefly

1804	Launching of Fulani jihads by Uthman dan Fodio
1804	Abolition of slave trade by Denmark
1806	British seizure of Cape region from Dutch
1807–1833	Abolition of slave trade in Britain and its territories
1816	Beginning of Shaka's Zulu Empire
1838	Great Trek by South African Boers
1842	Ending of trans-Atlantic slave trade by most European nations
1847	First American freed slave settlement in Liberia
1874–1901	British-Ashante wars
1878	Belgian colonization in Congo
1884–1885	Berlin Conference
1884–1885	Discovery of gold in South Africa
1898	French defeat of Samory Toure
1899–1902	Boer (South African) War
1905	Maji Maji Rebellion in Tanganyika
1912	Founding of African National Congress in South Africa

into the eastern Congo River Basin. In 1873 the British convinced the Zanzibar sultan to close the island's slave market, and as compensation Britain imported vast amounts of ivory, which was used for making piano keys, billiard balls, and cutlery handles. While fewer slaves were now exported, slavers still raided African villages to acquire the labor needed to carry the huge ivory tusks to the coast for export, often in well-armed caravans of up to one thousand people. The British gained control of Zanzibar in 1890, but some slave trading continued in parts of East and Central Africa until the early 1900s.

New Societies and Explorations

Between the later 1700s and later 1800s, the diminishing importance and then ending of the trans-Atlantic slave trade gradually changed the relationship between Africans and Europeans, fostering several new African societies, exploration of Africa by Western adventurers, and increased commerce between Europeans and Africans. As the demand for slaves waned, Europeans became more interested in acquiring African natural resources.

Even before slavery was abolished in the Americas, freed slaves there who returned to Africa from the Americas had established several West African states and port cities. The black founders of these states, and the whites who helped finance them, had both humanitarian aims and commercial goals, wanting to give freed slaves opportunities to run their own lives while also setting up new centers of Western trade. Thousands of freed slaves also settled in coastal towns of the Gold Coast (modern Ghana), Nigeria, and Dahomey, where some became merchants engaged in trade with the Americas.

 **Africa South of the Sahara** (*http://www-sul.stanford.edu/depts/ssrg/africa/*). A valuable site that contains links relevant to African history.

The two largest settlements of freed slaves emerged in Sierra Leone and Liberia. Spurred by abolitionists, in 1787 the British settled four hundred former slaves around the fort at Freetown, which became the core of their colony of Sierra Leone. Over the next few decades, the British shipped more former slaves to Freetown. Freed slaves from the United States were first shipped to Liberia in 1847 and were joined by others after the Civil War. Although Liberia remained an independent state governed by

by Arabs from the eastern Arabian state of Oman—continued longer than the trans-Atlantic trade. In 1835 the Omani leader, Sayyid Sa'id (SIGH-id SIGH-eed) (r. 1806–1856), moved his capital to Zanzibar, an island just off the coast of modern Tanzania, and built a commercial empire of ivory and slaves that flourished for forty years. To obtain slaves and ivory, Omani and Swahili merchants opened or expanded overland trade routes through Tanzania

> **❝As the demand for slaves waned, Europeans became more interested in acquiring African natural resources.❞**

the descendants of former slaves, its economy was dominated by U.S.-owned rubber plantations. In both Sierra Leone and Liberia, local Africans often resented the new settlers, who were mostly English-speaking Christians, because they occupied valuable land and often dominated commercial and political power.

The decline of the trans-Atlantic slave trade, which had caused turmoil and made travel dangerous in parts of Africa, also made Africa more accessible to Western explorers. Europeans wanted to discover whether the great African rivers such as the Nile and the Congo were navigable for commercial purposes. Adventurers were obsessed with finding the source of Africa's greatest river, the Nile, and they finally located Lake Victoria in 1860. The most famous explorer, David Livingstone (1813–1873), spent more than two decades traveling in eastern Africa, where he collected information and opened the region to Christian missionary activity and trade with the West.

From John H. Hanson, *Migration, Jihad, and Muslim Authority in West Africa* [Bloomington and Indianapolis: Indiana University Press, 1996]

African Muslim Warrior While Western pressure on coastal societies increased, several Muslim peoples expanded their influence in the West African interior. Some military forces, having acquired Western arms in exchange for slaves and gold, conquered regional empires that flourished for a century or more.

Livingstone and other European adventurers claimed to have "discovered" inland societies and geographic features, but these European explorers discovered little that Africans and Arabs did not already know, and they usually followed long-established trading routes. The ethnocentric stereotype of intrepid white explorers struggling through virgin territories is a myth, but it shaped Western views. Explorers publicized their findings and spread the notion of "Darkest Africa," which was seen as savage and in need of salvation.

With Africa more open in the 1800s, European traders began to obtain various raw materials needed by the West, such as peanuts, palm oil, gold, timber, and cotton, competing with dynamic West African merchants who, with the end of the slave trade, had set up cash crop plantations. With superior financial resources and governmental support, European companies eventually gained the upper hand over West African merchants. As a result, by 1890 in the trading port of Lagos, once a center of African commerce, only one rich African merchant was still in business.

Islamic Resurgence

Some major developments within Africa in this era derived largely from forces within African societies, such as tensions within Islamic societies of the Sudan that fostered militant expansion. The most notable example, the Fulani jihad (holy war), was part of a larger religious ferment in West Africa that had begun in the Intermediate Era when expanding Islam encountered African traditions. Many West Africans had embraced Islam by blending the religion with their own customs and sometimes animist beliefs. Conflicts broke out sporadically in parts of West Africa in the seventeenth and eighteenth centuries, often involving the Fulani, a pastoral and trading people who lived in communities scattered across the western and central Sudan. By the 1790s, religious conflicts between devout Muslims and those who mixed Muslim and African traditions had spread to the Fulani in the prosperous Hausa states of northern Nigeria.

One of these Fulani, Uthman dan Fodio (AHTH-mun dahn FOH-dee-oh) (1754–1817), a respected Muslim scholar and ardent follower of Sufi mysticism, criticized the tolerant attitude of many Hausa rulers toward religion, called for the conversion of non-Muslim Fulani, and proclaimed the goal of making Islam central to Sudanic life. His magnetic personality and Islamic zeal soon attracted a Fulani and Hausa following. Uthman's attacks on high taxes and social injustice, and his promise to build a government that would spread Islam and purify it of animist beliefs, alarmed Hausa rulers, who tried to restrict his activities. After an attempt was made on his life, Uthman mobilized his followers and launched a jihad in 1804. After conquering the Hausa states and then nearby territories, he created the Sokoto (SOH-kuh-toh) Caliphate, based in the city of Sokoto, and ruled much of what is today northern Nigeria.

> "Europeans used deceptive treaties, offered bribes, divided up states, and convinced African leaders that resistance was futile."

Uthman's jihad, and the vision of a purified Islam he offered, sparked others to take up his cause, and during the early 1800s, several other jihadist states, often led by Fulani religious scholars turned state builders, formed in the Sudan. The Islamic revival sparked by the jihads, which continued into the 1880s, allowed a more orthodox Islam to spread widely. As a result, just as Western influence was increasing in some parts of Africa, the Sudan was becoming even more Islamic. But by the later 1800s, as leaders entrenched their powers and forgot Uthman's reformist vision, the Fulani states declined, and Sokoto's power waned in the face of French and British expansion. Nevertheless, Islam remained a vital force in the Sudanic zone.

European Conquest

Several factors contributed to the acceleration of European conquests in Africa in the late 1800s (see Map 21.1). First, Western companies sought government help to compete with African traders and to pressure states to admit Western merchants. Second, advances in tropical medicine, especially the use of quinine for malaria, freed Europeans from high tropical mortality rates. Third, the invention of more powerful weapons gave Europeans a huge military advantage over African forces. Europeans used deceptive treaties, offered bribes, divided up states, and convinced African leaders that resistance was futile. When faced with resistance, however, Europeans used ruthless force.

 Interactive Map

The Belgian Colonization of the Congo

King Leopold of Belgium took the lead in colonization. In 1878, he hired Henry Stanley (1841–1904), a Welsh-born American and former Confederate soldier who became famous for his travels and published writings on traveling in central Africa. Stanley was familiar with the Congo River Basin, which King Leopold now commissioned Stanley to acquire for Belgium.

Soon other European powers joined the scramble to obtain colonies. In 1884–1885, the colonizing nations held a conference in Berlin to set the ground rules for colonization. For a claim to be recognized, the colonizer had to first give notice to the other Western powers of its intent and then occupy the territory with a military presence. Agents of European governments, such as Stanley working for Belgium, asked African chiefs, most of whom knew no Western languages, to sign treaties of friendship in these languages, but the treaties actually gave the land to European countries. To Africans the Westerners' concept of private ownership was alien, making it easy for European agents to manipulate them. If chiefs refused to sign, they were threatened with war. Fearing a slaughter and hoping to manipulate conditions for their own benefit, many chiefs signed. A Nigerian writer lamented in 1891 that the slavers' forcible possession of Africa's people had only been replaced by the European governments' forcible possession of Africa's land.

The "Pax Britannica"

Further weakening the African response, the colonial scramble came at a time when famine, drought, and epidemics of smallpox and cholera were killing millions, especially in eastern Africa. One French missionary reflected the despair: "Why so many calamities in succession? Why?"[4] They also were overwhelmed by the military disparity in weapons and tactics. Using powerful industrialized weapons such as the British Gatling and Maxim machine guns, Westerners willingly slaughtered thousands. In Kenya, British military expeditions attacked villages who resisted. A British officer in Kenya wrote home in 1902 about ordering the destruction of a Gikuyu village because an Englishman had been killed nearby. As a result, every adult villager was either shot or bayoneted, and the British burned all of the huts and then razed the banana farms to the ground. Apparently without irony, the British called their policy of establishing order the "Pax Britannica," or British peace. For most Africans, these were bitter years indeed.

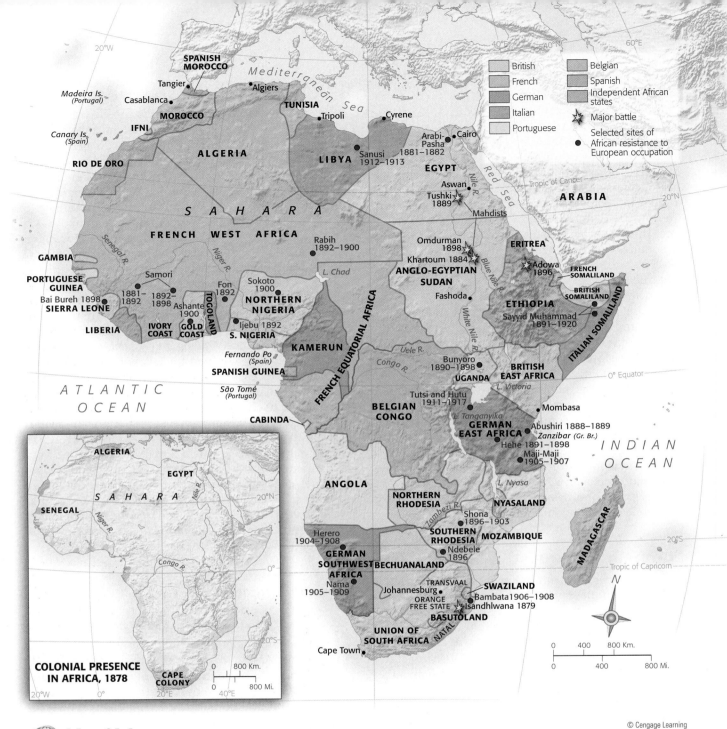

Legend:
- British
- French
- German
- Italian
- Portuguese
- Belgian
- Spanish
- Independent African states
- ✦ Major battle
- • Selected sites of African resistance to European occupation

SPANISH MOROCCO
Tangier
Madeira Is. (Portugal)
Casablanca
MOROCCO
IFNI
Canary Is. (Spain)
RIO DE ORO
Mediterranean Sea
Algiers
TUNISIA
Tripoli
Cyrene
LIBYA
Sanusi 1912–1913
ALGERIA
SAHARA
FRENCH WEST AFRICA
Arabi-Pasha 1881–1882
Cairo
EGYPT
Aswan
Tushki 1889
Mahdists
ARABIA
Tropic of Cancer
Red Sea
Nile R.
GAMBIA
Senegal R.
Niger R.
Rabih 1892–1900
L. Chad
Omdurman 1898
Khartoum 1884
ANGLO-EGYPTIAN SUDAN
Fashoda
Blue Nile R.
White Nile R.
ERITREA
Adowa 1896
FRENCH SOMALILAND
BRITISH SOMALILAND
PORTUGUESE GUINEA
Samori
Sokoto 1900
ETHIOPIA
Sayyid Muhammad 1891–1920
Bai Bureh 1898
1881–1892
1892–1898
Fon 1892
NORTHERN NIGERIA
ITALIAN SOMALILAND
SIERRA LEONE
Ashante 1900
TOGOLAND
LIBERIA
IVORY COAST
GOLD COAST
Ijebu 1892
S. NIGERIA
KAMERUN
Fernando Po (Spain)
SPANISH GUINEA
São Tomé (Portugal)
FRENCH EQUATORIAL AFRICA
Uele R.
Congo R.
Bunyoro 1890–1898
UGANDA
BRITISH EAST AFRICA
0° Equator
L. Victoria
Mombasa
ATLANTIC OCEAN
CABINDA
BELGIAN CONGO
Tutsi and Hutu 1911–1917
L. Tanganyika
GERMAN EAST AFRICA
Abushiri 1888–1889
Zanzibar (Gr. Br.)
Hehe 1891–1898
Maji-Maji 1905–1907
INDIAN OCEAN
ANGOLA
NORTHERN RHODESIA
Zambezi R.
L. Nyasa
NYASALAND
MOZAMBIQUE
Shona 1896–1903
SOUTHERN RHODESIA
Ndebele 1896
MADAGASCAR
20°S
Tropic of Capricorn
GERMAN SOUTHWEST AFRICA
Herero 1904–1908
BECHUANALAND
SWAZILAND
Bambata 1906–1908
Nama 1905–1909
Johannesburg
TRANSVAAL
ORANGE FREE STATE
Isandhlwana 1879
BASUTOLAND
NATAL
UNION OF SOUTH AFRICA
Cape Town
N
0   400   800 Km.
0   400   800 Mi.

Inset map:

ALGERIA
EGYPT
SAHARA
Nile R.
SENEGAL
Niger R.
Congo R.
0°
20°S
COLONIAL PRESENCE IN AFRICA, 1878
CAPE COLONY
0   800 Km.
0   800 Mi.
20°W   0°   20°E   40°E

© Cengage Learning

Map 21.1
Africa in 1914

Before 1878, the European powers held only a few coastal territories in Africa, but in that year they turned to expanding their power through colonization. By 1914, the British, French, Belgians, Germans, Italians, Portuguese, and Spanish controlled all of the continent except for Ethiopia and Liberia.

Finally, after centuries of rivalries and slave wars, Africans could not unite for common defense. Europeans took advantage of the political instability, pitting state against state and ethnic group against ethnic group. For example, the region that became Nigeria had been the home of various independent kingdoms, such as the predominantly animist Yoruba, the Muslim Hausa-Fulani, and village-based stateless societies such as the Igbo. Capitalizing on divisions among them, between 1887 and 1903, the British conquered or otherwise annexed these diverse societies, creating the artificial political unit they called Nigeria, because it occupied both sides of the lower Niger River.

Partition and Resistance

By 1914, European powers had partitioned the entire continent of Africa except for Ethiopia and Liberia. The French empire was concentrated in North, West, and Central Africa and extended across the Sahara from Senegal in the west to Lake Chad in North-Central Africa. The British had four colonies in West Africa, including Nigeria, but they built most of their empire in eastern and southern Africa. The four German colonies were scattered, while Italy concentrated on the Horn region of Northeast Africa, including Somalia and Eritrea, and on Libya in North Africa.

Cecil Rhodes Despite the Berlin Conference, European nations competed fiercely for territories. German colonization of Tanganyika inspired Britain to move into Kenya, Uganda, and Zanzibar, partly to block Germany. In South Africa, the brash British imperialist Cecil Rhodes (1853–1902), a clergyman's son who had made millions in the South African diamond mining industry, wanted to push British power north, outflanking the Portuguese and Germans. Rhodes was largely responsible for extending British influence into the territory he arrogantly named Northern and Southern Rhodesia. British settlers migrated to Southern Rhodesia (today's Zimbabwe) and Kenya, solidifying the British hold on the region.

African Resistance While many Africans had little hope of repulsing the well-armed Europeans, others offered spirited resistance to European conquest and occupation. As a result, it took decades for Europeans to conquer and occupy some territories, such as the western Sudan, where the Mandinka leader Samory Toure resisted for decades. Ethiopia,

fortified by high mountains that were difficult to penetrate, was not conquered until the 1930s. In 1896, Emperor Menelik (MEN-uh-lik) II (1844–1914), a reformer, easily defeated an invasion force of 10,000 Italian troops with a French-trained army of 80,000 men.

Read about Samory Toure, the Mandinka king and resistance leader of West Africa.

In the West African region known as the Gold Coast (today's Ghana), the Ashante kingdom offered particularly strong political and military resistance. The Ashante, like many African states, expanded in the early 1800s, clashing with the British, who sought to protect their coastal forts. In 1874, after more British–Ashante conflict over the coastal settlements, the British secured control of the coastal zone but were unable to push very deep into the interior. The British then deliberately fomented a civil war in the remaining Ashante territories to undermine the state, but the Ashante king refused to surrender. In 1896, three thousand well-armed British troops finally occupied the Ashante capital, Kumasi, and exiled the king. However, resistance continued, and the British did not manage to incorporate the Ashante into their Gold Coast colony until 1901.

Sometimes resistance was led by religious leaders. In West Africa, the mystical Sufi brotherhoods sometimes rallied Muslim opposition to the French or British. In Senegal the defiant Wolof people turned to Muslim clerics for leadership, and especially to Amadu Bamba Mbacke (AH-mah-doo BOM-ba um-BACK-ee) (ca. 1853–1927), who had founded a peaceful Sufi order, the *Murids* ("learners seeking God"). Eventually the French realized that they could only rule Senegal with the cooperation of the Murids and reached a compromise: Amadu Bamba acknowledged French administration but was free to expand the Murids, which remain a powerful influence among Senegalese Muslims.

LO² The Making of Settler Societies

While this era saw Europeans advancing in both Asia and Africa, only in Africa did they take over large tracts of land as settlers. The largest settler colony, South Africa, experienced an unusual history: over three centuries of white supremacy introduced by the Dutch colonizers and perpetuated by the British. The first Dutch settlement, Cape Town, was established at the Cape of Good Hope in 1652. Over the next two centuries, Dutch control gradually expanded along the coast and into the interior at the expense of the indigenous Bantu-speaking African peoples, who strongly resisted. European immigrants also settled in British East Africa, the Rhodesias, and the Portuguese colonies. Asian migrants joined them, often as traders.

Europeans and South Africans

From the beginning, South Africa was shaped by conflicts between European settlers and the African peoples whose ancestors had lived in the region for centuries. The Dutch settlers, known as Boers (Dutch for "farmers"), established a system of white supremacy in South Africa based on white rule over non-whites that enforced as much physical separation of the groups as possible. The system became even more rigid among those Boers who boarded wagon trains and migrated east along the coast and into the interior, a journey they called trekking, to find good farming land and to avoid governmental oversight. Trekking led to chronic conflict between the migrating Boers and the Bantu-speaking Xhosa (KHO-sa) people, farmers and pastoralists who already lived in the eastern Cape region. The two groups collided in the late 1700s and fought for nearly half a century. Many thousands died, mostly Xhosa.

The trek became the common way for Boers to flee restraints by any government. In 1806, the British annexed the Cape Colony, giving the Boers even more reason to migrate into the interior. Boers viewed white supremacy as sanctioned by their strict, puritanical Calvinist Christian beliefs, and the slave system also ensured them a cheap labor supply for their farms and ranches. By ending South African slavery, the British harmed the Boer economy. Later, the British granted the right to vote and hold office to Africans and mixed-descent people, known as coloreds, privileges that the Boers considered heresy.

Education, Civilization, and "Foreignization" in Buganda Learn what one African leader thought about the influence of European civilization on the native culture of his people.

Shaka Zulu and Moshoeshoe

In addition to the British, Boers faced conflict with the largest Bantu-speaking South African group, the Zulus. In the early 1800s, some Zulu peoples began a military expansion under an ambitious military genius, Shaka (ca. 1787–1828), whose exploits in war allowed him to become a powerful chief. Planning to gain dominance over the whole region, he united various Zulu clans in Natal (nuh-TALL), the region along South Africa's Indian Ocean coast, into a powerful nation, raising a disciplined army of some 40,000 warriors and developing effective new military tactics. In 1816, he began invading other groups' territories, and the resulting wars killed thousands of Africans, both Zulus and non-Zulus, and wreaked widespread disruption. Eventually Shaka grew more despotic and was assassinated by his brother as the Zulu empire fell. Ironically, by depopulating large areas of the mineral-rich interior plateau, Shaka's wars made it easier for the Boers to move in later.

Some leaders of Bantu-speaking groups found effective ways to avoid conquest by the Zulus and Boers. Perhaps the most successful was Moshoeshoe (MOE-shoo-shoo) (b. ca. 1786), who created a kingdom for his branch of the Sotho (SOO-too) people. With the region in turmoil from warfare because of the Zulu and Boer expansion, Moshoeshoe moved his people to an easily defended flat-top mountain in 1824. There he strengthened his community by taking in African refugees regardless of their ethnic origin and integrating them into his people. The king emphasized not only military defense but also diplomacy, skillfully cultivating friendship with the British as a counterweight to the Boers. While neighboring Africans fell under Boer rule, British support for Moshoeshoe allowed his Sotho kingdom to remain independent until 1871.

History and Cultures of Africa (http://www.columbia.edu/cu/lweb/indiv/africa/cuvl/cult.html). Provides valuable links to relevant websites on African history.

British–Boer Conflict and White Supremacy

In the decades after British annexation of the Cape, conflict between the Boers and the British intensified, eventually leading to a system of white supremacy in South Africa. In 1838, about one-fifth of all the Boers, alienated by British policies in the Cape Colony, began what they called the Great Trek, boarding their wag-

> From the beginning, South Africa was shaped by conflicts between European settlers and the African peoples whose ancestors had lived in the region for centuries.

ons and, with their sheep and cattle, heading in well-armed caravans of several hundred families north into the interior. After many hardships, including fighting with Zulus, they moved into the high plateau of what is now northern South Africa and created two independent Boer republics, Transvaal (TRANS-vahl) and the Orange Free State. Although the Bantu peoples battled the Boers for decades, they were conquered and forced to work on Boer farms. As the Boers consolidated control, their ideas of keeping themselves separate from Africans grew stronger. The evolving Boer ideology considered black Africans an "inferior race" hostile to European values. Devaluing Africans and despising the British, the Boers committed themselves to maintaining their identity and culture whatever the cost.

> "The evolving Boer ideology considered black Africans an 'inferior race' hostile to European values."

The Boer War

However, the discovery in the Boer republics of diamonds in 1867 and gold in the 1880s spurred the British to seek control over Boer territories, and their attempts to annex the Boer republics led to the South African War (1899–1902), often called the Boer War. The war culminated in British victory but also created chronic Boer resentment of the British. During the war, the Boers employed guerrilla tactics, acting as civilians by day and raiding British targets at night. To eradicate local support for the Boer commandos, the British burned Boer farms, destroyed towns, and interned thousands of Boers, including women and children, in concentration camps, where 26,000 died of disease and starvation. These brutalities discredited the war in Britain. Moreover, the British relied on African troops for victory, and thousands of Africans died fighting the Boers in hopes that the British would be less oppressive. But, when the war ended, Africans found they had merely exchanged one set of white masters for another.

Creating South African Society

After the Boer War, British and Boer leaders worked out a compromise in which the South African government became essentially a collaboration between the two groups, restoring Boer rights and strengthening white supremacy policies. To win Boer cooperation, the British extended discriminatory Boer laws; Africans were valued chiefly as cheap unskilled labor for the white-owned economy. Britain's racist policies became a constant source of humiliation and tension for Africans, and continued resistance gradually led the British to build a police state. Furthermore, despite the political compromises they had made, British–Boer tensions simmered as thousands of British settlers arrived, eventually becoming one-third of the white population. Asserting their long-established position in the country, the Boers began to style themselves Afrikaners (people of Africa) and their Dutch-derived language Afrikaans.

Three Peoples Interact

Domination by the Boers and the British reshaped South African life and culture in the later 1800s and early 1900s. Africans were recruited into the white-owned economy and often became Christian. Thousands of Africans moved to cities, especially the Transvaal mining center of Johannesburg, thus becoming removed from their farming villages and transformed into salaried workers. They experienced dreadful work conditions on white-owned factories, farms, and particularly in the mines, where hundreds of miners died each year. The Zulu poet B. W. Vilakezi described the miner's life in the early 1900s: "Roar, without rest, machines of the mines, Roar from dawn till darkness falls. To black men groaning as they labor, Tortured by their aching muscles, Gasping in the fetid air."[5]

> 66 Africans often resisted Western domination by adapting their cultural forms to changing conditions. 99

Africans often resisted Western domination by adapting their cultural forms to changing conditions. For example, Zulu warriors reworked dance tunes and turned them into songs to protest white military incursion. The Sotho people gradually transformed their tradition of poetry praising influential people and ancestors into songs expressing the fears and experiences of male migrants working in the mines and the women left behind in the villages. Educated urban Africans, who formed a middle class of professionals and traders, also found ways to oppose

The Great Trek Many Boers migrated into the South African interior in wagon trains. These migrants, known as Trekkers, endured hardships but also eventually subjugated the local African peoples, taking their land for farming, pasturing, and mining.

WAGGON ASCENDING THE UNCOMMOSS HILL, NATAL.

Mansell/Time & Life Pictures/Getty Images

white supremacy. One of these, the Johannesburg lawyer Pixley ka Isaka Seme, a graduate of Columbia University in New York, helped found the African National Congress in 1912 to promote African rights and spur Africa's cultural regeneration. Some Bantu composers creatively mixed Christian hymns with traditional Xhosa or Zulu choral music. The African National Congress adopted one such hymn, "God Bless Africa," as their official anthem of hope.

Like South Africa, several other colonies restricted African civil and economic rights, particularly Portuguese-ruled Angola and British-ruled Kenya and Southern Rhodesia. These colonial governments reserved for immigrant white farmers not only the best land, such as the fertile Kenyan highlands that were once dominated by the Gikuyu people, but also the most lucrative crops, such as coffee. African farmers also faced barriers in obtaining bank loans to compete with white farmers and were unable to gain any political power. Laws limited contact between whites and Africans except as employers and hired workers.

Asian minorities also became part of colonial societies. Beginning in the 1890s, Indians arrived to build railroads, work on sugar plantations, or become middle-level retail traders. Indians became the commercial middle class of East Africa and occupied a key economic niche in South Africa, the Rhodesias, Mozambique, and Madagascar. Cities such as Nairobi in Kenya, Kampala in Uganda, and Durban in South Africa had substantial Indian populations, and their downtowns were dominated by Indian stores, restaurants, and Hindu temples. In West and Central Africa, Lebanese occupied the middle levels of the economy as shopkeepers in cities and towns. Many black Africans resented the growing influence and wealth of the Asian immigrants, a sentiment that the British exploited to their own advantage.

LO³ The Colonial Reshaping of Sub-Saharan Africa

The experience of living under Western colonial domination from the 1880s to the 1960s reshaped sub-Saharan Africans' politics, society, culture, and economy. Colonialism created artificial states and transformed Africans into subject peoples who enjoyed few political rights. It also allowed Western business interests to penetrate the continent and integrate Africa into the global system as a supplier of valuable raw materials.

Colonial Governments

The colonial policies devised in European cities introduced new kinds of governments in Africa, as each colonizing power sought the best way to achieve maximum control at minimum expense. Two broad types of administration emerged: direct rule and indirect rule. Under direct rule, the administration was largely European, even down to the local level, and chiefs or kings were reduced to symbolic roles. Under indirect rule, the Europeans gave the traditional leaders of a district, the kings or chiefs, considerable local power but kept them subject to colonial officials. In general, indirect rule, which left much of the original society intact, caused less disruption than direct rule, but African leaders were required to consult with the local European adviser on many matters. The advisers enforced colonial law and order, collected taxes, and supervised public works. Because Europeans lacked enough officials to administer a large colony such as Nigeria or Tanganyika, this form of rule was inspired by pragmatism, but it weakened village democracy and did not benefit African societies.

Nigeria, an unwieldy colony that contained some 250 distinct African ethnic groups, provided an example of both kinds of administration. Indirect rule was taken to its fullest extent in largely Muslim northern Nigeria, leaving the traditional Hausa-Fulani courts and social structure largely undisturbed. By contrast, the British governed southern Nigeria chiefly through direct rule, with the result that greater change occurred in the south, including the introduction of Christian missions and cash crop farming. Peoples such as the Igbo and Yoruba successfully adapted to these changes that transformed their regions. The Yoruba successfully blended aspects of their indigenous culture, such as a rich artistic tradition and polytheism, with imported cultural traditions, such as English literature and Christianity, maintaining a high degree of tolerance for divergent views and rejecting helplessness.

> "The colonial policies devised in European cities introduced new kinds of governments in Africa, as each colonizing power sought the best way to achieve maximum control at minimum expense."

> 66 To maintain their privileged position, Europeans also imposed a color bar that kept Africans out of clubs, schools, and jobs reserved for Europeans. 99

Although supporters of colonialism defended Western rule as providing "a school for democracy," the rationale clearly differed from reality. By 1945, fewer than 1 percent of Africans enjoyed political rights or access to democratic institutions. Meanwhile, traditional African leaders enforced European policies if they wanted to keep their positions. Africans often viewed these privileged and wealthy leaders as little better than paid agents of colonialism.

Disrupting African Societies

The boundaries that European colonizers drew up to partition Africa into colonies created artificial countries that often ignored traditional ethnic relationships. Modern countries such as Nigeria, Ghana (the former Gold Coast), Congo, and Mozambique were colonial creations, not nations built on shared culture and identity. Colonizers ignored the interests of local people, sometimes dividing ethnic groups between two or more colonial systems. For example, the Kongolese, once masters of a major African kingdom, were split between Portuguese Angola and the Belgian and French Congos. At the same time, rival societies were sometimes joined, creating a basis for political instability later.

Ethnicity and Ethnocentrism

To maintain their privileged position, Europeans also imposed a color bar that kept Africans out of clubs, schools, and jobs reserved for Europeans. Europeans typically considered Africans unfit to rule themselves and badly in need of Western leadership. An ethnocentric British scholar argued in 1920 that "the chief distinction between the backward and forward peoples is that the former are of colored skin."[6] Such views ignored several thousand years of African governments, ranging from centralized kingdoms to village democracies, as well as participation in Eastern Hemisphere trade networks from ancient times. Racist ideology spawned the French and Belgian idea of the "civilizing mission," which viewed Africans as children who could attain adulthood only by adopting French language, religion, and culture.

The colonizers often misunderstood African societies and ethnic complexities. The British tended to identify people of similar culture and language as "tribes," such as the Yoruba of Nigeria and Gikuyu of Kenya, even though these peoples were actually collections of subgroups without much historical unity. Despite loose cultural homogeneity, the Yoruba were traditionally divided into several competing states, each with its own king, while the Gikuyu had few political structures higher than the village. In reality, African peoples such as the Yoruba, Gikuyu, Igbo, Xhosa, and Mandinka were ethnic groups, not unlike the politically divided inhabitants of early modern Europe.

Christianity in Africa

Christian missionaries also reshaped African culture and religious life. Christian missions established most of Africa's modern hospitals and schools, institutions that helped Africans but also reflected Western views. Mission doctors practiced Western medicine and denounced African folk medicine. Mission schools taught new agricultural methods, simple mathematics, reading, writing, and Western languages, thus giving a small group of educated Africans the skills they could use in the colonial economy and administration. Critics complained that the mission schools, as an Igbo writer put it, "miseducated" and "de-Africanized" them, perpetuating their status as "hewers of wood and haulers of water"[7] who were unable to challenge their subservience to Europeans. Furthermore, the Africans who attended mission schools and adopted Western ways often became divorced from their traditional African communities.

> "The transformation of African economic life was at least as significant as the political reorganization."

Yet modern education reached only a small minority of Africans. Before 1945, only 5 percent of children attended any government or mission school. The schools typically produced clerks in governments and businesses or cash crop farmers, although a few graduates became teachers, doctors, lawyers, and journalists. The first modern African college was established in Sierra Leone in 1827. But before 1940, the few Africans who could attend a university had to do so usually in Europe or the United States.

Millions of Africans did adopt Christianity, but its impact varied widely. Some Africans became devout Catholics or Protestants, while others only partially embraced Christianity, adopting those beliefs they liked, such as biblical calls for justice and equality, while rejecting others. Some African churches combined Christian doctrines with African practices and beliefs. Hence, in 1901 some Nigerians left the Anglican Church to form their own church, which condoned men having more than one wife. Yorubas, tolerant of diverse religious beliefs, often just added the Christian and Muslim gods to their polytheistic pantheon. Chrstianity also impacted women's lives, reducing women's traditional religious roles and promoting monogamy. Christian leaders sometimes asked men to give up multiple wives, leaving these women without support. Yet, women often welcomed monogamy and favored Christian social values, such as education for girls.

Africans in the World Economy

The transformation of African economic life was at least as significant as the political reorganization. Extracting wealth from a colony required tying its economy more closely to that of the colonizer. Colonial governments imposed economic policies to transform Africans into producers for the world market, hence rejecting the subsistence agriculture that, while having sustained Africans for centuries, now could not produce enough revenues for the government or investors. Requiring taxes to be paid in cash promoted a shift from food cultivation to growing cash crops such as cotton, cocoa, rubber, and palm oil or mining copper, gold, oil, chrome, cobalt, and diamonds. Authorities sometimes resorted to forced labor, most notoriously in the Belgian Congo, where more than half of the Congo's population died from overwork or brutality over a twenty-year period. An American missionary reported in 1895 that the Belgian policies "reduced the people to a state of utter despair. Each town is forced to bring a certain quality [of rubber]. The soldiers drive the people into the bush. If they will not go they are shot down, and their left hands cut off. The soldiers often shoot poor helpless women and harmless children."[8]

Through such measures as these, colonial Africa became linked to the West and the world economy, but often this global economy left Africans vulnerable. Western businesses and planters exercised considerable political influence, while African livelihoods became subject to the fluctuations of global commodities. Colonies also became markets for Western industrial products, displacing village handicrafts, and many Africans lost their economic self-sufficiency. With the growth of an automobile culture in the West, an oil-drilling industry also emerged along the West African coast from southern Nigeria to northern Angola, making these societies dependent on oil exports. Colonies often became economic monocultures dependent on the export of one or two major commodities, such as copper from Northern Rhodesia (now Zambia), cocoa from the Gold Coast, peanuts from Senegal, and cotton from Sudan. Many colonial policies made it difficult for Africans to diversify their economies.

Defining Gender Roles in Colonial Africa

The opportunities and demands of the colonial economy touched nearly everyone in some way, profoundly affecting the lives of both men and women. As men were frequently recruited or forced to migrate to other districts or colonies for mining or industrial labor, a permanent pattern of labor migration became established. This migration disrupted family and village life, helping to further destabilize African society. The male migrants often lived in crowded dormitories or huts that offered little privacy, enjoyed few amenities other than drinking beer in makeshift bars, and were able to visit their families back home for only a few days per year.

African women faced a different combination of hardship and opportunities. In many African societies, women had long enjoyed considerable autonomy, playing a major role as traders and farmers. Now, however, as men migrated for work or took up cash crop farming, women were left with all food production, which was less lucrative than the men's work. The Baule women of Ivory Coast, who had long profited from growing cotton and spinning it into

IN THE RUBBER COILS.

Scene—The Congo "Free" State.

Rubber Coils in Belgian Congo The Belgians colonized the Congo hoping to exploit its resources. This critical cartoon, published in the British satirical magazine *Punch* in 1906, shows a Congolese ensnared in the rubber coils of the Belgian king Leopold in the guise of a serpent. Rubber was the major cash crop, introduced by the Belgians to generate profits.

thread, lost their position to Baule men when cotton became a cash crop and textiles an export item. Many women traders who had dominated town markets now faced competition from Indians or Lebanese. But thanks to education, self-help, and ambition, some African women gained skills to support themselves as teachers, nurses, and merchants, but many poor women were overwhelmed by the challenges of trying to preserve their families while fulfilling new responsibilities.

African Resistance and the Colonial Legacy

Africans responded to colonialism in various ways. The Igbos of Nigeria capitalized on change by taking up lucrative cash crop farming or using education to forge careers as professionals or clerks. Other Africans dealt with change by enriching traditional ways. The imaginative Yoruba artist Olowe of Ise (oh-LO-way of ee-SAY) (ca. 1875–1938) emphasized Yoruba themes and ideals in the woodcarvings, elaborately carved doors, and other objects he sculpted for Yoruba kings. Some Africans negotiated change by mixing Western and African ideas, such as the Black Zion movement in South Africa, which maintained that Jesus was African, while also promoting African traditions such as faith healing.

Many Africans, however, chose noncooperation. Tax evasion and other forms of passive protest were rampant, especially in rural areas, while other Africans chose a more activist strategy and formed labor unions. Although unions were usually illegal in colonial systems that protected Western-owned businesses, strikes were common, especially among mine workers, who protested unsafe working conditions or long hours and were often imprisoned for their activism.

Sometimes distress and anger led to more drastic resistance as rebellions punctuated colonial rule. The Maji Maji Rebellion, for example, broke out in German-ruled Tanganyika in 1905 and was suppressed only after a bitter two-year struggle. The disenchanted Maji Maji peasants preferred to be subsistence farmers and grow their own food rather than be exploited commercial farm workers. These feelings led to a rebellion involving thousands. The rebels occupied some towns and sprinkled their bodies with magic water in hopes it would make them immune from bullets, but the Germans, using machine guns against rebels armed only with spears, soon regained the towns. Finally in 1907, the Maji Maji were defeated, at the cost of 26,000 African lives; however, the resistance caused the Germans to end forced labor.

Whether colonialism stimulated modern development or retarded it is one of the central questions of modern African history. Some historians contend that colonialism increased the productive capacity of the land, built cities and transportation networks, brought advances in technology, stimulated Africans to produce more wealth than they ever had before, and created rich opportunities for beneficial trade with the outside world. Other historians, however, point out that colonial rulers stole land, exploited labor, gained profitable access to raw materials, shifted profits back to Europe, limited Africa's eco-

nomic growth, and created artificial, unstable countries. Although economic growth occurred, colonial Africa enjoyed little development or balanced growth that benefited the majority of the people. The profits from plantations and mines supported European industrialization and enriched European businesses, leaving sub-Saharan Africa the most impoverished region of the world at the end of the colonial era.

LO⁴ Imperialism, Reform, and the Middle Eastern Societies

Between 1750 and 1914, most Muslim societies suffered repeated challenges from the growing power of western Europe and Russia, even the Ottoman Empire, which fell behind the industrializing West. Expanding European empires ate at the fringes of Persia and the shrinking Ottoman domain, and European economic penetration and cultural influences reshaped Middle Eastern life. The response of Muslims to these changes differed from society to society.

> 66 Perceiving Ottoman decline, the major European powers schemed to outflank each other while building up their influence in the weakening empire. 99

Challenges to the Ottoman Empire

For one thousand years, Islamic influence had spread throughout much of Afro-Eurasia. Muslims dominated the trade routes until the Early Modern Era, and large Islamic states stretched from Morocco to Indonesia. The Ottoman Turks forged a huge empire in southeastern Europe and western Asia, as well as gaining a strong influence across North Africa, while Safavid Persia and Mughal India also exercised regional power. But the rising influence of western Europeans posed a threat to the Islamic states. By 1750, as a result of both Western pressure and internal problems, the Ottoman power had diminished, the Safavids had fallen, the Mughals had lost most of India, and the Dutch ruled much of Indonesia. After 1750, the Islamic world faced new dangers.

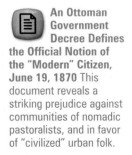 **An Ottoman Government Decree Defines the Official Notion of the "Modern" Citizen, June 19, 1870** This document reveals a striking prejudice against communities of nomadic pastoralists, and in favor of "civilized" urban folk.

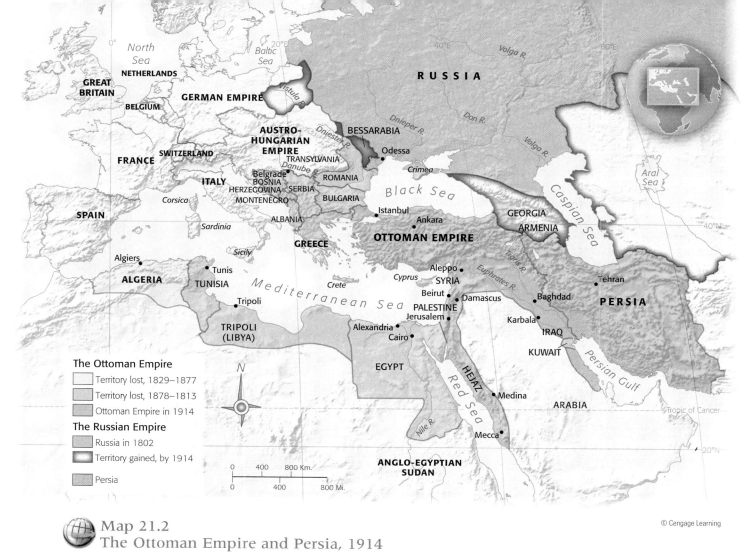

 Map 21.2
The Ottoman Empire and Persia, 1914

The Ottoman Empire once included much of southeastern Europe, western Asia, and North Africa. By 1914, it was restricted largely to parts of western Asia.

© Cengage Learning

In the nineteenth century, rising pressure from European nations, especially Russia, undermined the Ottoman Empire and its more than 60 million people (see Map 21.2). Since the 1500s, the Russians had been slowly expanding south toward the Black Sea, and in 1768 they defeated Ottoman forces and gained control over part of the northern Black Sea coast. Between 1792 and 1829, they extended this control to include the Crimean peninsula and the largely Christian Caucasus state of Georgia. In 1853, Czar Nicholas I characterized the weakening Ottoman Empire as "the sick man of Europe," a reputation that would stick.

Perceiving Ottoman decline, the major European powers schemed to outflank each other while building up their influence in the weakening empire. With European support, the Greeks, Serbs, Romanians, and Bulgarians rebelled and threw off Ottoman power in the 1800s. The Greek revolt, which enjoyed support from Britain, France, and Russia, revealed Ottoman weaknesses (see Chapter 19). A combined Ottoman-Egyptian force had nearly defeated the Greeks when an Anglo-French fleet and the Russian army intervened, shifting the military balance. The 1829 treaty that ended the war recognized Greek independence and gave autonomy to the Ottoman territories of Serbia and Moldavia.

Along with military setbacks, the Ottoman state also had more difficulty satisfying the desires of the empire's multiethnic population. The Turks had long benefited from the empire's ethnic diversity, using the varied peoples to enrich their state. Non-Muslim minorities played major roles in Ottoman commerce, the professions, and government. Moreover, the Ottomans had generally been tolerant of ethnic and religious minorities such as Kurds (mostly Sunni Muslims), Jews, and Arab Christians. To respect minority cultures and keep them from combining politically, the Ottomans allowed each group to basically rule itself through its own religious establishment, such as the Greek Orthodox Church. Christians and Jews felt particularly secure in the major Ottoman cities; Jews in much of the empire enjoyed more security and prosperity than they did in Europe. Multiethnic Istanbul was described in 1873 as "a city not of one nation but of many. Eight or nine languages are constantly spoken in the streets and five or six appear on the shop fronts."[9]

Armenian Nationalism

Despite the accommodation to ethnic diversity, some ethnic minorities became restless. Deteriorating Turkish relations with the Christian Armenians in eastern Turkey and the Caucasus led to a conflict between the two groups. Armenians had generally remained loyal Ottoman subjects, and some held high positions in the government. But during the 1800s, nationalist and socialist ideas percolating in Europe filtered into the Armenian communities and influenced some Armenians to want their own state. Acting on these nationalistic feelings, Armenians founded their own schools, libraries, hospitals, and presses and looked to Europe and North America for financial and moral support, while some extremists made terrorist attacks on Ottoman targets. The conflict intensified, with deadly consequences for the Armenians. In the 1890s and early 1900s, the Ottoman government responded to increasing Armenian assertiveness by seizing Armenian property, killing more than 100,000 Armenians, and exiling thousands more. Many Armenians moved to North America to escape the persecution, but those who remained continued to suffer.

Ottoman Reform and Modernization

Growing internal problems and military setbacks spurred Ottoman efforts to reform and modernize in order to match Western power. To survive, Ottoman sultans tried hard to build a modern, more secular, and more centralized government. However, various groups, including the Islamic religious leaders, the privileged military force known as Janissaries, local officials in Anatolia, and governors of distant Arab provinces benefited from weak central authority, so the process of centralization proved a challenge.

CHRONOLOGY

The Middle East, 1750–1914

1792–1812	Russian control of northern Black Sea lands
1794–1925	Qajar dynasty in Persia
1798–1799	French occupation of Egypt
1805–1848	Rule of Muhammad Ali in Egypt
1829	Greek independence from Ottoman Empire
1840	French colonization of Algeria
1859–1869	Building of Suez Canal
1882	British colonization of Egypt
1890s–1915	Turkish genocide against Armenians
1897	First Zionist conference
1899	British protectorate over Kuwait
1905–1911	Constitutional revolution in Persia
1907–1921	Russian and British spheres of influence in Persia
1908	Young Turk government in Ottoman Turkey
1908	Discovery of oil in Persia
1911–1912	Colonization of Libya and Morocco

Gradually, the system changed as Ottoman leaders and thinkers recognized the need to obtain knowledge and aid from the Christian West. One of the first reformist sultans, Mahmud II (MACH-mood) (r. 1808–1839), asserted central authority over local leaders. Mahmud slowly built a modern state and an army trained by Prussian officers. His successors set up new schools that taught European learning and languages, and by 1900 the University of Istanbul had become the Muslim world's first modern institution of higher education. The Ottomans also replaced many older Islam-based laws with laws based on French codes and increasingly marginalized Islam, demoralizing conservatives.

The growth of a more centralized government and a modern, secular Ottoman nationality continued through the 1800s, aided by the introduction of railroads and telegraphs. To foster a national identity, in 1846 Ottoman rulers declared all citizens equal before the law, announcing that "the differences of religion and sect among the subjects is something not affecting their rights of citizenship. It is wrong to make discriminations among us."[10] In the 1880s, a modernizing group known as the Young Turks emerged in the military and the universities. Their goal was to make Turkey a modern nation with a liberal constitution, and by 1908, when the Young Turks led a military coup that deposed the old sultan, Islam had faded as a political influence. The Young Turks espoused Turkish nationalism and sought to unite all Turkish peoples in western and central Asia, but under the facade of parliamentary government, they ruled as autocrats and military modernizers. During World War I, as an ally of Germany and Austria-Hungary, the Young Turks embraced a Turkish ethnic identity, secularization, and closer ties to the Western world at the expense of Islamic connections. After their defeat in World War I, the Ottoman Empire was dissolved and largely fell under British or French rule.

> "However, while Muhammad Ali's programs added to Egypt's power and wealth, they did not ultimately protect Egyptian independence and foster development."

Young Turks
A modernizing group in Ottoman Turkey that promoted a national identity and that gained power in the early twentieth century.

Egypt: Modernization and Occupation

The most extensive effort to deflect Western pressure through modernization came in Egypt, but only after Ottoman influence waned. The Ottomans, who occupied Egypt in 1517, had governed the province through the Mamluks, a Muslim caste of Turkish origin whose misrule gave French general Napoleon Bonaparte an excuse to invade the country by the later 1700s. While claiming to liberate the Egyptians, Bonaparte hoped to exploit Egypt's agriculture to provide grain for France. When Bonaparte abandoned his Egyptian adventure in 1801, Egypt came under the rule of Muhammad Ali (r. 1805–1848), a Turkish-speaking Albanian who had led the Ottoman forces that helped eject the French.

Muhammad Ali

After being appointed viceroy by the Ottoman sultan, Muhammad Ali moved to centralize his power in what was effectively now an independent country. However, European powers, who feared his ambitions, required him to officially remain loosely bound to the weakening Ottoman state. The charming sultan impressed Europeans with his talents: "If ever a man had an eye that denoted genius, [he] was the person. Never dead nor quiescent, it was fascinating like that of a gazelle; or, in the hour of storm, fierce as an eagle's."[11]

Muhammad Ali introduced ambitious reforms to transform Egypt into a European-style state with an effective army. He increased trade and moved to foster an industrial revolution by using government revenues from increased agricultural exports to establish factories, foundries, and shipyards. The Egyptian leader established a western-style military and arms industry. He also replaced Islamic with French legal codes, sent Egyptians to study technical subjects in Europe, encouraged the establishment of the first Arab newspapers, and laid the foundation for a Western-influenced state educational system. These changes have led historians to credit Muhammad Ali with founding Egypt as a modern nation-state.

However, while Muhammad Ali's programs added to Egypt's power and wealth, they did not ultimately protect Egyptian independence and foster development. Because Egypt had to import iron and coal, industrialization proved a challenge, and the Egyptian economy became more shackled to European finance. In 1838 the British obtained free trade within Ottoman domains. The resulting influx of cheap British commodities stifled Egypt's textile industry and its cottage handicraft manufacturing. Although the Egyptian cotton industry was stimulated in the 1860s by the American Civil War, which cut exports from the United States to Europe, Europeans were more interested in procuring Egyptian raw cotton for processing in their own mills than they were in buying finished textiles.

The British Seize Europe

Following the European model, Muhammad Ali turned then to seeking resources and markets through the conquest of neighboring societies. Egyptian armies moved south into Nubia and the

Muhammad Ali Meets European Representatives Muhammad Ali, the Egyptian sultan who tried to modernize his state, cultivated ties with Western nations. This painting shows the sultan in 1839 meeting with representatives from several European governments.

eastern Sudanic lands along the Nile River, which they made into an Egyptian colony, and also into the Ottoman territories of Arabia, Palestine, Syria, and Greece. But a northern thrust alarmed the European powers, inspiring them to destroy Egypt as a rival in the region and to gain control of the Suez Canal, which was built as a French–Egyptian collaboration between 1859 and 1869. The 100-mile-long canal—a magnificent technological achievement whose construction had cost the lives of thousands of Egyptian workers—linked the Mediterranean and Red Seas, greatly decreasing the shipping time between Europe and Asia. In 1875, Britain gained control of the canal when Muhammad Ali's grandson, the sultan Ismail, was forced by his country's skyrocketing national debt to sell Egypt's large share in canal ownership.

Eventually, to preempt the ambitions of other European powers, the British decided to seize Egypt using military force. By the 1870s, Egypt was bankrupt and deeply in debt to European financiers and governments. In addition, some in the country's political and commercial elite, including many Coptic Christians, were oriented toward Western ideas and welcomed the British. But most Egyptians, being chiefly influenced by conservative Islamic ideas and leaders, opposed the growing Western influence. In 1882, increasing local unrest and threats to European residents provided an excuse for the British to bombard Egypt's major port, Alexandria, and then invade the country. Thus, several decades after Muhammad Ali's death, Egypt became part of Britain's growing worldwide empire.

The Mahdi Uprising

Soon after gaining control of Egypt, the British had to deal with a challenge coming from the Sudanic region straddling the Nile River to Egypt's south (today the nation of Sudan). In 1881, a militant Arab Muslim in the Sudan, Muhammad Ahmad (1846–1885), the son of a shipbuilder, declared that he was the Mahdi (MAH-dee) ("the Guided One") and pledged to restore Islam's purity and destroy the Egyptian-imposed government, which he accused of corruption, lax morality, and subservience to European advisers. He recruited an army that defeated the Egyptian forces and their British officers, after which he formed an Islamic state. However, in 1898, British and Egyptian forces defeated the Mahdists and formed a new state known as the Anglo-Egyptian Sudan, which was effectively a British colony.

Persia: Challenges and Reforms

Persia, increasingly known as Iran, had long played a central role in the Islamic world, but in the 1700s, it faced new problems under the Qajars (KAH-jars), who took control after the Safavid collapse earlier in the century. The Qajars ruled an impoverished country that had suffered from years of civil war and anarchy, and early Qajar rulers were unable to resolve most of Persia's problems, instead becoming noted for greed, corruption, and lavish living. The majority of Persia's people, including the Qajar rulers, were Shi'ites, but the population also included Christian Armenians, Jews, Zoroastrians, and Sunni Kurds, all of whom sought to increase their autonomy. Shi'ite clerics, however, enjoyed great influence and wealth. Independent of any government, the top Shi'ite clerics engaged in power struggles with the Qajar shahs, arguing that a virtuous and learned Shi'ite scholar should rule Persia and that few Qajar rulers fit that description. Meanwhile, Shi'ites persecuted as heretical the Bahai (buh-HI) religion. Founded in 1867 by the Persian Bahaullah (bah-hah-oo-LAH) (1817–1892) as an offshoot of Persian Shi'ism, Bahai called for universal peace, the unity of all religions, and service to others. Shi'ites killed many Bahais and forced their leaders into exile.

Persia and the West Persia also faced continuous pressure from Russia and Britain. By the 1870s, Russia had gained territory on both sides of the Caspian Sea, and British power steadily grew in the Persian Gulf and along Arabia's Indian Ocean coast. British entrepreneurs controlled a monopoly on Persian railroad construction, banking, and oil. The Anglo-Iranian Oil Company (later British Petroleum), which struck oil in 1908, became Persia's dominant economic enterprise, but profits went chiefly to Britain. Persians disliked the powerful British economic role, which they considered a humiliation.

> **Bahai**
> An offshoot of Persian Shi'ism that was founded in 1867; Bahai preached universal peace, the unity of all religions, and service to others.

The weakness of the central government, combined with foreign pressure, led to political reforms. Some Qajar shahs provided an opening for change when they attempted to restore central government power. In the later 1800s, they rebuilt an army, set up a Western-style college, introduced a telegraph system, and gave Christian missionaries the right to establish schools and hospitals. However, these reforms threatened the conservative Shi'ite clergy, who hoped to thwart modernization.

> ❝ From 1905 to 1911, Persia enjoyed a constitutional revolution that fostered a brief period of democracy. ❞

From 1905 to 1911, Persia enjoyed a constitutional revolution that fostered a brief period of democracy. The more liberal Shi'ite clergy, allied with merchants in the capital, Tehran, Armenians, and Western-educated radicals, imposed a democratic constitution that sought to curb royal power by setting up a parliament elected by several major groups and granting freedom of the press. Soon more than four hundred newspapers were published. When a conservative, pro-Russian shah took power in 1907 and attempted to weaken the parliament, liberal newspapers, writers, and musicians lampooned him and his allies.

The progressive direction did not last, however. Britain and Russia formed an alliance and increased pressure on Persia to grant them more influence, straining the progressive leadership. As a result, the constitutionalist forces soon split into pro-Western nationalists seeking separation of religious and civil power, land reform, and universal education, and Shi'ite clerics and nobles who had become alarmed at the secular direction. As violence increased in 1911, the conservative royal government closed down the parliament and ended the democratic experiment. By then, however, Britain and Russia, stationing troops in southern and northern Persia, respectively, had reduced Persia's political and economic independence.

Ottoman Outposts

Declining Ottoman power and growing Western activity eventually had an impact on the Arab provinces of the eastern Ottoman Empire, especially Syria and Lebanon. Despite their diverse ethnic and religious mosaic, which included Arab and Armenian Christians, Sunni and Shi'ite Arabs, and Sunni Kurds, the peoples of these two adjacent territories had mostly lived in autonomous peace under Ottoman rule. A British writer commented on the generally stable conditions and social harmony in the late 1700s, writing that in Lebanon "every man lives in a perfect security of life and property. The peasant is not richer than in other countries, but he is free."[12]

Modernization in Lebanon, Syria, Iraq, and Kuwait

However, in the 1850s, poverty and a stagnant economy began to foster occasional conflicts in Syria and Lebanon, and as a result the densely populated region around Mount Lebanon came under the influence of several Western powers. For example, the French developed a special relationship with the Maronites (MAR-uh-nites), Arab Christians who sought a closer connection with the Roman Catholic Church, and American Protestant missionaries established a college in the main Lebanese city, Beirut, in 1866 that spread modern ideas. By the later 1800s, the weak economy had also encouraged emigration from Syria and Lebanon, especially Lebanese Christians, who often left as families for the United States. By 1914, perhaps 350,000 Arabs from Syria and Lebanon had emigrated to the Americas.

Change also came to Iraq, the heart of ancient Mesopotamia, which lacked political unity and had not prospered under Ottoman rule. The Ottomans divided Iraq into three provinces: (1) a largely Sunni Arab and Kurdish north, (2) a chiefly Sunni Arab center, and (3) a Shi'ite Arab–dominated south. Iraqis suffered from major floods and repeated epidemics of plague and cholera. A British official described Iraq as "a country of extremes, either dying of thirst or of being drowned."[13] Iraq also lacked order, foreign capital, and a transportation system such as railroads or steamships on the rivers, and the literacy rate remained extremely low.

Although the challenges were daunting, Western interest in this Ottoman backwater grew. European travelers were unanimous that Iraq had great economic potential: navigable rivers, fertile land, a strategic location, access to the Persian Gulf, and minerals. To gain a foothold in the region, in 1899 the British established a protectorate over the small neighboring kingdom of Kuwait (koo-WAIT) at the west end of the Persian Gulf. In the early 1900s, the Ottomans and foreign investors poured money into Iraq as they came to believe that it might have considerable oil; however, World War I temporarily halted such efforts.

The French in Northwest Africa

Northwest Africa also experienced European colonization. The Arabic-speaking societies along Africa's Mediterranean coast from Libya to Algeria had never been under firm Ottoman control, and their proximity to Europe made them natural targets for colonization. In 1840 the French embarked on full-scale colonization of Algeria, in part to divert the French public from an unpopular home government. Abd al-Qadir (AB dul-KA-deer), an energetic Algerian Muslim cleric, used Islamic appeals to unite Arab and Berber opposition to the French. His resourceful followers quickly learned how to make guns. The French captured Abd al-Qadir in 1847, but the fighting continued for years. Facing determined resistance, the French attempted to demoralize the Algerians by driving peasants off the best land and selling it to European settlers. To diffuse opposition, they also relocated and broke up tribes. Yet various anti-French revolts, often spurred by appeals to Islamic traditions, erupted until the 1880s. The ruthless French conquest and suppression of rebellions cost tens of thousands of French and hundreds of thousands of Algerian lives.

French policy reshaped Algerian society. The French intended, as an official wrote in 1862, to impose French culture, settlers, and economic priorities on the Arabs. General Bugeaud, the conqueror of Algeria, conceded in 1849 that "the Arabs with great insight understand very well the cruel revolution we have brought them; it is as radical for them as socialism would be for us."[14] Between the 1840s and 1914, more than 1 million immigrants from France, Italy, and Spain poured into Algeria, erecting a racist society similar to that of South Africa. The European settlers eventually elected representatives to the French parliament as Algeria was incorporated into the French state. The mainstay of the settler economy, vineyard cultivation and wine production, displaced food crops and pasture, an economic change that mocked Islamic values prohibiting alcoholic beverages.

Gradually, European power in Northwest Africa increased. In Morocco, a coastal country west of Algeria, Sultan Mawlay Hassan (r. 1873–1895) skillfully worked to preserve the country's independence by playing rival European powers off against each other. However, the French and Spanish, attracted by Morocco's strategic position, by 1912 had divided the country between them. Tunisia, just east of Algeria, had long enjoyed considerable autonomy under

Ottoman rule, and in 1881 France sent in troops to occupy Tunisia. Libya, a sparsely populated, mostly desert land between Tunisia and Egypt, was conquered by the Italians in 1911 and 1912, killing one-third of Libya's people. European colonialism now dominated the whole of North Africa.

> "The revivalists rejected what they considered the corruption of true Islam and embraced what they regarded as God's word in the Quran and the sayings of the Prophet Muhammad."

LO⁵ Middle Eastern Thought and Culture

West Asian and North African societies responded to the challenges facing them in three ways. One response was to form vibrant Islamic revivalist movements that promoted a purer version of Islamic practice rooted in early Muslim tradition. The second response involved reform movements that attempted to combine Islam with modernization and secularization. The early stirrings of Arab nationalism constituted a third response. While governments struggled, revivalist, reform, and nationalist movements pumped fresh vitality into Islamic culture but failed to offer an effective resistance to Western economic and military power.

Islamic Revivalism and the Rise of the Wahhabis

Political crises in the Middle East helped spark influential movements of Islamic revivalism, which sought to purify Islamic practices by reviving what their supporters considered to be a purer vision of Islamic society than the existing one. The revivalists rejected what they considered the corruption of true Islam and embraced what they regarded as God's word in the Quran and the sayings of the Prophet Muhammad. They also reaffirmed the ideal of the theocratic state of the early caliphs in Mecca, which blended religion and government. Muslim revivalists despised Sufism and what they viewed as other corrupting influences. Heeding this criticism, several Sufi brotherhoods

 Middle East Studies Internet Resources (*http://www.columbia .edu/cu/lweb/indiv/ mideast/cuvlm/index .html*). A useful collection of links on the Middle East.

eventually moved away from mystical beliefs toward an emphasis on the original teachings of the Prophet Muhammad.

While political leaders lost prestige and authority, religious leaders allied to merchant and tribal groups seized the initiative to spread revivalist thought. Carried by scholars, merchants, and missionaries, revivalist Islam spread from the Middle East to societies in every other part of the Islamic world, fostering debates over the role of Islam and how to meet the Western threat. Groups seeking to impose revivalist goals on others sometimes used violence, interpreting the early Muslim idea of jihad, or struggle for the faith, as a call to wage holy war against those Muslims who blended Islamic and local traditions. During the 1800s, revivalist movements stiffened resistance against French colonization in Algeria and West Africa, British colonization in Sudan, and Dutch colonization in Indonesia.

Wahhabism: An Islamic Puritan Movement

Revivalism had its greatest impact in Arabia, where it spurred a militant movement in the 1700s known as Wahhabism (wah-HAH-bi-zuhm). The movement's founder, Muhammad Abd al-Wahhab (al-wah-HAHB) (1703–1792), led a long campaign to purify Arabian Islam. Al-Wahhab had left his home in central Arabia to study Islamic theology in Medina and Iraq, where he adopted a strict interpretation of Islamic law. Returning home, he preached against those who were lax in their religious practice and promoted intolerance toward all alternative views, such as Sufism and Shi'ism. In 1744, his campaign gained a key ally, Muhammad Ibn Saud (sah-OOD), a tribal chief who helped al-Wahhab put together a fighting force to expand their influence.

Wahhabi power ebbed and flowed. During the later 1700s, the Wahhabis took over parts of Arabia and then advanced into Syria and Iraq, where they destroyed the Iraqi city of Karbala (KAHR-buh-luh), the major Shi'ite holy site, to demoralize Shi'ites. By 1805, the Wahhabis controlled Mecca and Medina, Islam's two holiest cities, where they horrified non-Wahhabi Muslims by massacring the residents and trying to destroy all sacred tombs in order to prevent saint worship. Their actions represented a major threat to conventional Islam. In response, Muhammad Ali, the governor of Egypt, used his European-style army

> "Some Muslim thinkers promoted modernization as a strategy for transforming Islamic society in response to the challenges of rising Western power and weakening Muslim governments."

and modern weapons to push the Wahhabis back from the holy cities. Despite these setbacks, Wahhabi ideas and zeal spread widely during the 1800s as Western power undermined Middle Eastern governments. Yet many Muslims condemned Wahhabi intolerance, extremism, and such practices as the forced veiling of women.

The History and Doctrines of Wahhabis

Read Abdullah Wahhab's response to critics about the beliefs of the Muwahhidin.

The Founding of Saudi Arabia

In 1902, the still-allied descendants of al-Wahhab and Ibn Saud launched a second great expansion. The head of the Saud family, Abdul Aziz Ibn Saud (1880–1953), sent Wahhabi clergy among the Bedouins to convince them to abandon their nomadic ways and join self-sufficient farming communities. The Wahhabi Bedouin communities adopted extreme asceticism and a literal interpretation of the Islamic legal code, the Shari'a. Wahhabi clergy beat men for arriving late for prayers, and Wahhabi men pledged to die fighting for their beliefs. In 1925, the Saud family established Saudi Arabia, a state based on the Shari'a, and discovery of oil in 1938 gave the Saud family and their Wahhabi allies the wealth to maintain their control.

Modernist Islamic Thought

Islamic revivalism as reflected in the rigid Wahhabi movement was only one of several strands of Islamic thought that emerged during the Modern Era. Some Muslim thinkers promoted modernization as a strategy for transforming Islamic society in response to

the challenges of rising Western power and weakening Muslim governments. While Wahhabis rejected modernity, modernist ideas grew stronger among Muslim intellectuals, who argued that Muslims should reject blind faith and reconcile Islam with fresh ideas, social change, and religious moderation.

Modernists detested many conservative Muslim traditions, including the restricted role of women. For example, Qasim Amin (KA-sim AH-mean), a French-educated Egyptian lawyer, argued in 1898 that the liberation of women was essential to the liberation of Egypt, that acquiring their "share of intellectual and moral development, happiness, and authority would prove to be the most significant development in Egyptian history." Women reformers such as Bahithat al-Badiya (buh-TEE-that al-buh-DEE-ya) echoed these sentiments (see Witness to the Past: Egyptian Women and Their Rights). Some radical reformers identified the veil as symbol of female oppression and urged its abolition.

Muslim modernists such as Muhammad Ali in Egypt believed that introducing change would be a straightforward process. They believed that by buying weapons and machines they could strengthen their armies and industries to deflect Western pressure, enrich their countries, and avoid domestic unrest. But their visionary ideas proved impractical and out of step with their largely conservative populations.

By the later 1800s, the challenges increased as Western technical and economic capabilities grew. Like European Enlightenment thinkers they often admired, some Muslim modernists struggled with how to reconcile faith and reason. They worried that the reforms needed to spur modernization required adopting Western philosophical and scientific theories, which were often contrary to Islamic beliefs about society, God, and nature. For example, capitalism undermined the Quranic prohibition against charging interest on loans, and the concept of human rights challenged slavery, which was still widespread in the nineteenth-century Muslim world. Belief in equality contradicted the low status of Muslim women, and the Western notions of popular sovereignty and the nation troubled those who believed that only God could make laws or establish standards, which the state must then administer. Some

Egyptian Women and Their Rights

One of the leading women writers and thinkers in early twentieth-century Egypt, Bahithat al-Badiya (buh-TEE-that al-buh-DEE-ya) (1886–1918), advocated greater economic and educational rights for women in a rapidly changing society. She wrote at a time when Egyptian nationalists were demanding independence from Britain and a modern state, and intellectuals were debating the merits of modernity as opposed to tradition. In 1909, in a lecture to an Egyptian women's club associated with a nationalist organization, Bahithat offered a program for improving women's lives. Struggling against male and Islamic opposition to women's rights, she sought a middle ground between Islamic conservatism and European secular liberalization.

Ladies, I greet you as a sister who feels what you feel, suffers what you suffer, and rejoices in what you rejoice. . . . Complaints about both men and women are rife. . . . This mutual blame which has deepened the antagonism between the sexes is something to be regretted and feared. God did not create man and women to hate each other but to love each other and to live together so the world would be populated. . . . Men say when we become educated we shall push them out of work and abandon the role for which God has created us. But isn't it rather men who have pushed women out of work? Before, women used to spin and to weave cloth for clothes, . . . but men invented machines for spinning and weaving. . . . In the past, women sewed clothes . . . but men invented the sewing machine. . . . Women . . . [made bread] with their own hands. Then men invented bakeries employing men. . . . I do not mean to denigrate these useful inventions which do a lot of our work. . . . Since male inventors and workers have taken away our work should we waste our time in idleness or seek other work to occupy us? Of course, we should do the latter. . . .

Men say to us categorically, "You women have been created for the house and we have been created to be breadwinners." Is this a God-given dictate? . . . No holy book has spelled it out. . . . Women in villages . . . help their men till the land and plant crops. Some women do the fertilizing, haul crops, lead animals, draw water for irrigation, and other chores. . . . Specialized work for each sex is a matter of convention, . . . not mandatory. . . . Women may not have to their credit great inventions but women have excelled in learning and the arts and politics. . . .

Nothing irritates me more than when men claim they do not wish us to work because they wish to spare us the burden. We do not want condescension, we want respect. . . .

If we had been raised from childhood to go unveiled and if our men were ready for it I would approve of unveiling those who want it. But the nation is not ready for it now. . . . The imprisonment in the home of the Egyptian woman of the past is detrimental while the current freedom of the European is excessive. I cannot find a better model [than] today's Turkish woman. She falls between the two extremes and does not violate what Islam prescribes. She is a good example of decorum and modesty. . . . We should get a sound education, not merely acquire the trappings of a foreign language and rudiments of music. Our education should also include home management, health care, and childcare. . . . We shall advance when we give up idleness.

Thinking About the Reading

1. How does Bahithat evaluate women's roles and gender relations in Egypt?
2. What does her moderate advice to Egyptian women suggest about Egyptian society and the power of patriarchy?

Source: Bahithat al-Badiya, "A Lecture in the Club of the Umma Party, 1909," trans. by Ali Badran and Margot Badran, in *Opening the Gate: A Century of Arab Feminist Writing*, ed. by Margot Badran and Miriam Cooke, (Bloomington: Indiana University Press, 1990), pp. 228–238. Copyright © 1990 by Indiana University Press. Reprinted with permission of Indiana University Press.

Cairo Opera House Hoping to demonstrate modernization, Egyptian leaders built an opera house in Cairo in the 1860s. One of the first pieces staged was an opera by Italian composer Giuseppe Verdi to celebrate the opening of the Suez Canal in 1869.

reformers doubted whether Islam, with its universalistic idea of a multiethnic community guided by God, was compatible with nationalism, which emphasized the unity of one group of people defined by a common state. The Moroccan historian Ahmad ibn Khalid al-Nasri feared that Western ideas tainted reforms. Writing of military cadets being trained in Western weapons and tactics, he worried that "they want to learn to fight to protect the faith, but they lose the faith in the process of learning how."[15] What role, the modernizers wondered, could clerics and the Shari'a have in a world of machines and nations?

Egypt-based thinkers took the lead in arguing the compatibility of Islam with modernization. The Persia-born activist and teacher Jamal al-Din al-Afghani (1838–1895), for example, preached innovative concepts of Islam. Al-Afghani favored reason and science; in his view, rigid interpretations of Islam combined with local traditions contributed to Arab backwardness. He lamented that, partly because of intolerance to new ideas, "the Arab world still remains

buried in profound darkness."[16] But al-Afghani also promoted resistance to Western power. His strong criticisms of British activity in Egypt and Persia, as well as of Arab leaders he viewed as puppets, led to his exile to Paris, where he published a weekly newspaper that promoted his views.

The Roots of Arab Nationalism

During the 1800s, a pan-Arab national consciousness developed in response to foreign domination by the Ottoman Turks and then by the British and French. But Arab identity was murky, divided by differences in religious and group affiliation. Arabs were predominantly Sunni Muslims, but some, particularly in the Persian Gulf and southern Iraq, were Shi'ites, and others, especially numerous in Egypt, Lebanon, and Syria, were Christians. They did not all have the same agenda or face the same problems. Even within the same society, Arabs were often divided into feuding patriarchal tribes that sometimes disliked rival tribes as much as they disliked Ottoman or European over-lords, while other Arabs remained loyal to Ottoman rule. Furthermore, in 1876, hoping to defuse ethnic nationalism, the Ottomans introduced a new constitution and gave the Arabs seats in the legislature based on their large population in the empire. Thus a pan-Arab or pan-Muslim movement remained unrealistic.

Yet, some thoughtful Arabs began to envision self-governing Arab nations free of Ottoman or Western domination. Arab nationalism emerged from a literary and cultural movement in Syria in the later 1800s. Some of the pioneering writers were Lebanese Christians, one of whom published a poem calling on Arabs to "arise and awake." The writings of modernist Muslim scholars were also influential, although they posed a conflict between a pan-Islamic approach and a stress on Arab identity and language. Arab nationalist groups formed all over the Ottoman Empire in response to Ottoman centralization, but before World War I, they had little public influence.

> ❝ Yet, some thoughtful Arabs began to envision self-governing Arab nations free of Ottoman or Western domination. ❞

The Zionist Quest

While Middle Eastern societies struggled to respond to the Western challenge, the Zionist movement (see Chapter 19) introduced another. In the Jewish ghettoes of eastern Europe, some thinkers began a quest for a homeland for their long-persecuted people, who had been living in a diaspora scattered around the world since being forced by the Romans to leave Palestine nearly two millennia earlier. Prayers in Jewish synagogues for worshiping "next year in Jerusalem," the ancient Hebrew capital in Palestine, had endured for centuries. While many European Jews rejected Zionism, identifying instead with the country where they lived; for others, Zionism functioned like nationalism, offering promises of a Jewish state. The first Zionist conference, held in Basel, Switzerland, in 1897, identified Palestine, then under Ottoman rule, as the potential Jewish homeland. For centuries, some Jews had visited or settled in Palestine, and perhaps 20,000 lived there in 1870, but the Ottomans refused to give Zionist leaders permission to organize a massive settlement of Jews, because many would likely come from the Ottomans' bitter enemy, Russia.

Soon militant Zionists began promoting Jewish migration to Palestine without Ottoman permission or the support of European governments. By 1914 some 85,000 Jews, most of them newcomers from Russia and Poland, lived in Palestine alongside some 700,000 Arabs. The immigrants established dozens of Jewish collective farms, each known as a kibbutz, whose members shared their wealth and promoted Hebrew as a common language. Immigrants also built the first largely Jewish city, Tel Aviv, purchasing land from absentee Arab and Turkish landowners. The Zionists had a flag, an anthem, an active Jewish press, and the support of international Zionist organizations, but because Jewish aims and institutions had no legal recognition in Palestine, the stage was set for future conflict with Palestinian Arabs, who resented the newcomers and their plans for a Jewish state.

kibbutz
A Jewish collective farm in twentieth-century Palestine that stressed the sharing of wealth.

 Listen to a synopsis of Chapter 21.

CHAPTER 22

South Asia, Southeast Asia, and Colonization, 1750–1914

Learning Outcomes

After reading this chapter, you should be able to answer the following questions:

LO¹ How and why did Britain extend its control throughout India?

LO² How did colonialism transform the Indian economy and foster new ideas in India?

LO³ How did the Western nations expand their control of Southeast Asia?

LO⁴ What were the major political, economic, and social consequences of colonialism in Southeast Asia?

> 66Rice fields are littered with our battle-killed; blood flows or lies in pools, stains hills and streams. [French] Troops bluster on and grab our land, our towns, roaring and stirring dust to dim the skies. A scholar with no talent and no power, could I redress a world turned upside down?99

—**Protest by Vietnamese poet Nguyen Dinh Chieu against French conquest, late nineteenth century[1]**

In 1858 the French, seeking to expand their empire in Asia, attacked Vietnam with military force, and over the next three decades, they conquered the country against determined resistance. A blind Vietnamese poet, Nguyen Dinh Chieu (NEW-yin dinh chew) (1822–1888), became a symbol of the Vietnamese resistance to the French when he wrote an oration honoring the fallen Vietnamese soldiers after a heroic defense in a battle in 1862: "You preferred to die fighting the enemy, and return to our ancestors in glory rather than survive in submission to the [Westerners]." The French retaliated by seizing Chieu's land and property. The poet remained unbowed, and in verse spread throughout the land, Chieu rallied opposition. He heaped scorn on his countrymen who collaborated with the French occupiers and advised them to maintain the struggle for independence: "Everyone will rejoice in seeing the West wind [colonialism],Vanish from [Vietnam's] mountains and rivers."[2] Chieu overcame the handicaps of blindness to become a physician, scholar, teacher, and renowned writer and bard, famous for his epic poems sung in the streets. Earning the admiration of his countrymen for his loyalty to family, king, and country, Chieu rejected the French offer of a financial subsidy and the return of his family land if he would rally to their cause.

By providing deadly new weapons and increasing the need for resources and markets, the Industrial Revolution in Europe and North America (see Chapters 19–20) set in motion an intensive Western penetration of other regions, including India and Southeast Asia. With enhanced military, economic, and technological power to assert their will, between 1750 and 1914, a few Western nations brought nearly all

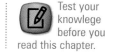

Test your knowlege before you read this chapter.

What do you think?

Europeans typically believed that Western colonialism improved inferior Asian and African societies.

Strongly Disagree						Strongly Agree
1	*2*	*3*	*4*	*5*	*6*	*7*

<<**Dipenegara** This painting shows Prince Dipenegara, a Javanese aristocrat who led a revolt against the Dutch colonizers in the 1820s, reading, with several attendants at hand.

of southern and eastern Asia under direct colonial or indirect neocolonial control. Western domination destroyed traditional Asian political systems, reoriented Asian economies, transmitted the ideas and technologies of Western life, and posed challenges for societies and their world-views. In turn, Asian workers produced resources that spurred Western economic growth.

Asians struggled with some success to reshape their relationship with the West. The unyielding resistance to imperialism exemplified by Nguyen Dinh Chieu gave hope to colonized people in Africa and the Middle East. While European power was too great to be overthrown in this period, eventually the Indians, Vietnamese, and Filipinos, among others, used the Western concept of nationalism to assert the rights of their peoples for self-determination.

LO¹ Forming British India

By the early 1700s, the Muslim Mughals who ruled much of India (see Chapter 18) were in steep decline, challenged by both Indians and Europeans. In the sixteenth and seventeenth centuries, the splendor of the Mughal court and India's valuable exports had attracted the Portuguese, Dutch, and British. As the Mughals lost power by the 1800s, the British took advantage of a fragmented India, controlling both India and the island of Sri Lanka. British conquest was in keeping with the history of South Asia, which had often been conquered by outsiders from Western and Central Asia. But unlike the Asian invaders, who often became assimilated into Indian society by adopting Hinduism or Buddhism or spreading Islam, the British maintained their own separate identity and cultural traditions.

Indian Trade, the West, and Mughal Decline

Europeans had long coveted South Asia for its spices and textiles, which had been a part of regional commerce for millennia. The Portuguese were the first

Europeans to trade directly with India. In 1498, they established a base at Goa (GO-uh), and for a century they sought to control the trade from India and Southeast Asia to the West. Soon Dutch traders arrived, eventually destroying Portuguese power in South and Southeast Asia (although Goa remained a Portuguese colony until 1961). The Dutch concentrated on Sri Lanka and, farther east, Indonesia. The British also took action, and by 1696, the British East

CHRONOLOGY

South Asia, 1750–1914

1744–1761	Anglo-French struggle for Coromandel coast
1757	Battle of Plassey
1764	British acquisition of Bengal
1774–1778	Warren Hastings governor of Bengal
1793	New land policy in Bengal
1799	British defeat of Mysore
1802	British colonization of Sri Lanka
1816	British protectorate over Nepal
1819	British occupation of all Maratha lands
1820s	Beginning of British Westernization policy
1839–1842	First Anglo-Afghan War
1849	British defeat of Sikhs in Punjab
1850	Completion of British India
1857–1858	Indian rebellion
1858	Introduction of colonial system in India
1877	Founding of Muslim college at Aligarh
1878–1880	Second Anglo-Afghan War
1885	Formation of Indian National Congress
1903	British invasion of Tibet
1906	Formation of Indian Muslim League

India Company possessed three fortified trading stations in India: at the towns of Calcutta in Bengal, Madras (today known as Chennai) on the southeastern coast, and Bombay (today called Mumbai) on the west coast. Meanwhile, the French formed a small colony in Pondicherry, a town near the British base at Madras.

Europeans encountered a fragmenting India. By 1750, the Mughals were corrupt and weak, because many Indians had already broken away from Mughal control. During the later 1700s, Mughal factions quarreled and different rivals claimed the throne, but the Mughal government controlled little beyond Delhi, and the countryside became increasingly disorderly. Without a powerful imperial state to control it, Indian society—with its diverse cultures, castes, languages, regions, and religions—lacked strong national cohesion and was unable to effectively resist European encroachments.

With the Mughals losing their grip, groups like the Marathas (muh-RAH-tuhs) and the Sikhs built powerful new states. The Marathas were a loosely knit confederacy led by Hindu warriors from west-central India, and the Sikhs were a religious minority in northwest India; both of these groups competed with new Muslim states that were often set up by Mughal governors whose allegiance to the Mughal emperor was nominal. By 1800 the Marathas ruled much of western India, and the Sikhs, under their leader, the dynamic Ranjit Singh (RUN-ji SING) (1780–1839), had conquered the Punjab and Kashmir in the northwest. In southern India, the Mughal collapse left a power vacuum that both Britain and France attempted to fill by supporting their respective Indian allies in the struggle for regional advantage. Ultimately, however, none of the rising Indian states, including the Marathas and Sikhs, gained enough power, acquired enough weapons, or forged enough cooperation to repulse the West.

The Founding and Expansion of British India

The British posed the gravest challenge to India, especially in Bengal, India's richest and most popu-

> "Ultimately, however, none of the rising Indian states, including the Marathas and Sikhs, gained enough power, acquired enough weapons, or forged enough cooperation to repulse the West."

lous region. Bengal was ruled by Muslim governors who mostly ignored the Mughal government in Delhi. When local Indian governments resisted an expansion of the British presence into their lands, the British resorted to military force.

Siraja Dowlah

In the mid-1700s, the Bengali ruler, Siraja Dowlah (see-RAH-ja DOW-luh) (ca. 1732–1757), considered the British bothersome leeches on his land's riches. Soon after becoming ruler, Dowlah alienated Western merchants and even his own more cautious officials, and in 1757 he rashly attacked British trading stations. After capturing the main station, Calcutta, Dowlah's forces placed 146 captured British men, women, and children in a crowded jail known as the Black Hole of Calcutta. The next day only 23 of them staggered out, the rest having died from suffocation and dehydration.

Robert Clive

Their rage and determination now fired, the British dispatched a force under Robert Clive (1725–1774) to regain Britain's holdings. A former clerk turned into a daring war strategist, the ambitious Clive and his 3,200 soldiers defeated some 50,000 Bengali troops at the Battle of Plassey in 1757 and recaptured Calcutta, marking the dawn of the British epic in India. Clive allied with Hindu bankers and Muslim nobles who were unhappy with Siraja Dowlah, who was executed, and by 1764, Clive controlled Bengal.

The British government, following a policy of mercantilism to acquire wealth for the state, allowed the British East India Company to govern Bengal and other parts of India, as they were acquired, and to exploit the inhabitants while sharing the profits with the British government. The British showed a lust for riches equal to that of the Spanish conquistadors in the 1500s. As governor of Bengal (1758–1760,

Black Hole of Calcutta A crowded jail in India where more than one hundred British prisoners of a hostile Bengali ruler died from suffocation and dehydration in 1757. This event precipitated the beginning of British use of force in India.

sepoys
Mercenary soldiers recruited among the warrior and peasant castes by the British in India.

1764–1767) for the Company, Clive launched an era of organized plunder, allowing British merchants and officials gradually to drain Bengal of its wealth while Company officials, including Clive, lived like kings in Calcutta. After 1760, the cry of "Go East," inspired by Clive's rags-to-riches story, fueled British imperialist ambitions. As they expanded their control of more Indian territory, the British became a new high caste, and, much like the former Mughal rulers, expected the Indians to serve them. Eventually the British Parliament accused Clive of corruption and fraud. Although cleared of the charges, a depressed Clive committed suicide at the age of forty-nine.

Warren Hastings

To transform the economic chaos left by Clive into a more profitable order and to consolidate the British position, the Company appointed Warren Hastings to serve as governor-general (1774–1778) of Bengal. Hastings redesigned the revenue system, made treaty alliances, and also pursued outright annexations to safeguard the British bases. A scholarly man who was influenced by Enlightenment thought, Hastings saw his task as a holding operation of limited ambitions, arguing against full colonization. In contrast to other British officials, Hastings respected the people he governed, advising one of his successors that, like the English, many Indians had a strong intellect, a sound integrity, and honorable feelings and should enjoy the same equal rights as the English colonizers. His successors, however, often disregarded his advice.

Success in Bengal fueled further British expansion in the subcontinent. In 1773, the British government gave the Company authority to administer all British-controlled Indian territories. Nonetheless, the Company still saw its role as mainly commercial. In 1794, the British Parliament forbade further annexation and declared territorial expansion to be repugnant to the honor and the policy of the nation. But despite the ban, governor-generals after Hastings continued to authorize the occupation of more areas of India, often against opposition, to prevent trade

disruption or to counteract rival European nations. Some imperialists talked about Britain's sacred trust to reshape the world, viewing the extension of British authority—and with it British culture, Christianity, and free-trade policies—as a great blessing for Asians.

Administering the British *Raj*

The reality, however, was often something other than a blessing. In acquiring more Indian territory, the British mixed military force, extortion, bribery, and manipulation. Because India was so diverse, British agents and merchants could play off one region against another, Hindu against Muslim, and were aided by Indian collaborators, especially ambitious businessmen. From India's warrior and peasant castes—

Virtual Library: South Asia (*http://www.columbia.edu/cu/libraries/indiv/area/sarai/*). A major site on India.

mostly Hindus but also some Muslims—the British recruited mercenary soldiers, known as sepoys, under the command of British officers. By 1857, there were nearly 200,000 sepoy troops in the Company military force, greatly outnumbering the 10,000 British officers and soldiers.

During the late 1700s and early 1800s, the British imposed their control over much of western, central, and northern India. They defeated the French on India's southeastern Coromandel coast after a series of imperial conflicts from 1744 to 1761. The Maratha confederacy, which controlled much of western and central India, was divided by rivalries. In 1805, the British occupied the Marathas' northern territories and entered Delhi, and took the remaining Maratha lands in 1819. They then turned their attention to the states of northwest India, where the Rajputs (RAHJ-putz), a Hindu warrior caste, were no longer the feared fighters they had been in earlier centuries and now signed treaties giving Britain claims on their lands. Only the Sikhs remained a threat to the British, but the death of the Sikh leader, Ranjit Singh, in 1839 shattered the Sikhs' unity and undermined their powerful military state. In 1849, after a series of bloody British-Sikh wars, Britain finally triumphed, stationing troops in the many small independent principalities scattered around India. By 1850, the British ruled all Indians

> **❝** The British showed a lust for riches equal to that of the Spanish conquistadors in the 1500s. **❞**

Clive Meets Indian Leaders In this painting, Robert Clive meets the new Bengali official, Mir Jafir, after the British victory in the 1757 Battle of Plassey. Clive supported Mir Jafir's seizure of power from the anti-British leader, Siraja Dowlah.

 Interactive Map

directly or through princes who collaborated with them (see Map 22.1).

South Asia Under the East India Tea Company

British expansion in India eventually led to interventions in neighboring societies, including Sri Lanka, the large, fertile island just south of India that the British called Ceylon. Fearing that the French might establish a base there, the British acquired the territory from the Dutch, controlling the entire island by 1815. The British transformed Sri Lanka, seizing rice-growing land from peasants to set up coffee, tea, and rubber plantations and recruiting Tamil-speaking workers from southeast India as laborers. By 1911, the Tamil laborers and their families made up 11 percent of the Sri Lankan population. Largely isolated on plantations, the Tamils maintained their own customs and Hindu religion and had little contact with Sri Lanka's majority population, the Buddhist Sinhalese. By the end of the 1800s, some educated Sinhalese, having turned to nationalism, considered both the British and the Tamils unwanted aliens. Sinhalese–Tamil tensions simmered for generations.

Map 22.1
The Growth of British India, 1750–1860
Gradually expanding control from their bases at Calcutta, Madras, and Bombay, the British completed their military conquest of the final holdout states by the 1850s.

Fearing that the Russians, who were conquering Muslim Central Asia, intended to expand into South Asia by land, the British also attempted to secure India's land borders. First they turned to Nepal, a kingdom just north of India in the Himalayan Mountains. Nepal's Hindu ruling caste, the Gurkhas (GORE-kuhz), were fierce fighters who

had sometimes invaded north India. British victory over the Gurkhas in 1814–1816 turned Nepal's monarchy into a British protectorate. Soldiers recruited from Nepal, also known as gurkhas, became a special military force for Britain and were employed on battlefields around the world in support of British objectives.

The Afghan Wars

Afghanistan, a mountainous region just west of India, seemed the most vulnerable to Russian expansion. An ethnically diverse region that had enjoyed only short periods of political unity, Afghanistan seemed an unlikely candidate to become a viable independent state. However, Afghans, among them the devoutly Islamic Pashtun tribes in the south, possessed the fighting skills to oppose Europeans who were bent on conquest. In the first Afghan War (1839–1842), Pashtuns massacred most of the 12,000 retreating British and Sepoy troops and the British civilians, including women and children. Undeterred, the British fought the second Afghan War (1878–1880) and replaced a Pashtun leader who favored the Russians with one who gave Britain control of Afghanistan's foreign affairs. With an ally as ruler, the British concluded that Afghanistan could not be annexed by military force.

The Westernization of India

The British East India Company gradually tightened its control of India and began to impose Western values on Indians. After Hastings, the Company shifted from sharing government with local rulers to becoming the sole power and administering India through British officials. In typically arrogant colonial language that ignored centuries of Indian achievements, Sir Thomas Munro, governor of Madras from 1820 to 1827, claimed that the British must maintain their rule until the Indians abandoned their "superstitions" and became "enlightened" enough to govern themselves. Reflecting these views, the Company promoted a policy of Westernization, a deliberate attempt to impose Western culture and ideas.

Westernization began in the 1820s and was strongly influenced by Christian evangelism. British officials, often disregarding Indian religious and cultural sensitivities, encouraged Christian missions and tried to ban customs they disliked. Many Indians rejoiced when they banned *sati*, the northern custom of widows throwing themselves on their husband's funeral pyre. But there was less Indian enthusiasm for British attempts to tinker with Muslim and Hindu law codes that were rooted in religious beliefs. The British also established schools that taught in English rather than an Indian language. This policy was spurred by Lord Macaulay (1800–1859), a reformer and firm believer in Western cultural superiority who considered it pointless to teach Indian languages, declaring in 1832 that "a single shelf of a good European library is worth the whole native literature of India and Arabia."[3] Some Indians considered English education a threat to both Hindu and Muslim customs, while others welcomed the English-medium schools because they opened Indian students to a wider world. The first English institution of higher education, the Hindu College in Calcutta, was founded by Indians in 1818.

Orientalism and William Jones

Not all the British in India found Indian culture to be backward. Some British admirers of Indian culture, reflecting what came to be called Orientalism, showed a scholarly interest in India and its history. Warren Hastings, for example, encouraged the study of Indian culture, languages, and literature, learning Greek, Latin, Persian, and Urdu himself. One of his officials, William Jones (1746–1794), who mastered Arabic, Persian, and Sanskrit, became the most influential Orientalist scholar, but his views often reflected

British East India Company Court This painted wood model shows an Indian court presided over by an official of the British East India Company.

an attempt to fit India into Western concepts of history and religion. Jones's ideas shaped European scholarly understanding of Indian history for generations, yet by the later 1800s, Orientalist cosmopolitanism and respect had largely been replaced by British nationalism and intolerance.

Ram Mohan Roy

The encounter between India and the West, as well as the British reforms, also fostered a Hindu social reform movement and philosophical renaissance under the brilliant leadership of the Bengali scholar Ram Mohan Roy (1772–1833). After seeing his sister burn to death on a funeral pyre, and concerned about what he saw as the harmful side of customs such as *sati* and caste divisions, Roy began a British-Indian dialogue in hopes of adopting certain Western ways to reform and strengthen Hinduism. To better understand the world by studying non-Hindu religions, Roy mastered their source languages—Hebrew and Greek for Christianity, Arabic and Persian for Islam—and thus became the world's first modern scholar of comparative religion. He founded secondary schools, newspapers, and an organization working for reform of Hindu society and beliefs. Viewing the British positively as promoters of knowledge and liberty, Roy wanted Britain to promote modernization while also seeking Indian advice.

Transforming the Indian Infrastructure

In order to make India more profitable, the British East India Company built roads, railroads, and irrigation systems; most significantly for rural Indians, they revised the land revenue collection, the principal source of public finance. The British viewed Indian rural society as stagnant, unable to provide the tax revenues needed to support British administration. Despite high taxes, bandits, and sometimes warfare, in precolonial times Indian villages generally provided economic security by promoting cooperation among their residents. Land belonged to the royal families, but peasants had the hereditary right to use it. British observers recognized the village system as self-sufficient and stable over time, but they destroyed it anyway when the Company began collecting taxes from farmers in money rather than, as had been common for centuries, a portion of the crop. Under this system, peasant farmers became tenants to landlords and were denied their hereditary rights to use the land. Many landlords sold their land rights at a good profit to businessmen, often city dwellers, who became absentee landlords and grew rich from the crops grown by the peasants. The Company also encouraged a switch from food crops to cash crops such as opium, coffee, rubber, tea, and cotton, often grown on plantations rather than peasant farms. The emphasis on money sacrificed a large measure of the stability and security peasants had once enjoyed.

Resistance: The 1857 Revolt

Despite Indian reform movements such as Roy's, Indians, especially once-prosperous families and peasants alike who lost wealth and stability, usually resented the British East India Company's Westernization and its associated economic policies. Furthermore, Sepoys increasingly resented the aggressive attempts of British officers to convert them to Christianity. Uprisings were recurrent, and in 1857 one revolt, sparked by Sepoy outrage, spread rapidly and offered a serious challenge to British authority.

Indian Railroad Train The railroads built during British rule carried both resources and passengers. This lithograph shows a Sikh signalman at the station and a train conveying Indian women and a European.

Sepoys stationed in Bengal became offended by new army rifle cartridges, which had to be bitten off with the teeth before being rammed down the gun barrel and were rumored to be greased with beef and pork fat, violating the religious dietary prohibitions of both cow-revering Hindus and pork-avoiding Muslims. The revolt, later called the first War of Independence by Indian Nationalists, began among the sepoys in the army and was soon supported by peasant and Muslim uprisings, along with a few members of Hindu and Muslim princely families. The revolt was confined largely to north and northeast India. Because no rebel leaders envisioned a unified Indian nation, British observers argued that the rebels had limited and selfish goals. But Muslims and Hindus alike felt that their customs and religions were being threatened, and they called for a joint defense of their religions against their common British enemy.

The rebels captured Delhi and besieged several cities, but they could not hold them for long. The desperate struggle involved ruthless tactics; both sides committed massacres. For example, rebels murdered one thousand British residents when they occupied the city of Kanpur. On the other side, when British troops recaptured Delhi, they became berserk and engaged in widespread raping, pillaging, and killing. The Muslim poet Ghalib mourned: "Here is a vast ocean of blood before me. Thousands of my friends are dead. Perhaps none is left even to shed tears upon my death."4 Anti-British sentiment was not widespread enough, however, to overcome the rebels' problems: inadequate arms, weak communications, and lack of a unified national strategy. When the British captured the last rebel fort, held by the Rani of Jhansi, in 1858, she was killed and the rebellion collapsed, although a few small rebel groups fought skirmishes with the British until 1860.

LO² The Reshaping of Indian Society

The 1857 revolt prompted the British to replace the British East India Company government with direct

> "The British divide-and-rule policy helped maintain British power but also exacerbated hatreds that remain today."

> ❝ India became the brightest 'jewel in the imperial crown,' a source of fabulous wealth. ❞

colonial rule. To address the symptoms of deep discontent, the 1858 Government of India Act transferred sovereignty to the British monarch. In 1876, Queen Victoria was proclaimed Empress of India, head of the government known as the British *Raj*, named for the ancient title of Hindu kings. India became the brightest "jewel in the imperial crown," a source of fabulous wealth. The policies pursued by the British Raj reshaped Indian society, sparking new economic, intellectual, and social patterns, and eventually inspiring a new sense of the Indian nation.

Colonial Government and Education

The British *Raj* bore many similarities to the Mughal system it had replaced. The top British officials, the viceroys, lived in splendor in Delhi. They made efforts to win Indian support by pomp and circumstance, including Mughal-style ceremonies and building a new capital at New Delhi, next to the old Mughal capital of Delhi, with gigantic architecture dwarfing even the monuments of the Mughals. After 1857, British officials mistrusted Indians but, like the Mughals before them, strategically preserved the Indian princes' privileges and palaces in exchange for promoting acceptance of British policies.

Borrowing Mughal practices, the British ruled through a mix of good communications, exploitation of Hindu-Muslim rivalries, and military force. The British connected India with a network of roads, bridges, and railways, and by 1900 India had more than 25,000 miles of track, the fourth largest rail system in the world. The British also deliberately pitted the Hindu majority against the Muslim minority by favoring one or the other group in law, language, and custom. For example, Hindus protested that the main Muslim language, Urdu, was used in many North Indian courts and that Muslim butchers were allowed to kill cows, considered sacred animals by Hindus. The British divide-and-rule policy helped maintain British power but also exacerbated hatreds that remain today. Local revenue supported a huge army of 200,000 men who were needed to keep the peace in India and fight British battles abroad.

In their efforts to rule, the British also introduced policies of discrimination against Indians and defensive frontier security. The British typically believed that Western colonialism improved inferior Asian and African societies. Indians were excluded from European-only clubs and parks as well as high positions in the bureaucracy, and enjoyed no real power or influence. Colonial Britain also concerned itself with border security and Russian ambitions, invading Tibet in 1903 and compelling Tibetan leaders to agree not to concede territory to Russia or any other foreign power. Lord Curzon (viceroy from 1899 to 1905) remarked that "we do not want their country . . . but it is important that no one else should seize it, and that it should be turned into a sort of buffer state between the Russian and Indian Empires."[5]

The *Raj* also continued the Westernization policy of the British East India Company, promoting British and often Christian values through an expanded English-medium education system. Thanks to these schools, English became the common language for educated Indians. However, only a privileged minority could afford to send their children to the English schools. By 1911, only 11 percent of men and 1 percent of women were literate in any language. Nonetheless, the schools fostered change by introducing new ideas like Christianity, consumerism, and Western philosophy. These Indians sent their sons and a few daughters to British universities, where notions like "freedom" and "self-determination of peoples" stood in sharp contrast to conditions in India. Returning students asked why the British did not practice such ideas in their colony. The growing British-educated professional class organized social, professional, and political bodies concerned with improving Indian life and acquiring more influence in government.

Economic Transformation

The British also transformed the Indian economy. Before 1700, Mughal India had been an economic powerhouse and manufacturing center, and the world leader in producing cotton textiles. India still produced one-quarter of all manufactured goods in 1750. The disparity between urban and rural wealth

> "By turning once self-sufficient peasants into tenants, the British planted the roots of one of contemporary India's greatest dilemmas, inequitable land distribution."

was narrower than in most societies. However, two centuries later, conditions had changed, as British policies, which were designed to drain India of its wealth to benefit Britain, harmed the Indian economy.

The Impact of the British System

The land tax system first introduced by the British East India Company in parts of India exploited the peasantry. By turning once self-sufficient peasants into tenants, the British planted the roots of one of contemporary India's greatest dilemmas, inequitable land distribution. As peasants lost their land rights and came to depend on the whims of landlords, they often fell hopelessly into debt. Furthermore, required now to pay taxes in cash, peasants had to grow cash crops such as cotton, jute, pepper, or opium rather than food. As a result, famine became more common, killing millions as food supplies and distribution became more uncertain.

Other changes also affected rural life. The introduction of steamships freed shipping routes and schedules from the vagaries of monsoon winds, and the opening of the Suez Canal in 1869 made it easier and much faster to ship raw materials from India to Europe, increasing the demand for these resources. The return ships brought to India cheap machine goods, which undermined the role of village craftsmen such as weavers and tinkers. As imported goods displaced artisans and farmers shifted to cash crops, the village economy came to be based on cash transactions. The quest for revenues and the priorities of commerce also ravaged the physical environment.

British trade policies also caused the decline of Indian manufacturing. The British discouraged Indian manufacturing by taxing Indian-made goods passing between Indian states and by prohibiting the import of industrial machinery. Meanwhile, British products flooded the country, destroying the livelihood of many skilled craftsmen, who were left with little choice but to become farm laborers. Yet industrial activity did not disappear from India between 1815 and 1914, and, despite many barriers, a few Indians found ways to prosper. British entrepreneurs established the world's largest jute-manufacturing industry, while Indians continued to compete with British imports by manufacturing cotton textiles and initiating a modern iron and steel sector. Unable to get British funding, some entrepreneurs raised money among Indian investors, and then used their wealth to promote scientific education.

Resistance to British Economics

By the late 1800s, the limits on India's industries became a subject of heated controversy. Indian critics alleged that tariffs protected British industries while strangling Indian industries that might have competed with them. While the British claimed that their rule improved India, the gap between British and Indian wealth grew: by 1895, the per capita income in Britain was fourteen to fifteen times higher than India's. Indian scholars attacked what one called "The Drain" of wealth and argued that British policies gave India "peace but not prosperity; the manufacturers lost their industries; the cultivators were ground down by a heavy and variable taxation; the revenues were to a large extent diverted to England."[6] Defenders of British policies replied that British rule brought investment, imported goods, railroads, and law and order. But critics questioned whether these innovations benefited most Indians or rather resulted in more systematic exploitation by increasingly prosperous British merchants and industrialists.

Population Growth and Indian Emigration

The plight of the Indian peasant was worsened by population growth. Despite the deadly famines, under British rule the Indian population rose from perhaps 100 million in 1700 to 300 million by 1920. The British imposed peace and improved sanitation and health. A similar population increase occurred in Europe at the same time, but growing numbers of Europeans could be absorbed by industrialization or emigration to the Americas and Australia. Unlike Europe, India enjoyed neither an industrial revolution nor an increase in farm productivity. Indian landlords had a stake in the cash crop system and wanted no innovations that might threaten their dominance.

As a result, the number of people far outstripped the amount of available food and land, creating dire poverty and widespread hunger.

As these problems mounted, millions of desperately poor Indians were recruited to emigrate to other lands. Plantations throughout the colonized world wanted Indian labor. Many Indians saw no alternative to leaving, but travel was hazardous. Most Indian emigrants were destined for plantations growing cash crops such as sugar, tea, or rubber and were indentured, meaning they had signed contracts that obligated them to work for a period of years (usually three to five) in order to repay their passage. Between 1880 and 1930, around a quarter million people per year, both men and women, left India. Few returned. The mortality rates for the indentured workers were so high and the indenture terms so unfavorable that critics considered the system another form of slavery.

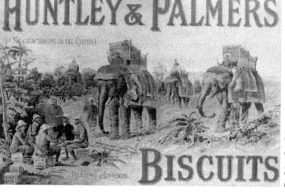

The resulting diaspora made Indians one of the most recognizable global societies. Cities such as Nairobi in Kenya, Rangoon in Burma, and Port of Spain in Trinidad had large Indian neighborhoods. Indians now had key economic roles in many countries. Indian trade networks, usually based on family or caste ties, reached around the Indian Ocean and Pacific Rim. The future leader of the Indian nationalist movement, Mohandas Gandhi (GAHN-dee), then a young law school graduate, experimented with his ideas of nonviolent resistance to illegitimate power while working among Indians in South Africa. Today people of Indian ancestry make up half or more of the populations of Mauritius, Trinidad, Guyana, Suriname, and Fiji and are substantial minorities in Sri Lanka, Malaysia, Singapore, Burma, Kenya, and South Africa.

Indian Thought and Society

In the later 1800s, Indian intellectuals responded to British rule and ideas in several ways. A small group of well-educated Indians wanted to combine the best of East and West. They sought reforms of customs, such as the ban on widow remarriage, that they saw as corruptions of Hinduism, but their influence waned after 1900. Another group, including the nationalist poet Rabindranath Tagore (RAH-bin-drah-NATH ta-GORE) (1861–1941), called attention to the glories of the Hindu past and argued that

Witness to the Past

Challenging British Imperialism with Spiritual Virtues

On the last day of the nineteenth century, Rabindranath Tagore wrote a poem in Bengali protesting the brutal imperialism of the war Britain was waging against the Boers in South Africa, driven, Tagore believed, by British nationalism. The poem suggested that the patient cultivation of the "spiritual virtues" of India and the East would become a force in the world after the reckless power of Western imperialism, sparked by nationalism, had lost its control over humankind. In this, he echoed the views of many Hindu nationalists and reformers that Hinduism and India had a special devotion to peace and spiritual insights that could benefit the Western world. For this poem and other influential writings, Tagore won the Noble Prize for literature in 1913.

The last sun of the century sets amidst the blood-red clouds of the West and the whirlwind of hatred.

The naked passion of self-love of Nations, in its drunken delirium of greed, is dancing to the clash of steel and the howling verses of vengeance.

The hungry self of the Nation shall burst in a violence of fury from its own shameless feeding, for it has made the world its food.

And licking it, crunching it, and swallowing it in big morsels, It swells and swells,

Till in the midst of its unholy feast descends the sudden shaft of heaven piercing its heart of grossness.

The crimson glow of light on the horizon is not the light of thy dawn of peace, my Motherland.

It is the glimmer of the funeral pyre burning to ashes the vast flesh—the self-love of the Nation—dead under its own excess.

The morning waits behind the patient dark of the East, Meek and silent.

Keep watch, India.

Bring your offerings of worship for that sacred sunrise.

Let the first hymn of its welcome sound in your voice and sing

"Come, Peace, thou daughter of God's own great suffering.

Come with thy treasure of contentment, the sword of fortitude, And meekness crowning thy forehead."

Be not ashamed, my brothers, to stand before the proud and the powerful, With your white robe of simpleness.

Let your crown be of humility, your freedom the freedom of the soul.

Build God's throne daily upon the ample barrenness of your poverty.

And know that what is huge is not great and pride is not everlasting.

Thinking About the Reading

1. How does Tagore perceive nationalism?
2. How does he believe India should respond to Western power?

Source: From *Sources of Indian Tradition, vol. 2,* William Theodore De Bary, ed. Copyright © 1958 Columbia University Press. Reprinted with permission of the publisher.

India needed nothing from the West (see Witness to the Past: Challenging British Imperialism with Spiritual Virtues). One thinker, Swami Vivekananda (SWAH-me VIH-vee-keh-NAHN-da) (1863–1902), was particularly influential in his concern for ending both British cultural and political domination: "O India, this is your terrible danger. The spell of imitating the West is getting such a strong hold upon you. Be proud that thou art an Indian, and proudly proclaim: 'I am an Indian, every Indian is my brother.'"[7] His writings and lectures gave Indians great pride in their own culture.

Sayyid Ahmad Khan and Islamic Modernism

Like Hindus, Muslims were forced to rethink their values and prospects, leading some to embrace Islamic revivalism and others to embrace modernity. To Muslims, India seemed increasingly dominated by European and Hindu values and ideas. In response, some Muslims traveled to the Middle East in pursuit of Islamic knowledge. The most dogmatic and militant form of Islamic revivalism, Wahhabism (see Chapter 21), became popular in the northwest frontier and Bengal. Opposed to modernization, especially progressive ideas such as women's rights, the revivalists clashed with other Muslims, Christians, Sikhs, and Hindus. In contrast to revivalists, Muslim modernists, led by the cosmopolitan Sayyid Ahmad Khan (1817–1898), wanted Muslims to gain strength to achieve power. Khan argued that "the more worldly progress we make, the more glory Islam gains." He wanted to show that Islam was compatible with modern science, and in 1877 he founded a college at Aligarh (AL-ee-GAHR) that offered Western learning within a Muslim context. Aligarh graduates dominated Muslim political activity in India until independence.

Changes in Caste and Gender Roles

India's caste system was also affected by British colonialism. Before the colonial era, Hindus in Bengal, Punjab, and south India generally saw the formal differences among varied castes as of only moderate importance for groups and individuals. From the early 1800s, however—and owing partly to British attempts to win support from high-caste Hindus—British policies sharpened caste identities, classifying people largely through their caste affiliations. In the nineteenth century, much of India became more caste conscious than ever before, with upper castes stressing their uniqueness and lower castes wanting to emulate the upper castes to improve their social status. Hindu thinkers became divided about the caste system. Some social reformers called for abolishing caste, while defenders of Hindu culture praised the ideals of conduct and morality embedded in the caste system.

Gender relations also changed during colonial times. Traditionally, women and men had performed separate but interdependent roles within a household governed by men, but farming families faced a loss of work as land came under the control of absentee landlords who emphasized growing cash crops rather than food. Lower-caste men in north India who sought to emulate the upper castes often placed more restrictions on their women, including forcing some into purdah, or seclusion.

At the same time, however, new opportunities arose for other women. More girls attended school, and many became teachers, nurses, and midwives. The first women doctors graduated in the 1880s. Indian and British reformers sought to improve the lives of Indian women and foster greater equality between the genders. A new marriage act in 1872 provoked controversy by providing for both civil marriage and marriage across caste lines. The British tried incremental reforms, such as banning sati, allowing widow remarriage, and raising the age of female consent from ten to twelve. Both British and Indian reformers tended to support the idea of marriage as based on love but also encouraged wives to show their husbands and children self-sacrificing devotion.

The Rise of Nationalism

British rule under the *Raj* fostered national feelings and bitterness as Indians became more connected to the outside world. By 1900, Indians were publishing six hundred newspapers in various languages, which reported on world events, such as the Irish struggle for independence from England, the Japanese defeat of Russia in war, and the U.S. conquest of the Philippines, all of which inspired Indians to oppose British rule.

In 1885 nationalists formed the Indian National Congress, which worked for peaceful progress toward self-government. But the Congress, as it came to be known, mostly attracted well-educated professionals and merchants of brahman backgrounds and had few working-class or peasant members. British officials were scornful of the Congress, doubting the possibility of Indian unity in such a diverse society. Constitutional reforms in 1909 brought a measure of representative government, but Indians still lacked true legislative and financial power. Growing frustrations led impatient members to form a more aggressive nationalist faction within the Congress. By 1907, this radical group, led by a former journalist of Maratha background, Bal Gangadhar Tilak (1856–1920), transformed the Congress from a gentleman's pressure group into the spearhead of an active independence movement. A fierce opponent of Western influences, Tilak defended Hindu orthodoxy and custom, using religion as a vitalizing force for the nationalist movement. But many politically aware Indians disliked Tilak and remained wary of the Congress. Some feared that democratic values threatened their aristocratic privileges.

cultivation system
An agricultural policy imposed by the Dutch in Java that forced Javanese farmers to grow sugar on rice land.

Muslims perceived the Hindu-dominated Congress, particularly radical leaders like Tilak, as anti-Muslim. In 1906, the All-India Muslim League was founded with the goal of uniting a population scattered in pockets all over the country. Hindus constituted 80 percent of India's population; Muslims were a majority only in eastern Bengal, Sind, north Punjab, and the mountain districts west of the Indus Valley. The Muslim League's first great victory came in 1909, when British reforms guaranteed some seats in representative councils to Muslims, setting a precedence for minority representation and enraging the Congress. Hindu-Muslim rivalries continued to complicate the nationalist movement throughout the twentieth century.

LO³ Southeast Asia and Colonization

Southeast Asian societies had long flourished from trade and had formed strong, often dynamic, states, but by the 1700s, most faced increasing political and economic challenges from Western powers. During the 1800s, the challenges became more threatening, and by 1914, all of the major Southeast Asian societies except the Siamese had come under Western colonial control. The major changes came in Indonesia, Vietnam, and Burma, where the Dutch, French, and British, respectively, increased their power, and in the Philippines, which by the end of the 1800s was controlled by the United States. Thus Southeast Asian societies became tied, more than ever before, to the larger world but lost their political and economic independence.

Dutch Colonialism in Indonesia

Between 1750 and 1914, the Dutch expanded their power in the Indonesian archipelago. They already controlled the Spice Islands (Maluku) of northeast Indonesia and the large island of Java, territories that supplied them with great wealth. In 1799, the Dutch government replaced the Dutch East Indies Company with a formal colonial government that was charged with reenergizing the administration of its scattered territories in Java and Sumatra.

In 1830, Dutch administrators introduced the cultivation system, an agricultural policy that forced farmers on Java to grow sugar on their rice land. The

government profited by setting a low fixed price to pay peasants for sugar, even when world prices were high. The cultivation system enriched the Dutch but ultimately impoverished many peasants. A Dutch critic of the system described the results: "If anyone should ask whether the man who grows the products receives a reward proportionate to the yields, the answer must be in the negative. The Government compels him to grow on *his* land what pleases it; it punishes him when he sells the crop to anyone else but it."[8]

 East and Southeast Asia: An Annotated Directory of Internet Resources (*http://newton.uor.edu/Departments&Programs/AsianStudiesDept/general.html*). This site offers many links on Southeast Asia.

Dutch-owned plantations growing sugar and other cash crops replaced the cultivation system in the 1870s.

In the later 1800s, the Dutch turned their attention to gaining control, and exploiting the resources, of the Indonesian islands they had not already conquered, such as Borneo and Sulawesi (see Map 22.2). The Dutch created Indonesia as a country by uniting the thousands of scattered societies and dozens of states of this vast, diverse archipelago into the Dutch East Indies. But the colony, governed from Batavia (now Jakarta) on Java, promoted little common national feeling and remained a collection of peoples with diverse languages and distinctive cultures. Later this diversity made it difficult to build an Indonesian nation with a common identity.

> "The Dutch created Indonesia as a country by uniting the thousands of scattered societies and dozens of states of this vast, diverse archipelago into the Dutch East Indies."

Interactive Map

plural society
A medley of peoples who mix but do not blend, instead maintaining their own cultures, religions, languages, and customs.

The British in Malaya and Burma

At the same time as the Dutch were expanding their power, the British became more politically and economically active in the southern part of the Malay Peninsula, later known as Malaya, and eventually they subjugated the varied Malay states. British Malaya originated in coastal port cities. Seeking a naval base in the eastern Indian Ocean, the British East India Company purchased Penang (puh-NANG) Island, off Malaya's northwest coast, from a cash-strapped Malay sultan in 1786. This action marked the first stage in creating a regional British sphere of influence. In 1819, a visionary British agent of the British East India Company, Jamaican-born Thomas Stamford Raffles (1781–1826), capitalized on local political unrest to acquire sparsely populated Singapore Island, at the tip of the Malay Peninsula. A fine harbor and strategic location made Singapore the base for Britain's regional thrust and a great source of profits. By the 1860s, the city built on Singapore, with a mostly Chinese population, had become the key China–India trade link and crossroads of Southeast Asian commerce. After obtaining the port city of Melaka from the Dutch in 1824, Britain now governed the three Malayan ports as one colony, known as the Straits Settlements.

British Rule in the Malay States

From their coastal ports, the British extended their influence into the Malay states. British merchants in the Straits Settlements pressured British authorities to intervene in the Malay states to acquire resources and markets. Adding to these challenges for the British was the steady immigration of Chinese to western Malaya, where they contracted with local Malay rulers to mine tin and gold, competing with British merchants. Chinese settlers established towns such as Kuala Lumpur (KWAH-luh loom-POOR), which later grew into major cities.

To facilitate access to these Malayan states, by the 1870s the British used order and security as their rationale for forcing various sultans to accept British domination. Britain soon achieved formal or informal control over nine sultanates, which, together with the Straits Settlements, became British Malaya. These actions eventually resulted in the artificial division of the historical Malay world into two countries, British Malaya (now part of Malaysia) and the Dutch East Indies (now Indonesia). The British also colonized the northern third of Borneo, creating the states of Sabah (British North Borneo) and Sarawak and imposing a protectorate over the old sultanate of Brunei.

British rule changed Malaya. Economic development occurred largely along the west coast, where the British encouraged the planting of pepper, tobacco, oil palm, and especially rubber. As thousands of Chinese and Indian immigrants settled there to work, Malaya developed a mining- and plantation-based economy that produced tin and rubber for Western resource and market needs. Malay villagers, pressured by British taxes to take up rubber planting, became integrated into the world economy and lost their traditional self-sufficiency. At the same time, the British maintained the Malay sultans and aristocracy as symbolic and privileged leaders of the Malay states. Thus a plural society developed, a medley of peoples—Malays, Chinese, and Indians—that mixed but did not blend.

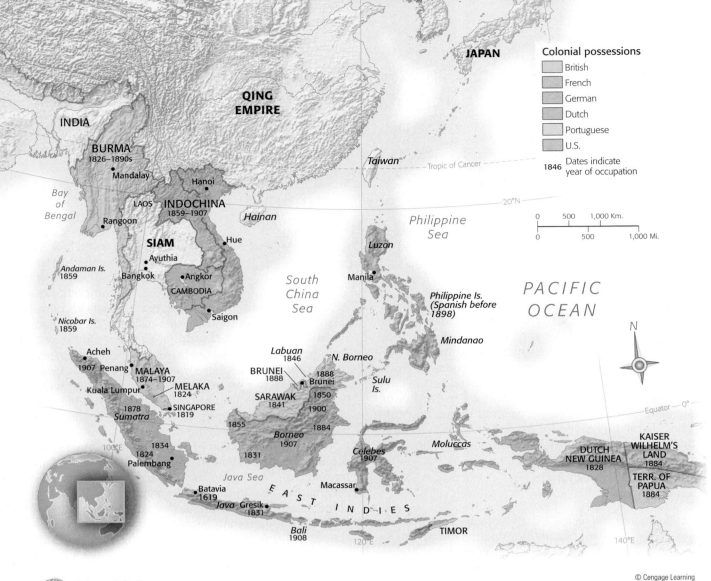

Map 22.2
The Colonization of Southeast Asia
Between 1800 and 1914, the European powers gradually conquered or gained control over the Southeast Asian societies that had not been colonized in the Early Modern Era. Only Siam remained independent.

© Cengage Learning

British Rule in Burma
As they expanded their power in India and Malaya, the British coveted Burma's rich lands and worried about Burmese claims to border regions. In three wars between 1824 and 1886, the British conquered Burma (today Myanmar). After the first two brutal wars, the British controlled much of southern Burma, leaving the Burman kings in control of only the north. As with the French in Vietnam, it took decades to colonize the country and overcome resistance. Vastly differing cultures and clashing strategic interests produced violent British-Burmese conflict.

The gradual loss of independence disrupted traditional society and proved devastating to the Burmans, the country's majority ethnic group. As they lost territory in the first two military defeats, Burmans began to feel an impending doom. Fear for the future was expressed in a frenzied cultural activity, including drama, love poetry, and music. For instance, Myawaddy (mee-ya-WAH-dee) (1761–1853), a government minister, soldier, scholar, and musician from a prominent noble family, tried to salvage Burman traditions by writing plays set in villages and collecting folk songs from the Burmans and other ethnic groups in the kingdom. The court, fearing that the Burmese heritage might disappear if the British triumphed, also compiled *The Glass Palace Chronicle*, a history of Burma from earliest times.

Between 1853 and 1878, a new Burmese king, the idealistic Mindon, tried to salvage his country's prospects by pursuing modernization and cultural renewal and seeking good relations with the British. However, worried that he might succeed in strengthening Burma, the British tried to humiliate Mindon and his government; Mindon in turn attempted to break down barriers between the court and the Burmese people. As the Burmans had feared, in 1886 the British completed their conquest, taking control of the government and exiling the royal family. When some Burmese resisted British rule, the British, in what they called "pacification," retaliated by destroying whole villages and executing rebel leaders. The Burman aristocracy and the royal system they had administered were destroyed, and Burma became a province of British India, a humiliating fate for this proud people.

Vietnam: Colonization and Resistance

For centuries a major power in Southeast Asia, Vietnam fell to French colonialism after a bitter struggle. In the 1700s, Vietnam was beset by growing problems, including civil war and rebellion. While a new dynasty reestablished some stability, it was unable to thwart the aggressive actions of the French, who colonized Vietnam against stiff resistance. The unpopular French regime changed Vietnamese society by introducing competitive capitalism into once-cooperative communities, linking the Vietnamese to the uncertainties of the world economy, undermining traditional politics, and otherwise exploiting the Vietnamese people.

The Tayson Rebellion

The Vietnamese state faced many challenges between 1750 and 1850. One challenge emerged with the Tayson Rebellion, launched in 1771 by three brothers from Tayson, a village in southern Vietnam. Social revolutionaries committed to a unified Vietnamese nation and fed up with corruption and misrule, the Tayson brothers and their thousands of armed followers fought for thirty years against the Vietnamese emperors and their French allies. In 1788 the Taysons defeated their foes and reestablished the national unity fractured in the long civil wars. They also sponsored economic expansion and rallied the people against a Chinese invasion.

The Nguyen Dynasty

A little more than a decade later, in 1802, Nguyen Anh (NEW-yin ahn) (1761–1820), the leader of a princely family based in Hue, led a force that defeated the Taysons and established a new imperial dynasty with French assistance, but the Nguyen dynasty he founded was unpopular and unable to address the social and economic inequalities that had inspired the Tayson Rebellion. *The Tale of Kieu*, a 3,300-line poem written by diplomat Nguyen Du (no relation to the dynasty) in the early 1800s, reflected a growing criticism of the greed and hypocrisy of upper-class Vietnamese and articulated the mistreatment of the Vietnamese people. But the internal challenges facing the Nguyen were soon eclipsed when the French conquered Vietnam. In 1858, the militarily powerful French, hoping to gain more commerce by controlling the Mekong and Red River trade routes to China, began what they arrogantly called a "civilizing mission" to spread French culture and Christianity and launched a bloody campaign of conquest against a determined but badly outgunned imperial Vietnamese resistance. In a quarter century of conflict, the French first conquered the south and then moved north, facing Vietnamese opposition the whole way.

Nguyen Quang Bich and the Can Vuong Rebels

By 1884, the French had conquered Vietnam but still had to consolidate their gains before they could impose their goals on the country. Consolidation proved more difficult than expected, as they faced prolonged resistance. It took the French another fifteen years to suppress the heroic efforts of thousands of poorly armed rebel groups known as the can vuong (kan voo-AHN) ("aid-

> 66 In the 1700s, Vietnam was beset by growing problems, including civil war and rebellion. 99

can vuong ("Aid-the-king") Rebel groups who waged guerrilla warfare for fifteen years against the French occupation of Vietnam.

the-king"), who resisted fiercely. One of the rebel leaders, the mandarin Nguyen Quang Bich, rejected any compromise with the French: "Please do not mention the word *surrender* any more. You cannot give any good counsel to a man who is determined to die." [9] The can vuong rebels became powerful symbols of resistance for later generations of Vietnamese fighting colonialism and foreign invasion. In suppressing the can vuong struggle, the French massacred thousands.

The French Federation of Indochina

In 1897, the French created the Federation of Indochina, so named because their Southeast Asian colonies were located between India and China. The federation was an artificial unit linking Vietnam, which the French broke into three separate territories, with newly acquired Cambodia and the diverse societies the French combined to create the colony of Laos. Both Cambodia and Laos had very different social, cultural, political, and historical legacies from those of Vietnam and relatively little in common with each other.

The French maintained their rule by force while allowing French commercial interests and settlers to exploit natural resources and markets. Following the pattern of European colonization elsewhere, the colonial regime destroyed the traditional autonomy of the Vietnamese villages by appointing leaders, often from outside, rather than allowing villages to select their own leaders, the traditional system, and by greatly increasing the tax burden to finance colonial administrative costs. Under French rural policies, many peasants lost their land or access to communal lands, and perhaps half of the cultivated land was turned over to private landowners, investors, and rubber planters, mostly French. France also made rice a major export crop, but the expanded production favored large landowners rather than peasants.

Siamese Modernization

The Siamese (today known as the Thai) were the only Southeast Asian country that retained their independence, a success that resulted from certain favorable conditions and wise leadership. In the early 1800s, when the British began pressuring Burma, Siam was a strong, flexible state under the vigorous new Bangkok-based Chakri dynasty, founded in 1767. Seeing Burma's dilemma, able Chakri kings mounted a successful strategy to resist Western pressures. With Britain and France, who both coveted Siam, preoccupied with controlling neighboring societies, Siamese

Bastille Day Parade in Vietnam This painting, by an unknown Vietnamese scholar, subtly criticizes the unpopular French colonization by satirizing the annual French holiday. A French man is shown with his arm around a Vietnamese woman, while unarmed Vietnamese lantern-bearers are being commanded by a French official.

leaders had time to counter a possible Western threat by strengthening government institutions, improving their economic infrastructure, and broadening their popular support in their diverse kingdom.

The farsighted Siamese kings who ruled during the late nineteenth and early twentieth centuries understood the changes in Southeast Asian politics and the rise of Western power, and they promoted a modernization policy designed to ensure political independence and economic growth: they yielded to the West when necessary and consolidated what remained. The price of political independence for Siam was giving up its claims over Laos and transferring northern Malaya to Britain. Siamese leaders also agreed to commercial agreements that opened the country to Western businesses. Nonetheless, the Siamese retained some control over their future. Finally, to minimize conflict with each other, British and French leaders opted to leave Siam as a buffer between British Burma and French Indochina.

WWW
Southeast Asia Guide (*http:// www.library.wisc .edu/guides/SEAsia/*). An easy-to-use site on Southeast Asia.

Two kings and their advisers were most responsible for Siam's success in avoiding colonization and modernizing the kingdom. The first, the scholarly, peace-loving King Mongkut (MAHN-kut) (r. 1851–1868), who had served as a Buddhist monk and teacher for several decades, was probably the most perceptive leader of his time in Southeast Asia. An outspoken man who had studied science and had learned to read Latin, Mongkut signed treaties with various Western powers, often with terms unfavorable for Siam, and invited Western aid to modernize his kingdom. To foster goodwill and provide his heirs with an understanding of the West, Mongkut hired the wives of Christian missionaries to teach English to his wives and sons.

The second king, Mongkut's son, Chulalongkorn (CHOO-lah-LONG-corn) (r. 1868–1910), who had traveled in Asia, built on his father's foundation by emphasizing diplomacy and modernization. Chulalongkorn started a broad reform program that included abolishing slavery, centralizing government services, strengthening the bureaucracy, establishing a Western-style government education system, and stimulating economic growth by encouraging the immigration of Chinese merchants and opening new land for rice production. These measures helped Siam successfully resist the colonizing intentions of the Western powers. When Chulalongkorn died in 1910, Siam (today called Thailand) was still independent.

The Philippines, Spain, and the United States

The Spanish had colonized the Philippines much earlier than the Dutch, French, and British had acquired territory in Southeast Asia (see Chapter 18). However, by the 1870s, Spanish rule had decayed and local resentment had grown. Philippine nationalism sprouted in the struggle against the Spanish, eventually generating an armed revolution that inspired other colonized Asian peoples. But the Filipino nationalists soon faced a more powerful foe, the United States. The military intervention of the United States during the revolution had momentous consequences, as the Americans helped defeat Spain but then crushed the revolutionary movement, replacing Spain as the colonial power.

The Filipino Nationalist Movement

As happened in the Spanish colonies in Latin America (see Chapter 19), hostility toward the corrupt, repressive, and economically stagnant rule of Spain had simmered for decades in the Philippines. Educated, local-born Filipinos of Spanish, indigenous, and mixed-descent (mestizo) background resented colonial power, the privileged immigrants from Spain, and the domination of the Catholic Church.

The Philippine nationalist movement arose to bring together all of the diverse societies of the islands and to oppose continued Spanish domination. Gradually, resentment of Spain turned nationalists toward revolution, which broke out in 1896. One dissident, Emilio Aguinaldo (AH-gee-NAHL-doe) (1870–1964), a small-town mayor of Chinese mestizo background, called on the Filipinos to rebel: "Filipinos! Open your eyes! Lovers of their native land, rise up in arms, to proclaim their liberty and independence." The revolutionaries welcomed women into their movement, even while they maintained conventional gender attitudes, viewing a woman as, in the words of one leader, a "helper and partner in the hardships of life."[10] Despite the revolutionary's heroic efforts, however, by 1897 the Spanish had contained the revolution, though they failed to capture all the leaders or to crush scattered resistance.

George Dewey and American Intervention

The situation changed dramatically in 1898 when the U.S. fleet, commanded by Admiral George Dewey, sailed into Manila Bay and destroyed the Spanish navy, causing thousands of

Spaniards to flee Manila. Americans had engaged in occasional naval skirmishes in Southeast Asia throughout the 1800s, and the American intervention in the Philippines reflected decades of American activity in Southeast Asia as Americans sought resources and markets. But not until the Spanish-American War in 1898 did the United States assert its military power on a large scale in the region. The fighting between U.S. and Spanish forces began in the Caribbean before expanding to the Philippines. The U.S. attack on Manila rejuvenated the revolutionaries led by Aguinaldo, who received initial American support and soon controlled much of the country. The revolutionaries declared independence and established a republican government with a semidemocratic constitution, but U.S. leaders had other plans for the country.

> 66 Colonial governments varied widely, although Europeans always held ultimate political authority. 99

The Philippine-American War

Taking up Rudyard Kipling's call to assume world responsibilities and "the white man's burden," U.S. President William McKinley called for colonization of the Philippines, ignoring the deep Filipino desire for independence. McKinley proclaimed: "It is our duty to uplift and civilize and Christianize and by God's Will do our very best by [the Filipinos]."[11] McKinley, who admitted he could not locate the Philippines on a world map, underestimated the Filipino opposition to the U.S. occupation. Some 125,000 American troops fought during the four-year Philippine-American War, and more than 5,000 Americans and some 16,000 Filipinos died in battle. Another 200,000 Filipinos died from famine and disease generated by the conflict.

American soldiers were surprised and demoralized by the ferocity of Filipino resistance. In many districts, Filipino soldiers enjoyed the active support of most of the local population. With peasant help, the elusive revolutionaries lived off the land and practiced a harassing form of guerrilla warfare. Both sides committed atrocities, including torture. Angered by American deaths there, U.S. General Jacob Smith ordered his men to turn Samar Island into a "howling wilderness," to "kill and burn. The more you kill and burn the better you will please me."[12] The reports caused Americans at home to become deeply split on the war. Strong supporters, especially in the business community, coveted Philippine resources and markets, and U.S. newspapers urged the slaughter of all

Filipinos who resisted. The writer Mark Twain excoriated such motives in his 1900 rewriting of "The Battle Hymn of the Republic": "Mine eyes have seen the orgy of the launching of the Sword; He is searching out the hoardings where the strangers' wealth is stored; He hath loosed his fateful lightnings, and with woe and death has scored; His lust is marching on."[13]

By 1902, after the revolutionaries were defeated and many wealthy Filipinos, to protect their interests, had decided to support U.S. rule, the United States declared the Philippines an American colony. The Americans attempted to reshape the society of those they paternalistically called "our little brown brothers," using the United States as the preferred model. They established an elected legislature filled mostly by Filipinos, but its decisions had to be approved by U.S. officials. In contrast to most Western colonies, the American colonial government fostered education, literacy, and modern health care, and the schools produced a large number of Filipinos who were fluent in English. But American rule generally ignored peasant needs while perpetuating the power of the Filipino landowners, who supported U.S. rule.

LO⁴ The Reshaping of Southeast Asia

Colonialism in Southeast Asia had many parallels to that in India and Africa. Although some Southeast Asians benefited, many others experienced worsening living conditions. From a global perspective, colonialism linked Southeast Asia more firmly to a Western-dominated world economy. But colonial policies also affected local political, social, intellectual, and cultural life. Like Indians, Southeast Asians responded to the challenges of colonialism in creative ways.

Colonial Governments

Colonialism destroyed the political autonomy of Southeast Asians. The only colony with much self-government was the U.S.-ruled Philippines, which had an elected legislature. The British did allow Malayans some participation in city or state government and, in 1935, formed a legislature in Burma that included both elected and appointed members. France and the Netherlands, however, although democracies themselves, allowed little democracy in their colonies.

Colonial governments varied widely, although Europeans always held ultimate political authority. As in sub-Saharan Africa (see Chapter 21), Europeans introduced either direct or indirect rule. Direct rule removed traditional leaders, such as the Burmese kings, or made them symbolic only, as with the Vietnamese emperors. Direct rule was used in Burma, the Philippines, Vietnam, and parts of Indonesia. By contrast, in Malaya, Cambodia, Laos, and some parts of Indonesia, Europeans applied indirect rule, governing a district through the traditional leaders, such as Malay sultans, Cambodian kings, or Javanese aristocrats. Whether governing directly or indirectly, the colonial authorities played off one ethnic group or one region against another, in the process creating problems that persisted after independence and made national unity difficult. Colonial boundaries in Southeast Asia ignored traditional ethnic relationships and rivalries, laying a basis for political instability. Countries such as Burma, Indonesia, and Laos were artificial creations of European colonialism rather than organic unities with more or less culturally similar populations.

Southeast Asia in the World Economy

As in India, the transformation of economic life was at least as significant as that of conquest and political reorganization. Southeast Asians had long participated in world trade as exporters of valuable resources, from spices and sugar to tin and gold. Because subsistence food farming could not produce enough revenues for colonial governments or investors, it was supplanted by cash crop farming, replacing the earlier age of commerce. Extracting mineral or agricultural wealth meant that Western businessmen controlled the top level of the economy, including the banks, import-export companies, mines, wells, and plantations. Gradually, as Southeast Asia came to be integrated into the world economy as a producer of raw materials and consumer of Western food and manufactured goods, it became one of the world's most valuable economic areas.

> "Many colonies developed monoculture economies that were dependent on the export of one or two major commodities, such as rubber and tin from Malaya, rice from Burma, or rubber and rice from Vietnam."

Colonial taxation policies encouraged people to grow cash crops, such as rubber, pepper, sugar, coffee, tea, opium, and palm oil; cut timber; mine gold and tin; and drill oil. Many colonies developed monoculture economies that were dependent on the export of one or two major commodities, such as rubber and tin from Malaya, rice from Burma, or rubber and rice from Vietnam. The world price for these exports fluctuated with unstable global demand, fostering a local economy that prospered or floundered depending on decisions made in Europe or North America. These economic activities also had an impact on the natural environment, as forests were cleared for plantations or logged for timber to be shipped out of the region.

For many Southeast Asians, rubber growing became the key factor in shaping their lives. The invention of the first bicycles and then automobiles opened up vast markets for rubber tires. To meet this need, the British introduced rubber cultivation to Malaya, and it then spread to Sumatra, Borneo, southern Thailand, Vietnam, and Cambodia. Thousands of acres of forest were cleared for rubber growing, mostly on European-owned plantations. Malaya became the world's greatest exporter of natural rubber, supplying more than half of the world supply by 1920. To produce rubber, plantation workers suffered long hours, strict discipline, monotonous routine, and poor food. A Vietnamese writer, on witnessing a French-owned rubber estate, said that "every day one was worn down a bit more, cheeks sunken, eyes hollow. Everyone appeared almost dead."[14]

Economic growth had major consequences for everyone but did not benefit all equally. For a small minority, especially the European colonizers and the local officials and merchants who cooperated with them, it brought wealth, but for most Southeast Asians, the results of economic growth were mixed. For instance, the Javanese peasants who grew sugar initially earned new income, and some took advantage of improved irrigation facilities to grow more rice as well as the required sugar. When peasants came to depend on sugar profits for survival, they often became impoverished because of rising costs. By 1900, some Dutch officials admitted that colonial rule had reduced many Javanese to complete poverty.

Java Coffee Plantation This painting from the nineteenth century shows a European manager supervising barefoot laborers who are raking and drying coffee beans, a major Javan cash crop.

Population Trends and Immigration

In addition to exploiting resources and developing economic monocultures, colonial policies also sparked rapid population growth. In 1600, perhaps 20 to 25 million people lived in Southeast Asia. By 1800, this number had grown to 30 or 35 million, and by the late 1930s, it was around 140 or 150 million. The greatest increases came on Java: in 1800, some 10 million people lived on Java, and this figure grew to 30 million by 1900 and 48 million by 1940. Dutch policies contributed to population growth directly or indirectly by fostering better health care and largely maintaining social order. As a result, people lived longer. Economic incentives also encouraged larger families to provide more labor for the fields. Fast-growing populations, especially in Java, Vietnam, and the Philippines, resulted in smaller farm plots and more landless people.

Immigration from other Asian regions also contributed to population growth. Between 1800 and 1941, millions of Chinese and smaller numbers of Indians immigrated to Southeast Asia to work as laborers, miners, planters, and merchants. Chinese immigrants chiefly came from poor, overcrowded coastal provinces in southeast China and typically were males whose goal was to make enough money to return to their native villages wealthy and respected. While some did achieve this goal and many eventually opened shops in Southeast Asia with their earnings, others remained too poor to return to China and spent their lives as laborers, miners, or plantation workers.

Other Chinese who did prosper as merchants, planters, and mine owners decided to remain in Southeast Asia. Through enterprise, cooperation, and organization, they dominated retail trade, becoming the commercial middle class in every colony except Burma. Some cities, such as Kuala Lumpur and Singapore, were largely Chinese in population; other cities also had substantial Chinese communities. The Chinese who settled permanently married local women or brought families from China. By adjusting to local conditions, the Chinese became a permanent presence in Southeast Asian life.

British Malaya attracted Indian settlers as well as Chinese, creating a more complex ethnic configuration. Indian immigrants had come to the Straits Settlements cities for decades as traders, craftsmen, and workers. Beginning in the 1880s, people from the Tamil-speaking region of southeast India were imported to work on Malayan rubber plantations, where they experienced the harshness of plantation life. The Chinese and Indians together eventually outnumbered the Malays, sparking Malay fears of being overwhelmed by immigrants. The British, to maintain their control, skillfully maintained the political separation of the three groups and discouraged cooperation among them.

Social and Cultural Changes

Colonial policies altered the lives of men and women, whether rural or urban, immigrant or local-born, in Southeast Asia. Economic changes particularly affected women, who had traditionally played a major economic role in local society as farmers, traders, and weavers and often enjoyed considerable independence from men. Now, as men took up cash crop farming, the responsibility for growing the family's food was often largely left to women, increasing their workload. Economic change also robbed many women of their key role as small traders in the local marketplace, decreasing their status as income earners for the family. The expansion of textile imports also affected women's status. After 1850, when inexpensive industry-made textiles began pouring in from Europe, people began to switch from using local handwoven cloth to imported goods, slowly forcing women out of the business.

Gender Roles and Urbanization

Women did not face their problems passively, however. Some joined movements to assert their rights. Siamese feminists opposed polygamy and supported girls' education. An inspirational Javanese woman, Raden Adjeng Kartini, also founded schools for girls and fostered Indonesian women's awareness of their situation. Today many Indonesians honor Kartini as a heroine whose writings and life influenced the rise of Indonesian feminism and nationalism. Southeast Asia already had large cities, but the coming of Western rule encouraged more rapid urbanization. Cities such as Manila, Jakarta, Rangoon (today known as Yangon), Singapore, Kuala Lumpur, and Saigon (today Ho Chi Minh City) attracted immigrant populations from other societies, such as the Chinese, and migrants from nearby districts. Ethnic variety characterized colonial towns and cities, which offered a diverse assortment of food stalls and restaurants, private schools that catered to different ethnic groups, and buildings erected by different religious sects. Nearly every city contained Muslim mosques, Buddhist, Hindu, and Chinese temples, and Christian churches. Some descendants of Chinese and Indian immigrants assimilated into the surrounding culture; friendships and even marriages crossed ethnic lines. For example, much of Thailand's political and economic leadership today has some mix of Chinese and Siamese ancestry, a result of cultural assimilation or intermarriage.

Read about Kartini, the inspirational social activist and teacher who represented a feminist consciousness new to Indonesia.

Educational and Cultural Transformation

Colonial governments differed in their commitment to education and assimilation. Most colo-

> "Colonial policies altered the lives of men and women, whether rural or urban, immigrant or local-born, in Southeast Asia."

nies left education to the Christian missions. As a result of the influence of mission schools, some Vietnamese, Indonesians, and Chinese became Christian, and hill peoples frequently did so, though few Theravada Buddhists or Muslims abandoned their faiths. A few colonies set up government schools, such as the U.S.-ruled Philippines and independent Siam. At the other extreme was French Vietnam, which spent little public money on schools. In general, in both the mission and government schools, the Western emphasis on individualism conflicted with traditional community values and loosened the social fabric.

Some communities developed alternatives to Western education. Buddhist and Muslim groups, which had sponsored schools for centuries, expanded their schools to enroll more students and teach them from a non-Western perspective. Other schools mixed Eastern and Western ideas. For example, in 1922 a mystical Javanese religious organization established schools that provided an alternative to both Islamic and Christian instruction. These schools emphasized Indonesian arts such as music and dance but also used Western ideas; for example, they encouraged students to express their own ideas and stressed social equality and the psychological development of their students. Many graduates became nationalist leaders.

Southeast Asians also expressed their sentiments in new cultural forms. For instance, on Java, musicians mixed European string instruments with the rhythms of the largely percussion Javanese gamelan orchestra to create a romantic new popular music, *kronchong*, which became widely popular on the island. Later in the early twentieth century, Western composers who observed performances by Javanese and Balinese gamelan orchestras incorporated gamelan influences into their music.

In most colonies, a modern literature developed that reflected both alienation from colonial rule and an awareness of rapid social and cultural change. But its criticism of the colonial regime was suppressed, forcing authors to make their points indirectly. For example, Vietnamese writers used historical themes from precolonial times or critiques of Vietnamese society to discuss contemporary conditions. This evasion was necessary to avoid censorship or even arrest for dissent.

Listen to a synopsis of Chapter 22.

CHAPTER 23

East Asia and the Russian Empire Face New Challenges,

1750–1914

Learning Outcomes

After reading this chapter, you should be able to answer the following questions:

LO¹ What were the causes and consequences of the Opium War?

LO² Why did Chinese efforts at modernization fail?

LO³ What factors aided Japan in the quest for modernization?

LO⁴ How did the Meiji government transform Japan and Korea?

LO⁵ What factors explain the expansion of the Russian Empire?

BBThe sacred traditions of our ancestors have fallen into oblivion. Those who watch attentively the march of events feel a dark and wonderful presentiment. We are on the eve of an immense revolution. But will the impulse come from within or without?cc

—A Chinese official, 1846[1]

In 1820, Li Ruzhen (LEE Ju-Chen) (1763–1830) published a satiric novel that boldly attacked Chinese social conditions, knowing that it would expose him to criticism from conservatives who favored the status quo. Set in the Tang dynasty a millennium earlier, *Flowers in the Mirror* was a complex novel that explored, among other themes, the relationship between the sexes. In one section of *Flowers,* Li describes a trip by three men to a country in which all of the gender roles that had been followed in China for centuries have been reversed. In this country, men suffer the pain of ear piercing and footbinding and endure hours every day putting on makeup, all to please the women who run the country. One of the men, Merchant Lin, is conscripted as a court "lady" by the female "king":

> In due course, his [bound] feet lost much of their original shape. Blood and flesh were squeezed into a pulp and then little remained of feet but dry bones and skin, shrunk to a dainty size. . . . With blood-red lipstick, and powder adorning his face, and jade and pearl adorning his coiffure and ears, Merchant Lin assumed, at last, a not unappealing appearance.[2]

Li seemed an unlikely man to address so starkly and sympathetically the low social status and daily challenges faced by women. A conventionally educated Confucian scholar who had failed the civil service examinations, Li became a writer on various nonfiction subjects. Growing Western intrusion, unchecked population growth, domestic unrest, political corruption, and growing opium addiction spurred Chinese scholars such as Li to reassess the relevance of Chinese traditions, such as outmoded civil service examinations, the

Test your knowlege before you read this chapter.

What do you think?

The responses of China and Japan to the Western threat were remarkably similar.

Strongly Disagree						Strongly Agree
1	2	3	4	5	6	7

<<**Treaty Between Japan and China** After an industrializing Japan defeated a declining China in a war over Japanese encroachments in Korea (1894–1895), diplomats from both nations met to negotiate a peace treaty. This painting shows the Chinese and Japanese representatives, easily identified by their different clothing styles, discussing the terms.

inequality of wealth, and women's footbinding. The growing dissatisfaction with China's practices that Li's provocative book represented, combined with Western intervention in China, set the stage for the immense revolution that would eventually transform this ancient society.

Like the Chinese, the Japanese also faced challenges, even before Western ships forced the nation open in the 1850s. Soon the old system fell, and in the 1870s, Japan's new leaders began an all-out program of modernization in an effort to prevent Western domination. By 1900, the Japanese had heavy industry, a modern military, and a comprehensive educational system. Emulating the Western imperialist countries, they also sought their own resources and markets abroad and soon colonized their neighbor, Korea, which had not modernized.

Although historically linked more closely to Europe than to Asia, Russia also became a factor in Asian politics after it expanded across Siberia to the Pacific. Perched on the borders of Europe, East Asia, and the Islamic Middle East and Central Asia, Russia engaged with societies in each of these regions through trade, warfare, and conquest. After it became dominant in parts of eastern Europe, pushed its borders southward into Ottoman territories, and conquered the Central Asian states, Russia was the largest territorial power in Eurasia.

LO¹ The Zenith and Decline of Qing China

Established by the Manchus, pastoralist invaders from Manchuria, the Qing (ching) (1644–1912) was the last dynasty in China's long history, the final phase

> "In the eighteenth century, Qing China was still one of the world's largest, most insular, most powerful, most prosperous, and most technologically sophisticated societies."

of China's 2,000-year-old imperial system. After reaching its zenith in the eighteenth century, Qing China experienced severe challenges and eventual decay in the nineteenth century. Several catastrophic wars resulted in unequal treaties with the West that increased Western penetration, and dynastic decline fostered major rebellions. Meanwhile, China's economy underwent changes, Christian missionaries posed a challenge to Chinese culture, and increasing poverty prompted millions of Chinese to seek their fortunes abroad. This decline in world standing had as much to do with Europe's rise as with China's failures.

Qing China in an Imperial World

In the eighteenth century, Qing China was still one of the world's largest, most insular, most powerful, most prosperous, and most technologically sophisticated societies, but troubling signs of decay developed. Although the Manchus had followed the political example of earlier Chinese dynasties, they were more despotic. Manchus dominated the top government positions and forbade intermarriage with the Chinese. While the Chinese accepted Manchu rule—as they had tolerated alien rule in the past—they resented the ethnic discrimination. There were other problems as well. Like various earlier dynasties, the Qing had built a great empire by occupying frontier regions and consolidating China's borders, but doing so stretched Qing military power and proved economically costly.

Qing Prosperity

Despite the challenges, the Qing generally maintained domestic prosperity for nearly two centuries. Chinese opened new lands for settlement and introduced crops from the Americas that provided additional food sources, such as corn, sweet potatoes, and peanuts. The volume of domestic trade grew in the 1700s, spurred by new textile factories, increased copper mining, and more money in circulation in the world's largest commercial economy. In 1830, China still accounted for one-third of world manufacturing, and in the 1850s, a British observer called the Chinese the world's greatest manufacturing people.

Internet Guide to Chinese Studies (*http://www.sino.uni-heidelberg.de/igcs/*). An excellent collection of links, maintained by a German university.

As a result of its prosperity and agricultural growth, China's population doubled from 150 million in 1700 to 300 million by 1800, and then rose to 432 million by 1850. Peasants responded to population pressure by finding additional marginal land to farm and expanding their use of irrigation and fertilizer. But population growth still outstripped the growth of the food supply, straining resources and fostering corruption, which increased Chinese resentment of the Qing government. Although in the 1700s living standards in the more developed regions of China were probably comparable to those of the more affluent parts of western Europe, in the 1800s they deteriorated, partly because of overpopulation.

Chinese culture and society became more conservative under the Manchus. In 1783, the Qing government prohibited books and plays that it considered treasonable to the Manchu state or subversive to traditional Chinese values. The Qing introduced harsher laws against unconventional behavior, such as homosexuality, which Chinese governments had generally tolerated for centuries, and increased social pressures on women to conform to such gender expectations as refusing to remarry after they became widows. The Qing mandated that public meetings be held every month in which an imperial edict be read out. It emphasized Confucian notions of moral virtue, heaping honor on filial sons, loyal officials, philanthropists, and faithful wives. Because increasing numbers of women were literate, the government published instructional books containing historical writings, some of them more than two millennia old, on female obligations. Women were advised not to look around when walking, laugh aloud, talk loudly, or sway their skirts when standing.

> 66 Widespread corruption, increasing poverty, drug trafficking, and local uprisings all added to increasingly severe economic problems. 99

Western Pressure and Qing Decline

China faced problems during the later Qing period and showed clear signs of dynastic decline by 1800. Widespread corruption, increasing poverty, drug trafficking, and local uprisings all added to increasingly severe economic problems. As political, economic, and social conditions deteriorated at home, European nations exerted pressure on the Qing government to grant them more privileges. China had encountered Western adventurers, traders, and missionaries already in the sixteenth and seventeenth centuries. Traders from Portugal, Russian, the Netherlands, and Great Britain had made inroads in the 1700s, and Westerners increasingly wanted more access, including freedom to travel inside China.

Chinese Isolationism

The Chinese debated how much contact with the West to allow. Chinese merchants in coastal cities, who had long traded with Southeast Asia, often supported contact because they could make fortunes by trading with the Europeans. Nevertheless, being largely self-sufficient in food and resources, China did not need foreign trade, and Qing emperors were unwilling to make concessions to the more open trade system desired by the Europeans. Before 1800, the Qing restricted trade to a few ports such as Guangzhou and Siberian outposts, and

Edict on Trade with Great Britain Learn why elaborate gifts brought by a British delegation and bestowed personally by Lord Macartney on Emperor Qianlong failed to convince the Emperor to accept Britain's trade proposals.

CHRONOLOGY

China, 1750–1915

1644–1912	Qing dynasty
1839–1842	Opium War
1842	Treaty of Nanjing
1850–1864	Taiping Rebellion
1856–1860	Arrow War
1894–1895	Sino-Japanese War
1898	100 Days of Reform
1900	Boxer Rebellion
1911	Chinese Revolution
1912	Formation of Chinese Republic
1915	Japan's 21 Demands on China

they refused diplomatic relations on an equal basis with the West. In the 1600s, Catholics and all other missionaries were expelled and prohibited from working in China. The Chinese knew little of the Western world and were confused by the diverse nationalities of the European peoples, whom they disparagingly called "foreign devils." Chinese leaders viewed European merchants as barbarians bearing tribute, and they required visiting diplomats to perform the humiliating custom of *kotow*, in which they prostrated themselves before the emperor.

> "The opium trade undermined the country's social fiber and impoverished thousands of families."

ter written by the Qing emperor Qianlong (chee-YEN-loong) (r. 1736–1795) to King George III of Britain following a British trade mission in 1793 requesting more access. The emperor denied Britain permission to establish an embassy but commended the king for his respectful spirit of humility in sending tribute: "It behooves you, O king, to display ever greater devotion and loyalty in the future, so that by perpetual submission to our throne, you may secure peace and prosperity for your country hereafter."[3]

World-Views of East and West

Chinese and European world-views were also incompatible. The British righteously saw themselves as benefiting China by opening the country to free trade. A British official wrote in 1821 that governments should let the stream of commerce flow as it will. China's attitude toward foreign trade and the outside world was well exemplified in a let-

The Opium Trade and War

Half a century after Emperor Qianlong blithely dismissed the British request with these words, the tables were turned. Their humiliating defeats in two wars in the mid-1800s forcibly jarred the Chinese from their complacency and made clear that the world was changing. These wars forced China to open its doors and to rethink traditional values and institutions.

Guangzhou During the eighteenth century, the Western traders in China were restricted to one riverside district in Guangzhou (Canton), where they built their warehouses, businesses, and homes in European style.

Photograph Courtesy Peabody Essex Museum, E79708 View of Guangzhou ca. 1800

Cultivating an Addiction

In the late 1700s, the British, taking the lead in the China trade, badly wanted more Chinese silk and tea, which had become valued revenue sources for British merchants. But China, desiring little from the West, accepted only precious gold and silver bullion as payment. Between the 1760s and 1780s, the import of silver into China increased more than 500 percent, causing an unfavorable trade disparity for the British. British found a solution in opium, an addictive drug that was grown in India and the Middle East. In the 1720s, the Chinese discovered that they could smoke opium for pleasure by mixing it in a pipe with tobacco. A highly addictive drug, it produced severe withdrawal symptoms such as cramps and nausea.

The British began to grow opium as a cash crop in the Bengal region of India in the 1700s, and soon British and American traders began smuggling opium into China. The Western drug smugglers and the governments that supported them, being concerned only with profits, were indifferent to the terrible moral and social consequences of their enterprise; by 1838, there were 5 to 10 million Chinese addicts. The opium trade undermined the country's social fiber and impoverished thousands of families. One Chinese official concluded that "opium is nothing else but a flowing poison [which] utterly ruins the minds and morals of the people, a dreadful calamity."[4]

Chinese Reaction to Opium Importation

The corrupt opium trade system at Guangzhou fostered conflict. China outlawed the opium trade in 1729, but to continue bringing in their huge profits from this trade, during the 1830s the British doubled opium imports while also pressing for reform of the trading system. Chinese leaders responded by further isolating the Western traders and mounting an attack on the opium trade. The emperor appointed the mandarin Lin Zezu (lin tsay-shoe) (1785–1850) to go to Guangzhou as commissioner and end the opium trade. Lin, an incorruptible Confucian moralist, concluded that if the opium traffic was not stopped, China would become poorer and its people weaker. Lin ordered his officials to raid the Western warehouses, where they seized and destroyed 20,000 chests of opium worth millions of dollars.

The Opium War

Lin's seizure of opium outraged Western traders, and Britain declared war. The following Opium War (1839–1842), as the British

called it, proved disastrous for China. The British fleet raided up and down the Chinese coast, blockading and bombarding ports, including Guangzhou. Although China had one of the world's most formidable military forces in 1600, since then Europeans had greatly surpassed China in naval and military technology. The British won most of the battles of the war, and when defeat was certain, dozens of Qing officers committed suicide. The lost battles forced the Chinese to assess the Western threat. While a few were concerned with the inadequacy of Chinese technology, most officials and other educated Chinese remained scornful of all things Western. One official wrote to the emperor that "the English barbarians are a detestable people, trusting entirely to their strong ships and large guns." Average Chinese felt similarly: one placard in Canton in 1841 was addressed to "rebellious barbarian dogs . . . We are definitely going to kill you, cut your heads off, and burn your bodies in the trash."[5]

In 1842, after the British made preparations to blow down the walls of the major city of Nanjing, along the Yangzi River in central China, the Qing were forced to sign the Treaty of Nanjing, which gave Britain permanent possession of Hong Kong, a sparsely populated coastal island downriver from Guangzhou; opened five ports to British trade; abolished Chinese trade monopolies; set fixed tariffs so that China no longer controlled its economic policy; and gave the British extraterritoriality, or freedom from local laws. The Chinese were also forced to pay Britain the war costs. Soon other Western countries signed treaties with China that gave them the same rights as the British. Each successive treaty expanded foreign privileges.

extraterritoriality Freedom from local laws for foreign subjects.

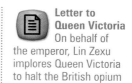

Letter to Queen Victoria On behalf of the emperor, Lin Zexu implores Queen Victoria to halt the British opium trade in China.

The Treaty System

The Opium War became to the Chinese a permanent symbol of Western imperialism and soon led to other wars and treaties that opened China to the West. After the Opium War, Westerners, especially the British, remained dissatisfied with the amount of trade, and the Chinese sought to evade their obligations. Another conflict, often known as the Arrow War (1856–1860), soon developed over a dispute aboard a Chinese ship, *The Arrow*, registered in Hong Kong. France also entered the war, using the mysterious murder of a French priest as an excuse. Facing two formidable powers, China was again defeated and forced to sign new treaties that favored the West. This treaty opened more ports on the coast and along rivers to Western traders, established foreign embassies in Beijing, and permitted Christian missionaries further access. Again forced to pay the war costs, China fell deeper into debt. The Arrow War also undermined China's position as a regional power, as it was forced to give up its claim to Vietnam, a long-time vassal state being colonized by France, and to acquiesce in the Russian takeover of eastern Siberia.

By restricting China's control of its economy and limiting Chinese power to make rules for Western residents, the treaty system deprived China of some of its autonomy. It also led to the formation of international settlements, zones in major Chinese cities set aside for foreigners in which no Chinese were allowed. They were in effect foreign cities with foreign governments in major ports such as Guangzhou and Shanghai. For example, a small island on the riverfront adjacent to downtown Guangzhou became the home of Western merchants, officials, and missionaries. It boasted mansions, warehouses, clubs, and churches built by and serving Westerners. Chinese were clearly unwelcome except as servants.

The Opium and Arrow Wars and the treaty system they fostered forced the Chinese to debate how best to respond to the new dangers the country faced. Some Chinese officials and other scholars understood the need for China to learn from the West. A few scholars argued that the Chinese should seriously study science, mathematics, and foreign languages. These views influenced the provincial official and reformer Zeng Guofan (zung gwoh-FAN) (1811–1872), who recommended making modern weapons and steamships. But, failing to see the magnitude of the challenges, few mandarins showed interest.

While scholars debated, Western cultural influence increased, and China's problems multiplied. To pay for the wars, the government had to raise taxes, causing many peasants to lose their land. The dispossessed often turned to begging or banditry. Natural disasters further demoralized the country. Between 1800 and 1850, the Yellow River flooded twenty times and then changed course, wiping out hundreds of towns and villages. Christian missionaries opened most of China's Western-type schools and hospitals, providing educational and health benefits to those Chinese who had access to them, but posing a challenge to Chinese religions. The missionaries and other Western residents, often ethnocentric and seeing themselves as agents of what they considered to be a superior Western and Christian civilization, tended to view the Chinese as depraved heathens and mocked their culture. Chinese generally distrusted not only the Christian missionaries but also the several hundred thousand Chinese who became Christian.

The Taiping Rebellion

Deteriorating conditions, government corruption, and the increasing Western presence eventually generated the Taiping Rebellion (1850–1864), the most critical of several midcentury upheavals against the Qing (see Map 23.1). Guangdong (GWAHNG-dong) province, on the southeast coast, experienced particularly severe social and economic dislocations that increased popular unrest. The rebellion began in a remote area and was fueled by economic insecurity, famine, loss of faith in government, and a desire for social change. The leader, Hong Xiuquan (hoong shee-OH-chew-an) (1813–1864), preached a doctrine blending Christianity and Chinese thought advocating for an equal distribution of goods, communal property, and equality between men and women. Hong established a sect, the Taipings (Heavenly Kingdom of Great Peace), that rejected Confucian traditions, and he prohibited opium use, polygamy, footbinding, prostitution, concubinage, and arranged marriages. In 1850, Hong launched a rebellion, invoking Chinese nationalism: "We raise the army of righteousness to liberate the masses for the sake of China."[6] Soon he had attracted millions of supporters from among the poor and disaffected.

The Taipings enjoyed early success, but ultimately their efforts failed and weakened China. Taiping armies conquered large parts of central and southern China, but the Taipings suffered from conflicts within their leadership, and their hostility to traditional Chinese culture cost them popular support. Ultimately most of the educated elite rallied to the Qing and organized provincial armies to oppose the Taipings. Westerners often sympathized with the Taipings because of their Christian influences and progressive social message, but they knew that a Qing victory would benefit Western nations. Hence, various Western nations aided the Qing as they defeated the Taipings and aborted the process of dynastic renewal.

The conflict left China in shambles. Many provinces had been devastated, and 20 million Chinese

Interactive Map

had been killed. An American missionary described the destruction: "Ruined cities, desolated towns and heaps of rubble still mark their path. The hum of busy populations had ceased and weeds and jungle cover the land."[7] The Qing were now deeper in debt to the West and compelled to adopt even more conciliatory attitudes.

Economic Change and Emigration

China's encounters with the West generated several economic changes. The extension of Western businesses into the interior stimulated the growth of the Chinese merchant class and small-scale Chinese-owned industries, such as match factories and flour mills. The Chinese merchants, however, disliked Western economic domination and the Qing government, which offered little resistance to Western imperialism. Gradually, a new working class, including women, labored in mines, factories, railways, and docks. The gulf between peasants in the interior and the merchants and workers in the coastal cities was vast.

China Under Western Control

The unequal treaties enabled Western economic penetration into China, increasing the incorporation of China

Map 23.1
Conflicts in Qing China, 1839–1870

During the mid-1800s, Qing China experienced repeated unrest, including several major rebellions. The largest and most destructive, the Taiping Rebellion, engulfed a large part of southern and central China between 1850 and 1864.

© Cengage Learning

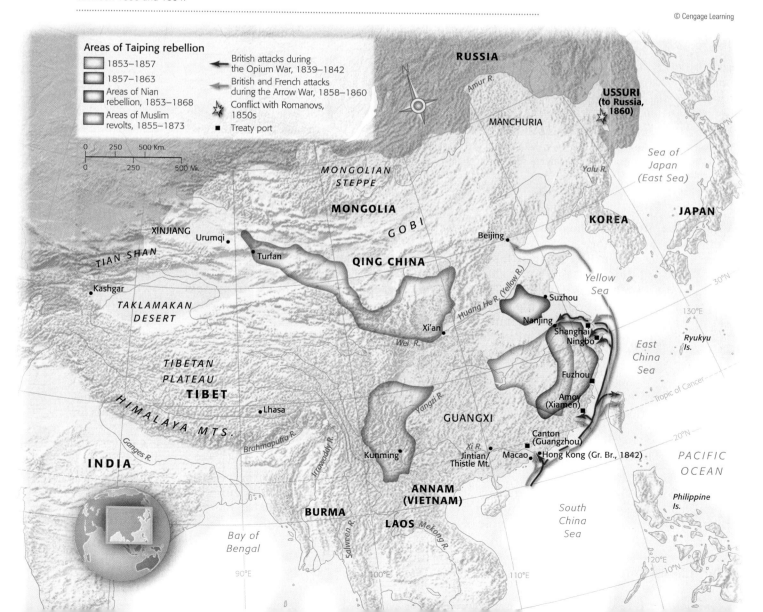

Rattan Factory in Guangzhou This photo, taken around 1875, shows Chinese men and women workers, mostly of peasant background, in a factory making rattan, along with the factory's European owners.

into a world economy dominated by the West. Westerners often ran Qing government agencies, banks, railroads, factories, and mines and guarded them with Western police. By 1920, foreign companies controlled most of China's iron ore, coal, railroads, and steamships, and Western businessmen became inspired by the notion of the vast China market. As happened in Southeast Asia, imported British textiles frequently displaced Chinese women from textile production, which peasant women had done for centuries to supplement family incomes. The Qing, already deeply in debt to Western governments and banks, had little money left for building China's economic institutions.

The Coolie Trade

Deteriorating economic, social, and political conditions in hard-hit coastal provinces, combined with natural disasters, prompted millions of Chinese to emigrate between the 1840s and 1920s, usually to places where Western colonialism and capitalism were opening new economic opportunities (see Chapters 20 and 22). The Chinese who emigrated formed the basis for local middle-class Chinese business communities. The majority left China as part of the notorious "coolie trade," a labor system known as such because Westerners called the emigrant workers, whether Chinese or Indian, "coolies," a derogatory term. Under this system, desperate Chinese, usually peasants, became indentured workers in faraway places, signing contracts that required them to labor for years on plantations, in mines, or on railroad lines to repay their passage. They endured discrimination and harsh working conditions in alien lands.

Chinese had migrated to Southeast Asia for centuries, but the increased emigration now greatly enlarged the Chinese diaspora to a global scale. The societies where Chinese settled, especially in Southeast Asia, became more closely connected to China through economic and social networks than

ever before. Chinese emigrants often returned to their native villages with wealth earned abroad, but others never earned enough money to return to China as they originally hoped. Others established small businesses and settled permanently abroad. The emigrants and their descendants, while often sustaining Chinese culture and language, also mixed Chinese and local customs. Today some 30 million people of Chinese ancestry live outside of China, the large majority of them in Southeast Asia.

LO² From Imperial to Republican China

The rebellions, government stagnation, poverty, and growing Western demands brought about a crisis for the Qing. Some Chinese still concluded that China should reaffirm its traditional ways and reject the West, but others increasingly recognized the need to absorb Western technologies and progress. As challenges mounted and China lost a war with Japan, some organized revolutionary movements. In the early 1900s, revolutionaries successfully overthrew the imperial system to form a republic, but these developments did not solve China's problems.

Pressures on Late Qing China

China's educated elite divided over how much China should modernize its society: conservatives argued against borrowing Western models, whereas liberals wanted moderate reforms. The conservatives, who dominated the bureaucracy, advised that China hold fast to traditions, protecting itself with Confucian moral conduct. Believing China could learn nothing from Westerners, they opposed railroads, underground mines, and other innovations, because these disrupted the harmony between humanity and nature, disturbed the graves of the ancestors, and put boatmen and cart drivers out of work. One conservative wrote that it was "better to

> "Liberals, believing China had to adopt certain Western ideas to survive, sponsored impressive government innovations."

> 66 Foreign pressures also contributed to China's decline as Chinese leaders developed a siege mentality in the face of Western threats. 99

see the nation die than its way of life change."[8] Conservatives were convinced that new technologies undermined social, economic, and even political values.

Liberals, believing China had to adopt certain Western ideas to survive, sponsored impressive government innovations. They streamlined central and regional governments, set up a foreign ministry, formed a college to train diplomats, established industries, and sent some students to schools in the West. Liberals also sought to modernize military forces, building arsenals and shipyards. By 1894, China had a better-trained army and sixty-five warships. Few liberals, however, wanted radical transformation: as one noted, "China should acquire the West's superiority in arms and machinery, but retain China's superiority in Confucian virtue."[9] Perhaps naively, liberals believed they could adopt Western tools while rejecting Western ideas.

The reforms failed to save the Qing, because the technological innovations themselves generated new problems. Newly built warships and railroads then needed coal to make steam to power them, which meant they needed improved coal-mining technology. Technical expertise was in short supply, and the Confucian social order was disrupted. The innovations were also expensive, further complicating the economic problems of a Chinese government that was forced to pay war reparations and to finance a growing debt to Western nations and banks. The problems became worse as China's poorly led, bureaucratic, and overly conservative government failed to make necessary changes. From 1861 to 1908, the imperial government was dominated by the Empress Dowager Ci Xi (zoo shee) (1835–1908), a concubine of the old emperor; on the emperor's death, Ci Xi had become the regent of the child emperor who replaced him. Forceful and intelligent, she was also covetous and irresponsible, squandering military funds to construct the magnificent Summer Palace, just outside Beijing, for her imperial retreat. Some historians identify the ineptitude of Manchu leaders such as Ci Xi as a major factor in China's failure to modernize.

Foreign Pressures on Late Qing China

Foreign pressures also contributed to China's decline as Chinese leaders developed a siege mentality in the face of Western threats. Some foreign powers dominated particular regions as spheres of influence, such as Britain in Guangdong and Germany in Shandong, acquiring resources, establishing enterprises, and manipulating local governments. The United States, Britain, France, and Germany exercised their power over China through gunboat diplomacy, the use of superior firepower to impose a country's will on local populations and governments. The term comes from the use of Western gunboats to patrol some of China's rivers and seacoasts in the late 1800s and early 1900s, interceding to protect Western businessmen, missionaries, and diplomats whose activities generated Chinese hostility. Sovereign Chinese rights and the people's outrage at foreign intrusion counted for little. But gunboats were only part of the story: Americans also promoted free trade, generously funded Christian missionaries, and donated to humanitarian causes such as flood relief and orphanages.

Despite the limits on its autonomy, China never became a full Western colony, such as India or Vietnam, perhaps because too many foreign powers were involved. The United States, which had become one of the most powerful and prosperous Western nations in the late 1800s, discouraged full colonization by promoting what it termed an "open door" policy that allowed equal access by all of the foreign powers to China's vast markets and resources. The open door enabled the Western nations and, eventually, Japan to avoid conflict among themselves and to acquire the economic fruits of empire without the high costs of conquering and governing China.

Chinese Study Maxim Gun After the Taiping Rebellion, the Qing emperor sent two Chinese mandarins to England to examine and purchase new weapons. In this photo, they examine a Maxim gun, one of the first machine guns that gave Western nations a great military advantage.

Late Qing Reforms and Wars

Between 1890 and 1916, the growing foreign challenge now included Japan, which was rapidly industrializing. In search of resources and markets to exploit, in the 1890s, Japan began intervening in Korea, long a vassal state of China. The Koreans asked China for assistance, and the resulting Sino-Japanese War (1894–1895) ended in a humiliating defeat for China. The Qing were forced to pay an indemnity and to recognize Korean independence, and in 1910, Korea became a Japanese colony. Other holdings such as Taiwan were also lost. The defeat by Japan proved a blow to Chinese pride and to the credibility of the Qing rulers.

These crises brought a group of progressive reformers to the attention of the young Manchu emperor, Guangxu, and, in 1898, under their influence, he called for dramatic changes, later known as the 100 Days of Reform, which included a crash program of economic modernization.

The Boxer Rebellion

But the Empress Dowager Xi Ci and her conservative allies blocked the proposals, arrested the reformers, and placed the emperor under house arrest. The ensuing tensions led to the Boxer Rebellion, a popular movement in 1900 that aimed at driving the foreigners out of China, but that resulted in an even stronger Western presence. The Qing gave strong backing to the Boxers ("Righteous Harmony Fists"), an anti-Western, anti-Christian secret society comprising mostly poor peasants. The Boxers attacked foreigners in north China, occupied Beijing, and besieged the foreign embassies. The Qing declared war on all of the foreign powers with which it had been forced to sign unequal treaties. In response, the British, Americans, French, and other powers put aside their differences and organized an international force that routed the Boxers, occupied Beijing, and forced the Qing to pay another huge indemnity and to permit foreign military forces to stay in China. The Russians used the rebellion as an excuse to occupy Manchuria.

The string of defeats generated final frantic efforts at reform and modernization, setting the stage for more dramatic transitions. Fearing China might soon be divided into colonies, the chastened Manchus now began more serious reform efforts,

> "The Boxers attacked foreigners in north China, occupied Beijing, and besieged the foreign embassies."

looking to Japan for models. The Qing abolished the 2,000-year-old Confucian examination system, set up modern, Western-style schools, and sent 10,000 students to Japan. The Qing also formed new government departments, allocated more money to the military, and strengthened provincial and local governments.

Liang Qichao and Liberal Reform

Liberals who had criticized the Qing reformers for going too slowly now became more influential. Many reformers had read and even translated European literature and scholarship, including that of Enlightenment writers, and were deeply impressed by Japan's modernization in the later 1800s. The leading liberal reformer, Liang Qichao (1871–1929), represented change within tradition. A scholar and journalist, Liang promoted a modernization that blended Confucian values and Western learning. He also believed China should industrialize, form a constitutional government, and focus on the idea of nation instead of culture.

Chinese Nationalism and Revolutionary Movements

For some Chinese inspired by nationalism, most importantly Sun Zhong Shan, better known as Sun Yat-Sen (soon yot-SEN), the fiasco of the Boxer Rebellion showed the futility of trying to change China by reform from above and prompted them to organize a revolution from below that could sweep the Manchus from power. Inspired by the Taipings, Meiji Japan (see next section), and the West, Sun Yat-Sen (1866–1925) mixed tradition and modernity; he did not come from an upper-class mandarin background and had no commitment to the traditional system. Convinced that the Qing system was hopeless, Sun decided to devote his life to politics and became the chief architect of the Chinese Revolution.

 Experience nationalism and imperialism through the eyes of either a Chinese citizen or a British official in the early to mid-1800s in this interactive simulation.

In 1895, Sun founded an anti-Manchu secret society that was dedicated to replacing the imperial system with a Western-style republic, and branches were set up in China, Japan, and Hawaii (see Witness to the Past: Planning a Revolutionary New China). Facing arrest in China for treason, Sun traveled extensively, recruiting support among Chinese merchants in Southeast Asia and North America, Chinese businessmen in the treaty ports, Chinese students in Japan, and sympathetic military officers. Sun and his followers thought of themselves as nationalists, more interested in China as a nation than as a culture. The cause of dramatic change also attracted feminists such as Qin Jin (Chin Chin) (1877–1907), who left her arranged marriage for study in Japan and then started a women's magazine and pursued political activity, expressing the hope that one day China would see free women "blooming like fields of flowers."[10] Later she was executed as a revolutionary.

Sun developed his program into what he termed the "Three Principles of the People." The first principle, nationalism, involved overthrowing the Manchus, restoring ethnic Chinese to power, and reclaiming China's historical greatness. For his second principle, he favored republicanism, an elected representative government rather than the constitutional monarchy sought by the liberal reformers. The third principle, people's livelihood, envisioned an equitable economic status for all. Eventually the day would come, he hoped, when the Chinese could look over their shoulder and find the West lagging far behind.

Revolution: Launching the Republican Era

Sun was traveling in the United States raising money for his cause when, on October 10, 1911, some Chinese influenced by Sun's ideas began the uprising. Soldiers in the Yangzi River city of Wuhan (woo-hahn) in central China mutinied against the Qing government and were soon joined by sympathizers in other cities. Within two months, the revolutionary soldiers controlled provinces in central and southern China. As the authority of the Qing government quickly crumbled outside their power base in the north, Sun returned to China for the first time in sixteen years. From their capital in Beijing, the Manchus hesitated, then asked an ambitious general, Yuan Shikai (yoo-AHN shee-KAI) (1859–1916), to deal with the revolutionaries. In control of a large army and in touch with both sides, Yuan decided to replace the dynasty with his own rule, playing the Manchus off against the revolutionaries.

The Guomindang and the End of the Qing Dynasty

The revolution had wide popular support, because many Chinese hated the Manchus. Sun's nationalist message spread rapidly, as he now reorganized his anti-Manchu secret society into a political party, the Guomindang (gwo-min-dong) (Chinese Nationalist Party), which gathered varied nationalists and liberal reformers into the fold. However, although widely respected, Sun was not a forceful leader, and the revolutionaries could agree only on opposing the Manchus.

Two centers of power now existed. General Yuan Shikai held the dominant position in the north and considerable influence over the Qing leaders in Beijing. The revolutionaries controlled the Yangzi Valley and parts of south China, and they made plans to establish a provisional republican government. Sun sought a compromise to save China from civil war, offering to make Yuan president of the republic if Yuan arranged for the abdication of the five-year-old Qing emperor. Yuan agreed, and in February 1912 the Qing dynasty, and with it the 2,000-year-old imperial system, was ended. In March 1912, a republic was established in Nanjing, on the Yangzi River in east-central China. In a move symbolizing a change of direction for China, the new government adopted the Western calendar. But Sun had underestimated Yuan's ambitions. While a modernizer, Yuan hoped to restore an autocratic system with himself at the top. He soon moved the capital back to Beijing in the north.

The new republic began with some signs of liberal accomplishment, including a constitution written by Sun that provided for a two-chamber parliament and a president. In early 1913, a restricted electorate chose a national assembly and provincial assemblies in the first and most open general election in China's long history. Sun's Guomindang, identified with nationalist revolution, won a majority of seats but lacked a consensus about the directions of change. A new women's suffrage movement, influenced by its counterparts in Europe, pressed for equal rights.

Yuan Shikai and the Chinese Civil War

In part because of Yuan Shikai's ambitions, however, the republican system failed to bring stability and liberty, dashing the hopes of Sun and his colleagues. Convinced that China needed a strong leader and government, Yuan considered Sun and the Guomindang formidable obstacles. He had Guomindang leaders assassinated, bought off, or, in the case of Sun, forced into exile. Yuan soon outlawed the Guomindang, suspended parliament, and banned the women's suffrage movement. He enjoyed the support of much of the army, the imperial bureaucracy, and the foreign powers, who preferred a strongman to the democratic uncertainties of Sun. Sun and his closest followers moved to Japan, embittered and

Planning a Revolutionary New China

In 1905, various radical Chinese groups met in Japan and merged into one revolutionary organization, the Tongmen Hui (Chinese Alliance Association), led by Sun Yat-Sen, then based in Tokyo. Most of the members were drawn from among the 10,000 Chinese students enrolled in Japanese universities. Unhappy with the Qing government and impressed by modernizing Japan, they sought to change China through revolution. In their founding proclamation, which was influenced by Western thought, they set out their agenda, visionary but vague, for a three-stage passage from military to constitutional government and a more equitable society.

Since the beginning of China as a nation, we Chinese have governed our own country despite occasional interruptions. When China was occasionally occupied by a foreign race, our ancestors could always . . . drive these foreigners out . . . and preserve China for future generations. . . . There is a difference, however, between our revolution and the revolutions of our ancestors. The purpose of past revolutions . . . was to restore China to the Chinese, and nothing else. We, on the other hand, strive not only to expel the ruling aliens [Manchus] . . . but also to change basically the political and economic structure of our country. . . . The revolutions of yesterday were revolutions by and for the heroes; our revolution, on the other hand, is a revolution by and for the people . . . everyone who believes in the principles of liberty, equality, and fraternity has an obligation to participate in it. . . .

At this juncture we wish to express candidly and fully how to make our revolution today and how to govern the country tomorrow.

1. Expulsion of the Manchus from China. . . . We shall quickly overthrow the Manchu government so as to restore the sovereignty of China to the Chinese.

2. Restoration of China to the Chinese. China belongs to the Chinese who have the right to govern themselves. . . .

3. Establishment of a Republic. Since one of the principles of our revolution is equality, we intend to establish a republic . . . all citizens will have the right to participate in the government, the president of the republic will be elected by the people, and the parliament will have deputies elected by and responsible to their respective constituencies. . . .

4. Equalization of Land Ownership. The social and economic structure of China must be so reconstructed that the fruits of labor will be shared by all Chinese on an equal basis. . . .

To attain the four goals . . ., we propose a procedure of three stages. The first . . . is that of military rule . . . [in which] the Military Government, in cooperation with the people, will eradicate all the abuses of the past; with the arrival of the second stage the Military Government will hand over local administration to the people while reserving for itself the right of jurisdiction over all matters that concern the nation as a whole; during the . . . final stage the Military Government will cease to exist and all governmental power will be invested in organs as prescribed in a national constitution. This orderly procedure is necessary because our people need time to acquaint themselves with the idea of liberty and equality . . ., the basis on which the republic of China rests. . . . On . . . restoring China to her own people, we urge everyone to step forward and to do the best he can. . . . Whatever our station in society is, rich or poor, we are all equal in our determination to safeguard the security of China as a nation and to preserve the Chinese people.

Thinking About the Reading

1. How does the proclamation use Western revolutionary and nationalist ideas?
2. How will revolution build a new China?

Source: Pei-Kai Cheng and Michael Lestz with Jonathan D. Spence, eds., *The Search for Modern China: A Documentary Collection* (New York: W.W. Norton, 1999), pp. 202–206.

demoralized, as Yuan became increasingly autocratic and announced plans to found a new dynasty.

Yuan's plans, however, were put on hold by current problems in China, including constant pressure from foreign powers, the secession of regions occupied largely by non-Chinese, and bankruptcy. Yuan was forced to borrow heavily from foreign governments to keep the country afloat. Tibet and Mongolia expelled their Chinese administrations. World War I also posed a challenge. Although China remained neutral, Japan, allied with Britain, occupied the German sphere of influence in the Shandong peninsula on China's east coast. Japan then presented Yuan with 21 Demands, including control of Shandong, more rights in Manchuria, and the appointment of Japanese advisers to the Chinese government, which infuriated the Chinese people. His imperial restoration plans aborted, a humiliated Yuan died in 1916, and China fell into the abyss of prolonged Civil War. Yuan's years in power had wrecked the republican institutions, and his submission to Japan's 21 Demands suggested that China was even weaker than before.

> "Like China, Japan faced foreign pressures, but Japan successfully met the challenge of the Western intrusion, while China gradually lost some of its autonomy."

LO³ Japan and Korea Under Challenge

In the second half of the nineteenth century, Japan met the Western challenge more successfully than China, rapidly transforming itself into a powerful industrialized nation. Although it had serious internal problems, Japan also possessed significant strengths that allowed it to achieve success. The shoguns—military dictators from the Tokugawa family ruling in the name of the emperor—had governed Japan since 1600 and had kept a tight hold on Japanese society. When the first Western ships arrived, the Japanese and Koreans, largely shut off by policies of seclusion from the outside world, were just as far behind the West in military and industrial technology as China, India, and other Asian societies had been. Their choices, however, caused different historical outcomes.

Tokugawa Japan and Qing China

Like China, Japan faced foreign pressures, but Japan successfully met the challenge of the Western intrusion, while China gradually lost some of its autonomy. The differences between these two ancient neighbors, historians argue, help explain the different outcomes. Geography played a role. Japan, being compact and linguistically homogeneous, had a strong sense of national unity and of loyalty to the emperor as a national symbol, whereas China's vastness created difficulties in communications and linguistically divided the country. In China, sentiments of loyalty were restricted largely to the family, and the Chinese were slow to assimilate new ideas, whereas Japan had a long tradition of readily borrowing from outside. As a result, Japanese leaders could more easily import and adopt new ideas, technologies, and institutions.

The two neighbors also differed in the influence of their merchants and in their political and military systems. The Japanese merchant class was assertive and was rapidly expanding its scope and power, whereas in China the commercial energies had reached their height centuries earlier, only to be contained and restricted by the government. Furthermore, in contrast to China's centralized empire, the Japanese government was pluralistic; the Tokugawa shogun, based in Edo (today's Tokyo), had to balance the interests of the various daimyo, the influential leaders of regional

CHRONOLOGY

Japan and Korea, 1750–1914

1392–1910	Yi dynasty in Korea
1600–1867	Tokugawa Shogunate
1853	Opening of Japan by Perry
1854	Treaty of Kanagawa
1867–1868	Meiji Restoration
1894–1895	Sino-Japanese War
1904–1905	Russo-Japanese War
1910	Japanese colonization of Korea and Taiwan

landowning families, while keeping the Kyoto-based emperor powerless. The Japanese military leaders, the samurai, still held a respected position in Japanese society. Never having been successfully invaded, the Japanese felt vulnerable when they encountered the well-armed Westerners. They prized political independence far more than cultural purity, while the Chinese were used to foreign rule and prized their Confucian traditions more than political independence. Thus Japanese leaders were far more sensitive to the Western threat than were the Chinese elite.

Late Tokugawa Advantages and Challenges

Japan also benefited from the energy and openness to new ideas of late Tokugawa society. Its many schools resulted in high literacy rates, and several schools specialized in so-called Dutch learning acquired from Dutch traders, including sciences such as medicine, physics, and chemistry. Whatever their status and occupation, the Japanese demonstrated a pattern of hard work, thrift, saving, and cooperation—attributes that lent themselves to modernization.

 The Floating World of Ukiyo-e: Shadow, Dreams, and Substance (*http://www.loc.gov/exhibits/ukiyo-e/*). Japanese prints at the Library of Congress.

Culture in Tokugawa Japan

Tokugawa Japan also enjoyed a thriving urban and artistic life. Cities such as Edo and Osaka, already among the world's largest, offered a flourishing commerce and diverse entertainments. Tokugawa arts produced creations that achieved renown worldwide, such as ceramics, jewelry, furniture, painting, and woodblock prints. Ando Hiroshige (1797–1858) concentrated on Tokyo scenes and landscapes emphasizing nature. The treatment of atmosphere and light in Japanese color prints influenced European impressionist painters of the later 1800s, such as Vincent Van Gogh, who admitted that he strove to emulate Japanese landscape painting.

Despite the richness of their society's culture, by the early 1800s, some Japanese sensed internal decay. The Tokugawa were blamed for the nation's growing domestic problems, including inflation, increasing taxes, and social disorder. In addition, there was the gradual impoverishment of the samurai, whose salaries had been cut over the years, and many ordinary Japanese experienced widespread famine and starvation in the 1830s. The growing social tensions and resentments reached a breaking point, fostering urban riots, peasant revolts, and various plots to depose the Tokugawa shogun.

Addressing the Western Threat

While worried about domestic unrest, Japanese officials were more concerned about the growing Western presence in the region, which they correctly perceived would impact Japan. They knew that Russians had been active in Siberia and the North Pacific since the 1700s and that British ships had sailed along Japan's coast. In 1825, the shogun ordered that whenever a foreign ship was sighted approaching the coast, the samurai should fire on it and drive it away. After China's defeat in the Opium War, Japan's shocked leaders encouraged the samurai to develop new, more effective weapons and contemplated starting a navy. The Japanese considered the Westerners to be money-grasping barbarians who did not understand the proper rules of social behavior and who would contaminate the national spirit. As the samurai vowed to fight to the death to resist Western invasion, this feeling of nationalism grew, putting pressure on the shogun to implement reforms to strengthen the country. At the national level, leaders broke up merchant monopolies, established a bureau to translate Western books, and reduced the number of government officials to save money, but these reforms largely failed to energize the system. Some provincial governments, especially in the southwest, were more aggressive in their efforts to modernize. Samurai in several of these domains learned how to cast better guns and to produce iron suitable for making modern cannon, and one even constructed an electric steam engine in the 1850s.

 Read about Ando Hiroshige, the Japanese artist who gained a worldwide reputation for his work that reflected a distinctly Japanese vision of landscape and urban life.

> 66 Despite the richness of their society's culture, by the early 1800s, some Japanese sensed internal decay. 99

The Opening of Japan and Political Crisis

The need for change was made urgent by external forces that arose in the 1850s when the Americans directly challenged Japan's exclusion policy. In 1853, a fleet of eleven U.S. warships commanded by Commodore Matthew Perry sailed into Tokyo Bay and delivered a letter to the shogun from the U.S. president, Millard Fillmore, demanding that the Japanese sign a treaty opening the country or face war when Perry returned the following year. Their three steamships shocked the Japanese with their ability to move against the wind and tide. The shogun, remembering the Opium War, granted Perry's demands in the Treaty of Kanagawa (1854) and then accepted the blame for the nation's humiliation. The treaty opened two ports to U.S. trade and allowed for the stationing of a U.S. consul. By 1856, American diplomats demanded a stronger commercial treaty, the opening of more ports, extraterritoriality, and the admission of Christian missionaries. The shogun reluctantly agreed; he soon signed similar treaties with the Dutch, British, French, and Russians.

> "From ancient times, the peoples of the mountainous Korean peninsula had been shaped by their location between powerful China and Japan."

reforms. The Japanese, who had already become interested in Western science and technology, however, saw these government innovations as too little and too late. Across Japan the Tokugawa shogun was now widely perceived as weak. The shogun's strategy of avoiding confrontation led a respected poet to complain angrily: "You, whose ancestors in the mighty days, Roared at the skies and swept the earth, Stand now helpless to drive off wrangling foreigners—How empty your title, 'Queller of the Barbarians.'"[11] Furthermore, the Western powers continually made new demands. By the 1860s, the Japanese seemed to be repeating the experience of China, gradually losing control of their political and economic future.

Challenges to the Korean Kingdom

Although it was faced with growing problems in this era, Korea had chosen relative isolation, similar to Tokugawa Japan. From ancient times, the peoples of the mountainous Korean peninsula had been shaped by their location between powerful China and Japan. Over the centuries, Koreans had mixed China's religions, political structure, and writing system with their own customs but maintained a strong national identity and political independence. Like China, Korea became a unified state presided over by a series of family dynasties ruling with a Confucian ideology.

The last of the Korean dynasties, the Yi (yee) (1392–1910), ruled the state they called Choson (choh-SAN) for more than five centuries, favoring powerful landlord families. By officially closing off Korea from the outside world after the Manchus invaded and pillaged the capital in the early 1600s, the Yi earned Choson the label of "the Hermit Kingdom." However, as in Tokugawa Japan, seclusion from the outside world was not absolute. Korea still traded with China. Better irrigation technologies and new strains of rice from China increased agricultural productivity. Korean scholars also visited China, and on their return some wrote books favorably contrasting Chinese society with what they considered Korea's overly rigid and inequitable social system. A few Koreans met Westerners in China and found their ideas and technologies to be of interest. Several strong kings in the 1700s fostered a renewed culture

Western Incursion

Like China, Japan experienced a forcible intrusion from the West that held the seeds of potential colonization. Although the changes still limited the Westerners' movement in Japan, most Japanese leaders saw that Japan was the loser in these dealings. Western merchants soon arrived, flooding the nation with cheap industrial goods to create a market and destroy native industries, as they had done earlier in China and India. International settlements restricted to foreigners were established in Japan's major port cities. Westerners enjoyed ever-increasing economic and legal privileges, and escalating domestic disunity held the potential for enhancing Western power. Western encroachment provoked a crisis for the Tokugawa government and a national debate about whether Japan should accommodate Westerners more or use military force to expel the intruders. One such faction proclaimed, "Revere the Emperor, Expel the Barbarians."

The Failure of the Shogunate

Shaken by the Western presence, the Tokugawa government launched efforts at modernization. It established a shipbuilding industry, promoted manufacturing, and promoted western education

of learning; some thinkers, to promote justice, examined social conditions by studying the peasants.

However, by the early 1800s, Choson, like Qing China and Tokugawa Japan, began to succumb to stress. As in Japan, the rigid social structure crumbled as the economy grew. Korea's population doubled to some 9 million between 1669 and 1800, increasing pressure on the land. With Buddhism losing influence, some Koreans turned to Christianity. Although officially prohibited, a few French and Chinese Christian missionaries nevertheless illegally entered Korea and spread their message. During the 1800s, Korea also experienced recurrent famines and increased political instability, including peasant uprisings. The Choson government blamed and persecuted Christians and missionaries for causing social turmoil.

The challenges to Korea caused some Koreans to consider their options. As in China and Japan, Korean intellectuals debated the value of Western learning, and some pushed for reforms of the traditional political and social system. With the Yi refusing direct commercial negotiations with the West, Korean military forces drove away French and American ships seeking to open Korea to Western trade, and in 1871, they repulsed a U.S. naval force. The Yi also worried about Russian expansion to the north, in eastern Siberia. By the later 1800s, Korea seemed in need of rejuvenation.

LO⁴ The Remaking of Japan and Korea

The ultimate Japanese response to Western intrusion was radically different from China's, allowing Japan to avoid colonialism and become the only non-Western nation to successfully industrialize and achieve Western standards of living before World War II. This transition owed much to a revolution that ended Tokugawa rule in 1868 and created a new government that fostered dramatic reforms. By the early 1900s, a powerful Japan had increased its influence in the wider world. Meanwhile, Korea was forced to abandon several centuries of isolation and eventually became a Japanese colony.

Tokugawa Defeat and the Meiji Restoration

By the 1860s, the deteriorating situation in Japan led to a revolution against the Tokugawa shogu-

nate, known as the Meiji Restoration (1867–1868), because it was carried out in the name of the emperor, whose reign name was Meiji (MAY-gee). The anti-Tokugawa leaders, united mostly by their hatred of the status quo, had varied goals and perspectives. Some were avid Westernizers, others extreme nationalists. Most were ambitious outsiders of samurai background who were alienated from the Tokugawa power structure. Although they came from privileged families, they were unafraid to ally with commoners, especially merchants, and generally were pragmatic men who understood that protecting Japan from foreign domination required radical change.

Meiji Restoration
A revolution against the Tokugawa shogunate in Japan in 1867–1868, carried out in the name of the Meiji emperor; led to the successful modernization of Japan.

Demise of the Tokugawa Shogunate

As public respect for the shogun faded, Japanese dissidents turned to the relatively powerless Meiji emperor as an alternative. While the shoguns had exercised power from Edo, the imperial family had lived in Kyoto two hundred miles to the south. In 1868, anti-Tokugawa leaders, backed by military force, seized the imperial palace in Kyoto and convinced the emperor to dismiss the shogun and decree the restoration of his own rule. The decree ousted the Tokugawa family from their land and positions, opened the government to men of talent, appointed the rebels as advisers to the emperor, and announced that "all matters shall be decided by public discussion" and "the evil customs of the past shall be broken off. Knowledge shall be sought throughout the world."¹² The Tokugawa family and their supporters fought back, sparking a bitter one-year civil war that cost many lives. Ultimately, however, the rebel forces prevailed and crushed all armed resistance.

> 66 As public respect for the shogun faded, Japanese dissidents turned to the relatively powerless Meiji emperor as an alternative. 99

Meiji Reforms

The Meiji regime took shape early, launching a crash program of modernization in just thirty years. Among the major changes introduced by the new leaders, Japan joined the world community and agreed to honor all treaties. The imperial residence was moved from Kyoto to Tokyo

> "The new political system had democratic trappings, but reformers were divided on how much democracy to foster."

(formerly Edo), a much larger and more dynamic city. Perceiving change as a necessary evil, the Meiji leaders pragmatically sought ways to achieve national unity, wealth, defense, and equality with the West. Meiji reformers combined Western models with Japanese traditions to build a distinctive form of industrial society that diffused the threat of colonialism. Despite its flaws, the system introduced by the Meiji proved productive for Japan.

 Explore Japan through the eyes of a young man during the Meiji Restoration in this interactive simulation.

Meiji leaders needed to establish an effective governmental structure and secure the loyalty of the population. One of their first acts was to form a State Council to advise and control the emperor. They then recruited both samurais and commoners into the new bureaucracy while convincing the regional daimyo families to give up control of their land, and the peasants living on it, in exchange for appointment as regional governors with guaranteed salaries. Freeing the peasants made it easier for them to move to cities in search of work, which had been illegal under the Tokugawa. The government employed thousands of Western advisers and workers who gave advice but were required to train Japanese assistants to replace them when their contracts expired. Because it financed these programs through tax revenues, Meiji Japan did not need foreign loans, hence avoiding the debt trap that ensnared most Latin American and Middle Eastern societies as well as China.

The new political system had democratic trappings, but reformers were divided on how much democracy to foster. The Japanese had no tradition of political freedom and had to invent a new word for the concept. In 1889, the Meiji leaders wrote the first constitution in Japanese history and formed a constitutional monarchy symbolically headed by the emperor. The constitution introduced an independent judiciary and a two-house parliament that was elected by the 450,000 men who were tax-paying property holders. Parliament chose members for the cabinet, which made policy and supervised the government apparatus, and the first political parties were formed in the 1880s.

"Rich Country, Strong Army"

Using the slogan "rich country, strong army," the government stressed industrial development and enhanced communications by building railroads and telegraphs. Anxious about Western imperialism in Asia, the Japanese concluded that military power was necessary to assert Japanese interests, so to build up the armed forces, including a modern navy, Meiji leaders drafted commoners as soldiers, once a profession limited to samurai. By breaking down the former distinction between samurai, merchant, and peasant, the military draft promoted social leveling, literacy, and nationalism among the peasants who joined. Compared with China, the Meiji leaders enjoyed more freedom to reshape and strengthen their nation. The various Western powers, largely preoccupied elsewhere, saw Japan mainly as a potential ally against each other.

State Capitalism: A New Economic Model

Meiji policies fostered a modern economy and society. In building an economic foundation, the Japanese created a new model of political economy, state capitalism, an economic system in which the state takes a leading role in supporting business and industrial enterprises and then regulates and closely monitors the economy once it is privatized. An example was Mitsui (MIT-soo-ee), a family-owned company whose business interests dated back to Tokugawa times. The most powerful corporations, the zaibatsu, dominated the national economy and maintained especially close ties to the government. They believed economic independence from the West to be patriotic. State capitalism and the growth of industry often favored city people over the rural peasantry; capital for industrialization was obtained by squeezing the peasants through the land tax. In exchange, however, the government spurred agricultural productivity by providing new seeds, improving land use, and supplying better irrigation.

First Commercial Bank in Edo During the Meiji era, the banking industry grew. This bank, built in Western style in Edo, was owned by the Mitsui family, which also owned large stores, breweries, factories, coal mines, and other enterprises. Mitsui was one of the major business conglomerates in Japan, with branches all over Asia.

The new economic structure perpetuated the traditional group orientation and social controls of Japanese society. Most Japanese identified closely with the company that employed them, and the economy flourished by exploiting Japanese workers. The government kept wages deliberately low so that scarce capital could be devoted to building factories, shipyards, and railroads. Ultimately, the sacrifices paid off by creating new jobs and fostering national wealth, but life in the Meiji era was not easy for most Japanese. For example, as in the United States and Europe, the textile mills mainly employed women, half of them below the age of twenty and 15 percent younger than fourteen, chiefly recruited from rural villages. The young factory women, paid half the salary of male workers, worked twelve-hour shifts, interrupted only by one half-hour meal break.

Mill workers experienced high death, physical abuse, and diseases such as tuberculosis caused by crowded working conditions.

Social Reform in Meiji Japan

Meiji reforms also fostered social change by attacking the rigid Tokugawa class system. New laws allowed people, regardless of background, to change occupations and move freely. They also stripped the samurai of their monopoly on military occupations, leading many to become lawyers, teachers, or journalists—and others to become perennial political dissenters. To involve Japanese of all backgrounds in modernization, the regime constructed a universal school system based on those in European nations such as Germany and paid for by both taxes and tuition. By 1900, Japan was training its own scientists, engineers, and technicians.

Meiji policies stimulated debate about the value of various social patterns. Some reformers blamed the traditional family, ruled firmly by senior men, for discouraging personal independence, but generally the Meiji sought to preserve gender roles. Confucian books popular in Japan claimed that the lifelong duty of women was obedience to men. Meiji policies promoted the idea of "Good Wife, Wise Mother" to strengthen families by having mothers stay at home with their children. But some women, such as activist Fukuda Hideko, rejected such models and argued that "virtually everything [for women] is coercive and oppressive, making it imperative that we women rise up and develop our own social movement."[13]

Westernization and Expansion

During the Meiji era, the Japanese became acquainted with Western philosophy, social theory, economic thought, literature, and fashions, all of which influenced Japanese society. The peak of Westernization came in the 1870s. In these years, the Japanese adopted the Western calendar, added European words to the Japanese language, became familiar with chairs and couches, began eating more meat, raised the Tokugawa ban on Christianity, shook hands rather than bowing, and often married in the Western style. Many Japanese equated all of this with progress.

Observers, foreign and Japanese, debated the impact of the Meiji reforms. Many Westerners were amazed at the dramatic transformation in Japan, but Japanese literature reflected the difficulty of life in a transitional era. In 1911, a Japanese novelist worried about a "nervous collapse" that would devastate the society as a result of the cultural confusion. By the later 1880s, the mania for Western fads had abated, and the Meiji leaders began to foster a synthesis of old and new. By the 1890s, there was a renewed emphasis on traditional values, including the ancient myths about the Japanese people arising from the gods and the divinity of the emperor. The Japanese were never slavish imitators of the West or alienated from their own traditions. In the Meiji view, a new culture combining East and West could be produced and taught to the people, just as had been done in earlier centuries with Korean and Chinese influences. The dramatic changes Japan experienced, however, created tensions within Japanese society and between Japan and other nations that ultimately fostered a more imperialistic foreign policy.

The Sino-Japanese and Russo-Japanese Wars

Eventually, Meiji Japan fought two wars (see Map 23.2). China and Japan battled each other in the Sino-Japanese War (1894–1895) over their competing influence in Korea, which Japan had long coveted for its fertile land but now also

 Interactive Map

viewed as a market for Japanese products. The war resulted in a smashing Japanese military victory and consequent dominance in Korea, as well as in the Chinese island of Taiwan, both of which the Japanese transformed into outright colonies in 1910. Impressed by Japanese military capabilities, Britain forged an alliance with Japan that endured through the Meiji era. Britain's rival, Russia, also had ambitions in Korea. Furthermore, Russia had acquired a foothold in resource-rich Manchuria, a nearby Chinese-controlled region Japan wanted to exploit. The rising tensions led to the Russo-Japanese War (1904–1905), during which the Japanese seized a Russian-held Manchurian port and then destroyed the Russian fleet sent out from Europe.

The Glory and End of Meiji Japan

The Japanese victory over Russia electrified the world and contributed to the great awakening of Asian nationalism. For the first time, a non-Western nation had defeated a major European power, giving hope to societies under Western domination. The triumph in the war further enhanced the pride of the Japanese people in their nation and confirmed that Japan had, in three decades, become a world power. Among the fruits of victory was the transfer to Japan of some Russian holdings in Manchuria and control of the southern half of Sakhalin island, off the Siberian coast.

The Meiji era, which came to an official end with the death of the Meiji emperor in 1916, had achieved stunning successes. Japan had secured national security and a position as a powerful regional power. The Meiji leaders had negotiated an end to the unequal treaties and had formed an alliance with the powerful British. Japan's wealth and influence were still less than that of the major industrial powers—the United States, Britain, France, and Germany—but Japan was now an industrial nation, on a par with countries such as Russia and Italy. With 50 million people, it prepared to play a bigger role in regional and world affairs. But as the country faced new challenges and setbacks in the next decades, many Japanese wisfully remembered the Meiji as a time of vitality, courage, and hope: "Snow is falling, Meiji recedes in the distance."

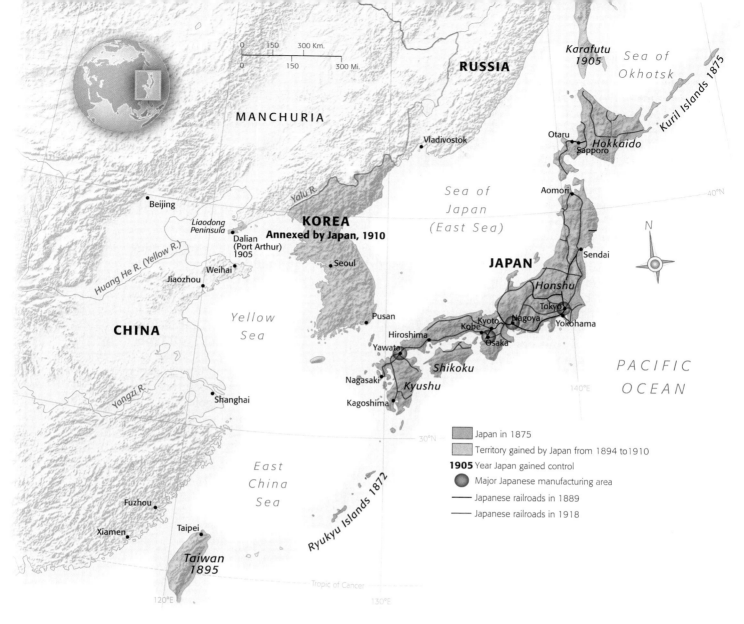

© Cengage Learning

Map 23.2
Japanese Modernization and Expansion, 1868–1913
Japan undertook a crash modernization in the later 1800s. By 1910, its military power had increased, and it had won a war with Russia and colonized Korea, Taiwan, and Sakhalin (then known as Karafutu).

Korean Transitions Under Japan

Rising Japanese power shaped modern Korea. This pattern began in 1876, when Meiji Japan, adopting the model used by the United States to open Japan, sent a naval expedition to Korea that forced the Yi government to open five ports and sign unequal treaties that gave Japan a strong role in Korea's economy. The growing Japanese influence in Korea compelled the Yi government to introduce reforms, such as toleration of Christianity, and sign trade agreements with Western nations. Many Korean peasants, impoverished by Japan's imperialist policies and drought, joined the Tonghak ("Eastern Learning"), a protest movement with an eclectic ideology not unlike the Taipings in China, that mixed Confucianism, Buddhism, Christianity, and hatred of Japan and the West. Spurred by famine, the movement grew into the nationwide Tonghak Rebellion against the Yi government in 1894. When Korea's longtime ally, China, sent in troops to help the Yi government repress the rebellion, China's rival, Japan, responded by also sending in a force and capturing the Korean capital, Seoul, holding the Yi royal family hostage to gain influence over the Korean government.

The desire of both China and Japan to capitalize on the Tonghak Rebellion led to the Sino-Japanese

War (1894–1895), which resulted in a humiliating Chinese withdrawal and a stronger presence on the part of the Japanese after they stamped out Korean resistance. Some 18,000 Koreans, mostly peasants who rallied to the Yi government, died in fighting the Japanese. Japan forcibly annexed Korea in 1910, transforming it from the "hermit kingdom" into a Japanese colony and ending the decrepit Yi dynasty. One resistance leader expressed the widespread Korean despair: "I was unable to repel our nation's enemies, or hold back our 4000 year long civilization from falling to the ground."[14]

Between 1910 and 1945, Korea was a heavily exploited, harshly ruled Japanese colony. It endured Japanese racism and brutal suppression of Korean nationalism and culture, although the Japanese also increased educational opportunities and built a modern economy. The Japanese seized Korean land for Japanese companies and restricted civil liberties. Nonetheless, Koreans continued to protest and resist. In 1919, the Japanese police brutally crushed peaceful demonstrations by men and women calling for independence, killing or injuring some 24,000 demonstrators and arresting 47,000. Resentment simmered as repressive measures, such as forcing students to speak only Japanese, increased. Koreans often looked for inspiration in Western ideas, including Christianity and Marxism. Many Koreans, however, rejected Western ideas, believing the best strategy was to strengthen Confucianism. There was no dominant nationalist thread.

Japanese relations with Koreans became even more exploitative during World War II. Korean men were conscripted as soldiers and workers, and young Korean women, termed by the Japanese "comfort women," were forced to serve as sex slaves for Japanese soldiers. Even today many Koreans have a deep antipathy for Japan as a result of colonial repression and exploitation.

LO⁵ Russia's Eurasian Empire

Between 1750 and 1914, Russia built a vast Eurasian empire stretching 3,200 miles from the Baltic Sea to the Bering Straits, in the process creating more intensive ties to Asian societies. The expansion continued through the 1800s, making Russia a hemispheric power controlling vast amounts of land. Located on the fringe of Europe, Central Asia, and the Middle East, Russia was influenced by all three regions. Russian society was characterized by autocratic governments, alternating periods of reform and reaction, a feudal-style rural system, and chronic discontent. During this era, Russia played an increasingly critical role in both Asian and European politics.

Europeanization and Czarist Despotism

Russians had long debated whether they belonged to the European tradition or had a unique heritage, and these debates were reflected in Russian politics. Influence from western Europe was particularly strong during the long reign of Catherine the Great (r. 1762–1796). Influenced by the Enlightenment, Catherine denounced slavery, hailed liberty, and patronized the arts and literature. She also presided over a golden age of opulence for the nobility, but Catherine's policies led to worsening social ills and imperialist expansion. Despite her liberal views, she could not encourage freedom among the common people, especially the disgruntled peasantry, because she needed support from the landed aristocracy. Instead, Catherine extended serfdom to Ukraine and denounced the French Revolution as irreligious and immoral. Continuing the expansionism of her predecessors, Catherine's energetic foreign policy added Poland and Finland to Russia's realm and annexed the Crimean peninsula in 1783, where Russia built a major naval base.

> **66** Located on the fringe of Europe, Central Asia, and the Middle East, Russia was influenced by all three regions. **99**

Russian History Index: The World Wide Web Virtual Library (*http://vlib.iue.it/ hist-russia/Index.html*). Useful links on Russian history.

To maintain power, the czars who followed Catherine, whether Westernizers or not, often relied on the brutal despotism common in Russian history. Czar Nicholas I (r. 1825–1855) feared alienating the aristocracy, suppressed the restless Poles, and formed a secret police force to harass, imprison, or eliminate opponents. Nicholas also expanded the empire further by invading Hungary and seeking dominance over the Ottomans to secure access for transport of Russia's grain exports through the Black Sea to the Mediterranean. He encouraged Slavic rebellion in the Balkans, which provoked Britain and France and led to the Crimean War of 1854. Some 250,000 soldiers on all sides died in the war. Armies of conscripted

Catherine the Great Resplendent in her royal robes, Catherine the Great triumphantly enters one of the ports of the Crimean peninsula recently captured from the Turks. Catherine presided over an expansion of the Russian Empire and efforts at modernization.

Russian serfs were no match for modern British and French forces, and Russia was defeated and forced to withdraw from Ottoman territory.

Nicholas's successor, Czar Alexander II (r. 1855–1881), was more oriented to western Europe and followed a reformist domestic policy, emancipating the serfs in 1861 and decentralizing government. But many serfs were unable, as required by the new law, to pay the landowners for the lands they wanted to use, and discontent grew throughout the later 1800s.

Russian Expansion in Asia

During this era, the Russians became more engaged with Asia, expanding their power in Siberia, the Caucasus, and Central Asia to form the largest contiguous land empire in the world (see Map 23.3). By the early 1800s, the Russians were anxious to counter British and French expansion in Asia and the Pacific. With Qing China in decline, Russians occupied the Amur Basin, and in 1860 gained official Chinese recognition of their claims in exchange for helping negotiate the end of the Arrow War pitting China against Britain and France. They also acquired a coastal zone that allowed them to satisfy their long-held goal for an ice-free port on Siberia's Pacific shore, to be used as a base for Russian commercial and military activity in the Pacific Basin. There the Russians built the city of Vladivostok ("Ruler of the East").

For several centuries, the Russians had also expanded around the Black Sea, seeking an outlet to the Mediterranean Sea and its maritime trade routes. Between 1800 and the 1870s, the Russians extended their control south through the mountainous Caucasus on the east of the Black Sea, absorbing Armenia and Georgia, both largely Christian, as well as Muslim Azerbaijan (az-uhr-bye-JAHN). Sometimes they faced fierce resistance in the Caucasus: they needed four decades to conquer the strongly Islamic

 Interactive Map

Chechens (CHECH-uhnz). The Russians triumphed in 1859 by ravaging Chechen lands, herds, and crops and beheading their captives. These atrocities fostered a Chechen hatred of Russian rule.

The Russians also colonized Muslim Central Asia, the first step in gaining direct access to the Indian Ocean trade and preventing Britain from establishing influence in the region from their base in India. By 1864, the Russians controlled all the lands of the Kazakh (KAH-zahk) people, east of the Caspian Sea, and looked south to the old Silk Road cities of Turkestan. Although they remained vigorous centers of Islamic learning and Sufism, diminished overland trade and warfare with Persians, Russians, and rival states had caused economic decline in most of these Central Asian states. By the 1870s, Russia's military capabilities had enabled it to dominate Turkestan. They also coveted Afghanistan, which eventually became a buffer between British India and Russian Central Asia. Czarist policy in Central Asia and the Caucasus promoted economic changes that chiefly benefited Russians. The czars

CHRONOLOGY

Russia and Central Asia, 1750–1914

1762–1796	Reign of Catherine the Great
1800–1870s	Russian conquest of Caucasus and Turkestan
1861	Emancipation of Russian serfs
1891–1915	Building of Trans-Siberian Railroad
1904–1905	Russo-Japanese War
1905	First Russian Revolution

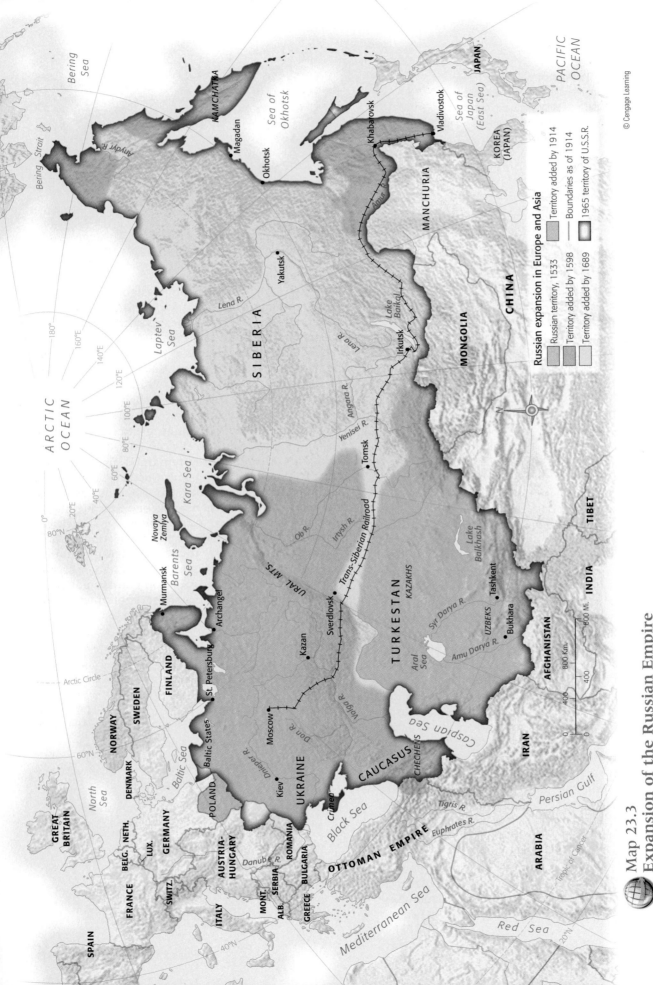

Map 23.3
Expansion of the Russian Empire

Between the 1500s and 1914, Russia gradually gained control of Siberia, Turkestan, the Caucasus, Ukraine, Poland, the Baltic states, and Finland, becoming the world's largest contiguous territorial empire.

Russian expansion in Europe and Asia

- Russian territory, 1533
- Territory added by 1598
- Territory added by 1689
- Territory added by 1914
- Boundaries as of 1914
- 1965 territory of U.S.S.R.

© Cengage Learning

also gradually introduced a policy of Russification, the promotion of Russian language and culture for the non-Russian peoples. This policy sparked resentment and spiritual revival among many Muslims.

Weakness in Imperial Russia

Russian expansion brought problems along with the gains: its sheer size hindered governance, fostered corruption, and prevented the ready exploitation of its vast resources. In addition, colonization of non-Russian lands made Russian leaders permanently fear rebellion, and they needed a huge army to maintain security in the colonized territories. The world's longest railroad, the Trans-Siberian, built between 1891 and 1915, fostered Russian settlement of eastern Siberia and helped Russian traders penetrate Manchuria and Korea. But this expansion brought conflict with Japan, generating the Russo-Japanese War (1904–1905). Russia's defeat in that war humiliated the country and its last czar, Nicholas II (r. 1894–1917).

Russian Changes and Revolution

Territorial expansion and political reforms created economic growth and fostered instability. Spurred by the acquisition of the Caucasus and Central Asian markets, Russia enjoyed increased industrialization during the later 1800s and ranked fifth in the world as an industrial power by 1914. With this came discontent among workers, who often resented the exploitation they faced. Women, particularly in the upper classes, also chafed under their traditional roles and sought more education and opportunities. Political and economic reformers were often influenced by western European ideas, but the appeal of these ideas caused Russian thinkers to torment themselves over their national identity and goals. Opposed to the Westernizers were the Slavophiles, who rejected what they saw as decadent Western models and defended Russian culture, such as respect for the Russian Orthodox Church. Slavophiles often advocated that Russians unite with other Slavs in eastern Europe and the Balkans to confront the West. One proponent of pan-Slavism wrote in 1871 that Russia was never an integral part of Europe, having different and, in his view, superior traditions.

 Make a decision to join the military or go to university under the rule of the autocratic Russian government in this interactive simulation.

Whether reformers or conservatives, Westernizers or Slavophiles, Russians were proud of their rich literary and artistic tradition. Novelists such as Fyodor Dostoyevsky (dos-tuh-YEF-skee) (1821–1881) and Leo Tolstoy (tuhl-STOI) (1828–1910) created enduring masterpieces, including Tolstoy's epic novel, *War and Peace* (1869), which profiled two noble families during the Napoleonic Wars. One of Russia's most honored composers, Pyotr Tchaikovsky (chi-KOF-skee) (1840–1893), traveled widely in Europe and wrote popular operas and ballets, including *Swan Lake* and *The Nutcracker*.

Despite such cultural accomplishments, Russian discontent with the autocratic system and the rising costs of empire building increased through the 1800s, resulting in violent resistance. To crush opposition, over the decades the czars sent thousands of dissidents to remote Siberian prison camps, where many died of illness, starvation, overwork, or the harsh climate. Repression fueled resentment of the government. Some anti-czar Russians joined the illegal Socialist Revolutionary Party, founded in 1898, that used terror to strike against the regime. In 1905, the sacrifices imposed on common people by the Russo-Japanese War sparked a major socialist-led revolutionary movement involving widespread violence. The unrest began when 100,000 factory workers in the capital, St. Petersburg, went on strike and then mounted a protest march demanding equality before the law, freedom of speech, and other progressive goals. Russian troops opened fire on the peaceful marchers, killing some 200 and wounding hundreds more. The violence shattered public support for the czar and fueled increasing revolutionary activity, which soon spread to the armed forces. The revolutionaries were split in their goals, a division that enabled the government to crush the uprising, executing thousands of rebels and burning prorebel villages. But the czar bowed to public demands and allowed an elected national assembly with limited powers. In defeat, the socialist movement fractured into hostile factions. However, conflicts among Russians simmered, and in 1917, they produced the greatest upheaval in Russia's history, which ended the czarist system (see Chapter 24).

 Listen to a synopsis of Chapter 23.

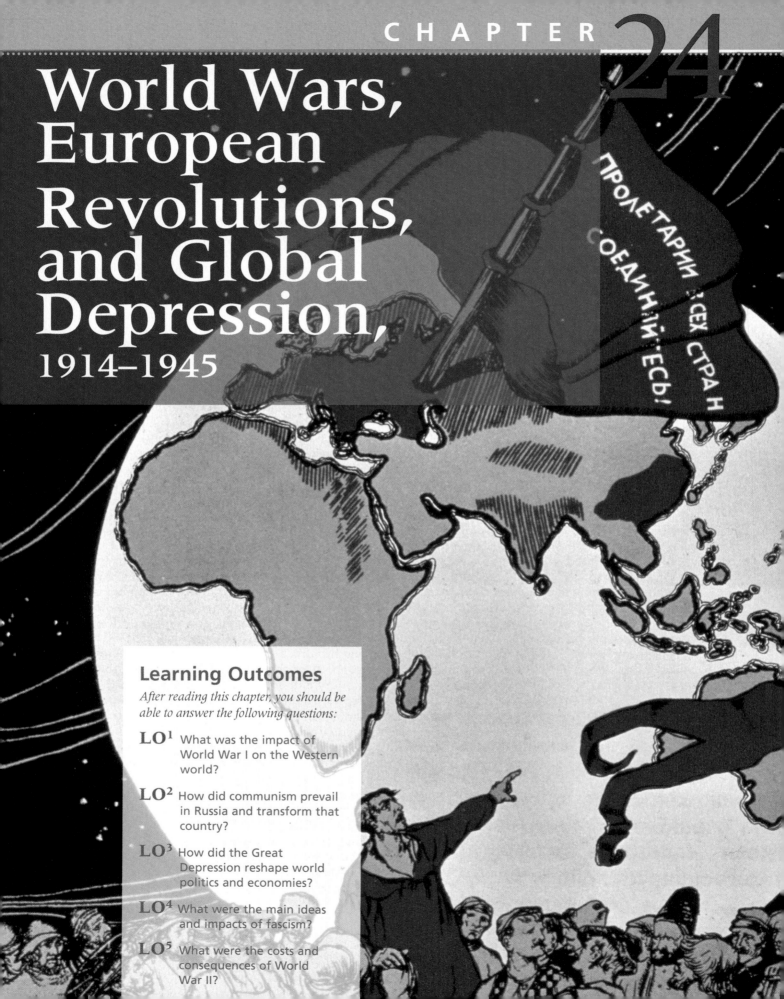

World Wars, European Revolutions, and Global Depression, 1914–1945

Learning Outcomes

After reading this chapter, you should be able to answer the following questions:

LO¹ What was the impact of World War I on the Western world?

LO² How did communism prevail in Russia and transform that country?

LO³ How did the Great Depression reshape world politics and economies?

LO⁴ What were the main ideas and impacts of fascism?

LO⁵ What were the costs and consequences of World War II?

> **❝**My beautiful, pitiful era. With an insane smile you look back, cruel and weak, like an animal past its prime, at the prints of your own paws.**❞**
>
> —Osip Mandelstam, Russian poet[1]

By April 1917, the French army had been fighting the Germans for more than two and a half years. World War I was creating growing casualty lists and inflicting tremendous hardship on soldiers on both sides. A new French commander, General Philippe Pétain (peh-TANH) (1856–1951), implemented a strategy to minimize French casualties. Pétain regarded his soldiers as more than cannon fodder, a view that made him popular with the fighting men, but he was overruled as the French launched another frontal assault on the well-fortified German lines. The result was a military disaster that caused perhaps 120,000 deaths and broke the fighting spirit of the French troops. Mutinies broke out in the units, ranging from minor infractions of code to violent disturbances. Pétain emerged from World War I a French hero, but he was later excoriated for serving as the nominal head of the Vichy French government under hated Nazi occupation in World War II. Pétain died in prison, a broken man looking back on three tumultuous decades (1914–1945) that had brought so much distress and destruction to the world. Two brutal world wars, a mighty revolution in Russia, a terrible economic depression with worldwide consequences, and the rise of new ideologies all occurred during what Russian Jewish poet Osip Mandelstam aptly described as a "beautiful, pitiful era."

In the years before World War I, some Europeans had believed that the world was poised for a peaceful, prosperous new age of international cooperation in which the horrors of war would be ended forever. The hopes of the idealists were dashed by two world wars that challenged the Western world-view of liberalism and rationalism that had captured the European imagination since the Enlightenment; and the faith in progress was shattered by dictatorship in Russia, economic collapse, and organized slaughter. The disarray in Europe, combined with the spread of new ideologies and technologies, helped undermine Western political influence in the world, except for that of the rising Western power, the United States.

Test your knowlege before you read this chapter.

What do you think?

The world wars weakened Europe's global position while increasing American influence and authority.

Strongly Disagree   Strongly Agree

1   2   3   4   5   6   7

[1]Quoted in Anne Applebaum, *Gula: A History* (NY: Doubleday, 2003), p. 3.

◀◀Global Communism The communist leaders of the Soviet Union hoped that their revolution in Russia in 1917 would inspire similar revolutions around the world, ending capitalism and imperialism. This poster reflects the dream of a triumphant communism.

Museum of the Revolution, Moscow/The Bridgeman Art Library International

LO¹ The Roots and Course of World War I

In August 1914, when war broke out between the major powers of Europe, the British foreign secretary remarked, "The lights are going out all over Europe. We shall not see them again in our lifetime."² The conflict pitted two alliances: Britain, France, and Russia formed the Triple Entente, which later included Serbia, Japan, Italy, Portugal, Romania, Greece, and eventually the United States. These nations, also known as the Allies, faced the Central Powers: Germany, Austria-Hungary, the Ottoman Empire, and Bulgaria. The leaders of the countries involved saw the conflict as nothing short of a struggle to control the global system, with its industrial economies and colonial empires. The Great War, as many Europeans called it, was history's first total war, an armed conflict between industrialized powers that lasted four terrible years. The war brought down empires and dynasties, made the United States a world power, and weakened western Europe's hold over the colonial world. And the end of the conflict made a second major war almost inevitable.

 **The Great War** (*http://www.pitt.edu/~pugachev/greatwar/ww1.html*). A useful site on World War I with many essays and links.

> "In the early 1900s, before World War I began, Europeans enjoyed affluence, social stability, and growing democracy; there were few signs of a major war involving the key European powers."

Preludes to War

In the early 1900s, before World War I began, Europeans enjoyed affluence, social stability, and growing democracy; there were few signs of a major war involving the key European powers. The productive European economies benefited from their links to each other and their access to resources and markets in other parts of the world. Whatever their nationality, Europeans looked to the future with confidence, felt superior to the rest of the world, and enjoyed their prosperity. Thanks to imperialism and industrialization, Europeans now consumed new products such as chocolate and rubber tires, and rising populations expanded markets. Between 1880 and 1910, the population grew 43 percent in Germany, 26 percent in Britain, and more than 50 percent in Russia.

European emigration to the Americas and Australia increased markets there for European goods, and improved transportation made it easier to move people, natural resources, and manufactured products over long distances. European capital financed South African gold and diamond mines, Malayan rubber plantations, Australian sheep stations, Russian railways, and Canadian wheat fields, and every sector of the growing U.S. economy.

Economic and Political Competition

But the prosperity, interdependence, and idealism of the era had their limits, and other conditions worked against them to breed tensions and resentments. The quest for imperial glory increased competition between the major European powers for economic and political influence. Britain, France, and Germany were the wealthiest, most powerful nations and fierce rivals with large overseas empires in Africa, Asia, the Pacific, and the Caribbean. Most Europeans still considered wars necessary struggles rather than terrible evils; they also stood by their national interests. The chief of the German General Staff told the German chancellor, "I hold war to be inevitable, and

CHRONOLOGY

World War I, 1914–1919

1908	Austria-Hungarian annexation of Bosnia-Herzegovina
1914	Outbreak of conflict
1916	Battle of Verdun
April 1917	U.S. intervention
March 1917	Fall of czarist government in Russia
March 1918	Brest-Litovsk Treaty
November 1918	End of conflict
1919	Paris Peace Conference

the sooner the better. Everyone is preparing for the great war, which they all expect."[3]

Britain, France, and Germany's fierce economic rivalry, in particular, had stoked the fires of war during the scramble for colonies in the late 1800s. Because they began empire building later than Britain and France, the Germans resented those nations' political control of much of the world and the resources and markets it gave them access to. Germany rapidly industrialized and challenged Britain for economic dominance in overseas markets. Britain, which had commanded the seas for a century, became concerned in 1900, when Germany began building a naval fleet. The growing rivalries led to the manufacture or acquisition of heavier weapons, an increase in the size of armies, and the formation of alliances. France and Russia shared Britain's hostility toward an increasingly aggressive Germany, which in turn felt encircled by these three hostile powers. Austria-Hungary, Germany's most loyal ally, and the Ottoman Empire shared German dislike of Russia. The growing nationalist agitation for self-determination by the many ethnic minorities within these multinational European empires added to the combustible mix.

Tensions in the Balkans

Austria-Hungary faced a particularly difficult challenge in governing the restless Czech, Slovak, and Balkan peoples within its empire. Conflict in the Balkans, the mountainous region in southeastern Europe, was fostered by the rivalries between nations and tensions between Balkan ethnic groups. The Balkans were coveted by the Ottomans (who lost most of their Balkan territory between 1908 and 1913), Russia, and Austria-Hungary. In 1908, Austria-Hungary annexed Bosnia-Herzegovina (boz-nee-uh-HERT-suh-go-vee-nuh), a Balkan territory containing three often-feuding Slavic peoples—Croats, Serbs, and Muslims—and also coveted by the neighboring country of Serbia. If their ally Germany could restrain the major Serbian ally, Russia, the leaders of Austria-Hungary thought war with Serbia over their conflicting Balkan claims might salvage their decaying empire, which once ruled large parts of Europe.

A Preventable Conflict?

Whether World War I could have been prevented is a controversial question for historians. The German monarch, Kaiser Wilhelm II (r. 1888–

> ❝Tensions in the Balkans led to war in 1914.❞

1918), who saw himself as a king with divine rights and answerable only to God, deserves some share of blame. He and other political and military leaders underestimated the human costs and long-term consequences of conflict. Although overstating the case, a key British leader later mourned that "the nations slithered over the brink into the boiling cauldron of war without a trace of apprehension or dismay."[4]

The Course of the European War

Tensions in the Balkans led to war in 1914. The pretext was a political dispute between Austria-Hungary and Serbia over the assassination of the Austrian archduke Franz Ferdinand (1863–1914), the heir to the Habsburg throne, and his wife, Sophie, in Sarajevo (sar-uh-YAY-vo), the capital city of Bosnia-Herzegovina, for an official visit. Although he advocated a conciliatory policy toward the Slavic minorities in the empire, the archduke symbolized continuing Austro-Hungarian domination to Serbs. The group behind the assassination, the Black Hand, were Bosnian Serbs who wanted to end Austrian rule in their land and merge Bosnia with Serbia. Pushed by anti-Slav hardliners in the government, Austria-Hungary responded to the assassination by declaring war on Serbia, Russia's ally. Germany followed suit to support Austria-Hungary, its militarily weaker ally, and Britain, France, and Russia declared war against Germany. Several months later, Ottoman Turkey, long a rival of Russia, joined the Central Powers, closing off British and French access to the Black Sea.

 **Mud and Khaki, Memoirs of an Incomplete Soldier** Read from the memoirs of a British soldier, and imagine the horrors of trench warfare and poison gas in World War I.

A Long, Brutal Conflict

European leaders expected a short war, lasting perhaps six months; instead they got a long, brutal conflict, the most devastating war in history to that point. This was the first fully industrialized war, as whole economies geared for war and modern military technology invented more efficient and indiscriminate ways of killing, including long-range artillery, poison gas, flamethrowers, and aerial bombing. The war massacred a generation of men, doomed youth cut down by shrapnel that tore flesh to pieces, high explosives that pulverized bone, and gas that seared the lungs. The German soldier turned writer Erich Maria

Remarque remembered the "great brotherhood [caused by] the desperate loyalty to one another of men condemned to die." The surviving soldiers were often maimed mentally or physically. Thousands suffered from shellshock, a horrific nervous condition that made normal life difficult or impossible. The war also generated disease and starvation among civilians.

The Western Front

The war on the western front in Belgium and northern France was largely one of soldiers huddling in muddy trenches, gas masks at hand, and using artillery and machine guns to pound the enemy troops in their trenches. In hopes of a breakthrough, one or another general ordered attacks across the barbed wire–filled ground, known as "No Man's Land," between the opposing trenches, which resulted in countless casualties. But for all the sacrifices required of soldiers, the front lines moved little in four years. The cataclysmic Battle of Verdun (vuhr-DUN), a fortress in northeastern France, in February 1916 symbolized the senseless slaughter of the war on the western front. The French stopped a surprise German assault, but more soldiers may have been killed per square yard at Verdun than in any other battle in history, with nearly 1 million French and German casualties. But despite the carnage, and the courage of the soldiers on both sides, Verdun had little impact on the war itself. By 1917, more effective offensive tactics using large armored tanks put more pressure on the German lines.

The Eastern Front

The war became global in scope (see Map 24.1). In the east, Germany and its allies quickly overran Serbia and Romania and pushed deep into western Russia against poorly organized Russian armies. By 1917, Russian morale was cracking.

Interactive Map

The war had killed or wounded more than 7 million Russians and caused massive dislocations, starvation, and disease. Originally a German ally, Italy switched sides in 1915 but lost heavily in several unsuccessful battles. In the Middle East, fighting took place over a wide area. Initially, the Ottomans took a heavy toll on the Allied troops that were sent to invade Turkey and occupy the Gallipoli Peninsula, the gateway to Istanbul. But an Arab uprising begun in 1916 and a British invasion of Ottoman-controlled Iraq forced the Ottoman forces to fight in western Asia and eventually to retreat from that area. Some fighting also broke out in East Africa, as the British and South Africans invaded the German colony of Tanganyika. On the other side of the world, Japan, a British ally, occupied German-held territory in China and the Pacific.

John Nash, *Over the Top* This painting, by the British artist John Nash, shows the trench warfare common on the western front during World War I. Here Allied soldiers leave their trenches to attack across "No Man's Land" on a snowy day.

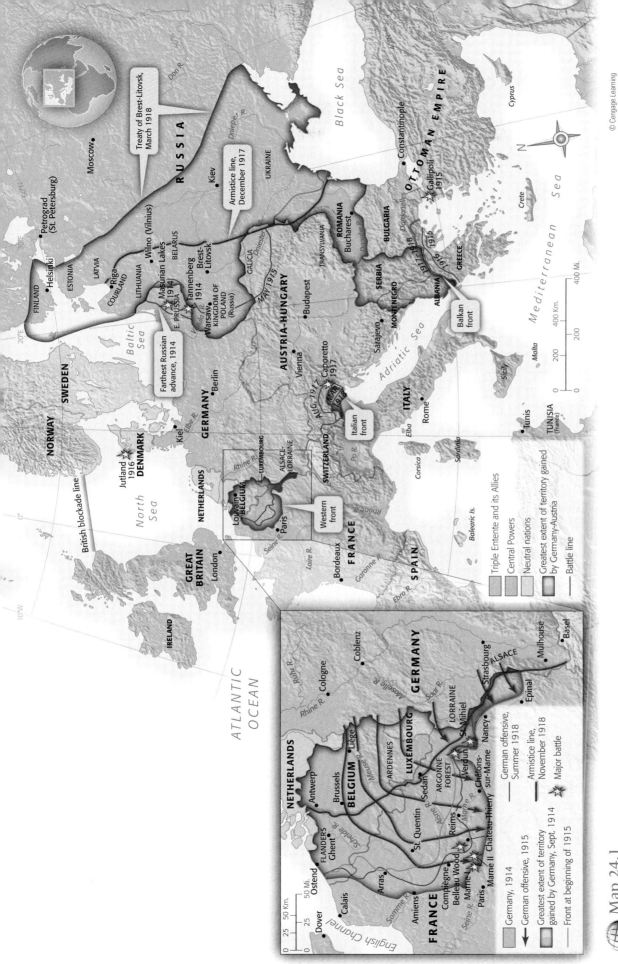

Map 24.1
World War I

World War I pitted the Triple Entente of Britain, France, and Russia, and its allies, against the Central Powers: Germany, Austria-Hungary, and the Ottoman Empire. The worst fighting occurred along the western front and in eastern Europe and Russia. The intervention of the United States in 1917 against the Central Powers proved decisive.

© Cengage Learning

Main map labels:

ATLANTIC OCEAN

British blockade line

North Sea

IRELAND

GREAT BRITAIN
London

NORWAY

SWEDEN

Baltic Sea

FINLAND
Helsinki

Petrograd (St. Petersburg)

Moscow

R U S S I A

Treaty of Brest-Litovsk, March 1918

Don R.

Dnieper R.

Kiev

UKRAINE

Armistice line, December 1917

ESTONIA
LATVIA
Riga
COURLAND
LITHUANIA
Wilno (Vilnius)
BELARUS
Brest-Litovsk

Farthest Russian advance, 1914

Masurian Lakes
Tannenberg 1914
1914
E. PRUSSIA
Warsaw
KINGDOM OF POLAND (Russia)

GALICIA
MAY 1915
Dniester R.

NETHERLANDS

Kiel
DENMARK
Jutland 1916

GERMANY
Berlin

Elbe R.
Rhine R.
LUXEMBOURG
ALSACE-LORRAINE

BELGIUM
Louvain

Western front

Paris

FRANCE
Bordeaux
Garonne R.
Loire R.
Seine R.

SPAIN
Ebro R.

SWITZERLAND

Vienna
AUSTRIA-HUNGARY
Budapest

AUG. 1917
Caporetto 1917

Italian front

ITALY
Rome
Po R.
Rhone R.

TRANSYLVANIA
ROMANIA
Bucharest
Danube R.

SERBIA
Sarajevo
MONTENEGRO

BULGARIA

Balkan front
ALBANIA
1917–18

GREECE
1915
1916

Dardanelles
Gallipoli 1915

OTTOMAN EMPIRE
Constantinople

Black Sea

Mediterranean Sea

Crete

Cyprus

Corsica
Sardinia
Balearic Is.
Elba
Sicily
Malta
Tunis
TUNISIA (France)

Adriatic Sea

0   200   400 Km.
0   200   400 Mi.

Legend:
- Triple Entente and its Allies
- Central Powers
- Neutral nations
- Greatest extent of territory gained by Germany-Austria
- Battle line

Inset map labels:

English Channel
Dover
Calais
Ostend
FLANDERS
Ghent
Antwerp
Brussels
BELGIUM
Liège
Amiens
Arras
Somme R.
St. Quentin
Compiègne
Reims
Belleau Wood
Marne I
Paris
Marne II
Château-Thierry
Chalons-sur-Marne
Seine R.
Aisne R.
Marne R.
Meuse R.
Scheldt R.

NETHERLANDS
Rhine R.
Ruhr R.
Cologne
Coblenz
GERMANY
Moselle R.
Saar R.

LUXEMBOURG
ARDENNES
Sedan
ARGONNE FOREST
Verdun
St. Mihiel
LORRAINE
Nancy
Strasbourg
ALSACE
Epinal
Mulhouse
Basel

FRANCE

0   25   50 Km.
0   25   50 Mi.

Inset legend:
- Germany, 1914
- German offensive, 1915
- Greatest extent of territory gained by Germany, Sept. 1914
- Front at beginning of 1915
- German offensive, Summer 1918
- Armistice line, November 1918
- Major battle

The United States Enters the War

Although the Germans won more battles than they lost, eventually the tide turned against them. Over time, the economic power of the Allies proved decisive. The Allies had superior wealth, better weapons, and more troops. The use of sea power was also crucial in determining the course of the war. Britain and Germany possessed the world's two most powerful navies, and they engaged each other in the North Sea and the eastern Mediterranean. The Germans used their submarines to break Allied supply lines, but their attacks on British and U.S. ships carrying supplies to Britain brought a reluctant United States into the war.

U.S. Intervention: The End of the War

Two fateful developments in 1917—the Russian Revolution, discussed later in this chapter, and the intervention of the United States—altered the conflict. The Russian Revolution overthrew the czarist government and took Russia out of the war in early 1918. Freed from the eastern front, German armies made breakthroughs against the British and French forces in the west. As a German victory seemed more likely, U.S. military leaders, politicians, and businessmen all pressed for intervention. U.S. companies and banks had a big stake in an Allied victory, because Allied defeat might have prevented payment on orders for American products and investments in the British and French economies. Americans were also enraged by German submarine attacks on U.S. merchant ships. After maintaining a perilous neutrality for three years, President Woodrow Wilson committed the United States to war, linking the military commitment to idealistic American values when he told Congress that "the world must be made safe for democracy. We are the champions of the rights of mankind."[5]

The U.S. intervention proved decisive in securing an Allied victory. Beginning on April 17, 1917, some 300,000 American troops poured into Europe and were warmly welcomed in Allied nations. Supported by the United States, the Allies blockaded German ports, creating severe economic problems. As U.S. troops and resources arrived, an Allied offensive pushed the German forces back. Soon Germany's allies began surrendering. The deteriorating conditions demoralized

> "Although powerful Western nations still dominated world politics and the world economy, the war also changed the old global order and began a new one."

Germans. Its overextended army in disarray, and suffering food and fuel shortages at home, Germany was forced to agree to peace in November 1918. Kaiser Wilhelm II and the Austro-Hungarian emperor both abdicated, ending two long-standing European monarchies. The Allies dictated the peace terms.

Consequences of World War I

World War I undermined the power of Germany and shifted more influence to the victors: Britain, France, and the United States. It reshaped Europe politically and rearranged the colonial empires. World War I and its aftermath also affected the societies of Asia and Africa, destroying their hopes for achieving independence or self-rule. Although powerful Western nations still dominated world politics and the world economy, the war also changed the old global order and began a new one.

The Treaty of Versailles

The Paris Peace Conference of 1919, held in the former royal palace in the Paris suburb of Versailles (vuhr-SIGH), reshaped Europe and resulted in the Treaty of Versailles. The U.S. president, Woodrow Wilson, went to Paris hoping to use his nation's growing power to sell an agenda promoting freedom, stability, and conciliatory treatment of Germany, known as the Fourteen Points, to skeptical British and French leaders. Favoring political freedom and stability, however, Wilson had to compromise with the hardline French, who wanted to punish Germany. The final treaty required Germany to partly dismantle its military; abandon its Asian, African, and Pacific colonies; and shift land to its European neighbors, leaving 3 million ethnic Germans outside of Germany in countries such as Czechoslovakia and Poland. The Treaty of Versailles also forced Germany to pay huge annual payments, known as reparations, to the Allies to compensate for their war costs. In short, Germany was left virtually disarmed and bankrupt. The new German leader, Friedrich Ebert, fretted: "The armi-

 Comments of the German Delegation to the Paris Peace Conference on the Conditions of Peace, October 1919 Read Germany's response to the Treaty of Versailles, which deprived it of its colonies, 13 percent of its land, and 10 percent of its population.

stice will not produce a just peace. The sacrifices imposed on us must lead to our people's doom."[6]

The Human Cost of the War

The war had taken an appalling human toll on both sides. Altogether 9 to 10 million soldiers and another 10 million civilians died, leaving a generation of European men decimated. The brutality radicalized many workers and peasants, especially in eastern Europe, and leftist political parties—Socialists and Communists—gained strength. In 1914, Europeans had gone to war with patriotic enthusiasm, but by 1918, some philosophers and writers concluded that the slaughter had destroyed the Western claim to moral leadership in the world. Pacifist, antiwar sentiments grew. The French writer Henri Barbusse, a soldier himself, reflected bitterly: "Shame on military glory, shame on armies, shame on the soldier's calling that changes men by turns into stupid victims and ignoble brutes."[7]

Reconfiguring Europe

The war destroyed several old states and created new ones. Four empires—the Russian, Ottoman, Austro-Hungarian, and German—collapsed. As a result of the Russian Revolution of 1917, Communists gained power in Russia, launching a new political and economic system. President Wilson, believing that ethnically homogeneous nation-states could prevent nationalist rivalries, convinced the Paris Peace Conference to redraw national boundaries to give ethnic minorities their own states. In eastern Europe, Poland, Czechoslovakia, Yugoslavia, and Finland were carved out of the ruins of the German, Austro-Hungarian, and Russian Empires, but most of the new states placed various ethnic groups within arbitrary boundaries, leading to tensions that would contribute to World War II's beginning. The appeal of self-determination also inspired uprisings in Britain's longtime colony, Ireland, and in 1921, Parliament was forced to grant most of the island special status within the British Empire as the self-governing Irish Free State.

However, the victorious powers ignored the principle of self-determination for their farther-flung colonies. Woodrow Wilson advocated democracy and human rights, but in seeking to strengthen Britain and France, he decided to support the preservation of their colonies in Asia, Africa, the Pacific, and the Caribbean. The peace settlement transferred Germany's African colonies to the victors, and Britain and France also gained control of the Middle Eastern societies formerly ruled by Ottoman Turkey. The peace settlements of World War I, by ignoring the political struggles of colonized peoples, thus spurred opposition to the West in Asia and Africa. The deaths of thousands of Asian and African colonial subjects who were conscripted or recruited to fight for Britain, France, or Germany in World War I sparked even deeper resentments. Thus, World War I was one of the key factors in the rise of nationalism, the desire to form politically independent nations, in the colonies between 1918 and 1941 (see Chapter 25).

The global system shaped by colonial empires and Western economic power survived, but European prestige and influence weakened. The war undermined European economies, allowing the United States to leap ahead of Europe. Wilson wanted an open world economy in which American industry could assert its new supremacy. Because European nations had borrowed money from the United States to finance the war, they now owed the United States $7 billion. This war debt allowed the United States, long a debtor nation, to become a creditor nation. By 1919, it was producing 42 percent of all the world's industrial output and had replaced Britain as the banker and workshop of the world.

Wilson also proposed and helped form a League of Nations, the first organization of independent nations to work for peace and humanitarian concerns. But Wilson could not persuade the U.S. Congress, controlled by the largely isolationist Republican opposition, to approve U.S. membership in the league. Hence, the only nation with the power and stature to make the League work stayed outside, leaving Britain and France alone to deal with European and global issues.

> " The Russian Revolution had deep roots in Russian history under the czars, the hereditary rulers. "

LO² The Revolutionary Path to Soviet Communism

The Russian Revolution, a major consequence of World War I, was a formative event of the twentieth century, shaping European and world history, politics, and beliefs. In the wake of the revolution, Russia provided a testing ground for communism, which fostered a powerful state that reshaped Russian society and provided an alternative to the capitalist democracy dominant in North America and western Europe.

The Roots of Revolution

The Russian Revolution had deep roots in Russian history under the czars, the hereditary rulers (see Chapter 23). Controlling a huge Eurasian empire, Russia had enjoyed some limited industrialization, but the powerful and wealthy landed aristocracy opposed further modernization. Socially and economically, Russia was still a somewhat feudalistic country. Although serfdom had been legally abolished in the nineteenth century, peasants often remained subject to the dictates of landowners and enjoyed little social mobility or wealth. Only revolution could forge a decisive change in Russian society.

Growing discontent among intellectuals, the floundering middle class, underpaid industrial workers, and peasants fomented radical movements. All of these groups hated the autocratic czarist system and the privileges enjoyed by the hereditary aristocracy. In 1905 a revolution broke out, only to be brutally crushed by the government, but it left a revolutionary heritage for the Bolsheviks, the most radical of Russia's antigovernment groups, who transformed the revolutionary socialist views promoted by Karl Marx in the mid-1800s into a dogmatic communist ideology. The Bolsheviks started as one faction of a broader socialist movement that split into several rival parties in 1903. The founder and leader of the Bolsheviks, Vladimir Lenin (LEN-in) (1870–1924), was strongly influenced by the works of Karl Marx. Most of the Bolshevik leaders, including Lenin, had spent time as political prisoners in harsh Siberian labor camps for opposing the government, and they were embittered toward the czarist system. They espoused a goal of helping the downtrodden workers and peasants redress the wrongs inflicted upon them by the rich and privileged. A new society, forged by revolutionary violence, could bring about a more equitable distribution of wealth and power for all. Lenin and the Bolsheviks favored a small, disciplined revolutionary organization that would work for workers' interests but abide by the decisions made by the leaders, a system known as the party line.

When World War I broke out, the Russian people rallied around the unpopular czarist government, seeing it as a patriotic war of defense against the

 Russian History Index: The World Wide Web Virtual Library (*http://vlib.iue.it/hist-russia/Index.html*). Contains useful essays and links on Russian history, society, and politics.

Lenin The Bolshevik leader Vladimir Lenin stirred crowds with his fiery revolutionary rhetoric, helping to spread the communist message among Russians who were fed up with ineffective government, war, and poverty.

hated Germans, their longtime rivals for dominion in eastern Europe. Only the Bolsheviks opposed the war, which they saw, with some justice, as an imperialistic struggle over markets and colonies. But the war soon lost its allure as Russian military forces collapsed in the face of German armies. Russia lacked the economic power and military and political leadership to compete.

The Bolshevik Seizure of Power

By 1917, the Russian people were sick of war and seeking change, sparking two revolutions. The first revolution erupted in March when riots and strikes caused by food shortages and other problems led to the toppling of the czar and the establishment of a provisional government led by Aleksandr Krenesky (kuh-REN-skee) (1881–1970). But the new provisional government leaders refused to provide the two things most Russians wanted: peace and land. Because of their commitments to the Allies, they vowed to continue fighting the highly unpopular war and declined to redistribute land from the old aristocracy to the peasantry until the war ended.

The political situation became chaotic. While the increasingly discredited provisional government asked for time, radicals organized soviets, local action councils that enlisted workers and soldiers to fight the factory owners and military officers, undermined government authority. The strongest soviet, in the capital, St. Petersburg, had between two thousand and three thousand members and was headed by an executive committee. As the soviets and the government jockeyed for control of St. Petersburg, the Germans, hoping to undermine the Russian provisional government, helped Lenin, in exile in Switzerland, to secretly return to Russia hidden in a railroad boxcar. Using the slogans of "peace, bread, and land" and "all power to the soviets," Lenin rapidly built up Bolshevik influence in the soviets. The provisional government became increasingly discredited and weak.

In October 1917, the Bolsheviks and their 240,000 party members staged an uprising and grabbed power from Kerensky's crumbling provisional government. Aided by the soviets, the Bolsheviks seized key government buildings in St. Petersburg, including the czar's Winter Palace, and pushed other, more moderate parties and soviets aside. Lenin claimed that his goal for Russia was to transfer power from the capitalists to the working class. The Bolsheviks renamed themselves the Communist Party and gained popular support by pulling Russia out of the war. In the Treaty of Brest-Litovsk, negotiated with Germany in March 1918, Russia gave up some of its empire in the west to Germany, abandoning the Ukraine, eastern Poland, the Baltic states, and Finland. They also moved the capital from St. Petersburg, which they renamed Leningrad, to Moscow.

Civil War, Lenin, and a New Society

Once in power, the communist regime had to develop a strategy for dealing with the postwar world. In 1919, Lenin, hoping to protect Russia's revolution by promoting world revolution, organized the Communist International, often known as the Comintern, a collection of communist parties from around the world. It would battle the U.S. vision, articulated by Woodrow Wilson, of promoting capitalism and democracy. Before World War II, however, the United States had the

> 66 By 1917, the Russian people were sick of war and seeking change, sparking two revolutions. 99

greater success in spreading its influence, partly because it helped stabilize postwar Europe with economic, political, and food assistance to promote pro-capitalist, anticommunist governments. The prospect of world revolution that would foster the spread of communism soon faded.

The Russian Civil War

The communists were further tested by the Russian Civil War (1918–1921). Conservative, anti-communist forces—who called themselves White Russians in contrast to the communists' military force, the Red Army—included the czarist aristocracy (among them large landowners), generals who were angry at losing their dominance, and a few pro-Western liberals favoring democracy. Heavily funded and armed by Western nations, which were alarmed by the Revolution, the White Russian armies fought the communist forces in the fringe areas of the Russian Empire in the three years following World War I (see Map 24.2). The outside intervention added an international flavor to the Russian Civil War. This intervention had come chiefly from Japan, Britain, France, and the United States. Soon recognizing the whole intervention effort as a quagmire, Wilson lamented that it was harder to get out than it was to go in. U.S. and other Western troops were finally removed in 1920, in some cases after soldiers mutinied. The Western intervention helped to solidify the communist government, which was widely seen by Russians as fighting a nationalist war against foreign powers seeking to restore the old discredited czarist order. Although the communists initially looked vulnerable, they eventually gained the advantage, defeating the White Russians and even reclaiming some of the territory lost in the Brest-Litovsk Treaty, including the Ukraine.

Interactive Map

The USSR Emerges

By 1922, the Communist Party controlled much of the old Russian Empire, but the civil war had left the country in dire straits. Russia's leaders renamed their nation the Union of

Legend:
- Boundary of Russian Empire 1914
- Area controlled by the Bolsheviks, August 1918
- Treaty of Brest-Litovsk, March 1918
- White Russian forces
- Non-Russian anti-Bolshevik forces
- Territory lost to Russia, 1914–1921
- Soviet territory, 1922
- Boundaries, 1922

Map 24.2
Civil War in Revolutionary Russia (1918–1921)

The communist seizure of power in Russia in 1917 sparked a counteroffensive, backed by varied Western nations and Japan, to reverse the Russian Revolution. The communists successfully defended the Russian heartland while pushing back the conservative offensive.

Soviet Socialist Republics (USSR), in theory a federation of all the empire's diverse peoples—such as Kazakhs, Uzbeks, Armenians, and Ukrainians—but in actuality largely controlled by Russians, and hence, to opponents, essentially a continuation of the Russian Empire built by the czars. Soon the USSR turned from world revolution to building what the leaders termed "socialism in one country"—the USSR—using coercion against reluctant citizens if necessary. Yet party leaders did not have a blueprint for transforming Russian society.

Because they had no model of a communist state, the Soviet leaders experimented while using their secret police to eliminate opponents, among them liberals and moderate socialists. The basis for Soviet communism was Marxism-Leninism, a mix of socialism (collective ownership of the economy) and Leninism, a political system in which one party holds a monopoly on power. Lenin initially favored centralization and nationalization of all economic activity, but he was forced by peasant opposition to adopt the New Economic Policy (NEP), a pragmatic approach that mixed capitalism and socialism. The NEP brought economic recovery and included limited capitalism in agriculture, allowing peasants to sell their produce on the open market. But the economy produced few consumer goods, so the peasants had no incentive to sell their produce for profit, because there was little to buy with the money they earned.

Communist Bureaucracy

The long Russian tradition of authoritarian, bureaucratic government under the czars and an obedient population provided a foundation for communist dictatorship. The communists were a small party, and most party leaders were, like Lenin, intellectuals from urban middle-class backgrounds who knew little of Russia's largest social class, the peasants. To regenerate the economy, they eventually adopted not popular control of farms and enterprises by workers and peasants, but a top-down managerial system staffed by officials chiefly of middle-class origin. Peasants and workers became just employees, not partners. Increasingly, the Communist Party and state became bureaucratic. The middle class was now largely composed of state employees, managers, and bureaucrats with salaries and privileges that were denied to the masses and dedicated not to fostering social change but to maintaining their own power. Lenin criticized the bloated bureaucracy and warned, accurately, that his probable successor, Joseph Stalin (STAH-lin) (1879–1953), had dictatorial tendencies. He hoped to reform the party but died in 1924.

Stalinism and a Changed Russia

Lenin's successor, Joseph Stalin (1879–1953), was a master bureaucrat who reshaped Soviet communism and Russia. Born in the Caucasus province of Georgia, the son of a shoemaker, he adopted the name Stalin ("Man of Steel") after joining the Bolsheviks. Stalin outmaneuvered his party rivals to succeed Lenin in 1924, and came to power as the peasants increasingly turned away from the Communist Party. Stalin urged a hard line against those who resisted state policies, eliminated all of his competition in the party, and became a dictator. The system he imposed, known today as Stalinism, included state ownership of all property, such as lands and businesses, a planned economy, and one-man rule.

Stalin: The "Man of Steel"

In 1928, Stalin ended Lenin's NEP and introduced an economic policy based on an annual series of plans for future production, known as Five-Year Plans, formulated by state bureaucrats. The Five-Year Plans produced basic industrial goods, such as steel and coal, but few consumer goods. Stalin also launched a massive crash industrialization program and withdrew the country from the global political and economic system. Under Stalin, the Soviet Union mobilized its own resources, refusing foreign investment. In order to introduce machines to increase farm production, Stalin strengthened the party's grip on the rural sector by collectivizing the land and turning private farms into commonly owned enterprises, in the process destroying the wealthier small farmers, the *kulaks*, as a class. Peasants who refused to join the collective farms were often exiled to Siberia.

The 1930s and 1940s were hard years for the Soviet people, filled with terror. Stalin's rule was marked by purges, or campaigns to eliminate actual or potential opponents; forced-labor camps for

Marxism-Leninism
The basis for Soviet communism, a mix of socialism (collective ownership of the economy) and Leninism.

New Economic Policy (NEP)
Lenin's pragmatic approach to economic development, which mixed capitalism and socialism.

Stalinism
Joseph Stalin's system of government, which included state ownership of all property, such as lands and businesses, a planned economy, and one-man rule.

gulags
Russian shorthand for harsh forced-labor camps in Siberia.

socialist realism
Literary and artistic works that depicted life from a revolutionary perspective, a style first introduced in Stalin's Russia.

Great Depression
A collapse of the world economy that lasted in varying degrees of severity through the 1930s.

suspected dissidents; and the widespread use of the secret police (known as the KGB), which spied on and sometimes terrorized the people. Stalin also deported millions of people to the harsh forced-labor camps in Siberia known as gulags (Russian shorthand for State Camp Administration). From 1929 until 1953, some 18 million people passed through the massive gulag system, and about 4.5 million of these never returned home. Gulag inmates toiled, starved, and died building railroads, cutting timber, or digging canals.

Not even beloved artists were spared the repression if they were Jewish, especially given Stalin's embrace of long-standing Russian anti-Semitism. One of Russia's most revered poets, Osip Mandelstam (MAHN-duhl-stuhm) (1891–1938), a Jew whose comment on the era begins this chapter, died in the gulag in 1938. By the early 1950s, the dead and jailed from Stalin's policies numbered around 40 million people, casualties of twenty-five years of repression.

Passive Resistance and Industrialization

The repression also came at a high economic cost. Peasants often destroyed their equipment and livestock as a protest against forced collectivization, and agriculture suffered from these losses for decades. Peasants adopted a stance of passive resistance, doing just the minimum to survive. Russia's annual food production between 1928 and 1980 was less than in 1924. Because agriculture stagnated, the government could not use the surplus to finance industrialization. Instead, it squeezed the urban workers, who became alienated and passively resisted, voicing their feelings in the common expression: "The government pretends they are paying us so we pretend we are working."

Even as the agricultural economy stagnated and the terror continued, however, the communists were reshaping Russian society by introducing modern ideas. Industrialization raised national economic power and the gross national product (GNP), the annual total of all economic activities, to second in the world by 1932. The Five-Year Plans successfully mobilized the population for industrialization, aided by government; as with Meiji Japan, the state, rather than private capital, was the main agent for change. The workforce that was engaged in industrial production nearly tripled between 1928 and 1937. Mass education raised the literacy rate from 28 percent in 1900 to more than 90 percent by the 1980s. Better medical care raised life expectancy from thirty-two in 1914 to seventy in 1960. The transformation in one decade, due in part to the nation's abundant natural resources, was impressive.

The Soviet Model

The USSR was the first society to leave the capitalist world order, industrialize rapidly under direct state control, and establish a new, socialist society. Stalin promoted official atheism and forced artists and writers to glorify Soviet life, a style known as socialist realism. His model held the promise of catching up to the West in a short time and to do so without capitalism, although it came at a high cost in human rights and lives. The USSR's pervasive system of political repression and state control, which was far greater even than that of the czars, limited its appeal to other societies. The USSR can be seen as a combination of Marxist ideology and czarist despotism, driven in turn by the missionary impulse derived from Christianity. The latter gave Soviet leaders the notion of spreading their "true faith" to the world.

> 66 Europe's very slow and painful recovery from the war fostered political opposition movements that weakened many European governments. 99

LO³ The Interwar Years and the Great Depression

In Europe after World War I, peace had brought a great questioning of the old order. By the early 1920s, western Europe had stabilized, and much of the European continent had come under democratically elected governments. Meanwhile, the United States, though suffering severe economic inequalities, enjoyed prosperity. Western affluence, however, was dramatically undermined by the significant event of the 1930s, the Great Depression, a collapse of the world economy that lasted in varying degrees of severity throughout the 1930s. The global extent of the Depression, rooted in developments in Europe and North America after

World War I, illustrated the economic interdependence of the world's societies. The distress caused by the Depression, which affected both industrialized nations and those countries and colonies supplying raw materials, in turn fostered radical political movements.

Europe and Japan in the 1920s

The 1920s was a decade of political, economic, and social change throughout western Europe. Europe's very slow and painful recovery from the war fostered political opposition movements that weakened many European governments. Where these governments were under conservative leaders from the middle and upper classes, the demands of workers for better conditions or unions were usually crushed. The resentment resulting from this repression, however, caused socialist and social democratic parties, such as the British Labor Party, to grow stronger; these parties worked to extend the rights and protections of workers through legislation.

Economic Instability in Europe For various reasons, some European countries remained politically and economically unstable. For instance, under a new democratic government, the Weimar (VIE-mahr) Republic, Germany struggled with high unemployment, a devastated economy, and the punishing conditions of the Versailles treaty. Costly reparations caused hyperinflation in Germany, which in turn stimulated the growth of extremist political groups. German prosperity was essential to spur the European economy, so the Allies reduced reparations and the United States extended loans, but the Weimar regime continued to face domestic challenges. Meanwhile, certain multiethnic, eastern European countries such as Czechoslovakia, which mixed Czechs and Slovaks with Germans, Poles, Hungarians, and Ukrainians, experienced significant political tensions.

Some western European countries enjoyed a degree of economic recovery that curbed inflation and unemployment. To stimulate their economies, Europeans borrowed U.S. mass production processes, and with growing middle-class prosperity, more Europeans could afford the improved versions of earlier inventions such as cars, radios, and refrigerators. Labor unions also gained strength, helping certain workers achieve an eight-hour day. The center of gravity shifted to the cities and a fast-growing new white-collar class that tended to oppose the socialism that was popular with the working class. Yet Europe's economies were more and more bound up with the world economy, in which they lost ground to

CHRONOLOGY

Europe, North America, and Japan, 1919–1940

1919–1920	First Red Scare in United States
1921	Irish Free State
1921	Formation of Italian fascist movement
1926	Formation of fascist state in Italy
1929–1941	Great Depression
1931	Japanese occupation of Manchuria
1933–1945	Presidency of Franklin D. Roosevelt
1933	Nazi electoral victory in Germany
1933–1938	Anti-Jewish legislation in Germany
1935–1936	Italian conquest of Ethiopia
1936	Start of fascist government in Japan
October 1936	Hitler–Mussolini alliance
1936–1939	Spanish Civil War
1937	Japanese invasion of China
March 1938	Austrian merger with Germany
1938	German annexation of western Czechoslovakia
August 1939	Nazi-Soviet pact
September 1939	German invasion of Poland
1940	Tripartite Pact between Germany, Italy, and Japan

the United States and Japan. Between 1913 and 1928, Europe's share of world exports fell from 53 to 45 percent, a drop that spurred competition for world markets among European nations.

New Social Patterns Emerge Social change also marked the 1920s, especially in the cities. Europeans developed new patterns of leisure and consumption. In European cities, affluent people found entertainment at nightclubs, cabarets, and dance halls and shopped at large department stores. Religious observance declined, because many Europeans felt abandoned by God on the battlefields or rejected Christianity as passé.

Gender patterns showed signs of change, too. The new fashion for women emphasized short hair and a boyish figure, while the "new woman," as the popular designation made her, also sought financial independence through paid work. The war had killed millions of young men, leaving fewer men to marry or hire. To fill this gap, women moved into office jobs, and the female secretary replaced the male clerk. More women also became lawyers, physicians, and even members of parliaments. In many countries, women fought for and often achieved legislation guaranteeing women's suffrage and other rights. As gender standards changed, once-shocking attitudes became common, including an openness about sexuality and rejection of traditional marriage. Such freedoms were challenged in the 1930s, when a return to traditional female roles in European nations brought bans on abortion and birth control.

Read about Yoshiya Nobuko, the popular Japanese writer and gender rebel.

> "In many countries, women fought for and often achieved legislation guaranteeing women's suffrage and other rights."

Japanese Prosperity After the War

Japan was also reshaped by industrialization, democratic politics, and liberalization during the 1920s, generating prosperity and new possibilities for the growing middle class. Powerful business interests dominated the democratic system that had been formed only a few years earlier, and the resulting corruption and volatility disillusioned many Japanese. Internationally, Japan played a visible role in the world. Even before World War I, Japan had acquired imperial holdings in Taiwan and Korea, and as a British ally in World War I, Japan also gained control of the German colonies in the Pacific. Japan's assertive role in the world, however, also created enemies. Tensions with the United States increased, fostered in part by Japanese bitterness toward the blatant racist discrimination against Japanese immigrants in the United States, and by U.S. hostility to Japanese ambitions in Asia and the Pacific.

Shifting Social Morals, Conservative Reaction

Nevertheless, a wave of Western influence permeated the cities. Urban middle-class Japanese were influenced by popular culture from the United States, and baseball became a popular Japanese sport. Young women questioned the Japanese tradition of the submissive female and dominant male. A leading feminist, Kato Shidzue (KAH-to shid-ZOO-ee) (1897–2001), became a strong proponent of family planning after having sojourned in the United States, and later turned to socialism and promotion of equal political rights for women. Conservatives, however, were troubled by shifting social mores. The working classes and rural population were alienated from the Westernized culture of the cities and did not share in the economic prosperity. Perplexed by the divide between traditional and modern values, Japanese thinkers and artists pondered national and cultural identity. For example, the writer Akutagawa Ryunosuke (1892–1927) combined Western and Japanese traditions by adding psychological dimensions to ancient folktales. His influential short story *Rashoman* tells of a rape and murder from several eyewitness perspectives.

The United States in the 1920s

In the postwar United States, Americans became more conservative and isolationist. Anticommunism prompted by the Russian Revolution and growing middle-class prosperity launched the triumph of conservative forces as Americans developed a powerful hostility for socialism of any kind. In 1919–1920, widespread public fear of communism, known as the "Red Scare," generated the first in a series of government crackdowns on dissidents, including suppression of strikes, harassment of labor unions, arrests of political radicals, and deportation of foreigners. The Red Scare froze attitudes toward the Soviet Union and communist movements for generations, as the United States pursued a long-term policy of isolating the USSR from international contact. Not until 1933 would the United States soften its policy of isolation toward the Soviet Union by extending diplomatic recognition.

Domestic government policies often turned a deaf ear to problems affecting the less affluent.

Strikes for better wages by desperate workers, many of whom had joined left-wing unions, proliferated, but federal, state, and local governments all helped employers fight labor unions in the Appalachian coal fields, Detroit auto plants, and South Atlantic textile mills. Another source of tension was the widespread resentment of the United States Congress for passing Prohibition, which outlawed alcohol. Political leaders also ignored terrorism, including lynchings, by white racists against African Americans in the South. Meanwhile, several million African Americans, in what was later called the Great Migration, moved from southern states to the north and west in the 1920s in search of jobs and security. Farmers were devastated by a postwar drop in demand and suffered throughout the decade, but they received little help from the federal government. Finally, the 1920s saw the passage of restrictive immigration policies that sought to exclude undesirable populations.

In contrast to the less affluent, for the top half of the U.S. population, these years were the "Roaring 20s," the hedonistic era when high society let down its inhibitions. Jazz music, rooted in southern black culture, became so popular that the era was often known as "the Jazz Age." Women, who had been active in labor unions, social reform movements, and religious organizations for decades, finally won the vote in 1920, which allowed more of them to enjoy a larger public role.

In contrast to Woodrow Wilson's idealistic globalism, Republican leaders in the 1920s proclaimed an isolationist U.S. foreign policy, ostensibly avoiding interference in other nations' affairs; but despite the rhetoric, interventionism was often practiced. Always pushing outward, restless American citizens sought new Christian converts, commercial markets, and business investments. U.S. presidents justified numerous military interventions to punish opponents and reward allies, especially in Latin America. U.S. Marines remained in Nicaragua for decades (1909–1933), and El Salvador, Haiti, Mexico, and the Dominican Republic all experienced major U.S. military incursions between 1914 and 1940.

Economic Collapse and American Reform

The major spur to change in the interwar years was the Great Depression. The crisis began in the United States in the fall of 1929, when prices on the New York Stock Exchange fell dramatically, ruining many investors. This crash ultimately precipitated a worldwide economic disaster that was unprecedented in intensity, longevity, and spread, affecting industrial and agricultural economies alike. The Depression lasted until 1941.

Causes of the Great Depression

Global factors helped foster the Great Depression. The flow of wealth into the United States intensified existing imbalances in the world economy in trade and investment. Because the United States was generally self-sufficient, it was less dependent on world trade than Britain had been when it was the world's leading economic power. With its growing population and rising standard of living, the United States enjoyed raw materials, thriving industry, and consumer markets within its borders. The nation also maintained protectionist policies and refused to shift to an aggressive free-trade position until well into the 1930s. Furthermore, the world banking and credit structure was very unstable, partly because, unlike Britain in the 1800s, the United States did not use its unmatched economic power to make sure the world economy worked efficiently. Yet U.S. banks, too anxious for profits, became overextended in loans to Britain, France, and Germany.

Conditions within the United States also played a role in generating the Great Depression. A "get-rich-quick" philosophy had led to risky loans and reckless investments. Income was increasingly distributed unevenly: by 1929, the top 20 percent of American families earned 54 percent of the income, whereas the bottom 40 percent earned 12.5 percent. As more wealth gravitated to fewer hands and more people fell into poverty, purchasing power declined, while more consumer products became available, causing a glut. Many manufacturers could not sell enough products at home or abroad to stay in business or avoid layoffs. These problems led to the stock market crash, followed by bank failures. As U.S. banks faced ruin, they called in their debts from western European banks, triggering a chain reaction of bank failures in North America and Europe. In the United States, the GNP fell by one-half in four years; industrial output fell by 50 percent; and unemployment rose from 3 to 25 percent of the labor force by 1932. All areas of the U.S. economy were hurt, and the misery was widespread.

Global Impact of the Great Depression

Global consequences were also severe. Some 30 percent of Germans were out of work by 1932, and German industrial output declined by half. A French politician summed up the disaster in his nation: "The oceans were deserted, the ships laid up in the silent ports, the factory smokestacks dead, long lines of

> "Hungry Americans flocked to breadlines and soup kitchens for food and milk supplied by charitable organizations."

workless in the towns, poverty throughout the countryside. Nations . . . shared the common lot of poverty."[8] Societies in Asia, Africa, Latin America, and the Caribbean were devastated as demand for raw materials such as rubber, tin, and sugar plummeted. Only the more insular USSR avoided major pain.

The Great Depression in the United States

The Great Depression brought severe economic distress to the wealthiest industrialized nation, the United States. Homeowners and farmers saw banks foreclose on their property. Migrant workers moved around in a futile search for jobs. Hungry Americans flocked to breadlines and soup kitchens for food and milk that was supplied by charitable organizations. Parts of the Midwest and Southwest became a Dust Bowl, as terrible drought and disappearing topsoil put agriculture badly out of balance. Farm income dropped 50 percent between 1929 and 1933, causing 3 to 4 million people, mostly former farmers, to head to the West Coast, especially California, after selling or losing their land. Panic, despair, and disillusionment seized the country.

Roosevelt's New Deal Reforms

The turmoil caused a turnaround in U.S. government policy and economic theory, as well as a change of leadership. Anger and discontent drove the Republicans from office in 1933 and brought in a new president, Democrat Franklin Delano Roosevelt (1882–1945). Roosevelt expressed optimism, telling the nation that they had nothing to fear but fear itself. He introduced the New Deal, a new government policy of liberal reform within a democratic framework to

Depression Breadline During the Depression, breadlines, such as this one in New York City, were common in the United States as millions of unemployed and desperate people sought food from social service providers, including religious groups.

WORLD'S HIGHEST STANDARD OF LIVING

There's no way like the American Way

alleviate the suffering caused by the Great Depression. His reforms included regulations on banks and stock exchanges to prevent future depressions and public welfare programs, such as public works jobs and social security that guaranteed retirement income for workers. For the first time in U.S. history, the federal government took responsibility for providing pensions and other supportive help to citizens. Roosevelt also legalized strikes and supported the organizing of workers to fight for better working conditions.

The direct involvement of the federal government in helping to alleviate social and economic problems altered the United States. Although it did not end the Depression, the New Deal made government popular and modified the pain enough that radicalism began to wane. By defusing the appeal of socialism and communism, the New Deal reforms, many historians conclude, probably saved U.S. capitalism. In the later 1930s, when the recovery faltered, Roosevelt used the ideas of the British economist John Maynard Keynes (1883–1946), who advocated deficit spending by governments to spur economic growth, a policy known as Keynesian economics. However, it was the mobilization of military forces and manufacturing during World War II that finally ended the Depression.

Global Depression's Impact

By devastating the economies of Europe and Japan, the Depression shattered the illusion of stability and challenged the weaker, less entrenched democratic systems. In most European countries, one-quarter to one-third of people were jobless. Germans often faced malnutrition, and hunger marches became common in Britain. A French observer described Paris as an "abyss of misery, suffering, and disorder, the theaters nearly empty, factories shut, businesses bankrupt; grey faces and bad news everywhere."[9] Countries developed public works programs to create jobs and also discouraged imports, further reducing international trade. Weimar Germany, whose democracy was fragile, had an enormous reparations debt and was in no position to launch a New Deal–style recovery.

European and Japanese Responses

Some other nations did discover remedies to gradually relieve the distress. Although British heavy industry recovered only modestly, newer industries such as automobiles and electronics showed rapid growth, and increased consumer demand for these products gradually turned around the British economy. The Scandinavian nations of Denmark, Norway, and Sweden had the most success by pursuing what came to be known as "the Middle Way," a combination of undogmatic socialist economics with long-established democratic traditions based on community action. By increasing government intervention in the economy, the social democrats ensured full employment and protected people from hardship.

The Depression hit Japan even harder than Europe and the United States, making clear its near-total dependence on foreign trade. As the world economy collapsed, many foreign markets closed and unemployment skyrocketed. Japan's foreign trade was cut in half in two years, forcing Japan's 100 million people to dramatically reduce consumption not only of luxuries but also of necessities, such as food and fuel. Unlike Britain, France, and the United States, Japan had no access to the resource-rich Western colonies in Southeast Asia. To resolve the nation's problems, Japanese leaders, becoming more authoritarian, turned to radical solutions, including expansion abroad and building a heavy arms industry at home.

The Rise of Mass Culture

Tempered by the trauma of war and then by the Depression, Western culture went in new directions during the interwar years. One major trend was the rise of mass culture, popular entertainments attuned to the tastes of a wide segment of the population and disseminated by the new mass media of radio and motion pictures. During the 1920s, radio stations appeared and the recording industry grew. By 1930, 40 percent of U.S. families owned a radio; by 1940, 86 percent did. The number of radios in Britain increased fivefold between 1926 and 1939.

Changing Artistic, Literary, and Scientific Perceptions

Western artists and writers responded to the twentieth century in new ways. The innovative and versatile Pablo Picasso (pi-KAH-so) (1881–1973), a Spaniard who settled in Paris, helped invent cubism, a form of painting that rejected visual reality and emphasized instead geometric shapes and forms that often suggested movement. The Irishman James Joyce (1882–1941), who had enjoyed no formal education

cubism

An early-twentieth-century form of painting that rejected visual reality and emphasized instead geometric shapes and forms that often suggested movement.

fascism

A twentieth-century ideology that typically involved extreme nationalism, hatred of ethnic minorities, ruthless repression of opposition groups, violent anticommunism, and authoritarian government.

but became close to many of the nation's leading thinkers and writers, broke traditional rules of grammar, and his books were often banned for using obscenity. In England, Virginia Woolf (1882–1941) converted the novel from a narrative story into a pattern of internal monologues, a succession of images, thoughts, and emotions known as stream of consciousness. Her 1929 novel, *A Room of One's Own*, championed women's growing economic independence.

The social and natural sciences also developed during the first half of the twentieth century, allowing for a greater understanding of human behavior and the physical world. Sigmund Freud (froid) (1856–1939), an Austrian Jewish physician, developed the field of psychoanalysis, a combination of medical science and psychology, and shocked the world by arguing that sex was of great subconscious importance in shaping people's behavior. In physics, Albert Einstein (1879–1955) radically modified the Newtonian vision of physical nature and rejected the absolutes of space and time. Einstein spent the rest of his life seeking a unifying theory to explain every physical process in the universe. He failed to achieve that goal, but some of the ideas he developed contributed to ongoing attempts by physicists to explain the universe.

LO⁴ The Rise of Fascism and the Renewal of Conflict

By devastating the economies of Germany and Japan, the Great Depression helped spread a new ideology in these countries. Although its form varied from country to country, this ideology, fascism, typically involved extreme nationalism, hatred of ethnic minorities, ruthless repression of opposition groups, violent anticommunism, and authoritarian government. Fascist movements began as political parties headed by charismatic leaders who supported military expansion. Fascism was an assault on the liberal values and rational thinking of the Enlightenment. It came to power in Italy, Germany, and Japan and also influenced China and several eastern European and Latin American nations.

> 66 Mussolini and his movement soon forged a new Italy. 99

Fascism in Italy and Germany

First emerging in Italy in 1921 in the aftermath of World War I, fascism was a response to the inadequacies, corruption, and instability of democratic politics there, as well as to the economic problems caused by World War I. Domestic unrest increased as Italy's peasants sought a more just society, workers demanded the right to form unions, and the economy slumped. Fascism arose from a pragmatic alliance of upper-class conservatives in the military, bureaucracy, and industry with discouraged members of the middle class who faced economic hardships. Both groups feared the possibility of Communist revolution. The middle class chiefly furnished the mass support for fascism. Benito Mussolini (MOO-suh-LEE-nee) (1883–1945), a blacksmith's son, one-time teacher and journalist, and former socialist and World War I veteran, founded the Italian fascist movement, which advocated national unity and strong government (see Witness to the Past: The Doctrine of Fascism).

Benito Mussolini

Mussolini and his movement soon forged a new Italy. A spellbinding orator, Mussolini had a talent for arousing mass enthusiasm by promising a vigorous and disciplined Italy. He especially attracted war veterans with his nationalistic rhetoric, accusing socialists of being unpatriotic and using an ancient Roman symbol, the *fasces*, a bundle of sticks wrapped around an ax handle and blade, to symbolize the unity and power he wanted to bring Italy. Mussolini won the support of the Italian king, the Catholic Church, landowners, industrialists, and the lower middle class, from which the fascists organized a uniform-wearing paramilitary group, the Blackshirts, who violently attacked, murdered, and intimidated opponents. In 1922, the king asked Mussolini to form a government. By 1926, Mussolini had killed, arrested, or cowed his opponents, turned Italy into a one-party state with restricted civil liberties, and created a cult of personality around himself. Despite the brutality, many Italians believed Mussolini was restoring social order.

The Rise of Hitler

Fascism became dominant in Germany after the Depression undermined the weak, democratic Weimar Republic that was already straining under the Versailles treaty's terms.

The Doctrine of Fascism

Benito Mussolini gradually developed an ideology for his movement that appealed to the Italian people's nationalistic emotions. The following excerpt comes from an essay under Mussolini's name that was published in an Italian encyclopedia in 1932. In fact, the true author was a Mussolini confidant, the philosopher Giovanni Gentile. The essay reflected Mussolini's vision of fascism as the wave of the future, in which the individual would subordinate her or his desires to the needs of the state.

Fascism, the more it considers and observes the future and the development of humanity quite apart from political considerations of the moment, believes neither in the possibility nor the utility of perpetual peace. It thus repudiates the doctrine of Pacifism—born of the renunciation of the struggle and an act of cowardice in the face of sacrifice. War alone brings up to its highest tension all human energy and puts the stamp of nobility upon the peoples who have the courage to meet it. . . . Fascism [is] the complete opposite of . . . Marxian Socialism, the materialist conception of history. . . . Above all Fascism denies that class-war can be the preponderant force in the transformation of society. . . .

After Socialism, Fascism combats the whole complex system of democratic ideology, and repudiates it, whether in its theoretical premises or in its practical application. Fascism denies that the majority, by the simple fact that it is a majority, can direct human society; it denies that numbers alone can govern by means of periodic consultation. . . . The democratic regime . . . [gives] the illusion of sovereignty, while the real effective sovereignty lies in the hands of other concealed and irresponsible forces. . . .

But the Fascist negation of Socialism, Democracy, and Liberalism must not be taken to mean that Fascism desires to lead the world back to the state of affairs before 1789 [the French Revolution]. . . . Given that the nineteenth century was the century of Socialism, of Liberalism, and of Democracy, it does not . . . follow that the twentieth century must also be the century of Socialism, Liberalism, and Democracy: political doctrines pass, but humanity remains. . . .

The foundation of Fascism is the conception of the State, its character, its duty, and its aim. Fascism conceives of the State as an absolute, in comparison with which all individuals or groups are relative, only to be conceived of in their relation to the State. . . . The Fascist state is itself conscious, and has itself a will and a personality. . . . The Fascist state is an embodied will to power and government, the Roman tradition is here an ideal of force in action. . . . Government is not so much a thing to be expressed in territorial or military terms as in terms of morality and the spirit. It must be thought of as an Empire—. . . a nation which directly or indirectly rules other nations. . . . For Fascism the growth of Empire, . . . the expansion of the nation, is an essential manifestation of vitality, and its opposite a sign of decadence. . . . But Empire demands discipline, the co-ordination of all forces and a deeply felt sense of duty and sacrifice; this fact explains many aspects of the practical working of the regime, the character of many forces in the State, and the necessarily severe measures which must be taken against those who would oppose this spontaneous and inevitable movement of Italy in the twentieth century, and would oppose it by recalling the outworn ideology of the nineteenth century.

Thinking About the Reading

1. Why does fascism reject pacifism, socialism, and liberal democracy?
2. What role does the state play under fascism?

Source: B. Mussolini, "The Political and Social Doctrine of Fascism," *Political Quarterly*, IV (July–September, 1933), pp. 341–356. Copyright © 1993 by Blackwell Publishing. Reprinted with permission by Blackwell Publishing.

The German people, who had an authoritarian political tradition and an economy in shambles, shared a widespread resentment of the World War I reparation payments. The Nazi Party, led by Adolph Hitler (1889–1945), offered a strategy for regaining political and economic strength and efficiency and for keeping workers under control. Hitler was an Austrian-born social misfit and frustrated artist who joined the German army in World War I. Already nurturing a hatred of Jews and labor unions, he became involved in right-wing German politics and, in 1920, helped form the Nazi Party, which promised to halt the unpopular reparations payments imposed by the Treaty of Versailles.

Hitler and the Nazis capitalized on the Great Depression to increase their strength. With economic collapse, the industrial workers moved left toward the communists, while the middle classes moved right toward the growing Nazi movement. Many Germans were willing to believe, as Hitler claimed, that Germany's problems could be blamed on unpopular minorities, especially the Jews, and foreign powers. Hitler understood propaganda and how to use

> "Hitler and the Nazis capitalized on the Great Depression to increase their strength."

a few basic ideas, such as anti-Semitism, and he made up "facts" to gain support. Hitler developed a powerful slogan: "one people, one government, one leader."

Nazism and Its Ideology

The Nazis won the largest number of seats in the 1932 elections, garnering nearly 14 million votes, and after 1933, Hitler tightened his grip on power, imposing ideological conformity, suppressing all dissent, and greatly expanding the army, thus solving the terrible unemployment problem. Massive government work-creation schemes eradicated unemployment by 1936. By 1939, Germany's GNP was 50 percent higher than it had been in 1929, mainly because of the manufacture of heavy machinery and armaments. But Hitler also sought to purify Germany racially, passing a series of anti-Semitic laws between 1933 and 1938. Hitler banned marriage and sexual relations between Jews and so-called Aryan Germans and eventually stripped German Jews of their citizenship.

Hitler's Motorcade In this photo from 1938, Adolph Hitler, standing stiffly in his car, salutes members of a paramilitary Nazi group, the Brownshirts, who parade before him at a Nazi rally in Nuremburg.

Japanese Militarism and Expansion

During the 1930s, Japan and Germany came to resemble each other fairly closely, even if their forms of fascism were very different. Although Japan never developed a mass-based Fascist Party like the Nazis, Japanese politics turned increasingly nationalistic and imperialistic. Japanese leaders often blamed foreign nations, especially the United States and the USSR, for Japan's problems. As in Nazi Germany, big business supported military expansion to gain resources and markets for exploitation.

Soon Japan turned more aggressive and authoritarian. In 1931, it invaded and gained control of the Chinese province of Manchuria. The League of Nations imposed no stiff penalties on Japan, a failure that helped to discredit that organization. The Japanese military, in alliance with big business and bureaucratic interests, now played a key role in the Japanese government. By 1936, the military controlled Japan and, as in Nazi Germany, imposed a fascist government that promoted labor control, censorship, the glorification of war, police repression, and hatred of foreign powers (the West). In 1937, a military skirmish outside of Beijing provided an excuse for Japan to launch a full-scale invasion of China, which prompted the United States to impose an oil embargo on Japan. By 1938, Japan controlled most of eastern China. When Japan signed a pact with Germany and Italy in 1940, the United States and Britain introduced stronger economic sanctions, including an oil embargo. Japan now faced economic collapse or war.

The Road to War

During the later 1930s, international tensions rose and various alliances formed. The United States, Britain, and France, known as the Allies, led a group of western European democracies that wanted to preserve the European state structure, the global economy, and the Western colonial system in Asia and Africa. The fascist countries, led by Germany, Italy, and Japan, known as the Axis Powers, sought to change the political map of Europe and Asia and gain dominance in the world economy. The prelude to another world war was also marked, as it had been for World War I, by diplomatic problems caused in part by a massive arms buildup all over Europe.

> **" The fascist countries, led by Germany, Italy, and Japan, known as the Axis Powers, sought to change the political map of Europe and Asia and gain dominance in the world economy. "**

Axis Imperialism

The big problem for the Allies was dealing with the imperialism of the Axis nations. Hitler pursued an aggressive foreign policy to dominate eastern Europe and unite the several million ethnic Germans separated by shifting state boundaries. In 1936, Hitler's troops occupied the Rhineland, German territory west of the Rhine River that had been demilitarized after World War I. Demonstrating how fascism had made Italy a strong power, in 1935, Italy invaded and brutally conquered the last independent African kingdom, Ethiopia. The League of Nations voted ineffective sanctions against Italy. Hitler and Mussolini forged a close alliance in 1936, but the later Tripartite Pact of 1940, linking Germany and Italy with Japan for mutual defense, was a marriage of strategic necessity, strained and wary.

The Spanish Civil War

Civil war in Spain heightened European tensions by drawing in foreign intervention and pitting competing ideologies against each other. Liberals and conservatives had struggled for two centuries to shape Spanish politics, and by the 1930s, Spain was polarized between left and right. During the 1936 elections, Spain's Republicans—a left-wing coalition of liberals, socialists, and communists promising reforms—edged out the National Front of conservatives, monarchists, and staunch Catholics. Alarmed, the right rallied around the fascist military forces led by General Francisco Franco (1892–1975), launching the Spanish Civil War (1936–1939). The Loyalist government forces, aided by the USSR, ultimately lost to Franco's fascists at a huge cost in lives on both sides. The war had an international flavor. Germany and Italy helped the Spanish fascists with weapons and advice, and several thousand volunteers from North America and varied European nations fought for the Loyalist cause. But the governments of the Western Allies refused to support the Loyalists, whom they viewed as too radical. The German bombing of Guernica (GWAR-ni-kuh), a village in northern Spain that was inhabited largely by Basque people, caused an international outcry and prompted Pablo Picasso to paint a celebrated testament to the atrocity.

The Failure of Appeasement

In the late 1930s, the Allies led by Britain followed a policy of appeasement toward fascist aggression. They were not yet prepared for war, and the catastrophe of World War I, in which several million young British and French men had died, meant that many saw another war as too terrible to contemplate. Yet war became inevitable. In 1938, Hitler turned his attention to eastern Europe, taking over Austria and then Czechoslovakia. As the war clouds approached, Hitler declared: "We shall not capitulate—no never! We may be destroyed, but if we are, we shall drag a world with us—a world in flames."[10] In August 1939, Hitler and Stalin signed the Nazi-Soviet Pact, a nonaggression agreement, and then Hitler launched an invasion of Poland, forcing France and Britain to declare war against Germany.

LO⁵ World War II: A Global Transition

Historians have sometimes viewed the years from 1914 to 1945 as one continuum, with World War II a continuation and amplification of World War I. Both wars shared some of the same causes, including nationalist rivalries, threats to the European balance of power, and a struggle to control the global economic system. But there were differences, too. For one, World War II also involved a three-way ideological contest between democracy, fascism, and communism. For another, the trench warfare and modest aerial bombing of World War I was superseded by the far more widespread aerial bombing and mobile armies used in World War II, with civilians now fair game.

World War II began as a European conflict, and for the first two years, major battles were confined largely to Europe, the North Atlantic, and North Africa. The firestorm soon became global, however, creating almost a separate war fought in East and Southeast Asia and the western Pacific. The conflict became the most costly war in world history, bringing staggering misery and ultimately killing some 50 million people. The war resulted in some of history's worst genocides and the use of the deadliest weapons ever known. It marked a major transition that reshaped world politics and international relations.

Cataclysmic War and Holocaust

In September 1939, Europe plunged into armed struggle, and in the next year, Germany and its allies

CHRONOLOGY

World War II, 1939–1945

1939	Beginning of war in Europe
June 1941	German invasion of Soviet Union
December 1941	Japanese bombing of Pearl Harbor; invasion of Southeast Asia
1942	Battle of Midway
1944	Allied landing at Normandy
July 1944	Bretton Woods Conference
February 1945	Yalta Conference
April 1945	Allied invasion of Germany
August 1945	U.S. bombing of Hiroshima and Nagasaki

overran nearly all of Europe, except for valiant Britain and neutral Switzerland and Sweden (see Map 24.3).

 Interactive Map

Germany imposed puppet regimes in the conquered territories, including the Vichy (VISH-ee) government in France headed by World War I hero, General Philippe Pétain, described in the chapter-opening vignette. The conquered countries were exploited by Germany, and millions of civilians were enslaved to work on German farms and in factories.

Churchill and Allied Resistance

But Germany failed to achieve all of its strategic objectives. Led by Prime Minister Winston Churchill (1874–1965), the heroic British withstood a blitz of aerial bombing in 1940 and German submarines in the Atlantic. Italian efforts to carve out a Mediterranean empire faltered, compelling the Germans to divert military resources to North Africa and Greece. Also frustrating Nazi goals were underground movements that emerged all over Europe to fight the Nazis.

In June 1941, the conflict expanded eastward. Germany broke its nonaggression pact and invaded Russia, driving deeply into the country. After misjudging German intentions and reeling from the invasion, the Soviet leader, Joseph Stalin, joined the anti-Axis alliance and received aid from the United

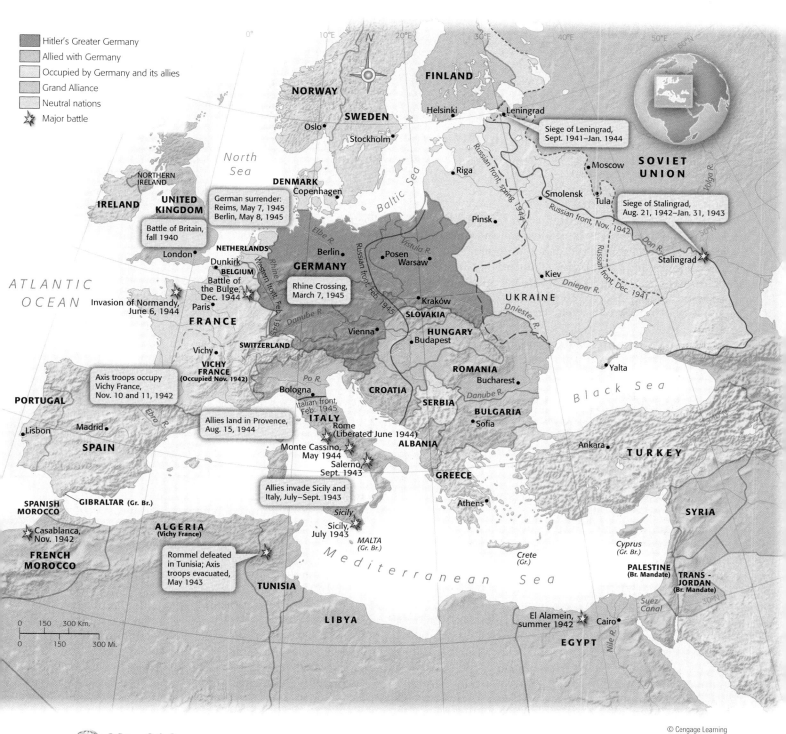

Key:
- Hitler's Greater Germany
- Allied with Germany
- Occupied by Germany and its allies
- Grand Alliance
- Neutral nations
- ★ Major battle

Siege of Leningrad, Sept. 1941–Jan. 1944

Siege of Stalingrad, Aug. 21, 1942–Jan. 31, 1943

German surrender: Reims, May 7, 1945 Berlin, May 8, 1945

Battle of Britain, fall 1940

Rhine Crossing, March 7, 1945

Battle of the Bulge, Dec. 1944

Invasion of Normandy, June 6, 1944

Axis troops occupy Vichy France, Nov. 10 and 11, 1942

Allies land in Provence, Aug. 15, 1944

Monte Cassino, May 1944

Salerno, Sept. 1943

Allies invade Sicily and Italy, July–Sept. 1943

Casablanca, Nov. 1942

Rommel defeated in Tunisia; Axis troops evacuated, May 1943

El Alamein, summer 1942

Russian front, spring 1944

Russian front, Nov. 1942

Russian front, Dec. 1941

Russian front, Feb. 1945

Western front, Feb. 1945

Italian front, Feb. 1945

Map 24.3
World War II in Europe and North Africa

The Axis Powers, led by Germany and Italy, initially occupied much of Europe, and in 1941 they invaded the Soviet Union, but they were unable to hold their gains against the counteroffensive of the United States, Britain, the Soviet Union, and the Free French forces.

> "German racist nationalism led to horrific campaigns of extermination against unpopular minorities and conquered peoples."

German resistance, faced retribution. The Nazis sent Bonhoeffer to a concentration camp in 1943 and hanged him in 1945.

Globalization of the War

Conflict between Japan and the United States eventu-

States and Britain that helped the USSR resist. It was an alliance of convenience, since the Western leaders and Stalin mistrusted each other. By winter 1941, German forces had reached the outskirts of Moscow and encircled another major city, Stalingrad. But although Germany had superior military forces, it ultimately failed to capture the major Russian cities, because the Red Army began an effective counterattack. The turning point came in February 1943, as the Soviet Red Army stopped the Germans at Stalingrad (today Volgograd). By the summer, German forces began a long, humiliating retreat from Russia.

The Holocaust

> 66 Conflict between Japan and the United States eventually globalized the war. 99

German racist nationalism led to horrific campaigns of extermination against unpopular minorities and conquered peoples. Hitler ordered what he called the "final solution" of the "Jewish Question." The term Holocaust came to be used for the Nazis' deliberate murder of Jews and Romany (Gypsies), one of the worst genocides, or deliberate mass killings of a target group, in history. Ultimately, some three-quarters of Europe's Jews were killed in the Holocaust. During 1942, the Germans had erected death camps, such as Bergen-Belsen (BUR-guhn-BEL-suhn) in western Germany and Auschwitz (OUSH-vits) in western Poland, targeting especially the large Jewish populations of Germany, Poland, and Ukraine. But Jews everywhere in Nazi-occupied Europe—Vichy France, the Netherlands, Hungary, Russia—were rounded up and put in death camps, where they were killed in gas chambers, starved, or worked to death. In addition to the 6 million Jews and half a million Romany (Gypsies) murdered in the Holocaust, the Nazis were responsible for the deaths of 11 million Slavs (including over 3 million Poles) and half a million other Europeans, including German communists, socialists, anti-Nazi Christians, and homosexuals.

Only a few brave Germans dared to resist or subvert Nazi policies and actions. Those who did, such as the Lutheran theologian Dietrich Bonhoeffer (BON-ho-fuhr) (1906–1945), a strong critic of Nazism and anti-Semitism who supported the underground

ally globalized the war (see Map 24.4). On December 7, 1941, what President Franklin D. Roosevelt called "a date which will live in infamy," Japanese navy ships and planes attacked the U.S. naval base at Pearl Harbor, Hawaii, destroying a considerable portion of the U.S. Pacific fleet, killing 2,400 Americans, and ending U.S. neutrality. Japanese leaders sought to defeat the Western colonial powers, especially the United States. At the same time they were attacking Pearl Harbor, Japanese military forces launched an invasion of Southeast Asia. Within several months, they controlled most of the region, having forced the United States out of the Philippines and jailed the British and Dutch residents of their respective colonies. For its industrial economy, Japan badly needed the resources of Southeast Asia, especially the oil and rubber of the Dutch East Indies (Indonesia). The Japanese already controlled eastern China after their invasion of 1937. Preoccupied with war in Europe, the Western powers were unable to resist the Japanese advance.

 Interactive Map

The 1941 Pearl Harbor attack outraged Americans who were once reluctant to go to war. A patriotic wave swept the country as America entered the war on both fronts, with early efforts aimed at defeating the Nazis in Europe. The war affected all segments of American society, especially women and ethnic minorities, in various ways. Six million women joined the workforce as the government encouraged women to do their "patriotic duty" in jobs that were once considered unladylike, such as on factory assembly lines. Some 5 million blacks left southern rural areas in the 1930s and 1940s and often found jobs in northern and western cities. After defeating fascism abroad, more white Americans were sympathetic to the demands of black organizations that they now wanted democracy in the United States, especially in the segregated South.

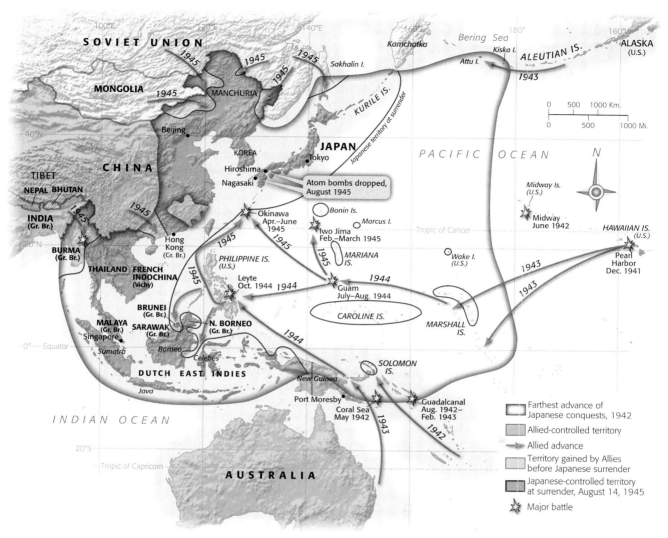

 **Map 24.4**
World War II in Asia and the Pacific

© Cengage Learning

After invading China in 1937, Japan disabled the U.S. fleet at Pearl Harbor in 1941 and in 1941–1942 occupied most of Southeast Asia and the western Pacific. The United States and its Allies pushed back the Japanese forces from their bases in the Pacific and bombed Japan from those bases, but Japan did not surrender until 1945, when the United States dropped atomic bombs on Hiroshima and Nagasaki.

The Decision to Use the Atomic Bomb
Learn why President Truman was advised to drop atomic bombs on Japan, from the chairman of the committee that gave him that advice.

But racism aimed at 110,000 Japanese Americans fueled one of the greatest invasions of civil liberties in U.S. history, as the U.S. government rounded them up, seized their property, and sent them to sparse internment camps in remote areas for the duration of the conflict. Their property was never returned. Many of these Americans were U.S.-born or naturalized citizens living in western states who had faced discrimination for decades. No evi-

dence of espionage by any Japanese American was ever discovered.

The End of the War

The U.S. entry in the war on the Allied side changed the shape of the conflict. The Axis forces had been triumphant through 1942, as Germany dominated much of Europe and North Africa, and Japan controlled most of Asia east of India and large areas of the western Pacific. In 1943, however, the tide began to turn. The Germans were defeated in North Africa, and Allied landings in Italy knocked that country out of the war. In June 1944, British and American forces landed on five beaches at Normandy, on the Atlantic coast of France, and with the help of the anti-Vichy Free French forces under General Charles DeGaulle (duh GAWL) (1890–1970), began pushing the Germans back.

The Defeat of Germany

The Axis forces were now on the defensive in Europe, but Germany was defeated only by massive Allied ground offensives and aerial bombardment, which stopped German armed forces and demoralized the civilian German population. The British fire-bombed several German cities and killed thousands of civilians. The Soviet Red Army pushed the Germans back in the east, while U.S. and British forces pushed the battered German army back from the west. Through the winter, the German war economy collapsed. In spring 1945, as British and U.S. armies moved into Germany from the west and the Soviet Red Army from the east, Hitler committed suicide in his underground bunker in Berlin, and Germany surrendered. Soon newsreels of the liberation of the concentration camps revealed to the whole world the full extent of Nazi atrocities.

 Experience the consequences of World War II through the eyes of one of three characters in this interactive simulation.

The Atomic Bomb and the Surrender of Japan

The Japanese defeat was even more dramatic than that of the Nazis in Europe. In June 1942, the United States stopped the Japanese Pacific advance at the battle of Midway Island, west of Hawaii, and began an offensive to isolate the Japanese bases in the Pacific. By mid-1944, it had pushed the Japanese out of most of the western Pacific islands, from which it launched bombing raids on Japan. By early 1945, U.S. forces, aided by the Australians and British, started to retake Southeast Asia and China from Japanese forces. The invasion of the small Japanese island of Okinawa (oh-kee-NAH-wah), in the Ryukyus just south of Japan, cost the lives of 10,000 American troops and 80,000 Japanese civilians, suggesting to U.S. officials what an invasion of the main Japanese islands might entail. Devastating as the war had been, however, Japan resisted American demands for total surrender.

> "World War II had heavy costs and large-scale consequences."

In August 1945, the United States forced the issue by dropping an atomic bomb on the Japanese city of Hiroshima. The bomb demolished most of the city and killed 80,000 people; thousands more were maimed or died later from injuries or radiation. Three days later, an American plane dropped a second bomb on Nagasaki, killing another 60,000 Japanese civilians. The Japanese emperor, Hirohito (HEAR-oh-HEE-toe) (1901–1989), opted for surrender on August 15. He went on the radio to ask his people to "suffer the insufferable, endure the unendurable," and cooperate with the U.S. occupation. For the first time in its long history, Japan had been defeated and successfully invaded. Disgraced, more than five hundred military officers committed suicide. World War II had come to an end.

Historical Reflections

Historians differ on whether it was necessary militarily to drop the atomic bombs on Japan, causing so many civilian deaths and forever changing the nature of war. Many contend that the Japanese would have fiercely resisted an American invasion, and hence the bombs ultimately saved many American and Japanese lives, while others argue that the United States used their terrible new weapon as a warning to the Soviet Union about U.S. capabilities, intended to dissuade Stalin from any expansionist ideas. In any case, Japan lost the war primarily because it overstretched its forces and failed to convert Southeast Asian resources into military and industrial products fast enough to defeat the larger, wealthier United States. Its brutal treatment of the Chinese and Southeast Asians, such as the 1937 "Rape of Nanjing," in which thousands of Chinese were massacred by Japanese troops, caused most Southeast Asians to look on the Japanese as perhaps even worse than the Western colonizers they had replaced.

The Costs and Consequences of Global War

World War II had heavy costs and large-scale consequences. It took a terrible toll in lives: approximately 15 million military and 35 million civilian deaths. Soviet Russia, which lost more than 20 million people, or 10 percent of its population, now had one more bitter memory in a long history of invasions by countries to the west. Poland and Yugoslavia both lost more than 10 percent of their people. Britain lost 375,000 people and France 600,000. Strategic bombing blasted parts of every major German city to rubble. In Asia, more than 2 million Japanese military personnel and probably 1 million Japanese civilians died, and 7 million Chinese were killed or wounded. Fighting on both fronts, some 300,000 American military personnel died. The European and Asian countries involved were economically devastated.

The war cleared the way for new global economic arrangements. In 1944, U.S. president Roosevelt summoned representatives of forty-four countries to a conference held in Bretton Woods, New Hampshire, to establish the postwar world economic order. The Bretton Woods Conference set up the International Monetary Fund and the World Bank, both dominated by the United States, to provide credit to states requiring financial investment for major economic projects. Bretton Woods also fixed currency exchange rates and encouraged trade liberalization, both policies that benefited the United States most.

World War II transformed world politics, removing the twin threats of German Nazism and Japanese militarism. In contrast to World War I, the victorious Allies were more generous toward the vanquished, giving the defeated nations massive aid and guidance to speed economic recovery. U.S. forces occupied Japan for several years, while Germany was temporarily divided into sectors controlled by Russia, Britain, France, and the United States. The war also fostered political changes in Asia. Chinese, Korean, and Vietnamese communists took advantage of Japanese occupation to gain support for their movements, and Western colonial rule was undermined throughout Southeast Asia (see Chapter 25).

Allied leaders also developed new political institutions and links for the postwar world. In February 1945, Roosevelt, Churchill, and Stalin met at a conference at Yalta (YAWL-tuh), in Russia's Crimean peninsula, to determine the postwar political order. The conference agreed to set up a world organization, the United Nations, and also divided Europe into anticommunist and communist spheres of interest. Western leaders, drained by war and seeking postwar stability in Europe, reluctantly agreed to Stalin's demand that the Soviet Union be allowed to dominate eastern Europe by stationing troops there and influencing its governments.

The aftermath of war also fostered a new rivalry between the two emerging superpowers, the United States and the USSR, that complicated the new global political order. The United States, which had not fought on its own soil, emerged from the war politically and economically stronger, becoming the dominant world power. But the USSR emerged from the war as a military power with imperial ambitions.

U.S. Air Force/AP Images

Bombing of Nagasaki This photo shows the awesome power of the atomic bomb dropped by the United States on the Japanese city of Nagasaki in August 1945, three days after the atomic bombing of Hiroshima. Some 60,000 Japanese died in the Nagasaki bombing.

U.S. leaders realized their nation would have to help reconstruct Europe and Japan to restore political stability and thwart Soviet ambitions there.

The political history of the world between 1945 and 1989 would revolve around the conflict between these two competing superpowers. Rapidly rebuilding after the war, the USSR installed communist governments throughout eastern Europe, including one in the eastern part of Germany under Soviet occupation. Indeed, World War II increased the appeal of communism worldwide and led to the establishment of communist regimes in Yugoslavia and North Korea. Both Soviet and U.S. leaders tended to look at the world through the lens of their World War II experience. For the USSR, that meant paranoia about any threat from the West and the need for military power. Americans tended to find a repeat of Hitler's aggression anywhere in the world they experienced a political threat, and they often sought to assert their power proactively. The U.S.–Soviet rivalry created a world very different from that existing before World War II.

Listen to a synopsis of Chapter 24.

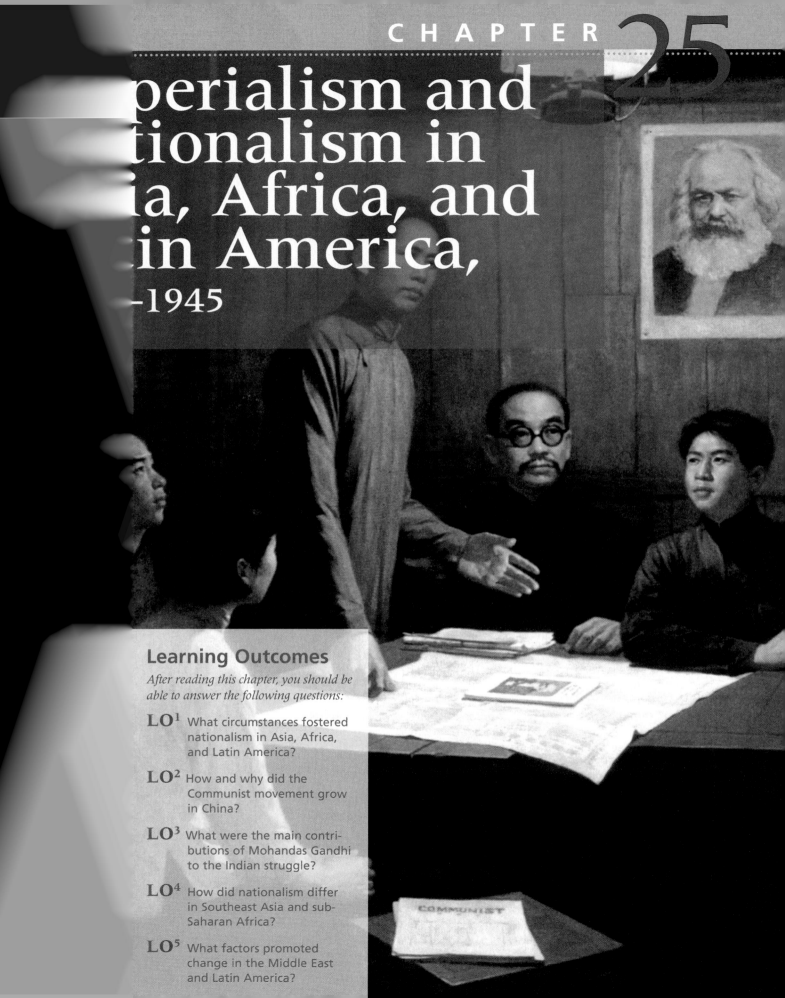

CHAPTER

25

perialism and
tionalism in
ia, Africa, and
in America,
–1945

Learning Outcomes

*After reading this chapter, you should be
able to answer the following questions:*

LO¹ What circumstances fostered
nationalism in Asia, Africa,
and Latin America?

LO² How and why did the
Communist movement grow
in China?

LO³ What were the main contributions of Mohandas Gandhi
to the Indian struggle?

LO⁴ How did nationalism differ
in Southeast Asia and sub-
Saharan Africa?

LO⁵ What factors promoted
change in the Middle East
and Latin America?

> 66What unhappiness strikes the poor, Who wear a single worn-out, torn cloth. Oh heaven, why are you not just? Some have abundance while others are in want.99
>
> —**Peasant folk song protesting colonialism in Vietnam**[1]

In 1911, Nguyen Tat Thanh, a young man from an impoverished village in French-ruled Vietnam, signed on as a merchant seaman on a French ship; he would not return to his homeland for another thirty years. Nguyen hated colonialism and was dreaming of an independent nation of Vietnam. While abroad, he worked as a cook in London and photo retoucher in Paris, spending his free time reading books on politics and working with Asian nationalists and French socialists to oppose colonialism, especially in Vietnam. Nguyen became famous among Vietnamese exiles for his efforts to address the delegates at the Paris Peace Conference after World War I about the self-determination of peoples, but the major Western powers, unwilling to consider any change in their colonial domains, refused to permit his entry.

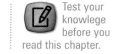
What do you think?

Nationalism became a strong force for change in Western-dominated societies in Asia, Africa, and Latin America.

Strongly Disagree					Strongly Agree	
1	2	3	4	5	6	7

Becoming disillusioned with Western democracy, the Vietnamese exile helped found the French Communist Party and spent time in the Soviet Union, becoming convinced that communism was the most effective strategy for promoting self-determination and nationalism. Later, under a new name, Ho Chi Minh ("He Who Enlightens"), he led the communist forces in Vietnam in their long struggle against French colonialism and then against the Americans. Ho became a worldwide symbol of national assertion, opposition to Western imperialism, and sympathy for the plight of peasants.

Between 1914 and 1945, nationalistic Asians such as Ho Chi Minh challenged the imperialism that had reshaped Asian and African politics and economies in the late nineteenth and early twentieth centuries. Rapid, often destabilizing change sparked nationalism aimed at escaping Western domination or control, especially after World War I weakened the European powers. Nationalist forces were awakened in colonies from Indonesia to Egypt to Senegal, becoming especially strong in India and Vietnam, and the Great Depression

<< **Mao Zedong Organizing Communists in China** This later artist's rendition shows the young Mao Zedong, the future Chinese Communist leader, organizing a communist group in his native province, Hunan, around 1921. A portrait of Karl Marx decorates the wall.

Photo12/The Image Works

generated further anger against the imperial system. In some societies in these regions, those seeking to overturn the status quo, such as Ho Chi Minh, mobilized large followings from discontented people. Despite frequent protests, the Western powers were able to retain their empires until after World War II, when nationalist movements became even stronger and made a return to the imperialist era impossible.

> "To cover the costs of managing the colonies, the colonial governments used a variety of methods that increased resentment, including higher taxes and forced labor."

LO¹ Western Imperialism and Its Challengers

The events that rocked the industrialized nations between 1914 and 1945—two world wars, the Russian Revolution, and the Great Depression—also affected the nonindustrialized societies of Asia, Africa, and Latin America, who enjoyed little power in the global system. But developments in nonindustrialized societies also owed much to local dynamics. When social and economic changes resulting from colonialism proved destabilizing, many disenchanted Asians and Africans adopted nationalism and Marxism to strengthen their own societies and resist Western colonizers.

The Impact of Colonialism

The colonialism imposed by Western nations on most Asians, Africans, and West Indians between 1500 and 1914 had a major impact. The slaughter of millions of people during World War I undermined Western credibility and whatever moral authority Western peoples claimed to possess. Thousands of colonial subjects conscripted in Asia and Africa as soldiers and workers died in the war effort. Both France and Germany drafted men, often through harsh and arbitrary methods, while Britain sent Africans and Indians. Some 46,000 Kenyans died fighting for Britain, and at least 25,000 West Africans perished helping France on the front lines. British and French officials had muted African resistance to the draft by promising democratic reforms, special treatment for war veterans,

and compensation for the families of deceased soldiers, but these promises were not carried out.

Colonialism also reshaped societies, often with harmful political, economic, and social results. As discussed in Chapters 21 and 22, colonization had resulted in the creation of artificial states that often ignored the ethnic composition of the territory or the historical configuration and economic bases of states in the region. As a result, colonies such as Dutch-ruled Indonesia, British Nigeria, and the Belgian Congo incorporated diverse and often rival ethnic groups who had little sense of national unity.

To cover the costs of managing the colonies, the colonial governments used a variety of methods that increased resentment, including higher taxes and forced labor. Forced labor was common in the African colonies, such as in Portuguese-ruled Mozambique, where men and women who could not pay the required taxes were sent to plantations and mines to work. Among the worst abuses by colonial regimes in Southeast Asia were their opium and alcohol monopolies, which enriched government coffers by requiring villagers to purchase designated amounts of these products. By 1918, opium sales accounted for one-third of all colonial revenues in Vietnam, and some Vietnamese became addicted to opium. Furthermore, most of the colonies developed economies that locked them into the almost exclusive production and export of one or two primary commodities. These economic limitations hampered later economic diversification.

Colonized peoples also disliked the arrogance of the Western colonizers. Europeans and North Americans assumed that their societies were superior, above those of other peoples of the world. This ethnocentric, often racist attitude was enshrined in the Covenant for the new League of Nations formed after World War I, which considered the colonized peoples not yet able to govern themselves in the modern world. Exploiting their unequal power, the Western officials, businessmen, and planters in the colonies commonly enjoyed mansions, servants, and private clubs, while many local people lived in dire poverty, underfed and malnourished.

At the same time, colonial governments built a modern communications and economic infrastructure that often spurred economic growth. The

Exporting Resources from Indonesia Small boats brought cash crops grown in eastern Java, part of the Dutch East Indies, to the port of Surabaya, from where they were shipped to Europe.

governments of British India, Dutch Indonesia, and British East Africa financed railroads that facilitated the movement of goods and people. Colonialism also fostered the growth of cities like British Kenya's capital, Nairobi, which grew to more than 100,000 people by 1944. Port cities founded by Western colonizers, such as Hong Kong on the China coast and Cape Town in South Africa, became key hubs of world trade. Improved health and sanitation contributed to rapid population growth in colonies such as India, Indonesia, the Philippines, and Vietnam, but this population growth outstripped economic resources, exacerbating poverty and, for Indians and Indonesians, stimulating emigration. In short, while defenders of colonialism boasted of their contributions, critics questioned how much they benefited Asians and Africans.

Competing Ideologies

The capitalism introduced by the West spurred resentment and anticolonial nationalism. Some non-European merchants, such as the Chinese in Southeast Asia and the Lebanese in West Africa, did

> 66 As a result of capitalism's excesses and failures, ideologies of resistance, including nationalism and Marxism, grew in influence in the colonized world. 99

profit from the growing economic opportunities. But colonial social and economic policies that promoted the spread of the capitalist market also destabilized rural villages, fomenting opposition to these policies.

The commercialization of agriculture transformed traditional, often communal, landowning arrangements into private property systems that converted land into a commodity to be exploited on the free market. Lacking the money or connections to compete, many peasants fell into dire poverty.

The Failure of Capitalism

The Great Depression of the 1930s was further reason for colonized peoples to conclude that global capitalism was a failure. The downturn brought economic catastrophe to many nonindustrialized societies as demand for their resources in the industrialized nations plummeted. Collapsing prices for rubber, sugar, and coffee crops harmed Southeast Asians. In Latin America, Argentina saw livestock and wheat prices collapse, and Cuba was staggered by falling sugar prices. As exports declined, colonial revenues also fell. Unequal landowning, growing mass poverty, limited economic opportunities for displaced peasants, and foreign control of the economy produced political unrest and anticapitalist activism.

Nationalism

As a result of capitalism's excesses and failures, ideologies of resistance, including nationalism and Marxism, grew in influence in the colonized world. In time, movements for change became movements for independence. Nationalism became especially popular among the educated middle class—students, lawyers, teachers, merchants, and military officers. Colonial powers set up few universities, but those that existed, such as the University of Rangoon in British Burma (today's Myanmar), offered a venue for nationalist-government conflicts and campus protests. To anticolonial leaders, nationalism promoted a sense of belonging to a nation that transcended parochial differences such as social class and religion. But the "nation" sometimes existed only in people's imagination: in the multiethnic colonies of Africa, Southeast Asia, and the Caribbean, it was difficult to overcome ethnic antagonism and rivalries to create a feeling of nationhood.

Marxism

Some Asians, Africans, and Latin Americans who sought radical change, such as Ho Chi Minh, mixed nationalism with Marxism, the ideas of socialism and revolution advocated by the nineteenth-century German Karl Marx. For them, Marxist ideas provided an alternative vision to colonialism, capitalism, and discredited local traditions and leaders. Young Asians, Africans, and West Indians studying abroad often adopted Marxism after facing bleak employment prospects and political repression back at home. Some of them gravitated to the most dogmatic form of Marxism, the communism practiced in the Soviet Union by the Bolsheviks (see Chapter 24), which required the leadership of a centralized revolutionary party. Radical nationalists, especially in Asia, also adopted revolutionary ideas developed by the Russian communist leader, Vladimir Lenin. Lenin saw the world as divided between imperial countries (the exploiters) and dominated countries (the exploited). Lenin's view appealed to radical nationalists who sought to make sense of their subjugation to the West. Although communist nations, among them the Soviet Union, also proved capable of blatantly imperialistic policies, during the first four decades of the twentieth century, Lenin's theory of capitalism-based imperialism seemed to offer validity.

Lengthening the Imperial Reach

At the same time that anti-imperialist feelings were rising between 1900 and 1945, the Allied victors of World War I were expanding their imperial reach and continuing to intervene in less-powerful nations. After the defeat of Germany and its Ottoman ally, Britain and France took control of the former Ottoman colonies in western Asia and the German colonies in Africa. Some of these societies, such as oil-rich Iraq, had valuable resources. Likewise, Australia and Japan occupied the German-ruled Pacific islands. Supported by colonial governments, Europeans continued to settle in Algeria, Angola, Kenya, South Africa, and Southern Rhodesia and to dispossess local people from their land. Moreover, while the war had ended, Western military conquests in Africa had not. In 1935–1936, Italy invaded and brutally conquered the last independent African state, Ethiopia, killing some 200,000 Ethiopians. The Ethiopian forces faced a fully mechanized and mobile Italian army, and, despite their spirited defense of the mountainous terrain, they succumbed to superior Italian aerial bombing and firepower. Italy's fascist dictator, Benito Mussolini, argued that it was a war to spread "civilization" and "liberate Africans"; in fact, he hoped to settle Italians in Ethiopia.

Meanwhile, the major Western power after World War I, the United States, continued to exercise influence in the Americas. During the Mexican Revolution, President Woodrow Wilson sent thousands of U.S. troops into Mexico to restore order and thereby protect large U.S. investments, particularly in the oil industry. American attitudes favoring the spread of democracy and capitalism in the world also played a role in the interventions, with Wilson

> " At the same time that anti-imperialist feelings were rising between 1900 and 1945, the Allied victors of World War I were expanding their imperial reach and continuing to intervene in less-powerful nations. "

arguing that he would teach the Latin American republics to elect good leaders. The United States' desire to protect U.S. investments by maintaining stability in Central America meant supporting the governments led by landowners and generals, such as the notoriously corrupt Nicaraguan president, Anastasio Somoza (1896–1956). Repeated U.S. interventions in the region left an aftertaste of local resentment against what Central Americans called "Yankee imperialism."

LO² Nationalism and Communism in China

The Chinese Revolution of 1911–1912, which ended the 2,000-year-old imperial system (see Chapter 23), had led to a republic that Chinese hoped would give the nation renewed strength in the world, but these hopes were dashed when China lapsed into warlordism and civil war, with a central government in name only and subject to pressure from the West and Japan. China's domestic failures and continuing Western imperialism sparked a vigorous nationalism as well as the formation of a communist party and China's eventual reunification.

Warlords, New Cultures, and Nationalism

During the demoralizing Warlord Era (1916–1927), China was divided into territories controlled by rival warlords, local political leaders that had their own armies. The warlords extracted revenue as their armies terrorized the local population. They were a mixed lot. Some called themselves nationalists and reformers and were interested in promoting education and industry; others took bribes to carry out policies favoring merchants or foreign governments. Meanwhile, high taxes, inflation, famine, accelerating social tensions, and banditry made life difficult for most Chinese.

The New Culture Movement

Radical new currents arose out of the people's despair. Cities became enclaves of revolutionary ideas for Chinese society and governance. New schools and universities opened, and schools for girls became more common. Thanks to educational opportunities, by the 1920s, many women worked as nurses, teachers, and civil servants, especially in cities. Exposure to Western ideas in universities, especially those run by Christian missionaries, led some Chinese students to question their own cultural traditions. such as footbinding, which largely disappeared except in remote rural areas by 1930.

During this time, Chinese intellectuals supported the New Culture Movement, which sought to erase the discredited past and sprout a literary revival. The movement originated in 1915 at Beijing University, China's intellectual mecca that hired radical professors and encouraged a mixing of Chinese and Western thought. There a group of professors began publishing the literary magazine *New Youth*, which became the chief vehicle for attacking China's traditions, including Confucianism, and advocating for republican government, equality, and scientific progress.

warlords
Local political leaders with their own armies.

New Culture Movement
A movement of Chinese intellectuals started in 1915 that sought to wash away the discredited past and sprout a literary revival.

CHRONOLOGY

China, 1911–1945

1911–1912	Chinese Revolution
1915	Beginning of New Culture Movement
1916–1927	Warlord Era
1919	May Fourth Movement
1926–1928	Northern Expedition to reunify China
1927	Guomindang suppression of communists
1927–1934	Mao Zedong's Jiangxi Soviet
1928–1937	Republic of China in Nanjing
1931	Japanese occupation of Manchuria
1935–1936	Long March by Chinese communists
1937–1945	Japanese invasion of China

The 21 Demands and the May Fourth Movement

Chinese rage against Western and Japanese imperialism increased in the aftermath of World War I. Although China had remained neutral, Japan, allied with Britain, took over the German sphere of influence in the Shandong peninsula of eastern China. In 1919, with the war over, Japan presented China with 21 Demands, including control of Shandong, increased rights in Manchuria, and appointment of Japanese advisers to the Chinese government. The 21 Demands and the decision by the Western allies to allow Japan to take over Shandong provoked a radical nationalist resurgence among students and workers, known as the May Fourth Movement, which opposed imperialism and the ineffective, warlord-controlled Chinese government. Shouting that China's territory could not be given away, the protestors also decried social injustice and government inaction. Capitulating to the protests, the Chinese government refused to sign the Versailles treaty that followed World War I. The new communist government running the Soviet Union openly sided with China, winning admiration among the Chinese.

Some Chinese also began studying communism, finding in it new promise for organizing change. In 1921, professors and students at Beijing University, many of whom had been active in the New Culture and May Fourth Movements, organized the Chinese Communist Party (CCP). Some of the party founders were European- or Japanese-educated reformers who admired Western science and culture, while others were nationalists who despised Western models. The communists recruited support by forming peasant associations, labor unions, women's groups, and youth clubs. Soviet advisers encouraged the party to organize among the urban working class but otherwise largely neglected the Chinese communists.

The Chinese Nationalist Party

The Guomindang (gwo-min-dong), or Nationalist Party, also called for the reunification of China. It was led by Sun Zhongshan, better known as Sun Yat-sen (soon yot-SEN) (1866–1925), who had led the revolutionary movement that overthrew the Qing dynasty

> **Chinese rage against Western and Japanese imperialism increased in the aftermath of World War I.**

but had then been forced into exile (see Chapter 23). Receiving no help from the Western nations, Sun forged closer ties to the Soviet Union, which sent advisers and military aid. In the mid-1920s, Sun's Guomindang and the Chinese communists worked together, in an alliance known as the United Front, to defeat warlordism and prevent foreign encroachment. However, Sun's ideology grew less democratic and more authoritarian, and he came to believe that China's 400 million people were not ready for democracy. Sun died in 1925, and the new Guomindang leader, Sun's brother-in-law, Jiang Jieshi (better known in the West as Chiang Kai-shek) (1887–1975), was more conservative. Chiang was a pro-business soldier and a patriot but indifferent to social change. He began developing a close relationship with the United States while building a modern military force.

The Republic of China

Between 1926 and 1928, the Guomindang forces and their communist allies succeeded in reunifying China with a military drive known as the Northern Expedition, during which they defeated or co-opted the warlords. The foreign powers recognized Chiang's new Republic of China, but the new government was wrought with conflict. Whereas communist and leftist Guomindang leaders sought social change and mobilization of workers, the right wing, led by Chiang, was allied with the antiprogressive Shanghai business community. Chiang expelled the communists from the United Front in 1927 and began a reign of terror against the leftists, killing thousands of them; those who survived went into hiding.

The Modernization of China

From 1928 to 1937, Chiang's Republic of China, based at Nanjing (nahn-JING) along the Yangzi River in east-central China, launched a program to modernize China. The Republic's leaders, many of them Western-educated Christians, fostered economic development and forged a modern state. They built railroads, factories, a banking system, and a modern army, streamlined the government, fostered public health and education, and adopted new legal codes that strengthened women's rights. The regime also negotiated an end to most of the unequal international treaties imposed by the Western nations and Japan in the 1800s. The U.S. government, closely allied with Chiang's regime, provided generous political and financial support for modernization efforts. Spurred by the idealistic desire to help the Chinese by reshaping them along American lines, Americans felt a paternalistic responsibility for China and funded schools, hospitals, orphanages, and churches.

Yet the Republic faced domestic challenges. While the urban elite in big coastal cities prospered, Chiang was unable or unwilling to deal with the growing poverty of the peasantry.

 Our Attitude Toward Modern Civilization of the West A Chinese professor rejects the idea that Eastern civilization is more "spiritual" than the "materialistic" West.

Commercialization of agriculture gradually shifted more land to landlords, and by 1930, about one-half of China's peasants lacked enough land to support their families. Adding to the problems, Chiang also tolerated government corruption and rewarded his financial backers in the commercial sector. As unhappiness with the government grew, Chiang, influenced by European fascism, built an authoritarian police state that brutally repressed all dissent.

Conflict with Japan

China also faced problems with Japan. In 1931, Japanese forces seized Manchuria, the large northeastern region rich in mineral resources and fertile farmland, and set up a puppet government under the last Manchu emperor, Henry Pu Yi (1906–1967) (see Map 25.1). Japan gradually extended its military and political influence southwest toward the Great Wall that separated Manchuria from northern China. Unable to match Japanese military power, Chiang was forced to follow a policy of appeasement. His attempts to strengthen the Chinese military diverted scarce resources from economic development, and his reluctance to fight Japan left him open to charges that he was unpatriotic.

Interactive Map

Ding Ling and Chinese Radicalism

During the years of warlordism and then the Republic, the challenges facing China were reflected in cultural life. Disillusioned by China's weakness in the world and continued political despotism, many intellectuals lost faith in both Chiang's regime and Chinese traditions. Din Ling (1904–1985), one of China's first feminist writers and a participant in the May Fourth Movement, became alienated from the Republic when the Guomindang killed her political activist husband. After this, Ding dedicated her writing to the revolutionary cause, but she was later persecuted by the communists for the radicalism in her writing.

Chinese Communism and Mao Zedong

As the communists who survived Chiang's terror worked to rebuild their movement, one of the younger party leaders, Mao Zedong (maow dzuh-dong) (1893–1976), pursued his own strategy to mount the revolution he now saw as necessary to replace the Chiang regime and reshape China. From a peasant family led by a domineering father who badly abused Mao's mother, Mao had run away from home to attend high school. In 1918, he moved to Beijing, where he came to embrace communism. In 1927, as Chiang attempted to eliminate communists, Mao fled to the rugged mountains of Jiangxi (kee-ON-see) province in south-central China, where he set up a revolutionary base, known as the Jiangxi Soviet after the political action groups of early-twentieth-century Russia (see Chapter 24). There he organized a guerrilla force to fight the Guomindang. Rejecting the advice of Soviet advisers to depend on support from the urban working class—as the communists had done in Russia in 1917—Mao opted instead to rely on China's huge peasantry, arguing that without the peasants, no revolution could succeed.

Mao Assembles His Red Army

In Jiangxi, Mao built an army out of peasants, bandits, and former Guomindang soldiers and mobilized the local population to provision and feed the army. Mao believed that violence was necessary to oppose Chiang, having earlier written that "a revolution is not a dinner party.... A revolution is an act

> "In Jiangxi, Mao built an army out of peasants, bandits, and former Guomindang soldiers and mobilized the local population to provision and feed the army."

Jiangxi Soviet A revolutionary base, established in 1927 in south-central China, where Mao Zedong organized a guerrilla force to fight the Guomindang.

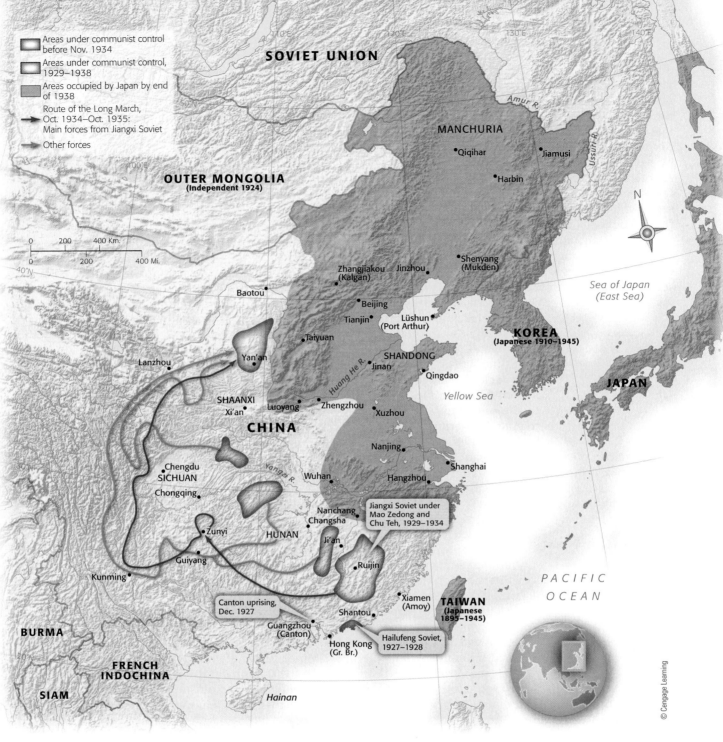

Legend:
- Areas under communist control before Nov. 1934
- Areas under communist control, 1929–1938
- Areas occupied by Japan by end of 1938
- Route of the Long March, Oct. 1934–Oct. 1935: Main forces from Jiangxi Soviet
- Other forces

SOVIET UNION

MANCHURIA

Qiqihar

Jiamusi

Harbin

OUTER MONGOLIA
(Independent 1924)

Baotou

Zhangjiakou (Kalgan)

Jinzhou

Shenyang (Mukden)

Beijing

Tianjin

Lüshun (Port Arthur)

KOREA
(Japanese 1910–1945)

Sea of Japan
(East Sea)

Taiyuan

Lanzhou

Yan'an

SHANDONG

Jinan

Qingdao

Yellow Sea

JAPAN

SHAANXI

Luoyang

Zhengzhou

Huang He R.

CHINA

Xi'an

Xuzhou

Nanjing

Chengdu

SICHUAN

Wuhan

Shanghai

Chongqing

Yangzi R.

Hangzhou

Jiangxi Soviet under Mao Zedong and Chu Teh, 1929–1934

Zunyi

Nanchang

Changsha

HUNAN

Ji'an

Ruijin

PACIFIC OCEAN

Guiyang

Kunming

Xiamen (Amoy)

TAIWAN
(Japanese 1895–1945)

Canton uprising, Dec. 1927

Shantou

BURMA

Guangzhou (Canton)

Hong Kong (Gr. Br.)

Hailufeng Soviet, 1927–1928

FRENCH INDOCHINA

SIAM

Hainan

© Cengage Learning

Map 25.1
Chinese Communist Movement and Chinese-Japanese War

Japan occupied much of northern and eastern China by 1939. In 1935–1936, the Chinese communists made the famous 6,000-mile Long March from their base in Jiangxi in southern China to Yan'an in north-west China.

of violence by which one class overthrows another."[2] Between 1928 and 1934, Mao expanded the Jiangxi Soviet by setting up communist-led local governments and redistributing land from the rich to the poor. As Chiang's repression intensified, top Chinese Communist Party leaders, who had once scorned Mao, moved to the Jiangxi Soviet. Increasingly alarmed by Mao's growing base and communist inroads in other parts of China, Chiang had his army blockade the Jiangxi Soviet to keep out essential supplies. This move forced Mao to reluctantly abandon his base.

The Long March

In 1935, Mao and 100,000 soldiers and followers broke through the blockade and, in search of a safer base, began the Long March, an epic journey in which Mao's Red Army fought their way 6,000 miles on foot and horseback through eleven provinces. During the one-year venture, the communists crossed eighteen mountain ranges, forded twenty-four rivers, and slogged through swamps, averaging seventeen miles per day; they lost 90 percent of their people to death or desertion. Finally, in late 1936, the ragtag survivors arrived in a poor northwestern province, where they moved into cavelike homes carved into the hills around the dusty city of Yan'an (YEH-nan). The Long March saved the communists from elimination by Chiang, making Mao the unchallenged party leader. Mao celebrated the achievement: "The Long March is the first of its kind in the annals of history [and has] proclaimed that the Red Army is an army of heroes."[3] Although the communists were still vulnerable to Chiang's larger, better-equipped forces, Chiang would be forced to shift his military priorities when the Japanese invaded China in 1937.

Long March An epic journey, full of hardship, in which Mao Zedong's Red Army fought their way 6,000 miles on foot and horseback through eleven Chinese provinces in the mid-1930s to establish a safe base of operation.

Japanese Invasion and Communist Revolution

The Japanese invasion of China in 1937 and the disastrous Chinese-Japanese war that followed altered China's politics, as Chiang had to divert money from modernization to the military. Mao captured the patriotic mood of the country by proposing a united front against Japan, and Chiang had little choice but to agree, relieving pressure on Mao's Yan'an base. But by the end of 1938, Japanese forces had swept over most of the eastern seaboard and controlled the best farmland and the industrial cities. War and occupation undermined Chiang's government and allowed the communists to strengthen, thus setting the stage for major changes in Chinese politics in the later 1940s.

The Long March This painting glorifies the crossing, over an old iron-chain bridge, of the Dadu River in western Sichuan province by the communist Red Army during the Long March. This successful crossing, against fierce attacks by Guomindang forces, was a key event in the communists' successful journey to northwest China.

people's war
An unconventional struggle that combined military action and political recruitment, formulated by Mao Zedong in China.

Maoism
An ideology promoted by Mao Zedong that mixed ideas from Chinese tradition with Marxist-Leninist ideas from the Soviet Union.

The Impact of the Second World War on China

The challenges of World War II caused many Chinese to lose faith in the Republic. Chiang's government was forced to relocate inland to Chongqing (CHUNG-king), a city protected by high mountains on the Yangzi River in west-central China. A mass migration of Chinese fleeing the Japanese followed. Unlike the modern, cosmopolitan coastal cities, Chongqing was a city with no bright lights or French restaurants and a depressing climate of fog and humidity. Fatigue, cynicism, and inflation discouraged the Guomindang and its followers. Virtually broke, Chiang's government had to squeeze the peasants in the areas it still controlled for tax revenues to support an army of 4 to 5 million men. Militarily ineffective, politically repressive, and economically corrupt, Chiang's government offered limited resistance to the Japanese, killed and imprisoned opponents of Guomindang rule, and put the personal gain of its leaders above the economic well-being of China's people.

Under such conditions, the communists at Yan'an were able to improve their prospects. Used to poverty, they had a more disciplined army than Chiang's with a higher morale. While Chiang's much larger forces had the main responsibility to fight the Japanese, the communists mounted guerrilla bands, mostly peasants, to harass the occupiers. These guerrillas engaged in an unconventional struggle, which Mao called "people's war," that combined military action and political recruitment. Communist activists set up village governments and peasant associations and encouraged women's rights. The communist message of social revolution, now blended with nationalism, offered hope for a better life to the downtrodden. Thousands of Chinese, including students, intellectuals, writers such as Ding Ling, and workers, flocked to Yan'an to join the communist cause. By 1945, the party had 1.2 million members.

The Victory of Maoism

The experiences of the communist leaders at Yan'an, marked by war

66 *Nationalist opposition to the British Raj, which had been building for decades, was spurred by the severe dislocations caused by World War I.* 99

and popular mobilization to support revolution, fostered the development of what later came to be known as Maoism, an ideology promoted by Mao that mixed ideas from Chinese tradition with Marxist-Leninist ideas from the Soviet Union. Mao emphasized the subordination of the individual to the needs of the group (a traditional Chinese notion), the superiority of political values over technical and artistic ones, and belief in the human will as a social force. Mao also contended that political power grows out of the barrel of a gun and that the Communist Party must command the military. To combat elitism, Mao introduced mass campaigns in which everyone engaged in physical labor that benefited villages, such as building dams and roads. Mao expressed faith that the Chinese people had the collective power and creativity to build a new society.

During World War II, Mao's communists built the foundation for revolution by gaining domination over much of rural north China. Hence, when the war ended, the Chinese communists were able to succeed in their revolutionary efforts: in the late 1940s, they won a bitter civil war, and in 1949, they established a communist government.

LO³ British Colonialism and the Indian Response

In India, as in China, resentment of Western imperialism, despotic government, and an inequitable social order sparked a powerful nationalist movement. Those who hoped that the end of World War I would bring them self-determination could see that British rhetoric about democracy and freedom did not apply to India. Growing organized opposition to British colonialism led to unrest that forced the British to modify some of their colonial policies. At the same time, growing nationalism eventually led to separate Hindu and Muslim nations after World War II.

British Policies, Ghandi, and Mass Resistance

Nationalist opposition to the British *Raj*, which had been building for decades, was spurred by the severe dislocations caused by World War I. To pay for the war, the British raised taxes and customs duties on

Indians, policies that sparked several armed uprisings. In addition, more than 1 million Indian soldiers fought for Britain in France and the Middle East, and 60,000 of these were killed. Many Indians expected a better future because of the sacrifices they had made, but the British dashed all hopes of major political change by declaring in 1917 that they would maintain India as an integral part of the British Empire. However, British prestige suffered irreparable damage from the losses incurred by war and was no longer the imperial giant it had formerly seemed.

The Amritsar Massacre

Growing problems, including a severe economic slump after the war, heightened Indian discontent and alarmed the British, causing them to clamp down on dissent and political activity and to maintain the laws that had been imposed during the war. In 1919, in the Punjab city of Amritsar, British officers suppressed a demonstration by massacring four hundred protesters and wounding one thousand others, including women and children. Throughout India, the Amritsar massacre was greeted with outrage, which intensified when the British hailed the officer in command as a national hero. Prominent Indians, many once pro-British, were appalled at the cruelty, which shook their faith in British rule. The Nobel Prize–winning writer Rabindranath Tagore (tuh-GAWR) (1861–1941) wrote, "The enormity of the measures taken up for quelling some local disturbances had, with a rude shock, revealed to our minds the helplessness of our position as British subjects in India."[4]

The Emergence of Gandhi

The unrest brought to the fore new Indian nationalist leaders, most importantly Mohandas K. Gandhi (GAHN-dee) (1869–1948). After getting his law degree in Britain, Gandhi lived for twenty-two years in South Africa, where the British colonial regime practiced racial segregation and white supremacy (see Chapter 21). To assert the rights of the Indian immigrants in South Africa, Gandhi developed tactics of nonviolent resistance, noncooperation with unjust laws and peaceful confrontation with illegitimate authority. After returning to India in 1920, he became the president of the main nationalist organization, the Indian National Congress. Gandhi's message of resisting the colonial regime nonviolently led him to mount mass campaigns against British political and economic institutions. Inspired by his example, huge numbers of ordinary people joined his movement, shaking the foundations of British colonial rule.

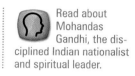

Read about Mohandas Gandhi, the disciplined Indian nationalist and spiritual leader.

Gandhi's doctrine of nonviolence was derived from ideas that had been introduced 2,500 years earlier by the Jains and Buddhists, two of India's religious groups, and also from Quakerism, a pacifist Christian movement Gandhi had encountered in England. Nonviolence—Gandhi often called it passive resistance—was, he wrote, "a method of securing rights by personal suffering; it is the reverse of resistance by arms."[5] Gandhi believed that violence, embodying hate and irrationality, was never justified. The enemy was to be met with reason, and if he responded with violence, this had to be endured in good spirit, requiring severe self-discipline. Gandhi made mass civil disobedience, involving such tactics as marches, sit-ins, and boycotts, the most effective expression of nonviolence. Disobedience also involved hunger strikes, peaceful violation of law, and refusal to pay taxes. Gandhi's Congress colleague, Jawaharlal Nehru (JAH-wa-HAR-lahl NAY-roo), placed Gandhi's strategy in perspective: "Gandhi was like a powerful current of fresh air that made us stretch ourselves and take deep breaths, like a Whirlwind that upset many things but most of all the working of people's minds."[6]

Thanks to Gandhi's efforts, during the 1920s, the Congress developed a mass base that was supported by people from all of India's cultures, religions, regions, and social backgrounds. His tactics bewildered the British, who, while claiming to uphold law, order, and Christian values, clubbed hunger strikers, used horses to trample nonviolent protesters, and arrested Gandhi and other leaders. Still, they

nonviolent resistance Noncooperation with unjust laws and peaceful confrontation with illegitimate authority, pursued by Mohandas Gandhi in India.

CHRONOLOGY

South Asia, 1914–1945

1919	Amritsar massacre
1930	Gandhi's Great Salt March
1931	London Conference
1935	Government of India Act
1937	Provincial elections
1942	Gandhi's Quit India campaign

were forced to make concessions. One of Gandhi's Indian critics told British officials in 1930 that the Congress "has undoubtedly acquired a great hold on the popular imagination."[7]

> "While resistance against British rule continued, a growing Hindu–Muslim division posed a problem for Indian nationalism."

The Great Salt March

The suffering caused by the Great Depression that began in 1929 led to a new Gandhi-led campaign in 1930, beginning with what Gandhi called the Great Salt March. During this event, Gandhi and several dozen followers marched to the west coast, where they produced salt from the Indian Ocean seawater in violation of British laws. Gandhi's action and arrest captured the popular imagination, setting off a wave of demonstrations, strikes, and boycotts against British interests. In quelling the unrest, the British killed 103, injured 420, and imprisoned 60,000 resisters. They released Gandhi a few months later, and he agreed to halt civil disobedience campaigns if the British would promote Indian-made goods and hold a conference to discuss India's political future.

Hindu–Muslim Division

While resistance against British rule continued, a growing Hindu–Muslim division posed a problem for Indian nationalism. Although some Muslims supported the largely Hindu Indian National Congress, others questioned their role in India. While Gandhi respected all religions and welcomed Muslim support, Muslim leaders mounted their own nationalist organizations to work for a potential Muslim country. In 1930, student activists in Britain called their proposed Muslim nation Pakistan, meaning "Land of the Pure" in the Urdu language spoken by many Indian Muslims. Accounting for some 20 percent of British India's population and largely concentrated in the northwest and Bengal, Muslims occupied all niches of society but were divided by social status, ancestry, language, and sect. The great majority were Sunni, but some were Shi'a.

Nehru and Indian Independence

While Muslim leaders often focused on the need for a state that enshrined their religious values, Congress leaders were chiefly Western-oriented Hindu intellectuals who wanted a secular, modern India. The forty-year-old Jawaharlal Nehru (1889–1964), who succeeded Gandhi as Congress leader in 1929, was the strongest advocate of a secular state. Born into a wealthy brahman family, educated in the West, and endowed with unusual charisma, Nehru had a passion for the welfare of the common people and demanded complete freedom from British domination. But while Gandhi wanted to reshape colonial society, Nehru and other Congress leaders focused more on political independence. Few Indian nationalists, whether Hindu or Muslim, shared the Chinese Communist goal of radical social transformation as a necessary part of economic development.

Muhammed Ali Jinnah and the Muslim League

By the 1930s, the main rival to the Congress was the Muslim League, led by the Western-educated Bombay lawyer Muhammed Ali Jinnah (jee-NAH) (1876–1948), a dapper figure who always spoke English. Jinnah promoted a Two Nations Theory, arguing that Islam and Hinduism were different social orders and that it was a naive Congress dream that the two groups could ever forge a common nationality. Jinnah developed the Muslim League into a mass political movement in competition with the Congress. He cultivated good relations with the British and convinced regional Muslim leaders, some once pro-Congress, to support the Muslim League. The Congress tried to marginalize the Muslim League and refused to form a coalition with it, which proved to be a mistake in the long run. The competing visions of the Congress and the Muslim League complicated British efforts to introduce representative government institutions. The two rival organizations clashed in 1931, when, as a result of Gandhi's agreement to suspend civil disobedience, Indian leaders and British officials met in London to discuss expanded elections. Although Congress objected, Muslims and other minorities did win electoral rights in India's many provinces.

The electoral agreement also did not end anticolonial unrest and counterviolence by the British. However, in 1935, their power in retreat, the British introduced a new constitution that allowed some 35 million Indians who owned property, including 6 million women, to vote for newly formed provincial legislatures. In the first provincial elections, in 1937, the Congress won 70 percent of the popular vote and the majority of seats, defeating the Muslim League even for seats reserved for Muslims. More Indians also rose to leadership positions in the army, police, and civil service. However, British officials argued that the communal divisions necessitated the continuation of British rule to maintain order, and Jinnah, battered but not broken by the disappointing Muslim League electoral performance, redoubled his efforts to unite Muslims against the Congress.

The "Quit India" Campaign

World War II was the deciding event in the path to Indian independence, but it also reshaped the nationalist dialogue by increasing the Hindu–Muslim divide. The British committed Indian troops to the war without consulting Congress leaders, who protested that cooperation must be between equal partners and by mutual consent. In 1942, fearing that the British had no intention of ending their colonial rule, Gandhi mounted a campaign calling on the British to "Quit India." In response, the British arrested Ghandi, Nehru, and the entire Congress leadership and 60,000 party activists, jailing many of them for the duration of the war. World War II harmed the rural poor and urban workers, as prices for essential goods soared. At the same time, famine in Bengal killed 3 million to 4 million people. In response to these hardships, Nehru's main rival for Congress leadership, the militant Bengali Marxist Subhas Chandra Bose (1895–1945), allied with imperial Japan and organized an Indian National Army, recruited largely from among Indian soldiers and Indian emigrants in Southeast Asia. His army invaded India from Japan-held Burma to attack the British. The invasion failed, but many Indians saw Bose and other Indian National Army leaders as national heroes.

The Partitioning of India

Meanwhile, the arrest of Congress leaders meant that Jinnah could consolidate the power of the Muslim League. Jinnah demanded the creation of a separate Muslim state, Pakistan, based on the provinces where Muslims were the majority. Rejecting Muslim separatism, the jailed Gandhi urged Muslims to resist what he termed the suicide of partition. But Gandhi's plea was futile, and British efforts to bring the factions together also failed. After World War II, the struggle between Indian nationalists and the British, and between Hindus and Muslims, resumed, leading to the end of British rule and the creation of two separate independent nations, predominantly Hindu India and a chiefly Muslim Pakistan carved out of the Muslim-majority areas of British India.

Social Change: Caste and Gender Relations

Nationalist politics, economic dislocations, and the stresses posed by rapid population growth had an enduring effect on India's social structure. India's population grew from 255 million in 1871 to 390 million in 1940. The trends that had reshaped the caste system beginning in the 1800s continued, particularly affecting the untouchables, the most powerless group in Hindu society and perhaps one-fifth of India's population. Although Gandhi, a high-caste Hindu, advocated for more dignity for untouchables, increasing attention to caste identities often resulted, tragically, in more discrimination. Untouchable leaders such as Dr. Bhimrao Ramji Ambedkar (BIM-rao RAM-jee am-BED-car) (1893–1956) subsequently launched movements to assert rights for their people. Ambedkar rose from one of the lowest groups, the sweepers who cleaned village streets, to earn a Ph.D. and a law degree from major U.S. and British universities. On his return to India, he started schools, newspapers, and political parties. Ambedkar successfully lobbied the government to promote upward mobility and benefits for the untouchables.

Attitudes toward women were also changing. Hindus increasingly favored widow remarriage, once forbidden, to help offset what they believed to be the higher Muslim birthrate. But while the feminist movement remained weak and had little support among Muslim and peasant women, many women joined the Congress and some demanded a vote equal to men for representative institutions, such as provincial legislatures. With British assent, all of the legislatures granted women the franchise between 1923 and 1930. Gandhi himself, unable to escape patriarchal attitudes, promoted women's traditional roles as wives, mothers, and supporters of men. Impressed by his wife Kasturbai's advocacy of

> **"** Nationalist politics, economic dislocations, and the stresses posed by rapid population growth had an enduring effect on India's social structure. **"**

nonviolence, Gandhi believed women were especially suited to passive resistance. He wrote paternalistically that women were the embodiment of humility, sacrifice, and silent suffering. But some women with a more militant vision of change joined men in terrorist organizations aimed at undermining colonialism, like Pritilata Waddedar (1911–1932), a brilliant Bengali university graduate, who led and died in an armed raid on a British club that reportedly boasted a sign: "Dogs and Indians not allowed."

LO⁴ Nationalist Stirrings in Southeast Asia and Sub-Saharan Africa

As in India, the challenges posed by European colonialism were also being addressed by nationalist movements and protests in Southeast Asia and sub-Saharan Africa. In 1930, the Indonesian Nationalist Party, struggling against Dutch colonialism, urged Indonesians to join the cause of national freedom and build a new nation. The plea symbolized the nationalist response in several other Southeast Asian colonies, especially French-ruled Vietnam. Although in sub-Saharan Africa organized nationalist movements, often based on ethnicity, were comparatively weaker politically, they did have meaningful cultural impact.

Changing Southeast Asia

The first stirrings of Southeast Asian nationalism came in the Philippines in the late 1800s, but the revolution was thwarted by Spain first and then the United States. In the Philippines, the U.S. promise of eventual independence tended to reduce radical sentiments. By 1941, nationalism also had a large following in Vietnam, British Burma, and parts of Indonesia, all places that had suffered particularly oppressive colonial rule and where independence would come only through force. Compared to these colonies, nationalism was weaker in French-ruled Cambodia and Laos and in British Malaya, all colonies that had experienced less social, economic, and political disruption.

One of the stronger nationalist movements arose in Burma (today's Myanmar). Despite having limited self-government by the 1930s, including an elected legislature, the colony's majority ethnic group, the Burmans, viewed British rule as oppressive. They also resented Christian converts and the large, often wealthy Indian community, which had immigrated

to Burma and dominated the economy. These resentments fostered the rise of nationalism among university students. The nationalists used Theravada Buddhism, the faith of most Burmese, as a rallying cry to press for reform, and some favored women's rights. When the Japanese invaded Burma in 1941, many Burmans welcomed them as liberators.

Although Siam (today's Thailand) was not a colony, nationalism grew there out of tensions between the aristocratic elite and the rising middle class that were exacerbated by the Great Depression. In 1932, military officers of middle-class background, who called themselves nationalists, took power in a coup against the royal government. The Siamese king, whose family had ruled the country since the late 1700s, agreed under pressure to become a constitutional, mostly symbolic monarch. Military leaders then ran the government throughout the 1930s, pursuing nationalist policies, renaming the country Thailand ("Land of Free People"), and urging the Thai people to live modern lives. During the late 1930s,

Thailand forged an alliance with rising imperial Japan, and introduced features of a fascist regime, militarizing the schools and suppressing dissent.

Nationalism in Vietnam and Indonesia

The most powerful nationalist movement in Southeast Asia emerged in Vietnam as a result of its destabilization during French colonial rule, when peasant lands were seized. The earliest nationalists seeking an end to French rule were led by the passionately revolutionary Phan Boi Chau (FAN boy chow) (1867–1940). Phan was born into a family of mandarins who had served the Vietnamese emperors as officials for generations, and he was educated in Confucian learning. By the time of his death in a French prison, Phan had inspired Vietnamese patriotism and resistance. But a younger generation of urban, French-educated intellectuals took a more radical approach—terrorism—assassinating colonial officials and bombing French buildings. One such uprising in 1930 brought about a French reign of terror against all dissidents, which destroyed the major nationalist groups except for the Vietnamese communists.

 WWW
Southeast Asia Guide (*http:// www.library.Wisc .edu/guides/SEAsia/*). An easy-to-use site on Southeast Asia.

Ho Chi Minh and the Indochinese Communist Party

The rise of Vietnamese communism during the repression owed much to Ho Chi Minh, a mandarin's son and former sailor turned left-wing political activist, as described at the start of the chapter. Ho had spent many years organizing the communist movement among Vietnamese exiles in Thailand and China. Ho came to believe that nothing less than Marxist revolution would provide an alternative to the discredited imperial system, an unjust society, and French rule. In 1930, Ho and his colleagues established the Indochinese Communist Party, which united anticolonial radicals from

> "The most powerful nationalist movement in Southeast Asia emerged in Vietnam as a result of its destabilization during French colonial rule, when peasant lands were seized."

Vietnam, Cambodia, and Laos. They linked themselves to the patriotic traditions of the earlier Vietnamese rebels, who for 2,000 years had led resistance first to Chinese conquerors and then to the French.

One Vietnamese Marxist, writing in 1943, exemplified the links with the past: "And, so it seems we are not lost after all. Behind us we have the immense history of our people. There [are] still spiritual cords attaching us."[8] Remembering Vietnam's long history of resistance to foreign occupation, Vietnamese communism took on a strongly nationalist flavor. In 1941, Ho established the Viet Minh, or Vietnamese Independence League, a coalition of anti-French groups that waged war against both the French colonizers and the Japanese, who occupied Vietnam during World War II.

Indonesian Nationalism

Nationalist activity also emerged in the Dutch East Indies. Diverse organizations sought freedom from Dutch control while calling for the unity of the Indonesian populace, which included hundreds of ethnic groups. One strategy was to adopt a unifying language, a lingua franca widely used as a common tongue among diverse groups that also had their own languages. Nationalist intellectuals began using Malay, which gradually became the language of the press and educational institutions.

Nationalist ideas competed with and sometimes reshaped Indonesian religious traditions. For example, some Muslims, impressed with but also resenting Western economic and military power, sought to reform and purify their faith. Reformers stressed the five pillars of Islam, devalued the writings of religious scholars after

> 66 Nationalist ideas competed with and sometimes reshaped Indonesian religious traditions. 99

Viet Minh
The Vietnamese Independence League, a coalition of anti-French groups established by Ho Chi Minh in 1941 that waged war against both the French and the Japanese.

lingua franca
A language widely used as a common tongue among diverse groups with different languages.

Muhammad, and favored the segregation of men and women in public, a custom long ignored by most Indonesians. In 1912, Javanese batik merchants who mixed these reformist religious ideas with nationalism established the colony's first true political movement, the Islamic Union, which by 1919 had recruited 2 million members.

After 1917, the Russian Revolution inspired radical Marxists in the Dutch East Indies. They formed the Indonesian Communist Party in 1920, which grew rapidly by attracting support chiefly from nondevout Muslim peasants and labor union members in Java. Overestimating their strength, the communists sparked a poorly planned uprising in 1926, which was crushed by the government and led to the execution of its leaders.

The destruction of the communists left an opening for other nationalists. The Indonesian Nationalist Party, led mostly by Javanese aristocrats who rejected Islamic reform ideas, was established in 1927 to promote a new national identity. Sukarno (soo-KAHR-no) (1902–1970), the key founder, designed a flag, wrote an anthem, and created a slogan for an independent Indonesia: "one nation—Indonesia, one people—Indonesian, one language—Indonesian." The Dutch authorities arrested Sukarno in 1929 and exiled him to a remote island prison for the next decade, making him a nationalist symbol and increasing his popularity (see Witness to the Past: Sukarno Indicts Dutch Colonialism). However, without his leadership, the Indonesian Nationalist Party grew more slowly throughout the 1930s.

Japanese Occupation: The Remaking of Southeast Asia

The occupation of Southeast Asia by Japanese forces during World War II from 1941 to 1945 boosted nationalism and weakened colonialism. Before 1941, colonial authority had remained strong. Then, in a few weeks in late 1941 and early 1942, everything changed. Japan had already bullied Thailand and the French colonial regime in Vietnam, which now took orders from the pro-Nazi Vichy government in France (see Chapter 24), to allow the stationing of Japanese troops. Then the bombing of Pearl Harbor in 1941 was quickly followed by a rapid Japanese invasion of Southeast Asia. With superior naval and air strength, the Japanese easily overwhelmed the colonial forces. Within four months, they controlled major cities and heavily populated regions, shattering the mystique of Western invincibility and expelling European and American officials. As an Indonesian writer later

remembered, the Japanese occupation "destroyed a whole set of illusions and left man as naked as when he was created."[9] The Japanese talked of "Asia for the Asians," but this rhetoric also masked the Japanese wartime exploitation of natural resources such as rubber and oil.

Indonesia Under the Japanese

Japanese domination was brief, less than four years, yet it led to significant changes. For example, in many places, conflicts between ethnic groups increased because of selective repression. In Malaya, Japanese policy that favored the majority Malays allowed Malay government officials to keep their jobs, while members of the Chinese minority often faced property seizures and arrest, creating antagonism between Malays and Chinese that persisted long after the war. By destroying the link to the world economy, the occupation also caused economic hardship. Western companies closed, causing unemployment, while Japanese forces seized natural resources and food. By 1944, living standards, crippled by severe shortages of essential goods such as food and clothing, were in steep decline. Southeast Asians suffered also from harassment by the Japanese police as well as forced labor: Javanese men became slave laborers and Filipinas, called "comfort women" by the Japanese, served the sexual needs of Japanese soldiers. As their war effort against the United States faltered, the desperate Japanese resorted to even more repressive policies to keep order and acquire resources.

Although often harsh, Japanese rule also offered some political benefits for Southeast Asians, such as promotion into government positions that were once reserved for Westerners. In addition, the Japanese—seeking to purge the area of Western cultural influences—closed Christian mission schools, encouraged Islamic or Buddhist leaders, and fostered a renaissance of indigenous culture and an outpouring of literature. The Japanese also promoted Southeast Asian nationalism, at least indirectly, because of their recruitment of Southeast Asian leaders to lend legitimacy to their rule. The Japanese freed nationalist leaders such as Sukarno from jail and gave them official positions, if little actual power. The nationalists enjoyed a new role in public life and used the Japanese-controlled radio and newspapers to foster nationalist beliefs. The Japanese also recruited young people into armed paramilitary forces, which became the basis for later nationalist armies in Indonesia and Burma that resisted the return of Western colonialism after World War II.

Sukarno Indicts Dutch Colonialism

Sukarno, the fiery Indonesian nationalist, was skilled at articulating his criticisms of colonialism. A splendid orator, he attracted a large following through his use of Indonesian, especially Javanese, religious and cultural symbols and frequent historical references in his speeches. Arrested by the Dutch in 1930, Sukarno delivered a passionate defense speech, known as "Indonesia Accuses," at his trial that became one of the most inspiring documents of Indonesian nationalism. Sukarno stressed the greatness of Indonesia's past as a building block for the future.

The word "imperialism" . . . designates a . . . tendency . . . to dominate or influence the affairs of another nation, . . . a system . . . of economic control. . . . As long as a nation does not wield political power in its own country, part of its potential, economic, social or political, will be used for interests which are not its interests, but contrary to them. . . . A colonial nation is a nation that cannot be itself, a nation that in almost all its branches, in all of its life, bears the mark of imperialism. There is no community of interests between the subject and the object of imperialism. Between the two there is only a contrast of interests and a conflict of needs. All interests of imperialism, social, economic, political, or cultural, are opposed to the interests of the Indonesian people. The imperialists desire the continuation of imperialism, the Indonesians desire its abolition. . . .

What are the roads to promote Indonesian nationalism? . . . First: we point out to the people that they have had a great past. Second: we reinforce the consciousness of the people that the present is dark. Third: we show the people the pure and brightly shining light of the future and the roads which lead to this future so full of promises. . . . The P.N.I. [Indonesian Nationalist Party] awakens and reinforces the people's consciousness of its "grandiose past," its "dark present" and the promises of a shining, beckoning future.

Our grandiose past? Oh, what Indonesian does not feel his heart shrink with sorrow when he hears the stories about the beautiful past, does not regret the disappearance of that departed glory! What Indonesian does not feel his national heart beat with joy when he hears about the greatness of the [Intermediate Era] empires of Melayu and Srivijaya, about the greatness of the empire of Mataram and Madjapahit. . . . A nation with such a grandiose past must surely have sufficient natural aptitude to have a beautiful future. . . . Among the people . . . again conscious of their great past, national feeling is revived, and the fire of hope blazes in their hearts.

Thinking About the Reading

1. What is Sukarno's evaluation of imperialism?
2. How does he think Indonesians should capitalize on their past?

Source: Harry J. Benda and John A. Larkin, eds., *The World of Southeast Asia: Selected Historical Readings* (New York: Harper and Row, 1967), pp. 190–193. Copyright © 1967 Harper and Row. Reprinted with permission of John A. Larkin.

Organizing an Opposition

Some Southeast Asians dared to actively oppose Japanese rule, especially in Vietnam. Vietnamese communism might never have achieved power so quickly had it not been for the Japanese occupation, which discredited the French administration and imposed great hardship on most of the population, a fact that the communists used to their advantage. The Viet Minh, led by Ho Chi Minh, were now armed and trained by American advisers, who, after the United States entered the war and needed local allies, had been sent to help anti-Japanese forces. In 1944, the Viet Minh moved out of their bases along the Chinese border and expanded their influence in northern Vietnam, attracting thousands of poor peasants to the anti-French nationalist cause while attacking the Japanese occupiers with guerrilla tactics. The Viet Minh rapidly gained popular support and recruits, thanks partly to a 1945 Japanese policy that exported scarce food to Japan while a famine killed 2 million Vietnamese.

Japanese fortunes waned as the United States gained the upper hand in the war, opening the way for political change in Southeast Asia. U.S. bombing of Japanese installations in Southeast Asia alerted local people that the regional balance of power was changing. Tired of economic deprivation and repression, few Southeast Asians regretted Japan's defeat, and some, especially in Malaya, British Borneo, and the Philippines, even welcomed the return of Western forces. Before World War II, the United States had promised to grant independence to the Philippines and did so in 1946, turning the country over to pro-U.S. leaders, but often the returning Westerners faced growing political volatility. The end of war set the stage for dramatic political change in Vietnam, Indonesia, and Burma, as nationalist forces resisted any return to the prewar status quo and successfully struggled for independence in the late 1940s and early 1950s.

Nationalism and Resistance in Africa

The roots of the African nationalist struggle had been planted in the decades before World War II, but lacking the mass base of Vietnamese or Indian nationalists, protests were less disruptive in Africa than in Southeast Asia and India. One obstacle was that imperial regimes in Africa did not permit enough African participation in government or education to produce a large educated class that could assume the responsibilities and burdens of nationhood.

The Question of National Identity

The artificial division of Africa was the most significant hindrance to nationalist organizing. All over Africa, the colonial regimes, by using divide-and-rule strategies to govern diverse ethnic groups, had made it difficult to create viable national identities. For example, Nigeria, in West Africa, was an artificial creation, the result of the late-nineteenth-century British colonization of diverse and often rival ethnic groups. While some Pan-Nigerian nationalists sought unity, most of the Nigerian nationalist organizations found their greatest support only among particular regions or ethnic groups within Nigeria. In the 1940s, a prominent leader of one of the major ethnic groups,

> "The artificial division of Africa was the most significant hindrance to nationalist organizing."

the Yoruba, complained that "Nigeria is not a nation [but] a mere geographical expression."[10]

West African nationalist currents were strongest in the growing, usually multiethnic cities, such as Lagos in Nigeria, Accra in the Gold Coast, and Dakar in Senegal. These became the breeding grounds of new ideas. City life, which offered a wide range of economic activities, also encouraged the growth of trade union movements, which sponsored occasional strikes to protest colonial policies or economic exploitation. However, rural people, especially farmers, also asserted their rights. For example, during the 1930s, cocoa growers in the British-ruled Gold Coast held back their crops from the government to protest low prices.

Henry Thuku and the African Nationalist Movements

African nationalism was sparked by World War I and the unfulfilled expectations for better lives in its aftermath. During the war, the British, French, and Germans had all drafted or recruited men from their African colonies to fight on European battlefields, where thousands died. When the survivors returned home, the promises the colonial powers had made to them about land or jobs proved empty. For example, Kenyan soldiers came back from the war to find that British settlers had seized their land. In response, Harry Thuku (THOO-koo) (ca. 1895–1970), a middle-class Kenyan and member of Kenya's largest ethnic group, the Gikuyu, created an alliance of diverse Kenyan ethnic groups in 1920 to confront the British. When the British arrested Thuku in 1922, rioting led by Gikuyu women broke out, and the British fired on the rioters, killing more than twenty of them.

Inspired in part by Harry Thuku's movement, nationalist organizations developed in various colonies in the 1920s and met with occasional success, especially in West Africa. These urban-based organizations, led mainly by Western-educated Africans, were formed in part to press for more African participation in local government. Among these was J. E. Casely Hayford (1866–1930), a lawyer and journalist in the British Gold Coast (today's Ghana) who was influenced by Gandhi. Some Africans, including Casely Hayford, favored a Pan-African approach and sought support across colonial borders; they did not view colonial boundaries as the basis for nations. But both nationalists and Pan-Africanists were unable to overcome the divide among rival ethnic groups within each colony and the gap between the cities and the villages. Furthermore, some African merchants, chiefs, and kings profited from their links to the colonizers and discouraged protests. Because of all these challenges, the urban nationalists had little influence before World War II.

Emergence of the African National Congress

In South Africa, the racial inequality and white supremacy established by the Dutch in South Africa and largely maintained by the British remained in place during most of the twentieth century, sparking nationalism that led some to resist oppression. The early South African nationalists, such as the founders of the African National Congress (usually known as the ANC, established in 1912), came from the urban middle class. The ANC encouraged education and preached African independence from white rule but did not directly confront the government until the 1950s. More militant African resistance also flourished, though, especially in the mining industry, where strikes were endemic throughout the twentieth century despite severe government repression.

Music and Protest

Colonial rule did, however, generate new cultural trends that allowed people to express their views, which were often critical, about colonial African life. For instance, during the 1930s, a musical style, highlife, arose in the Gold Coast and soon spread into other British West African colonies. It was carried chiefly by guitar-playing sailors and was an urban-based mix of Christian hymns, West Indian calypso songs, and African dance rhythms. Although the music was closely tied to dance bands and parties, some highlife musicians began addressing social and political issues, and this trend grew with nationalism. The very term *highlife* signified both an envy and disapproval of the Western colonizers and rich Africans, who lived in luxury in mansions staffed by servants. Many highlife songs were sung in pidgin English, a mixture of African and English words and grammar that spread throughout British West Africa as a marketplace lingua franca among ethnically diverse urban populations.

Given a white supremacist government that was anxious to suppress dissent, South African protest was often expressed in music, although usually veiled to avoid arrest. Even hymns in African churches had a protest element, because they were sung using African rather than Western vocal traditions. Knowing that few whites understood lyrics sung in African languages, African workers filled the mining camps and labor movements with political music, offering

highlife
An urban-based West African musical style mixing Christian hymns, West Indian calypso, and African dance rhythms.

pidgin English
The form of broken English that developed in Africa during the colonial era.

African Jazz Band Jazz from the United States had a wide following in the world in the 1920s, 1930s, and 1940s. Jazz especially influenced the music of black South Africans, some of whom formed jazz groups, such as the Harmony Kings.

messages such as "we demand freedom" and "workers unite." In the cities, jazz, which was developed originally by African American musicians across the Atlantic, became a form of resistance to the culture of the white racist Afrikaners. The preferred music of the small, educated black professional and business class, jazz ultimately became a symbol of black nationalism in South Africa.

LO⁵ Remaking the Middle East and Latin America

The peoples of both the Middle East and Latin America were also influenced by nationalism between 1914 and 1945. While North Africans, like sub-Saharan Africans and Southeast Asians, experienced Western colonial rule, Arabs in much of western Asia had been controlled for five hundred years by the Ottoman Turks, and under their rule the region was stagnating economically by the 1800s. European influence intensified after World War I, when the Ottoman colonies in western Asia were transferred to Britain and France, sparking nationalist resentment among the western Asian Arabs. Latin Americans, mostly Christians, achieved their independence in the nineteenth century and shared few recent experiences with colonized Arabs, Africans, and Southeast Asians, but two world wars and the Great Depression in the twentieth century caused turmoil, fostered dictatorships, and, as in other regions, spurred feelings of nationalism.

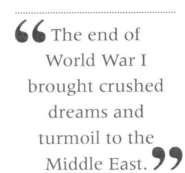

> "The end of World War I brought crushed dreams and turmoil to the Middle East."

Estado Novo History of the Middle East Database (http://www.nmhschool.org/tthornton/mehistorydatabase/mideastindex.php). A useful site on history, politics, and culture.

The Ottoman Aftermath

World War I was a watershed for Middle Eastern societies, because it dismantled the region's major state, the Turkish-dominated Ottoman Empire, and reshaped Arab politics. In the war, the Turks favored their long-time ally Germany because it shared their hatred of Russia, but the Ottomans and their European allies lost the war. The resulting breakup of the Ottoman Empire led to the emergence of a new, very different Turkish nation.

Syrian and Arab Nationalism

The hardships during World War I spurred Arab nationalism against Ottoman rule. Unrest in Syria brought on fierce Ottoman repression, as the Ottomans sent nationalist dissidents into exile and hanged others for treason. The most serious challenge to Ottoman rule came in Arabia, where Sharif Hussein ibn Ali (1856–1931), the Arab ruler of the Hejaz—the western Arabia region that included the Muslim holy cities of Mecca and Medina—shifted his loyalties in the war from the Ottomans to the British, who promised to support independence for the Arabs in Ottoman territory. In 1916, with British assistance, Sharif Hussein launched an Arab revolt against the Turks, attacking Ottoman bases and communications. The British invaded and occupied southern Iraq, an Ottoman province, which had a strategic position between Arabia, Syria, and Iran and was thought to have oil.

The end of World War I brought crushed dreams and turmoil to the Middle East. Arab nationalists such as Sharif Hussein did not know that during the war the eventually victorious European Allies—Britain, France, and Russia—had made secret agreements to dismantle the Ottoman Empire that ignored Arab interests. When the war ended, British troops occupied much of Iraq and Palestine, and French troops controlled the Syrian coast.

World War I caused great suffering to diverse Ottoman societies. The Caucasus peoples, especially the Christian Armenians, desired independence. Suspecting them of aiding Russia, the Turks turned on the Armenians living in eastern Anatolia. More than 1 million Armenians were deported, chiefly to Syria and Iraq, while perhaps another 1 million died of thirst, starvation, or systematic slaughter by the Ottoman army; some historians consider it a genocide. The violent assault created a permanent Turkish-Armenian hostility. After the war, the Russians regained control of the Caucasus, including Armenia. In a different context, hunger and disease also affected millions of Arabs in the Ottoman Empire, with 200,000 dying in Syria alone during the war.

A Writer for al-Asima, the Syrian Government Newspaper, Seeks to Establish the Popular Idea of the "Nation" The Syrian people are urged to put aside their differences and to embrace a common future based on a glorious past.

The Dismemberment of the Ottoman Empire

The Versailles treaty that ended World War I brought major political change, including dismemberment of the Ottoman Empire (see Map 25.2). Turkey's neighbors—the Greeks, Italians, and Armenians—made claims on Anatolia and adjacent islands, and European Zionists asked for a Jewish national home in Palestine (see Chapter 21). The Allies ended Ottoman control of Arab territories and suggested eventual independence to the Kurds, a Sunni Muslim people, distinct from both Arabs and Turks, who inhabited a large, mountainous region of Western Asia and were also the dominant ethnic group in southeast Turkey. Both Syria and Iraq declared their independence from the Ottoman Empire, but the League of Nations, dominated by Western countries, awarded France control over Syria and Lebanon, and Britain control over Iraq, Palestine, and Transjordan (today Jordan), under what the League called mandates.

Interactive Map

In theory, mandates were less onerous for local people than colonies because they allowed for administrative assistance for a limited time, but Arabs often wanted to build their own governments and shape new social systems. Arab nationalists in Syria proposed a democratic government, but French forces quickly occupied the country and exiled nationalist leaders. The Allies also ignored the desire of the Kurdish people for their own nation. Despite British proposals for such a change, the Kurds remained divided between Turkey, Persia (Iran), Iraq, and Syria, thus becoming the world's largest ethnic group without their own state.

Kemal Ataturk and Turkish Reform

While all of the former Ottoman territories experienced change after World War I, the heart of the empire, Turkey, saw the most revolutionary changes. The disastrous defeat in the war and the humiliating agreements that followed left the Turks helpless and bitter. But under the leadership of the daring war hero and ardent nationalist later known as Kemal Ataturk (kuh-MAHL AT-uh-turk) (1881–1938), the Turks enjoyed a spectacular postwar resurgence. In 1919, Ataturk began mobilizing military forces in eastern Anatolia into a revolutionary organization to oppose the Ottoman sultan, who was discredited by defeats, and to restore dignity to the Turks. Ataturk accepted the loss of Arab lands but wanted to preserve the Turkish majority areas and the eastern Anatolia districts inhabited chiefly by Kurds.

After establishing a rival Turkish government in the central Anatolia city of Ankara, Ataturk led his forces in fighting both the sultan's government in Istanbul and the foreign occupiers, especially the Greek forces that had moved deep into Anatolia. He finally pushed the Greeks back to the Aegean Sea, and eventually Turkey and Greece agreed to a population transfer in which many Greeks living in Turkish territory moved to Greece and the Turks dwelling in Greek lands moved to Turkey. In 1922, Ataturk deposed the Ottoman sultan and set up a republic with himself as president. He was a controversial figure among Turks, particularly devout Muslims, because Ataturk dismissed Islamic culture as an inferior mix of age-old mentalities. He favored modernization, announcing that "our eyes are turned westward. We shall transplant Western institutions to Asiatic soil. We wish to be a modern nation with our mind open, and yet

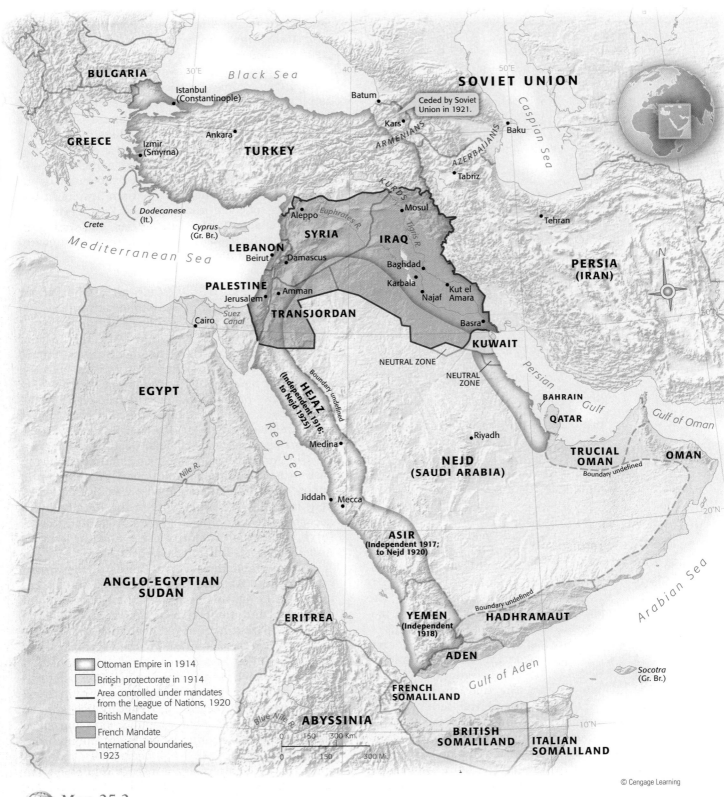

Map 25.2
Partition of the Ottoman Empire

Before 1914, the Ottoman Turks controlled much of western Asia, including western Arabia. After World War II, the League of Nations awarded Iraq, Transjordan, and Palestine to Britain. Syria and Lebanon were given to France, and western Arabia was ruled by Arabs. Eventually, the Saudi family, rulers of the Najd, expanded their rule into western Arabia and created Saudi Arabia.

Map labels:

BULGARIA
Black Sea
SOVIET UNION
Istanbul (Constantinople)
Batum
Ceded by Soviet Union in 1921.
Kars
Caspian Sea
GREECE
Ankara
TURKEY
ARMENIANS
Baku
Izmir (Smyrna)
AZERBAIJANIS
Dodecanese (It.)
Tabriz
Crete
KURDS
Cyprus (Gr. Br.)
Euphrates R.
Aleppo
Mosul
SYRIA
Tigris R.
IRAQ
Tehran
Mediterranean Sea
LEBANON
Beirut
Damascus
Baghdad
PERSIA (IRAN)
Karbala
PALESTINE
Amman
Najaf
Kut el Amara
Jerusalem
TRANSJORDAN
Basra
Cairo
Suez Canal
NEUTRAL ZONE
KUWAIT
NEUTRAL ZONE
EGYPT
HEJAZ (Independent 1916; to Nejd 1925)
Boundary undefined
BAHRAIN
Riyadh
QATAR
Gulf of Oman
Red Sea
Medina
TRUCIAL OMAN
OMAN
Nile R.
NEJD (SAUDI ARABIA)
Persian Gulf
Boundary undefined
Jiddah
Mecca
ANGLO-EGYPTIAN SUDAN
ASIR (Independent 1917; to Nejd 1920)
Arabian Sea
Socotra (Gr. Br.)
Blue Nile R.
ERITREA
YEMEN (Independent 1918)
HADHRAMAUT
Boundary undefined
ABYSSINIA
ADEN
FRENCH SOMALILAND
Gulf of Aden
BRITISH SOMALILAND
ITALIAN SOMALILAND

Legend:
Ottoman Empire in 1914
British protectorate in 1914
Area controlled under mandates from the League of Nations, 1920
British Mandate
French Mandate
International boundaries, 1923

0 150 300 Km.
0 150 300 Mi.

© Cengage Learning

to remain ourselves."[11] Ataturk claimed that secularization and the emancipation of women were in keeping with the pre-Islamic Turkish tradition.

In the 1920s, these ideas were put into action through a dazzling series of reforms that challenged Muslim traditions and promoted modern Western practices. Ataturk abolished Islamic religious schools and courts, and he removed reference to Islam as the state religion from the constitution. His government resembled a parliamentary democracy and earned the popularity of many urban dwellers, but he exercised near-dictatorial power and alienated the Kurdish minority by suppressing their language and culture. Ataturk left a deeply changed nation, but many of the reforms he introduced were never adopted in the villages, where Islam remained a strong influence.

> "Ataturk abolished Islamic religious schools and courts, and he removed reference to Islam as the state religion from the constitution."

1925, at the urging of Shi'ite clerics, Reza Khan abandoned the republican government and formed the Pahlavi (PAH-lah-vee) dynasty, with himself as shah, or king.

Although restoring a royal government, Reza Khan, like Ataturk in Turkey, set his country on a path toward modernization and, in 1935, renamed his nation Iran, a symbolic break with the past. The shah created a large national army through conscription, introduced a Western law code, and built infrastructure and government

Modern Iran, Egypt, and Iraq

During this era, major changes also occurred in the other major Middle Eastern countries. Like Turkey, Persia, later known as Iran, moved toward modernization, though with fewer permanent changes, and Egyptians and Iraqis turned toward nationalism in response to British attempts to maintain power in those countries.

The Pahlavi Dynasty in Iran

After World War I, Britain was given the power to impose a protectorate over Persia under which the Persian government was maintained but was forced to accept British loans, financial controls, advisers, and military forces. However, Persian opposition prompted the British to withdraw their troops in 1919 and seek a new approach. Britain supported General Reza Khan (REE-za kahn) (1877–1944), a soldier from a modest background who wanted to end the corrupt, ineffective royal dynasty, establish a secular republic, and address economic underdevelopment. In 1921, Reza Khan took control of the government with British backing, ending the monarchy. He was supported by secular Shi'ites, who had long struggled for a more democratic and open society. In 1924, an influential local magazine praised Reza Khan for freeing the country from having a king and expressed the hope that soon it would escape the domination of the powerful Shi'ite clergy. But in

Ataturk Wedding Dance The Turkish leader Kemal Ataturk promoted and adopted Western fashions while defying Muslim customs. In this photo from around 1925, Ataturk dances with his daughter at her Western-style wedding.

factories. He further strengthened the economy and Iran's political reputation by taking control over the oil industry. The regime also made social changes that outraged Muslim conservatives, such as outlawing the veiling of women in public and encouraging men to wear Western hats and clothes.

But while merchants and the middle class supported Reza Khan's policies, there was little improvement for poor Iranians, who mostly despised the government. Ultimately, the shah had less success in transforming Iran than Ataturk did in Turkey. Reza Khan's support for Germany during World War II prompted an Anglo-Russian occupation of Iran, which the Allies needed as a supply route. Humiliated, the shah abdicated in favor of his twenty-two-year-old son, Muhammad Reza Pahlavi (REH-zah PAH-lah-vee) (1919–1980), and went into exile. The son ruled until 1979.

Wafd and Egyptian Nationalism

In Egypt and Iraq, British control fostered nationalist Arab resistance. In Egypt during World War I, the British had imposed martial law and drafted peasants to build roads and railroads and dig trenches in war zones. Egyptians resented these policies and the thousands of British soldiers stationed in their country during the war. After the war, nationalists unsuccessfully sought an end to British domination. The leading nationalist party, the *Wafd*, was a secular movement seeking independence, representative government, civil liberties, and curtailed powers for the pro-British monarchy.

British missteps led to political change. In 1919, the British arrested the Wafd's leader, Saad Zaghlul (sod ZOG-lool) (ca. 1857-1927), and other Wafd leaders. Enraged Egyptians responded with strikes, student demonstrations, sabotage of railroads, and the murder of British soldiers. The anti-British movement united rich and poor, Muslims and Coptic Christians, men and women, and forced the British to release Zaghlul, who then went to the Paris Peace Conference to plead for national self-determination. Like Vietnam's Ho Chi Minh, he was ignored. Postwar unrest forced Britain to grant Egypt limited independence in 1922, controlling Egypt's defense and foreign affairs until 1936, the official end of its occupation. But Britain still kept thousands of troops along the Suez Canal, and it also shared with Egypt the administration of Sudan, the territory bordering Egypt on the south. Resentment of the continuing British presence increased during World War II.

Faisal and the British Administration of Iraq

The British also struggled to control Iraq, an artificial creation that united three Ottoman provinces, each dominated by a different group: Sunni Kurds, Sunni Arabs, and Shi'ite Arabs. Describing their occupation as a "liberation," the British promised to bestow on the Iraqis an efficient administration, honest finance, impartial justice, and security; in reality they discouraged self-government, and British occupation soon embittered many Iraqis. In 1920, Shi'ite clerics seeking an Islamic state proclaimed a holy war against the British, prompting various Shi'a and Sunni tribes to rise in rebellion. The British suppressed the rebellion, but at a great cost in money and lives: some ten thousand Iraqi and four hundred British died in the fighting. The British kept their own casualty lists low by relying heavily on aerial bombing, which flattened whole villages.

Shaken by the fierce resistance, the British changed direction in Iraq. They introduced limited self-government that allowed Iraqi participation in an appointed Council of State. The skilled diplomacy of a pro-Arab British archaeologist, writer, and diplomat, Lady Gertrude Bell (1868–1926), defused tensions. Seeking a king for Iraq who would be content to "reign but not govern," as Bell put it, in 1921 Britain installed a member of the Hashemite (HASH-uh-mite) royal family of Mecca, Sharif Hussein's son Faisal (1885–1935). In 1930, Faisal convinced Britain to grant Iraq independence, but only after he agreed to accept continued British military bases and government advisers. By then the British had found oil in Iraq, making them unwilling to cut their ties. Many Arabs considered Faisal and his Hashemite successors to be British clients serving British interests, but Iraqi politics after 1930 was shaped by a series of Sunni Arab military strongmen who dominated the kings and strongly influenced government policies.

Islam and Zionism

The stranglehold of European power and Western culture remained concerns of most Middle Eastern societies during the era. Although various colonized peoples struggled to free themselves, nationalist success came slowly. In the absence of political success, religion became a focus of attention. Arabs debated the merits of Westernization, the role of Islam in their societies, and the challenge posed by Zionism, an encounter that fostered long-term hostility between Muslims and Jews.

Middle Eastern leaders and intellectuals envied Western economic development, such as industrialization and a wealth of consumer goods, but disagreed about how many Western cultural, political, and social patterns should be adopted. Some sought wholesale transformation; some favored Islamic tradition; and still others sought a middle path between the two, such as mixing Western and Islamic laws. Between 1923 and 1930, Western-style constitutions, which provided for civil liberties and an elected parliament, were adopted in Egypt, Iraq, Lebanon, Transjordan, and Syria. But these parliaments were limited in their duties and unrepresentative. Real power usually remained in the hands of European officials or powerful kings, and most Arab politicians had little respect for civil liberties. Arabs did make progress in education, public health, industrialization, and communications, but change came slowly. The Egyptian literacy rate rose from 9 percent in 1917 to only 15 percent in 1937.

Social Changes in Egypt

Some women also asserted their rights and sought social change. One of these was the Egyptian Huda Shaarawi (HOO-da sha-RAH-we) (1879–1947). From a wealthy Cairo family, Huda had been married off at age thirteen to a much older cousin. Finding the marriage confining, Huda organized nonviolent anti-British demonstrations by women after World War I and then publicly removed her veil in 1923, shocking Egyptians. She founded and led the Egyptian feminist movement, which succeeded in raising the minimum marriage age for girls to sixteen and increasing educational opportunities for women.

The debates over Westernization fostered new intellectual currents in the Islamic world, some pro-Western, others anti-Western. Representing the former approach, a blind Egyptian author, Taha Husayn (1889–1973), educated in traditional Islamic schools but also at the Sorbonne in Paris, became the key figure of Egyptian literature in the era. In his writings, he challenged orthodox Islam and, in 1938, proclaimed that Westernizing Arab culture, which he favored, would fit with Egypt's traditions, which he described as a mix of Pharaonic, Arab, and Western cultures. "I want," he wrote, "our new life to harmonize with our ancient glory."

The Growing Influence of Wahhabism

In contrast, the popular reaction against Westernization came with a new Egyptian religious movement, the Muslim Brotherhood, and the strengthening influence of Wahhabi Islam. The Muslim Brotherhood was founded in 1928 by schoolteacher Hasan al-Banna (1906–1949). Al-Banna despised Western values, arguing that it "would be inexcusable for us to turn aside from the path of truth—Islam—and so follow the path of fleshly desires and vanities—the path of Europe."[12] Expressing a widespread resentment against Western influence, such as films, bars, and modern, figure-revealing women's fashions, the Brotherhood soon developed a following in Sudan and western Asia.

The puritanical Wahhabi movement came to dominate Arabia when tribal chief Abdul Aziz Ibn Saud (sah-OOD) (1902–1969) expanded the power of the Saudi family (see Chapter 21). By 1932, his forces had taken western Arabia and the Islamic holy cities of Mecca and Medina from the Hashemites and formed the country of Saudi Arabia. As king, Abdul Aziz began strictly enforcing Islamic law by establishing Committees for the Commendation of Virtue and the Condemnation of Vice to police personal behavior. At the same time, the Saudis welcomed material innovations from the West, such as automobiles, medicine, and telephones. In 1935 oil was discovered in Saudi Arabia, which contained the world's richest oil reserves. The resulting wealth chiefly benefited the royal family and their allies, the Wahhabi clergy.

Zionism: Jewish Nationalism

The roots of a long-term problem for Arab nationalists were planted in Palestine as the Zionist movement, which sought a Jewish homeland for the Jewish people, compelled many in the Jewish ghettoes of Europe to move there (see Chapters 19 and 21). The Zionist slogan—"a land without a people for a people without a land"—was supported by the British government in 1917 with the issuance of the Balfour Declaration, a letter approving the establishment of Palestine as a national home for the Jewish people. But the Zionist slogan had a flaw: Palestine was not a land without a people. Palestinian Arabs had lived there for many centuries, building cities, cultivating orchards, and herding livestock. A Zionist

Muslim Brotherhood An Egyptian religious movement founded in 1928 that expressed popular Arab reaction to Westernization.

Balfour Declaration A letter from the British foreign minister to Zionist leaders in 1917 that gave British support for the establishment of Palestine as a national home for the Jewish people.

leader later conceded that Jewish settlers were surprised to find people there. In Arab eyes, Jewish immigrants were European colonizers planning to dispossess them.

In the 1920s and 1930s, thousands of European Jews migrated to Palestine with British support, some of them fleeing Nazi Germany. By 1939, the Palestine population of 1.5 million was one-third Jewish. Although Jewish settlers established businesses, industries, and productive farms that contributed greatly to Palestine's economic development, Arabs feared becoming a vulnerable numerical minority in what they considered their own land. Zionist organizations began buying up the best land from absentee Arab landlords who disregarded the customary rights of villagers to use it, uprooting thousands of Arab peasants. As tensions increased, violence spread; sometimes hundreds of Arabs and Jews were killed in armed clashes.

> "Economic downturns led to political instability, which paved the way for governments led by military dictators, known as caudillos."

The Balfour Declaration Learn which questions were considered—and which were ignored—as Britain prepared to support the Zionist movement.

In 1936, a major Arab rebellion fostered a three-year civil war. All Arab factions united to oppose plans for establishing an independent Palestine. Concluding that the Arab–Jewish divide was unbridgeable, Britain proposed a partition into two states and the removal of thousands of Arabs from the Jewish side. Both groups rejected the proposal. In 1939, Britain placed a limit on Jewish immigration and banned land transfers, but the Holocaust during World War II reinforced the Jewish desire for a homeland where they could govern themselves.

Politics and Modernization in Latin America

While Islamic societies grappled with colonialism and the encounter with the West, Latin America, with economies reliant on a few natural resource exports such as beef, copper, coffee, and sugar, became more vulnerable to global political and economic crises. Latin Americans paid a price for their openness to the

Latin American Resources (*http://www .oberlin.edu/faculty/ svolk/latinam.htm*). An excellent collection of resources and links on history, politics, and culture.

world economy as foreign investment fell and foreign markets closed during the Great Depression in the 1930s, cutting the foreign trade of some countries by 90 percent. Economic downturns led to political instability, which paved the way for governments led by military dictators, known as caudillos.

A Continent of Dictators

During the Great Depression, dictators came to power all over the region (see Map 25.3). In 1930–1931, armed forces overthrew governments, among them elected ones, in a dozen Latin American

Interactive Map

nations, including large countries such as Peru, Argentina, and Brazil. Some of the new governments, such as those in Argentina and Brazil, were influenced by European fascism. Dictators often increased their governments' role in the economy, such as by beginning industries to provide products that were normally imported. They also used their power to amass huge fortunes for themselves and to repress dissent. In El Salvador, for example, President Maximiliano Hernandez Martinez massacred 30,000 protesting Indian peasants. Cubans suffered under brutal dictatorships for most of the era. In 1934, the United States encouraged a coup by Sgt. Fulgencio Batista (fool-HEN-see-oh bah-TEES-ta) (1901–1973), who dominated Cuba for the next twenty-five years as a right-wing dictator.

The challenges of the era also affected Chile, one of the most stable and open Latin American nations. Although the military had occasionally seized power for short periods, Chile had generally enjoyed elected democratic governments and highly competitive elections involving several parties. The dislocations of the Great Depression led to unity for the squabbling leftist and centrist parties, which formed the Popular Front and came to power in the 1939 elections. Their reformist government, supported by labor unions, sponsored industrialization.

A growing women's movement allied with the left also brought some change. Chilean feminists won some basic legal rights and benefits for mothers, but they could not get most of their social agenda, including abortion rights, approved, in part because of opposition by conservative Chilean women.

© Cengage Learning

![globe icon] Map 25.3
South and Central America in 1930

By 1930, Latin America had achieved its present political configuration, except that Britain, France, and Holland still had colonies in the Guianas region of South America, and Britain controlled British Honduras (today's Belize) in Central America.

Vargas and the Brazilian New State Movement

As elsewhere in Latin America, Brazil experienced political change that was often tinged with nationalism. In the 1920s middle-class reformers challenged domination by a corrupt ruling class that they felt did not listen to the common people or assert Brazil's national interests in the world. Their proposals for a more liberal society included official recognition of labor unions, a minimum wage, restraints in child labor, land reform, universal suffrage, and expansion of education to poor children. Eventually, the Great Depression reshaped Brazilian politics, prompting a civilian-military coup by Getulio Vargas (jay-TOO-lee-oh VAR-gus) (1883–1954) in 1930. A former soldier, lawyer, and government minister, Vargas launched the Estado Novo ("New State"), a fascist-influenced, modernizing dictatorship that ruled until 1945 and practiced torture and censorship to repress opponents. But the Estado Novo also sponsored modernizing reforms that made Vargas widely popular with the lower classes. Gradually, the dictator became more populist and nationalist. He was deposed by the army in 1945 after he had begun moving to the left, leaving behind acute tensions between right-wing and left-wing Brazilians.

Mexican Reforms Under Cardenas

As in Chile and Brazil, strongly progressive and nationalist ideas emerged in Mexico. After the turmoil of the decade-long Mexican Revolution (see Chapter 20), which ended only in 1920, Mexico badly needed funds for reconstruction but faced sharply reduced export earnings and a deepening economic slump. President Plutarcho Elias Calles (KAH-yays) (r. 1924–1928) put the political system on a solid footing by creating a new party that brought together various factions, yet most Mexicans saw little improvement in their lives. In 1934, Mexicans launched a new era by electing Lázaro Cárdenas (car-DAYN-es) (r. 1934–1940), an army officer with socialist leanings, as president. Peasants had grown cynical about the promises by leaders during the Mexican Revolution to supply them with land. Cardenas fulfilled this promise by assigning land ownership to the *ejidos* (eh-HEE-dos), the traditional agricultural cooperatives, who now apportioned land to their members. As a result, some 800,000 people realized their dream, but economic turmoil caused the payments and services the government had promised to evaporate.

Cárdenas did introduce reforms that made him wildly popular with other Mexicans. He encouraged the formation of a large labor confederation that led to a higher standard of living and more dignity for urban workers. Cárdenas also nationalized the oil industry, spurring celebrations in Mexico and outraging U.S. leaders. Workers gained a role in managing both the oil industry and the railroads. The president supported women's rights, arguing that working women had the same right as men to participate in electoral struggles. Although he was popular among the working classes, wealthy Mexican landowners and merchants, as well as U.S. political and business leaders, hated Cárdenas. He was followed by more moderate leaders who reversed support for the ejidos, favoring instead individual farmers, and ignored women's rights (Mexican women could not vote until 1953). These leaders also cooperated with the United States on immigration issues. During World War II, Mexico and the United States signed an agreement to send more Mexican workers north to fill the job positions in industry, agriculture, and the service sector left vacant by drafted American men. The flow northward of poor Mexicans, legal and illegal, became a floodtide after the war.

 Speech to the Nation In this excerpt from a radio address given in 1938, President Lázaro Cárdenas announces his decision to nationalize the Mexican oil industry.

Cultural Nationalism in Latin America and the Caribbean

Cultural nationalism influenced Latin American and Caribbean societies. A Brazilian literary trend known as Modernism sought to define a distinct national expression by exploring the country's rich cultural heritage. Rather than emulating European literary trends, modernist writers used forms and ideas reflecting Brazil's uniqueness. For instance, the poet, novelist, and critic Mario de Andrade (1893–1945) mixed words from various regional dialects and Native American, African, and Portuguese folklore into his work. Brazilian musicians also incorporated folk music: the composer Heitor Villa-Lobos's music (vee-luh-LO-bose) (1890–1959) expressed the national character that was inspired by Afro-Brazilian and Indian religious rites and urban music. The popular music and dance known as *samba* became not only a world symbol of Brazilian society but also a way for the Afro-Brazilian lower classes to express themselves.

The progressive spirit of the times also spurred literary and artistic movements throughout Latin America. In Chile, writers combined radical politics with cultural renaissance. The work of Marxist-influenced Chilean poet Pablo Neruda (ne-ROO-duh) (1904–1973) bristled with anger over economic inequalities. Sometimes governments retaliated against dissident artists; Neruda wrote some of his greatest poetry while in hiding or exile. Mexico produced several great painters, including Diego Rivera (rih-VEER-a) (1885–1957), a Marxist who became one of the most famous artists in the Western Hemisphere. His huge, realistic murals depicted the common people, especially peasants and workers, struggling for dignity. His wife, Frida Kahlo (KAH-lo) (1907–1954), the daughter of a German Jewish immigrant, specialized in vivid, even shocking paintings that were created mostly from her own experience and often expressed the physical and psychological pain suffered by women.

A cultural renaissance also occurred in the Caribbean, where intellectuals sought to create an authentic West Indian identity. In part this involved overcoming negative attitudes toward acknowledging Africa, as the ancestral home of most West Indians. Afro-Caribbean intellectuals, such as the Trinidadian Marxist C. L. R. James (1901–1989), sought to rebuild Afro-Caribbean pride by celebrating African roots, which he argued were a major contributor to the distinctive West Indian culture. James was a well-traveled historian, prolific writer, and activist who was equally at home in the Caribbean, Europe, Africa, and North America. His ability to combine Afro-Caribbean nationalism with an internationalist perspective inspired intellectuals around the world.

 Listen to a synopsis of Chapter 25.

Candido Portinari, *Coffee* Portinari, one of the finest Brazilian painters of the 1930s and 1940s, often portrayed urban and rural labor, reflecting his leftwing political views. He had grown up the son of Italian immigrants on a coffee plantation near Sao Paulo. This painting from 1935 shows plantation workers carrying heavy bags of coffee, much of which will be exported.

Museo Nacional Bellas Artes, Rio de Janeiro/Art Resource, NY

Societies • Networks • Transitions

Global Imbalances in the Modern World, 1750–1945

A world traveler in the nineteenth century could not help but notice the imbalances in wealth and power between the world's societies, imbalances that became even wider in the early twentieth century. The modern world was shaped in part by revolutions and innovations in western Europe and North America. In these societies, capitalism and industrialization fostered wealth and inspired new technologies, such as the steamships and railroads that conveyed travelers, resources, and products over great distances. But the new technologies also included deadly new weapons, such as repeating rifles and machine guns, that enabled the Western conquest of Asian and African societies, reshaping the world's political and economic configuration. Just as Spain and Portugal controlled Latin America until the early 1800s, a half-dozen Western nations ruled, or influenced the governments of, most Asian, African, and Caribbean peoples by 1914. Western domination of the global economy fostered investment but also facilitated a transfer of vast wealth to the West.

While several Western societies exercised disproportionate power in this era, other societies were not passive actors. Societies borrowed ideas, institutions, and technologies from each other, though redefining them to meet their own needs. Societies such as Siam (later Thailand), Persia (later Iran), Turkey, and, most spectacularly, Japan successfully resisted colonialism and, borrowing Western models, introduced some modernization. In fact, resistance to Western power was endemic in the global system, even in colonized societies such as Vietnam, Indonesia, India, and South Africa, where local peoples actively asserted their own interests. The movement of products, thought, and people, on a larger scale than ever before, transcended political boundaries, connecting distant societies. Europeans avidly imported Asian arts, Africans embraced Christianity, and peasants from India settled in the South Pacific and the West Indies. By the 1930s, people around the world, often using borrowed Western ideas such as nationalism and Marxism, were challenging Western political and economic power.

Imperialism, States, and the Global System

The world's governments changed greatly during the Modern Era, fostering new types of empires and states. A more integrated international order, dominated by a few Western nations and, eventually, also by Japan, was built on the foundation of the varied Western and Asian empires that had been the main power centers during the Early Modern Era. Societies worldwide grappled with the global political trends that affected people's well-being and livelihoods.

Global Empires

Powerful societies had formed empires since ancient times, but over the centuries, successive empires grew larger and more complex. In the mid-1700s, more than two-thirds of the world's people lived in one of several large, multiethnic empires whose economies were based largely on peasant agriculture. These empires stretched across the Eastern Hemisphere from Qing China and the Western colonies in Southeast Asia, such as Dutch Java and the Spanish Philippines, to the Ottoman, Russian, and Habsburg Empires. In the Americas, the huge Spanish Empire, Portuguese Brazil, and British North America all resembled the Eurasian empires in their multiethnic populations and agrarian base, although much of the agriculture was done by unfree labor. In addition to empires, there were strong states such as Tokugawa Japan, Siam, and the Ashante kingdom in West Africa. All empires and states depended on a command of military power, especially gunpowder weapons, and on world trade.

Many of the empires of the mid-1700s had crumbled by the early twentieth century. The Spanish, Portuguese, and British lost most of their territories in the Americas, and the Habsburg and Ottoman Empires were dismantled after World War I. In their place,

Queen Victoria as Seen by a Nigerian Carver
This wood effigy of the British monarch was made by a Yoruba artist in just-colonized Nigeria in the late nineteenth century.

Pitt Rivers Museum, Oxford University

modern empires had emerged. Between 1870 and 1914, a huge portion of the globe, divided up into colonies or spheres of influence by the West, was incorporated into a Western-dominated world economic system. The influential British imperialist and author Rudyard Kipling summarized the rationale for exercising imperial power: "That they should take who have the power, And they should keep who can."[1]

Like empires throughout history, modern imperial states, whatever their democratic forms at home, punished dissent in their colonies. Sometimes protests, such as those led by Mohandas Gandhi in India, forced Western colonizers to modify their policies; more commonly, protest leaders, such as Gandhi, Harry Thuku in Kenya, and Sukarno in Indonesia, were jailed or exiled. Some observers recognized the failure of democratic countries to encourage democracy in their own colonies, as a nineteenth-century English wit charged about his nation's treatment of Ireland: "the moment the very name of Ireland is mentioned, the English seem to bid adieu to common feelings, common prudence and common sense, and to act with the barbarity of tyrants and the fatuity of idiots."[2]

Nationalism and Revolutions

Whether parts of empires or not, societies all over the world struggled to become nations with self-government and common identities. But Western peoples formed the most powerful nations. Many European nations were formidable forces because of their strong government structures and democratic practices that fostered debate; they also enjoyed economic dynamism, possessed advanced weapons, and engaged in fierce rivalries with each other. Across the Atlantic, most Latin American nations struggled to achieve prosperity and internal unity, but the United States matched European capabilities and shared similar imperial ambitions by the later 1800s. By contrast, few people in colonized areas shared any sense of common identity, let alone a national mission; colonial governments were unpopular and usually viewed by the colonized as illegitimate. By drawing up arbitrary colonial borders, often without regard to ethnic connections or economic networks, colonies like Nigeria, Indonesia, and the Congo lacked any national cohesion. The ethnic diversity of most colonies inhibited the formation of nationalist movements.

Still, despite the barriers, nationalism spread, often encouraged by travel, exile, or education. The Venezuelan Símon Bolívar, the Filipino Jose Rizal (rih-ZALL) (1861–1896), and the Vietnamese Ho Chi Minh (1890–1969), all disenchanted with colonial restrictions, embraced a nationalist agenda while living in Europe. Yan Fu, a Chinese student living in England in the 1870s, recalled spending "whole days and nights discussing differences and similarities in Chinese and Western thought and political institutions."[3] Back in China, Yan Fu translated the work of liberal British thinkers and used it to spread nationalism and other Western ideas in China. But nationalists seeking to confront Western power did not all look to the West for inspiration. By 1900, rapidly modernizing Japan was a model nation for many Asians.

But nationalism was not always an imported sentiment. Many Asians had a sense of identity similar to nationalism long before the nineteenth century. People in Korea, Japan, and Vietnam, for example, had long enjoyed some national feeling based on shared religion, a common language, bureaucratic government, and the perception of one or more common enemies. African kingdoms such as Ashante (ah-SHAN-tee), Oyo (OH-yo), and Buganda (boo-GONE-da) enjoyed some attributes of nationhood.

Reflecting such national feeling, in 1898, Hawaii's last monarch, Queen Liliuokalani (luh-lee-uh-oh-kuh-LAH-nee), pleaded with the United States not to colonize the islands, since her people's "form of government is as dear to them as yours is precious to you. Quite as warmly as you love your country, so they love theirs."[4] U.S. leaders ignored her pleas and annexed Hawaii. To protect their power, colonizers labored hard to crush local traditions and to counter nationalism through the use of divide-and-rule strategies, such as the British encouragement of the Hindu–Muslim divide in India. Formerly well-defined states lost their traditional cohesion as they now became parts of empires.

Some societies needed major rebellions and revolutions to reject discredited orders and create new nations. The American and French Revolutions of the later 1700s began an Age of Revolution and inspired people elsewhere to take up arms against unjust or outdated governments. In the U.S. case, disgruntled colonists overthrew British rule and became known around the world as exponents of political freedom. During the mid-nineteenth century, the Taiping (TIE-ping) Rebellion against China's Qing dynasty and the Indian Rebellion against the British East India Company provided fierce challenges to established governments in the world's two most populous societies before ultimately failing. Early in the twentieth century, other revolutions overturned old governments and built nations in Mexico, Turkey, and China; the Chinese revolution ended 2,000 years of imperial control and established the foundation for a modern republic. The Russian Revolution of 1917 installed the world's first communist government, inspiring communist movements and revolutionary nationalists around the world.

The aftermath of World War I brought new revolutionary upheavals and ideologies. Old states collapsed in eastern Europe, fascism spread in Germany and Japan in the economic shambles caused by the Great Depression, and Spain erupted in civil war. In 1914, Marxism—the revolutionary socialist vision developed by Karl Marx (1818–1883)—had relatively little influence outside of Germany and Russia, but by 1945, the ideology had mass support in many places, including China, Korea, Indonesia, and Vietnam. Karl Marx had supplied the critique of class struggle and capitalism and offered Communism as a better way.

Now the Russian leader, Vladimir Lenin (1870–1924), fomented a revolution in 1917, and the Chinese communist leader Mao Zedong (maow dzuh-dong) (1893–1976) contributed a vision of a new, unselfish socialist society, writing that "the people are the sea, we [communists] are the fish, so long as we can swim in that sea, we will survive."[5] By combining communism with nationalism, the Vietnamese revolutionary Ho Chi Minh provided a workable model to overthrow colonialism. The ideas of Lenin, Mao, and Ho made Marxism a major vehicle for change after World War II.

Change in the Global System

During the Modern Era, the global system expanded and changed as Western political and military influence increased. Networks of trade and communication linking distant societies grew, but Western nations benefited more from their exchanges. Aided by this power, Western culture dominated local traditions, especially in Western colonies. For example, children in the U.S.-ruled Philippines, a tropical and predominantly Catholic land, learned English from books showing American youngsters throwing snowballs, playing baseball, and attending Protestant church services. In some cases, this deliberate Westernization reshaped beliefs and ways of life, as occurred among the Filipinos and the Igbos of southern Nigeria. However, Western cultural influence was weak in other colonized societies, especially Muslim ones such as Egypt or the Hausa of northern Nigeria.

There were winners and losers in the new global system. In 1750, Western overseas expansion, including military conquests, had already reshaped the Americas and some regions of Africa and southern Asia. Chinese, Indians, and western Europeans were the richest peoples at this time: collectively they accounted for 70 percent of all the world's economic activity and 80 percent of its manufacturing. China remained the greatest engine of the world economy. Britain was the rising European power, but it faced challenges from France, Russia, Spain, and the Ottoman Empire. The more economically developed districts and the major cities within the two wealthiest countries, Britain and China, apparently enjoyed similar living standards, such as abundant food and long life spans, until at least 1800.

By 1914, however, after a century and a half of Western industrialization, imperial expansion, and colonization, the global system had become more divided than ever before into rich and poor societies. India was now among the poorer countries, and China had suc-cumbed to Western military and economic influence, falling well behind the West. Meanwhile, a few Western nation-states—especially Great Britain, the United States, Germany, and France—had grown rich and influential. Because of their unparalleled military power, all four of these nations ruled colonial empires, from which they extracted valuable resources; played a leading role in world trade; and spread their cultures and ideas. Also among the richest nations, but having less international power, were a few other western European countries, including the Netherlands, Belgium, and Switzerland.

A middle category of countries—Canada, Japan, Russia, Italy, Portugal, and Spain—had a weaker economic base and less military power than those of the richest nations, but they still enjoyed economic and political autonomy. A third category of countries were those that were economically poor and militarily weak, either ruled directly as Western colonies, such as India, Indonesia, Nigeria, or Jamaica, or under strong political and economic influence as neocolonies, such as China, Thailand, and Iran. Economically, Latin American countries, relative to the rich North American and western European nations, were also poor.

Living conditions and governments in the rich countries differed dramatically in 1914 from those in the poor societies. Capitalism fostered growth in Europe and North America, although it took many decades for the benefits to reach the common people. The rich countries, such as Britain and the United States, were highly industrialized and enjoyed well-diversified economies and large middle classes. Many of their people lived in cities and, owing to mass education systems, became literate. These countries also boasted efficient, well-financed, constitutional governments. Rich countries were typically democratic and fostered public discourse of diverse political opinions, such as socialism and feminism. These patterns were also common in the less powerful Western nations and in Japan.

By contrast, the poor societies, especially Western colonies in Asia and Africa, where many people worked the lands owned by foreign landlords or planters, were not industrialized and people earned meager wages. Economic growth was often determined by foreign investment and markets rather than by local needs. For example, rather than growing food for the local community, farmers in Honduras, in Central America, grew bananas for the U.S. market while farmers in French-ruled Senegal, in West Africa, raised peanuts for export. Politically, a small upper class—African chiefs, Indian princes, Javanese aristocrats—played a political role by cooperating with Western rulers. Only a small minority of people had access to formal education, economic opportunity, and political decision making.

Their general poverty and lack of economic and political options did not mean that people in poor societies were always miserable. Celebrating their survival skills in the early 1900s, the Indian writer and thinker

Rabindranath Tagore (rah-BIN-dra-NATH TUH-gore) (1861–1941) found both triumphs and tragedies in Indian peasant life, which "with its everyday contentment and misery, has always been there in the peasants' fields and village festivals, manifesting their very simple and abiding humanity across all of history—sometimes under Mughal rule, sometimes under British rule."[6]

In the colonies, heavy Western cultural influence, such as the policies the French called their "civilizing mission" in Vietnam and West Africa—by which they tried to impose French ways on people they regarded as culturally inferior—was combined with psychological trauma as once-proud peoples succumbed to foreign rule and its racist restrictions. An anti-imperialist African organization complained in 1927 that colonialism had abruptly cut short "the development of the African people. These nations were later declared pagan and savage, an inferior race."[7] Although Western Christian missionaries often found eager converts, nationalists frequently accused them of undermining traditional beliefs. Western domination, however, did not preclude cultural and scientific achievements by colonized people. For example, although their country was a British colony, various Indian mathematicians and scientists won international renown, including Nobel Prize–winning physicist Sir Chandrasekhara Raman (CHAHN-dra-SEE-ker-ah RAH-man) (1888–1970) of Calcutta.

Between 1914 and 1945, the global system underwent further changes. Conflicts became world wars, fought on a greater scale than ever before and on battlefields thousands of miles apart. The United States became the world's richest, most powerful nation. Because of its defeat in World War I, Germany temporarily lost wealth and power. Germany, Italy, and Japan—all middle-ranking nations by the 1930s—challenged the rich nations—Britain, France, and the United States—during World War II. Several Latin American nations and Turkey enjoyed enough economic growth and stability of government to move into the middle-ranking category by the 1940s. Yet most of the societies of Asia, Africa, Latin America, and the Caribbean remained poor colonies or neocolonies.

The World Economy

Even before the Western overseas expansion that occurred between 1500 and 1914, trade had taken place over vast distances. Chinese, Indian, Arab, and Armenian merchants had long dominated the vigorous Asian trade, and for centuries Chinese silks and porcelains and Southeast Asian and Indian spices had reached Europe, the Middle East, and parts of sub-Saharan Africa. European explorers wished to locate the source of these riches, and after 1500, the Portuguese, Dutch, and British played key roles in this trade, beginning the rise of the world economy. European influence on the world economy increased in the 1700s and 1800s when Western traders, supported by their governments, sought new natural resources and

markets in the tropical world, thereby creating a truly global economic exchange. By 1914, the entire world was enmeshed in a vast economic exchange. People often produced resources or manufactured goods—Middle Eastern oil, Indonesian coffee, British textiles—for markets thousands of miles away. Europe's Industrial Revolution, which provided manufactured goods to trade for resources, dramatically reshaped the Western economies in the 1800s but only slowly spread to other regions.

The Inequality of Global Economic Exchange

Economic exchange between societies within the world economy did not proceed on an even playing field. As had been the case for empires throughout history—Assyrian, Roman, Chinese, Inca, Spanish, Dutch—imperialism and colonialism remained the means for transferring wealth to the imperial nations, which used that wealth to finance their own development. The imperial powers, seeking to enhance the value of their colonial economies, also used their control of world trade to shift cash crops like coffee that were indigenous to one part of the world to another.

Gearing economic growth chiefly to the needs of the imperial powers impeded economic development that might have benefited everyone. Many colonies developed economies that produced and exported only one or two primary resources, such as rice and rubber from French Vietnam or sugar from Spanish Cuba. Most of these resource exports were transformed into consumer goods, such as rubber tires and chocolate candies, and sold in stores in Western nations, to the profit of their merchants. For instance, chocolate, whose use for over two millennia was confined to elites in Mexico, gained an eager market among all classes throughout the Western world by the nineteenth century. Meanwhile, the Western manufactured goods exchanged for these resources, especially textiles, found markets in Africa, Asia, and Latin America. Although much of this exchange was largely exploitative, some colonized men and women managed to capitalize on it. For example, Omu Okwei (OH-moo AWK-way) (1872–1943), an Igbo, made a fortune trading palm oil for European imported goods, which she distributed widely in Nigeria through a vast network of women traders.

Societies specializing in producing one or two natural resources were especially vulnerable to a changing world economy. To take one case, British Malaya was a major rubber exporter, but most of its rubber plantations were British-owned, and Malayans had little influence over the world price of rubber, which was determined largely by Western consumers and corporations. The rise and fall of rubber prices affected not only the rubber tappers and their families but also the shops, often owned by Chinese immigrants, who sold them goods. Thus the livelihoods of people all over the world increasingly became subject to chronic fluctuations in the world markets.

The world economy widened the wealth gap between societies. In 1500, the differences in per capita income and living standards between people in the richer regions—China, Japan, Southeast Asia, India, Ottoman Turkey, and western Europe—had probably been minor. And these peoples were roughly only two to three times better off materially than the farmers and city folk of the world's poorest farming societies. By 1750, however, while China, western Europe, and British North America enjoyed similar levels of economic production, the wealth gap between them and others was increasing. By 1900, the wealth gap between the richest and poorest societies had grown to about 10 to 1. This trend accelerated throughout the twentieth century, in part because the wealth produced in Western colonies seldom contributed to local development.

Unequal economic exchange also fostered conflict. Wars erupted as one country threatened another's access to markets and resources. For example, British free-trade policies caused the Opium War with China in the mid-1800s. The Qing government worked to end both the legal and illegal opium trade, but, as the leading opium supplier, Britain needed to protect the opium exports to China from British India, and its defeat of China hastened Chinese decline. In addition, World War I was at least partly caused by the bitter imperial competition among European nations.

The Spread of Industrialization

The Industrial Revolution, which began in Britain in the late 1700s, was not just a Western development. China and India had once been the world's leading manufacturing countries, and knowledge of Chinese mechanical devices probably stimulated several British inventions. Between 1750 and 1850, however, Britain took the lead in modern industrialization, and by the mid-1800s, it produced about half of the world's manufactured goods, while China and India fell behind. Various other European nations, the United States, and Japan industrialized in the later 1800s. Only these few nations increased their resources and weapons as a result of industrialization, and hence only a few became world powers. Some of the profits from colonialism and other overseas activities stimulated European industrialization. For instance, the Dutch based some of their industrial and transportation growth on profits earned from selling coffee and sugar grown by peasants in their Indonesian colony. But even in Europe, agriculture and other nonindustrial activities, such as trade, remained economically important. By 1881, only 44 percent of the British, 36 percent of the German, and 20 percent of the American labor force were employed in industrial or industry-related occupations.

Industrialization gradually spread beyond Europe and North America, but it was highly uneven in its impact and pace. Western policies commonly discouraged colonists from maintaining or opening industries that might compete with Western manufacturers. For instance, India had been the world's greatest textile manufacturer for centuries, but British colonization gradually diminished the indus-

try through tax and tariff policies, opening the way for British-made textiles to dominate the Indian market. The British saw India not only as a market for their goods but also as a source of cash crops. Hence, in 1840, a British official boasted that his nation had "succeeded in converting India from a manufacturing country into a country exporting raw materials."[8] The once-flourishing Indian textile center of Calcutta lost two-thirds of its population between 1750 and 1850 as its manufacturing declined.

Several nations sought to foster development by setting up manufacturing operations. China, Persia, Egypt, the Ottoman Empire, and Mexico introduced textile industries in the nineteenth century. However, the British used tariffs, or stiff duties on imports to Britain, to stifle many of these industries, thereby opening doors for the export of British fabrics and clothing to these countries. Between 1900 and 1945, there was a resurgence of efforts at industrialization in various nations—China, Argentina, Brazil, and Australia—but agriculture remained the economic foundation for most of their population.

Before 1880, few industrial cities had emerged outside of northwestern Europe and North America, but, in a global economy, other urban places had grown dependent on the Industrial Revolution for their livelihood. Shanghai thrived as the commercial gateway to central China's interior; Singapore served as the economic hub for much of Southeast Asia; and Alexandria was the import-export center for Egypt and the upper Nile basin.

Frontiers and Migrations

The rise of a modern world economy, and its constant quest for resources, markets, and labor, accelerated migration. Modern transportation networks and rapid population growth propelled the movement of peoples. Between 1800 and 1900, the world population grew from 900 million to 1,500 million, with two-thirds of these people living in Asia. While some people escaped poverty and overcrowding by moving into frontier regions, many others, more than 100 million between 1830 and 1914, left for distant lands. Some, such as enslaved Africans who were transported to the Americas, were taken from their homes unwillingly. In contrast, millions of Europeans and Asians sought, and often found, better opportunities in other countries.

Settling Frontiers

From ancient times, people left overcrowded lands to move into sparsely settled frontiers, such as Bantu-speaking Africans, who had taken their ironworking and farming technologies from West Africa into the sparsely populated lands of central, eastern, and southern Africa long ago. Similar movements continued in modern times. White Americans moved westward across the North American continent, subduing and killing off the Native American peoples and seizing their land. In Australia, New

Zealand, and South Africa, European colonists also disrupted local peoples. In South America, Brazilians moved from the Atlantic coast westward into the rain forests and grasslands, setting up farms after pushing out local Indians.

Remote from central government controls and traditional social structures, the frontier fostered innovations. Frontier social conditions were often more flexible and offered new opportunities. Cultures met and mixed, and people of different groups intermarried. Cultural blending produced hybrid social groups such as the Russian Cossacks, western American cowboys, and Argentine gauchos. The cowboys and gauchos, who chiefly herded cattle for ranchers, combined European and self-sufficient Native American customs. Eventually, however, the frontier pioneers were absorbed into formal states.

African and European Population Movements

The largest population movements of the era involved the involuntary transport of African slaves across the Atlantic to the Americas and the chiefly voluntary migration of European emigrants to the Americas, southern Africa, Australia, and New Zealand. The Africans, shipped in chains and filth, typically faced brutal lives shortened by harsh conditions. In contrast, most of the Europeans chose to leave their homelands to seek a better life, and often succeeded.

The trans-Atlantic slave trade reached its height between 1760 and 1800. During these years, more than 70,000 people per year were herded onto crowded slave ships and shipped from Africa. The great majority of Africans were landed in Brazil and the Caribbean islands, where people of African ancestry today account for a large part of the population. The gradual abolition of slavery in the Americas eventually ended the trans-Atlantic trade, but the longtime slave trade from East and Central Africa to the Middle East continued until the end of the nineteenth century. By the early 1900s, slavery had declined significantly or been abolished in Africa, the Middle East, and Southeast Asia, largely as a result of the efforts of humanitarian organizations, churches, and both Western and local abolitionists.

During the Modern Era, the European migration across oceans to the Americas and the South Pacific

Interactive Map

dwarfed other population movements (see map). Unlike the African slaves, many European emigrants were escaping poverty or political repression and expected to improve their lives abroad. While the ships carrying the emigrants were often crowded and unhealthy, Europeans did not arrive in chains, with no possibility of freedom. The emigrants represented Europe's ethnic diversity but came largely from the British Isles, Germany, Italy, Spain, Poland, and Russia. Between 1500 and 1940, some 68 million people left Europe, creating new societies in the Americas, Australia, New Zealand, and southern Africa. The result of this large population movement was a Europeanization of societies, as European cultures were implanted far from their ancestral homes. The tendency to look toward Europe for inspiration was especially strong in Argentina, Chile, Canada, Australia, and New Zealand. In these societies, many immigrants and their descendants tended to maintain their native languages, churches, and social customs and to identify with their homelands. As a result, the numerous Italians in Argentina's capital, Buenos Aires, often spoke Italian, while Anglo-Argentines sent their children to private English-medium schools.

Modern World History Resources (*http://www.histore-search.com/modworld.html*). Has links to sites on many topics and regions.

Immigrants contributed much to their new lands. For example, in the United States, the Scottish-born Andrew Carnegie (1835–1919) helped build the iron and steel industry and with his philanthropy sponsored libraries. Others found different ways to improve their new societies, such as Lithuanian-born left-wing activist Emma Goldman (1869–1940), who emigrated to the United States in 1885. She was later arrested and deported for being an advocate for slum-dwellers and for opposing U.S. entry into World War I.

Asian Migrations

During this era, peoples from eastern and southern Asia also emigrated in large numbers, usually by ship to distant shores. They went in response to the demand among Western colonies and American nations for a labor force for the mines and plantations that supplied their wealth. As a result, Chinese mined tin in Southeast Asia and gold in California and Australia, while Indians worked on rubber plantations in British Malaya and sugar plantations in South Africa. Immigrants often died from overwork or ill health and, as happened with Chinese in California, sometimes suffered from violent discrimination. Yet, many Asians prevailed to raise families in their new nations. Today approximately 40 to 45 million Asians live outside of their ancestral homelands. Chinese and Indians constituted the great majority of Asian migrants, and their descendants became a vital presence in the world economy as merchants, miners, and plantation workers. Today the majority of Chinese in Southeast Asia, the South Pacific and Indian Ocean islands, the Caribbean, and Latin America are engaged in commerce.

Pushed by poverty, overpopulation, or war, people also emigrated from Northeast and Southeast Asia, forming cohesive communities in new lands. Numerous Japanese and Koreans left their homelands between 1850 and 1940. Some settled in Hawaii to work on pineapple plantations or in the canning industry. Many Japanese migrated to the Pacific Coast of the United States and Canada, some taking up farming. When the United States and Canada restricted Japanese immigration in the early 1900s, the Japanese emigrant flow turned to

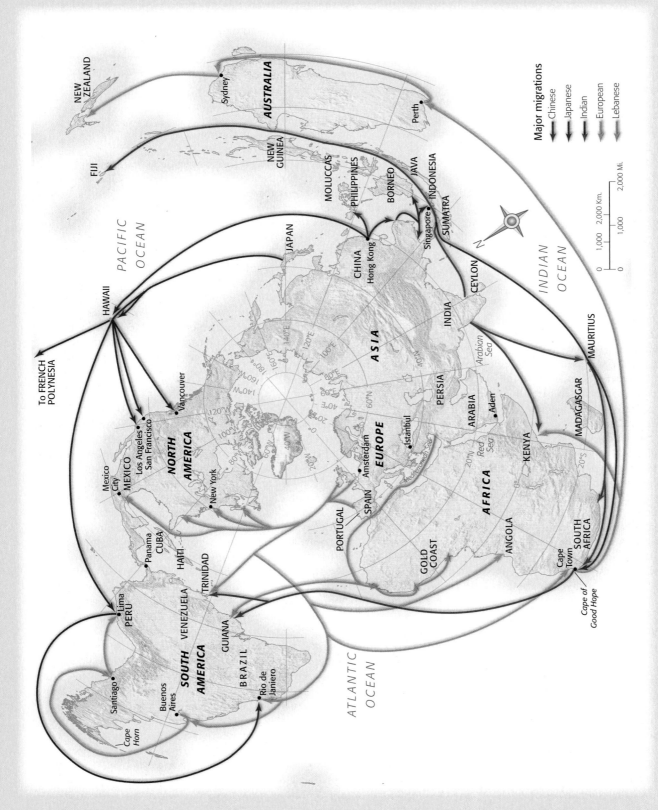

Asian and European Migration, 1750–1940

During this era, millions of Europeans emigrated to the Americas, South Africa, Australia, and New Zealand. Millions of Asians, especially Chinese and Indians, left their homes to work or settle in Southeast Asia, Africa, the Pacific islands, and the Americas.

Major migrations

- Chinese
- Japanese
- Indian
- European
- Lebanese

Singapore's Chinatown By the early 1900s, Singapore, a major Southeast Asian port and commercial crossroads, was predominantly Chinese in population. The bustling streets were lined by shops, workers' quarters, theaters, and brothels.

Latin America, especially Peru and Brazil. Between 1875 and 1940, Indonesians, mostly Javanese, were recruited to work on plantations in Malaya and British North Borneo but also in Dutch Guiana (today's Suriname), in South America, and on the French-ruled South Pacific island of New Caledonia. Some 50,000 Javanese today live in Suriname. After the United States colonized the Philippines, Filipinos began migrating to Hawaii and the U.S. Pacific coast as factory workers or farm laborers. Today 1.5 million Filipinos live in the United States.

The Spread of Technology and Mass Culture

The modern global system owed much to innovations in technology. Improved methods of communication and transportation allowed people, ideas, and products to travel farther and faster than ever before, enhancing networks of power and exchange. More effective military technologies enabled a few societies to gain control of others and combat rival powers. Finally, the increasing connections around the world enabled ideas and products to spread across borders.

Communication and Transportation

For much of history, communication over long distances had been slow, depending largely on beasts of burden carrying riders or pulling wagons, and later on sailing ships. In 500 B.C.E., a message carried by successive riders on horses could travel the 1,800-mile length of the Persian Empire in nine days. Two millennia later, in the 1600s, it took Dutch ships some nine months to sail from Amsterdam to Dutch-ruled Java to deliver news and orders. Then in the nineteenth century, thanks to the Industrial Revolution, communications changed dramatically. In 1844, the first telegraph messages were exchanged between Washington and Baltimore. By 1870, the cables had reached from Britain to India. The invention of the telephone in 1876 and radio in 1895 further increased the potential for communications. As the possibilities and advantages of broadcasting over great distances became apparent, the New Zealand premier proposed in 1911 that Britain build an empirewide radio network because of "the great importance of radio for social, commercial, and defensive purposes."[9] By the 1920s, radio transmissions had become commonplace in industrial nations, and British broadcasts could reach Canada, South Africa, India, and Australia.

Some technologies conveyed people and commodities as well as messages, transforming peoples' lives around the world. Railroads were built all over the world to carry goods and passengers, and as trains reached stations, telegraph messages smoothed their journeys by passing on traffic and weather information. By 1869, railroads connected the Pacific and Atlantic coasts of North America, and by 1903, anyone determined to make the long journey could ride the 9,000 miles between Paris and Siberia's Pacific coast. While railroads extended land networks, shipping lines that employed steamships linked the world. The opening of the 105-mile-long Suez Canal in 1869 and the 51-mile-long Panama Canal in 1914, both of which cost the lives of thousands of workers during their construction, greatly reduced travel times for many sea journeys and also made it easier and cheaper to ship resources from Asia and Latin America to Europe and North America. Now it only took a few weeks to sail from China or Singapore to New York or London.

In the early 1900s, motor cars and buses continued the revolution in land transportation begun by railroads, allowing people to more easily commute to city jobs and downtown stores or to travel between cities. After World War I, thousands of middle-class Europeans and North Americans owned their own cars, and in the 1930s, the first commercial air flights began, making long-distance journeys even faster. Transportation depended increasingly on fossil fuels, first coal and then oil. The use of vehicles fueled by oil increased the strategic importance of oil-rich regions, such as the Middle East, Indonesia, Mexico, and the Gulf Coast of the United States.

Technologies of Warfare

New technologies included those devoted to warfare that made it easier to kill more people and from a greater distance. Most of these weapons remained largely a monopoly of Western nations and Japan during this era, and thus contributed to the imbalances in global power. White adventurers and settlers used the rifle invented by the American Philo Remington (1816–1889), which was effective at 1,500 yards, to defeat, and seize the lands of, the Native Americans and the Australian Aborigines. Effective rifles also proved devastating in Africa against warriors armed only with spears and arrows. The British-born American explorer Henry Morton Stanley boasted of his use of repeating rifles and terrorism to destroy a hostile Congo village that had greeted him with spears and arrows: "I skirmish in their streets, drive them pell-mell into the woods beyond; with frantic haste I fire the huts, and end the scene by towing their canoes into midstream and setting them adrift."[10]

Military weaponry quickly improved, including more powerful repeating guns. In 1861, an American doctor, Richard Gatling (1818–1903), invented what quickly came to be known as the Gatling gun, which could fire up to three thousand rounds of ammunition per minute. The first totally automatic machine gun, spitting out eleven bullets per second, was invented in 1884 by Hiram Maxim (1840–1916), an American working in Britain, and gave the British an unparalleled military advantage. As a result of such innovations, during World War I the Allied and Central powers inflicted terrible casualties on each other. The Western nations had also by this time developed the first armored tanks and increasingly relied on battleships at sea. Air power became central to combat in the Spanish Civil War and World War II. The methods of warfare were now more indiscriminate in their targets and lethal than ever before in history. In 1945, the United States used the most deadly weapon in history, the atomic bomb, to force Japanese surrender and end World War II.

The Spread of Mass Cultures

The revolution in communications and transportation technologies contributed to the creation and spread of mass cultures, popular entertainments appealing to a large audience that often crossed class divisions and national borders. People were increasingly exposed to cultural products and activities that were common in other regions of their countries or imported from abroad. The emerging mass media, such as newspapers and radio, were centered in rapidly growing cities like New York, Paris, Istanbul, Buenos Aries, and Tokyo. These media disseminated mass culture, reporting on film stars and sports events or playing popular music. As literacy rates rose, the print media gained particular influence. India alone supported six hundred different newspapers in several dozen languages in 1900. Popular books competed with classic works of philosophy and religion for the hearts and minds of readers.

By spreading cultural influences into other societies, mass communications and increased travel sometimes fostered Westernization. Orchestras playing Western classical music appeared in various Asian societies, including India, China, and Japan, by the early 1900s. Films and popular music from the United States had an even larger international audience. American film stars such as Charlie Chaplin, born in Britain, became known throughout the world, and U.S.-born jazz musicians often made a living playing the nightclubs of Europe and Asia, where they inspired local musicians to take up jazz. Many societies adopted and excelled in Western sports. For example, Indians became skilled in British cricket; India's Prince Ranjitsinhji (RAHN-jeet-SING-jee) (1872–1933) became one of the world's best players. European football, also known as soccer, became an international sport that was played all over the world.

Influences from non-Western cultures also spread widely, contributing to creative cultural mixing. In the eighteenth and nineteenth centuries, growing Western interest in Chinese painting, Japanese prints, Indonesian gamelan music, and African woodcarvings influenced Western arts. Later, in the 1930s, Indian films and Indian popular music became popular in Southeast Asia and the Middle East, and Cuban music, a mix of African and Western traditions, developed a large following in West and Central Africa, where it blended with local styles. People found ways to combine imported ideas, whatever their source, with their own traditions. For instance, in his lyrical suite, *Bachianas Brasileiras*, of 1930, the Brazilian composer Heitor Villa-Lobos (HAY-tore VEE-ya LOW-bos) (1887–1959) adapted the Baroque influences of German composer Johann Sebastian Bach (1685–1750) to Brazilian folk and popular music.

The reach of organizations and social movements expanded, as did awareness of the world. Some organizations developed a global focus. For example, the Red Cross, a Christian organization formed in nineteenth-century Switzerland to alleviate human suffering by helping war victims, eventually became an international movement devoted to humanitarian aid around the globe (in the Islamic world it became the Red Crescent). Social movements also crossed borders. For instance, women in China, Japan, Indonesia, Egypt, and Chile, inspired in part by feminist movements in Europe and North America, sought to adapt the notions of women's rights and education to their own societies. The winning of women's suffrage resulted from the efforts of women worldwide. In the United States, Susan B. Anthony (1820–1906) cofounded the key national and international organizations working for women's suffrage, while across the Pacific in 1924, Ichikawa Fusae (ITCH-ee-KAH-wa foo-SIGH) (1893–1918) formed the major women's suffrage group in Japan, which won the right to vote in 1945.

Global crises now became more widely known, and people followed world events in newspapers and radio newscasts. An avid news follower, the Trinidad calypso singer who humorously called himself Atilla the Hun, appraised the devastation in the world of the later 1930s:

> All we can hear is of unrest, riots, revolutions; There is war in Spain and China. Man using all his skill and ingenuity making weapons to destroy humanity. In the [Italian invasion of Ethiopia] it is said, over six hundred thousand maimed and dead. The grim reaper has taken a gigantic toll. Why all the bloodshed and devastation, Decimating the earth's population? Why can't this warfare cease? All that the tortured world needs is peace.[11]

Soon after Atilla's plea, World War II raised the level of violence even further, providing a fitting end to a turbulent, violent era during which the world's people had become more closely linked into a common global system.

 Test your understanding of the material covered in Part V.

Suggested Reading

Bayly, C. A. *The Birth of the Modern World, 1780–1914*. Malden, MA: Blackwell, 2004. A brilliant, detailed study.

Cohen, Robin. *Global Diasporas: An Introduction*. Seattle: University of Washington Press, 1997. A brief, valuable survey.

Cook, Scott B. *Colonial Encounters in the Age of High Imperialism*. New York: Longman, 1996. Examines Western imperialism.

Curtin, Philip D. *The World and the West: The European Challenge and the Overseas Response in the Age of Empire*. New York: Cambridge University Press, 2000. An interesting study of reactions to European imperialism.

Hobsbawm, Eric. *The Age of Extremes: A History of the World, 1914–1991*. New York: Pantheon, 1994. A masterful overview, especially strong on social and cultural history.

Hoerder, Dirk. *Cultures in Contact: World Migrations in the Second Millennium*. Durham, NC: Duke University Press, 2003. A comprehensive, detailed summary of migrations and diasporas.

Marks, Robert B. *The Origins of the Modern World: A Global and Ecological Narrative*. Lanham, MD: Rowman and Littlefield, 2002. A concise, readable examination of some major themes.

Neiberg, Michael S. W*arfare in World History*. New York: Routledge, 2001. Good coverage of this era.

Ponting, Clive. *The Twentieth Century: A World History*. New York: Henry Holt and Company, 1998. Thematic study.

Stavrianos, Leften S. *Global Rift: The Third World Comes of Age*. New York: William Morrow, 1971. A provocative, innovative study.

Wesseling, H. L. *The European Colonial Empires, 1815–1919*. Harlow, United Kingdom: Pearson, 2004. A useful overview of the entire colonial enterprise by a Dutch scholar.

Wolf, Eric R. *Europe and the People Without History*. Berkeley: University of California Press, 1982. A thought-provoking analysis of the Western impact on the wider world from 1400 to 1914.

PART VI

Global Systems:

Interdependence and Conflict in the Contemporary World, Since 1945

NORTH AND CENTRAL AMERICA
The United States became the world's richest nation and greatest political, economic, and military power. It led the Western alliance against the Soviet Union, fighting major wars in Korea and Vietnam and intervening in other nations. After 1990 the United States had no major rival but confronted international terrorism, which prompted it to send military forces into Afghanistan and Iraq. Mexico's economic growth lagged, fostering emigration to the United States, while the Cuban Revolution brought communists to power, provoking U.S. hostility.

ARCTIC OCEAN

CANADA

NORTH AMERICA

UNITED STATES

MEXICO

CUBA

ATLANTIC OCEAN

VENEZUELA

PACIFIC OCEAN

Amazon

BRAZIL

ANDES

SOUTH AMERICA

CHILE

ARGENTINA

SOUTH AMERICA
The South American nations, often troubled by tensions between the political left and right, struggled to achieve political stability and economic growth. Some nations, such as Brazil, Argentina, and Chile, alternated between democratic, reformist regimes and brutal military dictatorships. U.S. intervention helped overthrow several leftist governments. After 1990 Argentina faced economic collapse; Brazil and Chile, mixing capitalism and socialism, enjoyed growth; and Venezuela turned to the left.

© Cengage Learning

EUROPE

Although western Europe recovered quickly from World War II, the imperial Western states were unable to maintain control of their colonies. The western European nations forged stable welfare states, providing a social safety net, and moved toward close cooperation and economic unity among themselves. The Soviet Union became a global superpower, controlling eastern Europe, but at the end of the 1980s it and its communist satellites collapsed. Germany, divided after World War II, was reunified, and Russia sought a new role in the world.

WESTERN ASIA

Nationalists gained control of the western Asian nations but faced new challenges. Israel, a new Jewish state in Palestine, won wars against Arab neighbors, and Arab-Israeli hostilities have remained a source of tension. Some nations, such as Turkey, pursued modernization. An Islamic revolution reshaped oil-rich Iran, which fought oil-rich Iraq in the 1980s. Saudi Arabia and several Persian Gulf states flourished from oil wealth. After 2001 U.S.-led forces invaded and occupied Afghanistan and Iraq but, while removing despotic governments, struggled to restore stability.

EASTERN ASIA

Coming to power through revolution in 1949, communists transformed China, creating a socialist society and fighting the United States during the Korean War. After 1978 new communist leaders mixed free markets with socialism and fostered modernization, turning China into an economic powerhouse. Japan recovered rapidly from World War II, embracing democracy and becoming an economic giant. Borrowing Japanese models, South Korea and Taiwan industrialized. North Korea remained a repressive communist state.

ARCTIC OCEAN

RUSSIA

BRITAIN
GERMANY
FRANCE
EUROPE
ITALY
Danube
TURKEY
IRAQ   IRAN
ALGERIA
PAKISTAN
SAUDI
ARABIA
INDIA
Nile
Ganges R.
HIMALAYAS
ASIA
CHINA
KOREA   JAPAN
TAIWAN
VIETNAM
THAILAND
BANGLADESH
MALAYSIA

AFRICA
NIGERIA
Niger R.
Congo R.

ATLANTIC OCEAN

INDIAN OCEAN

INDONESIA

ANGOLA

AUSTRALIA

SOUTH
AFRICA

NEW ZEALAND

AFRICA

As Arab and African nationalism grew stronger, colonies became independent nations, sometimes, as in Algeria and Angola, through revolution. In North Africa, Egypt promoted Arab nationalism and became a regional power but faced economic problems. Most of the new sub-Saharan African nations, which were artificial creations of colonialism, struggled to maintain political stability and foster economic development, but South Africans finally achieved black majority rule.

SOUTHERN ASIA AND OCEANIA

Britain granted independence to predominantly Hindu India but also to largely Muslim Pakistan, which eventually split when Bangladesh seceded. India enjoyed democracy and economic progress, but Pakistan and Bangladesh often fell under military rule. In Southeast Asia, the U.S. and British colonies gained independence peacefully while Indonesians triumphed through revolution. Vietnamese communists first defeated the French and then the United States. Malaysia, Singapore, and Thailand developed economically. Australia and New Zealand established closer links to Asia, and most of the Pacific islands gained independence from Western colonialism.

CHAPTER 26

The Remaking of the Global System,

Since 1945

Learning Outcomes

After reading this chapter, you should be able to answer the following questions:

LO¹ How did decolonization change the global system?

LO² What roles did the Cold War and superpower rivalry play in world politics?

LO³ What were some of the main consequences of a globalizing world economy?

LO⁴ How did growing networks linking societies influence social, political, and economic life?

" One heart, one destiny. Peace and love for all mankind. And Africa for Africans. **"**

—Bob Marley, reggae superstar[1]

In April 1980, when the new African nation of Zimbabwe (zim-BAHB-way) (formerly Southern Rhodesia) celebrated its independence from British rule, Bob Marley, a reggae music star from Jamaica and a symbol of black empowerment, performed at Zimbabwe's national stadium. Marley's experience there reflected many of the political and cultural trends of the later-twentieth-century world. Marley had been invited to appear in part because his songs, such as "Stir it Up" and "Get Up Stand Up," often dealt with issues such as poverty, racial prejudice, and human rights that resonated with thousands of Zimbabweans in the audience, who had endured decades of uncaring British colonial and then white minority government.

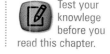 Test your knowlege before you read this chapter.

But Marley's concert was disrupted by the local police, who used tear gas to disperse thousands of black Zimbabweans who gathered outside the overcrowded stadium. The next night, Marley ignored threats of violence against him by local white racists and gave a free concert for 40,000 Zimbabweans, many of them unemployed. Although the free concert encountered no major problems, the violence of the previous night and the threats to his life had shown Marley that the social ills and ethnic hatreds he knew in Jamaica occurred elsewhere in the world as well. In Zimbabwe, where these ills ran particularly deep, they would not be solved by the nation's newly won independence under a black majority government.

An eloquent advocate of political and cultural freedom whose music was enjoyed by millions of fans around the world, Marley and his music touched hearts and minds across racial, political, religious, class, and cultural barriers. Reggae was a truly world music, an intoxicating mix of African, Caribbean, and North American traditions. To the world, Marley personified reggae's progressive politics and spiritual quest. His career reflected a world that was interconnected as never before and in great flux. Since World War II, the pace of change quickened and the global economy grew dramatically. Economic and

What do you think?

The global community has largely been successful in its efforts to deal with growing economic and environmental problems.

Strongly Disagree						Strongly Agree
1	2	3	4	5	6	7

<<"Our World Is Not for Sale" In 2004, tens of thousands of activists from all over the world, under the banner of "Our World Is Not for Sale," marched on the streets of Mumbai (formerly Bombay), India's largest city, to protest economic globalization, racial and caste oppression, and the U.S.-led war in Iraq.

cultural networks linked societies ever more closely, while people, ideas, technologies, and products flowed across porous borders. World politics were turbulent, reflecting the conflict between the United States and the Soviet Union (USSR), the world's two most powerful nations, and the struggle of African, Asian, and Latin American countries for decolonization and development. Since 1989, when the Soviet bloc collapsed, the world has groped toward a new political configuration while dealing with mounting challenges.

> "The nationalism that spread through Europe and the Americas in the 1800s became a powerful force in the colonized world in the 1900s."

LO¹ Decolonization, New States, and the Global System

The contemporary world was affected by Western imperialism's aftermath. After World War II, Asia, Africa, and Latin America became the major battlegrounds between the United States and the Soviet Union; these two nations had so much military, political, and economic might in comparison to other countries that they were known as superpowers. The struggle of Asian, African, and Latin American societies to end Western domination and to develop economically also shaped the postwar era. Nationalist movements proliferated, some seeking deep changes through social revolution. The former colonies also became part of a dynamic global system marked by continued imbalances in wealth and power.

Nationalism and Decolonization

The nationalism that spread through Europe and the Americas in the 1800s became a powerful force in the colonized world in the 1900s. Three basic types of nationalist movements developed between the early 1900s and the 1960s. In the first type, which occurred in most colonized societies, the nationalist goal was the end of colonial rule but not necessarily major social and economic change. The second type of nationalist movement, mounted by social revolutionaries inspired by Marxism, wanted not only

political independence but also a new social order free of Western economic domination. In China, for example, the communist movement led by Mao Zedong sought to reorganize Chinese society while limiting contact with the world economy and the United States. Making up a third type were the nationalist movements by long-repressed nonwhite majorities in white settler colonies such as Algeria and Zimbabwe. Whatever the type of nationalist movement, the dislocations caused by the Great Depression and World War II intensified anti-Western and anticolonial feelings.

....

Colonialism Succumbs to Nationalism

Colonialism gradually crumbled, often after confronting nationalist resistance led by charismatic figures such as Mohandas Gandhi in India, in the three decades after World War II. By the 1950s, most of the Western colonizers realized that the increased military force required to maintain their political control was too expensive. In 1946, the United States began the decolonization trend by granting independence to the Philippines. In the later 1940s, the British gave up their rule in India and Burma, and the Dutch abandoned Indonesia. Between 1946 and 1975, most of the Western colonies in Asia, Africa, and the Caribbean achieved independence (see Map 26.1).

Interactive Map

Some colonizers accepted decolonization only after attempts to quell nationalist uprisings had failed. The Dutch intended to regain their control of Indonesia, a source of immense wealth, after World War II but faced violent, nationalist resistance. In 1950, after losing many soldiers, the Dutch granted Indonesia independence. Similarly, the French had no plans to abandon their profitable colonies in Vietnam and Algeria, but uprisings by revolutionaries in these

Map 26.1 >> Decolonization

Between 1946 and 1975, most of the Western colonies in Asia, Africa, and the Caribbean won their independence, with the greatest number achieving independence in the 1960s. Decolonization reshaped the global political map.

1960 Year independence achieved

Former ruler
- Great Britain
- France
- Netherlands
- Italy
- Belgium
- Portugal
- United States
- Other

ATLANTIC OCEAN

PACIFIC OCEAN

INDIAN OCEAN

Tropic of Cancer

Tropic of Capricorn

Equator 0°

Mediterranean Sea

Black Sea

Caspian Sea

Arabian Sea

Bay of Bengal

GREAT BRITAIN
NETHERLANDS
BELGIUM
FRANCE
ITALY
SPAIN
PORTUGAL

JAPAN

NORTH KOREA 1948
SOUTH KOREA 1948 (From Japan)

PHILIPPINES 1946

PAPUA NEW GUINEA 1975 (From Australia)

TIMOR-LESTE 1999 (From Indonesia)

INDONESIA 1949

BRUNEI 1984 (From Gr. Br.)

SINGAPORE 1965 (From Malaysia)

MALAYSIA 1963

CAMBODIA 1953

SOUTH VIETNAM 1954

NORTH VIETNAM 1954 (Unified 1975)

LAOS 1949

MYANMAR (BURMA) 1947

PAKISTAN 1947; BANGLADESH 1973

SRI LANKA (CEYLON) 1948

MALDIVES 1975 (From Gr. Br.)

INDIA 1947

PAKISTAN 1947

MAURITIUS 1968 (From Gr. Br.)

SEYCHELLES 1976 (From Gr. Br.)

COMOROS 1975 (From France)

MADAGASCAR 1960

OMAN 1971

UNITED ARAB EMIRATES 1971

QATAR 1971

BAHRAIN 1971

KUWAIT 1961

P.D.R. OF YEMEN 1967 (Unified 1990)
YEMEN

IRAQ 1932

JORDAN 1946

SYRIA 1944

LEBANON 1944

ISRAEL 1948

CYPRUS 1960

MALTA 1964 (From Gr. Br.)

EGYPT 1922

LIBYA 1951

TUNISIA 1957

ALGERIA 1962

MOROCCO 1956

WESTERN SAHARA 1975 (Morocco) (From Spain)

MAURITANIA 1960

MALI 1960

NIGER 1960

CHAD 1960

SUDAN 1956

ERITREA 1993 (From Ethiopia)

DJIBOUTI 1977

ETHIOPIA

SOMALIA 1960

CAPE VERDE 1975 (From Port.)

SENEGAL 1960

GAMBIA 1965

GUINEA-BISSAU 1974

GUINEA 1958

SIERRA LEONE 1961

LIBERIA 1820s

CÔTE D'IVOIRE 1960

BURKINA FASO 1960

GHANA 1957

TOGO 1960

BENIN 1960

NIGERIA 1960

CAMEROON 1960

EQUATORIAL GUINEA 1968 (From Spain)

SÃO TOMÉ AND PRÍNCIPE 1975 (From Port.)

GABON 1960

REPUBLIC OF CONGO 1960

CENTRAL AFRICAN REPUBLIC 1960

DEM. REP. OF CONGO 1960

UGANDA 1962

KENYA 1963

RWANDA 1962

BURUNDI 1962

TANZANIA 1961

ANGOLA 1975

ZAMBIA 1964

MALAWI 1964

MOZAMBIQUE 1974

ZIMBABWE 1980

NAMIBIA 1990 (From South Africa)

BOTSWANA 1966

SWAZILAND 1968

LESOTHO 1966

SOUTH AFRICA (Republic 1961)

0   1,000   2,000 Km.
0   1,000   2,000 Mi.

N

colonies forced them to leave. In Vietnam, the communist forces led by Ho Chi Minh fiercely resisted French power, and heavy U.S. aid to the French could not prevent a humiliating French defeat in 1954. The ultimately successful anticolonial struggles by the Indonesian, Vietnamese, and Algerian nationalists had electrifying global effects, giving hope to colonized peoples elsewhere.

The Superpowers

Both superpowers sought to capitalize on the nationalist surge. The Soviet Union generally supported nationalist movements, sometimes supplying arms to revolutionaries. The Soviets also offered economic aid and diplomatic support to Asian and African countries that achieved independence and had strategic value, such as India and Egypt, or valuable resources, such as oil-rich Iran and Indonesia. The United States followed a mixed policy on decolonization. Wanting access to trade and outlets for investment in Asia and Africa, the United States encouraged the Dutch to leave Indonesia and urged independence for some British colonies in Africa, but Americans also opposed communism and the spread of Soviet influence. Consequently, where nationalism was led by communists or had a leftist orientation, as in French-ruled Vietnam, the United

African Independence In 1961, the British monarch, Queen Elizabeth II, made an official visit to newly independent Ghana, the former British colony of the Gold Coast. Here she walks under a ceremonial umbrella with the Ghanaian president, Kwame Nkrumah.

CHRONOLOGY

Global Politics, 1945–1989

1945	Formation of United Nations
1946–1975	Decolonization in Asia, Africa, Caribbean
1946–1989	Cold War
1949	Communist victory in China
1950–1953	Korean War
1954	Vietnamese defeat of French
1955	Bandung Conference
1959–1975	U.S.–Vietnam War
1959	Communist victory in Cuba
1962	Cuban Missile Crisis
1968	Widespread political protests
1975	End of Portuguese Empire

States supported continued colonial power, no matter how unpopular among the colonized people.

Colonialism did not completely disappear. By the 1980s, one major territorial empire, the USSR, remained, and it strained to repress the nationalist demands of the Baltic, Caucasus, and Central Asian peoples it ruled. The Soviet Empire was largely dismantled between 1989 and 1991, when the Soviet Union's communist system collapsed, although Russians still controlled some unwilling subjects, such as the Chechens, a Muslim people in southern Russia. At the beginning of the twenty-first century, Britain, France, and the United States still controlled small empires. Britain and France retained direct control of a few islands and some outposts, notably British Gibraltar, a strategically valuable naval base at the entrance to the Mediterranean Sea, and French Guiana, on the northeast coast of South America. The territories, mostly self-governing, linked to the United States included Puerto Rico, the Virgin Islands, American Samoa, and Guam.

Neo-Colonialism

Decolonization often resulted in neocolonialism, a continuing strong political and economic influence by the former colonizers. This happened in the Philippines, where Americans maintained a major role in the economy and influenced Philippine governments and popular culture. Similarly, the French controlled much of the economy and advised the government in the African nation of Cote d'Ivoire (COAT dee-VWAHR), and many Ivoirians favored French cuisine, literature, and language. Disenchantment with the continuing strong Western presence prompted some Asian and African intellectuals to advocate "decolonizing the mind," to escape what Bob Marley called a "mental slavery" that kept formerly colonized people in awe of Western power, wealth, and culture. "Decolonizing the mind" sometimes meant building a nationalist culture reflecting local traditions or abandoning the use of Western languages in people's writing.

Social Revolutionary States

During the twentieth century, revolutionary activity erupted in Asia, Africa, and Latin America, intensified by the drive to end colonialism and other forms of Western domination. In most cases, this revolutionary activity engaged peasants, who were often impoverished by the loss of their lands or the declining prices for the cash crops they grew. Revolutionary intellectuals, often Marxist, capitalized on this unhappiness to mobilize support, although those who joined their movements did not always embrace the more radical ideas. Understanding this, Amilcar Cabral (AM-ill-car ka-BRAWL) (1924–1973), the revolutionary leader in Portugal's West African colony of Guinea Bissau (GIN-ee bi-SOU), advised his Marxist colleagues to "always bear in mind that the people are not fighting for ideas, for the things in anyone's head. They are fighting to win material benefits, to live better, and in peace, to see their lives go forward, to guarantee the future of their children."[2] Between 1949 and 1980, social revolutionary regimes came to power through force of arms in Algeria Vietnam, China, Cuba, and many other countries. Opposed by the United States and often mistrusted by western European regimes, these states necessarily looked to the USSR for political, economic, and military support.

> "Decolonization often resulted in neocolonialism, a continuing strong political and economic influence by the former colonizers."

Planned Economies

Social revolutionary states had uneven relations with the world economy and the capitalist nations. Influenced by Stalinism, which fostered state-directed economic growth in the USSR in the 1930s, these states usually chose to withdraw from the world economy in order to limit outside interference, renounce foreign debts, and assume control of their economic direction. They created planned economies in which economic decisions were made centrally, by governments, rather than through free markets, as in capitalist societies.

Social revolutionary approaches brought mixed results. Some countries saw their goals sidetracked by civil wars or by rebellions supported by Western powers. For example, in Angola, a country in southwest Africa, South Africa and the United States provided financial and military support to rebels who fought the Marxist-dominated government for more than two decades. The civil war cost more than 200,000 lives, ruined much of the country, and forced the Angolan government to devote most of its resources to the military rather than to supporting its people. After the fighting ended in the late 1990s, the Marxists still held power, but Angolans were poorer than ever: half of the nation's children suffered from malnutrition. In contrast, between 1949 and 1978, communist-run China was able to increase its economic potential and reduce social problems, but at a heavy cost in repressing dissent and limiting personal freedom.

After 1978, China dramatically modified its socialist economy with market forces, such as by allowing foreign investment and free enterprise, which sparked even more rapid growth. The shift of China, followed by Vietnam, toward market economies and greater participation in the world economy in the 1980s suggested that revolution may have helped nations to gain control of their resources but was ultimately insufficient to raise living standards. Yet, China and Vietnam also found that capitalism and free markets could create more wealth than socialism but did not necessarily lead to an equitable distribution of wealth, fostering explosive social tensions.

A New Global System

During the later twentieth century, observers often divided the world into three categories of countries,

"During the later twentieth century, observers often divided the world into three categories of countries, each one having a different level of economic development."

each one having a different level of economic development. One category, the First World, comprised the industrialized democracies of western Europe, North America, Australia–New Zealand, and Japan. The Second World referred to the communist nations, led by the USSR and China. The Third World was made up of most societies in Asia, Africa, Latin America, and the Caribbean that were marked by mass poverty and a legacy of Western colonization or neocolonialism. Some experts added a fourth category, the Fourth World, or the poorest societies, which had very small economies and few exploitable resources, such as Laos, Bangladesh, Haiti, and Mali.

Economies in Transition

The notion of different worlds of economic development helped bring to light the roles played by different countries in global politics and economics between 1945 and the late 1980s, when the Western nations and the communist bloc, both wealthy and powerful compared to other societies, competed for influence in the rest of the world. However, critics argued that lumping the world's societies into a few categories was highly misleading. Furthermore, during the 1980s and 1990s, the global system was changing, complicating attempts to categorize nations. Countries such as Malaysia, South Korea, Dubai, and Chile, once grouped with the Third World, achieved rapid economic growth, and the communist systems that had defined the Second World often collapsed.

Post-War Japan

At the economically developed end of the global sys-
tem, most Western nations and Japan enjoyed new heights of prosperity from the 1960s through the 1980s. After World War II, the United States offered generous aid to Europe and Japan, helping them to recover from the destruction created by the war; this aid promoted further economic growth in industrialized countries that already had literate, skilled, and mostly urban populations, well-funded governments, and diversified economies. Japan's economy increased fivefold between 1953 and 1973, the fastest economic growth in world history. As Western and Japanese businesses invested heavily around the world, international trade soared. Japan and West Germany became the second and third largest capitalist economies. By the 1970s, several Western nations, including West Germany, Sweden, Canada, and Australia, had standards of living similar to those in the United States, and most had far less inequality in the distribution of wealth and income than did the United States.

Prosperity in the West

Although economic growth rates often slowed after 1990, Western prosperity relative to the rest of the world continued. By 2004, the Human Development Report—an annual study by the United Nations that rates the quality of life of the world's 177 nations—ranked, in order, Norway, Sweden, Australia, Canada, and the Netherlands as the most livable nations; following these were Belgium, Iceland, the United States, Japan, and Ireland. The report ranked thirty-six nations, mostly in sub-Saharan Africa, as having a low quality of life, with massive poverty, inadequate health care, and low rates of literacy. Tanzanian president Julius Nyerere (nye-RE-re) put the gap between rich and poor nations in perspective: "While the United States is trying to reach the moon, Tanzania is trying to reach its villages."[3]

Some nations had more resources and political stability to secure their citizens' lives, while poorer nations faced greater challenges in building stable nation-states. Richer nations usually benefited from democracy and allowed voters to freely choose their leaders. Democratic governments controlled social tensions, and generous welfare systems prevented mass poverty. Many western European states, Canada, and New Zealand adopted ambitious welfare systems, including comprehensive national health insurance. The European welfare states promoted a high degree of social justice and equality, while violence occurred in nations that had abandoned communism and its safety net of free or low-cost education, health care, and housing. The fighting between ethnic groups in Yugoslavia in the 1990s sometimes resulted in brutal atrocities and the forced expulsion of minorities. Only a few non-European nations, such as Sri Lanka and oil-rich Brunei, tried to mount welfare states with free education and health care, but they struggled to pay for them.

LO² Cold War, Hot Wars, and World Politics

A new global political configuration emerged after World War II: two major superpowers, the United States and the Soviet Union, each developed a system of allies in their competition for international influence. The confrontation between the two superpowers fostered the Cold War, a conflict lasting from 1946 to 1989, in which the United States and the USSR competed for allies and engaged in occasional warfare against their rival's allies rather than with each other directly. The United States enjoyed much greater influence than the USSR in the global system and boasted more allies. While the Cold War did not lead to a military conflict in which U.S. and Soviet military forces fought each other, it produced chronic mutual tension and led to covert and military interventions around the world.

> ❝ After World War II, U.S. concern shifted from opposing Nazi Germany and imperial Japan to countering the USSR. ❞

The Cold War: Division and Conflict

During the Cold War, the world took on a bipolar political character. Nations practicing capitalism and democracy, led by the United States, called themselves the Free World; those marked by socialist authoritarianism, led by the USSR and known as the Soviet bloc, were on the other side. For more than four decades, U.S.–USSR relations, and the struggle of each superpower to gain an advantage over its rival, dominated international affairs. While seeking to contain the spread of communism, the United States enhanced its own influence, while the USSR worked to spread communism and undercut American influence. Various other countries, in Asia, Africa, and Latin

America, sought to forge a third bloc, asserting their interests while navigating the dangerous shoals of superpower demands. In 1955, leaders from twenty-nine nonaligned Asian and African countries held a conference in Bandung, Indonesia, to oppose colonialism and gain recognition for what they called a Third World bloc, but they had trouble maintaining unity in the decades to follow.

Cold War
A conflict lasting from 1946 to 1989 in which the United States and the USSR competed for allies and engaged in occasional warfare against their rivals' allies rather than against each other directly.

....

The Ascendancy of the United States

Although Britain had been the world's leading economic, political, and military power in the nineteenth century, the United States became the world's most powerful nation in the twentieth, enjoying far greater wealth, military power, and cultural influence than any other nation, including the USSR. In 1945, the United States already had 1,200 warships, 3,000 bombers, and the atomic bomb; produced half of the world's industrial output; and held two-thirds of the gold. Americans seemed willing to bear a heavy financial and military burden to sustain their leading role in world affairs and to promote U.S. economic growth. U.S. President Dwight D. Eisenhower (g. 1953–1961) defended his nation's foreign policy, which included interventions against unfriendly governments, as necessary to obtain raw materials and preserve profitable markets.

....

Spread of Communism

After World War II, U.S. concern shifted from opposing Nazi Germany and imperial Japan to countering the USSR. Americans now perceived their wartime ally as a rival for influence. By 1948, the Soviets controlled all of eastern Europe and were allied with communist governments in Mongolia and North Korea. The U.S. policy of preventing the emergence of communist regimes became globalized: first, Americans tried unsuccessfully to prevent communists from coming to power in China in the late 1940s; then they became involved in the Korean War (1950–1953) to fight successfully the North Korean effort to forcibly reunify the Korean peninsula. Yet, despite

> "Insurgencies became common as unconventional warfare, such as sniping, sabotaging power plants, and planting roadside bombs, proliferated."

U.S. efforts, communist regimes came to power in China in 1949, North Vietnam in 1954, and Cuba in 1959. Furthermore, waging the Cold War and seeking to contain communism with military force, including a long war in Vietnam, financially burdened the United States, costing it between $4 trillion to $5 trillion and some 113,000 American lives between 1946 and 1989.

The Cold War fostered misunderstandings and tensions between the superpowers. Remembering centuries of invasions from the West, Soviet leaders occupied eastern Europe as a buffer zone and considered the United States and its western European allies a lethal danger; their combined military power greatly exceeded that of the USSR. American leaders mistrusted the USSR and despised communism, which challenged two of America's most treasured values, democracy and market economies. Americans viewed themselves as protecting freedom, while the Soviets claimed that they were helping the world's exploited and impoverished masses and acting as the beacon of anti-imperialism.

The Long Telegram This critique of the Soviet Union's ideology, authored by an American diplomat in 1946, profoundly influenced the foreign policy of the United States.

Interpreting the Cold War

Some historians believe the Cold War brought a long period of peace and stability, while others point to some eighty wars, often related to superpower rivalry, between 1945 and 1989 that resulted in 20 million deaths and perhaps 20 million refugees. The Cold War rivalries also transformed world politics by dragging emerging nations, already damaged by their long, humiliating subservience to Western colonialism, into upheavals that bankrupted economies and devastated entire peoples. In place of a USSR–U.S. war, a series of smaller conflicts occurred involving surrogates, governments, or movements allied to one superpower and fighting the troops from the other superpower. During two of the major conflicts, in Korea and Vietnam, U.S. troops battled not Soviet armies but allied communist forces that were Soviet surrogates. In Vietnam, the Soviets sent military supplies and advisers to help the Vietnamese communists, led by Ho Chi Minh, fight first the French and then the United States, which had helped install a pro-Western government in South Vietnam after the French defeat. The communists gained control of the entire country in 1975. Americans also used surrogates, such as when they supplied Islamic groups fighting the Soviets in Afghanistan in the 1980s.

In this warfare, rebels often used low-technology weapons and military strategies if those methods provided the most practical options available. Insurgencies became common as unconventional warfare, such as sniping, sabotaging power plants, and planting roadside bombs, proliferated. Insurgents fighting superpower forces often resorted to guerrilla warfare, an unconventional military strategy of avoiding full-scale direct confrontations in favor of small-scale skirmishes. In Vietnam, for example, communist guerrillas staged hit-and-run attacks on American patrols and field bases and planted land mines, explosives that detonated when stepped on, on trails used by American troops.

The Cold War fostered interventions—both covert and military—by both superpowers to protect their interests. The USSR sent military forces into Poland, Hungary, and Czechoslovakia to crush anti-Soviet movements and into Afghanistan to support a pro-Soviet government. The Afghanistan intervention was a disaster for the Soviet Union: heavy losses and humiliating withdrawal in 1989 contributed to its collapse. The Soviets, Chinese, and Cubans also gave aid to communist movements around the world, establishing a strong presence in nations such as Indonesia, India, and Chile, where they participated openly in politics. They also launched insurgencies against governments in several countries, such as Peru, Malaysia, and the Philippines, that ultimately failed to mobilize enough local support and were crushed.

For its part, the United States actively sought to shape the political and economic direction of Asian, African, and Latin American societies through generous aid and promoting human rights. Americans donated food, disaster and medical assistance, technical advice, and support to democratic organizations. But other efforts destabilized or helped overthrow governments that were deemed unfriendly to U.S. business and political interests, including regimes in Brazil, Chile, and Guatemala.

Intervention in Iran and Vietnam

The earliest U.S. intervention came in 1953 in oil-rich Iran, which was governed by a nationalist but noncommunist regime that nationalized British- and U.S.-owned oil companies operating in Iran, companies that sent most of their huge profits abroad, paid their Iranian workers less than fifty cents per day, and offered them no health care or paid vacations. In response to the nationalization, Britain and the United States imposed an economic boycott on Iran, making it hard for Iran to sell its oil. American agents recruited disaffected military officers and paid Iranians to spark riots that paralyzed the capital, forcing the nationalists from power and leading to a pro-U.S. but despotic government. The deposed Iranian leader, Mohammad Mossadeq, argued that he faced U.S. wrath for trying to remove "the network of colonialism, and the political and economic influence of the greatest empire on earth [the U.S.] from this land."[4] For the first time ever, the United States had organized the overthrow of a foreign government outside the Western Hemisphere.

To critics, the U.S. actions and other superpower interventions constituted a new form of imperialism. The interventions often proved costly as well. In Vietnam, for example, the communist-led forces achieved a military stalemate that cost the United States vast sums of money, killed some 58,000 Americans, and forced it to negotiate for peace and withdraw, harming U.S. prestige in the world. The war also had spillover effects: it created economic problems in the United States, cost the lives of several million Vietnamese, and required the USSR and China to spend scarce resources to supply their communist allies.

The Nuclear Arms Race and Global Militarization

The arms race between the superpowers and increasing militarization around the world became major components of the Cold War. Both superpowers developed nuclear weapons, explosive devices that owe their destructive power to the energy released by either splitting or fusing atoms. These weapons were the most deadly result of the technological surge that can be traced back to Albert Einstein, Sir Isaac Newton, and the scientific discoveries of the seventeenth and eighteenth centuries. A nuclear explosion produces a powerful blast, intense heat, and deadly radiation over a wide area. The nuclear weapons era began when the United States built the first atomic bombs and dropped two of these bombs on the Japanese cities of Hiroshima and Nagasaki to end World War II. In the following decades, both the United States and the USSR developed even more deadly nuclear warheads. The growth of nuclear arsenals was only the most dangerous part of a larger trend toward increased militarization. Both superpowers and the rest of the world feared the devastating power of nuclear weapons of mass destruction.

nuclear weapons Explosive devices that owe their destructive power to the energy released by either splitting or fusing atoms.

 Global Problems and the Culture of Capitalism (*http://faculty.plattsburgh.edu/richard.robbins/legacy/*). An outstanding site, aimed at undergraduates, with a wealth of resources.

> 66 The growth of nuclear arsenals was only the most dangerous part of a larger trend toward increased militarization. 99

The Nuclear Threat

Fortunately, these weapons were never used after 1945, although the world was close to a nuclear confrontation on several occasions. For example, in the early 1950s, as French colonial forces were losing the fight against communist-led insurgents in Vietnam, the Eisenhower administration in the United States offered atomic bombs to the French, who wisely declined the offer. In 1962, after discovering that the USSR had secretly placed nuclear missiles in Cuba, just 90 miles from Florida, President John F. Kennedy (1917–1963) demanded they be removed but vetoed a U.S. invasion that might have sparked all-out nuclear war. Some of Kennedy's advisers recommended that he attack Cuba with nuclear weapons. He rejected this advice, but his firm stance against missiles in Cuba created a tense crisis. Ultimately, the Soviets withdrew them, averting disaster. In response to a U.S. attack on his boat during the crisis, a Soviet submarine commander armed a missile carrying a nuclear weapon and aimed it at the United States, but he was talked out of firing it by other Soviet officers.

A Balance of Terror   Nuclear weapons shaped global politics. The Cold War fostered a balance of terror, with both superpowers unwilling to use the awesome power at their command for fear the other would retaliate. Historians debate whether the nuclear arms race helped preserve the peace by discouraging an all-out U.S.–USSR military confrontation or instead unsettled international politics and wasted trillions of dollars. Various other countries, including Britain, France, China, India, and Pakistan, also constructed or acquired nuclear bombs, while countries like Iran and North Korea began programs to do the same. In the 1970s, the two superpowers negotiated two treaties to limit further arms proliferation, and in 1987, they signed a treaty to reduce existing nuclear weapons. Nevertheless, more nations sought nuclear capability, provoking concerns about proliferation. But some outside the West argued that the monopoly on such weapons by a few powerful nations was unfair, and Middle Eastern leaders worried about Israeli nuclear efforts.

The Cost of the Cold War   The proportion of total world production and spending devoted to militaries grew dramatically during the Cold War. By 1985, the world was spending some $1.2 trillion annually on military forces and weapons, more than the combined income of the poorest 50 percent of world countries. The two superpowers together, with 11 percent of the world population, accounted for 60 percent of military spending, 25 percent of the world's armed forces, and 97 percent of its nuclear weapons; both the United States and USSR had stockpiles of thousands of nuclear weapons. They both also sold conventional weapons to other countries with which they had friendly relations.

Conflict in the Post-War World   Whether or not related to Cold War rivalries, the varied wars caused enormous casualties, with civilians accounting for some three-fourths of the dead. Two million people died during the Chinese civil war (1945–1949), 800,000 during the violent partition of India (1948), 2 million during the American-Vietnamese War, 1 million during the Nigerian civil war (1967), and more than 2 million in the Cambodian violence from 1970 to 1978. Millions of these deaths resulted from genocide, the deliberate killing of whole groups because of their ethnic or religious origin. Genocide, which had been practiced for centuries, reached its most organized campaign with the Nazi holocaust against the Jews during World War II (see Chapter 24). In the later twentieth century, genocides continued: in the 1990s, members of the Hutu majority slaughtered people belonging to the Tutsi minority in Rwanda (roo-AHN-duh), a Central African country, while extremist Serb Christians, seeking to maintain their political power, killed Bosnian and Albanian Muslims in Yugoslavia, in a policy they called "ethnic cleansing." The Yugoslav killings were finally stopped when the United States and western European nations sent in troops to restore order and punished the worst violators of human rights.

Global Organizations and Activism

During the Cold War, more than ever before in history, public and private organizations emerged with a global reach and mission to promote political cooperation and address various causes. The largest attempt by most of the world's sovereign nations to cooperate for the common good, the United Nations, was founded in 1945 with fifty-one members and became a key forum for global debate and diplomacy. The founding members agreed that the United Nations came about to "save succeeding generations from the scourge of war, reaffirm faith in fundamental rights, and respect international law."[5] As colonies gained independence and joined, the organization grew to more than one hundred members by the mid-1960s and to nearly two hundred by 2000. Pursuing cooperation on humanitarian aims, it developed agencies, such as the World Health Organization, that monitored diseases, funded and fostered medical research, and promoted public health, as well as the United Nations Children Fund, or UNICEF, which promoted children's welfare and education around the world. U.N.-sponsored health and nutrition programs helped increase average life expectancy from 45 in 1900 to 75 in 2000, and greatly reduced the risk of mothers dying in childbirth.

Role of the United Nations   The United Nations influenced international relations by discouraging, although not preventing, states from using force whenever they desired. To gain support for military actions, nations often felt it necessary to make their case before the policy-making Security Council; sometimes they received

support, but nations determined to go to war often ignored widespread disapproval by the U.N., as the United States did when it invaded Iraq in 2003. The Security Council sometimes voted to send peacekeeping troops into troubled countries. Each of the five major powers of 1945—the United States, China, Britain, France, and the USSR—received permanent seats with veto power in the Security Council. Both superpowers vetoed decisions that challenged their national interests. For instance, the United States often vetoed resolutions aimed at penalizing its ally, Israel, and also blocked, for more than two decades, the Chinese Communist government from occupying China's seat in the United Nations. But western nations found it more difficult to shape policies after Afro-Asian nations became the majority in the United Nations.

U.N. Peacekeepers in Congo The United Nations has regularly sent peacekeepers into troubled countries such as the Congo. This photo, from 2003, shows U.N. troops from Uruguay guarding a U.N. office while a Congolese woman and her four children, displaced from her village by factional fighting, seek U.N. help.

Toward a Global World-View

Since World War II, groupings of nations also cooperated to improve global conditions by forging international agreements and treaties. For example, most nations ratified an agreement banning biological weapons, such as deadly diseases like anthrax, in 1972. In 1997, most nations signed the Kyoto Protocol, pledging to begin reducing the harmful gases that contribute to global warming. But the United States and several other industrial nations impeded international cooperation by refusing to approve the modest efforts made by these agreements to reduce weapons, promote environmental stability, and establish accountability for international crimes.

Human Rights Watch (*http:// www.hrw.org/ wr2k3/introduction .html*). The website of a major human rights organization that reports on the entire world.

Private organizations and activists, chiefly based in western Europe, also worked for issues of peace, social justice, health, refugees, famine, conflict resolution, and environmental protection. Organizations such as Doctors Without Borders, which sent medical personnel to societies facing famine or epidemics, and Amnesty International, which worked to free political prisoners, were supported chiefly by private donations. In addition, leaders from different religious faiths worked for world peace, justice, and humanitarian concerns. For example, the Dalai Lama (DAH-lie LAH-ma) (b. 1935), the highest Tibetan Buddhist spiritual leader, won the Nobel Peace Prize in 1989 for his efforts—through speeches, writings, and conferences—to promote human rights and nonviolent conflict resolution.

World Politics Since 1989

Between 1989 and 1991, the Soviet bloc disintegrated and the communist regimes in eastern Europe and the former USSR collapsed, ending the Cold War and the bipolar world it had defined. Both U.S. and Soviet leaders deescalated tensions between the two superpowers in the later 1980s. When the Cold War ended, the United States became the sole superpower. Yet many scholars concur with George Kennan (1904–2004), the architect of the U.S. policy to contain communism in the 1940s, who concluded that no country "won" the Cold War, because it was fueled by misconceptions and nearly bankrupted both sides. Other nations, especially Japan and West Germany, protected from potential enemies by U.S. military bases, benefited from the conflict by investing heavily in economic growth rather than their own defense. By 2001, the United States had a larger annual military budget than the ten next-largest military spenders combined and was the major supplier of arms to the rest of the world.

> "Globalization has increased the interconnectedness between societies; events occurring or decisions taken in one part of the world affect societies far away."

War in the Persian Gulf

The first major post–Cold War challenge for the United States came in 1991 when Iraq's brutal dictator, Saddam Hussein (1937–2006), ordered his army to invade and occupy Iraq's small, oil-rich neighbor, Kuwait. The United States had supported Saddam and provided his military with weapons in the 1980s, when Iraq was fighting a war against Iran, whose Islamic government the United States opposed. Now the United States organized an international coalition, funded chiefly by Arab nations, and, in the Gulf War of 1991, rapidly defeated the Iraqis and pushed them out of Kuwait. In the aftermath of the quick victory over Iraq, U.S. president George H. W. Bush proclaimed a "new world order"—a new global system, led by the United States, that was based on American values.

Regional and Religious Conflicts

The end of the long, costly rivalry between capitalist countries and communist societies, however, did not result in universal peace or the triumph of American political values. Instead, the 1990s saw what some observers called a new world disorder. Ethnic and nationalist conflicts exploded in massive violence in Yugoslavia, eastern Europe, and Rwanda. States with weak or dysfunctional governments, such as Haiti in the Caribbean and Somalia in Northeast Africa, also experienced chronic fighting and civil war. Rising tides of religious conflict complicated politics in countries such as India, Indonesia, Algeria, and Nigeria. Militant Islam demonstrated its potency in Iran, Sudan, and Afghanistan and led some extremists to form terrorist groups to fight moderate Islamic regimes, Israel, and Western nations. By the early 2000s, Islamic radicals posed a greater challenge in Southeast Asia and the Middle East than the declining communist movements. The ambitions of aggressive dictators, such as Iraq's Saddam Hussein and the communist regime in North Korea, fostered regional tensions. The promise of a peaceful new world order foundered on the shoals of proliferating regional, nationalist, religious, economic, and ethnic conflicts.

LO³ Globalizing Economies, Underdevelopment, and Environmental Change

In the decades after 1945, the world economy was increasingly characterized by globalization, a pattern in which economic, political, and cultural processes reach beyond nation-state boundaries. This trend reduced barriers between countries and turned the world into a more closely integrated whole. However, it came with some major problems, including the widening inequality of nations, ever-increasing pollution, and a warming climate.

The Transnational Economy and Economic Institutions

Globalization has increased the interconnectedness between societies; events occurring or decisions taken in one part of the world affect societies far away. For example, rising or falling prices on the Tokyo or New York stock exchanges quickly influence stock markets elsewhere. Similarly, the decision by U.S. or British governments to sell supplies of stockpiled rubber, hence depressing world prices, affects the livelihood of rubber growers in Malaysia, Sri

CHRONOLOGY

Global Politics Since 1989

1989–1991	Dismantling of Soviet bloc and empire
1997	Kyoto Protocol on climate change
2001	Al Qaeda attack on United States
2003	U.S. invasion of Iraq

The Globaliza-
tion Website
(*http://www
.emory.edu/SOC/
globalization/*). A
useful site with many
resources and essays on
globalization.

Lanka, Brazil, and the Congo.
Not all of the transnational
economic activity has been
legal: heroin and cocaine sold
in North America and Europe
originates largely in Asia and
Latin America and is smuggled by transnational criminal syndicates. Whatever the
problems, economic globalization became a fact of
contemporary life and had numerous impacts on
the world's societies.

After World War II, economic globalization involved the spread of market capitalism as well as flows of capital, goods,
services, and people. The United States,
now the axis of the world economy, has
been the major proponent of globalization, with its leaders arguing that open
markets and conditions favorable to
investment and trade foster prosperity.
By 2000, the United States produced nearly
one-third of the world's goods and services;
Japan, with the next largest economy, accounted for
around one-sixth. International observers described
the impact of U.S. leadership metaphorically: when
the United States sneezes, the rest of the world
catches cold.

The Uneven Impact of Globalization

Despite the growth of the
world economy, some
argue that globalization
promises riches it does
not always deliver, distributing the benefits unequally.
Economic growth in a country does not, by itself,
improve the living conditions of the majority of people; better conditions also require well-functioning
governments, secure rights, and social services.
Globalization brought more advantages to some
nations, and some people within nations, than to
others. By the 1990s, two nations, the United States
and China, were gaining the most from the trend
toward removing trade barriers and fostering competitive markets worldwide. Both absorbed investment capital, aggressively acquired natural resources
from around the globe, and supplied diverse products
to growing foreign markets. China became the world's
third largest economy as its factories turned out
clothing, housewares, and other consumer goods.
However, not all Chinese have benefited equally:
workers have struggled to win rights, economic security, and safe working conditions.

Globalization's impact has been uneven. By the
early twenty-first century, a few other nations, such
as India, Ireland, Singapore, and South Korea, had, like

the United States and China, also capitalized on globalization, becoming centers of high technology. But
not all countries enjoyed such success. By the 1990s,
even Japan and some European nations struggled
to compete in the globalizing economy, while many
Asian and African nations fell deeper into poverty. As
United Nations Secretary General Kofi Annan (KO-fee
AN-uhn), a Ghanaian, put it in 2002: "Our challenge
today is to make globalization an engine that lifts
people out of hardship and misery, not a force that
holds them down."[6]

Although experiencing occasional setbacks, the Western industrial nations and
Japan have generally maintained a favorable position in the global economy. They
control most of the capital, markets, and
institutions of international finance,
such as banks, and their corporations
also own assets in other nations. The
capitalist systems in the industrialized
nations have ranged from the laissez-faire
approach, featuring limited government
interference, common in the United States, to
the mix of free markets and welfare states in western
Europe, to the closely linked government–business
relationship in Japan and South Korea. These contrast
with the economies in many former colonies, especially in Africa, where power holders, who are often
closely linked to foreign or domestic business interests, preside over largely poor populations.

Globalization and the Third World

Some once-poor countries
have exploited the trans-
national economy to their
advantage, achieving
spectacular growth. If revenues are not stolen by corrupt leaders, as has happened in places like Iraq and
Nigeria, possession of oil provides an economic foundation for national wealth. A few oil-rich nations,
such as the Persian Gulf states of Kuwait and the
United Arab Emirates, use oil revenues to improve the
material lives of their citizens. Various Asian countries, much like Japan in the late 1800s, have combined capitalist market economies, cheap labor, and
powerful governments to orchestrate industrialization. At the same time, they have ensured political
stability and attracted foreign investment by repressing political opposition. These countries have favored
export-oriented growth, producing consumer goods—
clothing, toys, housewares—for sale abroad, especially in the richer, consuming nations of Europe and
North America.

Asian countries using this development strategy improved their position in the global system.
In the 1980s and 1990s, China, South Korea, Taiwan,

Corbis

Malaysia, Thailand, and Singapore fostered the fastest-growing economies in the world and considerable prosperity. Often the growing middle class and labor leaders have demanded a larger voice in government and political liberalization. By the 1990s, Indonesians, South Koreans, Taiwanese, and Thais had replaced dictatorships with democratic governments that were chosen in free elections. The Asian systems became models for successful development by mixing capitalism, which is useful for creating wealth, with socialism, which can distribute wealth equitably.

International Lending and Trade Agreements

Various institutions shaped the transnational economy. The international lending agencies formed by the World War II Allies in 1944 to aid postwar reconstruction played crucial roles, especially the World Bank, which funded development projects such as dams and agricultural schemes, and the International Monetary Fund (IMF), which regulated currency dealings and helped alleviate severe financial problems. The IMF, which had the right to dictate economic policies to countries borrowing from it, favored Western investment and free markets, often at the expense of government funding for social services such as schools and health clinics. Borrowers failing to make these changes risked loss of IMF loans. Especially in Latin America and Africa, countries fell deeply into debt, often having to devote 40 to 50 percent of their foreign income just to pay the interest on their loans.

Trade agreements and trading blocs also shaped the world economy, reflecting an economic connectedness among nations that was unprecedented in world history. In 1947, twenty-three nations established the General Agreements on Trade and Tariffs (GATT), which set general guidelines for the conduct of world trade and rules for establishing tariffs and trade regulations. The inauguration of the World Trade Organization (WTO) by 124 nations in 1995 marked a new phase in the evolution of the postwar economic system, replacing GATT. By the early twenty-first century, several communist nations with market economies, including China and Vietnam, had joined

the WTO. The WTO had stronger dispute-resolution capabilities than GATT, and a member country could not veto a WTO decision that declared one of its regulations, such as environmental protection, to be an unfair restriction on trade. Various regional trading blocs also formed, such as the European Union.

Multinational Corporations

Giant business enterprises, known as multinational corporations because they operate all over the world, gained a leading role in the global marketplace. Some three hundred to four hundred companies, two-thirds of them U.S.-owned, dominated world production and trade. By the early 1980s, the multinationals had together become the third largest economic force in the world, exercising great influence over governments. By 2000, half of the world's one hundred largest economic entities were countries and half were multinational corporations.

The multinational corporations set the world price for various commodities, such as coffee, copper, or oil, and could play off one country against another to get the best deal. They also could easily switch manufacturing and hence jobs from one country to another. Multinationals have created millions of jobs in poor countries. Supporters argue that moving jobs from high-wage to low-wage countries, a pattern known as outsourcing, fosters a middle class of managers and technicians and offers work to people with few other job prospects. Critics reply that most of these jobs pay low wages, require long hours, and often offer little future. For example, the U.S.-based Nike Corporation, praised for creating needed jobs by making shoes in

> " Increasing competition from Asia and Latin America challenged Western and Japanese dominance in industrial activity. "

CHRONOLOGY

The Global Economy and New Technologies

1947	Formation of GATT
1947	Invention of transistor
1958	Invention of silicon microchips
1995	Formation of World Trade Organization

The Global Economy Cambodian Buddhist monks, following ancient traditions, collect their food from the devout in the capital city, Phnom Penh, while advertising for American cigarettes entices Cambodians into the global economy, despite government concerns about the health danger posed by tobacco products.

Vietnam, is also criticized because the Vietnamese employees, mainly women, work in unhealthy conditions, face sexual harassment from their male supervisors, and are fired if they complain.

The Spread of Industrialization

The industrialization that had transformed Europe and North America in the nineteenth century spread to other parts of the world, especially to Asia and Latin America, during the later twentieth century. Increasing competition from Asia and Latin America challenged Western and Japanese dominance in industrial activity. For example, the U.S. share of world industrial production fell from 50 percent in 1950 to below 30 percent in the late 1980s. Americans built more than 75 percent of all cars in 1950 but less than 20 percent by the early 1990s. Consumers worldwide now had more choice.

The Third Industrial Revolution

Technological innovations since 1945 spurred economic growth. The so-called Third Industrial Revolution came about through the creation of unprecedented scientific knowledge of new technologies that were more powerful than any invented before. These new technologies made the creations of the first Industrial Revolution, which began in the late 1700s, and the second Industrial Revolution of the later 1800s seem obsolete. With the new innovations, traditional smokestack industries such as steel mills in industrialized nations were displaced by nuclear power, computers, automation, and robotry. The technological surge also brought rocketry, genetic

Third Industrial Revolution The creation since 1945 of unprecedented scientific knowledge of new technologies more powerful than any invented before.

> "Uneven economic growth contributed to a growing gap between rich nations and poor nations, often described as developing."

engineering, silicon chips, and lasers. Space technology produced the first manned trips to the moon and unmanned crafts exploring the solar system. The British poet Archibald MacLeish observed: "To see the Earth as we now see it, small and blue and beautiful in that eternal silence [of space] where it floats, is to see ourselves as rulers on the Earth together."[7]

The Green Revolution

The Third Industrial Revolution has had potentially dramatic consequences for people around the world. For example, the Green Revolution has fostered increased agricultural output through the use of new high-yield seeds and mechanized farming, such as gasoline-powered tractors and harvesters. Farmers with the money to take advantage of these innovations can shorten the growing season, thus raising two or three crops per year. But not all farmers benefited from the Green Revolution. In countries such as India, the Philippines, and Mexico, the Green Revolution, which requires more capital for seeds and machines but fewer people to work the land, has often harmed poor peasants whose labor was no longer needed or who could not afford the investment.

United Nations Environment Program (*http://www.unep.org/ geo2000/ov-e/index .htm*). Provides access to United Nations reports on the world's environmental problems.

The Internet and Globalization

Industry and other economic activities have also become globalized. By the 1990s, more than two hundred export processing zones—industrial parks occupied largely by foreign-owned factories paying low taxes and wages—had been established around the world. For example, factories in northern Mexico, usually U.S.-owned, made goods, such as clothing, largely for the U.S. market and employed nearly half a million workers, mainly women. But not all of the new jobs were in factories. During the later twentieth century, the service and information exchange industries also grew. More people worked in service enterprises, such as fast-food restaurants, while others established transnational computer networks, such as AOL and Google, to help people use the Internet for communication and knowledge acquisition. By the 1990s, India, responding to these trends, was graduating thousands of people each year who were fluent in English and skilled in computer technology, becoming a world center for offshore information and technical services.

Outsourcing

Yet, the opportunities of industrialization and its globalization have come with risks. Hoping to better compete in the world economy, businesses have moved factories to countries with low wages and costs. As North American and western European companies have sought more profits, they have outsourced, or relocated, the jobs once held by several million workers to foreign countries with cheap labor costs and eager workers, such as India and Mexico. For example, in 1990, the U.S. clothing maker Levi Strauss closed its plant in San Antonio, Texas; laid off 1,150 workers, most of them Mexican American women; and relocated the operation to Costa Rica. Viola Casares, one of the fired workers, expressed the despair: "As long as I live I'll never forget how the white man in the suit said they had to shut us down to stay competitive."[8] Between 1981 and 1990, Levi Strauss, losing markets to lower-priced competitors, closed fifty-eight U.S. plants with more than 10,000 workers while shifting half of its production overseas.

Underdevelopment

Uneven economic growth contributed to a growing gap between rich nations and poor nations, often described as developing. The gap was already wide in 1945, since colonialism often did little to raise colonial people's general living standards. A Guyanese historian concluded that "the vast majority of Africans went into colonialism with a hoe and came out with a hoe."[9] Many Asian, African, and Latin American economies grew rapidly in the 1950s and 1960s, when the world economy boomed. In the 1970s and 1980s, however, as the world economy soured and the world prices for many exports collapsed, the growth rates of these economies declined. Then the world economy revived for a few years, only to experience a dramatic downturn in the later 1990s and early 2000s.

Western Investment

Economic growth has not always fostered development, growth that benefited the majority of the population. With economic globalization growing, rich countries pressure or encourage other nations to open their economies to foreign corporations and investment. Some nations, especially in East and Southeast Asia, have prospered from this investment, earning money to build schools, hospitals, and highways, but elsewhere Western investment often has done little to foster locally owned businesses. In Nigeria, for example, as in colonial times, British-owned enterprises have controlled banking, importing, and exporting, and foreign investment has gone mainly into cash crops and oil production, controlled largely by Western companies, such as Royal Dutch Shell. Furthermore, foreign investment and aid has often been misused to support projects favored by influential politicians or siphoned off to corrupt leaders, bureaucrats, and military officers.

Obstacles to Development

While some nations have become richer, others have become poorer. Most poor nations have suffered from some combination of rapid population growth, high unemployment, illiteracy, hunger, disease, corrupt or ineffective governments, and reliance on only a few exports, chiefly natural resources. A United Nations conference on the Environment and Development in 1997 bluntly concluded: "Too many countries have seen economic conditions worsen, public services deteriorate, and the total number of people in the world living in poverty has increased."[10] By the 1990s, the richest one-fifth of the world's people received 80 percent of the total income, while the poorest one-fifth earned less than 2 percent. Furthermore, the policies of rich countries often penalized poor countries (see Witness to the Past: An Agenda for a New Millennium). Despite preaching the benefits of free trade, rich nations have often blocked or restricted exports from poor nations into their own markets while heavily subsidizing their own farmers. Hence, wheat farmers in the West African country of Mali, however industrious, cannot compete with French or U.S. wheat farmers, who can sell their crops at much lower prices because of the financial support from their governments.

Rich and Poor in Brazil The stark contrast between the wealthy and the poor in many nations can be seen in the Brazilian city of Rio de Janeiro. Seeking jobs in expanding industries, millions of migrants flock to the city, building shantytown slums and squatter settlements in view of luxury high-rise apartment and office buildings.

Local Economic Strategies in the Third World

Despite the challenges they have faced since World War II, the nations outside of Europe and North America can boast of achievements. Between 1960 and 2000, they reduced infant mortality by half and doubled adult literacy rates. China, Sri Lanka, Malaysia, and Tanzania have been particularly successful in providing social services, such as schools and clinics, to rural areas. Various countries have developed their own locally based development strategies, such as local cooperative banks that provide credit to farmers and store grain for later consumption by villagers. However, such food supplies did not last long when

Witness to the Past

An Agenda for the New Millennium

In 2000, the United Nations called together the 188 member states for a summit at its headquarters in New York City to discuss the issues facing the world during the new millennium. In the following document, distributed before the summit, the United Nations secretary general, Kofi Annan of Ghana (GAH-nuh), laid out his vision for the organization and the challenges it faced in a world that had changed dramatically since the organization's formation more than five decades earlier.

If one word encapsulates the changes we are living through, it is "globalization." We live in a world that is interconnected as never before—one in which groups and individuals interact more and more directly across State frontiers. . . . This has its dangers, of course. Crime, narcotics, terrorism, disease, weapons—all these move back and forth faster, and in greater numbers, than in the past. People feel threatened by events far away. But the benefits of globalization are obvious too: faster growth, higher living standards, and new opportunities—not only for individuals but also for better understanding between nations, and for common action.

One problem is that, at present, these opportunities are far from equally distributed. How can we say that the half of the human race which has yet to make or receive a phone call, let alone use a computer, is taking part in globalization? We cannot, without insulting their poverty. A second problem is that, even where the global market does reach, it is not yet underpinned by rules based on shared social objectives. In the absence of such rules, globalization makes many people feel they are at the mercy of unpredictable forces. So, . . . the overarching challenge of our times is to make globalization mean more than bigger markets. To make a success of this great upheaval we must learn how to govern better, and . . . how to govern together. . . . We need to get [our nations] working together on global issues—all pulling their weight and all having their say.

What are these global issues? . . . First, freedom from want. How can we call human beings free and equal in dignity when over a billion of them are struggling to survive on less than one dollar a day, without safe drinking water, and when half of all humanity lacks adequate sanitation? Some of us are worrying about whether the stock market will crash, or struggling to master our latest computer, while more than half our fellow men and women have much more basic worries, such as where their children's next meal is coming from. . . . I believe we can halve the population of people living in extreme poverty; ensure that all children—girls and boys alike, particularly the girls—receive a full primary education; and . . . transform the lives of one hundred million slum dwellers around the world.

The second main [issue] is freedom from fear. Wars between States are mercifully less frequent than they used to be. But in the last decade internal wars have claimed more than five million lives, and driven many times that number of people from their homes. . . . We must do more to prevent conflicts from happening. Most conflicts happen in poor countries, especially those which are badly governed or where power and wealth are very unfairly distributed between ethnic or religious groups. So the best way to prevent conflict is to promote [fair representation of all groups in government], human rights, and broad-based economic development.

The third [issue] is . . . the freedom of future generations to sustain their lives on this planet. Even now, many of us have not understood how seriously that freedom is threatened. We are plundering our children's heritage to pay for our present unsustainable practices. We must stop. We must reduce emissions of . . . "greenhouse gases," to put a stop to global warming. . . . We must face the implications of a steadily shrinking surface of cultivable land, at a time when every year brings many millions of new mouths to feed. . . . We must preserve our forests, fisheries, and the diversity of living species, all of which are close to collapsing under the pressure of human consumption and destruction. . . . We need a new ethic of stewardship to encourage environment-friendly practices. . . . Above all we need to remember the old African wisdom which I learned as a child—that the earth is not ours. It is a treasure we hold in trust for our descendants.

Thinking About the Reading

1. What does Annan see as the major global issues of the new millennium?
2. How are the problems he outlined connected to each other?

Source: United Nations, *The Millennium Report* (*http://www .un.org/millennium/sg/report/state.htm*). Reprinted with permission of the United Nations.

severe drought caused major famine, as occurred in 2005, bringing widespread starvation.

Women, Children, and Economic Innovation

Women and their children have faced the harshest problems as modern economic growth has destroyed the traditional cycles of peasant life and undermined the handicrafts that once provided incomes for women. It has also fragmented families: men sometimes have to find work in other districts or countries, leaving their wives to support and raise the children. For example, in Africa, men migrate each year from Burkina Faso to the cocoa plantations and logging camps of the Ivory Coast, and from Mozambique to the mines of South Africa. Meanwhile, migrant work is becoming more feminized. Women leave India, Sri Lanka, and the Philippines to work as domestic servants for rich Arabs in the Persian Gulf states and Saudi Arabia, some facing sexual harassment or cruel employers. Asian and Latin American women are also recruited to work in homes and businesses in North America and Europe, some of them ending up in sweatshops or brothels.

Experts once assumed that schemes to foster economic development would benefit both genders, but women have generally been left behind because of their inferior social and political status. According to United Nations studies, women do 60 percent of the world's work and produce 50 to 75 percent of the world's food, yet they own only 1 percent of the world's property and earn 10 percent of the world's income. While many poor women earn money from growing food, engaging in small-scale trade, or working as domestic servants, most of women's labor—food preparation, cleaning, child rearing—is unpaid and done at home.

Internet Discussion of Marriage and Education for Saudi Women, 1996 Read a range of views on the challenges faced by Saudi women in matters of education, employment, and married life.

Some nations have fostered economic development that helps women and children through bottom-up policies relying on grassroots action: the efforts of common people. The founder of the Grameen Bank in Bangladesh, the economist Muhammad Yunus (b. 1940), felt that the conventional economics taught in universities ignored the poverty and struggles occurring in his nation's villages. Learning that conventional banks did not make loans to the poor, in 1983 Yunus opened the Grameen Bank, which makes credit available on cheap terms to peasants, especially women, for small-scale projects such as buying the tools they needed to earn a living. For example, a borrower might buy a cell phone that villagers could use to make business or personal calls, paying the borrower for each call, or purchase bamboo to make chairs. His bank eventually made loans of less than $100 to more than 2 million people. Only less than 2 percent of borrowers defaulted. The newly empowered women, earning an income for their families, now enjoyed higher social status.

Population, Urbanization, and Environmental Change

Rapid population growth and overcrowded cities became manifestations of global imbalance. With too many farmers competing for too little land, rural folk often had to abandon farming and often ended up in crowded cities—Jakarta in Indonesia, Calcutta in India, Cairo in Egypt, Mexico City—where they survived any way they could, often living in shantytowns or worse. Population growth and the resulting expansion of settlement into marginal lands posed unprecedented environmental challenges and increased competition for limited resources. These trends and the enormous surge of economic activity fueled by the use of fossil fuels have changed the world's environment.

The "Population Bomb"

During the past fifty years, the world's population has grown faster than ever before in history (see Map 26.2). Two thousand years ago, the earth had between 125 and 250 million people. At the end of World War II, the population had risen to 2.5 billion, and by 2006, it had more than doubled to 6.5 billion people.

Interactive Map

But fertility rates began dropping in much of the world during the late twentieth century, with the biggest declines occurring in industrialized nations. The reasons for the decline were the introduction and widespread use of artificial birth control, better health care, and larger numbers of women entering the paid workforce. By 1990, more than half of the world's couples with women of reproductive age practiced some form of contraception. Nonetheless, in the 1990s, nearly 100 million people were born each year. Demographers now envision a world population of some 9 to 9.5 billion by 2050, and some experts fear such major population growth could lead to increasingly severe social, economic, and environmental problems for the world.

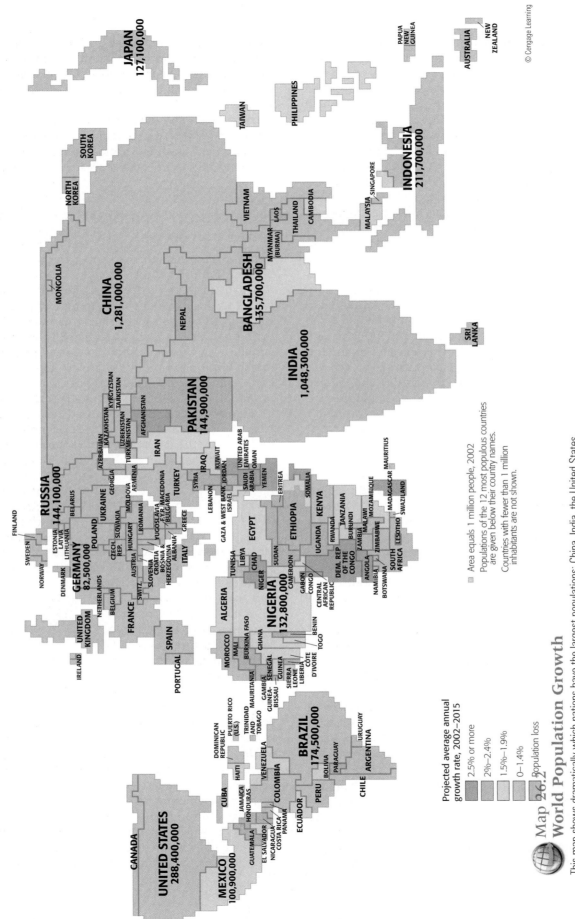

Map 26.2
World Population Growth

This map shows dramatically which nations have the largest populations: China, India, the United States, Indonesia, and Brazil. It also shows which regions experience the most rapid population growth: Africa, South Asia, and Central America.

Projected average annual growth rate, 2002–2015

- 2.5% or more
- 2%–2.4%
- 1.5%–1.9%
- 0–1.4%
- Population loss

- ■ Area equals 1 million people, 2002
  Populations of the 12 most populous countries are given below their country names.
  Countries with fewer than 1 million inhabitants are not shown.

© Cengage Learning

Population growth has been more rapid in some world regions than in others. Most of it has occurred in Asia, Africa, and Latin America. By 2000, three of the five countries with the largest populations were in Asia; China and India had the highest number, with around 1 billion people each. While Asia has continued, as it has for millennia, to house at least 60 percent of humanity, Europe's share of population fell from one-quarter in 1900 to one-eighth. Because of their falling birthrates, various European nations and Japan have declining and aging populations, which put a growing burden on those of working age to support elderly populations. Italy and Spain, both predominantly Roman Catholic nations that once had high birthrates, now have the world's lowest fertility rates. North American birthrates have also dropped, but the decline has been offset by immigration.

Nonetheless, the Western nations and Japan, enjoying high rates of resource consumption, have done more harm to the environment than countries with large populations but low consumption rates. At the same time, population growth has diminished the possibility for economic development in overcrowded nations that are already struggling. By 2000, more than 1 billion people around the world were desperately poor and unable to obtain basic essentials, such as adequate food. The Green Revolution, sparking dramatic increases in food production, averted mass famine, but by the 1990s, harvests reached a plateau, producing only small food increases or sometimes even decreases in food supplies. Furthermore, by the 1990s, fish catches were declining steeply, partly because of overfishing by Western and Japanese fleets using high-technology equipment.

Controlling Population Growth

The most effective tool to slow population growth, birth control, has been controversial, especially when this involves abortion, which is condemned as taking life by varied religious groups. Predominantly Islamic and Roman Catholic nations often discourage birth control as contrary to their religious beliefs, which oppose artificial curbs on pregnancy and favor large families. Prompted by these religious objections, some nations, including the United States under Republican presidents, have opposed international family planning organizations. But other nations have pursued vigorous population control programs. China dramatically reduced fertility, especially in the cities, through policies that promoted one child only per family; couples who flouted the laws faced stiff fines or, sometimes, forced abortions. The most successful campaigns to limit growth have targeted

women by giving them better education, health care, and a sense of dignity independent of their roles as mothers. Thus, as rural women in Bangladesh opened small businesses, which contributed to family incomes, they had fewer children.

During the twentieth century, people increasingly lived in cities. In 1900, cities held some 10 percent of the world population; that figure rose to 50 percent by 2000. Cities often grew into vast metropolises. In 1950, Western cities, headed by New York, dominated the list of the world's ten largest cities; fifty years later, the rankings had changed dramatically as Asian and Latin American cities dominated the list. Tokyo, the world's largest city with 28 million people, was followed by Mexico City, Bombay (India), São Paulo (Brazil), and Shanghai (China). Huge traffic jams made driving in Bangkok, Tokyo, Mexico City, and Lagos a nightmare. Struggling to provide needed services, cities usually dumped raw sewage into bays and rivers. By the early twenty-first century, cities were responsible for 75 percent of the world's resource consumption and produced 75 percent of its trash.

An Expanding World and Environmental Concerns

Industrialization, population growth, and urbanization have also affected environments and contributed to a warmer, drier global climate. Over the twentieth century, societies increased their industrial output twentyfold and their energy use fourteenfold. Western industrial nations and Japan have faced the environmental consequences of this output, such as air and water pollution, for several generations. Once-poor nations that became richer, such as China, South Korea, and Malaysia, paid the cost in noxious air, toxic waste, stripped forests, and warmer climates. Some environmental disasters have devastated large populations. For example, in 1957, an explosion in a nuclear waste dump in Russia killed some 10,000 people, contaminated 150 square miles of land, and forced the evacuation of 270,000 people. Meanwhile, by the 1990s, scientists were reporting a massive die-off among varieties of frogs and some ocean species, a catastrophe perhaps caused by pollution and ecological instability.

Read about Wangari Maathai, the Kenyan environmental activist who won the Nobel Peace Prize.

Deforestation and Desertification

Deforestation provides one sign of environmental destruction. In the twentieth century, half of the world's rain forests were cut down, as commercial loggers obtained wood for housing, farmers sought to convert forests into farms, and poor people obtained firewood. This destruction continues at a furious pace today; an area larger than Hungary is cleared each year. Between 1975 and 2000, one-quarter of the Central American rain forest was turned into grasslands, where beef cattle—raised chiefly to supply North American fast-food restaurants—now graze. Deforestation has had enormous long-term consequences, ranging from decreasing rainfall to loss of valuable pharmaceuticals, including those that might cure cancer or other illnesses. Millions of species of plants and animals have disappeared in recent decades, and by 2000, more than 11,000 species of plants and animals were threatened with extinction. Some scientists estimate that one-quarter to one-half of all current species could disappear by 2100. The destruction of forests, which absorb the carbon dioxide that heats up the atmosphere, has contributed to global warming.

The destruction of arable lands has arisen as another severe problem. Desertification, the transformation of once-productive land into barren desert, has increased with government, market, and population pressure to expand agriculture onto marginal land. During the past half-century in Africa, some 20,000 square miles of land became desert every year, much of it between the Sahara Desert and West Africa's coastal forests. To combat the resulting farming failures, Africans have used more pesticides, fertilizers, and irrigation, but these too often have long-term negative consequences. Drier climates diminish water supplies. One of Africa's largest lakes, Lake Chad, has lost 90 percent of its water since 1975. Deforestation and desertification also undermine farming by causing soil erosion, because with less vegetation to absorb water, rains wash away fertile topsoil and cause severe flooding. Drought has become a regular reality in Africa, forcing millions to become refugees in other lands.

Environmental Interventionism

To counter environmental decay, movements have emerged in different nations. Some, such as the Sierra Club in the United States and the Malaysian Nature Society, appeal chiefly to middle-class people. Others, such as the Chipko tree protection movement in India and the Greenbelt movement in Kenya, bring middle-class urbanites and rural peasants together in a common cause. The United Nations established an environmental program that issues regular reports warning that environmental destruction threatens the long-term health of the planet and its people.

LO⁴ New Global Networks and Their Consequences

During the late twentieth century, the world became connected in unprecedented ways, leading to talk of a global village, an interconnected world community in which all people, regardless of nationality, share a common fate. Globalization has reshaped politics and cultures as well as economic patterns, fostering not only the movement of money, products, and labor, but also of people, diseases, cultures, and religions. Increasingly, the world is marked by both unity and diversity, common influences mixing with local traditions. These transitions and encounters have not always gone smoothly, but they have often been creative.

> 66 Today, many people live in nations filled with immigrants and their descendants from the four corners of the globe. 99

Migration and Refugee Flows

Today, many people live in nations filled with immigrants and their descendants from the four corners of the globe. In western Europe, which is increasingly reliant on immigrant labor, 30 million people arrived between 1945 and 1975, chiefly from North Africa, West Africa, Turkey, South Asia, and the Caribbean. Similarly, 3.5 million Colombians moved to neighboring Venezuela, and 4 million Mexicans legally entered the United States, many filling low-wage jobs. Immigrants have often settled in Western nations, rapidly transforming cities such as Vancouver, Los Angeles, Sydney, and Paris into internationalized hubs of world culture and commerce. Cosmopolitanism—a blending of peoples and cultures—flavors cities that are closely linked to the world economy, such as Hong Kong, Singapore, São Paulo (POU-lo), London, and Dubai.

In many societies, the immigrants' presence has triggered tension and debates. Although economists argue that migrants usually make rather than take jobs, local people have often felt threatened by the newcomers and resent their continuing attachment to their own languages and cultural traditions. While the globalization of trade and jobs dissolves economic boundaries, governments increasingly impose tighter border controls in an effort to discourage illegal immigration. For example, the United States has devoted more resources to patrolling the long border with Mexico but has been unable to stop the flow of Latin Americans flocking north.

By the late twentieth century, the world contained some 100 million voluntary migrants to foreign countries, and the great majority moved for economic rather than political reasons. Many migrants—some from impoverished regions such as Central America and South Asia, others from more prosperous nations such as South Korea and Taiwan—have sought better economic opportunities in the industrialized West. Filipinos are an especially mobile people, migrating for short periods to other Southeast Asian nations and the Middle East and more permanently to North America. Some 8 million Filipinos lived abroad by 2002. Moving to a faraway, alien society is often traumatic, for both the migrant and the family members left behind.

Political turbulence, wars, genocides, and government repression have created some 20 million refugees. Desperate people have fled nations engulfed in political violence, such as Sudan, Guatemala, Afghanistan, and Cambodia, and drought-plagued states such as Ethiopia and Mali. Cubans, Chinese, Laotians (lao-OH-shuhnz), and Vietnamese, among others, have fled communist-run states that restricted their freedoms. Others, such as Haitians, Chileans, and Congolese, have escaped brutal right-wing dictatorships or corrupt despotisms. Millions of refugees have remained for decades, even generations, in squalid refugee camps: for example, many Palestinians who fled conflict in Israel have lived in refugee camps in neighboring Egypt, Jordan, and Lebanon (LEB-uh-nuhn) for more than five decades. Facing increasing numbers of people seeking refugee status, by the 1990s many nations, especially in Europe, became more cautious in granting political asylum.

The Global Spread of Disease

Diseases, whether confined chiefly to a local area or traveling the routes of trade and migration, have produced major pandemics, or massive disease outbreaks, throughout history. Today, although modern medicine has eliminated diseases that had long plagued humanity, some, such as cholera and malaria, still bedevil people who have little access to health care. Cholera still kills several thousand peo-

ple per year in poor countries, and malaria, spread by mosquitoes, debilitates millions of people in tropical regions. Both U.N. agencies and private organizations, such as Doctors Without Borders, have worked hard to reduce health threats and treat victims, but the travel of migrants, tourists, businesspeople, armies, truck drivers, sailors, and others continues to spread diseases.

The AIDS Epidemic The most deadly contemporary scourge affecting nations rich and poor, autoimmune deficiency syndrome (AIDS), is caused by a virus known as human immunodeficiency virus (HIV). AIDS spreads through sexual contact, needle sharing by drug addicts, and blood transfusions. Poverty, which forces many women into prostitution, is also a factor in the spread of AIDS. By 2005, some 42 million people around the world were infected with either HIV or AIDS, and 3.1 million died annually from AIDS, about one-third adult women, who were often infected by their husbands. In some African districts, parental deaths left some 30 percent of children orphans, and as much as 30 percent of the adult population of some African nations was HIV-positive.

By contrast, the disease is less catastrophic in countries with less poverty and better health care and communications. Only 0.2 percent of Americans were infected, and the rate was even lower in Europe. The pandemic has presented an obstacle to economic development and has proved to be a particular disaster in India, Southeast Asia, and east, central, and southern Africa. Because most AIDS victims are in their twenties and thirties, in the worst-affected countries the disease has killed or incapacitated the most highly trained and economically active section of the population. Treating AIDS patients also puts an added stress on the limited resources available for health care. AIDS victims are often rejected by their families and communities, dying alone and neglected by society.

Cultures and Religions Across Borders

The spread of cultural products and religions across national borders and the creative mixing of these with local traditions have been hallmarks of the modern world. These trends have developed within the context of a global system in which people and ideas meet. In societies around the world, popular culture—commonly produced for commercial purposes and spread by the mass media, such as radio, television, and films—has become a part of everyday life for billions of people. Spurred by globalization, religions have struggled for relevance but have also found new believers and adapted to new environments (see Map 26.3).

Interactive Map

Cultural Synthesis

> "The spread of cultural products and religions across national borders and the creative mixing of these with local traditions have been hallmarks of the modern world."

Societies have long exchanged cultural influences that have enriched local traditions. In the modern era, Western influences have been pervasive; yet, some of the modernization around the world that seems to reflect Westernization has remained superficial. The Internet, movies, pop music, and shopping malls that encourage consumption have attracted some youth in Asia, Africa, and Latin America, but their influence on the broader society, especially in the rural areas, is often more limited. No common world culture has emerged in this era. At the same time, Western technologies sometimes have served local needs. India, for instance, developed the world's largest film industry, producing some 1,000 films per year by 2002, three times more films than the United States or Japan. Modern media have reshaped people's lives, especially in cities, giving many societies a certain common denomination of experience.

The mixing of cultures and the increasing role of the mass media have been reflected in popular music. Anglo-American pop music styles, such as rock, jazz, and rap, all African American forms though having African roots, have found audiences all over the world. Vaclav Havel (vah-SLAV hah-VEL), the leader of the movement that overthrew Czech communism, credited the U.S. rock musician Frank Zappa with inspiring him to become an activist. Using the power of their celebrity and the mass media, Western pop stars have also raised awareness on issues such as racism, political prisoners, famine, and African poverty. Bono, the lead singer for the Irish rock band U2, campaigns tirelessly among political leaders for causes such as debt relief for poor nations. Many forms of music have mixed indigenous and imported influences, often from outside the West. For example, Congolese popular music, which borrowed Latin American dance rhythms, gained audiences throughout Africa and Europe in the 1980s. Indian film music and Arab folk music have influenced the popular music of Southeast Asia and East Africa.

Religion and Globalization

Although in the modern era, secular thought has become more popular than ever before in history, more than three-quarters of the world's people identify with one or another universal religion with roots deep in the past. By 2000, the world contained almost 2 billion Christians, 1.3 billion Muslims, 800 million Hindus, and 350 million Buddhists. Nearly 900 million practiced a local faith, such as animism or Daoism, or professed no religion (see Map 26.3). Religion sometimes has become the basis for national identity, as in chiefly Roman Catholic Poland and Ireland and in Muslim Bangladesh and Pakistan.

Religious leaders have debated how much, if at all, their faiths need to change to better engage the contemporary world. Serious efforts at reform came, for instance, in the Catholic Church in the 1960s when Pope John XXIII (pope 1958–1963) liberalized church practices, such as having the mass in a vernacular language rather than Latin, and encouraged a more active dialogue with other churches and religions. Meanwhile, a movement arose among Catholic clergy and laypeople in Latin America, called liberation theology, that cooperated with socialist and communist groups to improve the lives of the poor. Muslim liberals and militants also confronted each other over which directions Islam should take, arguing over such issues as the role of women, relations with non-Muslims, and whether states with Muslim majorities should make Islamic law the basis of their legal systems.

The easy spread of ideas in the globalized world has worked to the advantage of portable creeds that are not dependent on one culture or setting. In many places, notably Africa, religions tied to local culture, usually some form of polytheism or animism, have faded, while two universal religions, Christianity and Islam, fortified by missionary impulses, have gained wider followings in developing nations. At the same time, organized religion and its influence have declined in East Asia and much of the West. Communists discouraged religious observance in China, while increasing numbers of Japanese found neither their traditional faiths nor imported religions as relevant. Meanwhile, Christian churches in

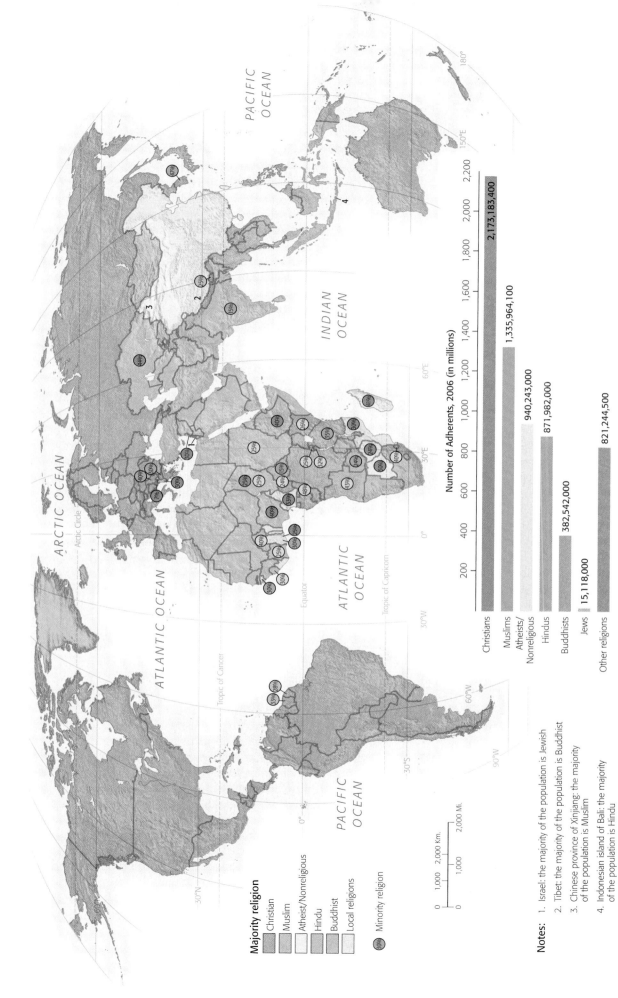

Majority religion

- Christian
- Muslim
- Atheist/Nonreligious
- Hindu
- Buddhist
- Local religions

50% Minority religion

Number of Adherents, 2006 (in millions)

Religion	Adherents
Christians	2,173,183,400
Muslims	1,335,964,100
Atheists/ Nonreligious	940,243,000
Hindus	871,982,000
Buddhists	382,542,000
Jews	15,118,000
Other religions	821,244,500

Notes: 1. Israel: the majority of the population is Jewish
2. Tibet: the majority of the population is Buddhist
3. Chinese province of Xinjiang: the majority of the population is Muslim
4. Indonesian island of Bali: the majority of the population is Hindu

Map 26.3
World Religions

Christianity has the most believers and is the dominant faith in the Americas, Oceania, Europe, Russia, and central and southern Africa. Most people in the northern half of Africa, western Asia, and Central Asia embrace Islam. Hindus are concentrated in India, and Buddhists in East and Southeast Asia.

© Cengage Learning

Europe, Canada, and Australia experienced dramatic drops in attendance and membership between 1960 and the early twenty-first century. Traditional church attitudes have also competed with changing social attitudes. Even predominantly Catholic nations in Europe have legalized abortion and moved toward equal rights for homosexuals, policies opposed by the Catholic Church. Both the Netherlands, once a center for a puritanical form of Protestantism, and Spain, before the 1970s one of the staunchest Catholic nations, have approved same-sex marriage.

Religion and Oppression

Long a source of conflict, religion continues to sow tensions between members of different faiths. Hundreds of people were killed or wounded in Nigeria when rival Christians and Muslims sporadically battled for control of several cities. Meanwhile, tensions between Muslims and Hindus sparked sporadic violence in India. Catholics and Protestants opposed each other in Northern Ireland and Uganda, while Sunni and Shi'a Muslims occasionally fought in Pakistan and western Asia. In Iraq, where some 60 percent of the population is Shi'a, the Sunni dictator, Saddam Hussein, restricted Shi'ite religious holidays, executed Shi'ites who opposed his regime, and allowed few Shi'ites into the government. After his regime was toppled by the 2003 U.S. invasion, conflicts between Shi'ites and Sunnis erupted, complicating U.S. efforts to restore political stability.

The Fundamentalist Backlash

Religious militancy has grown among some believers. Some Muslim militants have turned the old notion of *jihad*, or struggle within believers to strengthen their faith, into a campaign for holy war against unbelievers and countries or groups they consider anti-Muslim. The militants, often known as Islamists or jihadis, appeal especially to the young and poor, who are often unemployed and embittered toward their governments and the West. The more puritanical Muslims despise the sexuality and rebellion portrayed in Western television programs and movies.

Some Christians, especially in the United States, Latin America, and Africa, have turned to literal interpretations of the Bible, an approach labeled as fundamentalist, and formed proselytizing churches. These churches have often opposed secular culture, rejected scientific findings they deemed incompatible with biblical accounts, and condemned left-wing political and social movements. Christian and Islamic militancy has sparked similar movements in Buddhism, Hinduism, and Judaism, pitting the zealous believers against those with moderate, tolerant views.

Global Communications

A worldwide communications network has been a chief engine of globalization. The introduction of radio in the early 1900s and then tape recording and television in mid-century laid the basis for this network. These were followed by the invention of the transistor by three American physicists in 1947, which allowed for the miniaturization of electronics. In 1953, portable transistor radios became available and soon reached even remote villages, opening them to the news and culture of the wider world. Even villages without electricity could use transistor radios and cassette players.

Technological breakthroughs provided the foundation for more rapid and widespread communications. For decades, U.S., British, and German engineers gradually built a foundation for computer technology. The first general-purpose computers were built in 1948. In 1958, the first silicon microchips began a computer revolution that led several decades later to the first personal computers. By 2000, the world had more than 150 million personal computers with Internet access, 330 million Internet users, and 1.6 billion web pages, all part of a vast network often termed the information superhighway. Every minute, 10 million electronically transmitted messages, or e-mail, are dispatched via computer. E-mail allows people in different countries, however distant, to communicate instantly with each other. An interested reader in Hong Kong, Ghana, or Finland can access online newspapers such as the *New York Times* or the *Deccan Herald* in India. Along with computers, the rise of 24-hour cable news networks able to reach worldwide audiences, such as U.S.-based CNN (Cable News Network) and the Arab-language Al Jazeera, based in the Persian Gulf state of Qatar, widened access to diverse views.

The rapid evolution of media and information technology has had many consequences. For one, the development of cellular phones, e-mail, and the Internet means that information can be transmitted around the globe beyond the reach of governments, undermining their power to shape their citizens' thinking. In 2006, some U.S.-based Internet providers faced criticism for helping repressive governments such as China control the information flow and identify dissidents. Another major consequence is that technologies have enhanced the value of education and of English, which has gradually become a world language. By 2004, some three-quarters of all websites were in English. Perhaps one-quarter of the world's people know some English, and Asian countries with educated people fluent in English, such as India and Singapore, have an advantage in competing for high-technology industries. These major trends have also enhanced the global exchange of scientific ideas, but in the poorest nations, only a lucky few have satellite dishes, fax machines, and networked computers, and these promising technologies have not changed the lives of peasants and low-wage workers.

Global Movements

Increasing links between far-flung peoples have allowed for social and political movements to transcend borders. A wide variety of transnational organizations has emerged to promote issues such as the treatment of political prisoners, women's rights, and antiracism. As an example, Amnesty International, based in Britain, publicizes the plight of people who have been imprisoned solely for their political views and activities, such as the Burmese opposition leader Aung San Suu Kyi (AWNG sahn soo CHEE), organizing letter-writing and pressure campaigns to seek their release. Other movements have addressed globalization. For instance, the World Social Forum was formed in 2001 and has met annually in Brazil to oppose globalizing free-market capitalism and call for workers' rights and environmental protection.

Global Protest Movements

As the world became more closely linked, social or political movements or upheavals in one nation or region sometimes spread widely. For example, during the 1960s, students, workers, and political radicals in various nations organized protests against the U.S. war in Vietnam, racism, unresponsive governments, capitalism, and other concerns. In 1968, demonstrations, marches, and strikes intensified around the world. These movements were not coordinated

Internet Cafe in Thailand In this photo, a waiter at a cyberspace café, operated by the Swiss multinational ice cream company, Häagen Dazs, in Bangkok, Thailand, helps a young Thai woman navigate one of the café's computers.

> "As the world became more closely linked, social or political movements or upheavals in one nation or region sometimes spread widely."

and addressed largely local grievances, but young protesters were often influenced by the same writers, music, and ideas. To varying degrees, the turbulence affected more than a dozen countries, from the United States and Mexico to France, Czechoslovakia, and Japan. When thousands of demonstrators shouting "Mexico, Freedom" took to the streets of Mexico City to demand democracy and protest police brutality, the police opened fire, killing dozens of protesters and shocking the world. In the wake of the 1968 activism, movements focused on environmental awareness, peace, workers' rights, homosexual rights, and feminism grew in popularity.

Women in a Global Age

Women have been particularly active in seeking to expand their rights. Although most women's organizations work within national boundaries, some activists have placed women's issues on the international agenda, but do not always agree on solutions. In the United Nation's fourth World Conference on Women, held in China in 1995, the 40,000 delegates disagreed sharply on priorities. Delegates from rich nations wanted to expand women's employment options, social freedom, and control over their bodies, while Asian, African, and Latin American delegates were often chiefly interested in making their families more healthy and economically secure. Yet, despite disagreements, women have worked across borders on issues affecting all societies, such as preventing violence against women.

In 2005, Mukhtaran Bibi (MOOK-tahr-an BIH-bee), an illiterate woman from an impoverished Pakistani village, gained worldwide sympathy for her resistance to male brutality. As part of a village dispute, the tribal council had ruled that she be gang-raped to punish her family. Instead of following custom by ending the "disgrace" through suicide, however, she bravely pursued the rapists in court. They were convicted, and she used the money awarded to her by the court to start two village schools, one for boys and one for girls. When a higher court then overturned the men's convictions, her courageous refusal to accept the verdict caused an international outcry. While the Pakistan government tried to suppress the controversy, men and women around the world rallied to her cause. Mukhtaran Bibi inspired millions everywhere with her courage and faith in education and justice.

Global Terrorism

Terrorism, small-scale but violent attacks aimed at undermining a government or demoralizing a population, intensified in the late twentieth and early twenty-first centuries, expanding to global dimensions and reshaping world politics. For centuries, various groups and states used terrorism to support their goals. After 1945, Palestinians under Israeli control, Basque nationalists in Spain, and Irish nationalists in Britain, among others, engaged in terrorism for their causes. Some states also carried out or sponsored terrorism against unfriendly governments or political movements. The United States sponsored terrorism against leftist-ruled Nicaragua in the 1980s, helping form a military force, known as the Contras, that often attacked civilian targets, such as rural schools, daycare centers, and clinics operated by the government.

While terrorism has often remained local in scope, an increasingly interconnected world has spurred some terrorist organizations to operate on a global level, forming networks that have branches in many countries. The most active of these networks, formed by militant Islamists, have exploited communication and transportation networks to operate across national borders, capitalizing on widespread Muslim anger at Israel and U.S. foreign policies. Muslim terrorist groups became increasingly active during the 1970s and 1980s in Egypt, Algeria, and Lebanon, attacking politicians, police, Western residents and tourists, and Israeli and U.S. targets.

As a result, terrorism became a growing threat to life in the Middle East. To oppose Israeli occupation of Arab lands and demoralize Israelis, Palestinian militants strapped explosives to their bodies and detonated them in Israeli buses and businesses. Outraged by the killing and wounding of hundreds of Israeli civilians—both Jewish and Arab—the Israelis responded with force, killing or arresting Palestinians and expelling families of suspected militants from their homes, often bulldozing the houses into rubble. The poet Hanan Ashrawi (HA-non uh-SHRAH-wee), a

Christian Palestinian nationalist, condemned the suicide bombings but also lamented the earlier Israeli destruction of her family's property: "Have you seen a stone house die? It sighs, then wraps itself around its gutted heart and lays itself to rest."[11] Divided by politics, Israelis and Palestinians have shared the bitter experience of grieving for those lost in the chronic violence.

Osama Bin Laden and Al Qaeda

The Soviet military intervention in 1979 to support a pro-Soviet government in mostly Muslim Afghanistan provided the spark for forming a global network of Islamist terrorists. Islamic militants from the Middle East and Pakistan flocked to Afghanistan to assist the Muslim Afghan insurgents resisting the Soviets. In 1988, the most militant of the foreign fighters began to come together in a jihadi organization known as Al Qaeda ("The Base"). Al Qaeda's main leader was the Saudi Osama bin Laden (b. 1957), who came from an extremely wealthy family—his Yemen-born father had made billions in the Saudi construction industry—and had been trained as an engineer. Bin Laden used his wealth to support the Afghan rebels, mostly devout Muslims,

 Declaration of Jihad Against Americans Occupying the Land of the Two Holy Mosques Read a speech given by Osama bin Laden to his followers in Afghanistan, and soon published worldwide.

who were also funded and armed by the United States. After the Soviets abandoned Afghanistan in 1989, bin Laden used his supporters to set up Al Qaeda cells in Saudi Arabia, whose government he viewed as corrupt, and to target Egypt and Iraq, whose secular regimes suppressed Islamic militants. To recruit, support, and communicate with members, Al Qaeda used modern technology, publicizing their cause by setting up websites, using e-mail and satellite phones, and releasing videotapes to cable news networks of bin Laden's messages.

Eventually, Al Qaeda looked beyond the Middle East for targets. In the mid-1990s, the Afghanistan-based bin Laden began to plot terrorist efforts against his former ally in the Afghan resistance, the United States, whose military bases in Saudi Arabia, support for repressive Arab governments, and close alliance with Israel enraged many Arabs. Bin Laden argued that "to kill the Americans and their allies is an individual duty for every Muslim who can do it in any country in which it is possible to do so."[12] Most Muslims rejected such violent views, but Al Qaeda or related groups sponsored attacks on U.S. targets, such as the embassies in Kenya and Tanzania, causing hundreds of casualties.

September 11, 2001

On September 11, 2001, Al Qaeda members hijacked four U.S. commercial airliners and crashed them into New York's World Trade Center and the Pentagon near Washington, D.C., killing more than three thousand people, mostly civilians. The attacks shocked Americans, who were unused to terrorism at home, as well as people everywhere who opposed indiscriminate killing. U.S. president George W. Bush responded by declaring a war on terrorism. U.S. forces attacked Al Qaeda bases in Afghanistan, and then occupied the country, whose government, controlled by Islamists who had fought the Soviets, shielded bin Laden, but the United States failed to capture bin Laden and still faced resistance from Islamic militants.

In 2003, the United States, claiming that Saddam Hussein's Iraq was closely linked to Al Qaeda and possessed weapons of mass destruction, invaded Iraq, removed Saddam's brutal, despotic government, and imposed a U.S. military occupation. Britain provided the chief support for the U.S. effort. The U.S. troops, however, found no evidence of any ties between Saddam and Al Qaeda or any weapons of mass destruction. The occupation sparked an insurgency, including suicide bombings, and unleashed sectarian divisions that hindered U.S. efforts—supported by many Iraqis—to stabilize and rebuild Iraq. While most of the insurgents were Iraqis, mostly Sunni Muslims fearing domination by the Shi'ite majority, Islamists from other countries flocked to Iraq to attack Americans and help destabilize the country. The U.S. invasion and occupation, and the resistance to it, killed tens of thousands of Iraqi civilians, resulted in more than 25,000 U.S. casualties, alienated many U.S. allies and, like the earlier U.S. conflict in Vietnam, was unpopular around the world. Meanwhile, capitalizing on anti-U.S. sentiment among Muslims, Al Qaeda spawned loosely affiliated terrorist groups, often operating without direct Al Qaeda guidance.

Terrorism by militant Muslims had direct and indirect consequences for societies around the world. Al Qaeda or related groups launched terrorist attacks on several continents, from Spain and Britain to Indonesia, Kenya, and Morocco. Nations with despotic governments, such as China, Egypt, and Uzbekistan, used the threat of terrorism as a reason to restrict civil liberties. Human rights concerns faded amid the Western obsession with terrorism.

 Listen to a synopsis of Chapter 26.

CHAPTER 27

East Asian Resurgence,
Since 1945

Learning Outcomes

After reading this chapter, you should be able to answer the following questions:

LO[1] How did Maoism transform Chinese society?

LO[2] What factors explain the dramatic rise of Chinese economic power in the world since 1978?

LO[3] How did Japan rise from the ashes of defeat in World War II to become a global economic powerhouse?

LO[4] What policies led to the rise of the "Little Dragon" nations and their dynamic economies?

> " Once China's destiny is in the hands of the people, China, like the sun rising in the east, will illuminate every corner with a brilliant flame, and build a new, powerful and prosperous [society]. "
>
> —**Mao Zedong, Chinese communist leader**[1]

On October 1, 1949, the Chinese Communist leader Mao Zedong (maow dzuh-dong) (1893–1976) was driven into downtown Beijing, China's capital, accompanied by a dusty band of the People's Liberation Army. Mao, fifty-five years old, the son of a peasant family, had spent the previous twenty-two years living in remote rural areas. The Republic of China, the government headed by Jiang Jieshi (better known in the West as Chiang Kai-shek) (1887–1975), had lost to Mao's troops, and the president had fled to the large offshore island of Taiwan. Wearing a new suit, Mao climbed to the top of the Gate of Heavenly Peace, the entrance to the Forbidden City of the Qing emperors overlooking Beijing's spacious Tiananmen Square. Millions of Chinese jammed the square to hear their new ruler announce the founding of a new communist government, called the People's Republic of China. Referring to a century of corrupt governments, humiliation, and domination by Western nations and Japan, Mao thanked his allies and firmly proclaimed: "The Chinese people have stood up. Nobody will insult us again."[2]

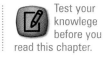
Test your knowlege before you read this chapter.

What do you think?

The late twentieth century witnessed a striking resurgence of Asian economic and political power.

Strongly Disagree   *Strongly Agree*

| 1 | 2 | 3 | 4 | 5 | 6 | 7 |

Pacific Rim
The economically dynamic Asian countries on the western edge of the Pacific Basin: China, Japan, South Korea, Taiwan, and several Southeast Asian nations.

The formation of the People's Republic marked a watershed in the history of China, the rest of East Asia, and the world. The new government brought to an end a century of severe instability. Its communist leaders were committed to the revolutionary transformation of the society, while making China respected abroad once again. Given China's size and population—1.3 billion by 2005—any major transition there had global significance. By the early twenty-first century, China, with a booming economy, had reclaimed some of the political and economic status it had lost two centuries earlier.

Chinese were not the only East Asians to enjoy a resurgence with a global impact. In the 1980s, observers referred to the **Pacific Rim**, the economically dynamic Asian countries on the edge of the Pacific

Wally McNamee/Corbis

≪ **The China Stock Exchange** The East Asian nations enjoyed an economic resurgence in this era. Since the 1980s, China has boasted the world's fastest growing economy and a booming stock exchange.

> "The key question confronting the Chinese communists after 1949 was how to achieve rapid economic development in an overpopulated, battered country."

Communist Triumph, Economy, and Government

Basin: China, Japan, South Korea, Taiwan, and several Southeast Asian nations. These observers also predicted that the twenty-first century would be the Pacific Century, marked by a shift of global economic power to the Pacific Rim, whose export-driven nations seemed poised to dominate a post–Cold War era where economic power outweighed military might. Although economic crises and changing world politics have challenged the Pacific Century concept, China, Japan, and their neighbors have remained major players in the global system.

LO¹ Mao's Revolutionary China

The Chinese Revolution that brought the Chinese communists to power in 1949 was one of the three greatest upheavals in modern world history, on line with the French Revolution of 1789 and the Russian Revolution of 1917. China's revolution remade a major world society while restoring China's international status. The communists built a strong government that made China the most experimental nation on earth, veering from one innovative policy to another in an attempt to renovate Chinese life. The People's Republic of China created a new model of economic development different from both Western-dominated capitalism and the highly centralized Soviet communism, but the path was littered with conflict and repression. Furthermore, the Chinese, like all societies, were products of their history. Even under communist rule, China remained partly an ancient empire and partly a modern nation, and its leaders often behaved much like the emperors of old in their autocratic exercise of power.

The U.S. defeat of Japan in 1945 removed the common enemy of both of China's major political factions, Mao's communists and Chiang Kai-shek's nationalist government, sparking a fierce civil war between them. Chiang disdained Mao as an unpolished peasant, while Mao despised Chiang for favoring the rich, yet both men shared patriotism, an autocratic style, and hunger for power. Chiang's 3.7-million-man army vastly outnumbered the 900,000 communist troops and enjoyed lavish military aid from the United States. The communists, aided by the Soviet Union (USSR), concentrated on north China and Manchuria. In trying to block Mao's forces, Chiang overstretched his supply lines; meanwhile, a rapid decline in the value of Chinese currency demoralized the population. The Chinese sought change, and many of them came to view the communist movement as a more honest alternative to Chiang's Nationalist Party. In the villages that they controlled, the communists promoted a social revolution, known as the "turning over," by encouraging villagers to denounce local landlords, transferring land from richer to poorer peasants, replacing government-appointed leaders with elected village councils, and protecting battered wives.

The military and political tide turned against the Republic. In 1948, Chiang's troops in Manchuria surrendered to the communists. To revive Chiang's prospects, and recognizing the growing unpopularity of his regime, the United States pressured him unsuccessfully to broaden his political base with democratic reforms. Through 1949, the communists took the major cities of north China and pushed Chiang's army south. Finally, Chiang fled to the island of Taiwan, along with thousands of troops and 2 million supporters. On Taiwan, with massive U.S. aid, the leaders of the relocated Republic of China developed a successful capitalist strategy for economic growth. Meanwhile, mainland China moved in a different direction.

Rebuilding China's Economy

The key question confronting the Chinese communists after 1949 was how to achieve rapid economic development in an overpopulated, battered country. Two decades of war had ruined the economy, leaving little capital for industrialization. Unlike Britain and France in the nineteenth century, China had no overseas empire to exploit. The new leaders did not want loans and foreign investment that might reduce their independence and lead to a debt trap. Furthermore, they faced a powerful enemy: propelled by alarm at Mao's policies and anticommunist Cold War concerns, the United

> "By the late 1950s, Mao, growing disenchanted with Stalinism, introduced a second model of development, known as Maoism, that synthesized Marxist and Chinese thought."

communes Large agricultural units introduced by Mao Zedong that combined many families and villages into a common system for pooling resources and labor.

States launched an economic boycott to shut China off from international trade, refused diplomatic recognition, and surrounded China with military bases. Isolated, China created its own models of economic and political development.

Between 1949 and 1957, China followed the Soviet model of central planning known as Stalinism: heavy industry, a powerful bureaucracy, and a managerial system. China received some Soviet aid in the 1950s, but otherwise the Chinese communists financed development through self-reliance and withdrew from the global system. The state emphasized austerity and acquired capital from the people by making them work hard for low wages, in hopes that future generations would live better. In the Stalinist years, the communists abolished private ownership of business and industry and transferred land to poor peasants. Soon they began collectivizing the rural economy into cooperatives, in which peasants helped each other and shared tools. As in the Soviet Union, the emphasis on state directive fostered the rise of a new privileged elite in the government and in the ruling Communist Party, which cracked down on dissent.

 Internet Guide to Chinese Studies (*http://www.sino.uni-heidelberg.de/igcs/*). An excellent collection of links, maintained at a German university.

CHRONOLOGY

China Since 1945

1945–1949	Chinese civil war
1949	Chinese communist triumph
1949–1957	Stalinist model
1950	Occupation of Tibet; new marriage law
1950–1953	Korean War
1957–1961	First use of Maoist model
1958–1961	Great Leap Forward
1960	Sino–Soviet split
1966–1976	Great Proletarian Cultural Revolution
1972	Nixon's trip to Beijing
1976	Death of Mao Zedong; arrest of Gang of Four
1978	Four Modernizations policy; normalization of U.S.–China diplomatic relations
1978–1989	Market socialism
1978–1997	Deng Xiaoping era
1989	Beijing Massacre; introduction of market Leninism
1997	Return of Hong Kong to China

The Emergence of Maoism

By the late 1950s, Mao, growing disenchanted with Stalinism, introduced a second model of development, known as Maoism, that synthesized Marxist and Chinese thought. Under Maoism, which was China's guiding ideology from 1957 to 1961 and then again from 1966 to 1976, the Chinese people were mobilized for development projects, such as building dams, pest elimination, and massive tree-planting campaigns. Mao reorganized the rural economy into communes, large agricultural units that combined many families and villages into a common administrative system for pooling resources and labor. The communes raised agricultural productivity, eliminated landlords, and promoted social and economic equality. Mao located industry in rural areas, thus keeping the peasants at home rather than fostering movement to cities, as happened in other countries.

The Great Leap Forward

The most radical Maoist policy was the Great Leap Forward (1958–1961), an ambitious attempt to industrialize China rapidly and end poverty through collective efforts. Farmers and workers were ordered to build small iron furnaces in their backyards, courtyards, and gardens and to spend their free time turning everything from cutlery to old bicycles into steel. The slogan "Achieve More, Better, Faster" swept through the nation. But the poorly conceived campaign, pushing the people too hard, nearly wrecked the economy and, along with disastrous weather, caused 30 million people to starve. These failures undermined Mao's influence, bringing more moderate policies in the early 1960s.

As in the USSR, the Communist Party, led by Mao as chairman, dominated the political system; party members occupied all key positions in the government and military down to village leaders. Using the slogan "Politics Takes Command," the communists made political values pervasive. All Chinese were required to become members of political discussion groups, but party activists monitored the discussions and reported dissenters. Political education was integrated into the schools, work units, and even leisure activities. The party also sought to eradicate inequalities and emphasized the interests of the group over those of the individual.

Explore life as a Chinese villager during the Mao period of the Great Leap Forward and decide whether to work in government or agriculture in this interactive simulation.

Honoring Chairman Mao Since the beginning of communist rule in China in 1949, this giant portrait of Mao Zedong, the chairman of the Chinese Communist Party, has hung on the Gate of Heavenly Peace, the entrance to the Forbidden City of the Qing dynasty emperors, in the heart of Beijing.

Peter Guttman/Corbis

Officials and intellectuals had to perform physical labor, such as spreading manure to fertilize farm fields, so that they would understand the experience of the workers and peasants.

Five Guarantees

Mao's system required massive social control, enabled by a vast police apparatus; millions suspected of opposing the communists were harassed, jailed, exiled, or killed. Even communist sympathizers, such as the outspoken feminist writer Ding Ling (1902–1986), were purged after falling out of official favor. In exchange for accepting its policies, the state promised everyone the "five guarantees" of food, clothes, fuel, education, and a decent burial. But thousands of people, wanting more personal happiness than the system allowed, fled to British-ruled Hong Kong over the years.

Maoist China in the World

The communists restored China's status as a major world power (see Map 27.1), with only some setbacks, and pursued a foreign policy that maximized stability at home. Mao reasserted Chinese sovereignty in outlying areas of China, and in 1950 sent armies to occupy Tibet, whose people, although conquered and incorporated into China by the Qing dynasty in the 1600s, had broken away from China in 1912. Most Tibetans opposed Chinese rule, sparking periodic unrest. The Chinese suppression of a Tibetan revolt led the highest Tibetan Buddhist leader, the Dalai Lama (DAH-lie LAH-mah) (b. 1935), to flee to India in 1958. In exile, the Dalai Lama became a defiant symbol of Tibetan resistance to Chinese rule, traveling the world to rally support for the Tibetan cause while promoting Buddhist ethics and world peace, for which he won the Nobel Peace Prize in 1989.

Interactive Map

The Korean War

In 1950, China, which supported the communist North Korean government installed in 1948, was drawn into the Korean War between the USSR-backed North Korea and United Nations forces sent to defend pro-U.S. South Korea. When the United Nations forces pushed the North Korean army toward China's border, and the U.S. commander, General Douglas MacArthur, talked reck-

> ❝ Political education was integrated into the schools, work units, and even leisure activities. ❞

lessly of occupying North Korea and carrying the offensive into China, the Chinese, feeling endangered, entered the conflict. Mao caught U.S. leaders by surprise by dispatching 300,000 troops into Korea, and the Chinese forces pushed United Nations troops back south. The war produced huge casualties on both sides, including several hundred thousand Chinese, and reinforced the hostility and mutual fear between China and the United States.

When the Korean War ended in a stalemate in 1953, the United States, seeking to halt communist expansion, signed a mutual defense treaty with Chiang Kai-shek's regime on Taiwan. The substantial U.S. forces stationed in Taiwan and South Korea joined the thousands of U.S. troops that had remained in Japan, Okinawa, and the Philippines after World War II, while the U.S. Navy patrolled the waters off China, making for a formidable U.S. military presence in East Asia. But the ability to achieve a stalemate in Korea with the powerful United States improved China's international position. In the 1950s, China, allied with the USSR, basically withdrew from the global system, maintaining limited trade with only a handful of Western nations.

The Sino–Soviet Split

China adapted to changing global politics. In the late 1950s, tensions between China and the USSR grew. Chinese leaders did not share the Soviet view that what was good for the USSR was necessarily good for international communism. The Soviet policy of "peaceful coexistence" with the West enraged Mao, who labeled the United States "a paper tiger." Mao also opposed the 1956 decision of the Soviet leader, Nikita Khrushchev (KROOSH-chef), to reveal the excesses of Stalinist police-state rule in Russia, raising the issue of abuse of power by communist dictators. By 1960, the Sino–Soviet split was official; the USSR withdrew advisors and technicians, even the spare parts for the industries they had helped build. The Chinese built up their military strength, tested their first atomic bomb, and occasionally clashed with Soviet forces on their border. To counterbalance the power of the United States and the USSR, China sought allies and influence in Asia and Africa. Yet, despite fierce rhetoric, Chinese leaders generally followed a cautious foreign policy.

RUSSIA

KAZAKHSTAN

UZBEKISTAN

TURKMENISTAN

KYRGYZSTAN

TAJIKISTAN

AFGHANISTAN

PAKISTAN

I N D I A

Indian claim

Chinese line of control

NEPAL

BHUTAN

(INDIA)

BANGLADESH

Lhasa

T I B E T

Q I N G H A I

X I N J I A N G

M O N G O L I A

I N N E R   M O N G O L I A

HEILONGJIANG

Harbin

JILIN

LIAONING

Dalian

BEIJING Beijing
Tianjin
TIANJIN

HEBEI

SHANDONG

Yellow
Sea

NORTH
KOREA

SOUTH
KOREA

JAPAN

Sea of Japan
(East Sea)

GANSU

NINGXIA

SHANXI

Dazhai

Huang He R.
(Yellow R.)

HENAN

JIANGSU

Nanjing

SHANGHAI

ZHEJIANG

Hangzhou

East China
Sea

SHAANXI

Xian

Yanan

Yangzi R.

HUBEI

ANHUI

Wuhan

Yangzi R.

CHONGQING

S I C H U A N

Chengdu

GUIZHOU

HUNAN

Changsha

JIANGXI

FUJIAN

Xiamen

TAIPEI

Taipei

TAIWAN

PHILIPPINES

Tropic of Cancer

20°N

Y U N N A N

GUANGXI

Xi R.

GUANGDONG

Guangzhou

Shenzhen
HONG KONG
MACAO

HAINAN

South
China
Sea

VIETNAM

LAOS

THAILAND

BURMA
(MYANMAR)

Bay of Bengal

PACIFIC
OCEAN

N

← Nationalist retreat
1948–1949

--- Boundary uncertain

0   150   300 Mi.
0   150 300 Km.

© Cengage Learning

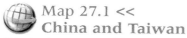

Map 27.1 <<
China and Taiwan

China is a huge country, divided into many provinces, and occupies a large part of eastern Eurasia. In 1949, the government of the Republic of China, defeated by the Chinese communists, moved to the island of Taiwan, off China's Pacific coast.

Nixon and Normalization

During the 1970s, Chinese foreign policy changed dramatically. The change was symbolized by U.S. president Richard Nixon's trip to Beijing in 1972, the first official contact between the two nations since 1949. The two nations shared a hostility toward the USSR; moreover, the bitter U.S. experience fighting communist forces in Vietnam and the gradual withdrawal of U.S. forces from that country had opened the door to foreign policy rethinking in both the United States and China. Chinese leaders perceived the United States as stepping back from Asian military and political commitments, and hence as a diminishing threat. The United States now agreed to quit blocking Chinese membership in the United Nations and, in 1978, normalized diplomatic relations with China. The Chinese also developed better relations with noncommunist nations in Southeast Asia and Africa.

Mao's Cultural Revolution: A New Society

Mao was a complex figure. He was, for example, a self-proclaimed feminist who promoted women's rights, but he was also a sexually promiscuous man who married several times. A poor public speaker with few close friends, he could nevertheless inspire millions to follow his lead. Power-hungry and ruthless, he made many enemies. Although many of his initiatives ultimately failed or resulted in misery for millions of people, he played a powerful role in modern world history, leading the communists to victory, reunifying China, focusing public attention on rural people, and placing his stamp on the world's most populous nation. That impact was particularly strong when Maoism was China's guiding ideology.

Dissatisfied with China's development by the early 1960s, in the mid-1960s Mao sought to regain his dominant status by resurrecting Maoism and offering a vision of a new society that harnessed the collective power of the people. In Mao's vision, individuals, inspired by the slogan "Serve the People," subordinated their own needs to the broader social order. His allies emphasized the cult of Mao and his revolutionary thoughts. This campaign laid the foundation for a major social movement inspired by Mao's thoughts.

The Cultural Revolution

For a decade, between 1966 and 1976, massive turmoil generated by Mao convulsed and reshaped China like a whirlwind. The Great Proletarian Cultural Revolution, as it was called, was a radical movement that represented Mao's attempt to implant his vision, destroy his enemies, crush the stifling bureaucracy, and renew the revolution's vigor. The movement's major supporters—young workers and students known as Red Guards—roamed around cities and the countryside in groups, smashing temples and churches and attacking and arresting anti-Mao leaders. Mao told them to destroy the party and government headquarters and that rebellion was justified. A Mao personality cult spread. The students carried copies of a little red book containing short quotations from Mao's writings, and one observer noted that "giant portraits of [Mao] now hung in the streets, busts were in every chamber, his books and photographs were everywhere on display."[3]

After the Revolution: Reform in Maoist China

The turmoil affected everyone. The chaos of these years caused serious economic problems, disrupting industrial and agricultural production and closing most schools for two years. The upheaval also resulted in thousands being killed, jailed, or removed from official positions, and millions of others were sent to remote rural areas. Anti-Mao officials, intellectuals, and people with upper-class backgrounds faced public criticism, followed by punishment if they failed to admit their political crimes. Soon even Mao was dampening down the radical fervor.

Great Proletarian Cultural Revolution A radical movement in China between 1966 and 1976 that represented Mao Zedong's attempt to implant his vision, destroy his enemies, crush the stifling bureaucracy, and renew the revolution's vigor.

Red Guards Young workers and students who were the major supporters of the Great Proletarian Cultural Revolution in Mao's China.

 One Hundred Items for Destroying the Old and Establishing the New Read this document of support for Mao's socialist ideology and commitment to destroy the old ways of Chinese thinking by a student group of Red Guards.

Despite such extremism, the communist movement to reshape Chinese society largely succeeded. Mao promoted a model of social equality, known as the Iron Rice Bowl, in which the people shared resources—food, draft animals, farm equipment—and the peasants enjoyed status and dignity. Maoism generally improved life for the poorer Chinese, especially in the thousands of villages. An emphasis on preventive medicine included the training of villagers, known as barefoot doctors, as paramedics. As a result, most Chinese now enjoyed decent health care, where once famine and disease were dominant. Mass education raised literacy rates to the levels of those in industrialized nations. Peasants often appreciated the changes.

Women and the Family under Maoism

The communists also tried to overturn centuries-old, Confucian-influenced hierarchical relationships, including patriarchy, by raising the status of women. Two changes profoundly affected women's lives. First, a new marriage law in 1950 abolished arranged marriages, forbade men from taking concubines, and made divorce easier. Second, a land reform empowered women economically by expanding their property rights. Women now enjoyed legal equality with men and greater access to education. Consequently, women played a stronger public role, and more women worked for wages. Yet few held high national positions, and rural areas remained more conservative than the cities in social matters. In general, however, communism changed the family system, often to the advantage of both women and men. An emphasis on love matches rather than arranged marriages fostered closer emotional ties, and fathers spent more time with their families than had been common a generation earlier.

Religion and the Arts in the New China

As with social patterns, the communists often undermined traditional beliefs and culture. Calling religion a bond enslaving people, Mao moved to control religious behavior and marginalize religious institutions such as Christian churches, Buddhist monasteries, and Islamic mosques. By the 1970s, only a small minority of Chinese openly practiced religion. Only Buddhist, Christian, and Muslim leaders who cooperated with the state maintained their positions. Determined to use the arts as a weapon in the class struggle, Mao sought to foster a "people's art" created by and for the common people. Government policies broadened popular participation in creating art, literature, and music. For example, during the Great Leap Forward, party activists went out to collect literature written by common people. In Shanghai alone, 200,000 people produced 5 million poems. Everyone was urged to work hard for a better future and a new society. The politicization of the arts reached its peak during the Cultural Revolution, and opera and ballet became central for the new revolutionary art.

Woodcut by Ku Yuan, from Mei-shu, 1944

Chinese Political Art This woodcut, carved during the Chinese civil war of the late 1940s, was typical of the political art made during Mao's era. Entitled "Support Our Common People's Own Army," the woodcut shows Chinese peasants working together with the communist military forces.

The End of the Maoist Era

After Mao died in 1976, the Chinese took stock of Mao's legacy. The communists could claim many achievements. They had restored China to great power status and renewed the confidence of the people after thirteen decades of exploitation and invasion by Western nations and Japan. China was no longer a doormat; it even had nuclear weapons. The communists also took much of the sting out of poverty. Most Chinese, though enjoying little material surplus, could satisfy their basic food, housing, and clothing needs. The economy in 1976 was healthier and more broadly based than in 1949, and food was more evenly distributed. Public health and literacy rates had risen substantially.

Tension Under the Surface

Mao's policies, however, had also resulted in failures and political repression. China may have gained control of its economic destiny, but it was still poor by world standards. Mao had discouraged free enterprise and individual initiative. On city streets, few private cars interfered with the bicycles that most Chinese used to get to work or go shopping. Chinese wanted greater material benefits, such as better housing and more consumer goods. In addition, the fierce punishment of dissenters and the turmoil of the Great Leap Forward and Cultural Revolution had ruined numerous lives, and government coercion and corruption were resented. The unfulfilled promises, and the chaos of the Cultural Revolution, disillusioned young Chinese. Bitter disagreements had ripped the Communist Party leadership apart. Mao and his radicalism were often blamed for the problems; many were ready for change.

LO² Chinese Modernization

With Mao gone, Deng Xiaoping (dung shee-yao-ping) (1904–1997), a longtime Communist Party leader who had often clashed with Mao, came to power in 1978 and rejected Mao's view of a self-sufficient, ideologically pure China outside the world economy. Deng believed China needed to modernize its economy and embrace new technology in order to become a major power. In 1978, Deng announced the policy of Four Modernizations: the development of agriculture,

> "From 1978 to 1989, Chinese leaders pursued market socialism, a mix of free enterprise, economic liberalization, and state controls that produced economic dynamism."

market socialism
A Chinese economic program used between 1978 and 1989 that mixed free enterprise, economic liberalization, and state controls and that produced economic dynamism in China.

industry, military, and science and technology to turn China into a powerful nation by 2000. His pragmatic policies eventually transformed China into an economic powerhouse.

Economic Reform and Political Repression

From 1978 to 1989, Chinese leaders pursued market socialism, a mix of free enterprise, economic liberalization, and state controls that produced economic dynamism. This pragmatic approach was more concerned with economic results than socialist values. Twice purged for opposing Mao, Deng was fond of a Chinese proverb: "It doesn't matter whether a cat is black or white, only if it catches mice." China began to import technology, foreign expertise, and capitalist ideas to spur manufacturing for the global market and stimulate productivity. Deng improved ties with the United States, Japan, western Europe, and noncommunist Southeast Asia. Dazzled by China's huge potential market for their own products, Western companies were delighted to do business with the Chinese.

Capitalist Ideas in China

Introducing capitalist ideas, the government gradually allowed private enterprises, and ultimately both private and state-owned enterprises were competing with each other. In agriculture, Deng replaced Mao's communes with the contract system in which peasants could bid on and lease (but could not buy) land to work it privately. In many districts, this free market led to soaring productivity and prosperity, with per capita income in rural areas rising fourfold in the first decade. Tapping a skilled, industrious, but cheap labor force, hundreds of Western and Asian companies set up manufacturing operations, producing goods such as clothing and toys. China became a consumer society in the 1980s; even in small cities, shops stocked Japanese televisions and Western soft drinks. Over the next twenty-five years, the economy quadrupled in size, and foreign trade increased ten times over.

A Reawakening of Culture

Deng also loosened political and cultural controls, arguing that liberation of thought and open-mindedness were essential for progress. Western popular culture, especially films, rock music, and discos, won a huge audience; books and magazines from around the world became available; and foreign travelers backpacked in remote areas. Intellectuals, journalists, and artists enjoyed greater freedom; people who had been long silenced or imprisoned were heard from again. Deng also increasingly tolerated religion, allowing Buddhist temples, Muslim mosques, and Christian churches to reopen.

 East and Southeast Asia: An Annotated Directory of Internet Resources (*http://newton.uor.edu/Departments&Programs/AsianStudiesDept/*). A superb set of links, maintained at the University of Redlands.

Cultural figures, cowed during Mao's time, began to test the limits of free expression. Novels and short stories revealed the depth of suffering during the Cultural Revolution. Writers reflected a widespread public cynicism about politics; Chinese-made films won international acclaim, even as they contended with wary government censors. Rock musicians, especially Cui Jian (sway jen), a former trumpeter with the Beijing Symphony, became a major voice for alienated urban youth. One fan commented that "Cui Jian says things we all feel, but cannot say."[4]

Problems with Market Socialism

But although most Chinese applauded the ideological loosening and the growing economic options, the dramatic changes under Deng Xiaoping showed a dark underside in the later 1980s. Many districts had seen few benefits from the reorganization of rural life. Chinese authorities imposed one policy for the vast nation rather than allowing districts and villages to find a policy that worked for them. Under Deng's market socialism, some villagers benefited more than others, opening a gap between newly rich and poor. Prices rose rapidly. Corruption increased as bureaucrats and Communist Party officials lined their own pockets. Divisions among political leaders also deepened: Stalinists and Maoists viewed economic liberalization as undermining one-party rule, and the fall of communism in eastern Europe and the USSR in 1989 alarmed hardliners. But reformers, seeing strong controls as inhibiting initiative, pushed democracy as "the fifth modernization." In response, party leaders opposed to liberalization called for cracking down, arresting dissidents. The most famous dissident, a former Red Guard named Wei Jingsheng (way ching-sheng) (b. 1950), spent years in jail.

Tiananmen Square and the Beijing Massacre

In 1989, the tensions in Deng's China reached a boiling point, generating massive protests and subsequent government repression. Thousands of protesters, led by university students and workers, took over Tiananmen Square in Beijing, calling for the resignation of the most unpopular hardline leaders, an end to corruption, and a transition to a democratic system. The party hardliners, in alliance with Deng, purged the moderate party leaders and ordered the army to clear out the demonstrators in what became known as the Beijing Massacre. Sending in tanks, the army killed hundreds and arrested thousands, while millions around the world watched the violence on television. But many Chinese outside the cities, valuing stability more than vague promises of a better world, applauded the government crackdown. The protesters had miscalculated the prospects of democracy in a country with an authoritarian political tradition.

> *Cultural figures, cowed during Mao's time, began to test the limits of free expression.*

Economic Change and Political Challenge

After the Beijing Massacre, the communists modified market socialism into market Leninism, a policy whereby the Chinese state asserted more power over society, while also fostering an even stronger market orientation in the economy. The communist leadership reestablished control in political, social, and cultural spheres, tolerating less dissent than they had in the 1980s, but the economy became further privatized. China now did not fit either the communist or the capitalist model; the party eventually labeled it a socialist market economy.

Dissent and Suppression

However, the control of the Leninist, or one-party, state was not absolute. In some local elections, communist officials did permit competition between candidates, allowing nonparty members to run for office. Many dissenters were able to spread their message. For example, opponents of the environmentally damaging Three Gorges Dam project, constructed to control the Yangzi (yahng-zeh) River and provide electrical power, publicized their views, although they had little success in halting the expensive project, which forced several million people to relocate. However, the Chinese state, often arbitrary in its actions, did use the military and police to intimidate dissidents. China may execute more than 100,000 people per year, mostly criminals but including some accused of economic misbehavior or political opposition. Anxious to preserve national unity, China's leaders also suppressed dissent in Tibet and among Muslim Turkish groups in Xinjiang (shin-jee-yahng), in far western China.

China's Economic Rebirth

After 1980, despite the ebb and flow of party domination, China enjoyed the fastest economic growth in the world, often 10 percent per year, abetted by a get-rich-quick mentality among many Chinese. China's exports increased fifteenfold between 1980 and 2000. After 1989, the communist leadership sought popular support by offering consumer goods and wealth rather than political reform, providing shops with ample consumer goods and households with spending money. In the early days of reform, people aspired to the "three bigs": bicycle, wristwatch, and sewing machine. By 2000, they wanted televisions, washing machines, and video recorders. As a result of the economic growth, the urban middle class grew rapidly. By 2005, China had already moved ahead of Germany as the third largest economy in the world. Some experts have argued that the United States and China are the two countries that have most benefited from economic globalization.

Problems in Prosperity

Although the economic reforms beginning in 1990 have improved living standards for many Chinese, they have also produced numerous downsides. Economic dynamism has occurred largely in a few coastal provinces and special economic zones, where towering skyscrapers and huge, upscale shopping malls dot the landscape of cities such as Shanghai and Shenzen. Elsewhere, however, conditions have often deteriorated. Unemployment grows dramatically as state enterprises close and inflation skyrockets. Although laws make it illegal to migrate to another district without government permission, millions of peasants seeking jobs have nonetheless moved to cities, where they struggle. Another problem is that China has become the number-two producer of greenhouse gases that cause global warming, although its output, about one-eighth of the world total, is only half that of the United States. Water supplies have become badly overstretched, and, with private cars clogging the city streets where bicycles once dominated, smog blankets the cities.

Wealth and Resentment

Political and economic changes have influenced other areas of Chinese life. In the cities, the newly rich entrepreneurs—enjoying luxury cars, access to golf courses, and vacations abroad—have lives that are alien to most Chinese. By 2004, some 236,000 Chinese were millionaires. Even the middle class, chiefly working in business, can aspire to some of these benefits; even teachers, professors, and doctors leave their low-paying state jobs to open businesses or join foreign corporations. The wealthy flaunt their affluence, and the poor resent it. By 2005, peasant protests against seizure of village land to build polluting factories, luxury housing, and golf courses had become frequent. Meanwhile, the shift to market forces leaves millions unable to afford medical care and schooling for their children. Thanks to the decline in health care, especially in rural areas, experts estimate that between half a million and 1.5 million Chinese have HIV or AIDS. Yet, despite reduced job security and social services, people are now freer than before to travel, change jobs, enjoy leisure, and even complain.

As the Chinese society and economy have rapidly changed, the Communist Party has faced problems

> "The communist leadership reestablished control in political, social, and cultural spheres, tolerating less dissent than they had in the 1980s, but the economy became further privatized."

Mao could never have anticipated. A Communist Party that once viewed itself as the protector of workers and peasants now welcomes wealthy businessmen into its ranks. Yet, after Deng's death in 1997, the party split between hardliners and younger reform-minded leaders lost legitimacy; powerful provincial leaders whose first priority is economic growth increasingly ignore Beijing. The rapid economic growth raises questions as to whether Chinese leaders can resolve the increasing inequalities and spread wealth more equitably to check the growth of social tensions.

Social Change, Gender, and Culture

Chinese usually define human rights in terms of the right to property, food, and housing rather than the freedom of individuals to do as they like. Popular participation in government and unfettered free speech are lower priorities than order for average Chinese, but economic growth and the quest for wealth have led to a rapid increase in crime and links between criminal groups and government officials. The close connection between government and business corruption, underworld activity, and financial success has led to Chinese talking about the "Five Colors," or surest roads to riches: (1) Communist Party connections, (2) prostitution, (3) smuggling, (4) illegal drug dealing, and (5) criminal gangs. Mao's China had been one of the world's safest countries, but after 1978, desperate people turned increasingly to crime as the way to get ahead; drug dealing became rampant once again, serving the growing number of people who used narcotics for escape. Maintaining Confucian and Maoist attitudes, Chinese often view wealth as corrupting and mistrust rich business interests.

The New Woman in China

The recent economic and social changes offered women opportunities but also posed problems. Women's economic status has often improved, but many still face restricted gender expectations. The feminist journalist Xue Xinran (shoe shin-rahn) wrote that "Chinese women had always thought that their lives should be full of misery. Many had no idea what happiness was, other than having a son for the family."[5] Rather than remaining in their villages, millions of rural women prefer to migrate to the cities, providing much of the labor force for the new factories that have helped turn China into

China-Profile: Facts, Figures, and Analyses (*http://www.china-profile.com*). Offers useful information on China today.

an economic giant. Women commonly work long hours, and few occupy high positions in the national government, Communist Party, large businesses, or rural communities.

Women have also faced other new hardships. Since by the 1980s China already had 1 billion people, one-fifth of humankind, Deng Xiaoping introduced a one-child-per-family policy to try to stabilize the population and limit growth toward a maximum population of 1.4 billion. But the policy encouraged and sometimes mandated abortion, and, since traditional attitudes favoring sons remained, also resulted in widespread killing of female babies. With more boys than girls being born and raised, an imbalance in numbers between the sexes developed, resulting in a growing trade in the abduction and sale of women to desperate men who were unable to find wives.

Western Influence

Because of China's growing contacts with the larger world economy, Chinese society is affected by global entertainment and consumer culture. Western popular culture, which spread to China in the 1980s, has become a powerful force among youth. Every city has discos and clubs offering Western music, and Chinese imitators of Anglo-American bands have found a vast teen audience. Chinese consumers in many places are served by numerous McDonald's outlets, Hard Rock Cafes, Wal-Marts, and some 85,000 Avon agents selling American cosmetics and beauty products. Partly because of greater contact with the outside world, homosexuals, who faced discrimination under Mao, have been slowly coming out, especially in the cities, where gay bars are common. But Western culture is not the only outside influence. South Korean popular culture and consumer products—music, clothing, television dramas, movies, cosmetics—became very fashionable among young Chinese in the early 2000s, and much of the conversion of millions of Chinese to evangelical Christianity is a result of the thousands of South Korean Protestant missionaries in the country.

Read about Xue Xinran, one of China's most successful and innovative journalists, who explored the lives of Chinese women.

Those Chinese with enough money to afford satellite dishes and personal computers linked to the Internet have gained access to ideas around the world. To restrict the free flow of information and exposure to dissident writings, state officials have tried to crack down on cyberspace, passing laws restricting Internet use, but websites and blogs—

some 14 million are available to Chinese—proliferate rapidly, making monitoring difficult. The government sometimes shuts down newspapers and magazines whose reporting is too daring, but brave journalists and officials have risked punishment by openly criticizing censorship. Another source of knowledge about Western ideas comes from the several hundred thousand Chinese, including the children of high officials, who have studied in Western universities.

Falun Gong

Policies toward religion have been inconsistent. After temples and churches reopened in the 1980s, the government tolerated millions of Chinese turning to the faith of their ancestors: Buddhism, Christianity, Daoism, or Islam. But the government has cracked down on movements that are deemed a threat or that refuse to accept official restrictions. For instance, it has arrested leaders and members of the assertive, missionary *Falun Gong* meditation sect, a mix of Daoist, Buddhist, and Christian influences, and has tried to close down rapidly proliferating Christian churches that have remained independent of government approval. While the Chinese remain a largely secular people, both Falun Gong and the independent churches have millions of followers who seek a deeper spiritual existence and sense of community.

China in the Global System

China's relations with the wider world have been colored by its historical experiences, but in recent years, Chinese have seen their nation stand tall, strong, and increasingly rich. In 1997, they celebrated the peaceful return of Hong Kong from British colonial control. Hong Kong, a prosperous enclave whose towering skyscrapers, bustling shopping malls, and dynamic film industry made it a symbol of East Asian capitalism, was incorporated under the policy of "one nation, two systems." Despite China's occasional interference in Hong Kong politics, a vocal pro-democracy movement in Hong Kong helps to maintain the territory's freedoms. In 1999, Portugal also returned its small coastal colony of Macao, which it had first occupied in the 1500s, to Chinese control.

Since 1976, China has pursued a pragmatic foreign policy designed to win friends and trading partners but to also avoid entangling alliances. China has exercised regional influence by trading extensively with neighbors. It gradually improved relations with the United States and USSR, and cultivated diplomatic relations with other nations, while avoiding close ties that might limit its options. It also became increasingly active in the world community, joining international organizations such as the World Trade Organization. Some 200 million Chinese children study English.

The post-Mao foreign policy enhanced national power while accepting the constraints imposed by the global system. By the twenty-first century, China enjoyed tremendous influence in the world economy. Taking advantage of a cheap but resourceful labor force, thousands of foreign investors have come from the West, Japan, Southeast Asia, South Korea, and even Taiwan, opening factories and negotiating joint ventures with Chinese firms. Meanwhile, China has supported the U.S. economy, becoming the major buyer of the treasury bonds that financed the growing U.S. national debt in the early 2000s. Chinese enterprises have begun buying up companies based on manufacturing and natural resources in other nations. Thus China has become the world's most successful newly industrializing economy, buttressed by a vast resource base and a huge domestic market.

Yet China has met roadblocks in enhancing its global power, among them uncertain relations with its neighbors. The Chinese government, still claiming Taiwan as an integral part of China, continues to threaten that island with forced unification. Although economic and social links between China and Taiwan developed unofficially beginning in the 1980s, few in the island nation, which enjoys democracy and a much higher standard of living, want a merger with the mainland in the near future. Meanwhile, Chinese relations with Japan fluctuate: the two nations need each other economically but are also natural rivals, the Chinese remaining resentful of Japanese brutality during World War II. In contrast to sporadic Chinese–Japanese tensions, China has improved relations with once-bitter enemies such as South Korea and anticommunist countries such as Malaysia, the Philippines, and Australia. In many of these and other countries, large numbers of people are learning Chinese, and some 90,000 foreign students study in China. Nonetheless, historical resentment of Japan and the West provides a strong foundation of Chinese nationalism, which sometimes provokes anti-Japan or anti-U.S. protest demonstrations.

China's tremendous size, population, natural resources, military strength, national confidence, and sense of history have made it a major global power but with a much lower overall standard of living than that of North America, western Europe, Japan, and several industrializing Asian nations. Using such factors as literacy, life expectancy, and per capita income, the 2004 United Nations Human Development Report placed China only 94th out of 177 nations in overall quality of life. Nonetheless, China has been returning to its historical leadership as the Asian dragon and a major engine of the global economy. As during the long period of Chinese power and prosperity between 600 and 1800 C.E., China is once again a major force in world affairs.

LO³ The Remaking of Japan

Japan rose from the shambles of World War II to economic dynamism (see Map 27.2). In August 1945,

Interactive Map

Japan's major cities were largely destroyed by U.S. bombing and its economy ruined. The Japanese people were psychologically devastated. Yet, within a decade, the country had recovered, and after several decades of the highest economic growth rates in world history, Japan became the world's second largest economy. A system stressing cooperation rather than individualism provided the basis for economic and social stability in an overcrowded land. But by the 1990s, Japan was experiencing political and economic uncertainty.

> **"The post–World War II occupation by the United States aided Japan's recovery."**

Occupation, Recovery, and One-Party Democracy

The post–World War II occupation by the United States aided Japan's recovery. In the wake of defeat, the Japanese people felt disoriented. The emperor, Hirohito (here-o-HEE-to) (1901–1989), still a revered figure, asked them to cooperate with the Allied occupation forces, and they did. Japan was placed under a U.S.-dominated military administration, the Supreme Command of Allied Powers (SCAP), which was tasked with rebuilding rather than punishing Japan. The victorious World War II Allies also broke up Japan's empire. Japan lost Korea, Taiwan, and Manchuria, while the United States took control of the Ryukyu Islands, which were returned to Japan in the 1970s, and Micronesia. SCAP's mission was to demilitarize and democratize Japan, using the United States as the model, and to aid economic recovery. SCAP dismantled the Japanese military, removed some civilian politicians, and tried and hanged seven wartime leaders as war criminals. Fearing that punishing the emperor—a member of an imperial family that was more than 1,500 years old—would destabilize Japan, U.S. officials did not charge Emperor Hirohito with war crimes, but he was forced to renounce his godlike aura and become a more public figure.

Post-War Japan

SCAP fostered political and social changes; soon, a thriving political democracy took root. A new constitution guaranteed civil liberties and weakened the central government. It also had a unique feature: the document stated that the Japanese people forever renounced war as the nation's sovereign right. The first democratic elections, held in 1946, involved various competing political parties. For the first time in Japanese history, all adult citizens, including women, could vote. Women won other rights as well but were only partly freed from traditional expectations. U.S. officials hoped to foster further democratization, but, after the communist victory in China and the outbreak of the Korean War, the United States shifted its emphasis to integrating Japan into the anticommunist Western alliance, symbolized by the signing in 1951 of a formal U.S.–Japan peace treaty. U.S. military bases have remained in Japan ever since.

Economic Recovery

Under SCAP the economy gradually recovered, using the same sort of quasi-capitalist system—a mix of government intervention and free markets—that Japan had had between the 1870s and the early 1930s. Land reform heavily subsidized the peasantry, making them strong government supporters and bringing unprecedented prosperity to the rural areas. SCAP also attempted to break up entrenched economic power, but these efforts were less successful; as before World War II, large industrial-commercial-banking combinations, or conglomerates, still dominated business, making Japan more competitive in the world economy, but workers gained the right to unionize.

Democracy Returns

The policies implemented during the SCAP occupation, which officially ended in 1952, were most successful where U.S. and Japanese desires coincided or when the policies fit with the nation's traditions. Democratic government fit both criteria: the Japanese had enjoyed several decades of democracy before the Great Depression,

Map 27.2

Japan and the Little Dragons

Japan fostered the strongest Asian economy through the second half of the twentieth century, but in recent decades the Little Dragons—South Korea, Taiwan, Hong Kong, and Singapore—also have had rapid economic growth.

and many Japanese longed for a return to it. Borrowing from abroad also fit with Japanese tradition. For several millennia, the Japanese had been open to acquiring ideas from outside and adapting them to their own traditions. In the late 1940s, with conditions stabilized, Japanese leaders embarked on a strategy of capitalizing on peace to strengthen the nation.

Politics in a One-Party Democracy

Despite stresses, Japan's democratic political system flourished. As in many western European countries, a variety of political parties, including communists, Buddhists, and right-wing nationalists, competed for parliamentary seats. But since the early 1950s, one major party, the center-right Liberal Democratic Party (LDP), has dominated Japanese politics, applying generally conservative, pro-business, and pro-U.S. policies. The electoral system imposed by SCAP gave greater weight to rural voters, the conservative backbone of LDP support, rather than the more liberal urban voters. Prime ministers learned to negotiate with varied opposition parties as well as with diverse factions within the LDP. Nonetheless, critics believe that a political system dominated by one party and a few wealthy kingpins is at best a partial democracy.

However, the need to finance political careers and raise money for elections fostered political corruption. Powerful corporations and criminal gangs

> "Despite stresses, Japan's democratic political system flourished."

were leading financial contributors. Bribery scandals sometimes forced political leaders to resign. In 1993, the LDP fragmented in factional disputes, and various opposition parties gained support for several years. But in 2001, the LDP returned to power under a reform leader.

To protect its shores, Japanese leaders forged a military alliance with the United States, but the alliance brought Japan problems as well as benefits. Thanks to this alliance, which allowed U.S. bases in Japan, Japan's military spending remained meager compared with that of the United States and the USSR. This ability to devote more resources to the civilian economy and industrial development was a major reason for Japan's rapid economic growth. Despite these benefits of the military alliance with the United States, some leftist parties, labor unions, and militant student groups long opposed the U.S. presence, which they viewed as neocolonialism. Japanese also feared that U.S. military interventions made Japan a potential target for U.S. enemies. Remembering the horrors of World War II, especially the atomic bombings of Hiroshima and Nagasaki that killed some 200,000 Japanese, many Japanese favored pacifism and believed that Japan's economic strength protected them from attack. Yet, with U.S. support, Japan began increasing its military spending in the 1980s, and by 2001 it had the fourth largest military budget in the world, ahead of China. The decision of Japanese leaders in 2004 to send soldiers to support, in noncombat activities, the U.S. war effort in Iraq was widely unpopular in Japan and, to critics, violated the constitutional ban against engaging in war.

The Japanese Economy

Adapting capitalism to its own traditions, Japan has achieved phenomenal economic growth. Wartime destruction had required the rebuilding of basic industries using the latest innovations. Investing in new industries and high-tech fields, the Japanese became the world leaders in manufacturing products such as oil tankers, automobiles, watches, and televisions. From the 1960s through the 1980s, Japan's annual growth rate was three times higher than that of other industrialized nations; by 2000, Japan produced some 16 percent of the world's goods and services, twice that of third-place Germany. What some called Japan's economic miracle was particularly impressive considering the country's lack of natural

CHRONOLOGY

Japan Since 1945

1946–1952	SCAP occupation of Japan
1946	First postwar Japanese elections
1951	U.S.-Japan peace treaty
1960s–1989	Era of rapid Japanese economic growth
1989	Beginning of Japanese economic downturn
1993	Fragmentation of Liberal Democratic Party
1997	Asian financial collapse

Japanese Protest Political demonstrations are common in Japanese cities. During this protest in 2001, liberals and leftists criticized new middle-school textbooks, approved by the Education Ministry, that, the critics claimed, distorted history by emphasizing nationalist viewpoints and downplaying Japanese atrocities in World War II.

resources. Japan has limited productive farmland and no major rivers to produce hydroelectric power, so the Japanese must import minerals needed for industry, such as iron ore, tin, and copper. Oil obtained from Alaska, Southeast Asia, and the Middle East powers Japan's transportation.

The Japanese became known for innovative technologies and high-quality products. Among those technologies was its magnificent mass-transit sys-

tem, including the state-of-the-art bullet trains that whisked passengers around the country at 125 to 150 miles per hour and were always on time. Electronics manufacturers such as Sony, Atari, and Nintendo invented entertainment-oriented products that became part of life on every continent. In addition, millions of people, from Boston to Bogotá to Bombay, drove Toyotas, Hondas, and other Japanese-made cars.

By the 1980s, the Japanese enjoyed living standards equal to those of most western Europeans. With unprecedented affluence, the Japanese became Western-style consumers; everyone now sought to own cars, televisions, washing machines, and air conditioners. The Japanese also enjoyed the world's highest average life expectancy: seventy-nine or eighty years. A more varied diet, including more meat and dairy products than their ancestors had, produced taller, healthier children. Western foods and beverages became popular, and coffeehouses and bars dotted most streets in commercial and entertainment districts. The rural areas also shared in the prosperity, although life there remained harder. But there was an underside to Japanese economic success: many workers had to make do with part-time jobs offering few benefits, and a small but growing underclass of people had no permanent jobs or homes.

Japan's capitalist economy has differed in fundamental ways from those of other industrial nations. It was a form of mercantilism, a cooperative relationship between government and big business that became known as Japan, Inc. (Japan Incorporated). Under this system, the national government and big business worked together to manage the economy. The government regulated business, setting overall guidelines, sponsoring research and development, and leasing the resulting products or technologies to private enterprise. Most Japanese businesses accepted the government guidelines because they took a longer-term view of profitability than was common in the West. But government–business cooperation occurred chiefly in international trade, the country's lifeblood, and it was made easier by the economic dominance of large Japanese conglomerates. As in many other countries, the government aided Japanese businesses by erecting protectionist barriers and bureaucratic hurdles that impeded foreign businesses in the Japanese market.

Economic growth has generated new problems. As in the West, industrialization fosters wealth but also harms the environment. As cities grew,

Japan, Inc.
The cooperative relationship between government and big business that has existed in Japan after 1945.

"Despite the popular, contemporary image of the timid Japanese female, women have become more assertive."

developers cleared farmland and forests. Pollution of rivers and bays wiped out coastal fishing. Smoggy air, produced by automobile exhaust mixing with pollutants from smokestacks, is rampant; thousands of people have died or been made ill by toxic waste dumped by factories. In addition to declining environmental health, many younger people resent the long hours and sacrifices expected of employees in Japanese companies.

But Japan's business and factory life has played a role in Japanese success. The system takes advantage of Japanese cultural values, such as conformity, hard work, thrift, and foresight, while adding new innovations. The 30 percent of workers employed in larger Japanese companies have often enjoyed lifetime job security and generous welfare benefits such as health insurance, recreation, housing, and car loans. When a corporation has faced financial trouble, top managers usually accept responsibility for the problems, cutting their own pay rather than firing workers.

Japanese Society, Culture, and Thought

Urbanization and affluence have contributed to social change. Sixty percent of Japanese now live in cities of more than 100,000 people. With nearly 30 million people, Tokyo is the world's largest city. With car ownership so popular, some of Tokyo's legendary traffic jams take police several days to untangle. Rush hour on the subways has evolved into "crush hour," with city employees equipped with padded poles pushing commuters into overflowing cars to enable subway train doors to close. Yet, despite Mafia-like organized crime syndicates, Japan's cities are the safest in the world; experts attribute low rates of violent crime in part to strict gun control.

Life in Japan, Inc.

The economy has changed men's lives, especially in the growing middle class. University-educated men typically want to become salaried white-collar office workers for major corporations. Japanese observers describe the salaryman, an urban middle-class male business employee who commits his energies and soul to the company, accepts assignments without complaint, and takes few vacations. Many men working in white-collar jobs are also known as "7-11 husbands" because they leave for work at 7 A.M. and do not return until 11 P.M. After work they and their office mates socialize in restaurants, bars, and nightclubs while their wives take care of the home.

Women and Family Life

Meanwhile, while earning more money, gaining legal protections, and enjoying greater freedom, women still struggle for full equality in a hierarchical society obsessed with patriarchy and seniority. Most women are expected to marry and then retire from the workforce in their early twenties to raise children. According to one young woman, when she and other women graduated from a top Japanese university, "our bright appearance [for the graduation ceremonies] in vividly colored kimonos [traditional robes] was deceiving. Deep in our hearts we knew that our opportunities to use our professional education would be few."[6] As single women began to support themselves, the average age of marriage for women rose from twenty-two in the 1950s to twenty-seven in the 1990s. Accordingly, marriage rates have declined, alarming politicians.

Despite the popular, contemporary image of the timid Japanese female, women have become more assertive. Working against the patriarchal grain of society, feminist organizations and several prominent women's leaders have publicized women's issues, and working women have lobbied companies for equal treatment and pay. Some women have moved into middle management or prestige occupations, such as law, journalism, college teaching, and diplomacy. Yet, women also largely remain outside political and economic power, and only a few attain positions of political leadership.

Family life has gradually changed. Although the traditional arranged marriage remains common, increasing numbers of men and women select their own spouse. Also reflecting a rise in personal freedom, more Japanese get married late or opt to end unhappy marriages in divorce, a rare decision before World War II. Studies have suggested that, while

Japanese Women Commuters A female passenger boards a train compartment reserved for women in a subway station in Tokyo. Tokyo's subways are usually jammed with passengers, and special cars allow women to travel without fear of possible sexual harassment.

many wives are lonely and resentful with their husbands seldom home, the majority prefer spending their growing leisure time away from their husbands. The decline of marriage has also had an impact on homosexuals, making it easier for them to find social acceptance.

Urbanization, Population, and Immigration

Urban housing remains cramped, and the elderly complain of neglect by their children, who have no room for them in their small homes. Birth control and abortion had been widely practiced in overcrowded Japan for centuries; the renewal of these practices after World War II, along with lower marriage rates, has enabled Japan to stabilize its population at 120 million for several decades. Yet declining birthrates also pose an economic dilemma. By 2000, Japan had a birthrate well below replacement standards but did not promote immigration to provide new workers. By 2005, foreigners, mostly Chinese and Koreans, numbered some 2 million in Japan, less than 2 percent of the total population. By contrast, foreigners accounted for 5 percent in Britain, 10 percent in Germany, 12 percent in the United States, and 22 percent in Australia. Paying for benefits and services for the retired has imposed an increasing strain on those working. Despite laws banning discrimination, Japanese leaders have largely failed to elevate the status of the *Burakumin,* a despised underclass for centuries, who number some 1 to 3 million people and traditionally did jobs that were considered unclean.

Education

Youth face their own kinds of pressures. The rigorous education system, which produces a well-trained workforce, is based on stiff examinations. The entrance exam for

A Japanese Generation Gap

The rapid pace of change since World War II has fostered growing generation gaps in many nations. In 1993, the Japanese essayist Yoshioka Shinobu (born in 1948) discussed the differences in perceptions between his "baby boomer" cohort born in the decade after 1945 and those Japanese of the next generation. Yoshioka's experiences reflected the exciting era of social experimentation during his teenage years in the 1960s. By contrast, young people in the 1970s faced a tighter economy and less official tolerance of radical ideas and organized political protests.

Whenever I hear someone mention Japan's baby boomers, . . . I think back to a conversation I had . . . [in] 1976 at a rock concert. . . . The band had the latest sound equipment, but its talent was no match for its technology. Bored, . . . I struck up a conversation with two young girls. . . . They had run away from home . . . because they were sick of school, and had come to Tokyo in search of adventure. . . . They had lied about their ages to get part-time jobs, were sharing a tiny apartment, and from time to time went out to concerts. . . . I told them I thought they must be having the time of their lives.

"Your generation had it good," one of the girls answered. "When you ran away from home, there was rock music, underground theater, demonstrations, all kinds of things—you could do whatever you wanted. Our generation has to walk a tightrope, . . . and there's nothing to catch us if we fall. We lose our balance, we die. You guys might have walked a tightrope too, but you had a safety net below. If you didn't like it up on the rope, you could always dive down and let yourself be caught in midair. You could do whatever you wanted to."

She had hit home. So that's how we look in the eyes of someone ten years younger, I thought. My generation . . . had an entirely different understanding of itself. [We] . . . had many names . . .: the baby boomers, the Beatles generation, the anti-Vietnam [War] generation. . . . [Our radical student movements] did much to discredit the established political system, but our generation was more than just a new political force. We began new trends in music, theater, art, and social customs . . . that defied the existing structure of authority and social conventions. In those days, nothing was worse than a willingness to capitulate to the "system" and adopt its narrow conventions.

Consequently, we tried our hands at everything. Singers of traditional [music], who had put in years of hard work climbing the rigid, hierarchical ladder before they were allowed to perform publicly, suddenly found themselves displaced by our barely rehearsed bands and spontaneous concerts. Some put on plays in . . . tents set up in vacant lots, ridiculing the empty and imitative formalism of Japan's commercial theater. Others . . . took off nearly penniless to wander about in foreign countries—their adventureousness helped make travel abroad commonplace.

The two girls were saying that these experiences . . . were only possible because we had a safety net underneath us. . . . The girls had a point. When [my] generation was growing up, the . . . confusion of the early postwar years had given way to spectacular economic growth. . . . This . . . engendered confidence in liberal politics and democratic government, and it also created a willingness to forgive the unruliness of the younger generation. . . . If we were arrested [in antiwar demonstrations] it did not worry us much. . . . The runaway girls told me that the age of such optimism was over. . . . Between my generation and the next, attitudes toward change took a 180-degree turn. For us, changes in society and the individual were exciting and intrinsically valuable. For the younger generation, however, change is frightening and the source of insecurity.

Thinking About the Reading

1. How did Yoshioka's generation contribute to change?
2. What does the essay tell us about Japan's connection to the wider world?

Source: Shinobu Yoshioka, "Talkin' 'bout My Generation," in Merry L. White and Sylvan Barnet, eds., *Comparing Cultures: Readings on Contemporary Japan for American Writers* (Boston: Bedford Books of St. Martin's Press, 1995), pp. 119–122. Reprinted with permission by Yoshioka Shinobu.

the top universities is so rigorous that it is known as "exam hell." The Japanese school year is also longer than that in most other nations. These varied pressures, and the expectations of conforming to the values of mainstream society, have encouraged youth rebellion. University students have often supported left-wing political organizations that protest issues such as U.S. military bases or the destruction of farmland to development. Eventually, however, most young people return to the mainstream upon graduation from university and take jobs in the corporate world. Some who cannot conform emigrate elsewhere in search of a more free-spirited life (see Witness to the Past: A Japanese Generation Gap) .

Defining Japanese Identity

As they have done over the past two centuries, the Japanese have continued to blend traditional and modern cultures and beliefs, East and West. With old values and traditions under stress, Japanese artists and writers now ponder whether the historical process of synthesizing foreign and local ideas has been the nation's salvation or its bane. In 1993, a prominent writer observed: "We are up to our necks in Western culture. But we have planted a little seed. We are beginning to re-create ourselves."[7] Others contend that Japanese needed to become less inward and more global-minded.

The questions about Japanese identity are often analyzed in films and literature that have achieved worldwide recognition. While the Japanese film industry, the world's third largest, produces escapist, action films that gain a large audience at home and abroad, it also makes thought-provoking masterpieces that force audiences to reflect on Japanese life. One of the most skillful directors, Kurosawa Akira (kur-o-SAH-wa a-KEER-a) (1910–1998), was celebrated for films mixing a distinctive Japanese style and setting with universal themes. *Rashomon* (1950), for example, deals with the relativity of truth by examining one event, the killing of a feudal lord and the violation of his wife by a bandit, through varied eyes, including the murdered lord, the wife, the bandit, and a woodcutter who witnessed the act. The Japanese have the world's highest literacy rate (99.9 percent) and the largest numbers of newspaper readers, magazine subscribers, and bookstores per capita. Japan boasts several world-famous novelists, Kawabata Ysunori (ka-wa-BAH-ta yoo-suh-NOOR-ee) (1899–1972) being the first Japanese, in 1968, to receive the Nobel Prize for literature.

Continuity has long characterized Japanese popular culture. Every sport, art form, and religion that has appeared in the past 1,500 years still attracts followers. For example, Japanese remain passionate about sumo wrestling, a sport going back centuries, in which two large Japanese men attempt to push each other out of a small ring. At the same time, change is also characteristically Japanese. While performances of kabuki or bunraku, theatrical forms that appeared in the 1600s, still attract devoted audiences, and young Japanese women often master the even older tea ceremony, many more Japanese follow professional baseball teams consume Japanese comics, or *manga* (MAHN-gah), and animated films, or *anime* (AN-ih-may), that are popular worldwide. Modern Japanese, especially young people, have avidly adopted cultural forms from around the world.

A Secular Society

Industrialization and urbanization have accelerated the declining influence of organized religion. Some Japanese remain deeply religious: militant Buddhist groups claim several million followers, and various new religions based on Buddhist or Shinto traditions, or a mix of the two, have flourished by addressing material prosperity and family problems. Nonetheless, the contemporary Japanese are a largely secular people. In census questionnaires in 2000, while most Japanese described themselves as Buddhists, Shintoists, or both, less than 15 percent reported any formal religious affiliation. The weak influence of organized religions and their moral systems has not resulted in social breakdown, however. Japanese remain among the world's most law-abiding, peaceful citizens, but morality now is mostly derived from the fear of bringing shame on the family or group rather than fear of retribution by gods or ancestors. The reluctance to disgrace the family suggests that Confucianism, the Chinese ethical system that was imported into Japan 1,400 years ago, remains influential.

Japan in the Global System

The Japanese have had to readjust their views of the economy and international relations over the past several decades. Like their North American and European counterparts, Japanese companies have sought cheaper labor overseas, a practice that has cost Japan jobs. In 1989, the Japanese economy went into a severe downturn, due in part to overvalued stocks that caused a crisis on the Tokyo Stock Exchange, but also to global recession and competition from newly industrializing nations in Southeast Asia. Many Japanese investors went bankrupt, confidence was shaken, and more than 1 million workers were laid off. Only in the early 2000s did Japanese leaders, beginning to overcome political and bureaucratic inertia, introduce policies that fostered higher growth rates and renewed business confidence, but the recovery remained incomplete.

While comfortable as an economic powerhouse, the Japanese remain reluctant to assert their political and military power in the world, remembering how the attempt to dominate eastern Asia brought them disaster during World War II. Japan's main concerns are the continued health of the world economy and access to overseas resources and markets, the two pillars on which its prosperity has depended. Japan maintains a strategic alliance with its major trading partner, the United States, but the two nations have also remained keen economic rivals and engage in occasional trade disputes. Japanese leaders have also worked to promote peaceful exchange with China and South Korea, two countries with long memories of Japanese imperialism. Relations with China have been particularly strained, as the Chinese have demanded that Japan accept responsibility for World War II atrocities in China, such as the murder and injury of thousands of civilians known as the Rape of Nanjing, a Chinese city. Resurgent Japanese and Chinese nationalisms clash. As China and several other Asian nations rise economically, Japan faces more competition.

LO⁴ The Little Dragons in the Asian Resurgence

While China and Japan were rising to regional and global power, a few of their East Asian neighbors also achieved economic development. Known as the Little Dragons because their societies were strongly influenced by the region's dominant Chinese culture, these neighbors—South Korea, Taiwan, Singapore, and Hong Kong—built rapidly growing, industrializing economies. Except for Hong Kong, a British colony until 1997 and a bastion of free enterprise, these societies largely followed the Meiji Japan model of state-directed capitalism, which involved government intervention into otherwise free-market economies. They were also inspired by Japan's resurgence

after World War II. All the Little Dragons shared a Confucian cultural heritage that emphasized hard work, discipline, cooperation, and tolerance for authoritarian governments. They all achieved an export-oriented industrialization that dramatically raised incomes, reduced poverty, and forged high standards in health and education. For South Korea, however, this development came only after a brutal war that left a hostile, rigidly communist North Korea on the border, and Taiwan had to find its own path in the shadow of China.

The Korean War

The Korean War (1950–1953) was rooted in the Korean nationalism that, despite fierce repression, simmered during a half-century of harsh Japanese colonial rule, which was imposed in 1910 (see Chapters 23 and 24). While introducing some economic modernization, the Japanese arrested or executed Korean nationalists, conscripted Korean women to serve Japanese soldiers, and relocated thousands of Korean workers to Japan. To maintain their rule, the Japanese manipulated divisions within Korean society. Christians constituted one influential group that grew in number

> " To maintain their rule, the Japanese manipulated divisions within Korean society. "

CHRONOLOGY

The Little Dragons Since 1945

1948–1994	Kim Il-Sung's leadership of North Korea
1950–1953	Korean War
1954	U.S.–Taiwan mutual defense treaty
1980s	South Korean democratization movement
1989	First democratic elections in Taiwan
1989–1991	Collapse of Soviet bloc and Soviet Union
1997	Asian financial collapse
1998	Beginning of South Korean "sunshine policy"

during the twentieth century. By the 1940s, one-fifth of Koreans had become Catholics or Protestants. Inspired by Soviet modernization, another group of Koreans had gravitated toward communism during colonial times. In contrast to these who imported ideas, a majority of Koreans maintained their adherence to Buddhism and Confucianism, regarding these traditional beliefs as central to Korean identity. Although Christians, communists, and traditionalists commonly hated Japanese rule, and members of all groups worked underground to oppose it, they could not cooperate, and no unified nationalist movement emerged.

Kim Il-Sung and Syngman Rhee

Japan's crushing defeat by the United States in 1945 meant political liberation for Korea and a chance to reestablish the nation free of foreign interference. But the United States quickly occupied the southern half of the peninsula and the Soviet Union the north, bisecting Korea and making it a hostage to the Cold War. As the USSR and the United States imposed rival governments, unification quickly became impossible, alarming nationalists of all stripes. With Soviet help, in 1948, communists led by the ruthless Kim Il-Sung (KIM ill-soon) (1912–1994) formed a government in North Korea. A clever strategist who had lived for years in the USSR, Kim quickly built a brutal communist system, eliminated his opponents, and reorganized rural society. But the impatient Kim disastrously overestimated the revolutionary potential of the south, and he also misjudged the Americans, who were determined to stop the spread of Soviet influence.

The United States helped create and then supported a South Korean state headed by Rhee Syngman (REE SING-man) (1865–1965), better known in the West as Syngman Rhee. A longtime nationalist and politically conservative Christian from a powerful landlord family, the autocratic, inflexible Rhee imprisoned or eliminated his opponents and sparked a rebellion by leftist movements, which United States troops helped crush. Although less repressive than Kim's North Korean regime, Rhee's South Korea held some 30,000 political prisoners.

The Korean War and the Superpowers

These developments set the stage for the Korean War (see Map 27.3), a conflict that shaped East Asian politics for half a century. Both Korean states, threatening to reunify Korea with military force, had initiated border skirmishes. In this highly charged context, North Korea, probably with

 Interactive Map

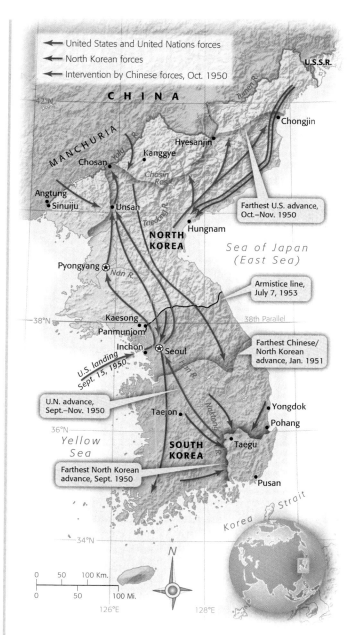

© Cengage Learning

Map 27.3
The Korean War

In 1950, North Korean forces crossed the 38th parallel and invaded South Korea, but they were then pushed back north by United Nations forces led by the United States. The intervention of China in support of North Korea pushed the United Nations forces south and produced a military stalemate, preserving the border between North and South Korea at the 38th parallel.

tacit Soviet and perhaps Chinese approval, invaded the South in 1950. The United Nations, then dominated by Western nations, approved a request by the United States to lead a military intervention to support South Korea, thus turning a Korean crisis into a

Cold War confrontation. U.S. President Harry Truman secretly planned a strike on North Korea with atomic weapons if North Korea's ally, the USSR, entered the war. But while the Soviets gave military supplies and advice to the North Koreans, they sent no combat troops.

The initiative shifted back and forth. United Nations troops, aided by U.S. air power, quickly pushed the North Koreans back across the north-south border. But U.S. general Douglas MacArthur's (1880–1964) decision to invade North Korea and push toward the Chinese border sparked a massive intervention by Chinese troops that drove back United Nations troops and turned a likely U.N. victory into a bitter stalemate. U.S. leaders had misjudged the Chinese willingness and capacity to fight. When the war ended in 1953 with peace talks, the boundary between the Koreas remained in the same place it was before the war but was now a heavily fortified zone. The war was a stalemate, but both sides claimed victory.

> 66 The postwar rise of South Korea was nearly as dramatic as that of Japan. 99

The Cost of the Conflict

The war proved costly in human terms, involving perhaps 1 million military dead and 1 or 2 million civilian Korean deaths. The U.N. forces suffered some 43,000 killed and more than 100,000 wounded, 90 percent of them Americans. South Korean military casualties numbered more than 100,000 dead and 160,000 wounded, and the North Koreans lost more than 300,000 soldiers. Chinese casualties were also high, more than 400,000 dead. The fighting also generated millions of Korean refugees who wandered the countryside during the war, and both North and South Korea were left in economic shambles.

The Remaking of South and North Korea

The postwar rise of South Korea was nearly as dramatic as that of Japan. Closely allied to the United States, the South Korean governments evolved from highly repressive military dictatorships in the 1950s to liberal democracies with free elections after the early 1990s. All regimes aimed at economic development. The United States protected the South Korean regimes from any North Korean threats by permanently stationing troops and supplying generous economic and military aid. Five decades after the war, some 40,000 U.S. troops and more than one hundred U.S.-owned nuclear weapons remained in South Korea.

Mixing government intervention and free markets, South Korea has enjoyed enormous economic growth. The nation invested heavily in the Middle East, Southeast Asia, and Russia, often to secure oil supplies, while exporting automobiles and electronic products. By the mid-1990s, South Korea had joined the ranks of advanced industrial nations, the first non-Western nation to make that transition since Japan in the late nineteenth century. Having acquired a standard of living South Koreans could only have dreamed of two decades earlier, with nearly full employment and universal literacy, the country became a high-technology model. Prosperity reshaped society. Both boys and girls received free education through age twelve. South Korean women benefited from new job options, often in the professions and business; marriage rates declined and average births per woman fell dramatically from 6 in 1990 to 1.6 in 2005.

Economic growth has also fostered political change. Democracy movements had begun in the 1960s, but they often faced government repression. In 1980, the dictatorship brutally crushed an uprising in a southern province that began when some five hundred people demonstrated, demanding an end of martial law; in response, paratroopers landed and began slaughtering the protesters and local people who got in their way. Hundreds of thousands of enraged Koreans then drove the troops out of the city, only to face a much larger force, which shot their way into the city, killing more than two thousand people. Eventually, political tensions diminished. During the later 1980s, governments fostered more liberalization, tolerated a freer press, and made overtures toward former enemies in the USSR and China. By the early 1990s, four decades after the Korean War ended, the South Korean people had forced a change in direction. With the growth of the middle class and organized labor, democracy flowered, though it was sometimes sullied by political corruption.

 Little Dragons Asian Studies (*http://coombs.anu.edu.au/WWWVL-AsianStudies.html*). A vast online resource maintained at Australian National University, with links to hundreds of sites.

But while the country fostered economic dynamism, political participation, and personal freedom, problems arose. Many rural people and unskilled workers did not share in the prosperity, and factories expected long hours from poorly paid workers. Thousands of Koreans, many of them middle class, emigrated to the United States. Furthermore, while South Koreans often welcomed the security provided by U.S. bases, others viewed the bases as an affront to Korean nationalism. Koreans on both sides of the demilitarized zone yearned for reunification. After years of hostility, North and South Korea finally achieved a wary peaceful coexistence. A dialogue begun in the later 1990s resulted in limited cross-border trade and allowed a few South Koreans to visit family members in North Korea they had not seen since the early 1950s. Televised images of South Koreans tearfully embracing aging parents or siblings mesmerized the nation. In 2000, South Korean president Kim Dae-jung (kin day-chung) (b. 1925), a liberal reformer, visited North Korea, an event that would have been unthinkable a decade earlier. Yet national reconciliation remains a distant dream.

South Korean Economic Growth One of South Korea's major, most diverse enterprises, the Hyundai Corporation, formed in 1976, engages in shipping, manufacturing, and trade, producing, among other products, chemicals, machinery, and information and telecommunications equipment. The ships in this company dry dock are being readied to carry Hyundai-made cars to distant markets around the world.

Stalinism in North Korea

North Korea's leaders chose a completely different path from that taken by South Korea. The communist leader Kim Il-Sung's decision to reunite Korea with force, which led to the Korean War, proved a mistake that devastated the country, though North Korea quickly recovered with aid from China and the USSR. From 1948 until his death in 1994, Kim was the nation's president, head of the Communist Party, and commander of the armed forces. He also created a personality cult around himself as the "Great Leader." To ensure loyalty and deflect blame for failures, Kim purged 70 percent of communist cadres and jailed or executed thousands of dissidents.

North Korea adopted a mix of Stalinism and Maoism to shape the economy and society. Soviet-style economic planning and central direction emphasized heavy industry and weapons at the expense of consumer goods. As a result, North Koreans did not enjoy the rising living standards of South Koreans. To inspire the population to work hard, Kim invented a political philosophy of self-reliance that was heavily influenced by Mao Zedong's policy of relying on a country's own strength and limiting contact with the

world economy. North Korea benefited from a favorable industrial base built during Japanese colonial times, since it contained more than three-quarters of Korea's factories and mines. For several decades, the North Korean economy outshined its South Korean rivals. The huge military establishment, however, drained these resources.

Politically, North Korea stressed group loyalty, ultranationalism, and independence from foreign influence, following the model of Korea's hereditary Yi dynasty and Confucian bureaucracy of the early nineteenth century. A small government and military elite, isolated from the bleak existence of the peasantry and workers, enjoyed special privileges and controlled the people by using regimentation and restricting information. The government required each citizen to register at a public security office and urged people to spy on their families and neighbors. To prevent people from hearing contrary views or unapproved culture, the only radios allowed were fixed to receive only the government station. Political prisoners and people caught trying to flee to China or South Korea faced long terms in harsh concentration camps or even execution.

By the 1990s, the regime faced stresses that resulted in increasing international isolation. The economy declined rapidly, thanks to poor management, commodity shortages, and rigid policies. Satellite photos of the Korean peninsula at night revealed the stark differences in electrical power between a brilliantly lit South Korea and a completely dark North Korea. U.S. diplomatic pressure isolated the regime, while efforts to strike back, such as assassination attempts on South Korean leaders, earned North Korea a reputation as an unpredictable terrorist state. When the Soviet bloc collapsed in 1989, Russia and China demanded that North Korea pay cash for oil and other imports.

North Korea's problems increased after Kim Jong-Il (chong-ill) (b. 1942), known as the "Dear Leader" as well as for his reputation as a playboy, succeeded his deceased father in 1995. When the nation soon faced mass starvation, Kim requested and received food aid from South Korea and Japan, and as the food shortages continued, the United Nations also sent food, much of it supplied from the United States. Even with the aid, many people died or were malnourished. Thousands of North Koreans fled to China to find food and work. Observers predicted the regime would collapse, but it avoided that fate. Thanks to isolation and tight information control, most North Koreans believed the state's propaganda.

North Korea became a concern in both regional and world politics. By the late 1990s, its military force was twice as large as South Korea's and apparently had a capability for building nuclear weapons. But with both Koreas possessing lethal military forces, war became less likely. This perception encouraged the search for common ground in pursuing national unification. The economic disasters of the 1990s, especially food shortages, softened the North Korean position, and after 1998, South Korea actively sought better relations to reduce the threat from its dangerous northern neighbor and its unpredictable leader.

Taiwan and China

The triumph of the Chinese communists on the mainland in 1949 led to the relocation of Chiang Kai-shek and his Nationalist government to the mountainous, subtropical Taiwan island, where he reestablished the Republic of China. Two governments claiming to represent China created a long-term diplomatic problem for the world community. Both the governments of the People's Republic on the mainland and of the Republic on Taiwan regarded the island as an integral part of China rather than a separate nation; this "one China policy" was endorsed by most of the world. Taiwan's people built a prosperous society but

remained divided about the nation's future and its long-term relationship to China.

Taiwan's Place in Asia

Taiwan had only become a part of Chinese territory in the seventeenth and eighteenth centuries, when the Qing dynasty claimed the island and Chinese began settling the island in large numbers, relegating the small Malay-speaking native population to mountain districts. In 1910, Taiwan became a Japanese colony. Japan ruled Taiwan less harshly than it did Korea, financing industrialization that produced a higher standard of living. After World War II, China reclaimed the island, but in 1947, local resentment of Chiang's heavy-handed regime led to an island-wide uprising. Chiang dispatched 100,000 troops from the mainland, who killed 30,000 to 40,000 Taiwanese in quelling the unrest.

As Chiang's Republic of China collapsed in 1948–1949, the president and 2 million mainlanders moved to Taiwan, taking with them their government, the Nationalist Party, the remaining military forces, the priceless art collections of the national museum, and China's national treasury. These mainlanders and their descendants eventually constituted some 15 to 20 percent of the total island population, which numbered 23 million by 2005. The minority mainlanders dominated politics, the economy, and the military. The majority Taiwanese, although Chinese in culture and language, often considered the mainlanders colonizers. Chiang viewed Taiwan as a temporary refuge, because he hoped to reconquer the mainland and then return there. But after his death in 1972, mainlanders cultivated better relations with the Taiwanese.

Taiwan's Economic Boom

Learning from their defeat in China, and using we generous U.S. aid, the Republic's leaders promoted rapid industrial and agricultural growth and a more equitable distribution of wealth. As a result, the peasantry prospered. As in South Korea and Meiji Japan, the economy mixed capitalism and foreign investment with a strong government role. Light industry and manufacturing eventually accounted for half of Taiwan's economic production and the bulk of exports. Taiwan became the world's third largest producer of computer hardware. Between the early 1970s and the late 1990s, it enjoyed more years of double-digit growth than any other nation. By the 1980s, the economic indicators far surpassed those on the mainland, including a per capita annual income of $8,000, approximately 99 percent of households owning a color television, 92 percent literacy, and a life expectancy of seventy-five years. Rapid development, however, also brought problems, including environmental destruction, traffic congestion, political corruption, and a severe economic slowdown in 1997.

> "Many of the East and Southeast Asian nations forged closer economic cooperation, with Japan and China forming the hubs."

Modernization in Taiwan

Modernization has challenged Chinese values and traditions. The small roadside cafés selling noodle soup and meat dumplings, a beloved mainstay of local life for generations, are often unable to compete with U.S. fast-food restaurants and convenience stores. While Confucian values, such as the emphasis on hard work, have fostered the material success of the Little Dragons, some Taiwanese have worried that Confucian ethics, including respect for parents and concern for the community rather than the individual, are threatened. In response, the Taiwan government has supported traditional Chinese culture by mandating the teaching of Confucian ethics in the schools. Despite the modernization, traditional Chinese culture remains stronger in Taiwan than in the mainland. More than 90 percent of the people describe themselves as, like their ancestors, Buddhists, Daoists, Confucianists, or a mix of the three ancient traditions.

Like South Korea, Taiwan until the later 1980s followed the authoritarian Little Dragon political model. For several decades, Chiang Kai-shek and his family controlled the island with a police state and made it illegal to advocate making Taiwan permanently independent of China. For four decades, Chiang's political party, the Nationalists, ruled as the sole legal party, but in 1989, nudged by a growing middle class seeking liberalization, they permitted opposition candidates to run in elections. Gradually, the regime recognized civil liberties, including the freedom of speech and press. The 2000 elections swept into office the Democratic Progressive Party (DPP), largely supported by the native Taiwanese; many party leaders, reflecting widespread Taiwanese opinion, advocated that Taiwan become a separate nation, a stance that angered both the Nationalist leaders on Taiwan and the communist leaders on the mainland. However, by 2005, elections showed reduced support for the DPP.

Taiwan and the Mainland

China has remained Taiwan's permanent challenge. Fearing an invasion to forcibly annex the island, Taiwan lavishly funded its military, kept a large standing army, and bought the latest fighter jets and gunboats, at the same time maintaining a defense alliance with the United States and allowing U.S. bases. But in 1978, the United States recognized the People's Republic as China's only government, embraced the one-China policy, and withdrew diplomatic recognition from its longtime ally, the Republic of China on Taiwan. However, the United States remains diplomatically and economically tied to Taiwan. In the later 1980s, Taiwan and China began to improve relations; trade has grown substantially, and many people from Taiwan have visited the mainland. However, doubts about whether China will move toward political liberalization, as well as alarm at occasional Chinese military exercises being conducted near Taiwan, have precluded any serious negotiations on reunification. Thus Taiwan's political future remains an open question.

The Little Dragons in the Global System

The rise of the Pacific Rim, including China, Japan, and the Little Dragons, in the late twentieth century reshaped the global system. The one-quarter of the world's population living along the western edge of the Pacific Basin established policies that allowed them to outpace the West and the rest of the world in economic growth while maintaining political stability. By the 1990s, the Little Dragons had diversified into high technology, thereby posing an economic challenge to Japan and the West.

Some economic trends suggested that the Pacific Rim nations were becoming an Asian counterpart to the European Community. Many of the East and Southeast Asian nations forged closer economic cooperation, with Japan and China forming the hubs. But in 1997, an economic meltdown hit South Korea, Taiwan, Japan, and the industrializing economies of Southeast Asia. As businesses closed, unemployment soared. By the early 2000s, South Korea and Taiwan had regained some of their dynamism but still faced challenges. But on the global stage, China and Japan will undoubtedly play major roles in the years to come, and in many respects, East Asia has returned to its historical role as a key engine of the world economy.

 Listen to a synopsis of Chapter 27.

CHAPTER 28

Rebuilding Europe and Russia,
Since 1945

Learning Outcomes

After reading this chapter, you should be able to answer the following questions:

LO¹ What factors fostered the movement toward unity in western Europe?

LO² How did the rise of welfare states transform western European societies?

LO³ What factors contributed to political crises in the Soviet Union and eastern Europe?

LO⁴ How did the demise of the communist system contribute to a new Europe?

❝This [united] Europe must be born. And she will, when Spaniards say "our Chartres," Englishmen "our Cracow," Italians "our Copenhagen," and Germans "our Bruges." Then Europe will live.**❞**

—Spanish writer Salvador de Madariaga, 1948[1]

Jacques Delors (deh-LOW-er) faced a challenge. Born in 1925, this French banker's son turned socialist politician had lived through a tumultuous time. Now, after holding high economic positions in the French government, he had dedicated himself to building a united Europe. In 1985, he became president of the European Commission, established to further European political cooperation. His goal was to reconcile national loyalties with support for a united Europe. In December 1991, Delors convened the leaders of twelve European nations, already closely linked through a common economic market, in the Dutch city of Maastricht. Communicating his sense of mission, he prodded them to transform the economic and political alliance begun in the late 1940s, and expanded in the 1950s, into a more comprehensive union.

Test your knowlege before you read this chapter.

What do you think?

Inherent weaknesses in the Soviet system caused its ultimate demise.

Strongly Disagree					Strongly Agree	
1	2	3	4	5	6	7

This meeting on Europe's future took place in the same month that the Soviet Union (USSR) dissolved. With their biggest communist rival no longer a threat, European leaders created a new European Union that would stretch from the Atlantic to the western frontier of Russia, allowing people to cross borders without passports and permitting trade goods to pass freely from country to country. A single currency, the *euro*, would also unite these states. Persuaded by Delors, conference leaders signed the Maastricht Treaty, and it was later ratified by voters in all member nations. While facing bumps in the road, the European Union, given the centuries of European strife that preceded it, was nonetheless a huge achievement.

From 1945 until 1990, three themes dominated European history: (1) the Cold War shaped by the United States and the USSR, the world's rival superpowers; (2) the rebirth of western European wealth and power; and (3) the movement toward European unity represented

◀◀ Fall of the Berlin Wall In 1989, as communist governments collapsed in eastern Europe, peaceful protesters climbed on top of the Berlin Wall, which had already been decorated with graffiti. The wall, which divided communist East and democratic West Berlin, was soon torn down.

> "Emotionally traumatized by the war and its atrocities, Europeans also saw their prestige in tatters around the world."

by the Maastricht Treaty. The trauma of two world wars had fostered a drive for unity by consensus of the nation-states involved rather than through military might. This movement accelerated after 1989, when the governments allied to the USSR collapsed and communism was largely abandoned, opening the way for a new, interconnected Europe in a post–Cold War world in which the United States held dominant power.

LO¹ Western Europe: Revival and Unity

Western Europe emerged from the ashes of World War II economically and morally bankrupt, yet made a rapid recovery with aid from the United States. Most western European societies reestablished working multiparty democracies that accorded personal freedom to their citizens. Beginning in 1947, however, Europe was split into two mutually hostile camps, western and eastern Europe, each with a different model of postwar reconstruction and rival military forces. Gradually, West Germany, France, and Britain served as the core of a rebuilt, increasingly unified European community and were able to regain influence in the world.

Recovery and the Remaking of Nations

World War II had devastated Europe in the 1940s. Some 50 million lives were lost; major cities were reduced to rubble; and Europe's economic potential was cut by some 50 percent. Transportation, food, housing, and fuel were in short supply. The chaos of war and the redrawing of political boundaries after the war caused massive displacement, including 10 million Germans who were forced to leave eastern Europe. Emotionally traumatized by the war and its atrocities, Europeans also saw their prestige in tatters around the world. War crimes trials held by the victo-

rious Allies in Nuremberg, Germany, in 1946 condemned Nazi leaders to death and declared crimes against humanity, especially genocide, to be indefensible. A Dutch thinker wrote that the old Europe was dead and beyond redemption.

The Marshall Plan

Economic growth provided the foundation for a new Europe. In 1947, the U.S. secretary of state, former general George Marshall (1880–1959), who had directed the U.S. army through World War II, proposed that the United States assist in restoring the economic health of Europe. This initiative, the Marshall Plan, created a recovery program aimed at preventing communist expansion and spreading liberal economic principles, such as free markets. Between 1948 and 1952, the United States offered $13 billion in aid, about half going to Britain, France, and West Germany. In exchange, American business enjoyed greater access to European markets. The Marshall Plan restored agricultural and industrial production while bolstering international trade. The rapid economic resurgence from 1948 to 1965 was unmatched in world history except for Japan's recovery in the same years (see Chapter 27).

The European Movement

The British leader Winston Churchill (1874–1965), who served twice as prime minister (1940–1945, 1951–1955), predicted the coming Cold War in 1946, warning "an iron curtain" had descended, dividing capitalist western Europe from communist eastern Europe. This Cold War division, however, as Churchill also predicted, helped stimulate a western European movement for cooperation. Eight hundred delegates met at the Hague, in Holland, in 1948, where they called for a democratic European economic union and the renunciation of national rivalry, generating what soon became the "European Movement."

After the war, western Europeans made a commitment to sustain parliamentary democracy. This was true for both the republics and the surviving constitutional monarchies, including Belgium, Britain, the Netherlands, and the Scandinavian nations, where kings and queens remained symbols of their people but held little power. Four major states—France, Italy, West Germany, and Britain—were the most influential in postwar western Europe. Longtime dictators

New political alignments emerged. Given the frequent conflicts between France and Germany in the past, political stability in western Europe depended on improved relations between these two nations, as well as on German recovery from war. Charles De Gaulle (1890–1970), the French Resistance general who largely dominated French politics between 1947 and 1969, overcame centuries of hatred by making French–German reconciliation the cornerstone of French policy. Similarly, the West German leader, Konrad Adenauer (ODD-en-HOUR) (1876–1967), sought a more cooperative relationship with France. This reconciliation was furthered in the 1960s by West German chancellor Willy Brandt (1913–1992), a fervent anti-Nazi who accepted German responsibilities for the war and the new borders imposed after the war, which awarded a large chunk of German territory to Poland. The improved French–German relationship owed much to economic growth. West Germany's economy rapidly expanded in the 1950s and 1960s, benefiting from a collaborative relationship with France.

opposed to change were overthrown and replaced by democrats in Spain, Portugal, and Greece in the 1970s. The end of colonial empires, and the loss of revenues from them, also reshaped European politics.

Politics in Post-War Europe

New political parties and movements took shape. On the right, parties calling themselves Christian Democrats, which had been closely tied to the Catholic Church before World War II, freed themselves from

Basque Terrorism The extremist Basque nationalist movement, the ETA, has waged a terrorist campaign against the Spanish government for decades. They have assassinated dozens of people and exploded bombs at government targets in cities and towns, resulting in the sort of destruction shown here after one attack.

AP Images/EFE/Javier Belver

Greens
A twentieth-century political movement in western Europe that rejected militarism and heavy industry and favored environmental protection over economic growth.

British Commonwealth of Nations
A forum, established by Britain in 1931, for discussing issues of mutual interest with its former colonies.

> "In the thirty years after World War II, most European colonizers abandoned their efforts to quell nationalist movements in Asia and Africa and started to leave their colonial territories."

Nationalism and the End of Colonialism

In the thirty years after World War II, most European colonizers abandoned their efforts to quell nationalist movements in Asia and Africa and started to leave their colonial territories. The British, whose empire had occupied an area 125 times larger than Great Britain, realized that imperial glory was past. In 1947, they bowed to the demands of Indian nationalists and recognized the independence of India. The Dutch, facing a determined nationalist resistance, reluctantly abandoned their lucrative colony, Indonesia, in 1950. By the mid-1960s, the British had turned over most of their colonies in Africa, Asia, and the Caribbean to local leaders, retaining control of only a few tiny outposts. Post-imperial Britain continued financial assistance and capital investment to many former colonies and maintained a more formal connection with them through the British Commonwealth of Nations, which the British established in 1931 and which comprised fifty-three states by 2000.

By contrast, the French and Portuguese only grudgingly recognized the inevitable. In the mid-1940s, nationalist rebellions broke out in French-controlled Algeria and Vietnam, which France attempted to quell at the cost of much bloodshed. In his criticism of France's use of torture against rebels in Algeria, the French philosopher Jean-Paul Sartre asserted that "France is struggling in the grip of a nightmare it is unable either to flee or to decipher."[2] In 1954, unable to defeat communist-led rebels, the French withdrew from Vietnam, and in 1962, they left Algeria. Eventually, France established close relations with most of its former colonies, including an enduring economic connection that critics considered a form of neocolonialism, or indirect domination. Portugal wasted lives and wealth violently resisting decolonization, but after democrats overthrew the longstanding fascist dictatorship, it granted its African colonies independence in 1975.

Europe and NATO in the Cold War

Beginning in 1946, the Cold War—shaped by rivalry between the two superpowers, the United States

clerical patronage. Still emphasizing Christian values and protecting the traditional family, these conservative parties were influential in a half-dozen countries, including West Germany and Italy. But because of corruption, these parties had lost considerable support by the 1990s. At the same time, parties on the left competed for support. The social democratic parties, which favored generous welfare programs to provide a safety net for all citizens, came to power in several countries soon after the war and moved toward state ownership of large industries such as steel and railroads. Eventually most of these parties, such as the British Labor Party, abandoned state ownership and economic planning for free markets. Meanwhile, the western European communist parties, with whom the social democrats had largely avoided cooperation, declined rapidly, maintaining a substantial following only in France, Italy, Portugal, and Spain. By the 1980s, a new political movement had had an impact: the Greens favored environmental protection over economic growth and militarism.

Western Europe was not immune to civil unrest. The desire of ethnic minorities for their own nations spurred unrest and terrorism in Spain and Northern Ireland. A chronic ethnic conflict embroiled Spain, where the Basque people, who live mostly in the north and speak a distinct language, sought either autonomy within, or independence from, Spain. An underground Basque independence movement, known as ETA (for "Basque Homeland and Freedom"), has carried out assassinations, bombings, and other terrorist acts against people linked to the Spanish government. Similarly, for decades in Northern Ireland, Catholics and Protestants fought for self-determination, causing a state of civil war as thousands died in terrorist violence. A power-sharing agreement resolved the conflict in the early twentieth century, but tensions remained.

and the USSR—influenced the various European nations' roles in the world. The USSR helped install communist governments in eastern Europe and East Germany, while the United States assumed the burden for protecting western Europe. In 1947, the U.S. president, Harry Truman (president 1945–1953), formed a policy, known as the Truman Doctrine, that asserted that the United States was the leader of the free world and was charged with defending countries threatened by Soviet pressure.

A World Divided

Strong European and U.S. fears of possible Soviet attack led to the formation in 1949 of the North Atlantic Treaty Organization, commonly known as NATO, a military alliance that linked nine western European countries with the United States and Canada. NATO allowed coordination of defense policies against the USSR and its communist allies, known as the Soviet bloc, in case of attack. Permanent U.S. military bases were set up in NATO countries, especially West Germany. The Soviets responded in 1955 by forming the Warsaw Pact, a defense alliance that linked the communist-ruled eastern European countries with the USSR (see Map 28.1). By the 1980s, senior officers in NATO and the Warsaw Pact had spent their careers preparing for a war that never came.

 Interactive Map

The Cold War and NATO were partly a response to the postwar division of Germany. Each of the four World War II allies—the United States, Britain, France, and the USSR—had an occupation zone in Germany and had also divided up the pre-1945 German capital, Berlin. In 1948, the three Western powers united their occupation zones. Angered by this move, the USSR blockaded Berlin to prevent supplies from reaching the city's Western-administered zone by land through Soviet-controlled East Germany. For a year, the allies supplied the city by airlift to the Berlin airport. In 1949, the USSR stopped the blockade and allowed the creation of the Federal Republic of Germany, or West Germany, while forming its own allied government, the German Democratic Republic, or East Germany. By 1954, West Germany was fully sovereign and soon joined NATO.

Reassessing Alliances

In the 1960s, Cold War fears slackened in Europe as the danger of actual war faded, leading western Europeans to reappraise their foreign policies. Some Europeans, especially in Britain, promoted the U.S. alliance, while others grew to resent U.S. power. Most Europeans opposed the American war in Vietnam, which American leaders justified as an effort to stop the spread of communism in Asia, as well as U.S. interventions to overthrow left-leaning governments in Latin America. The West German chancellor Willy Brandt, a Social Democrat, began rethinking Cold War attitudes in 1969. Although Brandt was strongly anticommunist, his policy of ostpolitik ("eastern politics") sought a reconciliation between West and East Germany and an expanded western European dialogue with the USSR. This policy led to a thaw in West Germany's relations with the Soviet bloc and gave hope to eastern Europeans who wanted more freedom. Gradually, western Europeans, by building their own military forces, became less reliant on U.S. power and played a larger role in NATO. Despite such differences, however, the alliance and NATO remained strong.

> " In the 1960s, Cold War fears slackened in Europe as the danger of actual war faded, leading western Europeans to reappraise their foreign policies. "

Truman Doctrine
A policy formed in 1947 that asserted that the United States was the leader of the free world and was charged with protecting countries like Greece and Turkey from communism.

NATO
(North Atlantic Treaty Organization) A military alliance, formed in 1949, that linked nine western European countries with the United States and Canada.

Soviet bloc
In the twentieth century, the Soviet Union and the communist states allied with it.

Warsaw Pact
A defense alliance formed in 1955 that linked the communist-ruled eastern European countries with the USSR.

ostpolitik
("Eastern politics") A West German policy, promoted by Chancellor Willy Brandt, that sought a reconciliation between West and East Germany and an expanded dialogue with the USSR.

From Cooperation to European Community

As a result of wartime economic destruction, increasing U.S. political and economic power, and the costs of decolonization, during the 1940s, Europeans lost influence to the United

© Cengage Learning

Legend:

Participants in the Marshall Plan

$ Member of NATO,* formed in 1949

Member of COMECON,** formed in 1949, and the Warsaw Pact, organized in 1955

Member of the European Common Market, formed in 1958

Iron Curtain

* North Atlantic Treaty Organization
** Council for Mutual Economic Assistance

0   200   400 Mi.
0   200   400 Km.

ICELAND
Reykjavik
Joined Common Market, 1973
Arctic Circle
20 W

ATLANTIC OCEAN

North Sea

IRELAND
Dublin
Joined Common Market, 1973

UNITED KINGDOM
London
U.S. loan of $3.5 billion, 1946
Exploded first atomic bomb, 1952
Joined Common Market, 1973

NORWAY
Oslo

SWEDEN
Stockholm

FINLAND
Helsinki

DENMARK
Copenhagen
Joined Common Market, 1973

Baltic Sea

NETHERLANDS
Amsterdam
BELGIUM
Brussels
LUX.
Joined Common Market, 1973

WEST GERMANY
Bonn
Joined NATO, 1955

EAST GERMANY
West Berlin
East Berlin
Berlin blockade, 1948–1949

POLAND
Warsaw

UNION OF SOVIET SOCIALIST REPUBLICS
Moscow
Exploded first atomic bomb, 1949

40 E
60 N

20 E

Volga R.
Don R.
Dnieper R.

Caspian Sea

FRANCE
Paris
Exploded first atomic bomb, 1960
Withdrew from NATO, 1966

SWITZ.
Bern

AUSTRIA
Vienna
Joined NATO, 1955
Zones of occupation ended, 1955

CZECHOSLOVAKIA
Prague
Communist coup, 1948
U.S.S.R. invasion, 1968

HUNGARY
Budapest
Revolution, 1956

ROMANIA
Bucharest
Danube R.

Black Sea

ITALY
Rome

Corsica
Sardinia

YUGOSLAVIA
Belgrade
Tito-Stalin schism, 1948

ALBANIA
Tiranë
Left COMECON, 1961
Withdrew from WP, 1968

BULGARIA
Sofia

GREECE
Athens
Truman Doctrine, 1947
Joined NATO, 1952
Joined Common Market, 1981

TURKEY
Ankara
Truman Doctrine, 1947
Joined NATO, 1952

CYPRUS
Nicosia

40 N

PORTUGAL
Lisbon
Joined Common Market, 1986

SPAIN
Madrid
Joined NATO, 1982
Joined Common Market, 1986

Balearic Is.

Mediterranean Sea

Sicily

N

Post–World War II Europe was divided by Cold War politics into communist and non-communist blocs. Most western European nations joined the NATO defense alliance. Western Europeans also cooperated in economic matters. By 1989, the Common Market had expanded from six to eleven members. The Soviet bloc counterpart, COMECON, had eight members.

States. The Bretton Woods agreement on international monetary cooperation, negotiated by representatives of forty-four countries in 1944, reshaped the world economy by making the U.S. dollar, pegged to the price of gold, the staple currency for Western nations. Faced with declining economic influence in the world, Europeans concluded they had no choice but to cooperate with each other.

In 1949, ten western European nations formed the Council of Europe, which sought to operate on the basis of a shared cultural heritage and democratic principles. In 1950, the Council produced the European Convention on Human Rights, the root of a Europe-wide justice system and court. But some leaders wanted more, especially Jean Monnet (MOAN-ay) (1888–1979), a French economist and former League of Nations official who was often called the "Father of United Europe," and French prime minister Robert Schuman (1886–1963), a strong proponent of French–German reconciliation. The two men wanted to make further war in Europe not only unthinkable but impossible. To encourage better economic coordination, they devised a plan for a European Coal and Steel Community (ECSC), which was finally formed with the signing of the Treaty of Paris in 1951. The ECSC promoted European economic stabilization and became the beginning of a framework for unity and peace. But some European nations, including Britain, feared loss of economic independence and declined to join.

The Common Market

Building on the foundation of the ECSC, the Common Market, later known as the European Community (EC), was formed in 1957 with six members: France, Italy, West Germany, the Netherlands, Belgium, and Luxembourg. The new organization included a customs union to remove tariff barriers between members, thus opening frontiers to the free movement of capital and labor. The members also set a plan for preserving peace and liberty by pooling economic resources, and they called upon other Europeans to join in their efforts. Soon others did: the EC added Britain, Ireland, and Denmark in 1973.

The EC created unprecedented economic unity in the world's largest free-trade zone, but it only slowly generated political unity. The founders dreamed of a united Europe: societies that depend on one another, they reasoned, will not go to war. But the EC weathered many disagreements as member nations squabbled to get the best deal for their own farmers or businesses, and the British periodically threatened to quit the grouping. Every member economy had to adapt to the laws of the marketplace, dumping uncompetitive industries. Despite such challenges, the EC greatly reduced old national tensions. The members eventually established an elected European Parliament, based in Brussels, Belgium, to devise policies that encouraged cooperation and standardization.

The European Community fostered unprecedented economic growth in the 1960s (see Map 28.2). With higher wages and greater purchasing power, families bought automobiles, washing machines, refrigerators, and televisions. Interactive Map More people worked in the service sector and fewer in agriculture. The middle classes grew rapidly, while blue-collar workers shared middle-class aspirations. Consumer markets reached from Europe's sprawling cities into remote villages, transforming them. Europeans invested in railroads and mass transit—subways and commuter trains—to make transportation more convenient. Yet prosperity did not eliminate all poverty or regional disparities. For example, industrialized northern Italy remained much wealthier than largely agricultural southern Italy.

Economic Breakdown

Despite the growing cooperation and the successes it fostered, western Europe still faced mounting economic problems. Europeans were hurt by American decisions that led to the dismantling of the Bretton Woods international monetary system. In 1971, with the U.S. economy undermined by the war in Vietnam, President Richard Nixon devalued the U.S. dollar, the staple currency of the Western nations, and ended its parity with gold. These moves destabilized world trade, triggering soaring prices and trade deficits. Then in 1973, European economies were brought to a standstill by a quadrupling of oil prices, followed by a short embargo on oil exports by the major oil-producing nations, which were angered by Western support of Israel. Frustrated motorists waiting in long lines at gas stations showed how vulnerable prosperity could be in the global system—and that noxious

GDP per capita

- Over $40,000
- $30,000–40,000
- $25,000–29,999
- $20,000–24,999
- $15,000–19,999
- $10,000–14,999
- Under $10,000

© Cengage Learning

Map 28.2
Europe's Gross Domestic Product

The gross domestic product, or the official measure of the output of goods and services in a national economy, provides a good summary of a nation's economic production. In the early twenty-first century, Norway, Ireland, and Switzerland were the most productive European countries on a per capita basis, while former Soviet bloc nations had the weakest performance.

air, toxic waste, and other environmental concerns were the apparent price of industrialization.

Cooperation also could not avert other economic problems deriving from global economic patterns. The end of cheap energy and growing competition from industrializing Asian nations and Japan hurt local European industries and workers. Aging fac-

tories, often decaying and inefficient, scaled back operations or closed, causing high unemployment in industrial cities such as Birmingham and Manchester in England. Jobless young people, living in bleak rowhouses or apartments and surviving on welfare payments, sometimes turned to drugs or crime. By 1983, unemployment rates in western Europe had risen to 10 percent. Some Europeans, blaming their problems on immigrant workers, gave a boost to right-wing, anti-immigrant parties. Capitalizing on the economic problems, free-market conservatives often regained political power, and once in power, they penalized striking workers and weakened labor unions.

> "By the 1990s, both white-collar and blue-collar Europeans worked fewer hours each year than their counterparts in the United States and Japan."

LO² Western European Societies and Cultures

In the ashes of World War II, the wartime British prime minister, Winston Churchill, wrote, "What is Europe? A rubble heap, a charnel house, a breeding ground for pestilence and hate."[3] Seeing the need for change, western European nations embarked on various experiments to improve the quality of life for all of their citizens. The main experiment was the blending of capitalism and socialism. The economic boom from the late 1940s to the 1970s allowed most western European states to construct social welfare programs that fostered political stability, ensured public health, and eliminated poverty for most citizens. Gender relations, family life, and sexual attitudes were also reshaped, while musicians, philosophers, and churches addressed the changing times.

Social Democracy

The rise of western European welfare states—government systems that offer their citizens a range of state-subsidized health, education, and social service benefits—and the high quality of life they fostered, owed much to an influential political philosophy called social democracy. Social democracy derived from socialists in the early 1900s, who eventually promoted a mixing of liberal democracy, market economies, and a safety net for workers. Since 1945, social democratic parties have governed or been the dominant opposition in many Western countries.

Since the 1940s, social democracy has meant a mixed capitalist-socialist economy, a commitment to parliamentary democracy and civil liberties, support for labor unions, and the goal of moderating the extremes of wealth and poverty. As a result, workers in northern and central Europe gained more rights and protections than workers anywhere else in the world. In West Germany, for example, they received generous pensions and gained seats on the boards of directors of the enterprises that employ them. Whatever their occupation, Europeans have often valued leisure at the expense of work. By the 1990s, both white-collar and blue-collar Europeans worked fewer hours each year than their counterparts in the United States and Japan.

Advantages and Disadvantages

Citizens in nations influenced by social democracy have received generous taxpayer-funded benefits from the state. Europeans tend to define welfare not just as assistance to the poor, as Americans do, but as protections to ensure that everyone enjoys better living standards and opportunities. Free education through the university level (but with stiff university entrance exams) has helped people from working-class and farming backgrounds to move into the middle and upper classes. Governments also subsidize housing for the elderly, child care and support, and unemployment insurance. Extensive mass transit makes travel and commuting affordable for all. Meanwhile, socialized medicine, such as the British National Health Service, which opened in 1948, removed the fear of serious illness and greatly improved public health. Northern European nations now have the most equitable distributions of income in the world and have nearly eliminated slums and real poverty.

These successes have come at some cost. Although the welfare states help create social stability, when economic growth rates level off, the states cannot meet all of the fresh demands placed on them. Funding the welfare programs has required high taxes, often half of a citizen's annual income, and worker protections inhibit companies' flexibility. Furthermore, many people with modest incomes, especially immigrants, live in drab apartment blocks or houses, often far from potential jobs and schools. Still, the Scandinavian nations, which were poor a century ago, have claimed both the strongest social

Swedish Father and Child Swedes have been the most innovative Europeans in social policy, including adopting in 1975 a law requiring employers to grant parental leave. While women mainly take advantage of the law, some men, including this man with his child, take off the full allotted time.

democratic governments and the world's most prosperous societies. The annual Human Development Report, issued by the United Nations, ranked Norway and Sweden as having the highest quality of life in the world in 2004.

Conservative Reaction

Beginning in the 1980s, the welfare states experienced more problems related to a downturn of the world economy. For decades, governments had paid for social services by borrowing against future exports, a strategy known as deficit spending. But falling export profits placed the welfare systems under strain, forcing cutbacks in benefits, and also prompted nations to cut spending for military defense. To enhance their competitiveness, companies began downsizing, thus putting pressure on generous unemployment programs. In some countries, conservative parties gained power and began to modify the welfare systems, as did the British government led by Prime Minister Margaret Thatcher (governed 1979–1990), a free-market enthusiast.

But the conservative regimes did not dismantle welfare state institutions such as national health insurance, which remained hugely popular. Furthermore, the economic problems, unlike those caused by the Great Depression of the 1930s, did not bring violence or political instability. While occasionally a political party with an anti-immigrant or anti–European Union platform has gained a following, the welfare state provides stability. Even most free-market conservatives have accepted its broad framework, although they seek to make it more efficient and cost effective.

> 66 Beginning in the 1980s, the welfare states experienced more problems related to a downturn of the world economy. 99

EUROPA—Gateway to the European Union (*http://europa.eu/index_en.htm*). Provides information on many topics.

Social Activism, Reform, and Gender Relations

Western European societies changed dramatically in the decades since 1945. A serious challenge to mainstream society came in 1968, when youth protests broke out in France that were aimed at the aging, autocratic president Charles De Gaulle, an antiquated university education system, and the unpopular U.S. war in Vietnam, France's former colony. University students took to the streets, fighting pitched battles with police, who responded with teargas. Inspired by the student protesters, industrial workers called a general strike, bringing some 10 million workers into the streets. Although De Gaulle outmaneuvered the protesters by rallying conservatives, raising workers' wages, and calling for a new national election, the protests begun in Paris soon spread to Italy and West Germany. Lacking strong public support, Europe's student protests soon fizzled. Still, De Gaulle resigned a year later after the public rejected, in a referendum, his proposals to reorganize the French government.

Crime and Punishment in Post-War Europe

Europeans also dealt with social problems common to all industrialized nations, such as drug and alcohol abuse and high divorce rates. But European attitudes and responses to the problems were often different from those in other countries. In contrast to the United States, for example, which has harshly punished drug use and trafficking, by the 1980s, western European legal systems generally treated drug use and minor drug sales as social and medical issues rather than criminal ones. Other laws in Europe also differed from those elsewhere in the world. Europeans generally opposed and abolished capital punishment, and most European nations enacted strict gun-control laws, which fostered low rates of violent crime.

The Sexual Revolution

Read about Simone de Beauvoir, the French feminist and philosopher who had a profound influence on the contemporary women's movement.

Attitudes toward marriage and gender relations also shifted in Europe. After World War II, governments tried to revitalize traditional cultural attitudes, such as the view that women were chiefly homemakers and that families should have many children. But in the 1960s and 1970s, changing

> "The lives of both men and women were affected by the changes in work, politics, and family life that the women's movements helped foster."

attitudes toward sexual activity, often known as the sexual revolution, began to undermine conventional practices. The contraceptive pill, which remained illegal in some Catholic countries until much later, gave women control over their reproduction and sexuality. Changing social attitudes moderated the social shame of divorce, extramarital sex, and unmarried cohabitation, and pornography and obscenity laws were relaxed.

Inspired by feminist thinkers such as the French philosopher Simone de Beauvoir (day bow-VWAR), women's movements grew in strength across Europe and, by the 1970s, pressed their agendas more effectively. Feminists in general wanted legal divorce, easier access to birth control, the right to abortion, and reform of family laws to give wives more influence; they first found success in Protestant countries but later made headway in Catholic nations. In 1973, Denmark, which had legalized some limited abortions in the 1930s, became the first nation to allow abortion on request. Although Pope John Paul II (pope 1978–2005) reiterated the long-standing church ban on contraception, abortion, and divorce, many Catholics ignored their church on these matters. During the 1970s and 1980s, most Catholic nations, including Italy and Spain, followed the earlier examples of France, Britain, and Germany and legalized both divorce and abortion.

Changing Attitudes toward Women, Marriage, and Homosexuality

The lives of both men and women were affected by the changes in work, politics, and family life that the women's movements helped foster. Women increased their political power in part because they had won the right to vote and constituted a majority of the electorate. Men and women now shared the responsibility for financially supporting their families: by the 1980s, women were half the workforce in Sweden, one-third in France and Italy, and one-quarter in conservative Ireland. Women moved into the professions, business, and even politics, at various times heading governments in Britain, Germany, Iceland, and Norway. Even Ireland, where patriarchy remained strong, in 1991 elected its first woman president, social democrat Mary Robinson (b. 1944), who was an outspoken law professor, feminist, single parent, and supporter of homosexual rights. As they became wage earners, women became less dependent on men. Yet, so few women had been able to achieve high corporate positions even in egalitarian Norway that, in 2006, Norway's social democratic government outraged business leaders by requiring that 40 percent of the board members of large private companies must be women.

As a result of less rigid gender roles, marriage patterns and attitudes about homosexuality also gradually changed. In the 1970s, the popular culture still held up the model of the married heterosexual couple, but by the 1980s, more men and women than before remained single. In 1998, 15 percent of women and men between twenty-five and twenty-nine years old in western Europe lived on their own. Increasing personal independence and mobility fostered small nuclear families instead of the large extended families of old, especially in northern Europe. Homosexuals also began to enjoy equal rights. Organizing to change discriminatory laws and attitudes, reform movements began in Switzerland in the 1930s and, after World War II, in several other countries. Nonetheless, in the 1950s, many governments continued to prosecute homosexuals: for example, in West Germany between 1953 and 1965, some 99,000 men were convicted under still-existing Nazi-era laws prohibiting homosexual activity. Laws opposing homosexual behavior began to be reformed or eliminated during the 1960s and 1970s, and most societies developed more tolerant attitudes. By 2001, most of northern Europe had passed laws recognizing domestic partnerships, and discrimination against homosexuals had ebbed. Several nations, including the Netherlands, Belgium, and Spain, legalized homosexual marriage in the early twenty-first century.

Immigration: Reshaping European Cultures

Population movements had been a feature of western European history for centuries, but in the later twentieth century, this pattern took a new turn as several million immigrants settled in various European countries. In response to economic growth that created labor shortages in northern Europe in the 1950s and 1960s, people from poorer southern Europe migrated north in search of better jobs and pay. They were soon joined by Turks, Algerians, Moroccans, and people from West Africa and the Caribbean, who were fleeing even harsher poverty. Meanwhile, many Indians, Pakistanis, and Bangladeshis sought a better life in their former imperial power, Britain, while emigrants

left the former Dutch colonies for the Netherlands. By 1974, 10 percent of the working population of France and West Germany were foreign-born.

The Impact of Immigration

The immigration reshaped European societies. By the early twenty-first century, immigrants constituted 10 percent of the population of Germany, 6 percent in France, and 5 percent in Britain. Major European cities such as Paris, London, and Berlin took on an international flavor. Islamic culture flourished in cities such as Hamburg (Germany) and Marseilles (France), where Arab- and Turkish-language radio stations had large audiences. Indian and Pakistani sundry goods and grocery shops and restaurants became features of English city life. People of Asian and African descent were elected to parliaments in countries such as Britain and the Netherlands.

The immigration also posed problems of absorption into European society, especially fostering tensions between whites and the nonwhite immigrants. Over the years, as Turks, Arabs, Africans, and Pakistanis arrived to do the low-paying jobs nobody else wanted and then settled down, they and their local-born children faced discrimination and sometimes violent attack by right-wing youth gangs. Neo-Nazis in Germany sometimes set fire to immigrant apartment buildings, and young toughs in England boasted of "Paki-bashing," or beating up people from the Indian subcontinent. While older immigrants often clung to the cultures and attitudes they brought from their Asian or Middle Eastern villages, such as a husband's authority over his wife and the preference for arranged marriages, their children struggled to reconcile the contrast between their conservative traditions with the materialistic, individualistic, secular societies of Europe.

After 1989, vanishing jobs put both immigrants and local people on the unemployment rolls or in competition for scarce work. Despite the economic problems, illegal immigration also increased. In 2001, perhaps 700,000 people fleeing extreme poverty or harsh repression illegally entered the European Union. Since the mid-1990s, anti-immigrant (especially anti-Muslim) movements have emerged even in famously tolerant countries like Denmark and the Netherlands, especially after the terrorist attacks against the United States in 2001, which shocked Europeans. Facing particular hostility since 2001, some Muslims, rejecting Western culture as immoral and

 European Union in the US (*http://www.eurunion.org/eu/*). Provides a wealth of data on the European Union.

criticizing the Islam brought by their parents from North African, Turkish, or South Asian villages as corrupted by Sufi mysticism, have become more devout than their parents. The most alienated Muslim youth, seeking a purpose in life, have turned to militant Islamic groups for direction.

Importing American Culture

Despite such social challenges, western Europeans enjoyed a resilient cultural life that was enriched by immigrants and imports. The influence of mass culture from the United States became more widespread than before the war. American cigarettes, Coca-Cola, and chewing gum symbolized postwar fashions, while African American jazz musicians often settled in Europe in the 1950s and 1960s to escape racism at home. Young people also enjoyed popular entertainments from outside of North America, such as Caribbean reggae music, Latin American dances, and Japanese animated films. Yet Europeans often treasured entertainers who reflected local culture, such as the waiflike French singer Edith Piaf (1915–1963), who was known for her sad, nostalgic songs.

Rock music helped define youth cultures, allowing young people to embrace an exciting, edgy music that their parents often disliked. After rock emerged in the United States in the mid-1950s, it rapidly gained a huge following in Europe, where American rock stars such as Buddy Holly, Elvis Presley, and Chuck Berry enjoyed massive popularity. By the 1960s, European musicians inspired by U.S. rock and blues had reshaped popular culture. The Beatles, young working-class men from Liverpool, England, matured as musicians and became the symbols of the younger generation for a decade. Beatlemania, as their impact was called, reached around the world.

Eventually, rock music introduced more personal reflection and social commentary. By the mid-1970s, a new style of rock, called punk, appeared that expressed social protest. Punk became especially influential in Britain, where working-class youth faced limited job options. The provocative songs of a leading British punk group, the Sex Pistols, deliberately insulted the monarchy and offended the deeper values of British society, much to the delight of their fans. As punk's energy dissipated, it was replaced in the 1980s by escapist dance music, but influenced later musicians significantly.

African and Asian Cultures in Europe

Cultural forms from Asia and Africa also influenced European culture. For example, in Britain the popular bhangra music emerged from a blending of Indian folk songs with Caribbean reggae and Anglo-American styles, such as rock, hip-hop, and disco. Using a mix of Indian and Western instruments, bhangra became popular with both white and Indian youth in Britain. By the 1980s, bhangra had spread to the Indian diaspora communities in continental Europe, North America, and the Caribbean, sustaining Indian identity. By the early 2000s, bhangra's appeal had widened, becoming a truly world music.

Cultural life was influenced not only by the wave of cultural imports but also by local developments. The creative cinema of France, Italy, and Sweden developed a global audience by depicting psychological and social dilemmas common to all people in a rapidly changing world. Literature also reflected political change. Writers known as postcolonialists sought to escape the world-view shaped by Western colonialism and dominance. For example, the India-born British writer Salman Rushdie (b. 1947), a Cambridge University–educated former actor from a Muslim family, criticized Western society, especially the Western treatment of Asian peoples. At the same time, however, he challenged what he considered the antimodern sensibilities of Islamic culture. His books, especially *The Satanic Verses* (1988), a critical look at Islamic history, created an uproar among conservative Muslims, even inspiring the rulers of Iran to issue death threats, forcing Rushdie to go into hiding.

bhangra
A popular music that emerged in Britain from a blending of traditional folk songs brought by Indian immigrants with Caribbean reggae and Anglo-American styles, such as rock, hip-hop, and disco.

existentialism
A European intellectual approach contending that truth is not absolute but constructed by people according to their society's beliefs.

Thought and Religion

Philosophy flourished in postwar Europe, continuing a secularizing trend that had been strong for more than a century. For several decades after the two world wars, Europeans struggled to understand their horrors, which seemed to contradict the emphasis on rational thought and tolerance that had been building in Europe since the Enlightenment. In seeking answers, some turned to new philosophies, while others struggled to reconcile religious faith and modern life.

Jean Paul Sartre

Existentialism, a philosophy whose speculation on the nature of reality reflects disillusionment with Europe's violent history, became an influential school of secular thought. The French philosopher Jean Paul Sartre (sahrt) (1905–1980) and the French feminist thinker Simone de Beauvoir (1908–1986), his longtime partner, transformed existentialism into a philosophy with wide appeal. Sartre argued that individuals are defined by a reality that they tend to view as the work of fate or imposed by others. He advised people to find their own meaning and not let others determine their lives. In his view, people must accept responsibility for their actions, and this should lead to political engagement to create a better society. Sartre became active in left-wing political movements, such as those promoting world peace and banning nuclear weapons. Sartre provided a philosophy that every individual could act upon and that reached across political boundaries. During his life, Sartre achieved a level of fame unusual for a philosopher; when he died in 1980, thousands of people attended his funeral.

Deconstruction and Postmodernism

Meanwhile, like existentialism, other influential philosophies debated the nature of reality. Marxism fostered an understanding of social class and gender inequality, but as a political philosophy it lost many followers after the 1960s. In contrast to Marxism, which offers a certitude about truth and the workings of society, an approach called deconstruction, pursued by the Algeria-born Frenchman Jacques Derrida (DER-i-dah) (b. 1930), claimed that all rational thought could be taken apart and shown to be meaningless. Derrida questioned the entire Western philosophical tradition and the notion, still popular in Europe and North America, that Western civilization was superior to other cultures. Inspired by Derrida's questioning of accepted wisdom, by the 1990s, literature and scholarship were influenced by the intellectual approach known as postmodernism, which contends that truth is not absolute but constructed by people according to their society's beliefs. Even scholars, postmodernists argue, cannot completely escape the prejudices of their gender, social class, ethnicity, and culture. Other thinkers, among them many Marxists, rejected the postmodernist notion that truth is relative and objectivity impossible.

Rethinking Religion

While philosophy flourished, organized religious life declined. The horrors of World War II and postwar materialism had destroyed many people's faith. Churchgoing declined precipitously, leaving churches in many cities semideserted. Polls in the 1990s showed that, whereas some two-thirds of Americans had a moderate or strong religious faith, less than half of western Europeans did. Meanwhile, conflicts between rival Christian churches, once a source of tension, lost their intensity. Formed in 1948, the World Council of Churches, based in Switzerland, brought together the main Protestant and Eastern Orthodox churches. Appalled by the Holocaust that had been perpetrated by the Nazis against the Jews, Christian thinkers began acknowledging their faiths' relationship to Judaism by referring, for the first time in history, to Europe's *Judeo-Christian* heritage. Although the Jewish population in Europe decreased sharply because of the Holocaust and post–World War II emigration to Israel and the Americas, Jews remained a key religious minority. Christians had also to deal with another faith: by 2000, immigration and conversions had made Islam the second largest religion in France, Belgium, and Spain after Roman Catholicism.

The Roman Catholic Church, which remained largely conservative but still politically influential, had to address the changes in European societies. Pope John XXIII (pope 1958–1963) began a comprehensive reform with the convocations of church leaders known as the Second Vatican Council (1962–1965), or Vatican II. Vatican II launched the most radical church changes since the Council of Trent in the mid-1500s had responded to the Protestant Reformation. It no longer required Latin in the liturgy, and it removed blame from the Jews for the death of Jesus. Even after Vatican II, however, many Catholics followed only the church teachings that suited them, widely ignoring, for example, the ban on artificial birth control, while some conservative Catholics turned to more traditionalist movements opposing Vatican II.

Vatican II: The Catholic Church Engages the Modern World Read how Pope John XXIII opened the Second Vatican Council, at which the Catholic Church reformed itself in significant ways.

LO³ Communism in the Soviet Union and Eastern Europe

Like western European countries, the Soviet Union changed after World War II. For several generations during the Cold War, the USSR was the major political, military, and ideological rival to the North American and western European nations. The USSR was the last great territorial empire and enjoyed substantial natural resources while maintaining a powerful state and a planned economy. But by the 1980s, the Soviet system was showing signs of decay.

The Soviet State and Economy

The USSR emerged from World War II as the world's number-two military and economic power, no mean achievement given the ravages of war in that land: 20 million killed, millions left homeless, cities blasted into rubble, the countryside laid waste. The trauma of that war helps explain the hostility toward the West:

> "The lives of both men and women were affected by the changes in work, politics, and family life that the women's movements helped foster."

CHRONOLOGY

The Soviet Union and Eastern Europe, 1945–1989

1945–1948	Formation of communist governments in eastern Europe
1948	Yugoslavia split from Soviet bloc
1953	Death of Stalin
1955	Formation of Warsaw Pact
1956	Khrushchev de-Stalinization policy
1956	Uprising in Hungary
1957	Launch of *Sputnik*
1960	Sino–Soviet split
1961	Building of Berlin Wall
1962	Cuban Missile Crisis
1968	Prague Spring in Czechoslovakia
1979–1989	Soviet war in Afghanistan
1980	Formation of Solidarity Trade Union in Poland
1985	Gorbachev new Soviet leader

Russians resented the sacrifices they had been forced to make because of Germany's conflict with Britain and France. These experiences reinforced traditional Russian paranoia, fostered by two centuries of invasions by Germany or France, and led Russians to maintain a huge defense establishment and their power in eastern Europe, keeping the region as a buffer zone between them and western Europe.

Stalin and the Soviet Bloc

The USSR in the early postwar years reflected the policies of its leader, Josef Stalin (STAH-lin) (1879–1953). Stalin believed that, because of their key role in the victory over Nazism and the Russian occupation of eastern Europe, the Soviets could deal as equals with the West. He therefore left Soviet armies in eastern Europe and helped establish communist governments there. Stalin also kept control of the Baltic states of Estonia, Latvia, and Lithuania, formerly independent nations that the Soviets occupied in World War II. Thus was created the Soviet bloc of nations, divided from the West by an "iron curtain" of heavily fortified borders. In 1949, the USSR gained a key ally with the communist victory in China (see Chapter 27). By 1949, Soviet scientists, helped by information collected by spies in the United States, had built and tested an atomic bomb, enabling the USSR to keep pace with the United States in the emerging arms race.

Stalin's years in power had been brutal for the Soviet people. The paranoid dictator, imagining potential enemies everywhere, maintained an iron grip on power. From the late 1920s through the early 1950s, millions of Soviet citizens were exiled to Siberia, and hundreds of others, including top Communist Party officials and military officers Stalin suspected of disloyalty, were convicted of treason in show trials and then executed. After World War II, the Communist Party maintained its tight rein on the arts, education, and science. For instance, party officials banned the poetry of Anna Akhmatova (uhk-MAH-tuh-vuh) (1888–1966), who had courageously recorded the

 Russian History Index: The World Wide Web Virtual Library (*http://vlib.iue.it/hist-russia/Index.html*). Contains useful essays and links on Russian history, society, and politics.

agonies of Stalin's purge victims, and detained her in a filthy hospital. Stalin's government also stepped up Russification, the effort to spread Russian language and culture in the non-Russian parts of the empire, especially Muslim Central Asia.

Khrushchev and De-Stalinization

The death of Stalin, who had achieved god-like status in the USSR, in 1953 sparked dissidence and rethinking, which led to modest political change. Stalin's successor, Nikita Khrushchev (KROOSH-chef) (1894–1971), was critical of Stalin's dictatorial ruling style and crimes and courageously began a process of de-Stalinization in 1956. Khrushchev sought to cleanse communism of the brutal Stalinist stain in order to legitimize the system among his people and around the world. Some of his criticism of Stalin circulated underground throughout the Soviet bloc, stirring up dissent in eastern Europe. In Poland, workers went on strike, and hundreds died or were wounded when the government suppressed it with force.

While it began a political thaw at home, de-Stalinization opened a split in the communist world that led eventually to China breaking its alliance with the USSR in 1960 and perhaps planted the seed for the unraveling of the Soviet Empire and system three decades later. Khrushchev promised that, under his leadership, the Soviet standard of living would eventually equal that of the United States. It never happened, but Khrushchev produced some achievements, especially in technology. In 1957, the USSR shocked the United States and the world by launching Sputnik, the first artificial satellite to orbit earth, and in 1961, cosmonaut Yuri Gagaran (guh-GAHR-un) (1934–1968) became the first man to fly aboard a rocket ship into earth orbit. Along with these achievements, however, came some old-style Soviet repressiveness: in 1957, Khrushchev prevented novelist Boris Pasternak (PAS-ter-NAK) (1890–1960) from publishing the novel *Dr. Zhivago*, a critical look at

> "Kruschchev sought to cleanse communism of the brutal Stalinist stain in order to legitimize the system among his people and around the world."

> ❝ Russians, having a long tradition of tolerating authoritarianism, learned how to survive its constraints, cooperating just enough with unpopular policies to avoid trouble. ❞

Crisis in Communism

the Bolsheviks during the Russian Civil War (1918–1921), which won a Nobel Prize in 1959 after being smuggled to the West.

The Brezhnev Era

In 1964, Khrushchev was deposed, and a much more staunch repression returned under Leonid Brezhnev (1906–1982), a cautious bureaucrat who imposed a Stalinist system in which the state had a hand in everything. Brezhnev led the country for the next two decades (1964–1982), and under him the Soviet state, run mostly in secret by a group of elderly, bureaucratic men, was intolerant of dissent, although less brutal than in Stalin's time. The secret police (KGB) monitored thought and behavior. Russians, having a long tradition of tolerating authoritarianism, learned how to survive its constraints, cooperating just enough with unpopular policies to avoid trouble. Active dissidence came from a few marginalized intellectuals and artists, some of whom found themselves in the remote prison camps, known as the Gulags, of Siberia. Many died there, but some persecuted intellectuals made notable achievements.

In 1970, the writer Alexander Solzhenitsyn (SOL-zhuh-NEET-sin) (b. 1918), a Red Army veteran imprisoned by Stalin in the Gulags for nine years, was forbidden to receive the Nobel Prize for literature. His novel, *One Day in the Life of Ivan Denisovich*, had exposed the harsh life in the labor camps. Another well-known dissident, Andrei Sakharov (SAH-kuh-rawf) (1921–1989), a physicist who had helped develop the first Soviet atomic bomb but became disillusioned with the government, won the Nobel Peace Prize in 1975 after advocating for an end to the arms race, but he was not allowed to attend the ceremonies.

The Soviets had achieved notable successes, but they had also experienced severe economic problems. The Five-Year Plans introduced by Stalin beginning in 1928 had rapidly transformed the USSR into a fairly modern society. To encourage more economic progress in the postwar years, Soviet leaders had three tools: the Communist Party, the bureaucracy, and the military. By the 1980s, however, all three had proved inadequate to the task. The authoritarian party tolerated little dissent and fostered rigidity. The overcentralized bureaucracy often bungled planning and management. The military, large but inefficient, was held together by brutal discipline, promoted incompetent officers, and wasted resources. In 1987, a West German college student deliberately exposed the flaws by piloting his small, single-engine plane unnoticed right through Soviet air security to land in Red Square, where he was arrested by astonished police.

Increasingly, the economy struggled. The Soviets spent vast sums to achieve nuclear and military parity with the United States, devoting much of their budget to a massive defense establishment, sucking investment from other scientific and technological projects. Some of the retail economy was carried out through the black market, where people often bought food and clothes from illegal vendors operating out of backrooms or on street corners. Worker absenteeism and indifference, caused by the practice of paying workers regardless of effort, made for inefficiency. The economy also took a blow from failure to innovate high technology. The Soviets completely missed the personal computer revolution sweeping the West beginning in the 1980s. And although they were better off than many Asians, Africans, and Latin Americans, most Soviet citizens lived well below North American and western European standards.

The environment also suffered. Industrial pollution led to dying forests and lakes, toxic farmland, and poisoned air. Diverting rivers for farming and power caused the Aral Sea, once nearly as large as North America's Lake Michigan, to practically dry up, and it also diminished the world's largest inland body of water, the Caspian Sea. In 1986, the nuclear power station at Chernobyl in the Ukraine exploded, causing numerous deaths and injuries, releasing radiation over a wide area of Europe, and revealing the Soviet Union's inadequate environmental protections. ·

As disillusionment set in, by the 1970s fewer Soviet citizens believed in the communist future. The Soviet people joked cynically: "Under capitalism man exploits man; under communism it's the other way around." In a society that Soviet leaders claimed was classless, the contrast between the wealth of the party, government, and military elite and that of everyone else was striking. Communism had fostered a favored elite, and social decay was evident everywhere: drab working-class lives, rampant corruption and bribery, the shortage of goods, high rates of alcoholism, and demoralized youth abounded.

Aral Sea As water from the rivers that supplied it was diverted for agriculture and industry, the Aral Sea in Soviet Central Asia lost more than half its water between 1960 and 2000. This photo shows a stranded boat where rich lake fisheries once existed.

The Soviet Union in the Cold War

The Cold War ebbed and flowed. The tensions between the United States and the USSR reached a height in the late 1940s through late 1950s. During the Korean War (1950–1953), the Soviets sent supplies to communist North Koreans who were fighting the South Koreans and the United States. Stalin's successors promoted a less aggressive policy, known as "peaceful coexistence," toward the West. From the late 1950s through late 1970s, the tensions between the superpowers eased somewhat, even though Soviet-backed forces took control of North Vietnam in 1954, and Cuba joined the communist camp in 1959.

However, there were also stumbling blocks to better relations. In 1961, the Soviet ally, East Germany, built a high, 27-mile-long wall around the part of Berlin administered by West Germany to prevent disenchanted East Germans from fleeing to the West. The wall became a potent symbol of the Cold War's divisiveness. In 1962, a crisis caused by the secret placing of Soviet nuclear missiles in Cuba, ninety miles from Florida, and by the demand by the United States that the missiles be removed brought the two superpowers to the brink of nuclear war. The Soviets withdrew the missiles, easing tensions. The Soviets also challenged the United States by helping arm the communist forces fighting U.S.-supported governments in South Vietnam, Laos, and the Philippines in the 1950s and 1960s.

The Soviet role in the world reflected national interest rather than communist ideology alone. The Soviets generally subordinated the global crusade for communism to the normal pursuit of allies, security, and political influence. To gain allies, they supported nationalist and revolutionary movements in Asia, Africa, and Latin America. On the whole, however, the Soviets followed pragmatic policies, usually sending military force only when their direct interests were threatened. They could do nothing when China broke with the USSR in 1960 and became a rival for influence in international communism. In contrast, they tolerated no opposition to Soviet power in the east European satellites, moving quickly to suppress revolts in Poland and Hungary in the 1950s, liberalizing tendencies in Czechoslovakia in 1968, and dissident movements in Poland in the 1970s and 1980s. The Brezhnev Doctrine asserted Moscow's right to interfere in the satellites to protect communist governments and maintain the Soviet bloc.

Eventually, however, military interventions proved costly. In 1979, Soviet armies invaded Afghanistan, on the southern border of the USSR, to prop up a pro-Soviet government. But in the 1980s, the United States, along with Arab nations and Pakistan, actively aided the Afghan rebels, mostly militant Muslims, who were fighting the secular Afghan regime and the Soviet occupation. Ultimately, Afghanistan, where the mountain and desert terrain made fighting difficult, proved a disaster for the USSR, costing 13,000 Russian lives and billions of dollars. Unable to subdue the opposition, the Soviets withdrew their forces in 1989. These difficulties of maintaining their hegemony contributed to a major reassessment of the Soviet system in the second half of the 1980s.

Soviet Society and Culture

Soviet society changed over the decades. After World War II, population growth surged, from 180 million in 1950 to 275 million by the late 1980s. The Soviet people were far healthier, better paid, and more educated than their predecessors had been in 1917. Citizens enjoyed social services that were unimaginable fifty years earlier, such as free medical care, old-age pensions, maternity leaves, guaranteed jobs, paid vacations, and day-care centers. In exchange for security, however, people knew they had to accept state power and the subordination of individual rights. These conditions reshaped gender relations, religion, and ethnic relations while also fostering resistance that was expressed through new forms of literature and music.

Women and the Family

The experiences of Soviet women reflected the provision of education and social services. While few women served in the Soviet hierarchy, most women were in the paid workforce, in both low-end and highly skilled jobs; for example, some three-quarters of doctors were women. Young women in rural areas, where people made less money than city workers, often migrated to the cities in search of a better life. Worried that the floodtide of female migrants to cities would diminish the next generation of farmers, the state tried, with limited success, to discourage the migration. While rural women faced an especially hard life, those in cities also faced demoralizing challenges: every day women of modest means stood in long lines in shops to buy food and necessities, washed clothes and dishes in the bathroom sink, and often prepared meals in communal kitchens. Meanwhile, women increasingly divorced abusive husbands, and the state legalized abortion. As a result, the average family became smaller. By the 1980s, both the birthrate and life expectancy were falling rapidly. While officially promoting gender equality, the state also used the schools to perpetuate the Russian stereotype that women were weak and passionate while men were strong and rational. Sometimes feminist activists were harassed, arrested, or even deported.

Religion and the Soviet State

In religious life, the state marginalized faith but did not eliminate it. Successive Soviet leaders promoted atheism and denounced Christianity as superstition, and the Russian Orthodox Church, for centuries a key focus of Russian life, became an informal agent of the state; the clergy, closely watched by the secret police, carefully avoided any suggestion of dissent. Still, Russians often attended church and nurtured their faith. In the 1980s, when the state became more tolerant, millions returned to the church, which performed mass baptisms and countless weddings. Yet Russia remained a largely secular society.

Ethnic Tensions

Soviet social conditions and state policies also affected ethnic relations. Relations between ethnic Russians and the diverse ethnic minorities, ranging from Christian Armenians to Muslim Uzbeks, deteriorated, provoking discontent. Restless ethnic minorities chafed at political, economic, and cultural domination by Russians, who constituted only about half of the Soviet population by the 1980s. In Central Asian Soviet republics such as Kazakhstan and Uzbekistan, newly built industrial cities attracted millions of ethnic Russian migrants, who monopolized most of the managerial and professional positions. Compared to neighboring regions of Asia, communism did bring relatively high living standards to Soviet Central Asia, but many Muslim peoples, such as the Uzbeks and Tajiks, resented the Russification of their cultures. The Baltic peoples (Lithuanians, Latvians, Estonians), forcibly annexed into the USSR during World War II, also hated Russian domination and the policy that replaced local languages with Russian. Some Jews, who were scattered around the country, sought the freedom to openly practice their religion or to emigrate to Israel or North America.

The Cultural Underground

Soviet state policies forced cultural creativity largely underground. Intellectuals duplicated and exchanged

RIA-Novosti

Soviet Rock Band For Soviet youth, rock music became a way of escaping the restrictions of Soviet life. This long-haired rocker from the 1980s wears a shirt with the communist symbol, the hammer and sickle, but the lyrics of rock bands often addressed the problems of Soviet life.

copies of forbidden books and magazines in secret; anti-Stalinist poets explored the breathing space between the official line and prison. Both imported and local versions of rock music became a major vehicle for presenting alternative ideas about life or criticizing the communist system. By the mid-1960s, some young Russians were modeling themselves on the Anglo-American youth counterculture symbolized by "hippies," wearing jeans and miniskirts and listening to the Beatles or their Soviet clones. For Soviet youth, rock music remained virtually the only escape from an oppressive society. Some 160,000 underground rock and jazz bands existed in the Soviet Union by the 1980s. Few musicians dared to challenge the system directly, but they explored the fringes, mocking the bureaucracy or the absurdity of Soviet life. Considering Western rock music to be degenerate and immoral, the authorities subjected innovative musicians to restrictions, although few faced arrest.

Eastern Europe in the Soviet System

Imposition of communist rule sealed the fate of eastern Europe for forty years. Soviet forces stayed in the region after World War II, installing communist governments and incorporating them into the Soviet bloc. Political parties were abolished, churches persecuted, and nationalistic leaders purged. In 1949, the communist nations formed COMECON (Council for Mutual Economic Assistance), which more closely integrated the Soviet and eastern European economies. Communism fostered economic development, especially in Romania and Bulgaria, which had little industrialization before World War II. But many eastern Europeans, especially in the more industrialized Czechoslovakia, Poland, and East Germany, aspired to living standards closer to those in western Europe. To supply consumer goods and finance industrialization, the governments took out loans and built up huge debts. As in the USSR, increased industrial activity created dirty air and toxic waste. Meanwhile, while the Soviets treated the satellite countries as neocolonies and exploited their resources, they also had to give them generous subsidies to maintain control.

Soviet Satellites Of all the eastern European communist nations, Yugoslavia followed the most independent path, breaking with the USSR entirely in 1948. In 1945, the Yugoslav Communist Party, led by Marshal Josip Broz Tito (TEE-toe) (1892–1980), who had been the widely popular leader of the local anti-Nazi resistance, won national elections. Tito wanted to avoid Soviet domination, so his government cooperated with them while also maintaining friendly relations with the West. For several decades, Tito's unique form of communism, which experimented with worker rather than manager control of factories, created enough prosperity and popular support to neutralize his nation's powerful ethnic divisions.

The refusal of eastern European populations to support Soviet domination fostered unrest. Poland, with its strong Catholic allegiances, was the most restless satellite, with its workers demanding more public input into the government. In 1956, Hungarian leaders tried to break with rigid communism by reinstating private property, inviting noncommunists into the government, and declaring the country neutral. When

> "By the 1970s, few Asian, African, or Latin American revolutionaries looked toward Moscow for inspiration."

a worker's council called for socialism that was adapted to Hungary's more liberal conditions, a Soviet bloc force occupied Hungary and executed the anti-Soviet leaders. Nonetheless, Hungary remained open to the West and was more tolerant of dissent than other Soviet satellites. Hungary's blend of state influence and free markets, known as market socialism, created the most prosperous Soviet bloc economy.

Dubcek and Walesa Other disgruntled eastern Europeans also defied Soviet power. In Czechoslovakia in 1968, the reform-minded leader Alexander Dubcek (DOOB-check) (1927–1993), during what was called the "Prague Spring," sought to shift to a more liberal "communism with a human face." Alarmed that the Czechs might start a dangerous trend, the Soviets sent Warsaw Pact troops into the country and replaced Dubcek and his supporters with repressive Soviet puppets. In Poland, the independent Solidarity trade union openly challenged the communist system. The union was formed in 1980 when, in response to high food prices and growing economic inequality, shipyard workers led by Lech Walesa (leck wa-LEN-za) (b. 1943), an electrical engineer, went on strike. As food prices continued to increase, thousands of women also took to the streets, and the dissidents then formed Solidarity, which aimed at economic liberalization. The movement was banned after the government declared martial law. Nonetheless, even though it was illegal, Solidarity had 9.5 million members by 1981 and worked for political as well as economic goals.

With political avenues closed off, young east Europeans used rock music as a protest vehicle. The result was often further repression. Government leaders prohibited performances by the more daring rock bands. Some East German musicians, among them the leading singer-songwriter Wolf Biermann (b. 1936), also a poet and novelist, were forced into exile; he wrote, "The German darkness descends over my spirit. It darkens overpowering in my song. It comes because I see my Germany so deeply torn."[4] These attitudes set the stage for later change.

Soviet Decline and Reform

Soviet problems mounted, forcing a reappraisal of the political and economic system and the nation's place in the world. The USSR had steadily lost ground in world affairs to the United States and economic ground to Japan and West Germany. Communist China went its own way in 1960 and became a bitter rival. The war in Afghanistan and the economic subsidizing of the east European satellites drained Soviet wealth. By the mid-1980s, the USSR had few close remaining allies outside of the Soviet bloc, which was restless. Soviet power in the world had always been mostly military, whereas the United States and its Western allies also had cultural, economic, technological, and even linguistic influence. All over the world, people studied English or French, not Russian. Some observers found more power in rock music, videos, fast food, youth fashions, and news networks than in the Soviet Red Army. By the 1970s, few Asian, African, or Latin American revolutionaries looked toward Moscow for inspiration.

 Letter to Comrades Brezhnev, Kosygin, and Podgorny Read a letter sent by prominent intellectuals to the Soviet leadership, urging a gradual democratization of the country as the only cure for its ills.

This declining international influence, combined with spiraling social and economic problems and a stifling bureaucracy, ultimately led to the rise of younger, reform-minded Soviet leaders who introduced dramatic change. The thaw of the 1970s had given Soviet leaders more contact with the outside world and an appreciation of the growing technological gap between them and the West. The planned economy that had powered a largely peasant society into a superpower now seemed a severe drag. In 1985, Mikhail Gorbachev (GORE-beh-CHOF) (b. 1931) became Soviet leader. While hoping to preserve the basics of the Soviet system, he understood the need to liberalize the economy, decentralize decision making, and relax ideological controls. However, Gorbachev inherited a Communist Party that allowed no political competition and managed a planned economy, run from the top with little room for individual initiative. With such a rigid system, the Soviet leader concluded, the USSR could never match the United States as a superpower.

Gorbachev introduced a dazzling series of reforms to reenergize the Soviet Union. He developed closer relations with the West, abandoning their decades-long ideological struggle. In 1987, the Treaty of Washington between the United States and the USSR lessened the threat of nuclear war by having both countries destroy their short- and long-range missiles. With his glasnost ("openness") policy, Gorbachev democratized the political system, including free elections, a real parliament that included noncommunist parties, the release of most political prisoners, and deemphasis of the role of the Communist Party. Gorbachev also loosened state control of the media, the arts, and scholarship, and let it be known that he would not maintain the unpopular communist governments in eastern Europe. They toppled or collapsed in 1989.

Admitting the faults of Soviet communism, Gorbachev also liberalized the economy, using market mechanisms in a policy known as perestroika ("restructuring") (see Witness to the Past: Restructuring Soviet Society). But the economic changes failed to take off. The intelligentsia wanted democratization, while the working classes preferred consumer goods, which did not come. Top bureaucrats proved resistant to changes that might threaten their role. Conservatives in the Communist Party and the secret police also opposed reforms that might undermine their power. Soon the Soviet system collapsed.

glasnost ("openness") The policy introduced in the Soviet Union by Mikhail Gorbachev in the 1980s to democratize the political system.

perestroika ("Restructuring") Mikhail Gorbachev's policy to liberalize the Soviet economy using market mechanisms.

 The Last Heir of Lenin Explains His Reform Plans: Perestroika and Glasnost Read President Gorbachev's analysis of the Soviet Union's decline, and his prescriptions for reform.

CHRONOLOGY

Europe, 1989–Present

1989	End of communist regimes in eastern Europe
1990	Reunification of Germany
1991	Breakup of Soviet Union
1991–2000	Yeltsin era in Russia
1991–2000	Crises in Yugoslavia
1991	Signing of Maastricht Treaty
2004	Expansion of European Union into eastern Europe

Restructuring Soviet Society

In 1987, Mikhail Gorbachev, the head of the Soviet Communist Party and government, published a book, *Perestroika*, outlining his policy of economic restructuring. His goal was to transform the inefficient, stagnant Soviet economy into one based on a decentralized market orientation similar to the market socialism of Hungary and China. The new policy gave greater autonomy to local government officials and factory managers and attempted to democratize the Communist Party. Causing a sensation, the book was ranked by some observers as the most important publication of the late twentieth century. By the early 1990s, with Gorbachev removed from office, the policy was eclipsed, but the book remained a testimony to the problems that led to the Soviet system's collapse. In this excerpt, Gorbachev defines *perestroika*.

Perestroika means overcoming the stagnation process, breaking down the braking mechanism, creating a dependable and effective mechanism for acceleration of social and economic progress and giving it dynamism.

Perestroika means initiative. It is the comprehensive development of democracy, socialist self-government, encouragement of initiative and creative endeavor, improved order and discipline, more glasnost (openness), criticism and selfcriticism in all spheres of our society. It is utmost respect for the individual and consideration for personal dignity.

Perestroika is the all-round intensification of the Soviet economy, the revival and development of the principles of democratic centralism in running the national economy, the universal introduction of economic methods, the renunciation of management by injunction and by administration methods, and the overall encouragement of innovation and socialist enterprise.

Perestroika means a resolute shift to scientific methods, an ability to provide a solid scientific basis for every new initiative. It means the combination of the achievements of the scientific and technological revolution with a planned economy.

Perestroika means priority development of the social sphere aimed at ever better satisfaction of the Soviet people's requirements for good living and working conditions, for good rest and recreation, education and health care. It means unceasing concern for cultural and spiritual wealth, for the culture of every individual and society as a whole.

Perestroika means the elimination from society of the distortions of social ethics, the consistent implementation of the principles of social justice. It means the unity of words and deeds, rights and duties. It is the elevation of honest, highly-qualified labor, the overcoming of leveling tendencies in pay and consumerism.

This is how we see perestroika today. This is how we see our tasks, and the substance and content of our work for the forthcoming period. It is difficult now to say how long that period will take. Of course, it will be much more than two or three years. We are ready for serious, strenuous and tedious work to ensure that our country reaches new heights by the end of the twentieth century.

Thinking About the Reading

1. What did Gorbachev mean by *perestroika*?
2. What problems did the policy aim to solve?

Source: Mikhail Gorbachev, *Perestroika* (New York: HarperCollins, 1987), pp. 34–35. Copyright © 1987 by Mikhail Gorbachev. Reprinted by permission of HarperCollins Publishers.

LO⁴ Communist Collapse: A New Russia and Europe

For four decades, the Cold War had provided the context for European politics. With the breakup of the communist bloc of nations in 1989 and the USSR in 1991, the political and economic face of Russia and Europe was reshaped. The collapse of these communist regions created hope but also uncertainties. Russia struggled to rebuild and to revive its power, but the capitalism introduced proved destabilizing. While Yugoslavia was torn apart by wars and Germany was reunited, Europeans had to redefine their identity. Western Europe pushed toward unification, but it still had to resolve the conflicting forces of nationalism and cooperation. Most Europeans now chose governments through multiparty elections and pursued individual freedom. By the beginning of the twenty-first century, Europe helped shape the age of globalization.

A New Russia and New Nations

A major development of twentieth-century history was the sudden collapse of the Soviet empire and communism in Europe. In 1985, there had been 5 million Soviet soldiers stationed from East Germany to Siberia's Pacific coast; six years later, the Soviet Union and its satellite nations had unraveled, without a shot being fired. Although the collapse was not a complete surprise, its pace was astonishing. While outside factors played a role in fostering the collapse, Soviet economic decline was probably the decisive cause. The result was a blending of new ideas from the capitalist, democratic West with Soviet-era traditions.

Boris Yeltsin

The collapse revealed the failure of the Soviet system, which was founded on one-party rule and strongly shaped by the political repression and centralized economy of Stalinism. Democratic governments and decentralized capitalism—dominant in North America, western Europe, and Japan—had adjusted better to global changes than the planned economies of communist states, and nationalist yearnings among non-Russians within the empire had sapped the foundation of empire. Mikhail Gorbachev's greatest contribution was to face up to the fact of failure. But by 1991, unable to control the forces unleashed, he resigned as the Communist Party leader and was replaced by Boris Yeltsin (YELT-sin) (b. 1931), a communist bureaucrat turned reformer who had strong U.S. support. Yeltsin ended seven decades of communist rule, and in response, Russians toppled statues of Lenin and restored czarist names to cities that had been renamed during the Soviet era.

Yeltsin acquiesced in the breakup of the USSR, a symbol of the nation's demise as a superpower, while maintaining the unity of the largest Soviet republic, Russia, which stretched from the Baltic Sea through ten time zones to the eastern tip of Siberia (see Map 28.3). Glasnost had opened a Pandora's Box. Ethnic hatreds,

 Interactive Map

> "In 1985, there had been 5 million Soviet soldiers stationed from East Germany to Siberia's Pacific coast; six years later, the Soviet Union and its satellite nations had unraveled, without a shot being fired."

oligarchs Well-placed former communists who amassed enough wealth to gain control of major segments of the post-Soviet Russian economy.

long suppressed by military force or alleviated by the government-provided safety net, soon exploded to the surface. In 1991, all of the fourteen Soviet republics outside of Russia declared their independence. However, many of the former Soviet republics were now led by former communist officials, whose autocratic ruling style resembled the old Soviet system.

Most of the new states have struggled to achieve economic self-sufficiency and political stability. Some states have been engulfed in conflict between rival ethnic or nationalist groups or have fought each other over territorial claims, as did Christian Armenia and Muslim Azerbaijan. But the results of revolutions are usually unpredictable. In Central Asia, inhabited largely by Muslims, some nominal and others devout in their faith, militant Muslims have launched insurgencies against the secular post-Soviet governments, seeking to replace them with Islamic states. Indeed, Islam gained support among the disenchanted and marginalized, especially jobless young men, in Central Asia. Islamic fervor has forced or prompted many women to don the headscarf and behave modestly. Meanwhile, millions of ethnic Russians in the former Soviet republics faced resentment for their relative affluence and ties to the former colonizer.

Difficulties for Yeltsin

Yeltsin had difficulty solving Russia's problems in the 1990s. Hoping to end economic stagnation, he took the advice of Russian free-market enthusiasts and of U.S. advisers, who often knew little of Russian culture, and introduced a strategy known as "shock therapy": rapid conversion of the planned economy to market capitalism. This produced more consumer goods and a growing middle class, but organized crime groups and a few well-placed former communists, known as oligarchs, gained control of major segments of the Russian economy. At the same time, Yeltsin faced secession movements within the Russian federation, especially in Chechnya, a largely

Map 28.3
The Dissolution of the Soviet Union

In 1991, the leaders of Russia, who had abandoned communism, allowed the other fourteen republics to leave the Soviet Union, bringing an end to a vast federation that had endured for more than seven decades. Still, Russia remained the world's largest nation in geographic size, stretching across ten time zones.

Muslim Caucasus territory that Russia had annexed in the 1870s. In 1994, this oil-rich region declared independence. Fearing that recognizing Chechnya's independence would encourage other secession movements, Yeltsin tried to crush the Chechen separatists, drawing the Red Army into a quagmire with thousands of casualties on both sides.

The economic pain of the Russian people was widespread. Millions of workers—and more women than men—lost their jobs as inefficient, obsolete Soviet industries closed. Arguing that the communists had destroyed the family by encouraging women to work, conservatives advocated that women stay at home and tend to family obligations. With the end of free higher education, families preferred to devote their limited money for schooling on their sons. Some

desperate women turned to prostitution for survival. Even when their enterprises did not close, factory workers, miners, and state employees, such as teachers, were often not paid for years. Yeltsin dismantled parts of the welfare state; as a result, public health deteriorated. By 1992, inflation was 2,500 percent, devastating people who lived on pensions and fixed incomes.

Stabilization under Vladimir Putin

In 2000, with the Russian economy near collapse and free markets discredited, Yeltsin resigned in disgrace and was replaced by Vladimir Putin (b. 1952), who ended shock therapy and changed the nation's direction. A former secret police colonel who kept a portrait of the modernizing eighteenth-century czar Peter the Great in his office, Putin supported capitalism and democratic reforms, but also pursued policies that were more authoritarian and nationalist than Yeltsin's. Political liberalism faded as Putin took control of much of the media, muffling opposition media outlets, and prosecuting some oligarchs for corruption. The state has also taken over many large private companies, turning the economy into a form of state capitalism not unlike Meiji Japan. Company managers profit while the public pays for losses. The economy made a modest recovery because of improved tax collection and higher prices for two leading Russian exports, oil and natural gas.

Putin brought back stability after fifteen years of turbulence, marrying the old autocratic government with a new, more outward-looking attitude. The Russian Orthodox Church—for centuries closely connected to Russian national identity and political power— regained some of the influence it had lost under communism. In many parts of Russia, Muslims—some 15 percent of the nation's population—and Christians have peacefully adapted to each other. Putin also sought good relations with Germany, France, the United States, and China. In Putin's Russia, however, the contrasts between rich and poor became stark. While Moscow's wealthiest cavorted in fine restaurants and glitzy casinos, towns often went without heat and power. Corruption, poverty, unaccountability, weak legal institutions, and the festering war in Chechnya stifled development. Polls showed that a majority of Russians preferred the communist years. A respected Russian historian harked back to Peter the Great and Catherine the Great, advising Russians, "Our future lies in openness to the entire world and in enlightenment."[5] It remained unclear whether Russia would follow that path.

The New Eastern Europe

The changes in the USSR resonated throughout eastern Europe. In the late 1980s, the Soviet leader, Mikhail Gorbachev, who admired the Hungarian market socialism model, was no longer willing to protect the corrupt, largely unpopular eastern European communist governments. These governments began to fail as democratic movements that were once underground surfaced. Hungary adopted a demo-

> **Political liberalism faded as Putin took control of much of the media, muffling opposition media outlets, and prosecuting some oligarchs for corruption.**

cratic system; Solidarity came to power in Poland; and East Germans streamed across the border into West Germany, an exodus that led to the dismantling of the Berlin Wall. People around the world watched on television as Berliners gleefully knocked down the Berlin Wall, the symbol of Cold War division. Soon the East German regime and the other east European communist governments had collapsed or been overthrown. In Czechoslovakia, the playwright Vaclav Havel (vax-LAV hah-VEL) (b. 1936), who had been frequently arrested for his pro-democracy activities, was elected president after massive demonstrations forced the communist leaders to resign in a largely peaceful transfer of power known as the "Velvet Revolution." Havel announced, "Your government, my people, has been returned to you."[6]

Poland and the Czech Republic

Democratic or semidemocratic governments were installed, seeking to replace centralized planned economies with market forces, but the rapid move to capitalism proved destabilizing. East Europeans took up voting enthusiastically, yet they also experienced the challenges of change. As in the former Soviet Union, the end of communism uncorked ethnic hatreds and rivalries going back centuries: Slovaks seceded from the Czechs, forming their own country, while Romanians repressed the large Hungarian minority. Millions were thrown out of work as obsolete factories closed; shops were full of attractive goods, but few people had the money to buy them. Only Poland and the Czech Republic enjoyed robust economic growth. In addition, certain protections of the communist welfare system, such as free education, health care, and subsidized housing, were removed, causing misery. Finally, by 2000, salaries caught up with prices in some places, but pockets of high unemployment remained, and the gap between rich and poor widened.

The political environment changed as diverse political parties competed for power. Capitalizing on widespread interest in rebuilding the social safety net, former Communist Party members who now called themselves reform communists won some national elections, especially in Poland and Hungary. They competed for power with free-market advocates, pro-Western liberals, and right-wing nationalists.

In a striking repudiation of the Soviet legacy, reform communists often supported joining the European Union and even the NATO military alliance. Anticommunists had few regrets of the changes since 1989: Adam Michnik, a leader of Polish Solidarity, concluded that "without the slightest hesitation it is much better to live in a country that is democratic, prosperous and thus boring"[7] than under the communist regime.

> "Democratic or semidemocratic governments were installed, seeking to replace centralized planned economies with market forces, but the rapid move to capitalism proved destabilizing."

responded with ferocity, prompting another NATO imposed settlement in 2000. Thousands of NATO troops remained in Bosnia and Kosovo, a symbol of eastern Europe's unresolved challenges.

Toward European Unity

Two themes have dominated western Europe in the years after 1989. One was the reunification of Germany. With the fall of communism and the Berlin Wall, the East German state collapsed, and Germany was quickly reunified in 1990, but challenges endured. Europeans also have

Yugoslavia

Interactive Map

The greatest instability came to Yugoslavia, a federation of states that self-destructed in bloody civil wars between ethnic groups (see Map 28.4). Created artificially for political convenience by diplomats after World War I, Yugoslavia contained antagonistic ethnic and religious groups. The largest, the nationalistic Orthodox Serbs, wanted to dominate the federation, while the Catholic Croats and Slovenians and the Bosnian and Albanian Muslims wanted independence for the regions they dominated. After the long-term federal leader, Tito—the product of a mixed Croat–Serb marriage whose autocratic policies limited dissent and kept the lid on ethnic hatreds—died in 1980, Yugoslavia became a seething cauldron of ethnic conflict.

The violence began in 1991, when the Serb-dominated Yugoslav army tried to stop two states, Slovenia and Croatia, from breaking away from the federation. In response, the United Nations sent in peacekeeping troops to secure their independence. In 1992, the Muslim majority in another Yugoslav state, Bosnia, declared independence, a move opposed by the minority Serbs and Croats there. Bosnian Serb militias, aided covertly by the largest Yugoslav state, Serbia, massacred thousands of Muslims, introducing a new term for genocide, "ethnic cleansing," and leading the United Nations to send more peacemakers. As the violence continued, U.S. air strikes under NATO auspices forced the Serbs to accept a peace treaty in 1995. The Bosnia conflict had killed 200,000 people and generated 4 million refugees. In 1999, violence returned when the Albanian majority in Kosovo, the southern region of Serbia, revolted and the Serbs

The Velvet Revolution Protesters took to the streets in Prague, Czechoslovakia, to protest communist government and demand democracy. These protests, known as the Velvet Revolution for their peaceful nature, were led by Vaclav Havel, pictured on the poster carried by a protester.

PRESIDENTEM

Peter Turnley/Corbis

continued moving toward continental unity, a second theme, but this movement also faced setbacks.

German Reunification

The hasty German reunification disappointed its proponents. For many East Germans, merging with the prosperous West Germany promised access to a materially comfortable life they could only dream of before. But reunification cost billions and threw the German economy into a tailspin. Before reunification, West Germany had enjoyed a long boom. A decade later, however, the reunified nation of 80 million people, suffering from Europe's slowest economic growth, was stuck in deep recession. Many workers in the former East Germany lost jobs as obsolete factories closed. By 2004, the unemployment rate in the east was twice as high as in the west. Some disillusioned youth turned to right-wing, often neo-Nazi, groups to express their anger against foreigners and immigrants.

The European Union

Worried by Germany's problems, western European leaders believed that hastening unification was the best strategy to

Map 28.4
Ethnic Conflicts in Eastern Europe

Many of the nations in central and eastern Europe contain substantial ethnic minorities, and tensions between various groups have often led to conflict. In Yugoslavia, the conflicts between the major ethnic groups—Serbs, Croats, Bosnian Muslims, and Albanians—led to violence and civil war at the end of the twentieth century.

© Cengage Learning

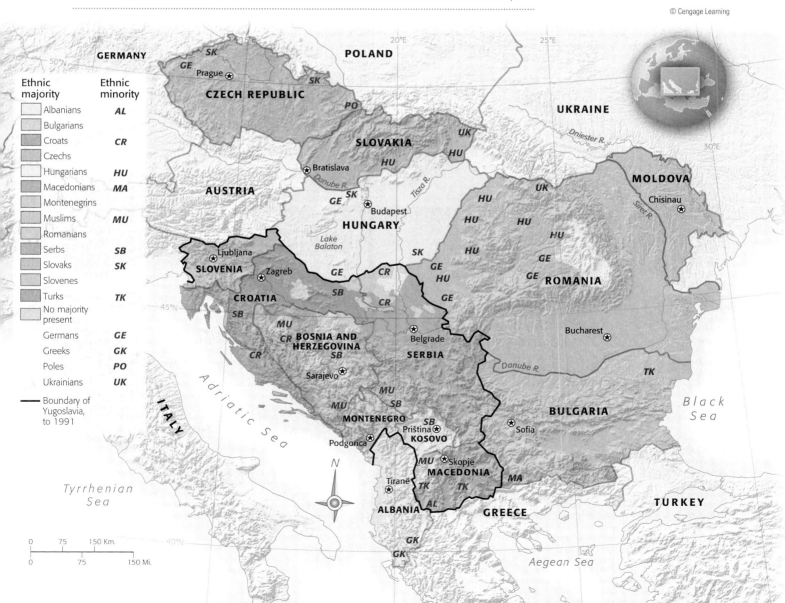

stabilize post-communist Europe. The Maastricht Treaty, which recognized a single currency, the euro, and a central bank, set a goal of achieving economic and monetary union by 2000. It required budgetary and wage restraint as a prelude to monetary union. The treaty pledged to promote balanced and sustainable economic progress by strengthening economic and social cohesion. By 2002, eleven of fifteen signers of the treaty had adopted the euro as their currency, an index of unity. Millions of Europeans were multilingual, moving easily between cultures, and young Europeans often studied in other European countries, factors that aided unity.

The European Union (EU) doubled its membership from twelve nations in 1993 to twenty-five in 2004, when various eastern European nations joined, including the Czech Republic, Poland, and Hungary. The EU became a bloc of nearly 400 million people, encompassing most of Europe and enjoying a combined economic power equal to that of the United States. Some of the members, such as Sweden, have continued to show steady economic growth. Conducting one-quarter of the world's commerce, the EU became one of the dominant economic forces in the world.

Challenges of Assimilation

However, the European Union hit several major road bumps. Critics had long called the EU a faceless bureaucracy with innumerable rules that compromised national independence and threatened national traditions. Indeed, two of Europe's most prosperous nations, Norway and Switzerland, declined membership, fearing the loss of national identity and the cost of subsidizing poorer members. The EU leaders have been cautious in admitting those former Soviet bloc states that have weak economies and autocratic leaders. Turkey, a largely Muslim nation, has long sought membership, fostering a EU debate about how to define Europe and whether non-Christian nations have a role in it. This debate spilled over into the effort by European diplomats to prepare a constitution for the Union. Amid much controversy, the constitution proposed in 2004 rejected any mention of Europe's Christian heritage. But in 2005, voters in two of the most pro-unity countries, France and the Netherlands, fearing loss of control to the EU bureaucracy, shocked EU leaders by rejecting the constitution. This rejection, along with the accelerating global recession in 2008–2009, raised questions about the EU's future.

Increasing unity did not resolve, and may have contributed to, political, economic, and social problems caused by a changing global economy. The economic austerity policies of the 1990s unsettled welfare states and provoked government changes. Social democrats, who had governed eleven of the sixteen western European nations in the early 1990s, now jockeyed with centrists, free-market conservatives, Greens, anti-immigrant nationalists, and the fading communists for power. Attempts to roll back social benefits sometimes set off massive protests and long strikes. While many Europeans preferred to

European Economic Power
Business and political leaders from India and the European Union met in a summit in 2005 to increase trade relations, reflecting the growing economic power of both India and western Europe.

maintain the welfare state even at the cost of slower economic growth, both the German and French governments replaced the thirty-five-hour workweek with the forty-hour workweek to increase their economic competitiveness. Yet, some large companies continued to downsize and cut or export jobs. In 2006, thousands in France rioted against loosening job protections.

Europeans also faced other challenges. By 2000, Europe, which a century earlier had been overcrowded and the world's greatest exporter of people, had a declining population, due mainly to the world's lowest birthrate: 1.2 children per woman. Yet, concerned about a much higher birth rate among Muslims, Europeans became increasingly hostile to immigration from the Middle East. Tensions simmered, and in 2005, rioting and vandalism by young Arab and African residents in France, many of them unemployed, caused much damage and heightened awareness of the challenges of assimilation. The European population decline also posed a long-term economic problem, because with more people retiring from than entering the workforce, younger workers had more responsibility for financing government services, such as pensions and health care, for the growing population of elderly. Thus Europeans still struggled to define their place in a changing world.

Europe and Russia in the Global System

With the end of the Cold War, Russia, western Europe, and the former Soviet bloc states searched for new roles in the world. Russia sought to maintain good relations with the EU, the United States, China, and the nearby Islamic nations, such as Iran, but also continued to act in its own self-interest. By 2004, NATO had added many of the former Warsaw Pact nations, discomforting Russia. Western Europeans seemed more reluctant than Americans to devote vast sums to the military or to send their armed forces into combat. The crises in Yugoslavia showed European weakness, with the United States pressing NATO for intervention and then leading the effort to restore order.

European relations with the United States became complicated. Various European nations, as part of a NATO commitment, sent troops to Afghanistan after the 2001 terrorist attacks on the United States and shared the goal of combating international terrorism. But most Europeans mistrusted the U.S. desire to invade oil-rich Iraq in 2003, believing it had little to

do with fighting terrorism and fearing it would destabilize the Middle East. As a result, major European nations such as France and Germany criticized the U.S. invasion and occupation. Although their people strongly opposed the war, some close U.S. allies, such as Italy, Poland, and Spain, sent small token forces, but only Britain had a sizeable military presence in Iraq. This participation ultimately cost British prime minister Tony Blair his popular support, and he resigned in 2007. In 2008, the election of U.S. president Barack Obama, a critic of the war, harkened a new era of U.S.–European relations.

Europeans also disagreed on how best to respond to international terrorism, especially the threat posed by militant Islamic groups. The substantial Muslim immigrant populations in Europe complicated European nations' policies on the Middle East. By 2000, 19 million immigrants, including 13 million Muslims, made up 6 percent of the total EU population. Islamic militancy spread among some people of Arab or South Asian ancestry in Europe, and the major terrorist network, Al Qaeda, had a presence in several nations. Deadly terrorist attacks on commuter trains in Madrid in 2004 and the London subway in 2005, which killed several hundred people, convinced many Europeans that Western military interventions in the Middle East might increase rather than diminish the terrorist threat. In 2006, shocked Europeans found how tense Muslim–Western relations had become when offensive cartoons satirizing the Islamic prophet Muhammad, published by a right-wing, anti-immigrant Danish newspaper, caused massive riots and demonstrations around the Muslim world, resulting in hundreds of deaths and attacks on Danish embassies and business interests.

With the move toward closer political and economic integration, Europe became much more than a collection of separate countries sharing certain cultural traditions and history. Europeans still played key roles in resolving world problems. European nations took the lead in developing international treaties on issues such as climate change, biological and chemical weapons, international criminal courts, and genocide. Some European workers also led movements against the economic globalization they saw as costing jobs and livelihoods. Though their region is no longer the powerful colossus it had been in the nineteenth century, Europeans are carving out a new place in the world.

 Listen to a synopsis of Chapter 28.

CHAPTER 29

The Americas and the Pacific Basin:

New Roles in the Contemporary World, Since 1945

Learning Outcomes

After reading this chapter, you should be able to answer the following questions:

LO¹ How did the Cold War shape U.S. foreign policies?

LO² How and why are the societies of the United States, Canada, and Australia similar to and different from each other?

LO³ Why have democracy and economic development proven to be difficult goals in Latin America?

LO⁴ How have Latin American and Caribbean cultures been dynamic?

❝ It's curious. Our generals listen to the [U.S.] Pentagon. They learn the ideology of National Security and commit all these crimes [against the Argentine people]. Then the same [American] people who gave us this gift come and ask, "How did these terrible things happen?**❞**

—**President Raul Alfonsin of Argentina, 1984**[1]

The women appeared one day in 1977 at the historic Plaza de Mayo, adjacent to the presidential palace in Buenos Aires, Argentina. For several years, Argentina's military regime had been waging a bloody campaign to eliminate dissidents, killing or abducting some thirty thousand people and arresting and torturing thousands more. Some of those targeted may have belonged to outlawed leftist groups, but many simply held progressive political ideas. Soon the women's ranks swelled to more than one hundred at each weekly vigil, making their silent protest impossible to ignore. A year later, they numbered more than one thousand. These mothers and grandmothers pinned photographs of missing family members to their chests, silently demanding answers: where were their children, husbands, pregnant daughters, and grandchildren, some of them newborn infants?

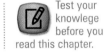

Test your knowlege before you read this chapter.

What do you think?

During the Cold War, the United States did not interfere in Latin American affairs.

Strongly Disagree   Strongly Agree

1   2   3   4   5   6   7

The "Mothers and Grandmothers of the Plaza de Mayo," as they came to be known, dared to challenge one of Latin America's most brutal tyrannies. Their courageous protest inspired others in Argentina and around the world with hope and moral outrage at repression by military forces. The protest illustrates how some Latin Americans addressed the authoritarian governments under which they lived, as Latin American countries often shifted back and forth between dictatorship and democracy in the decades following World War II. Many Latin Americans came to resent the United States, which often supported despotic governments that repressed their people while welcoming U.S. investment. The gatherings in Buenos Aires continued weekly until 1983, when the regime fell and a civilian government began to investigate the disappearances, but most

<< **A Naturalization Ceremony** Seeking political freedom or economic opportunities, immigrants flock to the United States and many become citizens. At this ceremony, eight hundred residents, representing eighty-eight countries, took the oath of citizenship in Columbus, Ohio, in April 2005.

Argentineans never learned the fates of their loved ones.

The United States remained the hemisphere's dominant power during this period while gradually expanding its global influence. Wars in Korea and Vietnam were part of the U.S. effort to shape the global system while also opposing the expansion of communism. After World War II, the United States became the global workshop, banker, preacher, and police officer. It enjoyed unrivaled supremacy, a combination of military might, economic power, and political-ideological leadership that was contested only by the Soviet Union between 1946 and 1989. After 1989, the United States became the world's only remaining superpower. U.S. society increasingly differed from those of Canada and the Pacific Basin countries of Australia and New Zealand.

LO¹ The United States as a Superpower

By virtue of its size, power, and wealth, the United States has played a major role in the world after World War II, promoting human rights and freedom, lavishing aid on various allies, and providing leadership in a politically fragmented world. During the Cold War (1946–1989), U.S. policies were shaped by competition with the Soviet bloc for allies and strategic advantage. While people around the world admired American democratic ideals, prosperity, and technological ingenuity, the U.S.-led wars, interventions, support for authoritarian allies, frequent neglect of human rights, and the globalization of capitalism fostered widespread hostility toward the United States. After the Cold War, the United States and its allies faced new challenges, especially the rise of international terrorism.

> "World War II was a watershed for the United States, accelerating political centralization and economic growth."

> ❝ The Cold War produced an expectation of permanent conflict between two competing ideologies: communism and capitalist democracy. ❞

The Postwar United States and the Cold War

World War II was a watershed for the United States, accelerating political centralization and economic growth. At the same time, it compelled Americans to accept international involvements and thus promoted an activist foreign policy. By the later 1940s, observers began referring to both the United States and the USSR as superpowers because of their unrivaled political, economic, and military might. As U.S.–Soviet rivalry increased, the two superpowers sought to block each other from gaining influence in other countries.

The American Century

The victory over Nazism and Japanese militarism reinforced Americans' confidence and sense of mission. In 1941, Henry Luce, the publisher of one of the most influential news magazines in the United States, *Time*, declared that the twentieth century would be the American Century, and that Americans must accept their duty and opportunity to exercise influence in the world. After the war, the U.S. government pursued a strategy for expanding its economic influence, rebuilding defeated Germany and Japan, establishing global financial networks, lavishing aid on western Europe, and using U.S. military forces to protect U.S. allies in Asia. The United States also opposed radical nationalist movements, especially communist-led revolutionary groups, in Asia, Africa, and Latin America.

For several decades, as the U.S. economy soared, the notion of an American Century seemed realistic. Among the great powers, only the United States had not been bombed or financially drained, and therefore it was able to keep intact a modern industrial system. The United States alone could produce, on a large scale, the consumer goods needed by others. In 1950, it accounted for 27 percent of total world economic output. By becoming the engine of the world economy, Americans experienced an economic boom that lasted until the late 1960s and helped finance an activist U.S. foreign policy. Americans forged close trade links with Canada, western Europe, and Japan while sponsoring large-scale foreign aid programs and investment, especially in Asian and Latin American countries.

Such aid and investment often supported cash-crop agriculture and mining, reinforcing the economic dependence of developing nations by promoting unbalanced economic growth. Later, U.S. investment developed light industry, especially textile factories, that utilized cheap labor in countries such as Mexico and Thailand. Asian, African, and Latin America countries became key U.S. markets, acquiring more than one-third of American exports by the 1990s, while American consumption of ever-more foreign imports, from Japanese cars to Middle Eastern oil, contributed to a chronic trade imbalance. By 2005, imports were 57 percent larger than exports as Americans lived beyond their means, and globalization led to outsourcing of manufacturing and jobs.

> **domino theory**
> A theory that envisioned countries falling one by one to communism and that became a mainstay of U.S. policy during the Cold War.

The Cold War

The Cold War with the USSR shaped U.S. foreign relations. American leaders saw the Soviet Union as pursuing global aggression and fostering political unrest. Although they had good reason to worry about the Soviet state, which was headed by a ruthless dictator, Joseph Stalin, and possessed formidable military might, U.S. leaders and intelligence analysts often overestimated the Soviet threat. The Cold War produced an expectation of permanent conflict between two competing ideologies: communism and capitalist democracy. Given this assumption, the U.S. government became obsessed with secrecy and control. Two key U.S. institutions carrying out the anti-Soviet strategy, the Central Intelligence Agency (CIA) and the National Security Council, both established in 1947, operated in top secrecy, with little congressional oversight and ever-larger budgets, reaching a total of $40 billion per year for all intelligence agencies by the 1980s. By the early 1950s, the domino theory, which envisioned countries falling one by one to communism, became a mainstay of U.S. policy.

 WWW-VL: History: United States (*http://vlib.iue.it/history/USA/*). A virtual library, maintained at the University of Kansas, that contains links to hundreds of sites.

McCarthyism

Anticommunism intensified within the United States when U.S. senator Joseph McCarthy (1909–1957), a hard-drinking former judge, capitalized on Cold War fears and began to identify suspected communists in the government, the military, education, and the entertainment industry. His campaign, which became known as McCarthyism, led to the firing or blacklisting of not only a handful of secret communists but also thousands of Americans who held left-wing political views, which were condemned as "un-American" in the early 1950s. McCarthy called hundreds of people,

"Between 1945 and 1975, U.S. power was unmatched in the world, and the United States maintained military bases on every inhabited continent and in dozens of countries around the world."

from movie actors to State Department officials, before his Senate committee, ruining the lives of many innocent people before his popularity waned in 1954. That same year, the U.S. Senate finally censured McCarthy for recklessly charging top military leaders with treason.

Multilateralism vs. Unilateralism

For much of the Cold War era, a broad consensus emerged around opposing the spread of communism and Soviet power, though strategies differed. Some leaders pursued multilateralism, an approach in which the United States sought a coordination of foreign policies with allies in western Europe, Japan, and Canada, avoiding activities that might enflame world opinion against the United States. In contrast, most policymakers, and the presidents they served, favored unilateralism, a foreign policy in which the United States acted alone in its own perceived national interest even if key allies disapproved. The Cold War–driven consensus stifled those who questioned the rationale, tactics, and cost of an activist policy. But by the later 1960s, debates raged over controversial decisions such as military action in Vietnam, undermining the consensus and provoking increasing dissent.

Containing Communism

The main U.S. strategy, known as containment, was aimed at preventing

communists from gaining power, and the USSR from getting political influence, in other nations. An influential, top-secret government report, known as NSC-68, prepared by the National Security Council in 1950, provided the rationale for activist policies: "The issues that face us are momentous, involving the fulfillment or destruction not only of this [U.S.] Republic but of civilization itself."[2] NSC-68 sanctioned any tactics, including assassination, in the anticommunism struggle, and inspired a massive, expensive military buildup. The Soviets matched the U.S. military buildup, creating a constant escalation of military spending and ever-more-sophisticated weapons. Under a policy known in the United States as Mutually Assured Destruction, or MAD, the United States and the USSR used the fear of nuclear weapons to deter each other. Some historians believe that MAD prevented a direct military confrontation between the two rivals that might have sparked World War III.

Defense spending reshaped the U.S. economy. Despite the warning of U.S. president Dwight Eisenhower (g. 1953–1961), a chief commander during World War II, to guard against the growing influence of what he termed the military-industrial complex, an alliance of military leaders and weapons producers, defense became an enormous business. It employed one-fifth of the U.S. industrial workforce and one-third of scientists and engineers by the 1960s, while costing U.S. taxpayers hundreds of billions per year. The United States also sold weapons to allied nations, among them despotic regimes, some of which used the weapons against their own people. The United States also trained these regimes' military officers and police forces, who often used the tactics they learned to eliminate dissidents.

Three Decades of U.S. Supremacy

Between 1945 and 1975, U.S. power was unmatched in the world, and the United States maintained military bases on every inhabited continent and in dozens of countries around the world (see Map 29.1). The United States employed military force and covertly aided governments to suppress opposition or, as in Chile in 1973, helped over-

Interactive Map

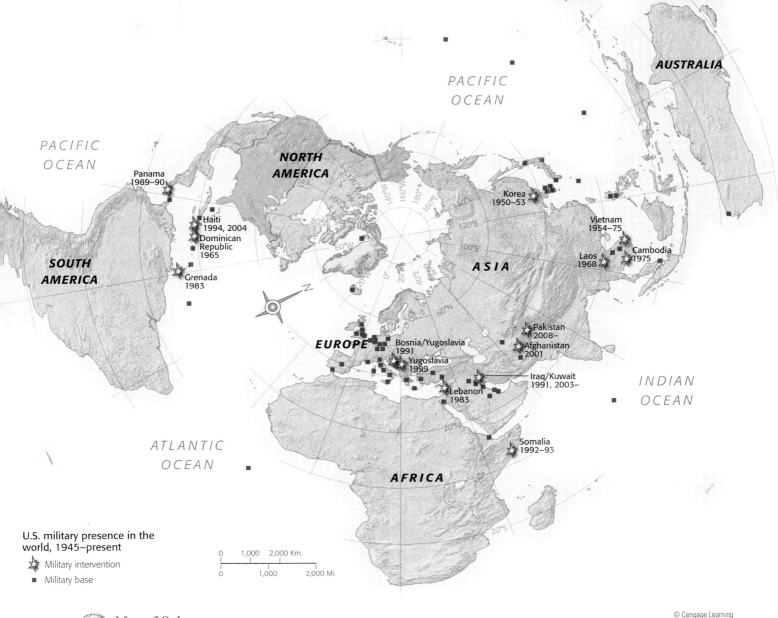

U.S. military presence in the
world, 1945–present

✦ Military intervention

■ Military base

Panama
1989–90

Haiti
1994, 2004

Dominican
Republic
1965

Grenada
1983

Korea
1950–53

Vietnam
1954–75

Laos
1968

Cambodia
1975

Pakistan
2008–

Afghanistan
2001

Bosnia/Yugoslavia
1991

Yugoslavia
1999

Iraq/Kuwait
1991, 2003–

Lebanon
1983

Somalia
1992–93

PACIFIC
OCEAN

PACIFIC
OCEAN

NORTH
AMERICA

SOUTH
AMERICA

ATLANTIC
OCEAN

EUROPE

ASIA

AUSTRALIA

AFRICA

INDIAN
OCEAN

0   1,000   2,000 Km.

0   1,000   2,000 Mi.

© Cengage Learning

**Map 29.1
U.S. Military Presence in the World, Since 1945**

As the major superpower, the United States maintained several dozen military bases outside of North
America, while engaging in military operations in Latin America, Africa, Asia, the Middle East, and Europe.

throw governments that were considered unfriendly
to U.S. interests, even if, as in Chile, these governments
were democratic and had been freely elected. Some
foreign observers applauded U.S. efforts to suppress
left-wing governments and movements that might
have favored the USSR or Communist China, whereas
others were hostile to U.S. power and criticized the
United States for practicing superpower imperialism.

Yet U.S. power, especially its economic leadership, became less dominant between the mid-1970s
and the early 1990s. Reasons for this change included
the rise of a rebuilt western Europe and Japan to eco-

nomic power, the military strength of the USSR, the
economic challenge from industrializing nations
such as South Korea and China, and the damage done
to the U.S. economy and prestige by the unsuccessful,
widely unpopular war in Vietnam. Also a factor was
the economic price Americans paid for global power.
Over four decades the Cold War cost the U.S. government around $4 trillion, and while growing U.S.
defense budgets of the 1980s did help undermine the
Soviet Union, it also transformed the United States
from a creditor nation into the world's largest debtor
nation, leaving Americans with ballooning federal

budget deficits. Only in the 1990s, under President Bill Clinton (g. 1993–2001), did the U.S. government temporarily eliminate the budget deficits that had accelerated between the 1960s and the 1980s.

Wars in Korea and Vietnam

In 1949, the Chinese communist victory in China, a country whose longtime government had been allied with and armed by the United States (see Chapter 27), alarmed Americans. Communist expansion, and the U.S. determination to halt it, led to the Korean War (1950–1953), which was followed a decade later by a more massive U.S. intervention in another Asian society, Vietnam. The conflict in Vietnam was the longest war the United States had ever waged (1963–1975).

The Korean War was sparked when North Korea, ruled by a brutal communist regime allied to the USSR, invaded South Korea, a U.S. ally, with the goal of forcibly reunifying the Korean peninsula (see Chapter 27). The anticommunist mood in the United States, already inflamed by the communist victory in China, made it politically unthinkable for President Harry S Truman not to oppose the North Korean thrust. But Truman never consulted the U.S. Congress, which had the constitutional responsibility to declare war; officially, Korea was a police action under U.N. sponsorship rather than a war, a precedent that allowed future presidents to commit U.S. military forces without congressional approval.

Furthermore, the Soviet support of North Korea with arms and advice, and the intervention of the communist Chinese on the North Korean side, deepened American fear of communist expansion. However, despite the 38,000 Americans killed and over 100,000 wounded, the war ended in stalemate. For the first time since the War of 1812, the United States had failed to decisively win a major military conflict. North Korea remained a rigid communist state, and South Korea did not become a democracy until the 1980s, more than three decades after the war.

The domino theory, which predicted a communist sweep throughout Southeast Asia, and the desire to keep valuable Southeast Asian resources in friendly hands, provided the rationale for financing the French effort to maintain colonial control (1946–1954) in Vietnam. When that effort failed, U.S. involvement increased, leading eventually to the U.S. military fighting Vietnamese communist forces armed by the USSR and China (see Chapter 31). Few U.S. leaders comprehended the depth of Vietnamese anti-Western nationalism and the country's long history of resistance to foreign invaders. As a growing communist-led insurgency, backed by North Vietnam, challenged a widely unpopular, U.S.-supported South Vietnamese government, the U.S. president, Lyndon B. Johnson (g. 1963–1969), committed military forces and launched an intensive air war against targets in North and South Vietnam and later in neighboring Cambodia and Laos. U.S. troop totals topped off at 550,000 by 1967. Between 1963 and 1975, 2.5 million Americans served in Vietnam; 58,000 died and 300,000 were wounded there.

As support within the United States for the war ebbed with military stalemate and increasing casualties in what seemed a quagmire, Johnson's successor, President Richard Nixon (g. 1969–1973), gradually withdrew U.S. forces and negotiated a political settlement with North Vietnam. But a policy throughout the war of spending lavishly on both "guns and butter"— military and domestic needs—generated huge budget deficits and other economic problems with which the United States struggled from the later 1960s into the 1990s. The war in Vietnam ultimately cost U.S. taxpayers around $1 trillion, as well as the nation's diplomatic prestige and credibility around the globe.

The United States and the Developing Nations

Decolonization, nationalism, the U.S.–Soviet struggle, and persistent poverty combined to make the Asian, African, and Latin American societies prone to crises, sometimes drawing in the United States. The United States often favored decolonization that presented opportunities to U.S. business; for example, it successfully pressured the Dutch to abandon Indonesia. However, the United States opposed independence for colonies, such as French-ruled Vietnam, where communists or other leftists dominated the nationalist movements. After decolonization, Americans offered generous aid to friendly nations and to victims of famine or natural catastrophes. U.S. assistance also sparked the Green Revolution in agriculture, which led to improved food production in countries such as India, Mexico, and the Philippines. However, Cold War challenges often involved the United States in long-term confrontations with communist-led revolutions, and U.S. leaders also staged interventions to help their allies oppose left-leaning governments in Iran, Chile, and Guatemala.

In some U.S. interventions, presidents dispatched troops to overturn a government or to support one side in a civil war or revolutionary situation. U.S. leaders used the threat of communism as the rationale for these actions, but some interventions removed democratic governments, as in Guatemala and Chile, or suppressed democratic movements. For example, President

On Patrol in Vietnam U.S. soldiers sought out National Liberation Front fighters and supporters in the villages, rice fields, and jungles of South Vietnam. They could not easily tell friend from foe and warily dealt with local people.

Lyndon Johnson, claiming that Americans would not permit another communist government alongside Fidel Castro's Cuba in the Western Hemisphere, dispatched twenty thousand U.S. Marines into the Dominican Republic in 1965 to support a military government that was under attack by the democratically elected leaders they had recently overthrown. The elected leaders, while left-leaning, were noncommunist reformers who had wide popular support.

Former Dominican president and the leader of the antimilitary movement, Juan Bosch (1909–2001), declared that "this was a democratic revolution smashed by the leading democracy in the world."[3] In addition to military interventions, the United States also provided friendly governments or anti-leftist groups with weapons, military advisers, intelligence agents, and funding. For example, in Laos from 1960 to 1975, during what was known as the CIA's "secret war" because the U.S. role was kept hidden from Congress and the U.S. public, Americans recruited an army from the Hmong hill peoples to fight communist Laotian and North Vietnamese forces (see Chapter 31).

A final type of intervention involved covert destabilization, which involved American agents working underground to help undermine or spark the overthrow of governments seen as hostile to U.S. interests. Covert actions even included arranging for assassinations of government leaders. U.S. clandestine activity, which undermined elected left-leaning democratic governments in Iran in the 1950s and Thailand and Chile in the 1970s, brought brutal dictatorships to all three countries. U.S. Secretary of State Henry Kissinger defended the U.S. encouragement of a military coup against the democratically elected, leftist Chilean government—a government that respected civil liberties—by explaining, "I don't see why we need to stand by and watch a country go communist due to the irresponsibility of its own people."[4] This attitude that the United States knows best has often infuriated people in other nations. Only in the mid-1970s,

preemptive war
A U.S. doctrine, triggered by the 2001 terrorist attacks, that sanctioned unilateral military action against potential threats.

with congressional hearings on covert activities, did Americans learn of the U.S. role in Chile and other interventions.

The United States in the Global System after 1989

The demise of the Soviet bloc in 1989 and the dissolution of the USSR in 1991 left the United States the dominant world power, although the European Union and the rising East Asian nations also enjoyed growing influence in the global system. But the lack of a rival superpower did not mean the end of challengers, among them international terrorists. The United States used its unsurpassed military and economic power to maintain a global presence and intervene in several countries, but Americans also paid a price in blood and treasure for activist foreign policies and global leadership.

American Foreign Policy after the Cold War

The United States now struggled to find a new role in a world characterized by what observers called a "New World Disorder" because of an outbreak of small, deadly conflicts. During the early 1990s, for example, President Bill Clinton (g. 1993–2001) sent a small number of U.S. troops, under United Nations auspices, to stabilize Somalia, a famine-racked northeast African state involved in a civil war. The intervention turned out badly, however, when the forces of a local warlord paraded the mutilated bodies of dead U.S. soldiers through the streets, forcing a U.S. withdrawal. In the aftermath, Americans were reluctant to assert power in other places where civilians were being slaughtered by the thousands, such as Rwanda and Liberia. However, working with European allies, Clinton did send U.S. forces to help end the deadly civil wars in the former Yugoslavia, and sought to resolve other foreign policy problems through diplomacy. In the 1990s, the Clinton administration reestablished diplomatic ties with Vietnam and lifted the trade embargo, which it viewed as punitive and counterproductive for U.S. business.

Radical Islam: The Taliban and Al Qaeda

Cold War policies sometimes came back to haunt the United States. In the 1980s, it had given military and financial aid to the Islamic rebels fighting Soviet troops and the pro-Soviet government in Afghanistan (see Chapter 30). Some of this aid went to Arab volunteers, among them the Saudi militant Osama bin Laden (b. 1957), who were fighting alongside the rebels. After the Soviets left Afghanistan in defeat in 1989, Muslim militants, the Taliban, defeated the other factions and imposed a rigid Islamic state, offering refuge for bin Laden's global terrorist network that became Al Qaeda ("the Base"). Al Qaeda now plotted terrorist attacks against the United States and its allies, sometimes using leftover U.S. weapons.

Farther west, Iraq's ruthless dictator, Saddam Hussein, used weapons acquired from the United States, his ally against Iran in the 1980s, to threaten Iraq's neighbors and repress dissident groups. In 1991, the United States led a coalition of nations that pushed invading Iraqi forces out of Kuwait during the Gulf War and then later protected the Kurds in northern Iraq from Saddam's reprisals. The intervention in oil-rich Kuwait was part of a consistent U.S. policy over the decades to protect the flow of oil from the Middle East to the West.

September 11, 2001

The terrorist attack launched by Al Qaeda on the World Trade Center in New York and the Pentagon in Washington, D.C., in September 2001, which killed nearly three thousand Americans, shocked the nation and led to a reshaping of both domestic and foreign policies. The new U.S. president, George W. Bush (b. 1946), introduced policies, such as preventive detention and monitoring of libraries, designed to prevent possible domestic terrorism. By attacking buildings that symbolized U.S. economic and military power to people around the world, the terrorists—young Muslim fanatics mostly from two close U.S. allies, Egypt and Saudi Arabia—hoped to capitalize on widespread anti-U.S. feelings. However, people in most countries, even if they disliked the United States and its power, deplored the bombings and the loss of innocent life.

The Bush Doctrine

The attacks prompted President Bush to declare a war on international terrorism using military force, but terrorist networks had no clear command structure or military resources and could not be influenced by diplomacy. With international support, the United States invaded Afghanistan to destroy Al Qaeda terrorist bases and displace the militant Islamic government that tolerated their presence. Bush announced a new doctrine of preemptive war that sanctioned unilateral military action against potential threats, and he named Iraq, Iran, and North Korea as comprising an "axis of evil" that threatened world peace (see Witness to the Past: Justifying Preemptive Strikes). The Bush doctrine advocated that the United States maintain overwhelming military superiority over all challengers. Critics perceived the Bush doctrine as a recipe for acquiring an American empire through military action, a violation, they charged, of international law.

The concern with international terrorism led to a resumption of unilateralist U.S. foreign policies, in which the United States acted without widespread international support. Rejecting opposition from the United Nations and key U.S. allies, in 2003 the Bush administration used faulty or manipulated intelligence to claim that Iraq possessed weapons of mass destruction and aided Al Qaeda. American forces invaded and occupied Iraq, ending Saddam Hussein's brutal regime, but the U.S. forces found no weapons of mass destruction or evidence of a Saddam–Al Qaeda link; furthermore, the Bush administration had planned poorly for restoring stability in Iraq, a nation rich in oil but troubled by ethnic and religious divisions that exploded into civil war. A mounting insurgency by Iraqis and suicide bombings largely linked to foreign terrorists, who now flocked to Iraq to fight Americans, caused thousands of U.S. casualties, and complicated political and economic reconstruction.

By 2006, basic services, such as electricity, and oil production had still not been restored to prewar levels, and violence continued to plague Iraqi society. The spiraling costs of the Iraq occupation and other expenses, combined with large tax cuts, ballooned U.S. budget deficits that could not be sustained long term without serious damage to the U.S. economy. The unpopular Iraq war, charges that the United States tortured suspected terrorists, and the U.S. rejection of several international treaties, such as that on global warming, further alienated Western allies and divided the American people.

Wars in Iraq and Afghanistan

Flexing its military might rather than diplomatic influence, the United States had assumed heavy burdens, sending troops to Afghanistan, Iraq, and elsewhere while maintaining military bases in several dozen countries and islands around the world. By 2004, the United States accounted for half of all military spending worldwide, spending as much on its military and weapons as all other nations combined, and it also accounted for about half of all arms sales to the world's nations.

> " Living in the world's richest nation, many Americans benefited from a growing economy and widespread affluence. "

The United States plays a vital role in world governance through its diplomatic engagements, vast military deployments, and buttressing of the global economy, a fact appreciated by many nations because the cost is largely borne by U.S. taxpayers. Yet the global recession that began in the United States in 2007 revealed systemic weaknesses in the American economy. Although anti-U.S. sentiment grew in the early twenty-first century, President Barack Obama was elected in 2008 on the promise of a new direction in American diplomacy. In his inaugural address, President Obama pledged a more principled course: "Our security emanates from the justness of our cause; the force of our example; the tempering qualities of humility and restraint."[5] Nevertheless, since the Romans two millennia ago, no other nation has been as dominant in military, economic, political, and social realms as the United States has been after 1990.

LO² The Changing Societies of North America and the Pacific Basin

In the years following World War II, the United States and Canada in North America and Australia and New Zealand in the southwestern corner of the Pacific Basin—all originally settled by people from the British Isles—shared a general prosperity, similar social patterns, and many cultural traditions, but they also played different roles in the world. Besides exercising more political, economic, and military power than these other nations, the United States had a stable democracy and a rapidly changing society. The United States, Canada, and Australia all attracted millions of immigrants from around the world, linking their cultures more closely to other nations.

Prosperity, Technology, and Inequality in the United States

Living in the world's richest nation, many Americans benefited from a growing economy and widespread affluence. During the nation's most prosperous

In the wake of the shocking terrorist attacks on the United States in September 2001, the administration of President George W. Bush produced a document, the National Security Strategy of the United States, that restated the U.S. desire to spread democracy and capitalism while announcing that the United States would act preemptively, striking first, unilaterally if necessary, against any hostile states that the Bush administration believed might be planning to attack U.S. targets. Depending on the observer, the document either reflected or exploited Americans' fear of terrorist attacks. In 2003, Bush used the preemptive strike rationale to order a military invasion and occupation of Iraq, which he claimed had weapons of mass destruction. After Saddam's fall, Bush offered a new mission: fostering democracy in Iraq as an example for the Middle East. To critics, however, the failure to find such weapons, the faulty intelligence about them, and the huge financial and human costs of the resulting occupation for both Americans and Iraqis all suggested the dangers of a preemptive strategy. Furthermore, they argued, many presidents before Bush had claimed to promote democracy abroad but had rarely done so, especially when they used military force to install a pro-U.S. government in another country.

The great struggles of the twentieth century between liberty and totalitarianism ended with a decisive victory for the forces of freedom—and a single sustainable model for national success: freedom democracy and free enterprise.... Only nations that share a commitment to protecting basic human rights and guaranteeing political and economic freedom will be able to unleash the potential of their people and assure their future prosperity.... Today the United States enjoys a position of unparalleled military strength and great economic and political influence. In keeping with our heritage and principles we do not use our strength to press for unilateral advantage. We seek instead to create a balance of power that favors human freedom.... We will extend the peace by encouraging free and open societies on every continent.

Defending our Nation against its enemies is the first and fundamental commitment of the Federal Government. Today, that task has changed dramatically. Enemies in the past needed great armies and great industrial capabilities to endanger America. Now, shadowy networks of individuals can bring great chaos and suffering to our shores for less than it costs to purchase a single tank. Terrorists are organized to penetrate open societies and to turn the power of modern technologies against us. To defeat this threat we must make use of every tool in our arsenal.... The war against terrorists of global reach is a global enterprise of uncertain duration.... America will hold to account nations that are compromised by terror, including those who harbor terrorists—because the allies of terror are the enemies of civilization.... Our enemies have openly declared that they are seeking weapons of mass destruction.... The United States will not allow these efforts to succeed.... And, as a matter of common sense and self-defense, America will act against such emerging threats before they are fully formed.... We must be prepared to defeat our enemies' plans. History will judge harshly those who saw this coming danger but failed to act. In the new world we have entered, the only path to peace and security is the path of action....

The struggle against global terrorism is different from any other war in our history. It will be fought on many fronts against a particularly elusive enemy over an extended period of time.... New deadly challenges have emerged from rogue states and terrorists.... Rogue regimes seek nuclear, biological, and chemical weapons.... We must be prepared to stop rogue states and their terrorist clients before they are able to threaten or use weapons of mass destruction against the United States and our allies.... The United States can no longer solely rely on a reactive posture as we have in the past.... We cannot let our enemies strike first.... We must adapt the concept of imminent threat to the capabilities and objectives of today's adversaries.... The greater the threat, the greater the risk of inaction—and the more compelling the case for taking anticipatory action to defend ourselves, even if uncertainty remains as to the time and place of the enemy's attack. To forestall or prevent such hostile acts by our adversaries, the United States will, if necessary, act preemptively.

Thinking About the Reading

1. How does the document reflect the tendency of U.S. leaders to claim a national goal of spreading U.S. political and economic models in the world?
2. What does the document offer as the rationale for preemptive actions?

Source: The National Security Strategy of the United States (http://www.whitehouse.gov/nsc/print/nssall.html).

decade, the 1960s, the production of goods and services doubled, and per capita income rose by half. Many Americans moved into new automobile, aerospace, service, and information technology industries. By 2000, the United States accounted for one-third of the world's total production of goods and services, more than twice as much as second-place Japan, and enjoyed a median annual family income of more than $40,000.

Americans also owned the majority of, and profited from, the giant multinational corporations, such as General Motors and Wal-Mart, that played ever-larger roles in the globalizing world economy. However, there were downsides to this growth. With 6 percent of the world population, Americans also consumed around 40 percent of all the world's resources and produced a large share of the chemicals, gases, and toxic wastes that pollute the atmosphere, alter the climate, and destroy the land. A major world study in 2005 ranked the United States twenty-eighth in meeting sustainable environmental goals, well behind most developed and developing nations.

A Winner-Takes-All Economy

Beginning in the 1970s, a growing economy improved the lot of some people, but it hurt millions of others. Americans celebrated innovations in medicine, space research, transportation, and particularly electronics. Space satellites greatly improved weather forecasting, communications, and intelligence gathering. Computers and handheld devices revolutionized life with their convenience and versatility. But as computers and robots increased efficiency, they also replaced many workers. In the 1980s, one-third of industrial jobs disappeared. Industrialists won corporate bonuses for relocating factories and exporting jobs to Latin America or Asia, devastating factory-dependent American communities. By the early 2000s, although life for the majority of Americans remained comfortable compared to that in most other nations, unemployment for men was the highest it had been in five decades. Some economists referred to a winner-takes-all economy that produced ever-more millionaires but also a struggling middle class and, at the bottom of the social ladder, more

> "Except for the richest 1 percent of Americans, whose earnings skyrocketed, average incomes fell between 2001 and 2006."

indigent and homeless people. Except for the richest 1 percent of Americans, whose earnings skyrocketed, average incomes fell between 2001 and 2006.

In contrast to western Europe, Canada, Australia, and New Zealand, the United States never developed a comprehensive welfare state. As a result, despite federal government efforts at abolishing poverty, a widening gap separated the richest one-third and the poorest one-third of Americans. The inequality of wealth in the United States grew dramatically after 1980, and by 1997, the top 1 percent of the population owned 20 percent of all the wealth. By 2004, 12.5 percent of Americans lived below the poverty line. In 2005, the devastating hurricane, Katrina, caused massive damage and flooding in the Gulf Coast, ruining New Orleans, rendering millions homeless, and killing several thousand people. It also starkly revealed America's poverty gap: most of the people who died or were only rescued days later were black and poor, unable to afford transportation out of the area. Partly because of the inequalities in wealth and health care, the United States ranked eighth—behind several European nations, Canada, and Australia—in overall quality of life in the 2004 United Nations Human Development Report.

Suburbia

Changes in the economy went hand in hand with the suburbanization of American life. In the decades following World War II, millions of people sought a better life in suburbia, the bedroom communities on the edges of major cities. Suburbs, occupied typically by white Americans, featured shopping malls and well-funded schools. Suburban developer William Levitt argued that no person who owned his or her own house and yard could be a communist, because he or she was too busy keeping up, and working to pay for, his or her property. The automobile, increasingly affordable for the middle class, combined with government-funded freeway and highway construction, made long commutes from the suburbs to jobs in the central city possible. City cores were increasingly dominated by the local-born poor, often nonwhite, or immigrants, while increasing use of fossil fuels and clearing land for housing and business development harmed the environment.

American Political Life: Conservatism and Liberalism

In the decades after World War II, fiscal conservatives, commonly big business groups favoring low taxes and opposing social welfare, allied with religious groups who disliked social and cultural liberalization, dominated the presidency and often the United States Congress and the judiciary. Liberals played a key role in U.S. political life chiefly in the 1960s and, to a lesser extent, the 1990s; they were generally supported by labor unions and groups that sought social change and a stronger government safety net.

American Society in the 1950s

The widespread desire for stability after the great Depression and a calamitous world war encouraged both a political and social conservatism throughout the 1950s. Americans who questioned the government or prevailing social norms faced harassment, expulsion from job or school, arrest, or accusations of being "un-American." Whatever their social class, more Americans than ever before married, producing a "baby boom" of children born in the years following the war. The mass media portrayed happy women in a world defined by kitchen, bedroom, babies, and home. Society expected homosexuals to remain deep in the closet, and those who did not faced taunting, beatings, or arrest.

The 1960s: A Decade of Change

American politics and society were reshaped again during the 1960s, becoming open to new ideas and lifestyles as liberalism became influential. The era saw many achievements, including the first people to walk on the moon and the idealism that created the Peace Corps, an agency that sent young Americans to help communities in developing nations, chiefly as teachers, health workers, and agricultural specialists. Presidents John F. Kennedy (g. 1961–1963) and Lyndon B. Johnson (g. 1963–1969) launched government programs to address poverty and racism. But the 1960s was also a decade of doubts, anger, and violence. Three national leaders were assassinated, including Kennedy, who was shot in the head while riding in a motorcade in 1963. The war in Vietnam, the civil rights movement for African Americans, and issues of environmental protection and women's empowerment divided the nation. The country's social fabric fragmented as pro-war "hawks" and antiwar "doves" competed for support. Riots and demonstrations punctuated the decade.

During the 1960s, a large segment of young people, chiefly middle class, rebelled against the values of their parents and established society. Some youth, especially high school and university students, worked to change society and politics, registering voters, holding "teach-ins" to discuss national issues, and going door to door to spread their cause. Other youth forged what they called a counterculture that often involved using illegal drugs and engaging in casual sex. The Summer of Love in 1967, during which young people from North America and elsewhere gathered in San Francisco to hear rock music and share camaraderie, and the Woodstock rock music festival of 1969, which attracted more than 300,000 young people, marked the zenith of both the youth counterculture and political activism.

The Conservative Era

In the 1970s, with the winding down of the war in Vietnam and widespread concern at the social excesses of the previous decade, the nation returned to more conservative values and politics. With the exception of the 1990s, when the moderate Bill Clinton (g. 1993–2001) held the presidency, conservatives maintained their dominance of American politics, the economy, and the social agenda until 2008. Religion remained a powerful force, with Americans being more likely to attend churches and profess strong Christian beliefs than most Europeans. By the 1980s, Christian conservatives, mainly evangelical Protestants but also many Catholics, became influential in public life, helping elect political conservatives to office. Some experts attributed the rise of Christian conservatism to a rejection of reason and tolerance. While Americans avidly consumed new technologies, polls showed that, because of religious conservatism, substantial numbers also mistrusted science.

Observers found much to deplore and much to praise in U.S. politics. Money from big corporations and other special interests increasingly played a major role, fostering corruption and

> ❝ The widespread desire for stability after the great Depression and a calamitous world war encouraged both a political and social conservatism throughout the 1950s. ❞

widespread political apathy. However, on the positive side, a free media exposed government corruption, including abuse of power by presidents. President Richard Nixon, facing impeachment, resigned in 1973 for sanctioning and then covering up illegal activities by his subordinates. The presidencies of both Ronald Reagan (g. 1983–1989) and Clinton were marred by congressional hearings examining their misdeeds. After the controversial, bitter 2000 and 2004 elections, Americans were sharply divided between the two major political parties and the divergent policies they supported.

Barack Obama: New Possibilities

In 2008, with two wars continuing in Afghanistan and Iraq and a severe recession threatening American prosperity, the Democratic Party won the White House and increased its majorities in the Senate and House of Representatives. President Obama's campaign inspired more Americans than ever before to get involved and vote, causing many observers to note that 2008 represented the beginning of a new political era. In the early months of his presidency, President Obama charted a pragmatic course, sidestepping the bitter partisanship of his predecessors, yet the challenges to Americans loomed ever larger.

American Society and Popular Culture

American society was changed by shifting patterns after World War II, especially suburbanization. Most suburbs lacked ethnic and cultural diversity and isolated residents from the stimulation, as well as the problems, of big-city life. Suburban living also intensified the trend, begun before World War II, toward two-parent, single-breadwinner nuclear families that lived apart from other relatives. Critics lambasted the conformity of life in the standardized suburban tract houses, while changing city life affected both ethnic and gender relations.

The Civil Rights Movement

The most significant social change came with the Civil Rights movement, which was organized by African Americans in the 1950s. Southern states maintained strict racial segregation, forcing blacks to attend separate schools and to even use different public drinking fountains than whites. Racism and poverty often encouraged African Americans in northern industrial cities to concentrate in run-down inner-city neighborhoods, known as ghettos. In 1954, the Supreme Court outlawed segregated schools, and one year later, in Montgomery, Alabama, Rosa Parks (1913–2005), a seamstress and community activist, bravely refused to give up her front seat on a bus to a white man, sparking a mass movement for change.

A black minister, Reverend Martin Luther King, Jr. (1929–1968), led a bus boycott to protest Parks' arrest and fine. Using the strategy of nonviolent resistance pioneered by Mohandas Gandhi in South Africa and India in the early twentieth century, King led a protest movement all over the South. While leading the 1963 March on Washington to demand equal rights for nonwhites, he presented his vision: "I have a dream. When we let freedom ring, all of God's children will be able to join hands and sing in the words of that old spiritual, 'Thank God almighty, we are free at last!'"[6] King's assassination by a white racist in 1968 shocked the nation, but by then the African American struggle for equal rights had inspired similar struggles by nonwhites elsewhere in the world.

Thanks to the efforts of King, Parks, and many others, African Americans gradually gained legal equality, and many became able to move into the middle and upper classes. The 2008 election of President Obama, the first African American to hold the nation's highest office, was a momentous and inspirational achievement. However, in the early twenty-first century, African Americans were still far more likely than whites to live in poverty, face unemployment, and be imprisoned.

A Multicultural America

In the later twentieth century, Americans became an increasingly multiracial, multicultural society. By 2006, the U.S. population of 300 million, the third largest total in the world after China and India, was more diverse than ever, and more than 10 percent were foreign-born. American life took on a cosmopolitan flavor as Latin American grocery stores, Asian restaurants, and African art galleries opened in communities throughout the country, and Spanish was widely spoken.

Ethnic groups grew through legal and illegal immigration. Millions of Latin Americans moved to the United States. By 2000, the Mexican American population alone numbered around 20 million and seemed poised to soon outnumber the 25 million African Americans. Several million Asians also relocated to the United States, especially from China, South Korea, India, and Southeast Asia. Immigrants also arrived from Europe, the Middle East, the Caribbean, and South Pacific islands. Many labored for meager wages

President Obama Inaugurated on January 20, 2009, President Barack Obama is the son of an American mother and Kenyan father. In the village of Kogelo, Kenya, the birthplace of Obama's father, revellers celebrated the historic occasion.

in crowded sweatshops in big cities, where bosses often ignored safety regulations. Immigration marginalized Native Americans even more than before. While many lived in cities, others remained isolated on reservations. Some of them joined movements to assert their rights, often seeking a return of lands seized by white settlers generations earlier, and a few tribes achieved prosperity by operating gambling casinos; however, most Native Americans remained poor.

The Feminist Revolution

Women's issues became more prominent in U.S. history. In the 1950s, few women worked for high pay, married women could not borrow money in their own names, there was no legal concept of sexual harassment, and men often joked of keeping women "barefoot and pregnant." Beginning in the 1960s, women led a feminist movement demanding equal legal rights with men and improved economic status. In 1963, Betty Friedan's (1921–2006) passionate book, *The Feminine Mystique*, identified women's core prob-

lem as a stunting of their growth by a patriarchal society. With slogans such as "Sisterhood Is Powerful," women came together in groups, such as the National Organization for Women (NOW), to fight against sexism. Thanks in part to feminists' efforts, the median income of women workers climbed from 62 to 70 percent of that of men, and the number of women with paid work more than doubled between 1960 and 2000. Women held governorships, served in Congress, and sat on the Supreme Court. By the twenty-first century, more women than men attended universities, some joining highly paid, traditionally male occupations such as law, university teaching, engineering, and medicine. However, most women with paid jobs struggled to juggle work with family and housekeeping responsibilities, and sexual harassment, domestic violence, and rape remained serious problems.

 Feminist Manifestoes From the Late 1960s Learn why feminists in the United States opposed all forms of patriarchy, and protested institutions like the Miss America Pageant.

Social and legal changes affected both women and men. Divorce became easier and more common; by the 1990s, more than half of all marriages ended in divorce, and single-parent households grew more frequent. Increasingly, men and women never married. Whatever their gender, Americans remained deeply divided on some women's issues, especially abortion, which was long common but illegal before being declared legal by the Supreme Court in 1973. Americans also disagreed about homosexuality. By the 1960s, gay men and lesbians actively struggled to end harassment and legal discrimination, gaining greater acceptance in society. Yet homosexuals still faced hostility and sometimes violence. During the early twenty-first century, Americans quarreled over allowing homosexuals to marry or establish legal partnerships, a pattern of acceptance that was common in Europe and Canada but opposed by many conservative Americans.

From Rock to Rap

Once importers of culture from Europe, Americans became the world's greatest exporters of popular culture products. U.S.-made films, television programs, books, magazines, and sports reached a global audience, and popular music, especially rock, helped spark a cultural revolution in the 1950s and 1960s. The first exhilarating blasts of rock 'n' roll, notably from the white singer Elvis Presley (1935–1977) and the inventive black guitarist Chuck Berry (b. 1926), delighted youth while often alarming adults. Rock was inspired by black music, chiefly rhythm-and-blues, but also by the country music of white southerners, and it became the heart of the youth movement of the 1960s. Albums by key rock musicians, such as the American folk singer-songwriter Bob Dylan and the British group The Beatles, conveyed messages that shaped political awareness. After the 1960s, rock lost its political edge but, evolving into forms such as punk, grunge, and heavy metal, remained at the heart of U.S. popular music. In the 1980s and 1990s, rap music, or hip-hop, emerged out of black ghettos. An eclectic mix of rock, soul, rhythm-and-blues, and Caribbean music, hip-hop expressed the tensions of urban black youth yearning for independence, dignity, sex, and fun.

The Canadian Experience

Canadians have remained proudly independent of their powerful southern neighbor while nurturing their political and social differences, such as by maintaining two official languages—English and French. Two parties, one liberal and one conservative, have dominated national elections, but smaller left-wing and right-wing parties also play key roles, often governing Canadian provinces. The Party Québécois (KAY-be-KWAH), for example, which supports French Canadian nationalism, is influential in French-speaking Quebec, a province that contains one-quarter of Canada's population, and periodically seeks the separation of Quebec from Canada (see Map 29.2).

Interactive Map

In 1985, the federal parliament, hoping to preserve a united Canada, responded to French Canadians' resentments against Canada's English-speaking majority by recognizing Quebec as a distinct society within Canada and granting more autonomy to all the provinces.

Canadians, 33 million strong by 2005, cannot ignore their proximity to the United States, which has almost ten times Canada's population and vastly more power in the world. Most of Canada's people live within 100 miles of the U.S. border, and thus have easy access to the U.S. mass media and other cultural influences. Canada has also formed a major trading partnership with its southern neighbor. Americans own some 20 percent of the Canadian economy, prompting some Canadians to welcome U.S. investment as a spur to economic growth and others to resent U.S. domination.

Free Trade and the Decline of Democracy

Read a cogent critique by Ralph Nader, a consumer advocate and political activist, of international free-trade agreements.

In 1994, the North American Free Trade Agreement (NAFTA) further bound the Canadian, Mexican, and U.S. economies. Yet, despite usually friendly U.S.–Canada relations, Canadians have often opposed U.S. foreign policies, including the wars in Vietnam and Iraq.

Despite occasional economic downturns, Canadians have enjoyed industrialization and prosperity, which in turn have fostered social stability. Agricultural, industrial, and natural resource exports have helped finance rising living standards; vast oil reserves have enriched western provinces. Canada has consistently ranked among the top five nations in the annual United Nations Human Development Index of quality of life, and has built a strong social safety net for its citizens, including national health insurance. Also, Canadians have generally been more liberal on social and economic issues than Americans, approving same-sex marriage, banning the death penalty, and, in some provinces, decriminalizing marijuana use. As the society has become more secular, organized religion has

© Cengage Learning

![globe icon] **Map 29.2**
Canada

The Canadian federation includes eleven provinces stretching from Newfoundland in the east to British Columbia and the Yukon in the west. In 1999, a large part of northern Canada, inhabited chiefly by the Inuit, became the self-governing region of Nunavut.

---

had a declining influence in public life, a trend especially notable in Quebec, where the Catholic Church once enjoyed great influence.

Canadian society has become increasingly diverse. The nation has welcomed several million immigrants from all over the world, many from Asia and the Caribbean. In 2005, one of those Caribbean immigrants, Haitian-born Michaelle Jean, a television journalist in Quebec, became Canada's governor general, the nation's official head of state. Unlike Americans, Canadians have adopted laws, especially the Multiculturalism Act of 1988, to allow ethnic minorities to maintain their cultures. Canadians have also recognized the rights of the indigenous Native Americans, known in Canada as the "First Nations," who have pressed land claims. To address the desire for autonomy of the Inuit people of the Arctic region, in 1999 the federal government transformed much of

northern Canada into the self-governing territory of Nunavut (NOO-nuh-voot), whose 27,000 people are mostly Inuit.

The Pacific Basin Societies

The diverse societies scattered around the Pacific Basin experienced major changes during this era as they adjusted to a new world. In the two largest, most populous countries, Australia and New Zealand, the majority population, descended from mainly British and Irish, settlers, had long identified with western European society, building economies that closely resembled those of the industrial West. But the rise of Asian economies prompted Australia and New Zealand to cultivate closer ties with East and Southeast Asian nations. Meanwhile, many Pacific islands that were once ruled by Britain, France, or

New Zealand became independent nations navigating in a globalizing world.

Australia

During this era, Australia became one of the world's most affluent nations, known to its people as the "lucky country" because of its abundant resources and high living standards. Thanks in part to a comprehensive system of social welfare, health care, and education, Australians have forged a quality of life that placed the nation third after Norway and Sweden in the United Nations Human Development Report for 2004. However, the nation has also faced economic and social problems, including a chronic high unemployment rate, enduring sexism, and areas of persisting poverty.

With 20 million people by 2005, Australia has become an increasingly diverse nation. In 1973, the federal government abandoned restrictions on nonwhite, especially Asian, immigration—known as the "white Australia" policy—that had been in place since 1901. The shift to a policy based on skills rather than ethnicity stimulated immigration from Asia and the Middle East, and predominantly Asian neighborhoods developed in major cities. Newcomers from Europe also continued to arrive, and by 2001, nearly one-quarter of Australia's people had been born abroad. Race relations improved as Aborigines, often poor and facing discrimination, gained some self-determination and land rights for their tribal territories. As a result, one group was able to block a dam project in the 1990s that threatened tribal land. Yet, those Aborigines living in cities, often in run-down neighborhoods, have struggled to find their place in the largely white-owned urban economy.

Changing global conditions have forced new economic thinking. With an economy based primarily on the export of natural and animal resources, such as minerals, wheat, beef, and wool, Australia needed secure outside markets. But the formation of the European Community and NAFTA threatened traditional markets in Europe and North America, raising questions about the nation's traditional link to Britain. Subsequently, Australians established closer trade links to nations in Southeast Asia, East Asia, and

Lion's Dance In recent decades, many Asians have settled in Australia. This Chinese lion's dance, in Melbourne's large Chinatown, celebrates the Chinese New Year.

the Pacific islands. By 2000, Asian nations accounted for some 60 percent of Australia's export market.

New Zealand

Like Australians, New Zealanders had long depended on British patronage, but they now had to adjust to changing global conditions. The nation's economy relied heavily on tourism and the export of agricultural products, mostly to Britain. When Britain joined the European Community, New Zealand's access to British markets was diminished, so New Zealand cultivated closer relations with the United States. However, these relations cooled after New Zealand refused to allow nuclear-armed U.S. ships to make visits to its ports. New Zealand then fostered economic cooperation with nearby Asian and Pacific countries, and by 2000, these countries accounted for one-third of the nation's trade.

New economic directions affected New Zealand's society. While experiencing rising unemployment, New Zealanders were supported by an elaborate social welfare system. Owing in part to expanded educational opportunities, women gained new economic roles and served in politics. In 1999, Helen Clark (b. 1950), a former university professor, became the nation's first female prime minister. Increased immigration from Asia and the Pacific islands and new recognition and rights for the native Maori minority reflected the fact that New Zealanders became more comfortable with ethnic diversity.

The Islanders

While Australians and New Zealanders had long enjoyed independence, the decolonization of the Pacific islands, spurred by the United Nations, had to wait until the 1960s. Between 1962 and 1980, nine independent Pacific nations were formed in Polynesia and Melanesia, and in 1990, the United States gave up control of some of its Micronesian territories. But even most independent islands retained close ties to their former colonizers. Some French-ruled islands, such as Tahiti and New Caledonia, became overseas departments of France, with representation in the French parliament, but many islanders still resented what they considered to be a disguised French colonialism. Whether nation or colony, islanders usually remained dependent on fishing, tourism, and the export of mineral and agricultural products.

Islanders have cooperated on common issues, collectively adapting to change while retaining some indigenous traditions. For example, Western Samoa, first ruled by Germany and then by New Zealand, has

an elected parliament, adopted from the West, but clan chiefs still govern the villages, as they have for centuries. But certain forces have undermined traditional village life. Poverty has fostered migration to island cities, such as Suva in Fiji and Pago Pago in American Samoa, and emigration to Australia, New Zealand, Hawaii, and the mainland United States. Some islands have also experienced ethnic or regional conflict as groups compete for political power and scarce land. Together the islanders fought high-technology fishing fleets from industrialized nations, especially Japan, that threatened their own low-technology fishing, and joined with Australia and New Zealand to declare the Pacific a nuclear-free zone. However, some problems affecting islands have defied solution. Because of rising sea levels, which threaten low-lying atolls and coastal plains, many islanders, such as the eleven thousand people on the Tuvalo islands in the central Pacific, will have to relocate over the next century.

LO³ Political Change in Latin America and the Caribbean

The Latin American and Caribbean peoples (see Map 29.3) had a different experience than North Americans and the Pacific Basin societies. Social inequality, economic underdevelopment, and the demands for change often generated revolutionary and progressive political movements in impoverished villages and shantytowns. Sometimes leftists gained power, launching reforms, though only in Cuba did they remain in power for decades. A few Latin American countries and most small Caribbean islands enjoyed a consistent democratic tradition; elsewhere, however, military leaders or autocratic civilians often dominated governments.

Interactive Map

Despotisms and Democracies

Latin American governments struggled to find the right mix of policies to raise living standards and expand political participation. Early in the century, the Mexican Revolution, for example, challenged the inequities in society and wealth but later lost most of its revolution-

Internet Resources for Latin America (*http://lib.nmsu.edu/subject/bord/laguia/*). This outstanding site, from New Mexico State University, provides information and links.

Map 29.3
Modern Latin America and the Caribbean

Latin America includes the nations of Central and South America and those Caribbean societies that are Spanish-speaking, including Cuba and the Dominican Republic. Brazil, Argentina, and Mexico are the largest Latin American nations. The peoples of the small Caribbean islands also formed independent states.

© Cengage Learning

ary vigor and ultimately failed to resolve Mexico's problems. At other times, paternalistic but authoritarian reformers mobilized workers and peasants for change, but they also failed to empower the mass of the population or significantly improve their lives.

Juan Perón and Argentina

The charismatic Juan Perón (puh-RONE) (1895–1974), a former army officer and hypnotic public speaker who was elected Argentina's president in

1946, was one of the major autocratic reformers. Perón soon marginalized the legislature and crushed his opposition. With help from his hugely popular wife, Evita Perón (1919–1952), an actress and proponent of social justice, the nationalistic Perón won the support of workers and the middle class by emphasizing industrialization and by having his government buy up banks, companies, and railroads that were often owned by unpopular foreign interests. Meanwhile, Evita promoted women's issues, but after she died in 1952, Perón's popular support waned. Corruption, growing unemployment, inflation, strikes, and human rights abuses led to his overthrow in 1955. Perón returned to power briefly in 1973–1974, but otherwise the military ruled Argentina for most of the 1950s through early 1980s, often killing opponents. Yet Perón's followers helped to achieve the restoration of democracy in 1983.

"Right-wing and left-wing forces jockeyed for power in Latin America for decades."

aspirations often opposed by whites.

Hugo Chavez and Venezuela

By the later 1990s, as disillusionment with capitalism increased, the left was regaining the political initiative. Mobilizing workers and peasants, who had benefited little from the country's oil wealth, the former general Hugo Chavez was elected president of oil-rich Venezuela and introduced socialist policies that alienated the wealthy and middle class but cheered poor Venezuelans, who supported his mar-

An Era of Turmoil

Right-wing and left-wing forces jockeyed for power in Latin America for decades. In the majority of countries from the 1950s through the late 1980s, right-wing military governments and despots ruled, suppressing labor unions, student protesters, and democracy activists to maintain stability. Some right-wing governments, especially in Central American countries such as El Salvador and Guatemala, organized informal armed units, known as death squads, to assassinate dissidents who were deemed threats to the regime. However, despite the repression, left-wing movements increased their strength. For example, by 1979, the Sandinistas, a revolutionary movement led by Marxists, had mobilized enough popular support to defeat the dictatorship, in power since the 1920s, and gain control of Nicaragua.

During the later 1980s, with right-wing authoritarian rule largely discredited because it was unable or unwilling to address mass poverty, many nations turned to democracy under centrist or moderate leftist leaders. But in most cases, the free markets these democratic governments introduced struggled to resolve severe challenges, allowing both right-wing and extreme leftist forces to increase in strength. Some nations also faced racial and ethnic tensions. In particular, the large Indian communities in Bolivia, Peru, Colombia, Mexico, and Guatemala, often allied with the left, increasingly sought equal rights, a fairer share of the wealth, and recognition of their cultures,

CHRONOLOGY

Latin America and the Caribbean, Since 1945

1946–1955	Government of Juan Perón in Argentina
1954	CIA overthrow of Guatemalan government
1959	Triumph of Fidel Castro in Cuba
1962	Cuban missile crisis
1964–1985	Military government in Brazil
1973	Overthrow of Chilean government
1973–1989	Military government in Chile
1979–1989	Sandinista government in Nicaragua
1983	Restoration of Argentina's democracy
1990	U.S. invasion of Panama
1994	Formation of NAFTA
1998	Economic collapse in many nations
2000	Election of President Vicente Fox in Mexico
2002	Election of President Lula da Silva in Brazil

ginalization of the congress and control of the courts. Chavez called his policies the Bolivaran Revolution, linking them to the nineteenth-century, Venezuelan-born liberator, Simón Bolívar. But the United States moved to isolate the dictatorial, pro-Cuba Chavez regime and support the opposition. During the early twenty-first century, voters who were desperate for more equitable economic and social policies also elected pragmatic leftist leaders in countries such as Argentina, Brazil, Chile, and Uruguay. These leaders often began the process—neglected by their cautious predecessors—of prosecuting the human-rights violations that occurred years earlier under military rule. But whether imported economic ideas will work for Latin Americans remains to be seen.

"By the later 1990s, as disillusionment with capitalism increased, the left was regaining the political initiative."

The United States in Latin America

The United States has had a powerful economic and political presence in Latin America since the nineteenth century, and, as the world's major superpower, it had even more of an impact in the second half of the twentieth century. The U.S. role in the region was complex, with the country serving not only as the neighborhood bully at times but also as a leading trading partner, a major source of investment capital, a supplier of military and economic assistance, and an inspiration to the region's democrats and free-market enthusiasts. As a result, many Latin American leaders maintained close relations with various U.S. administrations. U.S. popular culture, particularly films and music, influenced local cultures, while several million Latin Americans have moved to the United States legally or illegally. The United States gained favor in the region by transferring control of the Panama Canal—built by the United States in the early 1900s—to Panama in 1999, yet the agreement also allowed U.S. military bases to remain along the canal.

The United States intervened in Latin American and Caribbean countries under the banner of anti-communism. These interventions aroused much local resentment, as was illustrated by the earliest intervention, in Guatemala in 1954. A force led by exiled Guatemalan military officers, covertly organized, armed, and trained by the U.S. Central Intelligence Agency (CIA), overthrew a democratically elected reformist government that American

leaders accused of being communist, an unsupported claim. The government had angered U.S. business interests, especially the powerful United Fruit Company, by implementing land reform and encouraging labor unions. The United Fruit Company controlled much of the Guatemalan economy, especially the banana plantations, and had close ties to officials in the Eisenhower administration. The removal of the democratic regime was welcomed by wealthy Guatemalans and U.S. corporations with investments in Guatemala, but the new leaders proved to be murderous tyrants. Forming death squads, they killed more than 200,000 Guatemalans, especially poor Indian peasants and workers, over the next three decades. By 1990, 90 percent of Guatemalans still lived in poverty, and one-third of them lacked adequate food.

 Explore life in Nicaragua as a young agricultural worker in the 1970s through this interactive simulation.

The successful ousting of the Guatemalan government encouraged U.S. leaders to use their power elsewhere to further Cold War foreign policy objectives. Americans offered military assistance and advice to maintain friendly governments in power against the challenge of revolutionary movements in El Salvador, Honduras, and Colombia. As in Guatemala, the United States also used covert operations to help undermine or overthrow governments deemed too left-leaning, for example, in Brazil (1964), Chile (1973), and Nicaragua (1989). The American public was often unaware of the covert U.S. activities until years later. In 1990, U.S. troops invaded Panama to remove and arrest the dictator, Manuel Noriega (b. 1940), a longtime U.S. ally and well-paid CIA informant who was also implicated in human-rights abuses and in smuggling narcotics into the United States. In 1994, U.S. troops were sent to Haiti, the Western Hemisphere's poorest country, in support of a reform government that had replaced a brutal dictatorship. U.S. troops have remained in Haiti promoting stability as political rivalries continue, leaving Haitians poorer and more desperate.

 Latin American Network Information Center (*http://lanic.utexas.edu/*). Very useful site on contemporary Latin America, maintained at the University of Texas.

Mexico and Brazil: Models of Development?

The Mexican Revolution in the early twentieth century had led to hopes of reducing social inequality, but the nation's leaders soon turned to emphasizing economic growth over uplifting the poor majority. Mexico's limited democracy offered regular elections and some civil liberties, but one party, the Party of Revolutionary Institutions (PRI), controlled the elections and hence the government, often resorting to voter fraud. The PRI was led by businessmen and bureaucrats who fostered stability while deflecting challenges to their power monopoly for decades. In 1968, it shocked the nation by ordering police to open fire on a large demonstration, killing hundreds of university students and other protesters.

> "The Mexican Revolution in the early twentieth century had led to hopes of reducing social inequality, but the nation's leaders soon turned to emphasizing economic growth over uplifting the poor majority."

Vicente Fox and Mexican Reform

By the 1980s, the PRI began to falter. In the early 1990s, a peasant revolt in a poor southern state, Chiapas, revealed starkly the PRI's failure to redress rural poverty. The election of a reformist, non-PRI president, Vicente Fox, a pro-U.S. free-market conservative, in 2000 ended the seven-decades-long PRI monopoly on federal power. However, Fox proved unable to foster much economic or social change, and the PRI still held power in many states. By 2005, a more open and pluralistic political system had emerged, with stronger leftist and right-wing parties contending with the PRI for support. Whether the democratic processes fostered by Fox can be consolidated and endure remained to be seen.

NAFTA

Mexico's economic system also gradually opened, but without diminishing poverty. For decades, the PRI had mixed capitalism with a strong government role. However, the collapse of world oil prices in the 1980s damaged Mexico's development prospects, so PRI leaders replaced protectionist policies with open markets. In 1994, the North American Free Trade Agreement (NAFTA) helped integrate the U.S. and Mexican economies, and many U.S.-owned factories that employed thousands of workers opened on the Mexican side of the border. The majority of these workers, however, have been poorly paid young women. Elsewhere, peasant farmers, unable to compete with highly subsidized U.S. farmers, have often been ruined. Even the urban middle class feels the economic pain as wages stagnate. In 1980, Mexico's economy was nearly four times larger than South Korea's; by 2005, a dynamic South Korea had pushed ahead of Mexico. In addition, Mexico's population quadrupled between 1940 and 2000, pressuring the nation's resources. Because of poverty and overpopulation, thousands of desperate Mexicans continue to cross the border to the United States each year, legally or illegally, in search of a better life.

Brazil

Few Latin American nations have had as much promise and experienced as many problems as Brazil. Occupying half of the South American continent, and with a population in 2005 of some 186 million, Brazil is Latin America's colossus and has its largest economy. From the mid-1940s to the mid-1960s, the nation had a democratic government, which persisted for two decades despite increasing political tensions and periodic economic crises. In 1961, Joao Goulart (jao joo-LART) (1918–1976), a populist reformer supported by leftist groups, assumed the presidency. Under his rule, the economy stumbled, and efforts to organize the impoverished peasants and rural workers antagonized powerful landlords. Seeking to halt change and impose order, the military overthrew Goulart in 1964 and ruled Brazil for the next two decades under a harsh military dictatorship, which arrested some 40,000 citizens. Viewing Brazil as ripe for a communist takeover, the United States had encouraged the military coup. Businessmen and other wealthy Brazilians, fearing disorder, welcomed the change.

Between 1964 and 1985, authoritarian governments, headed by generals and supported by the United States, gave priority to economic growth and national security at the expense of social programs. Relying on brutal repression, the regimes imposed comprehensive censorship, outlawed political parties, and weakened workers' rights. Right-wing vigilante groups and death squads instilled terror, killing or torturing dissidents; one police squad assassinated more than one thousand people. The generals imposed a capitalist economic model recommended by American advisers encouraging free markets, industrialization, and foreign investment.

For a decade, the economy boomed, eliciting foreign praise of the "Brazilian miracle" as annual growth rates averaged 10 percent between 1968 and 1974 and exports soared. The United States and international lending agencies poured in $8 billion in aid. But the "miracle" depended on low wages and redistributing income upward to the rich and middle class: the top 10 percent of people enjoyed 75 percent of the income gain, while half of all households lived below the poverty line. Beginning in the 1960s, Brazilian governments encouraged land speculators and foreign corporations to open up the vast Amazon basin, the world's largest tropical rain forest and river system. The virgin forest was rapidly stripped for logging, farming, mining, and ranching, displacing many of the 200,000 Indians who lived off its resources.

By 1980, the "miracle" was fading as Brazil experienced an inflation rate of more than 100 percent, a massive foreign debt, and sagging industrial production. Meanwhile, numerous sectors of society demanded democracy, and the Catholic Church criticized human-rights violations. In 1985, the growing political liberalization climaxed with a return to democracy and the election of a civilian president. Under the successive democratic governments led by moderate reformers, however, many problems remained unresolved, because leaders feared that policies hurting big business might provoke a military coup. As economic problems increased, inflation soared to 2,500 percent by 1994. Responding to the gross inequality in rural land ownership, landless peasants seized land, but landowners hired gunmen to harass the militants. Social inequities, such as school dropout rates, malnutrition, bankrupt public health services, homelessness, and debt slavery, grew.

Although the economy revived in the later 1990s, Brazilians, wanting further reform, turned to the political left. In 2002, they gave leftist candidates 80 percent of the vote and elected as president socialist labor leader Luis Ignacio da Silva (b. 1944), known as Lula, a former metalworker and longtime dissident. While Lula has fostered faster economic growth, peasant and worker groups believe Lula's economic policies go too far in pleasing financial interests and international lenders. Despite the booming economy, by 2006, corruption scandals threatened the regime.

Revolutionary Cuba

In contrast to Mexico and Brazil, Cuba, led by Fidel Castro (b. 1927), built a society dominated by a powerful communist government. A one-time amateur baseball star who was nearly signed by a U.S. professional team but instead became a lawyer, Castro came to power in 1959, the victor of a revolution against a repressive, corrupt dictator who was long supported by the United States. Castro allied with the Cuban Communist Party and promised radical change, prompting thousands of upper- and middle-class Cubans to flee to the nearby United States. In 1961, the United States moved to isolate and then overthrow his regime by organizing a military force composed of Cuban exiles that landed on a Cuban beach, known as the Bay of Pigs. But the invasion had been poorly planned and enjoyed little popular support in Cuba. Castro's forces routed the invading exiles, a humiliation for the United States.

Needing a protector, Castro became a firm Soviet ally, thereby alarming the United States further. The Cuba–USSR alliance soon precipitated a major crisis. In 1962, U.S. air surveillance of the island revealed Soviet ballistic missiles with a 2,000-mile range and capable of carrying nuclear warheads. The U.S. demand that the missiles be removed sparked what became known as the Cuban missile crisis, during which the United States imposed a naval blockade on Cuba and considered an invasion of the island. With the threat of nuclear confrontation looming, the Soviets backed down and removed the missiles, but afterwards the United States, hoping to bring down Castro's regime, imposed an economic boycott that endured into the twenty-first century, cutting off Cuba from sources of trade and investment.

In the 1960s and 1970s, Castro tried innovative socialist policies, often known as Castroism, to stimulate economic development in Cuba while also tightly controlling its population. Castro called capitalism "repugnant, filthy, gross, alienating because it causes war, hypocrisy and competition"[7]; yet his own policies generated little surplus food and few consumer goods. Nonetheless, Castroism improved the material and social life of the working classes; the regime built schools and clinics, mounted literacy campaigns, and promoted equality for long-marginalized Afro-Cubans and women. In quality-of-life statistics, by the mid-1980s, Cuba, with the lowest infant mortality and

Castroism
Innovative socialist policies introduced by Fidel Castro to stimulate economic development in Cuba while tightly controlling its population.

highest literacy rates and life expectancy, ranked well ahead of other Latin American nations. In contrast to some Latin American dictatorships, the Cuban government did not form death squads or sponsor murders of dissidents, but Castro placed limits on free expression, jailing those who defied the ban. The jailed included brave writers, homosexuals, and those advocating free speech and elections. Seeking political freedom, better-paying jobs, or higher living standards, several hundred thousand Cubans have fled over the years, chiefly to the United States.

The Cuban Revolution had international repercussions. Castro exchanged dependence on the United States for dependence on the USSR, which, to maintain the alliance, poured billions of dollars of aid into the country. With the collapse of the USSR in 1991, however, Castro lost his patron and benefactor. Since then Cuba has struggled: the social welfare system has cracked, and the economy has crumbled despite efforts to introduce some market forces. Critics of U.S. policy, including most U.S. allies, have argued that the U.S. embargo helps Castro's regime by reinforcing strong anti-U.S. feelings and discrediting pro-U.S. dissidents. Many Cubans, while desiring a freer, more productive system, do not necessarily want the United States to determine their fate.

Chile: Reform and Repression

While Cubans sought to escape underdevelopment through revolution, Chileans, like Brazilians, tried a succession of strategies, from reform to dictatorship to democracy. Chileans enjoyed a long tradition of elected democratic governments sustained by a large middle class, high rates of literacy and urbanization, and mass-based political parties. Nonetheless, a wealthy elite of businessmen, military officers, and landowners held political power and suppressed labor unrest. Despite a growing manufacturing sector, Chile depended on the export of minerals, especially copper. By the 1960s, a stagnant economy widened the gap between rich and poor.

Salvador Allende

Chile shifted direction with the 1970 elections. Six liberal, socialist, and communist parties united in a left-leaning coalition, the Popular Unity, that was supported largely by small businessmen, the urban working class, and peasants. Their winning presidential candidate, Salvador Allende (ah-YEN-dee) (1908–1973), who had developed compassion for the poor while working as a medical doctor, promised a "Chilean road" to socialism, through constitutional means in a parliamen-

Castro Addressing Crowd A spellbinding orator, the Cuban leader, Fidel Castro, often recruits support for his government and policies by speaking at large rallies.

tary democracy. His regime took over, and paid compensation to, banks and a copper industry that had been dominated by powerful U.S. corporations. Land reform broke up underutilized ranches and divided the land among the peasant residents. Allende's government supported the labor unions and provided urban shantytowns with health clinics and better schools. Both employment and economic production reached the highest levels in Chilean history. The Popular Unity was also committed to the creation of a Chilean cultural renaissance. Democracy flourished and Allende enjoyed growing popularity.

However, the Popular Unity government also generated opposition. The rapid reforms produced shortages of luxury goods, fostering middle-class resentment. Allende's opponents controlled the mass media and judiciary and dominated the congress. At the same time, the U.S. president, Richard Nixon, worried about Allende's friendship with Cuba's Fidel Castro and feared that Allende's socialism without revolution could become a model for Latin America, threatening U.S. interests. The United States mounted an international economic embargo on Chilean exports, while the CIA undertook a disinformation campaign to discredit Allende and organized strikes to paralyze the economy.

American Intervention

In 1973, a military coup supported by the United States overthrew Allende, who died while defending the presidential palace from an assault. The military imposed a brutal military dictatorship led by General Augusto Pinochet (ah-GOOS-toh pin-oh-CHET) (b. 1915). Pinochet launched a reign of terror, suppressing rights and arresting some 150,000 Allende supporters and detaining and routinely torturing hundreds of political prisoners for years. The regime murdered thousands of dissidents, sometimes in front of other prisoners held in the national stadium, and buried the victims in unmarked mass graves. Thousands of Chileans fled the country. Advised by U.S. economists, Pinochet shifted to a free enterprise economy, similar to military-ruled Brazil's, that generated growth and moderate middle-class prosperity purchased at the cost of a monumental foreign debt and environmental degradation. But little of this wealth trickled down to the poor, whose living standards deteriorated.

Chilean Recovery

However, a severe economic crisis that undermined the regime's legitimacy led to a return to a civilian-led liberal democracy. Escalating social tensions and political protests prompted the junta to hold an election and restore democracy in 1989. The resulting center-left governments struggled to maintain middle-class prosperity while promoting a more equitable distribution of wealth. They retained free enterprise while making additions to health, housing, education, and social spending. These policies chipped away at poverty, and unemployment has plummeted. Tax increases and increased welfare have not stifled the annual economic growth of about 10 percent. Chile has become the most prosperous Latin American economy, enjoying a stable democratic system. Yet, many Chileans remain bitter toward the United States for having once helped install and perpetuate a brutal military regime.

LO⁴ Changing Latin American and Caribbean Societies

The societies of Latin America and the Caribbean, while facing daunting economic problems, have experienced distinctive social and cultural patterns. Rather than balanced economic growth, Latin American and Caribbean nations have often emphasized export of traditional natural resources such as oil, sugar, coffee, bananas, wool, and copper. Varied mixes of peoples and traditions speaking different languages often have little in common with each other. But the regions' peoples have fostered dynamic cultural forms that have found international popularity.

Latin American Economies

Although often enjoying economic growth, no Latin American nations have achieved the level of prosperity found in the industrialized West. Latin Americans forged rising literacy rates, lowered infant mortality rates, and more people than ever now own televisions, even in poor neighborhoods. Nonetheless, the world price for most of their natural resource exports usually has declined every year, leaving less money for economic development. To pay the bills, governments have taken out loans, eventually owing billions to international lenders. Rapidly expanding populations, growing at 3 percent per year, add to the social burden and cause environmental problems. Governments have treated indigenous peoples and the rain forests they inhabit as expendable resources.

Latin America has also suffered severe income inequality: by 2000, the top 10 percent of the population earned half of all income, and 70 percent of the people lived in poverty. In Brazil, half of the people have had no access to doctors, even while Rio de Janeiro has become the world's plastic surgery capital, with hundreds of cosmetic surgeons catering to wealthy Brazilians and foreigners. To survive, poor peasants in some nations have often turned to growing coca and opium for making cocaine and heroin. But the drug trade, largely sold to the U.S. market, fosters political turbulence and government corruption and profits only a few drug kingpins.

Agriculture has remained a mainstay of most Latin American economies. Landholding is usually concentrated in a small group of aristocratic families and multinational corporations, such as the U.S.-based United Fruit Company. By the 1990s, 60 percent of all agricultural land was held in large estates and farmed inefficiently, contributing to food shortages and malnutrition. Modern agriculture requires large investments for machinery, fertilizers, pesticides, and fuel, but growing beans and corn to feed hungry peasants supplies inadequate revenue.

> 66 Agriculture has remained a mainstay of most Latin American economies. 99

As a result, vast tracts of rain forests and land that once grew food crops have been transformed into beef cattle ranches. In Mexico, beef cattle consume more food than the poorest one-quarter of people.

Hardships in rural areas have generated migration to cities; by 2000, Latin America had become the world's most urbanized, with 75 percent of people living in cities and towns. The migrants live in festering shantytowns and can often find only poorly paid work. Half the urban population lack adequate water, housing, sanitation, and social services. But economic growth has also fostered growing middle classes, which have become one-third of the population in Argentina, Chile, and Uruguay and one-fifth in Brazil and Mexico.

Beginning in the 1980s, many Latin American nations, hoping to emulate the success of the United States, adopted neoliberalism, an economic model that promoted free markets, privatization, and Western investment. The model, encouraged by the United States, generated growth for a decade, but it failed to curb government corruption, install honest judicial systems, foster labor-intensive industries, or reduce the power of rich elites or dependence on foreign

U.S. Factory in Mexico Since the 1980s, growing numbers of U.S. companies have relocated industrial operations to Mexico, building many factories along the Rio Grande River that separates Mexico from Texas. In this factory, in Matamoros, Mexico, the mostly female labor force makes toys for the U.S. market.

Keith Dannemiller/Corbis

loans and investment. Free markets have often meant that a few people enjoyed fabulous wealth while most people remained poor. The nation that most ardently adopted neoliberalism, Argentina, saw its economy collapse in 1998; unemployment soared and, by 2001, half of the people lived in poverty. But although neoliberalism lost credibility, no other economic model, such as Cuban communism or Allende's socialism with democracy, had widespread support or a record of success in Latin America.

> "Beginning in the 1980s, many Latin American nations, hoping to emulate the success of the United States, adopted neoliberalism, an economic model that promoted free markets, privatization, and Western investment."

Latin America: Society and Religion

Political and economic change has modified social arrangements, especially in gender relations and family life. Although men dominate the governments, militaries, businesses, and the Catholic Church, women's struggles have managed to reduce gender inequality, and many women now work outside of the home. Factories relocating from North America attract young women, who are preferred to men because they accept lower wages and have been raised to obey. As women have entered the workforce, family life has undergone strains. By the 1990s, far fewer people married, especially among the poor. But divorce, banned by the Catholic Church, has remained difficult or impossible to get in some nations, and men still enjoy a double standard in sexual behavior. Although abortion is illegal everywhere in the region, Latin America has one of the world's highest abortion rates. Gay men and lesbians also struggle for acceptance, as homosexuality remains illegal in many nations, including Castro's Cuba.

> ❝ As gender expectations have changed, women have become more active in politics. ❞

As gender expectations have changed, women have become more active in politics. Between 1945 and 1961, women gained the right to vote. In 1990, Violeta Chamorro (vee-oh-LET-ah cha-MOR-roe) (b. 1919), a newspaper publisher, was elected president of Nicaragua, and she served until 1996. In 2006, Chileans showed a willingness to expand their political horizons by electing as president the pediatrician turned socialist politician Michelle Bachelet (BAH-she-let), a divorced mother of three whose father was murdered while she and her mother were jailed and tortured during the Pinochet years. Leading the victorious center-left coalition, Bachelet struck a blow for gender equity by filling half of her cabinet positions with women, including the key defense and economy ministries.

During military rule in Argentina, Brazil, and Chile, women political prisoners were kept naked and often raped. For instance, Doris Tijereno Haslam (b. 1943), an early member of the leftist Sandinista movement in Nicaragua who fought as a guerrilla commander, was twice arrested and badly tortured by the corrupt dictatorship of General Anastasio Somoza Debayle (1923–1967). After the Sandinista victory in 1979, she headed the national police and served in the congress. Women fought back against discrimination and violence, as in Mexico, where the feminist movement challenged inequitable laws and social practices. A 1974 law guaranteed women equal rights for jobs, salaries, and legal standing.

Another traditional foundation for Latin American society, religion, also was subject to change. In the 1960s, progressive Latin American Roman Catholics developed liberation theology, a movement to make Catholicism more relevant to contemporary society and address the plight of the poor. Priests favoring liberation theology, especially in Brazil, cooperated with Marxist and liberal groups in working for social justice until the Vatican prohibited the movement in the 1980s. On the whole, the Roman Catholic hierarchy remained conservative. Protestantism, chiefly evangelical or pentecostal, grew rapidly with increased missionary efforts, attracting converts with its participatory, emotional services. By the 1990s, Protestants numbered nearly 20 percent of the population in Guatemala and 8 percent in Brazil and Chile. The religious landscape of Latin America looked very different in 2000 than it had a century earlier.

Latin American and Caribbean Cultures

Latin America has fostered creative cultural forms that have reached a global audience. The mass media have both shaped and reflected the prevailing cultures. Inexpensive transistor radios became widely available, and by the 1980s, thousands of radio stations had sprouted all over the region. While most stations were privately owned, governments frequently sought to control their content. In 1950, television came to the main cities, eventually spreading widely. Immensely popular local television soap operas dominated prime-time viewing and gained a large market around the world.

Literature in Latin America

Literature has also flourished, with writers often criticizing or describing social conditions and government failures. Former journalist Gabriel García Márquez (MAHR-kez) (b. 1928), a Nobel Prize–winning Colombian novelist, developed an international audience for imaginative books full of what literary scholars called "magic realism," the representation of possible events as if they were wonders and impossible events as commonplace. His most famous work, *One Hundred Years of Solitude* (1970), charts the history of a Colombian house, the family who live in it, and the town where it was located, through wars, changing politics, and economic crises.

Some writers were critical of those holding power. For example, in Chile, the greatest epic poem of the leftist writer and former diplomat Pablo Neruda (neh-ROO-da) (1904–1973), *General Song*, published in 1950, portrays the history of the entire hemisphere, showing an innocent pre-Columbian America cruelly awakened by Spanish conquest. In 1971, Neruda won the Nobel Prize for literature, distressing those who viewed his radical views as a threat to Latin American society.

Music, Cinema, and Cultural Diversity

Like other peoples, Latin Americans have mixed local cultural traditions with imported influences. The Brazilian New Cinema movement, launched in 1955, tried to replace the influence of Hollywood films with films that reflected Brazilian life. One of the movement's finest films, *Black Orpheus* (1959), which gained an international following, employed a soundtrack of local popular music to examine the annual pre-Lenten Carnival in Rio de Janeiro's shantytowns and the extremes of wealth and poverty revealed in the different ways rich and poor celebrated Carnival. In the 1960s and 1970s, a musical style known as New Song, based chiefly on local folk music and closely tied to progressive politics and protest, gained popularity in a half-dozen countries, becoming especially influential in Chile. Seeking an alternative to the Anglo-American popular culture favored by elite Chileans, Chilean musicians have used indigenous Andean instruments and tunes. During the later 1960s, Chilean New Song pioneers such as Violeta Parra and Victor Jara (HAR-a) wrote or collected songs that addressed problems of Chilean society such as poverty and inequality. Parra (1918–1967) served as the bridge between the older generation of folk musicians and the younger generation of singer-songwriters.

Because of its left-wing connections, New Song was vulnerable to changing political conditions. In 1970, Chilean New Song musicians had joined the electoral campaign of Salvador Allende's leftist Popular Unity coalition, which sought to unseat a centrist administration. After Allende won the presidency, he encouraged the media to pay more attention to New Song and less to popular music from the United States. But in 1973, the Chilean military seized power and arrested, executed, or deported most of the New Song musicians. Before thousands of other detainees held in the national stadium, soldiers publicly cut off Victor Jara's fingers, which he had used to play his guitar, and then executed him, symbolizing the death of free expression in Chile and the government's fear of the power of popular culture.

Cultural diversity characterizes most Latin American nations, especially Brazil, where race remains a central social category. Like the United States, Brazil has never become a true racial melting pot. Race has often correlated with social status: whites dominate the top brackets, blacks the bottom, and mixed-descent Brazilians fall in between. The flexible Brazilian concept of race, however, differs from the biological concept that North Americans have. Dark-skinned people can aspire to social mobility by earning a good income since, as a popular local saying claimed, "money lightens." Furthermore, Afro-Brazilian culture has had a growing influence, and many whites have embraced aspects of black culture.

For Brazil, as for most Latin American nations, professional sports have become a popular enter-

Read about Violeta Parra, the Chilean New Song pioneer who came from a poor working-class background.

tainment and diversion from social problems. European football, or soccer, has been hugely popular for decades, uniting fans of all social backgrounds. Brazilians are proud of the international success of their national team, which won the World Cup championships five times between 1958 and 2002 by employing a creative, teamwork-oriented strategy, known as "samba football," that Brazilians have identified with the national spirit.

Rastafarianism and Reggae

With diverse populations of blacks, whites, and Asians, the Caribbean islands, like Latin America, offered an environment for creative cultural development, especially in religion and music. Jamaica's legacy of slavery and colonialism fostered the development of Rastafarianism, a religion mixing Christian, African, and local influences. The believers revered the emperor Ras Tafari of Ethiopia, the sole unconquered, uncolonized African state in 1930. Its followers, known as Rastas, adopted distinctive practices, including smoking ganja (marijuana), an illegal drug, and sporting dreadlocked hair, that outraged Jamaica's social and economic elite. As a movement of the black poor, Rastafarianism became identified in Jamaica and other Caribbean islands with radical groups seeking to redistribute wealth.

The most influential popular music to come out of the Caribbean had similar mixed origins. In the 1960s, Jamaican musicians created reggae, a style blending North American rhythm-and-blues with Afro-Jamaican traditions and marked by a distinctive beat maintained by the bass guitar. The songs of reggae musicians, who were often Rastas, promoted social justice, economic equality, and the freedom of people, especially Rastas, to live as they liked without interference by the police. The international popularity of reggae owed much to Bob Marley (1945–1981), a Rasta, and his group, the Wailers. Marley became the first international superstar to hail from a developing nation. His explosive performances and provocative lyrics offered clear messages: "Slave driver, the table is turned; Catch a fire, you gonna get burned."[8] After Marley's death from cancer in 1981, many reggae musicians watered down their message.

Latin America and the Caribbean in the Global System

Over the years, various Caribbean and Latin American leaders sought to increase regional economic coop-

eration. Commerce among Latin American nations more than doubled between 1988 and 1994. For example, the Southern Cone Common Market, formed in 1996, included six South American nations with more than 200 million people. Similarly, Caribbean countries cooperated in the Caribbean Community and Common Market, formed in 1973. Some U.S.–Latin American issues remain contested. For instance, while people in the United States have blamed Latin American drug cartels for smuggling illegal drugs into the United States, Latin Americans have often resented the U.S. interventions and economic impositions they consider Yankee imperialism. Latin American and Caribbean leaders have also feared being pushed aside in a world economy dominated by North American, European, and, increasingly, Asian nations.

Globalization influenced Latin Americans and their economies. Asian nations, especially China, Japan, Taiwan, and South Korea, captured a growing share of Latin America's traditional overseas markets while also investing in Latin America and the Caribbean. In a globalized economy, a hiccup in Tokyo or New York caused a stomach ache in Ecuador or El Salvador. Because most Latin American and Caribbean economies followed the track of the U.S. economy, they were particularly vulnerable to change in the United States.

When the 2001 terrorist attacks in the United States diverted U.S. attention to the Middle East, the sudden U.S. disinterest in Latin America and its problems sparked a regional economic downturn that reduced demand for Latin American exports. The economic gains made in the mid-1990s slipped away, and the one-fifth of Latin America's 500 million people who lived in extreme poverty by 2000 faced an even grimmer future. Only a few nations, such as Brazil and Chile, had much hope of improving their status in the global system.

Listen to a synopsis of Chapter 29.

Buffeted by political changes and economic crises, Latin Americans search for their identity and role in a world dominated by other societies.

Rastafarianism
A religion from Jamaica that arose in 1930 and that mixed Christian, African, and local influences; Rastafarianism attracted urban slum dwellers and the rural poor by preaching a return of black people to Africa.

reggae
A popular music style that began in Jamaica in the 1960s and that blended North American rhythm and blues with Afro-Jamaican traditions; reggae is marked by a distinctive beat maintained by the bass guitar.

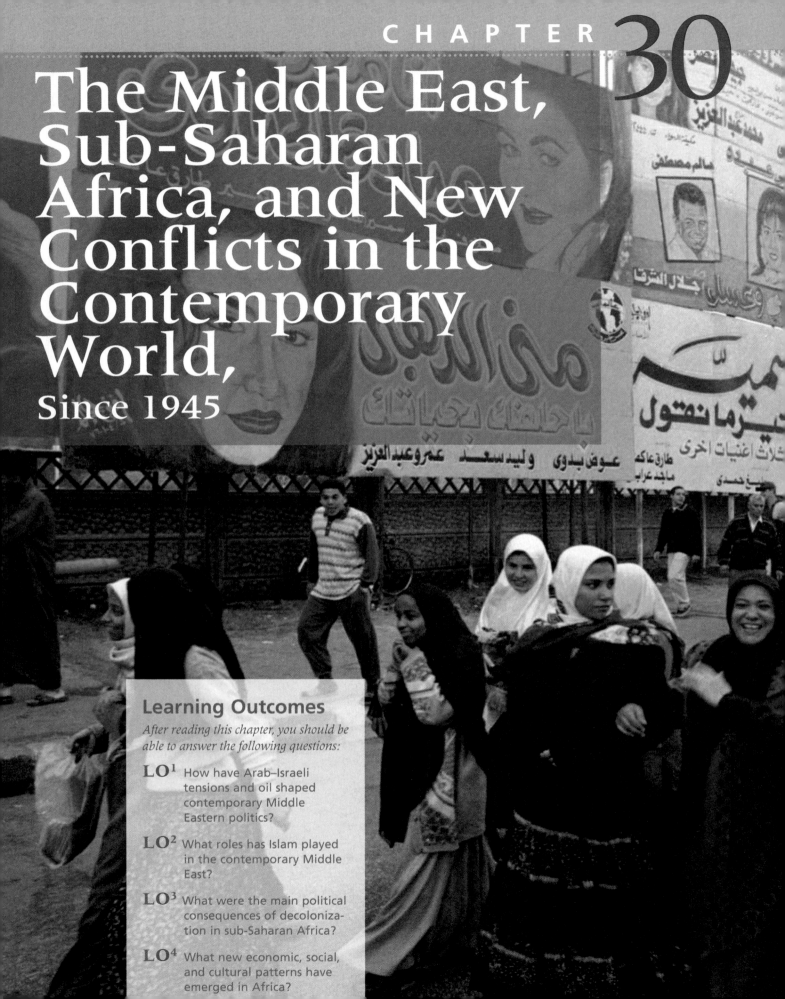

CHAPTER 30

The Middle East, Sub-Saharan Africa, and New Conflicts in the Contemporary World,

Since 1945

Learning Outcomes

After reading this chapter, you should be able to answer the following questions:

LO¹ How have Arab–Israeli tensions and oil shaped contemporary Middle Eastern politics?

LO² What roles has Islam played in the contemporary Middle East?

LO³ What were the main political consequences of decolonization in sub-Saharan Africa?

LO⁴ What new economic, social, and cultural patterns have emerged in Africa?

> **❝**I saw the Berlin Wall fall, [Nelson] Mandela walk free. I saw a dream whose time has come change my history—so keep on dreaming. In the best of times and in the worst of times gotta keep looking at the skyline, not at the hole in the road.**❞**
>
> —**"Your Time Will Come" by South African pop group Savuka, 1993**[1]

The writer Chinua Achebe (ah-CHAY-bay) (b. 1930) dissected the underside of African politics in a controversial 1987 blockbuster novel, *Anthills of the Savannah. Anthills* mercilessly depicts the immorality, vanity, and destructiveness of a military dictatorship much like the one Achebe had experienced in Nigeria. Nigerian military leaders overthrew a civilian government in 1983 and began arrest-ing people whose corruption was well known, but then pro-ceeded to jail anyone, including journalists, who questioned the regime's economic mismanage-ment and human-rights abuses. Just as the black and white musicians in the South African pop group, Savuka, could sing of dreams changing history and a new era beginning with the end of white minority rule, Achebe also offered a powerful message about the need for people to protest unaccountable, repressive power. The politi-cal and economic realities of contemporary Africa and the Middle East are reflected in these regions' cultures, as writers, musicians, and art-ists have used their art to spur political and social change.

Test your knowlege before you read this chapter.

The problems vividly described by Achebe for Nigeria—corruption, economic stagnation, combustible social tensions, and failed promises of democracy—have applied to most other nations in sub-Saharan Africa and the Middle East. The triumph of national-ism and decolonization reshaped Africa and the Middle East: between 1945 and 1975, country after country became independent or escaped from Western political domination. In contrast to various East Asian, Southeast Asian, and Latin American nations, however, African and Middle Eastern nations have often struggled to survive. While cultur-ally innovative, few of the nations have successfully resolved their social and economic problems. For some nations, Islam has become

[1]Written by Johnny Clegg. Publisher: HRBV Music/Thythm Safari

<< Modern vs. Traditional Wearing traditional clothing, including veils and head scarves, Egyptian women walk through downtown Cairo in 1998 in front of billboards promoting popular entertainers. The scene illustrates the encounter between Islamic customs and modern ideas in many Middle Eastern nations.

AP Images/Enric Marti

807

a rallying cry to assert political interests and preserve cultures. Global superpowers have manipulated governments and intervened to serve their own ends.

> "In the decade after World War II, nationalist governments in the Middle East replaced most of the remaining colonial regimes."

LO¹ The Middle East: New Nations and Old Societies

Few world regions have witnessed more turbulence in the past half-century than the Middle East, the predominantly Muslim nations stretching from Morocco eastward across North Africa and western Asia to Turkey, Iran, and Afghanistan. The major ethnic group, the Arabs, have dominated most of these nations, but Turks, Iranians, Kurds, and Israeli Jews also influence the region. After World War II, Middle Eastern societies ended Western colonization and asserted their own political interests, often under modernizing leaders. But within these societies, dictatorial governments have proliferated, and chronic political instability has been common. Centuries-old hostilities between Sunni and Shi'a Muslims simmer. Meanwhile, the Persian Gulf area, which contains much of the world's oil reserves, has become crucial to the global system.

The Reshaping of the Middle East

In the decade after World War II, nationalist governments in the Middle East replaced most of the remaining colonial regimes. The French abandoned control of Morocco, Tunisia, Lebanon, and Syria, while the Italians left Libya. However, Muslim guerrillas fought 500,000 French troops for eight years to bring independence to Algeria, which had a large European settler population. Some 250,000 Algerians died in the conflict before the French granted independence in 1962. Some Middle Eastern nations, such as Egypt and Morocco, had a long history of national identity, but many were fragile states. For example, after World War I, the British had formed the new states of Iraq, Jordan, and Palestine with arbitrary boundaries, while Afghanistan, Turkey, Lebanon, and Syria included contentious ethnic and religious groups.

Iran and Turkey, which had never been colonized, sought influential roles in the region and built formidable military forces. Both also abused their citizens' human rights, arresting dissidents and restricting ethnic minorities. Turkey, led largely by secular leaders, looked increasingly westward, joining NATO (the North Atlantic Treaty Organization), hosting U.S. military bases, developing democratic institutions, and applying for membership in the European Union. But Turkey's governments, while generally promoting a modern version of women's rights, have also suppressed the largest ethnic minority, the Kurds, who chiefly live in southeastern Turkey. Although the nation's 70 million people are largely Muslim, the government has also limited political activity by groups that favor an Islamic state.

After decolonization, hopes for development throughout the Middle East were soon dashed as vested economic interests and most of the Muslim clergy opposed significant social and economic changes. Many people remained mired in illiteracy, poverty, and disease. Turkey shifted from military-dominated to democratically elected governments by the 1980s, but the military remained powerful, and strict internal security laws resulted in the imprisonment of several thousand people for political offenses.

Lebanese could choose between many competing warlord or religious-based parties, and a new constitution in 2002 allowed both men and women in the small Persian Gulf kingdom of Bahrain (BAH-rain) to elect a parliament. But in most countries, elections were rigged, parliaments were weak, or governments made it difficult for opposition candidates to run. Furthermore, the United States and the Soviet Union, attracted by the region's oil and strategic location along vital waterways, soon filled the power vacuum created by decolonization. Arabs talked about uniting across political borders, but pan-Arab nationalism was never able to overcome political and sectional rivalries and meddling by the superpowers. In addition, many post-1945 challenges have made the Middle East a highly combustible region subject to strains.

Arab Nationalism and Egypt

Confrontation between Arab nationalism and the world's superpowers was acute in Egypt, a former British protectorate and the most populous Arab country. In 1952, a charismatic Egyptian leader, General Gamal Abdul Nasser (NAS-uhr) (1918–1970), led a military coup that ended the corrupt pro-British monarchy. Like many Egyptians, Nasser despised the British and the Egyptian leaders who collaborated with them. As an army officer with a commanding personality, he developed a vision of a new Egypt, free of Western domination and social inequality.

As Egypt's president, Nasser, a modernizer, promised to improve the lives of the impoverished masses and to implement land reform, ideas that made him a hero in the Arab world. To generate power and improve flood control, Nasser's regime used Soviet aid to build the massive Aswan High Dam along the Nile, completed in 1970. But his nonaligned foreign policy antagonized a United States that was obsessed with Cold War rivalry. Accusing the West of "imperialist methods, habits of blood-sucking and usurping rights, and interference in other countries,"[2] in 1956 Nasser's government took over ownership of the British-operated Suez Canal, a key passage that was built through Egypt in the nineteenth century. To Egyptians, foreign ownership of the canal had symbolized their subjugation; to Europeans, the canal was the lifeline that moved oil and resources to the West from Asia. To protect that link, Britain, France, and Israel sent in military forces to reclaim the canal, but diplomatic opposition by the pro-Egypt Soviet Union and the United States, which disliked Nasser but feared regional instability, forced their withdrawal. By standing up to the West, Nasser became an even greater Arab hero and a champion of nonalignment, or neutrality, between the two rival superpowers. However, the Israeli defeat of Egypt and its allies in a brief 1967 war humiliated Nasser. Furthermore, although Nasser had introduced social and economic reforms, they fostered little economic or military strength for Egypt.

Arab Human Development Reports (http://www.un.org/english). The general United Nations site contains links to the reports, issued annually beginning in 2002 and available online, that assess the successes and challenges facing the Arab nations.

Nasser's successors followed pragmatic, pro-U.S. policies, and in 1978 signed a peace treaty with Israel brokered by the U.S. president, Jimmy Carter. But a shift to capitalism and heavy U.S. aid largely has not improved living conditions. Egypt's leaders reversed Nasser's land reform and dismantled the socialist economy, allowing a few well-connected capitalists to acquire state property and become fabulously rich while the poorest became even poorer. With little oil and few resources other than the fertile lands along the Nile, Egypt suffers from high malnutrition and unemployment, low rates of literacy and public health, and a huge national debt. Islamic militants, feeding on these frustrations, challenge the secular but corrupt government.

Israel in Middle Eastern Politics

The conflict between Israel and the Arabs, especially the Palestinians, was the Middle East's most insurmountable problem for more than half a century. Under the influence of Zionism and its dream of a Jewish homeland, Jews had been emigrating from Europe to Palestine since the late 1800s, building cities and forming productive socialist farming settlements. The growing Jewish presence, however, triggered occasional conflicts with the Palestinian Arab majority. Then the Nazis' murder of 6 million Jews during World War II, and Jewish desire for a safe haven, set the stage for the birth of Israel. But the new nation never established a secure position or fostered allies within the region.

The Birth of Israel

When Jewish refugees, traumatized by the Holocaust, poured into Palestine from post–World War II Europe, moderate Jewish leaders negotiated with the British for a peaceful transfer of power to them in Palestine. Meanwhile, Zionist extremists, impatient with negotiations, used terrorism, such as bombings and assassinations, against the British, Arabs, and moderate Jews. At the same time, Arabs resorted to violent attacks on Jews. Unable to maintain order, Britain abandoned the territory in 1948, referring the Palestine question to the new United Nations as Jewish leaders proclaimed the establishment of the state of Israel. By establishing a multiparty parliamentary democracy and seeking to

rebuild shattered Jewish lives, the Israelis gained the strong support of Western nations and especially the United States, which pumped in several billion dollars in aid annually for the next five decades.

Arab Reaction to the Jewish State

The establishment of a Jewish state in Palestine led to full-scale war in 1948–1949 between Israel and its Arab neighbors, to whom Israel was a white settler state and a symbol of Western colonialism (see Map 30.1). As Palestinian Arabs fled the fighting and the continued terrorism against them by Jewish extremists, Israelis occupied their farms and houses. The Israelis won the war and expelled 85 percent of the Palestinian Arabs from Israel. While some Palestinian exiles became a prosperous middle class throughout the Middle East, most unhappily settled in squalid refugee camps in Egypt, Lebanon, Jordan, and Syria. They supported the Palestine Liberation Organization (PLO), a coalition of Arab nationalist, Muslim, and Christian groups led by Yasser Arafat (YA-sir AR-uh-fat) (1929–2004), an engineer from a wealthy Jerusalem family.

Arafat's pragmatic style united Arab factions, but neither the Western nations nor Israel officially recognized the PLO until the 1990s, prompting it to resort

Interactive Map

Dismantling Israeli Settlements Palestinians have viewed the settlements built by ardent Zionists in the West Bank and Gaza as a provocation. Israeli troops have sometimes been ordered to dismantle settlements and remove the enraged settlers by force. In 2005, all of the Israeli settlements were closed down in Gaza.

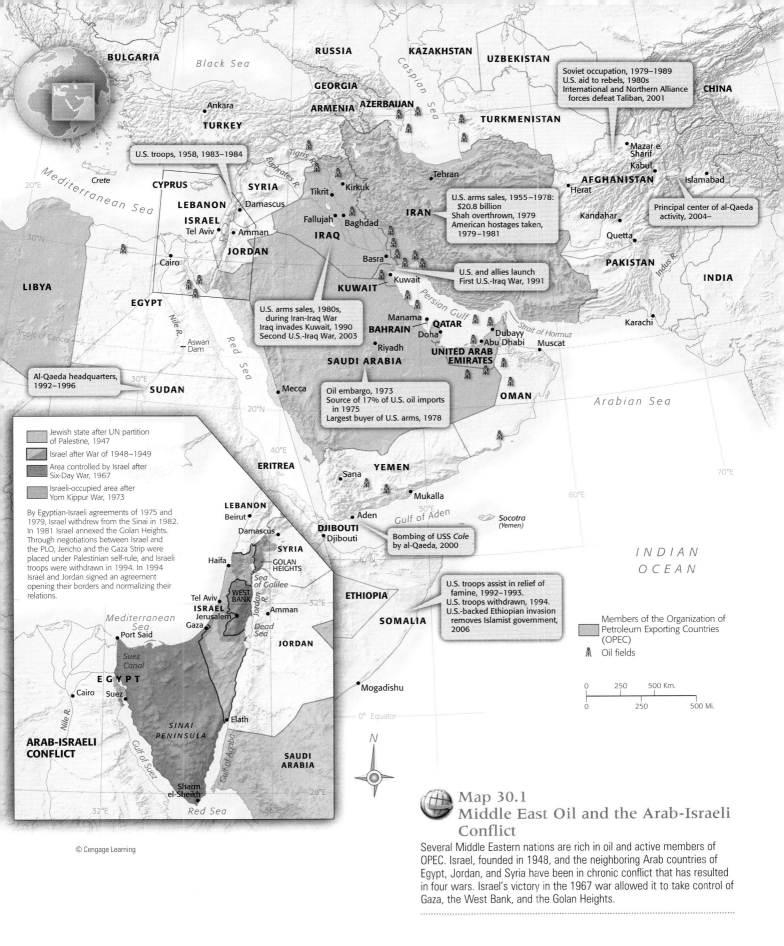

Map 30.1
Middle East Oil and the Arab-Israeli
Conflict

Several Middle Eastern nations are rich in oil and active members of
OPEC. Israel, founded in 1948, and the neighboring Arab countries of
Egypt, Jordan, and Syria have been in chronic conflict that has resulted
in four wars. Israel's victory in the 1967 war allowed it to take control of
Gaza, the West Bank, and the Golan Heights.

> "An Arab-Israeli War in 1967 further complicated regional politics, heightening conflict and reshaping Israeli society."

to terrorism against Israel. The Palestinians remaining in Israel participated in democratic politics but were disproportionally poor and often saw themselves as second-class citizens. Meanwhile, thousands more Jewish immigrants arrived, intensifying divisions in Israeli society between secular and devout Jews. Israelis, obsessed now with military security, devoted half of their total national budget to the military. A cycle of violence followed for years, with a PLO attack on Israeli civilians followed by Israeli reprisals. Mutual distrust and violence increased.

The 1967 War

An Arab-Israeli War in 1967 further complicated regional politics, heightening conflict and reshaping Israeli society. Responding successfully to an ill-advised attack led by Egypt and Jordan, Israel gained control of new territories that had once been part of Palestine: the West Bank, that part of Jordan on the western side of the Jordan River; the eastern half of Jerusalem; the Gaza Strip, a small coastal enclave of Egypt; and the Golan Heights, a Syrian plateau overlooking northeast Israel. The Israeli victory doubled the amount of land controlled by Israel, but the nation now contained 3 million Jews and 2 million Arabs, a combustible situation. Israel treated the Palestinians in the occupied territories as a colonized people, allowing them no political rights. In 1973, another Israeli war with Egypt and Syria proved costly to all sides.

Palestinian Resistance

Increasing Israeli control over the Palestinians in the occupied territories exacerbated the conflict. Although many Israelis wanted to trade occupied land for a permanent peace settlement, ultranationalist Israelis, with government support, began claiming and settling on Arab land, creating another problem: thousands of Jewish settlers, largely militant Zionists and religious conservatives, living amid hostile Arabs. Because

Arab and Israeli Soccer Players Discuss Ethnic Relations in Israel, 2000 Learn how Arabs and Jews get along in the world of professional soccer in Israel.

Israel has remained a democracy with a vibrant free press, Israelis have heatedly debated these policies and the general treatment of Arabs. In 1987, desperate Palestinians began a resistance known as the Intifada ("Uprising") against the Israeli occupation. Negotiations led in 1993 to limited self-government under the PLO in parts of the occupied territories, the basis for a possible Palestinian state, and a peace agreement between Israel and Jordan.

But after a series of political blunders, violence erupted again in 2000, returning the Israel–Palestine problem to center stage. Moderate Israelis and Palestinians lost hope as demoralizing Palestinian suicide bombings of civilian targets, such as restaurants and public buses, and Israeli reprisal attacks on Palestinian neighborhoods renewed fifty years of violence. Israel built a high-security fence separating it from the West Bank that also incorporated some occupied territory, enraging Palestinians. Yet, in 2005, tensions eased. After Yasser Arafat's death, his moderate party chose a less controversial leader, and the Israeli government closed the Israeli settlements in Gaza and disbanded several illegal settlements in the West Bank.

However, in 2006, the Palestinians gave the militant Islamic Hamas movement a majority of seats in the Palestinian parliament, alarming Israelis, because Hamas refused to recognize Israel's right to exist. Hamas owed its victory in part to its longtime social welfare activities and to hundreds of conservative Muslim women who campaigned door to door for the party; six of them won seats. The future of Israeli-Palestinian relations remained uncertain, as no basis for ensuring long-term peace has yet emerged.

Iran, Iraq, and Regional Conflicts

Rich in oil and strategically located along the Persian Gulf, Iran, once known as Persia, had been buffeted between rival European nations for a century. Outside interference in Iranian affairs continued after World War II, when a conflict developed between the young king, Shah Mohammed Pahlavi (pah-LAH-vee) (1919–1980), and nationalist reformers who were opposed to foreign domination. In 1951, nationalists came to power, reducing the shah to a ceremonial role; because Iran had been receiving little revenue from the British-dominated oil industry, the nationalists also took ownership of it. In response, Britain and its ally, the United States—considering the nationalists to be sympathetic to the USSR—cut off aid and launched a boycott, bringing Iran to near bankruptcy and fostering unrest. In 1953, American CIA agents secretly organized opposition among military leaders and paid disgruntled Iranians to riot against the nationalist government. In the turmoil, royalists overthrew the nationalist government and restored the unpopular shah to power, embittering many Iranians. Shah Pahlavi, a ruthless, pleasure-loving man who dreamed of restoring Persia as a great power, allied himself with the strongest superpower, the United States, and allowed U.S. companies to control the oil industry.

> ❝ Rich in oil and strategically located along the Persian Gulf, Iran, once known as Persia, had been buffeted between rival European nations for a century. ❞

(1902–1989), took power, eliminated leftists and moderates, and replaced the shah's secular policies with the Islamic Shari'a, which devout Muslims considered the law of God. As Iran became an Islamic state, thousands of Iranians fled abroad. Among the new restrictions, women were forced to wear veils and prohibited from socializing with men from outside their families. Like the shah, the clerics ruled by terror, suppressed ethnic minorities, such as the Kurds in the northwest, and executed opponents.

The Iranian Revolution fostered opposition from outside. The United States became bitterly opposed after Islamic militants seized the U.S. Embassy in Tehran in 1979 and held it and the U.S. diplomats for one year. Iran's Arab neighbors, who had always feared Iran's territorial size, large population, military strength, and regional ambitions, were also worried about Islamic militancy aimed at their more secular governments. Tensions were fueled by centuries of animosity between the mostly Sunni Arabs and the mostly Shi'ite Iranians. An Iranian program to develop nuclear power and, possibly, weapons, also concerned the international community.

Iran Under the Shah

Along with modernization, the shah's 35 years of rule also brought a huge military force built with oil revenues and political repression. The shah's promotion of a market economy and women's rights was admired in the West but failed to improve living standards for most Iranians. While corrupt elites siphoned off most of the money earmarked for development, including generous U.S. aid, 60 percent of peasants remained landless. Cities became overcrowded as Iranians abandoned destitute rural villages; the shah's policies and persistent inequalities fostered unrest. The shah's secret police eliminated opposition forcibly, imprisoning thousands of political prisoners. Conservative Shi'ite leaders opposed the modernization, such as the unveiled women and crowded bars, which they viewed as a threat to Muslim religion and culture. Then in 1979, the economy slumped. Strikes and protests forced the shah into exile and turned the United States and Iran into bitter foes.

 Get a glimpse into Iranian life in late 1970s Iran by choosing whether or not to support the Shah in this interactive simulation.

 **The Revolution That Failed Women** Read a critical analysis of the status of Iranian women before and after the Revolution.

Reform and Repression

Eventually, Iranian politics changed as the nation mixed theocracy with the trappings of democracy. A more open electoral process allowed opposition parties to win seats in parliament. Beginning in 1997, reformers gained a share of power. This, however, fostered a power struggle between moderate reformers, many of them clerics, and the hard-line clerics who controlled the judicial and electoral systems. With the economy floundering, the reformers sought closer ties to the outside world, democratization, and a loosening of harsh laws but found the United States unwilling to improve relations. Young people, resenting clerical leadership and Islamic laws, often supported reform and increasingly challenged restrictions on personal behavior. But the hard-liners maintained overall political power, banning reformist newspapers and disqualifying reformist political candidates. Shirin Ebadi (shih-RIN ee-BOD-ee) (b. 1947), a feminist Iranian

Khomeini and Revolution

With the shah's departure, an Islamic revolution began to reshape Iran. While some Shi'ite thinkers discouraged the clergy from political activism, others promoted clerical involvement in governing an Islamic state. The latter's views prevailed when militant Shi'ite clerics, led by the long-exiled Ayatollah Ruhollah Khomeini (roo-HOLE-ah KOH-may-nee)

lawyer and human-rights activist, won the Nobel Peace Prize in 2003 for bravely challenging the clerical leadership and favoring a reformist Islam. But in 2005, Iranians lost faith in the ineffective reformist leaders and elected a hard-line, anti-reform president who pledged to increase the nation's nuclear capabilities and restore conservative values.

Iraq proved another major source of regional instability. In 1958, the Iraqi army overthrew an unpopular monarchy and began more than four decades of ruthless military dictatorships. These governments, usually led by the Ba'ath ("Renaissance") Party—which favored socialism and Arab nationalism and strongly opposed Israel—fostered secular policies and some economic development, making Iraq one of the most prosperous Arab societies by the 1980s. Representing the Sunni minority of 20 percent, the Ba'ath ruled a nation with a restless Arab Shi'ite majority, located mostly in the south, and a disaffected Kurdish minority in the north. In 1979, army officer Saddam Hussein (1937–2006) took power in Iraq and proved even more brutal than his predecessors.

Saddam Hussein and the Iran-Iraq War

Alarmed by the Iranian Revolution, and hated by Ayatollah Khomeini, who considered Saddam's secular regime godless, Saddam launched a war against Iran in 1980, using poison gas against Iranian soldiers, but he was unable to achieve victory. The United States, with its vested interest in Iraq's oil—the world's second largest proven reserves—and hostility toward Iran, provided arms to Saddam's military. As the casualties mounted, both Iran and Iraq drafted teenagers to fight. The costs of war were staggering: more than 260,000 Iranian and 100,000 Iraqi dead and grave damage to the Iraqi economy, including major destruction in Iraq's main port, Basra.

The Persian Gulf War

When the war ended in 1988 with no victor, Saddam's actions fostered regional tension. The U.S. government continued to support his regime, but in 1991, Iraq invaded prosperous Kuwait, a former British protectorate ruled by an Arab royal family. The United States, worried that oil-rich Saudi Arabia might be next, formed a coalition and launched the Persian Gulf War (1991), which drove Iraqis from Kuwait and killed perhaps 30,000 Iraqi soldiers. But Saddam remained in power, persecuting dissidents and slaughtering Shi'ites and Kurds who rebelled after the Gulf War defeat. At least 30,000 Shi'ites and many thousands of Kurds died from the fighting. Still, Saddam's war-making capabilities were badly damaged, and the United States and United Nations eventually gave the Kurds in the north some protection and greater self-governance, while sanctions imposed by the United Nations restricted Iraq's power. Because of these sanctions and Saddam's economic mismanagement, the Iraqi people struggled to acquire food and medical supplies, and thousands died from the resulting shortages.

Saudi Arabia, Oil, and the World

The Persian Gulf War revealed the close connection between Saudi Arabia, a kingdom built on conservative Islam and oil, and the outside world, especially the United States, which had military bases and a strong economic stake in the kingdom. Comprising mostly bleak desert, Saudi Arabia possesses the world's largest known oil reserves. Beginning in the 1940s, the nation's leaders used oil revenues to fund modernization projects, building highways, hospitals, and universities. By the 1980s, the Saudis had achieved health and literacy rates that were high for the Middle East. Glittering shopping malls served affluent urbanites, yet outside the cities, poor Saudis often still traveled by camel and slept in tents.

Despite the modernization, Saudi political and social life has remained conservative, with the royal family exercising power and living extravagantly while tolerating corruption and quashing dissent. With the acquiescence of the Saudi royal family, the Wahhabis, followers of the most rigid form of Islam, maintain a stranglehold on Islamic thought, practice, and education. Wahhabis believe that women should stay at home and be controlled by men. A special police force patrols the streets and markets to punish women for violating the strict dress codes, which require them to be covered head to foot. In the 1990s, the religious police prevented unveiled female students from fleeing a school dormitory fire, causing dozens of the girls to burn to death. The Shi'ite minority, despised by the Wahhabis, have enjoyed few rights. Saudi and Western critics believe that the narrow Islam taught in Saudi schools promotes extremism and anti-Western sentiment.

Saudi Arabia's policies have strongly influenced world oil prices and availability. The kingdom was the major player in the formation in 1960 of OPEC

Oil Wealth Saudi Arabia contains the world's largest oil operations, mostly located on or near the Persian Gulf. A Saudi worker overlooks one of the nation's many refineries, which produces the oil exports that have brought the nation wealth.

(Organization of Petroleum Exporting Countries), a cartel designed to give the producers more power over the price of oil and leverage over consuming nations. OPEC's members range from Middle Eastern nations such as Algeria, Iran, and the United Arab Emirates to more distant countries such as Mexico, Nigeria, and Indonesia. In 1973, OPEC members, angry at Western support of Israel, reduced the world oil supply to raise prices, badly discomforting industrialized nations. After the embargo ended, the world price remained high, enriching OPEC members and forcing the United States and western Europe to conserve fuel. But in the 1980s, reduced oil consumption broke OPEC's power and prices plummeted, damaging the economies of most OPEC members.

Saudi Arabia remained the world's largest exporter of oil, but by the 1990s, the Saudi economy had soured. Between 1980 and 2000, income levels fell by two-thirds, while members of the royal family spent money lavishly and often violated Wahhabi restrictions with their high living abroad. Resentment of the royal family increased, as did dislike of the royal family's U.S. allies. Some Saudis have embraced militant Islam, a few joining terrorist groups such as Al Qaeda. Most of the young men who hijacked four U.S. airliners and crashed them into the Pentagon and World Trade Center in 2001 were Saudis, and their Al Qaeda leader, Osama bin Laden (b. 1957), became a militant Wahhabi after growing up in a wealthy Saudi family. Yet, thanks to oil, Saudi Arabia and the industrialized nations, especially the United States, have remained close allies despite vast differences.

LO² Change and Conflict in the Middle East

In 1979, the Islamic world celebrated thirteen centuries of Islamic history. For most of those centuries, Muslims had made brilliant contributions to the world, fostering extensive trade networks, spreading scientific knowledge, and founding powerful empires. By the nineteenth century, however, Western powers increasingly meddled with these societies, though the longer history and older traditions of Islam remained relevant into the present. Islamic societies also experienced social and cultural change, as new conflicts resulting from foreign interventions, Islamic militancy, and international terrorism reshaped the region's role in the global system.

Religion, Ethnicity, and Conflict

In parts of the Middle East, ethnic and religious hostilities have fostered long-term conflict. In Lebanon, for example, a long civil war resulted from rivalry between a dozen rival factions, Christian and Muslim, for control of the small state and its resources. In this deeply fragmented land, a national government existed largely only in name during the 1970s and 1980s. Lebanon's main city, Beirut, once a prosperous mecca for trade and tourism, was devastated by factional fighting. Israel, Syria, and the United States were all sucked into the chronic conflict. Syria stationed troops in the north and east, and Israel did the same in the south. In the 1980s, the United States intervened on behalf of a weak national government led by the largest, most pro-Western Christian faction. U.S. warships shelled areas around Beirut dominated by opposition, especially Shi'ite, factions while U.S. Marines secured the Beirut airport. The disastrous U.S. mission made the United States a focus of Arab rage and resulted in some five hundred U.S. deaths from suicide bombers. In the 1990s, the fighting ebbed, and Lebanon regained some stability but little unity.

Elsewhere, in the Sudan, a huge country linking the Middle East and sub-Saharan Africa, the Arab Muslim-dominated government used military force to control the rebellious African Christians and animists in the south, causing 2 million deaths. In 2005, the two sides agreed to end the conflict, but by then the Arab-controlled Sudan government faced a rebellion in Darfur, an impoverished western region where

> "Although deeply divided by clan and factional rivalries, Kurds had long sought either their own nation or self-government within their countries of residence."

> 66 Muslim liberals advocated improving women's lives through education, and some women activists argued that the Quran supported women's rights. 99

African Muslim farmers competed for scarce land with Arab pastoralists. To regain control, the government launched a genocide against the Africans. Thousands of people died from military assaults on their villages or from disease and starvation after they fled, many into neighboring Chad.

Another longtime ethnic conflict concerned Kurds, a large ethnic group—over 20 million strong—inhabiting mountain districts in Iran, Iraq, Syria, and Turkey. Although deeply divided by clan and factional rivalries, Kurds had long sought either their own nation or self-government within their countries of residence. This desire brought them into constant conflict with central governments. Kurdish rebel groups were especially active in eastern Turkey, where the Turkish government, hoping to build a national Turkish identity, repressed Kurdish culture and language. Kurds were also restless in oil-rich northern Iraq, where the dictator, Saddam Hussein, made Kurds a special target of his repression, launching air raids and poison gas attacks against Kurdish villages.

Gender, Religion, and Culture

Gender relations and family life have changed relatively little in the Middle Eastern societies. In a few nations, notably Turkey, Iraq, and Lebanon, urban women expanded their economic opportunities by running businesses and entering the professions. But compared with the rest of the world, most Middle Eastern women remained in the home, often secluded from the outside world, with their lives controlled by the men of their families.

Feminism in the Middle East

Male and female reformers have challenged women's subservient status for centuries, and a full-fledged feminist movement emerged in Egypt in the 1920s. Muslim liberals advocated improving women's lives through education, and some women activists argued that the Quran supported women's rights. Turkey, Tunisia, and Iraq adopted Western-influenced family laws allowing civil marriages and divorce, but conservative Muslims prevented their enactment in other Middle Eastern societies. Devout women often opposed secular feminism, arguing that women were best protected by strict Islamic law, but they also became activists when compelled to do so. For instance, Zainab Al-Ghazali (1917–2005) in Egypt founded an organization that built mosques, trained female preachers, and promoted an active women's role in public life; her staunch support of Islamic values upset not only liberal feminists but also Egypt's modernizing President Nasser, who had her jailed and tortured.

Liberal and conservative Muslims disagree on women's dress. Liberals often see the veil as a symbol of female subjugation, and many women have adopted Western dress. But since the 1960s, in secular nations such as Turkey and Egypt, women influenced by revivalist Islam have lobbied to wear the veil or head scarf as a symbol of piety. In Turkey, where the secular government has been wary of Islamic militancy, head scarves have been banned from schools. At the same time, attitudes toward homosexuality have generally become more repressive. In many countries, homosexual behavior, when discovered, frequently results in jail terms or even more severe punishments.

Tradition vs. Modernity

The clash between tradition and modernity in the Middle East has provided a fertile environment for creativity in religion, music, and literature. Islam has remained at the heart of Middle Eastern life, but, despite its message of peace, social justice, and community, it has often proved more divisive than unifying (see Map 30.2). Age-old divisions such as those between Sunni and Shi'a, liberal and conservative, secular and devout, Sufi and anti-Sufi, remain powerful, especially in western Asia.

 Interactive Map

Islamists and *Jihad*

Antimodern, usually puritanical militants known

as Islamists, who seek an Islamic state and are bitter rivals of secular Muslims, became increasingly influential, especially in Egypt, Algeria, Turkey, and Iran. The writings of the Iranian Ali Shariati (SHAR-ee-AH-tee) (1933–1977), educated in France but a critic of the West, influenced Shi'ites. He castigated Western democracy as subverted by greed but also blamed Islamic tradition for reducing women to, as he put it, the level of a washing machine. Egyptian writer Sayyid Qutb (SIGH-eed ka-TOOB) (1906–1966) sparked political Sunni Islam and redefined *jihad* ("struggle") as violent opposition to the West rather than, as most Muslim thinkers had taught for centuries, personal struggle to maintain faith. Inspired by thinkers like Qutb, the most extreme Islamists, known as *jihadists*, formed organizations such as the Muslim Brotherhood that plotted violence against their modernizing opponents.

 History of the Middle East Database (*http://www.nmhschool .org/tthornton/mehistory database/mideastindex .php*). A useful site on history, politics, and culture.

In a troubled world, the Islamic revival satisfies for millions a need for personal solace, a yearning for tradition, and a dream of a just political system as propounded by the earliest Muslims. While most people have rejected extremist groups, disillusionment with governments and resentment of Western power have prompted a growing turn to Islam for moral support. When elections are allowed, Islamic groups with their large followings tend to triumph over secular parties, as happened in Iraq, Egypt, and Palestine in 2005, a reason why pro-Western modernists often fear democracy. During the past several decades, Islamic influence has grown. Shi'ite activists in Iraq have closed bars and harassed unveiled women, while Sunni militants attack followers of Sufi mysticism, which they view as heresy. Islamists in Algeria, Egypt, and Saudi Arabia have mounted movements aimed initially at challenging their governments; some have become involved with international terrorist groups.

> "In a troubled world, the Islamic revival satisfies for millions a need for personal solace, a yearning for tradition, and a dream of a just political system as propounded by the earliest Muslims."

Muslims in total population
- Over 85%
- 51% to 85%
- 26% to 50%
- 11% to 25%
- 3% to 10%
- Under 3%
- League of Arab States

1. SENEGAL
2. GAMBIA
3. GUINEA-BISSAU
4. GUINEA
5. SIERRA LEONE
6. LIBERIA
7. CÔTE D'IVOIRE
8. GHANA
9. TOGO
10. BENIN
11. MAYOTTE (Fr.)
12. BOSNIA & HERZEGOVINA
13. SERBIA
14. MONTENEGRO
15. ALBANIA
16. MACEDONIA

© Cengage Learning

Map 30.2
The Islamic World

The Islamic world includes not only the Middle East—Western Asia and North Africa—but also countries with Muslim majorities in sub-Saharan Africa, Central Asia, and South and Southeast Asia. In addition, Muslims live in most other Eastern Hemisphere nations and in the Americas.

rai

("opinion") A twentieth-century pop music of Algeria based on local Bedouin chants, Spanish flamenco, French cafe songs, Egyptian pop, and other influences and featuring improvised lyrics that often deal with forbidden themes of sex and alcohol.

Music and Literature in the Contemporary Middle East

While Islamic militants have condemned music, dance, and other pleasures, many people have been fans of popular culture, especially music. Musicians often hope to encourage national unity or shape society, usually in a more liberal direction. The songs of peace and coexistence sung by hugely popular Lebanese singer Fairuz (fie-ROOZ) were sometimes credited with being the major symbol of hope in that turbulent, civil war–plagued land. Similarly, Israelis revered Yemen-born Shoshana Damari (1923–2006), whose optimistic songs encouraged Israeli unity by extolling the nation and its military forces. But in religiously dogmatic or ethnically divided states, popular music has sometimes stirred controversy. The Islamic government of Iran, which is opposed to women performing in public, tried to silence all female singers, including the vocalist and film star Googoosh (GOO-goosh), whose melancholic Westernized pop music had a huge audience in Iran during the 1960s and 1970s.

The rai ("opinion") pop music of Algeria is based on local Bedouin chants, Spanish flamenco, French café songs, Egyptian pop, and other influences, and its improvised lyrics often deal with forbidden themes of sex and alcohol. Rai holds great appeal to urban working-class youth in North Africa and to the offspring of Arab immigrants in France, but it is anathema to puritanical Islamic militants in Algeria.

Middle Eastern writers have used their literature to express ideas forbidden in politics and religion. For instance, the novels of the Egyptian Naguib Mahfuz (nah-GEEB mah-FOOZ) (b. 1911) have addressed social problems and questioned conservative religious values. Many of his writings have been banned in Egypt and other Islamic nations, but Mahfuz has achieved worldwide renown and in 1988 became the first Arab writer to win a Nobel Prize for literature. Iranian writers have often risked punishment by satirizing the failings of governments and business.

Turmoil in Afghanistan

Violence and extreme Islamic movements emerged in Afghanistan, fostering instability there for three decades. Afghanistan's diverse Muslim ethnic groups have little sense of national unity in this landlocked land of harsh deserts and rugged mountains. From the early 1800s until 1978, kings from the largest ethnic group, the Pashtuns, loosely governed the territory. In 1978, pro-communist generals seized power, forged close ties with the Soviet Union, and introduced radical social and economic reforms that challenged Islamic traditions. They implemented land reform, promoted women's education, and replaced

> "Afghanistan's diverse Muslim ethnic groups have little sense of national unity in this landlocked land of harsh deserts and rugged mountains."

Islamic law with a secular family law giving women more rights.

When conservative Islamic rebels, known as mujahidin ("holy warriors"), rebelled against the pro-Soviet regime, the Soviet Union invaded in 1979, launching decades of turbulence. The mujahidin, while poorly armed and divided, won small victories against the 150,000 Soviet troops. Both sides resorted to ruthless brutality; indiscriminate Soviet air attacks on the rebels created 5 million refugees and turned the population against the Soviet occupation. The United States, Pakistan, and Arab nations sent military and financial aid to the rebels, including the wealthy Saudi Osama bin Laden (b. 1957), a trained engineer turned Islamic militant. By the mid-1980s, Afghanistan had become an unwinnable quagmire for the Soviet forces, which withdrew in 1989. The pro-Soviet government collapsed, and rival mujahidin groups fought for control. With the USSR gone and the civil war over, the West offered little help to reconstruct the ruined country.

Afghanistan soon returned to global attention. As conflict between rival militias continued, a group of

Arab Art The large monument of Revolution, in Baghdad, sculpted by a major modern Iraqi artist, Jawad Salim (1920–1961), occupies a central place in the city. Commissioned in 1958 after the overthrow of the monarchy, it celebrates the Iraqi struggle for justice and freedom and often provided a motif for Iraqi poets.

SuperStock

Pashtun religious students known as the Taliban ("students") organized a military force to impose order and stamp out what they considered immoral behavior, such as rape and drinking, among the tribal factions fighting for control of the post-Soviet government. The Taliban conquered much of the Pashtun south and then seized the capital, Kabul, in 1996. Eventually they extended their influence north, where ethnic factions continued to resist them. The puritanical Taliban reversed the modernization of the pro-Soviet regime and introduced an especially harsh form of Islamic rule. Women in the capital, Kabul, who once wore jeans and T-shirts and attended universities, were now required to wear long black robes and stay at home. Education for women was banned, and alcohol disappeared from stores. Reflecting their intolerance and disdain for Afghanistan's pre-Islamic past, the Taliban also destroyed spectacular monumental Buddhas carved into a mountainside over a millennium ago, outraging the world.

International terrorist groups with a jihadist agenda began to form around Arab volunteers who had come originally to fight for the mujahidin cause. The Saudi Osama bin Laden became the leader and chief financial backer of the largest international terrorist group, Al Qaeda. Bin Laden called on Muslims to take up arms against the United States and other Western regimes, whom he called "crusaders" after the Christians who invaded the Middle East during the Intermediate Era: "Tell the Muslims everywhere that the vanguards of the warriors who are fighting the enemies of Islam belong to them."[3] In the late 1990s, these Islamic terrorist groups made Taliban-controlled Afghanistan their base, building camps to train more terrorists.

Islamic Militancy, Terrorism, and Western Interventions

The rise of international terrorism linked to Islamist groups and chiefly targeting Americans and Europeans soon resulted in a renewal of superpower intervention. After the Al Qaeda attacks on the United States in September 2001, the United States, with widespread world support, sent military forces into Taliban-ruled Afghanistan. Soon the United States and its allies had displaced the Taliban, destroyed the Al Qaeda bases, and installed a fragile pro-Western government. Many Afghans and most Muslims out-side of Afghanistan applauded the demise of the Taliban, but instability ensued: tribal warlords controlled large territories; the major Taliban and Al Qaeda leaders, including bin Laden, evaded the U.S. troops and went into hiding; and the United States and western Europe struggled to support the fledgling democracy. By 2005, a Taliban-led insurgency was growing in strength.

The Afghan war was followed by a larger conflict in Iraq. Charging that Iraq's dictator, Saddam Hussein, had weapons of mass destruction and was linked to Al Qaeda, the U.S. president George W. Bush, supported chiefly by Britain, ordered an invasion and occupation of Iraq in 2003 without support from the United Nations, many Western allies, and regional allies such as Turkey and Egypt. Massive looting followed the quick U.S. victory, as museums, ancient historical sites, power plants, armories, and communications networks were plundered. U.S. credibility suffered after the Americans found no nuclear, biological, or chemical weapons or any Saddam–Al Qaeda links. Nor had the Americans adequately planned for the problems of the postwar reconstruction. U.S. forces struggled to contain factional divisions and restore basic services, such as electricity and clean water, to Saddam-era levels. They also struggled to maintain order against a persistent resistance movement, and to defend against terrifying suicide bombings by newly arrived foreign jihadis linked to Al Qaeda. Many Iraqis, especially Shi'ites and Kurds, had hated Saddam's bloody regime and welcomed his demise, but Iraqis also often resented yet another Western occupation. While Arab liberals often hoped democracy would flower in Iraq and throughout the region, the occupation of an oil-rich Arab country, at a high cost in U.S. and Iraqi casualties, tied down the U.S. military and intensified anti-U.S. feeling around the world.

The Middle East in the Global System

The Middle East has been subject to explosive internal forces as well as changes in the global system. By the late twentieth century, observers argued that much of the Middle East had adjusted poorly to a rapidly changing world, lagging behind much of Asia and Latin America in development. In 2002, various Arab thinkers issued an Arab Human Development Report that outlined the economic and social failures of the Arab world, including the marginalization of women and the limited development in health and education (see Witness to the Past: Assessing Arab Development). Debate is also fostered by regional

Assessing Arab Development

Under the auspices of the United Nations Development Programme, a group of Arab scholars and opinion makers from the twenty-two member states of the Arab League, a regional organization, met to consider the Arab condition. In 2002, they issued the first of four planned reports that offered both a description of the Arab condition and a prescription for change. Hailed by Arab and non-Arab observers as a path-breaking effort by Arabs to foster a debate on the inadequacies of Arab development and local barriers to progress, the first document reported great strides in many areas but also unsolved problems. This excerpt is from the Executive Summary.

The Arab Human Development Report 2002 . . . places people squarely at the [center] of development in all its dimensions: economic, social, civil, political, and cultural. It provides a neutral forum to measure progress and deficits, propose strategies to policymakers, and draw attention to country problems that can benefit from regional solutions. It is guided by the conviction that solid analysis can contribute to the many efforts underway to mobilize the region's rich human potential. There has been considerable progress in laying the foundations for health, habitat, and education. Two notable achievements are the enormous quantitative expansion in educating the young and a conspicuous improvement in fighting death. For example, life expectancy has increased by 15 years over the last three decades, and infant mortality rates have dropped by two-thirds. Moreover, the region's growth has been "pro-poor": there is much less dire poverty (defined as an income of less than a dollar a day) than in any other developing region.

But there have been warning signs as well. Over the past twenty years, growth in per capita income was the lowest in the world except in sub-Saharan Africa. . . . If such trends continue [into] the future, it will take the average Arab citizen 140 years to double his or her income. . . . The decline in productivity has been accompanied by deterioration in real wages, which has accentuated poverty. It is evident that . . . Arab countries have not developed as quickly or as fully as other comparable regions. . . . The Arab region is richer than it is developed, . . . hobbled by a . . . poverty of capabilities and . . . opportunities. These have their roots in three deficits: freedom, women's empowerment, and knowledge. Growth alone will neither bridge these gaps nor set the region on the road to sustainable development.

The way forward involves tackling human capabilities and knowledge. It also involves promoting systems of good governance, those that promote, support and sustain human well-being, based on expanding human capabilities, choices, opportunities and freedoms, . . . especially for the poorest and most marginalized members of society. The empowerment of women must be addressed throughout. . . .

[The Report concludes that] People in most Arab countries live longer than the world average life expectancy of 67. However, disease and disability reduce life expectancy by between five and 11 years. Arab women have lower life expectancy than the world average. . . . Arab countries have made tangible progress in improving literacy: . . . female literacy rates tripled since 1970. Yet 65 million adults are illiterate, almost two-thirds of them women. . . . One out of every five Arabs lives on less than $2 per day . . . Arab countries had the lowest freedom score [in the world] in the late 1990s. . . . [Utilization] of Arab women's capabilities through political and economic participation remains the lowest in the world. . . . Serious knowledge deficits include weak systems of scientific research and development.

The Arab world is at a crossroads. The fundamental choice is whether its trajectory will remain marked by inertia, as reflected in much of the present institutional context, and by ineffective policies that have produced the substantial development challenges facing the region; or whether prospects for an Arab renaissance, anchored in human development will be actively pursued.

Thinking About the Reading

1. How have Arabs done in promoting freedom, women's empowerment, and knowledge?
2. What does the report consider the major improvements and the major failures and challenges of the Arab nations?

Source: Arab Human Development Report 2002: Creating Opportunities for Future Generations (UNDP, 2002), available online at http://www.rbas.undp.org/ahdr/press_kits2002/PRExec Summary.pdf. Reprinted with permission of the United Nations Development Programme (UNDP).

cable networks, such as Qatar-based Al Jazeera, as well as websites and blogs that spread awareness of political and social developments.

The region's economic record has been checkered. By 2005, the Middle East had the world's highest unemployment rate, 13.2 percent and, except for sub-Saharan Africa, the slowest economic growth and lowest productivity. Only Turkey has fostered much industrialization and high economic growth rates. Nations with oil, such as Algeria, Iran, and Libya, have remained dangerously dependent on oil revenues, and oil wealth has often led to political corruption. But some small Persian Gulf states like Dubai (doo-BUY) have used their oil wealth to become centers of global commerce. The growing need of industrializing nations such as China and India for oil ensures that the profits will flow to oil-rich nations for years to come. However, Middle Eastern nations that are without oil have struggled to build modern economies with limited resources.

Middle Easterners increasingly have hoped to preserve revered traditional patterns while finding ways to harmonize them with the realities of the modern world. The recent history of the Middle East, like that of India and sub-Saharan Africa, has challenged the widespread notion that contact with the modern world automatically erodes all traditional cultures and steers people inevitably toward Western models. Older patterns of life and thought, including Islam, have persisted in much of the region, and Islamic militancy has tapped a strand of unease with Western ideas. Many Muslims reject what they see as the materialistic, hedonistic values of Western culture. Iranians and Arabs have often agreed with the Indian Muslim poet Muhammad Iqbal (ik-BALL) (1873–1938), who wrote in 1927: "Against Europe I protest, And the attraction of the West: Woe for Europe and her charm, Swift to capture and disarm! Earth awaits rebuilding; rise! Out of slumber deep, Arise!"[4] Other Muslims, however, are wary of Islamic militancy, which has not delivered a better material life in the main country controlled by Islamists, Iran. Middle Eastern reformists such as the Iranian Reza Aslan have sought greater economic development, political freedom, and rights for women. Aslan criticized what he termed the "false idols" of bigotry and fanaticism and argued for a return to Islam's egalitarian roots.

> 66 Middle Easterners increasingly have hoped to preserve revered traditional patterns while finding ways to harmonize them with the realities of the modern world. 99

Interventions by outside powers, such as the United States, reflect the global importance of the Middle East, especially its oil wealth and strategic location among key waterways of world trade. Until cost-effective alternative power sources become common, all industrial economies need access to oil. While U.S. leaders hope democracy will spread, many experts worry that instability in Iraq might unsettle the entire region. Furthermore, few problems, including the Arab–Israel conflict, seem resolvable anytime soon. These challenges make the Middle East a focus of world attention and, some fear, a potential tinderbox.

LO³ Political Change in Sub-Saharan Africa

As in the Middle East, the rise of nationalism and the consequent wave of decolonization in Africa reduced Western political influence, reshaping societies and politics. Between 1957 and 1975, the colonial era ended in sub-Saharan Africa as countries became politically independent. In the early 1960s, as optimistic Africans celebrated their freedom and formed governments, the times were electric with change, and hopes for a better future were high. But with the end of colonial domination, institutions had to be built anew. The years since 1960 have been, in many respects, the most momentous in all of Africa's history. Africans still struggle to find the right mix of policies to resolve their problems.

Nationalism and Decolonization

Rising nationalism sparked decolonization. Between the late nineteenth century and the 1950s, the European colonial powers often maintained control through divide and rule of the different ethnic groups. For example, each of the major Nigerian ethnic groups—the Hausa, Yoruba, and Igbo (Ibo)—had little in common with each other and formed their own nationalist organizations, challenging those Nigerians who sought a united front. Independence sometimes came peacefully after negotiations between nationalist leaders and European rulers, but sometimes only after bitter struggles and violence.

The increasing problems posed for Western colonizers often encouraged them to transfer power peacefully. World War II had undermined Western credibility in the European colonies: many Africans felt revulsion against the Western powers and their pretensions of superiority. The British and French claimed to be fighting for freedom and democracy, but Africans noticed that these values seldom applied in the colonies. With Western vulnerability obvious, nationalist leaders negotiated for reforms in the 1940s. After the war, the British introduced local government in some African colonies, yet most colonial governments did little to prepare their societies for true independence.

> "Between the late nineteenth century and the 1950s, the European colonial powers often maintained control through divide and rule of the different ethnic groups."

pan-Africanism
The dream, originating in the early twentieth century, that all Africans would cooperate to eventually form some sort of united states of the continent.

Nkrumah's Pan-African Dream

The first change came in the British Gold Coast. In 1948, small farmers boycotted European businesses that were suspected of profiteering at their expense. The growing tensions led to riots in the towns. A rising leader in the Gold Coast, Kwame Nkrumah (KWAH-mee nn-KROO-muh) (1909–1972), who had been educated in the West, became convinced that only socialism could save Africa. In 1949, Nkrumah organized a political party, the first real mass organization in Africa, but he was soon arrested by the British, who viewed him as dangerous. Because of the continued unrest, however, the British allowed an election in 1951 for a legislative council, and Nkrumah's party won a huge majority. After negotiations, in 1957 the Gold Coast became independent and was renamed Ghana, after the first great West African kingdom over a millennium earlier. Nkrumah became the nation's first prime minister and the hero of Africa, preaching pan-Africanism, the dream that all Africans would cooperate to eventually form a united continent.

The anticolonial dam had now burst. By 1963, all of the British colonies in West Africa had become independent, largely through a combination of peaceful negotiations and strikes by workers. By contrast, the French at first failed to recognize change: they fought brutal but unsuccessful wars in the 1950s to keep Vietnam and Algeria from leaving the colonial fold. But France eventually gave its colonies the option of voting for a complete break or for autonomy within a French community of closely connected nations. Initially, only the West African colony of Guinea opted to expel the French completely, prompting the French to withdraw all economic aid. Later the French colonies became independent, though they usually maintained close ties to France.

 Comments on Algeria, April 11, 1961 Read excerpts of a press conference held by Charles de Gaulle, in which he declares France's willingness to accept Algerian independence.

CHRONOLOGY

Sub-Saharan Africa, 1945–Present

1948	Introduction of apartheid in South Africa
1949	First mass-based political party in Gold Coast
1952–1960	Mau Mau uprising in Kenya
1957	Independence for Ghana
1957–1975	African decolonization
1967	Assassination of Patrice Lumumba in Congo
1965–1980	White government in Southern Rhodesia
1967–1970	Nigerian Civil War
1975	Independence for Portuguese colonies
1991–1994	Civil war in Somalia
1994	Genocide in Rwanda
1994	Nelson Mandela first black president of South Africa
1998	End of Mobuto era in Congo

Mau Mau During the 1950s, Africans in Kenya, especially the Gikuyu, rebelled against British colonial rule. The British responded by detaining some 90,000 suspected rebels and sympathizers in concentration camps such as this, where many died.

Mau Mau Rebellion
An eight-year uprising in the 1950s by the Gikuyu people in Kenya against British rule.

Violence in Kenya and the Congo

Whereas peaceful power transfers worked in some colonies, widespread violence preceded or accompanied independence in others. For example, many British settlers had migrated to Kenya after both World War I and World War II, taking land from the Africans to establish farms. In 1952, many Gikuyu, Kenya's largest ethnic group, which had suffered the most land losses, began an eight-year uprising against British rule, known as the Mau Mau Rebellion. The British sent thousands of troops to Kenya and committed atrocities against pro–Mau Mau villages, ultimately killing 10,000 Gikuyu and detaining 90,000 others in harsh prison camps. Finally, the British released the nationalist leader, Jomo Kenyatta (ken-YAH-tuh) (ca. 1889–1978), a former herd boy who had studied anthropology in Britain. Negotiations resulted in Kenyan independence in 1963, and Kenyatta became the first freely elected prime minister. Britain also granted independence to Uganda and Tanzania. In Kenya, white settlers who had strongly opposed political rights for the African majority often remained, sometimes serving in the Kenyan government.

Violence also engulfed the Belgian Congo, a vast, natural resource–rich territory containing some two hundred ethnic groups that had been brutally subjugated during the colonial era. At independence, the Congo had only a few university graduates. The only Congolese leader with any national following, the widely admired and left-leaning visionary Patrice Lumumba (loo-MOOM-buh) (1925–1961), opposed the economic domination of Belgian business and mining interests. In 1959, riots broke out in Congolese cities, forcing the Belgians to announce the colony's first free elections, which were won by Lumumba's party. As the Lumumba took power, some Congolese troops mutinied and attacked whites.

Taking advantage of the chaos, Belgian-supported leaders in the mineral-rich Katanga region who opposed Lumumba announced their secession from the country. The United Nations sent in a peace-keeping force that restored order in the Congo. But Katanga leaders, with the complicity of Belgium and the United States, who feared that Lumumba favored the Soviet Union, abducted and murdered him in 1961. Both Belgium and the United States supported the Congo's new leader, General Joseph Mobuto (mo-BOO-to), who became a brutal and oppressive dictator. In 1971, Mobuto, who had given his country a new name, Zaire, also changed his name to Mobuto Sese Seko, "Mobuto the All Powerful."

Angola, Guinea-Bissau, and Mozambique

Portugal, ruled by a fascist dictator, had been reluctant to give up its African colonial empire. Revolts had broken out in its three colonies—Angola, Guinea-Bissau, and Mozambique—in the early 1960s, but the Portuguese launched military campaigns to crush them. Angola's liberation movement was divided into three rival factions based on the country's major ethnic groupings. Marxists led the major liberation movements in Mozambique and Guinea Bissau. The visionary leader of the Guinea-Bissau movement, Amilcar Cabral (AH-mill-CAR kah-BRAHL) (1924–1973), emphasized educating the people to empower them; he was assassinated by Portuguese agents in 1973. In 1974, however, Portugal's war-weary army ended the dictatorship in Portugal. The new democratic, socialist-led government granted the colonies their independence in 1975, but violence, insurgencies, and disorder reigned for years.

Zambia, Malawi, and Zimbabwe

The British colonies of the Rhodesias and Nyasaland in southern Africa, all containing white settlers who bitterly resisted efforts at equality for Africans, were among the last African colonies to gain independence under black majority rule. As African nationalists launched largely nonviolent resistance

"Whereas peaceful power transfers worked in some colonies, widespread violence preceded or accompanied independence in others."

> New African nations typically experienced political and economic challenges that fostered instability: coups, prolonged civil wars, and recurring famines.

campaigns in the colonies, the British granted independence to Zambia (Northern Rhodesia) and Malawi (formerly Nyasaland) in 1963. But the large white settler population in Southern Rhodesia declared independence from Britain in 1965 and installed a racist government that imposed stricter segregation. Africans in Southern Rhodesia took up arms against the white settler government in two rival Marxist-led liberation movements. By 1980, African resistance was so strong that the United States and Britain pressured the white government to allow elections, which were won by Robert Mugabe (moo-GAH-bee) (b. 1924), a former political prisoner who had transformed his guerrilla movement into a party. The country became independent as Zimbabwe.

Political Change and Conflict

A West African scholar called *nation* "a magical word meant to exorcise ethnic quarrels and antagonisms—and as such very precious,"[5] but, as he conceded, the magic usually failed to overcome disunity. New African nations typically experienced political and economic challenges that fostered instability: coups, prolonged civil wars, and recurring famines (see Map 30.3). Several million refugees fled violence, repression, and hunger, while corruption and ethnic divisions made dictatorship more common than democracy. During the 1990s, various countries crumbled into brutal anarchy.

 Interactive Map

Although new African nations typically started as parliamentary democracies, only a few sustained democratic systems. Militaries have often been the only groups that can govern effectively, since they have a shared ideology of leadership, good internal communications, and a tradition of discipline. However, military officers have also ruled with a heavy hand and often looted treasuries. Civilian leaders have often favored one-party states because, they

Map 30.3
Contemporary Africa and the Middle East

Sub-Saharan and North Africa contain more than forty nations. Six sub-Saharan African nations and Algeria in North Africa experienced anticolonial revolutions, and a dozen sub-Saharan nations have been racked by civil wars since independence.

argue, such parties incorporate all ethnic groups. While some of these one-party states, such as in the Congo (Zaire), have been despotisms, others have been relatively democratic. Some nations, such as Nigeria and Ghana, shifted back and forth between authoritarian military dictatorships and ineffective, corrupt civilian governments. Western-style democracy has had little chance to flower in these artificial, multiethnic countries that typically have a tiny middle class and numerous poor people. And, given the deteriorating economic conditions of the past thirty years, governments have had little money for public investment. Furthermore, many nationalist leaders have lost their credibility after a few years, such as Ghana's Kwame Nkrumah, once Africa's greatest hero, who was overthrown for mismanagement and died in exile.

Africa's Leaders: Visionaries, Pragmatists, and Tyrants

African leaders have been a mixed lot. Some have been highly respected, farsighted visionaries, such as Tanzania's Julius Nyerere (NEE-ya-RARE-y) (g. 1962–1985) and Mozambique's Samora Machel (g. 1975–1986), and pragmatic problem solvers, such as South Africa's first black president, Nelson Mandela. Although not all of their initiatives have succeeded, they have used political office largely to improve society rather than enrich themselves. Others have disappointed or brutalized their people. Some, such as the Congo (Zaire) dictator Mobuto (g. 1965–1997) and the Nigerian military dictator Sani Abacha (g. 1993–1998), have been ruthless crooks, arresting or murdering opponents and plundering public treasuries.

Read about Nelson and Winnie Mandela, the courageous South African freedom fighters and leaders in the struggle against apartheid.

During the 1970s in Uganda, then ruled by Idi Amin (EE-dee AH-meen) (1925–2004), a poorly educated general, some 300,000 people suspected of opposing Amin were killed, and thousands more were jailed or fled into exile. Even when their credibility has ended, many leaders have rigged elections or had compliant parliaments declare them presidents for life.

Political instability, conflict, and social unrest have grown as people have struggled for their share of the dwindling pie. The blatant corruption, conspicuous consumption, and smuggling in government and the business sector have increased inequalities and deepened public frustrations. Sub-Saharan Africa has the world's highest rate of income inequality. East Africans chastise the wabenzi ("people who drive a Mercedes Benz"), a privileged urban class of politicians, high bureaucrats, professionals, military officers, and businessmen who manipulate their connections to amass wealth. Political, military, and business elites have often squandered scarce resources on imported luxuries.

On the other hand, in some societies relations, between governments and the governed have improved. New grassroots and other nongovernmental organizations have worked for issues such as human rights and the environment. Ordinary people, especially women, have demanded and sometimes gained greater responsibility for improving their lives. For example, by 2000, some 25,000 local women's groups in Kenya had pushed for improved rights and other issues of interest to women, such as environmental protection. Because few Africans can afford health insurance, in countries such as Senegal, poor people have come together to form small mutual health organizations. Strong support from women voters helped Liberian economist Ellen Johnson-Sirleaf (b. 1939), a Harvard-trained banker and former United Nations official, become the first woman president in Africa in 2005, as Liberia sought to recover from a long civil war and then a corrupt dictatorship.

Endemic Problems

The combination of artificial boundaries, weak national identity, and economic collapse has produced chronic turmoil in several African nations, resulting in what one discouraged African observer called the dark night of bloodshed and death. For example, Liberia and Sierra Leone, once among the more stable countries, disintegrated in the 1990s as ethnic-based rebel groups challenged their country's government for power. In drought-plagued Somalia, when longtime military rule collapsed in 1991, the country divided into regions ruled by feuding, armed Somali clans. As the Somali economy disintegrated, causing thousands to starve to death, the United Nations dispatched a humanitarian mission. But some Americans in the United Nations force were killed, and the United Nations withdrew in 1994, unable to achieve a unified government. While the fighting lessened, Somalia remained a country in name only, controlled by warlords.

Sometimes hatreds have led to genocide, killing directed at eliminating a particular group. This happened in the small, impoverished, and densely populated state of Rwanda, most of whose population belonged to the majority Hutu and minority Tutsi ethnic groups. The German and then the Belgian colonizers had ruled through Tutsi kings. Soon after independence, the Hutu rebelled against the Tutsi-dominated government, slaughtering thousands of Tutsi and forcing others out of the country. In 1994, the extremist Hutu government in Rwanda began a genocide against the remaining Tutsi and moderate

Hutus, murdering more than 500,000 people. Tutsi exiles based in Uganda then invaded Rwanda, forcing the Hutu leadership and its followers into the neighboring Congo. More than 2 million Hutu fled. The new Tutsi-led government continued to face militant Hutu resistance groups based in the Congo, leading to Rwandan military incursions into the Congo.

Nigeria: Hopes and Frustrations

The hopes and frustrations of contemporary Africa are mirrored in Nigeria, which in 2005 was home to some 130 million people, about one-fifth of Africa's total population. Like many African countries, Nigeria contains an extraordinary variety of ethnic groups, languages, religions, and even ecologies. While some 250 ethnic groups live in Nigeria, about two-thirds of the people belong to the Hausa-Fulani, Igbo (Ibo), or Yoruba groups. Nigeria's oil wealth has brought income—80 percent of the nation's total revenues— but has also corrupted politics and increased social inequality.

Nigeria's history has frequently been punctuated by coups, countercoups, riots, political assassinations, and civil war rooted in regional and ethnic rivalries. Between 1967 and 1970, Nigeria endured a bloody civil war to prevent the secession of the Igbo-dominated and oil-rich southeast region. The religious divide between Christians, who dominate the south, and Muslims, who control the north, has also complicated politics. Following a Muslim revival among the Hausa-Fulani, northern states have often imposed strict Islamic law, antagonizing non-Muslims.

The Nigerian oil industry, while creating some prosperity, has also made Nigeria dependent on oil exports and spawned political and economic problems. A few politicians, bureaucrats, and businessmen have monopolized oil profits, fostering corruption, sometimes outright plunder of public wealth, and inequitable wealth distribution. By 2005, the top 20 percent of Nigerians received 56 percent of all the country's wealth, while the bottom 20 percent got only 4.4 percent. Sporadic protests, including sabotage of the oil pipelines, have been met with military force; protest leaders are accused of treason and sometimes executed. Disenchanted Nigerians refer to a "republic of the privileged and rich" and a "mon-

eytocracy." Oil money created high expectations in the 1970s, but the economic boom turned to bust in the 1980s when world oil prices collapsed, increasing economic hardship and social unrest and forcing the nation to take on massive foreign debt to pay its bills. Meanwhile, the debate about whether Nigeria should seek to adopt Western models or attempt to retain its own indigenous traditions has never abated.

The New South Africa

Another large country, South Africa, experienced conflict and inequality for more than three centuries. From World War II to the early 1990s, South Africa remained the last bastion of institutionalized white racism on the continent. The white population, some 15 percent of the total and divided between an Afrikaner majority (descendants of Dutch settlers) and an English minority, ruled the black majority (74 percent) and the Indians (2 percent) and mixed-descent Coloreds (9 percent). Aided by a ruthless police security system, the result was nearly unparalleled cruelty, a chilling juxtaposition of comfort for whites and despair for blacks.

Apartheid: Entrenched White Supremacy

South African white supremacy, in place for several centuries, became more systematic after 1948, when Afrikaner nationalists won the white-only elections and declared full independence from Britain. A top nationalist leader claimed: "We [whites] need [Africans] because they work for us but they can never claim political rights. Not now, nor in the future."[6] Their new policy, apartheid (uh-PAHRT-ate) ("separate development"), set up a police state to enforce racial separation and passed strict segregationist laws that reached into all aspects of peoples' lives. While white families usually lived comfortably in well-furnished apartments or houses, a typical house in Soweto, a dusty African suburb of Johannesburg, was bleak, with the residents using candles or gas lamps for lighting. Only one-quarter of the Soweto houses had running water and perhaps fifteen in one hundred enjoyed electricity.

Apartheid also created what white leaders called tribal homelands, known as bantustans, rural reservations where black Africans were required to live if they were not needed in the modern economy. The system allocated whites 87 percent of the nation's land and nonwhites the other 13 percent. Every year, thousands of Africans were forcibly resettled to the impoverished bantustans, which contained little fertile land and few jobs and services. Infant mortality rates in the bantustans were among the world's highest. Under this system, black families were fractured as men and women were recruited on annual contracts for jobs outside the bantustans.

Natural Resources and Economic Disparity

Rich in strategic minerals such as gold, diamonds, uranium, platinum, and chrome, South Africa became the most industrialized nation on the continent, but the wealth was monopolized by the white minority. By 1994, the ratio of average black to white incomes stood at 1 to 10, the most inequitable income distribution in the world. African unemployment reached 33 percent. Nonetheless, because of the country's mineral wealth and extensive foreign investment, the South African government enjoyed the support of several powerful industrialized countries, including the United States, Britain, and Japan, who feared that unrest or black majority rule might threaten their billions in investments and access to lucrative resources.

Resistance and Emergence of the African National Congress

Despite the repression, Africans resisted and often paid a price for their defiance. South African leaders forged the world's leading police state, with the world's highest rate of execution and brutal treatment of dissidents. Among the victims was Stephen Biko (1946–1977), a former medical student and resistance leader who was beaten to death in police custody. Hundreds of Africans were arrested each day for "pass law" violations and held for days or weeks before being released. Death squads of off-duty policemen sometimes assassinated black leaders, such as Victoria Mxenge (ma-SEN-gee), a lawyer who defended antiapartheid activists. Defying the government, strikes, work interruptions, and sabotage became common.

The African National Congress (ANC), long a voice for nonviolent resistance, emerged as the major opposition organization. The ANC remained multiracial, with some whites, Coloreds, and Indians serving in its leadership. In 1955, despairing of peaceful protest, a more militant ANC leadership had framed its inclusive vision in the Freedom Charter: "South Africa belongs to all who live in it, black and white."⁷ But the ANC was declared illegal, and government repression forced it underground, where it adopted a policy of violent resistance and trained young South Africans in exile how to use weapons. Several of its main leaders, including Nelson Mandela (man-DEL-uh) (b. 1918), spent as many as thirty years in prison for their political activities.

Women played an influential role in the ANC, often, like the men, facing arrest and mistreatment.

Mandela's Victory

Ultimately, moderation and realism in both the ANC and the ruling National Party brought a more just and democratic society. International isolation, economic troubles, the increasing incompatibility between apartheid's restrictions and a need for more highly skilled black workers, and growing black unrest forced the government to relax apartheid and release Mandela from prison. The two parties agreed on a new constitution requiring "one man, one vote." In 1994, white supremacy came to a stunning end in the first all-race elections in South African history, which installed Mandela as president and gave the ANC two-thirds of the seats in Parliament.

The ANC government enjoyed massive goodwill but has also faced daunting challenges in healing a deeply fragmented society while restoring the pride and spirits of African communities destabilized by apartheid. Mandela worked to find the right mix of racial reconciliation and major changes to benefit the disadvantaged black majority. In 1999, Mandela left office, a still-popular figure, and the ANC retained power in free elections. It improved services in black communities, raised black living standards, and created opportunities for Africans, fostering a growing black upper and middle class. Yet challenges linger: crime has rapidly increased, violent protests have broken out, and black unemployment has remained high. South Africa has one of the world's highest rates of HIV/AIDS, with some 5 million South Africans infected. Nonetheless, South Africa has become the model of progress for sub-Saharan Africa, and people everywhere hope that the nation succeeds in healing racial wounds while spreading the benefits of its wealth to all citizens.

LO⁴ Changing African Economies, Societies, and Cultures

In the decades since the 1960s, for many sub-Saharan African nations, achieving economic development and true independence has seemed a desperate struggle. African nations have tried various strategies to generate development to benefit the majority of people, but no strategy has proved effective over the long term. Economic problems have proliferated, but Africans have created new social and cultural forms as they reckon with their political and economic problems.

Economic Change and Under-development

Modern Africa has experienced severe economic problems. Africans have mostly supplied agricultural and mineral resources, such as cocoa and copper, to the global economy, but this has not brought widespread wealth. Only a few countries have enjoyed consistently robust economic growth or substantially raised living standards. Sub-Saharan Africa contained nineteen of the world's twenty poorest countries in 2004. With more than 670 million people (almost 13 percent of the world population) by 2004, this region accounts for only 1 percent of the world's production of goods and services, about the same as one of the smallest European nations, Belgium, with 10 million people. Half of the people live in poverty, earning less than $1 per day, the highest poverty rate in the world. Sub-Saharan Africa has also had the world's highest infant mortality rates and lowest average life expectancies.

Prospects: More People . . . Less Food

The economic doldrums have been linked to other problems. The region's economies have generally grown by 1 to 2 percent per year, but its population increase is the world's highest, more than 3 percent. Since 10 to 15 percent of babies die before their first birthday, parents have had an incentive to bear many children. At current rates, the population will double to 1.3 billion by 2025, but new jobs, classrooms, and food supplies will not keep pace. Only a few nations have enjoyed self-sufficiency in food production; most require food imports from Europe and North America. Women grow the bulk of the food, but the male farmers growing cash crops for export receive most of the government aid. Millions of Africans, perhaps one-third of them children, are chronically malnourished, and as a result often have permanent brain damage. Several million children die each year from hunger-related ailments. Severe drought and the drying up of water sources is a chronic problem in many regions, while less than half of school-age children attend school. Some 25 million girls receive no elementary education.

> "Africans have mostly supplied agricultural and mineral resources, such as cocoa and copper, to the global economy, but this has not brought widespread wealth."

Neo-Colonial Capitalism

To achieve economic development, Africans have sought viable economic strategies. The most common development model has been termed "neocolonial capitalism," because it involved close economic ties to the Western nations and free markets of some sort. The countries following this model favored the cash crops and minerals that had dominated the colonial economy, often at the expense of food production, and welcomed western European and U.S. investment and economic advice. A few countries prospered with this strategy, at least for a time, but the political consequences were often negative. Ivory Coast (or Côte d'Ivoire) and Kenya were among the most hospitable to a Western presence, and in the 1960s and 1970s, both countries enjoyed high rates of growth and rising incomes. Ivory Coast remained a major exporter of coffee and cocoa, while Kenya, with world-famous game parks, lived from tourism and the export of coffee, tea, and minerals. By the mid-1980s, both had per capita incomes about double the African average. But both countries eventually became one-party states that, while stable, grew despotic. Well-placed leaders plundered the economies, and the environment suffered. By the late 1990s, as world prices for coffee and cocoa collapsed, the economies experienced increasing stress, protesters demanded more democracy, the delicate ecologies became dangerously unbalanced, and crime rates soared. By the early 2000s, Ivory Coast was engulfed in civil war, while Kenyans had forced out a dictator and elected a reformist government that has failed to fulfill its promises.

The most disastrous example of neocolonial capitalism was the Democratic Republic of the Congo (known as Zaire between 1971 and 1997). A huge country, with 60 million people, Congo enjoys a strategic location in the center of Africa, rich mineral resources, and good land. But it became Africa's biggest failure. Over the years, the United States and Belgium poured billions of investment and aid into the Congo to keep President Mobuto Sese Seko in power. To the

African Studies Internet Resources (*http://www.columbia.edu/cu/lweb/indiv/africa/index.html*). Provides valuable links to relevant websites on contemporary Africa.

Congolese, however, Mobuto was unforgivingly corrupt, looting the treasury and foreign aid to amass a huge personal fortune—some $4 to $5 billion—while repressing his opponents. As a result, the Congo suffered one of the world's highest infant mortality rates, limited health care, and widespread malnutrition. In 1998, a long-festering rebellion gained strength, forcing Mobuto into exile, where he died. Rebels took over, but they have done little to foster democracy or development. The Congo was soon fragmented in civil war and interethnic fighting, and rebel groups controlled large sections of the sprawling country. Nearly 4 million Congolese died from the fighting and its side effect, the collapse of medical care, between 1998 and 2004, causing a humanitarian crisis.

Reason for Hope: Ghana and Botswana

The most recent showcases for economic success have been Ghana and Botswana. For several decades, after Kwame Nkrumah lost power, Ghana had experienced a roller coaster of corrupt civilian governments interspersed with military regimes. In the 1990s, the leaders gradually strengthened democracy and mixed capitalism with socialism. Ghana became increasingly prosperous: by 2000, it enjoyed one of the continent's highest annual per capita incomes, $1,600. Investment in schools resulted in one of Africa's most educated populations. Beginning as a failure like Ghana, Botswana, when it gained independence in 1966, exported nothing and was one of the world's poorest countries. Gradually, however, using ethnic traditions as a foundation, Botswanans carved out a successful democracy; the economy, health care, education, and protection of resources all steadily improved, despite deadly droughts. By 2000, Botswanans had fostered living standards higher than those of most African and many Middle Eastern, Asian, and Latin American societies, boasting an annual per capita income of more than $3,000, an economy growing by 11 percent per year, and a literacy rate of 70 percent. Unfortunately, the AIDS epidemic, which hit Botswana particularly hard, rapidly undermined economic and health gains.

African Socialisms

To foster development, some African nationalists have pursued revolutionary or reformist strategies.

They have concluded that the political and economic institutions inherited from colonialism could not spark economic development, because they transferred wealth and resources to the West. After independence, more wealth still flowed out of Africa than into it, and the disparity has increased every year. The radicals argued that, to empower Africans, it was necessary to reduce the colonial state to ashes and replace it with something entirely new.

Various social revolutionary regimes emerged from the long wars of liberation against entrenched colonial or white minority governments. Some Africans looked toward communist-ruled China or the USSR for inspiration. Marxist revolutionary governments came to power in Angola and Mozambique after the Portuguese left, but they struggled to implement socialism. To counter these governments, the white-ruled South African state sponsored opposition guerrilla movements, aided by a U.S. government wanting to overturn Marxist regimes, that kept these countries in civil war for several decades. During Angola's long civil war, more than 1.5 million people died. The war eventually ended, but Angola, which is blessed with coffee, oil, diamonds, and other minerals but plagued with corruption, still struggled to foster development. The civil war in Mozambique, one of the world's poorest nations, resulted in 1 million deaths and 5 million refugees. Since its war ended in 1992, the pragmatic Marxist leaders introduced free multiparty elections and liberalized the economy, raising the per capita income to $1,200.

One social revolutionary state, Zimbabwe, the former British colony of Southern Rhodesia, at first became Africa's biggest success story. The Marxist-influenced government, led by the liberation hero Robert Mugabe, a schoolteacher turned lawyer, proved pragmatic for more than a decade, respecting democratic processes and human rights, encouraging the white minority to stay, and trying to raise living standards and opportunities for black Zimbabweans. The country became one of the few food-exporting nations on the continent. Zimbabwe eventually faced severe problems, however, including tensions between rival African ethnic groups. Continuing white ownership of the best farmland produced resentment among land-hungry blacks.

During the 1990s, Mugabe, succumbing to the allure of power and wealth, became more dictatorial and used land disputes to divide the nation. As his

> **" To foster development, some African nationalists have pursued revolutionary or reformist strategies. "**

support among both whites and Africans waned, he rigged elections, harassed or jailed his opponents, and ordered the seizure of white-owned farms. By 2005, commercial agriculture had collapsed, the country was gripped by drought, life expectancy had dropped sharply, and Mugabe's police had demolished the homes and shops of poor blacks who favored the opposition. The nation, once one of Africa's most promising, veered toward catastrophe.

> "Exciting new musical genres have emerged as musicians have sought to make sense of their changing social identities, world-views, and lives."

Cities, Families, and Gender Relations

Modern Africa has seen rapid social change. Since the 1940s, more people have lived in cosmopolitan cities where traditional and modern attitudes meet, mix, and clash. Cities have grown rapidly: between 1965 and 2000, the percentage of sub-Saharan Africans living in urban areas doubled, from 14 to 30 percent, but people concentrate in one or two key cities for each country. Hence, Abidjan in Ivory Coast and Luanda in Angola each contain one-quarter of their country's population. With their modern office towers, theaters, and shopping centers, cities have become the centers for political and economic power as well as for cultural creativity and social change. In fact, cities have grown so fast that services such as buses, water, power, police, schools, and health centers cannot meet the needs of their populations. Such growth is exemplified by Nigeria's largest city, Lagos, which grew from less than 1 million in 1965 to a chaotic megalopolis of some 10 million by 2000.

The family, while remaining the primary social unit, has also changed. The extended family of the villages declined in the cities and was often replaced by the smaller nuclear family. Individualism increasingly challenged village communalism, where marriages were largely arranged by elders; in the cities, young people often arrange their own marriages. Traditionally, village men had an economic incentive to take more than one wife, since women did most of the routine farm work, but with no farming option, urban women have lost economic status, and men no longer need several wives. Men enjoy more educational opportunities than women and hence dominate the job market. Sometimes governments erected barriers against women in the economy: President Mobuto in the Congo stressed an authoritarian male model and discouraged women from seeking paid work, and in the 1980s, Nigeria's military regime blamed market women for high prices, raiding their stalls and beating them.

Nonetheless, gender roles have changed as women have become more independent, and a growing number served in governments and parliaments. Indeed, sub-Saharan Africa ranks ahead of the rest of the developing world in the percentage of women (16 percent) in legislative positions. For example, the Kenyan Grace Ogot (OH-got) (b. 1930) served in parliament while writing short stories in which her heroines confronted traditional values and change. Women have formed groups to work for society's improvement. For instance, the Nigerian Eka Esu-Williams (b. 1950), the daughter of a midwife, earned a Ph.D. in Immunology and pursued an academic career before forming Women Against AIDS in Africa in 1988. Women are usually left with self-employment in low-wage activity, such as the small-scale trade of hawking goods and keeping stalls in city markets, a female profession for centuries; domestic work as maids, cooks, or nannies; or hairdressing.

African Culture and Religious Change

Africans have reconstructed their cultures in creative ways. In the popular arts, especially music and literature, imported ideas are combined with African culture. Urbanization, the growth of mass media, and the mixing of ethnic groups and outside influences have all created a fertile ground for mixed popular music styles that have reflected social, economic, and political realities. Exciting new musical genres have emerged as musicians have sought to make sense of their changing social identities, world-views, and lives. Miriam Makeba (muh-KAY-ba) (b. 1932), the South African jazz and pop singer who was forced by the apartheid government to spend decades in exile, explained, "I live to sing about what I see and know. I don't sing politics, I sing truth."[8] The rise of varied African-based popular music styles has helped Africans adjust to change while affirming their spirit in the face of external influences and internal failures. For instance, the *juju* music of the Nigerian Yoruba reflects Yoruba traditions and values while mixing local and Western instruments, such as electric guitars.

Songs as a Weapon Against Injustice

African popular musicians reach an international audience, performing and selling recordings around the world. Perhaps the greatest African superstar, the Senegalese Youssou N'Dour (YOO-soo en-DOOR) (b. 1959), collaborates with leading Western musicians but remains true to his roots, living in Dakar and following his tolerant Sufi Muslim faith. Some musicians are highly political. The Nigerian Fela Kuti (1938–1997), whose music mixed jazz, soul, rock, and Yoruba traditions, used his songs as a weapon to attack the Nigerian government and its Western sponsors, and faced frequent arrest and beatings for his protests. Like Bob Marley, Fela gained worldwide fame for his use of music to attack injustice and influence politics.

African Literature: An Emerging International Force

As with popular musicians, writers have produced distinctive literatures by combining old traditions with new influences to comment on modern society. African literature has questioned the status quo, asserted African identity, and attempted to influence political change and economic development. Major figures have often written in English or French to better develop an international reputation. For example, the Nigerian Wole Soyinka (WOE-lay shaw-YING-kuh) (b. 1934)—a Yoruba poet, playwright, novelist, and sometime filmmaker who won the 1986 Nobel Prize for literature—mixes Yoruba mysticism with criticisms of Western capitalism, racism, cultural imperialism, and African failures. A former political prisoner, Soyinka has denounced repressive African leaders, including Nigeria's, with as much venom as he attacks Western imperialists, chastising "Nigeria's self-engorgement at the banquet of highway robberies, public executions, public floggings and other institutionalized sadisms, casual cruelties, wanton destruction."[9] The powerful criticism of governments offered by Soyinka and his Nigerian colleague Chinua Achebe has often forced both authors to live in exile.

Writers and artists have also tried to find authentic African perspectives. Negritude is a literary and philosophical movement to forge distinctively African views that first developed in the 1930s. The Senegalese writer and later the first president of his country after independence, Leopold Senghor, was a major negritude voice, attempting to balance

> **negritude**
> A twentieth-century literary and philosophical movement to forge distinctively African views.

African Cultural Expression Africans have developed diverse and vibrant popular music, often by mixing Western and local traditions. In Nigeria, juju music, played by bands such as Captain Jidi Oyo and his Yankee System in this 1982 photo, has been popular among the Yoruba people.

the Western stress on rational thought with African approaches to knowledge, such as mysticism and animism, long disdained by Europeans as superstition. One of the best-known writers in Francophone West Africa, Ousmane Sembene (OOS-man sem-BEN-ee) (b. 1923) of Senegal, was influenced more by Marxism than negritude. His writings, often set in the colonial period, show African resistance to Western domination and social inequality. Sympathizing with exploited people, his work also attacks Senegal's privileged elite, including greedy businessmen and government officials.

English-language literature has also flourished in South Africa and East Africa. For example, Kenyan Ngugi Wa Thiongo (en-GOO-gee wah thee-AHN-go) (b. 1938), a former journalist turned university professor who studied in England, has written several novels that explore the relationship between colonialism and social fragmentation, showing Gikuyu society struggling to retain its identity, culture, and traditions while adjusting to the modern world. His 1979 novel, *Petals of Blood*, portrays a Kenya struggling to free itself from neocolonialism but also beset with corruption. His attacks on the privileged local elite allied with Western exploitation earned Ngugi several terms in Kenyan jails and later forced him into exile.

Religion in Contemporary Africa

Africans have maintained a triple religious heritage: animism/polytheism, Islam, and Christianity. All of these faiths have many followers, although the older animism has lost influence, and the relations between the traditions are not always easy. With their links to wider worlds, Christianity and Islam are also globalizing influences, spreading Western or Middle Eastern political, social, and economic ideas. Africans often view religions in both theoretical and practical terms, refusing to divorce metaphysical speculation from everyday life. They adopt views that help them survive the changes of modern times, rejecting old ideas and adding new ones as needed. Religion has remained in constant flux.

Christianity became Africa's largest religion, attracting some 250 to 300 million followers by 2000, both the fervent and the nominal in faith. Some countries, such as Congo, South Africa, and Uganda, became largely Christian. Africans are prominent in the world leadership of the Anglican and Catholic churches. Christianity has proven a powerful force for social change. Believers often favor the liberation of women, and mission schools have educated many African leaders, influencing their worldviews. A growing number of independent churches,

some blending African traditions into worship and theology, have no ties to the older Western-based denominations; some African churches have enjoyed spectacular growth, with services that attract thousands of congregants each Sunday. Yet many Africans have viewed Christianity critically. According to a popular nationalist saying: "When the missionaries came the Africans had the land and the Christians had the Bible. They taught us to pray with our eyes closed. When we opened them they had the land and we had the Bible."[10]

More than 200 million black Africans follow Islam. About one-fourth of all sub-Saharan countries have Muslim majorities. Some revivalist and Wahhabi movements have gained influence, especially in northern Nigeria, where some states have imposed Islamic law, sparking deadly clashes with Christian minorities. But most Muslims and Christians remain moderate and inclusive. While politicians use religion as a wedge issue, and Christian-Muslim clashes have occurred in countries such as Ivory Coast, tolerance has more often marked relations among Christians, Muslims, and animists. Ethnicity often divides people more than religion.

Africa in the Global System

African developments have occurred in a global context. During the Cold War, some African countries gained aid from the superpowers, but the rivalry also fostered manipulation. Countries such as Congo and Angola often became pawns in the Cold War, with the superpowers helping to support or remove leaders. But with the Cold War over, the Western world has largely ignored Africa, and the wealth gap between African countries and the Western industrialized nations has grown even wider than during colonial times. Today the gap between the richest Western nations and the poorest African countries is around 400 to 1.

The World Economy

Global conditions have often proven counterproductive for Africans. Only when the world economy boomed in the 1950s and 1960s did African economies show steady growth. Since the 1970s, however, as the world economy soured and the world prices for many African exports collapsed, African economic growth rates steadily dropped. Western experts have encouraged a policy known as "structural adjustment," in which international lenders, such as the International Monetary Fund (IMF) and the World Bank, loan nations money on the condition that these nations open their economies to private investment and, to balance national budgets, reduce government spending for health, education, and farmers. The resulting hardship on average people increases unrest and resentment both of governments and of the Western nations that control the IMF and World Bank. This private investment also promotes a shift away from traditional farming to modern agriculture. But modern agriculture, with its reliance on tractors, chemical fertilizers, and new seeds, entails a large environmental and social cost.

By 1998, as a percentage of total output, African countries had the largest foreign debts in the world: $230 billion. At the same time, the world prices for most of Africa's exports, such as coffee, cotton, and tobacco from Tanzania and cocoa from Ghana, have steadily dropped since the 1960s. African farmers cannot compete with highly subsidized Western farmers and the tariff barriers erected in Europe, North America, and Japan against food and fiber imports from Africa. Increasingly desperate, countries such as Guinea-Bissau and Somalia have agreed to allow dangerous toxic waste, such as deadly but unwanted chemicals produced in the West, to be buried on their land in exchange for cash.

Africa's economic problems have had diverse roots. Some resulted from colonialism, which imposed economic policies that caused severe environmental destruction, such as desertification and deforestation, while incorporating the people into the world economy as specialized producers of minerals or cash crops for export rather than food farmers. Hence, Zambia relies on exploiting copper, Uganda coffee, Malawi tobacco, and Nigeria oil (95 percent). Nations have remained vulnerable to drops in world commodity prices for their exports. Since independence, bad policy decisions, poor leadership, corruption, unstable politics, and misguided advice from Western experts have also contributed to the

economic crisis. In addition, the rapid spread of HIV/AIDS has ravaged African nations, killing and affecting millions (see Chapter 26). In some nations, one-third of the population has HIV.

The Vision of a New Society

But although falling behind much of Asia and Latin America economically, Africans have had both successes and failures. Using foreign aid and their own resources, they have made rapid strides in literacy, social and medical services, including active birth-control campaigns, and road construction. Some nations, such as South Africa and Uganda, have a feisty free press. Africans have also attempted to work together to resolve problems. The African Union, formed in 2000 with 54 members, has sent peacekeeping troops into violence-torn countries such as Sudan. Many nations have moved toward more democratic systems and private enterprise. However, political leadership has often failed to root out corruption, restructure existing institutions, and foster food production. Millions still live in poverty. Africa suffers a particularly acute "brain drain" as academics, students, and professionals, seeking a better life, move to Europe or North America.

African history is not only an authentic, dynamic saga of indigenous African development but also part of a larger global process. Over the past half-century, Western influence has remained strong, and Africans have not enjoyed complete control of their destiny. The Ghanaian historian Jacob Ajayi (a-JAH-yee) laid out the challenge: "The vision of a new [African] society will need to be developed out of the African historical experience. The African is not yet master of his own fate, but neither is he completely at the mercy of fate."[11]

 Listen to a synopsis of Chapter 30.

CHAPTER 31

South Asia, Southeast Asia, and Global Connections,
Since 1945

Learning Outcomes

After reading this chapter, you should be able to answer the following questions:

LO¹ What factors led to the political division of South Asia?

LO² What have been the major achievements and disappointments of the South Asian nations?

LO³ What were the causes and consequences of the wars in Indochina?

LO⁴ How has decolonization and globalization shaped the new Southeast Asian nations?

❝This music sings the struggle of [humanity]. This music is my life. This is the revolution we have begun. But the revolution is only a means to attain freedom, and freedom is only a means to enrich the happiness and nobility of human life.**❞**

—Hazil, the Indonesian revolutionary nationalist in Mochtar Lubis's novel *A Road with No End* (1952)[1]

In 1950, a small, idealistic group of leading Indonesian writers published a moving declaration promoting universal human dignity: "We [Indonesians] are the heirs to the culture of the whole world, a culture which is ours to extend and develop in our own way [by] the discarding of old and outmoded values and their replacement by new ones. Our fundamental quest is [helping] humanity."[2] These writers hoped that Indonesia could combine the most humane ideas of East and West to become a beacon to the world, open to all cultures and showing respect for the common people. While delighted with independence, the writers warned against the dangers of a narrow nationalism that devalued other cultures.

Test your knowlege before you read this chapter.

What do you think?

Both South Asian and Southeast Asian nations faced widespread conflict in their quests for self-governance.

Strongly Disagree						Strongly Agree
I	2	3	4	5	6	7

The writers had been inspired by the irreverent Sumatran poet Chairul Anwar (CHAI-roll ON-war) (1922–1949), who believed the revolution had destroyed the old colonial society and opened up the possibility of building a new, open society. Anwar excited Indonesian writers with his path-breaking poems that stretched the possibilities of the Indonesian language. But he had died when just twenty-seven years old, leaving it to others, among them the liberal Sumatran author Mochtar Lubis (MOKE-tar LOO-bis) (b. 1920), whose work is quoted above, to carry on the campaign. The declaration's noble aspirations and recognition of Indonesia's connection to the wider world reflected a new sense of possibility as walls of colonialism were being knocked down.

But the writers' idealism was soon dashed by the realities of the early post–World War II years. While Southeast Asians longed for human dignity, other, more immediate goals took precedence,

<<**Commuting to Work** Vietnam has largely recovered from its decades of war and has experienced increasing economic growth. These women in Hanoi are commuting to work by bicycle.

From Frances FitzGerald, Vietnam: Spirits of the Earth. Photographer: Mary Cross

including securing independence, building new nations, and addressing economic problems. Despite false starts and conflicts, over the following decades, Indonesians and other nations of South and Southeast Asia sought, and sometimes found, answers to their challenges while increasing their links to global networks.

> "As violence flared, thousands of Hindus and Sikhs fled Pakistan for India, and thousands of Muslims fled India for Pakistan."

The societies of South and Southeast Asia, which changed dramatically without destroying tradition, offer striking contrasts with the wider world as well as with each other. Except for East Asia, this is the most densely populated part of the world: more than 1.5 billion people live in the lands stretching eastward from Pakistan and India to Indonesia and the Philippines. It is also a very diverse area, containing a wide array of languages, ethnic groups, religions, world-views, governments, and levels of economic development. This region of contrasts has played an important role in the world for more than four millennia and continues to be one of the cornerstones of the world economy.

LO¹ The Reshaping of South Asia

World War II undermined British colonial control and led to independence for the peoples of South Asia. The British, who were economically drained by the war and realizing that continued control of India would be costly, handed power over to local leaders. The first prime minister of independent India was Jawaharlal Nehru (NAY-roo) (1889–1964), whose idealism about India's independence was tempered by the realities of the challenges ahead. India's long struggle for independence, marked by the nonviolent philosophy of Mohandas Gandhi (1868–1948), had ironically ended with Gandhi assassinated and British India divided into several separate, often hostile countries—India, Pakistan, Bangladesh, and Sri Lanka. Each of the four nations had its achievements and failures, but the

geographically largest and most populous, India, has been the regional colossus and a major player in world affairs.

Decolonization, Partition, and the Nehru Years

The religious divisions of South Asia undermined regional unity. During World War II, relations between the British and the mainly Hindu leadership of the Indian National Congress ruptured (see Chapter 25). Taking advantage, and fearing domination by the much larger Hindu community in India, the Muslim League pressed its case with the British for a separate Muslim nation, to be called Pakistan. After the war ended, negotiations to bring the Congress and the Muslim League together in a common vision broke down in 1946 amidst widespread rioting and violence; in Calcutta alone, five thousand people died. Subsequently, the Muslim leader, Mohammed Ali Jinnah (1876–1948), announced that if India were not divided, it would be destroyed. In 1947, British negotiators reached an agreement with Congress and Muslim League leaders to create two independent nations, India and a Pakistan formed out of the Muslim majority areas of eastern Bengal and the northwestern provinces along the Indus River.

Religious Violence in India and Pakistan

The two nations emerged in hopefulness. In a speech to his new nation, India, Prime Minister Nehru proclaimed: "Long years ago we made a tryst with destiny, and now the time comes when we shall redeem our pledge. At the stroke of the midnight hour, when the world sleeps, India will awake to life and freedom."[3] A similar mood of renewal struck people in Pakistan, but the euphoria in both new nations proved short-lived, as partition sparked hatreds between local members of the majority faith, who felt empowered, and religious minorities, who feared discrimination. As violence flared, thousands of Hindus and Sikhs fled Pakistan for India, and thousands of Muslims fled India for Pakistan. Altogether some 5 million refugees crossed the India–West Pakistan border, and 1 million crossed

 **Virtual Library: South Asia** (http://www.columbia.edu/cu/libraries/indiv/area/sarai/). A major site maintained by Columbia University.

the India–East Pakistan border. About half a million refugees died from the religious violence.

Mohandas Gandhi

The sixty-eight-year-old Mohandas Gandhi labored to stop the killing. Moving into the Muslim quarter of Delhi, he toured refugee camps without escort, read aloud from the scriptures of all religions, including Islam's holiest book, the Quran, and confronted Hindu mobs attacking mosques. Finally, in desperation, and hoping to send a powerful message, Gandhi, who weighed only 113 pounds, began a fast that he said would last until all the violence in the city had stopped or he died. He quickly fell ill, but Gandhi's effort worked, allowing him to break off his fast. After the violence subsided, a substantial Muslim and Sikh minority remained in India and a Hindu and Sikh minority in Pakistan. But partition had been shattering. Furthermore, Gandhi's support for Muslim victims of Hindu violence outraged Hindu extremists, who regarded Gandhi as a traitor. In January 1948, one of them assassinated Gandhi, shocking the world.

India's Firm Foundation

Despite its bloody start, India was built on a solid political foundation. Britain bequeathed the basis for parliamentary democracy, a trained civil service, a good communications system, and an educated elite committed to modernization. India became a republic with a constitution based on the British model, led by a prime minister chosen by the majority party in an elected parliament. However, given its extraordinary diversity, India had difficulty building national unity. To accommodate the many religious minorities, regions, and diverse cultures, India adopted a federal system, with elected state governments, and was officially secular with complete separation of religion and state. Kashmir (CASH-mere), a mountainous Himalayan state on the India–Pakistan border, became a constant source of tension between India and Pakistan, because it had a Muslim majority but a Hindu ruler who opted to join India.

The Vulnerability of Pakistan

The new Pakistan confronted numerous problems. Its two wings were separated by a thousand miles of India. The nation's founding leader, Jinnah,

> 66 Despite its bloody start, India was built on a solid political foundation. 99

CHRONOLOGY

South Asia, 1945–Present

1947	Independence for India and Pakistan
1948	Assassination of Mohandas Gandhi; Sri Lankan independence
1948–1964	Nehru era in India
1950	Indian republic
1959	Sri Lanka's Sirimavo Bandaranaike first woman prime minister
1962	India-China border war
1971	Formation of Bangladesh
1975–1977	State of emergency under Indira Gandhi
1984	Assassination of Indira Gandhi
1988–1990	First Benazir Bhutto government in Pakistan
1993–1996	Second Benazir Bhutto government
1999	Military government led by Pervez Musharraf

died soon after independence, and his successor was assassinated. Before independence, Muslims had been overrepresented in the British Indian military, and the army now played a stronger role in Pakistan's politics than in India's. The loss of top civilian leaders, lack of a balanced economic base, massive poverty, and geographic division made Pakistan vulnerable to political instability and military rule.

India's first prime minister, Nehru, a close associate of Gandhi and the son of a respected early Indian nationalist, dominated Indian politics for sixteen years (1948–1964). A gifted speaker and brilliant thinker, Nehru enjoyed widespread popular support. The majority of Indians lived in overcrowded, unhealthy urban slums or dusty villages that lacked electricity and running water, but Nehru promised to address the nation's overwhelming poverty. He believed firmly in democracy, emphasizing

Muslims Leaving India for Pakistan During Partition As India and Pakistan split into two new nations in 1947, millions of Muslims and Hindus fled their homes to escape violence. This photo shows displaced Muslims, carrying a few meager belongings, jamming a train headed from India to Pakistan.

consent rather than coercion. While India lagged behind communist-ruled China in economic development, it developed a system of personal freedom. Believing in peaceful coexistence with neighbors and renouncing military aggression, Nehru helped to found the Non-Aligned Movement of nations, such as Egypt and Indonesia, which were unwilling to commit to either the U.S. or Soviet camps in the Cold War.

Nehru's Pragmatic Leadership

Nehru's policies derived from his complex ideals. Although the British-educated lawyer admired Western politics, literature, and economic dynamism, he also respected India's cultural heritage and moral strength. Raised a Hindu, Nehru was nevertheless a secularist who believed that Congress should represent, and promote justice for, all Indians. Although himself a high-caste brahman, he distrusted the influence of the Hindu priests. Nehru shared Gandhi's opposition to the caste system and fought gender inequalities. In 1955, after years of struggle, Nehru convinced parliament to approve new laws on untouchability and women's rights that provided penalties for discrimination. The lowest-ranking social group, untouchables, acquired special quotas in government services and universities, while Hindu women gained equal legal rights with men, including the right to divorce, property rights, and equal inheritance. But some laws that challenged centuries of tradition were often ignored in rural areas.

Nehru's government built the framework for productive economic change. Nehru introduced a planning system to foster modern technology and mixed capitalism and socialism, private capital and a strong state sector. He left established industries in private hands but set up public ventures to build power plants, dams, and irrigation canals. In the 1960s, the Green Revolution (see Chapter 26) fostered a dramatic rise in food production. Nehru employed five-year plans to make India independent of foreign suppliers for power, steel, basic commodities, and food. By the 1970s, India was one of the world's ten most industrialized nations and nearly self-sufficient in food.

Nehru's Mixed Record

But some of Nehru's policies proved failures. Government control of the private sector through regulations gave bureaucrats great power, fostered corruption, and shackled private enterprise. Nehru failed to cultivate good relations with Pakistan or with China, and in 1962, Chinese troops humiliated Indian forces during a border dispute. Nehru also failed to address unchecked population growth, which rose from 389 million in 1941 to 434 million in 1961. The government built schools and universities but failed to substantially raise literacy rates. Yet, when Nehru died in 1964, millions mourned the end of an idealistic era that had earned India respect in the world. Furthermore, Congress had no leader of comparable stature to follow Nehru.

The Making of Pakistan and Bangladesh

Pakistan faced greater challenges than did India. Jinnah had pledged to make the nation happy and prosperous, but the leaders who followed him had only limited success, in part because of tensions between ethnic groups who shared an Islamic faith but often little else. From the beginning, tensions flared between the nationalistic Bengalis, who dominated the east, and the Punjabis and Sindhis, who dominated the west. The two regions differed in language, culture, and outlook. The factionalized Pakistani parliament proved unworkable, providing an excuse for military leaders to take over the government in 1958. By 1969, dissatisfaction with military dictatorship led to riots, prompting martial law.

At the end of the 1960s, ethnic tensions came to a boil, eventually fracturing Pakistan into two nations, Pakistan and Bangladesh (see Map 31.1). The Bengalis in East Pakistan had felt they did not get a fair share of the nation's resources and political power. After the Awami League, a Bengali nationalist party, won a majority of East Pakistan's seats in national elections, in early 1971, Pakistani troops arrested the party leader, Sheikh Mujiber Rahman (shake MOO-jee-bur RAH-mun) (1920–1975). Then, hoping to crush Awami League support, troops opened fire on university dormitories and Hindu homes, causing hundreds of casualties.

 Interactive Map

> 66 At the end of the 1960s, ethnic tensions came to a boil, eventually fracturing Pakistan into two nations, Pakistan and Bangladesh. 99

Inspired by Sheikh Mujiber, the Awami League then declared independence. In response, troops from West Pakistan poured into East Pakistan, terrorizing the Bengali population with massacres, arson, and the raping of thousands of women. At least half a million Bengalis died at Pakistani hands, and 10 million desperate, starving Bengali refugees fled to India. World opinion turned against Pakistan. India appealed for world support of East Pakistan, armed the Bengali guerrillas, and, after an ill-advised Pakistani attack on Indian airfields, declared war and sent troops into both West and East Pakistan, rapidly gaining the upper hand. Fearful of India, Pakistan had long cultivated an alliance with China and the United States, both of which supplied it with military aid. American President Richard Nixon ignored the massive killing of Bengalis, and China threatened to intervene on behalf of Pakistan, but Soviet backing of India discouraged such a move. By the end of 1971, Pakistani troops in Bengal had surrendered to Indian forces, and the Awami League, led by Sheikh Mujibur, established a new nation, Bangladesh, in what had been East Pakistan.

Awami League A Bengali nationalist party that began the move from independence from West Pakistan.

The Indira Gandhi Era

With the sudden death of Nehru's respected successor in 1966, the Congress selected Nehru's daughter, Indira Gandhi (1917–1984), to be the nation's first woman prime minister. She had worked closely with her father while her husband (no relation to Mohandas Gandhi) served in parliament. A shrewd campaigner, Mrs. Gandhi enjoyed a decade and a half in power. When her support waned in the 1967 elections, she responded aggressively with policies to win back the poor. Her status was elevated by India's smashing military victory over archenemy Pakistan. But Mrs. Gandhi's war triumph and mounting domestic problems also fostered her use of increasingly harsh policies. Powerful vested interests ignored her reforms, the economy faltered, and many Indians turned against the Congress.

The Indian Crisis of 1975

In 1975, Gandhi declared a state of emergency, suspending civil rights,

Map 31.1
Modern South Asia

India, predominantly Hindu, is the largest South Asian nation and separates the two densely populated Islamic nations of Bangladesh and Pakistan. Buddhists are the majority in Sri Lanka, just off India's southeast coast. The small kingdoms of Bhutan and Nepal are located in the Himalayan mountain range.

closing state governments, and jailing some ten thousand opposition leaders and dissidents. Her actions were condemned, but some of her policies improved the economy. Meanwhile, her youngest son, Sanjay Gandhi (1946–1980), launched two controversial programs designed to reduce birth rates and clear out urban slums; these proved unsuccessful and were deeply unpopular. In 1977, Indira lifted the emergency and announced general elections. After thirty years in power, the Congress Party, and with it Indira Gandhi, was voted out of office and replaced by an uneasy coalition of diverse parties that included Hindu nationalists. But the coalition government solved few problems, and in 1980 it collapsed.

Sikh Rebellion of Amritsar

Indira Gandhi and the Congress returned to power in the 1980 elections, restoring the Nehru dynasty. But they also faced deep cynicism, growing unemployment, and unrest. In 1980, Sanjay Gandhi died in a plane crash, and Indira Gandhi elevated her eldest son Rajiv (1944–1991), an apolitical airline pilot, as her heir apparent. Mrs. Gandhi's final crisis broke out in the Punjab, India's richest state. The growing political consciousness of the Sikhs, whose religion mixes Hindu and Muslim ideas, had led to a desire for statehood. In 1983, armed Sikh extremists, demanding an independent Sikh homeland, occupied the Golden Temple at Amritsar (uhm-RIT-suhr), the holiest shrine in the Sikh religion, and turned it into a fortress. In 1984, the Indian army stormed the Golden Temple against fierce resistance. When the fighting ended, the temple was reduced to rubble and over one thousand militants and soldiers lay dead.

The End of Nehru's Dynasty

Violence had returned to Indian political life. The destruction of their holiest temple shocked the Sikhs and led to the shooting death of Indira Gandhi by two of her Sikh bodyguards. The assassination in turn generated rioting and attacks on Sikhs. Hindu mobs roamed Delhi, burning Sikh shops and killing Sikhs, often by pouring gasoline over them and setting them ablaze. The dead numbered in the thousands. Rajiv Gandhi, succeeding his mother at only forty years old, proved ineffective. In 1991, while campaigning in the southern city of Madras, he was blown up by a young Sri Lankan woman handing him flowers. Yet despite this tumult, India remained a functioning democracy and a thriving nation.

LO² South Asian Politics and Societies

South Asian societies changed beginning in the 1970s, each forging its own political role in the region. With a little more than 1 billion people by 2005 and 65 percent of the land in the subcontinent, the Republic of India rose to regional dominance. Indian governments began to liberalize the economy, stimulating growth. At the same time, growing Hindu nationalism has challenged the domination of India's Congress Party, threatening its secular vision. Meanwhile, India's neighbors in South Asia have struggled to achieve stability and economic development. Both Pakistan and Sri Lanka have experienced persistent ethnic violence, while India and Pakistan remain on bitter terms. Whatever the political tensions that divide them, however, they also share some life patterns, as ancient customs exist side by side with modern machines and ways of living.

> "India rejected the revolutionary path of China, instead promoting civil liberties and constitutional democracy."

Indian Politics

When India celebrated its fiftieth jubilee of independence in 1997, the nation's president reminded his people that India's challenge was to achieve economic growth with social justice. That goal remains elusive, but Indians can boast that, in politics, their country has maintained one of the few working multiparty democracies outside of the industrialized nation-states, one that fosters lively political debate and forces candidates to appeal to voters.

Democracy's Role in India

India rejected the revolutionary path of China, instead promoting civil liberties and constitutional democracy. To some observers, democracy provides a flexible system for accommodating the differing interests of the diverse population. Others, however, argue that democracy has intensified differences between groups. Certainly, tensions between Hindus and Muslims and between high-caste and low-caste Hindus, manipulated by opportunistic politicians, have complicated political life. There are also differences over how real the effects of democracy are in the presence of powerful economic and political elites. Some say that democracy has become only a safety valve for popular frustration, creating the illusion of mass participation that prevents a frontal attack on caste and class inequalities.

The Congress Party has remained nationally influential for more than five decades but has had to contend with rivals. On the left, several communist parties dominate politics in West Bengal in the northeast and Kerala in the southwest, repeatedly winning elections by promoting modernization and support for the poor within a democratic framework. On the right, several Hindu nationalist parties opposed the secular Congress, but with limited success until the 1990s. In the southern Indian states, various parties representing regional interests gradually gained strength, generally dominating state governments and becoming part of federal coalitions. These regional parties, often led by stars of the local film industries, have worked to protect local languages while preserving English as a national language. All of India's parties have suffered from corruption.

Since 1989, Indian politics has become more pluralistic. The Congress lost several elections to coalitions that included Hindu nationalists. The major Hindu nationalist party, the **Bharatha Janata** (BJP), gained influence in north India with a platform of state support for Hindu issues. The BJP slogan, "One Nation, One People, One Culture," confronts the Gandhi–Nehru vision of a tolerant multicultural state. By the late 1990s, India suffered from rising political corruption, violent secessionist movements in border regions, caste conflict, religious hostilities, and political fragmentation. In 2002, major Hindu–Muslim violence broke out again, leaving more than one thousand people dead and more than 100,000 terrified Muslims, burned out of their cities, huddled in tent camps.

In 2004, the Congress, led by Rajiv Gandhi's Italian-born, sari-wearing widow, Sonia Gandhi (b. 1946), a Roman Catholic who met Rajiv when both were students in England, capitalized on disenchantment among the poor and Muslims and unexpectedly defeated the ruling BJP-led coalition. She formed a new government committed to secularism and economic growth. A Pakistan-born Sikh economist, Manmohan Singh, became the first non-Hindu prime minister. A free press monitors Indian politics: in 2005, a television station's investigation of corruption forced several members of parliament to resign.

The Indian Economy in Transition

India has struggled to resolve problems inherited from colonial times:

> 66 India has struggled to resolve problems inherited from colonial times: economic backwardness, skyrocketing population growth, and crushing poverty. 99

economic backwardness, skyrocketing population growth, and crushing poverty. While Nehru's dream of eradicating these problems has not yet been realized, Indians can boast of many gains, especially its great success in strengthening its agricultural and manufacturing production. After 1991, Indian leaders dismantled the socialist sector of the economy built by Nehru while sparking economic revival. Reform, deregulation, and liberalization contributed to an economic growth rate of 6 to 7 percent per year by the late 1990s. Several cities, especially Bangalore and Bombay (Mumbai), became high-tech centers closely linked to global communications. Hundreds of international corporations, taking advantage of a growing, educated Indian middle class, have moved information and technical service jobs, such as call-in customer service and computer programming, from North America and Europe to India. India's boom has even prompted thousands of highly educated Indians living in North America and Europe to return to India and join its high-tech sector. Significant progress also has been made in agriculture. Since 1947, India has doubled food production, thanks largely to the Green Revolution of improved seeds and fertilizers. The nation now grows enough wheat and rice to feed the entire population, but persisting inequalities have prevented equitable distribution.

Population and Poverty: Ongoing Problems

Despite the economic revival, India's economy has not succeeded in delivering a better life to most Indians. More than half still live below the poverty line, and 40 percent lack an adequate diet. While China nears universal literacy, only half of Indians can read and write. Meanwhile, population growth eats away at the national resources: every year, 30 million Indians are born. By 2050, India will have 1.5 billion people, more than China. Ironically, success in doubling life expectancy contributes to overpopulation, which causes overcrowded cities, a lack of adequate sanitation, and insufficient health care. Millions of Indians sleep on city sidewalks for lack of money and housing. While affluent Indians increasingly buy fancy imported cars, many commuters ride on the roofs of jammed buses and trains.

Global Communications India's call centers provide low-paid English-speaking workers and high-speed telecommunications for customer service help lines around the world. Here, Indian employees are working at a call center in the southern Indian city of Bangalore.

The stark contrasts between the modern and traditional sectors of the economy have produced uneven development and raised questions as to who benefits from the changes. Successive Indian governments have been unable to challenge vested interests such as the powerful landlords. Meanwhile, poor peasants, unable to make a living from their small farms, fall further behind. Poverty fosters growing urban crime and rural banditry, especially in several densely populated northern states. The population below the official poverty line lacks purchasing power to sustain local industry. Economic growth and poverty ravage the environment as cities encroach on farmland and people cut down trees for firewood. The Chipko forest conservation movement, based on traditional and Gandhian principles and led mostly by women, is one of many groups working to protect the environment.

Indian Cities, Gender Patterns, and Cultures

In his will, India's first prime minister, Jawaharlal Nehru, asked that his ashes be scattered in the Ganges River, not because of the river's traditional religious significance to Hindus but because it symbolized to him India's millennia-old culture, ever-changing and yet ever the same. Such a pattern has indeed characterized India's society and culture. Ancient traditions such as caste, gender stereotypes, and family practices have persisted but in modified forms, and Indians make religion both central to their lives and a source of conflict. Indians have also used literature, film, and other cultural forms to examine their society and place in the world.

The Abiding Power of Tradition

The contrast between the villages, where 80 percent of Indians live, and the cities remains stark. The growing urban middle class enjoy recreations and technologies, from golf to video games, that are available to the affluent around the world. Whether they live in the Punjab, Calcutta, or Bangalore, educated urban young people are becoming more cosmopolitan, often listening to the same music and buying the same consumer goods, a homogenization that

> "The contrast between the villages, where 80 percent of Indians live, and the cities remains stark."

conservatives see as a threat to local cultures. Practices that ensure strict divisions between castes, such as avoiding physical contact or sharing food, are harder to maintain in cities than in villages, where caste remains more firmly rooted. At the bottom of the caste system, the untouchables, some 20 percent of India's population, still live difficult lives, even though government assistance and reforms have enabled some low-caste people to enter high-status occupations and positions. The grooves of tradition run deep, particularly in the rural areas, and changes can bring demoralization and disorientation as well as satisfaction.

 Internet Indian History Sourcebook (*http://www.fordham.edu/halsall/india/indiasbook.html*). An invaluable collection of sources and links on India from ancient to modern times.

However, in some regions, especially in cities, families have changed. Modern life has hastened the breakup of traditional extended families; some Indians now live in smaller, nuclear families. New forms of employment, which can cause family members to move to other districts or countries, have undermined family cohesion. A traditional preference for male babies, however, has continued, and today the ability of technology to determine the sex of a fetus has led many Indians who want male children to terminate pregnancies.

Women in Indian Society

Nehru had believed that India could progress only if women played a full part in the nation. Accordingly, new laws banned once-widespread customs such as polygamy, child marriage, and sati. Female literacy has risen, from 1 percent in 1901 to 27 percent in 2000, though it is still only half the male rate. But some changing customs have penalized women. For example, the practice of requiring new brides to provide generous dowries to their in-laws, once restricted to higher castes, has become common in all castes. As a result, especially in rural areas, reports have increased of families banishing, injuring, or killing young brides whose own families failed to supply the promised dowries. Notions of women's rights, common in cities, are less known in villages.

Yet many Indian women have benefited from education, becoming leaders in such fields as journalism, business, trade unions, the arts, and government. An antipatriarchy women's movement, growing for a century, has become more active since the 1970s, suggesting that women's issues will remain on the nation's agenda. Outside the big cities, however, women have remained largely bound by tradition, expected to demonstrate submission, obedience, and absolute dedication to their husbands. By 2004, AIDS grew rapidly as a health problem, a result largely of women being forced into prostitution to serve the sexual needs of increasingly mobile male workers such as long-haul truckers.

Religion, Politics, and Violence

Religion, like society, has changed, becoming intertwined with politics. Although Hindus form a large majority, India's population also includes 120 million Muslims, more than 20 million Sikhs, and nearly 20 million Christians. Religious differences have become politicized. Some upper-caste Hindus, for instance, particularly in the BJP, have used the notion of a Hindu nation to marginalize Muslims and low-caste Hindus. Civil unrest involving violent attacks on Muslims by militant Hindu nationalists has caused political crises. Yet, despite the tensions, Muslims occupy high positions in India's government, business, and the professions and play a key role in cultural expression. India's most famous modern artist, Tyeb Mehta (b. 1925), is a Shi'ite Muslim whose works, much of which address the Hindu–Muslim divide, sell all over the world.

Bollywood

Indians have also eagerly embraced modern cultural forms to express ideas. While Indian-born novelists such as Arundhati Roy (AH-roon-DAH-tee roy) and Salman Rushdie have achieved worldwide fame, a more popular cultural form in contemporary India has been film. India has built the world's largest film industry; it makes about one thousand movies per year, and finds audiences among both Indian emigrants and non-Indians around the world. The Mumbai film industry, known as Bollywood, has become India's largest, churning out films in Hindi. Many films, especially musicals, portray a fantasy world that enables

 Read about Raj Kapoor, Bollywood film star, and the first real superstar of Indian film.

viewers to forget their troubles. Religious divisions are muted in Bollywood, and the leading directors, writers, and stars often come from Muslim backgrounds. Voters in southern India have even favored stars of the local film industry as state leaders.

Islamic Politics and Societies

South Asia's two densely populated Muslim countries, Pakistan and Bangladesh, have struggled to develop economically and to maintain political stability. Both countries are divided between secular and devout Muslims, have alternated between military dictatorships and elected civilian governments, and have generally conservative cultures.

Containing 150 million people, more than 95 percent of them Sunni Muslims, Pakistan has had difficulty transforming its diverse ethnic and tribal groups into a politically stable, unified nation. The most long-lasting civilian leader, Zulkifar Ali Bhutto (zool-KEE-far AH-lee BOO-toe) (r. 1971–1977), a lawyer educated overseas, came to power with great ambitions. Although he came from a wealthy landowning family, he pursued socialist policies that were unpopular with the wealthy. Accusing him of corruption, the army took power and later executed Bhutto. The Soviet occupation of Afghanistan in 1979 and the Pakistan-supported Islamic resistance to the Soviets that followed (see Chapter 30) distracted Pakistanis from their unpopular military regime and brought more U.S. military aid to Pakistan.

Benazir Bhutto Pakistani politics has remained turbulent. In 1986, Bhutto's daughter, Benazir Bhutto (BEN-ah-ZEER BOO-toe) (1953–2007), a graduate of Britain's Oxford University, put together a movement to challenge the military regime. As unrest increased in 1988, Bhutto became prime minister. She was respected abroad but struggled to govern effectively. Accused of abuse of power, she was dismissed in 1990, returning to power after the 1993 elections. But critical problems persisted, including growing fighting between ethnic factions and attacks by militant Sunnis on the small Shi'a Muslim and Christian minorities. In 1996, she was once again removed. Bhutto was assassinated in 2007 in the midst of one last comeback campaign.

In 1999, the military took over, installing as president Indian-born General Pervez Musharraf (per-VEZ moo-SHAR-uff) (b. 1943), whose family had fled to Pakistan during the partition in 1947. He faced the same challenge as his predecessors: to halt factional violence, punish corruption, collect taxes from the wealthy, restore economic growth, and balance the demands of militant and secular Muslims. Although Musharraf allied with the United States after the 2001 Al Qaeda attacks and the resulting U.S. invasion of Afghanistan, many Pakistanis resent the West, in part because the United States, while seeking Pakistani help in the war on international terrorism, is reluctant to remove high tariff barriers against Pakistani textiles, a major export that accounts for nearly half of all manufacturing jobs. Experts argue that an expansion of this work might relieve the high unemployment rate and hence reduce the appeal of extremist Islam for desperate young men.

Repression of Pakistani Women Pakistani society and culture have remained conservative. Pakistan's founding leader, Jinnah, a cosmopolitan British-educated lawyer, had favored more rights for women, but national leaders who shared this view were reluctant to challenge the strong opposition to women's rights, especially in rural areas. In 1979, an Islamizing military government pushed through discriminatory laws that made women who were raped guilty of adultery, a serious offense. Women enjoyed far fewer legal rights than men and were more commonly jailed or punished than men for adultery. Women's groups who courageously protested in the streets faced military attacks. By the 1990s, things had changed little: only 10 percent of adult women were employed outside the home, and fewer than 20 percent were literate. The United Nations ranked Pakistan near the bottom of nations in women's equality.

Bangladesh: Political and Social Struggles Even more so than Pakistan, Bangladesh, overcrowded with 125 million people, has encountered barriers to development. Mostly flat plains, the land is prone to devastating hurricanes, floods, tornados, and famine. The nation's founder, Sheik Mujiber Rahman, had hoped that the nation he envisioned—secular, democratic, and socialist—would rapidly progress, but, after tightening his power, he was assassinated by the military. None of the governments after him, whether military or civilian, has had much success in resolving problems, and all have suffered from corruption. Several leaders have been assassinated.

After 1991, democracy became the main pattern, and the two largest parties have been led by women. The conservative Islamic and pro-capitalist Khaleda Zia (ZEE-uh) (b. 1945), the widow of an assassinated leader, heads one party, while the left-leaning Sheikh Hasina Wajed (shake ha-SEE-nah WAH-jed) (b. 1947), the daughter of the assassinated Sheik Mujibur Rahman, the nation's first prime minister, leads the Awami League. Sheikh Hasina escaped an assassination attempt in 2004. The two women, bitter rivals, have alternated as the nation's prime minister.

Despite political turbulence, however, Bangladesh has had more success than Pakistan. The nation has been a pioneer among developing nations in programs to eliminate poverty and now provides some formal education to 60 percent of its children. The Grameen Bank, which loans small amounts of money, particularly to poor women for starting a village business, has helped millions of people, earning world attention (see Chapter 26). A visionary activist, Fazle Hasan Abed, launched a movement to improve rural life through forming cooperatives. But the nation's per capita income remains $120 per year (35 cents per day), and only 35 percent of adults are literate. Nearly half the population live below the official poverty line. Conflict and instability continue to plague the country.

As in Pakistan, social and cultural issues have divided Bangladesh. Unlike Pakistan, Bangladesh is officially a secular state and has a large Hindu minority (16 percent). Although over the centuries the Bengalis incorporated Hindu and Buddhist influences as well as Sufi mysticism into their version of Islam, making them tolerant of opposing views, militant Muslim political movements seeking an Islamic state gained strength in the 1990s, heightening divisions among Muslims. The militants, allied with Khaleda Zia's party, succeeded in restricting women's rights. Islamic militants also pressured the government to prosecute feminist writers such as the medical doctor turned novelist Taslima Nasreen (b. 1962), who wrote critically of religion, conservative culture, and irrational, blind faith. Muslim militants condemned Nasreen's writing as blasphemy against Islam, a capital offense. Nasreen fled into exile in Europe to escape death threats.

Sri Lanka and Its Conflicts

Sri Lanka, an island nation of 20 million people, shares problems of ethnic conflict and poverty with its South Asian neighbors but, like India, has generally maintained a democracy. In 1948, the leaders of the majority ethnic group, the Sinhalese—some 75 percent of the population and mostly Theravada Buddhists—negotiated independence from Britain and inherited a colonial economy based on rubber and tea plantations. Laws passed by the Sinhalese-dominated government that discriminated against

the language and culture of the major ethnic minority, the Tamils, mostly Hindus, generated fighting between the two groups. A Tamil community had existed in northern Sri Lanka for generations, but many Sri Lankan Tamils descended from immigrants who were recruited from India in the nineteenth century to work on British coffee, tea, and rubber plantations.

In 1959, Sirimavo Bandaranaike (sree-MAH-vo BAN-dar-an-EYE-kee) (1916–2004), the Sinhalese widow of an assassinated leader, led her party to victory and became the world's first woman prime minister. Her enemies derided her as a "kitchen woman," yet she proved to be a strong leader and dominated her nation's politics in the 1960s and 1970s. Although she implemented socialist policies that improved economic and social conditions, Bandaranaike faced resistance from a communist-led rebellion among the poor. Sinhalese-dominated Sri Lankan governments sponsored textile and electronics manufacturing to reduce dependence on cash crop exports. While socialist policies discouraged free enterprise, they fostered the highest literacy rates (85 percent) and, by providing rice and free medical care to the poor, the longest life span (sixty-nine years) in South Asia. These policies benefited all of the nation's ethnic groups.

In 1983, a section of the Tamil minority seeking independence for their region began a rebellion that has kept the island in a constant state of tension. The assassination of top political leaders and communal fighting became common. In 1994, Chandrika Kumaratunga (CHAN-dree-ka koo-MAHR-a-TOON-ga) (b. 1945), the University of Paris–educated daughter of Sirimavo Bandaranaike, led her party to victory and became Sri Lanka's second woman leader. She sought both military victory over the Tamils and political peace but achieved neither, narrowly escaping an assassination attempt in 2000. Nearly 60,000 people, many innocent civilians, have died in twenty years of violence between Tamils and Sinhalese. The violence split the Buddhist clergy between those advocating peace and tolerance and those demanding defeat of the Hindu Tamils, whom they view as a threat to Buddhism. Although national reconciliation has proven elusive, the Sinhalese and moderate Tamils continue to practice democratic politics.

South Asia in the Global System

Since 1945, South Asian nations have grown in geopolitical and economic stature. Although Nehru strode the world stage as a major leader of the nonaligned nations, seeking a middle ground between the United States and the USSR, his successors lacked his international influence. However, in the past decade, India has become a center of advanced technology and one of the most industrialized nations outside of Europe and North America. Every year, Indian universities turn out thousands of talented engineers and computer scientists who have built up homegrown industries and have also helped staff the high-tech silicon valleys of North America and Europe. By the early twenty-first century, experts debated whether India or China might eventually compete for world economic leadership with the United States, whose multidimensional power Indian leaders admired. Some pointed to India's large number of English-speakers, solid financial system, and vibrant democracy as advantages. However, critics argued that to become a world power, India needed to contain social tensions and reduce poverty in the cities and villages.

South Asian technology and ingenuity have led to scientific achievements. In 1975, the Indian government launched into orbit its first satellite, named after Aryabhata (OUR-ya-BAH-ta), a major Indian scientist and mathematician who lived more than fifteen hundred years ago. In 1998, India openly tested its first nuclear bomb, triggering India–Pakistan rivalries and inspiring Pakistan to develop nuclear weapons. Since the late 1990s, the weapons experts of many nations and international organizations have worried about Pakistan's nuclear abilities, since Islamic militants, some with possible links to global terrorist networks, play a key role in local and national politics. In 2004, a top Pakistani nuclear scientist admitted to selling nuclear secrets to other nations.

Global and regional politics have intensified Indian-Pakistani rivalries. After U.S. president George W. Bush, in the wake of the 2001 terrorist attacks on the United States, justified preemptive military attacks against potential threats, some Indians, adapting that justification to their own ends, wondered why India should not preemptively attack Pakistan. But India–Pakistan relations have remained combustible: a coordinated terrorist attack on various sites in Mumbai, India in late 2008 killed or wounded hundreds of Indians. Still, after 2000 Indian and Pakistani leaders have promoted a thaw in relations, visiting each others' countries, co-sponsoring sports competitions, and giving hope that tensions might diminish.

South Asians have also made a distinctive contribution to world politics. Although maintaining traditional social patterns and cultural viewpoints, the four major South Asian nations, all democracies some or most of the time, have been led by women at various times. Hence, while women remain disadvantaged, they have enjoyed more high-level political power than in other nations. The political power of a few women is just part of the great complexity of this region.

LO³ Revolution, War, and Reconstruction in Indochina

From the 1940s through the 1970s, the peoples of the Southeast Asia region that the French called Indochina—Vietnam, Cambodia, and Laos— experienced the most wrenching violence as two powerful Western nations, France and the United States, attempted to roll back revolutionary nationalism. The end of World War II and the rise of the Cold War set the stage for two successive struggles with global implications. During the first struggle, known

CHRONOLOGY

Indochina, 1945–Present

1945	Formation of Viet Minh government in Vietnam
1946–1954	First Indochina War
1953	Independence of Laos, Cambodia
1961–1975	U.S.-Vietnamese War
1963	Assassination of South Vietnam president Ngo Dinh Diem
1964	Gulf of Tonkin incident
1968	Tet Offensive
1970	Overthrow of Prince Sihanouk in Cambodia
1975	Communist victories in Vietnam, Cambodia, Laos
1978	Vietnamese invasion of Cambodia

as the First Indochina War (1946–1954), the French attempted to maintain their colonial control of Vietnam against communist-led opposition, a conflict that eventually ended in French defeat. The second and more destructive war, in which the United States and its Vietnamese allies waged an ultimately unsuccessful fight against communist-led Vietnamese forces, also dragged in the peoples of neighboring Cambodia and Laos. When the turmoil ended, all of the societies involved had to rebuild.

> "Worried about the spread of communism, the United States shifted from supporting the Viet Minh during World War II to opposing all left-wing nationalists, including Ho and the Viet Minh."

The First Indochina War and Partition

For Vietnam, the first decade after World War II included an anticolonial revolution. In 1945, the Japanese army in southern Vietnam had surrendered to British forces, who moved into the major southern city, Saigon, and then prepared the ground for a French return to power. Meanwhile, the Viet Minh, a communist-led anti-Japanese guerrilla force that, armed and trained partly by the United States during the war, had occupied much of northern and central Vietnam during the Japanese occupation, captured the colonial capital in the north, Hanoi, and in 1945, declared the end of French colonialism. Although it only controlled the northern part of the country, the Viet Minh–led government, headed by Ho Chi Minh, became the first non-French regime in Vietnam in more than eighty years. In his address to a half-million jubilant Vietnamese who gathered in Hanoi's main square, Ho quoted the U.S. Declaration of Independence and added: "It means: All the peoples on earth are equal from birth, all the peoples have a right to live and to be happy and free."[4] In northern Vietnam, the Mandate of Heaven, an ancient concept that gave legitimacy to Vietnamese emperors, had now passed to the Viet Minh. Both French and American observers on the scene noted that the majority of Vietnamese supported the Viet Minh.

Resistance to Vietnamese Independence

However, Vietnamese independence faced formidable roadblocks. The French, desperate to retain their empire in Southeast Asia especially because of its rubber, rice, and tungsten, quickly reoccupied southern Vietnam. Meanwhile, the Republic of China sent its troops to disarm the remaining Japanese soldiers in northern Vietnam. This provocative move made the Vietnamese fear a permanent presence by their traditional enemy, China. The United States, an ally of both France and republican China, was alarmed at Ho Chi Minh's association with the USSR and communism. Worried about the spread of communism, the United States shifted from supporting the Viet Minh during World War II to opposing all left-wing nationalists, including Ho and the Viet Minh.

Vietnam remained tense. The French, refusing to accept Ho's government, had allies among Vietnamese Catholics and pro-Western nationalists. Ho negotiated with the French for recognition of Vietnamese independence in the north. The French did arrange for Chinese troops to withdraw but refused to give up their claims to northern Vietnam. Ho also appealed to the U.S. president, Harry Truman, for U.S. political and economic support for Vietnam's independence but received no answer. In 1946, Ho warned a French diplomat that a war would be unwinnable: "You will kill ten of my men while we will kill one of yours, but you will be the ones who will end up exhausted."[5] When the French ended peaceful negotiations, brutal warfare ensued.

The First Indochina War

During the First Indochina War from 1946 to 1954, the French attempted, with massive U.S. aid, to maintain their colonial grip. Sending in a large military force, the French pushed the Viet Minh out of the northern cities, but brutal French tactics alienated the civilian population. In rural areas, the Viet Minh won peasant support and new recruits by transferring land to poor villagers. As his forces became bogged down in what observers called a "quicksand war," a French general complained that fighting the Viet Minh was "like ridding a dog of its fleas. We can pick them, drown them, and poison them, but they will be back in a few days."[6] After a major military defeat in 1954, when Viet Minh forces overwhelmed a key French base, the French abandoned their efforts and went home.

The peace agreements negotiated at a conference in Geneva, Switzerland, in 1954 divided the country into two Vietnams, displeasing the Vietnamese people. The agreements left the Viet Minh in control of North Vietnam and called for elections in 1956 to determine whether the South Vietnamese wanted to join with the North in a unified country. Ignoring the Geneva agreements, which it had not signed, the United States quickly filled the political vacuum left by the French departure and helped install Ngo Dinh Diem (no dinh dee-EM) (1901–1963), an anticommunist who had been a long-time resident in the United States, as president of South Vietnam. With U.S. support, Diem refused to hold reunification elections. His government and Ho's North Vietnam differed dramatically. Ho's government built a disciplined state that addressed the inequalities of the colonial period. Land reform redistributed land from powerful landlords to poor peasants. However, the government's authoritarian style and socialist policies prompted nearly a million anticommunist North Vietnamese, mostly middle class or members of the Catholic minority, to move to South Vietnam, where President Diem, an ardent Catholic from a wealthy mandarin family, established a government based in Saigon. The United States poured economic and military aid into South Vietnam, but Diem's regime became increasingly unpopular, especially since he opposed land reform.

The Viet Cong

Soon the political dynamics intensified. By the late 1950s, dissidents in South Vietnam, including former Viet Minh soldiers, had formed a communist-led revolutionary movement, the National Liberation Front (NLF), often known as the Viet Cong. Armed by North Vietnam, the insurgency in South Vietnam grew, and the Diem government responded with repression, murdering or imprisoning thousands of suspected rebels. Adding to the anti-Diem mood, Buddhists resented the government's pro-Catholic policies, and nationalists generally viewed Diem as an American puppet. Meanwhile, the NLF spread their influence in rural areas, often assassinating government officials. By the early 1960s, the NLF, now aided by North Vietnamese troops, controlled large sections of South Vietnam, and thousands more American

troops, still called military advisers, became more involved in combat. In 1963, U.S. leaders, judging Diem ineffective, sanctioned his overthrow by his own military officers, who killed him. As the situation deteriorated, U.S. concerns about a possible Communist sweep through Southeast Asia provided the rationale for U.S. action. The stage was set for another war.

> 66 Despite their technological superiority, U.S. forces struggled to work with South Vietnamese leaders and find effective strategies to overcome the communists. 99

The American-Vietnamese War

By the mid-1960s, the United States had escalated the conflict into a full-scale military commitment (see Map 31.2). U.S. president Lyndon Johnson's (g. 1963–1969) excuse was an alleged North Vietnamese attack on a U.S. ship in the Gulf of Tonkin in 1964, which probably never occurred. Johnson and other U.S. leaders wanted to spread democracy and capitalism, but they had little understanding of the nationalism and defiance that had shaped Vietnam, a country with many historical reasons for mistrusting foreign powers.

 Interactive Map

Soon the war intensified, drawing in a larger U.S. presence and more North Vietnamese forces and expanding the violence across the country. In 1965, Johnson ordered an air war against targets in both South and North Vietnam and a massive intervention of ground troops, peaking at 550,000 Americans by 1968. Meanwhile, Diem was succeeded by a series of military regimes that never achieved credibility with the majority of South Vietnamese. Military supplies and thousands of North Vietnamese troops regularly moved south through the mountains of eastern Laos and Cambodia, along what came to be known as the Ho Chi Minh Trail.

America at a Disadvantage

Despite their technological superiority, U.S. forces struggled to work with South Vietnamese leaders and find effective strategies to overcome the communists. Because the South Vietnamese army, largely conscripts, suffered from high desertion and casualty

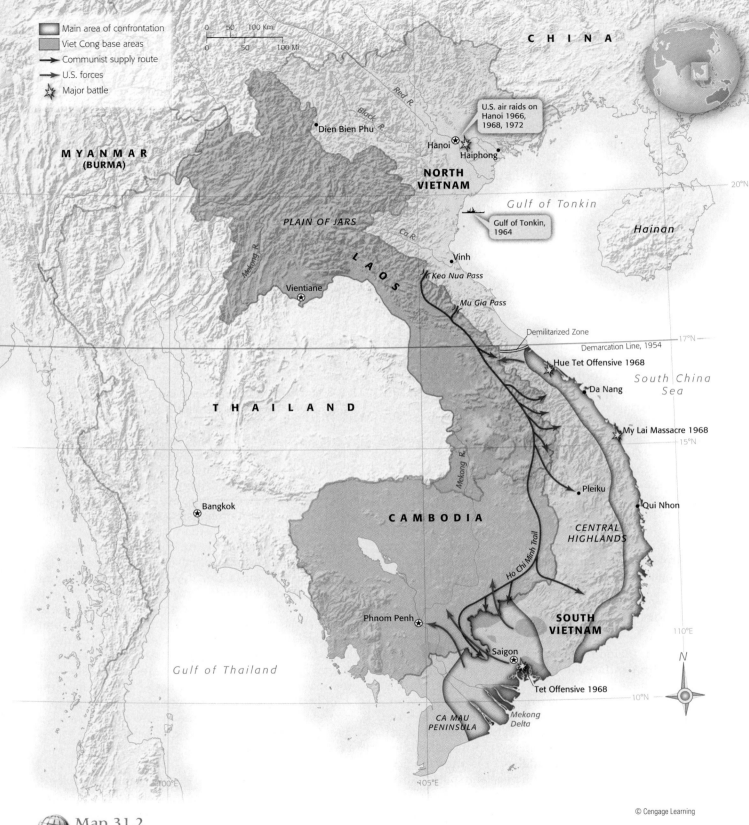

Main area of confrontation
Viet Cong base areas
Communist supply route
U.S. forces
Major battle

0   50   100 Km.
0   50   100 Mi.

CHINA

MYANMAR
(BURMA)

Red R.

Black R.

Dien Bien Phu

Hanoi
Haiphong

U.S. air raids on
Hanoi 1966,
1968, 1972

NORTH
VIETNAM

20°N

PLAIN OF JARS

Mekong R.

Ca R.

Gulf of Tonkin

Gulf of Tonkin,
1964

Hainan

Vientiane

LAOS

Vinh

Keo Nua Pass

Mu Gia Pass

Demilitarized Zone

Demarcation Line, 1954

17°N

THAILAND

Hue Tet Offensive 1968

South China
Sea

Da Nang

My Lai Massacre 1968

15°N

Mekong R.

Bangkok

CAMBODIA

Pleiku

Qui Nhon

CENTRAL
HIGHLANDS

Ho Chi Minh Trail

Phnom Penh

SOUTH
VIETNAM

110°E

Saigon

Gulf of Thailand

Tet Offensive 1968

10°N

CA MAU
PENINSULA

Mekong
Delta

100°E

105°E

N

© Cengage Learning

Map 31.2
The U.S.–Vietnamese War

From the early 1960s until 1975, South Vietnam, aided by thousands of U.S. troops and air power, resisted a communist-led insurgency aided by North Vietnam, which sent troops and supplies down the Ho Chi Minh Trail through Laos and Cambodia.

rates, Americans did much of the fighting. U.S. strategists viewed Vietnam chiefly in military terms: they measured success by counting the enemy dead and creating free fire zones, areas where civilians were ordered to evacuate so that U.S. forces could attack any people remaining as the enemy. Such policies made it difficult for the United States to win the "hearts and minds" of the South Vietnamese. Vietnam became the most heavily bombed nation in history, as the United States dropped nearly triple the total bomb tonnage used in World War II. The resulting destruction, combined with the use by U.S. forces of chemical defoliants to clear forests and wetlands, caused massive environmental damage. Thanks to the toxic chemicals sprayed on the land and water, Vietnam today has the world's highest rate of birth defects and one of the highest rates of cancer.

South Vietnamese had to choose sides. For procommunist Vietnamese, the American-Vietnamese War was a continuation of the First Indochina War to expel the French and rebuild a damaged society. For poor peasants, inequitable land ownership was the key issue of the war, and the communists gained peasant support by advocating land reform. Other South Vietnamese supported the pro-U.S. government or rejected both sides, repulsed by war's destruction and violence.

The Tet Offensive

By 1967, the U.S. military strategy had brought about a military stalemate, but a turning point came in 1968 with the Tet Offensive, in which communist forces attacked the major South Vietnamese cities during the Vietnamese new year. Although the communists suffered high casualties, Tet proved a major setback for the United States and caused Americans to reappraise the conflict. By the late 1960s, a majority of Americans had turned against the commitment to a seemingly endless, costly war with uncertain goals. Even the death of Ho Chi Minh in 1969 did not alter the situation. The United States began a gradual withdrawal of troops and negotiated peace agreements with North Vietnam. In 1973, U.S. ground forces left Vietnam but maintained air support. By 1975, the NLF and North Vietnam had defeated the South Vietnamese forces and reunified the country under communist leadership. As communist forces marched into Saigon, more than 70,000 South Vietnamese who had worked with the United States fled the country, most of them finding asylum in the United States. The devastating war cost the United States 58,000 dead and 519,000 physically disabled. Around 4 million Vietnamese were

killed or wounded—10 percent of the total population. By 1975, the fighting had ended, and Vietnam turned to reconstruction.

War and Reconstruction in Indochina

Laos and Cambodia became pawns in the American-Vietnamese War, eventually engulfed in its violence. Anticolonial sentiment had grown in both societies during and after the Japanese occupation of World War II. In 1953, the French granted Laos independence under a conservative, pro-French government dominated by the ethnic Lao majority. At the same time, Cambodia gained its independence from France under the popular Prince Norodom Sihanouk (SEE-uh-nook) (b. 1922), who won the first free election in 1955. The United States began an intervention in Laos in the late 1950s, intensifying an internal conflict between U.S.-backed anti-communist right-wingers, people favoring neutrality between the superpowers, and the Pathet Lao, revolutionary Laotian nationalists allied with North Vietnam. In 1960, right-wing forces advised and equipped by the U.S. Central Intelligence Agency (CIA) seized the Laotian government, controlling the south and the Mekong Valley, while the Pathet Lao gained control in the northern mountains.

The Cost of War in Laos

The fighting engulfed the entire nation. The pro-U.S. Laotian regime, bloated with corruption, had an ineffective U.S.-financed army. To overcome this disadvantage, Americans turned to the hill peoples for recruits, including the Hmong, who sought autonomy from the Laotian government. Promising them permanent U.S. support and protection, in 1960, the CIA recruited a secret army of some 45,000 soldiers that attacked North Vietnamese forces along the Ho Chi Minh Trail and fought the Pathet Lao. Ten percent of the Hmong population, some 30,000 people, died during a conflict that was largely unknown to the American public, while thousands of others fled into refugee camps. The war killed some 100,000 Laotians. In 1975, the Pathet Lao took full control of a war-weary Laos. Thousands of anti-communist Laotians fled into Thailand, many later moving to the United States and other Western nations.

> "Like Laos, Cambodia also became part of the Indochina conflict."

Prince Sihanouk and the Khmer Rouge

Like Laos, Cambodia also became part of the Indochina conflict. Its first president, the multitalented Prince Sihanouk, ruled as a benevolent autocrat, diplomatically maintaining Cambodian independence and peace. But during the 1960s, both the Vietnamese communists and the United States violated Cambodian neutrality, and the Khmer Rouge (kmahr roozh) ("Red Khmers"), a communist insurgent group seeking to overthrow the government and led by alienated intellectuals, built a small support base of impoverished peasants. In addition, military officers and big businessmen began to resent Sihanouk's dictatorial rule and desired to share in the U.S. money and arms flowing into neighboring states.

In 1970, Sihanouk was overthrown by U.S.-backed generals and civilians, beginning a tragic era in Cambodian history. With Sihanouk in exile, U.S. and South Vietnamese forces soon invaded eastern Cambodia in search of Vietnamese communist bases, and the resulting instability created an opening for the Khmer Rouge to recruit mass support. The pro-U.S. government lacked legitimacy and became increasingly dependent on U.S. aid for virtually all supplies, and the ineffective Cambodian army suffered from corruption and low morale. Meanwhile, U.S. planes launched an intensive, terrifying air assault through the heart of Cambodia's agricultural area, where most of the population lived. The bombing killed thousands of innocent civilians, and rice production declined by almost half. Amid the destruction, the Khmer Rouge rapidly enlarged its forces, recruiting from among the shell-shocked peasantry. From 1970 through 1975, between 750,000 and 1 million Cambodians, mostly civilians, perished from the conflict between the Khmer Rouge and the U.S.-backed government. In 1975, the Khmer Rouge seized the capital, Phnom Penh.

Reform and Healing in Vietnam and Laos

After years of war and destruction, Vietnam, Laos, and Cambodia began the challenging task of reconstruction. In the largest nation, Vietnam, socialist policies failed to revitalize the economy, and the reunification of North and South Vietnam proved harsh. Between 1978 and 1985, half a million refugees, known as "boat people," risked their lives to escape Vietnam in rickety boats, becoming easy targets for pirates. After spending months or years in crowded refugee camps in Southeast Asia, most of the refugees were resettled in North America, Australia, or France. In the 1980s, the Vietnamese government regrouped and introduced market-oriented reforms similar to those in China favoring private enterprise and foreign investment. These reforms increased productivity, fostered some prosperity in the cities, and ended the refugee flow. Emphasis on education more than doubled the 1945 literacy rates to 85 percent of adults, but the shift from rigid socialism also widened economic inequality, leaving most farmers living just above the poverty line. Politically, Vietnam, like China, remained an authoritarian one-party state, but restrictions on cultural expression loosened. Several former soldiers became pop music stars, and many writers addressed contemporary problems and the war's legacy in fiction.

Gradually, the communists expanded ties to the West and the world economy. In the late 1990s, the United States and Vietnam resumed diplomatic relations, and U.S. president Bill Clinton lifted the U.S. economic embargo. Bustling Saigon, now renamed Ho Chi Minh City, enjoyed especially dynamic growth and prosperity. Consumers in the United States now buy shrimp and underwear imported from Vietnam, while many Americans, including former soldiers and Vietnamese refugees, visit Vietnam.

Like the Vietnamese, Laotians also needed to deal with the divisions and destruction caused by the war. Many Laotians fled into exile, among them 300,000 Hmongs who settled in the United States. Since the 1980s, Laotian leaders have sought warmer relations with neighboring Thailand and China as well as with the United States, but rigid communists still dominate the one-party state. While several cities and districts have vibrant economies, attracting Western tourists, most Laotians remain poor.

Repression Under the Khmer Rouge

Cambodia has faced a far more difficult challenge than Vietnam and Laos, because war was followed by fierce repression. When the communist Khmer Rouge, hardened by years of brutal war, achieved

Honoring Ho Chi Minh These schoolgirls, dressed in traditional clothing and parading before Ho Chi Minh's mausoleum in Hanoi, are part of an annual festival to honor the leading figure of Vietnamese communism.

Vietnam's Intervention in Cambodia

The situation changed in 1978, leading to a new government. The Vietnamese, alarmed at Khmer Rouge territorial claims and the murder of thousands of ethnic Vietnamese in Cambodia, invaded Cambodia, and rapidly pushed the Khmer Rouge to the Thailand border. The Vietnamese invasion liberated the Cambodian people from tyranny and installed a less brutal communist government. But military conflict continued for years as a Khmer Rouge–dominated resistance, subsidized chiefly by China and the United States, controlled some sections of the country. Cambodia proved to be an endless sinkhole of conflict that drained scarce wealth and complicated Vietnam's relations with the West. In the early 1990s, a coalition government was formed under United Nations sponsorship that brought about change. The Khmer Rouge, which refused to take part, splintered and collapsed. While the resulting peace was welcomed by all, the government remained repressive and corrupt. Sihanouk returned from exile to become king but had little power and served largely as a symbol of Cambodia's link to its past. Life for many Cambodians remained grim, but some organized in support of more democracy and social reforms. Nevertheless, the new government has transformed a still-haunted Cambodia into a functioning society, kept afloat largely by Western tourism and aid.

power in 1975, they turned on the urban population with a fury, driving everyone into the rural areas to farm. The Khmer Rouge's radical vision of a propertyless, classless peasant society, combined with their violence against suspected dissenters, led to the flight of thousands of refugees into neighboring countries and what survivors called the "killing fields": the Khmer Rouge executed thousands of victims in death camps and shot or starved many others, indiscriminately. Ultimately, the Khmer Rouge and their brutal leader, Pol Pot (1925–1998), were responsible for the death of 1 to 2 million Cambodians.

LO⁴ New Nations in Southeast Asia

In addition to the Indochinese countries, the post–World War II nationalist thrust for independence produced other new nations in Southeast Asia (see Map 31.3), but the building of states capable of improving the lives of their people had only just begun. Indonesia, the Philippines, Burma, and the other new nations avoided the destructive warfare rocking Indochina

Interactive Map

1946 Year of independence

CHINA
INDIA
BANGLADESH
Mandalay
BURMA
(MYANMAR)
1947
Chiang Mai
Hanoi
LAOS
1949
NORTH
VIETNAM
1954
Rangoon
Vientiane
Dividing Line 1954–1975
THAILAND
(SIAM)
Hue
Bangkok
SOUTH
VIETNAM
1954
CAMBODIA
1954
Phnom Penh
Ho Chi Minh City
(Saigon)
Bay
of
Bengal
Guangzhou
Taiwan
Tropic of Cancer
Philippine
Sea
Luzon
PHILIPPINES
1946
Manila
Samar
Iloilo
Leyte
Cebu
Mindanao
Davao
Sulu
Sea
N. Borneo
PALAU
PACIFIC
OCEAN
20°N
South
China
Sea
Acheh
Penang
Medan
MALAYA
Kuala Lumpur
Melaka
SINGAPORE
1965
Kuching
SARAWAK
Sumatra
Palembang
BRUNEI
1984
M A L A Y S I A
1963
SABAH
Sulu Archipelago
Celebes
Sea
Borneo
Balikpapan
INDIAN
OCEAN
100°E
Jakarta
Bandung
Java
Jogjakarta
Bali
Java Sea
Surabaya
Bandjermasin
Makassar
Celebes
(Sulawesi)
Flores
I   N   D   O   N   E   S   I   A
1949
Moluccas (Malaku)
West Irian
East Timor
(TIMOR LESTE)
1999
120°E
PAPUA
NEW
GUINEA
1975
AUSTRALIA
140°E
Equator — 0°
N
0   500   1,000 Km.
0   500   1,000 Mi.

© Cengage Learning

Map 31.3
Modern Southeast Asia

Indonesia, covering thousands of islands, is the largest, most populous Southeast Asian nation. Southeast Asia also includes four other island nations, five nations on the mainland, and Malaysia, which sprawls from the Malay Peninsula to northern Borneo.

but did have to overcome economic underdevelopment, promote national unity, and deal with opposition to the new ruling groups. The years between 1945 and 1975 were marked by economic progress, Cold War–inspired conflict, and dictatorships; the years following brought even more change and growth. Some nations, including Indonesia, Malaysia, Singapore, and Thailand, have gained reputations as "tigers" because of their economic dynamism. At the same time, governments often have become authoritarian in an effort to ensure social stability.

Indonesia: The Quest for Freedom and Order

Indonesian independence came through struggle. The violent resistance to Dutch colonialism of the late 1940s, known as the Indonesian Revolution, was a bitter conflict in which the Dutch used massive violence to suppress the Indonesian nationalists, who fought back. In a short story about the brutal battle to control the east Javanese city of Surabaya, a nationalist writer noted that the revolutionary soldiers "killed [the Dutch soldiers] with great determination, spirit and hunger."[7] The United States, fearing regional instability, pressured the Dutch to grant independence in 1950.

Sukarno and Indonesian Nationalism

Indonesia still faced the challenge of fostering a unified nation. Given the diversity of islands, peoples, and cultures, Indonesian leaders became obsessed with creating national unity. During the 1950s and early 1960s, Indonesia was led by the charismatic but increasingly authoritarian president Sukarno (soo-KAHR-no) (1902–1970), the son of a Javanese aristocrat and a Balinese mother. A spell-binding orator who was able to rally popular support and bring different factions together, Sukarno worked to unite a huge nation in which villagers on remote islands and cosmopolitan city dwellers on Java knew little about each other. Despite his efforts, however, the multiparty parliamentary system became divisive in the 1950s. Regionalism grew as outer islanders resented domination by the Javanese, who constituted more than half of Indonesia's population and, many outer islanders believed, were favored by Sukarno. Sukarno's poorly implemented economic policies contributed to a severe crisis by the early 1960s and deepened divisions between communist, Islamic, and military forces.

Indonesia's 1965 Military Coup

By 1965, Indonesia had become a country of explosive social and political pressures. After a failed attempt by a small military faction with communist sympathies to seize power, a group of discontented generals arrested Sukarno, took power, and launched a brutal campaign to eliminate all leftists, especially the communists who had gained influence among poor peasants in Java. The resulting bloodbath, led by the army and Muslim groups, killed perhaps half a million Indonesians, including communists and members of the large, unpopular Chinese minority. Most communist leaders were killed or arrested; thousands of leftists were held in remote prison camps for years. Sukarno died in disgrace in 1970.

> Given the diversity of islands, peoples, and cultures, Indonesian leaders became obsessed with creating national unity.

Suharto's New Order

Between 1966 and 1998, the government, known as the New Order, headed by general-turned-president Suharto (b. 1921), a Javanese former soldier first in the Dutch colonial and then in the nationalist army, mixed military and civilian leadership to maintain law and order. Suharto used force to repress regional opposition in both East Timor, a small, former Portuguese colony where the mostly Christian population sought independence, and north Sumatra, where the fiercely Islamic Achehnese sought independence. However, although it limited political opposition, the New Order improved Indonesia's economic position and encouraged the rise of an educated urban middle class and vibrant popular culture. Per capita income, life expectancy, and adult literacy increased, aided by an annual economic growth rate of nearly 5 percent by the 1990s, although one-third of the population still earned less than a dollar per day.

East and Southeast Asia: An Annotated Directory of Internet Resources (http://newton.uor.edu/Departments&Programs/AsianStudiesDept/).

Islamic Challenges to Secular Indonesia

Yet, for all the economic productivity, the New Order also started some negative trends. During these years, Indonesia became economically dependent on exporting oil, which represented 80 percent of foreign earnings. When world oil prices declined in the 1980s, Indonesia was forced to accumulate an enormous foreign debt. Adding to the problems, the rapid development of mining, forestry, and cash crop agriculture took a toll on the environment. Furthermore, income disparities between classes and regions widened, while political and business

CHRONOLOGY

Non-Communist Southeast Asia, Since 1945

1945–1950	Indonesian Revolution
1948	Independence of Burma
1963	Formation of Malaysia
1965	Secession of Singapore from Malaysia
1965–1966	Turmoil in Indonesia
1966–1998	New Order in Indonesia
1997	Economic crisis in Southeast Asia

corruption became a major problem. The wealthy frolicked in nightclubs, casinos, and golf courses built across the street from slums or on land appropriated from powerless villages. Suharto, the son of poor peasants, became one of the world's most corrupt leaders, and he and his family acquired more than $15 billion in assets from their business enterprises and from access to public coffers.

Many Indonesians disliked the New Order. For some, Islam provided the chief vehicle for opposition. Some 87 percent of Indonesians are either devout or nominal Muslims, but few have supported militant Islamist movements like those in the Middle East and Pakistan. Suharto discouraged such Islamic radicalism as a threat to national unity in a country that also includes Christians and Hindus. However, devout Muslims have often opposed the government's secular policies and have desired a more Islamic approach to social, cultural, and legal matters, while a progressive, democratic strand of Indonesian Islamic thought has favored liberal reform. Muslim liberals tap into the traditional emphasis on harmony, consensus, and tolerance that was incorporated into Indonesian, especially Javanese, Islam; they thus offer a stark contrast to the more dogmatic Islam common in countries such as Pakistan and Saudi Arabia.

By the 1990s, Indonesian society was suffering from increasing class tensions, insecurities, student protests, and labor unrest, all of which set the stage for dramatic changes. When the economy collapsed, throwing millions out of work and raising prices for essential goods, riots throughout the country resulted to Suharto's resignation in 1998. With the longtime strongman gone, the country fell into turmoil, and protests and ethnic clashes proliferated. Many civilians, particularly among the urban middle class, wanted to strengthen democracy, and in 1999, free elections were held. Later, Megawati Soekarnoputri (MEH-ga-WHA-tee soo-KAR-no-POO-tri), the daughter of Indonesia's first president, Sukarno, became Indonesia's first woman president. Like her father, Megawati followed secular, nationalist policies but also showed little faith in grassroots democracy and resolved few problems. By 2004, popular support for her regime had ebbed, and she was defeated for reelection by a Javanese general.

> "Filipinos have struggled to create a clear national identity out of the diverse mosaic of local languages and regions."

The End of Suharto's New Order

The end of Suharto's New Order, and the disorderly democracy that replaced it, brought unprecedented freedom but also new problems. Removing New Order restrictions allowed long-simmering ethnic hostilities to reemerge, especially in East Timor and Acheh. Terrorist attacks in Indonesia, especially the bombing of popular tourist venues on Bali in 2003 and 2005, added to the growing tensions, raising questions about the long-term viability of Indonesian democracy. Complicating the political problems, in 2004, more than 100,000 Indonesians perished from earthquakes and a deadly tidal wave, or tsunami, that destroyed cities and washed away coastal villages on Sumatra. Efforts to recover from these major setbacks further undermined the economy.

Politics and Society in the Philippines and Malaysia

The Philippines achieved independence from the United States on July 4, 1946, though the two countries remained bound by close political and economic links. The new nation soon faced problems sustaining democracy. A small group of landowners, industrialists, and businessmen who had prospered under U.S. rule manipulated elected governments to preserve their power and to protect U.S. economic interests. Free elections involved so much violence, bribery, and fraud that disillusioned Filipinos spoke of them as decided by "guns, goons, and gold." Furthermore, nationalists often believed that continuing U.S. influence hindered the creation of a truly independent Filipino identity and culture. Filipinos have struggled to create a clear national identity out of the diverse mosaic of local languages and regions.

Political Instability and the Rise of Ferdinand Marcos

Economic inequality and social divisions have fueled conflict. The communist-led Huk Rebellion from 1948 to 1954 capitalized on discontent among the rural poor. Only heavy U.S. assistance to the government suppressed the rebellion. In the 1970s, the communist New Peoples Army (NPA) controlled many rural tenant farmers and urban slum dwellers. Religious differences have also led to conflict. While most Filipinos became Christian in Spanish times, the southern islands have large Muslim populations, some of whom have taken up arms to protest the Christian-dominated government. In 1972, President Ferdinand Marcos (1917–1989) used the restoration of law and order as an excuse to suspend democracy, and from 1972 until 1986, he ruled as a dictator. On Marcos's watch, economic conditions worsened, rural poverty became more widespread, the population grew rapidly, and political opposition was limited by the murder or detention of dissidents, censorship, and rigged elections.

The dictator and his cronies looted the country for their own benefit, amassing billions. In the capital, Manila, a tiny minority lived in palatial homes surrounded by high walls topped with bits of broken glass and barbed wire, while homeless families slept in bushes. The majority of rural families were landless, and child malnutrition increased. To escape poverty, Filipinos often migrated, temporarily or permanently, to other Asian nations, the United States, or the Middle East. Some 10 million Filipinos lived abroad by 2006.

Collapse of the Marcos Regime

The failures of the Marcos years led to massive public protests in 1986 that brought down Marcos and restored democracy. The opposition had rallied around U.S.-educated Corazon Aquino (ah-KEE-no) (b. 1933), a descendant of a Chinese immigrant, whose popular politician husband had been assassinated by Marcos's henchmen. In a spectacular nonviolent revolution under the banner of "people's power," street

People's Power Demonstration in the Philippines In 1986, the simmering opposition to the dictatorial government of Ferdinand Marcos led to massive demonstrations in Manila. Under the banner of "people's power," business people, professionals, housewives, soldiers, students, and cultural figures rallied to topple the regime.

Corbis

demonstrations involving
students, workers, busi-
nessmen, housewives, and
clergy demanded justice
and freedom. Marcos and
his family fled into exile in
the United States, which
had long supported his
regime. When thousands of
demonstrators broke into the presidential palace,
they found that the dictator's wife, Imelda Marcos, a
former beauty queen, had acquired thousands of
pairs of shoes and vast stores of undergarments,
symbolizing the Marcos's corruption and waste.
Corazon Aquino became president and reestablished
democracy.

Yet the hopes of democracy were dashed as
Filipino politics remained turbulent. The government,
while open to dissenting voices, continued to be dominated by the wealthiest Filipinos, mostly members
of the hundred or so landowning families. Corazon
Aquino, herself a member of one of these families,
voluntarily left office at the end of her term in 1992.
Her successors had rocky presidencies; one of these
men, a former film star with a reputation for heavy
drinking, gambling, and womanizing, was impeached
for corruption and vote-rigging. In 2001, another
woman, Gloria Macapagal-Arroyo (b. 1947), a Ph.D. in
economics and the daughter of a former president,
became president but also faced allegations of corruption. She was reelected in 2005 but faced constant
challenges questioning her legitimacy. Two decades
after the overthrow of Marcos, the public seems disillusioned with the results. Many Filipinos also resent
the continuing close ties to the United States.

Yet post-Marcos governments had successes and
failures. Democracy returned, a free press flourished,
and the economy improved after 1990, yet much of the
economic growth was eaten up by the region's fastest
population growth, because Filipinos maintained their
preference for large families. And none of the governments successfully addressed poverty or seemed
willing to curb the activities of influential companies
exploiting marine, mineral, and timber resources.
Differences in access to health care, welfare, and
related services continued to reflect the great gaps in
income between social classes and regions.

> "In Thailand, leaders
> sought to build a national
> culture based on Thai
> cultural values, including
> reverence for Buddhism
> and the monarchy, which
> had little formal power
> but symbolized the
> nation."

Diversity and Dictatorship in Thailand and Burma

Thailand and Burma
also struggled to create
national unity and stability. Although historical
rivals, the two countries
have shared certain pat-
terns. The majority eth-
nic groups, the Thais and
the Burmans, are both
Theravada Buddhists who
assert authority over a
variety of ethnic minorities, including sizable immigrant trading communities of Chinese and Indians.
Both countries also have experienced insurgencies
by disaffected ethnic, religious, or political factions.
However, while Burma had been a restless British
colony since the mid-1800s, Thailand (once known
as Siam) was the only major Southeast Asian country to avoid colonization. As a result, Thais have
had more control over their government, economy,
and culture than other Southeast Asians. Since the
1970s, the contrasts between prosperous Thailand
and stagnant Burma have become striking. Both
nations have had a long history of military dictatorship, but only the Thais, finding the repressive
atmosphere chilling, made a transition to more
open government.

**Political Turmoil in
Post-War Thailand**

In Thailand, leaders
sought to build a national
culture based on Thai cultural values, including
reverence for Buddhism and the monarchy, which
had little formal power but symbolized the nation.
Thai culture promotes respect for those in authority
and values social harmony. However, this conservatism has also fostered authoritarian governments
and bureaucratic inertia. Ethnic and religious diversity has also posed political problems. Thailand's
political history after 1945 was characterized by long
periods of military rule, often corrupt and oppressive,
followed by short-lived democratically elected or
semidemocratic governments. Not until the 1970s
would a true mass politics develop in Thailand, as
opposition movements challenged the long
entrenched military regime. Opposition gained sway
in part from Thais' resentment of the United States,
which supported the military regime and had military bases and some 50,000 troops in the country. The

presence of free-spending American soldiers created a false prosperity while also posing a challenge to Buddhist moralists, who were outraged by the sleazy bars, nightclubs, and brothels that often exploited poor Thai women.

Collapse of Military Rule

In 1973, antigovernment feelings boiled over, and the military regime was overthrown following student-led mass demonstrations that involved several hundred thousand people. The military strongman was forced to flee the country, and the collapse of military rule opened a brief era of political liberalization. For the first time in Thai history, democracy and debate flourished. But right-wing military officers and bureaucrats became alarmed at challenges to their power and privileges, and Thai society became increasingly polarized between liberals and conservatives. Finally, in 1976, bloody clashes between leftist students and right-wing youth gangs led to a military coup and martial law, which resulted in the killing or wounding of hundreds and the arrest of thousands of students and their supporters. The return of military power reestablished order, but the massacres discredited the military.

By the 1980s, Thailand had turned away from military dictatorship and developed a semidemocratic system combining traditions of order and hierarchy, symbolized by the monarchy, with notions of representative, accountable government. While most successful political candidates came from wealthy families, often of Chinese ancestry, the rapidly expanding urban middle class generally supported more democracy. A new constitution adopted in 1997 guaranteed civil liberties and reformed the electoral system, and a lively free press emerged.

Thailand has generally enjoyed high rates of economic growth since the 1970s. Despite a growing manufacturing sector, the export of commodities such as rice, rubber, tin, and timber remains significant. Although the Chinese minority, some 10 percent of the population, controls much of the wealth, Thais enjoy high per capita incomes and standards of public health by Asian standards, yet perhaps one-quarter are very poor, especially in rural areas. The economic "miracle," as some have called it, has, in many respects, been built on the backs of women and children, many from rural districts, who work in urban factories, the service sector, and the sex industry. Problems besides widespread poverty and sexual exploitation also challenge Thais. The economic collapse of 1997 that affected much of Asia also threw many Thais out of work. The rapidly growing, over-crowded capital, Bangkok, is one of the most polluted cities in Asia, and the nation's once-abundant rain forests disappear at a rapid rate, a fact lamented by Thai musicians and poets (see Witness to the Past: A Thai Poet's Plea for Saving the Environment). Health issues have arisen too: the AIDS rate skyrockets. Yet, despite their problems, Thais possess a talent for political compromise, and Buddhism teaches tolerance, respect for nature, and a belief in the worth of the individual. Thais have the basis for a democratic spirit, a more equitable distribution of wealth, and an environmental ethic.

Burmese Independence and Political Chaos

To the west of Thailand, Burma emerged from the Japanese occupation devastated, with whole cities blasted into rubble by Allied bombing. After the war, the British returned to reestablish their colonial control. However, facing a well-armed Burmese nationalist army and weary of conflict, they elected to negotiate independence with the charismatic nationalist leader Aung San (1915–1947). In 1948, the British left Burma, but newly elected Prime Minister Aung San was assassinated by a political rival. He was replaced by his longtime colleague, U Nu (1907–1995), an idealistic Buddhist who also supported democracy. Soon key ethnic minorities, fearful of domination by the majority Burmans, each organized armies and declared their secession from Burma. For the next four decades, the central government rarely controlled more than half the nation's territory as the ethnic armies and communist insurgents fought each other and the Burmese army. To fund themselves, insurgents often relied on the opium trade.

Burma Under Military Rule

In 1962, the army deposed U Nu and seized control. Skeptical of democracy for a fragmented nation, military rulers suspended civil liberties, seized economic control, imposed censorship, and devoted most government revenue to the military. However, by the 1980s, as a result of the military's oppressive control, economic stagnation and political repression had fostered dissent, and various secession movements continued. According to the United Nations, Burma became one of the world's ten poorest nations. Sparked by economic decline and political repression, mass protests in 1988, led by students and Buddhist monks, demanded civil liberties. These protests ended, however, when soldiers killed hundreds and jailed thousands of demonstrators. The regime increased its repression.

A Thai Poet's Plea for Saving the Environment

Angkhan Kalayanaphong (AHN-kan KALL-a-YAWN-a-fong), born in 1926, the most popular poet in Thailand for decades, also gained fame as an accomplished graphic artist and painter. His poems often addressed social, Buddhist, and environmental themes. In his long poem, "Bangkok-Thailand," he examines Thailand and its problems in the 1970s and 1980s. The author pulls no punches in condemning Thai society for neglecting its heritage; he skewers politicians, government institutions, big business, and the entertainment industry. In this section, Angkhan pleads for Thais to save the forest environment being destroyed by commercial logging.

Oh, I do not imagine the forest like that
So deep, so beautiful, everything so special.
It pertains to dreams that are beyond truth. . . .
Dense woods in dense forests; slowly
The rays of half a day mix with the night.
Strange atmosphere causing admiration.
Loneliness up to the clouds, stillness and beauty.
Rays of gold play upon, penetrate the tree-tops
rays displayed in stripes, the brightness of the sun.
I stretch out my hand drawing down clouds mixing them with brandy.
This is supreme happiness. . . .
The lofty trees do not think of reward for the scent of their blossoms. . . .
Men kill the wood because they venerate money as in all the world. . . .

The lofty trees contribute much to morals.
They should be infinitely lauded for it.
The trace of the ax kills. Blood runs in streams. . . .
You, trees, give the flattering pollen attended by scents.
You make the sacrifice again and again.
Do you ever respond angrily?
You have accepted your fate which is contemptuous of all that is beautiful.
But troublesome are the murderers, the doers of future sins.
Greedy after money, they are blind to divine work.
Their hearts are black to large extent, instead of being honest and upright.
They have no breeding, are lawless. . . .
Thailand in particular is in a very bad way.
Because of their [commercial] value parks are 'purified,' i.e., destroyed.
Man's blood is depraved, cursed and base.
His ancestors are swine and dogs. It is madness to say they are Thai.

Thinking About the Reading

1. What qualities does the poet attribute to the forest?
2. What motives does he attribute to the loggers and businessmen who exploit the forest environment?

Source: Klaus Wenk, *Thai Literature: An Introduction* (Bangkok: White Lotus, 1995), pp. 95–98. Copyright © 1995 Klaus Wenk. Reprinted with permission.

In 1990, Burma, now renamed Myanmar (my-ahn-MAH), allowed elections under international pressure, though with restrictions. Even though most of its leaders were in jail, the opposition quickly organized and won a landslide victory. Aung San Suu Kyi (AWNG sahn soo CHEE) (b. 1945), daughter of the founding president and an eloquent orator, returned from a long exile in England to lead the democratic forces. But the military refused to hand over power, put Aung San Suu Kyi under house arrest, and rounded up hundreds of opposition supporters.

Refusing to compromise and becoming a courageous symbol of principled leadership, Aung San Suu Kyi won the Nobel Peace Prize in 1991.

Today the military regime remains in power and still detains opposition leaders, including Aung San Suu Kyi. The generals cleverly manipulate politics while slightly relaxing their grip. Although many Burmese still dream of democracy, others have accommodated themselves to military rule, valuing stability. To expand the economy and thus increase its own revenues, the government began welcoming foreign investment. Western, Japanese, and Southeast Asian corporations invest in Burma, diminishing the willingness of other countries to punish Burma for gross human-rights violations.

Diversity and Prosperity in Malaysia and Singapore

Compared with some of its neighbors, governments proved more stable in Malaya after independence. After World War II, the British sought to dampen political unrest in Malaya as communist-led insurgents kept the colony on edge for a decade. In 1957, with the insurgency crushed, Malaya became independent as a federation of states under a government led by the main Malay party, UMNO (United Malays National Organization). However, the predominantly Chinese city-state of Singapore, a major trading center and military base, remained outside the federation as a British colony. In Malaya, the majority ethnic group, the Malays, nearly all Muslim, dominated politics, but the Chinese, one-third of the population, were granted liberal citizenship rights and maintained strong economic power. British leaders, seeing their colonial role in Singapore as well as in two northern Borneo states they controlled, Sabah and Sarawak, as burdensome, suggested joining them with Malaya in a larger federation, to be called Malaysia. This new, geographically divided Malaysia was formed in 1963.

Ethnic and Political Tension in Malaysia

In the years that followed, Malaysia struggled to create national unity out of deep regional and ethnic divisions. Singapore withdrew from Malaysia in 1965 and became an independent nation. Given the need to reduce political tensions, sustain economic growth, and preserve stability, the leaders of the key ethnic groups in Malaya—Malays, Chinese, and Indians—cooperated through political parties that allied in an UMNO-dominated ruling coalition, but below the surface, ethnic tensions simmered. After 1970, Malay-dominated governments pursued policies designed to reshape Malaysia's society and economy.

Over time, Malaysia and Singapore, both open to the world as they have been for centuries, have achieved exceptional political stability and economic progress. The two nations have shared a similar mix of ethnic groups, and both countries maintain democratic forms, but the ruling parties sometimes arrest or harass opposition leaders. After 1970, Malaysia has remained politically stable by maintaining a limited democracy and holding regular elections in which the ruling, modernizing Malay-led coalition of parties controls the voting and most of the media. The Chinese-dominated ruling party in Singapore has used similar strategies to maintain its hold on power. Because the print and broadcast media are controlled by the government or their allies in both nations, dissidents use the Internet to spread their views on their societies. Both countries have successfully diversified their economies and thus stimulated economic development, and they have also raised living standards and spread the wealth.

Religion and Prosperity in Malaysia

In Malaysia, religion has remained vital, including in politics, which has often divided the Muslim majority from the Christian, Hindu, Buddhist, and animist minorities. Islamic movements with dogmatic, sometimes militant views have gained support among some young Malays who are alienated by a Westernized, materialistic society. These movements, which discourage contact with non-Muslims and encourage women to dress modestly, often alarm secular Malays and non-Muslims. In response, Malay women's rights groups use Islamic arguments to oppose restrictions favored by conservatives. They find some support among the numerous women holding high government positions. Hence, Sisters in Islam, founded in the 1980s by the politically well-connected academic, Zainab Anwar, espouses an Islam supporting freedom, justice, and equality.

Supported by abundant natural resources, economic diversification, and entrepreneurial talent, Malaysia has become a highly successful developing nation, surpassing European nations like Portugal and Hungary in national wealth. High annual growth rates have enabled Malaysia to achieve a relatively high per capita income and to build light industry that employs cheap labor to make shoes, toys, and other consumer goods for export. Many of these workers are women; half of Malaysian women work for wages. The manufacturing sector has continued to grow rapidly, and oil and timber have become valuable export commodities. Malaysia recovered rapidly from the 1997 Asian economic collapse by imposing more government controls on the economy, ignoring Western economic advice.

But economic growth comes at the price of toxic waste problems, severe deforestation, air pollution, and social change. Violence between Chinese and Malays in 1969 resulted in the New Economic Policy;

Kuala Lumpur Dominated by new skyscrapers, including some of the world's tallest buildings, and a spectacular mosque, the Malaysian capital city, Kuala Lumpur, has become a prosperous center for Asian commerce and industry.

aimed at redistributing more wealth to Malays, it has fostered a substantial Malay middle class. Official poverty rates dropped from some 50 percent in 1970 to around 20 percent by 2000. Nevertheless, the gap between rich and poor remains and may have widened. In the bustling capital city, Kuala Lumpur, jammed freeways, glittering malls, and high-rise luxury condominiums contrast with shantytown squatter settlements and countless shabbily dressed street hawkers.

The Example of Singapore

Restricted to a tiny island, Singapore has done even better than Malaysia economically, despite few resources, and has become among the world's most prosperous nations. The predominance of Chinese, the descendants of immigrants during the past two centuries, makes Singapore unique in Southeast Asia. The Singapore government has mixed free-wheeling economic policies with an autocratic leadership that tightly controls the 5 million people and limits dissent. Singapore is run like a giant corporation, efficient and ruthless. People pay a stiff fine if they are caught spitting, littering, or even tossing used chewing gum on the street. Yet it is also one of the healthiest societies, enjoying, for example, the world's lowest rate of infant mortality. Singapore has devoted more of its national budget to education than other nations: everyone studies English in school, and the nation's approach to math education is widely admired. Businesspeople from around the world have flocked to this globalized city, just as they had flocked to the Straits of Melaka's trading states centuries ago.

Southeast Asia in the Global System

After the mid-1970s, a shift of economic direction allowed several Southeast Asians to develop and play a greater role in the world economy. By the 1990s, experts talked about a vibrant Pacific Rim that included the "tiger" nations as well as Japan, China, Taiwan, and South Korea (see Chapter 27). Some forecast a Pacific Century in which these nations would lead the world economically and increase their political strength.

To promote economic growth and political stability, Southeast Asian countries began cooperating as never before. Founded in 1967 by Malaysia, Indonesia, Thailand, Singapore, and the Philippines, ASEAN (Association of Southeast Asian Nations) was a regional economic and political organization aimed at fostering economic exchange among the non-communist Southeast Asian nations. ASEAN's priorities shifted after the end of the wars in Indochina in 1975, and Vietnam, Cambodia, Laos, Burma, and the tiny, oil-rich state of Brunei, on Borneo, became members. ASEAN emerged as the world's fourth largest trading bloc and provided a forum for the various nations to work out their differences and deal with the wider world.

Although Southeast Asians still export the natural resources they did in colonial times, some nations have seen major economic growth through industrialization and exploitation of other resources, including oil, timber, rubber, rice, tin, sugar, and palm oil. With these exports, as well as manufactured goods such as computer chips, clothing, and sports equipment, the region has fostered some of the fastest growing economies in the world. Malaysia, Thailand, Singapore, and, to some extent, Indonesia and Vietnam have become major recipients of foreign investment. Growth did bring challenges: In 1997, most Southeast Asian countries faced a severe economic crisis, part of a broader global collapse. Causes included poorly regulated banking systems, overconfident investments, and government favoritism toward well-placed business interests. By the early

2000s, however, as the crisis eventually bottomed out, several countries began to put their economies back on a rapid growth track.

Southeast Asians have also influenced global politics. Vietnamese communists under Ho Chi Minh, in their ultimately successful fifty-year fight against French colonialism, Japanese occupation, and then U.S. intervention, stimulated a wave of revolutionary efforts, from Nicaragua to Mozambique, to overthrow Western domination. Women have long played an influential role in Southeast Asia, and the political leaders such as Corazon Aquino in the Philippines and Aung San Suu Kyi in Burma have become inspirations to people worldwide. By the early twenty-first century, the Southeast Asian nations were shifting their focus from the United States to China, which they viewed as the rising world power with which they must cooperate for regional stability.

Engagement with the outside world has shaped modern Southeast Asia. Global influences and economic development have increasingly modified lives, especially in the cities. Yet even rural areas have become more connected to wider networks by televisions, outboard motors, motor scooters, and phones. Still, change has often been superficial. For every youngster who joins the fan club for a Western pop star, another identifies with an Islamic, Buddhist, or Christian organization, sometimes a militant one. Many people find themselves perched uneasily between the cooperative village values of the past and the competitive, materialistic modern world.

Listen to a synopsis of Chapter 31.

Societies • Networks • Transitions

The Contemporary World, Since 1945

The world has changed dramatically since 1945. Some observers have described these years as the most revolutionary age in history. All regions of the world have become part of a global system. The Indonesian thinker Soedjatmoko (so-jat-MOH-ko) described a world of collapsing "national boundaries and horrifying destructive power, expanding technological capacity and instant communication [in which] we live in imperfect intimacy with all our fellow human beings."[1] This interconnected and rapidly changing global society, and the people who shape it, have produced both great good and indescribable horrors.

The contemporary world has become a global unity within a larger diversity. Globalization has fostered or intensified networks of exchange and communication: international trade pacts and electronic fund transfers, jet-speed travel and cell phones. Yet, even as they have become more closely linked, nations have not been able to work together to meet the challenges facing humanity, such as poverty and environmental distress. No clear international consensus has emerged on maintaining strong local cultures in the face of global influences, correcting the widening gap between rich and poor nations, and achieving a better balance between environmental preservation and economic development. Solving these problems requires complex strategies and the joint efforts of many nations.

Globalization and Cultures

Over recent centuries, humans have built a web, or networked society—a global system that today encompasses most of the world's 6.5 billion people. All of these terms imply transnational connections and the institutions that foster them, such as the World Bank, the Internet, and religious missionaries. Around the world, people speak, with fear or enthusiasm, of globalization. Some observers see the trend as dangerous folly, others as a boon, and still others have mixed feelings.

Globalization and Its Impacts

The roots of globalization go deep into the past. During the first millennium of the Common Era, trade networks such as the Silk Road, which linked China and Europe across Central Asia and the Middle East, and the spread of religions such as Buddhism, Christianity, and Islam, connected distant societies. One thousand years ago, an Eastern Hemisphere–wide economy based in Asia and anchored by Chinese and Indian manufacturing and Islamic trade networks represented an early form of globalization. The links between the hemispheres forged after 1492—during which Europeans competed for a share of the growing trade in raw materials—expanded the reach of this economy. In the nineteenth century, the Industrial Revolution and European imperialism extended the connections even further, aided by technological innovations such as steamships and trans-oceanic cables.

 Globalization Guide (*http:// www.global isationguide.org*). A useful collection of essays and links.

The integration of commerce and financial services today is more developed than ever before. As the global system has become increasingly linked, societies have become more dependent on each other for everything from consumer goods and entertainments to fuels and technological innovations. For example, all over the world, people consume Chinese textiles, U.S. films, Persian Gulf oil, Indian yoga, and Japanese electronics. Videoconferencing allows business partners in Los Angeles, Berlin, and Hong Kong to confer instantaneously with one another. During the early twenty-first century, the world's most powerful nation, the United States, has become increasingly reliant on Asian nations, especially China, to finance its skyrocketing national debt.

Such interdependence, as well as the reach of political, cultural, and social events across distances, has had an increasing impact in a shrinking world. For instance, in 2005, when Hurricane Katrina devastated the Gulf Coast of the United States, the export of corn from the U.S. Midwest through the port of New Orleans was disrupted. Japan, a major consumer of that corn, then turned to South Africa for supplies, which deprived people in Malawi of South African corn, causing widespread starvation in Malawi. While globalization affects every country to some degree, the great bulk of world trade and financial flow and activity is concentrated in, and has the largest impact on, the peoples of North America, Europe, and a group of Asian nations stretching from Japan to India.

Furthermore, many observers believe that globalization is unmanageable. U.S. journalist Thomas Friedman has noted, "Globalization isn't a choice. It's a reality, and no one is in charge. You keep looking for someone to complain to, to take the heat off your markets. Well guess what, there's no one on the other end of the phone."[2] This powerlessness to affect massive global economic forces has become chillingly evident in the global recession that began in 2008. This impersonal globalization, operating independent of governments, has had major impacts on societies, politics, economies, cultures, and environments. The best way for governments to adapt seems to be by educating their citizens, especially their young people, for a new, more competitive world. Various Asian nations, such as India, Taiwan, and Singapore, have adapted to these changes deftly, pouring money into education, science, and technology. The Western nations that have successfully adjusted to globalization are mainly those, especially in Scandinavia, that have combined open markets with strong societal and environmental protections.

Global forces, symbolized by advertising for foreign-made goods and satellites miles up in the sky relaying information around the world, interact with local cultures. As a result, local traditions and products sometimes get replaced, and imported and local cultures blend. An example of blending comes from France, where, with its large Arab immigrant population, Arab entrepreneurs have prospered by selling fast-food hamburgers and pizza prepared according to Muslim requirements and adapted to Arab taste. People around the world consume global products, from fast food to fashionable footwear to action films, but still enjoy cultural traditions that are distinctly local, such as Thai boxing or sumo wrestling in Japan.

 **The Globalization Website** (*http://www .sociology.emory.edu/ globalization/*). A very useful site with many resources and essays related to globalization.

To flourish in an interconnected world, people have had to become aware of international conditions. In North America, activists seeking to fight inequality or preserve the environment have urged people to think globally but act locally. Acting locally, Brazilian environmental and citizens' groups work to save their rain forests, while environmentally conscious North Americans and Europeans support organizations, businesses, and political leaders committed to improving the global environment. Others argue that people must think and act both globally and locally—to embrace both global and local citizenship. But, despite greatly increased travel and migration, only a small minority of people have become true citizens of the world, comfortable everywhere. Moreover, world government remains a distant prospect at the beginning of the twenty-first century.

Cultural Imperialism: The Globalization of Culture

The inequitable relationship between the dominant West and the developing nations has compelled observers to examine global change. Arising from this effort has been the concept of cultural imperialism, in which the economic and political power of Western nations, especially the United States, enables their cultural products to spread widely. Some African writers have called this pattern a "cultural bomb," arguing that Western products and entertainments destroy local cultures. In this view, the developed countries export popular music, disco dancing, skimpy women's clothing, and sex-drenched films and publications reflecting these countries' own values and experiences. Other societies adopt these products, which modify or suffocate their own traditions. For instance, big-budget Hollywood films attract large audiences, whereas local films, made on small budgets, cannot compete, and the local film industries often die as a result. To survive, local filmmakers adopt the formulas used by successful Hollywood filmmakers: sex and violence. Critics of Western power argue that cultural exchange has been common throughout history, but in the modern world has become largely a one-way street, leading to domination by Western, especially Anglo-American, culture.

Popular culture produced in the United States, entertaining but also challenging to traditional values, has emerged as the closest thing available to a global entertainment. The Monroe Doctrine—the early-nineteenth-century declaration by Congress that the United States would interfere in Latin American political developments—has now become, in the view of certain wags, the "Marilyn Monroe Doctrine," after the famous American actress who, for many non-Americans, symbolized U.S. culture in the 1950s.

Some American icons have become symbols of a new global modernity and capitalism. In 1989, two young East Germans crossed the Berlin Wall and discovered their first McDonald's restaurant. One of them remembered, "It was all so modern, the windows were so amazing. I felt like a lost convict who'd just spent twenty-five years in prison. I was in a state of shock."[3] Not even the Chinese, with one of the world's most admired cuisines, were immune to the appeal of modern U.S. marketing techniques and convenience for harried urbanites, judging from the growing number of McDonald's franchises in Beijing. Yet, Chinese restaurants flourish around the world.

 Global Problems and the Culture of Capitalism (*http://faculty.plattsburgh .edu/richard.robbins/ legacy/*). An outstanding site, aimed at undergraduates, with a wealth of resources on many topics.

Still, popular American entertainments often face opposition. Governments, from the Islamic clerics running Iran to the more democratic leaders of India, have attempted to halt or control the influx of what they consider destabilizing, immoral pop culture. In 2005, representatives of many nations, meeting under the auspices of the United Nations cultural organization, agreed that all nations had the right to restrict cultural imports, outraging American political and entertainment leaders.

Forming New World Cultures

Whatever the real scope of cultural imperialism, a new world culture appears to be on the rise. The world is becoming one vast network of relationships as ideas, people, and goods move between its different regions. Mexican and Brazilian soap operas, Indian (Bollywood) films, Nigerian novels, Arab, African, and Caribbean pop music, and Japanese comics and electronic games have been popular all over the globe. And the cultural traffic flow is not one way. In North America, western Europe, and Australia, people take up Indian yoga, Chinese *tai qi,* and other Asian spiritual disciplines; patronize Thai, Indian, Chinese, and Japanese restaurants; enjoy Brazilian and African pop music; learn Latin American dances; and master Asian martial arts. In 1998, the Chinese cellist Yo Yo Ma, born in Paris and later a U.S. resident, founded the Silk Road Ensemble, which brings together Western, East Asian, and Middle Eastern musicians to tour the world playing music that mixes the instruments and traditions of both East and West.

The meeting of global and local cultures fosters hybridization, the blending of two cultures, a process that can be either enriching or impoverishing. Record stores in Western cities set aside some of their display space to sell a hybrid form called "world music," popular music originating largely outside of the West that mixes Western influences with local and other traditions. World music has introduced Western and global audiences to a rich variety of sounds, often rooted in Asian, African, Caribbean, and Latin American traditions. While reshaping music for a global market, world music has also given Asian, African, and Latin American musicians a larger audience. Just like Western pop stars, some world musicians—such as the Brazilian singer-songwriter Caetano Veloso, and the Senegalese Youssou N'Dour, the descendant of griots, who mixes guitars with West African talking drums—perform around the world.

Inequality and Development

Globalization, resulting from interconnections transcending the boundaries of nations, benefits some people but not all equally. The gap between rich and poor nations, and rich and poor people within nations, has grown and remains one of the world's major problems. In 1960, the richest one-fifth of the world's population had a total income thirty times the poorest one-fifth; by 2000, the ratio had more than doubled. The former Soviet leader Mikhail Gorbachev, a keen student of world affairs, has asked: "Will the whole world turn into one big Brazil, into countries with complete inequality and [gated communities] for the rich elite?"[4]

The North-South Gap

With the changes in the global system since World War II, nations on every continent have improved their liv-
ing standards, lowered poverty rates, and increased their stake in the global economy, which has more than quintupled in size since 1950. The average per capita income in the world grew 2.6 times in the same period, to some $5,000 per year. But the rising tide of the world economy has not lifted all ships, leaving some nations, especially in the southern lands near or below the equator, poor relative to the northern countries. The economies of these nations, known as underdeveloped nations, have stagnated or enjoyed only very modest growth, leaving the majority of their people in poverty. More than 1 billion people live in extreme poverty, with an income of less than $1 per day. The gap between the richest and poorest countries, often known as the North-South gap, has widened steadily (see map). For instance, the difference in average per capita incomes between industrialized and nonindustrialized nations grew from 2 to 1 in 1850 to 10 to 1 in 1950 to 30 to 1 by 2000. Today the industrialized North contains one-quarter of the world's population but accounts for more than three-quarters of its production of goods and services.

Interactive Map

The growing North-South disparity in consumption is striking. For example, while Americans, 5 percent of the world's population, consume 40 percent of the world's resources, people in a Bolivian valley experience an impoverished material life. According to a study of the valley: "In a man's lifetime, he will buy one suit, one white shirt, perhaps a hat and a pair of rubber boots. The only things which have to be purchased in the market are a small radio-record player, the batteries to run it, plaster religious figures, a bicycle, and some cutlery."[5] Food consumption also differs dramatically. On average, North Americans consume twice as many calories each day as Haitians and Bangladeshis. While overeating contributes to widespread obesity in industrialized nations, one-sixth of the world's people are chronically malnourished, often suffering permanent brain damage because of it, and lack access to clean water. Fifteen million children die each year from hunger-related ailments.

There are also other indicators of difference in wealth. The 10 percent of people who live in the most industrialized nations consume two-thirds of the world's energy. Literacy rates range from a low of 14 percent in Niger, in West Africa, to a high of 99 percent in some twenty wealthy countries. Life expectancy ranges from a high of eighty years in Japan to a low of thirty-seven years in Sierra Leone, in West Africa. More than 60 percent of the world's poorest people are women.

Challenges of Development

Of course, the experiences of the Asian, African, and Latin American nations involve more than the bleak story of poverty and underdevelopment. Life expectancy worldwide has grown by nearly half, and infant mortality has

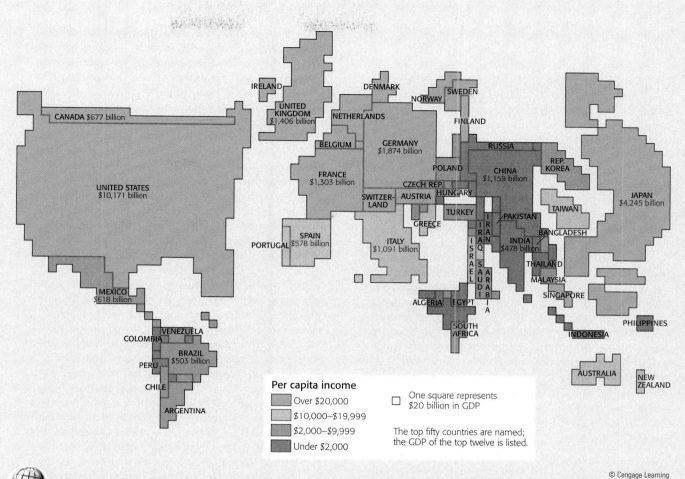

Per capita income

- Over $20,000
- $10,000–$19,999
- $2,000–$9,999
- Under $2,000

☐ One square represents $20 billion in GDP

The top fifty countries are named; the GDP of the top twelve is listed.

CANADA $677 billion
UNITED STATES $10,171 billion
MEXICO $618 billion
IRELAND
UNITED KINGDOM $1,406 billion
DENMARK
NORWAY
SWEDEN
NETHERLANDS
BELGIUM
GERMANY $1,874 billion
FINLAND
FRANCE $1,303 billion
POLAND
RUSSIA
REP. KOREA
CZECH REP.
HUNGARY
CHINA $1,159 billion
JAPAN $4,245 billion
SWITZER-LAND
AUSTRIA
TURKEY
PAKISTAN
TAIWAN
GREECE
IRAN
PORTUGAL
SPAIN $578 billion
ITALY $1,091 billion
ISRAEL
IRAQ
SAUDI ARABIA
INDIA $478 billion
BANGLADESH
THAILAND
MALAYSIA
SINGAPORE
ALGERIA
EGYPT
SOUTH AFRICA
INDONESIA
PHILIPPINES
VENEZUELA
COLOMBIA
BRAZIL $503 billion
PERU
CHILE
ARGENTINA
AUSTRALIA
NEW ZEALAND

© Cengage Learning

Global Distribution of Wealth

The countries of North America, northern Europe, and Japan have the most wealth and the world's highest per capita incomes, averaging more than $20,000 per year. At the other extreme, many people in South America and most people in the poor countries of sub-Saharan Africa, South Asia, and the Middle East earn less than $2,000 per year.

dropped by two-thirds since 1955. Some Asian and Latin American nations have achieved literacy rates comparable to those of some European nations. The number of countries the United Nations considers to have "high human development" grew from sixteen to fifty-five between 1960 and 2004. The rapidly industrializing nations of East and Southeast Asia have led the way: Singapore and South Korea achieved similar world economic rankings with such European nations as Italy, Greece, and Portugal. Several Latin American nations, Caribbean islands, and small oil-rich Persian Gulf states joined the top development category. Many rising nations—such as Malaysia, Thailand, India, and Brazil—formed a growing group of Newly Industrializing Countries (NICs), which have enjoyed high economic growth rates since the 1960s. Malaysia, for example, has dramatically reduced poverty rates, whereas India and Singapore have become centers of high technol-

ogy. Nor is technological innovation restricted to the well educated.

While some countries are on the rise, others struggle to spur economic growth that benefits all of the population. Valiant efforts have failed to substantially raise living standards for everyone. For instance, in much of Latin America, the wealthiest 20 percent have enjoyed huge income increases, whereas the poorest 40 percent have lost income. Capitalism supported by Western investment has helped a few countries, especially those that combine strong governments with social and economic reform, as in South Korea, Malaysia, and Thailand, but reliance on free markets and Western investment has often failed to sustain development. Little of the trickle-down of wealth from the rich to the poor—predicted by Western economists who favor free enterprise—has occurred. Instead, the result has often been trickle-out: the loss of a country's wealth to multinational corporations and international banks.

At the same time, alternatives to capitalism have not necessarily brought improvement. Communist and other social revolutionary countries have experienced severe problems. Some of these countries, such as Fidel Castro's Cuba and Mao Zedong's China, did a good job of delivering education and health care but were unable to create much wealth. Some communist countries, such as Angola and Vietnam, also sometimes faced civil wars and trade embargoes imposed by the West that drained their economies. Because in most cases neither capitalism nor socialism by itself proved the answer, most communist regimes eventually allowed private companies and Western investment while maintaining strong, centralized governments.

Since adopting this model after the end of the Maoist era, China, for example, has generated the world's most rapid economic growth; in recent years, Vietnam has tried to follow the same path. However, economic liberalization that dismantles government services has deprived millions of Chinese and Vietnamese of the free education and health care they enjoyed under socialism, fostering unrest. The formula of mixing capitalism and socialism has worked well in much of East and Southeast Asia. In these regions, a dynamic, largely unfettered private sector has evolved along with planning, land reform, investment in education, and other public policies to benefit the common people.

Envisioning a New World Order

The challenge of development is only a part of a larger contemporary question: how societies, working together, can forge a new, more equitable world order. Even after World War II, decolonization, and the rise of revolutionary states such as China, a few nations, mostly in the West and East Asia, still held disproportionate power and influence. The United States has played the key role and borne the major costs in managing the global system through military alliances (such as NATO), trade pacts (such as GATT), and international organizations (such as the World Bank). However, since the 1960s, observers have argued that fostering widespread economic development also requires addressing the inequalities within the global system and cooperating on international issues. The United Nations has been one major attempt at global cooperation but has had a mixed record.

The current world order contains many problems and the looming reality of limited resources, including water, food, and oil. Conflicts over resources in one nation often spill over into neighboring nations, complicating international relations. The prospect of fostering a more equitable sharing of world resources raises questions about the availability of resources. Experts worry that the world's resources and environment could not support a Western standard of living for all of the world. If every Chinese, Indian, Egyptian, and Peruvian, they argue,

consumed the same products and calories as Americans, Swedes, or Japanese, world resources would quickly diminish. For all 6.5 billion people in today's world to live at a western European standard of living would require a 140-fold increase in the consumption of resources and energy. Present oil supplies would run out in one or two decades, assuming the oil could be pumped and refined into petroleum that fast. Furthermore, most of the world's population growth is occurring in the developing nations, putting even more pressure on diminishing resources.

China's recent economic success shows the challenges ahead. By the early twenty-first century, a China rushing toward development had become a huge consumer of the world's industrial, agricultural, and natural resources, energizing global trade but causing shortages elsewhere. For example, world oil prices have soared since 2000 in part because of China's increasing energy appetite as Chinese—1.3 billion people, compared with 300 million Americans—switch from bicycles to cars. If the Chinese consumed as much oil per capita as Americans, their demand would exceed the present world production. China's living standards remain far below those of Japan and South Korea, but should they rise to that level in the next decade or two, China will further stress the supply chain. Assuming China does not experience a revolution, civil war, or economic collapse, experts expect it to have the world's largest economy by 2035 or 2040. As occurred in the industrializing West earlier, rapid Chinese development has also led to environmental degradation, including dangerous air pollution. People in nations such as China and India do not believe that the industrialized Western peoples have any more right to consume the world's resources than they do, and they want their fair share.

Resolving problems of underdevelopment, and the poverty it brings, requires change within individual countries, such as implementing land reform, curbing corruption, and reducing bureaucratic obstacles to enterprise. Many experts have advocated bottom-up development that involves peasants, workers, and women, rather than bureaucratic elites, in decision making. Such decisions would include shaping policies that provide families with adequate economic security, hence reducing the desire among parents for many children to ensure their support in old age. The Grameen Bank in Bangladesh, which loans money to poor women, is an outstanding example of such a bottom-up policy.

International cooperation is hobbled because the leaders of rich and poor nations often disagree on how to address global inequality. For economic and strategic reasons, Western nations want to protect their access to and heavy consumption of resources such as oil and copper and also worry about trade competition from Newly Industrializing Nations. In democratic nations, these leaders have had to answer to voters, who fear compromising their own prosperity. Beginning in the 1970s, various conferences and movements have debated modifying

Protesting Global Warming This demonstration by environmental activists concerned with global warming—a potentially dangerous trend caused by burning fossil fuels such as coal that produces more carbon dioxide—took place in Turkey.

the world economic order by, for example, stabilizing world prices for natural resource exports, which chiefly come from developing nations, so that governments could better anticipate annual revenues. Responding to a worldwide campaign to help poor nations, in 2005, the industrialized nations canceled the burdensome debts of the poorest nations. Yet critics wondered whether poor nations with corrupt governments would use increased revenues wisely, while Western nations are often resistant to changes that could threaten their powerful position in the world economy.

Sustainable Environments

The decades since the mid-twentieth century were unusual for the intensity of environmental deterioration and the centrality of human effort in sparking it. The industrialized nations especially had become used to rapid economic growth and were dependent on abundant cheap energy and fresh water, needs that led to unparalleled environmental destruction. By the dawn of the twenty-first century, the challenge of a changing environment became obvious. On every continent, but especially in Eurasia and North America, gas-guzzling vehicles, smoky factories, coal-fired power plants, and large farming operations produce large amounts of carbon dioxide and other

pollutants, contributing to rising average temperatures that scientists call global warming. This climate change, if it continues, may have a catastrophic impact on human life. Problems such as global warming raise the question of whether the natural environment can maintain itself in the long term and support plant, animal, and human life—a pattern known as sustainability.

Societies and Environmental Change

Human activity has altered environments since prehistory, sometimes with catastrophic results. Environmental collapse triggered by agricultural practices or deforestation helped undermine the Mesopotamians, Romans, and Maya, among others. But modern industrial societies and rapidly growing populations encroach on their natural settings even more heavily. Between the 1890s and the 1990s, the world economy grew fourteen times larger, industrial output twenty times, energy use fourteen times, carbon dioxide emissions seventeen times, water use nine times, and marine fish catches thirty-five times. These increases contributed to, among other pressing problems, air and water pollution, disposal of hazardous waste, declining genetic diversity in crops, and a mass extinction of plant and animal species. With their heavy economic production and consumption, people today are borrowing from tomorrow.

The atmosphere faces particular dangers, including a measurable warming. Earth's climate changed little, with only minor fluctuations, between the last Ice Age, which ended 10,000 years ago, and the end of the eighteenth century, when the Industrial Revolution began in Europe, but it has been changing fast over the past two centuries. Since 1985, the world has experienced the highest average annual temperatures on record and unprecedented droughts. Scientists now largely agree that global warming has been increasing, although they debate its causes and dangers. Without major efforts to curb warming, scientists forecast a rise of somewhere between an alarming 2.5 and a catastrophic 10.4 degrees by 2100, which, if it happens, will change human life dramatically.

Scientists speak of a Greenhouse Effect, the overheating of earth from human-made pollutants. The main culprits are gases such as carbon dioxide, chlorofluorocarbons, and methane, which accumulate in the atmosphere and trap heat. The amount of heat-trapping carbon dioxide in the atmosphere increased by one-third between 1900 and 2000, mostly from burning coal and oil. The greenhouse gases come largely from factory smokestacks, coal-fired power plants, and gasoline-powered vehicle exhausts. The United States accounts for some 25 percent of the carbon dioxide and up to 50 percent of the other polluting chemicals. Europe, Russia, Japan, and China produce much of the rest. Some pollutants also destroy the ozone layer, a gaseous region in the upper atmosphere that protects humans from the cancer-causing ultraviolet rays of the sun. Scientists discovered that the ozone depletion rate in the 1990s was twice as fast as was thought a decade earlier.

In the pessimistic scenarios, the consequences of rising temperatures for many of the world's peoples are devastating. Earth gets baked, rich farmland turns to desert, and forests wilt. Fresh water, already scarce, becomes even harder to find as lakes and streams dry up. Rising ocean temperatures damage fisheries and kill most protective coral reefs while also increasing the intensity of hurricanes. Tropical and subtropical nations find agriculture and life generally more difficult. In North America, farming becomes tougher in the southern United States, though more productive in a warming Canada.

Some peoples might face even more daunting challenges. Global warming has reduced the ice covering the Arctic Ocean by half in recent years, while thawing the adjacent land; these developments diminish the habitat for cold-adapted animals, such as polar bears, and threaten the livelihood and settlements of Arctic peoples. At the other end of the world, the West Antarctic ice shelf holds a vast amount of water, and in some places has already begun to melt. If this trend accelerates, it will raise sea levels enough over the next two centuries to cover much low-lying coastal land. This will have disastrous consequences for regions such as the U.S. Gulf Coast and Florida, the Low Countries of northwest Europe, Bangladesh and eastern India, and small island nations already now barely above sea level, including Tonga, Tuvalu, the Bahamas, and the Maldives.

Environmental Issues and Movements

The exploitation of the earth's resources for human benefit, which has accelerated since 1945, has undermined sustainability. While soil, forests, and fisheries are renewable resources if properly managed, mineral resources such as oil and copper cannot be replaced once they are used up. Oil experts disagree as to when all known recoverable oil reserves will become exhausted. Anticipating future resource and energy shortages, experts have for years recommended that industrial nations conserve oil by reducing dependence on it as the main fuel while developing renewable energy resources, such as solar, tidal, and wind power. Some nations have turned toward building more nuclear power plants, which are expensive and potentially dangerous but do less damage to the climate than burning fossil fuels. So far a few developing nations and some European countries have shown the most commitment to conservation and developing renewable energies.

Scientific conclusions about global warming and the need to reduce dependence on oil have often challenged powerful economic interests and upset governments that favor economic growth and worry about economic competition from rival nations. For example, since the 1970s, U.S. presidents and Congress, fearing possible negative effects on U.S. business, have often opposed environmental agreements, such as the Kyoto treaty of 1997, which was an effort, supported by most of the world's nations, to begin reducing greenhouse gases, as well as a European proposal seeking a 15 percent alternative energy use by 2010 (versus 1 percent today). Leaders of a few other powerful nations, including Japan, Russia, Britain, and China, have also been reluctant to cooperate with the world community on environmental issues. In 2005, 150 nations met in Montreal, Canada, and reaffirmed their commitment to the Kyoto treaty. To sustain environmental health, a Canadian statesman has argued, requires a "revolution in [our] thinking as basic as the one introduced by Copernicus who [in the 1500s] first pointed out that the earth was not the center of the universe."[6]

An environmental movement began in the West in the late nineteenth century, eventually sparking similar movements around the world. By the 1970s, organizations such as Greenpeace, Earth First!, and the Rainforest Action Network pressed for a global commitment to stop environmental destruction. In 1992, a UN–sponsored global conference in Rio de Janeiro issued a proclamation urging sustainable development: "Human beings are entitled to a healthy and productive life in harmony with nature."[7] But the realities of modern politics, national rivalries, and fierce economic competition continue to make such a change difficult.

Global Pasts and Futures

The study of history helps us understand today's news and views as they are reported in daily newspapers, broadcast on radio and television, and disseminated online. Historians often describe their work as involving a dialogue between past, present, and future. A few years ago, French scientist René Dubos argued: "The past is not dead history. It is living material out of which makes the present and builds the future."[8] Current global problems have their roots in the patterns of world history. While seeking to understand how the past shaped the present, historians also speculate on how current trends may shape the future.

Understanding the Global Past

World historians offer several ways of understanding the world of yesterday, today, and tomorrow. One view is that contacts and collisions between different societies produce change. Whether through peaceful exchange or warfare or perhaps both, when societies encounter other societies, they are exposed to different customs and ideas. Around two thousand years ago, thanks to advances in transportation and growing economies, increasingly mobile peoples began to encounter others far away, laying the roots for a global system to emerge after 1450. Historians also emphasize continuity, the persistence of social, cultural, political, and religious ideas and patterns, as well as change, the transformations in ways of life, work, and thought. Continuities are common. For example, many Christians, Muslims, Jews, Buddhists, and Hindus still look at the world through the prism of traditional religious values that were forged millennia ago and are still meaningful today. For instance, Islam increased its following from 400 million people in 1960 to 1.3 billion by 2004.

Yet changes, too, are everywhere. Thus most people, among them the devout followers of the old religions, also engage in activities, face challenges, and use forms of transportation and communication that were nonexistent a few generations ago. As a result, missionaries and clerics often use radio, television, and the Internet to spread their message. Another insight offered by global historians is that great transitions, such as the agricultural and industrial revolutions or, more recently, the rise of high technology, can turn history in new directions.

As a result of the spread of Western cultural influences, market economies, economic consumption practices, and individualistic values, some scholars see a growing standardization of the world's societies. Many people welcome this standardization as a sign of progress, whereas others perceive it as a threat to local traditions. Still others consider the claim that societies and cultures are standardizing inaccurate, seeing instead a real increase in differences, especially the growing gap between rich and poor nations. In fact, living standards in the world have not been standardized. While people in the rich countries usually own several expensive electrical appliances, from washing machines to plasma televisions, millions of people in the poor nations do not even have electricity. Still, thanks to contacts between distant societies, the Western value of materialistic indulgence has became common, even if it is often out of reach for the poorest half of the world's people.

The experiences of most societies over the past half century reveal a mix of change and continuity. For example, Western ideas have gained even greater influence in the world since 1945 than they had before. People in different lands have adopted Western ideas of government, such as constitutions and elections, although not necessarily the substance of democracy, along with Western-rooted ideologies and faiths: capitalism, socialism, nationalism, and Christianity. Western pop culture, from rock music to soft drinks and blue jeans, has spread widely, leading to the "Coca-Colazation" of the world stemming from Western economic power, including advertising. Yet influences from the West are usually strongest in large cities and penetrate less deeply into the villages in Africa, Asia, and the Middle East, where traditional ways reflect continuity with the past. As a result, city youth in Malaysia or Tanzania may follow the latest recordings from Western pop stars, but these recordings may be unknown to their rural counterparts. Yet the urban youth may also share with rural youth traditional views about family and faith, and rural youth may, like their city counterparts, own motorcycles, boom boxes, and cell phones that make their lives different from those of their parents.

As a result of the transition to globalizing technology, culture, and commerce, the contacts between societies and their interdependence have vastly increased since 1945. In different ways, nuclear weapons, multinational corporations, earth-circling satellites, World Cup soccer, and cable news networks draw people together, willingly or not. Closer contact, of course, does not necessarily mean friendly relations and a less dangerous world; it can also bring collisions. Guided missiles and planes carrying bombs can reach 10,000 miles from their base. Terrorist plots hatched in Afghanistan by Islamic militants who blame the United States for Middle Eastern problems killed Americans in New York City and Washington, D.C., in 2001. Some of the terrorists involved in planning or carrying out those and other attacks were once secular Muslims who went to Europe or the United States for college and, culturally disoriented and resentful of Western policies, became Islamic militants and then joined a terrorist organization with global reach and access to high technology such as satellite phones, computers, and the Internet.

The same technologies that allow people to instantly access and share information around the world also allows governments to spy on citizens and criminals to use cyberspace for their own purposes. Meanwhile, hackers can live anywhere and disrupt computer operations all over the world. Technology also threatens governments. In 2005, the search engine company, Google, made available a program, Google Earth, that can be freely downloaded and allows a user anywhere to see aerial and satellite photos of any location in the world. Governments from Algeria to India to Russia protested unsuccessfully that this violated their laws and revealed data, such as the layout of military bases, that they did not want available to the general public.

The contacts, changes, and transitions since 1945 have created a global village, a single community of exchange and interaction. In some regions, even remote villages have become part of this global village. By the 1960s, for example, people living in the once-isolated interior of the island of Borneo, divided between Indonesia and Malaysia, could access the outside world through battery-powered transistor radios and cassette players, and also by means of visiting traders, Christian missionaries, and government officials. Borneo's interior people also often left their remote villages to find work at logging camps, oil wells, or plantations as their rain forest environment and small farms rapidly disappeared, destroyed by international timber and mining operations that cut forests and stripped land. As once-remote peoples, like those in the Borneo interior, are brought into the global system, and ethnic minorities are incorporated into nations, they find it harder to maintain their cultures and languages. Half of all languages are in danger of dying out over the next several decades, and less than 1 percent of languages are used on the Internet.

Toward the Future

In 1974, the American economic historian Robert Heilbroner, asking what promise the future holds, doubted the permanence of modern industrial society and even democracy in the face of population explosion, environmental degradation, resource depletion, militarization, and the increasing economic desperation of people in the poorest countries. Heilbroner believed most people are not willing to sacrifice for the good of future generations. Like him, other experts often despair. The world's long history of war, inequality, and exploitation, even when seemingly offset by progress, does not foster optimism. Indeed, some respected experts predict human extinction if people do not adopt more sustainable ways, and scientific studies are more frequently pessimistic than optimistic about the future. One environmental analysis concludes: "Our generation is the first to be faced with decisions that will determine whether the earth our children inherit will be habitable."[9]

Yet, since World War II, humanity has produced many green shoots of hope. Western Europe moved rapidly to political and economic unity, defusing centuries of conflict. Eastern Europeans and Russians overturned dogmatic communist regimes, ending the long Cold War between the superpowers. The Scandinavian nations, one hundred years ago among the poorest European societies,

International Women's Day 2005 Women around the world became more willing to assert their rights. Activists from diverse Indian nongovernmental organizations who were interested in women's rights marched in New Delhi, India's capital, in 2005 to mark International Women's Day.

have virtually eliminated poverty, achieving the world's highest quality of life. Several Asian nations rapidly developed, dramatically improving living standards and national wealth. A century ago desperately poor, China has become not only able to feed and clothe its huge population but also to export industrial products to the world.

Thanks in part to global efforts, black majority rule came to South Africa. More than two dozen nations, including some in Asia, Latin America, and the Caribbean, have elected women presidents or prime ministers, and women, making their voices heard, have increasingly gained more power over their lives in many countries. Despite some notable conflicts, wars have become less common than before. Unlike the Cold War years between 1946 and 1992, when fighting between and within nations was frequent, between 1992 and 2005, the number of wars with more than one thousandbattle deaths per year declined by 80 percent.

Hopeful developments have also resulted from international cooperation. A large majority of nations have signed agreements to ban weapons of mass destruction, punish genocide, and reduce gases contributing to global warming. Drastic reductions in the arms race have diminished the threat of nuclear war. United Nations agencies have improved lives for children and women in many countries and spurred cooperation on environmental issues. Local nongovernmental organizations, often with international connections, have also become active, working for the rights of women, children, workers, and peasants and for a healthier environment. Human rights groups with chapters around the world have worked courageously to promote civil liberties and the release of political prisoners. Encouraged by environmental activists abroad, brave tribal groups in tropical rain forests have resisted the logging and mining destroying their habitats. Not least in its effects, the growing information superhighway now instantly links millions of computers with people, libraries, and other information sources around the world.

A history not only of cruelty and exploitation but also of compassion and sacrifice provides hope in navigating troubled times. Remembering when people behaved magnificently may foster inspiration to answer the challenges. The contemporary age offers ample examples of inspiring people: democracy activists such as Nelson

United Nations (*http://www .un.org*). The pathway to the websites of the many United Nations agencies, operations, and ongoing projects.

Mandela, Vaclav Havel, Mohandas Gandhi, and Aung San Suu Kyi; social activists such as Wangari Maathai, Dr. Martin Luther King, Jr., Shirin Ebadi, and Mukhtaran Bibi; cultural figures such as Wole Soyinka, Violeta Parra, Simone de Beauvoir, and Cui Jian; and figures who have built links between societies such as Jean Monnet, Bono, and the Dalai Lama. Historians sometimes view the past as a stream with banks. The stream is filled with people killing, bullying, enslaving, and doing other things historians usually record, while on the banks, unnoticed, women and men build homes, raise children, tend farms, settle disputes, pray, sing songs, sculpt statues, trade with their neighbors, and chat with travelers from other lands. Historians often ignore the banks for the stream, but what happens on the banks may be more reassuring.

Some observers, believing that cultural differences will increasingly drive international politics, forecast a clash of civilizations, such as between the Christian West and Islam, which are seen as irreconcilably opposed in world-views. But simplistic formulas miss the complexity of the global order. None of the great religions and the cultures that they shaped are monolithic, the divisions among

Christians or Muslims, Westerners or Middle Easterners, being as great as their differences with other traditions. No cultures or religions have a monopoly on values such as peace, justice, charity, tolerance, public discussion, and goodwill. In any case, nations generally shape their foreign policies according to their national interests rather than ideology. Wars over resources, such as oil and water, some observers claim, are more likely to occur than wars over cultural differences.

Other observers doubt that, whatever the tensions, any titanic military struggle like the two world wars of the twentieth century is inevitable; they expect that the world will cooperate on major issues and tolerate different concepts of economics, government, God, morality, and society for years to come. Furthermore, thanks to the many available information sources, people can become informed about why past societies, such as the Mesopotamians and Maya, destroyed their environments and collapsed, and how countries blundered into wars or failed to develop cooperative relations with their neighbors that maintained peace. These insights, if acquired, may help people today to avoid repeating the mistakes of the past and construct a better future.

Four centuries ago, the English playwright William Shakespeare wrote that the past is prologue to the present. The study of world history allows us to ask questions about the global future, because we understand the changing patterns of the global past, including the building of societies, their interactions through networks, and the great transitions that reshaped humanity. The contemporary age has been marked by a complex mix of dividing and unifying forces, unique societies differing greatly in standards of living but linked into a global system of exchange. People today cannot yet know with certainty where the path will lead, but they can help build it.

Nineteenth-century British novelist Lewis Carroll (1832–1898) suggested a way of looking at the problem in his novel *Through the Looking Glass*, about Alice in Wonderland. Lost and perplexed in Wonderland, Alice asked the Cheshire Cat: "Would you tell me, please, which way I ought to go from here?" The enigmatic cat pondered the query for a

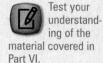

Test your understanding of the material covered in Part VI.

few moments and then replied: "That depends a great deal on where you want to get to."[10] Societies, working together, must chart that course into the future.

Suggested Reading

Baylis, John, et al., eds. *The Globalization of World Politics: An Introduction to International Relations*, 3rd ed. New York: Oxford University Press, 2004. Essays on world politics by British scholars.

Brown, Lester. *Plan B 2.0: Rescuing a Planet Under Stress and a Civilizaion in Trouble*. New York: W.W. Norton, 2006. A survey of the world's environmental and resource challenges and some possible solutions.

Hannerz, Ulf. *Transnational Connections: Culture, People, Places*. New York: Routledge, 1996. Interesting essays on cultures and networks in the age of globalization by a Swedish scholar.

Held, David, ed. *A Globalizing World? Culture, Economics, Politics*. New York: Routledge, 2000. An excellent collection of essays and readings on various aspects of globalization, compiled by British scholars.

Hobsbawm, Eric. *On the Edge of the New Century*. New York: The New Press, 1999. Thoughts on the past, present, and future by a British historian.

Kennedy, Paul. *Preparing for the Twenty-First Century*. New York: Random House, 1993. A study of how population, technology, and the environment shaped the contemporary world and various regions.

Mayor, Federico, and Jerome Bindé. *The World Ahead: Our Future in the Making*. New York: Zed Books, 2001. A comprehensive study, prepared by European scholars for the United Nations, of political, economic, social, cultural, and environmental trends.

Mazrui, Ali. *Cultural Forces in World Politics*. London: Heinemann, 1990. A challenging examination of world-views and patterns by a distinguished African scholar.

Newland, Kathleen, and Kamala Chandrakirana Soedjatmoko, eds. *Transforming Humanity: The Visionary Writings of Soedjatmoko*. West Hartford, CT: Kumarian Press, 1994.

Thoughtful essays on development, violence, religion, and other issues in the contemporary world by an influential Indonesian thinker.

Pieterse, Jan Nederveen, ed. *Global Futures: Shaping Globalization*. London: Zed Books, 2000. Provocative essays on world trends by scholars from around the world.

Sachs, Jeffrey. *The End of Poverty: Economic Possibilities for Our Time*. New York: Penguin, 2005. Controversial but stimulating discussion of global poverty issues.

Seager, Joni. *The Penguin Atlas of Women in the World*, revised and updated. New York: Penguin, 2003. Creative, indispensable examination of women around the world.

Sen, Amartya. *Identity and Violence: The Illusion of Destiny*. New York: W.W. Norton, 2006. Provocative critique by an India-born economist of the clash of civilizations idea.

Smith, Dan, and Ane Braein. *Penguin State of the World Atlas*, 7th ed. New York: Penguin, 2003. The latest edition of an invaluable map based reference providing an overview of world conditions.

State of the World. New York: W.W. Norton. Informative annual surveys of the world's environmental health that are published annually by the Worldwatch Institute in Washington, D.C.

Taylor, Timothy D. *Global Pop: World Music, World Markets*. New York: Routledge, 1997. A fine study of the world music industry and major musicians.

Index

American Empires. *See* Aztec Empire; Inca Empire

American Indians, North American, 370, 427, 434–435, 681; migration of, 2, 11, 12*(map)*; deaths/massacre of, 435, 528; disease and, 298, 305; intermarriage with Europeans, 440–441; lands of, 489, 490, 790; missionaries and, 432, 434, 438–439, 441, 481, 482; mound builders, 86, 100, 212–213, 297–298 *and map*; population decline, 413; relocations of, 526–527; British alliance with, 440, 441*(illus.)*; in Canada, 538, 539, 792; southwestern desert cultures, 296–297 *and map*; trade and contact, 294, 359; women in, 481; as First Nations, 430, 792

American Indians (Native Americans). *See also* Andean societies; Mesoamerica; as hunter-gatherers, 86; disease and, 370, 425, 427, 432, 435, 437, 479, 480*(illus.)*, 539; environment and movement of, 84–86; exploitation of, 447; forced labor of, 430, 439*(illus.)*; intermarriage by, 438, 481; as mineworkers, 442; as "Noble Savages," 383; egalitarian, 397; in Mexico, 533, 796; rural villages and, 535; in Latin America, 437, 438–439, 495, 497, 535, 796; as slaves, 440*(illus.)*

American Revolution, 488, 489–490; British colonialism and, 489, 677; Declaration of Independence, 489; France and, 490, 491, 522; Latin America and, 496; legacy of, 490; Patriots *vs.* Loyalists in, 489, 490

American Samoa, 692, 794

Americas (New World; Western Hemisphere). *See also* Andean region; Latin America; Mesoamerica; North America; South America; migrations to, 11, 12*(map)*, 84–86; extinction in, 20; agriculture in, 17, 19*(map)*; hunter-gatherers in, 14, 86; irrigation in, 20; chronology (40,000–600 B.C.E.), 85; Paleo-Indians in, 86; Eastern Hemisphere and, 84; migrations to, 84–86; exchange networks in, 72; Classical Era societies in, 197; spread of religious beliefs in, 223; trade and cultural contact in, 282, 360*(map)*; African slaves in, 292, 293; chronology (200 B.C.E.–1492 C.E.), 294; collapse of Classical era states in, 293–294; societies of, 293–298; European conquest of, 378; Dutch colonies in, 392; population of, 365; Spanish conquests in, 377*(map)*, 378, 445, 476; Columbus in, 353, 357; gunpowder empires in, 474; new food crops from, 374, 467, 479; slave trade in, 371, 413 *and map*, 414 *and illus.*;

origin of name, 430; Atlantic system and, 441; chronology (1650–1760), 441; Columbian exchange in, 435; silver from, 378, 463, 478; plantation slavery in, 444–446; Arab immigrants in, 562; Monroe Doctrine and, 527; European immigrants in, 517, 518*(map)*, 620; pop culture, 635, 759

Amharic language (Geez), 201, 291

Amharic people (Ethiopia), 201, 203, 407, 412

Amili, Baha al-Din Muhammad, 420

Amin, 461

Amin, Idi, 827

Amin, Qasim, 564

Amina of Zaria, 285, 405

Amistad (slave ship), 414

Amnesty International, 699, 715

Amon (Amon-Re), 49, 53, 54

Amorites, Babylonia and, 34

Amritsar (India): massacre in, 657; revolt (1983), 843; temple in, 453, 843

Amsterdam: stock exchange in, 372–373*(illus.)*; artists of, 395; as world trade hub, 378, 392, 475

Amur River Basin, 423, 476, 615

Analects (Confucius), 106, 107

Anasazi of American Southwest, 228, 296, 297*(map)*, 366, 427

Anatolia (modern Turkey), 69, 667. *See also* Ottoman Empire; Turkic (Turkish) peoples; Çatal Hüyük, 20*(illus.)*, 21, 22*(illus.)*; coinage in, 95; Indo-Europeans in, 23, 24*(map)*; Hittites in, 25, 34, 67, 96*(illus.)*; Lydia in, 127, 141; Persia and, 127, 195; Greeks in, 125, 127 (*See also* Ionian Greeks); Rome and, 177; Seljuk Turks in, 249, 347

Anaximander, 125

Ancestor worship, 439, 469; in China, 79, 114, 118; in Vietnam, 325; in Africa, 61, 205, 288, 291; Australian Aborigine, 215; in Japan, 275

Ancient foundation (4000–600 B.C.E.), 91–98; political, 95–96; social and cultural, 96–98; technological, 91–92, 93*(map)*; urban and economic, 92, 94–95

Andean societies, 2, 210, 359. *See also* Inca Empire; agriculture in, 18, 19*(map)*, 87; architecture of, 88; ceramics of, 88; Chavín, 89*(map)*, 91, 223; Chimu, 295–296; domesticated animals in, 20; human sacrifice in, 223; Moche, 211, 223; population of, 212; Tiwanaku, 100, 211–212, 223, 228, 293; mining in, 442

Andrade, Mario de, 675

Andrews, Emily Harding, 519*(illus.)*

An Duong (Vietnam), 166

Angkor Empire (Cambodia), 229; disintegration of, 323; kings of, 320, 321; slavery in, 363

Angkor Wat (Cambodia) temples, 321, 322*(illus.)*

Angles (Germanic tribe), 187

Anglicanism (Church of England), 383, 384*(map)*, 392, 393; Henry VIII and, 385; Methodism and, 520; in Africa, 554, 834

Anglo-Iranian Oil Company, 561

Anglo-Saxons, in England, 333

Angola, 687, 825; Portuguese and, 371; as Portuguese colony, 410, 415, 552, 553; queens of, 410, 411*(illus.)*; slaves from, 413*(map)*, 415; European colonialism in, 544, 650; Marxism in, 693; civil war in, 693, 831, 870

Angra Mainyu (demon-god), 130

Animals: *See also* Alpacas and llamas; Camels; Cattle; Horses; apes and primates, 7, 8; in cave paintings, 15*(illus.)*; domestication of, 5, 18, 19*(map)*, 20, 57; extinction of, 13; in Indus Valley, 39; sacrifice of, 238

Animism (spirit worship), 14, 98, 118; in Americas, 86; Shinto, in Japan, 122, 275; in Africa, 60, 204, 282, 284, 288, 291; in Korea, 120, 274; in Southeast Asia, 166, 168, 320, 323, 328; Islam and, 238, 282; in Melaka, 327; in Siam and Tibet, 362; on Java, 459; in Philippines, 459, 460; in Africa, 482, 546, 712, 816, 834; Islam and, 482, 546, 863

Anna Comnena, 348

Annan, Kofi, 701, 706

Anne Boleyn, 385

Antarctica, 539; global warming and, 872

Anthills of the Savannah (Achebe), 807

Anthony, Susan B., 685

Anticommunism, 632. *See also* Communism; Cold War, 695–696, 778; decolonization and, 692; Korean War and, 723, 782; McCarthyism, 779–780

Antigone (Sophocles), 226

Antigonids (Greece), 144 *and map*, 146

Antigua, 496

Anti-Semitism: *See also* Jews; in Europe, 386, 398, 505; in Nazi Germany, 638, 642; in Soviet Union, 630

Antwerp, 374, 375*(illus.)*; Bourse in, 373; Spanish sack of, 387

Anwar, Chairul, 837

Anwar, Zainab, 863

Anyang (China), 71, 76*(map)*, 77

Aotearoa, 541. *See also* New Zealand

Apache people, 528

Apartheid, in South Africa, 828–829, 832

Apes (primates), 7, 8

Apollo (god), 135; Delphic oracle and, 137

Appeasement: of fascists, 639, 640; of Japanese, 653

Aqueducts: Greek, 134; Roman, 174, 183; Aztec, 301

Aquinas, Thomas, 339, 346

Aquino, Corazon (Philippines), 859, 860, 865

Aquitane (France), 354(map)

Arab armies: See also Armed forces, Islamic expansion and; in Afghanistan, 237, 314; conquest of, 229; Tang China and, 258(map), 262

Arab empires. See Caliphates (Arab Caliphates); Sasanid Empire

Arab Human Development Report, 821

Arabia (Arabian Peninsula), 28, 416, 560. See also Saudi Arabia; camel domestication in, 23; beginnings of Islam in, 195; Wahhabism in, 563–564; revolt in, 666

The Arabian Nights, 241

Arabic alphabet, 246

Arabic language, 29, 247, 562, 714; in Africa, 288, 291, 292, 401; Quran and, 234, 246; spread of, 237, 238, 254

Arabic numerals, 162, 356

Arabic script, 246, 247, 254; African languages in, 285, 288; Urdu in, 318

Arab-Israeli conflict, 687, 811–814, 813(map), 818; suicide bombers in, 716–717

Arab League, 818(map), 821

Arab nationalism, 485, 563, 666; roots of, 566–567; in Syria, 667; in Egypt, 670, 687, 808–809; Zionism and, 671, 810

Arabs (Arab nations). See also specific nations; rise of, 194–195; in Sassanian Persia, 194–195, 237; Nabataean, 194–195; pastoral nomadism in, 194; Aksum and, 201; in East Africa, 288; in Hausa states, 285; navigation skill of, 249, 366; lateen sails of, 356; Greek thought and, 336; technology of, 376; mathematics of, 376, 381; in East Africa, 406; Omani, 411, 416, 474, 478, 545; slave trade and, 411, 415, 545; Ottomans and, 419, 558, 666; in Morocco, 422; trade routes of, 477(map); Christians, 558, 562, 566; immigrants to Americas, 562; Palestinian, 567, 671, 672, 810; Westernization and, 671; Gulf War and, 700; folk music (rai) of, 818; uprising by, 622, 666, 672; African farmers and, in Sudan, 816; in France, 775, 867

Arab traders (merchants):405, 478. See also Muslims, traders and merchants; in Europe, 162; in Africa, 205, 281, 284, 287, 289, 366; Islam and, 235; Muhammed as, 232–233; in Korea,

273; African slave trade and, 292, 339; in India, 317

Arafat, Yasser, 810, 812

Aragon (Iberia), 343

Aral Sea, drying of, 763 and illus.

Aramaic language, 129

Ara Pacis (Altar of Peace), 181(illus.)

Aratta (Mesopotamia), 31

Arawak-speaking people: Taino, 428–430; voyages of, 429(map); women, 428(illus.)

Archers. See Bows and arrows (archers)

Arches, Roman use of, 174

Archimedes, 145

Architecture. See also Construction materials and techniques; Housing; and specific types of buildings (e.g. pyramids, temples); Sumerian, 30, 31; Egyptian, 52; Mesoamerican, 88; Olmec, 89; Chavín, 90; Persian, 127; Southeast Asian, 166; Roman, 183; Aksumite, 201; Tiwanaku, 211–212; Islamic, 244 and illus., 247; Toltec, 294; Arab, in East Africa, 288; Pagan, 320; Angkor, 312, 322(illus.); Islamic, in Africa, 405(illus.); Ottoman, 418; Indo-Islamic, 453; Siamese, 475; in British India, 577; Russian, 348(illus.); skyscrapers, in Kuala Lumpur, 864(illus.)

Arctic peoples, 17; autonomy for, 792 and map; global warming and, 872

Argentina: African slavery in, 444; colonial, 442, 495; cattle ranching in, 442; European immigration to, 535, 681; independence of, 496, 497, 498(map); tango in, 535; dictatorship in, 532, 672; Great Depression in, 649; mothers' protests in, 777–778; under Peron, 795–796; pragmatic leftists in, 797; economy in, 686, 803

Aristarchus, 145

Aristocracy (nobility). See also Upper class (elites); Landowners; Sumerian, 30; Egyptian, 54; Chinese, 77, 78, 79, 110; Korean, 120, 273; Persian, 131; Greek, 133, 134; Hellenistic era, 144; Vietnamese, 165; Roman patricians, 174; Byzantine, 192; Aksumite, 201; Mande, 204; Maya, 208; Arab merchants, 235; Japanese, 274, 275, 277, 278; Yoruba, 286; Kongo, 293; military, in India, 308; Tibetan, 314; Aztec, 302; Hindu, in India, 318; on Java, 322, 328; Siamese, 324; English kings and, 343; European, 338, 375, 387; Lutheranism and, 383; Eastern European, 353, 379; Russian, 390, 614, 626, 627; English, 393; in Siam, 457, 660; Javanese, 462, 568–569(illus.), 662; French Revolution and, 491, 492; British India, 581; Burman, 585; Malay, 583; Latin American, 802

Aristophanes, 137

Aristotle, 22, 135, 218; Alexander and, 142, 155; science and, 136, 219; Islam and, 244, 247; European revival and, 346

Arizona, Pueblo peoples of, 212, 296

Arjuna, 45

Armed forces, United States. See also Military, United States; revolutionary, 490; in Hawaii, 530, 531; Indian wars and, 528; in Mexico, 527, 650; Philippine revolution and, 588; in Russian civil war, 627, 628(map); in World War I, 624; in Nicaragua, 536, 633, 651; in World War II, 642, 643–644 and map; in Yugoslavia, 698; in South Korea, 741, 742; in Caribbean, 797; in Vietnam War, 782, 783(illus.), 851–853 and map; Marines, in Lebanon, 816; in Middle East, 811(map), 820

Armed forces (soldiers; troops). See also Military; Navy; War; Warriors; Weapons and military technology; Mesopotamian, 30, 33, 95; Assyrian, 34, 35; Egyptian, 53; Chinese, 78, 96, 110, 111, 112, 119, 120; Greek, 133, 134, 140; Persian, 128, 140; Macedonian, 142; Mauryan India, 155, 156; Carthaginian, 176; of Alexander the Great, 127, 131; Roman, 146, 174, 175, 176, 177, 178, 181, 183, 184(illus.), 185, 220; Kushite, 198; Aksum and, 200; empires and, 220; Islamic expansion and, 194, 234, 237–238; Turkic, in Islam, 243; Aztec, 299; Crusades and, 250–251; gunpowder and, 252; Mongol, 243, 251, 317, 349, 364; Song China, 266; Timurid, 253, 318; Byzantine, 336; German, 335; Inca, 302; Indian, 308; Bulgar, 336, 347; Magyar, 336; Ottoman, 355; professional, in Europe, 388 and illus.; English civil war, 392; Moroccan, 404; Spanish, 431–433 and illus.; Safavid Persia, 420, 422; Aztec, 426; Chinese, 465, 613; Napoleonic wars, 493, 496; Portuguese, 449; French, 458, 543, 619; Siamese, 457, 458; Ottoman Janissaries, 418, 419, 558; Vietnamese, 569, 585; Boer War, 551; Zulu, 550; Egyptian, 559–560, 564; British, in Africa, 549; British India, 577; colonial Africa, 549, 555; Japanese, 471, 610; Mahdist, 543(illus.), 561; Mexican women, 533 and illus.; Chinese, 598, 601, 604; Russian, 557, 614–615, 617; World War I, 619, 621–622 and illus., 624; German, 624, 626; colonial, in World War I, 625, 648, 656–657, 664; Free French, 641(map), 644; Japanese, in World War II, 642, 643(map), 644,

662, 850; Nazi German, 638, 640–642 and map, 643–644; World War II, 640–644; Chinese warlords, 651; Italian, in Ethiopia, 650; Soviet (Red Army), 627, 642, 644, 645, 696, 769; Chinese (Red Army), 653, 654(map), 655 and illus., 719, 720, 723, 728; Iranian conscripts, 669; British, in Middle East, 666, 670; Latin America, 672; Japanese, 734; United Nations peacekeepers, 699 and illus., 772; Warsaw Pact, 766; Congolese, 824; Indian, 843; Indonesian revolution, 856; Pakistani, 839; Vietnam War, 851

Armenia (Armenians), 128, 667; merchants, 419, 479; in Ottoman Empire, 416, 418, 419, 420; Ottoman slaughter of, 558, 666; Christianity in, 254, 418, 421, 561, 666, 765, 769; in Persia, 420–421, 479; Russia and, 615, 629

Armor, body: Hyksos, 53; Roman, 177; Spanish conquistador, 425

Armored tanks, 622, 684

Arrhenius, Svante, 521

Arrow War (1856–1860), 597–598, 599(map), 615

Ars Pacis (Atlar of Peace), 181(illus.)

Art and artists. See also Painters and painting; rock art, 5(illus.), 10–11; clay seals, in India, 39 and illus.; Mesopotamian mosaic, 33(illus.); Nok (Nigeria), 60(illus.); Jomon Japan, 84(illus.); Olmec heads, 90 and illus.; Dutch, 372–373(illus.), 395, 455(illus.); Gandhara, 158; European Renaissance, 381–382, 383(illus.); Buddhist temple, 163(illus.); Meroë, 198; French, 388(illus.), 389, 397(illus.); Australian Aborigine, 215; Chinese, 117, 257, 263(illus.); Korean, 274; Italian, 381, 395; Japanese, 275, 279, 473 and illus, 607; African, 292; Hohokam, 296; Aztec, 301(illus.), 302; Chola India, 317(illus.); Angkor, 321; Mughal India, 453; Italian Renaissance, 355; in Ottoman Empire, 418; Persian, 363(illus.), 420, 421(illus.); realism in, 520; Chinese, 465, 466(illus.), 726 and illus.,728; socialist realism, 630; Yoruba, 556, 676(illus.); Mexican, 646–647(illus.); Iraqi, 819(illus.)

Artemesia of Halicarnassus, 128

Arthur legend, 347

Artillery, 474. See also Cannon; Ottoman, 419; Spanish, 432; Moroccan, 423; Mughal India, 453; in World War I, 621, 622

Artisans. See Craftspeople (artisans) and specific crafts

Aryabhata (Indian mathematician), 162

Aryabhata (satellite), 849

Aryans, 41–46, 95, 96; Vedas and, 41–42, 43; Indo-Aryan synthesis, 43–46; migrations of, 37(map), 41; religion of, 42–43; society of, 42; in South India, 159; in Sri Lanka, 159; metallurgy and, 93(map); Nazi Germany and, 638

Asceticism, 152, 153, 564. See also Buddhist; Christian monasteries

ASEAN (Association of Southeast Asia Nations), 865

Ashante kingdom, 474, 485, 676, 677; conflict with British, 549; slave trade and, 371, 413(map), 415, 475

Ashikaga shogunate (Japan), 279, 364, 471

Ashoka, 157–158 and illus., 159, 160; Buddhism of, 157, 220

Ashoka column, 157(illus.)

Ashur (Assyria), 34

Ashurbanipal, 35; library of, 34

Ashwari, Hannan, 716–717

Asia (Asians). See also Central Asia; East Asia; Eurasia; South Asia; Southeast Asia; spread of Buddhism in, 161(map); American silver in, 442; merchants, 454–455, 481, 550; Europeans and, 450; United States and, 530, 779; Western colonialism in, 508, 510; radical nationalism in, 650; World War II in, 643(map); new world economy and, 701–702; industrialization in, 703, 754; population growth in, 708(map), 709; decolonization in, 750; Australian trade and, 794; world trade and, 866

Asia Minor. See Western (southwestern Asia)

Asian immigrants, 680, 681–683 and map; in Australia, 540; in Latin America, 535; in East Africa, 552; as plantation workers, 531, 681, 683; in European parliaments, 758; in United States, 789

Aslan, Reza, 822

Aspasia, 137

Aspelta (Kush), 59 and illus.

Assembly: Sumerian, 95; Greek, 132, 133, 134; Centuriate (Rome), 174, 175; Netherlands, 392; Swedish, 393; colonial America, 489; Chinese, 604

Assembly-line production, 503

Assimilation. See Cultural assimilation

Assyrian Empire: administration of, 34, 35, 128; conquests of, 34–35, 68, 96; Egypt and, 54, 59; Israel and, 64, 65; metallurgy and, 93(map); Persian Empire and, 126

Astrolabe (navigation device), 376

Astrology, 95

Astronomy: Stone Age megaliths, 17, 23; Olmec, 89; Zapotec, 210; Greek, 158; Indian, 158, 162, 219, 311–312; Chinese, 115, 261, 264, 469, 470; Maya, 208–209; observatories, 17, 210, 248, 251, 273, 475; Korean, 273,

276, 277(illus.); European, 381, 396; Ottoman, 418

Aswan, 52; High Dam at, 809

Ataturk, Kemal (Turkey), 667, 669 and illus.

Atheism, in Soviet Union, 630

Athena (goddess), 134, 139(illus.)

Athens, 101. See also City-states, Greek (polis); Acropolis, 139 and illus.; Delian League and, 139; drama and literature of, 136–137; intellectual life of, 135–136; Macedonia and, 140, 142; navy of, 138, 139, 140, 141; Peloponnesian War and, 132(map), 138, 139–140(map); Persian Wars and, 138; politics in, 133–134; trade of, 140, 141

Atlantic, European exploration of, 376, 377(map), 427. See also Columbus, Christopher

Atlantic system (Atlantic economy): African slave trade in, 402, 410, 413(map), 414–415, 441–447; Columbian exchange, 435, 479–480; impact of, 446–447; Latin America and, 442, 444; North America and, 443(map), 445, 447; plantation zone and, 444–445 and illus.; slave life and African-American culture, 445–446

Atomic bomb: See also Nuclear weapons; in World War II, 643(map), 644, 645(illus.), 684, 697, 734; United States and, 695, 697; of China, 723, 727; in France and United Kingdom, 752(map); Soviet, 752(map), 761, 762

Atomic energy, 521

Aton (sun-god), 54

Attila the Hun (calypso singer), 685

Attila the Hun (conquerer), 187

Audiencias (courts) in Spanish America, 436

Augsburg Confession, 383

Augustine of Hippo, 190

Augustus Caesar (Octavian), 181(illus.), 183; Cleopatra and, 177–178

Aung San, 861

Aung San Suu Kyi, 715, 862, 865, 875

Aurangzeb (Mughal India), 451, 453–454

Auschwitz death camp, 642

Australia, 197, 537(map), 539; early humans in, 3, 10, 11, 12(map); hunter-gatherers of, 14, 17; Aborigines of, 92, 213, 214–215, 540, 793; Eurasian biota in, 480; Britain and, 510, 540, 793; foreigners in, 737; gold rush in, 514–515(illus.), 540; European settlers in, 485, 681, 792; immigration to, 514(illus.), 517, 518(map), 620, 785; China and, 731, 793(illus.); church decline in, 714; links to Asia, 540, 687, 792, 793–794; quality of life in, 694, 787, 793; in World War II, 644

Australopithecines (hominids), 8, 9(illus.)

(Nubia), 198; in Maya, 208; in China, 270

Batista, Fulgencio (Cuba), 672

Baule people of Ivory Coast, 555

Bay of Pigs invasion (Cuba, 1961), 799

Beans, 79, 87, 105, 211, 212, 293, 337

Beatles (musical group), 759, 765, 791

Bede (English theologian), 343

Bedouin tribes of North Africa, 232, 234, 564

Bedreddin, Seyh, 419

Beermaking, 18, 97

Beethoven, Ludwig von, 520

Beijing, 263, 465(illus.), 466, 598, 603, 604; Jesuits in, 469; Forbidden City, 719, 722(illus.); as Mongol capital, 267; Nixon in, 725; fast-food restaurants in, 867

Beijing Massacre (1989), 728

Beijing University, 651, 652

Beirut, Lebanon, 562; civil war in, 816

Belgian colonies. See also Belgian Congo; in 1913, 512(map); in Africa, 511, 512(map), 554; independence of, 691(map)

Belgian Congo, 547, 548(map). See also Congo; rubber plantations in, 554, 555 and illus.; rival ethic groups in, 553, 648; forced labor in, 554–555

Belgium, 678. See also Flanders; Antwerp, 373, 374, 375(illus.); Catholicism in, 387, 520; Habsburgs and, 504; industrialization in, 502; World War I in, 622, 623(map); quality of life in, 694, 830; monarchy in, 748; European Community and, 753

Belisarius, 191

Belize (British Honduras), 673(map)

Bell, Gertrude, 670

Bellini, Giovanni, 381, 418

Bells of Marquies, 97(illus.)

Benares (Varanasi), 154, 155, 313

Benedictines (religious order), 190, 333

Benedict of Nursia, 190

Benefices (land grants), 338

Bengal (Bengalis), 313, 451, 455, 479. See also Bangladesh; British and, 456, 571–572; famine in, 659; merchants of, 452; Muslims in, 581, 582, 658, 838; nationalism in, 841; opium in, 597

Bengali language, 42, 318

Benin, 283(map), 286–287, 371, 405, 415, 416; bronze artistry of, 286, 287(illus.), 406(illus.)

Benjamin of Tudela, 241

Benz, Karl, 521

Berbers, 57, 422, 562; Egypt and, 51; camels and, 60; caravan trade and, 60, 204, 292; Carthage and, 176; attack on Ghana by, 284

Berenicke (Egypt), 149, 226

Bergen-Belsen death camp, 642

Bering Strait land bridge, 11, 12(map), 85

Berlin: airlift to (1948), 751; immigrants in, 758; population of, 517

Berlin Conference (1884–1885), 547, 549

Berlin Wall, 764; dismantling of, 746–747(illus.), 771, 772

Bernhardt, Sarah, 519

Bernini, Gianlorenzo, 395

Bernstein, Eduard, 508

Berry, Chuck, 759, 791

Berry, Thomas, 5

Beverley, Robert, 440

Bhagavad Gita, 44, 45, 151, 152

Bhakti Hinduism, 312–313, 318, 452–453

Bhangra (Indian folk music), 759

Bharata tribe (India), 42

Bharatha Janata (BJP, India), 844, 846

Bhaskara, 311

Bhutto, Benazir, 847

Bhutto, Zulkifar Ali, 847

Bibi, Mukhtaran, 716, 875

Bible, the (Hebrew Bible), 63–64, 92, 140, 201, 223; garden of Eden in, 17, 98; creation story (Genesis), 6, 20–21, 36, 98; linear view of history in, 65–66; Greek translation, 144–145; New Testament (Gospels), 187; gender stereotypes in, 341; in Slavic languages, 349; of Gutenberg, 356; Luther's translation of, 383; literal interpretation of, 714

Biermann, Wolf, 766

Big Bang theory, 6

Big business. See also Corporations; capitalism and, 380, 467; monopoly and, 503, 529; in United States, 529, 788; in Japan, 639, 735; in Brazil, 799; in Cambodia, 854

Biko, Stephen, 829

Bill of Rights (England, 1689), 393, 492

Bill of Rights (United States, 1792), 490, 506, 522

Bini people (Benin), 286–287, 290

Bin Laden, Osama, 717, 815. See also Al Qaeda; in Afghanistan, 784, 819, 820

Biological weapons, 699

Bipedalism, hominids and, 8

Birmingham (England), 754; industrialization in, 500, 502(map)

Birth control, 14, 183, 835. See also Abortion; Catholics and, 709, 757, 760; contraceptives for, 707, 757; in Europe, 519, 632; women's movement and, 757; in Japan, 632, 737; in China, 709, 730; in India, 846

Birthrate, decline in, 709; in Europe, 775; in India, 842; in Japan, 737; in South Korea, 742; in Soviet Union, 765

Bishops, 342, 385; councils of, 189, 355; of Rome, 189, 193, 332, 348 (See also

Papacy); doctrinal consensus of, 224; appointment of, 333, 343; corruption of, 355

Bismarck, Otto von (Germany), 505

Bison (buffalo) hunting, 15(illus.), 86, 435, 528

Black Death, 251–252, 266, 479. See also Plague; in Europe, 229, 269, 350, 352(illus.), 365

Black empowerment, 689

Black Hand (Bosnian Serb group), 621

Black Hole of Calcutta, 571

Black Legend, Spanish colonials and, 437, 439

Black Orpheus (film), 804

Black Robes, 434. See also Jesuit missionaries

Black Sea region, 67; Greek colonies in, 125, 131, 132(map), 140, 141; Ottomans and, 417; plague in, 251, 365; Russia and, 390, 423, 481, 557 and map, 615; trade in, 356; Vikings in, 335

Blackshirts (Italian fascists), 636

Black Zion movement, 556

Blair, Tony, 775

Blake, William, 517

Blues (music), 446

Boat people (Vietnamese refugees), 854

Boats and boatbuilding, 92. See also Canoes; Ships and shipping; Ainu, 84; Pacific coast Indians, 86; Chinese, 114; Viking, 335 and illus.; colonial cash crops and, 649(illus.)

Bocaccio, Giovanni, 355

Bodhisattva(s), 160

Body armor, 53, 177; Spanish conquistador, 425

Body hair, 10

Body tattooing, 217

Boers (South Africa), 412–413, 550–551, 552(illus.)

Boer War (1899–1902), 550

Bolivar, Simon, 496–497 and illus., 499, 535, 677

Bolivarian Revolution, in Venezuela, 797

Bolivia: Spanish conquest of, 432; independence of, 497, 498(map); Indians of, 442, 796; silver mines in, 442, 476; regional wars and, 531; poverty in, 868

Bollywood (Indian) films, 846–847

Bologna (Italy) University, 346

Bolsheviks, 626–627 and illus., 650, 762. See also Communist Party (Soviet Union)

Bombay (Mumbai), 844; British in, 456, 571; globalization protest in, 688–689(illus.); population growth in, 709; film industry in, 846–847; terrorism in, 849

Bombs and bombing: *See also* Atomic bombs; Chinese, 278; British, in China, 597; in World War I, 621; in World War II, 640, 643*(map)*, 644, 645*(illus.)*, 662, 664, 732, 861; of Guernica, 639; Italian, in Ethiopia, 650; in Iraq, 670, 820; land mines, 696; in Lebanon, 816; NATO air strikes, 772; terrorist, 716–717, 749*(illus.)*, 750, 858; in Israeli-Arab conflict, 716–717, 810, 812; in Vietnam War, 853; of Cambodia, by United States, 854

Bondu kingdom (West Africa), 401

Bonhoeffer, Dietrich, 642

Boniface (missionary), 333

Boniface VIII, Pope, 345

Bono (U2 pop singer), 712, 875

Bon (Tibetan folk religion), 313

Bookkeeping, 22

Book of Changes (Yijing), 80

Book of Songs (China), 74

Book of the Dead, Egyptian, 55

Books, 404. *See also* Libraries; Literacy; burning of, in China, 110; in China, 80, 264; Maya codex, 207*(illus.)*, 209, 437; Timbuktu, 285; Aztec codex, 302, 433*(illus.)*; Buddhist, 307; encyclopedias, 247, 261, 271, 276

Borneo, 81, 82, 83*(map)*, 165; British colony in, 583, 664; Dutch control of, 583; in global system, 874; Islam in, 327 *and map*; Sabah and Sarawak, 583, 856*(map)*, 863

Bornu (West Africa), 283*(map)*

Borobodur (Java) temple mountain, 322

Borrowing, by Japanese, 274, 473, 606, 734. *See also* Cultural assimilation

Bosch, Juan, 783

Bose, Subhas Chandra, 659

Bosnia-Herzegovina, 621; ethnic conflict in, 772, 773*(map)*

Bosnian Serbs, 621, 698, 772, 773*(map)*

Bosporus, Straits of, 138, 423

Boston, 528; colonial, 445, 447, 489

Boston Tea Party, 489

Botswana (Southern Africa), 831

"Bottom-up" development, 870

Boudica (Celts), 185

Bourbon dynasty (France), 387, 394*(map)*, 491, 493

Bourgeoisie, 379, 508, 509. *See also* Middle class

Bourse market (Antwerp), 373

Bows and arrows (archers): Stone Age, 5*(illus.)*, 13; Aryan, 41; Chinese, 77; Roman crossbows, 177; American Indian, 213, 298, 684; Kushite, 198; Mongol, 267; English longbow, 353; in Congo, 684

Boxer Rebellion (China), 603

Boycotts. *See* Economic sanctions (boycotts; embargo)

Brahma (god), 46, 152, 312

Brahmanas (Hindu commentaries), 46

Brahmans (Hindu priests), 44, 220, 319, 452, 453, 581; as landowners, 152; oral traditions and, 41, 46, 312; as court advisors, 308; education and, 312; Nehru and, 840; in Southeast Asia, 166, 320, 321, 324

Brain, human evolution and, 7, 8, 10

Brain drain, in Africa, 835

Brandt, Willy (Germany), 749, 751

Brazil: independence of, 497, 498*(map)*, 499; monarchy in, 498*(map)*, 499, 532; Afro-Brazilians, 535, 536; slavery in, 532; coffee in, 445, 534, 535; European immigration to, 535; slavery outlawed in, 544; Japanese in, 535, 683; music and dance of, 535–536, 675; Great Depression in, 672; modernism in, 674; rubber in, 534, 701; pragmatic leftists in, 797; United States and, 697, 797; World Social Forum in, 715; dictatorship and democracy in, 672, 686, 798–799; liberation theology in, 803; rich-poor gap in, 705 *and illus.*, 802, 804; global system and, 805; culture of, 804; economic growth in, 869; rain forests of, 799, 867

Brazil, colonial: African slavery in, 410, 413*(map)*, 444.445–446, 495–496, 681; Afro-Brazilians, 495–496; cattle ranching in, 442; creoles in, 436; gold from, 442; maroon societies in, 446; mulattos in, 436, 481; Native peoples of, 427; Portuguese and, 377*(map)*, 430, 433, 436, 499; sugar plantations in, 433, 444, 445

Brazilwood (textile dye), 433

Brest-Litovsk, Treaty of (1918), 623*(map)*, 627

Bretton Woods Conference (1944), 645, 753

Brezhnev, Leonid, 762

Brezhnev Doctrine, 764

Bridges: land bridges, 11, 12*(map)*, 16, 85; in imperial China, 261, 263*(illus.)*, 264; in Inca Empire, 304

Bristol, England, 447

Britain, 17, 176. *See also* England; Great Britain; Celtic, 185; Roman, 177

British Commonwealth of Nations, 750

British East India Company, 392, 570–574. *See also* India, British rule of; in Bengal, 571; court of, 575*(illus.)*; direct rule and, 577; expansion of, 571–574 *and map*; Indian infrastructure and, 576; land tax policy of, 578; in Malaya, 583; Sepoy revolt and, 576–577, 677; trading stations of, 456; westernization and, 575, 576, 578

British Empire (British colonies), 371, 474, 477*(map)*, 485, 511. *See also*

British (English) North America; in 1913, 512*(map)*; Ireland as, 505–506; in Australia, 540; in Caribbean, 433, 445, 446, 496, 510, 536 (*See also* Jamaica); in Southeast Asia, 458*(map)*; Hong Kong, 723, 731, 740; Indian Ocean trade and, 450; Industrial Revolution and, 500; world trade and, 509–510, 678; Canadian self-rule, 537–538; Egypt and, 560, 561; end of slave trade in, 544; Guiana (Guyana), 434, 496, 535, 673*(map)*; New Zealand, 541; Kenya, 547, 549, 552, 824 *and illus.*; in Africa, 485, 548*(map)*, 550, 551, 824; Kuwait and, 562; Burma, 510, 584–585; Malaya, 583, 587, 863; in Pacific, 540; radio network, 684; in Southeast Asia, 584*(map)*; in Sudan, 543*(illus.)*, 561; in West Africa, 549, 823; independence of, 691*(map)*, 750, 823

British (English) exploration, 377*(map)*, 539

British (English) North America, 370, 378, 392, 439–441; Canada, 489; claims to, 377*(map)*, 430; Native Americans in, 441 *and illus.*; plantation slavery in, 444–445; Puritans in, 385; revolution in, 488, 489–490; slave rebellions in, 446

British Honduras (Belize), 673*(map)*

British immigrants: in Africa, 549, 824; in Australia, 540; in Canada, 538, 539; in New Zealand, 540

British merchants (traders), 401, 487; in India, 572, 579; in Latin America, 534; in Malaya, 583; China and, 597

British National Health Service, 755, 756

British Raj. *See* India, British rule of

Bronze: in Egypt, 53; tin for, 30–31, 81, 91; Central Asian, 40; in early China, 70*(illus.)*, 71, 75, 77 *and illus.*, 111; in East Asia, 83; in Southeast Asia, 81 *and illus.*; iron's advantages over, 21, 34, 92; in Mycenaean Greece, 67; Scythian, 127; Guinea kingdoms, 286, 287*(illus.)*; African art in, 292; Indian art in, 317*(illus.)*; Inca, 304; artisans of Benin, 406*(illus.)*

Bronze Age, 31, 91; in India, 36; life span in, 97

Bruegel, Pieter, art of, 381, 382*(illus.)*

Brunei, sultanate of, 583; oil wealth of, 695, 865

Bry, Theodore de, 440*(illus.)*

Bubonic plague, 191, 251–252, 269, 355, 365

Buddha (Siddhartha Gautama), 153–154, 218, 219; First Sermon of, 154, 155; relics of, 153*(illus.)*; statues of, 117*(illus.)*, 256*(illus.)*; reincarnation of, 324

712, 799, 803; liberation theology and, 712, 803; in Poland, 393, 520, 712, 766; conservatism of, 788; in Italy, 636, 709; in Spain, 520, 639, 709, 714; in Africa, 834; in Vietnam, 850, 851

Catholic missionaries, 539. *See also* Jesuit missionaries; in Africa, 293; in China, 469, 596; in East Africa, 412; in Kongo, 409, 410; in Mexico, 300; Native Americans and, 432, 436, 437, 438–439; in Philippines, 460; Spanish, on Guam, 431; in Vietnam, 457

Cattle (cattle ranching): domestication of, 36; early Saharan peoples and, 23, 57; oxen, 20, 39, 114*(illus.)*; Bantu, 61; Indian/Hindu taboos and, 42–43, 150–151; in colonial Americas, 442, 479; in South Africa, 205, 407, 412, 550, 551; in United States, 526, 528; cowboys, 526; in Australia, 540; gauchos, 681; in Central America, 710; deforestation and, 802; in Mexico, 802

Caucasus region, 8, 23, 194, 558; Parthians in, 146; Russia and, 557 *and map*, 615, 616*(map)*; Soviet control of, 692; oil in, 770

Caudillos (Latin America dictators), 532, 533, 672

Cavalry. *See* Horsemen (cavalry)

Cavazzi, Father, 411*(illus.)*

Cave paintings, 10, 14. *See also* Rock art; in Sahara, 5*(illus.)*; in Europe, 15*(illus.)*; in Baja California, 88; along Silk Road, 102*(illus.)*; in Ajanta (India), 163*(illus.)*

Celebrity, 712

Celibacy: monastic, 224; Aztec priests, 302; in India, 309; of Catholic priests, 383; Christianity and, 342–343

Celtic language, 393

Celtic peoples, 24; in France, 171, 176; Rome and, 172, 176; Gauls, 175, 177; in Ireland, 185; legends of, 347

Censorate agency (China), 260, 270

Censorship: in Japan, 639; in Brazil, 674; in China, 730–731

Central America, 2, 84, 484. *See also specific country;* independence of, 498*(map)*, 499; Maya of, 100, 206, 294, 427; Spanish colonies in, 370, 432; Spanish exploration of, 430; United States and, 536, 651; in 1930, 673*(map)*; deforestation in, 710; labor migration from, 711; death squads in, 796

Central Asia (Central Asians). *See also* Huns; Mongols (Mongolian Empire); Silk Road; Indo-Europeans in, 23, 24*(map)*; Oxus cities in, 40–41; Harappan trade and, 39, 40; early China and, 40, 75, 76, 79; Scythians, 127; trading cities of, 104, 113; Turks of, 106; imperial China and, 103, 109,

112, 117, 119, 222, 258*(map)*, 271; India and, 101, 149, 163; Buddhism in, 117, 118, 158, 159; Parthians and, 146; Silk Road trade and, 165; Kushan Empire in, 194; observatory in, 248; Mongol control of, 251; Timurids in, 253; Islam in, 314; trade routes in, 364; Islam in, 420, 423, 574, 615, 617, 769; Mughal India and, 451; Sufi Muslims in, 482; Russian expansion in, 390, 423, 574, 594, 615, 616*(map)*, 617; Soviet expansion and, 692, 762, 765

Centralization, 475. *See also* Kingship (emperors; monarchy); in early modern Europe, 375; in Egypt, 52; in China, 109, 110; in Japan, 472; in United States, 522; in Ottoman Empire, 558; in Soviet Union, 629, 769

Central Powers, World War I, 620, 621, 623*(map)*. *See also* Germany; Austria-Hungary; Ottoman Empire

Centuriate Assembly (Rome), 174, 175

Ceramics: *See also* Porcelain; Pottery; Andean, 88; Maya, 206; Japanese, 279; Persian, 421, 422*(illus.)*

Cervantes Saavedra, Miguel de, 382

Ceylon. *See* Sri Lanka

Cezanne, Paul, art of, 521

Chaco Canyon, Pueblo peoples at, 296, 297*(map)*

Chad, refugees in, 816

Chairs, in China, 114, 259

Chakri dynasty (Siam), 586–587

Chaldeans (Mesopotamia), 35, 64–65, 66*(illus.)*

Chamorro, Violeta, 803

Chamorro people of Guam, 215, 431

Champa (Chams), 166, 167 *and map*, 319*(map)*; matrilineal system in, 168; Vietnam and, 326

Chan Chan (Chimu), 296

Chandra Gupta II (India), 148*(illus.)*, 161

Chandragupta Maurya (India), 155–156

Chang'an (Xi'an), 78, 103, 259, 274; sack of, 262

Chaplin, Charlie, 684

Chariots, 92, 204; in warfare, 35, 53, 96, 174

Charlemagne, 338, 364; Christian church and, 331, 333; conquests of, 334*(map)*; morality and, 341

Charles I (England), 392

Charles Martel (Franks), 237, 333

Charles the Bald (West Francia), 334*(map)*

Charleston, colonial era, 447

Charles V (Holy Roman Emperor), 387

Charles X (France), 493

Chaucer, Geoffrey, 351, 352

Chavez, Hugo (Venezuela), 796–797

Chavín (Andes), 89*(map)*, 90, 94, 210, 211, 223

Chechnya, Russia and, 615, 692, 769–770, 771

Chemical industry, in Germany, 503

Chemical weapons, in Vietnam War, 853

Chemistry: Indian, 162; Chinese, 261

Cheops (Egypt), 52, 53*(illus.)*

Chernobyl nuclear disaster (1986), 763

Cherokee Indians, 440; removal of, 527

Chiang Kai-shek (Jiang Jieshi), 652–653, 655–656; defeat and withdrawal of, 719, 720, 744; U.S. alliance with, 723

Chiapas (Mexico) revolt in, 798

Chiefs (chiefdoms): Central Asian, 40; Mesoamerican, 88; pastoralist, 116; Japanese, 120; Celtic, 185; African, 204, 282, 286, 290, 447; Polynesian, 216; Maori, 541; Native American, 86, 298, 429, 538; Pacific Islander, 431, 794; Philippines, 328, 459, 460; African slavery and, 414, 446, 475; in colonial Africa, 547, 553; Zulu, 407, 550

Childbearing and childcare, 137. *See also* Children; Infant mortality; hunter-gatherers and, 14; agriculture and, 21, 97; infanticide, 134, 246; patriarchy and, 114; Moche, 211; African, 291; Aztec, 302; India, 309; in Sweden, 756*(illus.)*

Children. *See also* Family; Schools; in Sumer, 30; in Harappa (India), 38; filial piety and, 106, 107; in Greece, 133; vaccination of, in India, 163; sold into slavery, 245; in early modern Europe, 399; labor of, 508, 518–519; malnourished, in Africa, 693, 830, 831; United Nations and, 698

Chile, 686; native peoples of, 86; Spanish conquest of, 432; independence of, 497, 498*(map)*; regional wars and, 531; European immigration to, 535, 681; women's movement in, 672; refugees from, 711; communists in, 696; United States' intervention in, 697, 780–781, 782, 783–784, 797, 801; economy of, 694; reform and repression in, 800–801; democracy in, 801; music of, 804; women in politics, 803; global system and, 805

Chilies (vegetable), 435, 480

Chimalpahin Cuahtlehuanitzin, 425

Chimpanzees, 7

Chimu Empire, 228, 296; Inca conquest of, 302

China, early, 3, 71, 72–80; cosmology, 6; early hominids in, 8, 11; agriculture in, 17, 19*(map)*, 72–73; harvest song from, 18; ancestor worship, 79; slavery in, 77, 78, 79; bronze, 77 *and illus.*, 91; Central Asian nomads and, 40, 75, 76, 79; chronology (7000–600 B.C.E.), 73; cities of, 71, 76*(map)*, 94; government, 76–77; migration from, 82, 320;

China, *continued*

Neolithic, 73, 75; oracle bones in, 78; population growth in, 73, 75, 79; Shang dynasty, 71*(illus.)*, 75, 76–78; writing in, 75, 78, 79, 80*(illus.)*; Xia dynasty, 75; Zhou dynasty, 76*(map)*, 78–79, 98; Warring States period, 76*(map)*, 79, 104*(map)*, 105, 106, 109

China, imperial, 475. *See also* Han Empire; Qing Empire; Song Empire; Tang Empire, *and individual emperors;* nomadic peoples and, 116–117; population of, 105, 112, 114; Silk Road trade and, 103, 111*(map)*, 225, 258*(map)*; Axial Age, 104–109; Buddhism in, 101, 117–118 and illus.; Buddhist pilgrims from, 118, 149, 152, 223, 306–307 and illus., 313, 362; Central Asians and, 109, 112, 117, 119, 222; chronology (1122 B.C.E.–618 C.E.), 105; dynastic cycle and, 116; expansion, 110, 111–112 and map, 116, 463*(map)*, 465, 594; population of, 105, 112, 114, 118, 258, 262, 338, 365; Qin dynasty, 101, 104*(map)*, 109–111, 112; Roman Empire and, 112, 113, 178, 184, 222, 225; Sui dynasty, 118–119, 120, 122, 257, 258; Vietnam as colony of, 110, 112, 165, 166; warfare of, 220; Korea and, 101, 112, 119–120, 463*(map)*, 470, 608; manufacturing in, 264, 361, 371, 450, 478; chronology (1368–1689), 464; merchants in, 263, 266, 272, 356; Ming dynasty, 267, 270–272 and map, 325, 366, 463, 464, 466; Mongol conquest of, 266–270, 268*(map)*; American foods in, 594; American silver in, 463; economy of, 464, 476, 594; Enlightenment thinkers and, 398, 476, 482, 513; European traders in, 371, 596, 597; United States and, 527; Siam and, 481; chronology (1644–1915), 595; science and technology of, 376, 380, 396, 397; silk industry and trade in, 114, 269, 358; taxation in, 110, 116, 261, 263, 356; technological innovations from, 116, 355, 356, 365; trade of, 101, 113, 116, 257, 320–321, 323; trade routes of, 477*(map)*; Christian missionaries in, 371, 396, 469, 470, 482, 594, 598, 602, 651; Confucianism in, 466, 476, 482, 595, 603, 607; western challenge to, 469; women in, 114–115, 226, 264, 269, 362, 466, 482; world economy and, 466–469; Russia and, 423, 463*(map)*, 469, 476, 615; Taiwan and, 465, 469, 481; tea trade in, 463, 464, 466; Opium War in, 596–598, 599*(map)*; Yuan Shikai and, 604, 606; chronology (1911–1945), 651; nationalism in, 652; New Culture

Movement in, 651; Warlord Era (1916–1927), 651, 652

China, Japan and, 101, 119, 229, 485, 720; Yayoi era, 120–121; cultural borrowing, 257, 274; 21 Demands, 606, 652; Rape of Nanjing and, 644, 740; treaty between, 592–593*(illus.)*; Tokugawa era, 606–607; Manchuria and, 606, 612, 639, 652, 653, 654*(map)*; war between (1894–1895), 603, 612, 613–614; war between (1937–1945), 654*(map)*, 655; in World War I, 622; in World War II, 642, 643*(map)*, 644, 645, 656, 731

China, People's Republic of, 718–732. *See also* Communist Party (China); communist triumph in, 719, 720; AIDS in, 729; aid to communist movements by, 696; atomic weapons of, 698, 727; chronology (1945–1997), 721; Cultural Revolution in, 725–726, 727; economic planning in, 720–721; in global system, 701; Korean War and, 723, 741–742 *and map*, 782; Maoism in the world, 723, 725; United Nations and, 699; end of Maoist era, 726–727; one-child policy in, 709; market economy in, 693, 702, 728; modernization in, 727–732; population growth in, 708*(map)*, 709, 719; economic change, and politics in, 728–730; reform and repression in, 727–728; refugees from, 711; religion in, 712, 728, 731; social revolution in, 656, 690, 719, 720; social services in, 705; society, gender and culture in, 730–731; Soviet Union and, 721, 723, 761, 762, 767; Taiwan and, 724*(map)*; North Korea and, 743, 744; United States and, 721, 725, 727, 731; India and, 840, 841, 849; World Conference on Women (1995), 716; civil rights in, 717; oil needs of, 822; Pakistan and, 841; Southeast Asia and, 725, 727; cuisine of, 867; economic power of, 687, 870; pollution in, 729, 870

China, Republic of, 652–653, 850. *See also* Chiang kai-shek; Taiwan; Sun Yat-sen and, 603–605; civil war in, 606, 656, 698, 719, 720

Chinampas (Aztec gardens), 301

China (pottery). *See* Porcelain; Pottery

Chinese exploration (Zheng He), 271, 272*(map)*, 366, 426

Chinese immigrants, 594, 682*(map)*; in Canada, 539; coolie trade, 600–601; in United States, 529, 530; in Hawaii, 531; in Malaya, 583, 662, 680; railroads and, 529; in Singapore, 583, 590, 683*(illus.)*, 864; in Southeast Asia, 600, 681; in Thailand, 860, 861; in Japan, 737

Chinese language, 79, 83, 220, 731, 744

Chinese merchants (traders), 599; intermarriage of, 460*(illus.)*; in Philippines, 460 *and illus.*; in Southeast Asia, 587, 590, 595, 604, 649; European trade and, 595

Chinese Nationalist Party. *See* Guomindang party

Chinese writing, 75, 78, 79, 80*(illus.)*, 110, 119; Japanese and, 122, 274; in Korea, 273, 276

Chipko tree protection movement, 710, 845

Chishtiya (Sufi movement), 452

Chivalry, 232, 277, 308, 338

Cholas (India), 316*(map)*, 317, 323

Cholera, 547, 562, 711

Chongqing (China), 656

Choson Korea, 276, 470, 608–609

Christ. *See* Jesus (Christ)

Christian Church. *See also* Catholicism; Protestantism; *specific sect;* Byzantine Empire and, 348–349; Ethiopian, 407, 412; Germans in, 222, 333; Great Schism in, 355; heresy, 342; in medieval Europe, 229, 331, 332, 342–343; Reformation of, 380; rivalry among, 474; as social and political force, 342–343; conservatives in, 788

Christian Democrats (Europe), 749–750

Christianity (Christians). *See also* Bible, the; Christian church; Ethiopian Christianity; Orthodox Christianity; beginnings of, 187–190; crusading tradition of, 376; in India, 159, 160; Zoroastrianism and, 129, 131; in Nubia, 200, 202; Judaism and, 63, 65, 129; mystery religions and, 146, 189; Nestorian, 194, 232, 239, 247, 249, 259, 261, 364; paganism and, 189, 333; priests, 190, 342–343; spread of, 117, 172, 188*(map)*, 220, 222, 332, 354*(map)*; Islam and, 188*(map)*, 232, 233, 234, 235, 237, 239, 245; in Africa, 101; in Armenia, 254, 418, 421, 561, 666, 765, 769; in medieval Europe, 342–343; in Spain, 243–244; in 1450 C.E., 360*(map)*; morality and ethics of, 361; homosexuality and, 363; African, 407, 410, 411*(illus.)*; Safavid Persia, 421; slaves and, 415, 418; African American culture and, 446; Native Americans and, 442; Japanese, 472; Latin America, 436; Indian, 572, 576, 578, 846; Philippines, 588; West African, 546; Arab, 558, 562, 566; Ottoman, 557, 558; South African, 550, 551, 552; global dominance of, 712, 713*(map)*; Chinese, 598, 726, 728, 730; Korean, 740–741; African, 816; usury and, 340

Christian militancy. *See* Crusades

and, 515; Chinese nationalism and, 651; in Qing China, 476, 595, 603, 607; and patriarchy, in China, 726; in Taiwan, 745; cultural heritage of, 740

Confucius (Kong Fuzi), 106–108 *and illus.*; *Analects* of, 106, 107; Laozi and, 108, 218; *Spring and Autumn Annals*, 115

Congo, 553; as Belgian colony, 547, 548*(map)*, 553, 554–555 *and illus.*, 648; rubber in, 554, 555 *and illus.*, 701; United Nations troops in, 699*(illus.)*; foreign investment in, 830; refugees from, 711; hybrid pop music of, 712; Mobutu in, 825, 827, 830–831; Rwanda and, 828; as Zaire, 824, 825, 826, 830–831

Congo rainforest, Mbuti of, 13

Congo River, 56, 60

Congo River Basin, 56, 59, 288, 406, 415. *See also* Kongo; Belgium and, 547; exploration of, 546; ivory trade in, 545; Katanga, 205

Congregation of the Index, 385

Congress of Vienna, 493, 494*(map)*

Congress Party (India), 842. *See also* Indian National Congress; Nehru and, 840, 841

Congress (United States), 527, 530, 624; Cuba and, 536; League of Nations and, 625; Prohibition and, 633; Korean War and, 782; Democratic majority in, 789; Senate, 780; environmental agreements and, 872

Conquistadors of Spain, 431–433 *and illus.*

Conscription (military draft), 610; in Japan, 274, 277; of colonials, in World War I, 625, 648, 664; in Iran, 669; in Russia, 614–615; in Vietnam War, 851

Conservatives: in Latin America, 532; in Manchu China, 593, 595, 601; in Japan, 632; fascism and, 636; free market, in Europe, 756, 774; in Soviet Union, 767; in United States, 788–789; Islamic, in Middle East, 814, 817; Islamic, in Pakistan, 847; in Thailand, 860

Constantine (Rome), 186, 189

Constantinople, 191, 225, 259, 336. *See also* Istanbul; Santa Sophia Church in, 170*(illus.)*; as imperial capital, 186; Crusades and, 250, 251, 348; Ottoman conquest of, 254, 348; as Istanbul, 254, 348, 355; patriarchs of, 348, 350

Constituent Assembly (France), 492

Constitutional monarchy, 345; in Europe, 392, 393, 493, 499, 748; in Japan, 610; in Thailand, 660

Constitution(s): Swiss, 392; Iroquois, 435; United States, 435, 490, 492, 506, 522; Cherokee, 527; French, 492; Mexican, 534; Cuban, 536; Ottoman, 559, 567; Persian, 561; Philippines, 588; British India, 581, 658, 839; Chinese, 604; Japanese, 610, 732,

734; in Middle East, 671; Turkish, 669; European Union, 774; Bahrain, 808; South Africa, 829; Thai, 861

Construction materials and techniques. *See also* Architecture; Engineering; Housing; in ancient Egypt, 52, 53*(illus.)*; in Harappa, 38 *and illus.*; in early China, 71; moundbuilders, in Americas, 86, 88, 100, 212–213; in Great Wall of China, 110–111 *and illus.*; Japanese, 121; Nazca lines, 212; stone, in East Africa, 288, 289 *and illus.*

Consuls of Rome, 174, 175, 177

Consumer goods: in Europe, 379, 510, 753; in India, 845; in China, 727, 729, 730

Consumerism: in Japan, 735; in United States, 868

Containment policy, 696, 699, 780

Contraceptives, 14, 183, 707, 757. *See also* Birth control

Contras (Nicaragua), 716

Conversos (Christian converts), 437

Cook, James, 217, 539

Cooking methods, 9. *See also* Food (diet; nutrition); in China, 73, 79

Copernicus, Nicolaus, 381, 396

Copper, 21, 672, 870; bronze and, 30–31; coinage, 79; African, 203, 292; Aymara and, 212; East African, 289; Inca, 304; Native American trade in, 86, 225, 298; in Zambia, 555, 835; in China, 594; in Africa, 830

Copper Age, 91

Coptic Christians, 560, 670; Ethiopian Church, 195, 200, 202, 203

Coptic (Egyptian) language, 238

Cordoba (Spain), 243

Corn. *See* Maize (corn)

Corporations, 530. *See also* Business; foreign, in Latin America, 534–535; foreign, in poor countries, 705; Japanese conglomerates (zaibatsu), 610–611 *and illus.*, 732, 735, 736; multinational, 702–703, 787, 802; American, in Guatemala, 797; in South Korea, 743*(illus.)*

Corruption: in Ottoman Empire, 419; in colonial Latin America, 495; in Persia, 561; in Vietnam, 585; in China, 653, 728; in Russia, 617, 771; in South Korea, 742; in Taiwan, 745; in Europe, 750; in United States, 788–789; in Argentina, 796; in Brazil, 799; drug trade and, 802; in Iran, 813; in Africa, 825, 827, 831; in Nigeria, 807, 828; in Bangladesh, 847; in India, 841, 844; in Indonesia, 858; in Philippines, 860

Corsica, 173*(map)*, 174; Rome and, 176

Cortés, Hernán, 32, 425, 426, 429*(map)*

Cosmetics, 54; in Japan, 275

Cosmic order. *See also* Creation myths; in Africa, 60, 61; in China, 80; in Islam,

249; in Africa, 291; in Hinduism, 322 *and illus.*

Cosmopolitanism. *See also* Multiethnicity; in China, 117, 118; in Ionia, 141; Hellenistic era, 144–145; in Roman Empire, 178; in Persia, 194; in Aksum, 201; in East Africa, 205; in Islam, 231, 239, 243, 249, 254, 336; on Java, 461, 857; in Southeast Asia, 168, 320, 326, 328; in port cities, 361; Orientalist, 576; world economic linkages and, 710; in United States, 789; in Africa, 832; in Indian cities, 845

Cossacks (Russian warriors), 423, 681

Costa Rica, 704

Cote D'Ivoire. *See* Ivory Coast (Cote d'Ivoire)

Cotton (cotton industry), 242. *See also* Cloth and clothing; Textiles (textile industry); African, 57, 198, 203, 415; American, 88, 211, 212, 296, 304; plantations, 441, 478; spinning machines, 397; in China, 397, 464, 466; in colonial North America, 444; in India, 39–40, 309, 452, 478, 576, 578, 579; in Britain, 499, 501; mechanization in, 501; women workers in, 555; in United States, 522, 523; Egyptian, 559; in colonial Africa, 554, 555

Cotton gins, 464

Council of Europe, 753

Council of Nicaea (325), 189

Council of State (Iraq), 670

Council of Trent (1545–1563), 385–386, 760

Councils: Athens, 133, 134; of bishops, 192, 355; Iroquois, 435; of merchants, in Persia, 421; Yoruba women, 405

Councils of elders: in African villages, 282, 290; in Indian villages, 156, 309; in Sparta, 134

Counterculture (1960s), 765, 788

Counter Reformation, 385–386

Counterrevolution, in Europe, 492

Courtly love, 341

Covert actions, by United States, 783–784, 797. *See also* CIA (Central Intelligence Agency)

Cowboys, 526; Latin American gauchos, 681

Craftspeople (artisans). *See also* Metallurgy; *specific crafts;* early cities and, 21, 22; Mesopotamian, 27, 94; Egyptian, 52; Chinese, 78; Mauryan India, 157; Maya, 207; Hopewell, 213; Chinese, 264, 265; Korean, 273; African, 285, 286; at Cahokia, 298; medieval Europe, 339; Viking, 335; Safavid Persia, 421; Chinese, in Philippines, 460; European, 476; Japanese, 471; Javanese, 461; in British India, 578

Creation (origin) myths: Mesopotamian, 6; Hebrew (Genesis), 6, 20–21, 36; Indian, 42, 44; African, 61; in Americas, 86

Credit: *See also* Debt; Loans; Indian merchants and, 452; Great Depression and, 633

Creole elite, in Latin America, 436, 437, 495, 535; independence and, 496, 497, 499

Cresques, Abraham, 375

Crete: Minoan, 3, 63, 66, 67 *and illus.;* Greek city-states in, 132*(map)*

Crime: in China, 730; in Europe *vs.* United States, 757; criminal syndicates, 701, 736, 769

Crimea, 141, 365; Russia and, 557

Crimean War (1854), 614–615

Croatia (Croats), 621; ethnic conflict in, 772, 773*(map)*

Cro-Magnons (hominids), 11

Cromwell, Oliver (England), 392

Crops: *See also* Cash crops; Indonesian, in East Africa, 205; Islam and, 242; in Columbian exchange, 435; African-American exchange, 446; from Americas, in China, 594

Crossbows, 177. *See also* Bows and arrows

Crusades, 232, 348; Muslims and, 250–251, 345–346; papacy and, 250, 346

Cruz, Sor Juana Inez de la, 436, 476

Crystal Palace Exposition (London, 1851), 486–487 *and illus.*

Cuauhtemoc (Aztec), 432

Cuba, 444, 794; Columbus in, 429*(map)*; free blacks in, 446; Spain and, 430, 431, 432, 527, 534; sugar production in, 444, 534, 649–650, 679; independence movement in, 534; United States and, 527, 531, 534, 536; abolition of slavery in, 535, 544; aid to insurgents by, 696; Chinese in, 535; communism in, 696, 764, 799; dictatorship in, 672, 799, 800 *and illus.*; refugees from, 711, 800; Soviet Union and, 764

Cuban Missile Crisis (1962), 697, 764, 799

Cuban Revolution, 686, 799–800 *and illus.*

Cubism (painting style), 635

Cui Jian, 728, 875

Cultivation system, in Dutch Indonesia, 582–583

Cults. *See also* Ancestor worship; Gods and goddesses; Shrines; Mithraism, 145–146; Inca, 302; of Christian saints, 383; Devaraja, 319; Mao, in China, 722*(illus.)*, 725

Cultural assimilation: *See also* Cultural unity; Aryans in India, 41; in Southeast Asia, 82; China and, 117, 119, 167–

168; Indian castes and, 151; Islam and, 239, 241, 254; Mongols, in China, 267; Japanese borrowing, 274, 473, 606; in Manchu China, 464; of European Jews, 505

Cultural diversity. *See also* Cosmopolitanism; in hominid tool cultures, 9; in Egypt, 51; Persian Empire and, 127; Mediterranean basin, 141; in India, 152, 307; Roman Empire, 178; in sub-Saharan Africa, 197; Pacific Island societies, 213; in Islam, 242, 243; in Tang China, 259; in southern Africa, 287; in Austrian Empire, 393; in Southeast Asia, 308, 320; in India, 450, 839, 843; in Southeast Asia, 838; in Australia, 793

Cultural imperialism, 867

Cultural mixing, 685. *See also* Intermarriage; Mixed-descent people; in frontier, 681; in Latin America, 535–536; mass media and, 712

Cultural Revolution (China), 725–726, 727, 728

Cultural unity: in India, 43–44, 158; in China, 78, 79, 119; in Mesoamerica, 88; in Japan, 121; in Southeast Asia, 168; in Korea, 273; in Maya, 207; in Africa, 290, 292

Culture(s). *See also* Art and artists; Folk culture; Oral culture; Pop culture; Traditional culture *and specific cultures;* language and, 10; violence and, 14–15; Sumerian, 30; innovation, 96; Greek, 141, 144 (*See also* Greco-Roman culture; Hellenistic Age); religion and society, 223–224; trade and, 225–226; Ming China, 270–271; Mongol, 267, 269; Japanese, 275; Byzantine, 348–349; medieval trade and, 336; colonial Latin America, 436–437; African-American, 446; Javanese, 462; Middle Eastern, 563–567; colonial Africa, 553; Burman, 584–585; Latin American nationalism and, 674–675; Caribbean, 675; Japanese, 736; spread of mass culture, 635, 683, 685–685, 759; globalization and, 866–868; local *vs.* global, 867

Cuneiform writing, 31–32 *and illus.,* 68, 96*(illus.)*

Cunha, Euclides da, 535

Currency, 702. *See also* Coins (coinage); bars of precious metal as, 68; creation of, 95; Byzantine, 192; paper money, in China, 262; in African trade, 284; seashell-based, 86, 290, 292; Chinese decline, 720; exchange rates, 645; European *euro,* 747, 774; U.S. dollar, 753

Curzon, Lord (British India), 578

Customs, 14

Cuzco (Peru), 302, 432

Cynicism, 145

Cyprian, 222

Cyrillic alphabet, 349

Cyril (missionary), 349

Cyrus II (the Great, Persia), 127, 131, 141

Czars of Russia, 350, 389–390, 626. *See also specific czar*

Czechoslovakia, 624, 625; Protestants in 388; multiethnicity in, 631; Nazi invasion of, 640; "Prague Spring" in, 766; protests in, 716; Soviet domination of, 696, 752*(map)*, 764; Velvet Revolution in, 771, 772*(illus.)*; Slovak secession from, 771, 773*(map)*

Czech Republic (Czechs), 621; in European Union, 774; Havel and, 712

Da Gama, Vasco, 293, 377*(map)*, 408–409, 410

Dahomey, 545; slave trade and, 415, 475, 481

Daimler, Gottlieb, 521

Daimyo, in Japan, 279, 471, 472, 473, 606–607; Meiji restoration and, 610

Dakar, Senegal, 664, 833

Dalai Lama, 699, 723, 875

Damari, Shoshana, 818

Damascus, 251; Islam in, 240 *and illus.;* Italian merchants in, 253*(illus.)*

Dams: in Egypt, 809; in China, 729

Dance: in Africa, 292; Balinese, 324; in India, 39, 42, 317*(illus.)*; Sufi dervishes, 419; Argentine tango, 535; Brazilian samba, 446, 536, 675; Ghost Dance, 528; African, 665; Indian *bhangra,* 759

Dante Alighieri, 355

Danube River Basin, 185, 332

Daoism, 115, 168, 712, 745; Confucianism and, 101, 108, 118, 219, 261, 266; landscape painting and, 108, 466; Laozi and, 108, 118, 219; Li Po and, 262; Zen Buddhism and, 278; in Vietnam, 325; in China, 466, 731

Dar al-Islam, 248–249, 250*(map)*. *See also* Islam (Islamic world); East Africa and, 287

Darfur (Sudan) genocide in, 816

Dario, Ruben, 535

Darius III (Persia), 142, 143*(illus.)*

Darius I (Persia), 131; expedition to India, 127, 155; as lawgiver, 127; wars with Greece, 127–128, 138

Dark Age, in Europe. *See* Medieval Europe

Dark Age (Greece), 68

"Darkest Africa," 546

Darwin, Charles, 6–7, 513, 521

Da Silva, Luis Ignacio ("Lula"), 799

David (Hebrews), 223*(illus.)*

Da Vinci, Leonardo, 381

Death camps: in World War II, 642 (*See also* Holocaust); in Cambodia, 855

Death rites, 314. *See also* Burials; Tombs

Death squads: in Brazil, 799; in Central America, 796, 797; in South Africa, 829

De Beauvoir, Simone, 757, 760, 875

Debs, Eugene V., 530

Debt. *See also* Foreign debt; Loans; Reparations; War debt; of Roman plebians, 175; Egyptian, 560, 809; Chinese, 597, 598, 599, 600, 601; credit, 452, 633; Latin American and African, 702; of Indian peasants, 578; United States, 633, 731, 781–782, 866; canceled, for poor nations, 712, 871; in Eastern Europe, 766

Debt slavery: in Greece, 133; in Roman Empire, 175, 181

Decameron (Bocaccio), 355

Decentralization: *See also* Centralization; in Gupta India, 160

Decimal system, 77, 105, 115, 162

Declaration of Independence (United States), 489, 530, 850

Declaration of the Rights of Man (France), 492, 504

Decolonization, 690, 782; nationalism and, 690–693 *and map*, 822–825; after World War II, 750, 751; in Pacific region, 794; in sub-Saharan Africa, 822–825; and partition of India, 838–839, 840*(illus.)*

Deconstruction, Derrida and, 760

Deficit spending, 756

Deforestation, 709–710; of Greece, 20; Lebanon cedars, 52, 68; metallurgy and, 91; Kush and, 198; of Pacific islands, 215; in Greenland, 350, 427; in India, 479; on Fiji, 539; desertification and, 709, 710, 835; need for cropland and, 479, 589; in tropics, 710; cattle ranching and, 710; in Malaysia, 863; in Thailand, 861, 862; in Africa, 835; in Borneo, 874

De Gaulle, Charles, 644, 749, 757

Deities. *See* Gods and goddesses; *specific deities*

Del Castillo, Bernal Diaz, 300

Delhi, India, 422; Mughals in, 571, 577

Delhi Sultanate (India), 268*(map)*, 316–317; Hindu politics and culture in, 317; Tamerlane and, 318; tower in, 315*(illus.)*

Delian League (Greece), 139

Delors, Jacques, 747

Delos, as network hub, 225

Delphi, oracle of Apollo at, 137

Democracy. *See also* Parliamentary democracy; in Africa, 58; in ancient Greece, 133, 134, 136, 139–140, 142; Roman, 174; in African villages, 290; Protestantism and, 385; representative, 387; in England, 393; Locke and, 398; in North American colonies, 439, 488,

489; in United States, 515, 523, 696; constitutional, 506; village, 506, 553, 554; in Iran, 561; in Africa, 553; World War I and, 625; fascism and, 637; African Americans and, 642; capitalism and, 627, 650, 695, 779, 786, 851; in Chile, 672, 801; in Japan, 632, 732, 734; political stability and, 694; in Thailand, 702, 861; in South Korea, 702, 742; on Taiwan, 702; social, in Western Europe, 750, 755–756; in Indonesia, 702, 858; in Eastern Europe, 771–772 *and illus.*; in Soviet Union, 767; in Latin America, 777, 796; in Middle East, 812; in Philippines, 860; in Africa, 826, 830, 831; in China, 728, 731; in India, 839, 843, 849

Democratic Party (United States), 789

Democratic Progressive Party (Taiwan), 745

Democratic Republic of the Congo, 830. *See also* Congo

Demonstrations. *See* Protests; Student protests

Deng Xiaoping, reforms of, 727, 728, 730

Denmark (Danes), 171, 343, 493. *See also* Scandinavia; Lutheranism in, 388; Sweden and, 393; Norway and, 504; slave trade and, 413, 544; social democracy in, 635; abortion rights in, 757; anti-Muslim movement in, 758, 775; European Community and, 753; in Common Market, 752*(map)*

Depression (late 1800s), 503, 530. *See also* Great Depression

Derrida, Jacques, deconstruction and, 760

Dervishes, 245, 419, 482. *See also* Sufis

Descartes, René, 395, 396, 397, 466

Desertification, 20, 57, 709, 710. *See also* Drought; *specific desert;* in Africa, 479, 835

Deshima, Nagasaki Bay, 472

Despotism: *See also* Authoritarianism; Dictatorship; Tyrants; in Manchu China, 594; in czarist Russia, 630; in Africa, 826, 830–831

Dessalines, Jean Jacques, 496

Devaraja (Indian god-king), 319

Developing (poor) nations: American investment in, 779; United States interventions in, 782–783; Arab, 821; population growth in, 705, 870; globalization and, 866, 867; resources from, 871; debt relief for, 712, 871

Development: *See also* Economy; underdevelopment, 704–707, 830–831, 870; challenges of, 868–870; in Africa, 829–831; envisioning new world order, 870–871; inequality and, 868–871; North-South gap, 868, 869*(map)*

Dewey, George, 587

Diallo, Ayuba Suleiman, 401, 402

Diamonds, 75; African mines, 549, 551, 620, 829

Dias, Bartolomeu, 293, 357, 408

Diaspora, trade, 141, 168; Armenian, 421; Indian, 452; in Latin America, 535; Chinese, 600–601

Diaspora (dispersal): Jewish, 65, 189; Greek, 131; Bantu, in East Africa, 287–290

Diaz, Porfirio (Mexico), 533

Dickens, Charles, 520

Dictatorship, 136. *See also* Authoritarianism; Military dictatorship; in Rome, 177; shoguns, in Japan, 278; in French Revolution, 492, 493; in Latin America (caudillos), 484, 532, 666, 777; in Brazil, 674; in Soviet Union, 629–630, 723; in Turkey, 669; regional tensions and, 700; in South Korea, 742; United States' support for, 783; in Haiti, 797; in Philippines, 859–860; fascist, in Portugal, 825; in Congo (Zaire), 825

Diem, Ngo Dinh, 851

Diet. *See* Food (diet; nutrition)

Dilmun (Bahrain), 95

Ding Ling, 653, 656, 723

Dinosaurs, extinction of, 7

Diocletian (Rome), 186

Diogenes, 145

Dionysus (god), 135, 181

Dipenegara, Prince, 568–569*(illus.)*

Diplomacy: Chinese, 103, 112; in India, 156; Aboriginal, 214; Chinese and, 470; African queens and, 410; Muhammad and, 234; Aztec, 299; in Siam, 511; gunboat, in China, 602

Direct *vs.* indirect rule: in British India, 577; in colonial Africa, 553; in Southeast Asia, 589

Discrimination: *See also* Racism; in British-ruled India, 578; against homosexuals, 758

Disease. *See also* Black Death; Epidemics; Medicine (physicians); Plague; Small pox; domesticated animals and, 20, 87; American Indians and, 87; sub-Saharan Africa, 56; Indian medicine and, 163; in Columbian exchange, 435, 479–480; vaccines against, 163, 521; Islamic studies of, 247; tuberculosis, 298; in Kongo, 409; Native Americans and, 370, 425, 427, 432, 435, 437, 439, 479, 480*(illus.)*, 539; Pacific Islanders and, 431; in European cities, 399, 517; malaria, 56, 298, 412, 434, 511, 547, 711; sanitation and, 521; Australian Aborigines and, 540; cholera, 547, 562, 711; syphilis, 435, 480; tuberculosis, 298, 385, 435, 611; weaponized, 699; World Health Organization and, 698; in World War I, 622, 666; global spread of, 711; AIDS/HIV, 711, 729, 829, 831, 832, 835, 846

Diversity. *See* Cultural diversity; Ethnic diversity

Divination (oracles), 78, 137

The Divine Comedy (Dante), 355

Divine kingship: Egyptian, 53; in Africa, 198; Chinese Mandate of Heaven, 78, 115; in India, 159; in Teotihuacan, 210; Maya, 206; in Inca Empire, 302; in Southeast Asia, 319, 321, 322; of German Kaiser, 621

Divine right of kings, 389. *See also* Absolutism

Divorce: *See also* Marriage; in Egypt, 54; in Greece, 137; in Byzantium, 192; in Islam, 236; in Japan, 278; in India, 309; Henry VIII and, 385; Ottoman, 418; in China, 726; in Japan, 736; in Soviet Union, 764; in Europe, 757; in United States, 791; in Latin America, 803

DNA studies: early humans and, 7, 10, 11; Native Americans and, 85

Dr. Zhivago (Pasternak), 762

Doctors. *See* Medicine (physicians)

Doctors Without Borders, 699, 711

Dogon (West Africa) creation myth, 6

Domestication: in Americas, 210; of animals, 5, 18, 19*(map)*, 20, 23, 39, 81, 87; of plants, 17, 57, 61, 81, 87, 210; in ancient India, 36, 39; of sheep and goats, 5, 36, 57

Dominican religious order, 438

Dominican Republic, 531; United States and, 536, 633, 783

Dominion of Canada, 538–539. *See also* Canada

Domino theory, 782. *See also* Anticommunism

Dom Pedro II (Portugal), 499, 532

Don Quixote (Cervantes), 382

Don Son (Vietnam) bronze drums, 81 *and illus.*

Dorian Greeks, 67, 68, 69

Dostoyevsky, Fyodor, 617

Dowlah, Siraja, 571, 573*(illus.)*

Draft animals: *See also* Horses; Oxen; lack of, in Americas, 87; lack of, in Africa, 292

Drake, Francis, piracy of, 434

Drama (theater): Greek, 136–137; Indian, 163; Chinese opera, 265, 269, 271; Japanese, 279; shadow puppet, 322; Shakespeare, 382, 383; Japanese kabuki, 473 *and illus.*, 739; Burman, 584–585

Dravidian cultures, 159; Aryans and, 41, 43–44, 46

Dravidian languages, 39, 159

Dreamtime of Aborigines, 215

Dresden (Maya) Codex, 207*(illus.)*

Drought, 17. *See also* Rainfall; in Middle East, 16; in Sahara, 8, 57; Akkadian decline and, 32–33; in Aksum, 202; Maya collapse and, 209, 294; in Americas, 87, 212, 366; famine and, 707, 827; in India, 318; in Great Depression, 634; in Africa, 710, 830, 832; global warming and, 872

Drug trade. *See also* Opium trade; heroin, 701, 802; marijuana, 791, 805; coca (cocaine), 435, 701, 802; AIDS and, 711; Latin American, 802

Druids (Celtic priests), 185

Dubai (Persian Gulf state), 694, 710, 822

Dubcek, Alexander (Czechoslovakia), 766

Dubos, René, 873

Du Fu, 262

Dust Bowl (United States, 1930s), 634

Dutch East India Company, 392, 455, 461, 478, 582

Dutch Empire (Dutch colonies), 474, 477*(map)*. *See also* Indonesia, Dutch rule of; Netherlands (the Dutch, Holland); in Africa, 402; in Americas, 378, 433; in Brazil, 433; Guiana, 433, 446, 496; Indonesia, 371, 461–462; in Melaka, 450; wealth from, 447; in North America, 434; in South Africa, 371, 412–413, 481, 549, 550–551; in 1913, 512*(map)*; in Southeast Asia, 458*(map)*, 584*(map)*; Sri Lanka, 392, 455, 570; independence of, 691*(map)*; immigrants to Netherlands, 758

Dutch Guiana (Suriname), 433, 496, 673*(map)*; maroon society in, 446; plantation labor in, 535, 683

"Dutch learning", in Japan, 607

Dutch traders (merchants), 447; intermarriage by, 481; in Japan, 472, 607; in Siam, 458

Dutch West India Company, 434

Dylan, Bob, 791

Dynastic cycle, in China, 78, 114, 116

Dyula people of West Africa, 404, 405

Early modern world (1450–1750), 370–371; environmental changes, 479–480; gunpowder and warfare in, 476; missionaries and religion in, 482; new empires and military power in, 474–476; polycentrism in, 475–476; social and cultural change in, 480–482; world economy, 476–479

Earth First! (organization), 872

Earth mother, 181*(illus.)*, 304

Earthquakes, 6, 40, 66, 211

East Africa: *See also* Zimbabwe; human origins in, 7–8, 10; Great Lakes region, 57, 60, 205, 287; trade networks of, 101, 199*(map)*; Indonesians in, 205; ironworking in, 57, 58, 205; maritime trade in, 198, 205–206, 283*(map)*; Chinese voyages to, 271; coastal cities of, 229; spice trade of, 249; merchants in, 291; Swahili Coast, 283*(map)*, 288; Arabs in, 281, 288, 366; Bantu in, 205, 290; city-states of, 287, 363; slave trade and, 293, 363; Gikuyu people, 290; trading cities of, 403*(map)*, 406, 408; Portuguese in, 370, 378, 408, 410–411, 454; Arab traders in, 478; Asian immigrants in, 550; slave trade in, 408, 413*(map)*, 415, 544–545; upper class in, 827; World War I in, 622; British colonial, 510, 550, 649

East Asia, 371, 482, 485. *See also specific country*; early humans in, 9, 11, 12*(map)*; origins of agriculture in, 19*(map)*; Chinese influence in, 3, 76, 112, 116, 119, 229; migrations to Americas from, 85; Buddhism in, 117–118; Classical societies in, 101, 104; Confucianism in, 107, 362; Qing China and, 463*(map)*; foreign investment in, 705; decline of religion in, 712; economic resurgence in, 687, 719–720; "little dragons" in, 733*(map)*, 740, 745; United States military in, 723; capitalism in, 731; global system and, 784

Easter Island, 165, 216 and map, 217

Eastern Europe: early clothing in, 13; Mongol conquest of, 267, 268*(map)*; trade of, 341; Black Death in, 353; Byzantines and, 347, 349; Christianity in, 350, 362; chronology (600–1500), 347; peasants/serfs of, 356; serfdom in, 379; Ottoman control of, 419; grain from, 479; feudalism in, 517; World War I in, 625; Nazi conquest of, 639, 640; Russia and, 594; Soviet domination of, 645, 687, 695, 696, 751–752 *and map*, 766, 767; Soviet army in, 761; chronology (1945–1989), 761; end of Soviet domination in, 699; fall of Communism in, 728, 767, 771–772

Eastern hemisphere, 358; Africa in, 407; Americas and, 85, 87, 213; diseases from, 479–480; Islamic influence in, 237

Eastern Orthodoxy. *See* Orthodox Christianity

Eastern woodlands societies, North America, 297*(map)*, 298

Easter Uprising (Ireland, 1916), 505–506

East Francia, 335

East Germany, 771, 867; reunification and, 773; rock musician protests in, 766; Soviet Union and, 645, 751, 764

East India Companies. *See also* British East India Company; Dutch, 392, 455, 461, 478, 582; French, 455

East Timor, 856*(map)*, 857, 858

Ebadi, Shirin, 813–814, 875

El Salvador, 531; Indian massacre in, 672; United States military in, 633, 797; death squads in, 796

E-mail (electronic mail), 714

Emancipation, of serfs, 615. *See also* Freedom

Emancipation Proclamation (1862), 528

Embargo. *See* Economic sanctions (boycott; embargo)

Emperors. *See* Kingship (emperors; monarchy)

Empires. *See* Colonies (colonization); Expansion, *and specific empires and emperors*

Empiricism, 398. *See also* Science

Enclosure policy (England), 398

Encomienda (labor tax), 442

Encyclopedias, 247; Chinese, 261, 271; Korean, 276

Engels, Friedrich, 507, 509

Engineering, 849. *See also* Construction materials and techniques; Persian, 127; of Archimedes, 145; Sri Lankan, 159; Etruscan, 174; Funan, 167; Roman, 183; Yemenite, 195; Aksumite, 201; Chinese, 119, 261, 264; Chimu, 296; Inca, 304; Angkor, 321; Panama Canal, 536

England, 187, 343. *See also* Great Britain (England); first humans in, 9; Stonehenge in, 17; Greek explorer in, 171; Celts in, 185; cathedral in, 330(*illus.*); Christianity in, 333; population of, 338; slavery in, 339; Viking raids in, 335; watermills in, 337; Norman conquest of, 335, 343; Aquitane and, 354(*map*); peasant revolts in, 352; wars with France, 353

English colonies. *See* British Empire

English language: in Siam, 587; in Canada, 537, 538; in India, 575, 578, 704, 844; in Philippines, 588, 678; pidgin, 665; as world language, 714–715, 767; in China, 731; in South and East Africa, 834; in Singapore, 864

Enheduanna, 32

Enlightenment, 155, 397–398 *and illus.*, 500, 544, 572. *See also* Nirvana; salons of, 398(*illus.*); Catherine the Great and, 614; China and, 398, 476, 482, 513; North American colonists and, 439, 488, 489, 490; Latin American liberty and, 495, 496; liberalism and, 506, 636; rationalism of, 397, 496, 520, 564, 636, 759; Muslim modernists and, 564; Nietzsche and, 520; Mozart and, 520; fascism and, 636

Entrepreneurs: *See also* Business and businessmen; in Surat, 452; in China, 467, 729; British, 561, 578; globalization and, 867; in Malaysia, 863

Environment, the. *See also* Deforestation; Global warming; Pollution; evolution and, 6–7; extinction and, 7; hunter-gatherers and, 13, 86; transition to agriculture and, 15–17, 20–21; Mesopotamian, 28–29; in Indus Valley, 36–37, 40; Egyptian, 50–51; in sub-Saharan Africa, 56–57; in eastern Mediterranean, 63; Southeast Asia, 80–81, 319; Northeast Asia, 82–83; in Americas, 84–85, 86; Kush decline and, 198; Australian, 214; imperial decline and, 222; Anasazi collapse and, 296; medieval Europe, 332, 343; island fragility, 431; population growth and, 479; early modern world, 479–480; global warming and, 709; resource consumption rates and, 709; destruction of, 715, 801; in Japan, 735–736; Soviet Union and, 763; economic growth and, 845, 866; in India, 710, 845; in Indonesia, 857; in Kenya, 827; globalization and, 709, 867; United States and, 872; Vietnam War, 853; in China, 729, 870; in Western Europe, 750, 867; issues and movements, 872; sustainability of, 871–872

Epic of Gilgamesh, 35–36, 64, 98, 140

Epidemics, 116, 222. *See also* AIDS/HIV; Black Death; Plague; Small pox; in Roman Empire, 184; American Indians and, 298, 305, 432, 528; in Iraq, 562; in Africa, 547

Epitaphs, Roman, 182

Equal field system, in China, 260

Equality. *See* Egalitarianism (equality)

Equiano, Olaudah, 414

Eratosthenes, 145

Ericson, Leif, 305

Erie Canal (New York state), 523

Eritrea (northeast Africa), 58, 549

Estado Nuovo (Brazil), 674

Estates General (France), 491

Estonia, 761

Esu-Williams, Eka, 832

ETA. *See* Basques in Spain

Ethics: *See also* Morality; Hindu, 45; Axial Age, 105, 219; Confucian, 106

Ethiopia, 51, 283(*map*), 357, 403(*map*), 549; early hominids in, 8; iron ore in, 58; origins of farming in, 17, 57; trade of, 59; Aksum Empire, 196(*illus.*), 199(*map*), 200–203; Arabian politics and, 232; Italian invasion of, 511, 549, 639, 650; Rastafarians and, 805; refugees from, 711

Ethiopian Christianity, 223(*illus.*), 225, 407, 412; Coptic Christians, 195, 200, 202, 203, 560, 670

Ethnic conflict: in colonial Africa, 549, 553, 648, 650, 664, 665; in Dutch Indonesia, 648, 661; nationalism and,

664; in Caribbean, 650; in Yugoslavia, 695, 766; in colonial Southeast Asia, 589, 650; in Europe, 750; in former Soviet Union, 769; in Eastern Europe, 772, 773(*map*); in Latin America, 796; in Middle East, 816; in Pacific Islands, 794; in Afghanistan, 820; Rwandan genocide and, 827–828; in Pakistan, 841, 843; in Sri Lanka, 843; in Malaysia, 662, 863; in Burma, 860, 861; in Indonesia, 858

Ethnic diversity (minorities): *See also specific ethnic minorities;* in Southeast Asia, 82; in Hellenistic era, 144; Central Asian, 158; in Ottoman Empire, 418, 577–578; in Sudanic Africa, 282, 284, 285; in United States, 523, 528, 529, 789–790; in Congo, 677; in New Zealand, 794; World War I and, 621, 625; in Canada, 792; in Malaysia, 865

Ethnic identity, in Africa, 291

Ethnocentrism: in China, 272, 464, 598; of Europeans in Africa, 546, 553–554; Western culture and, 598; colonialism and, 648

Etruria, Italy, 173(*map*)

Etruscans, 171, 173(*map*), 174

Euclid, 145

Eunuchs, in imperial China, 271

Euphrates River Valley, 5, 16(*illus.*). *See also* Tigris-Euphrates Valley

Eurasia: early humans in, 8, 9, 11, 12(*map*); agriculture in, 17; Chinese economy and, 476; Columbian exchange and, 479–480; drought in, 33; traditions of, 36; ironworking in, 92; Indo-European migration in, 25, 92; growing trade of, 479; Silk Road and, 113; gunpowder empires in, 474; Axial Age empires in, 101; Classical Era societies in, 197; Tang China and, 258; Mongol conquest of, 267, 268(*map*); Byzantium and, 347–348; trade routes in, 222, 355, 359; Russian expansion in, 511, 512(*map*), 614–617 *and map*

Eurasians, in Java, 462

Euripedes, 134, 137

Euro (currency), 747, 774

Europe (1450–1750), 371, 373–399; in 1740, 394(*map*); absolutist and despotic monarchies, 389–390, 391(*map*); African slave trade and, 408, 413(*map*); American foods in, 480; arts and philosophy, 395–396; capitalism in, 374–375, 378–380, 398–399; changing states and politics in, 387–395; chronology, 379; cultural and social transformation, 395–399; Enlightenment in, 397–398 *and illus.*; expansion and capitalism in, 374–380; family and gender relations, 399; limited power of, 475;

Fundamentalist religions, 714

Fur trade: in Alaska, 539; beaver, in North America, 434; bison massacre and, 528; in Canada, 440, 539; Russian, 469, 539

Fusae, Ichikawa, 685

Gaelic language, 393

Gagaran, Yuri, 762

Gaius Marius, 177

Gaja Mada (Madjapahit), 322

Galileo Galilei, 396, 482

Galleons (ships), 376, 462–463

Gallipoli, World War I in, 622

Gambling, Aryans and, 42

Gamelan music, in Indonesia, 591, 684

Games, 31, 42. *See also* Ball games; Sports

Ganda people of Buganda, 406

Gandhara, 158

Gandhi, Indira (India), 841–843; assassination of, 843

Gandhi, Mohandas K., 153, 664, 677, 875; assassination of, 838, 839; caste system and, 659, 840; nonviolent resistance and, 579, 657, 789, 838; on Western civilization, 513; on women, 659–660

Gandhi, Rajiv, 843

Gandhi, Sanjay, 842, 843

Gandhi, Sonia, 844

Ganges Basin, 43, 46, 154, 158, 159

Ganges River (India), 845; pilgrims at, 152, 313

Gan Ying, 112

Gao of Songhai, 285, 292, 402

Garamante tribes, Saharan salt trade and, 204

García Márquez, Gabriel, 804

Garibaldi, Giuseppi, 505

Gast, John, painting of, 525*(illus.)*

Gathas (Zoroastrian scripture), 130, 131

Gathering, by women, 13, 16. *See also* Hunter-gatherers

Gatling, Richard, 684

Gatling gun, 547, 684

Gauchos (Latin American cowboys), 681

Gauguin, Paul, 521

Gauls (Celts), Rome and, 175, 177

Gaza, Israel and, 810*(illus.)*, 811*(map)*, 812

Geez (Amharic) language, 201, 291

Gender relations. *See also* Homosexuality; Marriage; Women; Sexuality; in early human society, 5, 8; in India, 39; labor division and, 22, 97; in China, 79, 114–115; in Persia, 131; in Greece, 136, 137; in India, 162; Roman, 183; Byzantine, 192; Maya, 208; Australian Aboriginal, 214; Classic Era, 226; in Islam, 236–237, 245–246; in African villages, 290; in imperial China, 264, 267, 593; in Korea, 276; Aztec, 302; in Americas, 304; Inca, 303; Hinduism

and, 311; universal religions and, 362–363; Enlightenment and, 398; changes in, 481–482; in colonial Africa, 555; Portuguese and, 455; female roles and, 518; in Philippines, 461, 587; in Japan, 473, 612; in colonial Southeast Asia, 590–591; in India, 452, 581, 659–660; in Europe, 399, 632, 757; in United States, 791; in Latin America, 803; in sub-Saharan Africa, 832

General Agreements on Trade and Tariffs, 702

General Song (Neruda), 804

Genesis (Hebrew Bible), 6, 20–21, 36, 97

Geneva, Calvinism in, 383, 385

Geneva Agreements (1954), 851

Genghis Khan (Temuchin), 251, 267, 317, 349, 364

Genoa, Italy, 336, 356, 374; Mamluk trade with, 252, 253*(illus.)*

Genocide, 640, 875; Armenian, 558, 666; Nazi Holocaust, 642, 672, 698, 748, 760, 810; in Rwanda, 698, 827–828; Serbian "ethnic cleansing," 698, 772; in Sudan, 816; in Cambodia, 698, 855

Gentile, Giovanni, 637

Gentry: *See also* Landowners; Chinese landlords, 465, 653; in eastern Europe, 517

Geoffrin, Maria-Therese, 397*(illus.)*

Geology, 6

Geometry: Chinese, 115; Greek, 125, 145; Nazca, 212; Arab, 247

George III (Britain), 596

Georgia (Caucasus), 557 *and map,* 615

Georgia (North America), 441; Sea Islands, 446; Cherokees of, 527

German colonies (German Empire), 485, 678; in 1913, 512*(map)*; in Africa, 511, 512*(map)*, 548*(map)*, 549, 556, 624, 625; in Pacific, 540, 584*(map)*, 622, 624, 632; in China, 602, 622; post-World War I, 624, 625

German Democratic Republic. *See* East Germany

Germanic traditions, 332

Germany (Germanic peoples). *See also* East Germany; Nazi Germany; West Germany; first humans in, 9; Roman Empire and, 101, 172, 184, 185; Byzantium and, 191; Christianity and, 222, 333; in Sicily, 243; killing of Jews in, 346; Magyars and, 336; papal authority and, 343; fragmentation of, 345; Franks, 187, 190, 333–335 *and map;* Saxons, 187, 335; serfdom in, 353; trade alliance of, 356; Lutheranism in, 383, 384*(map)*; baroque music of, 395; free thinking in, 385; in colonial America, 439; Napoleonic era, 493–494 *and map;* as great power, 487, 510; industrialization

in, 502, 503, 621; Jews in, 505; Social Democrats in, 508; unification of, 505; alliances of, 510; in United States, 518*(map)*, 530; in World War I, 559, 620–622, 623*(map)*, 624, 679; Weimar Republic, 631, 636; World War I reparations and, 624–625, 631; Great Depression in, 633, 634; Russian peace treaty with, 623*(map)*, 627; Spanish civil war and, 639; post-World War II division of, 645; Neo-Nazis in, 758, 773; immigrants in, 758; reunification of, 687, 768, 772, 773

Geronimo (Apaches), 528

"Get-rich-quick" mentality, 633, 729

Ghalib (Muslim poet), 577

Ghana (Gold Coast), 101, 199*(map)*, 549, 826. *See also* Ashante kingdom; trans-Saharan trade and, 282, 283*(map)*; gold trade in, 204, 284; slavery in, 204; Portuguese and, 293; Islam in, 282; Akan states in, 408; slaves from, 413*(map)*, 415; cocoa in, 555, 664, 835; colonial rule in, 553, 555, 664; freed slaves in, 545; highlife music in, 665; independence of, 691*(map)*, 692*(illus.)*, 823; nationalism in, 827

Al-Ghazali, Zainab, 817

Ghazni (Afghan sultanate), 314–315

Ghost Dance (Indian movement), 528

Gibraltar, 226, 389, 692

Gikuyu people (Kenya), 290; colonialism and, 547, 554, 664; Kenyan nationalism and, 814 *and illus.;* literature of, 834

Gilgamesh, 31*(illus.)*. *See also Epic of Gilgamesh*

Giza (Egypt), pyramids at, 52, 53*(illus.)*

Glacial period. *See* Ice Age

Gladiators of Rome, 181

Glasgow (Scotland) "tobacco lords," 447

Glasnost (openness) policy, 767, 768, 769

The Glass Palace Chronicle, 585

Global communism, 618–619 *and illus.*

Global corporations. *See* Multinational corporations

Global empires, 676–677. *See also specific empire*

Globalization. *See also* World economy; agricultural diversity and, 17–20 *and map;* defined, 700; early human migrations, 10–11, 12*(map)*, 13; protest against, 688–689*(illus.)*, 775; disease and, 711; immigration and, 711; Intermediate Era, 358, 361; Internet and, 704; outsourcing and, 702, 704, 779; Islamic, 241, 248–249; underdevelopment and, 706; China and, 729; of capitalism, 701, 715; multinational corporations and, 702–703, 787; religion and, 712; Third World and, 701–702; uneven impact of, 701, 866–867; western imperialism

market socialism in, 766, 768, 771; revolt in (1956), 752(map), 764, 766; in European Union, 774; in Romania, 771, 773(map)

Huns, 158, 194, 222; China and, 103, 112, 116; India and, 163; Rome and, 185, 187

Hunter-gatherers, 8, 13–15. See also Hunting; Aboriginal Australians, 540; transition to farming and, 5, 6, 16; Australian, 3, 14, 17, 214; cultural life and violence of, 14–15; egalitarian ethos of, 14, 58, 96; kinship and cooperation in, 13–14; !Kung people, 13, 58; Native Americans as, 426, 435; shifting cultivation and, 16; species extinction and, 13; in early Japan, 84; Native Americans as, 86, 87

Hunting: in Stone Age, 13; of buffalo (bison), 15(illus.), 86, 435, 528; by Mongols, 269(illus.)

Huron (American) Indians, 435

Hurricanes, in United States, 787, 866

Husayn, Taha, 671

Husayn (grandson of Muhammad), 240, 241, 421

Hussein, Faisal (Iraq), 670

Hussein, Saddam, 714; invasion of Kuwait by, 700, 784, 814; United States overthrow of, 717, 785, 820; Kurds and, 784, 814, 816

Hussein Ibn Ali, Sharif, 666

Hutu-Tutsi rivalry (Rwanda), 698, 827–828

Huygens, Christian, 397

Hybrid social groups, 681. See also Intermarriage; Mixed cultures

Hyksos (Semitic people), 53

Hypatia of Alexandria, 190, 226

Hyundai Corporation, 743(illus.)

Iberian Peninsula: exploration from, 376, 377(map). See also Portuguese exploration; Spanish exploration; Jews and Muslims expelled from, 422

Ibn al-Shatir, 381

Ibn Battuta, Abdallah Muhammad, 249, 362; in East Africa, 288; in Mali, 285; routes of, 250(map)

Ibn Khaldun, Abd al-Rahman, 231, 248, 251–252

Ibn Khalid al-Nasri, Ahmad, 543, 544, 566

Ibn Majid, Shihab al-Din Ahmad, 366

Ibn Rushd (Averroes), 246

Ibn Sina, Abu Ali al-Husain, 244, 247

Ice Ages, 8, 13. See also Stone Age; Bering land bridge in, 11, 12(map), 85; Little Ice Age, 350, 365–366, 374, 427, 479

Iceland, 305, 366, 392; quality of life in, 694; Vikings in, 336

Icons (religious images), 348

Ideas, spread of, 64. See also Intellectual life; Political thought; Silk Road and, 117; Islam and, 247; Mongol Empire, 269; in Americas, 304

Ideographs, Chinese, 79, 80(illus.), 274

Ideologies, 503–504. See also Capitalism; Marxism; Nationalism; Liberalism; Socialism; imperialist, 513; Nazism, 638; Maoism, 721–722, 725, 726

Idia (Bini), 290

Idrus Aloma (Kanem-Bornu), 404

Igbo people of Nigeria, 60, 61, 404, 678, 828; ancestral curse and, 401–402; slave trade and, 414, 415; colonialism and, 549, 554, 555; nationalism and, 822

Ignatius of Loyola, 385. See also Jesuit missionaries

Iliad (Homer), 67, 68–69, 98

Il-Khanid Persia, 251, 268(map)

Iltutmish, Sultan, 317

Immigration (immigrants). See also Migration (population movement); specific ethnic group or nationality; Arabs to Americas, 562; Armenian, 558; to Australia, 505, 514–515(illus.), 518(map), 785; to Canada, 538(illus.), 539; Chinese, in Taiwan, 465; in English North America; in Europe, 710, 755, 758–759, 775; European, in Ottoman Empire; Filipino, 530, 531, 683, 707, 711, 859; Japanese to Southeast Asia, 471; Jewish, 517, 567, 672, 760, 765, 812; Korean, 711, 737, 743; Mexican in United States, 674, 686, 711, 798; naturalization ceremony, 776–777(illus.); to North America, 434, 439, 517, 518(map), 558, 709; to United States, 529–530, 632, 633, 743, 760, 785, 789–790, 800

Imperialism (empires). See also Colonialism; Expansion; Western imperialism; specific empires; foundations of European, 378; Aztec, 426; in Africa, 415–416, 485; Ottoman, 418; industrialization and, 415–416, 508, 510, 620; expansion of, 511; global empires, 511, 513; national rivalries and, 510; new technologies and, 511; social Darwinism and, 513; Axis Powers, 639, 640; capitalism-based, 650; fascism and, 637, 639; Sukarno on, 663; United States ("Yankee"), 536, 651, 677, 697, 781, 805; Japanese, 740; cultural, 867

Impressionism (painting style), 521, 607

Inanna (goddess), 27, 28, 35

Inca Empire, 228, 298–299 and map, 358, 426, 429(map). See also Peru, colonial; administration, 302–303; Chimu and, 296; economy and gender,

303; engineering and science of, 304; Machu Picchu, 303(illus.), 304; roads in, 299(map), 304; Spanish conquest of, 370, 432–433

Incense, myrrh and, 49

Income inequality, 633. See also Wealth gap; in Britain and India, 579; in United States, 694, 787; in Latin American, 801–802; North-South gap, 868; in South Africa, 829; in sub-Saharan Africa, 827

Indentured labor, 439, 579, 600

Independence: See also Nationalism; Self-determination; Netherlands, 387; Swiss, 388; United States, 489–490; Latin American, 494, 496–499 and map, 535; Cuban, 534; Greek, 504–505, 506(illus.), 557; Irish, 505–506; Siamese, 586, 587; Korean, 608, 614; Philippines, 664, 690, 691(map); Indian, 658–659; Basque struggle for, 750; European colonies, 691(map); Vietnamese, 168, 325, 647–648, 691(map), 850; former Soviet republics, 769; former Yugoslavia, 772; sub-Saharan Africa, 824, 825; Bangladesh, 841

India. See also Hindus (Hinduism); earliest humans in, 11; epic literature of, 42, 44, 46, 149; agriculture in, 17, 19(map); Indo-Europeans in, 24(map), 25; social classes in, 28, 44; trade links of, 22, 32; chronology (7000–600 B.C.E.), 38; cyclical view of time in, 66; early cities in, 36–40; Indo-Aryan synthesis, 43–44, 46; economy, 43, 46, 156, 157, 158; Harappa in, 36–40; China and, 113; chronology (563 B.C.E.–550 C.E.), 150; Greek settlers in, 143; Chinese Buddhists (Faxian) in, 118, 162, 223, 306–307 and illus., 313, 362; gold coins, 148(illus.), 158, 161; Gupta Empire, 101, 160–164, 222; mathematics in, 162, 219, 247–248; Mauryan Empire, 43, 101, 154–158, 220, 221(map), 222; merchant class in, 149, 153, 157, 158; Persian expedition to, 127, 155; science and medicine in, 158, 162–163, 311–312; trade in, 157, 161, 221(map), 308, 317; village life in, 151 and illus., 155, 158, 309, 312, 318; Kushan Empire, 158, 159, 161(map), 194, 221(map); Delhi Sultanate, 268(map), 315(illus.), 316–317 and map; manufacturing in, 309, 361; Timurid attack on, 253

India, British rule of, 510, 575–582, 678. See also British East India Company; cash crops in, 578, 579, 581, 597, 680; caste and gender roles in, 576, 581; colonial government in, 577–578, 649; economic transformation in, 578–579; education in, 575, 578; expansion

Isaac (Hebrew), 63
Isabella (Spain), 353, 428, 430
Isaiah (Hebrew prophet), 65, 218
Isfahan, Persia, 420, 475; Afghan sack of, 421
Ishmael (Hebrew), 63
Ishtar (goddess), 35
Isis (goddess), 55, 145
Islamic clerics. *See* Muslim clerics
Islamic empires. *See* Caliphates; India, Mughal Empire in; Ottoman Empire
Islamic law (shar'ia), 245, 404, 558, 571; Quran and, 233, 239; in Afghanistan, 819, 820; in Nigeria, 828, 834; in Iran, 813; Wahhabism and, 563, 564, 671, 814, 834
Islamic militancy (Islamists), 758–759. *See also* Jihad; in Afghanistan, 696, 700, 764, 784; in Sudan, 700; Al Qaeda, 717, 775, 784, 820; September 11 (2001) attacks and, 775, 784; in Central Asia, 768; in Europe, 775; in Iran, 700, 813; in Middle East, 815, 822; Muslim Brotherhood and, 671, 817; Palestinian, 716–717; terrorism and, 775, 816, 820; in Bangladesh, 848; in Indonesia, 858; in Malaysia, 863; high technology and, 873
Islamic Revolution (Iran), 687, 700, 813
Islamic Union (Indonesia), 662
Islam (Islamic world), 231–254. *See also* Muslims; Pilgrims, Muslim; Quran; Shi'ism; Sufis; Sunni Islam; myths of, 36; emergence of, 195; in Africa, 282, 284, 285, 287, 288; meaning of word, 233; Zoroastrianism and, 129, 131, 141, 237, 238, 242; beliefs and society, 235–237; in Central Asia, 314; Christianity and, 188*(map)*, 232, 233, 234, 235, 237, 239, 245; chronology (570–1220 C.E.), 236; contributions of, 254; conversion to, 200, 234, 238, 239, 245, 253, 284; cosmopolitanism in, 231, 239, 243, 249, 254, 336; Eastern Hemiphere domination, 231–232; expansion of, 203, 229, 237–238 *and map*, 240, 242*(map)*, 248, 362; Five Pillars of, 235–236; gender relations in, 236–237, 245–246; globalization of, 248–249, 250*(map)*; chronology (1095–1492), 248; Hinduism and, 308, 310, 314; Ibn Batuta's travels in, 249, 250*(map)*, 285, 288, 362; in India, 229, 308, 314–316; Jews and, 65, 233, 234, 236, 238–239, 245; in 900 C.E., 360*(map)*; laws of (Shari'a), 233, 239, 245; umma, 233–234, 235, 238, 240, 241, 243; literature and art in, 246–247; Middle East and, 237, 239; Mongols and, 243, 364; morality and ethics of, 236, 240, 361;

mosques, 233, 240*(illus.)*, 247, 259; in Southeast Asia, 229, 323–324, 326–328; polygamy in, 233–234, 236, 245, 246, 363; schools and scholars, 239, 243, 244, 247, 248, 249, 254, 285; science and mathematics, 232, 244, 246–247; Shi'ite, 240–241, 243, 244, 247, 362; slavery in, 245, 363; Sufism, 244–245, 247, 318, 323; Sunni, 240–241, 243, 244, 323–324; theology and religious practice, 244–245; trade in, 249, 254; Turks, 243, 245; women in, 233–234, 236–237, 245–246 *and illus.*; Christian rivalry with, 376, 455, 457, 875; ideas and technology of, 380, 396; Ottoman, 384*(map)*, 387, 418, 419, 482; in Central Asia, 420, 423, 574, 615, 617; in Middle East, 402, 563–564, 807–808; in Africa, 404, 405*(illus.)*, 406, 411, 546; in Sudan, 546–547; modernism and, 560, 564–566, 581; Napoleon and, 543; in Southeast Asia, 459; spread of, 402, 818*(map)*, 873; revivalism, 563, 581; Wahhabism, 563–564, 581, 671, 815, 834; westernization and, 560, 564, 566; alcohol prohibition in, 562, 818, 820; change and conflict in, 815–816; Red Crescent in, 685; Turkish modernization and, 667, 669; in Europe, 758, 760; in Indonesia, 661–662, 857, 858; reformist, in Iran, 813–814; Zionism and, 670; birth control discouraged in, 709; in West Africa, 546; Western culture and, 560, 564, 566, 822; in China, 731; in Pakistan, 712, 847
Ismail, Sultan (Egypt), 560
Isma'il (Safavids), 420
Isolationism: Qing China, 595–596; seclusion policy in Japan and Korea, 606, 608; in United States (1920s), 632, 633
Israel, 63, 64, 250. *See also* Hebrews; Jews; Canaanites and, 92; allied with United States, 699, 717, 810; Arab-Israeli conflicts, 687, 809–812, 811*(map)*, 816; rebirth of, 810; immigration to, 765, 812; nuclear weapons of, 698; Palestinian terrorism and, 716–717; Western support for, 753, 815; Egypt and, 809; music in, 818
Issus, Battle of (333 B.C.E.), 143*(illus.)*
Istanbul, 254, 348, 355, 416, 419, 667. *See also* Constantinople; Greek independence and, 504; multiethnicity in, 558; trade in, 418, 478; University of, 558
Italian colonies, 512*(map)*, 563; in Africa, 511, 512*(map)*, 548*(map)*, 549; independence of, 691*(map)*, 808

Italy, trading cities of, 355. *See also* Genoa; Venice; Marco Polo and, 269
Italy (Italians), 67, 493, 504, 667, 678; climate and geography of, 172; Etruscans in, 173*(map)*, 174; Greek colonies in, 131, 132*(map)*, 173*(map)*, 174; Rome's conquest of, 175–176; artists of, 381, 395; Ostrogoths in, 187, 191; Lombards in, 333, 335; slavery in, 339; banking in, 340; universities in, 346; fragmentation of, 345; Renaissance in, 355; pasta in, 359; slavery in, 408; China and, 469 (*See also* Polo, Marco); merchants in Africa, 407; unification of, 505; women's rights in, 505; invasion of Ethiopia by, 511, 549, 639, 650; in World War I, 620, 621, 622; fascism in, 636, 637; immigrants, in Americas, 518*(map)*, 530, 681; Spanish civil war and, 639; in World War II, 641*(map)*, 643, 679; aging population in, 709; post-WWII politics in, 748, 750; European Community and, 753
Iturbide, Agustin de, 499
Ivan III, Czar (Russia), 350
Ivan IV the Terrible, Czar (Russia), 389, 391*(map)*
Ivory Coast (Cote d'Ivoire), 693, 707; despotism in, 830; export crops in, 555; religious conflict in, 834
Ivory trade, 58, 202, 281, 288*(illus.)*, 410; African, 402, 406, 408, 411, 415, 545
Iyalode ("mother of the town"), 405

Jacobins (France), 492, 493, 504
Jafir, Mir (Bengal), 573*(illus.)*
Jahan, Shah (Mughal India), 451, 453
Jahangir (Mughal India), 451, 452
Jainism, 152, 162, 657
Jakarta (Batavia), 458*(map)*, 461, 462 *and illus.*, 583, 591, 707
Jamaica, 497; sugar plantations in, 444; as British colony, 434, 496, 678; Columbus in, 430; maroons in, 446; Asians in, 535; Rastafarianism in, 805; reggae music of, 689, 805
James, C. L. R., 675
James, William, 523
James II (England), 392–393
Jamestown colony (Virginia), 434
Janissaries (Ottoman military), 418, 419, 558
Japan, China and, 80, 101, 119, 229, 485, 720; Yayoi era, 120–121; cultural borrowing and, 257, 274; 21 Demands, 606, 652; Manchuria and, 606, 652, 653, 654*(map)*; Rape of Nanjing and, 644, 740; revolutionary groups, 605; trade, 464, 602, 727; treaty between, 592–593*(illus.)*; Tokugawa era, 606–607; war between (1894–1895), 603,

612, 613–614; war between (1937–1945), 654(map), 655; World War I, 622; World War II, 642, 643(map), 644, 645, 656, 731

Japan, Inc., 736

Japanese-American internment, in World War II, 643

Japanese Empire (Japanese colonies), 512(map), 740. See also Japan, China and; fascism and militarism in, 639; Great Depression in, 635; Korea, 594, 603, 612, 613(map), 740–741; in World War II, 642, 643 and map, 644–645, 679; Southeast Asia in, 642, 643(map), 644, 660, 661, 662–664; Taiwan, 612, 613(map), 632, 744

Japanese language, 84, 614

Japan (Japanese), 3, 104, 678; early humans in, 9, 11; climate zones, 82–83; Ainu culture in, 83–84, 120; Jomon society in, 84 and illus., 120; Korean immigrants in, 83, 120; chronology (300 B.C.E.–710 C.E.), 119; isolation of, and cultural unity, 121; Yamato, 120(map), 121; Yayoi, 120–121; Buddhism in, 229, 256(illus.); chronology (645–1568), 273; feudalism in, 277–278, 364; women in, 275, 278; Heian period, 275, 276–77, 362; Mongol invasions and, 276(map), 278; Nara era, 274–275; Shinto in, 122, 275, 362; shogunates in, 278, 279; warrior class in, 276–278, 279, 362; Ashikaga shogunate, 470; Christian missionaries in, 371, 448(illus.), 471, 472; chronology (1338–1841), 470; civil war in, 471, 472, 476; closing of, 472; Europeans in, 471–472; invasion of Korea by, 470; Tokugawa, 371, 471, 472–473, 475, 606–608, 609; women in, 472–473, 482; education in, 594, 608, 735(illus.), 737, 739; immigrants from, 471, 530, 531, 535, 539, 632, 683; industrialization in, 499, 503, 594, 610, 612, 680, 703; Meiji era, 609–614; modernization in, 511, 594, 609–610, 613(map), 676, 677; seclusion policy in, 606, 608; social reform in, 611–612; United States and, 515, 780; alliance with Britain, 606, 612, 622, 632; war with Russia, 612, 617; woodblock art of, 473 and illus., 607, 611(illus.); World War I and, 620, 622; Russian civil war and, 627, 628(map); after World War I, 631, 632; borrowing by, 734; literacy in, 472, 476, 607, 610; nationalism in, 607, 609, 610, 612; Indian National Army and, 659; post-war rebuilding of, 687, 694; quality of life in, 694; women's rights in, 632, 685, 732; aging population in, 709, 868; decline of religion in, 712; democracy in,

732, 734; economic growth in, 694, 699, 701, 732, 734–736, 767, 781; remaking of, 732–740; generation gap in, 738; global system and, 701, 739–740; occupation and recovery, 732, 734; protests in (1960s), 716; Asian "Little Dragons" and, 733(map), 740, 745; society and culture, 736–739; environmental destruction in, 709; South African investment, 829

Jara, Victor, 804

Jati (castes) in India, 150, 452. See also India, caste system in

Java (Javanese), 81, 82, 83(map), 259, 378, 683; early humans in, 8–9; Buddhist temple in, 164(illus.); Indianization in, 166, 321–322; Islam in, 323, 328, 459, 858; Madjapahit Empire, 319(map), 322–323; maritime trade and, 326, 328; coffee in, 461, 590(illus.); cultivation system on, 582–583; as Dutch colony, 457, 458(map), 461–462, 582–583, 649(illus.), 683; revolt against Dutch in, 568–569(illus.); gamelan orchestra in, 591; Japanese occupation, 662; nationalism in, 663; domination of Indonesia by, 857; population growth in, 690

Jayarajadevi (Khmer), 321

Jayavarman (Angkor), 320

Jayavarman VII (Angkor), 321

Jazz music, 684; African Americans and, 446, 633, 666, 759; in Europe, 759; in South Africa, 665 and illus., 832; in Soviet Union, 765

Jean, Michaelle, 792

Jeanne d'Arc (France), 353

Jefferson, Thomas, 490, 525; Declaration of Independence and, 489; Locke and, 398

Jenne-Jenno (Mali), 203, 204

Jeremiah (prophet), 218

Jericho (Palestine), 29

Jerusalem, 64, 375; temple in, 189; Crusades in, 250, 251, 345, 346

Jesuit missionaries: in China, 396, 469, 470; in Ethiopia, 412; in French Canada, 434; in India, 385; in Japan, 385, 448(illus.), 472; St. Francis Xavier, 385, 472; in Uruguay, 438

Jesus (Christ), 101, 146, 170(illus.). See also Christianity; teachings and death of, 187–188; Islam and, 233

Jewelry (ornament): in Indus Valley, 38, 40; in Meroë, 198; in East Africa, 288; Cahokian, 298

Jews. See also Anti-Semitism; Hebrews; Israel; Judaism; as mapmakers, 375; Roman rule and, 65; return to Palestine, 64, 65, 127; Christianity and, 187–188, 189; Ethiopian Falasha, 201; diaspora of, 65, 189, 361; as bankers,

379; as merchants, 254, 261, 317; in Baghdad, 254; in China, 261; in Islamic Spain, 242; in Poland and Lithuania, 393; Islam and, 65, 233, 234, 236, 238–239, 245; persecution and slaughter of, in Europe, 251, 343, 345, 346; as moneylenders, 340; expulsed from France, 342; expulsed from Spain, 244, 353, 417, 478; in Morocco, 422; as merchants, 399, 419, 478; converso, in Spain, 436; in Ottoman Empire, 417, 418, 558; ghettoization of, 505, 567; immigration by, 517, 567, 672, 760, 765, 812; persecution of, in Europe, 386, 517; in Persia, 561; Russian poets, 619; Holocaust and, 642, 760, 810; Nazi Germany and, 638; Zionism and, 505, 567, 667, 671–672

Jiang Jieshi. See Chiang Kai-shek

Jiangxi Soviet (China), 653, 655

Jidi Oyo (pop musician), 833(illus.)

Jihad (holy war), 236, 563, 714, 817. See also Militant Islam; in Sudanic Africa, 546–547; in Iraq, 670; in Afghanistan, 820

Jin dynasty (China), 266

Jinnah, Muhammad Ali, 658, 659, 847; partition and, 838, 839

Jiroft (Iran), 31

Johannesburg, South Africa, 551

John I (England), 345

John Paul II, pope, 757

Johnson, Lyndon B., 783; poverty and racism programs, 788; Vietnam War and, 782, 851

Johnson, William, 441(illus.)

Johnson-Sirleaf, Ellen (Liberia), 827

John XXIII, Pope, 712, 760

Joint family, 42, 114

Joint-stock companies, 380, 392

Jomon culture (Japan), 84 and illus., 120

Jones, William, 575–576

Jonson, Ben, 386

Jordan River Valley, 17, 29

Jordan (Transjordan): Nabateans in, 194–195; Palestinians in, 711; British control of, 667, 668(map); Israel and, 811(map)

Joyce, James, 635–636

Juarez, Benito (Mexico), 533

Judah, 64–65

Judaism, 3, 63, 65, 714. See also Hebrews; Israel; Jews; Zoroastrianism and, 129, 141; Christianity and, 189, 235; converts to, 222, 249; in India, 159, 160; Judaeo-Christian heritage and, 760

Juju music (Nigeria), 832

Julius Caesar (Rome), 177

Jundishapur (India), 194

Junks (Chinese ships), 116, 469

Juno (goddess), 181

Laws (legal codes), 475. *See also* Islamic law (shar'ia); Chinese (*See* Legalism); Mosaic (Hebrew), 34, 63, 64, 65; Code of Hammurabi, 34, 35, 36, 95, 97; trade and, 95; Persian Empire, 127, 128; Code of Manu (India), 150, 162; Roman, 174, 175, 191, 343; Byzantine, 191; French Revolution and, 492; in Mughal India, 451; Ottoman reform and, 558; French, in Egypt, 559; racist, in colonial Africa, 551, 552; racist, in United States, 528; in British India, 575; Siamese, 324; western, in Iran, 669; gun control, 736, 757; international, 698, 785

League of Arab States, 818*(map)*, 821

League of Nations, 625, 639, 648; Middle East and, 667, 668*(map)*

Lebanon (Lebanese), 250. *See also* Phoenicia; cedars of, 52, 68; Shi'ite Islam in, 241; Ottoman rule in, 416, 562; Christians in, 562; in African towns, 552, 649; in Latin America, 535; French control of, 667, 668*(map)*; terrorists in, 716; Palestinians in, 711; civil war in, 816, 818; pop music in, 818

Le dynasty (Vietnam), 325, 326*(illus.)*

Legalism, in China, 110, 112; Confucianism and, 101, 109, 219, 220

Le Loi, 325

Lemoinnier, painting by, 397*(illus.)*

Lenin, Vladimir, 626 *and illus.*, 627, 650, 678

Leo Africanus, 404

Leo III, Pope, 331

Leopold (Belgium), 547, 555*(illus.)*

Leo X, Pope, 383

Lepanto, Battle of (1571), 387

The Leviathan (Hobbes), 395–396

Levi Strauss company, 704

Levitt, William, 787

Liang Qichao, 603

Liberal Democratic Party (Japan), 734

Liberalization: economic, in Poland, 766; in China, 745; in South Korea, 742; in Taiwan, 745; in India, 844

Liberals (liberalism): parliamentary democracy and, 504, 506–507; religion and, 520; in Latin America, 532; in China, 601; fascism and, 636, 637; in Brazil, 674; in Russia, 627, 629; in United States, 522, 634, 788; in Canada, 791; Muslim, 816–817, 858

Liberation movements, in Africa, 825

Liberation theology, 712, 803

Liberia, 545–546, 549; civil war in, 784, 827

Libraries: in Assyrian Empire, 34; in Sui China, 119; in Alexandria, 145; in India, 156; in Islamic Spain, 243, 247; in Persia, 247, 251; in Timbuktu,

285; in Christian monasteries, 332; in Fatimid Egypt, 362; in colonial Mexico, 436; Carnegie's philanthropy and, 681

Libya, 204, 822; Egypt and, 54; as Italian colony, 549, 563

Life expectancy, 13; of plantation slaves, 444, 445; in Soviet Union, 630, 765; United Nations programs and, 698; in Japan, 735; in Taiwan, 745; in Africa, 830, 832; in Arab countries, 821; in India, 844; in Indonesia, 857; North-South gap in, 868

Liliuokalani (Hawaii), 530, 677

Lima, Peru, 432, 436, 442

Lincoln, Abraham, 528

Lineage. *See* Matrilineal kinship; Patrilineal systems

Lingua franca, 661, 665

Lin Zezu, 597

Li Po, 262

Li Ruzhen, 593–594

Li Si (China), 109

Literacy, 705; in ancient China, 79, 98; in Meroë, 198; Islam and, 246–247; in Siam, 325, 457; European printing press and, 376, 383; of women, 472, 595; in Burma, 476; in Japan, 472, 476, 607, 610, 694, 739; in Soviet Union, 630; in Egypt, 671; in China, 595, 726, 727; in South Korea, 742; in Taiwan, 744; in Cuba, 799–800; in Arab countries, 821; in Africa, 831; in India, 844; in Latin America, 801, 869; in Indonesia, 857; in Sri Lanka, 848; in Vietnam, 854; North-South gap in, 868

Literature. *See also* Drama; Libraries; Poets and poetry; Printing technology; Writing; Mesopotamian, 35–36; Greek, 68–69; Indian, 163; Roman, 183; Korean, 274; medieval European, 346–347; English, 351, 352; Renaissance, 355, 382–383; American, 523; Brazilian, 535; Chinese, 269, 271, 466, 651, 726, 728; colonial rule and, 591; Romanticism *vs.* realism in, 520, 523; Vietnamese, 591; Japanese, 275, 612, 632, 739; Russian, 617; twentieth-century, 635–636; Egyptian, 671; Southeast Asia, 662; European postcolonialist, 759; Latin American, 804; Soviet Union, 762; Nigerian, 807; Indonesian, 837–838; in Middle East, 819; African, 833–834

Lithuania, 761. *See also* Poland-Lithuania; Catholicism in, 350, 393; Russia and, 389; serfdom in, 353, 379; Jews in, 505

Little Dragons of Asia, 733*(map)*, 740. *See also* Hong Kong; Singapore; South Korea; Taiwan; in global system, 745

Little Ice Age, 350, 365–366, 374, 427, 479

Liverpool, England, 447, 500, 759

Living standards (quality of life), 874; in Australia, 694, 787; in Canada, 694, 787, 791; in China, 729, 731, 870; in Japan, 735; in Mexico, 674; in Southeast Asia, 662; in South Korea, 742, 743; in Soviet Union, 762, 765; in Taiwan, 744; in Europe, 755, 766, 787; in Africa, 829, 830, 831; wealth gap and, 680, 694, 869, 873; Western, 694, 870; in Malaysia, 863

Livingstone, David, 546

Llamas and alpacas, 20, 87, 212, 304

Loans: *See also* Debt; interest (usury) on, 131, 340, 375, 379; to Europe, by United States, 633; to villagers, 707

Local culture, globalization and, 866, 867, 868

Locke, John, 398, 466, 489, 506

Loess (soil), 72

Lombards, in Italy, 333, 335

London: childhood mortality in, 399; Crystal Palace Exposition (1851), 486–487 *and illus.*; population of, 339, 374, 517; immigrants in, 710, 758; terrorism in, 775

Longbow, 353. *See also* Bows and arrows

Long March (China), 654*(map)*, 655 *and illus.*

Longshan culture (China), 75

Lord-vassal relations. *See also* Feudalism; in Japan, 277; in medieval Europe, 338–339

Lothal (India), 40

Lothar (Holy Roman Emperor), 334*(map)*

Louisiana, 434; moundbuilders in, 86, *and illus.*; Cajuns in, 440; mixed-descent people in, 481

Louisiana Purchase, 525, 526*(map)*

Louis IX (St. Louis, France), 345

Louis-Philippe (France), 493

Louis the German, 334*(map)*

Louis XIV (France), 389, 469; Siam and, 458, 482

Louis XVI (France): French Revolution and, 491, 492

Low Countries, 341, 378, 517. *See also* Belgium; Flanders; Netherlands; art in, 381; Spanish rule in, 387

Lowell, Massachusetts, strike in, 530

Loyalists: in American Revolution, 489, 490, 538; in Spanish civil war, 639

Luanda (Angola), 832

Luba kingdom (Congo), 406–407

Lubis, Mochtar, 837

Luce, Henry, 778

"Lucy" (australopithecene), 8

Luddites (protesters), 501

Lula (Luis Ignacio da Silva), 799

Lumumba, Patrice (Congo), 824–825

Lunda kingdom (Congo), 406–407, 410

Luther, Martin, 383; anti-Semitism of, 386

Mapmaking (cartography), 428, 470, 482; Babylonian, 92; Greek, 125; Polynesian, 217(illus.); in Europe, 375; Muslim Spain, 248; Ottoman, 396; Polynesian, 539; Portuguese, 357

Maratha confederacy (India), 454, 571, 572

Marconi, Guglielmo, radio and, 521

Marcos, Ferdinand (Philippines), 858–860

Marcos, Imelda, 860

Marcus Aurelius (Rome), 178, 180

Mari (Akkadian Empire), 32

Marianas Islands, 215, 216(map)

Marijuana, 791, 805

"Marilyn Monroe Doctrine," 867

Marine resources. See Fishing (fishermen)

Maritime exploration: See also Exploration (expeditions); Egyptian, 54; Austronesians, 82, 83(map), 101, 165, 213; of Europe, 476

Maritime trade. See Ships and shipping

Mark, Gospel of, 187

Mark Anthony (Rome), 177–178

Market economy, 378, 696. See also Capitalism; Free market; in Europe, 476; in China and Vietnam, 693, 854; Russian conversion to, 769

Market Leninism, 728–729

Markets. See also Merchants (traders); Trade; in Baghdad, 241; Cahokia, 298; Aztec, 300, 301; Antwerp, 373, 375(illus.); African, 405–406; Isfahan bazaar, 420, 421; in Goa, 455(illus.)

Market socialism: in China, 727–728, 768; in Hungary, 766, 768, 771; perestroika, in Soviet Union, 767–768

Market women: in Africa, 404, 834; colonialism and, 591, 679; in Southeast Asia, 292, 321, 324, 325, 457

Marley, Bob, 693, 805, 833; in Zimbabwe, 689

Maronite Christians, 562

Maroons (escaped slaves), 446

Marquesas Islands, 215–216 and map, 217, 540

Marriage. See also Divorce; Intermarriage; Polygamy; of slaves, 30; in China, 79; in India, 42, 162; in Persia, 131; Greek, 137; in Rome, 183; Islamic, 245; in imperial China, 114, 269; in Korea, 276; in Japan, 278; Aztec, 302; of slaves, 291; African women and, 290–291; in India, 309; in Siam, 324; Russian rulers and, 349; European monarchies and, 353; Flemish, 382(illus.); Henry VIII and, 385; in Europe, 342, 399, 632; Columbus and, 428; in India, 451; in Japan, 473, 612, 736–737; early modern era, 517–518; in British India, 581; love matches in, 518, 581; Indonesian women and, 459; in Egypt, 671; reform of, in China, 726;

in Japan, 736; in South Korea, 742; in Europe, 758; homosexuals and, 714, 758, 791; in United States, 791; sexual revolution and, 757; in Middle East, 817; in Latin America, 803; reform of, in India, 846

Marseilles (Massalia), 141, 171

Marshall, George, 748

Marshall, William, 338

Marshall Islands, 215, 216(map), 217(illus.)

Marshall Plan for Europe, 748

Martí, Jose, Cuba and, 534

Martial law: See also Military dictatorship; in South Korea, 742

Martin, Emma, 507

Martinique Island, 434

Marx, Karl, 507–508, 509; legacy of, 650, 678; Russian Revolution and, 626

Marxism, 507–508, 630; in Angola, 693, 831; in Vietnam, 661; nationalism and, 648, 650, 676; revolution and, 678; in Latin America, 675, 796; Maoism and, 721; deconstruction and, 760; in Mozambique, 825, 831; in Senegal, 834

Marxism-Leninism, 629, 656

Mary (mother of Jesus), 193, 293, 341–342; cult of, 383, 437, 460

Mary Tudor (England), 385

Massachusetts, 490, 527; Indians of, 298

Mass culture, spread of, 635, 683, 685–685, 759. See also Popular culture

Mass extinctions, 7, 20, 86

Mass media, 635, 711. See also Newspapers; Radio; Television; cultural synthesis and, 712; Internet and, 863; Latin American, 804; Russian control of, 771; in United States, 788, 789, 791

Mass production, 444, 501, 503, 529, 631

Mass transit: in Europe, 753; in Japan, 735, 737(illus.)

Materialism, capitalism and, 873

Maternal ancestry, DNA studies and, 10

Mathematical Principles of Natural Philosophy (Newton), 396

Mathematics: Sumerian, 32; in ancient Egypt, 55; Olmec, 90; trade and, 22; Chinese, 105; money and, 95; numbering systems, 32, 75, 162, 210, 247–248, 356, 376; concept of zero, 162, 209, 248, 311; decimal system, 77, 105, 115, 162; fractions, 55, 115; geometry, 115, 125, 145, 212, 247; Greek, 135, 141; value of pi (π), 115, 162; Hellenistic age, 145; trigonometry, 247; algebra, 115, 247; Indian, 162, 219, 311, 312, 376, 679; Islamic, 247–248; Maya, 209; Moche, 211; Arab, 376, 381; European, 376, 396, 475; Ottoman, 418

Matriarchy: vs. patriarchy, 200; in Southeast Asia, 320

Matrilineal kinship: Neolithic, 14; in India, 39, 46; Kushite, 59; erosion of, 97; in Southeast Asia, 168; Christianity and, 200; Aboriginal, 214; in Polynesia, 216; in Africa, 290; Khmer, 321; in Native American societies, 295, 298, 434; in West Africa, 402, 404, 405

Matthew, Gospel of, 187

Mau Mau Rebellion (Kenya), 814 and illus.

Mauritania, 59

Mauritius, 579

Mauryan Empire (India), 43, 101, 154, 156(map), 222; Ashoka and, 157–158 and illus., 159, 160, 220; decline of, 157–158; imperial state in, 155–156, 220; roads in, 157, 222; society and economy, 156–157; trade of, 221(map)

Mawlay Hassan, Sultan (Morocco), 562

Maxim, Hiram, 684

Maxim gun, 511, 547, 602(illus.), 684

Maximian (Rome), 186

Maximilian (Mexico), 533

Maya, 100, 206(map), 226, 427, 430, 435; Olmecs and, 89, 90; agriculture and architecture of, 206, 294; astronomy, 208–209; decline of, 213, 228, 294; emergence of, 206–207; Olmecs and, 89, 90, 206, 210, 223; politics and trade of, 207, 221(map); slavery in, 207; society and religion, 208, 223; Toltecs and, 295; writings of, 206–207, 209, 294; in Yucatan, 206, 294, 436, 437

May Fourth Movement (China), 652, 653

Mazzini, Giuseppe, 505

Mbanga (Congo), 290

Mbuti Pygmies (Congo), 13

Meadows of Gold and Mines of Gems (al-Mas'udi)

Mecca, 246, 563, 564, 666; Hashemites of, 670, 671; Ka'ba in, 232; Muhammad in, 233, 235 and illus.; pilgrimage (haj) to, 230(illus.), 232, 235–236, 239, 252, 284

Mechanization, 519; of agriculture, 517, 704; Luddite protest against, 501

Medes (Median Empire), 126, 128

Media. See Mass media; Newspapers; Radio

Medicine (physicians), 398, 475. See also Disease; Health care; American, 86; Egyptian, 55; Greek, 158; Indian, 158, 162–163; Islamic, 247; hospitals, 157, 247; Chinese, 264, 726; American (quinine), 293; Korean, 276; Inca, 304; in Kongo, 409; women in, 581, 764; mission hospitals, 554, 561, 598; modern era, 521; in colonial Africa, 547, 554; Ottoman, 418; in Soviet Union, 630, 764; Doctors Without

745; in Japan, 732; Korean War and, 741–742 *and map*; interventions by, 695, 751, 781*(map)*, 782–783, 822; worldwide (1945–present), 780, 781*(map)*, 785; in Turkey, 808; in Laos and Cambodia, 782, 854; in Vietnam War, 782, 783*(illus.)*; in Afghanistan, 785; in Iraq, 687, 714, 785; in Panama, 797; in Thailand, 860–861

Military dictatorship (military rule): in Japan, 639; in Latin America, 484, 531, 672, 686, 777; in Thailand, 660–661; in South Korea, 742; in Argentina, 796; in Brazil, 798–799; in Chile, 801, 804; human rights abuses and, 797, 807, 863; in Iraq, 670, 814; in Nigeria, 807; in Africa, 825, 826, 827; in Paksitan, 841; United States' arms sales to, 780, 784; in Burma and Thailand, 860–862; in Indonesia, 857–858

Military draft (conscription), 610; in Japan, 274, 277; of colonials, in World War I, 625, 648, 664; in Iran, 669; in Russia, 614–615; in Vietnam War, 851

Military-industrial complex, 780

Military technology. *See* Weapons and military technology

Mill, John Stuart, 506

Millet (grain), 17, 57, 203, 205, 290

Millet (nationality) system, 254

Mills: watermills, 264, 337; windmills, 337, 445*(illus.)*

Minamoto-no-Yoritomo, 278

Mindon (Burma), 585

Ming Empire (China), 267, 463, 464, 466; government and culture, 270–271; isolationism of, 271–272; Vietnam and, 325; Zheng He's voyages in, 271, 272*(map)*, 366, 426

Mining and minerals. *See also* Gold; Iron and steel industry; *specific metals;* in colonial Bolivia, 442; coal, in Britain, 499, 500, 501, 502*(map)*; in British Malaya, 583; imported, in Japan, 735; in colonial Africa, 554, 555; in South Africa, 551, 665, 829; in Congo, 824

Minoan civilization, 3, 63, 67 *and illus.;* trade of, 64*(map)*, 66, 67

Minorities. *See* Ethnic minorities; *specific minorities*

Mirabai, 453

Missionaries: Buddhist, 118, 157; Catholic, 293, 300; Christian, 293, 333, 362; messianism and, 65; Muslim, 362 *(See also* Islam, conversion to)

Missionary impulse, 630, 712. *See also* Catholic missionaries; Christian missionaries

Mississippi River (Valley), 86, 212; French exploration of, 434; native peoples, 228, 297–298 *and map,* 427

Mithraism, 145–146

Mithra (sun god), 146

Mitochondrial DNA. *See* DNA

Mitsui conglomerate, 610, 611*(illus.)*

Mixcoatl (Toltec), 294

Mixed-descent people: *See also* Mestizos; Mulattos; Eurasians, in Java, 462; in Latin America, 436, 495, 535; Metis, in Canada, 440, 539; in Portuguese communities, 455; coloreds, in South Africa, 550, 828, 829

Mobutu Sese Seko (Zaire), 825, 827; despotism of, 830–831, 832

Moche (Peru), 206*(map)*, 293; trade and culture, 211, 221*(map)*

Mocteczuma I (Aztec), 299

Mocteczuma II (Aztec), 302, 432

Modernization. *See also* Westernization; in Ottoman Empire, 558–559; in Burma, 585; in Egypt, 559, 560*(illus.)*, 566*(illus.)*, 809; Islam and, 560, 564–566, 581; in Japan, 511, 594, 607, 609, 613*(map)*, 676, 677; in Siam, 511, 586–587, 676; in Korea, 614; in Russia, 614, 615*(illus.)*, 626; in Brazil, 674; in China, 601, 603, 652–653, 727–732; in Turkey, 667, 669 *and illus.,* 676; opposition to, in Iran, 669–670; in Taiwan, 745; in Middle East, 817, 822; in Saudi Arabia, 814

Mogadishu (East African city-state), 287

Mogollon Indians, 212, 296, 297*(map)*

Mohenjo-Daro (Indus River Valley), 37, 38*(illus.)*

Moikeha, 217

Moldavia, 557

Moluccas. *See* Maluku (Moluccas)

Mombasa (East African city-state), 287, 290, 408, 411

Monarchy. *See* Kingship (emperors; monarchy)

Monasteries. *See* Buddhist monasteries; Christian monasteries

Monet, Claude, art of, 521

Monetary system. *See also* Currency; American metals in, 452; Bretton Woods, 645, 753; European Union, 774

Money, 95. *See also* Coins (coinage); Currency; Chinese paper, 262, 263

Moneylending. *See* Loans, interest on

Mongkut (Siam), 587

Mongols (Mongolian Empire), 364–365. *See also specific* khans and khanates; culture and networks, 267, 269–270; Islam and, 243; Buddhism and, 160, 267, 313; China and, 116, 272; conquest of China by, 266–270, 268*(map)*; conquest of Korea by, 274; invasion of Japan by, 276*(map)*, 278; Southeast Asia and, 323; heritage and networks of, 365; Russia and, 349–350;

innovation in Europe and, 355; military technology of, 267, 363*(illus.)*; sack of Baghdad, 243, 251; Timurids, 253, 318; breakup of, 423; China and, 463*(map)*, 465, 606; communism in, 695

Moniz, Donha Felipa, 428

Monnet, Jean, 753, 875

Monoculture economies, 442, 445. *See also* Cash crops; Plantation zone; in Latin America, 495; in American South, 528; in colonial Africa, 555; in Southeast Asia, 589

Monogamy, 304, 362. *See also* Marriage

Monomotapa (East Africa), 403*(map)*, 412

Monophysite theology, 232

Monopoly, 529; big business and, 503, 504

Monopoly trade: Chinese state, 109, 110, 467, 597; Dutch, in Southeast Asia, 461; empire building and, 510; British, in Persia, 561; Indian salt trade, 658; in colonial Southeast Asia, 648

Monotheism: Akhenaten and, 54; Hebrew, 63, 65, 98; Islamic, 233, 234, 240, 310, 314; in West Africa, 60, 98, 291; in Zoroastrianism, 129, 130; Islam and, 450

Monroe, James, 527

Monroe Doctrine, 527, 867

Monsoon winds, 76*(map)*; Indian fleets and, 164

Montaigne, Michel Eyquem de, 383

Monte Alban (Zapotec), 209–210, 293

Montenegrins, 773*(map)*

Montesque, Baron de, 489, 506

Monte Verde (Chile), 86

Montreal, 434, 440, 872

Morality (moral code), 98, 219. *See also* Ethics; Hebrews and, 65; Axial age thinkers and, 219; Buddhist, 154, 220, 361; Chinese, 78, 266; Christian, 190, 341, 361; Confucian, 106, 108, 115, 271; Islam, 236, 240, 361; power and, 381; Protestant, 385, 392; Confucian, 595, 601; Indian caste system and, 581; Japanese, 732

Morelos, Jose Maria (Mexico), 497, 499

Morgan, Henry, 434

Morgan, J. P., 529

Morocco, 176, 285, 420, 475, 808; expansion of, 404, 423; Sa'dian dynasty in, 422–423; European colonization of, 562; labor migration from, 758; terrorism in, 717

Moronobu, art of, 473 *and illus.*

Moros, in Philippines, 460

Moscow, 627, 642

Moses, 233; laws of, 34, 63, 64, 65

Moshoeshoe (Sotho), 550

Mosques, 247; in China, 259; in Damascus, 240(illus.); in Medina, 233; in Africa, 405(illus.); in Ottoman Empire, 418; in China, 728; in Kuala Lumpur, 864(illus.)

Mossadeq, Mohammad, 697

Mother goddess, 20(illus.), 181(illus.), 304. See also Mary, mother of Jesus; in India, 39, 312

Motherhood. See Childbearing and childcare

Mothers and Grandmothers of the Plaza de Mayo (Argentina), 777–778

Motion pictures. See Film industry

Moundbuilders: in North America, 86, 100, 212–213, 297–298 and map; in South America, 88

Movable type, 264, 356. See also Printing technology; in Korea, 276, 277(illus.)

Mozambique (East Africa), 287, 552, 707, 827; slaves from, 412; Portuguese in, 408, 410; as Portuguese colony, 412, 415, 648, 825; European colonialism in, 544, 553; forced labor in, 648; independence of, 691(map); Marxism in, 825; civil war in, 831

Mozart, Wolfgang Amadeus, 520

Mugabe, Robert (Zimbabwe), 825, 831–832

Mughal Empire. See India, Mughal Empire in

Muhammad Ali (Egypt), 559, 560(illus.), 564

Muhammad ibn Abdullah (Prophet), 235(illus.), 240, 417. See also Islam; Muslims; Quran; descent from, 420, 423; on gender relations, 236–237; life and message of, 232–235, 563; death of, 235, 237; successors to, 238, 245; Danish cartoon of, 775

Mujahidin (Afghanistan), 819

Mujiber, Sheikh, 841

Mulattos (mixed-ancestry): in Africa, 481; in Brazil, 436, 481; in colonial Latin America, 436, 446; in Latin America, 497, 532, 535

Multiculturalism Act of 1988 (Canada), 792

Multiethnicity: See also Ethnic diversity; Mixed-descent people; in Ottoman Empire, 418, 557–558; empire and, 676; in Eastern Europe, 631; in United States, 789–790

Multilateralism, 780

Multinational corporations, 802, 870; globalization and, 702–703, 787, 844

Multiregionalists, 9–10

Mumbai. See Bombay (Mumbai)

Mummification: in ancient Egypt, 54, 55; in Inca Empire, 302; in South America

Mumtaz Mahal (Mughal India), 453

Munro, Thomas (British India), 575

Murasaki Shibiku, 275

Murids (Sufi order), 549

Muscovy (Russian state), 349–350

Musharraf, Pervez (Pakistan), 847

Music: Stone Age, 14; in India, 42; in Egypt, 54; in early China, 73, 75, 97 and illus.; in Andean cities, 88; in Sumerian cities, 26(illus.), 97; in Greece, 137; in Gupta India, 163; in Meroë, 198; Chinese opera, 265, 269, 271; in Africa, 205, 287(illus.), 292; in Japan, 274; in Korea, 120, 277(illus.); Silk Road, 259(illus.); European baroque, 395; in Bali, 324; African American, 446, 633, 666, 712, 759, 791; folk songs, 585, 675, 684, 759, 791, 804; Romanticism, 520; African traditions, 535–536; Argentine tango, 535; Indonesian gamelan, 591, 684; Javanese kronchong, 591; Brazilian, 536, 675, 684; Burmese, 584–585; calypso, 446, 536, 665, 685; Caribbean, 446, 536, 665, 759, 791, 805; Italian opera, 566(illus.); Russian, 617; jazz, 446, 633, 665 and illus., 666, 684, 759, 765, 832; cultural mixing and, 684; popular, 712; protest and, 665–666, 759, 804, 807, 833; punk rock, 759, 791; reggae and Marley, 446, 536, 665, 689, 693, 759, 805; Chilean, 804; rap, 791; Western, in China, 728, 730; in Soviet Union, 765 and illus.; rock music, 765 and illus., 788, 791; in Middle East, 818; juju, of Nigeria, 832, 833(illus.); African pop music, 807, 832; world music, 868

Muskets, 449. See also Guns; in Japan, 472; in Mughal India, 453; of Safavid Persia, 420

Muslim Brotherhood, 671, 817

Muslim-Christian hostility, 342, 376, 455, 457; Crusades and, 250–251, 345–346, 362; in Middle East and Africa, 816; in Nigeria, 828, 834

Muslim clerics: in Senegal, 549; Shi'ite, in Iran (Persia), 561, 669, 813; Shi'ite, in Iraq, 670; in Algeria, 562; in Middle East, 808; in Iran, 867; Wahhabi, 564, 671

Muslim-Hindu relations, 308, 310, 314, 318–319, 714; in Mughal India, 450, 454, 482; in British India, 577, 677; Indian nationalism and, 581–582, 658–659; in partition of India, 659, 838–839; (1950s–present), 843, 844, 846

Muslim League (India), 582, 658–659, 838

Muslim merchants and traders, 232, 245, 282, 326, 328, 563; in Melaka, 457; slave trade and, 408

Muslims, 384(map). See also Islam; Pilgrims, Muslim; Spain, Muslim; Shi'ism; Sufis; Sunni Islam; agriculture

and, 242–243; meaning of word, 233; Chinese expansion and, 258(map); expelled from Spain, 244, 422; in Africa, 288; Spanish inquisition and, 343; in West Africa, 546(illus.); African animism and, 482, 546; in Balkans, 621; in Pakistan, 658, 659, 838–839, 840(illus.); in Philippines, 459, 460, 859; in United States, 523; Afghan rebels, 717; global spread of, 712, 713(map); in Chechnya, 692, 770; Rushdie and, 759; in Central Asia, 762; in Xinjiang, 465, 729; Turkish modernization and, 667, 669 and illus., 774; in China, 726; in Europe, 775; in Russia, 771; in Yugoslavia, 772, 773(map); in Indian film industry, 847; in Malaysia, 863

Mussolini, Benito, 636, 637; invasion of Ethiopia, and, 639, 650

Mutually Assured Destruction (MAD), 780

Muziris (Indian port), 149

Mwana Mkisi, Mombasa and, 290

Mxenge, Victoria, 829

Myanmar. See Burma (Myanmar)

Myawaddy, 584–585

Mycenaean Greeks, 3, 68, 69, 92; trade, 63, 64(map), 67

Myrrh (incense), 49

Mystery religions, 145–146, 189

Mysticism: See also Daosim; Sufis (Sufi mysticism); in India, 152; in China, 108; bhakti, in Hinduism, 312–313, 318, 452–453; African animism and, 834

Mythology: See also Epic of Gilgamesh; Sumerian, 30, 36; creation myths, 6, 20–21, 36, 42, 44, 61, 84; Indian, 42, 44; Egyptian, 55; sacred books and, 98; Aboriginal dreamtime, 215

Nabataean Arabs, 194–195

Nadir Shah (Persia), 421–422

NAFTA (North American Free Trade Agreement): Canada and, 791; Mexico in, 791, 798

Nagasaki, atomic bombing of, 643(map), 644, 645(illus.), 697, 734

Nahuatl-speaking people, 299, 425

Nairobi, Kenya, 552; growth of, 649

Najaf (Iraq), 241

Nalanda (India), 362; Buddhist monastery at, 162

Nam Tien (Vietnamese migration), 325–326

Nanak, Sikh guru, 453

Nanjing, 263, 466, 604, 652; Japanese destruction of, 644, 740; Treaty of (1842), 597

Naples, in Napoleonic era, 493

Napoleon Bonaparte, 493–494 and map; Haitian Revolution and, 496; in Egypt, 543–544, 559

inequality and, 97; in Persia, 131, 421; in Greece, 137; in Rome, 183; in Vietnam, 168, 325; Christianity and, 189; *vs.* matriarchy, 200; Arab clans, 232; religion and, 223, 226; in Inca, 303; in India, 42, 162, 309, 312, 317; in Southeast Asia, 320; religion and, 362; Islamic, 404–405, 459, 566; Ottoman, 418; colonial North America, 437, 441; Mughal India, 452, 453; Latin American, 497; women's rights and, 482, 497; Confucianism and, 726; in Japan, 121, 473, 736; feminism and, 790

Patricians (elite Romans), 174, 175

Patrilineal systems: Maya, 208; Aboriginal, 214; African, 288; Vietnamese, 325; Inca, 303; Indian, 452

Patriots, in American Revolution, 489, 490

Paul of Tarsus, 188–189

Pax Britannica (British peace), 547

Pax Romana (Roman peace), 178

Peace Corps, United States and, 788

Peanuts, 415, 480, 555, 594, 678

Pearl Harbor attack (1941), 642, 643*(map)*, 662

Peasants, 17, 517. *See also* Farmers; Rural Societies; Indian sudras, 44, 161; Egyptian, 53, 54; Chinese, 74, 79, 105, 111, 113–114, 260, 264, 271; Persian, 131; Vietnamese, 166, 325; Roman, 177, 181, 185–186; Byzantine, 192; Korean, 273, 274; Maya, 208; Japanese, 274, 275, 277, 279; Angkor, 321; animism and, 166, 320, 323; European (serfs), 336, 337*(illus.)*, 338, 340, 353, 356, 363, 364, 374, 379, 383; revolts by, 339, 352, 383; Black Death and, 350; Flemish, 382*(illus.)*; English enclosure and, 398; Safavid Persia, 420; Spanish taxes and, 447; Chinese, 464, 466, 595, 599, 600; Filipino, 460; Japanese, 472, 610, 732; Javanese, 323, 461, 462, 589, 662; revolt by, in Britain, 493; revolts by, in China, 464, 598, 603, 607; French Revolution and, 491, 492; Algerian, 562; Russian serfs, 389, 390, 614, 615; in Dutch Indonesia, 582, 680; taxation of, 447, 576, 578, 586; British India, 576, 577, 578, 679; Mexican, 497, 499, 533–534, 674, 675*(illus.)*, 795, 798; Palestinian Arab, 672; revolt by, in Korea, 609, 613; Russian Revolution and, 626, 627; Soviet collectivization and, 629, 630; World War I and, 625; poverty of, 649, 650; Chinese Communists and, 652, 653, 656, 726 *and illus.*; Italian fascism and, 636; Chinese land reform and, 720, 721, 727; Egyptian, 670; Vietnamese, 586, 647, 661, 851,

853; agriculture of, 676, 704; social revolutions and, 693; bank loans to, 707; Taiwanese, 744; revolt by, in Mexico, 798; Indian, 845; Iranian, 813; South American, 796, 799, 801; bombing of, in Cambodia, 854

Pedro I (Brazil), 499

Peisistratus, 134

Peloponnesian War (431–404 B.C.E.), 132*(map)*, 138, 139–140*(map)*

The Peloponnesian War (Thucydides), 140

Penang Island, 583. *See also* Singapore

Pentagon attack (9/11), 717, 784, 815

People's Liberation Army (China), 719

People's Power (Philippines), 859–860 *and illus.*

People's War, in China, 656

Pepin the Short (Franks), 333

Pepper trade, 149, 361, 452, 457, 578, 583, 589. *See also* Spice trade

Perestroika (restructuring), in Soviet Union, 767, 768

Pericles (Greece), 137, 139, 140, 141

Periplus of the Erythraean Sea, 202

Peron, Evita, 796

Peron, Juan (Argentina), 795–796

Perpetual motion machine, 311

Perry, Matthew, opening of Japan by, 608

Persepolis (Persia), 124–125*(illus.)*, 127, 142

Persia (Iran). *See also* Iran; Safavid Empire; Sassanian Persia; Zoroastrianism; Indo-Europeans and, 24*(map)*, 25; Arabian politics and, 232; Parthian Empire, 112, 144*(map)*, 145, 158, 179*(map)*, 220, 222; Seleucid, 144 *and map*, 146; Abbasid caliphate and, 241, 243; Il-Khanid, 251, 268*(map)*; commerce of, 420–421; poetic tradition in, 244–245, 246–247; Shi'ite Islam in, 241; women, 246*(illus.)*; Silk Road musicians, 259*(illus.)*; windmills in, 337; Mongol conquest of, 318, 363*(illus.)*; trade of, 359; East Africa and, 406; Ottoman Empire and, 557*(map)*

Persian Empire (Achaemenids), 101, 126–131, 219; Mesopotamia and, 33, 35; Egypt and, 54; Hebrews and, 65; chronology (1000–334 B.C.E.), 129; decline of, 131; Greeks and, 126, 127, 141; kingship in, 125*(illus.)*, 127–128, 220; multicultural legacy of, 126, 141; policies and networks, 128–129; Alexander the Great and, 126, 142–143 *and illus.*; regional character of, 126–128; revival of, 172; roads in, 126*(map)*, 222; trade of, 221*(map)*; tribute to, 127, 141; Zoroastrianism in, 129–131

Persian-Greek Wars, 127–128, 132*(map)*, 138, 140

Persian Gulf region: oil wealth in, 687, 701, 822, 866, 869; British power in, 561; migrant workers in, 707

Persian Gulf trade, 29, 194; Bahrain Island in, 31; Africa and, 363; Hormuz in, 249, 361, 366; Ottomans and, 417

Persian Gulf War (1991), 784

Persian language, 40, 254, 318, 420

Personal computers, 730–731. *See also* Computers

Peru, colonial, 436; Spanish conquest of, 432; Inca Empire in, 370, 426, 429*(map)*, 432–433; Indian revolt in, 495; intermarriage in, 438; silver from, 476

Peru (Peruvian societies), 696. *See also* Andean societies; Inca Empire; Caral, 88, 89*(map)*, 92; Chimu Empire, 228, 296, 302; Moche, 100, 211, 293; Nazca, 212; independence of, 497, 498*(map)*; regional wars and, 531; Chinese and Japanese in, 535, 683; Indians of, 87, 796; dictatorship in, 672

Pétain, Philippe, 619, 640

Petals of Blood (Ngugi), 834

Peter (apostle), 189

Peter I the Great, Czar (Russia), 389–390, 391*(map)*, 771

Petra (Jordan), 194–195, 225

Petrarch, Francis, 365

Phalanx (Greek battle formation), 133, 142, 174

Phan Boi Chau, 661

Pharoahs (Egypt), 52, 53*(illus.)*, 54, 129, 142

Phaulkon, Constantine, 458–459

Philadelphia, 490, 528

Philip II (France), 345

Philip II (Macedonia), 142

Philip II (Spain), 387, 460

Philippa, Senhora, 481

Philippines (Filipinos), 82, 83*(map)*, 165, 215, 378, 764, 865; Spanish discovery of, 377*(map)*, 431, 459; Catholicism in, 459, 460, 587, 678; galleon trade and, 462–463; Islam in, 402; Japan and, 471; Chinese merchant class in, 459, 460 *and illus.*, 478; as Spanish colony, 371, 457, 458*(map)*, 459–461, 478, 482, 587–588; United States and, 485, 511, 513, 530, 587–588; China and, 731; population growth in, 649, 859, 860; village-based societies in, 328; insurgencies in, 696; Japanese occupation of, 642, 643*(map)*, 662; nationalism in, 660; Western culture in, 678, 693; immigrants/labor migrations from, 530, 531, 683, 707, 711, 859; independence of, 664, 690, 691*(map)*; United States and, 660, 664, 690, 691*(map)*, 858, 860; Green Revolution in, 704, 782; Marcos regime in, 858–860; politics and society in, 858–860

Philip the Fair (France), 345

Philosophy (philosophers). *See also*
Confucianism; Daoism; Enlightenment;
Ideas; Intellectuals; Axial Age, 104,
105–109, 135–136, 218–219; Chinese,
79, 101, 104, 105–109, 466; Legalism,
in China, 101, 109, 110, 112, 219,
220; Greek, 135–136; Hellenistic, 145;
Hindu, 152, 312; Indian, 159; Stoicism,
145, 178, 180, 218; Islamic, 244, 247;
European, 380–381, 520; French,
397*(illus.)*, 398, 759–760; reason
and, 395; American, 523; Indian
Renaissance, 576, 579–580; "get-rich-
quick," 633, 729; African Negritude,
833–834
Phoenicia (Phoenicians), 49, 67–68.
See also Canaanites; Carthage
(Carthaginians); alphabet, 63, 67, 68,
69, 129, 141; Greeks and, 141, 174,
225; settlements of, 63, 64*(map)*, 176;
trade networks of, 3, 67, 68, 95, 140
Physicians. *See* Medicine
Physics, 381, 396; modern era, 521, 636
Piaf, Edith, 759
Picasso, Pablo, art of, 521, 635, 639
Pictograms: Sumerian, 31–32; Egyptian,
52; Chinese, 75, 79, 80*(illus.)*
Pidgin English, 665
Pilgrims (pilgrimages): Chinese Buddhist,
in India, 118, 149, 162, 223, 306–307
and illus., 313, 362; Christian, 345;
Hindu, 152, 313; in Mughal India,
453; Muslim, 230*(illus.)*, 232, 235–236,
239, 241, 245, 284, 358 (*See also* Ibn
Battuta, Abdallah Muhammad)
Pima and Papago Indians, 212
Pinochet, Agusto (Chile), 801, 803
Pi (π), 115, 162
Pirates (piracy), 167, 361, 463, 530;
in Indian Ocean, 165, 317, 456; in
Caribbean region, 434; China and,
272; English, 434; Japanese, 464, 471;
Portuguese, 469; in Southeast Asia, 854
Pixley ka Isaka Seme, 552
Pizarro, Francisco, Inca conquest and,
429*(map)*, 432–433
Plague, 34, 270, 318, 479. *See also* Black
Death; in Athens, 140; in Roman
Empire, 184; of Justinian, 191, 222,
332; bubonic, 191, 251–252, 269, 355,
365; in China, 464; in Iraq, 562
Planned economy, 693, 767, 769
Plantation zone. *See also* Cash crops;
Rubber and rubber plantations; Sugar
plantations; African slavery in, 410,
413, 414, 426, 444–445 *and illus.*; in
Americas, 413, 414, 426, 478, 480;
British industrialization and, 500; in
colonial Philippines, 460, 478; Haitian
Revolution and, 496; slavery in United
States, 522, 523, 528; in Latin America,
532, 534; in West Africa, 555; in British

India, 576; in Sri Lanka, 573; Asian
workers in, 531, 579, 681, 683; in
British Malaya, 583; in Hawaii, 683
Plant domestication. *See* Domestication,
of plants; *specific crops*
Plassey, Battle of (1757), 571, 573*(illus.)*
Plataea, Battle of (479 B.C.E.), 138
Plato, 20, 136, 141, 219; Socrates and,
135, 218
Platt Amendment (United States), 536
Playwrights. *See* Drama (theater)
Plebeians (Rome), 174–175
Plebiscites (elections), in Rome, 175
Pleistocene epoch. *See also* Ice Age
PLO. *See* Palestine Liberation
Organization
Plows, 15, 46; in China, 79, 114*(illus.)*;
ox-drawn, 20, 114*(illus.)*; in
Europe, 337
Plural society, in Malaya, 583. *See also*
Ethnic diversity
Plutarch, 177–178
Poets and poetry. *See also* Literature;
Mesopotamian, 32; Indian, 42, 44,
46, 149; Greek, 68, 137–138 (*See also*
Homer); Tamil, 159; Roman, 183; Arab,
232; European, 232, 341, 346; Persian,
244–245, 246–247; African, 285;
Chinese, 261–262, 265; Japanese, 274,
275; Indian, 310; Ottoman, 418; colonial
Mexico, 436; Mughal India, 452, 453;
Japanese, 473; Persian, 475; Chinese,
482, 726; Romantic, 520; American,
526; Zulu, 551; Arab nationalist, 567;
Nicaraguan, 535; in British India, 577;
Indian nationalist, 579–580; Vietnamese,
569, 570, 585; Russian Jew, 619, 630;
Soviet Russia, 761–762, 765; Chilean,
675, 804; Nigerian, 833; Indonesian,
837; Thai, 862
Pogroms (removals) of Jews, 517
Poison gas, in warfare, 621, 642, 814, 816
Poland-Lithuania, 393; Russia and, 395,
423, 492
Poland (Poles), 343, 387, 482, 644; Jews
in, 342; serfdom in, 379; Sweden
and, 393; Catholicism in, 393, 520,
712, 766; Russia and, 389, 390, 614,
627; frustrated nationalism in, 505;
immigrants from, 517, 530; Jews in,
567, 642; Germany and, 624, 749;
independence of, 625; Nazi Germany
and, 640, 642; serfdom in, 353; Soviet
domination of, 696, 764; Solidarity in,
766, 771, 772; worker's rights in, 762,
766; in European Union, 774
Police brutality: in Korea, 614; protests
against, 716; in Saudi Arabia, 814
Police state: *See also* Secret police; in
South Africa, 828–829; in Taiwan, 745;
in Zimbabwe, 832
Polis. *See* City-states, Greek (polis)

Political activists: Sartre on, 760; in
Thailand, 862, 863
Political corruption. *See* Corruption
Political independence. *See* Independence
Political parties: *See also* Communist
Party; in Chile, 672, 800–801, 804; in
China, 604; in Japan, 610; in Egypt,
670; in post-war Europe, 749–750; in
United States, 633, 709, 789; French
Canadian, 791; Green, 750, 774; in
India, 840, 841, 842, 844; in Iraq, 814;
in Mexico, 798; one-party states, in
Africa, 825–826, 830
Political prisoners: *See also* Prison camps;
Amnesty International and, 699, 715;
in Siberian gulags, 617, 629–630, 761;
in China, 728, 729; in North Korea,
743; in South Korea, 741; freed, in
Soviet Union, 767; in Chile, 801; in
Cuba, 800; in India, 842; in Iran, 813;
in Nicaragua, 803; in Africa, 829, 833;
in Turkey, 808
Political protest. *See* Protest
Political revolutions, 488. *See also* Age of
Revolution; Revolutions
Political rights. *See* Civil liberties (rights)
Political structure (political order). *See
also* Administration; Democracy;
Government; Monarchy; *and specific
institutions*; Sumerian, 30; African,
58; foundations of, 95–96; religion
and, 98; Persian, 128–129; Greek,
68, 132–134. (*See also* Democracy, in
Greece); Chinese, 79, 112, 116, 259,
266; Indian, 158, 308, 318; Khmer,
167; Roman, 174, 175, 177; Aksum,
203; Mande, 204; Axial Age reformers
and, 220; Islamic, 240, 243; African
village, 290; Mesoamerica, 293; North
American Indian, 298, 435; European,
338, 375; Ottoman, 417; Japanese,
277, 279, 471, 734; Safavid Persia,
420; industrialization and, 499; Latin
America, 436, 495, 532; in colonial
Africa, 554; Chinese, 656; global
(1945–1989), 645, 692; quality of life
and, 694; in United States, 788–789;
Mexican reforms, 798; and Islam,
in Middle East, 794–801, 808; and
conflict, in sub-Saharan Africa, 825–
828; Malaysian, 863
Political thought (ideology). *See also*
Conservatives; Democracy; Ideologies;
Legalism; Liberalism; Confucianism
and, 112, 219; Delhi India, 316;
of Hobbes, 395–396, 398; Italian
Renaissance, 380–381; of Locke, 398;
of Gandhi, 657; Cold War rivalry,
695–697
Politics: world (since 1989), 690, 698,
699–700; in postwar Europe, 749–750;
Chilean musicians and, 804; Indian,

546; in Malaysia, 700; in Sri Lanka, 573, 700–701, 848; World War II and, 642, 662

Rufisque, Senegal, 481

Ruhr district, Germany, 502

Ruling class. *See* Aristocracy; Upper class (elites). Austronesian, in Funan, 167; Roman, 178; Inca, 303; in Russia, 349

Rumi, Jalal Al-Din, 247

Rural areas (rural society). *See also* Farmers; Peasants; Villages; Jiroft (Iran), 31; Harappa, 40; Chinese economy and, 113–114; Greek city-states and, 132; in Japan, 276–277; medieval Europe, 332, 338; in England, 398; in British India, 575, 578; in United States, 525; African, 664; in Philippines, 460, 858–859; in Japan, 632, 732, 735; social services in, 705; urban pop culture and, 712; Chinese reforms and, 727, 728; in Bangladesh, 848; in India, 846; in Vietnam, 850, 851; in Thailand, 861

Rural-to-urban migration: *See also* Urbanization; in Europe, 517; in South Africa, 551; in China, 729, 730; in Soviet Union, 764; in Latin America, 802; in Iran, 813

Rus, 349. *See also* Russia

Rushdie, Salman, 759, 846

Russian language, 617, 762, 765

Russian Orthodox Church, 348*(illus.)*, 349–350, 362, 389, 617, 765, 771

Russian Revolution (1905), 617

Russian Revolution (1917), 617, 624, 625–627, 677; Bolsheviks and, 626–627 *and illus.*; roots of, 626–627

Russia (Russian Empire), 474, 678. *See also* Soviet Union (USSR); Byzantium and, 229; chronology (600–1500), 347; Mongols and, 349–350; Swedes in, 349; Vikings in, 335, 349; czars and despotism, 389–390; Central Asia and, 423, 594; Ottoman Empire and, 371, 419, 557 *and map*; Siberia and, 390, 391*(map)*, 423, 463*(map)*, 469, 481, 607, 609, 615; Napoleonic France and, 493, 494*(map)*; Poland-Lithuania and, 395, 423, 492; alliances of, 510; British India and, 575, 615; expansion of, 389–390, 391*(map)*, 394*(map)*, 423, 485, 511, 557*(map)*, 594; China and, 423, 463*(map)*, 469, 476; Greece and, 504, 557; Jews in, 505, 517, 567, 642; Persia and, 421, 561; sale of Alaska by, 525; Afghanistan and, 575, 615; as great power, 487; famine in, 517, 626; industrialization in, 617, 626; Manchuria and, 603, 612; unrest and revolution in, 624; in World War I, 620, 621, 622–623 *and map*, 626; civil war in (1918–1921), 627–628 *and map*,

762; peasants and serfdom in, 379, 517, 626; nuclear waste explosion in, 709; post-Soviet, 768–771, 775

Russification policy, 617, 762, 765

Russo-Japanese War (1904–1905), 612, 617

Rwanda, 58; genocide in, 698, 700, 784, 827–828

Ryukyu Islands, Japan and, 644, 732

Ryunosuke, Akutagawa, 632

Sabah, Borneo, 583, 863

Saba (Sheba, Yemen), 195, 201

Sacraments, in Christian Church, 342, 343

Sacrifice. *See also* Human sacrifice; in Vedic religion, 42; in Roman religion, 181; Hindu women and, 311; in Islam, 235, 238

Sa'dians (Morocco), 422–423

Safavid Empire (Persia), 371, 402, 420–422, 474; culture, 421; decline of, 421–422, 556; expansion of, 417*(map)*, 420, 454; Shi'ite Islam in, 420, 421, 422, 423; trading network, 420–421, 478, 479; women, 421, 422*(illus.)*

Sahara region. *See also* Trans-Saharan trade and caravan routes; rock art images in, 5*(illus.)*, 57; climate changes in, 8, 51, 57; migrants from, 51; desert expansion in, 57, 60, 877; pastoralism in, 23, 57

Sahel region, desertification in, 479

Saigon. *See* Ho Chi Minh City (Saigon)

Saikaku, Ihara, 473

Sailing (seafaring). *See also* Navigation; Ships and shipping; by Egyptians, 49; innovations for, 92; by Indonesians, 164*(illus.)*; coastal American trade, 211, 304; lateen sails for, 165, 249, 355; by Pacific Islanders, 82, 215, 217

St. Lawrence River, 537

St. Petersburg, 390 *and illus.*, 617; Bolsheviks in, 627

Sakhalin Island, 612

Sakharov, Andrei, 762

Salah al-Din (Saladin), 251

Salamis, Battle of, 138

Salaryman, in Japan, 736

Salavarrieta, Policarpa de, 497

Salerno University (Italy), 346

Salim, Jawad, 819*(illus.)*

Salons, in Paris, 397*(illus.)*

Salt trade, 94; in Egypt, 55; in India, 161; trans-Saharan, 204, 284; in Africa, 292; in India, 658

Salvador da Bahia, 433

Salvation: Hebrews and, 66; Hinduism and, 152; in Jainism, 153; Buddhism and, 118, 160, 278; mystery religions and, 145; Christians and, 224, 342; Protestantism and, 383

Samarkand (Silk Road city), 113, 225, 358; Islam in, 237, 314; observatory in, 248; Tamerlane in, 253, 318

Samba (dance), 446, 536, 675

Samoa, 82, 215, 216*(map)*, 511, 692, 794; Christianity in, 540

Samory Toure (Mandinka), 549

Samurai (Japanese warriors), 276–278, 279, 471, 472, 473; Meiji restoration and, 609, 610, 611; weaponry of, 607

Sandanistas (Nicaragua), 796, 803

Sanitation and sewers, 38 *and illus.*, 66, 521, 579, 649

Sankore (Timbuktu): mosque, 405*(illus.)*; University of, 404

San Lorenzo (Olmec center), 88, 90*(illus.)*

San Martin, Jose de (Cuba), 496, 497, 535

Sanskrit language, 42, 44, 163, 226, 312; in Tibet, 313

Santa Anna, Antonio Lopez de (Mexico), 532–533

Santa Sophia Church, 170 *(illus.)*, 192*(illus.)*, 193

Santo Domingo, Hispaniola, 431

Sao Paolo (Brazil), 433, 709, 710

Sappho, 137–138

Sarajevo, 621

Sarawak, Borneo, 856*(map)*, 863

Sardinia, 172; Carthage and, 173*(map)*, 174, 176

Sargon (Akkad), 32, 95

Sarte, Jean-Paul, 750; existentialism and, 759–760

Sassanian Persia, 158, 220, 222; Arabs and Islam in, 194–195, 237; Rome and, 146, 194, 195; Byzantine Empire and, 190–191, 192, 193*(map)*, 194, 195, 347; conquests of, 193*(map)*, 194, 202–203; religion and culture, 194, 242

The Satanic Verses (Rushdie), 759

Satellites: Russian, 762; communications and, 787; Indian, 849

Sati (widow burning), 39, 162, 311, 451, 453, 846; ban on, 575, 576, 581

Satraps (Persian Empire), 128, 131

Saud, Abdul Aziz Ibn (Arabia), 564, 671

Saud, Muhammad Ibn (Arabia), 563

Saudi Arabia, 668*(map)*; migrant workers in, 707; oil wealth of, 564, 671, 687, 814–815 *and illus.*; royal family of, 668*(map)*, 671, 814, 815; terrorism in, 717, 784, 815, 817; United States and, 784, 811*(map)*; Wahhabism in, 563–564, 671, 814

Savanna (grasslands): *See also* Sudanic Africa; pastoralism and, 23; in Africa, 8, 56, 203, 205

Savannah (city), colonial era, 479

Savuka (African music group), 807

Saxons, 187, 335

Sayyid Sa'id, 545

government, 76–77; society and culture, 77–78; technology, 77; writing in, 71, 78

Shankara, 312

Sharecropping, 528. *See also* Tenant farmers

Shar'ia. *See* Islamic law

Shariati, Ali, 817

Shawnee (American) Indians, 538

Sheba (Saba, Yemen), 195, 201

Sheep raising, 61, 63; domestication of, 5, 36, 57; in England, 398; in South Africa, 412; in Ireland, 505; in New Zealand, 541; in Australia, 620

Sheffield, industrialization in, 503*(illus.)*

Shen, Michael Alphonsus, 469

Shidzue, Kato, 632

Shifting cultivation, 16–17; in Africa, 57, 203, 287, 292; in Americas, 206, 294

Shi Huangdi (China), 109–110; tomb of, 111

Shi'ism (Shi'a Islam), 243, 247, 658. *See also* Sunni-Shi'ite rivalry; in Egypt, 362; in Safavid Persia, 420, 421, 423, 482; in Iraq, 562, 566, 717, 814, 817, 820; in Iran, 561, 669, 813; in Saudi Arabia, 814; in Lebanon, 816

Shinobu, Yoshioka, 738

Shinto religion (Japan), 122, 275, 362, 471, 739

Ships and shipping (maritime trade), 92. *See also* Canoes; Indian Ocean maritime trade; Mediterranean Sea trade; Navigation; Pirates; Sailing (seafaring); Mesopotamian, 31; Persian Gulf, 22; ancient Egyptian, 52; Indian, 40, 149, 159; boats, 84, 86; in China, 114, 116, 264, 271; Greek, 125, 131; imperial Chinese, 116; Indian Ocean vessels, 164*(illus.)*; Southeast Asian, 81, 101, 164–165, 166, 319; Etruscan, 174; Carthaginian, 176; Roman, 183; East African, 205, 287, 288; Australian societies and, 215; Austronesian, 217; Axial age linkages in, 225; Indian, 308; Sumatran, 323; Melakan, 327; in Antwerp, 373; Portuguese, 328, 357, 366, 376, 408, 410; rise of, 359–361 *and map*, 366; Viking, 335*(illus.)*; English, 376; East African ports and, 406; Dutch, 447, 455, 683; of Columbus, 426; Ottoman, 417; slave trade, 414 *and illus.*; in Morocco, 422; Russian, 423; Siam and, 459; Indonesians in, 461; Spanish (galleons), 376, 430–431, 459, 462–463; canals and, 510, 560, 578, 684; steamships, 501, 510, 511, 541, 578, 684, 866; in World War I, 624; South Korean, 743*(illus.)*

Shiva, 39, 46, 152, 313, 320, 453; as Lord of the Dance, 317*(illus.)*

Shock therapy, in Russia, 769, 770

Shogunates, in Japan, 278–279. *See also* Tokugawa shogunate; Kamakura, 278; Ashikaga, 279, 364, 471

Shona people, 289, 291, 406, 412

Shotoku (Japan), 122*(illus.)*

Shrines: Islamic (Ka'ba), 232, 236; Shinto, in Japan, 275; German pagan, 333

Siam (Siamese), 676. *See also* Thailand (Siam); slavery in, 363; Sukhothai in, 319*(map)*, 324; Buddhism in, 324–325, 457, 482; Chinese in, 481; diplomacy in, 511; Europeans in, 458–459, 475; France and, 458–459, 463, 482; Japan and, 471; literacy in, 457, 476

Siberia, 85, 616*(map)*; Ainu and, 84; early hominids in, 11; Russia and, 390, 391*(map)*, 423, 463*(map)*, 469, 481, 598, 607, 609, 615; prison camps *(gulags)* in, 617, 629–630, 761

Sicily, 66, 172; Black Death in, 350; Carthage and, 176; Greek colonization of, 67, 173*(map)*; Muslims in, 243, 254, 336

Siddhartha Gautama (Buddha), 117*(illus.)*, 118, 153–154. *See also* Buddhism; First Sermon of, 154, 155

Sidon (Phoenicia), 67

Siege weapons, 35, 96. *See also* Weapons and military technology; catapults, 267, 363*(illus.)*; Mongol, 267, 363*(illus.)*, 364

Sierra Club, 710

Sierra Leone, 545–546; college in, 554; ethnic conflict in, 827; life expectancy in, 868

Sihanouk, Norodom (Cambodia), 853, 854, 855

Sikhs, 453, 454, 846; British and, 571, 572; nationalism of, 843; partition of India and, 838, 839

Silesia, coal in, 502

Silk industry: Chinese, 73, 74, 113, 114, 269, 358, 462, 464, 466, 472, 478; Persian, 420

Silk Road, 41, 221*(map)*, 360*(map)*, 420, 423, 615, 866; Buddhism and, 118, 159, 161*(map)*; camels on, 103, 224*(illus.)*, 259*(illus.)*; caravans on, 102*(illus.)*, 113, 224*(illus.)*, 359*(illus.)*; cities on, 158, 159, 194, 225, 358; disruption in, 165; Sogdians and, 158; impact of, 158, 252, 358–359 *and illus.*; Islam and, 237; Roman Empire and, 113, 178, 183; Mediterranean trade and, 113; Mongols and, 251, 279, 355; China and, 103, 111*(map)*, 225, 258*(map)*; plague and, 251, 365; Sassanid Empire and, 193*(map)*; Tibet and, 313

Silk Road Ensemble (music group), 868

Silla (Korea), 120, 273

Silver, 211, 464; coinage, 95, 161, 263; Greek, 141; Persian, 128*(illus.)*, 131;

Roman, 183, 184, 225; mercantilism and, 380; Japanese, 471, 472; as medium of exchange, 597

Silver, from Americas, 378, 436, 443*(map)*, 495; Bolivian, 442, 476; in China, 463, 466, 478, 597; Inca, 304; in India, 452

Sima Qian, 115

Simony (sale of bishoprics), 343

Sinan, Pasha, 418

Sind, 127

Singapore, 680, 711; Chinese in, 583, 590, 683*(illus.)*, 864; English language in, 715; independence of, 691*(map)*; globalization and, 867; economic growth in, 733*(map)*, 740, 856, 865, 869; high technology in, 701, 715, 869

Singh, Manmohan, 844

Singh, Ranjit (Marathas), 571, 572

Sinhalese, in Sri Lanka, 159, 848; Buddhism and, 573

Sinicization (Chinese assimilation), 109

Sinn Fein (Ireland), 505–506

Sino-Japanese War (1894–1895), 603, 612, 613–614

Sisters in Islam (Malaysia), 863

Six Dynasties Era (China), 116

Skin color, racism and, 10, 415; in colonial Americas, 446; in Brazil, 481, 535; in colonial Africa, 554; in United States, 528, 535

Skyscrapers, in East Asia, 864*(illus.)*

Slave revolts, 496; in Haiti, 446, 544

Slavery, abolition of, 497, 681; in China, 465; in France, 492; in United States, 522, 523, 528; in Latin America, 535; in Siam, 587

Slave soldiery, Ottoman, 418, 419, 558

Slaves (slavery), 226. *See also* African slavery; in Mesopotamia, 30, 32, 35; in Egypt, 54; in China, 77, 78, 79, 105; in Persia, 131; in Greece, 133, 134, 137, 141, 226; in colonial Brazil, 433, 445–446; debt, 133, 181, 291, 302; Etruscan, 174; in Roman Empire, 181, 183, 226; in Dutch South Africa, 550; in Islam, 245, 363; Maya, 207, 208, 226; African, 245, 284, 285, 291, 363, 364; freedom for, 446 (*See also* Slavery, abolition of); in Aztec Empire, 302; in Southeast Asia, 321, 324, 363; European feudalism and, 339; Native Americans as, 438, 440*(illus.)*, 442; revolts by, in Americas, 446; in Siam, 457; in United States, 490, 522, 523, 528; women as, 523

Slave trade, 445. *See also* African slave trade; in Africa, 292–293; Atlantic system and, 413–414 *and map*, 446–447; economic impact of, 446–447; end of, 485; in sub-Saharan Africa, 291

Slavic language, 349

582; Indianization in, 321–322; Islam in, 323, 326, 327(map), 328; Islam on, 857; maritime trade of, 320, 323

Sumerians, 29–32, 95. *See also* Mesopotamia; economy and culture, 30–32; *Epic of Gilgamesh* and, 35, 36, 98; music of, 26(illus.), 97; Neo-Sumerian Empire, 33; writing and technology of, 31–32

Summer of Love (1967), 788

Sumo wrestling, in Japan, 739, 867

Sundiata (Mali), 284

Sun gods and goddesses: Amon-Re and Re, 49, 53, 54, 59; Japanese, 121, 278; Mithra, 146; Aztec, 300; Hindu, in India, 311(illus.); Inca, 302

Sunni Islam, 422; Kurds and, 561, 562, 667; in Ottoman Empire, 420; in Pakistan, 658, 847; in Southeast Asia, 323–324; in Iran, 423, 482, 813; in Iraq, 562, 670, 717, 814; Uzbeks and, 423

Sunni-Shi'ite rivalry, 240–241, 243, 244, 847; Arab nationalism and, 566, 808; in Iran, 423, 482, 561, 813; in Iraq, 562, 714, 717, 814, 817

Sun Yat-Sen (Sun Zhong Shan), 603–605, 652

Supernatural, belief in, 98. *See also* Religion(s); Native American, 86; Chinese, 79–80, 116; Greek, 134; African, 291; Southeast Asian, 325; Tibetan, 314

Superpowers, in Cold War, 645, 767, 778–784. *See also* Soviet Union; United States; Africa and, 834; conflict in, 690; Egypt and, 808, 809; interventions by, 697, 808; Korean War, 741–742 *and map*; 764; nationalism and, 692; nonaligned nations and, 695, 809; nuclear arms race, 697–698; rivalry between, 778; United Nations and, 698–699; United States as sole, 699, 769, 778, 797

The Suppliant Woman (Euripedes), 134

Supreme Command of Allied Powers (SCAP), 732, 734

Supreme Court (United States), 526–527, 789, 791

Surat (India), 452, 455, 456

Suriname (Dutch Guiana), 433, 579, 683

Survival of the fittest, 513, 529

Susa (Mesopotamia), 128

Susenyos (Ethiopia), 412

Sustainable environments, 871–872

Swahili Coast (East Africa), 283(map), 288, 289; trading cities, 406, 408, 410–411

Swahili language, 288, 291, 292

Sweden (Swedes), 640. *See also* Scandinavia; in Russia, 349; Lutheranism in, 388. 393; independence of, 393; wars with Russia, 389, 390, 393; Finland and, 504; women's education in, 519; social democracy in, 635; in European Union, 774; quality of life in, 756 *and illus.*

Sweet potatoes, 87, 88, 213, 594. *See also* Yams

Swimme, Brian, 5

Switzerland, 640, 678, 760; Calvinism in, 383, 385; as constitutional confederation, 392; higher education for women in, 519; nationalism in, 504, 520; Red Cross in, 685; independence of, 388, 774; homosexual rights in, 758

Swords. *See* Steel swords

Syphilis, 435, 480

Syracuse (Greece), fortifications of, 140

Syria (Syrians), 560, 564. *See also* Canaan; Phoenicia; Abu Hureyra in, 5, 15, 16(illus.); early farming in, 17; first cities in, 30; Egypt and, 53, 54; Persian Empire and, 127; Seleucid, 144; Rome and, 177, 194; Islamic caliphate in, 240; plague in, 251; Mamluks in, 252; Ottoman rule in, 416, 562, 666; immigrants from, 535; Christians in, 562; French control of, 666, 667, 668(map); Arab nationalism in, 567, 667; Palestinians in, 810; conflict with Israel, 811(map), 812, 816

Tacitus, 183

Tagore, Rabindranath, 579–580, 657, 679

Tahiti, 82, 83(map), 216 *and map*, 539, 540, 794

Tai Chen, 466

Taika reforms (Japan), 274

Taino people of Caribbean region, 428, 429–430; enslavement of, 430

Tai peoples, 320, 323. *See also* Thailand (Siam)

Taiping Rebellion, 598–599 *and map*, 603, 613, 677

Taiwan, 82, 687, 733(map); China and, 465, 469, 481, 745; Dutch in, 469, 476; as Japanese colony, 612, 613(map), 632, 744; democracy in, 702; labor migration from, 711; economy of, 720, 734(map), 740, 744, 745; Chiang Kai-shek in, 719, 720, 723, 744; China and, 724(map), 731, 744, 745; United States' aid to, 723, 744; globalization and, 701, 867

Tajiks (Tajikistan), 765

Taj Mahal, 247, 453

Talas, Battle of (751), 237, 241, 258(map), 262, 314

The Tale of the Kieu (Nguyen Du), 585

Taliban (Afghanistan), 784

Tamerlane, 253, 318

Tamil kingdoms, 159, 317

Tamil-speakers, 590; in Sri Lanka, 573, 848

Tanganyika: as German colony, 549, 553, 555; World War I in, 622

Tang Empire (China), 119, 257; Arab armies and, 237; changes in, and collapse of, 262; Eurasian exchange and, 258; government networks and growth, 258–260, 258(map); India and, 308, 312; Korea and, 120; pottery of, 259(illus.); religion, culture and technology, 260–262; Tibet and, 313

Tango (dance), 535

Tantrism (Tantric Buddhism), 313

Tanzania, 58, 705, 835; colonial, 824; early humans in, 9(illus.); Kilwa, 288; Nyerere in, 694, 827; Rhapta, 205

Tariffs. *See also* Protectionism; United States, 523, 528; British industry and, 579, 680; in Europe, 753, 835

Tartar states, 389, 423

Tasmania, 214

Tassili archers (Algeria), 5(illus.)

Tattooing, 217

Taxation, 475; Greek, 67; in early China, 79; in Egypt, 54, 176, 178; kingship and, 95; in Persian Empire, 128, 131; in India, 156, 161; in imperial China, 110, 116, 261, 263, 356; in Southeast Asia, 168; Byzantine, 192; in Islam, 234; in Roman Empire, 178, 183, 185, 220; of Korean peasants, 274; of Indian peasants, 309; in Delhi India, 317, 318; English kings and, 343, 345; in medieval Europe, 342; French monarchy and, 353; in Ottoman Empire, 419; Spanish, 447; in Mughal India, 451, 454; on Muslim merchants, 457; colonial cash crops and, 460; in China, 466, 651, 656; on Chinese merchants, 467, 468; French Revolution and, 491; in British North America, 489; in colonial Latin America, 496; in colonial Africa, 553, 556, 648; in British India, 576, 578, 579; in British Malaya, 583; in Japan, 610; in Russia, 771; United States' military and, 780, 782, 785; in welfare states, 755; in Chile, 801

Taylor, Harriet, 519

Tayson Rebellion (Vietnam), 585

Tchaikovsky, Pyotr, music of, 617

Tea ceremony, in Japan, 279, 471, 739

Tea trade, 510, 576, 579, 830; taxation on, 489; Chinese, 259, 262, 463, 464, 466; Ceylon (Sri Lanka), 511(illus.), 573, 848

Technology: *See also* High technology; Science(s); Tools; Weapons and military technology; Stone Age, 7, 13; first cities and, 21–22; Egyptian, 55; Indo-Aryan, 46; African farmers and, 60–61; in Korea and Japan, 83; Southeast Asian, 81; foundations for (4000–600 B.C.E.), 91–92; Chinese, 105, 115, 116, 262, 264, 266; Hellenistic age, 145; Roman Empire, 183; Mongols and, 269, 364, 365; Inca, 304; medieval Europe, 336–337, 356; Renaissance Italy, 355; Arab, 376; European, 376, 396–397; Chinese, 376, 464, 475; Ottoman, 419; Western European, 470; British, 475, 510; Industrial Revolution, 501; spread of, 683; innovation and, 703–704, 866

Tecumseh (Shawnee), 538

Tehran (Iran), 561

Telegraph, 559, 561, 610, 683; undersea cables, 511; wireless, 521. *See also* Radio; railroads and, 684

Telephone, 684, 714

Telescopes, 248, 396

Television, 711; cable news networks, 714, 822; Latin American, 804

Tell, William, Swiss nationalism and, 520

Tell Hamoukar, 30

The Tempest (Shakespeare), 373, 383

Temples, 98. *See also* Hindu temples; Mesopotamian, 30, 35; ancient Egyptian, 48*(illus.)*, 49; Olmec, 89; urban, 94; Greek, 139 *and illus.*; Japanese, 122; Buddhist, 122, 151*(illus.)*, 163*(illus.)*, 164*(illus.)*, 261*(illus.)*, 320, 362, 728; Jewish, 189; Kushite, 198; Roman, 183; Maya, 207; Moche, 211; Cahokia, 297; Aksum, 201; Inca, 304; Borobodur, 322; Aztec, 432; Sikh, in Amritsar, 453, 843

Temuchin. *See* Ghenghis Khan

Tenant farmers: in Europe, 374; in Philippines, 460; in India, 576, 578

Ten Commandments, 64, 65

Tenochtitlan (Mexico), 299, 300–301, 302, 436; Spanish conquest of, 425, 432

Teotihuacan (Mexico), 220, 299; collapse of, 293–294; pyramids, 209 *and illus.*, 210; Toltecs and, 295

Terrace farming, 18, 87, 292, 296, 304

Terracotta, 60*(illus.)*, 94*(illus.)*, 111, 203*(illus.)*

Terror and terrorism: *See also* Al Qaeda; in Assyrian Empire, 34, 35; in Aztec Empire, 302; Portuguese, 454; in French Revolution, 492; in Ottoman Empire, 558; racist, in United States,

633; in Russia and Soviet Union, 617, 629–630; in China, 651, 652; Bengali women and, 660; United States and, 686; global networks, 716–717, 784; in North Korea, 744; Basques, in Spain, 716, 749*(illus.)*, 750; George Bush's war on, 717, 786; in Europe, 775; September 11 (2001), 717, 775, 784, 873; in Chile, 801; in Arab-Israeli conflict, 810, 812; in Iran, 813; in Afghanistan, 820; in Bali, 858; in India, 849

Tet Offensive (Vietnam, 1968), 852*(map)*, 853

Texas, annexation of, 525, 526*(map)*, 527, 533

Textiles (textile industry). *See also* Cloth and clothing; Cotton; Silk; Egyptian, 176; in India, 161, 361; European, 374; Chinese, 397, 600; Persian, 421; dyes for, 433; Indian, 452, 454, 456, 463, 478, 680; innovation in, 475; British (English), 487, 499, 501, 679; spinning machines in, 397, 499; steam power for, 501; in New England, 523, 529*(illus.)*, 530; Egyptian, 559; women in, 437, 518–519, 529*(illus.)*, 530, 600, 611; woolen, in Europe, 304; Japanese, 611; Sri Lankan, 848

Thackeray, William, 501

Thailand (Siam), 17, 81, 167, 323, 678. *See also* Siam; independence of, 485; modernization of, 676; nationalism in, 660; AIDS prevention in, 861; Internet cafe in, 715*(illus.)*; military rule of, 860–861; United States and, 783, 860–861; Laos and, 853; Buddhism in, 860, 861; democracy in, 702, 861; economic growth in, 702, 856, 865, 869

Thales of Miletus, 125, 135, 218

Thatcher, Margaret (Britain), 756

Theater. *See* Drama (theater)

Thebes (Egypt), 49, 53, 55

Thebes (Greece), 140, 142

Theocracy: Mande, in Africa, 204; in Angkor, 321; in Switzerland, 385; in Safavid Persia, 420, 421; Islamic, 563; in Iran, 813

Theodora (Byzantium), 191, 226

Theology, 383, 395. *See also* Gods and goddesses; Monotheism; Polytheism; Hindu, 152; Christian, 190, 193, 348; Islamic, 244; liberation, 712, 803; Monophysite, 232

Thera, paintings from, 66, 67*(illus.)*

Theravada Buddhism, 159–160, 456; in Southeast Asia, 160, 229, 308, 323, 324–325, 362; monks, 160, 224; in Burma, 660, 860, 861; in Siam

(Thailand), 324–325, 457, 482, 860, 861; in Sri Lanka, 848

Thermopyle, Battle of, 138

Third Crusade (1189–1192), 251

Third Estate (France), 491, 492

Third Industrial Revolution, 703–704

Third World, 694, 695; *See also* Developing (poor) nations; globalization and, 701–702; local economies in, 705

Thirty Years War (1618–1648), 388 *and illus.*, 392

Thomas (apostle), 160

Thomas Aquinas, 339, 346

Three-field farming system, 337

Three Gorges Dam (China), 729

Three Kingdoms Era (China), 116

"Three Principles of the People" (Sun), 604, 605

Through the Looking Glass (Carroll), 875

Thucydides, 140

Thuku, Harry, 664, 677

Tiananmen Square (Beijing), 719, 728

Tian (supernatural force), 79–80

Tibet (Tibetans), *(map)*; Buddhism in, 160, 313–314, 316, 450, 699; immigration from, 320; British invasion of, 578; China and, 463*(map)*, 465, 606, 723, 729

Tiglath-pileser (Assyrian Empire), 34

Tigris-Euphrates Valley, 3, 5. *See also* Mesopotamia; first cities in, 27, 29, 30; geography of, 28; metallurgy in, 93*(map)*

Tikal (Maya city-state), 293

Tilak, Bal Gangadhar, 581–582

Timbuktu (Africa), 285, 402, 403*(map)*, 404; Moroccans and, 420; mosque in, 405*(illus.)*; trade in, 284, 292; University of, 362

Time. *See also* Calendar; Clocks; Hebrew view of, 65–66; Indian view of, 66

Timor, colonization of, 458*(map)*, 461

Timurids, 253, 318

Tin mines, 31, 81, 91, 164, 249, 583, 589, 634

Tito, Josip Broz (Yugoslavia), 766, 772

Tiv people of Nigeria, 290

Tiwanaku (Aymara), 100, 213, 220, 228, 293; architecture of, 211–212

Tlatelolco, Aztec market in, 300

Tlaxcalans, Aztec Empire and, 432

Tobacco, 429, 435, 447, 522, 583, 703*(illus.)*; in Atlantic economy, 443*(map)*; in China, 480; in Africa, 835; in Europe, 480; prohibition of, 453; slave labor for, 441, 445

Tobacco lords, of Glasgow, 447

Tocqueville, Alexis de, 487, 523

Tokugawa Ieyasu, 471, 472

consumption in, 868; terrorist attacks in, 775, 849; war in Afghanistan, 775, 819, 820; greenhouse effect and, 872

United States, economic sanctions by. *See* Economic sanctions (boycott; embargo)

Universal human dignity, 837. *See also* Human rights

Universal religions: *See also* Buddhism; Christianity; Hinduism; Islam; spread of, 222–224; triumph of, 361–362

Universal Soul, 152

Universal truth, 219, 223

Universities and colleges, 755. *See also* Student protests; in China, 112, 260, 266, 362, 651, 652; in colonial Latin America, 436, 442; Islamic, 243, 285, 362, 404, 581; women in, 519, 790; in Africa, 285, 362, 404, 554; in Istanbul, 558; in Lebanon, 562; in Persia, 561; in medieval Europe, 254, 339, 346, 362; in India, 156, 162, 362, 575, 578, 841, 849; nationalist movements in, 650; in Japan, 736, 739

Untouchables (pariahs), 44, 150, 151, 162, 318, 846; Gandhi and, 659, 840

U Nu (Burma), 861

Upanishads (Indian epic), 46, 152, 154, 312

Upper class (elites). *See also* Aristocracy (nobility); Warrior class; Wealth (wealthy); Egyptian, 54; Peruvian, 88; Indian, 44, 220, 309, 319. *See also* Brahmans; Greek oligarchy, 133; Hellenistic age, 144; Chinese (mandarins), 98, 112–113, 118, 260, 264; Roman, 177, 181, 185–186, 220; Byzantine, 192; empire and, 220; conspicuous consumption of, 378; Korean, 273; Japanese, 275–276; Kongo, 290; in Ottoman Empire, 418, 419; planter class, 444; Aztec, 302; family size and, 519; Inca, 303; Mughal India, 452; Chinese women, 466, 482; Southeast Asian, 323, 325; plague in Europe and, 350; Latin American creole, 436, 437, 496, 497, 499, 531–532, 535; United States, 522; Egyptian, 560; Vietnamese, 585; Italian fascism and, 636; Qing China, 468, 601, 607; colonialism and, 678–679; Soviet Union, 763; African urban, 827, 834; Indian, 839, 843

Ural-Altaic languages, 83, 336

Urban II, Pope, 250, 346

Urbanization. *See also* Cities and towns; Rural-to-urban migration; first cities and, 21–22; in Mesopotamia, 28; Harappan, 37–38; in Sudan, 59–60; in Americas, 88; in Southeast Asia, 166,

328; of Islam, 241–242; Maya, 206; capitalism and, 395; in Europe, 516, 517; in United States, 529–530; in Southeast Asia, 591; in Japan, 737; in Africa, 832

Urdu language, 318, 450–451, 577, 658

Ur (Sumeria), 33 *and illus.*

Uruguay, 87, 438, 497, 498*(map)*, 797; immigration to, 535

Uruk (Mesopotamia), 27, 29, 31 *and illus.*, 32, 35, 94

Usury (interest), 131, 340, 375, 379

Utah, Pueblo Indians in, 212

Uthman, Caliph, 239, 240

Uthman dan Fodio, 546–547

Utopian socialism, 507

Utrecht, Treaty of (1714), 388–389

Uxmal (Maya city), 294

Uzbeks (Uzbekistan), 41; Muslim, 765; terrorist threat in, 420, 423, 629, 717

Vaccinations, against disease, 163, 521

Vaisya (Indian merchant caste), 44, 452

Vajrayana Buddhism, 313

Valerian (Rome), 195

Vandals (Germanic tribe), 187, 191

Van Gogh, Vincent, 521, 607

Van Lang (Vietnam), 166

Van Linschoten, Jan Huygen, 455*(illus.)*

Vargas, Getulio (Brazil), 674

Varna, in India, 44, 150. *See also* Caste system, in India

Vassals, 338, 343. *See also* Lord-vassal relations; Tribute system

Vatican. *See also* Papacy (popes); Sistine Chapel in, 381; Second Council (1962–1965), 760

Vedanta (Hindu) tradition, 152, 312

Vedas (Hindu scripture), 44, 46, 223; Aryans and, 42–43; Brahmans and, 312

Vedic Age (India), 42–43, 46

Vega, Garcilaso de la, 438

Vegetarianism, in India, 150, 153, 157

Veiling of women. *See under* Women, seclusion of

Veloso, Caetano, 868

Velvet Revolution, in Czechoslovakia, 771, 772*(illus.)*

Venezuela: Spanish claims to, 430, 432; cattle ranching in, 442; independence of, 496, 497, 498*(map)*; European immigration to, 535; Colombians in, 711; oil industry in, 796; Chavez in, 796–797

Venice (Venetians), 348, 356, 387; as art center, 381; Byzantine trade rivalry with, 336; capitalism in, 374; decline of, 389; Mamluk trade with, 252, 253*(illus.)*; slave trade and, 245, 339

Veracruz, Mexico, 432

Verdi, Giuseppi, operas of, 566*(illus.)*

Verdun, Battle of (1916), 622

Verdun, Treaty of (843), 334*(map)*, 335

Vermeer, Jan, paintings of, 395

Vernacular languages, 42, 342, 355, 712

Verrazano, Giovanni da, 430

Versailles palace, 389

Versailles Treaty (1919), 631, 652, 667; Wilson and, 624–625; German reparations in, 636, 638

Vespucci, Amerigo, 430

Viceroyalties, 436. *See also* Spanish colonies

Vichy government (France), 641*(map)*, 642, 662; Pétain and, 619, 640

Victoria (Britain), 487, 507, 676*(illus.)*; as Empress of India, 577

Vienna, Congress of, 493, 494*(map)*

Vienna, Ottoman defeat in, 387, 416, 419

Viet Cong (National Liberation Front), 851, 852*(map)*, 853

Viet Minh (Vietnamese Independence League), 661, 663, 850, 851. *See also* Ho Chi Minh

Vietnam, French rule of, 598, 648, 823; Japanese and, 662; population growth in, 649; racism and, 679; nationalism in, 660, 661, 664, 677, 750; communism in, 661, 663, 865; United States and, 692, 696, 697, 782; independence and, 691*(map)*; revolution and partition of, 850–851

Vietnam (Vietnamese): maritime trade of, 82; bronze drum in, 81 *and illus.*; China and, 80, 110, 112, 165, 166, 167–168, 463*(map)*, 598; chronology, 165; independence of, 168; Champa and, 166, 167 *and map*; Funan and, 167; China and, 229, 258*(map)*, 262, 272, 325; expansion of, 323; Le dynasty in, 325, 326*(illus.)*; French in, 457; expansion of, 463; refugees from, 711, 853; market economy and, 693, 702, 854; Nike Corporation in, 702–703; U.S. trade embargo of, 784, 854, 870; working women in, 703, 836–837*(illus.)*; communism in, 850, 853, 854; invasion of Cambodia by, 855; reunification of, 854; in ASEAN, 865

Vietnam War (1963–1975): Nixon and, 725, 753; protests against, 757, 791; United States and, 696, 751, 780, 781; American army in, 782, 783*(illus.)*, 851–853 *and map*; Johnson and, 782, 851

Vijayanagara (India), 317

body armor, 53, 177; Greek phalanx, 133, 142, 174; in China, 78, 105, 252, 261, 264; Kushite, 198; Mongol, 267, 278, 363(illus.), 364, 365; flaming rockets, 261; gunpowder, 252, 261, 355, 356, 359, 365; African, 410; artillery, 419, 423, 432, 453, 521, 621, 622; Aztec, 433(illus.); European, 376, 476, 511, 547, 564, 597; Mongol, 476; Portuguese, 328, 410; Ottoman, 404, 417, 419, 420; of Safavid Persia, 420; shipboard, 376, 387, 449, 454, 474; Spanish conquistador, 425, 432, 433(illus.); steel swords, 361, 410, 461, 471; armored tanks, 622, 684; biological weapons, 699; World War I, 621, 622 and illus., 624; World War II, 640; poison gas, 621, 642, 814, 816; Cold War buildup, 697–698; landmines, 696; United States' sales of, 780, 784, 785, 811(map); chemical, in Vietnam War, 853

Weapons of mass destruction, 875. See also Nuclear weapons; alleged, in Iraq, 717, 785, 786, 820

Weather. See Climate and weather

Weaving (textiles): See also Cloth and clothing; Textiles; Egyptian, 54–55; Indian cotton, 40; Muslim, 246; Aztec, 302; Inca woolens, 302, 304; women and, 54–55, 246, 302, 437

Wei Jingsheng, 728

Weimar Republic (Germany), 636

Welfare state (welfare systems), 508, 694–695; in Europe, 517, 687, 702, 750, 755–756, 774–775, 787; end of, in Eastern Europe, 771; end of, in Russia, 770; Japan as, 736; New Zealand as, 787, 794

Wells Cathedral, England, 330(illus.)

Wen-Amon, 68

Wesley, John, Methodism and, 520

West Africa: See also Mali and specific country; Dogon creation myth, 6; agriculture in, 17, 19(map), 57; Atlantic system and, 441; Guinea Coast of, 56; iron working in, 58; monotheism in, 60; Carthaginian exploration of, 68, 176; North Africa and, 101; desertification in, 479; gold from, 177, 356; Kushite traditions in, 200; kingdoms of, 229; slave trade in, 371, 401, 413–414, 415, 481; Tiv people of, 290; Portuguese exploration of, 293, 339, 355, 357; red pepper trade of, 361; slavery and slave trade in, 293, 339; Portuguese exploration of, 407; Bondu kingdom in, 401; coastal trade

of, 403(map); gold from, 376, 405; cash crop plantations in, 555; early modern states in, 402, 403(map), 404–406; European trade with, 402, 405–406 and illus.; peanuts in, 480; hybrid social groups in, 481; Islam in, 546; Sufi mysticism in, 547, 549; new societies in, 545–546; World War I and, 648; nationalism in, 664; French in, 679; music of, 665, 868; immigrant labor from, 711, 758

West Bank, Israel and, 810(illus.), 811(map), 812

Western colonialism, 569–570, 696, 810. See also Western imperialism

Western Europe: See also Europe (1450–1750); Medieval Europe; church power in, 229; industrialization in, 499; Ottoman Empire and, 419; changes in (1920s), 631; world economy and, 476

Western Europe (1945–present). See also European Union; chronology, 749; from cooperation to community, 751–753 and map; European Movement, 748–749; humanitarian groups in; immigration in, 710, 755, 758–759; Marshall Plan for, 748; nationalism and decolonization, 750; NATO and Cold War in, 750–751, 752(map); China and, 727; politics in remaking of, 749–750; revival and unity in, 747–755; revolutions and; social democracy in, 750, 755–756; social reform and gender relations in, 756–758; societies and cultures, 755–760; thought and religion in, 759–760; unemployment in, 754–755; United States and, 696, 781; welfare states in, 695–696, 755–756

Western Front, World War I, 622 and illus., 623(map)

Western Hemisphere. See Americas, the (New World)

Western imperialism (Western domination): See also Colonialism; Imperialism; in Africa, 485; challenges to, 648–651; global economy and, 676, 677; globalization and, 511, 513; Ho Chi Minh and, 647–648; industrialization and, 508, 509; nationalism and, 580; resurgence of, 508, 509–513; Japan and, 607, 608, 610; China and, 599–600

Westernization (Western culture), 635; in British India, 575, 576, 578; in China, 601, 728, 730; neo-colonialism and, 693; in Russia, 389–390, 617; in Southeast Asia, 662; of Turkey, 667,

669 and illus.; in global system, 678, 679; Islam and, 560, 564, 566, 822; in Japan, 473, 612, 632, 739; Derrida's deconstruction of, 760; opposition to, in Iran, 670; in Middle East, 670–671; global culture and, 868

Western nations: See also Western Europe; United States; specific nations; immigrant labor in, 711; resource consumption of, 678, 709, 870; Russian civil war and, 627, 628(map); investment by, 705, 830; support for Israel, 753, 815; wealth of, 834

Western Samoa, 794

Western (southwestern) Asia, 3, 371, 485, 671. See also Middle East; hominids in, 8; origins of agriculture in, 17, 18, 19(map); goddess from, 20(illus.); Indo-Europeans in, 24(map); emergence of cities in, 22; folk traditions of, 36; Bronze Age in, 91; Persian Empire and, 129, 142; chronology (224–616), 191; Classical societies in, 101; China and, 158; Indian philosophers in, 159; Islamic conquest of, 229, 238 and map, 345; Mongol conquest of, 268(map); nationalism in, 687; Ottoman rule in, 666, 668(map); tradition vs. modernity in, 817

West Germany, 771; economic growth of, 699, 749, 767, 773; European Community and, 753; France and, 749; homosexuality in, 758; in NATO, 752(map); postwar reconstruction of, 748; reunification and, 773; as welfare state, 755; immigrants in, 758

West Indies. See Caribbean region

Westphalia, Treaty of (1648), 388

Whale hunting, 539

Wheat, 41, 57, 480; in Canada, 434, 539, 620; domestication of, 16, 17; Egyptian export of, 176, 178; government subsidies for, 705; in India, 37, 39, 46, 452, 844; in Islam, 242; in medieval Europe, 337

Wheelbarrow, 359

Wheels, 92. See also Chariots

White collar workers, 631, 736

"White man's burden," 513, 588

White Russians, 627, 628(map)

White supremacy, in South Africa, 412, 550–551, 552, 657, 665, 828–829. See also Racism

Whitman, Walt, 523

Widow burning. See Sati

Wilde, Oscar, 519

Wilhelm II, Kaiser (Germany), 621, 624

William and Mary (England), 387, 393
William I, Kaiser (Germany), 505
William of Normandy, 343
William of Orange, 387, 393
Wilson, Woodrow, 531; World War I peace and, 625; Fourteen Points of, 624; Russian communism and, 627; Latin America and, 650–651
Windmills, 337, 445(illus.)
Wine, 18, 97, 181, 562; in India, 42; in Mediterranean region, 63, 66, 140; in China, 262, 265
"Winner-take-all" economy, 787
Winthrop, John, 490
Witches, torture of, 399
Wollstonecraft, Mary, 492–493, 519
Wolof people of Senegal, 549
Women, 94, 342. See also Feminism; Fertility cults; Gender relations; Marriage; Matrilineal societies; Sexuality; agriculture and, 16; as Sumerian priestesses, 30, 32; Indian, 39, 42, 44; Israeli, 66(illus.); in ancient Egypt, 49, 54–55; in Minoan Crete, 67(illus.); Arawak, 428(illus.), 429; as shamans, in Korea, 83; literacy of, 79; pottery and, 97; in China, 79, 114–115; Ionian Greek queens, 128; Greek, 134, 138 and illus.; Vietnamese rebels, 168; Etruscan, 174; early Christianity and, 189, 193; Celtic warrior-queens, 185; in Japan, 275, 278; Roman, 183, 226; Korean queens, 273; education of, 226, 275; Kushite queens, 198, 200(illus.), 226; Native American, 298; footbinding, in China, 264, 269, 362, 466, 651; African queens, 285, 290; commerce and, 321, 324; in Islam, 233–234, 236–237, 245–246 and illus., 362, 402; in Southeast Asia, 320, 321; Burmese queens, 320, 363; Christian nuns, 332, 351, 436; in medieval Europe, 341–342, 351, 352; in Japan, 472–473, 482; in African politics, 404–405, 410, 411(illus.), 832; in African slave trade, 481; Latin American, 436, 437, 497; in American Revolution, 490; in Mexican Revolution, 533(illus.), 534; in Mughal India, 451, 453, 481; African colonialism and, 555; Native American, 439; Islamic modernization and, 564, 565, 806–807(illus.); as novelists, 636; Ottoman, 418; Persian, 421, 422(illus.); as poets, 453, 482; as prostitutes, 137, 234, 439, 585, 614, 662, 711, 769, 846, 861; sati (widow burning) and, 451, 453, 575, 576, 581; in Siam, 457; as slaves, 523; in Soviet Union, 764; Filipina, 461, 707; sexual

harrassment of, 703, 707, 737(illus.), 790; development and, 707; in Japan, 736–737; Argentinian protests, 777–778; protests by, in Poland, 766; Palestinian Muslim, 812
Women, education of, 226, 246, 275; in China, 465–466, 726; in Europe, 519; in Africa, 554; in Indonesia, 591; in Siam, 591; in Russia, 617; reduced fertility and, 709; in Japan, 736; in Afghanistan, 819; in Egypt, 816; in India, 846; in United States, 790
Women, seclusion of (purdah), 131, 246, 276, 318–319, 362; in India, 452, 581; in Safavid Persia, 421; and veiling, 421, 452, 565, 670, 813, 817; in Egypt, 671, 806–807(illus.); in Iran, 813; in Saudi Arabia, 814; in Afghanistan, 820
Women, work of: cloth production (weaving) by, 13, 54–55, 97, 246, 302, 304; in colonial Africa, 555; market women, 292, 321, 324, 325, 404, 457, 591, 679, 832; in medicine, 581, 764; textile industry, 437, 518–519, 529(illus.), 530, 600, 611; in Africa, 292, 404, 679, 830, 832; in World War II, 642; in China, 599, 600(illus.), 718(illus.), 726, 730; in Mexico, 704, 798, 802(illus.); in Europe, 399, 632, 757–758; in Japan, 736, 737(illus.); in South Korea, 742; in Soviet Union, 770; unpaid, 707; in United States, 790; in Vietnam, 703, 836–837 (illus.); as political leaders, 756, 790, 794, 803, 827, 874; in Malaysia, 863; in South and Southeast Asian politics, 841–843, 848, 849, 860, 862, 865
Women Against AIDS in Africa, 832
Women's rights, 840. See also Voting rights (suffrage) for women; to property, 30, 54, 134, 137, 162, 183, 192, 236, 418, 471, 736; Islam and, in Indonesia, 459; French Revolution and, 492–493; in Italy, 505; in United States, 524, 685, 788; in China, 656; in Egypt, 564, 565, 671; in Mexico, 533(illus.), 534, 674, 803; in Japan, 632, 685, 732; socialism and, 507; in Turkey, 669, 817; in Burma, 660; in China, 726; in Europe, 632, 757; in Pakistan, 716; in Latin America, 803; in Iran, 813; Islam and, 816–817, 863; in Africa, 827; in India, 840, 846, 874(illus.); in Malaysia, 863
Woodblock printing, 116, 261, 356; Chinese, 726(illus.); Japanese, 473 and illus., 607, 611(illus.); in Korea, 273
Woodstock music festival (1969), 788
Woolen trade, in Europe, 304

Woolf, Virginia, 636
Workers (working class), 79, 364. See also Labor; Peasants; Slaves; British industrialization and, 444; consumer goods and, 510; Marxist proletariat, 507, 508, 509; European, 510; families, 518–519; sexuality and, 517; World War I and, 625; Chinese, 599, 600(illus.), 652, 722, 725; rights of, 715; Italian fascism and, 636; Japanese, 632, 736; in Nazi Germany, 638; Russian, 617, 626, 627; Mexican, 674, 675(illus.), 795; South Korean, 742–743; Soviet Union, 629, 630, 763; Venezuelan, 796; European, 631, 753, 755, 775; in United States, 530, 789–790; Argentina, 796; Chilean, 800; Cuban, 799
Working women. See Women, work of
World Bank, 645, 702, 866; private investment and, 834–835
World Conference on Women (1995), 716
World Council of Churches, 760
World cultures, 868
World Cup (football), 805
World economy (global trade). See also Globalization; Amsterdam and, 373; colonial Latin America and, 442; Southeast Asia and, 462–463; China and, 466–469, 600; emerging, 476–479; British Empire and, 509–510; Latin America in, 534; colonial Africa in, 554–555; British Malaya and, 583; Vietnam and, 585, 854; European influence on, 631; Great Depression and, 630–631, 633–634; World War II and, 640, 645; Axis Powers and, 639; colonial ports in, 649; inequality in, 680; Western domination of, 676, 677; underdevelopment and, 704–705; Cambodia in, 703(illus.); China in, 693, 731, 732; Japan in, 740, 754; United States' supremacy in, 625, 778; Africa in, 830, 834–835; North-South gap, 868; environmental sustainability and, 871; crisis in (2008–2009), 774, 785
World Health Organization, 698
World history, foundations of, 91–98. See also Historians; political, 95–96; social and cultural, 96–98; technological, 91–92, 93(map); urban and economic, 92, 94–95
World music, 868
World politics. See also Cold War; since 1989, 690, 698, 699–700
World Social Forum (Brazil), 715
World Trade Center attack (2001), 717, 784, 815

To help you take your reading outside the covers of WORLD, each new text comes with access to the exciting learning environment of a robust eBook.

Working with Your eBook

You can read WORLD wherever and whenever you're online by paging through the eBook on your computer. But you can do more than just read. Your eBook also contains hundreds of live links to

 Primary source documents

 Interactive maps

 Web links for further investigation

 Interactive quizzes

 Audio resources

 Historical simulation activities

 Profiles of key historical figures

Each link takes you directly to the source or interactive feature. Your eBook also features easy page navigation, bookmarking, highlighting, note taking, a search engine, and a print function.

You can save your WORLD user name and password for future reference here:

User Name: _____ Password: _____

Access your eBook and other online tools by going here:

4ltrpress.cengage.com/world/

Click on the book you are using and enter the Student area of the site. Register using the access code on the card bound into your textbook. Click on the links and have fun exploring!

Add your own favorite websites here:

_____

_____

_____

_____

_____

_____

Key Terms

LO² hominids
A family including humans and their immediate ancestors.

Australopithecines
Early hominids living in eastern and southern Africa 3 to 4 million years ago.

Homo habilis
("Handy human") A direct ancestor of humans, so named because of its increased brain size and ability to make and use simple stone tools for hunting and gathering.

Homo erectus
("Erect human") A hominid that emerged in East Africa probably between 1.8 and 2.2 million years ago.

Homo sapiens
("Thinking human") A hominid who evolved around 400,000 or 500,000 years ago and from whom anatomically modern humans (*Homo sapiens sapiens*) evolved around 100,000 years ago.

Neanderthals
Hominids who were probably descended from *Homo erectus* populations in Europe and who later spread into western and Central Asia.

Cro-Magnons
The first modern, tool-using humans in Europe.

LO³ Paleolithic
The Old Stone Age, which began 100,000 years ago with the first modern humans and lasted for many millennia.

Mesolithic
The Middle Stone Age, which began around 15,000 years ago as the glaciers from the final Ice Age began to recede.

Neolithic
The New Stone Age, which began between 10,000 and 11,500 years ago with the transition to farming.

matrilineal kinship
A pattern of kinship that traces descent and inheritance through the female line.

animism
The belief that all creatures as well as inanimate objects and natural phenomena have souls and can influence human well-being.

polytheism
A belief in many spirits or deities.

shamans
Specialists in communicating with or manipulating the supernatural realm.

CHRONOLOGY

14 billion years	Big Bang
4.5 billion years ago	Solar system and earth
5–6 million years ago	Earliest proto-humans
400,000–200,000 B.C.E.	*Homo sapiens*
135,000–100,000 B.C.E.	Modern humans
100,000 B.C.E.	Modern humans in Eurasia
100,000–9500 B.C.E.	Stone Age
9500–8000 B.C.E.	Beginning of agriculture
3500–3200 B.C.E.	First cities in western Asia
3000 B.C.E.	Introduction of bronze
1500 B.C.E.	Introduction of iron

LO¹ How have various human societies sought to understand the formation of the universe, earth, and humanity?

- To fully understand human history, it is helpful to first examine the origins of our planet, the beginning of life on earth, our prehuman ancestors, and their creation stories.

- Constant changes in geology and climate influenced the adaptation and survival of species such as humans, which are closely related to chimpanzees and other great apes; they eventually became dominant because of their use of intelligence.

LO² According to most scientists, what were the various stages of human evolution?

- Early hominids first evolved in Africa 4 to 6 million years ago; of them, *Homo habilis* was most successful because it used simple stone tools.

- *Homo erectus* developed more refined tools and migrated to Eurasia and throughout Africa.

- *Homo sapiens* had larger brains and evolved into modern humans, who developed language and spread throughout the world.

LO³ How did hunting and gathering shape life during the long Stone Age?

- During the Paleolithic and Mesolithic eras, people lived in small groups of hunters and gatherers.

- Hunting and gathering groups were usually close-knit and egalitarian, though violence was not unknown.

LO⁴ What environmental factors explain the transition to agriculture?

- The end of the last great Ice Age and increased population density led people to shift gradually from hunting and gathering to farming.

- Settled farming could support much denser populations and allowed for food storage, but it also led to new health problems and environmental damage.

- Farming probably began in the area of southwestern Asia known as the "Fertile Crescent."

LO⁴ horticulture
The growing of crops with simple methods and tools.

LO⁵ pastoral nomadism
An economy based on breeding, rearing, and harvesting livestock.

tribes
Associations of clans that traced descent from a common ancestor.

Indo-Europeans
Various tribes who all spoke related languages that derived from some original common tongue and who eventually settled Europe, Iran, and northern India.

LO⁵ How did farming and metallurgy establish the foundations for the rise of cities, states, and trade networks?

• Highly productive farming and new technology allowed for the formation of the first cities, which became centers of trade.

• People in cities developed forms of recordkeeping and writing.

• Pastoral nomads, or herders, played an important role in spreading culture across Eurasia, though most eventually took up farming.

2 Ancient Societies in Mesopotamia, India, and Central Asia, 5000–600 B.C.E.

Chapter in Review

Key Terms

LO¹ Fertile Crescent
A large semicircular fertile region that included the valleys of the Tigris and Euphrates Rivers stretching northwest from the Persian Gulf, the eastern shores of the Mediterranean Sea, and, to some scholars, the banks of the Nile River in North Africa.

ziggurat
A stepped, pyramidal-shaped temple building in Sumerian cities, seen as the home of the chief god of the city.

patriarchy
A system in which men largely control women and children and shape ideas about appropriate gender behavior.

cuneiform
("wedge-shape") A Latin term used to describe the writing system invented by the Sumerians.

LO³ Harappan
Name given to the city-states and the widespread Bronze Age culture they shared that were centered in the Indus River Valley and nearby rivers in northwest India between 2200 and 1800 B.C.E.

Dravidian
A language family whose speakers are the great majority of the population in southern India.

Shiva
The Hindu god of destruction and of fertility and the harvest.

steppes
The plains of Central Asia.

LO⁴ Aryans
Indo-European-speaking nomadic pastoralists who migrated from Iran into northwest India between 1600 and 1400 B.C.E. (see pastoral nomadism).

Vedas
The Aryans' "books of knowledge," the principal source of religious belief for Hindus: a vast collection of sacred hymns to the gods and thoughts about religion, philosophy, and magic.

Sanskrit
The classical language of north India, originally both written and spoken but now reserved for religious and literary writing.

Mahabharata
("Great Bharata") An Aryan epic and the world's longest poem.

CHRONOLOGY

3200	first cuneiform writing
3000–2300 B.C.E.	Sumerian city-states
2350–2160 B.C.E.	Akkadian Empire
2600–1750 B.C.E.	Harappan city-states
2200–1800 B.C.E.	Oxus cities
ca. 2000	*Epic of Gilgamesh* written in cuneiform
1800–1595 B.C.E.	Old Babylonian Empire
1790–1780	Hammurabi's Law Code
1900–1750	Harappan society collapses
1600–1400 B.C.E.	Aryan migrations
ca. 1600–1200	Hittite Empire
1500–1000 B.C.E.	Aryan Age
1115–605 B.C.E.	Assyrian Empire
ca. 626–539	Chaldean (Neo-Babylonian) Empire
ca. 539–330	Persian Empire
1000–450	Height of Indo-Aryan synthesis
800–600	Compilation of *Upanishads*

LO¹ Why did farming, cities, and states develop first in the Fertile Crescent?

- The first urban societies of Mesopotamia developed in the Tigris-Euphrates Basin.
- Sumerian society was hierarchical and patriarchal.
- The earliest writing system was the cuneiform system.
- The world's first empire, the Akkadian Empire, was founded by Sargon.

LO² What were some of the main features of Mesopotamian societies?

- The Babylonians, Hittites, Assyrians, and Chaldeans created empires in Mesopotamia.
- Surviving documents, including Hammurabi's Code and *The Epic of Gilgamesh*, indicate Mesopotamian values and perspectives, including a pessimistic view of life.
- The Assyrian Empire, known for its brutality, dominated a large region.

LO³ What were some of the distinctive features of the Harappan cities?

- The earliest Indian urban society emerged in the Indus River Valley around 2600 B.C.E.
- The Harappans had well-planned cities with advanced sanitation, a culture that gave women high status, and a written language.
- Harappan cities enjoyed extensive foreign trade with western and Central Asia.
- The steppes of Central Asia were home to mostly nomads, but evidence of an urban society has been discovered on the Oxus River.

LO⁴ How did the Aryan migrations reshape Indian society?

- The Indo-European Aryans, a cattle-raising tribal people, migrated into north India 3,500 years ago.
- The Vedas, written in Sanskrit, are religious writings that reveal information on the Aryan religion and their patriarchal culture.
- Eventually Aryans built kingdoms in the Ganges River Basin.

LO⁵ Indo-Aryan synthesis
The fusion of Aryan and Dravidian cultures in India over many centuries.

brahmans
The Universal Soul, or Absolute Reality, that Hindus believe fills all space and time.

kshatriyas
Warriors and landowners headed by the rajas in the Hindu caste system.

vaisyas
The merchants and artisans in the Hindu caste system.

sudras
The mostly poorer farmers, farm workers, and menial laborers in the Hindu caste system.

caste system
The four-tiered Hindu social system comprising hereditary social classes that restrict the occupation of their members and their relations with members of other castes.

pariahs
The large group of outcasts or untouchables below the official Hindu castes.

Bhagavad Gita
("Lord's Song") A poem in the Mahabharata that is the most treasured piece of ancient Hindu literature.

Brahmanas
Commentaries on the Vedas that emphasize the role of priests (brahmans).

Upanishads
Ancient Indian philosophical writings that speculate on the ultimate truth of the creation of life.

LO⁵ How did Indian society and the Hindu religion emerge from the mixing of Aryan and local cultures?

- Aryan and local cultures mixed together over the centuries and eventually produced a unique four-tiered caste system.

- The *Bhagavad Gita*, which emphasizes one's earthly duty and the soul's immortality, became the most treasured piece of Indian literature.

- Hinduism developed over many centuries, its central teachings collected in a series of sacred texts, including the *Brahmanas* and the *Upanishads*.

3 Chapter in Review

Key Terms

LO¹ pharaohs
Rulers of ancient Egypt.

hieroglyphics
The ancient Egyptian writing system, which evolved from pictograms into stylized pictures expressing ideas.

ma'at
Ancient Egyptian term for justice, the correct order of things.

monotheism
The belief in a single, all-powerful god.

LO² Sudan
A grassland region stretching along the southern fringe of the Sahara Desert from the western tip of Africa to the Nile valley.

desertification
The transformation of once-productive land into useless desert.

LO³ Bantu
Sub-Saharan African peoples who developed a cultural tradition based on farming and iron metallurgy, which they spread widely through great migrations.

LO⁴ messianism
The Hebrew belief that their God, Yahweh, had given them a special mission in the world.

CHRONOLOGY

8000–5000 B.C.E.	Earliest agriculture in the Sahara and Nubia
2663–2195 B.C.E.	Old Kingdom
2066–1650 B.C.E.	Middle Kingdom
2000 B.C.E.–1000 C.E.	Bantu migrations
2000–1500 B.C.E.	Possible time frame for Abraham
2000–1400 B.C.E.	Minoan Crete
1550–1064 B.C.E.	New Kingdom
1800–1500 B.C.E.	Nubian kingdom of Kerma
1600–1200 B.C.E.	Mycenaea
1300–1200 B.C.E.	Hebrew Exodus from Egypt
900 B.C.E.	Rise of Kush
900–800 B.C.E.	Mande towns
1200–800 B.C.E.	Greek "Dark Age"
1000–722 B.C.E.	Hebrew kingdoms
750 B.C.E.	Carthage colony established by Phoenicians

LO¹ What were some unique features of ancient Egypt?

- The regular flooding of the Nile River provided a highly fertile valley and a dependable growing season and led Egyptians to develop a strong central government to make the most of their agricultural system.

- The pyramids were built by the Egyptian pharaohs of the Old Kingdom, thought to be descendants of the sun-god.

- During the Middle Kingdom, the Egyptian capital moved from Memphis to Thebes, and the New Kingdom was a time of Egyptian expansion and eventual decline.

- Though wealthy Egyptians enjoyed lavish lifestyles, even the poor were relatively comfortable, and women had greater independence and rights in Egypt than in any other ancient society.

- Ancient Egyptians had great technical skill in architecture, medicine, and preserving the dead, because they believed they could obtain immortality if their bodies were mummified.

LO² How did environmental factors help shape ancient sub-Saharan African history?

- African geography is extremely varied, ranging from jungles with abundant rainfall to deserts like the Sahara with practically no rainfall.

- Small-scale agriculture flourished in Africa, though animal domestication was rare.

- Sub-Saharan Africans worked with iron at the same time or before they worked with bronze or gold.

LO³ What were some achievements of the ancient Nubian, Sudanic, and Bantu peoples?

- Early sub-Saharan societies were linked by trade and loosely organized, without centralized rule.

- Nubia had a close relationship with Egypt, which eventually destroyed the Nubian kingdom of Kerma; later, the Nubian kingdom of Kush increased in power as Egypt declined and became a major trading hub linking the peoples of Africa to the Mediterranean.

- Caravan routes through the Sahara allowed for trade and for links among widely separated African peoples.

- The Bantus spread widely throughout Africa, mixing their culture and traditions with those of local peoples.

LO⁴ What were the contributions of the Hebrews, Minoans, Mycenaeans, Phoenicians, and Dorian Greeks to later societies in the region?

- Mountainous Greece favored the development of many small, independent communities, rather than one homogenous community.

- The Hebrews' religious writings, emphasizing monotheism, morality, messianism, and meaning in history, have had a tremendous impact on religious history.

- Minoan Crete was the first great Mediterranean sea power and had a well-developed urban infrastructure.

- The Mycenaeans are remembered for their military might; the Phoenicians' legacy included their maritime trade and an alphabet that served as the basis for later European alphabets.

- The Homeric epics, the *Iliad* and the *Odyssey*, greatly influenced the emerging Greek society, which was a synthesis of Mycenaean and Dorian Greek peoples.

4

Around the Pacific Rim: Eastern Eurasia
and the Americas, 5000–600 B.C.E.

Chapter in Review

Key Terms

LO¹ loess
The dust blown in from the Mongolian deserts that enriched the soils of northern China.

LO² Mandate of Heaven
A Chinese belief from ancient times that rulers had the support of the supernatural realm as long as conditions were good, but rebellion was justified when they were not.

dynastic cycle
The view of Chinese historians that dynasties rise and fall in a cyclical fashion, largely based on the collection of taxes and the morale of the government and the armies.

Yijing
The Book of Changes, an ancient Chinese collection of sixty-four mystic hexagrams and commentaries upon them that was used to predict future events.

LO³ Lapita
The ancient western Pacific culture that stretched some 2,500 miles from just northeast of New Guinea to Samoa.

Jomon
The earliest documented culture in Japan, known for the ropelike design on its pottery.

LO⁴ Clovis
A Native American culture dating back some 11,500 to 13,500 years.

mound building
The construction of huge earthen mounds, often with temples on top, by some peoples in the Americas from ancient times to the fifteenth century C.E.

Mesoamerica
The region stretching from central Mexico southeast into northern Central America.

Olmecs
The earliest urban society in Mesoamerica.

Chavín
The earliest-known Andean urban society.

CHRONOLOGY

40,000–20,000 B.C.E.	possible earliest migrations to Americas (disputed)
11,500–9500 B.C.E.	beginning of Clovis culture
10,000–300 B.C.E.	Jomon culture
8000–6000 B.C.E.	agriculture begins in Southeast Asia
8000 B.C.E.	agriculture begins in Mesoamerica and Andes
7000 B.C.E.	agriculture begins in Yellow River Basin, China
5000–3000 B.C.E.	Yangshao culture
4500–2000 B.C.E.	Bronze Age begins
4000–2000 B.C.E.	Austronesian migrations
3000–2200 B.C.E.	Longshan culture
3000–1600 B.C.E.	Peruvian cities
1752–1122 B.C.E.	Shang dynasty
1200–300 B.C.E.	Olmecs
1200–200 B.C.E.	Chavín
1122–221 B.C.E.	Zhou dynasty
1000–800 B.C.E.	first Southeast Asian states

LO¹ How did an expanding Chinese society arise from diverse local traditions?

• Early Chinese society was concentrated inland from the sea and was frequently fragmented into various states.

• In the cold, dry Chinese north, crops such as wheat and millet were grown, whereas in the wetter, warmer south, rice was dominant.

• As time passed, the widely diverse Chinese peoples began to knit themselves together into one broad society with traditions that persist to this day.

LO² What were some key differences between the Shang and Zhou periods in China?

• The western Shang established an authoritarian state, with the king playing the role of father to the entire country.

• Under the Shang, society became increasingly stratified, divided up into a dominant aristocracy, a middle class, farmers and laborers, and slaves.

• After a slave rebellion overthrew the Shang, the Zhou established a more widespread, less centralized empire, introducing the concepts of rule by the "Mandate of Heaven," and of the dynastic cycle.

• A common written language provided a unifying link for the Chinese. One of the first Chinese books was the *Yijing*, which was related to the idea of the universal opposing forces, yin and yang.

LO³ How did the traditions developing in Southeast and Northeast Asia differ from those in India and China?

• The peoples of Southeast Asia established early maritime trading networks, while inland geographic boundaries led to the development of extremely diverse cultures.

• Extensive migration occurred among China, Southeast Asia, and the Pacific islands.

• Korea and Japan, while being strongly influenced by the Chinese, were shaped by different environments and created unique cultures, languages, and societies.

LO⁴ How do scholars explain the settlement of the Americas and the rise of the first American societies?

- The lands of the Western Hemisphere are smaller in area than those of the Eastern Hemisphere and are constructed on a north-south axis rather than an east-west one. Native American peoples probably migrated from Eurasia to North America from Siberia to Alaska at least 12,000 years ago, and possibly between 20,000 and 40,000 years ago.

- Early American peoples survived by hunting, gathering, and fishing, as well as trading over large distances. Mutual cooperation, earth worship, personal connections with guardian spirits, and shamanism were common in early American cultural life.

- In response to the challenges posed by different climates, American peoples domesticated more different plants than all the peoples of the Eastern Hemisphere.

- Lacking draft animals, Americans came up with ingenious approaches to farming, but the absence of draft animals also meant that Native Americans were not exposed to many diseases before the arrival of Europeans and Africans after 1492 C.E.

- Various technological breakthroughs led to the development of urban societies in Mesoamerica and the Andes, including Caral, America's first known city.

- The Olmecs of Mesoamerica and the Chavín of South America were early urban societies that served as patterns for later American urban societies.

Eurasian Connections and New Traditions in East Asia,
600 B.C.E.–600 C.E.

Chapter in Review

Key Terms

LO¹ Confucianism
A Chinese philosophy based on the ideas of Confucius (ca. 551–479 B.C.E.) that emphasized the correct relations among people; became the dominant philosophy of East Asia for two millennia.

The Analects
The book of the sayings of Confucius (ca. 551–479 B.C.E.), collected by his disciples and published a century or two after his death (see Confucianism).

filial piety
The Confucian rule that children should respect and obey their parents (see Confucianism).

Daoism
A Chinese philosophy that emphasized adaptation to nature; arose in the late Zhou era.

Legalism
A Chinese philosophy that advocated harsh control of people by the state; became the dominant philosophy during the Qin dynasty (221–207 B.C.E.) and was later tempered by Confucianism.

LO² Sinicization
The process by which Central Asian invaders maintained continuity with China's past by adopting Chinese culture.

mandarins
Educated men who staffed the imperial Chinese bureaucracy from the Han dynasty until the early twentieth century.

scholar-gentry
A Chinese social class of learned officeholders and landowners that arose in the Han dynasty and continued until the early twentieth century.

Silk Road
A lively caravan route through Central Asia that linked China with India, the Middle East, and southern Europe that began during the Han dynasty (207 B.C.E.–221 C.E.) and continued for many centuries.

sericulture
Silk making, which arose in ancient China.

LO⁴ Shinto
("Way of the gods") The ancient animistic Japanese cult that emphasized closeness to nature; enjoyed a rich mythology that included many deities (see animism).

CHRONOLOGY

1122–221 B.C.E.	Zhou dynasty
550–350 B.C.E.	Height of Axial Age in China
221–206 B.C.E.	Qin dynasty
108 B.C.E.–313 C.E.	Chinese colonization
300 B.C.E.–552 C.E.	Yayoi culture
206 B.C.E.–220 C.E.	Han dynasty
222–581 C.E.	Three Kingdoms and Six Dynasties
350–668 C.E.	Koguryo Empire
589–618 C.E.	Sui dynasty
514–935 C.E.	Silla State in southern Korea
552–710 C.E.	Yamato state
538 C.E.	Buddhism introduced to Japan
604 C.E.	first Japanese constitution

LO¹ What were the distinctive features of the Chinese philosophies that emerged during the late Zhou period?

- Despite being marred by chronic civil warfare, China became the most populous society on earth, and its economy evolved rapidly during the Warring States Period.

- The belated development of iron technologies, as well as many other breakthroughs, finally made China competitive with western Asia.

- Instability resulting from military conflict led intellectuals to question the basic tenets of society. Three Chinese philosophies from this period—Confucianism, Daoism, and Legalism—have influenced Chinese government and culture through two millennia.

LO² How was Chinese society organized during the Han, and how was China linked to the rest of Eurasia?

- Through military conquest and the application of Legalist principles, the Qin dynasty unified the warring states into a new centralized, imperial China.

- Both the Han dynasty and the Roman Empire reached their peaks at about the same time. Han government was characterized by a blending of central and local authority and a softening of Legalism with Confucian humanism.

- The diplomatic and military expansion under Han rulers set the stage for expanded Eurasian trade, but rural peasant labor continued to be the foundation of the economy.

- The family structure became the central social institution; its patriarchal hierarchy, codified in law, put the needs of the group above the needs of the individual.

- Han innovations included the development of paper, mathematical and medical breakthroughs, and the establishment of Chinese historiography.

LO³ What outside influences helped shape China after the fall of the Han?

- Spurred by invasions of nomadic peoples from the north, the population shifted south, but the invaders were assimilated by existing Chinese government structures.

- Buddhism took root in China during this tumultuous period, spreading along the trade routes from India and melding with existing Confucian thought.

- The Chinese attitude toward religion was characterized by an easy interchange of beliefs, in which individuals drew from a variety of perspectives depending on their need.

- Like the Qin before them, the Sui rulers also reunited China using harsh measures but made lasting contributions, such as the Grand Canal.

LO⁴ How did the Koreans and Japanese assimilate Chinese influences into their own distinctive societies?

- Like most of China, Korea and Japan were agricultural societies, a similarity that facilitated the easy transmission of Chinese culture.

- Korea's proximity to China, along with the alternating military dominance of one culture over the other, led to the adoption of Chinese writing and other technologies in Korea.

- Both Buddhism and Confucianism permeated Korean culture from China and were blended with the native belief system of animism, keeping Korean culture distinctive.

- The flow of ideas and people from Korea and China to Japan introduced Buddhism, writing, and other influences into Japan, but the Japanese culture, arts, and religion remained distinctive, due in part to Japan's lack of space and the social problems of overcrowding.

6 Western Asia, the Eastern Mediterranean, and Regional Systems, 600–200 B.C.E.

Chapter in Review

Key Terms

LO1 Achaemenid
The ruling family of the Classical Persian Empire (ca. 550–450 B.C.E.).

satrap
("Protector of the kingdom") An official in the Classical Persian Empire (ca. 550–450 B.C.E.) who ruled according to established laws and procedures and paid a fixed amount of taxes to the emperor each year.

Zoroastrianism
A monotheistic religion founded by the Persian Zoroaster that later became the state religion of Persia. Its notion of one god opposed by the devil may have influenced Judaism and later Christianity (see monotheism).

Ahura Mazda
(the "Wise Lord") The one god of Zoroastrianism.

LO2 polis
A city-state in Classical Greece; each polis embraced nearby rural areas, whose agricultural surplus then helped support the urban population.

oligarchy
Rule by a small group of wealthy leaders.

tyrant
Someone who ruled a Greek polis outside the law, not necessarily a brutal ruler.

Sophists
Thinkers in Classical Greece (fifth century B.C.E.) who emphasized skepticism and the belief that there is no ultimate truth.

Socratic Method
A method of asking people leading questions to help them examine the truth of their ideas; introduced by the Greek philosopher Socrates (469–399 B.C.E.).

metaphysics
The broad field of philosophy that studies the most general concepts and categories underlying ourselves and the world around us.

LO3 Delian League
A defensive league organized by Greek cities in the fifth century B.C.E. to defeat the Persians.

Peloponnesian War
A long war between Athens and Sparta and their respective allies in 431–404 B.C.E. that resulted in the defeat of Athens.

trade diaspora
Merchants from the same city or country who live permanently in foreign cities or countries.

CHRONOLOGY

ca. 594 B.C.E.	Solon's reforms in Athens
550–530 B.C.E.	Kingship of Cyrus the Great
525–523 B.C.E.	Persian conquest of Egypt
521–486 B.C.E.	Kingship of Darius I
499–479 B.C.E.	Greco-Persian Wars
460–429 B.C.E.	Periclean era in Athens
431–404 B.C.E.	Peloponnesian War
338 B.C.E.	Macedonian conquest of Greece
336–323 B.C.E.	Reign of Alexander the Great
330 B.C.E.	Alexander's occupation of Persia

LO1 How did the Persians acquire and maintain their empire?

• The Persian Empire, centered on a trade crossroads, lasted for only two centuries, but it was larger than any empire that preceded it.

• The Persians often won the support of peoples they had conquered through their respect for native cultures and their institution of the rule of law.

• The monotheistic Persian religion, Zoroastrianism, may have contributed some key ideas to Judaism, Christianity, and Islam.

• Although the Persian Empire was conquered by Alexander the Great in 330 B.C.E., it had begun to decline over a century earlier, suffering civil unrest and dissension among the ruling family.

LO2 What were some features of Greek governance, philosophy, and science?

• The mountainous, maritime geography of Greece fostered the development of multiple city-states rather than one centralized state.

• The polis system of governance allowed extensive political rights for aristocratic citizens. But eventually, increased trade and the rise of the infantry reduced the power of Greek aristocrats.

• The two most powerful Greek city-states, Athens and Sparta, developed distinctive systems: Athens emerged as a radical democracy for the minority who were citizens, while Sparta focused on its military strength and had the strongest army in Greece.

• The Greeks were notable for their commitment to using reason to understand the world. Three of the greatest Greek philosophers were Socrates, who believed in absolute truths; Plato, who described an ideal society in the Republic; and Aristotle, who explored human nature and the workings of the physical world.

• Greek drama tended to focus on tragedy and reflected both realities and criticisms of its class and gender divisions.

LO3 In what ways did Persians and Greeks encounter and influence each other?

• Early in the fifth century B.C.E., the Persians attacked the Greeks several times, but the Greeks, against great odds, fended them off.

• Following the Greek victory over the Persians, Athens' growing arrogance eventually led to the Peloponnesian War between Athens and Sparta, which ended with Spartan victory.

• Herodotus, who wrote of the Greco-Persian Wars, and Thucydides, who wrote of the Peloponnesian War, were the first historians to write critical and analytical history.

• The eastern Mediterranean and western Asia were zones of intense trade and cultural mixing.

LO⁴ Hellenism

A widespread culture flourishing between 359 and 100 B.C.E. that combined western Asian (mainly Persian) and Greek (Hellenic) characteristics.

Cynicism

A Hellenistic philosophy, made famous by the philosopher Diogenes (fourth century B.C.E.), that emphasized living a radically simple life, shunning material things and all pretense, and remaining true to one's fundamental values (see Hellenism).

Stoicism

A Hellenistic philosophy begun by Zeno in the third century B.C.E. that emphasized the importance of cooperating with and accepting nature, as well as the unity and equality of all people (see Hellenism).

Mithraism

A Hellenistic cult that worshiped Mithra, a Persian deity associated with the sun; had some influence on Christianity.

LO⁴ What impact did Alexander the Great and his conquests have on world history?

• After the Peloponnesian War, no Greek city was strong enough to unite the rest of the Greek peninsula, but King Philip II of Macedonia was, conquering several Greek cities.

• King Philip's son Alexander established a vast empire and trading network that linked the Mediterranean, western Asia, and India, and spread Hellenism, a mix of Greek and Persian culture.

• Hellenism was marked by rigorous scientific inquiry, philosophies such as Cynicism and Stoicism that urged people to take life as it came, and mystical religions that influenced Christianity.

7 Classical Societies in Southern and Central Asia, 600 B.C.E.–600 C.E.

Chapter in Review

Key Terms

LO¹ Brahman
The Universal Soul, or Absolute Reality, that Hindus believe fills all space and time.

Vedanta
("Completion of the Vedas") A school of Classical Indian thought that offered Hindus mystical experience and a belief in the underlying unity of all reality.

Jainism
An Indian religion that believes that life in all forms must be protected because everything, including animals, insects, plants, sticks, and stones, has a separate soul and is alive; arose in 500 B.C.E. as an alternative to Hinduism.

Buddhism
A major world religion based on the teachings of the Buddha that emphasized putting an end to desire and being compassionate to all creatures.

nirvana
("the blowing out") A kind of everlasting peace or end of suffering achieved through perfection of wisdom and compassion (see Buddhism).

monasticism
The pursuit of a religious life of penance, prayer, and meditation, either alone or in a community of other seekers.

LO² Kushans
An Indo-European people from Central Asia who conquered much of northwest India and western parts of the Ganges Basin and constructed an empire (50–250 C.E.) that also encompassed Afghanistan and parts of Central Asia.

Theravada
("Teachings of the Elders") One of the two main branches of Buddhism, the other being Mahayana, that arose just before the Common Era. Theravada remained closer to the Buddha's original vision.

Mahayana
("the Greater Vehicle to salvation") One of the two main branches of Buddhism; a more popularized form of Buddhist belief and practice than Theravada. Mahayana Buddhism tended to make Buddha into a god and also developed the notion of the bodhisattva.

bodhisattva
A loving and ever-compassionate "saint" who has postponed his or her own attainment of nirvana to help others find salvation through liberation from birth and rebirth (see Buddhism, Mahayana).

CHRONOLOGY

563–483 B.C.E.	Life of the Buddha
322–185 B.C.E.	Mauryan Empire
269–232 B.C.E.	Reign of Ashoka
200 B.C.E.–50 C.E.	Division of Buddhism into Theravada and Mahayana Schools
111 B.C.E.–939 C.E.	Chinese colonization of Vietnam
39–41 C.E.	Trung Sisters' Rebellion in Vietnam
50–250 C.E.	Kushan era
ca. 75–550 C.E.	Funan
ca. 100–1200 C.E.	Era of Indianization
ca. 192–1471 C.E.	Champa
320–550 C.E.	Gupta era
450–750 C.E.	Zhenla states

LO¹ What ideas did Buddhism take from Hinduism, and what ideas were unique?

- The Indian caste system, which began to take form in the Classical Era, became hereditary and placed limits on one's occupation, diet, religious practice, and social interactions.
- New spiritual movements within Hinduism, such as yoga and Vedanta, challenged priestly control and emphasized the goal of escaping the ego.
- Although Hinduism was extremely inclusive, the two movements of Jainism and Buddhism split off from it, and Buddhism in particular became globally influential.

LO² How did the Mauryas shape Indian society, and how, in turn, did classical India influence the world beyond South Asia?

- Through the conquests by Darius and Alexander the Great, northwest India experienced significant influence from the West.
- After Alexander's retreat, Chandragupta established the first imperial Indian state, the centralized, autocratic Mauryan Empire, which included the Indus and Ganges Basins and excelled in crafts and trade.
- King Ashoka, Chandragupta's grandson, became a pacifist convert to Buddhism, which he helped to spread to Sri Lanka, Southeast Asia, and Afghanistan. Several decades after Ashoka died, the Mauryan Empire broke down.
- Trade, migrations, and invasions led to cultural exchange between post-Mauryan Indians and many other peoples, including the Kushans from Central Asia.
- Buddhism split into Theravada, a more traditional form, and Mahayana, a more accessible form, but declined in popularity in India while spreading to Central Asia, China, and Southeast Asia, where it flourished.

LO³ What were the main achievements of the Gupta era?

- Under the decentralized Gupta Empire, based in northern India, the government attained prosperity while pursuing progressive tax policies and religious tolerance.
- Over time, the status of Indian women declined, particularly in the north.
- During the Gupta era, science, mathematics, literature, and the arts all thrived.
- The Gupta Empire was greatly weakened by Hun invasion, and soon thereafter it collapsed.

LO⁴ Indianization

The process by which Indian ideas spread into and influenced many Southeast Asian societies; a mixing of Indian with indigenous ideas.

LO⁴ How did Southeast Asians blend indigenous and foreign influences to create unique societies?

- Austronesians engaged in wide-ranging maritime trade and also settled over a wide area, from Madagascar, off the coast of Africa, to the Pacific islands of Polynesia.
- Southeast Asians were influenced by both Chinese and Indian culture, but they retained distinct aspects of their native cultures.
- Some principal states in this era were Funan, Zhenla, and Champa on the southeast Asian mainland.
- Vietnam showed great resistance in its long struggle against Chinese colonization.
- Southeast Asian societies tended to be multiethnic and able to blend diverse elements into cultural unity.

8 Chapter in Review

Key Terms

LO¹ patricians
The aristocratic upper class who controlled the Roman Senate.

Centuriate Assembly
A Roman legislative body made up of soldiers.

consuls
Two patrician men, elected by the Centuriate Assembly each year, who had executive power in the Roman Republic.

plebeians
The commoner class in Rome.

tribunes
Roman men elected to represent plebeian interests in the Centuriate Assembly.

Pax Romana
("Roman Peace") The period of peace and prosperity in Roman history from the reign of Augustus through that of Emperor Marcus Aurelius in 180 C.E.

LO² Romance languages
Languages that derive from Latin, such as French, Italian, and Spanish.

LO³ Nicene Creed
A set of beliefs, prepared by the council at Nicaea in 325 C.E., that became the official doctrine of the early Christian church.

LO⁴ Manicheanism
A blend of Zoroastrianism, Buddhism, and Christianity, founded by Mani (216–277 C.E.), that emphasized a continuing struggle between the equal forces of light and dark.

CHRONOLOGY

509 B.C.E.	Roman Republic
264–146 B.C.E.	Punic Wars
60–58 B.C.E.	Julius Caesar completes conquest from Rhine to Atlantic
31 B.C.E.–180 C.E.	*Pax Romana*
7–6 B.C.E.–30 C.E.	Life of Jesus
251 C.E.	Germans defeat Roman armies, sack Balkans
313 C.E.	Legalization of Christianity
240–272 C.E.	Founding of Sassanian Empire
395 C.E.	Division of eastern and western empires
451 C.E.	Huns invade western Europe
455 C.E.	Vandals sack Rome
330 C.E.	Founding of Constantinople
476 C.E.	Official end of western Roman Empire
527–565 C.E.	Reign of Justinian
607–616 C.E.	Sassanians conquer Syria, Palestine, and Egypt

LO¹ How did the Romans develop and maintain their large empire?

- The agricultural plenty of Italy allowed for the development of larger states than had been possible in Greece, and the Mediterranean Sea allowed for Roman expansion.
- Following the Etruscans, who had formed the first urban society in Italy, Rome formed a republic, in which citizens ruled the state.
- After a major defeat by the Gauls, Rome defeated Carthage, its primary rival, in the Punic Wars and then conquered an empire.
- With the shift from Roman Republic to empire, military leaders gained power, farmers grew impoverished, and the people had less voice in government.
- The *Pax Romana*, which began with Augustus, was a time of peace, prosperity, and cosmopolitan living, but also of imperial rule and a passive populace.

LO² What were some notable accomplishments of Roman life, and what factors contributed to Rome's decline?

- The Romans set long-lasting legal standards and offered allegiance to a wide variety of gods, many of them borrowed from other peoples. Their society was patriarchal and highly stratified.
- Rome served as a nexus for trade and communication, and it excelled in architecture and engineering.
- Beset by a range of problems, including uneasy succession, economic imbalance, overexpansion, climate change, and disease, the Roman Empire began to decline.
- The Celts, who were fierce warriors, posed a threat to the Romans, but they were eventually pushed back to rugged areas of the British Isles. The Germans exerted continued pressure on the Roman Empire from the north.
- The Roman Empire had trouble fielding enough soldiers or gathering enough money to fend off the German threat, because many of its poor had traded their rights for protection by the rich, and many of the rich had left the cities to live on their estates.
- The Roman Empire fell in 476 C.E., but an offshoot, the Byzantine Empire, lasted for another thousand years.

LO³ How did Christianity develop and expand?

- Christianity was born in Palestine, an area with a tradition of rebellion against Rome, and grew out of the Jewish prophetic tradition.
- Jesus opposed excessive legalism and ceremony, but scholars debate whether he saw himself as divine or the "son of God."

- Paul was instrumental in spreading and shaping Christianity after Jesus's death, as well as in arguing that one did not have to be Jewish to become a Christian. By 400 C.E., Christianity became the official Roman religion.
- In defending Christianity against its critics, Augustine of Hippo distinguished between Christians, who would be saved, and non-Christians, who would be damned.

LO⁴ How did the Byzantine and Sassanian Empires reinvigorate the eastern Mediterranean world?

- Justinian ruled the Byzantine Empire as an absolute monarch. More urban and wealthy than western Europe, the Byzantine Empire served as a trading hub for goods from across Europe and Asia.
- Byzantine culture became more Greek and less Roman, and the Byzantine church denied the authority of the pope and came to emphasize ritual and doctrine to a greater degree than did the Roman church.
- The Sassanians revived the strength of Persia, and adopted Zoroastrianism as a state religion.
- Arab culture began to rise out of tribes of pastoral nomads, the trading cities of Petra and Palmyra, and the farming-based kingdoms of Yemen.

9

Classical Societies and Regional Networks in Africa, the Americas, and Oceania, 600 B.C.E.–600 C.E.

Chapter in Review

Key Terms

LO¹ Meroitic
A cursive script developed in the Classical Era by the Kushites in Nubia that can be read only partly today.

Coptic Church
A branch of Christianity that had become influential in Egypt and became dominant in Nubia between the fourth and sixth centuries C.E.

Aksum
A literate, urban state that appeared in northern Ethiopia before the Common Era and grew into an empire and a crossroads for trade.

Geez
The classical Amharic written language of Ethiopia, a mixture of African and Semitic influences.

LO² Ghana
The first known major Sudanic state, formed by the Soninke people of the middle Niger valley around 500 C.E.

Mande
Diverse Sudanic peoples who spoke closely related languages, shared many customs, and dominated the western Niger River Basin and adjacent areas of West Africa (see Sudan).

griots
A respected class of oral historians and musicians in West Africa who memorized and recited the history of the group, emphasizing the deeds of leaders.

Nilotes
Ironworking pastoralists from the eastern Sudan who settled in East Africa in the Classical Era and there had frequent interactions with the Bantus (see pastoral nomadism).

LO³ Maya
The most long-lasting and widespread of the classical Mesoamerican societies, who occupied the Yucatan Peninsula and Northern Central America for almost 2,000 years.

Teotihuacan
("the City of the Gods") The largest city in the Americas and the capital of an empire in central Mexico during Classical times.

CHRONOLOGY

2000 B.C.E.–1000 C.E.	Bantu migrations into Central, East, and South Africa
800 B.C.E.–350 C.E.	Kush
1100–150 B.C.E.	Early Maya society
600 B.C.E.–1100 C.E.	Tiwanaku Empire in the Andes
1500–1000 B.C.E.	Micronesian settlement of Marianas
1100–800 B.C.E.	Settlement of Fiji, Samoa, and Tonga
400 B.C.E.–800 C.E.	Aksum kingdom in Ethiopia
300 B.C.E.	Beginning of maritime trade to East African coast
400 B.C.E.–1000 C.E.	Monte Alban in Mexico
300 B.C.E.–1200 C.E.	Polynesian settlement of Pacific
200 B.C.E.	Founding of Jenne-Jenno
300 C.E.	Introduction of Christianity to Kush and Aksum
200 B.C.E.–600 C.E.	Hopewell mound-builders
200 B.C.E.–700 C.E.	Moche
200 B.C.E.–750 C.E.	Teotihuacan
ca. 500 C.E.	Founding of Ghana
100–900 C.E.	Anasazi society in southwest North America
400–600 C.E.	Polynesian settlement of Hawaii
800–1000 C.E.	Polynesian settlement of New Zealand

LO¹ What were some of the similarities and differences between Kush and Aksum?

- The kingdom of Kush in Nubia, with its capital city of Meroë, was a major African iron producer and crossroads of trade between sub-Saharan Africa and the Mediterranean.
- Kush was influenced by Egypt but was also remarkable for its rich culture, its fearsome warriors and absolute monarchs, and its strong laws and traditions.
- Aksum, in the Ethiopian highlands, had contact with Egypt and Arabia, may have forged links with the Hebrews, and after a time eclipsed Meroë as the region's primary trade center.
- Aksum's king converted to Christianity as a means of establishing closer relationships with Rome, Byzantium, and Egypt.
- Like Kush, Aksum may have declined in part because of climate change, but it was also hurt by the Islamic conquest of its neighbors; unlike Kush, however, the society endured for another 2,000 years.

LO² How did the spread of the Bantus reshape sub-Saharan Africa?

- The Sudan region included trading hubs such as Jenne-Jenno, but the population in the Classical Era was not dense enough to require a powerful state; Ghana was the first state to arise, probably around 500 C.E.
- The Garamante peoples controlled the extensive caravan routes through the Sahara Desert to bring salt from the African Mediterranean coast to Sudan, which exported gold in return.
- The Bantu peoples, equipped with iron tools, continued to migrate south and east, mixing with and sometimes pushing out other peoples, and they made their way to South Africa by the third century C.E.
- Indonesian mariners settled on the East African coast and, to a greater extent, in Madagascar, where a mixed Indonesian–Bantu culture survives to this day. Favorable trade winds facilitated the slow growth of contact between East Africa and southwestern Asia, India, and Southeast Asia.

LO⁴ Moche
A prosperous, powerful state that formed along the northern Peruvian coast from 200 B.C.E. to 700 C.E.

LO⁵ dreamtime
In Aboriginal Australian mythology, the distant past when the spiritual ancestors gave order and form to the universe at the world's creation.

LO³ What were some of the similarities and differences between the Maya and Teotihuacan?

- The Maya society on the Yucatan Peninsula lived largely on corn, developed comprehensive writing and numbering systems, and built impressive buildings and large pyramids. A few cities, such as Tikal, came to dominate Maya society, but there was no overarching Maya state.

- The Maya tried to please their gods through human sacrifice and self-purification. Religion also motivated them to study astonomy and devise very accurate calendars.

- The Zapotecs built the city and state of Monte Alban, and another urban center arose at Teotihuacan, which grew into one of the largest and best-designed cities in the world.

LO⁴ How did the Mesoamerican, Andean, and North American societies compare and contrast with each other?

- In Peru and Ecuador, coastal and interior peoples created an interdependent trading network stretching from Mexico to Chile.

- In the Andes, Chavín was succeeded by Moche, whose pottery depicts a violent culture of war and sacrifice but also of advanced metalwork and architecture.

- In the desert Southwest of North America, the Hohokam, Anasazi, and Mogollon people developed extensive irrigation systems, and their cultural artifacts show some Mesoamerican influence.

- Supported by corn and expanded trade networks, mound-building cultures spread across eastern North America.

LO⁵ How were Australian and Pacific societies shaped by their environments?

- Aboriginal Australians developed great understanding of natural phenomena and were very successful hunters and gatherers for thousands of years.

- Aborigines across Australia believed in the dreamtime of the mythic past and felt that spirits and ghosts inhabited much of the physical world.

- Austronesian peoples from Southeast Asia took to the sea and settled on various Pacific islands, developing into Micronesian and Polynesian cultures.

- An extensive trading network developed among the Pacific islands and, despite their isolation from each other, the islands' cultures remained quite homogenous.

Key Terms

LO¹ Bedouins
Tent-dwelling nomadic Arab pastoralists of the seventh century C.E. who wandered in search of oases, grazing lands, or trade caravans to raid.

Ka'ba
A huge sacred cube-shaped stone in the city of Mecca to which people made annual pilgrimages.

Quran
("Recitation") Islam's holiest book; contains the official version of Muhammad's revelations, and to believers is the inspired word of God.

Hadith
The remembered words and deeds of Muhammad, revered by many Muslims as a source of belief.

hijra
The emigration of Muslims from Mecca to Medina in 622.

umma
The community of Muslim believers united around God's message.

Allah
To Muslims the one and only, all-powerful God.

caliphate
An imperial state headed by an Islamic ruler, the caliph, considered the designated successor of the Prophet in civil affairs.

Ramadan
The thirty days of annual fasting when Muslims abstain from eating, drinking, and sex during daylight hours, to demonstrate sacrifice for their faith and understand the hunger of the poor.

haj
The Muslim pilgrimage to the holy city of Mecca to worship with multitudes of other believers from around the world.

jihad
Effort to live as God intended; a spiritual, moral, and intellectual struggle to enhance personal faith and follow the Quran.

LO² sultan
A Muslim ruler of only one country.

Shari'a
The Islamic legal code for the regulation of social, economic, and religious life.

madrasas
Religious boarding schools found all over the Muslim world.

Sunni
The main branch of Islam comprising those who accept the practices of the Prophet and the historical succession of caliphs.

CHRONOLOGY

622	Hijra of Muhammad to Medina
634–651	Arab conquests in Middle East
632–661	Rashidun Caliphate
661–750	Umayyad Caliphate
750–1258	Abbasid Caliphate
711–1492	Muslim states in Spain
732	European victory at Battle of Tours
705–715	Islamic conquests of Afghanistan and Central Asia
1096–1272	Christian Crusades in Middle East
1258	Mongol seizure of Baghdad and end of Abbasid Caliphate
1218–1360	Mongol conquests in Central and western Asia
1300–1923	Ottoman Empire
1453	End of Byzantine state
1369–1405	Reign of Tamerlane

LO¹ How did Islam rise?
- Islam was born in Arabia, a harsh land where many people lived in cooperative tribes or clans.
- Islam's holiest book, the Quran, is believed to be a record of the divine revelations of God as told to the prophet Muhammad.
- Facing some opposition in Mecca and drawn to resolve a dispute in Medina, Muhammad and his followers moved there and won many new converts.
- Muhammad's teachings were monotheistic (like Christianity and Judaism) and emphasized equality and mutual respect among all peoples.
- Islam is based on the five pillars: profession of faith; formal worship; charity; annual fasting, or Ramadan; and the pilgrimage, or haj, to Mecca.

LO² What factors led to the rise of the Islamic states and what did those states achieve?
- Islam spread extremely rapidly via Arab conquest of the Middle East, North Africa, Central Asia, and parts of India and Europe, facilitated in part by the weaknesses of other empires.
- Arab identity and language gradually spread to many of the conquered peoples; Muslim leaders imposed Shari'a, a legal code that regulated social, economic, and religious life.
- In the tumultuous period of the early Rashidun Caliphate, Islam began to split into two branches: the Sunni majority branch and the Shi'a dissident branch, who believed Ali was the only successor to the Prophet.
- The Umayyad dynasty, which succeeded the Rashidun Caliphate, was led by men with no connection to Muhammad who extended the empire into Byzantine lands.
- Under the Abbasid Caliphate, Baghdad became a cosmopolitan hub of trading and culture.
- As they expanded, Arabs adopted the imperial ruling structures of the peoples they conquered and were targeted by numerous invaders, including the Mongols.
- Spain and Sicily were ruled by Muslims for several centuries, although Christians gradually reclaimed them and failed to maintain the tolerance of the Muslim rulers.

LO³ What were the major concerns of Muslim thinkers and writers?
- Sufism, a mystical approach to Islam that emphasized flexibility and a personal connection with God, drew both Sunni and Shi'ite followers.
- Although the Quran and most Muslim societies restricted women, some Muslim societies did not, and both Muslims and non-Muslims have debated the origins and benefits of such practices as wearing a veil.

Shi'a
The branch of Islam that emphasizes the religious leaders descended from Muhammad through his son-in-law, Ali, whom they believe was the rightful successor to the Prophet.

LO³ Sufism
A mystical approach and practice within Islam that emphasized personal spiritual experience.

calligraphy
The artful writing of words.

LO⁴ Dar al-Islam
("Abode of Islam") The Islamic world stretching from Morocco to Indonesia and joined by both a common faith and trade; arose between the eighth and the seventeenth century.

millet
The nationality system through which the Ottomans allowed the leaders of religious and ethnic minorities to administer their own communities.

- Literature, especially poetry, was very important in Islamic culture, as was calligraphy, the artful writing of words.
- Several academic disciplines flourished in the Islamic world. The Scientific Revolution would not have occurred without the help of Islamic mathematicians, who passed on to Europe Indian mathematics.

LO⁴ Why do historians speak of Islam as a hemispheric culture?

- Trade routes spread Islam throughout the hemisphere, eventually creating Dar al-Islam, an Islamic world stretching from Indonesia to Morocco, in which Arabs constituted a minority of Muslims.
- The series of Christian Crusades to win back the Judeo-Christian Holy Land from Muslims led to long-lasting animosity.
- The Mongols, led by Genghis Khan and Hulegu, one of his grandsons, ruthlessly attacked Muslims in Central Asia and sacked Baghdad, but the Islamic tradition endured throughout Mongol rule.
- The arrival of gunpowder from China allowed Muslim military states, such as the Mamluks and the Timurids, to gain power, while the Ottoman Turks established an extremely successful empire in the territory of the former Byzantine Empire by allowing subject minorities to administer their own affairs.
- By conducting and preserving a great deal of scientific and philosophical learning, the Muslims contributed much to European culture.

Key Terms

LO² neo-Confucianism
A form of Confucianism arising in China during the Song period (960–1279) that incorporated many Buddhist and Daoist metaphysical ideas (see Buddhism, Daoism).

qi
In Chinese thought, the energizing force pervading the universe.

LO³ kotow
The tribute-bearers' act of prostrating themselves before the Chinese emperor.

LO⁴ dyarchy
A form of dual government that began in Japan during the Nara period (710–784), whereby one powerful family ruled the country while the emperor held mostly symbolic power.

kana
A Japanese phonetic script developed in the Heian period (794–1184) that consisted of some forty-seven syllabic signs derived from Chinese characters.

LO⁵ samurai
("One who serves") A member of the Japanese warrior class, which gained power between the twelfth and fourteenth centuries and continued until the nineteenth.

Bushido
("Way of the Warrior") An idealized ethic for the Japanese samurai.

Shogun
("Barbarian-subduing generalissimo") In effect a Japanese military dictator who controlled the country in the name of the emperor; the first shogun took power in 1185, and the last one fell in 1868.

Zen
A form of Japanese Buddhism that emerged in the Intermediate Era; called the meditation sect because it emphasizes individual practice and discipline, self-control, self-understanding, and intuition.

Noh
Japanese plays that use stylized gestures and spectacular masks; began in the fourteenth century C.E.

Daimyo
("Great name") Large landowning territorial magnates who monopolized local power in Japan beginning during the Ashikaga period (1338–1568).

CHRONOLOGY

618–907	Tang dynasty
751	Battle of Talas
868	First woodblock print books
688–918	Silla
645	Taika reforms in Japan
710–784	Nara period
794–1184	Heian period
960–1279	Song dynasty
918–1392	Unification of Korea by Koryo
1167–1227	Life of Ghengis Khan
1279–1368	Yuan dynasty (Mongols)
1180–1333	Kamakura Shogunate
1368–1644	Ming dynasty
1405–1433	Voyages of Admiral Zheng He
1392–1910	Yi dynasty (Choson)
1338–1568	Ashikaga Shogunate

LO¹ What role did Tang China play in the Eurasian world?
- The Tang Empire was marked by ambitious expansion, a tolerant atmosphere of innovation, and stable governance maintained by keeping the emperor's authority in check and by rewarding high achievers through the civil service exam system.
- Buddhism reached its peak influence during the Tang, but it was greatly weakened when Emperor Wuzong seized Buddhist monasteries.
- During the Tang, the first book was printed using woodblocks. Poetry and other arts were very popular; while usually stressing Daoist harmony, they sometimes expressed criticism of the government.

LO² Why might historians consider the Song dynasty the high point of China's golden age?
- The Song dynasty was notable for its bustling urban life, educated elite, maritime trade, and advanced economy, but the status of women declined during this period.
- Song China made great advances in the manufacture of porcelain, ships, and bridges and in the prevention of disease.
- The Song's achievements did not lead to a major historical transition, because China at this time felt self-sufficient, was not interested in conquest, and ultimately failed to control the militant pastoral nomads peacefully.

LO³ How did China change during the Yuan and Ming dynasties?
- The ancient Chinese fear of Central Asian nomads was realized when the Mongols, under Genghis and Khubilai Khan, conquered China and established the Yuan dynasty, improving China's transportation system and moving the capital to Beijing.
- Because of lack of cooperation from Chinese scholars and bureaucrats, the Mongols established an international civil service, in which Marco Polo served.
- After the decline of the Mongols, the Chinese enjoyed three centuries of prosperity under the Ming dynasty, and their sense of well-being was displayed in Zheng He's grand sailing expeditions, which enhanced China's position among its neighbors.
- For reasons that are still debated, the Ming emperor suddenly ordered all overseas activity halted, and China turned inward, beginning an isolationist period that ended only in the 1800s.

LO⁴ How did the Koreans and Japanese make use of Chinese culture in developing their own distinctive societies?

- The Korean state of Silla was subordinate to China and borrowed a great deal from China's culture, adapting it to Korean traditions.

- The Koryo state was dominated by the aristocracy and saw the decline of Buddhist influence.

- In the Nara period, Japan borrowed heavily from Chinese culture, but its government was a dyarchy in which one powerful family dominated the emperor, and imports such as Buddhism were melded with native cultural features such as Shinto.

- In the Heian period, borrowing from China ended, foreign contacts were stopped, and a small elite group of women and men, who were concerned almost exclusively with the pursuit of aesthetic beauty, created some of Japan's best art and literature.

LO⁵ How did Korean and Japanese society change in the late Intermediate Era?

- The Yi, who ruled Korea after the Mongols, sought good relations with China and instituted the Chinese educational and civil service exam system.

- In Japan, the warrior class, or samurai, gradually attained supremacy over the emperor, and an organization based on lords and vassals became dominant.

- The Kamakura Shogunate began after the winner of a Japanese civil war was given the title of shogun, or military dictator, who ruled while the emperor retreated behind the scenes.

- Three enduring Buddhist sects developed in Japan: (1) Pure Land, which stressed equality; (2) Nicheren, which was militant; and (3) Zen, which stressed meditation, discipline, and simplicity.

- The Ashikaga Shogunate, which followed the Kamakura, had little power over the provinces, which became ruled by landowning lords called daimyo.

12 Chapter in Review

Key Terms

LO¹ mansa
("King") Mande term used by the Malinke people to refer to the ruler of the Mali Empire (1234–1550).

Swahili
Name for a distinctive people, culture, and language, a mix of Bantu, Arab, and Islamic influences, that developed during the Intermediate Era on the East African coast.

LO² oral traditions
Verbal testimonies concerning the past; the major form of oral literature in cultures without writing.

LO³ Quetzalcoatl
The feathered serpent, a symbol that goes back deep in Mesoamerican history.

LO⁴ chinampas
Artificial islands built along lakeshores of the central valley of Mexico and used by the Aztecs for growing food.

quipus
Differently colored knotted strings used by the Incas to record commercial dealings, property ownerships, and census data.

CHRONOLOGY

ca. 500–1203	Ghana
600–800	High point of Maya
700–1400	Anasazi
800–1475	Chimu Empire
900–1168	Toltec Empire
1000–1200	Rise of Hausa city-states
ca. 1000–1450	Zimbabwe kingdom
1050–1250	High point of Cahokia
1220–1897	Benin
1234–1550	Mali Empire
ca. 1375	Rise of Kongo kingdom
1464–1591	Songhai Empire
1428–1521	Aztec Empire
1440–1532	Inca Empire
1492	Columbus reaches Caribbean

LO¹ How did contact with Islamic peoples help shape the societies of West Africa?

- The kingdom of Ghana in the area south of the Sahara, known as the Sudan, benefited most from the Sahara caravan trade and gradually embraced Islam.

- The kingdom of Mali also grew fabulously wealthy because of the caravan trade, but like Ghana, it ultimately declined because of infighting and external threats. The Songhai, who split off from Mali, amassed great wealth from the demand for gold and slaves.

- Other kingdoms in the Housa region and south of the Sudan, on the Guinea coast, developed unique societies based on farming, mining, and trade.

- The Bantus continued to expand across eastern and southern Africa and established numerous coastal city-states that were greatly influenced by trade with Arabs. The East African coast became largely Muslim, though it retained a great deal of its native African culture.

- The fusion of Bantu, Arab, and Islamic culture yielded a new language, Swahili, and led to the adoption of many Arabic practices by East Africans.

- Zimbabwe rose to prosperity as a result of mining and built large granite buildings whose precise use is still debated by historians; the Kongo had a king who was in theory absolute and divine, though his powers were limited.

LO² What were some distinctive patterns of government, society, thought, and economy in Intermediate Africa?

- Many Africans lived in "stateless societies" in which family relationships and a variety of social networks organized people's lives.

- In addition to Muslims and Christians, many Africans were polytheistic, believers in multiple gods and spirits. Important knowledge was passed down orally by griots.

- African agriculture faced many challenges, including the difficulty of obtaining and using draft animals, poor soil, and irregular rainfall.

- Several million African slaves from across the continent were shipped to the Middle East during the Intermediate period, and the Portuguese lay the groundwork for the much larger European slave trade to the Americas.

LO³ What factors explain the collapse of the Early Intermediate Era American societies?

- American Classical states like the Maya survived longer than their counterparts in Eurasia, though they ultimately declined. The northern Maya continued on fitfully before collapsing by 1500.

- The Toltecs, a loose military empire based in central Mexico, adopted the cult of Quetzalcoatl, the feathered serpent.

- The Pueblo peoples of the American Southwest thrived on maize, grew and wove cotton, and were largely egalitarian and matrilineal.

- In the Mississippi and Ohio River Basins, mound-building cultures thrived on the fertile land and built some of the largest structures in the world.

LO⁴ How were the Aztec and Inca Empires different, and how were they similar?

- The Aztecs, productive farmers and traders, lived in a state of constant war and conquest, sacrificing thousands of enemy warriors a year, but their enemies helped the Spanish to conquer them.

- The Incas conquered a wide area in the Andes and had a hierarchical social structure, but they were far more inclusive and tolerant than the Aztecs. Trade was tightly controlled by the state, and sophisticated agriculture yielded an abundant food supply.

- Despite extremely limited contact between Andean societies and Mesoamerican ones, they were similar in terms of gender relations and warfare protocols.

Key Terms

LO¹ Rajputs
("King's sons") An Indian warrior caste formed by earlier Central Asian invaders who adopted Hinduism.

polyandry
Marriage of a woman to several husbands.

bhakti
Devotional worship of a personal Hindu god.

Vajrayana
("Thunderbolt") A form of Buddhism that featured female saviors and the human attainment of magical powers; developed in the Intermediate Era and became the main form of Buddhism in Nepal and Tibet.

Tantrism
An approach within both Buddhism and Hinduism that worshiped the female essence of the universe; developed in the Intermediate Era.

Lamaism
The Tibetan form of Buddhism, characterized by the centrality of monks (lamas) and huge monasteries.

LO² purdah
The Indian Muslim custom of secluding women.

LO³ Devaraja
("god-king") The title used by Indianized Southeast Asian rulers, who wished to be seen as a reincarnated Buddha or Shiva worthy of cult worship.

wayang kulit
Javanese shadow puppet play, developed during the Intermediate Era, based on Hindu epics like the *Ramayana* and local Javanese content.

LO⁴ Nam Tien
("Drive to the South") A long process beginning in the tenth century in which some Vietnamese left the overcrowded north to migrate southward along the coast of Vietnam.

CHRONOLOGY

600–647	Empire of Harsha
620–649	First Tibetan kingdom and introduction of Buddhism
711	First Muslim invasion of northwest India
192–1471	Kingdom of Champa
600–1290	Srivijaya Empire
846–1216	Chola dynasty
802–1432	Angkor Empire
939	End of Chinese colonization in Vietnam
1192–1526	Delhi Sultanate
1044–1287	Pagan kingdom in Burma
1336–1565	Vijayanagara state
1398-1399	Devastation of Delhi by Tamerlane
1238–1419	Sukhotai kingdom, Siam
1350–1767	Ayuthia kingdom, Siam
1403–1511	Melaka state
1428–1788	Le dynasty in Vietnam

LO¹ What were some of the main features of Hindu society at its height, and how did Hinduism and Buddhism change over time?

- In the Intermediate Era, India was fragmented into many small states; the north was influenced by earlier Central Asian invaders and the south by maritime trade with Southeast Asia. The village, based on cooperation and caste, remained the basic unit of Indian life.

- Indian merchants in the cities were heavily taxed, but India and China produced most of the world's manufactured goods in this era.

- Indian men had much more power than women, who were forced to marry early and earned respect through bearing children, particularly boys.

- The mathematician Bhaskara discovered perpetual motion, which influenced science in the West.

- Hinduism adapted to the needs of a wide variety of people, from the worldly to the scholarly, and helped establish a common culture throughout India. A renaissance led by religious thinkers Shankara and Ramanuja stimulated new ideas and practices, revitalizing the faith.

- Indian Buddhism declined generally, but it remained important in the northeast, where Vajrayana and Tantrism grew out of the interplay between Buddhism and Hinduism.

- Buddhism became the dominant religion in Tibet, where it became Lamaism, and many Indian Buddhist monks took refuge there to escape Islamic persecution.

LO² How did Islam alter the ancient Indian pattern of diversity in unity?

- Hindu warriors fended off Muslim invaders for a time, but they were eventually defeated; the invasion caused long-term Hindu resentment and also contributed to Buddhism's decline in India.

- The Islamic Delhi Sultanate brought unity to north India for the first time in centuries, but its rulers ranged from the enlightened to the tyrannical.

- Various Hindu monarchies, including the Cholas, maintained power in southern and eastern India, while Hindu traditions died out in the north.

- The Delhi Sultanate declined because of climate change and civil war, and north Indian unity was shattered by the invasion of Tamerlane.

- Muslim and Hindu beliefs were radically opposed and remained largely separate, despite some cultural interchange. Over time Muslim rulers came to tolerate Hindu subjects, many of whom eventually converted to Islam.

LO³ What political and religious forms shaped Southeast Asian societies in the Early Intermediate Era?

- Southeast Asian kingdoms—multiethnic and shaped by trade and immigrants for centuries—were strongly influenced by India, and, as in India, their rulers considered themselves god-kings, although their power was limited in the provinces.

- The Indianized kingdom of Angkor controlled a large swath of Southeast Asia and completed advanced civil engineering projects. Hindu priests played a very important role in Angkor, and the social structure was extremely rigid.

- On Java, a highly stratified Indianized society that championed harmony developed, while on Sumatra, Srivajaya became a powerful commercial empire.

- Southeast Asians fended off the Mongols, but new peoples such as the Tai invaded and destroyed Angkor, and the gradual introduction of Theravada Buddhism and Sunni Islam challenged the hierarchical order and displaced Indian influence in many states.

LO⁴ What was the influence of Theravada Buddhism and Islam on Southeast Asia?

- Siamese states such as Sukhotai and Ayuthia were Theravada Buddhist monarchies that valued individualism and peacefulness, offered women a fair amount of freedom, and were permeated by Buddhist values.

- Despite gaining freedom from Chinese rule, Vietnam retained a great deal of Chinese cultural influence.

- Inhabitants of the Malay and Indonesian archipelagoes embraced Islam, grafting it onto Hinduism and Buddhism to create many different patterns of Islamic belief.

- Southeast Asia became an international crossroads, attracting visitors from all over—including, eventually, the Portuguese.

Key Terms

LO 1 medieval
A term first used in the 1400s by Italian historians to describe the centuries between the classical Romans and their own time.

feudalism
A political arrangement characterized by a weak central monarchy that ruled over smaller states or influential families that were largely autonomous but owed service obligations to the monarch; prevailed in medieval Europe.

vassal
In medieval Europe, a subordinate person who owed service to a lord.

benefices
In medieval Europe, grants of land from lord to vassal.

fief
In medieval Europe, the thing granted in a feudal contract, usually land (see feudalism).

knights
In medieval Europe, armored military retainers on horseback who swore allegiance to their lord.

chivalry
The rigid code of behavior, including a sense of duty and honor, of medieval European knights.

manorialism
The medieval European system of autonomous, nearly self-sufficient agricultural estates.

serfs
In medieval Europe, peasants legally bound to their lord and tied to the land through generations.

LO 2 guilds
In medieval Europe, collective fraternal organizations of craftsmen and merchants designed to protect the economic interests of their members.

usury
The practice of loaning money at interest; considered a sin in medieval Europe, although necessary to commerce.

courtly love
A standard of polite relationships between knights and ladies that arose in the 1100s in medieval Europe. Courtly love was celebrated in song by wandering troubadours.

excommunicate
To expel a person from the Roman Catholic church and its sacraments.

Holy Inquisition
A church court created in 1231 in medieval Europe to investigate and eliminate heresy; inquisitions continued into the 1600s.

CHRONOLOGY

750–1200	Viking attacks in Europe
632	First Arab expansion into Byzantine Empire
768–814	Reign of Charlemagne
756–1492	Muslim states in Spain
843	Treaty of Verdun
825	First Swedish Viking bases in Russia
988	Russian conversion to Christianity
955	Defeat of Magyars
986	Otto the Great's revival of Holy Roman Empire
1066	Norman conquest of England
1054	Schism between Roman and Byzantine churches
1096–1444	Crusades
1198–1216	Pope Innocent III
1231	Beginning of Inquisition
1265	First English Parliament
1337–1453	Hundred Years' War
1237–1241	Mongol invasions
1348–1350	Peak of Black Death
1420	Beginning of Portuguese exploration of Africa
1453	Fall of Constantinople to Turks

LO 1 What institutions and technologies shaped medieval European societies between 500 and 1000?

• With the decline of the Roman Empire, the Christian church became a power in its own right with influence over, and protection from, German kings. Christians more aggressively spread their faith, assimilating pagan practices and sometimes persecuting non-Christians.

• During this time, the Papal States were created, Charlemagne's Carolingian empire temporarily united much of Europe, and Otto the Great began the tradition of calling Germany the Holy Roman Empire.

• The Vikings of Scandinavia raided European lands for more than four centuries, eventually settling in Iceland, Greenland, and various European territories. European merchants engaged in growing trade with Muslims, who introduced Europeans to Classical Greek, Indian, Arab, and Persian ideas.

• Technological advances such as the moldboard plow, the horseshoe, and the horse collar improved agriculture, as did the three-field system, and the watermill helped improve European industry.

• Feudalism was a medieval political arrangement in which a king gave nobles the right to rule over sections of his territory in exchange for their allegiance.

LO 2 How did the Christian church influence medieval religious, political, and intellectual life?

• Medieval society was patriarchal and considered women to be inferior to men; the ideal of courtly love applied largely to extramarital affection or unrequited love.

• Much of the tensions in medieval society were caused by intolerance for "outsiders": non-Christians and heretics, homosexuals, Muslims, and Jews, all of whom were treated harshly.

• The church and its priests had a great deal of power over people's lives, but many priests were unqualified or incompetent. Some popes were more powerful than kings, and they also orchestrated the Holy Inquisition, which killed thousands of "nonbelievers."

• Christians adopted the Jewish belief in progress over time and the belief that everything in the world was for the use of humans, a view that influenced later industrialization.

simony
In medieval Europe, a practice whereby wealthy families paid to have their sons appointed bishops.

Magna Carta
("Great Charter") An agreement signed by King John of England in 1215 that limited the feudal rights of the English king and his officials while protecting the rights of the church, lords, and merchants.

LO⁴ Renaissance
("Rebirth") A dramatic flowering in arts and learning that began in the Italian city-states around 1350 and spread through Europe through the 1500s.

humanism
The name for the European Renaissance philosophy, which emphasized humanity, worldly concerns, and reason rather than religious beliefs.

- Spurred on by a mix of religious idealism and greed, Christians mounted a series of Crusades to wrest the "Holy Land" from Muslim control, thereby creating long-standing resentment among Muslims.

- A mix of religious and secular topics were studied at urban universities, where theologians struggled to reconcile faith and reason.

LO³ How did Byzantine society differ from that of western Europe?

- The Byzantines were under almost constant attack by their neighbors, including Sassanian Persians, Bulgars, Slavs, and even Christians from western Europe, but Byzantium survived until it was conquered by the Turks in 1453.

- Byzantium's culture and Orthodox Christianity survived, because they were spread through war and trade to many eastern European peoples, including Russians, Bulgars, Serbs, and many Ukrainians.

- The Russians, who had adopted Orthodox Christianity, were attacked by the Mongols but emerged as one of the strongest societies in eastern Europe.

LO⁴ What developments between 1300 and 1500 gave Europeans the incentive and means to begin reshaping the world after 1500?

- The Black Death killed one-third of Europe's people and reduced the power of western European nobles while increasing the power of eastern European nobles.

- French rulers increased their power in the Hundred Years' War, England's Tudor dynasty later made England a world power, and Spanish Christians gradually drove out the Muslims, while in Germany and Italy the nobility remained strong.

- The church entered a decline in power and prestige, and the papacy was weakened by the Great Schism. At the same time, Renaissance artists and writers rediscovered classical influences and championed worldly concerns, individualism, and realism rather than spirituality.

- Major technological developments, influenced by ideas imported from China and the Muslim world, included the printing press and guns.

- After the Black Death, Europe's population soared and its merchants grew increasingly successful and powerful.

- The Portuguese were the first to begin exploring the West Coast of Africa for slaves, gold, and other trade goods, and their adventures eventually led to Columbus's voyage to the Americas.

Key Terms

LO¹ capitalism
An economic system in which property, exchange, and the means of production are privately owned.

bourgeoisie
The urban-based, mostly commercial, middle class that arose with capitalism in the Early Modern Era.

commercial capitalism
The economic system in which most capital was invested in commercial enterprises such as trading companies, including the world's first joint-stock companies.

mercantilism
An economic approach that emerged in Early Modern Europe based on a government policy of building a nation's wealth by expanding its reserves of precious metals.

LO² Reformation
The movement to reform Christianity that was begun by Martin Luther in the sixteenth century.

Protestants
Groups that broke completely with the Roman Catholic Church as the result of the Reformation.

Counter Reformation
A movement to confront Protestantism and crush dissidents within the Catholic Church.

LO³ absolutism
A form of government in which sovereignty is vested in a single person, the king or queen; monarchs in the sixteenth and seventeenth centuries based their authority on the theory of the divine right of kings (i.e., that they had received their authority from God and were responsible only to Him).

LO⁴ baroque
An extravagant and, to many, shocking European artistic movement of the 1600s that encouraged release from restraints of thought and expression.

Scientific Revolution
An era of rapid European advance in knowledge, particularly in mathematics and astronomy, that occurred between 1600 and 1750.

Enlightenment
A philosophical movement based on science and reason that began in Europe in the late seventeenth century and continued through the eighteenth century.

empiricism
An approach that stresses experience and the testing of propositions rather than reason alone in acquiring knowledge.

CHRONOLOGY

1350–1615	Renaissance
1517–1615	Protestant Reformation
1588	Defeat of Spanish armada
1600–1750	Scientific Revolution
1618–1648	Thirty Years' War
1675–1800	Enlightenment
1641–1645	English Civil War
1688–1689	English Glorious Revolution

LO¹ **How did exploration, colonization, and capitalism increase Western power and wealth?**

- Europe's political decentralization, improved technologies, and increased exploration allowed for the growth of cities and the development of capitalism.

- Motivated by "Gold, God, and Glory," Europeans, led by the Spanish and the Portuguese, set up colonies in the Americas, Africa, and Asia.

- Contesting medieval Christian attitudes, capitalism took hold in western Europe, while eastern European leaders resisted it and instead mandated serfdom.

- Commercial capitalists, assisted by the mercantilist policies of their countries, increased their market power by pooling resources in such organizations as joint-stock companies.

LO² **How did the Renaissance and Reformation mark a crucial cultural and intellectual transition?**

- Renaissance humanists questioned the authority of the Catholic Church and challenged accepted truths of morality, science, and astronomy. Renaissance artists and writers such as Michelangelo and Shakespeare and Cervantes aimed to represent humanity more realistically.

- Martin Luther criticized the corruption of the Catholic Church and set the Reformation in motion; it was propelled by others like John Calvin, whose ideas were taken up by the Puritans, and King Henry VIII of England, who made England Protestant.

- In the Counter Reformation, the Catholic Church attempted to reassert its dominance, but ultimately it focused on converting non-Europeans.

- Religious conflicts sparked several wars between Catholic and Protestant nations as well as continued conflicts with the Muslim Ottoman Empire.

LO³ **What type of governments emerged in Europe in this era?**

- Europeans fought a series of wars, some religiously motivated and some not; for example, in the Thirty Years' War, which involved many countries, Catholic France triumphed over the Catholic Habsburgs.

- Absolutist monarchs included Louis XIV of France, who lived in astounding luxury and wielded great power, and Russian czars Ivan the Terrible and Peter the Great.

- Representative governments arose in the Netherlands, where the Dutch instituted a decentralized republican system of government, and in England, where political power became more equally shared between the monarch and Parliament.

- Amidst the ongoing political turmoil in Europe, Austria and Prussia became major powers, Sweden saw its fortunes rise and fall, and Poland and Lithuania came under Russian power.

LO⁴ **How did major intellectual, scientific, and social changes help to reshape the West?**

- The extravagant baroque style that followed the Renaissance emphasized artistic freedom, while Dutch painters eschewed religious themes for natural ones.

philosophes
The intellectuals who fostered the French Enlightenment.

enclosure
Arising in Early Modern Europe, the pattern in which landlords fenced off common lands once used by the public for grazing livestock and collecting firewood.

- Bacon and Descartes emphasized the role of reason in science and philosophy, respectively, while Thomas Hobbes developed a pessimistic political philosophy.
- Advances in astronomy, particularly those made by Galileo, greatly antagonized Catholic officials, while Isaac Newton discovered fundamental laws of physics.
- Locke and Voltaire were among the prominent thinkers of the Enlightenment, a movement that favored reason over unquestioning faith.
- First in England and then elsewhere in western Europe, rural peasants were impoverished by landowners' greed and served as a ready source of labor for industry. In addition, the economic role of women declined, as, in many cases, did their social standing.

Key Terms

LO¹ **Darkest Africa**
Those areas of the African continent least known to Europeans but, in European eyes, awaiting to be "opened" to the "light of Western civilization."

LO² **racism**
A set of beliefs, practices, and institutions based on devaluing groups that are supposedly biologically different.

Boers
Dutch farming settlers in South Africa in the eighteenth century.

trekking
The migrations of Boer settlers in cattle-drawn wagons into the interior of South Africa whenever they wanted to flee government restraints.

Middle Passage
The slave's journey by ship from Africa to the Americas.

Atlantic System
A large network that arose with the trans-Atlantic slave trade; the network spanned western and Central Africa, the east coast and southern region of English North America, the Caribbean Basin, and the northern and eastern coastal zones of South America.

imperialism
The control or domination, direct or indirect, of one state or people over another.

colonialism
Government by one society over another society.

LO³ **janissaries**
("new troops") Well-armed, highly disciplined, and generally effective elite military corps of infantrymen in the Ottoman Empire.

LO⁴ **Cossacks**
Tough adventurers and soldiers from southern Russia who were descendants of Russians, Poles, and Lithuanians fleeing serfdom, slavery, or jail.

CHRONOLOGY

1300–1923	Ottoman Empire
1482–1497	Portuguese encounters with East Africa
1507–1543	Rule of Alfonso I in Kongo
1526–1870	Trans-Atlantic slave trade
1501–1736	Safavid Persia
1514–1517	Ottoman Conquest of Syria, Egypt, and Arabia
1520–1566	Suleiman the Magnificent
1591	Destruction of Songhai
1554–1659	Sa'dian Morocco
1652	Dutch settlement of Cape Town
1682–1699	Ottoman wars with Habsburg Austria
1715	Beginning of Russian conquest of Turkestan

LO¹ **How did the larger sub-Saharan African societies and states differ from each other in the sixteenth century?**

- Songhai, the last great Sudanic kingdom with its trading city Timbuktu, produced many scholars of Islam, and its society was relatively open to contributions from women.

- West African states were extremely varied and included the strict Islamic kingdom of Kanem-Bornu, the Hausa traders, the Yoruba in western Nigeria, and the kingdom of Benin.

- In Bantu-speaking East Africa, coastal city-states such as Kilwa and Malindi grew wealthy from trade; the Shona exported gold and ivory; Buganda traded extensively with East African coastal cities; and Kongo on the Atlantic coast was one of the first African states to be visited by Europeans.

- Enslavement of many peoples was widespread when western Europeans began to obtain African slaves.

LO² **What were the consequences of African–European encounters in this era, especially the trans-Atlantic slave trade?**

- Early Portuguese relations with Africa included cooperation with the Kongo kingdom, conflict with the Khoikhoi, and failed attempts to trade with East African coastal city-states.

- Under Christian King Alfonso I, Kongo attempted to emulate Portugal, but relations soured as the Portuguese began to enslave large numbers of Kongolese to work on sugar plantations in Africa and Brazil, and eventually the Portuguese conquered both Angola and Kongo, which then became the major source of slaves for the trans-Atlantic slave trade.

- In their ultimately unsuccessful attempt to dominate Indian Ocean trade, the Portuguese established control over the East African coast, but they failed to dominate Africa's gold trade and eventually lost influence.

- Dutch settlers in southern Africa, later called Boers, imposed white supremacy over the lands they seized but lived in close contact with their imported African and Asian slaves.

- Millions of West African slaves were shipped to North America on the horrific journey known as the Middle Passage, because they were the cheapest form of labor available to work the farms and mines. Many slaves died, committed suicide, or mutinied en route.

- The slave trade led to racist views, as many Europeans justified the practice by claiming that Africans were inherently inferior.

- The slave trade destabilized and harmed many African societies, but some prospered by selling neighboring peoples into slavery.

- As a result of the slave trade, European nations established imperial and colonial control over much of Africa, and their impression of Africa shifted from respect to condescension.

LO³ What factors made the Ottoman Empire such a powerful force in the region?

- Under Suleiman the Magnificent, the Ottoman Empire stretched across vast areas of the Middle East, North Africa, and southeastern Europe, and it controlled the overland trade routes between Europe and the Indian Ocean.

- Leaders of the Ottoman Empire were chosen on the basis of merit, not birth, and even Christians served as administrators and soldiers.

- The Ottoman Empire was culturally and religiously diverse and attracted a range of artists and thinkers from across Eurasia, though some believe that state influence on Islam caused it to become more close-minded.

- Though the Ottoman Empire remained strong through much of the seventeenth century, its military discipline, weaponry, and political stability soon began a gradual decline, while European power and influence grew.

LO⁴ How did the Persian and Central Asian experience differ from that of the Ottomans?

- Under the leadership of a charismatic boy named Isma'il, the Safavids, originally from Azerbaijan, conquered Persia and made the Persians convert from Sunni to Shi'a Islam.

- Under the Safavids, Persia was a major exporter of silk and remained a major conduit of trade.

- The Safavid Empire patronized art and literature, and Safavid artists became famous for their miniature painting and their carpet weaving.

- Safavid religious leaders, increasingly relying on their own authority rather than that of the Quran, eventually became more influential as the power of Safavid rulers declined and then collapsed.

- Morocco, the far western outpost of Islam, absorbed many fleeing Iberian Muslims and grew into a powerful state that, under the Sa'dians, eventually defeated the Portuguese.

- With the aid of the Cossacks, Russia engaged in a large territorial expansion to create a land-based empire, coming into conflict with Siberian and Islamic Central Asian peoples, including the Uzbeks in Turkestan.

Key Terms

LO² conquistadors
The leaders of Spanish soldiers engaged in armed conquest in the Americas.

LO³ Columbian Exchange
The transportation of diseases, animals, and plants from one hemisphere to another that resulted from European exploration and conquest between 1492 and 1750.

audiencias
Judicial tribunals with administrative functions that served as subdivisions of viceroyalties in Spanish America.

creoles
People of Iberian ancestry who were born in Latin America.

mestizos
Groups in Latin America that blended white and Indian ancestry.

mulattos
Groups in Latin America that blend African ancestry with white and Indian ancestry.

Black Legend
The Spanish reputation for brutality toward Native Americans, including the repression of native religions, execution of rebels, and forced labor.

Metis
People in Canada of mixed French and Indian descent.

LO⁴ haciendas
Vast ranches in Spanish America.

encomienda
("Entrustment") The Crown's grant to a colonial Spaniard in Latin America of a certain number of Indians from whom he extracted tribute.

monoculture
An economy dependent on the production and export of one chief commodity.

development
Growth in a variety of economic areas that benefits the majority of people; the opposite of monoculture.

plantation zone
A group of societies with economies that relied on enslaved African labor; the plantation zone stretched from Virginia and Kentucky southward through the West Indies and the east coast of Central America to central Brazil and the Pacific coast of Colombia.

CHRONOLOGY

1492	First Columbian voyage
1494	Treaty of Tordesillas
1497	Cabot's landing in North America
1500	Portuguese claim of Brazil
1519–1521	Magellan's circumnavigation of the globe
1521	Spanish conquest of Aztecs
1535	Spanish conquest of Incas
1604	French settlement in Canada
1607	English settlement in Virginia
1627	Colony of New France
1759	English defeat of French in Quebec

LO¹ How did encounters between Europe and the Americas increase in the 1500s?

- In 1500, many American peoples lived by hunting, gathering, and fishing, while others lived in the widespread, often repressive empires created by the Incas and the Aztecs.

- From 1000 on, Norse from Greenland intermittently settled in Newfoundland, and other Europeans may have crossed the Atlantic in search of fish.

- Beginning in 1492, Christopher Columbus's travels and his discovery of Atlantic wind patterns opened up exploration of the Americas. Columbus gradually gave up on the idea that he had discovered an Atlantic route to Asia, which was later discovered by Magellan.

- European nations divided up the Western Hemisphere according to the Treaty of Tordesillas, and as Europeans explored the Americas, some seeking riches and others converts, their diseases and weapons decimated native populations.

- Pacific Island societies, which ranged from the highly stratified Hawaiians to subsistence atoll inhabitants, were generally not visited by Europeans in the 1500s.

LO² How did Europeans conquer and begin settling the American societies?

- The Spanish under Cortés were able to conquer the Aztecs because of their superior weaponry, their alliances with other American peoples, and a smallpox epidemic that ravaged the Aztecs.

- From their base in Mexico, the Spanish pushed north and south, proceeding to rule much of South America with great cruelty.

- The Portuguese fended off attempts by the French and the Dutch to colonize Brazil and enslaved many of its Indians.

- The Spanish, Portuguese, Dutch, French, and English all struggled for colonial control of the Americas, with pirates from each country preying on other countries' ships.

- The English established colonies in what is now the eastern United States, while the French did so in eastern Canada, New Orleans, and the Mississippi River Basin.

- Many North American colonies thrived on fish and fur, while others practiced agriculture, and all eventually pushed native peoples off their lands.

LO³ What were the major consequences of European colonization of the Americas?

- As a result of American colonization, people, diseases, commodities, and many animal and plant species were exchanged between Europe and the Americas in what is called the Columbian Exchange.

- The Spanish exploited the resources of their American colonies and ruled them harshly, inspiring several rebellions and earning the label of the "Black Legend," though other countries sometimes used similar methods.

- In the Spanish American colonies, a recognizable culture developed, more rigidly Catholic than in Europe and featuring American-born Spanish (creoles) and mixed-race peoples (mestizos and mulattos).

- In their attempts to convert Native Americans to Catholicism, the Spanish and Portuguese often trampled on Native American customs and crushed resisters harshly. As English and French colonists vied for authority, Indian tribes were often caught between the warring powers.

LO^4 What impact did the trans-Atlantic slave trade and emerging Atlantic system have on European and American societies?

- Using Indian labor, Spanish colonists became wealthy at first through ranching and mining gold and silver, but their economies eventually suffered from a lack of diversification.

- Plantations run with African slave labor and focused on producing a single product—sugar in Latin America and the Caribbean, cotton in southeastern North America—also eventually created impoverished societies. Sugar became a fundamental part of the European diet.

- Areas of the Americas with the greatest natural resources ended up being the poorest, while those with the least natural resources, such as the northern English colonies, were forced to develop more broad-based economies and became wealthy and well developed.

- African slaves in the Americas were treated as commodities, and resistance to slavery was rarely successful. But elements of African religion, music, language, and agriculture all found their way into American cultures.

- The slave trade and plantation economies helped spur European capitalism and were extremely profitable to Europeans and North American colonists.

- Spain and Portugal wasted the wealth they derived from their colonies, but the Dutch and the English invested it wisely and, as a result, gained an advantage over other world powers.

Key Terms

LO¹ Urdu
A language developed in Mughal India that mixed Hindi, Arabic, and Persian and was written in the Persian script.

Sikhs
("Disciples") Members of an Indian religion founded in the Early Modern Era that adopted elements from both Hinduism and Islam, including mysticism.

LO² Hispanization
The process by which, over nearly three centuries of Spanish colonial rule beginning in 1565, the Catholic religion and Spanish culture were imposed on the Philippine people.

Moros
The Spanish term for the Muslim peoples of the southern Philippines.

Indios
The Spanish term for Filipinos, who for the most part held the lowest social status.

LO⁴ ukiyo-e
Colorful Japanese woodblock prints that celebrated the life of the "floating world," the urban entertainment districts of Tokogawa Japan.

bunraku
The puppet theater of Tokugawa Japan.

kabuki
The all-male and racy drama that became the favored entertainment of the urban population in Tokugawa Japan.

haiku
The seventeen-syllable poem that proved an excellent vehicle for discussing the passage of time and the change of seasons in Early Modern Japan.

CHRONOLOGY

1350–1767	Ayuthia
1368–1644	Ming dynasty
1392–1573	Ashikaga Shogunate
1392–1910	Yi dynasty in Korea
1498	Arrival of Vasco da Gama in India
1511	Portuguese conquest of Melaka
1526–1761	Mughal India
1557	Portuguese base at Macao
1556–1605	Reign of Akbar
1565	Spanish conquest of Philippines
1592–1598	Japanese invasions of Korea
1600	Founding of British East India Company
1603	Tokugawa Shogunate founded
1639–1841	Japanese seclusion policy
1640s	Dutch conquests in Ceylon
1644–1912	Qing dynasty
1688	Siamese expulsion of French
1689	Treaty of Nerchinsk

LO¹ **What were the major achievements and failures of the Mughal Empire?**

• The Muslim Mughal Empire attained great riches and, especially under Akbar, maintained an enlightened rule over religiously diverse India, but it began to decline after the fall of Akbar.

• The Indian economy, already strong, expanded greatly as extensive foreign trade brought an influx of silver and enriched entrepreneurs.

• Tensions existed between Indian Muslims and Hindus, though some were able to bridge the gap through mysticism or alternative sects such as the Sikhs.

• The Mughal decline hastened under Aurangzeb, a harsh and corrupt ruler who was particularly resented by non-Muslims. Meanwhile, Portuguese traders gained a significant share of trade with India.

• The Portuguese, Dutch, French, and English all competed for dominance in trade with India, with the English growing increasingly strong by the mid-eighteenth century.

LO² **How did Southeast Asia become more fully integrated into the world economy?**

• Increased trade in Southeast Asia led to greater political centralization and increased the influence of major world religions such as Islam and Buddhism. Europeans were attracted by Southeast Asia's riches and resources.

• Theravada Buddhism thrived in Siam, while Islam flourished on the Malay Peninsula, where an orthodox form took hold, and in the Indonesian archipelago, where it blended with local traditions.

• The Spanish conquered the Philippine Islands and eventually succeeded in converting local people to Christianity, though the Filipinos shaped Christianity to their own ends.

• The militaristic Dutch came to dominate Southeast Asia, particularly Java, which they turned into a highly profitable coffee exporter, but whose culture they did not attempt to transform.

• As a result of European colonization, Southeast Asia entered the world economy, though European speculators often focused on making quick money rather than strengthening the region's economy for the long term.

LO³ What factors enabled China to remain one of the world's strongest societies?

- During the Ming dynasty, China maintained its economic power, but it turned increasingly inward and anti-foreign and was ultimately undermined by plague, famine, and pressures from Japan.

- The Qing dynasty was established by foreign Manchus, who assimilated to many Chinese ways, amassed the greatest Eurasian land empire since the Mongols, and added Taiwan to China's holdings.

- Chinese neo-Confucians incorporated elements of Buddhism and Daoism into their thinking and emphasized reason, but over time neo-Confucianism discouraged the growth of new ideas.

- China's economy remained extremely strong but never developed full-scale capitalism or industrialization, perhaps because it lacked an exploitable overseas empire, and perhaps because the government failed to encourage entrepreneurship.

- China had fitful encounters with Europeans, including Portuguese traders who irked Chinese authorities and established a colony at Macao, and missionaries who had little success and were ultimately banned for undermining Chinese traditions. The Russians also sought influence in the area north of China.

LO⁴ How did Korea and Japan change during this era?

- The Chinese helped Korea to rebuff a 1592 Japanese invasion, but as a result Korean culture began to liberalize and shed some customs borrowed from China.

- Ashikaga Japan saw tremendous economic and population growth, but it was undermined by a lengthy civil war, during which Europeans introduced guns and Christianity, upsetting Japan's social order.

- The Tokugawa Shogunate ended Japan's civil war, restored strict order, and expelled Europeans, with the exception of a small group of Dutch traders who were uninterested in missionary work.

- Despite the Tokugawa leaders' attempt to halt change, the Japanese economy grew rapidly, tensions in Japanese society increased, and Japan's culture flourished.

- Tokugawa Japan was quite stable, but its rigidity hampered its growth and made it vulnerable when Western powers returned in the mid-nineteenth century.

Chapter in Review

Key Terms

LO¹ Age of Revolution
The period from the 1770s through the 1840s when revolutions rocked North America, Europe, the Caribbean, and Latin America.

Jacobins
A radical faction in the French Revolution that believed civil rights had to be set aside in a crisis; the Jacobins executed thousands of French citizens.

LO³ Industrial Revolution
A dramatic transformation in the production and transportation of goods that transformed western Europe from the 1770s to the 1870s.

laissez faire
Restriction of government interference in the marketplace, such as laws regulating business and profits.

Luddites
Anti-industrialization activists in Britain who destroyed machines in a mass protest against the effects of mechanization (see Industrial Revolution).

LO⁴ ideology
A coherent, widely shared system of ideas about the nature of the social, political, and economic realm.

nationalism
A primary loyalty to, and identity with, a nation bound by a common culture, government, and shared territory.

nation-states
Politically centralized countries with defined territorial boundaries.

Zionism
A movement arising in late-nineteenth-century Europe that sought a Jewish homeland.

liberalism
An ideology of the Modern Era, based on Enlightenment ideas, that favored emancipating the individual from all restraints, whether governmental, economic, or religious.

parliamentary democracy
Government by representatives elected by the people.

socialism
An ideology arising in nineteenth-century Europe offering a vision of social equality and the common, or public, ownership of economic institutions such as factories.

proletariat
The industrial working class.

CHRONOLOGY

1770s–1870s	First Industrial Revolution
1775–1783	American Revolution
1776	Adam Smith's *Wealth of Nations*
1776	The American Declaration of Independence
1789–1815	French Revolution
1791–1804	Haitian Revolution
1800	British Act of Union
1804	Crowning of Napoleon as emperor of France
1810–1826	Spanish-American wars of independence
1815	Defeat of Napoleon at Battle of Waterloo; Congress of Vienna
1848	Marx's *The Communist Manifesto*; waves of uprisings across Europe
1859–1870	Unification of Italy
1862–1871	Unification of Germany
1870–1914	Second Industrial Revolution

LO¹ What were the major consequences of the American and French Revolutions?

- Many North American colonists, inspired by Enlightenment thinkers, chafed against British rule and pushed for independence, while other Americans, including many Indians and black slaves, sided with the British.

- After a first failed attempt at confederation, the thirteen American colonies agreed upon a system that balanced federal and state powers, but the American Revolution did little to change the social order and did not extend equal rights to blacks, women, and Indians.

- The French Revolution achieved some of its progressive goals and was an inspiration to some societies, but it led to a period of war and widespread terror.

- In the tumultuous aftermath of the French Revolution, Napoleon Bonaparte seized power, implemented some reforms, and sought to conquer Europe, but his eventual defeat led to the Congress of Vienna, at which many pre-Revolution boundaries were restored. Throughout the first half of the nineteenth century, other revolutions led to gradual progress.

LO² How did the Caribbean and Latin American revolutions compare with those in Europe and North America?

- Spain controlled its American colonies tightly, leaving little room for intellectual freedom or economic mobility, and put down many revolts through the end of the eighteenth century.

- After more than a decade of revolutionary struggle, the Afro-Haitian slaves won their freedom from the French, but they soon fell under the control of an African-born despot.

- Rising dissatisfaction among South Americans, particularly creoles, led to successful independence movements throughout the continent, though the newly free nations had trouble forming democratic governments.

- After Mexico obtained its independence, the coalition that had opposed the Spanish fell apart, while members of the Portuguese royal family who fled to Brazil helped it to obtain its independence peacefully.

LO³ How did industrialization reshape economic and social life?

- The Industrial Revolution began in England and gradually spread throughout western Europe and North America. Industrial capitalism centered on manufacturing, and economic philosophers such as Adam Smith advocated laissez faire, the idea that the market, if left alone, would improve everyone's standard of living and create ever-increasing wealth and progress.

- As technology played an increasingly important role in the economy and in people's lives, with machines constantly evolving and being put to new uses, some people marveled at the technological change while others, such as the Luddites, resisted it.

- The Second Industrial Revolution ushered in an age of specialization and mass production, and it favored monopolistic corporations that could afford enormous investments in new technology.

LO⁴ How did nationalism, liberalism, and socialism differ from each other?

- With the rise of nationalism, the inhabitants of a given country came to identify with each other as distinct from, and often better than, the inhabitants of other countries.

- Greece attained nationhood through revolution, Italy through a unification movement, and Germany through collective war against others, while the Poles, the Irish, and the Jews struggled unsuccessfully to form nations.

- Liberalism, which favored maximizing individual liberty, was particularly influential in Britain and the United States of America.

- Socialism aimed to achieve economic equality through common ownership of industry, and its major proponent, Karl Marx, argued that history is driven by class struggle and that capitalism would inevitably give way to a communist society.

- Social Democrats, who rejected Marx's revolutionary ideas and instead favored working to better the lot of workers within a capitalist democracy, managed to greatly improve working conditions by the early 1900s.

LO⁵ What factors spurred the Western imperialism of the later 1800s?

- The Industrial Revolution led Great Britian, and later other western nations, to seek new territories for resources and markets. The result was a renewed scramble for colonial domination.

- As the world became connected by economic and political networks, many African, Asian, and Pacific peoples struggled for their independence, but the technological advantage of Western nations often proved insurmountable.

- Westerners rationalized imperialism and colonization as good for the colonized, who were offered the fruits of Western culture in exchange for their independence.

Key Terms

LO¹ feminism
A philosophy that became strong in the twentieth century, promoting political, social, and economic equality for women with men.

romanticism
A philosophical, literary, artistic, and musical movement that questioned the Enlightenment's rationalist values and instead glorified emotions, individual imagination, and heroism.

modernism
A cultural trend that openly broke with romanticism and other traditions by embracing progress and welcoming the future.

LO² Manifest Destiny
Americans' conviction that their country's institutions and culture, regarded as unmatched, gave them a God-given right to take over the land.

sphere of interest
An area in which one great power assumes exclusive responsibility for maintaining peace and attempts to monopolize the area's resources.

LO³ caudillos
Latin American military strongmen who acquired and maintained power through force between the early nineteenth and mid-twentieth centuries.

samba
A Brazilian popular music and dance that arose in the early twentieth century.

calypso
A song style in Trinidad that often featured lyrics addressing daily life and topical subjects.

LO⁴ dominion
A country that has autonomy but owes allegiance to the British crown; developed in the early twentieth century.

CHRONOLOGY

1763	British defeat of French forces in North America
1770s	Cook expeditions to Polynesia, Australia, and New Zealand
1788	First British penal colony in Australia
1803	Louisiana Purchase
1812–1814	U.S.-British War of 1812
1823	Monroe Doctrine
1823–1889	Abolition of slavery
1846–1848	U.S.-Mexican War
1840s–1890	Western colonization of Pacific islands
1859	Publication of Charles Darwin's *On the Origin of the Species*
1861–1865	Civil War, abolition of slavery
1862–1867	French occupation of Mexico
1867	Canadian Confederation
1869	Completion of transcontinental railroad
1875–1884	War between Chile and Peru-Bolivia
1885–1898	Cuban revolt against Spain
1889	Brazilian republic
1896	Women's suffrage in Finland
1898–1902	Spanish-American War
1898	Annexation of Hawaii
1898–1902	Spanish-American War, colonization of Philippines
1901	Platt Amendment to Cuban constitution
1901	Australian Commonwealth
1905	Publication of Albert Einstein's general theory of relativity
1907	New Zealand self-government
1910–1920	Mexican Revolution
1914	Panama Canal

LO¹ How and why did European social, cultural, and intellectual patterns change during this era?

- In Europe, better crops and health care produced higher populations, which led to increasing urbanization, impoverishment, and emigration.

- As Europe became more industrialized and interconnected, the nuclear family and love marriages became increasingly common, while women, who were initially relegated to the home, began to gain legal rights and economic opportunities.

- While some Protestants attempted to stamp out behavior they considered sinful, Europeans as a whole became more secular, and the Catholic Church's influence declined.

- Cultural trends such as romanticism, realism, and modernism emerged, while advances in science and technology led to improved medical care, the theory of evolution, greater understanding of the physical world, and new sources of energy.

LO² How did westward expansion, industrialization, and immigration transform American society?

- Politically, the United States balanced individual liberty with systems designed to check disorder; economically, it balanced protectionist and free-market interests.

- A distinctive American culture developed that celebrated democracy and practicality but also was influenced by the persistence of African slavery.

- Americans gradually expanded west, taking advantage of abundant natural resources, going to war with Mexico, inflicting great suffering on Native Americans, and exerting its influence in Latin America.

- The Civil War killed hundreds of thousands, did tremendous damage to the South's economy, and freed the slaves, though discrimination and segregation continued for at least another century.
- American industry advanced rapidly, producing immense wealth for a small number of tycoons, helping others to prosper, and creating difficult, hazardous work for many.
- Millions of immigrants poured into the United States, seeking opportunity and often finding discrimination, while social movements sought better treatment for workers and greater rights for women.
- In the interests of promoting and protecting American business interests, the U.S. military intervened in the affairs of many foreign countries and territories, most notably in the Spanish-American War, which brought the United States its first formal colonies.

LO³ What political, economic, and social patterns shaped Latin America after independence?

- After gaining independence from Spain, Latin American nations were plagued by instability, undemocratic governments, and socioeconomic inequality along racial lines.
- After a disastrous period as a republic, a brief occupation by the French, and a pro-business dictatorship, a long, violent revolution finally led to political stability in Mexico.
- Latin American economies tended to focus on the export of one or two natural resources, which created instability and made them susceptible to foreign domination.
- The abolition of slavery and the arrival millions of immigrants from Europe, India, Japan, and elsewhere transformed Latin American societies, and new cultural forms emerged from its diverse peoples.
- The United States repeatedly intervened in Latin American affairs, most directly in Cuba, whose diplomatic affairs it dominated for three decades, and Panama, through which it built the Panama Canal.

LO⁴ Why did the foundations for nationhood differ in Canada and Oceania?

- Over time, Canada became increasingly independent of Britain and overcame the challenges of its French and English speakers and threats from the neighboring United States.
- Western nations, starting with Britain and France but later including Russia, the United States, and Germany, colonized the Pacific islands and exploited their natural resources.
- Starting as penal colonies, British settlers in Australia and New Zealand clashed with indigenous peoples but eventually prevailed, establishing the two countries as dominions of the British Empire.

21 Chapter in Review

Key Terms

LO³ direct rule
A method of ruling colonies whereby a largely European colonial administration supervised all activity, even down to the local level, and native chiefs or kings were reduced to symbolic roles.

indirect rule
A method of ruling colonies whereby districts were administered by traditional (native) leaders, who had considerable local power but were subject to European officials.

LO⁴ Young Turks
A modernizing group in Ottoman Turkey that promoted a national identity and that gained power in the early twentieth century.

Bahai
An offshoot of Persian Shi'ism that was founded in 1867; Bahai preached universal peace, the unity of all religions, and service to others.

LO⁵ Islamic revivalism
Arab movements beginning in the eighteenth century that sought to purify Islamic practices by reviving what their supporters considered to be a purer vision of Islamic society.

Wahhabism
A militant Islamic revivalist movement founded in Arabia in the eighteenth century.

kibbutz
A Jewish collective farm in twentieth-century Palestine that stressed the sharing of wealth.

CHRONOLOGY

1794–1925	Qajar dynasty in Persia
1805–1848	Rule of Muhammad Ali in Egypt
1806	British seizure of South Africa from Dutch
1840	French colonization of Algeria
1842	Ending of trans-Atlantic slave trade by most European nations
1859–1869	Building of Suez Canal
1874–1901	British-Ashante wars
1878	Belgian colonization of the Congo
1882	British colonization of Egypt
1884–1885	Berlin Conference on colonialism
1897	First Zionist Conference
1899–1902	Boer War
1908	Discovery of oil in Persia
1911–1912	Colonization of Libya and Morocco

LO¹ How did Western nations obtain colonies in sub-Saharan Africa?

- Opposed by many Europeans on humanitarian and religious grounds and losing its economic usefulness, African slavery was phased out by the end of the nineteenth century.

- With the end of the slave trade, Europeans began to explore Africa's interior and to take advantage of its vast store of natural resources.

- At the same time, tensions increased between purist and moderate West African Muslims, and Uthman dan Fodio, who led the Fulani jihads, established the Sokoto Caliphate, which became a strong presence in the Sudan.

- European nations rapidly colonized Africa by engaging in deceptive negotiations, by threatening and often carrying out acts of violence, and by exploiting existing rivalries among groups of Africans.

- By 1914, all but a small portion of Africa had been divided up among the European powers, which squabbled over control of various territories and sometimes met fierce resistance from Africans, such as the Ashante.

LO² How did white supremacy shape South Africa?

- Dutch settlers of South Africa, called Boers, pursued a policy of white supremacy despite more liberal British policies. South Africa was also shaped by the conquests of Shaka, a Zulu leader.

- The Boers fled inland to escape British control, but when diamonds and gold were discovered in the Boer republics, the British instigated and won the South African War, after which they agreed to enforce white supremacist policies in order to gain Boer cooperation.

- Blacks suffered greatly in white-dominated South Africa, but many resisted through poetry, music, dance, and political organizations such as the African National Congress. Indians and other Asians came to form the middle class in many African societies.

LO³ What were some of the major consequences of colonialism in Africa?

- African colonial governments served the interests of the colonizers, though the colonizers' involvement in local affairs varied between forms of direct and indirect rule.

- Colonizers divided Africa into countries with artificial boundaries, disrupting cultures and exacerbating hostilities among peoples. And while Christian missionary schools provided a small minority of Africans with skills they could use in the white world, they largely ignored and often damaged the native African culture.

- As African economies came to depend on a single commodity desired by Europeans, colonized Africans lost their subsistence skills, were sometimes forced into near slavery, and were often forced to work far from home.

- While some Africans resisted European rule, colonization transformed the continent, did little to materially improve African lives, and prevented Africans from building diversified and strong economies.

LO⁴ What political and economic impact did Europe have on the Middle East?

- After 1750, the Ottoman Empire's power began to wane under pressure from Russia and western Europe and also from the Armenians, who exerted pressure from within the empire for greater autonomy.
- The Ottomans modernized their army, adopted French-style laws, and became increasingly secular, but their decline continued until the empire was broken apart in World War I.
- After Napoleon left Egypt, an Ottoman-appointed governor, Muhammad Ali, attempted an ambitious and somewhat successful program of modernization; ultimately, however, Britain gained control of the Suez Canal and made Egypt a colony.
- Persia, fragmented under the rule of the Qajars, came to be dominated economically by Britain, and interference by both Britain and Russia helped to end a brief period of progressive rule.
- Westerners became increasingly influential in Syria, Lebanon, and Iraq, and successfully colonized Northwest Africa: first Algeria, where settlers established a racist society; then Morocco, which was shared by France and Spain; and finally Tunisia and Libya.

LO⁵ How did Middle Eastern thought and culture respond to the Western challenge?

- One response to European pressure was Islamic revivalism, which was most influential in Arabia, where militant followers of al-Wahhab and Ibn Saud favored theocracy and eventually formed Saudi Arabia.
- Some intellectuals tried to modernize their religion, but modern European ideas such as equality continued to clash with Islamic practices such as slavery and the subjugation of women, and Western nationalism was at odds with the idea of a universal brotherhood under God.
- Some tried to inspire pan-Arab nationalism, but religious divisions and rivalries made this a difficult task.
- Muslims were also challenged by European Zionists, who moved to Palestine despite Ottoman objections, and Palestinian Arabs, setting the stage for future conflict.

Chapter in Review

Key Terms

LO¹ Marathas
A loosely knit confederacy led by Hindu warriors from west-central India; one of several groups that challenged British domination after the decline of the Mughals.

Black Hole of Calcutta
A crowded jail in India where more than one hundred British prisoners of a hostile Bengali ruler died from suffocation and dehydration in 1757. This event precipitated the beginning of British use of force in India.

sepoys
Mercenary soldiers recruited among the warrior and peasant castes by the British in India.

Westernization
A deliberate attempt to spread Western culture and ideas.

Orientalism
An eighteenth- and nineteenth-century scholarly interest among British officials in India and its history that prompted some to rediscover the Hindu classical age.

LO³ cultivation system
An agricultural policy imposed by the Dutch in Java that forced Javanese farmers to grow sugar on rice land.

plural society
A medley of peoples who mix but do not blend, instead maintaining their own cultures, religions, languages, and customs.

can vuong
("Aid-the-king") Rebel groups who waged guerrilla warfare for fifteen years against the French occupation of Vietnam.

CHRONOLOGY

1757	Battle of Plassey
1788–1802	Tayson rule in Vietnam
1802	British colonization of Sri Lanka
1819	British colony in Singapore
1824–1886	Anglo-Burman Wars
1839–1842	First Anglo-Afghan War
1850	Completion of British India
1857–1858	Indian Rebellion
1858	Introduction of colonial system in India
1858–1884	French conquest of Vietnam
1869	Opening of Suez Canal
1878–1880	Second Anglo-Afghan War
1885	Indian National Congress
1885–1886	Completion of British conquest of Burma
1898–1902	United States conquest of Philippines
1903	British invasion of Tibet
1906	Formation of Indian Muslim League
1908	Dutch defeat of last Balinese kingdom

LO¹ How and why did Britain extend its control throughout India?

- Fragmented after the decline of the Mughals, India was unable to resist encroachment by the Portuguese, Dutch, British, and French.

- In reaction to the Black Hole of Calcutta, the British under Robert Clive took over Bengal and proceeded to plunder its riches; although his successor, Warren Hastings, was more respectful, many governor-generals disregarded Indians' rights.

- Though initially opposed by the French, the British East India Company gradually expanded its control over India by employing local collaborators and playing groups off against each other, and by 1850, Britain controlled all of India.

- The British expanded into Sri Lanka, Nepal, and Afghanistan with varying success, and tried to make Indians more Western by abolishing customs they considered backward.

- By having peasants pay their taxes in cash rather than in crops, the British began to shift India from a barter economy to a money economy, a change that undermined centuries of rural stability.

- Though some Indians supported Westernization, periodic revolts occurred, and in 1857, the sepoys began a large rebellion that led to much bloodshed and eventually Indian defeat.

LO² How did colonialism transform the Indian economy and foster new ideas in India?

- After 1857, the British monarchy ruled India through the British *Raj,* which built palatial buildings, a large railroad system, and an expanded English-language school system, spreading western ideals such as nationalism and sowing the seeds for an Indian revolution against Britain.

- Britain stifled Indian industry by using India as a market for British industrial products, and it turned Indian peasants into tenants who had to grow cash crops for Britain rather than their own food, thus destroying the centuries-old village economy and exacerbating famine and poverty.

- As the Indian population increased, many poor Indians were driven to work all over the world in indentured servitude, while other Indians emigrated to work as laborers, merchants, and moneylenders.

- While some Hindus and Muslims wanted to combine the best in British and Indian culture, others sought to revive more traditional practices. The caste system became more rigid under British rule, and women facing greater restrictions in some cases and expanded opportunity in others.
- As Indian nationalists began to unite in their opposition to the British, the Hindu majority formed the Indian National Congress in 1885, but it was opposed by some aristocrats, who feared losing their privileges, and by Muslims, who formed the All-India Muslim League in 1906.

LO³ How did the Western nations expand their control of Southeast Asia?

- As the Dutch expanded their control over the Indonesian archipelago, they joined together vastly disparate cultures and disrupted the traditional economy, such as by forcing Javanese farmers to grow sugar on rice land and to sell it at unfairly low prices.
- The British expanded control over the Malay Peninsula and Burma, gaining key strategic trading centers while suppressing dissent and local traditions.
- After conquering Vietnam, the French faced fierce resistance from can vuong rebels, but they ultimately conquered the rebels and opened the country to exploitation by French commercial interests.
- Unlike the rest of Southeast Asia, Siam (now Thailand) avoided colonization because of its fortunate geographic location and its far-seeing leaders, who gave in to some Western demands and consolidated popular support.
- After defeating the Spanish in the Philippines and supporting local rebels, the U.S. government turned against the Filipinos and, after a bloody struggle, established a colony geared toward American economic needs.

LO⁴ What were the major political, economic, and social consequences of colonialism in Southeast Asia?

- Colonized Southeast Asian peoples were allowed varying degrees of autonomy, though in general they had very little and were frequently joined into countries with little ethnic or cultural unity.
- Economic life in colonies was reshaped to serve Western nations' needs for raw materials, especially rubber, and for markets for their goods, and in many cases it led to destruction of the natural environment and the impoverishment of native Indonesians.
- Millions of Chinese immigrated to Southeast Asia, where many prospered as merchants and retailers, while a smaller number of Indians came to work in Malayan rubber plantations.
- Economic changes caused by colonization especially affected women's lives, while education and cultural interchange between Westerners and colonized peoples produced new cultural forms, such as kronchong music.

Chapter in Review

Key Terms

LO¹ extraterritoriality
Freedom from local laws for foreign subjects.

international settlements
Special zones in major Chinese cities set aside for foreigners in the later nineteenth century where no Chinese were allowed; arose as a result of China's defeat in the Opium and Arrow Wars.

LO² gunboat diplomacy
The Western countries' use of superior firepower to impose their will on local populations and governments in the nineteenth century.

LO⁴ Meiji Restoration
A revolution against the Tokugawa shogunate in Japan in 1867–1868, carried out in the name of the Meiji emperor; led to the successful modernization of Japan.

state capitalism
An economic system in which the state takes a leading role in supporting business and industrial enterprises; introduced by the Meiji government in Japan.

zaibatsu
The most powerful Japanese corporations that dominated the national economy beginning during the Meiji regime and maintained an especially close relationship to the government.

LO⁵ Russification
A czarist policy in the nineteenth century that promoted Russian language and culture for non-Russian peoples; created resentment among many Muslims in Central Asia and the Caucasus.

Slavophiles
Nineteenth-century Russians who emphasized Russia's unique culture and rejected Western models.

CHRONOLOGY

1392–1910	Yi Dynasty in Korea
1600–1867	Tokugawa Shogunate in Japan
1762–1796	Reign of Catherine the Great
1800–1870s	Russian conquest of Turkestan and Caucasus
1839–1842	Opium War
1850–1864	Taiping Rebellion
1853	Opening of Japan by Perry
1861	Emancipation of Russian serfs
1867–1868	Meiji Restoration
1894–1895	Sino-Japanese War
1900	Boxer Rebellion
1904–1905	Russo-Japanese War
1905	First Russian Revolution
1910	Japanese colonization of Korea and Taiwan
1911	Chinese Revolution

LO¹ What were the causes and consequences of the Opium War?

- By the nineteenth century, China faced increasing problems as well as pressure from Westerners for greater trade opportunities, but the Qing refused to allow an open trading system, thus creating a severe trade imbalance between the West and the East.

- To solve this imbalance, the British began smuggling opium into China, and when China protested, the British defeated China in the Opium War and forced the Chinese to agree to highly unfavorable terms that allowed the British to trade in China.

- After another war, China was forced to set aside special areas exclusively for Westerners, called international settlements, and to also allow Christian missionaries into the country.

- Economic insecurity, famine, and Western interference eventually led to the Taiping Rebellion, a widespread and devastating revolt that was ultimately put down by the Qing with help from Western powers.

- China's economy was increasingly penetrated and transformed by Western powers, and millions of Chinese emigrated throughout the world, some to be indentured workers and others to go into business.

LO² Why did Chinese efforts at modernization fail?

- By the late 1800s, China's autonomy had been all but eliminated by gunboat diplomacy, under which Western powers ensured the safety of Westerners in China through the use of force. Conservatives and liberals, meanwhile, argued over the degree to which China should reform in the face of the Western challenge.

- After China lost its influence over Korea in the Sino-Japanese War and the Boxer Rebellion failed to rid China of foreigners, liberals moved to modernize and Westernize Chinese education and culture.

- Sun Yat-Sen, born to Chinese peasants but educated in Western schools, formed a secret society devoted to replacing imperial rule with a Western-style republic and set out three principles: nationalism, republicanism, and economic equality.

- A revolution inspired by Sun Yat-Sen succeeded in toppling the Qing dynasty with the assistance of General Yuan Shikai, but Sun's republic was short-lived, as Yuan seized power. Yuan's reign was weakened by Japanese encroachment and the loss of influence over areas such as Mongolia and Tibet, and after his death China entered a period of civil war.

LO³ What factors aided Japan in the quest for modernization?

- Japan was better able than China to deal with foreign pressures because of its compactness and homogeneity, its openness to outside ideas, its balance of power between groups of elites, its strong merchant class, and its sensitivity to foreign threats.

- Late Tokugawa Japanese culture was vigorous and open to Western learning, but internal decay in Japan led to riots, revolts, and subsequent reforms. However, when faced with a choice between war and opening Japan to American trade, the Japanese shogun chose trade, which led to the opening of Japan to the West.

LO⁴ How did the Meiji government transform Japan and Korea?

- After the Meiji Restoration, which overthrew the Tokugawa shogunate, Japanese samurai and other reformers established a regime that was dedicated to making Japan open to and competitive with the rest of the world.

- The Meiji regime modernized Japan by breaking down social distinctions, pursuing industrial and military strength, and establishing a constitutional monarchy.

- In the late 1800s, Meiji leaders worked to balance traditional practices with newly adopted Western ones, and Japan fought successful wars against both China and Russia. Japanese were torn between pride in Meiji successes and regret over traditions they had abandoned.

- Meiji Japan forced Korea to accept unequal trade agreements and, after defeating China in the Sino-Japanese War, turned Korea into a colony and ruled it harshly, brutally suppressing dissent and exploiting its men and women during World War II.

LO⁵ What factors explain the expansion of the Russian Empire?

- The Russian leader Catherine the Great paid lip service to Enlightenment values, but she presided over an era of royal opulence, territorial expansion, and expanded serfdom, and she was followed by the despotic Nicholas I, who led the nation to defeat in the Crimean War.

- Russian expansion brought it control of eastern Siberia, Muslim Central Asia, and the Caucasus states, although some peoples, such as the Chechens, fiercely resisted.

- Russia's economy expanded along with its territory, creating a discontented proletariat, and while many Russian thinkers embraced Western ideals, the Slavophiles argued for the superiority of traditional Russian culture. Some members of the proletariat joined terrorist groups and supported a revolution in 1905, which, while suppressed, led to reforms.

Key Terms

LO² **Bolsheviks**
The most radical of Russia's antigovernment groups in the early twentieth century, who embraced a dogmatic form of Marxism.

soviets
Local action councils formed by Russian radicals before the 1917 Russian Revolution that enlisted workers and soldiers to fight the factory owners and military officers.

Marxism-Leninism
The basis for Soviet communism, a mix of socialism (collective ownership of the economy) and Leninism.

New Economic Policy (NEP)
Lenin's pragmatic approach to economic development, which mixed capitalism and socialism.

Stalinism
Joseph Stalin's system of government, which included state ownership of all property, such as lands and businesses, a planned economy, and one-man rule.

gulags
Russian shorthand for harsh forced-labor camps in Siberia.

socialist realism
Literary and artistic works that depicted life from a revolutionary perspective, a style first introduced in Stalin's Russia.

LO³ **Great Depression**
A collapse of the world economy that lasted in varying degrees of severity through the 1930s.

Dust Bowl
Parts of the U.S. Midwest and Southwest during the 1930s where disappearing topsoil and severe drought threw agriculture badly out of balance.

New Deal
A new U.S. government program of liberal reform within a democratic framework introduced by President Franklin Roosevelt to alleviate suffering caused by the Great Depression.

cubism
An early-twentieth-century form of painting that rejected visual reality and emphasized instead geometric shapes and forms that often suggested movement.

LO⁴ **fascism**
A twentieth-century ideology that typically involved extreme nationalism, hatred of ethnic minorities, ruthless repression of opposition groups, violent anticommunism, and authoritarian government.

CHRONOLOGY

1914	Outbreak of conflict
1917	U.S. intervention; Russian Revolution
1918	End of conflict
1919	Versailles Treaty
1921	Irish Free State
1926	Fascist state in Italy
1929–1941	Great Depression
1933	Nazi triumph in Germany
1933–1945	Presidency of Franklin D. Roosevelt
1936–1939	Spanish Civil War
1937	Japanese invasion of China
1938	German takeover of Austria and Czechoslovakia
1939	German invasion of Poland; World War II begins
1940	Tripartite Pact Between Germany, Italy, and Japan
1941	Japanese attack on Pearl Harbor
1944	Bretton Woods Conference
1945	Allied invasion of Germany; atomic bombs dropped on Japan; war's end

LO¹ What was the impact of World War I on the Western world?

• The early 1900s in Europe were marked by great affluence and stability, expanding markets, and shared notions of culture, justice, and human rights, but imperial tensions and secret alliances sowed the seeds of conflict.

• Sparked by the assassination of Austrian archduke Franz Ferdinand in Sarajevo, the war soon involved Austro-Hungary, Germany, Britain, France, and the Ottoman Empire, all of which employed unprecedented military technology that caused millions of deaths.

• In 1917, Russia left the war and Germany seemed on the verge of victory when the United States entered the fighting, in part because of economic ties with France and Britain and in part because of outrage over German submarine attacks on U.S. ships.

• The United States helped the French and British win the war, but U.S. president Woodrow Wilson could not prevent the French from dictating punishing settlement terms for Germany.

• The horrors of World War I led to the radicalization of many Europeans; a growth of antiwar sentiment; the breakup of the Ottoman Empire and Germany; the breakup of much of the Russian and Austro-Hungarian Empires, which were carved into new countries; and the world dominance of the United States.

LO² How did communism prevail in Russia and transform that country?

• In March 1917, a spontaneous revolution overthrew the czar, but its urban liberal leaders could not satisfy the people's demand for reform and an end to the war, so radical soviets, including the Bolsheviks—a group of Marxist revolutionaries led by Vladimir Lenin—seized power, after which they removed Russia from the war.

• Lenin and the Bolsheviks soon faced the Russian Civil War, launched by the White Russians, who included defenders of the aristocracy and were funded and armed by Western nations that were disturbed by the Bolshevik revolution. The Bolsheviks prevailed, establishing Marxism-Leninism in the USSR, a brand of socialism achieved through ruthless one-party rule that failed to achieve a true connection between the masses and the government.

• Lenin's successor, Joseph Stalin, sent millions to forced-labor camps called gulags and imposed state ownership of all property and a planned economy, which led to decreased harvests and widespread misery. Rapid industrialization made the USSR the second largest world economy by 1932, but at the cost of many lives and limitations of human rights.

LO³ How did the Great Depression reshape world politics and economies?

- After the war, Germany experienced rapid inflation because of its postwar debt, Europe lost economic ground to the United States and Japan, and women entered the workforce and the political sphere.

- Many Japanese benefited from postwar economic growth, while Japan played a larger role in world affairs and clashed with the United States over its treatment of Japanese immigrants and Japanese ambitions in Asia.

- American fear of communism led to the "Red Scare" and a more conservative, isolationist phase in American politics, while the split widened between the poor, who suffered under government policies, and the affluent, who enjoyed the "Roaring 20s."

- Among the factors contributing to the Great Depression were trade protectionism, risky investment practices, and the uneven distribution of income. With millions of Americans jobless, homeless, and hungry, President Franklin Delano Roosevelt instituted the New Deal, greatly expanding the federal government's role.

- The Great Depression hit Europe and Japan even harder than the United States, rendering Germany unable to pay its heavy debts and causing Japan to become more authoritarian and expansionist, while Scandinavian nations emerged in better condition by combining socialism and democracy. Western artists, writers, and intellectuals responded to the challenges of modernity in new and innovative ways.

LO⁴ What were the main ideas and impacts of fascism?

- A new ideology, fascism, that developed in Italy and Germany out of economic collapse, stressed extreme nationalism, an authoritarian state, and hatred of minorities and leftists.

- Suffering from the Depression, resentful of post–World War I reparations, and fearful of socialism, many Germans supported Adolph Hitler's Nazi Party, which blamed problems on minorities such as the Jews and revived the economy through a military buildup.

- Japan became increasingly nationalistic and imperialistic, blamed its problems on foreigners, took over most of eastern China, and signed a pact with Germany and Italy.

- Tensions rose as Italy invaded Ethiopia, fascists took over Spain, and Germany took over Austria and Czechoslovakia; France and Britain declared war after Germany signed a nonaggression pact with the Soviet Union and invaded Poland.

LO⁵ What were the costs and consequences of World War II?

- Germany rapidly took over most of Europe and used it as a source of raw materials, but the British withstood extended bombing, and Germany wasted valuable resources on an ultimately unsuccessful invasion of the Soviet Union.

- Nazi Germany deliberately killed 6 million Jews and a half million Gypsies in death camps, along with millions of others; historians are divided on how much the German people knew about the death camps and how responsible they were for them.

- After Japan attacked Pearl Harbor, the United States entered the war in both Asia and Europe, and many women and blacks found work in professions that had until then been closed to them, while Japanese Americans were put in internment camps.

- After the United States entered the war, the Allies slowly began to win the war in Europe, and in the spring of 1945, with U.S. forces advancing from the west and the Soviets from the east, Hitler committed suicide and Germany surrendered. After Japan refused to agree to a total surrender despite serious setbacks, the United States dropped atomic bombs on Hiroshima and Nagasaki, killing, injuring, and sickening scores of thousands.

- More than 50 million military personnel and civilians were killed in World War II, but in its aftermath, Germany, Italy, and Japan were aided rather than punished, and the United States and Soviet Union emerged as the world's dominant powers.

Chapter in Review

Key Terms

LO² warlords
Local political leaders with their own armies.

New Culture Movement
A movement of Chinese intellectuals started in 1915 that sought to wash away the discredited past and sprout a literary revival.

May Fourth Movement
A radical nationalist resurgence in China in 1919 that opposed imperialism and the ineffective, warlord-controlled Chinese government.

Jiangxi Soviet
A revolutionary base, established in 1927 in south-central China, where Mao Zedong organized a guerrilla force to fight the Guomindang.

Long March
An epic journey, full of hardship, in which Mao Zedong's Red Army fought their way 6,000 miles on foot and horseback through eleven Chinese provinces in the mid-1930s to establish a safe base of operation.

people's war
An unconventional struggle that combined military action and political recruitment, formulated by Mao Zedong in China.

Maoism
An ideology promoted by Mao Zedong that mixed ideas from Chinese tradition with Marxist-Leninist ideas from the Soviet Union.

LO³ nonviolent resistance
Noncooperation with unjust laws and peaceful confrontation with illegitimate authority, pursued by Mohandas Gandhi in India.

LO⁴ Viet Minh
The Vietnamese Independence League, a coalition of anti-French groups established by Ho Chi Minh in 1941 that waged war against both the French and the Japanese.

lingua franca
A language widely used as a common tongue among diverse groups with different languages.

highlife
An urban-based West African musical style mixing Christian hymns, West Indian calypso, and African dance rhythms.

pidgin English
The form of broken English that developed in Africa during the colonial era.

CHRONOLOGY

1909–1933	U.S. military force in Nicaragua
1912	Formation of ANC in South Africa
1916	Arab revolt against the Turks
1916–1927	Warlord Era in China
1917	Balfour Declaration
1919	Amritsar massacre
1920–1922	Nationalist unrest in Kenya
1921–1979	Pahlavi dynasty in Iran
1922	Formation of Turkish republic by Ataturk
1926–1927	Communist uprising in Indonesia
1928–1937	Republic of China
1930	Indochinese Communist Party; Ghandi's Great Salt March; Independence for Iraq
1930–1931	Military governments throughout Latin America
1930–1945	Estado Novo in Brazil
1934	Fulgencio Batista Cuban dictator
1934–1940	Cardenas presidency in Mexico
1935	Government of India Act; Discovery of oil in Saudi Arabia
1935–1936	Conquest of Ethiopia by Italy; Chinese Communist Long March
1936	British–Egypt alliance
1936–1939	Civil war in Palestine
1941–1945	Japanese occupation of Southeast Asia
1942	Gandhi's Quit India campaign

LO¹ What circumstances fostered nationalism in Asia, Africa, and Latin America?

• World War I affected colonies in Asia, Africa, and the Caribbean as thousands of colonial subjects were forced to fight and die for France, Germany, and Britain, and promises of democratic reforms and veterans' benefits were not carried out.

• Colonial governments imposed heavy taxes and hard labor on the colonial peoples, a state of affairs that was defended by the Western idea that the colonial peoples could not yet govern themselves.

• When western capitalism disrupted traditional rural life in many colonies and caused further anguish during the Great Depression, many frustrated colonial subjects turned to nationalism and Marxism as alternatives.

• Despite local opposition, Western nations expanded their colonial reach between 1900 and 1945: Italy brutally conquered Ethiopia; France and Britain took over former Ottoman colonies; and the United States continued to meddle in Central America.

LO² How and why did the Communist movement grow in China?

• After the end of the imperial system, rival warlords controlled China during a period of civil war, and intellectuals formed the New Culture Movement, which called for a modernized China that fostered individualism and equality.

• Japan's aggressive demands after World War I enraged the Chinese, and some were attracted to communism, but Sun Yat-sen's successor, the pro-business Chiang Kai-shek, allied the nationalist movement with the United States.

• Chiang Kai-shek's Republic of China launched a modernization program, but it was hampered by a split with the communists, persistent rural poverty, and the Japanese seizure of Manchuria.

• Mao Zedong organized peasants into a communist revolutionary army and then led them on the punishing Long March in search of safety from Chiang Kai-shek's far stronger army, which might have triumphed had it not been diverted by a 1937 Japanese invasion.

- The Chinese people lost faith in Chiang's government as it squeezed them for taxes to support a failing war against Japan, while Mao's communists instilled hope through guerrilla warfare and a promise of equality and progress through shared sacrifice.

LO³ What were the main contributions of Mohandas Gandhi to the Indian struggle?

- In the aftermath of World War I, in which tens of thousands of their people died, Indians were angry that Britain denied them greater autonomy and imposed higher taxes to pay for the war, and resentment peaked with the massacre of hundreds of peaceful protesters at Amritsar.

- Mohandas Gandhi, the foremost Indian nationalist leader, promoted nonviolent resistance to British rule, including strikes, boycotts, and refusal to pay taxes, and won a massive popular following for the Indian National Congress.

- Although even his Indian supporters considered some of Gandhi's ideas naive and utopian, campaigns such as the Great Salt March were highly effective in winning concessions from the British.

- Feeling threatened by the predominantly Hindu National Congress, the Muslim League, led by Jinnah, argued that Indian Muslims should have a country of their own, which they called Pakistan. The Muslim League grew increasingly powerful, and eventually, after World War II, both Pakistan and India gained independence from Britain.

- Leaders of the untouchables, the lowest Hindu caste, pushed for and obtained greater opportunities, and women were given the right to vote and allowed somewhat more freedom.

LO⁴ How did nationalism differ in Southeast Asia and sub-Saharan Africa?

- Southeast Asian nationalism was strong in places such as Burma, which experienced harsh colonial rule, and even emerged as a rallying cry in Siam (Thailand), which was never colonized but where a military coup of middle-class background overthrew the royal government.

- Vietnamese resistance to French rule became more radical under the terrorist Vietnamese Nationalist Party, which the French harshly repressed, and the Viet Minh, a coalition led by the communist Ho Chi Minh. In the Dutch East Indies, a variety of groups representing Muslims, women, and communists worked toward independence, and of these the Indonesian Nationalist Party, which incorporated both Islam and Marxism, was most influential.

- Southeast Asians suffered greatly under Japanese occupation, but Japanese control of Southeast Asia during World War II also showed that Westerners could be defeated and primed the colonized peoples to resist recolonization by Westerners after the war was over.

- Although African nationalist movements were hampered by the existence of rival ethnic groups within artificial colonies, anger over the poor treatment of Africans who had fought in World War I inspired many, especially in cities, to work for independence.

LO⁵ What factors promoted change in the Middle East and Latin America?

- In the post–World War I breakup of the Ottoman Empire, Iraq, Syria, and Lebanon sought freedom but were instead colonized by Britain and France. Turkey revived under the leadership of Ataturk, who modernized the country and minimized the role of Islam.

- Reza Khan, the British-supported shah of Persia, attempted to modernize his country as Ataturk had Turkey, though with less success, while Britain, in reaction to violent opposition, granted Egypt and Iraq increasing independence.

- Arab leaders debated how to balance modernization with Islam; the most puritanical form of Islam, Wahhabism, came to dominate Saudi Arabia; and the return of Jews to Palestine caused great tensions with the Arabs who had lived there for centuries.

- Vulnerable Latin American economies were greatly damaged during the Great Depression, which led to instability and the rise of military dictators in many countries.

- Impoverished and frustrated after a long revolution, many Mexicans were pleased by the rule of Lazaro Cardenas, who gave land to agricultural cooperatives, nationalized industries, and supported women's rights, but who was followed by less progressive leaders.

- Latin American and Caribbean artists, musicians, and writers produced art that expressed their unique cultural perspectives.

Key Terms

LO¹ First World
A later-twentieth-century term for the industrialized democracies of western Europe, North America, Australia–New Zealand, and Japan.

Second World
A later-twentieth-century term for the Communist nations, led by the USSR and China.

Third World
A later-twentieth-century term for the societies in Asia, Africa, Latin America, and the Caribbean, which were shaped by mass poverty and a legacy of colonization or neocolonialism.

Fourth World
A later-twentieth-century term for the poorest societies, with very small economies and few exploitable resources.

LO² Cold War
A conflict lasting from 1946 to 1989 in which the United States and the USSR competed for allies and engaged in occasional warfare against their rivals' allies rather than against each other directly.

guerrilla warfare
An unconventional military strategy of avoiding full-scale direct confrontations in favor of small-scale skirmishes.

nuclear weapons
Explosive devices that owe their destructive power to the energy released by either splitting or fusing atoms.

LO³ globalization
A pattern in which economic, political, and cultural processes reach beyond nation-state boundaries.

multinational corporations
Giant business enterprises that operate all over the world; multinationals have gained a leading role in the global marketplace.

Third Industrial Revolution
The creation since 1945 of unprecedented scientific knowledge of new technologies more powerful than any invented before.

Green Revolution
A later-twentieth-century term for increased agricultural output through the use of new high-yield seeds and mechanized farming.

desertification
The transformation of once-productive land into useless desert.

CHRONOLOGY

1945	Formation of the United Nations
1950–1953	Korean War
1946–1975	Decolonization in Asia, Africa, and Caribbean
1959–1975	U.S.–Vietnam War
1946–1989	Cold War
1968	Widespread political protests
1962	Cuban Missile Crisis
1989–1991	Dismantling of Soviet bloc and Soviet Union
2001	Al Qaeda attack on United States

LO¹ How did decolonization change the global system?

• Between 1946 and 1975, most Western colonies achieved independence, though the United States continued to oppose communist anticolonial movements, and the Soviet Union's vast colonial empire endured until 1989.

• Western nations maintained a great deal of influence over many of their former colonies, which led some intellectuals to call for "decolonizing the mind."

• Revolutionary regimes, often inspired by Marxism, came to power in several Asian, African, and Latin American nations, though they met with mixed economic success.

• The division of the world's nations into First, Second, and Third Worlds grew blurry as some Third World nations developed First-World-level economies and the Soviet Union collapsed. Democratic countries tended to be more stable and offer more support to their citizens.

LO² What roles did the Cold War and superpower rivalry play in world politics?

• During the Cold War, the United States and the USSR struggled for world control, with the United States generally favoring democracy and capitalism, and the USSR supporting emerging communist regimes and movements.

• Though the United States and the USSR never fought directly, they were involved in dozens of wars and military interventions in other countries, such as Vietnam and Afghanistan.

• The United States and the USSR participated in a massive arms race, spending trillions of dollars on nuclear weapons, which led to widespread fear of mass destruction.

• The United Nations was formed with the goal of promoting world peace and human rights and to facilitate an international justice system.

• When the Soviet Union collapsed, the United States was the sole superpower, but religious extremism and ethnic and nationalist conflicts have ensured continuing conflict.

LO³ What were some of the main consequences of a globalizing world economy?

• Globalization has boosted world economies and has reaped great rewards for countries such as the United States and China, but it has not always benefited the lives of poor people and has also led to continued foreign domination of some groups and nations by others.

• The World Bank and the International Monetary Fund have lent money to developing nations but sometimes dictate economic policies to borrowers, while multinational corporations have become so large that they exert great influence over governments.

• Industrialization has spread throughout Asia and Latin America; the Third Industrial Revolution has created powerful new technologies; the Green Revolution has allowed for increased agricultural production; and the service and information industries have grown rapidly; but some globalization practices have produced hardships.

LO4 global village
A later-twentieth-century term for an interconnected world community in which all people, regardless of their nationality, share a common fate.

terrorism
Small-scale but violent attacks aimed at undermining a government or demoralizing a population.

- Despite worldwide economic growth, some countries remain underdeveloped and the gap between the wealthy and poor is striking; however, the developing world has made great improvements in infant mortality and adult literacy.

- Women have faced great problems in the modern economy as they have been drastically underpaid for their contributions, but grassroots programs such as the Grameen Bank have offered some increased economic opportunity.

- Over the past fifty years, the world population has exploded in developing countries, while fertility rates have dropped and populations have grown older in Europe, North America, and Japan.

- Industrialization and population growth have led to increased pollution and deforestation, which have led to massive extinction of plant and animal species and global warming.

LO4 How did growing networks linking societies influence social, political, and economic life?

- In the new global village, millions of people have immigrated to foreign countries seeking greater economic opportunity or an escape from insufferable conditions at home.

- Modern medicine has eliminated many diseases, but cholera and malaria are still a serious problem, and AIDS has seriously affected Africa, India, and areas of Southeast Asia.

- Western consumer culture has spread around the world, while musical forms from different cultures have mingled, and performers have expressed political and often controversial views.

- The world's major religious traditions have remained numerically strong, and some have worked to adapt to the modern world; many Muslims and Christians have grown more fundamentalist.

- Worldwide communication was facilitated by technologies such as radio, television, and the Internet, making a vast array of information available, despite efforts by some governments to limit its availability.

- Increased global communication led to political movements that transcended conventional borders, such as Amnesty International, the 1968 youth protests, and the women's movement.

- Terrorism, which had been used throughout the twentieth century by marginalized groups, became more deadly, culminating in the radical Muslim group Al Qaeda's 2001 attack on the United States.

Chapter in Review

Key Terms

LO¹ Pacific Rim
The economically dynamic Asian countries on the western edge of the Pacific Basin: China, Japan, South Korea, Taiwan, and several Southeast Asian nations.

Pacific Century
The possible shift of global economic power from Europe and North America to the Pacific Rim in the twenty-first century.

communes
Large agricultural units introduced by Mao Zedong that combined many families and villages into a common system for pooling resources and labor.

Great Leap Forward
Mao Zedong's ambitious attempt in the later 1950s to industrialize China rapidly and end poverty through collective efforts.

Great Proletarian Cultural Revolution
A radical movement in China between 1966 and 1976 that represented Mao Zedong's attempt to implant his vision, destroy his enemies, crush the stifling bureaucracy, and renew the revolution's vigor.

Red Guards
Young workers and students who were the major supporters of the Great Proletarian Cultural Revolution in Mao's China.

Iron Rice Bowl
A model of social equality in Mao's China in which the people, especially in the villages, shared resources and the peasants enjoyed status and dignity.

LO² market socialism
A Chinese economic program used between 1978 and 1989 that mixed free enterprise, economic liberalization, and state controls and that produced economic dynamism in China.

market Leninism
A policy followed after the Beijing Massacre in 1989, whereby the Chinese Communist state asserted more power over society while also fostering an even stronger market orientation in the economy than had existed under market socialism.

LO³ Japan, Inc.
The cooperative relationship between government and big business that has existed in Japan after 1945.

salaryman
A Japanese urban middle-class male business employee who commits his energies and soul to the company, accepts assignments without complaint, and takes few vacations.

CHRONOLOGY

1945–1949	Chinese civil war
1946–1952	U.S. occupation of Japan
1949	Chinese communist triumph
1950–1953	Korean War
1960	Sino–Soviet split
1960s–1989	Rapid economic growth
1966–1976	Great Proletarian Cultural Revolution
1978	Four modernizations policy
1997	Asian financial collapse

LO¹ How did Maoism transform Chinese society?

- After Japan was defeated in World War II, Chinese communists and nationalists fought a civil war in which Mao Zedong's communists triumphed over Chiang Kaishek's nationalists.

- To develop its economy, China first employed Stalinism, which featured central planning dominated by a bureaucratic elite, and then shifted to Maoism, which emphasized mass mobilization of the people, but under Maoism millions starved to death and many suffered under political repression.

- China reasserted itself as a world power, reclaiming Tibet, becoming involved in the Korean War, ultimately splitting with the USSR, and reestablishing formal relations with the United States in the 1970s.

- Frustrated with China's development, Mao led a decade-long cultural revolution that caused great economic problems and brought misery to many. He also reshaped Chinese society, improving literacy rates and health care, expanding the rights of women, and encouraging the people to produce their own literature and art.

- While Mao restored China as a world power and brought many out of poverty, after his death in 1976 many Chinese wanted to join the modern world and global economy.

LO² What factors explain the dramatic rise of Chinese economic power in the world since 1978?

- Under Deng Xiaoping, China opened up to Western economic ideas and investment, as well as to political, religious, and cultural currents that had been suppressed under Mao.

- Although many supported Deng's reforms, they led to increasing corruption, a growing gap between rich and poor, and, in 1989, a violent suppression of prodemocracy dissidents in the Beijing Massacre.

- Under market Leninism, the Chinese state increased political and social control while privatizing the economy, which grew briskly, though there was stagnation in many rural areas and environmental damage in others.

- The growth of China's economy has improved access to consumer goods and Western culture, but has also led to increased crime and drug use, and an effort to limit population has led to the killing of female babies.

- China has enjoyed a great recovery and return to world prominence in recent decades, though it still has uncertain relations with Taiwan and Japan, and its living standard remains much lower than many other countries.

LO³ How did Japan rise from the ashes of defeat in World War II to become a global economic powerhouse?

- After World War II, a U.S.-led occupation of Japan (SCAP) worked to rebuild Japan's economy while demilitarizing the country and encouraging the return of democracy, much of which was successful.

- The Liberal Democratic Party dominated Japanese politics for decades, and the constitutional statute preventing military development freed up resources to help fuel

LO⁴ Little Dragons
South Korea, Taiwan, Singapore,
and Hong Kong, which were strongly influenced
by Chinese culture and built rapidly growing,
industrializing economies in the twentieth
century.

the economy. The economy has grown at a phenomenal rate, though it has caused environmental problems and great personal sacrifices on the part of workers.

- Japan's cities have become increasingly congested, men are expected to devote all of their energy to work, women struggle for equality, and students face the pressure of an arduous education system.

- Japanese have managed to blend their traditions with modern and foreign influences and have maintained a high degree of social order despite low participation in organized religion.

- In the early 2000s, Japan's economy began to recover from a decade-long downturn, while in world politics, Japan has played an important role, though it has been hesitant to assert its power too forcefully.

LO⁴ What policies led to the rise of the "Little Dragon" nations and their dynamic economies?

- After World War II, communist North Korea, assisted by the USSR and China, fought a war with South Korea, assisted by a U.S.-dominated United Nations force, that caused thousands of deaths and devastation and ended with the same border that existed at the start of the war.

- South Korean governments have grown more tolerant of internal dissent and more open to relations with former enemies, such as communist North Korea and China, though their primary emphasis has been on economic growth.

- After the Korean War, North Korea recovered with support from the USSR and China and was ruled as a repressive communist dictatorship with a centrally planned economy, whose shortcomings led to widespread food shortages in the 1990s.

- With the communists ruling mainland China, nationalists took over Taiwan, which they ruled as a police state and turned into an economic powerhouse, but relations with mainland China have continued to be tense.

- China and the "Little Dragons" (Taiwan, South Korea, Singapore, and Hong Kong) grew rapidly in the late twentieth century, leading to predictions of increased Asian influence in the future.

Key Terms

LO¹ Marshall Plan
A recovery program proposed for western Europe by the United States that aimed to prevent communist expansion and to spread liberal economic principles.

Greens
A twentieth-century political movement in western Europe that rejected militarism and heavy industry and favored environmental protection over economic growth.

British Commonwealth of Nations
A forum, established by Britain in 1931, for discussing issues of mutual interest with its former colonies.

Truman Doctrine
A policy formed in 1947 that asserted that the United States was the leader of the free world and was charged with protecting countries like Greece and Turkey from communism.

NATO
(North Atlantic Treaty Organization) A military alliance, formed in 1949, that linked nine western European countries with the United States and Canada.

Soviet bloc
In the twentieth century, the Soviet Union and the communist states allied with it.

Warsaw Pact
A defense alliance formed in 1955 that linked the communist-ruled eastern European countries with the USSR.

ostpolitik
("Eastern politics") A West German policy, promoted by Chancellor Willy Brandt, that sought a reconciliation between West and East Germany and an expanded dialogue with the USSR.

LO² welfare states
Government systems that offer their citizens a range of state-subsidized health, education, and social service benefits; adopted by western European nations after World War II.

bhangra
A popular music that emerged in Britain from a blending of traditional folk songs brought by Indian immigrants with Caribbean reggae and Anglo-American styles, such as rock, hip hop, and disco.

existentialism
A European intellectual approach contending that truth is not absolute but constructed by people according to their society's beliefs.

postmodernism
A European intellectual approach contending that truth is not absolute but constructed by people according to their society's beliefs.

LO¹ What factors fostered the movement toward unity in western Europe?

• World War II devastated western Europe's population, infrastructure, and economy, but it enjoyed a remarkable period of rebirth, aided by extensive U.S. funding. New patterns in European politics included right-wing Christian Democrat parties, leftist social democrats, and the emergence of the Greens.

• A wave of decolonization followed World War II, though former colonizing nations usually maintained economic ties with their former holdings.

• The Cold War shaped European politics, with eastern Europe allied with the USSR and western Europe allied with the United States, but over time some European leaders advocated dialogue with the USSR.

• European countries joined together in the European Community, which became the world's largest free-trade zone and led to increased prosperity; however, the 1970s brought hard times, and European unity sometimes threatened to give way.

LO² How did the rise of welfare states transform western European societies?

• Western European governments have generally instituted the welfare state, a mix of capitalism and socialism in which citizens pay high taxes in exchange for an extensive safety net.

• In 1968, a wave of radical protest swept Europe, and over the decades European society was liberalized by the sexual revolution.

• The large numbers of immigrants who came to western Europe reshaped the cultures of many regions, while rock and later punk music became extremely popular among European youth.

• Philosophies such as existentialism, which urged people to control their own lives, and postmodernism, which claimed that complete objectivity is impossible, became popular in postwar Europe.

• Organized religion became less influential in postwar Europe, while tensions among branches of Christianity faded, Roman Catholicism liberalized, and Muslims became a significant portion of the European population.

LO³ What factors contributed to political crises in the Soviet Union and eastern Europe?

• Under Stalin, the USSR ruthlessly suppressed dissent; under Khrushchev, it moderated somewhat and focused on economic and technological development; under Brezhnev, it became more repressive again.

• Although the Soviet economy grew under communism, it suffered from lack of innovation, inept planning, and an overemphasis on the military, and it created a privileged class of Communist Party and military insiders.

- U.S.–USSR relations were strained by the Cuban Missile Crisis, the Berlin Wall, and Soviet support for communist Cuba and North Vietnam, but the USSR's foreign interventions were usually motivated by its national interest rather than a desire to spread communism.

- In exchange for limited freedom, Soviet citizens were offered extensive social services, but many non-Russians in Central Asia and the Baltics resented Russian cultural domination, while Soviet youth turned to rock music to express their rebellion.

- Much of eastern Europe was effectively colonized by the USSR, though Yugoslavia pursued an independent communist course, and citizens of Poland, Hungary, and Czechoslovakia mounted challenges to Soviet rule.

- With the USSR losing ground, Soviet leader Mikhail Gorbachev introduced reforms designed to democratize the USSR, to liberalize its economy, and to allow eastern European countries greater self-determination.

LO4 How did the demise of the communist system contribute to a new Europe?

- The collapsing Soviet bloc and Soviet decay created problems for Gorbachev, and he was replaced by Boris Yeltsin, who allowed independence for all the non-Russian Soviet republics, and pursued a rapid shift to capitalism.

- However, as a result of this "shock therapy," a small group of former Communist Party officials became extremely wealthy, while most Russians suffered economically. Yeltsin was replaced by the more authoritarian Vladimir Putin, who brought back some stability.

- With the fall of the USSR, formerly communist eastern Europe became more democratic, though many countries struggled economically and others suffered political upheaval, especially Yugoslavia, which experienced violent civil war and "ethnic cleansing."

- German reunification, celebrated at first, yielded mixed results, while the European Union grew to include twenty-five nations by 2004 but faced questions over whether to admit non-Christian nations and over what form its constitution should take.

- European nations struggled to navigate the evolving world economy, to deal with Islamic terrorism, and to work out relations with each other and with the United States.

Key Terms

LO¹ Intifada
("Uprising") A resistance begun in 1987 by Palestinians against the Israeli occupation of Gaza and the West Bank.

Ba'ath
A political party in the Middle East that favored socialism and Arab nationalism and strongly opposed Israel.

OPEC
(Organization of Petroleum Exporting Countries) A cartel formed in 1960 to give producers more power over the price of oil and leverage with the consuming nations.

LO² Islamists
Antimodern, usually puritanical Islamic militants who seek an Islamic state.

rai
("opinion") A twentieth-century pop music of Algeria based on local Bedouin chants, Spanish flamenco, French café songs, Egyptian pop, and other influences and featuring improvised lyrics that often deal with forbidden themes of sex and alcohol.

mujahidin
("holy warriors") Conservative Islamic rebels who rebelled against the pro-Soviet regime in Afghanistan in the 1970s and 1980s.

Taliban
("students") A group of Pashtun religious students who organized a military force in the 1980s to fight what they considered to be immorality and corruption and to impose order in Afghanistan.

LO³ pan-Africanism
The dream, originating in the early twentieth century, that all Africans would cooperate to eventually form some sort of united states of the continent.

Mau Mau Rebellion
An eight-year uprising in the 1950s by the Gikuyu people in Kenya against British rule.

wabenzi
("people who drive a Mercedes Benz") A privileged urban class in Africa since the mid-twentieth century of politicians, high bureaucrats, professionals, military officers, and businessmen who manipulate their connections to amass wealth.

apartheid
("separate development") A South African policy to set up a police state to enforce racial separation; lasted from 1948 to 1994.

bantustans
Rural reservations in South Africa where black Africans under apartheid were required to live if they were not needed in the modern economy.

CHRONOLOGY

1948	Formation of Israel
1948	Apartheid in South Africa
1954–1962	Algerian Revolution
1957–1965	African decolonization
1967	Arab–Israeli Six-Day War
1973	OPEC oil embargo
1975	Independence for Portuguese colonies
1979	Islamic revolution in Iran
1994	Black majority rule in South Africa
2003	United States invasion of Iraq

LO¹ How have Arab–Israeli tensions and oil shaped contemporary Middle Eastern politics?

- After World War II, nationalist governments replaced many colonial regimes in the Middle East, but the region has failed to develop many working multiparty democracies.

- Egyptian leader General Gamal Abdul Nasser threw off British influence, seized control of the Suez Canal, and pursued socialist policies, but neither he nor his pro-American successors brought prosperity to Egypt.

- Traumatized by the Holocaust, many Jews moved to Palestine after World War II and established the state of Israel, which led to a war between Jews and Arabs, a mass exodus of Palestinians into refugee camps, and enduring tensions.

- After the 1967 Arab-Israeli War, Israel occupied lands with a large Arab population and severely limited their freedom, while Palestinians became increasingly militant in their opposition.

- After nationalists overthrew the Iranian shah, the United States helped return him to power; he ruled ruthlessly until 1979, when he was overthrown by Islamic fundamentalists.

- From 1958 on, Iraq was ruled by ruthless military dictatorships dominated by the Sunni minority, and in 1979, Saddam Hussein came to power, launched a costly war against Iran, and then was attacked by the United States after invading Kuwait.

- Saudi Arabia grew extremely wealthy from oil sales, but many citizens have remained poor, and conservative religious leaders and their followers have criticized the Saudi royal family and its ties with the United States.

LO² What roles has Islam played in the contemporary Middle East?

- For several decades, Lebanon was divided among a variety of warring factions supported by foreign governments; in the Sudan, Arab Muslims fought with African Christians and launched a genocide against African Muslims; and the Kurds came into conflict with the governments of several Middle Eastern countries.

- Although some Middle Eastern women have attained greater freedom and adopted Western dress, many remain in the home, subject to male authority.

- Middle Eastern societies have been divided between Islamists and secular Muslims, and popular musicians and writers have raised the ire of religious conservatives.

- In Afghanistan, U.S.-supported Islamic rebels and Soviet-assisted communists fought for a decade until the Soviets withdrew, after which the Taliban took over much of the country and allowed terrorist groups such as Al Qaeda to base themselves there.

- After Al Qaeda's September 2001 attack on the United States, a U.S.-led invasion overthrew the Taliban and set up a weak pro-Western government; in 2003, the United States invaded Iraq, generating massive looting and persistent, violent opposition, even by Iraqis who hated Saddam Hussein.

- Middle Eastern societies have been torn between those who promote modernization and those who champion tradition, while the region has remained strategically important to outside powers.

LO⁴ negritude
A twentieth-century literary and philosophical movement to forge distinctively African views.

LO³ What were the main political consequences of decolonization in sub-Saharan Africa?

- European colonial rulers had played rival ethnic groups in Africa against each other, but after World War II, Ghana became the first colony to achieve independence.

- Most British colonies attained independence through peaceful means, but Kenya's transition was long and violent, as was that of the Belgian Congo, Angola, Guinea-Bissau, Mozambique, and Zimbabwe.

- After independence, many African nations were ruled by military dictatorships or corrupt civilians; many nationalist leaders lost favor over time; the gap between rich and poor widened; and some nations experienced ongoing violence, disorder, and genocide.

- Nigeria, home to rival ethnic and religious groups, has experienced civil war, coups, and corrupt military rule, and while its oil reserves have brought wealth to the elite, they have hardly benefited the poor.

- Under apartheid, a white minority in South Africa viciously suppressed the black majority, but the African National Congress, led by Nelson Mandela, ultimately won control of the government in 1994.

LO⁴ What new economic, social, and cultural patterns have emerged in Africa?

- African countries have struggled economically, with many being forced to import food and others, like the Congo, to enter into neocolonial relationships with Western powers, but Ghana and Botswana have managed to significantly improve their economies.

- Marxist revolutionary governments, which appealed to many Africans who wanted to erase the colonial legacy, came to power in Angola and Mozambique, both of which then entered into long civil wars, as well as in Zimbabwe.

- African cities have grown rapidly and often lack necessary services, individualism has grown more common, and women have lost some of the economic value they had in agricultural villages, though some have become successful professionals.

- African musicians, writers, and artists have drawn on local traditions as well as influences from the West to create original forms and works that criticize both Western encroachment and homegrown corruption.

- While animism has grown less influential in Africa, Christianity is the most popular religion but has been seen by some as connected to Western imperialism, while Islam is followed by 200 million Africans.

- The economic gap between Africa and the industrialized West continues to grow, and Western attempts to help Africa through the IMF and the World Bank often include requirements that harm the environment and the poor.

Chapter in Review

Key Terms

LO¹ Awami League
A Bengali nationalist party that began the move from independence from West Pakistan.

LO² Bharatha Janata (BJP)
The major Hindu nationalist party in India.

Bollywood
The Mumbai film industry in India.

LO³ National Liberation Front (NLF)
Often known as the Viet Cong, a communist-led revolutionary movement in South Vietnam that resisted American intervention in the American-Vietnamese War.

Tet Offensive
Communist attacks on major South Vietnamese cities in 1968, a turning point in the American-Vietnamese War.

Pathet Lao
Revolutionary Laotian nationalists allied with North Vietnam during the American-Vietnamese War.

Khmer Rouge
("Red Khmers") A communist insurgent group that sought to overthrow the government in Cambodia during the 1960s through the mid-1990s.

LO⁴ New Order
The Indonesian government headed by President Suharto from 1966 to 1998, which mixed military and civilian leadership.

ASEAN
(Association of Southeast Asian Nations) A regional economic and political organization formed in 1967 to promote cooperation among the non-communist Southeast Asian nations; eventually became a major trading bloc.

CHRONOLOGY

1945–1950	Indonesian Revolution
1946–1954	First Indochina War
1947	Independence for India and Pakistan
1948–1964	Nehru era in India
1948	Independence of Burma
1963–1975	U.S.-Vietnamese War
1966–1998	New Order in Indonesia
1971	Formation of Bangladesh
1975	Communist victories in Vietnam, Cambodia, Laos
1984	Assassination of Indira Ghandi
1997	Asian economic crisis

LO¹ What factors led to the political division of South Asia?

- After World War II, when majority Muslim Pakistan broke off from majority Hindu India, religious violence and a dispute over the territory of Kashmir set the stage for continued tension between the two countries.

- Nehru attempted to expand the rights of women and, through a mix of capitalism and socialism, vastly increased India's industrial and agricultural output, but the population expanded at a dangerously rapid rate, and not all policies were successful.

- East and West Pakistan were divided along ethnic lines, and a military crackdown on a Bengali nationalist party led to a bloody civil war in which India intervened on behalf of East Pakistan, which then became a separate country, Bangladesh.

- Nehru's daughter, Indira Gandhi, was prime minister for more than a decade, but she treated her opposition harshly and was assassinated in the midst of clashes between Hindus and Sikhs; her son and successor, Rajiv Gandhi, was also assassinated.

LO² What have been the major achievements and disappointments of the South Asian nations?

- India's multiparty democracy has endured despite religious and caste tensions, and the Congress Party has been consistently influential, though communist parties and Hindu nationalists also have large followings.

- Despite great advances in agricultural and industrial production, India still suffers from extensive poverty, and its rapidly growing population is likely to perpetuate this problem.

- While caste distinctions have remained strong in villages, they have broken down somewhat in cities; women have advanced in education and opportunity, though they are still less educated than men; and religion continues to be a source of tension.

- Pakistan has alternated between civilian and military governments and has been slow to grant women equal rights, while Bangladesh has battled poverty and has generally accepted religious minorities, though militant Muslim groups have gained influence in recent years.

- Since it became independent, Sri Lanka has been a democracy; it elected the world's first woman prime minister, and it has nurtured a well-educated, healthy population, but since 1983 the minority Tamils have fought for independence.

- India has produced talented engineers and computer scientists and made advances in technology, although its nuclear arms race with Pakistan has raised the worry of nuclear weapons being in the hands of Islamic terrorists.

- Though women's rights are not universal in South Asia, more South Asian women have achieved positions of great power than in other areas of the world.

LO³ What were the causes and consequences of the wars in Indochina?

- After World War II, Ho Chi Minh's communist Viet Minh took partial control of Vietnam and declared independence, but the U.S.-supported French fought back in the First Indochina War, which ended in Viet Minh victory.

- Instead of allowing an election to determine the future of South Vietnam, the United States installed Diem as president, but he was opposed by the communist National Liberation Front.

- Using a questionable attack as a pretext, the United States went to war to rid Vietnam of communism, but could not triumph over the communists, who gained control of Vietnam two years after the United States pulled out its ground forces.

- In Laos, the United States recruited Hmong hill people to fight the Pathet Lao revolutionaries, who took control of the country in 1975, while in Cambodia, the United States bombed areas occupied by North Vietnamese and supported a weak, dependent government, which was overthrown in 1975 by the Khmer Rouge.

- Vietnam struggled after the war, but in the 1980s, it opened up its economy, and by the 1990s, it had reestablished ties with the rest of the world, including the United States.

- Many Laotians fled into exile, while Cambodia endured vicious repression under the Khmer Rouge, who continued to wreak havoc even after a Vietnamese invasion pushed them out of power.

LO⁴ How has decolonization and globalization shaped the new Southeast Asian nations?

- After a hard-won independence from the Dutch, Indonesia struggled to attain unity under Sukarno, but a group of generals removed Sukarno from power.

- Under Suharto, the Indonesian New Order government repressed regional opposition and improved the economy, but Suharto was corrupt and forced to resign in 1997.

- After attaining independence, the Philippines remained strongly influenced by the United States and struggled with economic inequality and a Muslim insurgency. Under Marcos, the Philippines was divided between the very rich and the poor; eventually he was forced out, and the governments that followed were more democratic but still dominated by the wealthy.

- Thailand alternated between long periods of military rule and short periods of democratic or semidemocratic rule. Since the 1980s, its semidemocratic system has enjoyed economic growth.

- Burma endured decades of factional fighting and, since 1962, brutal military domination. In recent years, its corrupt regime has failed to take advantage of ample natural resources and has stifled its opposition.

- Malaysia has taken advantage of abundant natural resources to become highly successful, while Singapore, with fewer resources, thrives through a combination of economic freedom and political restriction.

- With their rapidly growing economies, the Southeast Asian "tigers" have inspired developing nations around the world, and while most of the region has modernized, tradition thrives in them as well.